Notable
Hispanic
American
Women

Notable
Hispanic
American
Women

FIRST EDITION

Diane Telgen and Jim Kamp, Editors

Foreword by Graciela Beecher,
President of the National Association of
Cuban-American Women of the U.S.A.

Gale Research Inc. • *DETROIT* • *WASHINGTON, D.C.* • *LONDON*

STAFF

Diane Telgen and Jim Kamp, *Editors*

Kathleen J. Edgar, Marie Ellavich, Denise E. Kasinec, Susan Reicha,
Deborah A. Stanley, and Thomas Wiloch, *Associate Editors*
Joanna Brod, David M. Galens, Margaret Mazurkiewicz, and Cornelia A. Pernik, *Assistant Editors*

Kevin Hile, *Contributing Editor*
Laurie Collier, Ronie-Richele Garcia-Johnson, Marion C. Gonsior,
Tom Pendergast, Paul Schellinger, and Deborah A. Straub, *Contributing Copy Editors*

James G. Lesniak, *Senior Editor*

Victoria B. Cariappa, *Research Manager*
Mary Rose Bonk, *Research Supervisor*
Reginald A. Carlton, Clare Collins, Andrew Guy Malonis, and Norma Sawaya, *Editorial Associates*
Patricia Bowen, Rachel A. Dixon, Shirley Gates, Sharon McGilvray, and Devra M. Sladics, *Editorial Assistants*

Mary Beth Trimper, *Production Manager*
Evi Seoud, *Assistant Production Manager*
Mary Kelley, *Production Assistant*

Cynthia Baldwin, *Art Director*
Arthur Chartow, *Cover Designer*
Yolanda Latham, *Keyliner*

∞™ The paper used in this publication meets the minimum requirements of American National Standard for Informational Sciences—Permanence Paper for Printed Library Materials, ANSI Z39.48-1984.

ISBN 0-8103-7578-8
Printed in the United States of America
Published simultaneously in the United Kingdom
by Gale Research International Limited
(An affiliated company of Gale Research Inc.)

Library of Congress Cataloging-in-Publication Data

Notable Hispanic American women / edited by Diane Telgen and Jim Kamp.
　　　　p. cm.
　　　Includes bibliographical references and index.
　　　ISBN 0-8103-7578-8: $59.95
　　　　1. Hispanic American women—Biography—Dictionaries. I. Telgen, Diane. II. Kamp, Jim.
E184.S75N68　1993
920.72'089'68073—dc20
　　[B]　　　　　　　　　　　　　　　　　　　　92-42483
　　　　　　　　　　　　　　　　　　　　　　　　CIP

10 9 8 7 6 5 4 3 2 1

Contents

Foreword

For centuries Hispanic American women have fought and are still fighting for the respect and recognition they deserve. Just a few decades ago, marriage was considered the most normal and satisfying mode of existence for the Hispanic American woman. "Machismo," or male dominance, still prevailing in many countries and areas of Latin America, is well described by the words of American actor Cary Grant in a film about a Latin American dictator: "Latin men like to keep their women poor, illiterate, and pregnant." Exaggerated or not, it is a fact that Hispanic American women historically had to tear down barriers within their immediate families before facing the outside world in their fight for self-determination and empowerment. As time went by Hispanic American women began to realize that, without denying the dignity and importance of their roles as wives and mothers, it was essential to play other important roles in the United States: They needed to acquire a voice in all areas of social, economic, and political issues in the country. Being confined to their homes or to low-paying jobs in garment factories was not sufficient for those Hispanic American women who decided to create a place for themselves and their daughters in a white, male-dominated world. They yearned to be heard in the nation's capital and elsewhere throughout the United States by participating in the political and policy-making process of the country.

Thanks to the pioneering efforts of Chicanas, Puerto Ricans, Cubans, and South and Central Americans, we today have the first Hispanic American Congresswoman in Washington, D.C.: Ileana Ros-Lehtinen, a Cuban American who garnered international attention when she won a seat in the U.S. House of Representatives. But before her came a myriad of Latino women who made outstanding contributions in the fields of education, fine arts, science, business, sports, leadership, and politics at local and state levels. This book is dedicated to these women, heroines in their own right, with the intention of revealing the struggle of Hispanic American women who have worked for a better future for themselves and for their daughters, overcoming the obstacles and heart-breaks along their respective paths.

From colonial times there have been extraordinary Latino women who raised their voices for women's rights. Some of the most prominent examples never lived in the United States, women such as Sor Juana Inés de la Cruz in Mexico, who was followed by Juana de Ibarbourou, Alfonsina Storni, and Gabriela Mistral, who was the first Latino woman to win the Nobel Prize in Literature in the New World. The Civil Rights Movement of the 1960s brought forth a number of Hispanic American women who decided to join fathers, brothers, and husbands and strive for equality and justice. Women like Puerto Rican educator Antonia Pantoja, founder of the National Puerto Rican Forum, ASPIRA, the Puerto Rican Association for Community Affairs, and the Puerto Rican Research Center; the Chicano organizer and activist Dolores Huerta of the United Farm Workers; and Puerto Rican actress and singer Rita Moreno, recipient of numerous awards for her talent and excellence in movies and television and on the stage, have all helped promote Hispanic American women in virtually all fields of human endeavor.

In recent times there has been a growing awareness of the achievements of Hispanic American women. The year 1992 has seen *Hispanic Magazine* institute for the first time the Latina Excellence

Awards. In 1992 the Hispanic Heritage Awards selected Antonia Pantoja as one of its recipients. The National Association of Cuban American Women, at its Ninth Annual Achievement Awards Dinner, honored not only Cuban American women such as Miriam Alonso, vice mayor of the city of Miami, but also Chicanas and Puerto Ricans such as Judy Canales, president of the Mexican-American Women's National Organization, and Arlene F. Gillespie, vice president of the National Puerto Rican Coalition. We can certainly say that the Hispanic American Women's Movement has come of age in the 1990s.

Controversy has sometimes surrounded the use of the term "Hispanic." Since a resident or citizen of the United States of Spanish ancestry may be Mexican, Puerto Rican, Cuban, Dominican, Peruvian, Venezuelan, etc., an umbrella or all-encompassing term had to be adopted to cover the unity in diversity. Some years back, the term "Latin American" was used and still is; since the 1980s, however, the term "Hispanic American" has gained popularity. The ambiguity continues. For some, the term "Latin" or "Latino" also includes people of Portuguese, French, and Italian heritage. Therefore, the word "Hispanic" is useful in designating residents of the United States who inherited the Spanish culture and language of the Conquistadors. Nevertheless, we cannot classify as Hispanic only those people whose ancestors came from Spain, for Hispanic Americans come in all shapes and colors. There are white Hispanics, black Hispanics, Indian Hispanics, and mixed-blood Hispanics. All speak and cherish, for the most part, the culture and even the religion of Spain, which as a country carried out the only successful crusade in the world—the Christianization of the territories discovered by Christopher Columbus and colonized by Spaniards. "Hispanic American" thus functions as an umbrella term to cover the diversity of residents of the United States who claim the language and culture of Spain as their own.

Hispanic American women have contributed in many ways to the betterment of society. Some have achieved notoriety on the national or international level, while others have had a positive impact locally, changing the world around them, improving life for all Hispanic women in this country. A female psychologist, for example, might not be known by the country at large, but she is recognized as an authority by her fellow psychologists. In addition to psychology, there are many other fields of knowledge that have benefitted from the achievements of Hispanic American women, including education, health, sports, science, or entertainment. Women who advance a field of human knowledge deserve to be recognized, primarily because they touch the lives of many women who have seen them as examples worth emulating and have subsequently gained national or even international fame.

Notable Hispanic American Women represents all those women whose lights, large or small, bright or dim, have shone and warmed the hearts of their daughters, friends, neighbors, and countrymen . . . women who struggled to gain excellence and attained it in a large or small sense . . . women who have made and who continue to make the world in which we live a better place for all of us, be it locally, nationally or worldwide.

Graciela Beecher
President, National Association of Cuban-American Women of the U.S.A.
President, Cuban-American Legal Defense & Education Fund

Introduction

In 1992, the "Year of the Woman," Gale Research Inc. published *Notable Black American Women* in an attempt to fill a reference void on minority women. The idea for the book stemmed from Henrietta W. Smith's 1988 article "Missing and Wanted: Black Women in Encyclopedias" (*School Library Journal*, February) in which Smith made a general call for better and more current coverage of black women. An overwhelming success with readers and reviewers alike, *Notable Black American Women* provided the impetus for *Notable Hispanic American Women*, another biographical volume adding to what would otherwise be a dearth of reference sources on minorities and women.

Based on a mixture of personal interviews, book studies, and/or articles from such periodicals as *Más, Nuestro Tiempo, Hispanic, Intercambios Femeniles, Hispanic Business,* and *Vista,* the entries in *Notable Hispanic American Women* feature historical and contemporary women from a broad range of professions, including medicine, labor, entertainment, business, law, sports, journalism, science, education, politics, religion, literature, and others. The nearly 300 entries range from 500 to 2500 words and cover the noteworthy personal, family, and career details that helped shape and define each woman's life. In addition, many of the longer entries are accompanied by a personal photograph.

Advisory Board Selected Entrants

To determine the "notables" among Hispanic American women, we assembled an advisory board of distinguished Hispanic American women (see p. xxxiii) to recommend and evaluate names. In general, the advisory board and the editors focused on women whose contributions on the local, national, or international level have positively impacted their respective fields of endeavor or society at large. Though we have made every attempt to include key figures, we make no claim to have isolated the "most notable" Hispanic American women—an impossible goal. We are pleased that most of the biographies we wanted to feature are included; however, time constraints, space limitations, and research and interview availability prevented us from listing a few other women deserving of inclusion. Our hope is that in presenting these entries, we are providing a basis for future research on an important segment of the American fabric: Hispanic American women.

We followed the U.S. Census Bureau in defining "Hispanic" women as those who identify their origin or descent as being from Mexico, Puerto Rico, Cuba, Spain, or any of the Spanish-speaking countries of Central or South America. In considering the term "American," we included not only U.S. citizens but those individuals who live and work in the United States and who have made contributions to American culture. In the case of historical figures, we extended this definition to include those territories that are now part of the United States.

Personal Interviews Ensure Timeliness and Accuracy

The scarcity of in-depth sources on Hispanic American women became evident during the compilation of this volume. For most of the entries that comprise *Notable Hispanic American Women,* telephone interviews were conducted to secure current information; in a number of cases, these interviews provided the *only* source of information. Consequently, this book contains a good deal of material that cannot be found anywhere else.

Numerous Points of Access

Entries in *Notable Hispanic American Women* are arranged alphabetically by surname. In cases involving compound surnames, we attempted to follow each entrant's preference in terms of alphabetizing under the first or second surname. For example, Blandina Cárdenas Ramírez is listed under "R" while Marlene Cintron de Frias is listed under "C". To facilitate access, cross references have been provided in the list of **Entrants** and in the main text for locating names involving compound surnames, hyphenated names, pseudonyms, and name variations. In addition to the alphabetical list of **Entrants** (see p. xi), there are listings of **Entrants by Occupation** (see p. xxi) and **Entrants by Ethnicity** (see p. xxix) to assist those seeking names from a given profession or heritage. Finally, there is an extensive subject index at the back of the book containing names, book titles, and general subjects, such as "Bilingualism," "Community involvement," "Discrimination," "Health and medicine," "Leadership," and hundreds of others.

Special Thanks

Many people helped in the preparation of *Notable Hispanic American Women*. In addition to the advisors, writers, and proofreaders, there were several individuals who made special efforts to make the present volume a reality: Ruth Carranza of *Intercambios Femeniles* helped during the planning and development stage by providing a list of qualified contributors with experience writing on Hispanic American women; Luis Vasquez of MAYA Hispanic Marketing and Communications and Diana Martinez of L.A. Media were generous in lending their expertise by taking on several writing assignments; Margo Gutierrez and Martha Cotera, both affiliated with University of Texas at Austin's renowned Chicano library, helped out time and again by locating research materials for our writers; Jim Evans played an important role in making sure last-minute assignments were completed; and Michelle Vachon generously agreed to track down information and write entries on women for whom very little research material existed.

Comments Welcome

Although we went to considerable lengths to ensure the accuracy of the information presented in this volume, we are aware that mistakes and/or omissions are inevitable. Therefore, we welcome all feedback related to the content of this first volume of *Notable Hispanic American Women* and will keep all comments and suggestions on file. A list of names for the second edition has already been started, and we welcome your recommendations of other names worthy of inclusion in future editions.

Please send comments and suggestions to:

> The Editors
> *Notable Hispanic American Women*
> Gale Research Inc.
> 835 Penobscot Building
> Detroit, MI 48226

Entrants

D

S

Occupation Index

Ethnicity Index

Advisory Board

Graciela Beecher
President, National Association of Cuban-American Women of the U.S.A.
President, Cuban-American Legal Defense & Education Fund

Jane Arce Bello
Executive Officer, Association of Hispanic Arts

Gloria Bonilla-Santiago
Associate Professor, School of Social Work, Rutgers University
Director, Hispanic Affairs Office, Rutgers University

Rhonda Rios Kravitz
Librarian, California State University, Sacramento
Past president, REFORMA (National Association
to Promote Library Services to the Spanish-Speaking)

Tey Diana Rebolledo
Professor of Spanish and Chicana Literature, University of New Mexico
President, National Association for Chicano Studies

Shirlene Soto
Professor of History, Chicano Studies Department, California State University, Northridge

Celia Gonzales Torres
Cofounder and past chair, National Network of Hispanic Women
Principal, Torres Enterprises

Michelle Vachon
Researcher and writer, *Hispanic Business*
Free-lance writer

Contributors

Anna Macias Aguayo, *Dallas Morning News*
D. D. Andreassi, *Observer and Eccentric,* Oakland County, Michigan
Sylvia P. Apodaca, Washington, D.C.
Graciela Beecher, National Association of Cuban-American Women of the U.S.A.
Cheryl Beller, Royal Oak, Michigan
Pamela Berry, Sterling Heights, Michigan
Gloria Bonilla-Santiago, Rutgers University
Julie Catalano, San Antonio, Texas
Andrés Chávez, L.A. Media, Los Angeles, California
Julia Edgar, *Daily Tribune,* Royal Oak, Michigan
Bill Evans, Walled Lake, Michigan
Sally Foster, Rochester Hills, Michigan
Ronie-Richele Garcia-Johnson, Ann Arbor, Michigan
Marian C. Gonsior, Westland, Michigan
Rosalva Hernandez, *Detroit News*
Jonathan J. Higuera, Washington, D.C.
Carol Hopkins, *Monthly Detroit*
Kelly King Howes, Gaithersburg, Maryland
Anne Janette Johnson, Haddonfield, New Jersey
Elena Kellner, *Los Angeles Times*
Robyn Kleerekoper, Southfield, Michigan
Jeanne M. Lesinski, Onalaska, Wisconsin
Dawn Levy, Washington, D.C.
Bruce MacLeod, *Macomb Daily,* Mt. Clemens, Michigan
Alma Renee Madrid, Colorado Springs, Colorado
Ann Malaspina, Astoria, New York
Sandra Márquez, *Hispanic Link*
Teresa Márquez, University of New Mexico General Library
Diana Martínez, L.A. Media, Los Angeles, California
Yleana Martinez, Cambridge, Massachusetts
Peg McNichol, Mt. Clemens, Michigan
Susan Lopez Mele, Washington, D.C.
Oralia Michel, L.A. Media, Los Angeles, California
Paul Miller, University of Miami
T. A. Niles, University of Miami
Lawrence J. Paladino, Detroit, Michigan
Suzanne L. Parker, Birmingham, Michigan
Silvia Novo Pena, Texas Southern University
Tom Pendergast, West Lafayette, Indiana
Stephanie Poythress, Rochester Hills, Michigan

Tey Diana Rebolledo, University of New Mexico
Margaret Rose, California State University, Bakersfield
Marilyn Stein, Royal Oak, Michigan
Michelle Vachon, *Hispanic Business*
Luis Vasquez-Ajmac, MAYA Hispanic Marketing and Communications
Ana Veciana-Suarez, *Miami Herald*
Carol von Hatten, St. Clair Shores, Michigan
Elizabeth Wenning, Tuscon, Arizona
Denise Wiloch, Canton, Michigan

Photo Credits

Photographs appearing in *Notable Hispanic American Women* were received from the following sources:

Courtesy of Marie Acosta-Colon: p. 1; Courtesy of the Ballet Nacional de Cuba Archives: p. 5; Courtesy of PolyGram Records, Inc.: p. 8; Lansing State Journal, courtesy of Yolanda Alvarado: p. 12; Photograph by Bill Eichner: p. 15; Courtesy of Lupe Anguiano: p. 23; © 1989 Elaine Mode: p. 26; Courtesy of Carmen Rivera-Babin: p. 35; Photograph by Wm. Stetz, courtesy of Judith Baca: p. 36; AP/Wide World Photos: pp. 38, 43, 46, 50, 75, 99, 131, 210, 236, 237, 278, 287, 293, 318, 341, 385, 416; Courtesy of Maxine Baca Zinn: p. 41; Courtesy of Cheryl Brownstein-Santiago: p. 62; Courtesy of Cecilia Preciado Burciaga: p. 64; University of Colorado News Bureau, courtesy of Cordelia Candelaria: p. 71; Archive Photos: pp. 81, 204; Courtesy of Sylvia Castillo: p. 85; Photograph by Bacharach Photographers, courtesy of Linda Chavez: p. 93; Courtesy of Chevron U.S.A. Products Company: p. 104; © Southwestern University: p. 113; Courtesy of Ralph Mercado Management: p. 115; Courtesy of Angela de Hoyos: p. 122; Courtesy of Jane L. Delgado: p. 128; Courtesy of Patricia Diaz Dennis: p. 134; Courtesy of Remedios Diaz-Oliver: p. 137; Photograph by Jose Villarrubia, courtesy of Rita Elizondo: p. 144; U.S. Department of Education, courtesy of Rita Esquivel: p. 147; Photograph by Alberto Tolot, © 1990 CBS Records Inc., courtesy of Epic Records: p. 149; Photograph by Clara Griffin: p. 151; Photograph by Marcella Scuderi: p. 161; Courtesy of Frances Josephine Garcia: p. 168; Courtesy of Juliet Garcia: p. 171; Courtesy of Mayor Norma G. Garcia: p. 173; Courtesy of Lena Guerrero: p. 189; Courtesy of Antonia Hernandez: p. 196; Photograph by Peter Schaff, courtesy of Marta Casals Istomin: p. 215; Courtesy of The José Iturbi Foundation: p. 218; Courtesy of Mari-Luci Jaramillo: p. 221; Courtesy of National Association for Hispanic Elderly: p. 226; Courtesy of Dr. Aliza A. Lifshitz: p. 230; Courtesy of Monica Lozano: p. 240; Courtesy of Wendy Lucero-Schayes: p. 243; Photograph by Neil Davenport, © 1991 Sony Music, courtesy of Columbia Records: p. 253; Courtesy of Vilma S. Martinez: p. 261; Courtesy of Margarita Melville: p. 268; Courtesy of Pat Mora: p. 280; Courtesy of Cherríe Moraga: p. 283; Courtesy of NASA: p. 297; Courtesy of Katherine D. Ortega: p. 303; Courtesy of Arte Público Press, University of Houston: p. 321; Courtesy of Blandina Cardenas Ramirez: p. 328; Courtesy of Pacific Gas and Electric Company: p. 337; Courtesy of Avance: p. 345; Courtesy of Helen Rodriguez-Trias: p. 348; Courtesy of Lina S. Rodriguez: p. 350; Courtesy of Elektra Entertainment: p. 353; UPI/Bettmann: p. 356; Courtesy of Lucille Roybal-Allard: p. 358; Courtesy of Irma Santaella: p. 370; Courtesy of Isauro Santiago: p. 373; Copyright © 1992 John Reilly Photography, courtesy of Miriam Santos: p. 377; Courtesy of Cristina Saralegui: p. 379; Illustration Services, University of California, Davis, courtesy of Adaljiza Sosa Riddell: p. 388; Courtesy of Marta Sotomayor: p. 391; Courtesy of Celia Torres: p. 401; Courtesy of Nydia Margarita Velázquez: p. 406; Photograph by Beatriz Schiller, courtesy of Nelly Vuksic: p. 413; Courtesy of City of Phoenix: p. 419; Courtesy of Carmen Zapata: p. 420.

Notable Hispanic American Women

A

Acosta, Romana Bañuelos
See **Bañuelos, Romana Acosta**

Marie Acosta-Colón
(1949-)
Arts advocate and administrator

Throughout her life, Marie Acosta-Colón has made a point of getting involved, be it on stage or off. Formerly active in the political theatre groups Grupo Mascarones and the San Francisco Mime Troupe, Acosta-Colón has become a prominent advocate for art funding and an experienced arts administrator. She has worked extensively for the California Arts Council and is the head of the Mexican Museum in San Francisco.

Acosta-Colón was born December 8, 1949, the second of five children in her family. Because her father was in the U.S. Navy, she lived in several states, including Hawaii, but most of her childhood was spent on the West Coast. Her father, Frank Acosta, is Native American; her mother, Beatrice, is Hispanic and a homemaker.

1968 Democratic Convention Sparks Political Activism

Acosta-Colón's political activism began during her college years when she was a political science major at Los Angeles Valley Junior College in Los Angeles, California. In the summer of 1968, she went to the Democratic National Convention in Chicago as a volunteer for presidential candidate Senator Eugene McCarthy. There she observed the violent police crackdown on anti-Vietnam war demonstrators that alerted the entire nation to the strength of anti-war sentiment that had been building in the late 1960s. Acosta-Colón recalled in an interview with Carol Hopkins that the convention—one of the most violent on record with bloody confrontations occurring between young demonstrators and Chicago police—changed her life. "The values I had grown up with were thrown into question, the beliefs in a government by the people and for the people. It was so obvious there was

Marie Acosta-Colón

injustice going on. I came back [to California] and discovered that the politics of the day dictated that I had to become a more active citizen."

Her early life had not prepared her for what she saw in Chicago. "My father was in the service, and when you're in the service, you're not inclined to find other families questioning your government's practices toward other people in your own country. You pretty much believe that government is good, that government is fair and that everything is wonderful." It was then, she decided, that she was going to try and right "social, political and economic inequities." She switched schools and attended California State University for two years, remaining active in the Chicano student movement.

Mexico, Acosta-Colón says, has always held a special place in her heart. In the summer of 1969, she traveled to Mexico City to study economics at the Universidad Nacional Autonoma de Mexico. Prior to this time, Acosta-Colón had been thinking about becoming a lawyer. Her Mexican summer altered her decision. "When I saw the discrepancy of poverty and wealth in Mexico, law didn't seem the fix." The young student was repelled by the stark differences, she says, between the "haves and the have-nots." In 1971, she returned to Mexico (she never graduated from college) and became an actress with Grupo Mascarones, a theater group which performed plays with political themes in Mexico and the United States. She remained in Mexico until 1974. Looking back, Acosta-Colón remembered her years there fondly. "It was one of the more vibrant moments of our history. Salvador Allende was in Chile; the Vietnam War was on. It was much more compelling for me to be in Mexico where the theater I was working with was the center for international cross-fertilization of ideas and creativity. We had some of the finest theater directors from Latin America [working with us]."

Because of its limited budget and personnel, the theatre group relied on its members to assist with some of the administrative tasks. In 1972, Acosta-Colón became the group's tour coordinator and company manager, responsible for publicity, sales, and booking. In retrospect, Acosta-Colón believes this early experience has given her a unique perspective for her work today. "If I'd gone through graduate school and studied for a business degree, I wouldn't have [the same awareness]. There's a whole other dimension of understanding the arts business if you've been an artist." In the mid-1970s in the United States, many Chicano theater groups were beginning to gain notoriety. With nearly four years of stage and administrative experience to her credit, Acosta-Colón began to consider returning to America. She heard of work available with a traditional Mexican troupe and with the San Francisco Mime Troupe. She chose the mime troupe, she said in an interview with Carol Hopkins, because of her history in Mexico. "It seemed to me more could be said with an international or mixed perspective than with a culturally specific one. The mime troupe included people from different communities, and the plays were very accessible to a lot [of people]." The Tony Award-winning San Francisco Mime Troupe, known for its strong social commentary, was Acosta-Colón's "family" for eleven years.

For six years she was a performer with the only mime troupe "that talked," said Acosta-Colón. "I had a variety of roles. We weren't given a script and told, 'Mold this character.' We had to form the character ourselves." Around this time, Acosta-Colón married. In 1978, her first child, Carlos Antonio Colón, was born. She later had another son, Nicolas. Having a young child made touring extremely difficult, Acosta-Colón stated. While the actress adapted to the changes in her life, fundamental changes were going on inside the mime group as well. The loosely organized troupe realized it needed more structure and decided to separate acting and business responsibilities in order to take pressure off of the performers. In 1980 Acosta-Colón became the troupe's general manager. She served in this capacity until 1985.

Theatre Experience Used to Promote Arts in California

During this period Acosta-Colón began serving on several arts-related panels and boards. In 1980 she was one of the founding members of the Arts Economic Development Consortium of San Francisco. For much of the 1980s she sat on several panels for the California Arts Council. From 1982 to 1984 she was a board member of the People's Coalition in San Francisco. Since 1984, Acosta-Colón has been a member of the Association of Performing Arts Presenters' National Task Force on Presenting and Touring. She continues to serve as a site evaluator for the National Endowment for the Arts as she has since she was first appointed in 1985. Her extensive background in the arts as an administrator, activist, and advocate has made her a valued participant on many boards. Acosta-Colón commented that "a lot of arts advocacy was brewing at the same time I became an administrator."

In 1986 she left the mime troupe and became project director of the Professional Management Assistance Project where she designed a statewide technical assistance program for multi-cultural arts organizations in California. Her work experience continued to grow. After many years of volunteering for the California Arts Council, Acosta-Colón was hired as a special assistant to the director in 1986. While working with the council, she coordinated California Dialogue II, the 1988 statewide conference of multi-cultural artists. In 1989, officials from San Francisco's Mexican Museum approached Acosta-Colón about becoming the art institute's third director. After some hesitation, she accepted the position. "For me the motivating factor was that this museum represented a unique opportunity for the Latino community," she told Hopkins. "Generally art and culture in this country are all based on Western European traditions. With this museum we have an opportunity of putting into place the contributions of an ethnic-specific community, one that has made great contributions to art and culture in this country."

The 17-year-old museum, located in San Francisco's Marina district, has a 19-member staff which oversees about 9,000 pieces ranging from pre-Columbian to Chicano art. Because space in the building is limited, only a small portion of the museum's collection can be exhibited at any given time. One of the museum's most notable collections belonged to former U.S. vice president and famed millionaire Nelson Rockefeller. During his lifetime of collecting, he sometimes purchased all of a Mexican artist's work at once, thereby obtaining obscure samples of some of Mexico's best craftspeople. After his death, Rockefeller's daughter chose the Mexican Museum as the recipient of his large and diverse collection of folk art. Under Acosta-Colón's leadership, the museum's budget has increased three-fold from around $550,000 to $1.5 million.

Reports indicate that more and more visitors are viewing the many exhibitions held at the Mexican Museum each year. Acosta-Colón is proud of the work she is doing. She strongly believes the Latino community needs a cultural place to call its own. "If people go through a civic or cultural center of a city and . . . not see something that reflects them, the sense of ownership and contribution and the sense of belonging aren't the same as for the people who take it for granted. I want the museum to be that for the communities in the United States that emanate from Latin America, Cuba, Spain, Puerto Rico, and Mexico," she declared to Hopkins. Acosta-Colón also acknowledged that the proximity of the cultural institution is also important—to be relevant, it should be located in or near the community whose art it reflects. It is Acosta-Colón's goal to one day build a new museum closer to San Francisco's Mission district, home to the majority of the city's Latinos.

Acosta-Colón has remained politically active in her community. In 1989, five artists and arts administrators gathered in her kitchen and formed the San Francisco Arts Democratic Club. When asked if she might ever run for an elected office, she noted that people often ask her that question. "I wouldn't rule it out, but I don't see it in the cards. I'm very active in San Francisco politics but very specifically with issues having to do with the arts and trying to encourage legislators to utilize and fund the arts."

Even with cutbacks in the arts nationwide, Acosta-Colón is hopeful about the future. "I think in hard times the arts is often more creative and more responsive and has more of a social conscience than when times are good." Acosta-Colón, a self-described intense worker, is still affiliated with several Bay area committees and boards. She is presently serving as an appointee on the mayor's task force on cultural affairs. In 1991, she was named Woman of the Year by California Assembly Speaker Willie Brown for his district. Even with all of her accomplishments, as she looks to the future, Acosta-Colón considers something she once left behind in the past. She contemplates returning to school in order to fulfill her dream of becoming a lawyer. She once believed that the law had not corrected many fundamental inequalities in society. While her perception has not changed greatly, Acosta-Colón believes that a law degree would be of great help in her continuing community efforts. She told Hopkins: "If there was anything I could wish for, it would be a fellowship so I could get a law degree. I think I need that in order to continue to contribute at a greater level. That [would give me] the educational validity . . . and flexibility I need for what I do next."

Sources:

Periodicals

Grantmakers in the Arts (newsletter), summer, 1992, p. 9.
Latin American Art, fall, 1990, pp. 95-98.
San Francisco Chronicle, May 26, 1991, p. E1.
San Francisco Independent, December 26, 1991, p. 3.

Other

Acosta-Colón, Marie, telephone interview with Carol Hopkins, September 1, 1992.

—*Sketch by Carol Hopkins*

Marjorie Agosín
(1955-)
Poet, writer, educator

Chilean poet Marjorie Agosín believes that her upbringing in an educated, Jewish household is what allows her to express themes of social injustice in her work. A former Fulbright fellow who teaches Spanish at Wellesley College in Massachusetts, Agosín writes poetry that gives voice to Latin American women who are silenced by the oppression of dictatorship. "My writing is linked to the speech of those who do not speak," she explained in an essay for *Brujula <> Compass*. "Gags, blindfolds, mute women, women of smoke make up my texts, but my texts come also from the stratum of the imagination." The author of numerous volumes of poetry, Agosín received the Good Neighbor Award from the National Association of Christians and Jews in 1987.

Agosín was born June 15, 1955, in Bethesda, Maryland, the daughter of Moises and Frida Agosín. At the time of Agosín's birth, her father was a visiting scientist at the National Institutes of Health. At the age of three, however, she returned with her family by boat to Chile, where they stayed until she was 15. Venturing back to the United States for one year so that her father could teach at the University of Georgia at Athens, the family learned of the changing political climate in their homeland. The Socialist President Salvador Allende was ousted and killed in a military coup and was replaced with the dictator Augusto Pinochet Ugarte. The family, staunch socialists, opted to remain in the United States.

Chilean Art Inspires *Scraps of Cloth*

Agosín graduated from Clark Central High School in Athens, Georgia, in 1973, before moving on to the University of Georgia, where she received a bachelor of arts degree in philosophy in 1976. In 1982 she was awarded a doctorate in Latin American literature from Indiana University at Bloomington. In 1990 she continued her studies as a Fulbright fellow in Argentina. On one of her trips to Chile while still a graduate student, Agosín discovered the world of women who sew *arpilleras*, small wall-hangings made of cloth. The images depicted in the *arpilleras* showed the misery and pleasures experienced by these shantytown dwellers whose lives were marred by poverty and the pain of the disappearance of their loved ones. Immediately recognizing that this art form was being subverted and used as a political tool, Agosín set herself the task of writing a book about these women, entitled *Scraps of Cloth*. The work was subsequently used as the basis for a documentary produced for Public Broadcasting Service (PBS).

During her career, Agosín has also penned other books. Her volumes of poetry include *Brujas y algo mas, Hogueras/ Bonfires, Women of Smoke,* and *Zones of Pain.* She has also coedited a book about Chilean author María Luisa Bombal, on whom she wrote her thesis, and has edited an anthology entitled *Landscapes of a New Land: Fiction by Latin American Women.* Agosín contributes book reviews regularly to the *New York Times, Boston Globe,* and *Christian Science Monitor,* and is a member of the advisory board of *Ms.* magazine.

Makes Frequent Visits to Chile

Agosín returns yearly to Chile, often visiting for as long as three or four months. Although she is based in the United States, she says she has never adjusted to life in North America. "The older I become, the more foreign I feel living here. But it's very good for a writer to feel like a foreigner," she told Yleana Martinez in a telephone interview. Part of her alienation, she suggests, may come from being raised as a socialist and living in a capitalist society.

Married to nuclear physicist John Wiggins and the mother of two children, Agosín explained to Martinez her reasons for writing. "It is important to tell people that I have had a privileged life, a wonderful family and education," she said. "But I have made use of that privilege to help those who don't have it. It is a theme in my work. I'm not taking these causes because it's fashionable, because a lot of people may think it's opportunistic, but because being Jewish makes you closer to the disadvantaged. In the U.S. (being Jewish) is associated with power, but in Latin America, it is a minority."

Sources:

Periodicals

Brujula <> Compass (Spanish-language; translation by Cola Franzen), January/February, 1992, p. 21.
Hispania, March, 1987; September, 1987.
Los Angeles Times Book Review, December 24, 1989.
World Literature Today, winter, 1982.

Other

Agosín, Marjorie, telephone interview with Yleana Martinez, August, 1992.

—*Sketch by Yleana Martinez*

Marilyn Aguirre-Molina
(1948-)
Public health activist, educator

There is a bumper sticker on the car that Marilyn Aguirre-Molina drives around her home in New Jersey. On it are the words "Think globally, act locally." The statement is more than decoration—it is a creed that the educator and community activist has lived by all of her adult life.

Aguirre-Molina was born in New York City in 1948, the daughter of working class parents and the granddaughter of first generation Puerto Rican immigrants. Surrounded by a large, close-knit family in East Harlem, she attributes warm recollections of home life as a deciding factor in her career choice. Aguirre-Molina told this contributor that her family's ethic was one of "Working with others to mutually meet our needs."

In search of an education to help her attain her goals, Aguirre-Molina attended Columbia University where she received a master's degree in 1976 and a doctorate in education in 1980. She applied her acumen to finding solutions to the problems that have plagued Hispanic communities. Her research through the years has been focused on the public health, morbidity, and mortality patterns among Latinos, with special emphasis on finding ways to reduce substance abuse. In the 1970s she became a director at the East Harlem Council for Human Services where she worked with teenagers struggling with drug, tobacco, and alcohol dependency. Working with the council gave Aguirre-Molina new perspective on research and evaluation. "I began to recognize the importance of documenting what communities do," she said.

After receiving her doctorate, Aguirre-Molina taught at a state college. In 1983, Rutgers University asked her to join its renowned Center of Alcohol Studies. Aguirre-Molina worked on program development for five years while also teaching public health in the school's graduate program. In 1988, the chairperson of the Department of Environmental and Community Medicine at the University of Medicine and Dentistry of New Jersey invited her to join their faculty as an assistant professor.

Aguirre-Molina works in two worlds. As she stated to this contributor, "I feel I've been able to bridge the gap—both teaching and remaining active in applied research." In addition to instructing first-year medical students, Aguirre-Molina is deeply involved in a major study of the Latino population in Perth Amboy, New Jersey. She and researchers are seeking ways to reduce risk factors among Latino adolescents by studying teen pregnancy, school failure, and drug and alcohol use. Aguirre-Molina is hopeful that the program will have a long-term impact on the community. In addition, her scholarship has been noted. Between 1988 and 1991, Aguirre-Molina received a fellowship from the prestigious W.K. Kellogg Foundation. The funding allowed her to study the economies and public health systems in countries like Cuba, South Africa, and Scandinavia.

Throughout all her work, Aguirre-Molina has remained vocally active in her community efforts. In 1989 she appeared on *The Today Show* taking a stand against alcohol and tobacco industries deliberately marketing their products to Latinos and African Americans. Together with her husband, Carlos Molina, she has written a book entitled *Latino Health: A Growing Challenge for the United States.* It is due out in January of 1993.

When she reflects on her accomplishments, Aguirre-Molina sees her life's work as broadening her understanding of so many things. Her bumper sticker decree "Think globally, act locally" is reflected in her perception of common problems. As she stated, "I see that what happens in a little community doesn't just happen in isolation. What happens in the world community has a major impact on everyone's lives."

Sources:

Aguirre-Molina, Marilyn, telephone interview with Carol Hopkins, August 12, 1992, Detroit, Michigan.

—*Sketch by Carol Hopkins*

Allard, Lucille Roybal
See **Roybal-Allard, Lucille**

Alicia Alonso
(1921?-)
Ballerina

Alicia Alonso has been fascinating audiences with her performances for more than fifty years. The winner of the Golden Medal of the Gran Teatro Liceo de Barcelona, the Grand Prix de la Ville de Paris, the "Anna Pavlova" Prize of the Dance University of Paris, and the Cuban Women's Foundation's highest award, the "Ana Betancourt," Alonso is

Alicia Alonso

a classic artist of the dance. She broke cold war barriers to dance *Giselle,* and she even went on to perform the same piece when she was blind. She brought ballet to Cuba and Cubans to the ballet as she established the Ballet Nacional de Cuba and a national ballet school. She has tirelessly fought to dance and to give others the opportunity to dance. She has done all this because, as she explained in 1979 in the *Saturday Review,* "I live when I dance. I live not just for myself. When I'm on stage with my dancers, I live with them. It is life."

The ballerina was born Alicia Ernestina de la Caridad del Cobre Martínez on December 21 (the year of Alonso's birth has been variously listed as 1917, 1921, and 1922). The petite girl with black hair and eyes was raised in the city of her birth, Havana, Cuba, by her parents Antonio Martínez and Ernestina (Hoyo) Martínez. Antonio Martínez was a lieutenant in the Cuban army, and he housed his family in the privileged section of the city known as the Vedado. Ernestina Martínez cared for her four children at home; Alicia Alonso credits her mother with encouraging her talent. She recalled in *Dance* magazine, "Mama used to put me in a room with a phonograph and a scarf. That would keep me quiet for a few hours, doing what I imagined was dancing." Alonso's parents did more than leave the girl to develop her talent alone; they provided her with dancing lessons. At the Sociedad Pro-Arte Musical in the capital, the young girl received her first dancing lessons. By age ten Alonso had her public debut when she danced in a waltz in *Sleeping Beauty.*

The best place, at that time, for a gifted dancer to learn and to begin a career was New York City. Alonso and her husband, Fernando Alonso, moved to that city soon after their marriage on February 19, 1937. While Fernando Alonso, a dancer Alicia met at the Sociedad, worked with New York's Mordkin Ballet Company, Alicia Alonso trained at the School of American Ballet and with some of the best private teachers of classical ballet, including Alexandra Fedorova, Anatole Vilzak, and—later in London—Vera Volkova.

Oddly enough, Alonso did not begin her dance career as a ballerina. Her first performances on stage were as a tap dancer in comedies in the late 1930s. In the musicals *Great Lady* and *Stars in Your Eyes,* the latter starring Ethel Merman and Jimmy Durante, Alonso danced as a chorine. By 1939 Alonso was chosen to join the American Ballet Caravan as a soloist and soon thereafter she signed with Ballet Theatre, or the American Ballet Theatre, as a ballet dancer. Alonso's talent was recognized, and she was given solo parts, such as that of the Bird in *Peter and the Wolf* and that of Carlotta Grisi in *Le Pas de Quatre.*

Vision Problems Hinder Career

Alonso was well on her way to success when severe problems with her vision halted her career. The ballerina's retinas detached, and she was temporarily blinded. The three operations performed to restore her vision were very delicate, and Alonso was confined to bed for one year. She could not turn her head, laugh, or even cry. Despite her physical problems, Alonso did not lose her passion for the ballet. She began to envision herself dancing; by this technique, she learned the movements necessary to dance *Giselle.* When the heavy bandages were removed and Alonso found that she could see, she first had to learn how to walk again. It was not long before she was dancing the very role she had rehearsed over and over again as she lay blind in bed.

At the Metropolitan Opera House in 1943, Alonso danced *Giselle* in place of Alicia Markova, who was ill. The ballerina's dance with Anton Dolin was lauded by the *New York Times* as "one of the most distinguished performances of the season." Alonso would become famous for her unique interpretation of *Giselle.* Her grandson, Ivan Monreal, would say of her years later that, when dancing with her in *Giselle,* he did not think of Alonso as his grandmother. He told the *Saturday Review,* "I think of her as Giselle.... Because she *is* Giselle."

After three years of dancing *Giselle* for Ballet Theatre with Dolin, André Eglevsky, and Igor Youskevitch, Alonso was honored with the position of principal dancer. She danced in contemporary ballets such as *Undertow, Fall River Legend, Theme and Variations, Romeo and Juliet, Aleko, Circo de España, Gala Performance, Billy the Kid, Petrouchka, Lilac Garden, Graduation Ball, Waltz Academy, On Stage!, Caprichos,* as well as in standard classics such as *Swan Lake,*

La fille Mal Gardée, Aurora's Wedding, Les Sylphides, and *The Nutcracker.* Alicia Alonso's reputation as a supreme dancer was growing.

Returns to Cuba to Form Ballet Company

In 1948 Alonso decided to return to her native Cuba to found her own ballet with her husband Fernando Alonso serving as the general director and his brother working as artistic director. The Ballet Alicia Alonso, as the company was called, provided Ballet Theatre dancers with work and inspired potential dancers and ballet enthusiasts alike throughout South America.

Alonso was not content with this success. Too many of Ballet Alicia Alonso's dancers were non-Cubans. Alonso wanted to give the young people of her native land the opportunity to excel as dancers. In 1950, with the proceeds from her South American tour, a subsidy from the Cuban Ministry of Education, and donations from patrons of the ballet, Alonso was able to open the Alicia Alonso Academy of Ballet in Havana. Alonso had recruited some of the world's best dancers to become instructors at her school; these instructors taught their enthusiastic students well, and soon, the ranks of Ballet Alicia Alonso were swelling with young Cuban dancers.

Alonso's dreams of bringing ballet to Cuba had come true. Her company, once consisting of more non-Cubans than Cubans, was now a showcase for Cuban talent. The company staged *Swan Lake, Don Quixote, Aurora's Wedding, Coppélia, Songoro Cosongo, La Fille Mal Gardée,* and, of course, *Giselle.*

Unfortunately, by 1956, Alonso found it necessary to disband her ballet company as well as her school. Fulgencio Batista's regime, which had granted an annual subsidy to Alonso's company, had been decreasing the amount of the subsidy every year. Alonso's dancers, determined to keep dancing despite their low pay, were forced to keep other jobs as well; they were consequently exhausted when it was time to dance. When the government promised Alonso $500 every month if she promised, in return, not to make public the problems with the unsatisfactory subsidy, Alonso refused. She decided that it would be better to shut down operations altogether, and she left the country to dance elsewhere.

Embarks on Tour behind Iron Curtain

Alonso next worked as a guest artist with the Ballet Russe de Monte Carlo for the next three years, during which time she was honored with an invitation to dance in the Soviet Union. This highly unusual invitation demonstrated the respect Alonso received throughout the world. No Western dancer had ever before been invited to dance behind the communist iron curtain in the Soviet Union during the cold war. For two-and-a-half months in the winter of 1957, Alonso toured cities including Moscow, Riga, Leningrad (now St. Petersburg), and Kiev as she danced in *Giselle* and *Swan Lake.* The great ballerina danced as a guest with the Leningrad Opera Ballet and even appeared on television in Moscow. After this exciting tour, Alonso returned to the United States.

After the Cuban Revolution in 1959, the prima ballerina Alicia Alonso decided to leave the United States and return to her native country. With so many Cubans fleeing their own country to live in America, Alonso's decision was almost unheard of; many people thought that she was making a mistake, and they told her so. Despite their concerns, Alonso was determined to become a part of the revolution that would, supposedly, bring opportunity to all. As a one-time principal dancer with Ballet Theatre in New York, the first Western ballerina ever invited to dance in the Soviet Union, the winner of *Dance* magazine's award for 1958, and the founder of the Ballet de Cuba, Alonso believed that she could make important contributions to her people now that Fulgencio Batista's regime was out of power.

Provides Dance Training to Cubans

Fidel Castro, eager to enrich Cuba with cultural and educational organizations, provided Alonso with $200,000 to begin again. She reopened her school, and her new ballet company, the Ballet Nacional de Cuba, was given official status and guaranteed backing by the federal government. Soon, the Ballet could count more than 100 members, and a system of dance schools had been established on the island. As every child was promised a free education in Cuba, any student who was talented and serious enough could receive ballet instruction. After an audition, a child could pass to an elementary level school which emphasized training in the arts. The next stage was Cubanacán, a beautiful academy of the arts near Havana. The final stage before actually entering the Ballet Nacional was training at Alonso's school of the Ballet Nacional de Cuba in Havana. Alonso explained the system in the *Saturday Review* in 1979: "A rural child has an equal opportunity with the city child. If there is dance talent, we will find it; if the child has a desire to dance, we will give him every chance to develop his talent." As one example of the system, *Saturday Review* reminded its readers that Jorge Esquivel, who was Cuba's premier danseur and Alonso's usual partner despite his youth, was once a "forgotten orphan."

The government's enthusiasm for Alonso's work enabled her to bring ballet to the Cuban people in other ways as well. Choreographers were encouraged to create original works for the Ballet Nacional, and the best of these works were performed along with the classics such as *Coppélia, La Fille Mal Gardée, The Nutcracker, Les Sylphides,* and again, *Giselle.* Those who stood more to gain from watching than from creating also benefitted from the government's support of the Ballet. The company traveled to perform in front of all kinds of audiences—the poor and the rich alike enjoyed the ballet in parks, schools, and even factories.

The only audience for which the company was prohibited from performing was the one in the United States. The Ballet Nacional de Cuba went instead to many countries which were, at the time, communist. The People's Republic of China, Mongolia, North Vietnam, and countries in Central and South America were treated to performances. Alonso herself traveled elsewhere as a guest artist with many companies. These included the Grands Ballets Canadiens and the Royal Danish Ballet. Alonso danced *Giselle* at Montreal's Expo 67 and received standing ovations. Although Alonso had been a star of Ballet Theatre in the United States, she was not allowed to dance there for some years. When cold war tensions were peaking, the U.S. State Department would not allow Alonso to enter the country because of her support for the communist administration of Fidel Castro.

Tours North America

It was not until 1971 that the Ballet Nacional de Cuba could make a North American tour. Alonso danced a piece from *Swan Lake, Oedipus the King, La Dame aux Camélias, Carmen,* and *Giselle.* After viewing Alonso's performance in *Giselle,* a critic from the *New York Times* reported, "In some respects the physical command is not so certain as it was years ago, but [Alonso] is now a far better dancer than she was. The nuances and grace notes that distinguish great classic dancing from the superbly accomplished are now very evident, and her musical phrasing is as individual as ever."

The fact that Alonso performed so beautifully was a testament to her great skill and talent; the dancer was almost completely blind. She had to be led onto stage— once she was there, she found her position with the aid of bright spotlights. After her performance she had to follow a voice to get off the stage. Alonso did not want people to view her performance in light of this handicap, and she insisted that the dance should be enjoyed without external considerations. Her vision was restored by Barcelona surgeons in 1972, and she was healthy enough to perform by 1975. During the latter half of the 1970s she danced as a guest performer throughout the United States, and of course, in Cuba with the Ballet Nacional.

Besides touring with the Ballet Nacional and on her own, Alonso has been involved in many other activities during the years since 1958. She has choreographed works such as *Ensayo sinfónica, The Circus, Lidia,* and *The Little Thief.* Alonso trains students and decides which should advance to the next level of the training system. She has been a member of the World Council for Peace since 1974, and she has served as vice president of the National Union of Cuban Writers and Artists. Alonso also does her share of the work that is delegated to all Cubans—she toils, along with members of the company, in the coffee fields to fulfill her agricultural duties. Alonso also spends time with her family. By 1977, she had divorced Fernando Alonso and married a writer and lawyer named Pedro Simon. Her daughter, Laura Alonso, is a soloist with the Ballet Nacional; she trains her mother every morning, correcting the veteran dancer as if she were a beginner when she misses a step.

In 1990, Alicia Alonso, at the approximate age of seventy years, gave a performance of the pas de deux from *Swan Lake*, Act II, at the American Ballet Theatre's fiftieth anniversary celebration. While it was "an excruciatingly slow and rickety performance," as Laura Jacobs wrote in the *New Leader*, it was also passionate. According to Jacobs, Alonso's "'40s technique of soft turn-out and sachet-like port de bras gave the ballet a glow that was missing from every performance by ABT's young beauties in their spanking new *Swan Lake* last spring." Despite her age, the beauty of Alonso's dance will never fade. Dancing, to the ballerina, is in fact what revives her. She was quoted in the *Saturday Review:* "Dance works on the total being. By that I mean the mind and the spirit as well as the purely physical parts, and I think of dance as the *total* antibiotic for healing."

Sources:

Periodicals

Dance, December, 1953; June, 1980, p. 117; November, 1981, p. 110; April, 1982, p. 118; June, 1982, pp. 74+; October, 1982, pp. 35+; January, 1983, pp. 97+; January, 1985, p. 72; August, 1987, p. 58; September, 1989, pp. 68-69; August, 1990, pp. 32+.
New Leader, March 5, 1990, pp. 21-22.
New York Times, November 3, 1943; June 21, 1971.
Saturday Review, January 6, 1979.
World Press Review, April, 1982, p. 62.

—Sketch by Ronie-Richele Garcia-Johnson

Maria Conchita Alonso
(1957-)
Actress, singer

Entertainer Maria Conchita Alonso has accomplished the formidable task of balancing a thriving career as a Hollywood film actress with success in Spanish pop music. In addition to making records and movies, she has worked as a magazine model and a television actress and has created her own film production company. For her contributions to both the entertainment industry and to the

Maria Conchita Alonso

Hispanic community, Alonso was named Hispanic Woman of the Year by the Mexican American Opportunity Foundation in 1990, and in 1992 she was named Hispanic Entertainer of the Year for the Cinco de Mayo celebration.

Alonso was born in Cuba to Jose and Conchita Alonso. The Alonso family, which includes older brothers Ricardo and Roberto (whom Alonso refers to as her "biggest fans"), emigrated to Venezuela when the actress was still a child. When she was growing up, Alonso's parents sent her to schools in France and Switzerland, and although she loved her years in Europe, she remains proud of both her Cuban blood and her Venezuelan upbringing.

Alonso's artistic calling came early. By age fourteen, she was modeling and doing television commercials. In 1971 Alonso was named "Miss Teenager of the World" and in 1975 she represented Venezuela in the "Miss World" Pageant. In an interview with the *Los Angeles Times,* she recalled her stay in London for the Miss World Pageant: "I love food. I love to eat. Because I was nervous about the contest, I ate and ate. So much so that when it came to the night of the contest, I couldn't even get into the dress I'd bought." She still walked away from the pageant as sixth runner-up. Her parents provided a balanced perspective on her success as a beauty contestant that helped Alonso in later endeavors. "They kept my feet firmly on the ground," she recalled in an interview. They helped her realize that "it's not looks, it's what is inside you, it's what you do with your life that's important."

Alonso returned to Venezuela and went on to star in ten Spanish-language television "soap operas" (shown throughout Latin America and the United States) while also carving a niche for herself as one of the hottest singers in Spanish pop-rock music. Although she quickly became a favorite with Hispanic audiences, she opted to expand her career and try her luck in the United States. In 1982 she moved from Caracas to Los Angeles. Her motto: "Dare to try new things." Her goal: the movies.

Move to Hollywood Pays Off

The gamble paid off when she was cast as Robin Williams's Italian immigrant girlfriend in the film *Moscow on the Hudson.* Her "simpatica" effervescence caught the eye of Hollywood filmmakers and landed her roles in nine more films, including *Colors,* starring Robert Duvall and Sean Penn, and *Running Man,* in which Alonso played opposite Arnold Schwarzenegger. Other movies featuring Alonso were *Extreme Prejudice, Touch and Go, Blood Ties, A Fine Mess, Vampire's Kiss, Predator II,* and *McBain.* Although not box-office blockbusters, the films established her as a capable actress in both comedy and drama who could hold her own against Hollywood's top leading men.

Alonso looks to Arnold Schwarzenegger (her co-star in *Running Man*) as a type of role model, a fellow foreigner in the American film industry. She considers him "number one in the world, yet he is a foreigner. . . . And with an accent heavier than mine. And with a name more difficult to pronounce than mine!" In a more serious tone she added, "I would like to reach the place Arnold's at, or even further. . . . I don't think he'll ever be nominated for an Academy Award because the type of movies he makes are not for that. I do want to be nominated for an 'Oscar.' In this aspect, I'd like to surpass him."

Alonso has worked as a television actress as well. In 1989 she starred in the short-lived NBC-TV series *One of the Boys,* which told the experiences of a young Hispanic girl newly arrived in the United States. When asked by this contributor if she enjoyed the experience, Alonso recalled: "We got ratings, but NBC didn't think it would be a long-running hit and they canceled it. I was happy because I don't want to do that type of television yet. Perhaps when I'm older, but for now I want to do my movies, my concert tours."

The entertainer's sparkling personality and witty repartee make her a favorite guest on the television talk-show circuit, where she is frequently asked about the difficulty of working in Hollywood as a Hispanic. She related to *Hispanic* magazine that when television host David Letterman once inquired if she minded playing Hispanic roles, Alonso replied, "Why not? That's what I am. The important thing is that they be good parts." When this contributor asked her if it was difficult for foreigners to find work in Hollywood, she pointed out, "It's difficult for any foreigner, but it's also difficult for someone from here. My best friend is an American actress and she works less than I. It's hard for

anybody, but even more so for a foreigner." Alonso does not believe being a Hispanic makes the challenge more difficult: "I always try not to say 'for a Hispanic' because I don't believe being Hispanic has anything to do with the fact we don't get much work. It has to do with being a foreigner, to speak with a different accent, to have a different 'look.'" Reflecting on the particular obstacles for a woman in acting, Alonso stated, "There are fewer roles for women than for men. And there are two or three actresses who usually corner the female role in movies."

Musical Talent Wins Grammy Nominations

As a singer and live performer, Alonso's musical career has kept pace with her film work. In 1988 she was nominated for Best Latin Pop Performance at the Grammy awards for the single *Otra Mentira Mas.* This was her second Grammy nomination. In 1985, she was short-listed for Best Latin Artist for her self-titled album *Maria Conchita.* The record was certified platinum internationally and her previous four albums, including *O Ella o Yo,* went gold. Another album, *Hazme Sentir,* coproduced by Alonso and K.C. Porter, garnered gold records in several countries after the release of only two singles. Alonso looks forward to recording in English, but has turned down offers from two separate labels because the companies were interested in a type of music that is different from what she likes to do. She explained to this contributor: "I believe it is preferable to start off doing what one likes; it's more difficult to change to what you want later. So I haven't yet signed a contract. I'm waiting to do what I want and to be in a position in which the contract be a good one instead of simply being 'just a contract.' I'll keep at it until it does happen."

In 1991 Alonso signed a 52-show contract with Channel 13, the Mexican government's commercial TV channel, to star in *Picante!* (which means "spicy"), a weekly prime time variety program. The show, coproduced by Alonso, was conceived and shaped to showcase her many talents—singing, dancing, acting, comedy, and interviewing guest stars. Because it coincided with the series' debut, and because she "felt like it," she appeared in the December 1991 issue of *Playboy, Mexico* which, according to Alonso, ran a set of "sexy but not nude" photos. Alonso had rejected prior offers from *Playboy, USA* because "they show more." In addition to her television work, Alonso created her first video in 1992. The dance and fitness program was released in Spanish as *Bailalo Caliente!* and in English as *Dance it Up!* She is currently working on an autobiographical video entitled *Asi Soy Yo.*

Reflecting on the unique challenges of maintaining two careers, Alonso admitted, "I'm very dispersed. My dedication is placed in many things." She also feels she's sacrificed some of her Hispanic career by doing American movies: "Yes, I've lost some ground. My name in the Hispanic market has maintained itself, but I've lost in the sense that other artists in the Latin market, for instance singers, that's all they do. And they spend 24 hours a day,

12 months a year doing that—their record, their concert tour, their promotions. They dedicate their mind, their energy, everything exclusively towards that goal. Same thing with Hispanic soap opera actors. They do one soap here, another there. That's the only thing they do. Instead I do too many things. . . . So, of course, I've probably lost some following. . . . In my movies, in my television program, in records, in modeling, in other side businesses I have."

Managing careers on two continents and in two diverse fields requires a discipline that Alonso explained to this contributor: "Patience and perseverance, and believing in yourself." And she offered this insight: "It important not to have a big ego. No Hispanic artist is likely to be valued or respected in the American market as they are valued and respected in the Hispanic market. That's why the majority of Latin stars don't do anything in the U.S. Because they can be a big star elsewhere, but be a nobody here. An artist's ego is very big and they can't take the rejection. I think you need a very tranquil ego, very controlled. You also have to be a hard worker."

Alonso, who is single, admitted to this contributor that she has sacrificed much of her private life in order to maintain multiple careers "because if you're not working on one thing, you're working on another." She does spend some time on avocational interests. An animal lover, Alonso has her two pet Yorkshire terriers travel with her whenever possible. She favors legislation protecting the rights of animals and several years ago changed her eating habits to become a semi-vegetarian. She also spends time at her homes in Los Angeles, Caracas, Miami, and Mexico City.

Speaking Out Brings Risks and Rewards

Both the Hispanic entertainment community and Hollywood insiders have labeled the multi-faceted artist a true fighter. Frank and outspoken, her effervescent free-spirited image tends to belie the intensity of her mission. This contributor asked Alonso if she ever fears that being vocal could bring negative repercussions to her career. As always, Alonso replied honestly: "I'd probably be very unhappy were I to shut my mouth. I never think of what could happen. If I considered the consequences, I maybe wouldn't do many things. But instead, I prefer simply to behave as I feel at that moment and forget about what could happen. And then, when things do happen, I think 'I blew it!'"

Alonso does concede that her maverick spirit has lost her some movie roles. She explained in an interview: "I find that my personality—because I am a bit rebellious, very spontaneous, very open—many producers don't see beyond that. I've had problems in getting certain roles because they don't realize that my personality can be the way it is, but as soon as I begin to act I can become whatever I want to be. It doesn't matter how I am in my daily life; what I can do as an artist is something else. When I act, I can become whatever my role requires."

But her spunk and ingenuity have also won her roles. Auditioning for the comedy movie *A Fine Mess*, where she was to play the Chilean wife of a gangster, Alonso's natural temperament caught producer Blake Edwards' attention. She drove up to the audition in a classic Jaguar convertible and, just as it rolled to a stop, the car burst into plumes of steam and smoke. Alonso leaped out, looked under the hood and, enveloped in clouds of smoke and steam, flung her arms up in frustration. Edwards found this so funny that he gave her the role on the spot.

Explaining her apparently boundless bravado, Alonso expressed to *Time* magazine that "we Latins have this fire inside us, in our hearts, in our skin, the flesh. You just go for it." She does not worry that her Spanish-flavored English may limit her roles. "Who cares? I know plenty of actresses who speak without accents. They're not working. I am."

Alonso's professional choices are not based on money but on personal instinct. Often one path is pitted against another. But she insists "that's the way it is and I don't want to change." She is constantly becoming involved in new projects, even in the business end of "show-business." A savvy entrepreneur, Alonso has formed a production company to develop film and television properties, in English and Spanish.

Alonso acknowledged that an important part of her success is that "I've always been 'Latina,' but with a very European mentality. My mother was an adventurer, very daring. She did not become a performer because her family wouldn't let her. My father had also been quite an adventurer and he told me to launch myself; that while one has health, energy and strength, one can conquer the world. The family's support is the most important."

And what will happen the day Maria Conchita Alonso accomplishes all her goals? With her customary honesty Alonso reflected for a moment and told this contributor: "Then I'll semi-retire. There's a conflict within me. I want to work in this business because I adore my career. But I also suffer a lot. There are many lonely and sad moments. So, even though I don't think I'll completely give up my career, I will slow down in order to have a life with my man, or for whatever other reasons." Maria Conchita Alonso—beauty queen, pop-rock singer, television star, film actress, business executive—declared to this contributor that she prefers to be known "as an all-around entertainer. As someone who can do it all. An artist."

Sources:

Periodicals

Hispanic, May 1989, pp. 14-16.
Hispanic Business, July 1992, p. 22.
Los Angeles Times, August 9, 1986.
Time, July 11, 1988, p. 72.

Other

Alonso, Maria Conchita, interviews with Elena Kellner, February 1992 and May 1992.

—*Sketch by Elena Kellner*

Linda Alvarado
(1951-)
Business owner

Linda Alvarado doesn't believe in following any traditional paths. As the only girl in a family of six children, she was accustomed to "hanging out with the guys." Years later, she is still doing so as president of the Denver-based general contracting firm Alvarado Construction, Inc., and part owner of the Colorado Rockies major league baseball team. In fields usually dominated by white males, Alvarado is one of only a few female executives.

Born Linda B. Martinez, she grew up in Albuquerque, New Mexico. Her father worked for the Atomic Energy Commission, and her mother was a homemaker. "It was a very positive environment," Alvarado told Carol Hopkins in a telephone interview. "Even though I was the only girl, the expectation for me was no different." She credits her parents with giving her "huge doses" of confidence and self-esteem and encouraging her to excel both in the classroom and in athletics. Active in both high school and college sports, she lettered in girls' basketball, volleyball, and softball and also ran track.

Launches Career in Construction Industry

Alvarado says she entered the construction industry "by default." After graduating from California's Pomona College, she was briefly employed there as a lab assistant in the botany department, where she "overwatered and drowned all the plants." She then took a job with a southern California development company as a contract administrator and learned all phases of the construction business, from preparing bids to assembling a contract. When interest rates skyrocketed, her employer decided to form a construction management group to speed up the process of getting new projects under way. Alvarado was transferred to the management group, and to her surprise, she liked it. She then went back to school and took classes in estimating, blueprint, and critical path method scheduling to expand her knowledge of the business.

In 1974, she and a partner established the Martinez Alvarado Construction Management Corporation. Within two years, she bought out her partner and soon became a general contractor. Now known as Alvarado Construction, Inc., the company boasts a list of accomplishments that includes dozens of projects such as commercial buildings, bus facilities, a convention center, and airport hangars. "I love what I do," enthuses Alvarado. She especially enjoys following a project from concept to construction. "There is enormous satisfaction knowing that one started from ground zero and has a terrific final project, something of great permanence and beauty."

Joins Ranks of Major League Baseball Team Owners

Outside the world of construction, Alvarado is a partner in the Colorado Rockies, a major league baseball team set to begin play in the 1993 season. When asked why she chose to become involved in baseball, she says she wanted to show that women can get involved in nontraditional fields. "I am entering it with money that I earned," she explains. "That is important, that we [women] participate in big business." Alvarado was also drawn to baseball because she views it as one sport where Hispanics have enjoyed tremendous success. "There are so many role models in [baseball]," she says. "I think [having a Hispanic team owner] brings the sport full circle."

As Alvarado reflects on her career, she believes her greatest challenge has been changing people's attitudes. "There is a perception that you had to be 6'2", burly, and have muscles like Popeye's to be a contractor," she notes. "These are myths. [It has sometimes been a problem] finding men who would forget the myths, men who know that this is a business that requires brains, not just brawn." She admits there are still "pockets of resistance," but they are gradually disappearing.

In the future, Alvarado envisions becoming more involved with development. "Our core business will always be construction. We're just finding new applications like design-built projects or turnkey projects. We're positioning ourselves so that if the construction industry changes and financing shrinks, we're not going to be inflexible."

Alvarado is a member of several Fortune 500 corporate boards. When she has had occasion to resign from a directorship, she recommends another Hispanic or a woman to replace her. "I'm not there because I'm good," she explains. "I'm there because someone ahead of me was great."

Sources:

Periodicals

Minority Business Entrepreneur, July/August, 1989.

Other

Alvarado, Linda, telephone interview with Carol Hopkins,
    September 15, 1992.

—*Sketch by Carol Hopkins*

Yolanda H. Alvarado
(1943-)
Journalist

Journalist Yolanda H. Alvarado has taken an active role
in local and world-wide efforts to improve conditions for
minorities, women, and the mentally ill. Prompted by her
dissatisfaction with the way her mentally ill daughter was
treated by experts in the field, she coordinated, published,
promoted, and distributed a booklet, *Mental Illness: A
Family Resource Guide,* that was used by mental health
agencies throughout Michigan. She has also founded a
Hispanic women's group, launched community outreach
programs to expose editors and reporters to concerns
among minorities, and rallied for women's issues at a
global summit of world leaders.

Alvarado was born September 27, 1943, to Maria Luisa
Vera and Raymond G. Hernandez. Both of her parents
were raised in Texas and struggled as migrant farm workers. Her father died while serving in Germany in World
War II when Alvarado was about six months old. She told
this interviewer that growing up poor and one of nine
children in Austin, Texas, was a good education. "I think I
always felt that I had to do my best, and I believe that having
grown up poor is what gave me the motivation to work to
make life better for other people," Alvarado reflected. "I
think poverty is a great teacher as far as sensitivity for other
people."

Some of the children Alvarado grew up with were not so
kind. Alvarado felt the painful sting of racism when she
attended school one year in Galveston, Texas. "And that is
another reason I became interested in minority causes,"
she stated in the interview. "The popular kids wouldn't talk
to me." She often socialized with the handicapped students
and the experience prepared her for much of her later
work.

Regardless of the struggles, Alvarado was always a high
achiever in school. When she was nineteen she finished in
the top five in a statewide secretarial test given in Texas. At
that point in her life she did not realize the significance of
the achievement, because she always expected to do well.
She told this interviewer that she "didn't know how to

Yolanda H. Alvarado

measure success, because success for me was getting where
you wanted to go."

Her marriages were not as successful, and after two
divorces, Alvarado was faced with the challenge of supporting herself and her three children. Alvarado told this
interviewer that she married her first two husbands because she "wasn't able to recognize what a supportive man
was, a man who lets you be who you are. I was single for
eighteen years [from 1974 to 1992]. In my first marriage
my husband thought he could date and in my second
marriage my husband was an alcoholic." While she struggled with her marital problems, Alvarado's children, Rosario,
Yul, and Joseph Omar always remained her top priority.
An article in Michigan's *Lansing State Journal* described the
importance she placed on her children: "Yolanda counts as
one of her proudest accomplishments raising three children as a single parent on the salary she earned as a
reporter."

Internship Opens Door to Journalism Career

Her career as a journalist was born out of necessity.
Alvarado told this interviewer that "[I] originally headed
out to be a secretary and completed business college. . . . I
got involved in journalism because I needed a way to
support three children." In a *Lansing State Journal* column,
"The Onlooker," Alvarado said: "After 18 months working
in Holland [Michigan] as a secretary for nine biology
professors at Hope College, I realized I would never be

able to support three children and myself on secretarial pay and child support." She sought financial aid, went on welfare, and became a full-time student at Hope. A year later, she began a job with a bilingual newspaper in Lansing and pulled herself off of welfare. But her meager nine thousand dollar annual pay was not sufficient. She knew she would have to make a change, and in 1974 she applied for an internship with the *Lansing State Journal.*

Alvarado reached a turning point in her life when she landed the internship position. But after three months on the job she realized she needed to go back to college if she was going to support her children, a goal that had been made more difficult when her ex-husband stopped sending child support payments. Alvarado submitted a letter of resignation to the newspaper. A few days later, however, her managers offered Alvarado a full-time job at the beginner's rate of reporter's pay. She worked as a reporter at the *Lansing State Journal* from 1974 to 1987, and she became a copy editor in 1987. During this time she also served as secretary, vice president, and president of the National Newspaper Guild in Michigan and worked toward her bachelor of arts degree at Spring Arbor College, where she graduated in 1988.

Alvarado realized that the internship had opened doors for her and she wanted to give other minorities a similar opportunity. In a *Lansing State Journal* column published in August 1986, Alvarado said that she considered internships "an excellent way for newspapers to acquire Hispanic reporters, still a rarity in Michigan. We probably number less than a half dozen." In an effort to raise these figures, Alvarado coordinated the Michigan State University Hispanic Journalism program. She also advocated hiring minorities in a 1989 article, "Copy Editor Seeks Diversity in the Newsroom," in the *Gannetteer,* a magazine distributed to employees of Gannett Services newspapers. "Maybe I helped in the early stages of Gannett thinking that [diversity in the newsroom] might be something that they would like," she told this interviewer. At the *Lansing State Journal* she also coordinated an outreach program where editors and reporters attended community meetings to learn about the concerns of minority groups.

This kind of commitment to social change was appreciated by many organizations who presented her with a number of awards. In 1985 Alvarado received the Diana Award in Communications from the YMCA. She also attended the National Hispana Leadership Institute, won the 1986 National Newspaper Guild Distinguished Service Award, and was named one of the top 100 Hispanic Women in Communications in 1987 by *Hispanic.* In 1990 Alvarado was honored with a Life Achievement Award by Hispanic Women in the Network.

Hispanic and Women's Rights Advocate Urges Change

Committed to making life better for Hispanics, Alvarado, a second generation Mexican American who speaks fluent Spanish, worked as vice president of the Michigan Coalition of Concerned Hispanics from 1987 to 1991 and developed a Hispanic agenda for Michigan. She concentrated on education, health, and migrant farm worker's issues. "I felt that being able to focus on specific concerns to address is important for Hispanics," Alvarado said to this interviewer. "Hispanics are oftentimes an invisible minority. Often people think of minorities as black versus white and they forget there are other minorities like Hispanic, Asian Americans, and Native Americans." She expressed her opinions about discrimination in a *Lansing State Journal* column: "It's disheartening to listen to the terms 'reverse discrimination' and 'quotas' being used as ammunition against career, job, and educational opportunities for minorities. . . . Decision-making bodies—public and private—should strive to reflect the population in the geographic area they serve."

Using her pen as her instrument for reform, Alvarado addressed concerns of both Hispanics and women in a 1989 *Vista* article, "Cracking the Old Boys Network." Research for the magazine article involved interviewing women throughout the country. The reporter asked her subjects how they perceived the ability of Hispanic women to overcome the prejudices perpetuated against them by men in positions of authority in the workplace. The suggestions were varied and included one idea from a woman who thought that learning to play golf would help. Alvarado told this interviewer that although strides have been made in recognizing discrimination in the workplace, Hispanic women continue to face challenges. "There were so many Hispanic women that were pigeon-holed into multicultural roles as opposed to other areas of management that would not involve doing community outreach or marketing to minorities," Alvarado told this interviewer. "That's great that companies are hiring people to do that. But, on the other hand it shows me that they're not diversified in having Hispanic women do a job that they would expect a non-minority woman to do."

Alvarado stated in her interview that she believes the various issues concerning women and Hispanics often overlap. "I feel the women's movement is a great training ground for Hispanic women in organizing and I also feel that a lot of women's concerns are Hispanic concerns." She addressed those issues from 1976 through 1980 while she served as president of the Mujeres Unidas de Michigan. Alvarado described the group to this interviewer as "the Hispanic women's version of the women's movement." Alvarado has also served on the board of directors for Michigan Protection and Advocacy and worked on the Michigan Civil Service Comparable Worth Task Force. The task force looked at the disparity of pay between the female dominated and male dominated jobs in civil services. "We came up with a strategy to equalize the pay and also to create a greater mix so that you don't have areas that are male dominated or female dominated as much," Alvarado told this interviewer.

Her work with women's groups continued when she was appointed by Governor William G. Milliken to the Michigan Women's Commission. Alvarado edited the organization's newsletter, *Michigan Women.* She also contributed to the 1980 Michigan Women's agenda platform as well as the agenda for the Midwest Hispanic Coalition, a tool for political action and community work. And she marked a milestone in Hispanic leadership when she founded and coordinated the Hispanic Women in the Network of Michigan in 1988. The group coordinated six state conferences for Hispanic women and offered leadership workshops.

Reform Activities Involve Local and Global Communities

Alvarado also wanted to initiate change when she became involved with the Michigan Independent Living Council, a group that identified concerns among people with handicaps and promoted strategies for reforms. Her diligence was acknowledged with the Sondra Berlin Award from the Michigan Handicappers Association in 1989. She saw another need for reform when she joined the Alliance for the Mentally Ill in Michigan. Once again, Alvarado took a painful personal experience and reached out to help others. "I have a daughter who has manic depression and I have been involved in the mental health arena quite a bit because of her illness," she told this interviewer. In addition to developing the booklet *Mental Illness: A Family Resource Guide,* Alvarado established a training program to help law enforcement personnel deal with the mentally ill.

Alvarado has found time for international issues as well. In 1990 she worked with the Women for Meaningful Summits, a coalition of women's groups, that drafted a report highlighting women's issues for a meeting between U.S. President George Bush and Soviet leader Mikhail Gorbachev. Alvarado, who chaired the children's committee on abuse and violence, was appointed a delegate to develop documents to be reviewed by Bush and Gorbachev. She wrote a column for the *Lansing State Journal* in June, 1991, that highlighted her two-week trip to the Soviet Union as a member of the ethnic women's delegation that met with the official Women's Soviet Committee in Moscow. "The words that best describe my two weeks in the Soviet Union are bittersweet and mind-boggling," she declared in the column. "I had envisioned cities void of aesthetic beauty. But walking into Red Square felt as though God breathed life into a page from a fairy-tale book. . . . I had believed that under socialism, heads of households all have jobs and own an equal amount of property. But beggars outside our hotels disproved the theory."

Alvarado has also had a hand in cultivating aesthetic beauty back home in Michigan. "One of the things that I used to be involved in was coordinating arts projects," she told this interviewer. "And the one that I was most proud of was coordinating Lansing's first electric parade on the Grand River." As a little girl she used to go to the Colorado River and watch the parade of lighted and decorated boats.

In the 1970s, when Lansing began to develop a river front walk, Alvarado decided she would recreate her memories. "I linked up with another person who was willing to coordinate a festival with the parade," she said in the interview. Alvarado oversaw all the details, including research on how many lights it takes for a boat float, what height boats needed to be in order to pass under the bridges, and what kind of security patrols and parking accommodations would be needed. She coordinated everything from start to finish and even recruited people to build floats. "I had to make everything sound as though it was a realistic thing," she said in the interview.

Alvarado is enthusiastic about all her work, whether it is local or global; for her it holds the same amount of significance. "I feel that I've learned to create social change and that it's great fun to do," she told this interviewer. "I feel I have skills to lead groups and identify issues and concerns. I enjoy playing the leadership role." When she was asked how she found time to work on so many different projects, Alvarado told this interviewer, she sets "a beginning time and when I feel I've accomplished what I set out to do I begin something new. I generally can accomplish several efforts at one time and it comes from community organizing in the early seventies. With experience it becomes quicker and you become more efficient. And also you become able to create more social change."

Sources:

Periodicals

Lansing State Journal, August 22, 1986; September 5, 1987; October 25, 1988; June 30, 1991; July 24, 1991.

Other

Alvarado, Yolanda H., telephone interview with D. D. Andreassi, August, 1992.

—*Sketch by D. D. Andreassi*

Julia Alvarez
Novelist, poet

In her poetry and prose, Julia Alvarez has expressed her feelings about her immigration to the United States. Although she was born in New York City, she spent her early years in the Dominican Republic. After her family's immigration to America, she and her sisters struggled to find a place for themselves in their new world. Alvarez has used her dual experience as a starting point for the exploration

Julia Alvarez

of culture through writing. Her most notable work, *How the Garcia Girls Lost Their Accents,* fictionally discusses her life in the two countries and the hardships her family faced as immigrants. The culmination of many years of effort, the novel is a collection of memoirs that features numerous memorable characters. The fifteen stories which make up the novel offer entertaining insights to a wide variety of potential readers that includes both Hispanics and non-Hispanics. Hispanic women especially may find that Alvarez's work voices many of their own concerns. The importance of this voice has been recognized, and *How the Garcia Girls Lost Their Accents* has received critical acclaim.

Background in the Dominican Republic

Reminiscing on her youth in an article in *American Scholar,* Alvarez wrote, "Although I was raised in the Dominican Republic by Dominican parents in an extended Dominican family, mine was an American childhood." As she described her family background, her father's once-wealthy family had supported the wrong side during the revolution while her mother's parents benefitted from their support of the people in power. They lived on her mother's family property. Life in the compound was somewhat communal; Alvarez and her sisters were brought up along with their cousins and supervised by her mother, maids, and many aunts. While this might have been an ideal arrangement, Alvarez's grandmother made living there difficult for their mother and father. The grandmother would not let her daughter forget that she had married a

poor man, nor did she accept reminders that he was only poor because of his family's loyalties during the revolution.

Although her own family was not as well off as their relatives, Alvarez did not feel inferior. None of the cousins were allowed to forget that she was born in America. Her father, a doctor who ran the nearby hospital, had met her mother while she was attending school in America. While such extravagances as shopping trips to America were beyond their financial means, Alvarez's family was highly influenced by American attitudes and goods. If her mother could not buy her daughters American clothing, she made sure that Alvarez and her sisters were as fashionable as their cousins. The children ate American food, attended the American school, and for a special treat, ate ice cream from the American ice cream parlor. American cars were bought at the American dealership, shopping was done at the American's store, and American appliances were flaunted in the compound. The entire extended family was obsessed with America; to the children, it was a fantasy land.

As Alvarez acknowledges in her article in *American Scholar,* her family's association with the United States may have saved her father's life. The members of her mother's family were respected because of their ties with America. Alvarez's uncles had attended Ivy League Colleges, and her grandfather was a cultural attaché to the United Nations. The dictator of the Dominican Republic, Rafael Leonidas Trujillo Molina, could not victimize a family with such strong American ties. He would not destroy them for their money, and he hesitated to struggle with them for political reasons. When Alvarez's father secretly joined the forces attempting to oust Trujillo, the police set up surveillance of the compound. It was rumored that, respected family or not, her father was soon to be apprehended. Just before the police were to capture her father in 1960, an American agent, known to Alvarez as Tio Vic, warned him; he ushered the family into an airplane and out of the country. Describing the scene as their plane landed in America in *American Scholar,* Alvarez wrote, "All my childhood I had dressed like an American, eaten American foods, and befriended American children. I had gone to an American school and spent most of the day speaking and reading English. At night, my prayers were full of blond hair and blue eyes and snow. . . . All my childhood I had longed for this moment of arrival. And here I was, an American girl, coming home at last."

American Experiences

Alvarez's homecoming was not what she had expected it to be. Although she was thrilled to be back in America, she would soon face homesickness, alienation, and prejudice. She missed her cousins, her family's large home in the compound, and the respect her family name demanded. Alvarez, her parents, and her sisters squeezed themselves and their possessions into a tiny apartment. As she related to *Brújula <> Compass,* the experience was like a crash: "The feeling of loss caused a radical change in me. It made me an introverted little girl." Alvarez became an avid reader, immersing herself in books and, eventually, writing.

Alvarez went on to college. She earned undergraduate and graduate degrees in literature and writing and became an English professor at Middlebury College in Vermont. She received grants from the National Endowment for the Arts and The Ingram Merrill Foundation in addition to a PEN Oakland/Josephine Miles Award for excellence in multicultural literature. She published several collections of poetry including *Homecoming,* which appeared in 1984, and by 1987 she was working on a collection of stories. When Alvarez published *How the Garcia Girls Lost Their Accents* in 1991, the 290-page novel received considerable attention. The past decade had seen a surge of ethnic novels, and *Garcia Girls* came to be known as an exemplary example of the genre.

How the Garcia Girls Lost Their Accents

Rather than a straight narrative, *How the Garcia Girls Lost Their Accents* is a reverse-chronological-order series of 15 interwoven stories chronicling four sisters and their parents. A comparison with Alvarez's article in *American Scholar* suggests that these stories are autobiographical; like her family, the Garcia family is Dominican and displaced in America. Like Alvarez and her sisters, the Garcia girls struggle to adapt to their new environment and assimilate themselves into the American culture.

The first group of stories is dated "1989-1972." Thus, the novel's first story seems to be its ending. Entitled "Antojos," which is Spanish for "cravings," this story is a memory of one of the sisters, Yolanda, and her return to the Dominican as an adult. Yolanda (whose story ends the novel and who acts as Alvarez's alter ego) has secretly decided to make her home here, having found life in the United States unfulfilling. When she ignores the warnings of her wealthy relatives and drives into the country for the guava fruit she has been craving, she faces disappointment. She is regarded as an American despite her native roots, and although she finds her guavas, her romantic journey is marred by her feelings as an outsider. Alvarez ends this story ambiguously—similar to the rest of the stories. The attempts of Yolanda and her sisters to lead successful lives in the United States are presented more as memory fragments than stories with definite beginnings and endings.

The next story focuses on Sofia, the youngest of the girls. At this point, however, the four girls are women, with husbands and careers. The details of Sofia's break with her father over her decision to take a lover before marriage are presented, and the events at a birthday party she prepared for her father are recounted. Sofia cannot be totally forgiven, nor can she ever return to the Dominican Republic; in the process of becoming an American girl of the 1960s, she has gone beyond the moral limits imposed by her father, who personifies life in the old world.

The third story relates some background information as it reveals a mother's perceptions of her four girls. During a family gathering, Mamita tells her favorite story about each of the girls, and the reader learns that Sandi spent time in a mental institution after almost starving herself to death. The fourth story about Yolanda reveals that she too had a mental breakdown of her own after a failed relationship, and in the next story she becomes the narrator. In "The Rudy Elmenhurst Story," Yolanda's tale of her reluctance to sleep with the dashing young man she loved because of his casual approach to the matter explains her ensuing trouble with men as well as her problems assimilating into American youth culture: "Catholic or not, I still thought it a sin for a guy to just barge in five years later with a bottle of expensive wine and assume you'd drink out of his hand. A guy who had ditched me, who had haunted my sexual awakening with a nightmare of self-doubt. For a moment as I watched him get in his car and drive away, I felt a flash of that old self-doubt."

The memories in the second section of the novel recall the years from 1960 to 1970. The girls are younger, and they are experiencing their first years as immigrants. Attempts they made to reconcile themselves to their new culture are challenged by their parents, who want their children to "mix with the 'right kind' of Americans," and the girls are threatened with having to spend time on the Island, which they have come to dread. In this section, the girls save their sister from a macho cousin's imposition, a pervert exposes himself to Carla, and Yolanda sees snow for the first time and thinks it is fall-out from a nuclear bomb.

The final story in this section, "Floor Show," focuses on Sandi's perception of events as the family spends a scandalous evening with an American doctor and his drunkenly indiscreet wife in a Spanish restaurant. Sandi is shocked and upset when this woman kisses her father and later dances with the flamenco dancers that the young girl so admires. Cautioned by her mother to behave at the important dinner, Sandi does as she is told and stays quiet until she is offered a flamenco doll by the American woman, who seems to understand her desire for it. "Sandi was not going to miss her chance. This woman had kissed her father. This woman had ruined the act of the beautiful dancers. The way Sandi saw it, this woman owed her something." The woman gave Sandi something more than the doll; her smile "intimated the things Sandi was just beginning to learn, things that the dancers knew all about, which was why they danced with such vehemence, such passion."

In the third and final section, "1960-1956," America is still a dream—the family is still on the island. The first story is divided into two parts and recalls the family's traumatic encounter with the *guardia,* or secret police, and their subsequent flight from their home. From that moment on, the tales regress to the girls' early memories of life in the huge de la Torre compound. Yolanda tells of the presents her grandmother brought the children from America and an ensuing encounter with her cousin, Sandi recalls her art lessons and the fright she had at the instructor's home, Carla remembers the mechanical bank her father brought her from F.A.O. Schwarz in New York and the maid who desperately wanted it.

Finally, Yolanda concludes the novel with one of her earliest memories—she stole a kitten (which she named Schwarz, after the famous toy store) from its mother and then abandoned it, even though she had been warned by a strange hunter: "To take it away would be a violation of its natural right to live." The mother cat haunted the girl until she left the island, and, as Yolanda confides in her narration, "There are still times I wake up at three o'clock in the morning and peer into the darkness. At that hour and in that loneliness, I hear her, a black furred thing lurking in the corners of my life, her magenta mouth opening, wailing over some violation that lies at the center of my art."

The praise Alvarez received for her first novel outweighed the criticism that a new novelist often encounters. The *New York Times Book Review* found that Alvarez "beautifully captured the threshold experience of the new immigrant, where the past is not yet a memory and the future remains an anxious dream." *Hispanic*'s critic wrote, "Well-crafted, although at times overly sentimental, these stories provide a glimpse into the making of another American family with a Hispanic surname." And the *Library Journal* reported, "Alvarez is a gifted, evocative storyteller of promise."

In early 1992, Alvarez told *Brújula <> Compass* that while she had a few ideas for her next work and thought she may write another novel, she was not certain what she would write. "That is the most passionate part of the process of writing. It is only possible to discover it as it is done; upon writing the ideas . . . a direction is found. A voice is discovered, the rhythm, the characters, but one cannot know beforehand." Her work is praised for its significance to Hispanic culture and to Hispanic women in particular. In the words of a critic for *Más*, Alvarez, along with the celebrated writer Sandra Cisneros, brings "a bilingual and bicultural vision" that highlights women's experiences.

Sources:

Books

Alvarez, Julia, *How the Garcia Girls Lost Their Accents*, Algonquin Books, 1991.

Periodicals

American Scholar, winter, 1987, pp. 71-85.
Atlanta Journal, August 11, 1991, p. A13.
Boston Globe, May 26, 1991, p. A13.
Brújula <> Compass (Spanish-language; translation by Ronie-Richele Garcia-Johnson), January-February, 1992, p. 16.
Hispanic, June, 1991, p. 55; September, 1992, pp. 36, 38.
Library Journal, May 1, 1991, p. 102.
Los Angeles Times, June 7, 1991, p. E4.
Más (Spanish-language; translation by Ronie-Richele Garcia-Johnson), November-December, 1991, p. 100.
New York Times Book Review, October 6, 1991, p. 14.
Nuestro, November, 1984, pp. 34+; March, 1985, pp. 52+; January-February, 1986, pp. 32+.
Publishers Weekly, April 5, 1991, p. 133.
School Library Journal, September, 1991, p. 292.
Washington Post, June 20, 1991, p. D11.

—Sketch by Ronie-Richele Garcia-Johnson

Linda Alvarez
Television newscaster

Every weekday afternoon at four o'clock, Linda Alvarez coanchors the news on Los Angeles television station KNBC. Although thousands of viewers throughout southern California are familiar with her face, few of them know her story. Originally a teacher, she broke into television as a weather reporter in Chicago and quickly moved into the newsroom. By 1992, she had won numerous awards—including six Emmys—for her broadcast skills as well as for her contributions to the community.

Alvarez seems to have inherited her determination to excel from her family. Seeking to improve their lives, her grandparents had moved from Mexico to Los Angeles when their son Ray (Alvarez's father) was just six years old. To earn a living, they made tamales and sold them from their car to workers in the city's garment district; in time, they saved enough money to open a restaurant.

Ray Alvarez was as determined to succeed as his parents. After graduating from high school, he joined the Navy and worked as a mechanic during World War II in the Pacific theater. Upon his return to the United States, the new citizen worked as a mechanic in a gas station, then became the station's manager and later its owner. Around the same time, he met and married Margarita Larios, a fourth-generation Californian of Mexican and Chilean descent. The couple's daughter, Linda Alvarez, was born in her grandmother's bedroom, one mile away from downtown Los Angeles.

Close Family Bonds Nurtured a Budding Talent

As a little girl, Alvarez helped her grandparents—peeling and tearing the corn husks they used to encase their tamales—and from them she learned to work hard and take pride in her efforts. From her gregarious father she learned the value of getting along with others. And from her book-loving mother she gained an appreciation of the written word, a sense of curiosity, and the desire to travel.

Alvarez did well in the strict Catholic schools she attended as a youngster. She graduated from Venice High School at the age of sixteen and made plans to enroll in college. Although her father wanted her to be a doctor, Alvarez was unsure about her future. She thought that she should understand more about the medical profession before making her decision, so she spent a year working as a receptionist in a doctor's office and earning money for college.

When Alvarez received a scholarship to attend the University of California at Los Angeles (UCLA), she decided to major in English and minor in Spanish and French. She loved to write, and because there were very few career options for women at the time, she decided to become a teacher when she graduated in 1963. She spent an additional year at UCLA earning her teaching credentials and then went to work at Venice High School. For two years, she taught English and Spanish, a job she enjoyed very much.

In her spare time after school, Alvarez taught Spanish to Peace Corps volunteers and was soon inspired to go to South America herself. In addition to teaching at the University of Carabobo in Venezuela, she set up her own English-language school.

Wins Teaching Position at the United Nations

Upon her return to the United States, Alvarez taught English, literature, and Spanish for two years at a public school in Westchester, New York. When she heard of openings for language teachers at the United Nations, she applied but was told that instructors would be hired to teach only their native languages and that she was therefore eligible to teach English but not Spanish. Alvarez reluctantly decided to try out for a job teaching English, but just moments before she was to deliver a sample lesson to a group of students and judges, she decided to do it in Spanish instead of English, figuring she had nothing to lose. The gamble paid off; Alvarez was praised as an exemplary teacher at the close of the auditions and was assured a job teaching Spanish.

Alvarez says that she herself learned two important lessons from that experience. The first was that she could take risks, and at several junctures in her career, she has done just that. The second lesson was even more revealing, and it has also influenced her greatly. After her audition, one of the interviewers who had expected to hear a lesson in English called Alvarez into his office and gave her a wry smile. "Do you know why you did that?" he asked, referring to her impromptu Spanish lesson. Alvarez was still too surprised at her own boldness to reply, so the interviewer

answered the question himself. "You like who you are when you are speaking Spanish," he said. With that simple observation, he verbalized something that Alvarez had never consciously realized, and she has not forgotten his words.

After a "wonderful" two-year stint teaching at the United Nations, Alvarez moved on. During a period when she was teaching in Hartford, Connecticut, throughout the regular school year, she spent a summer in Mexico City teaching at the Universidad Autonoma Nacional. She then went on to work for the Department of Health, Education, and Welfare in Chicago as a director of an adult basic education program in which immigrants were taught "survival" English.

Makes First Television Appearances in Chicago

It was while Alvarez was working in Chicago that one of her friends, the producer of the bilingual talk show "Nosotros" on Chicago's WTTW, noticed that she had no accent when she spoke either Spanish or English. The station offered her the chance to make public service announcements in both languages once a week, for which she was paid six dollars.

In addition to gaining media experience, Alvarez began to garner attention. Officials at Chicago's NBC-TV affiliate, WMAQ, let her know they had an opening for a weather person at their station. Although Alvarez had always enjoyed watching the news on television, she had never considered a career in the media; she certainly did not envision herself becoming the stereotypical "weather girl." But her supervisor pointed out that the weather reporting position could serve as a stepping-stone to other opportunities. She noted that Alvarez enjoyed teaching, and as a news reporter she would have the opportunity to inform and instruct thousands of people. That advice convinced Alvarez to try for the position, which she won.

But Alvarez knew that she had a lot of work to do if she wanted to become a bona fide news reporter. First, she had to excel as a weather person. Uncomfortable with the idea of giving weather reports without knowing what actually caused the conditions she was discussing, she began to study meteorology. And since she knew that she needed experience as a reporter, she asked endless questions of her colleagues and followed them around town on their assignments on her own time. Within six months, the woman whose knees had knocked during her first weather reports was hired as a reporter on a new news program at WMAQ. In another six months, Alvarez became cohost of a live, 90-minute, on-location talk show called "Chicago Camera." She spent three and a half years on the show and in the process learned how to think on her feet, how to interview, and how to condense ideas.

Still determined to make it as a news reporter, however, Alvarez took a fifty-percent pay cut to move to Los Angeles and cohost KNBC's "The Saturday Show." Then a television station in Phoenix contacted her about an opening as a general assignment reporter, and once again she decided to take yet another pay cut to accept the position. Within six months, she was an anchor for the five o'clock news. Within another year, she was reporting for the ten o'clock broadcasts as well, and within two years, she was an anchor for weekday news broadcasts at five o'clock, six o'clock, and ten o'clock. By 1983 Alvarez had also begun to produce documentaries on issues that were yet to become talk-show standards, including AIDS, sexual abuse, and gun control. On a more personal note, it was during her seven and a half years in Phoenix that she met and married cameraman Bill Timmer.

Returns to Los Angeles and Wins Coveted Coanchor Spot

In August, 1985, Alvarez was offered a position back in Los Angeles with KNBC-TV as a weekend coanchor. Pleased with the chance to return to her hometown as well as further her career, Alvarez happily accepted the offer. Before long she was coanchoring a half-hour weekday newscast at six o'clock. She held this position from September, 1986, until April, 1988, when she was promoted to an hour-long coanchor spot weekdays at four o'clock.

Alvarez's work for KNBC has been very exciting. She reported on the Mexico City earthquake from the Mexican capital in 1985, the Los Angeles earthquake in 1987, and the San Francisco Bay area earthquakes in 1989. She also covered Pope John Paul II's visit to Los Angeles and even traveled to Seoul, South Korea, to report on the 1988 Summer Olympic Games. In addition, she was the first American television journalist to interview Mexican President Carlos Salinas de Gortari at length at the presidential palace in Mexico City. Alvarez has also prepared a number of special programs for KNBC. One of these, a public affairs series entitled "Health Fax," won an Emmy Award in 1988.

Some of Alvarez's most satisfying pieces, however, are those she creates with the people of southern California. When she finds the opportunity to do so, she likes to report on minorities who are dedicated to helping their communities, especially young, inner-city teenagers who are working to make a difference in their neighborhoods. She is especially proud of a series of stories she did that focused on youths who have managed to "beat the odds," noting that such pieces combat stereotypes by allowing viewers to see aspects of the city's people that are usually ignored by the media.

Reaches Out to Young Hispanic Women

Given Alvarez's commitment to cover such stories, it is not surprising that she contributes to her community during her free time as well. Despite her busy schedule, she makes a point of serving on the boards of the YMCA of Metropolitan Los Angeles, the National Conference of Christians and Jews, Big Sisters of Los Angeles, and the Neighborhood Youth Association. She also speaks quite frequently to groups of young women in junior high school and high school about her life, her career, and the importance of setting goals and seeking help from those with more experience. In her talks, Alvarez credits her family, as well as the scholarship she received to attend UCLA, for giving her a "wonderful background." As she explained to interviewer Ronie-Richele Garcia-Johnson, "I don't think of myself as a minority. I think of myself as a Hispanic woman who has learned the value of working hard from [her family] and working smart from school. . . . I can choose what I want to do." Alvarez hopes that by sharing her own story with young women, she can encourage them to set goals and do the work necessary to achieve them.

Alvarez's professional and personal contributions have not gone unrecognized. By 1992, she had won a total of six Emmy Awards, the Ruben Salazar Media Award, several press club awards for news series and documentary reports, and certificates of commendation from Women in Communications, Women in Radio and Television, and the National Association of Hispanic Journalists, to name just a few. Alvarez has also been honored with the 1988 Silver Achievement Award for communications from the YWCA, the 1989 and 1990 John Swett Awards for media excellence in education reporting from the California Teachers Association, and a 1991 award for professional achievement and community service from the Women's Council and the Mexican American Legal Defense and Educational Fund (MALDEF). In 1992, Alvarez was lauded by the Variety Boys and Girls club and named as a Golden Woman of the Year.

Sources:

Alvarez, Linda, interview with Ronie-Richele Garcia-Johnson, September 1, 1992.

—Sketch by Ronie-Richele Garcia-Johnson

Luz Alvarez Martinez
(1942-)
Social activist

Luz Alvarez Martinez is director of an organization solely dedicated to Hispanic women's health issues, the Organizacion Nacional de La Salud de La Mujer Latina, or National Latina Health Organization (NLHO). For her, this is the fulfillment of a lifetime of efforts to provide educational and health services for Hispanic women. "One of my virtues is that I am very patient," said Alvarez

Martinez in an interview with this contributor. "I was not part of the women's movement or the Chicano movement of the late 1960s and early 1970s. At the time, I felt that it was important to devote all my time to my family. But I knew that one day I would be able to involve myself in issues outside of my family." She waited until her youngest son was in kindergarten before actively working towards her goal. It took her nine years to accomplish her dream, from 1977 when she returned to school until 1986, the year the organization was launched.

Alvarez Martinez was born on October 25, 1942, in Niles, California, the seventh of eleven children and a first-generation Mexican American. She grew up in an all-white neighborhood in San Leandro, near Oakland, California. "There were only two Mexican American and one Chinese families represented in grammar school." Later, she attended St. Elizabeth Catholic High School in Oakland. After graduation, she decided to stay in Oakland "because it was a culturally and ethnically diverse city," she explained in her interview. She worked as a stenographer for the Alameda County Probation Department.

At twenty-one, Alvarez Martinez married and enrolled in community college with the idea of doing social work among Hispanics. She had planned to continue studying while raising her family, but she changed her mind after the birth of her twin sons. "I wanted to be with them and be the major influence on their early development." So in 1977, when her fourth son entered kindergarten, the thirty-four-year-old mother went back to school. Immediately she became involved with school politics and the Women's Center and took a medic training course at the Berkeley Women's Health Collective, "a very feminist California clinic," she pointed out in her interview.

In 1981 she entered Hayward State University, near Oakland, to study nursing. This coincided with her divorce after seventeen years of marriage. Suddenly, she was a single mother of four, a full-time student and a part-time customer service coordinator for IBM. Despite her mother's financial help—"Asking her was hard, but she was so supportive"—the combined tasks proved too difficult for Alvarez Martinez. "I developed serious health problems," she recalled in her interview. In 1983, she dropped out of school and started working full time at IBM.

The same year an incident took place that reinforced her determination to create a health information service for Hispanic women. She had gone to the hospital for a tubal ligation. Before the operation, she discovered that two films, one in English and one in Spanish, were at the patients' disposal to help them make a decision. The English version mentioned the various contraceptive methods available, while the Spanish version emphasized sterilization. Alvarez Martinez later learned that economically disadvantaged women were often offered sterilization as the only possible birth control choice.

Establishes Bilingual Health Information Services

Also in 1983 Alvarez Martinez attended the first national conference of the Black Women's Health Project. "For the first time, I saw how powerful a group of women of color could be," she told this contributor. She met the Project's founder, Byllye Avery, and accompanied her to Kenya in 1985 for the United Nations International Women's Conference. And on International Women's Day 1986, during a workshop on Third World women's health issues, Alvarez Martinez and three other Hispanic women—Paulita Ortiz, Alicia Bejarano, Elizabeth Gastelumendi—decided to create a bilingual information service on physical and mental health issues for Hispanic women. A few months later, they received a grant that enabled them to launch the NLHO.

The organization aims to ensure quality health care for Hispanic women and to give them access to English and Spanish health information. The NLHO advocates giving women free choice of contraceptive methods, including abortion. Alvarez Martinez has supported women's total freedom of options since the 1960s, in spite of her Catholic upbringing. "I left the Church after the birth of my sons in 1964 when I was told that I could not practice birth control methods and be within the laws of Christ," she related in her interview. "I could not believe that a priest or an organization could tell me what I should do about family planning, that I was not intelligent, logical, or practical enough to make a decision for myself."

Alvarez Martinez plans to expand the organization to every state in the country. She also wants to open centers for battered Hispanic women—few existing centers offer services in Spanish. "No woman should stay in an abusive marriage because there is no choice," she stated in her interview. "We need to help each other."

Alvarez Martinez belongs to the Oakland chapter of the Mexican American Political Association, and is a founding member of the Democratic Party's Latin Political Action Committee in Sacramento, California. She is also a grandmother.

Sources:

Periodicals

Hispanic, March, 1991, p. 46.
New York Post, April 16, 1992, p. 2.

Other

Alvarez Martinez, Luz, interview with contributor Michelle Vachon, conducted on May 11, 1992.

—Sketch by Michelle Vachon

Hortensia Maria Alvirez
(1944-)
Entrepreneur

Hortensia Maria Alvirez started her public relations and marketing company in the back room of an apartment. But modest beginnings did not stop ABL Associates from flourishing into an international and multi-million dollar company. Alvirez's accomplishments are especially significant considering that there were few female corporate heads during the early 1970s when she began. Professionally and personally, Alvirez faced adversity and triumphed. When she was only twenty years old she was diagnosed with Hodgkin's disease, cancer of the lymph nodes. "I was in and out of treatment and I was told that I had six months to live," she recalled in a telephone interview with D. D. Andreassi. "I decided that would not be the case."

Alvirez was born December 10, 1944, to Hortensia Peréz de León and Mario Alvirez Pablos in Mexico City. While Alvirez was still a child, her mother divorced her father and set out to work in the United States. Deciding that the Southwest would be difficult because of discrimination, Alvirez's mother appealed to a maiden aunt who was an entrepreneur in Mexico City to help her get a job. The aunt sent de León to the United States with her one-year-old daughter to work for the Mexican Embassy at a Mexican electrical company. Alvirez's mother had twenty-five dollars in her purse and could not speak English. She was a "very strong woman," however, explained Alvirez in her interview, and taught her daughter by example. Alvirez was placed in a boarding school for working class mothers, and the school soon became her home. "I was taken care of by these lovely ladies, African American women," remembered Alvirez in her interview with Andreassi. "It was owned by a white woman. And I became a very American child very quickly." Alvirez's mother was only able to see her once a week, because she could not afford more frequent visits. "It was a very emotional experience, because I didn't have my mother," related Alvirez.

When she was five years old Alvirez began to live with her mother in downtown Washington, attending the first mixed school in Washington, D.C. During this time she experienced racism and bigotry, and one incident stands out in her memory. When she was ten years old a local druggist turned her away saying he didn't sell to "Spics." Having lived in an international town like Washington all her life, Alvirez had never before experienced such blatant prejudice. She pointed out in her interview that there are many opportunities in this country, but minorities and women still face problems of prejudice. Her view is that both groups have to learn to communicate effectively and use every God-given asset they have to the best of their ability.

While she was growing up Alvirez's grandfather insisted that she attend school in Mexico for part of the year. "I came from a family that put a lot of emphasis on education," Alvirez told Andreassi. She graduated from high school in Washington, D.C., and went to college in Mexico, graduating from the Universidad Autonoma de Mexico with a degree in commercial art in 1964. She also studied accounting, business, journalism, and writing, all of which prepared her for ABL Associates.

The same year she graduated from college, Alvirez's life took an unexpected turn—she was diagnosed with Hodgkin's disease. At one point during her treatment she was told that she only had six months to live, but she was determined to not give up hope. Alvirez underwent treatment at the National Institutes of Health in Washington, D.C., and she was among the first patients there to be successfully treated for Hodgkin's. "Through the work they did with me they were able to save other people," Alvirez related in her interview with Andreassi. When she beat the cancer, Alvirez said, she realized that she had to do something with her life "other than being a nice Latin girl who went to school and got married."

So, Alvirez went to work at several places as a research assistant and secretary. She commented in her interview that she "typed her way to the top" at Partners of the Alliance, which is the private sector affiliate of the Alliance for Progress, part of the government AID program. Alvirez, twenty-four years old at the time, was office manager, staff supervisor, personnel recruiter, and policy initiator. Her fluency in Spanish made her especially qualified for translating and setting up conferences in Latin America. The job thoroughly reinforced the work ethic she learned from her mother and gave her insight into women's roles— especially Latin professional women—outside the United States. She told Andreassi that she "turned around one day and saw these guys on the golf course, and I was running the business. I came to realize women did not have to be secretaries for the rest of their lives. There were few women who were success stories and very few who were corporate directors. I realized that I could do a lot more than I was told I could."

Founds ABL Associates

Alvirez began doing consulting work and decided she could do even more. She started ABL Associates, which offered research information as well as office and communication services. Then she began providing publicity services and public affairs in any language. Some of the company's clients in 1992 included the National Medical Association and the U.S. federal government. In 1992 she had ten employees and the company was earning four and half million dollars annually. "I know there are a lot more successful companies, but I am quite happy," she maintained in her interview.

In the meantime, Alvirez had married, given birth to two children, Lesley Alexis and Christian Adolfo (who were raised bilingually and biculturally), and gotten divorced. Her mother, whom Alvirez described as the "bulwark of the family," had remarried and had three children. "My mother stressed throughout all the years of sacrifice that we had to get an education and we had to work," Alvirez said in her interview with Andreassi. At the age of 70, her mother was director of budgeting at Westinghouse. "She's beautiful and she's such an incredible woman—she taught us how to work," Alvirez said. Emphasizing her mother's strong work ethic, Alvirez told Andreassi that she always objected to the Mexican stereotype of a man sitting against a building with a sombrero on his head. "As an immigrant, I'm a little different from the Ellis Island perspective. We had to become very modern very quickly without losing the intensity of the community."

Alvirez's accomplishments were recognized with an award from the Mexican American Women's National Association (MANA) in 1981. She was also one of the finalists in the 1989 Women of Enterprises, which is an award given annually by Avon Corporation. Her volunteer work includes serving as chair of MANA, as a member of the committee to promote Washington, D.C., and as a member of the mayor's (Washington, D.C.) overall economic development committee. She was also a member of the Women's Equity Action League, and a member of the public relations committee of the American Cancer Society in Washington, D.C. Alvirez served as chair of the advisory board of the First Women's National Bank of Washington, D.C., and she was one of the founding members of the first multicultural mental health committee of Washington, D.C., in 1974.

Alvirez explained to Andreassi that she would like to see herself as someone who is "able to accomplish something professionally and still give back to the community, or on a global basis—particularly in making this country successful. I'd like to feel I'm able to contribute to the tradition that will add to the value of this country and to help my people become stars."

Sources:

Alvirez, Hortensia Maria, telephone interview with D. D. Andreassi, October 16-19, 1992.

—Sketch by D. D. Andreassi

Amezcua, Consuelo González
See González Amezcua, Consuelo

Angeles Torres, Maria de los
See Torres, Maria de los Angeles

Lupe Anguiano
(1929-)
Educator, activist

While serving as the southwest regional director of the National Conference of Bishops in 1973, Lupe Anguiano moved into a San Antonio, Texas, housing project to work with women on welfare. It is a mission that is never far from the heart of the nationally acclaimed activist that *Ms.* magazine once called "both dreamer and pragmatist." Anguiano's work in San Antonio culminated in the "Let's Get Off Welfare" campaign, which featured a demonstration by more than 100 women demanding jobs, not government handouts. The community response to the campaign was overwhelming and led to jobs for 500 women in six months.

Six years later, Anguiano obtained private funding to found the National Women's Employment and Education Project, which explored alternatives to Aid to Families with Dependent Children (AFDC). "The goal was to develop a model program that would demonstrate an effective system of assisting women on AFDC and help them move from welfare to jobs," Anguiano told Pamela Berry in a telephone interview. "The goal was for it to be a model program for future national welfare policy change." She also observed, "My programs appeal to corporate America because they work," since they are based on a realistic approach to the employment process. Anguiano went on to create nine models in eight states, which she left in the control of the residents once they were up and running. Some of the models were still in existence more than a decade later.

Religious Background Guides Career Choices

A dedication to serving the needs of the disadvantaged is a thread that runs throughout Anguiano's life and career. Born in 1929 in La Junta, Colorado, to Mexican immigrants, Anguiano was brought up in a devout Roman Catholic household. She was named after Our Lady of Guadalupe, the patron saint of Mexico, and celebrates her birthday on her patron saint's feast day, December 12. In Mexico, girls born on the twelfth of any month are traditionally named Lupe. "I always grew up with a great love for Christ and for our faith," she said. "I received that love and that devotion not from the Catholic institution itself but rather from the love my father and mother had for

Lupe Anguiano

Christ." Anguiano's father, Jose Anguiano, was a laborer for the Santa Fe Railroad. While she was growing up, her mother, Rosary Gunwale Anguiano, would take Lupe, her three sisters, and two brothers to California each summer to pick crops. Eventually, her mother saved enough money to start a small shop in Satiety, California, that sold soda, ice cream, and candy. When her father retired from the railroad in 1937, the family moved to Satiety. The shop later grew into a grocery store run by one of her brothers.

Anguiano attended and graduated from California's Ventura Junior College in 1948 and entered religious life a year later. She was a Roman Catholic nun with Our Lady of Victory Missionary Sisters for 15 years, teaching religion and working at several parishes across the country. While living at a mission in Los Angeles, she campaigned against housing discrimination, coordinated youth programs, and organized committees to help improve the quality of life for poor people in the community. Her community work eventually led to her decision to leave the convent; she found religious life too restrictive to her desires to serve the community.

Her first post-convent job was as a counselor with a youth training and employment project. Within a year, she was recruited to be the East Los Angeles coordinator for the Federation of Neighborhood Centers, a job that involved organizing youth projects throughout the community. While working there, she was selected to be one of 30 delegates who were invited to come to the White House to speak with President Lyndon Johnson about the needs of Mexican Americans. Her presentation was so impressive that Vice President Hubert Humphrey suggested that she work with the administration to help improve education for Mexican Americans. From 1967-69, she served as a presidential appointee to the U.S. Office of Education, where she created the Mexican American Unit, later called the Hispanic Unit. She also assisted with the development and passage of the Bilingual Education Act.

After the passage of the act, Anguiano realized she was feeling homesick in Washington, D.C. "I was one of the few brown faces around here," she recalled in her interview. Then, in 1969, she received a call from César Chávez, the organizer of the United Farm Workers Union, asking her to work with him. For one year she worked as a volunteer for Chávez; her responsibilities included organizing a grape boycott in Michigan. At the end of the year, Anguiano worked briefly for the National Association for the Advancement of Colored People, as the southwest regional director of their Legal Defense and Education Fund, before being asked to return to Washington, D.C., in 1973. She assumed the position of program officer for the former U.S. Department of Health, Education, and Welfare. There she helped to monitor affirmative action programs. She also worked with a group of other women in the department to develop the "blueprint for American women" during the Equal Rights Amendment hearings. The blueprint was part of a national plan to improve the status of women as it related to health, education, and welfare. It was at this time that Anguiano began focusing on women on welfare. "I found that poor women on welfare were not coming out and speaking at the Equal Rights Amendment hearings so I started to look at where they were," she explained. "I saw they were on AFDC welfare."

Offers an Alternative to Women on Welfare

Anguiano put together a group of Hispanic women to talk to the group that was preparing the report on American women. "In doing research on welfare, I found that 90 percent of the families on AFDC are headed by women," she said in her telephone interview. "They are young—their average age was 28—and there were three and a half million of them." Anguiano strongly believed that the welfare system in the country needed to be reformed to focus more closely on the economic needs of the women. Learning that President Richard Nixon's administration was not overly receptive to the ideas she proposed, however, she decided that it was time to leave Washington, D.C.

Anguiano accepted a position coordinating Hispanic programs for the National Conference of Catholic Bishops in 1973, with the understanding that she would make welfare reform her main priority. Soon after, she launched her "Let's Get Off Welfare" campaign, which captured the attention of the media and generated a tremendous response from the community. "I already knew that women, more than anything, wanted and needed to go to work instead of being on welfare," she said. "The policy needed to be changed from income maintenance to an employment policy." An employment policy, she claimed, needed to be augmented by a social service support system that provided such benefits as child care. Anguiano organized the poor women in the community so that some were free to work outside of the home, while others cared for the children.

Following the public demonstration that was the highlight of the campaign, Anguiano received a flood of calls from community groups and businesses that wanted to aid her cause: the local Kiwanis Club provided the funds to train women to become cashiers for a local grocery chain; the local telephone company trained women to become customer service operators; and an airplane factory trained women as sheet metal operators. Of the 3,000 women who were trained throughout the course of the campaign, 90 percent were placed in jobs and 88 percent retained or improved their employment status.

By 1977, the project became so large that Anguiano decided to leave her position with the National Conference of Catholic Bishops to cofound National Women's Program Development, an organization that focused, in part, on programs for Native Americans. The following year she received her master's degree in education and administration from Antioch University in Yellow Springs, Ohio.

In 1979, she left the National Women's Program Development to found the National Women's Employment and Education Project in order to concentrate more fully on welfare reform. That same year she also started her own consulting firm, Lupe Anguiano and Associates. In 1991, as a consultant for her alma mater, Ventura Junior College, she did research and data analysis on the ethnic makeup of the student population to aid the college in its recruitment efforts, curriculum planning, and teacher training and development programs. "One of the things I discovered was out of about 9,000 [high] schools in California, only about 500 do not have students who are bilingual or multilingual—and yet the college [Ventura] was doing 'business as usual,'" she said. "There are 46 different languages spoken in California classrooms. It's not a situation of five years from now we're going to have a diverse population in the classroom—it is *now*." She recommended that the college change its strategy of recruiting teachers from various ethnic groups and instead train the existing teacher population to deal with a diverse student body. "I started to encourage the term diversity to be inclusive of whites, blacks, Hispanics, Asians, Native Americans. . . . We need to look at the population and the diversity and start pulling everybody together to work as a diverse team." In 1992 she was hired as a consultant to the U.S. Department of Personnel Management, Division of Affirmative Recruitment, to develop a model program for what she calls "diversity recruitment."

Despite her widening interests and activities, Anguiano has not given up her dream of welfare reform. She intends to write a book on the welfare system and her experiences in trying to reform it. "Being on welfare is being on poverty; it is not enough," she stated in her interview. "It is a degrading and dehumanizing system that must be changed." Anguiano views her work with welfare reform as being part of an overall effort to bring out the best in people. "What I want to do is be part of a movement to encourage the acceptance of diversity both in the country and the world," she said. "I want us to look at prosperity from the standpoint of not being patronizing to others but challenging people to create a new world of love and prosperity."

Anguiano has received a long list of awards and honors for her work throughout the years, including the Best of American Award from the Federation of Republican Women, the Brindis Award from the Hispanic Women's Caucus, the Wonder Woman Award by Warner Communications, and the President's Volunteer Action Award, which was presented to her at the White House in 1983. In addition to her awards, Anguiano was commended by several institutions for her work. She was named one of America's 100 Most Important Women in 1989 by the *Ladies' Home Journal* and one of the 100 Most Influential Hispanics for the 1980s by *Hispanic Business Magazine*. She was included in "A Gallery of Women," a traveling national exhibit by Adolph Coors Company, from 1985-87, and featured in a CBS television spot, "An American Portrait," commemorating the Statue of Liberty centennial in 1986. She also appeared on a CBS commemorative calendar that same year.

Anguiano credits much of her success to being in the right place at the right time. "I feel that I have been very blessed, in looking back at my life, that I have been placed in very important locations and areas of concern," she said. "I also think that I have been very blessed with great vision."

Sources:

Periodicals

Intercambios, spring, 1991, pp. 19-20.
Ms., September, 1985.

Other

Anguiano, Lupe, telephone interview with Pamela Berry, August 8, 1992.

—Sketch by Pamela Berry

Miriam Angulo
(1955-)
Bank vice president, consultant

By the age of 31, Miriam Angulo was a senior vice president at CenTrust, a large Miami, Florida, bank; four years later she became the chief financial officer for Bank United, also in Miami. Within a year, she had struck out on her own as a strategic planner and consultant for international business firms. She attributes her swift rise to the ranks of upper management to hard work and adaptability. "I have been very fortunate to have had a quick career path," she said in a telephone interview with Pamela Berry. "I think hard work had a lot to do with it, also being able to anticipate changes and prepare for them so it seemed like you were there before anyone else was."

Angulo was born in 1955, in New York City, to Hispanic parents of diverse backgrounds. Her father, Jose Felipe Martinez, was a Cuban immigrant who worked as an engineer and general contractor. Her mother, Anna Beatriz Castro Martinez, was born in the United States to Venezuelan parents. She worked as a deputy controller for a Venezuelan firm. Being comfortable with change is a trait that Angulo may have inherited from her parents. On a vacation to Florida when Angulo was a teenager, her family "fell in love with Florida and the next thing I knew I was in Florida." Her parents believed that the Miami area would provide a better quality of life for their children than their home in the New York borough of Queens. The family moved to Coral Gables, southwest of Miami, in 1970, and Angulo still lives there.

Upon graduating from high school, Angulo attended the University of Miami and received a bachelor's degree in business in 1977 and an M.B.A. the following year. Angulo began her banking career at Southeast Bank in Miami, where she worked from 1978 to 1984. She was hired as an accounting systems analyst and ended her employment there as an operations research officer. That same year, 1984, she married Jose Miguel Angulo, who works for the State of Florida. They have two children, a son and a daughter.

After leaving her post at Southeast Bank, Angulo went to work for CenTrust. She worked there from 1984-90, starting as a financial analyst and eventually being promoted to senior vice president in charge of long-term strategic planning. "That was probably the most exciting job I ever had," she said. "It was a wonderful opportunity—I was given the opportunity to work and I did OK." In 1990, Angulo became the senior vice president and chief financial officer for Bank United, where she worked one year. After she left Bank United in 1991, she started her own full-

time consulting and accounting practice. She had previous experience in the field, having operated a part-time practice, but she now felt that she had the proper means to develop the practice and also spend more time with her family. "I thought in the long run it was going to help me balance out my family life because on the other career track I was never home," she said. "This helped me bridge my home life with my career."

The majority of Angulo's work as an independent accountant/consultant has involved business planning and international strategic planning. She has worked extensively with development organizations in Central America, developing long-term strategic plans to help businesses and industries grow. Her main career goal is to continue expanding her business. "One of the major reasons I decided to take the leap was our marketplace has changed significantly, so it comes down to adapting to the marketplace," she related in her interview. "I saw the great growth potential [of being an independent consultant]. There's an opportunity to develop my entrepreneurial spirit—which I think is there."

Sources:

Angulo, Miriam, telephone interview with Pamela Berry, August 11, 1992.

—Sketch by Pamela Berry

Año Nuevo Kerr, Louise
See Kerr, Louise Año Nuevo

Mari Carmen Aponte
(1946-)
Attorney

With a passion for acting and a deep commitment to the Hispanic community, Mari Carmen Aponte became a lawyer with a mission: to be a visible and contributing member of society. Aponte chose law because, as she said to Luis Vasquez-Ajmac during an interview, "it was a natural blend to combine my acting abilities with my caring

Mari Carmen Aponte

arts in theatre from Villanova University in Villanova, Pennsylvania.

After her master's degree in 1970, Aponte moved to Camden, New Jersey, where she taught high school. Aponte's experience in Camden became a turning point in her professional career. At a time when no bilingual programs existed in high school, she became acutely aware of the unaddressed educational needs of Hispanic children. Because she wanted to make a difference, Aponte ultimately decided that going to law school was a way of making changes within the system in a far more effective way than teaching.

In 1976, Aponte completed her J.D. from Temple University School of Law in Philadelphia. She feels strongly about the role of education in her life. As she revealed in her interview, "Having access to education changed my life and can change the lives of so many younger Hispanics. Hispanics with credentials," she continued, "can enjoy the bounty of the American dream. Education is of primordial importance."

Upon completing her law degree in 1976, Aponte remained in Philadelphia and established Clark & Aponte, a law firm for the general practice of law including civil and criminal defense matters. Concurrently, from 1977 to 1979, she acted as associate counsel for Blue Cross of Greater Philadelphia. As associate counsel, Aponte was responsible for the defense of subscriber suits and guidance of legal processes. She also provided interpretation of and counsel on the impact of federal, state, and local regulations. In addition, she developed and implemented a system by which approximately 70 percent of the litigation was handled in-house by Blue Cross staff, thereby netting substantial savings in legal fees for the company.

White House Fellowship Broadens Career

The year 1979 was another turning point in Aponte's life, both professionally and personally. With the encouragement of friends and colleagues, Aponte applied for a White House fellowship in hopes of getting first-hand experience in the process of governing the nation. Among the 3000 promising young Americans seeking the fellowship, Aponte was awarded the White House fellowship by President Jimmy Carter in 1979. Serving as special assistant to Moon Landrieu, then Secretary of Housing and Urban Development, Aponte assisted in the development of policy and overall department strategy in several program areas. Frequently, Aponte travelled with Landrieu to Hispanic communities and often represented him at meetings of major public interest groups concerning neighborhoods and community projects.

Aponte made many contacts while working under the Secretary of Housing and Urban Development. More im-

for the Hispanic community. It requires acting experience and a lot of passion and commitment." Aponte's commitment to her work has garnered her several awards and honors. In 1979, for example, she was selected Most Outstanding Puerto Rican in Pennsylvania by the Puerto Rican Tri-State Congress. In 1980, she was chosen as Outstanding Young Woman in America, was honored by the Philadelphia City Council for community service, and was selected by the Philadelphia Jaycees as Outstanding Young Leader of the Year in Philadelphia, Pennsylvania. In addition to receiving numerous fellowships and honors, Aponte founded and has maintained a successful and growing law firm in Washington, D.C., for eight years.

Aponte was born October 22, 1946, in San Juan, Puerto Rico. The oldest of two, she is the daughter of René Aponte, now deceased, and María Cristina Rodríguez, both professionals. Her mother taught high school English and later taught at the University of Puerto Rico. Her father, an engineer by profession, was the driving force in her upbringing. She describes him as an "overachiever" who set high expectations for his two daughters.

From a well-educated family, Aponte felt that she had no choice but to attend college and become a professional. In 1968, Aponte obtained a bachelor of arts in political science from Rosemont College in Rosemont, Pennsylvania. While in college, Aponte discovered she had a knack for acting and eventually pursued a master of fine portantly, she gained confidence in herself. By the time the fellowship ended, Aponte felt comfortable with the high-level politics and policy making that goes on in the White House. In describing her fellowship experience to Vasquez-Ajmac, she stated, "The White House fellowship was my year as Cinderella. . . . I felt blessed."

In 1981 Aponte resumed her law practice by joining Powell, Goldstein, Frazer & Murphy and worked as an associate until 1982. While at the firm, Aponte researched, filed pleadings, and litigated civil matters in local courts. She also counseled business, educational, and charitable organizations in tax and general corporate matters.

Since January 1983, Aponte has been a partner of Aponte & Tsaknis (formerly Pena, Aponte & Tsaknis, P.C.) in Washington, D.C. Aponte's firm, as she described it to Vasquez-Ajmac, "is a product of a dream of having a Hispanic law firm downtown." Although immigration, family, and criminal law are important to Aponte, she wanted to get away from these traditional areas of practice when she founded her law firm. "It's just that the diversity of our community needs to be reflected in the community at large, and I thought that we needed a Hispanic law firm that could do corporate work, civil litigation, and transactional work." Of the firm's successes, Aponte is particularly proud of the fact that she has a joint venture with a 500-lawyer national law firm and maintains an excellent relationship with the partners. "Traditionally, you do not see in minority law firms joint ventures with big prestigious law firms. That is an achievement we are very proud of." Aponte remarked that her firm has been able to make the joint venture work by approaching corporate clients and bringing diversity to the table.

Another achievement of which Aponte is very proud is the quality of work she has been able to attract. Aponte's firm has attracted clients like Aetna Life and Casualty, White Consolidated Industry, and Resolution Trust Corporation, to name a few. Aponte revealed that her firm is becoming involved in a project that is going to undertake complex litigation regarding pensions of a failed bank. "That is going to be a significant project," Aponte noted in her interview, "not only in terms of time but also in terms of the complexity of the issue. There are issues that have not been litigated before, so they will be rather important." Aponte's firm also counsels non-profit clients on tax-related matters.

Although the law firm of Aponte & Tsaknis is a product of a dream, Aponte thought that the process of achieving her dream would be easier. What kept her going despite difficulties and adversity was her sense of duty to the Hispanic community. Being able to keep her law firm open and growing was, in her mind, a reflection on the Hispanic community. Courage, commitment, intelligence, and happiness with self were also factors that Aponte cited as contributing to her success.

Active professionally, Aponte has been appointed to many committees and associations throughout her career. She has been involved with such organizations as the Philadelphia Bar Association, the American Bar Association, and the Hispanic Bar Association, for which she was president in 1983 of the District of Columbia chapter. Since 1989, Aponte has also been serving as chair of the American Bar Association's Minority Women Subcommittee of the Commission on Minorities. Aponte's Bar admissions include the Supreme Court of the United States, the United States Court of Appeals for the District of Columbia, the United States District Court for the Eastern District of Pennsylvania, the United States District Court for the District of Columbia, the Supreme Court of Pennsylvania, and the Washington, D.C., Court of Appeals.

Strives to Eliminate Negative Stereotypes

Aponte's commitment to the Hispanic community is one of pride and devotion. She cares what other people think about the Hispanic community and aims to dispel negative stereotypes. She believes that if Hispanics become visible and contributing members of society, it will be easier for other Hispanics to become leaders in their chosen careers. To the extent that this can happen, Aponte related to Vasquez-Ajmac, "it won't be a surprise to find a Hispanic on the board of directors of a major corporation." Aponte says individuals like writer Carlos Fuentes and actor Raúl Julia are "carrying the torch for Hispanics, making Hispanics look good."

Conscientious and civic-minded herself, Aponte has also dedicated time and effort to many community activities. At various times she has devoted her time to the Housing Association of Delaware Valley, Jefferson Hospital's Mental Health and Mental Retardation Center, International Young Lawyers Association, and the Puerto Rican Legal Defense and Education Fund. In addition, President Carter appointed Aponte to the Commission on Presidential Scholars, and from 1983 to 1991 Aponte was elected to the Board of Directors of the National Network of Hispanic Women.

At age forty-six, Aponte, who resides in Washington, D.C., is not about to retire. In the future, Aponte hopes to become an even stronger voice for the Hispanic community within the State Democratic Committee, an elected position. "At this time," she said to Vasquez-Ajmac, "there is nobody Hispanic in the State Democratic Committee." She added, "I will raise the issues of concern to Hispanics."

Sources:

Aponte, Mari Carmen, interview with Luis Vasquez-Ajmac, April 15, 1992, Washington, D.C.

—Sketch by Luis Vasquez-Ajmac

Concha Maria de Concepción Arguello
(1791-1857)
Pioneer, nun

Concepción Arguello, a California pioneer and nun, is generally remembered for her romance with a Russian count. Concha Maria de Concepción Arguello was born in 1791 in Yerba Buena, California, when it belonged to Spain as part of Mexico. She was one of Jose Arguello's nine children. As the owner of Pancho de las Pulgas, a 35,000-acre estate, Jose Arguello became acting governor of both upper and lower California. Apparently, Arguello's power and wealth were key to the interest of Count Nikolai Rezanof in his daughter, Doña Concepción.

Rezanof was "the first Russian explorer who showed definite designs upon any part of California," *Appleton's Cyclopedia of American Biography* reports. Rezanof came to the California territory in 1806 to establish commercial ties for the Russian colony of Sitka, which is now part of Alaska, and to set up a Russian colony. It is speculated in *Appleton's* that Rezanof asked for Arguello's hand in marriage in the hopes of obtaining help from her respected and influential family.

In *These Were the Women: U.S.A., 1776-1860,* Mary Ormsbee Whitton suggests that Concepción, only 15, became enamored of the Count during his visit to her father's house on a mission to buy provisions for the Czar's starving colonies up north. "Such trade agreements had to be approved at long distance by the viceroy in Mexico. Not 'til May was the young count's errand completed. Then he left, bound all the way to St. Petersburg to obtain the Czar's consent to his marriage with this beautiful young Spaniard."

Rezanof never came back, and it wasn't until 1842 that Concepción, now 51, heard from a visiting explorer that her betrothed, on a long journey across Siberia, had been thrown from his horse and killed. The heart-broken Arguello never married. Instead, eight years after she heard of Rezanof's death, she decided to become a nun with the Third Order of St. Francis in the World. Arguello applied to the order after three Dominican sisters arrived to found Santa Catalina at Monterey, which shortly became St. Catherine's at Benecia. Arguello took her final vows in 1852.

As a nun, Arguello's duties were "to teach native Californians and Indians the truths of our holy faith," according to Whitton's study. Tradition has it that she traveled throughout California to spread her faith. Roman Catholic Church papers, however, "connect her chiefly with the Mission Soledad, 'Thousands of acres of barren brown plain' 30 miles south of Monterey near the Salinas River."

A memorial was erected in Concepción Arguello's honor in the convent garden at Benecia, where she died in December, 1857. She had become the convent's first mother superior and became known to the poor of old California as *La Beata*—"The Blessed One."

Sources:

Books

Appleton's Cyclopedia of American Biography, edited by James Grant Wilson and John Fiske, Volume 1, D. Appleton & Co., 1888, p. 89.

Whitton, Mary Ormsbee, *These Were the Women: U.S.A., 1776-1860; The Story of Women Who Helped Make American Culture,* Hastings House, 1954, pp. 258-259.

—*Sketch by Lawrence J. Paladino*

Lucie Arnaz
(1951-)
Actress

Lucie Arnaz is the daughter of famous Hollywood stars Lucille Ball and Desi Arnaz, but she has earned a name for herself as a stage, television, and movie actress. Even though her acting career began on her mother's long-running television show *Here's Lucy,* Arnaz felt most comfortable on stage. She told *Ladies' Home Journal,* "It's my medium, where I feel most at home, and I love it!" The critics have also applauded her stage performances. In 1979 she won the Los Angeles Drama Critics Award for *They're Playing Our Song.*

Arnaz was born July 17, 1951, in Los Angeles, California, to Lucille Desiree Arnaz III (who used Lucille Ball as her career name) and actor, band leader, and producer Desiderio Alberto Arnaz (more popularly known as Desi Arnaz). He was born in Santiago, Cuba, and with his mother he fled to Miami, Florida, during the revolution of the 1950s. Arnaz was in front of audiences even before she was born. Her mother was five months' pregnant when she and Desi made the pilot for *I Love Lucy,* the classic television show that audiences around the world have watched for decades in syndication. Ball enjoyed the same success with the television show, *Here's Lucy,* which included her daughter in the cast. The mother-daughter team, however, was not always on good terms. Arnaz often described her relationship with her mother as strained, and when they worked together they were even more tense. "My boss was my mother!" Arnaz told *McCall's*. "We would drag the work stuff home and the mother-daughter stuff to work." In an attempt to become independent, she moved to her own apartment. When Arnaz was 20 she married Phillip Menegaux, but they divorced not long after. Years later she married Laurence Luckinbill and had three children, Simon, Joe, and Kate. She also has two stepsons that Luckinbill brought to the marriage.

In the meantime, Arnaz continued her acting career. In 1972 she made her stage debut in *Cabaret* with the San Bernardino Civic Light Opera. Five years later she was Kathy in *Vanities* at the Mark Taper Forum in Los Angeles, and the following year she starred as Annie Oakley in *Annie Get Your Gun*. She worked three seasons with the John Kenley Theatres in plays such as *Once Upon a Mattress, Li'l Abner* and *Bye Bye Birdie*. She also acted in several films, including *Billy Jack Goes to Washington* in 1977 and *The Jazz Singer* in 1980.

In addition to stage and film acting, Arnaz was able to display her versatility in her broadcast work. On television she appeared in such varied programming as *Marcus Welby, Timex Presents Words and Music, Ed Sullivan's Clown Around, Death Scream,* and *The Dating Game*. She also hosted *Southern California Easter Seals Telethon* and a radio show, *Tune in with Lucie*.

Despite her success as a guest performer, Arnaz's attempts to follow in her mother's footsteps and star in a television series did not go well. Shows like *One More Try, The Lucie Arnaz Show,* and *Sons and Daughters* met with sharp criticism. One review in *Variety* opined that *Sons and Daughters* was "glutted with cardboard characters and stilted situations.... Arnaz comes off shrill as Tess, who should be the most sympathetic character." Although Tess was unpopular with the critics, Arnaz identified with the character, who was a compulsive cleaner and organizer. In *Ladies' Home Journal* she said, "Like me, [Tess] sometimes doesn't stop long enough to enjoy what she's completed."

Although her forays into film and television met with mixed success, Arnaz continued to flourish in the medium with which she is most comfortable: the stage. Describing her 1991 performance in *Rainbow and Stars* at the Rockefeller Plaza, a *New York Times* critic said that Arnaz has the "kind of voice that overcomes as it slices its way through the rafters of Broadway theaters. And when the singer and actress lets loose in the comic numbers of her cabaret act, she is something to see."

Sources:

Periodicals

Ladies' Home Journal, October 1990, p. 48.
McCall's, May 1991, p. 23.
New York Times, April 1991, p. C16.

Variety, January 21, 1990.

—Sketch by D. D. Andreassi

Dolores S. Atencio
(1955-)
Attorney, association president

While she always knew that she would become a lawyer, Dolores S. Atencio never expected to become the successful leader that she is today. The woman who, as a child, had "everything going against" her and "every reason to fail" has become the president of the Hispanic National Bar Association (HNBA). In 1991 *Hispanic Business Magazine* named Atencio one of the 100 most influential Hispanics. Through her achievements she has opened doors for other Hispanic women as well as promoted the entrance of Hispanics into previously inaccessible arenas. In an equally powerful and influential role, Atencio is also a mother. Her status as a parent has intensified her devotion to increasing Hispanic influence in the United States. Just as her mother saw the importance of education in securing a woman's place in the world, Atencio, a self-described feminist, wants to create a better environment for the Hispanic woman her young daughter will grow up to be.

In an interview with Ronie-Richele Garcia-Johnson, Atencio recalled that, as a child, her family was very poor. Her mother, Lupe, and her father, Robert, were high school sweethearts. When Lupe, just 17 years old, found that she was pregnant, she and Robert dropped out of high school and married. Not long after Atencio was born in Pueblo, Colorado, on August 15, 1955, Robert Atencio's alcoholism destroyed the marriage. The Atencios separated; with her mother, Dolores moved in with her grandparents.

Atencio's mother sought work. In addition to her lack of education and experience, Lupe, who was dark-skinned, faced another obstacle as she attempted to provide for her daughter: sexual and racial discrimination. She was forced to work long and hard hours for low pay. Lupe wanted a better life for her daughter and took steps to secure an independent and comfortable future for her daughter. Lupe thus encouraged Dolores to become a lawyer. Her mother reasoned that she could enjoy a fulfilling career and simultaneously take a stand against the injustice her mother faced every day. Dolores Atencio happily accepted this idea. She recalls that she always knew she would be a lawyer. With this goal in mind, Atencio worked very hard in school. By the time she reached high school, she "single-mindedly" began to pursue her dream career. She earned outstanding grades and was enthusiastic in her extracurricular activities (she was a cheerleader every year). Handily managing a busy schedule, Atencio graduated with honors in 1973.

Atencio decided to attend Colorado College, a private liberal arts institution, upon her graduation from high school. During her freshman year she met her first husband, who was also a Chicano, and they dated throughout their college years. Atencio did very well in college and became active with the MeCHa organization. Just after receiving a bachelor's degree in political science from Colorado College in 1977, Atencio was married. She went on to study law at the University of Denver College of Law. The attorney recalls that she did not do as well academically in law school as she had in her undergraduate years. Also, she recalls that "many of us [Chicanos] were isolated and felt content with getting through." It was not a good attitude, nor one she would advocate, she said, but Chicano students at the time "didn't want to be judged" with standards which were foreign to them. Atencio did, however, make significant contributions to the student community during those years. She was the cochair of the Chicano Law Student Organization, and she became actively involved with the Democratic party. Out of necessity, Atencio also worked as a law clerk every year she was in school.

Begins Career in Legal Profession

Upon her graduation from law school in 1980, Atencio's first marriage ended. She had been forced to make a choice between her career and her marriage, and, as she told Garcia-Johnson, she chose her career. She had worked long and hard to become a lawyer, and she was not about to sacrifice her dream just when it was becoming a reality. In 1981 Atencio was admitted to the Colorado Bar. From July of that year until July 1982, she worked as a staff attorney in the Denver offices of the Colorado Rural Legal Services. Her work with the organization was part of the now defunct Reginald Heber Community Lawyer Fellowship Program, which recruited new law graduates who had been active in their communities. The program paid the fellows a salary in return for 20 percent of their time, which had to be contributed to communities and issues outside their regular work place. Atencio's next job was as an assistant attorney general for Colorado's Criminal Appellate Division. In this position from July 1982 to May 1985, Atencio specialized in criminal appellate litigation. This job required a great amount of research and writing and also exercised Atencio's analytical and oratory skills.

In addition to working at the Attorney General's Office, Atencio was committed to her community. The 1983 recipient of an Outstanding Young Woman Award served as a member of both the Hispanic education advisory committee for Denver public schools and the Community Technical Skills Center board of directors; as the president of the Mi Casa Women's Center board of directors; and as a member of the Latin American Research and Service

Agency board of directors from 1983 to 1985. Atencio was also involved with the National Institute for Trial Advocacy in 1985. She won an American Express Award for Community Involvement that year.

Launches Radio Station in Denver

While working at the attorney general's office, Atencio befriended a paralegal named Florence Hernandez-Ramos. Hernandez-Ramos was the director of a unique project. For 12 years, community groups had been unable to utilize an available radio frequency. When the right to make use of it was given to the Hispanic community, Hernandez-Ramos, along with her sister, Mercedes Hernandez, was determined to get radio station KUVO on the air. Hernandez-Ramos asked Atencio to organize a fundraiser for the project. She accepted the offer. For KUVO, she organized the first statewide Chicano artshow in Colorado. She became so enthusiastic about the radio station that she decided to leave the attorney general's office to work on the project full-time. "It was an unusual thing to do," Atencio recalled. "My first task was to raise my own salary." Although the three Hispanic women, Hernandez-Ramos, Hernandez, and Atencio, knew nothing about radio, they were determined to give the Hispanic community a voice in metropolitan Denver. Their persistence and hard work were rewarded when, in 1985, they successfully established KUVO, Denver's first public bilingual radio station.

Atencio served as KUVO's development director from 1985 to 1987. She was responsible for advising the station and drafting contracts, as well as overseeing the fundraising and public relations that would ensure the fledgling station's survival. Her efforts resulted in success—in 1992 KUVO enjoyed its seventh year of broadcasting jazz, the blues, and a variety of Hispanic music.

During Atencio's years at the radio station, she met her second husband, David Martinez, a journalist who would become the director of communications for the Colorado Housing and Finance Authority. The couple married. Also during that time, Atencio received a Kellogg Foundation fellowship. This enabled her to develop an expertise outside her chosen profession of law for three years. After creating her own individual learning plan, she studied Hispanic management and ownership of broadcast facilities and visited such outlets in the United States, Puerto Rico, Cuba, Spain, and Mexico. During this time Atencio also purchased a minority ownership in the Denver Univision affiliate television station.

In May of 1987, Atencio left the radio station. Her daughter, Simone Atencio-Martinez, was six months old, and Atencio had made the decision to be with her. Atencio also missed law and began to practice at home on a part-time basis. She continued her research as a Kellogg National Leadership fellow and joined the Colorado State Board of Social Work Examiners, on which she served until 1990.

Works to Benefit Hispanic Women Lawyers

Simone was soon old enough to be left with a sitter, and her mother was ready to once more practice law full-time. Atencio went to work for the Colorado Bar Association from 1988 to 1990 as the director of legal and public services. In this position, and as a liaison to the specialty bar associations, she helped organize the first statewide minority women lawyers conference in September, 1989. This conference proved to be an important one for minority women in the legal profession. As a result of it, the Colorado Coalition of Minority Women Lawyers and the Women's Section of the Colorado Hispanic Bar Association were established.

This period in Atencio's life became especially busy. As Convention Chair for the HNBA, she was responsible for the organization's national convention in Denver. In May of 1990, Atencio was approached by the Denver Grand Prix Auto Race, Inc. They needed an attorney with administrative background to negotiate agreements and leases with the owners of property along the race track, as well as write corporate and sponsorship contracts. Although Atencio knew very little about auto racing, she accepted the challenge to deal with public officials and private business. Two weeks after the first race she helped organize, the HNBA convention took place. "Basically," she told Garcia-Johnson, "I was a mad woman that summer."

Around the time that she began to work for the Denver Grand Prix, Atencio was approached by a friend who encouraged her to run for president of the HNBA. The friend was an excellent reference for Atencio's candidacy. In addition to being president-elect of the Colorado Hispanic Bar Association in 1990, this friend held other high profile positions in the Colorado legal community. At first, Atencio hesitated to run for president. She wondered if she was qualified for or had the time to invest in such an important responsibility. When her friend pointed out that, if she won, Atencio would be only the second woman ever to hold the office, and that, if she did not win, the possibility of a woman securing the presidency in the near future was unlikely, Atencio decided to run. It was important to her that women held leadership roles, and if she had the opportunity to become one of those leaders, she should take it. Atencio won the election and became the president-elect of the HNBA from 1990 to 1991. From September 1991 to September 1992, she served as that organization's national president. In that capacity, she was responsible for leading Hispanic lawyers as they dealt with significant legal issues.

Addresses Legal and Economic Concerns

Atencio was very concerned about the potential effects of the early 1990s recession on the United States's 16,000 Hispanic attorneys, especially the ten percent of that number who were women. As she explained in *Vista,* "Since Hispanics tend to practice singly or work in small law firms, they're really vulnerable. There is a great need for their services, but less opportunity for them to make money." Without that money, Atencio asserts, Hispanics in law will not achieve the influence and standard of living that they have earned and fewer young Hispanics will choose law as a profession.

Atencio took steps to strengthen the economic base of Hispanics. In January of 1991 she led a delegation of HNBA lawyers to Mexico City to meet with the President of Mexico, Carlos Salinas de Gortari, his cabinet members, and government and business leaders to discuss the American Free Trade Agreement. Atencio has met with U.S. Attorney General William Barr, FBI Director William Sessions, former Chief of Staff John Sununu, Legal Counsel C. Boyden Gray, and various other elected officials. She became a National Institute of Justice Peer/Grant Reviewer in 1991. All of this activity resulted in Atencio being named one of the country's 100 most influential Hispanics by *Hispanic Business Magazine* in October, 1991.

Atencio says that she takes a pro-active approach to being president of the HNBA. This tactic has been very successful. In mid-1992, under Atencio's leadership, the HNBA successfully lobbied the Federal Senate Judiciary to consider more Hispanic judges as they selected appointments to the Federal Bench. Before that time, just two percent of the Federal Judiciary was Hispanic. The six Hispanics that the HNBA endorsed were considered and three women were confirmed. With the help of the HNBA, who insisted that she be considered, Sonia Sotomayor became the first Latino (male or female) federal bench judge in New York. In addition to facilitating the appointments of Hispanics to positions that many feel they should have secured long ago, the HNBA is also working to promote the futures of potential Hispanic lawyers by ensuring the availability of scholarships to minority law students.

Atencio worked with the Denver Grand Prix until it filed for bankruptcy in September, 1991. Since November, 1991, Atencio has worked as an attorney specializing in business and corporate law and was associated with the law firm of Pryor, Carney & Johnson. She is a member of the Colorado Second Judicial District Performance Evaluation Commission and chairs the Budget Committee of the Colorado Bar Association. Beginning in July of 1992, she served on the Colorado and Denver Bar Associations' Joint Management Committee. In addition, she is also a fellow of the American Bar Association Foundation.

Despite her hectic schedule, Atencio devotes herself to her family. No matter how busy she is, she always makes time for her young daughter. She takes Simone along when she travels and even brings her to meetings. Atencio believes that including Simone in various activities will introduce the child to exciting places and enthusiastic people, giving Simone more confidence than Atencio had as a child. Her experience as a working mother has made her even more interested in "feminist issues," especially those that affect Hispanic women.

Although she has attained considerable respect and power, Atencio is modest about her success and sometimes regrets that she has not spent time as a public defender. She told Garcia-Johnson, "My career has gone places that I never even dreamed it would go." Her mother, who wanted her child to right the wrongs she encountered as a poor minority, has good reason to believe that Dolores Atencio has begun to do just that. Through her work in community service and the legal forum, Atencio defends and upholds the rights of Hispanics.

Sources:

Periodicals

Vista, January 27, 1991, p. 8.

Other

Dolores Atencio, telephone interview with Ronie-Richele Garcia-Johnson, August, 1992.

—Sketch by Ronie-Richele Garcia-Johnson

Paulette Atencio
(1947-)
Traditional storyteller, businesswoman

Paulette Atencio can make large successes come from small opportunities. She runs a profitable baking and catering business that grew out of providing after-school snacks to her children and their friends, but she is also widely known as a teller of traditional Hispanic stories, or *cuentos.* They are mostly oral tales from her native New Mexico that she has collected and published in her book, *Cuentos from My Childhood,* which she also produced on an audiocassette format. Atencio's knack for storytelling emerged one afternoon when she had to keep the children she was babysitting occupied. She decided to tell them stories that her mother used to tell. Atencio has since told her stories for audiences, both children and adults, from Nashville to Alaska. Her stories combine Hispanic tales with elements of more universal myths. Atencio creates stories which document elements of traditional Hispanic life in New Mexico while contributing to the world's folk narrative tradition.

Atencio is the youngest of Ricardo and Raquel Duran's ten children. She grew up in a small rural town called

Penasco in northern New Mexico. Throughout her childhood, Atencio listened to her mother's *cuentos* around the family hearth. In this manner, the traditions of the town and the Hispanic culture of New Mexico were passed on to another generation. Atencio told interviewer Andrés Chávez that the value she sees in traditional storytelling comes in part from its ability to evoke childhood. "I think that most people like to daydream about the times when they were young and what storytelling did for them. I think it's a very rewarding experience. Even the older people like storytelling. They come in and they laugh and they play. It's like they're little children all over again." Atencio also feels that traditional storytelling can instill values and promote good behavior. As she explained to Chávez, "The world is changing so much; everybody is in a hurry and television has to do the entertaining or little children have to entertain themselves. When we were growing up it wasn't like our parents had to get after us or hit us, it was through their storytelling, it set an example. Every story has a moral and there is always a lesson to be learned from it."

Atencio is planning a second volume of her *cuentos.* She is also working with the "Artist in Residence" program for the State of New Mexico, and she says that she may run for political office in the future. Whatever her future plans yield, Atencio hopes that she will be remembered for her positive contributions. As she told Chávez, "I want the good things that I have done to outweigh the bad. I believe that only then will I find beautiful things waiting at the end of the rainbow. I believe that is what life is all about."

Sources:

Atencio, Paulette, interview with Andrés Chávez, September 28, 1992.

—Sketch by Andrés Chávez

Awilda López, Mara
See **López, Mara Awilda**

Yamila Azize
(1953-)
Women's studies scholar, researcher

Yamila Azize, director of the Women's Studies Program at the University of Puerto Rico, has overseen many important studies, one of which had a particularly difficult beginning. After many fruitless attempts to secure matching funds for her research project on women's health issues, Azize nearly gave up. It was on Holy Thursday, she recalled in an interview, that she finally received a $35,000 grant offer from the Ford Foundation. "I was working alone at my office when I received a call from the Ford Foundation at a moment when we were desperately seeking money for abortion research," she stated in a telephone interview with Pam Berry. "I have a joke that then I believed in God!" The research findings, published in 1992, impacted Puerto Rican public policy on abortion. "Our data and research brought some light and knowledge to an issue like abortion that traditionally has not been researched in Puerto Rico," she said. "Our main focus has been to approach abortion as a health issue and not a moral issue."

This was not the first time that Azize, an associate professor with the university's Cayey College, had conducted important academic research. The previous year, she had received a Ford Foundation grant to examine the curriculum of five colleges within the university from a gender perspective and recommend curriculum changes that would reflect women's issues and accomplishments. The resulting curriculum proposal, submitted in 1992, has been used by the University of Puerto Rico and other universities to effect curriculum change. "It focuses on the core curriculum that all students must take, so it made us able to affect students who traditionally don't enroll in specialized women's studies classes," she said.

Azize's interest in academic life began when she was a child. She was born in 1953 to parents who placed a high priority on education. Azize's father, Miguel Azize, was a property appraiser, born in Puerto Rico of Lebanese parents. Her mother, Francesco Vargas, was a patient advocate at a hospital. They sent Azize to a prestigious private school where the student was further inspired by her elementary school principal, who was a noted author of children's literature. "She motivated me to start writing poems and to get enchanted with knowledge in all its manifestations," Azize said.

After obtaining a bachelor's degree in literature from the University of Puerto Rico in 1975, Azize received a five-year fellowship from the Ford Foundation to pursue graduate studies at the University of Pennsylvania. She received her master's degree in 1976 and her doctorate in 1980,

both in romance languages. "It was a big challenge for me to share with students from different places and to see that I was able to finish my degree in another country," she said.

After graduation, Azize became an assistant professor at the University of Puerto Rico's San German Campus. She was promoted to associate professor and director of the Women's Studies Program at the university's Cayey College in 1988. There she became involved in academic work and community activities related to women's issues. The Women's Studies Program, under her direction, worked with community leaders to establish a counseling clinic for poor women. The clinic offers free counseling on such issues as domestic violence, rape, and incest.

One of Azize's many other projects has been to develop an extensive collection of resource materials on women's issues for the university's library—the largest such collection in Puerto Rico. She has also written a book on the history of feminism in Puerto Rico, *La mujer en la lucha,* which has been printed three times and is scheduled to be published in English. Azize has proposed a study of gender bias in the courts, which she is conducting with the endorsement of the Puerto Rican Supreme Court.

Despite her professional accomplishments, Azize feels that her most important accomplishment is a personal one: breaking free from traditional lifestyle patterns by remaining single and committed to feminist issues. In an interview she stated, "To try to have an independent criteria to organize my personal and professional life—that's one of my constant struggles."

Sources:

Periodicals

San Juan Star, November 15, 1990, p. 6.

Other

Azize, Yamila, telephone interview with Pam Berry, August 22, 1992.

—*Sketch by Pam Berry*

B

Maria Teresa Babín
(1910-1989)
Educator

When Maria Teresa Babín died in 1989, literary and academic communities mourned her passing. Babín was a professor of Spanish and Puerto Rican studies in Puerto Rico and the United States, as well as a renowned literary critic, essayist, and creative writer. "Puerto Rican cultural life suffered a great loss with the death of Dr. Maria Teresa Babín on Dec. 19, 1989," according to a memorial tribute published in *La revista del Centro de Estudios Avanzados de Puerto Rico y El Caribe*. Her literary studies were filled with insights into the culture of Puerto Rico and its people. An accomplished researcher, she conducted important studies on such Puerto Rican literary notables as Julia de Burgos, Augusto Malaret, and Luis Palés Matos. Her most important works were studies of the life, poetry, and prose of Federico García Lorca, one of Spain's most cherished poets and dramatists.

Babín's scholarly instincts were nurtured early on. Born in 1910 in Ponce, Puerto Rico, Babín was encouraged by her Puerto Rican mother, Joaquina Cortes de Babín, to study literature and pursue a higher education. Her father, Emmanuel Babín, was born in the French colony of Guadeloupe; he managed workers on a sugar cane plantation. Babín received her bachelor's degree in Spanish from the University of Puerto Rico in 1939 and her master's degree in Hispanic studies from U.P.R. in 1939. From 1932-40, she taught Spanish and French in high schools in Puerto Rico and the United States.

While developing her academic career, Babín entered the writing profession by composing articles on literature, education, and politics, as well as critical essays on the work of such Puerto Rican and Spanish authors as Miguel Meléndez Muñoz, Fernando Sierra Berdecía, Manuel Méndez Ballester, René Marqués, Emilio S. Belaval, Carmelina Vizcarrondo, Ana Roqué de Duprey, Francisco Gonzalo Marin, and Manuel Joglar Cacho. Her articles and essays were published in various professional journals and newspapers, including *Brújula, Ateneo Puertorriqueño, El mundo, El imparcial, Puerto Rico ilustrado, La democracia,* *Revista Hispanica moderna, Repertorio Americano, La torre,* and *Revista del Instituto de Cultura Puertorriqueña*.

In 1940, Babín accepted a position as associate professor of Spanish and chair of the department at the University of Puerto Rico's Rio Piedras campus. Towards the end of her tenure at the university, she collaborated on the second edition of the *Columbia Encyclopedia*, writing articles in English on Spanish literature. Six years later, Babín moved to the United States and became an instructor of Romance languages at Hunter College, now part of the City University of New York. A short time later she began writing what would become one of her major literary projects, a book entitled *Introducción a la Cultura Hispánica*, which was published in 1949. This book was praised by many critics and was used as a textbook at several colleges and universities in the United States.

Studied Life and Works of Federico García Lorca

When Babín obtained her doctorate from Columbia University in New York City in 1951, her doctoral thesis as well as her master's thesis were on the life and works of Federico García Lorca. As Babín's research developed so did her interest in the great Spanish author—so much so that Lorca became the subject of four other Babín books, *Federico García Lorca y su vida, El mundo poética de Federico García Lorca, García Lorca—Vida y obra,* and *La prosa mágica de García Lorca*. While studying at Columbia University, she met her first husband, Estevan Vicente, an artist who was born in Spain.

After earning her doctorate, Babín became an assistant professor of Spanish at New York University's Washington Square College and continued to write many articles, critical essays, and several books. However, Federico García Lorca was not the only subject of her literary attention. In 1956, *Fantasía Boricua: Estampas de mi terra* was published. The book contained fantasies and images, or estampas, of her native land, interwoven with major events, such as the celebration of Christmas in Puerto Rico, the great hurricane of 1899, and the importance of fishing and harvesting sugar cane. *La hora colmada*, a theatrical fable, was published in 1960. Other works during this period include an anthology of the verses of Francisco Gonzalo Marin and *Panorama de la cultura Puertorriqueña*, both published in 1958.

The 1960s was a period of growth for Babín—both personally and professionally. In 1964, she married her

Maria Teresa Babín

Unión Mujeres Americanas literary prize, 1962, and the Literary Prize of the Year from the Instituto Puertorriqueño, 1970.

Sources:

Books

La revista del Centro de Estudios Avanzados de Puerto Rico y El Caribe, Department of Puerto Rican Studies, Center for Advanced Studies on Puerto Rico, 1989, p. 25.

Rivera de Alvarez, Josefina, *Diccionario de literatura Puertorriquent,* Instituto de Cultura Puertorriquent, 1974, pp. 158-161.

Other

Rivera, Carmen, telephone interview with Pam Berry, September 9 and 10, 1992, San Juan, Puerto Rico.

—Sketch by Pam Berry

second husband, Jose Nieto, a Spanish-born college professor. In 1967, a book entitled *La gesta de Puerto Rico* was published, as well as *Antologia poética de Evaristo Ribera Chevremont,* written with Jaime Luis Rodriguez. And Babín left Washington Square College to join the faculty of Lehman College of the City University of New York Graduate Center. It was during her tenure at Lehman College, 1969-72, that Babín founded and headed the first Department of Puerto Rican Studies in the United States.

In 1970, Babín took on the additional duties of professor of Spanish at the City University of New York Graduate Center; she was named professor emeritus in 1978. Once again, Babín blended her academic duties at both Lehman College and City University with her writing career and produced a number of notable literary works, including four well-received books: *The Puerto Ricans' Spirit: Their History, Life and Culture, La poesia gallega de García Lorca, Estudios Lorquianos,* and *Genio y figura de Nemesio R. Canales.*

Although busy with her various full-time teaching positions and writing assignments, Babín also found time to share her extensive knowledge and love of Puerto Rican culture and literature with others by lecturing at numerous universities across the United States and consulting with various universities, organizations, and government agencies. Babín received numerous awards and honors for her work, including several prestigious prizes for her writing, the Instituto de Literatura Puertorriqueña literary prize, 1954, the Ateneo Puertorriqueño literary prize, 1955, the

Judith F. Baca
(1946-)
Artist, muralist, professor

Judith Francisca Baca has risen from the role of premiere muralist of the streets of Los Angeles to that of an international chronicler. In more than two decades of painting large-scale projects, Baca has sought to display the history and culture of a variety of races in her artwork. In addition to her work as a muralist and community organizer, Baca helped found the Social and Public Art Resource Center (SPARC) in Venice, California, an organization dedicated to the promotion and cultivation of Latino artists. Baca's stature in the art world rose with her project the "Great Wall," the largest outdoor mural in the world. Her next large-scale public art project, the "World Wall," which is a study of envisioning a world without fear, includes participation by international artists and has been displayed in locations as diverse as Gorky Park in Moscow and the Smithsonian Institution in Washington, D.C. "A pivotal figure since the early 1970s is Chicano muralist, teacher, and community activist Judy Baca," wrote Paul Von Blum in *Z Magazine.* "Her combined efforts as a muralist and artistic director of SPARC have brought her national acclaim. . . . (Her) initial projects established Baca as a major public artist whose work encompassed a communal process culminating in vivid, socially conscious imagery."

Judith F. Baca

Baca, a second-generation Chicana, was born September 20, 1946, in south central Los Angeles. Growing up in the Huntington Park neighborhood, she was brought up in a strong female household, which included her mother, grandmother, and two aunts, one of whom was mentally retarded. While Baca's mother, Ortensia Baca ("She dropped the 'H' because she didn't like the Anglos calling her 'Hortense,'" Baca said in a telephone interview with Yleana Martinez), worked at a tire factory, Baca was raised primarily by her grandmother. Although she did not know her father, a musician named Valentino Marcel, Baca was very happy. She recalled: "It was a very strong, wonderful, matriarchal household. I was everybody's child. I had a wonderful playmate in my grown-up aunt who wasn't grown up in her head. It was like she was five, my age, only she was big."

When Baca was six her mother married Clarence Ferrari and moved to Pacoima, where Baca would spend her formative years. She remembers that she spoke English poorly in elementary school and felt very alien in the school. She missed living in a Spanish-speaking household with her grandmother, who stayed behind in south central Los Angeles. Out of this alienation, however, came her first opportunity to practice art. Her teacher allowed her to sit in a corner and paint while the rest of the class carried on.

Baca graduated in 1964 from Bishop Alemany High School, a Catholic school in Mission Hills, California, run

by the Sisters of St. Joseph Carondelet. A year later, she would marry at the age of 19. The marriage would last six years. She returned to her alma mater to teach after receiving a bachelor's degree in art in 1969 from California State University in Northridge. That same year, she embarked on her first cooperative art venture when she rounded up a number of ethnically diverse students to paint a mural at the school. It was "a method to force the group into cooperation," she said, a method she would employ time and again in her future projects.

Baca's days at the high school were numbered. Baca became involved with the peace movement against the war in Viet Nam and participated in marches, alongside many of the nuns who also taught at the school. A change in the school's administration resulted in a notorious incident, the purge of the "Alemany Eighteen," she said. Ten nuns, Baca, and seven other lay teachers were fired for their anti-war activities. Shortly thereafter the rest of the nuns withdrew from operating the school in protest of the action. Baca said she was "quite traumatized" by the event, for she believed her teaching career was over.

However, Baca soon found employment in a special program for artists with the City of Los Angeles Cultural Affairs Division. Baca traveled from schools to parks, teaching art, eventually forming her own group, "Las Vistas Nuevas," she said. The group, made up of 20 kids from four different gangs and neighborhood groups, painted her first mural for her, in Hollenbeck Park. "The city was amazed at the work I was doing," she recalled, "putting up murals with kids who'd run directors out of neighborhood centers. The city let me do my own thing."

Inspired by *Los Tres Grandes* Mexican Muralists

Shortly after the completion of the Hollenbeck Park mural, someone handed her a book on "Los Tres Grandes"— Diego Rivera, David Alfaro Siqueiros, and José Clemente Orozco—the famous Mexican muralists, and Baca began to learn about the Mexican tradition of mural painting. In the mid-1970's, she did go to Mexico to take classes in mural materials and techniques at Siqueiros's studio and traveled around the country looking at the murals. "The precedence of all mural painting in America lies with Los Tres Grandes," she said in an interview with Ann Malaspina. Baca is firmly fixed in that tradition. "I believe taking art to the people is a political act," she said, echoing her forebears. "I am a Mexican mural painter in the true sense, but I took it to the next level. To keep an art form living, it has to grow and change."

Back in Los Angeles, with the support of the city firmly behind her, Baca expanded her program into the Citywide Mural Project. At least 250 murals were painted under her supervision. Baca can rightfully claim to be the first in Los Angeles to work with multicultural youth to produce murals. "Walls were already used as community billboards in

L.A., so the extension of graffiti to images was not that big a leap to make," she said in her telephone interview.

Her most ambitious project during the 1970s was the "Great Wall," a half-mile long narrative mural painted on the Tujunga Wash drainage canal in San Fernando Valley. Its subject is Los Angeles' multi-ethnic history from neolithic times up to the 1950s and encompasses such events as the Freedom Bus Rides, Japanese American Internment during World War II, the great Dust Bowl Journey, and the infamous Zoot Suit Riots of 1942. The "Great Wall" was painted over five summers in nine years. Baca developed the concept, hired people, and helped raise money for the project, which she likened in a telephone interview to "developing a military encampment."

Baca began to see the value in working with diverse groups to create public art. "It still is the only example of interracial work that focuses on working on racial differences in Los Angeles. It was not only a mural program, but it addressed ethnicity and acknowledged the differences between cultural groups," she said. Using the "Great Wall" project as a model, Baca went on to found in 1976 the Social and Public Art Resource Center (SPARC), in Venice, California. The non-profit, multicultural art center continues a program of involving artists, community groups and youth to present and preserve murals and other public art. The internationally recognized alternative art center also houses an archive of more than 16,000 slides of public art from around the world.

"World Wall" Mural Established Reputation

In 1987 Baca embarked on an even grander project, "World Wall: A Vision of the Future Without Fear." Its themes of global importance, war, peace, and cooperation grew out of brainstorming sessions with people selected to provide cultural diversity and expertise in areas of concern to the project. The portable mural is made of seven 10-by-30-foot panels to be painted by Baca and arranged in a 100-foot semi-circle. With four panels completed, the piece premiered in Finland in June 1990. It then traveled to the Soviet Union, where it was displayed in Gorky Park. The mural includes seven panels to be painted by artists from the countries in which it will be displayed. These additional panels will be hung on the outer circle.

For Baca, the jump from producing murals with neighborhood groups to working with artists from around the world was a natural transition. "My idea was that what we had learned with the interracial work in Los Angeles could be applied to an international scope, from the neighborhood to the global," she said. "The World Wall is an attempt to push the state of arts in muralism so that the mural creates its own architecture. It makes its own space and can be assembled by any people anywhere." Second, she asked the participating artists to act as visionaries, to envision the future without fear, she said. The mural, when completed, "will be a world-wide collaboration." The titles of the panels painted by Baca are "Triumph of the Heart," "Nonviolent Resistance," "New World Systems," "Balance," "Human Based Technology," "Missiles to Starships," and "Triumph of the Hands." The panels will use striking imagery to present specific allegories.

In her artist's statement for "World Wall," Baca wrote: ". . . Many of us read Jonathan Schell's *Fate of the Earth*, in which he said that we must imagine the eventuality of nuclear war before we can change our destiny. It occurred to me later that it was not imagining destruction that was so hard to us but rather imagining peace. One of the students on the 'World Wall' team said, 'Is peace everyone sitting around watching TV?' If we cannot imagine peace as an active concept, how can we ever hope for it to happen?"

Creating the World Wall—especially working with children—was a labor of love. In *Artweek*, Baca recounted an exercise she often did with her young assistants. She asked them to gather in a large circle and hold out their hands. "And then you'd see all these wonderful little hands, these little brown fingers, stubby Asian hands, slim-fingered white hands, all these various hands," Baca recalled. Then she would tell the teenagers: "We need every hand here. We have nine weeks and we have 350 feet of wall, it's these hands that will make that."

Despite her success on numerous levels, Baca has struggled with raising funds for her work. In an interview with the *Los Angeles Times*, Baca said it was "ironic" that she had received more support for the "World Wall" from abroad than on a local level. She said other countries have sponsored visits for her and her assistants by providing free accommodations and other arrangements but that she had been turned down by several influential U.S. foundations and art councils. However, she did secure funding from groups including the Rockefeller Foundation, the Women's Foundation, and Arco. "The intention is to create a dialogue of a vision of the future where there will be a world without fear," she told the *Los Angeles Times*. "As artists, we have the power of spreading ideas, and this is a way in which the power of ideas can move around the world," she said.

Baca's art reflects her commitment to addressing social ills. This interest, she claims, stems from being raised by her grandmother, whom she described as being a very religious person and the neighborhood's resident healer. She can recall that her grandmother used herbs and prayer to make her well. She believes that her artwork exhibits much of the conscientiousness instilled in her by her grandmother through the images of healing and making the family work. "[My work] focuses on social struggles, issues, and ills that come about from racism," she said.

Baca holds a master's degree in art from California State University at Northridge and is a full professor of art at the University of California at Irvine.

Sources:

Books

Lippard, Lucy, *Mixed Blessings: Art for a Multicultural America,* Penguin Books, 1988.

Periodicals

Artweek, October 6, 1979, p. 5; November 14, 1991, pp. 10-11; November 21, 1991, pp. 10-11.
Life, December, 1980, pp. 87-90.
Los Angeles Times, April 5, 1991, p. F16.
Von Blum, Paul, "Women Political Artists in Los Angeles: Judy Baca's Public Art," *Z Magazine,* October, 1991, pp. 70-74.

Other

Baca, Judith F., telephone interview with Yleana Martinez, August, 1992.
Baca, Judith F., interview with Ann Malaspina, August, 1992.
Mesa-Bains, Amalia, "El Mundo Femenino: Chicana Artists of the Movement—A Commentary on Development and Production," contained in *CARA: Chicano Art—Resistance & Affirmation (1965-1985),* sponsored by UCLA, Wight Gallery, 1991.

—Sketch by Yleana Martinez

Polly Baca

Polly Baca
(1943-)
Politician, activist

Polly Baca is a pioneer in the growing field of Hispanic woman politics. A Colorado State Senator for 12 years, Baca was the first woman chair of the House Democratic Caucus, and in 1985 she was elected chair of the Senate Democratic Caucus. She was the first woman and only minority woman to be elected to the Colorado Senate and the first Hispanic woman to serve in leadership in any State Senate in the United States. A long-time activist at the local, regional, and national levels with civic groups, she is nationally known for her leadership skills and motivational presentations.

Baca was born in Greeley, Colorado, in 1943. She is the daughter of Spanish Americans José Manuel, a former migrant farm worker, and Leda Sierra, a strong and fiercely independent woman. From her mother Polly learned that "a woman must be her own person, independent and able to care for herself," Baca stated in a 1988 interview with contributor Gloria Bonilla-Santiago.

Encounters Racism as a Child

One of Baca's early memories is from grade school, where she first began to notice racial discrimination. She and her family went to church and saw little girls inside in white dresses; somehow, Baca knew she wanted to be seated with them. But the ushers came and told her family they had to sit on the side aisle because they were "Mexican Americans." The center aisles were reserved for the Anglos who went to that church. In her interview, Baca recalled clearly the experience: "They assumed we were Mexican American from the other side of the tracks. They didn't want us there. My mother forced my father to move into a low-income, racially mixed neighborhood, but it was not the Spanish neighborhood. We called it the Spanish American colony because we were from Colorado and from the old Spanish families. My mother was the strength in my family."

At fourteen, Baca's father was killed in an accident, and shortly after her mother died. She literally had to assume the role of an adult even though she had no role models. She raised her three younger brothers using common sense. She loved them and she did what she thought her mother would have done. Motivated by her neighbor, Baca finished high school and won a scholarship to attend college. She recollected in her interview that she "wanted to go to Colorado State University and major in physics. My chemistry teacher told me about Madame Curie and told me I couldn't succeed in public life because I was 'Mexican American,' but I could in the scientific field because they had to judge you by what you were. So that's what I decided to be, a physics major. The principal at that high school was very bigoted. She tried to discourage me from applying to the state university."

Although Baca began university studies with a major in physics, she was soon drawn back to her ninth-grade desire to enter a field of power—law and politics. She plunged into campus politics, taking the vice presidency, and later the presidency, of the university Young Democrats; she was also secretary for her freshman class. Active as a volunteer for congressional campaigns, Baca was a student volunteer of the Viva Kennedy Clubs for John F. Kennedy and worked as an intern for the Colorado Democratic Party.

After receiving her B.A. in political science in 1962, Baca was recruited to work as an editorial assistant for a trade union newspaper in Washington, D.C. Shortly after, she was recruited to work for President Lyndon Johnson's administration as a public information officer for a White House agency. Next she joined the national campaign staff of the late Senator Robert F. Kennedy in his bid for President of the United States in 1968. That same year she served as the director of research and information for the National Council of La Raza in Phoenix, Arizona, where she met her husband, Miguel Barragán, a Chicano activist and former priest. The marriage produced two children, Monica and Mike, before ending in divorce. A few years later, adding to a long list of "firsts," Polly became an assistant to the Chairman of the Democratic National Committee. Shortly after, she opened a public relations business in Adams County after returning to Colorado, where her professional experiences blossomed into her political career.

Wins Election in Colorado

In 1974, Polly Baca won Colorado's 34th district seat in the state's House of Representatives, and four years later she was elected to the Colorado State Legislature as the first Hispanic woman senator. In 1977, she was elected the first woman chair of the House Democratic Caucus, and in 1985, she was elected chair of the Senate Democratic caucus. She was the first minority woman to be elected to the Colorado Senate and the first Hispanic woman to serve in leadership in any State Senate in the United States.

In her interview Baca recalled a personal note Senator Edward Kennedy sent to her with his best personal wishes during her legislative campaign, saying, "We need more representation of the Chicano community in public office as we need more women, and Polly's the best of both. . . . She will represent a progressive, bright, and effective

addition to the state legislature, one who will speak for all the people of her district."

As a freshman legislator in the Colorado House of Representatives, Polly broke an old rule of the seniority system which imposed a "watch and wait" attitude on first termers. In the 1975 session of the Colorado Legislature, she introduced nine House bills and carried six Senate bills in the House. Two of these House bills and three of Senate bills were passed by both houses and signed into law by the governor. Throughout her term she sponsored 201 more House bills and 57 additional Senate bills. Of these, 156 passed both houses and are now law. Some of her most notable bills are Senate Bill 118, providing for the protection of deposits of public monies held by the state and national banks (1986); Senate Bill 87, providing authority to the Colorado district courts to enforce foreign subpoenas, (1985); Senate Bill 139, concerning assessment of civil money penalties by the state banking board, (1985); House Bill 1117, continuing the short-term-loan revolving fund in the division of housing, (1985); House Bill 1336, regulating the operation of non state post-secondary institutions in Colorado by the Colorado Commission of Higher Education, and many others.

As the *Denver Post* summarized, Baca was known in Colorado as "a democratic senator representing 63,000 Adams County residents. On the other hand, she is the Colorado politician who has the closest ties to the nation's Democratic Leadership in Washington, D.C. . . . In fact, Barragan, has better, more open links to the White House than Gov. Dick Lamm and other Democratic leaders in Colorado." Throughout her work Baca won the respect of many leaders in the state of Colorado and nationally. By any standards, she must be judged a good policy maker.

Part of her success is attributable to her many volunteer and civic activities, which she has pursued throughout her career and which she views as a basic training ground for any politician. These activities included Chicano and minority activism, party politics, women's rights, professional and business development, and political and community organizing. Locally, she worked on the Board of Trustees of Labor's Community Agency, the Latin American Research and Service Agency, the Mile High United Way, and she has been on the Policy Advisory Council on the Division of the State Compensation Insurance Fund. On a broader scale, she served on the boards of the National Chicano Planning Council and Mexican American Legal Defense and Education Fund (MALDEF) and many others.

Baca told the *Denver Post* that she is especially proud of her part in the founding of the National Congress of Hispanic American Citizens, better known as "El Congreso," the country's first and only full-time Latino lobby at the nation's Capitol. Her experience at the state legislative committee level reads like a Who's Who of committee assignments: Rules; Business Affairs and Labor; Finance; Local Government; Agriculture, National Resources and

Energy; Transportation; School Finance; State Affairs; Health, Environment, Welfare and Institutions; Legislative Audit; and Education. Baca's legislation, moreover, has always been people-oriented. For example, in 1986 Polly Baca introduced innovative legislation to correct inequitable financial burdens on Colorado property tax-payers, while still providing quality education. In addition, she introduced legislation to protect public monies in state national banks. In 1980 and again in 1984, she was elected Co-Chair of the Democratic National Convention and chaired the Colorado delegation to the 1978 Democratic Mid-term Conference. Baca also gladly shared her extensive foreign affairs experience as a participant and panelist to major international conferences in Columbia, Mexico, the USSR, Israel, Egypt, Lebanon, Canada, Belgium, and West Germany.

It was her track record of performance and success at the national level as senator that motivated her to be a candidate for the U.S. Congress in 1986. In a personal interview for *Hispanic Women Breaking Ground and Barriers,* Baca commented on the disappointment she felt after losing the race: "I've had two great pains in my life. The divorce was rejection by a male . . . that's how I perceived it. The other was when I lost my race for Congress. This was rejection because I was an Hispanic woman. That's the only reason I lost that race. It's a great deal of pain. I don't know of a pain that is greater and that's why people don't take risks. It's a lack of confidence that you can't succeed or the willingness to withstand the rejection if you fail."

After the long campaign, Baca retired from public office and became President of Sierra Baca Systems, a consulting firm specializing in program development and assessment, leadership training, issue analysis and motivational presentations. In addition, Baca has frequently appeared as a political commentator on both television and radio. She is nationally known for her leadership skills and for breaking ground in the area of politics for Latinas in the United States.

In 1988, she was honored as one of the original 14 members to be inducted into the National Hispanic Hall of Fame and being listed in the World Who's Who of Women. Though Baca has no political aspirations at present, she continues to be active with national civic groups and serves on a bipartisan Commission on National Political Conventions. More recently, Baca has been devoting her time to heading up the Colorado Institute for Hispanic Education and Economic Empowerment, whose mission is to "create a pool of Hispanic leaders who are sensitive to cultural differences and gender issues, and who will jump on the fast track to leadership positions," according to Mercedes Olivera in *Vista.* "If we are to have social cohesiveness as a nation," Baca related in *Vista,* "I feel strongly that we have to value the other people, their value system, culture, history. If we honor those differences, then we can look at the human thread that unites us all as human beings."

Sources:

Periodicals

The Collegian (Colorado State University), May 29, 1962, p. 1.
Dateline Young Democrats, April/May, 1967, pp. 1-6.
Denver Catholic Register, June 30, 1981, pp. 1-5.
Denver Post, October 21, 1979, pp. 1, 37, 39.
La Voz (Denver), January 8, 1980, p. 8.
Vista, February 4, 1992, p. 24.

Other

Baca, Polly, "Hispanic Women as a Moving Force in Government and the Public Sector," speech presented at Hispanas Unidas: The Force of San Antonio Conference, San Antonio, TX, March 24, 1984, pp. 1-3.
Baca, Polly, interview with Gloria Bonilla-Santiago, New York, NY, December 30, 1988, Cherry Hill, NJ.
Baca-Barragan, Polly, "Public Policy and the Chicano Population," prepared for the Stanford Center for Chicano Research, Stanford University, March 5, 1982, unpublished paper, pp. 1-10.
"Polly Baca for Congress: Neighborhood Campaign Materials," Thornton, Colorado, 1986. p. 1.
Neighborhood Campaign News, *Bills and Resolutions Successfully Introduced by Senator Baca and Enacted into Law,* 1986, p.4.

—*Sketch by Gloria Bonilla-Santiago*

Maxine Baca Zinn
(1942-)
Sociologist

As an undergraduate at California State College (now California State University) at Long Beach, Maxine Baca Zinn sat in on sociology classes and listened to professors discuss minorities. A Chicana who grew up in Santa Fe, New Mexico, the future sociologist could not identify with what her professors were saying. "They didn't describe social life as I experienced it," she recalled in a telephone interview with Yleana Martinez. "So I decided to set the record straight." Baca Zinn, credited with being one of the very first to conduct sociological work on Latino families and Mexican American women, has been lovingly referred to by her colleagues as one of "the foremothers of Chicana feminism." Since 1990 she has taught sociology at Michigan State University in East Lansing, where she resides with her husband, Alan Zinn, and their son, Prentice.

Maxine Baca Zinn

Baca Zinn's studies in family sociology have earned her a reputation as a pioneer in the field of family, race, and ethnic relations. She has published widely in scholarly journals on the topic of Mexican American families. She has read her findings at numerous professional conferences and association meetings. In addition, she has received several awards honoring her for her research, including the 1990 Outstanding Alumnus Award from the College of Social and Behavioral sciences of her alma mater, California State University, Long Beach, and the 1989 Cheryl Miller Lecturer Award on Women and Social Change, which is cosponsored by Sociologists for Women in Society and Loyola University of Chicago. In 1988 Baca Zinn received a special recognition award for contributions to the Western Social Science Association, where she had served as president from 1985 to 1986.

Maxine Baca was born June 11, 1942, in Santa Fe, New Mexico, to Presente and Louise Duran Baca. After graduating from high school, she entered California State College at Long Beach, earning a bachelor of arts degree in sociology in 1966. Two years later she returned to her home state to begin graduate studies at the University of New Mexico, where she also worked as a graduate teaching assistant. She received her master's degree in sociology in 1970, and was inducted to the Phi Kappa Phi Honor Society in 1971. Later that year she entered the doctoral program in sociology at the University of Oregon, where she held a graduate teaching fellowship through 1973. Also in 1973, she was

awarded a dissertation fellowship from the Ford Foundation. She received her Ph.D. from the University of Oregon in 1978.

Meanwhile, she moved to Michigan in 1975 to begin teaching at the University of Michigan at Flint, where she has been honored several times for her teaching. In 1975 she received a Faculty Special Merit Award and in 1982 the Faculty Achievement Award for Scholarly or Creative Achievement. One year later she was given the Distinguished Faculty Award from the Michigan Association of Governing Boards. In the summer of 1984 Baca Zinn was a visiting scholar at the Center for Research on Women at Memphis State University in Memphis, Tennessee, where she would return in the spring of 1987 as a research professor in residence.

While on leave from the University of Michigan at Flint, Baca Zinn worked as a visiting professor of sociology at the University of California at Berkeley, a guest professor of sociology at the University of Connecticut, and a distinguished visiting professor in Women's Studies at the University of Delaware. She was named a senior research associate at the Julian Samora Research Institute at Michigan State University in 1990.

Baca Zinn, a member of the American Sociological Society, was elected to that organization's governing council in 1992. She said her election to the ten-member council came as a surprise because all 13,000 members of the society vote to select the council. This victory, she said, is an indication of how the studies she has conducted have "pushed the margin." She does not claim this accomplishment as stemming from her unique insight into the field of race and family studies. Rather, she regards it as testimony to the importance of the work. "Society is becoming so diverse that the old ways of thinking do not work any more," she commented.

Challenges Prevailing Views of Minorities

Baca Zinn's dedication to the area of ethnic families was formed in the late 1960s and early 1970s. Her early work, she said, revolved around changing myths about minority people. "I wanted to move away from the 'blaming the victim' stance. I then found, as I did more and more scholarship, that when you change models and explanations of minorities, you have to change the whole explanation of how society works—and change explanations of white people as well." This led to her becoming more interested in "the whole global picture," she said. She has found that there is a connection between the circumstances of different classes and races: "Economically privileged people are where they are largely because of where minorities are now."

As a young sociologist, Baca Zinn began conducting what she termed "oppositional scholarship," questioning the mainstream view that minorities are their own worst enemy. But as her studies took her more deeply into the world of women, especially that of Mexican American women, she found that her "oppositional scholarship" approach could not apply: "When you add women and minorities (to the research), you have to change the explanations of social relations." She compared her discovery to a recipe that cannot be adapted. "The metaphor is that you can't just add women and stir. Like when you have a recipe, and then go on with it as usual. When you add women and minorities . . . you have to explain and rethink the position and explanation of European Americans."

In one of her earliest articles, "Chicanas: Power and Control in the Domestic Sphere," published in 1975 in *De Colores: Journal of Emerging Raza Philosophies,* Baca Zinn sought to examine Chicanas' roles as depicted until then in sociological literature. She writes that the "passive, submissive, Mexican woman is a creation of social scientists and journalists who have taken for granted the idea that women are dependent and unproductive creatures." Baca Zinn provides several examples that attack the prevailing notion that Chicanas are dependent. She concludes that there is sufficient sociological literature on the Mexican American family that reveals that women control family activities, despite the patriarchal orientation of Chicano life. She notes that Chicano families are indeed mother-centered, and that Chicanas have developed alignments with other women which nurture a collective sense of their own worth. Baca Zinn calls upon her sisters to replace the stereotype of the passive Chicana "with concepts of diverse women whose responsibility for the physical and cultural survival of Chicanos is acknowledged and seriously examined."

Baca Zinn's studies on Mexican American women have brought her closer to her goal of making sociology more "minority inclusive." She believes there are more and more scholars "revising the past," offering new interpretations of the sociological framework of minorities and their families. However, her mission has been an arduous one. As a self-proclaimed "marginal intellectual," she works within the system by publishing scholarly articles, by having her views publicly aired at association gatherings, and through mentoring students—particularly Latinas and women of color.

Analyzes Chicana and Latina Feminism

Her interests now lie in analyzing what it means to be a Chicana feminist. Baca Zinn believes that the ideals of feminine liberation differ among the racial groups. "I think that Chicana and Latina feminism is very much overlooked," she declared. "We are looking at how Chicanas and Latinas are claiming their own feminism, but how? That's one of the difficult issues. The question is, what is Chicana-Latina feminism, and how does it differ from Black feminism? I'm working on some ideas."

As she and her fellow sociologists with the same objective have continued to break down stereotypes, the work, she believes, has become more theoretical. Baca Zinn cherishes her tight social network of sociologist friends, which includes men, white women, and women of color. "We really have invented a new 'women of color feminism.' It doesn't take white women's experiences as the starting point for theorizing and analyzing women's lives. It takes the lives and experiences of women of color and uses that as a standpoint. We all think of ourselves as marginal intellectuals, like outsiders," she noted. She added, "We're really challenging the boundary of mainstream scholarship."

Sources:

Periodicals

De Colores: Journal of Emerging Raza Philosophies, winter, 1975, pp. 19-31.

Other

Baca Zinn, Maxine, telephone conversation with Yleana Martinez, August, 1992.

—*Sketch by Yleana Martinez*

Joan Baez
(1941-)
Singer, songwriter, activist

Singer, songwriter, and activist Joan Baez was an important part of the fabric that made up the 1960s experience. During the decade she appeared on the cover of *Time* magazine, sang to a crowd of 350,000 gathered at the Lincoln Memorial for Martin Luther King, Jr.'s "I Have a Dream" speech, toured with legendary entertainer Bob Dylan, campaigned against the Vietnam War, and performed at Woodstock. Despite her connection with so many of the important events and personalities of the sixties, she refuses to see herself as a symbol of that era. In a *Rolling Stone* interview with Mike Sager she maintains that she would rather be seen as an example "of following through on your beliefs, using your talents to do so."

Baez's beliefs and her talents have brought her considerable fame during a 30-year career that found its start in early childhood influences. She was born Joan Chandos Baez on January 9, 1941, in Staten Island, New York, to

Joan Baez

Joan Bridge Baez, originally from Scotland, and Albert Baez, who came to the United States from Mexico. From her parents the singer inherited both a rich multicultural background and the nonviolent Quaker religious beliefs that inspired her own interest in issues of peace and justice. Her father was a physicist whose moral concerns caused him to turn down lucrative defense work and devote his life to academic research. Commenting on the consequences of her father's decision in her 1987 autobiography *And a Voice to Sing With,* Baez notes: "We would never have all the fine and useless things little girls want when they are growing up. Instead we would have a father with a clear conscience. Decency would be his legacy to us."

Because of her Hispanic roots, Baez was introduced to racial inequality at a young age. In her autobiography she recalls being taunted as a child because of the color of her skin and relates her experiences in junior high school where she felt isolated from both the Mexican and Anglo children. She writes: "Few Mexicans were interested in school and they were ostracized by the whites. So there I was, with a Mexican name, skin, and hair: the Anglos couldn't accept me because of all three, and the Mexicans couldn't accept me because I didn't speak Spanish." She was also considered strange because of her pacifist beliefs. While other students spoke with fear of the Soviet Union and the echoed anticommunist feelings firmly held by most adults at the time, Baez took an antimilitary stance that she learned from family discussions and Quaker activities.

Baez admits that loneliness was an important factor in her desire to become a singer. Seeing music as a path to popularity, she spent a summer developing her voice and learning to play the ukulele. She soon gained a reputation as an entertainer and made her first stage appearance in a school talent show. She was also known among her peers as a talented artist who could sketch Disney characters and paint school election posters with ease. At 14 she wrote a short, self-illustrated essay entitled "What I Believe" in which she related her beliefs on many topics. The essay expresses many of the truths that would serve as a moral guide for Baez's actions throughout her life. The excerpt she includes in her autobiography ends with her musing "I think of myself as hardly a speck. Then I see there is no use for this tiny dot to spend its small life doing things for itself. It might as well spend its tiny amount of time making the less fortunate specks in the world enjoy themselves."

Discovers Folk Scene in Boston

A family move from California to the Boston area after her high school graduation provided the circumstances that eventually allowed Baez to help "the less fortunate specks" mentioned in her essay. Although she started classes at Boston University, intellectual pursuits were quickly superseded by her growing interest in folk music. Bolstered by the popularity of such folk musicians as Pete Seeger and the Kingston Trio, the genre had experienced a revival during the late 1950s. Coffee houses that featured local singers became popular gathering spots for college students throughout the country. At first Baez and a roommate sang duets ("Fair and Tender Maidens" was their specialty) at coffee houses in the Boston area, but Baez soon went solo. She accepted an invitation to perform two nights a week at Club Mt. Auburn 47, a Harvard Square jazz club that was hoping to add folk enthusiasts to its clientele.

In 1959, Baez had gathered enough of a following to record her first album, titled *Folksingers 'Round Harvard Square,* that she recorded with two friends. That same year she sang for a couple of weeks at The Gate of Horn, a Chicago nightclub. While there she met popular folk singer Bob Gibson, who invited her to appear with him at the first Newport Jazz Festival that August. Her three-octave soprano voice captivated the festival crowd of 13,000 and made her an instant celebrity. Although she returned to her coffee house engagements after the festival, Baez sensed the increasingly important role that music would play in her life. In *And a Voice to Sing With* she notes that after her Newport appearance she realized that "in the book of my destiny the first page had been turned, and that this book could no longer be exchanged for any other."

Turning down more lucrative deals with larger record companies, Baez chose to sign her first contract with Vanguard, a small label known for its quality classical music recordings. Her first solo album, simply titled *Joan Baez,* was released near the end of 1960. The album was made up entirely of traditional folk songs, including "All My Trials" (an often requested favorite among Baez fans) and "The House of the Rising Sun," a song previously popularized by Huddie Ledbetter (Leadbelly), a black blues singer. A song in Spanish as well as the popular Scottish ballad, "Mary Hamilton," were also included. The album was a success, reaching the number three spot on the sales charts. Near the time of the record's release, Baez moved to California's Pacific coast.

From her new home in California, Baez often commuted to the East coast, playing colleges with other folk artists in auditoriums seating two to five hundred people. In November 1960, she played her first solo concert to an audience of 800 in New York City. By 1963, her third album had come out and she was playing at the Forest Hills Music Festival and Hollywood Bowl with ten to 20,000 in attendance. As her career seemed to take over her life, she began to think about the essay that she wrote as a teenager and what was truly important to her. In her autobiography she writes, "I was in a position now to do something more with my life than just sing. I had the capacity to make lots and lots of money. I could reach lots and lots of people. It would be a while before this sentiment would take root and grow into something tangible, but the intent was now evident and becoming stronger by the day."

Becomes Active in Vietnam War Protest

The Vietnam War protest became the cause to which Baez would devote an increasingly larger amount of energy as the sixties progressed. In 1964, she announced that she would stop paying the 60 percent of her federal income tax that she figured went to financing the U.S. Defense Department. The following year she founded the Institute for the Study of Nonviolence (now called the Resource Center for Nonviolence) in Palo Alto, California. Her political beliefs at times affected her career. In 1967, citing the singer's strong antiwar stance, the Daughters of the American Revolution (DAR) refused Baez the permission to play at their Constitution Hall in Washington, D.C. When news of the refusal received sympathetic coverage in the press, Secretary of the Interior Mo Udall gave Baez permission to play an outdoor concert at the base of the Washington Monument, where an estimated 30,000 people came to hear her sing. Several months later she was arrested and jailed for her active opposition to the Vietnam War draft. The following year she married David Harris, a leader in the draft resistance movement.

Baez's social activism during the sixties sometimes overshadowed the reason for her rise to fame: her voice. From the beginning of her career, reviewers had struggled to describe its quality. In two early reviews appearing in the *New York Times,* music critic Bob Shelton referred to Baez's voice first as "a soprano voice, surprisingly never trained, that has a purity, penetrating clarity and control that not a few art singers would envy," later adding that it was "as lustrous and rich as old gold." The writer of a *Time* cover story on Baez discovered in her voice "distant reminders of black women wailing in the night, of detached madrigal singers performing calmly at court, and of saddened gypsies trying to charm death into leaving their Spanish caves." In *And a Voice to Sing With* Baez refers to her voice as her "greatest gift" closely followed by a "second greatest gift," that of "a desire to share that voice, and the bounties it has heaped upon me, with others."

Bob Dylan and Woodstock

Despite her increasing involvement in political concerns, Baez shared her voice with others in concert appearances and on numerous albums during the 1960s. Reluctant to leave traditional melodies behind, she slowly added more contemporary music to her repertoire. Her fourth album, *Joan Baez in Concert Part Two,* released in 1963, included a Bob Dylan song, "Don't Think Twice, It's All Right." That same year she helped Dylan's career by inviting him to appear with her during her concert tour. The two singers eventually toured together with equal billing and Baez later recorded *Any Day Now,* a double-album of Dylan tunes. She further expanded the scope of her musical offerings during the decade with *Baptism,* an album of spoken and sung selections from the poetry of Arthur Rimbaud, Federico García Lorca, James Joyce, and others, and an album of country and western music called *David's Album.* In one of the highlights of her career, Baez appeared at what many consider to be the pinnacle of 1960s culture, the Woodstock Music Festival. The five-day event was held in 1969 in upstate New York and brought together some of the most important and influential musicians of the decade. The concert drew more than 500,000 people with its theme of "five days of peace, love, and music."

The seventies saw Baez emerge as a songwriter on her album *Blessed Are . . .,* which featured several songs based on her experiences as a wife and mother, including "A Song for David" and "Gabriel and Me," a lullaby written for her son. In 1971 Baez and Harris were divorced and she decided to end her association with Vanguard. "The Night They Drove Old Dixie Down," a cut off her last Vanguard album, *Blessed Are . . .,* became one of the most popular songs of 1972 and Baez's biggest commercial success. Continuing her political activism that same year, she and a small group of friends toured (what was then North) Vietnam to witness the effects of the continuing war on the Vietnamese people. During 11 of the 13 days, Baez stayed in the capital city of Hanoi, where the United States carried out the heaviest raids of the war. On her return home, Baez edited 15 hours of tapes she had recorded during her trip and made them into her 1973 album, *Where Are You Now, My Son?,* a very personal plea for an end to the war.

Baez remained active with political and social concerns in the United States as well. The same year as her Vietnam visit, she organized a gathering of women and children who joined hands around the Congress building in Washington, D.C., to protest continued U.S. involvement in

Vietnam. 2,500 marchers, who had to brave flood waters left in the wake of Hurricane Agnes, linked arms around Congress while simultaneous demonstrations took place in San Francisco, Palo Alto, Minneapolis, and Boise. Since 1973, Baez has served on the national advisory board of Amnesty International, a worldwide organization that works for the release of people imprisoned for their religious or political beliefs, and she was instrumental in founding Amnesty West Coast, the group's California branch. In 1979 she founded Humanitas International (for which she still serves as president). Based in Menlo Park, California, the organization promotes human rights, disarmament, and nonviolence through seminars and other educational opportunities.

Career Sees Resurgence

In her autobiography, Baez notes how sometime during the late 1970s she "began the painful and humiliating process of discovering, ever so slowly, that though I might be timeless in the world of music, at least in the United States I was no longer *timely.*" Her waning popularity received a boost in 1985 when she was asked to open the U.S. portion of Live-Aid, a multi-act rock concert designed to raise funds for relief of African famine victims. In 1986 she took part, along with fellow musicians Sting, U2, and Peter Gabriel, in the "Conspiracy of Hope" concert tour celebrating Amnesty International's 25th anniversary. In 1987 she released *Recently,* her first album to appear in the United States after an eight-year hiatus. The album included such diverse offerings as the old standard "Let Us Break Bread Together," a South African chant, "Asimbonanga," and a cover of Peter Gabriel's "Biko," which tells the story of slain South African activist Steven Biko.

In 1987, *And a Voice to Sing With* was reviewed in a number of major periodicals in the United States and once again brought Baez's life and music to the attention of the national media. In the book, and in the interviews that followed its publication, Baez spoke of the materialism she saw pervading society. In a *Christian Science Monitor* review Amy Duncan referred to the fact that "Baez writes a bit dispiritedly about the '80s, and decries particularly the 'me generation' mentality and what she sees as a lack of ethical and humanitarian values." In a conversation with Alvin P. Sanoff appearing in *U.S. News & World Report,* Baez contrasted the politically concerned music of her early career to the music of today, stating, "The prevailing ethos is: No negative thoughts, and everything is beautiful!" Baez continued, "You just jog, eat enough of the right yogurt, and everything is going to be all right."

Social historian Barbara Goldsmith characterized Baez's work as the story of not just one person but of an entire society. "Baez's 20-year metamorphosis from popular folk singer to 80's survivor provides an instructional tale from which one could extrapolate the changes in values in our society in the past two decades," Goldsmith wrote in the *New York Times Book Review.* Whatever changes Goldsmith

detected in Baez's value system, Baez herself minimizes. As Cathleen McGuigan pointed out in *Newsweek,* "Baez's music may have gone out of style, but according to her book, she never altered her art or her politics to suit fashion." In the preface to *And a Voice to Sing With* Baez appears proud of the fact that despite what she has been through, her "social and political views have remained astoundingly steadfast." She continues: "I have been true to the principles of nonviolence, developing a stronger and stronger aversion to the ideologies of both the far right and the far left and a deeper sense of rage and sorrow over the suffering they continue to produce all over the world."

Baez continues to attract public attention with both her voice and her activism. In a 1989 *New York Times* review of a Baez concert that coincided with the 30th anniversary of *Joan Baez's* release, Stephen Holden wrote: "Her voice, though quite different in texture from the ethereal folk soprano of her first albums, remains a powerful instrument." In celebration of the anniversary, Baez released *Speaking of Dreams,* an album of social commentary. In addition to maintaining her music, she continued to dedicate her time to causes in which she believes. In the late 1980s Baez toured Israel and the occupied territories of the Middle East seeking a peaceful end to the conflict there. In 1991 she announced plans to develop low-income housing on 140 acres of land in northern California. She has survived what she calls in her autobiography, "the ashes and silence of the 1980s," and appears to be firm in her dedication to do what she can to make life easier for "the less fortunate specks in the world."

Sources:

Books

Baez, Joan, *Daybreak,* Dial, 1968.
Baez, Joan, *And a Voice to Sing With,* Summit Books, 1987.

Periodicals

Christian Science Monitor, September 3, 1987, p. 21.
Los Angeles Times, February 3, 1991, p. K1.
Newsweek, July 20, 1987, p. 62.
New York Times, November 7, 1960; November 13, 1961; December 12, 1989, p. C24.
New York Times Book Review, June 21, 1987, p. 30.
Rolling Stone, November 5, 1987, p. 163.
Time, June 1, 1962, p. 39; November 23, 1962, p. 54.
U.S. News & World Report, June 29, 1987, p. 60.

—Sketch by Marian C. Gonsior

Bains, Amalia Mesa
See **Mesa-Bains, Amalia**

Lourdes G. Baird
(1935-)
State attorney general, judge

Although Lourdes G. Baird had what she described to the *Los Angeles Times* as a "rather Spanish colonial upbringing," she was not inclined to perform as the traditional "colonial" wife and mother. Instead, after bearing three children the homemaker decided to go back to school, and she is now one of five women in the United States serving as an attorney general. While her late mother would "be very surprised" if she knew of Baird's prestigious position, Baird's colleagues are not; her work as an attorney and as a judge has been repeatedly praised.

The *Los Angeles Times* wrote of her reputation, "Baird is widely praised in legal circles for her judgment, fairness, administrative skills, her sense of humor and her ability to relate to a wide variety of individuals and groups." Baird was so well suited to a position of high authority that two Republicans—a U.S. senator and the president of the United States—nominated the Democrat for the office of U.S. attorney general for the Central District of California. She was, in fact, nominated ahead of three highly qualified Republican male candidates. Considering that this Hispanic woman began her career late in life, it is a testament to her abilities that she presides over the largest federal judicial district in the nation. With her determination and consequent success, Baird provides an inspirational example for both Hispanics and women.

Baird was born the seventh child of James C. Gillespie and Josefina Delgado on May 12, 1935, in Quito, Ecuador. Gillespie's career required a move to Los Angeles and the family relocated there when Baird was just one year old. Because her mother was a devout Catholic, Baird was educated in Catholic, all-girl schools. She told the *Los Angeles Times*, "There's something in retrospect that was great about going to an all-girls high school." Because the nuns who ran the schools provided positive role models and encouragement to the girls, the Catholic schools instilled independence in Baird's character and led her to enjoy sports. The impact the schools had on Baird is evident in how she works and plays; one of the most powerful women in the United States still hikes, runs, and skis despite being in her fifties.

Baird married businessman William T. Baird in December, 1956, after graduating from Immaculate Heart High School and spending time in secretarial school. Together the couple had three children, William Jr., Maria, and John. Baird stayed home to take care of the children for 11 years. By the time John, their youngest child, entered

Lourdes G. Baird

elementary school, Baird had decided that it was time for her to go to school as well.

Education and Early Judicial Career

Baird became a part-time student at Los Angeles City College. Admitting one of her fears about going back to school, Baird recalled in the *Los Angeles Times* that she was afraid that her "Blue Chip stamps would fall out of my purse and I'd be discovered for what I was." Five years later, the homemaker had earned her associate of arts degree. With her confidence renewed, she transferred to the University of California at Los Angeles. By 1973, Baird had received her B.A. in sociology, and was headed for law school at the same university. Although her marriage faltered—she and her husband divorced in 1975—Baird did well in law school. After graduation, she passed the California Bar exam the first time she took it. She was 41 years old.

Baird began her career in 1977, working for William D. Keller as an assistant prosecutor in the United States Attorney's Office. In 1983, she became a private attorney as a partner in the firm Baird, Munger & Myers. By 1986 she had become a judge in the East Los Angeles Municipal Court, maintaining that position until 1987. After an appointment by Governor George Deukmejian in 1987, Baird served as a Los Angeles Municipal Court judge. With Deukmejian's next appointment, Baird became the Los Angeles Superior Court judge in 1988. She held that office, in which she worked in the Juvenile Court on abuse and custody cases, until 1990.

These were not the only experiences Baird would bring to her post as attorney general; her activity in social and civic organizations complimented her career. She has been involved with the California Women Lawyers Association since 1980, and she served as the UCLA School of Law Alumni Association president from 1981 to 1984. From 1983 to 1986 Baird worked on the Ninth Circuit Court of Appeals advisory committee and specialized as a Ninth Circuit Judicial conference lawyer representative. In 1986, she became a member of the Mexican-American Bar Association, the Latino Judges Association, and the National Association of Women Judges and remains a member of these organizations.

Nominated for Attorney General Post

When a position opened for the U.S. attorney general in California's Central District, Baird's long resume was scrutinized. Special qualifications were needed to become attorney general for the largest federal district in the nation—with its seven counties and 14 million people, the district was rife with drug trafficking, money laundering, savings and loans scams, and even cases of defense industry fraud. In addition, the new attorney general would also oversee more than 150 lawyers. When Republican U.S. Senator Pete Wilson nominated Baird for the position in November 1989, observers were pleasantly surprised. It was not that Baird was unqualified for the position—she was clearly an excellent judge—it was that a Republican had nominated her, and that, if she were confirmed, she would be the first U.S. attorney in many years who was a member of the party opposing the president. While Senator Wilson was praised for his decision, some remarked that the choice reflected his political savvy; the nomination would garner Hispanic, Democratic, and female supporters for the Senator, who was a gubernatorial candidate at the time. The *Los Angeles Times* endorsed Baird's nomination in an editorial in early December with the headline, "Baird for US Attorney? Of Course."

The president, and later, the senators, who were to ensure Baird's appointment to the office of U.S. attorney general, had to consider Baird's opinions as well as her reputation. A Republican turned Democrat, Baird believed the death penalty to be justifiable in certain cases. She was in favor of equal rights for women and increasing child care options for families. Baird would not tell the *Los Angeles Times,* however, her stand on abortion. She was quoted as saying, "My duty is to enforce federal law and it's not up to me to judge what I like and don't like."

After a formal background check by the FBI, it took President George Bush six months to nominate Baird for the position. When Baird heard the news of her nomination by President Bush, she was thrilled. "I'm delighted," she told the *Los Angeles Times.* "I know there are incredible

challenges out there [in the district]." The newspaper believed that Baird was ready for those challenges, and urged voters to support her in her bid to retain her seat on the Superior Court in another editorial.

The *Los Angeles Times* reviewed Baird's career and provided the opinions of several of her peers regarding her possible performance as attorney general. She was lauded by Judge Paul Boland, who had watched Baird handle more than a year's worth of child abuse cases, and by Robert Brosio, the interim U.S. attorney general. Assistant U.S. attorney William F. Fahey, head of the government fraud unit and a coworker of Baird's in the early 1980s, remarked in the *Los Angeles Times,* "I think she'll be a great leader." Baird herself felt good about the cases she had worked on as a prosecutor, and later as a judge, for the government.

One person who did not favor Baird's nomination, Lew Gutwitz, reminded the media of a case which exemplified Baird's tough stance towards criminals. Gutwitz, a lawyer who had defended American Indian activist Leonard Peltier in 1979, thought that Baird had been "meanspirited" during the proceedings. Peltier had been imprisoned for consecutive life sentences for killing two FBI agents. He later escaped from a federal prison in Lompoc, California, insisting that he had to escape to avoid being killed by the government. When U.S. District Judge Lawrence T. Lydick did not allow Peltier's attorneys to defend the convict on the basis of the alleged government conspiracy, the attorneys attempted to circumvent the decision. Baird and her cocounsel, Robert Biniaz, objected to these activities, and their objections were sustained by the district judge. Peltier was finally convicted, and, despite Gutwitz's objections, Baird was proud of her contribution to that outcome. The entire Peltier case was brought to new light in the early 1990s with the release of director Michael Apted's documentary film *Incident at Ogalala.*

One-and-a-half months after Bush's action, Baird's nomination for the position of U.S. attorney general of the Central District of California was confirmed by the U.S. Senate. When the silver-haired woman was sworn into office by U.S. District Judge Manuel L. Real in mid-July, 1990, Baird was 55 years old. Her proud children were grown—William Jr. was working in television in Los Angeles, Maria was a mother herself and living in Berkeley, California, and John was a student at the University of California at Santa Cruz. While Baird had proven that it is possible to achieve success as a woman, a mother, and a Hispanic, she also demonstrated the benefits of returning to school to find a rewarding career after raising a family.

From Drug Issues to the Rodney King Trial

After her confirmation, Baird was eager to begin work on the many different problems that awaited her in a district notorious for its criminal activity. She would deal with cases in an area that ranged from San Luis Obispo to

San Bernardino. As she told the *Los Angeles Times,* she was anxious about the drug abuse situation in the district. "Crime is rampant. My experience on the bench has indicated to me the horror of drugs—the main problem in the United States." She continued discussing the relationship of drug abuse to alcohol abuse, "Drugs pervade the society. I'm not a prophet of doom, but I can't tell you how it's going to be overcome." While the new attorney general intends to fight drug abuse with tough sentencing, she also states that more treatment facilities are needed to rehabilitate drug users.

Observers hoped that Baird would deal with another thorny issue. The mayor of Los Angeles, Tom Bradley, had been the subject of a federal grand jury investigation for some time. His relationship with a local bank was questionable, and there was some indication that he might have benefitted from insider stock knowledge. The attorney general would have to decide whether to bring federal charges against the mayor. Another issue surfaced after Baird was sworn into office in July of 1990. The Los Angeles district attorney's office and the Los Angeles Sheriff's Department had allegedly misused jailhouse informants; the grand jury they faced could not reach a verdict. Once again, Baird would be responsible for investigating the process as well as the problem.

Dealing with such issues meant that Baird would have to restructure the attorney general's office itself. The office would be dealing with a higher percentage of cases than when Baird worked there as an assistant attorney. These cases were becoming more and more complex. Additional attorneys would have to be hired to handle the savings and loan fraud cases. Finally, the new attorneys, along with the veteran attorneys, would have to be organized to work efficiently.

In April of 1992 Baird became involved in one of the most controversial cases to surface in the 1990s. In March of 1991 a black motorist named Rodney King was stopped by several white police officers. What ensued remains controversial and hotly debated, but a videotape emerged that showed the police officers savagely beating King. What motivated the beating remains an issue that may never be resolved. The officers were brought to trial and eventually acquitted. The black community in Los Angeles erupted in a rage, sparking one of the worst riots in U.S. history. When the smoke cleared, 60 people were dead and more than 800 million dollars in damage had been wrought. Much of the legal community expressed dissatisfaction with the verdict, citing a clear violation of King's civil rights. In the wake of the acquittal and riot, Baird headed up a new prosecution of the officers. Civil rights infraction charges were leveled not only at the officers who beat King but at the officers who looked on but failed to interfere with his beating. Baird's prosecution and administrative skills would figure prominently in the new case.

With a district as large and as densely populated as the Central District of California, Baird has a busy schedule. Although Baird is over 50 years old, Baird's career is still young. Observers cite her past achievements in predicting her future performances and successes—whether she serves justice as attorney general or moves on to a position of even more authority.

Sources:

Periodicals

Detroit Free Press, August 6, 1992, p. 3A; August 9, 1992, p. 2F.
Los Angeles Times, November 30, 1989, p. B1; December 4, 1989, p. B6; May 15, 1990, p. B1; May 21, 1990, p. B6; July 11, 1990, p. B6; July 19, 1990, p. B1.

—*Ronie-Richele Garcia-Johnson*

Laura Balverde-Sanchez
(1951-)
Chief executive officer

When Laura Balverde-Sanchez and her husband Joe bought the El Rey Sausage Company in 1983, the Los Angeles company was headed toward bankruptcy. In 1992—with Balverde-Sanchez at the helm as president and chief executive officer of the reorganized New El Rey Sausage Co.—sales were expected to hit $6 million, ten times what they were in 1983. El Rey is a leading producer of chorizo, the spicy Mexican sausage. Since Balverde-Sanchez and her husband bought the company, they have added more food lines, including fried pork rinds, salsa, and cheese. "Not everyone is made to go into business for themselves," she was quoted as saying in the *Los Angeles Times Magazine.* "It's cutthroat and I don't advocate it for everyone because you will get divorced and will lose your sanity." Fortunately, Balverde-Sanchez was half-joking. She did stay married, and she and the business are sanely thriving.

Balverde-Sanchez's grit, determination, and willingness to take risks can be traced to her early childhood. Born in Los Angeles, California, in 1951, she comes from a family with a strong work ethic. As the *Los Angeles Times Magazine* noted, her mother, a sewing machine operator, insisted, against all odds, that the family move from East Los Angeles to Monterey Park in 1959 so they could own their own home. To do so, her parents had to work twice as hard. Growing up, she and her two siblings were dropped off at a day care center at 6:30 a.m. and picked up every day at 6:00 p.m. After dinner, she helped her mother with her work.

Her mother, Elvira Santoyo Huerto, immigrated from Mexico, and her father, Ubaldo Huerto, is a machinist who helps keep the El Rey machinery running. Her grandfather owned a ranch in Baha, California, where Balverde-Sanchez worked during the summers while she was growing up. "My earliest recollection of any significant influences that had a long-term impact on my business was of my parents, grandfather, and uncles making do with what they had," she told Pam Berry in an interview. "On the farm—the ranch—if a battery went dead on a piece of farm equipment, you borrowed one from the car so you could thrash and harvest before the sun went down."

After graduating from high school, Balverde-Sanchez attended California State College in Los Angeles for one year before transferring to the University of California, Los Angeles, where she received a bachelor's degree in psychology in 1973. She has also completed work toward a master's degree in public administration at the University of Southern California. According to the *Los Angeles Times Magazine,* she worked four part-time jobs to pay for her education while carrying a full load of classes.

Upon graduation, she began teaching English as a second language. In 1974, she was hired by the Los Angeles Unified School District, where she taught in the night school program for eight years. During the day, she held full-time corporate jobs. She was a management staffing representative for General Telephone of California for three years and later a personnel manager for Foremost Foods in Los Angeles.

Bought Sausage Company

In 1981, after working her way up the corporate ladder for about a year and a half, she learned she had a tumor. Although the growth turned out to be benign, the discovery caused her to reevaluate her life and career direction. She had always wanted to own her own store (her grandfather had owned a general store), so she quit her job at Foremost and opened an antique shop in Hancock Park. In 1982, she married Joe Sanchez, a grocer and owner of an independent chain of food markets. The couple bought El Rey Sausage Co. in 1983 as an investment. When the company started to lose money, she was asked by the board of directors to run it herself. She has never looked back since.

Balverde-Sanchez's early years with the company were difficult. According to *Good Housekeeping,* "She would arrive at work each morning at five. She'd blend spices, mix them with the meat, put 500 pounds of mixture into the stuffer, check casings, package the sausages, label the packages, then cart the boxes to the cooler." She also had to sell the product and manage operations. Balverde-Sanchez recalled in the *Los Angeles Times* one particularly difficult day when she had to admit to her accountant that she did not know how to read a balance sheet: "I was really

in tears," she said. "I said, 'Show me what numbers need to get bigger and what numbers need to get smaller.'"

A year later, the right numbers were getting bigger and she was beginning to turn the business around. Within five years, sales revenues reached $4.5 million. Although her hard work has meant certain sacrifices in her lifestyle, Balverde-Sanchez manages to keep a humorous perspective on things. As she told the *Los Angeles Times Magazine,* "It's hard to be austere. Women my age are into fur coats, nice jewelry. I'm into electric pallet jacks." Her plans for the future include adding new products and delegating more job responsibilities to free up her leisure time. "I see the business as a little calf," Balverde-Sanchez said in the *Los Angeles Times Magazine.* "I'm feeding it, taking good care of it—because someday someone might take an interest in us and buy us out."

Sources:

Periodicals

Good Housekeeping, July, 1988, p. 70.
Los Angeles Times, December 15, 1987, Section 4, p. 1.
Los Angeles Times Magazine, December 4, 1988, pp. 32-34.

Other

Balverde-Sanchez, Laura, telephone interview with Pam Berry, August 12, 1992.

—Sketch by Pam Berry

Romana Acosta Bañuelos
(1925-)
Businesswoman, former U.S. Treasurer

Romana Acosta Bañuelos began what would become a highly successful business with an aunt and a tortilla machine, founded a bank, and became the Treasurer of the United States. No one would argue against the idea that Bañuelos has achieved the American dream. Bañuelos, however, is not one to rest on her laurels, so despite her success, she has continued to rely on her sound business judgement and to work as hard ever on a number of challenging projects.

Bañuelos was born on March 20, 1925, in Miami, Arizona, a small mining town. Her parents were born in Mexico and the family was poor. In 1933, as the effects of the Great Depression were still being felt throughout the country, Arizona officials told a number of Mexican families, includ-

Romana Acosta Bañuelos

ing the Bañuelos family, that they had to return to Mexico. According to the authorities, the economic situation was not improving and since jobs were scarce, the family would be better off in their own homeland of Mexico. The families were informed that if they would leave, the cost of transporting themselves and their furniture to the border would be paid. Bañuelos told an interviewer for *Nuestro:* "They told us we could come back anytime we wanted to, as soon as the economy got better. So my mother and father believed what they were told, and we left."

The family moved to Sonora, Mexico, to work on a small ranch that relatives owned. There, Bañuelos rose early with her parents to tend to the wheat, corn, potatoes, and peanuts that her father had planted. She also helped her mother as she made the empanadas (turnovers) which her mother sold to local restaurants and bakeries. Bañuelos explained to *Nuestro* that her mother was a excellent role model as a resourceful businesswoman: in addition to marketing her baked goods, she decided to raise chickens. "My mother was the type of woman that taught us how to live in any place and work with what we have."

Versatility Key to Bañuelos's Achievements

Perhaps this inherent versatility has allowed Bañuelos to become the success that she is today. Although she had married, borne two sons, and divorced by the time she was nineteen years old, she did not hesitate to set high goals for herself and to make the most of her life. As a young single

mother, Bañuelos packed up her children and returned to her native country, the United States. Upon her arrival in Los Angeles, she found a job, began to work, care for her family, and save money. By the time she was twenty-one years old, she had remarried and saved four hundred dollars. With this savings, and the help of an aunt, a tortilla machine, a grinder, and a fan, the ambitious Bañuelos set up a tortilla factory in the heart of downtown Los Angeles. At the end of their first day in business, in 1949, she and her aunt had made thirty-six dollars.

Business gradually picked up as Bañuelos and her aunt persuaded restaurant and store owners to buy their tortillas. The small company they began, Ramona's Mexican Food Products, Inc., was booming by the mid-1960s. By 1979, Ramona's employed 400 people, distributed 22 different food products, and the company's sales had soared to 12 million dollars annually. While consumers were familiar with the brand name of Ramona's, by 1990 the largest independent Mexican food processing plant in the state of California, and the trademark woman wearing a huge sombrero, some people confusedly referred to Romana Bañuelos incorrectly as Ramona. The company, however, was named after an early Californian folk heroine named Ramona, and not Romana herself.

As soon as Bañuelos's business began to succeed, she began to think of the plight of other Hispanics that were less fortunate than herself. She is a founder and trustee of Ramona's Mexican Food Products, Inc. Scholarship Foundation, which assists high school graduates of Mexican-American heritage in their educational goals. Bañuelos also turned her focus on those Hispanics who wanted to start their own businesses. She realized that, if Hispanics could increase their financial base, they could increase their political influence. Toward this goal of community empowerment, in 1965 Bañuelos, along with some partners, started the Pan-American National Bank. By 1969, Bañuelos had become the chairperson of the board of directors of the bank, and had received recognition from her peers in the business world. She was named the Outstanding Business Woman of the Year in November, 1969, and during that same year, Mayor Sam Yorty presented Bañuelos with a commendation award from the board of supervisors of the county of Los Angeles. Bañuelos's banking venture became another huge success for her. By 1979, according to *Nuestro,* Pan-American National Bank held deposits of $38,864,000 and assets of $41,472,000. By 1992, Bañuelos had served as chair of the bank's board of directors for three terms of office.

It was Bañuelos's business talent, however, rather than the power created by the collection of money in the Pan-American National Bank, that wielded political influence for Bañuelos during the early 1970s. After Richard Nixon was elected president of the United States, she was asked by the Republican party members if they could place her name on the list of possible candidates for the position of

Treasurer of the United States. Although she thought that she had no chance to win the nomination and confirmation, she decided to allow herself to be considered for the office. To her surprise, President Nixon selected Bañuelos as his candidate for U.S. Treasurer and started the nomination process in motion.

Nomination to Become U.S. Treasurer Jeopardized

Before Bañuelos could really savor the fact that she had been nominated for the position of U.S. Treasurer, Ramona's Mexican Food Products, Inc., was raided by U.S. immigration agents. Instead of the usual, quiet inspection, the agents loudly stormed through the building. The raid received broad media attention and seemed to damage Bañuelos's chances of securing the appointment. President Nixon, however, continued to support Bañuelos, who immediately claimed that the raid had been politically motivated. Called before a Senate investigative committee, Bañuelos argued that the Democratic party was responsible for setting in motion the chain of events that resulted in the raid. Later testimony corroborated these claims, and the Senate committee ruled that Bañuelos had been unfairly targeted to cause embarrassment for the Nixon administration.

Despite the upsetting and unfair raid, Nixon's appointment of Bañuelos was confirmed. She resigned her position at the Pan-American National Bank to go to Washington, D.C., to serve as a public official. On December 17, 1971, she took the oath of office and became the Treasurer of the United States as well as the highest ranking Mexican-American in the United States government during this administration. Bañuelos enjoyed her time as U.S. Treasurer. "It was a beautiful experience," she told *Nuestro.* "I will always be grateful to President Nixon."

In February of 1974, Bañuelos resigned as U.S. Treasurer so she could devote more time to her family, businesses, and philanthropical projects. She was recognized in 1975 with a honorary doctorate of business administration from the City University of Los Angeles. In 1976, she was included in the Library of Human Resources as one of the United States's "Valuable Resources" by the American Bicentennial Research Institute for her professional and civic contributions to the country. The East Los Angeles Community Union honored her with the Board of Directors Woman Achievement Award in 1977.

In recent years, Bañuelos has divided her time between Ramona's Mexican Food Products, Inc., and the Pan-American National Bank. While Romana works as the president of Ramona's, her children Carlos A. Torres, Ramona A. Bañuelos, and Martin A. Torres are involved in the day-to-day business operations of the company in various positions. Bañuelos is also currently serving as the president of the Pan-American National Bank.

Sources:

Books

Who's Who among Hispanic Americans, 1992-93, Gale, 1992.

Periodicals

Nuestro, June/July, 1979, pp. 34+.

—*Sketch by Ronie-Richele Garcia-Johnson*

Maria Gertrudes Barcelo
(1800-1852)
Entrepreneur

Maria Gertrudes Barcelo, the notorious "La Tules," is one of the most colorful and fascinating legends from an era known for extravagant personalities. An aggressive entrepreneur of posh gambling palaces and an astute businesswoman, Barcelo found fame and a sizeable fortune in the male-dominated old Southwest.

Born in 1800 in the state of Sonora in northern Mexico to a privileged family, Barcelo was well educated by her parents. Shortly after Mexico won its independence from Spain in the early 1820s, Barcelo and her family moved to the village of Valencia in New Mexico. Whether her desire for independence was the result of education or her own self-sufficiency cannot be determined, but Barcelo was ahead of her time in both the financial acumen and a feminist consciousness she displayed as a young woman. When she married at the age of 23, she refused to relinquish either her right to make contracts or the deeds to her property to her husband as custom dictated. Furthermore, Barcelo retained and used her maiden name.

Casinos Bring Fame and Fortune

Seeking better financial opportunities, Barcelo and her husband relocated to the Santa Fe area. In 1825, she began operating a game of chance in the Ortiz Mountains, where she came to be nicknamed "La Tules." After several years, Barcelo saved enough to purchase her own monte bank casino in Santa Fe. The gambling house soon became one of the most popular casinos in Santa Fe and favored by society's elite. Customers were drawn not only by the "magnificent pier-glass mirrors" and the "brussels carpets" described by Twitchell in *Old Santa Fe,* but by the reputed beauty and the charm of the best monte dealer in Santa Fe, the notorious "La Tules."

In 1837, new taxes, increased government centralization, and the revised Mexican constitution caused an uprising in which the governor, Albino Perez, was assassinated. General Manual Armijo suppressed the uprising and was appointed Governor of New Mexico by President Santa Ana. As Barcelo gained fortune and fame, she advanced in Santa Fe society and soon became a great favorite in official Mexican circles. She was transformed from the infamous "La Tules" to the acclaimed Señora Dona Gertrudes Barcelo. The new governor was attracted to Barcelo and it was reputed that she not only became his mistress but was the power behind the throne. During the early 1840s, Barcelo prevailed over the fashionable society of Santa Fe.

Gambling Empire Includes Trade and Investment

Barcelo did not limit her enterprises to gambling houses, but became involved with trade and investing, as well. In 1843, she sent $10,000 to the United States to be invested in goods. During the late 1820s, traders and settlers from the United States began to relocate in the Mexican dominion. Early chronicles provide insights into the cultural clashes between the native Mexican population and the Anglo Americans who moved to the Southwest. The popularity of dancing and gambling across all Mexican classes seemed incomprehensible to many straight-laced Anglos and the infamous "La Tules" remained an enigma to many Anglos. A contemporary eyewitness and diarist, Susan Shelby Magoffin, described her as "a stately dame of a certain age, the possessor of a portion of that shrewd sense and fascinating manner necessary to allure the wayward, inexperienced youth to the hall of final ruin."

In 1846, Santa Fe, occupied by General Kearny in response to the United States declaration of war on Mexico, established a civilian government. The Mexican War, fought primarily in old Mexico, ended in 1848 with the Treaty of Guadalupe Hidalgo which ceded all of New Mexico to the United States. By 1850, New Mexico joined the United States as a "free" (non-slave holding) state. During the United States military occupation of New Mexico, Barcelo sided with the American forces and was a very popular figure among the military officers. During the occupation, Barcelo received information regarding a conspiracy from one of her servants. She relayed the information to American military and civilian authorities. In addition, she provided a substantial loan to the United States occupation forces for supplies. The loan terms required that one of the officers escort her to a military ball. Colorful and flamboyant to the end, Barcelo arranged that her own funeral be one of the most expensive and ornate in Santa Fe history. She was buried with full church honors in 1852.

Driven by ambition, but aided by beauty and skill, Barcelo advanced to the inner circles of Mexican society in Santa Fe. As a successful businesswoman catering to the pastimes of both Mexicans and Anglos, she enjoyed great, if not universal, popularity and achieved wealth and political influence. Her legacy as one of the great characters of the wild west lives on even today.

Sources:

Books

Bernard, H. Russell, and Duncan Livie Isauro, editors, *Introduction to Chicano Studies,* second edition, Macmillan, 1982.

Drumm, Stella, editor, *Down the Santa Fe Trail and into Mexico: The Diary of Susan Shelby Magoff in 1846-1847,* Yale University Press, 1926.

Duffus, R. L., *The Santa Fe Trail,* Tudor, 1934.

Gregg, Josiah, *Commerce of the Prairies,* University of Oklahoma Press, 1954.

Robinson, Cecil, *With the Ears of Strangers: The Mexican in American Literature,* University of Arizona Press, 1963.

Twitchell, Ralph Emerson, *Old Santa Fe: The Story of New Mexico's Ancient Capital,* Rio Grande Press, 1963.

—*Sketch by Sally Foster*

Santa Barraza
(1951-)
Educator, artist, painter

Along with such renowned Chicano artists as Carmen Lomas Garza, Amado Peña, Jr., and Cesar Martinez, Santa Barraza is recognized as one of a group of Texas Chicano artists who organized in the 1970s to bring due regard to Chicano art. The descendant of Karankawa Indians, Spanish colonials, and Mexican grantees, Barraza crafts mixed media work, blending symbols from her cultural heritage with Catholic imagery. Her art has been exhibited the world over, including Mexico, Italy, England, and Japan. In a catalog for an exhibition of her work which appeared in 1992 at the Galeria Posada in Sacramento, California, curator Tere Romo wrote: "By tapping into pre-conquest symbols, personal memories, and sacred artforms such as the *retablo* (ex-voto), Santa re-affirms the value of Mexican artistic traditions and their power to nurture and sustain our cultural identity on this side of the border. It is through this 'cultural art of resistance' that she has fought off assimilation, found her strength as a woman, and her voice as an artist."

Barraza was born April 7, 1951, in Kingsville, Texas, the daughter of Joaquin Barraza and Frances Contreras Barraza.

She received bachelor's and master's degrees in fine arts from the University of Texas at Austin, in 1975 and 1982 respectively. Between studies she helped found Mujeres Artistas del Suroeste (MAS) in 1976, one of the first nonprofit organizations dedicated exclusively to promoting Chicana and Latina visual artists. In 1981 she opened the Diseño Studio, the first Chicano art gallery in Austin, Texas. She left Texas in 1985 to pursue a teaching post at La Roche College in Pittsburgh. In 1988 she began teaching art at Pennsylvania State University.

Organizes Chicano/Mexican Artists Conference

During her years in Austin, Barraza was instrumental in organizing a groundbreaking international conference between Chicano and Mexican artists in 1979. The *encuentro*, entitled the Conferencia Plastica Chicana, is credited with eventually producing a greater rapport between the two groups. At first, however, the conference nearly ruptured when visiting artists from Mexico City's prestigious San Carlos Academy of Art questioned whether Chicano art was indeed a legitimate art form. In a telephone interview with Yleana Martinez, Barraza said the issue proved quite controversial because the visiting artists reached a consensus that Chicano art was "underdeveloped." The Chicano conference sponsors countered that their work was indeed a young art movement, and that not many Chicanos had much access to higher education and formal art training as had their Mexican counterparts.

Barraza believes that appreciation for Chicano art has come a long way since then. Groups such as MAS and the Social and Public Art Resource Center (SPARC) in Venice, California, have helped initiate a boom in Latino art. In a catalog for the 1991 exhibit, "CARA: Chicano Art: Resistance & Affirmation (1965-1985)," the art scholar Amalia Mesa-Bains wrote: "(Barraza's) personal experience of continuity and history placed (her) in the pivotal role of cultural chronicler."

Barraza is adamant that her work is created not for a mainstream audience, but for her beloved *raza*. She has chosen as her medium *retablos*—sheets of galvanized steel on which she paints brightly colored evocative images of virgins, folk-art healers, Mexican revolutionary figures like general Pancho Villa and 'adelitas,' and the ever-present maguey plant. For Barraza, the maguey represents a powerful cultural symbol for life and Mestizo heritage. "It is a symbol of resurrection and rebirth," she said. "It gives you pulque, it gives you things to eat. It provides nutriment, medicine, and makes paper for codices, fiber for huipiles and clothing."

Sources:

Books

Catalog for Exhibition of Works by Santa Barraza, Galeria Posada (Sacramento, CA), 1992.

Lippard, Lucy, *Mixed Blessings: Art for a Multicultural America*, Penguin, 1988.

Mesa-Bains, Amalia, "El Mundo Femenino: Chicana Artists of the Movement—A Commentary On Development and Production," in *CARA: Chicano Art: Resistance & Affirmation (1965-1985) Catalog*, sponsored by UCLA, Wight Art Gallery, 1991.

Periodicals

Performing Arts Magazine, July, 1991, p. 12.

Other

Barraza, Santa C., telephone interview with Yleana Martinez, August, 1992.

—Sketch by Yleana Martinez

Petra Barreras del Rio
(1952-)
Art museum director

Petra Barreras del Rio took on many challenges when she became executive director of El Museo del Barrio, a New York City art institution. Not only did she have to raise museum funds during an economic recession, but as a Puerto Rican woman, Barreras del Rio also had to overcome the forces of discrimination. A trained art historian, she dedicated herself to El Museo's mission: to promote contemporary Puerto Rican and Latin American artists and make their work accessible to a broad public.

Even as a child, Barreras was a lover of museums. She was born in San Juan, Puerto Rico, on October 30, 1952. Her father, Francisco Barreras, was a farmer and politician; her mother, Josefa del Rio, worked as a teacher. Barreras had no interest in becoming an artist, but at an early age, she became a frequent visitor to San Juan's two major museums. "I remember visiting the museums and being totally in awe of the work and excited by it," she recalled in an interview. As a teenager, Barreras del Rio was sent on a tour of Spain and France. "The things I remember most vividly are the museums," she said. "I decided to make a career of it."

In 1973, Barreras del Rio graduated magna cum laude from the University of Puerto Rico, Rio Piedras, with a B.A.

in Puerto Rican art and art history. She won a Ford Foundation Fellowship for graduate studies at New York University's Institute of Fine Arts in Manhattan. In 1977, she received her M.A. in European Painting and Museum Training from the Institute. While studying in Manhattan, Barreras del Rio began leading bilingual Spanish-English gallery talks at the Metropolitan Museum, located near the college campus. In 1977, she served as a curator at El Museo del Barrio, a Hispanic art museum, and then returned to the Metropolitan to work as an assistant museum educator in the Community Education department. At the Metropolitan, she developed special programs, gallery and slide talks, panel discussions, and lectures for Spanish-speaking museum visitors.

In 1980, Barreras del Rio was hired by the New York State Council on the Arts. For the next six years, she served as a program analyst for the Visual Artists Program, reviewing and making recommendations on grant requests. In her job, she was able to visit arts institutions all over the state and learn how they balanced budgets and achieved artistic goals. "It was a good experience to see how government agencies prepare their recommendations," declared Barreras del Rio.

Named Head of El Museo del Barrio

The art historian was hired as the executive director of El Museo del Barrio in 1986. The museum, which was founded in 1969, is the largest institution in the country devoted to Hispanic art and the only one with a special focus on Puerto Rican artists. Operating on a fraction of the budget of its more famous Fifth Avenue neighbors like the Metropolitan Museum of Art and the Solomon R. Guggenheim Museum, El Museo has, in its young history, become a vital player in the contemporary art world.

The museum was founded as part of an alternative public school and located in a brownstone on 116th Street. El Museo was named after its East Harlem neighborhood, which was predominately Puerto Rican and known as El Barrio, the Spanish word for "district." "It was felt that there was not enough art in other museums in the city that was relevant to Puerto Ricans in El Barrio," recalled Barreras del Rio. In 1977, El Museo moved to its current site at 1230 Fifth Avenue and 104th Street, on the edge of Spanish Harlem, where the sights and sounds of the neighborhood have a definite Caribbean flavor. The museum rents a portion of the city-owned Heckscher Foundation building, a massive edifice, which sits directly across Fifth Avenue from Central Park. The museum's main gallery, which displays its current exhibits, is spacious, open, and sunny.

Barreras del Rio brought to the executive director position the right combination of expertise in Puerto Rican art history, experience in bilingual arts education, and inside knowledge of museum financing. "It was a special time for

El Museo. In the mid-1980's, the city was starting to feel its economic base was not that strong and many changes were happening at El Museo," said Barreras del Rio. El Museo relies on city and state funds for a large portion of its budget.

The museum's permanent collection of over 8,000 objects includes drawings, prints, posters, paintings, videos, films, sculptures, photographs, and folk art. About 75 percent of the work is by contemporary Puerto Rican artists; Latin American artists living in the United States also display their pieces. El Museo has an extensive collection of Puerto Rican santos, small hand-carved and painted folk icons with religious significance. Schoolchildren are welcomed at El Museo for gallery talks and arts education programs, which comprise a major effort by the museum.

El Museo is dedicated to promoting Latino artists who are not widely known. The museum frequently provides artists their first opportunity for a one-person show and catalogue. "We give higher visibility to Latino artists than they've received until we've shown them," Barreras del Rio explained. The museum also helps artists by purchasing their work and providing artist-in-residence opportunities. Because of this emphasis, the museum has gained a reputation as a repository for fresh and exciting Latino art. "Many curators and people who study art history come to our archive on Latino artists," noted Barreras del Rio.

Funding Cuts and Gender Bias Complicate Work

Like many arts institutions in the 1990s, El Museo has faced serious financial problems. In 1992, the museum closed during August to save money. Barreras del Rio has been forced to scale back programming, while mounting a new drive for individual donations to replace cutbacks in public and philanthropic funds. Further complicating Barreras del Rio's job is the fact that many people are not comfortable with a Hispanic woman at the helm of a large arts organization. "Despite the public perception, most museum directors are men. That is something that will be changing, but it's still unusual to be a woman in this job in this day and age," stated Barreras del Rio. On fundraising visits, she often brings along a male member of her board of directors. "In certain areas of philanthropy that are more conservative, men seem more reliable than women," she commented.

Barreras del Rio earned a Museum Management Institute Certificate from the Getty Fund and American Federation of the Arts in 1989. Also that year, she received a Mayor's Award of Honor for Arts and Culture. She is a member of the Alumni Association at the Institute of Fine Arts, a board member of the Art Table, and a member of advisory panels for the National Endowment for the Arts' Expansion Arts and Challenge Grant Program. She is also an advisory board member at the Sculpture Center and the Center for American Cultural Studies at Columbia University. In addition she is a member of the American Association of Museums and the Cultural Institutes Group.

While at El Museo, Barreras del Rio has edited museum publications on the artists Taller Alma Boricua, Edgar Franceschi, and Ravael Montanez Ortiz. When looking to her future, the administrator, who lives in New York City, is interested in continuing her work in art curating, research, and teaching.

Sources:

Periodicals

Art in America, February 1980, pp. 69-70.

Other

Barreras del Rio, Petra, interview with Ann Malaspina, September 15, 1992.

—Sketch by Ann Malaspina

Graciela Beecher
(1927-)
Educator, executive

Graciela Beecher drew upon her experience as a language teacher and Cuban exile to found the Latin American Educational Center in Fort Wayne, Indiana, in 1976. The center's initial purpose was to help Hispanic immigrants adapt to life in the United States by offering services such as classes in English as a second language. It has since expanded its services to provide assistance to minorities and people from non-Spanish speaking countries. During the 1970s, the center served the needs of many Vietnamese, Cambodian, and Laotian people who were brought to the country by religious charitable organizations. "Since I was an exile myself I could understand their problems and communicate with them quite well," Beecher told this contributor in a telephone interview.

For Beecher, the role of educating others comes naturally; she considers herself a "born teacher." Born in Havana, Cuba, in 1927, she was brought up in an affluent family that lived in the shadow of her prominent grandfather, Jose Antolin del Cueto, who is considered the "father of civil law in Cuba," according to Beecher. At various times during his distinguished career, he was a chief justice, president of the University of Havana, and dean of the university's college of law. "When I went to some conventions of language professors in the States, I would run into lawyers who studied under my grandfather and they wanted to shake my hand," Beecher said. "He was regarded as something extraordinary." Beecher's father, Manuel Fernandez Bilbau, was also a lawyer, and her mother, Maria Teresa del Cueto, was a homemaker.

Beecher studied languages at the University of Havana prior to being offered a fellowship to study and teach at Memphis State University in Memphis, Tennessee. She received a bachelor's degree with a major in French from Memphis State in 1949. She followed up that accomplishment by obtaining a doctorate in education from the University of Havana two years later.

Before studying in Tennessee and for several years after returning to Havana, Beecher taught languages for the Havana Community School System. In 1954, she and a colleague decided to found a two-year business school, which they named Oxford Academy. Beecher was president of the school until 1961. In 1961, Beecher accepted a job offer from St. Francis College in Fort Wayne, Indiana. She eventually became chairman of the language department before leaving in 1976 to found the Latin American Educational Center, where she is executive director.

Today, the federally funded program focuses on providing educational career counseling for minorities, as well as English as a second language. "We want to help people continue their education in one way or another," she said. "If they dropped out of high school then we want to get them back in high school or help them get their GED. The idea is to prepare people to keep on studying. We don't want to give them a fish, we try to teach them how to fish." In 1988, the center produced a series of 12 videotapes and an accompanying book entitled "The Road Less Travelled: Three Generations of Cuban American Women." The video and book have been distributed to universities across the country.

Despite her varied accomplishments, Beecher gets her greatest career satisfaction out of being a teacher. "Helping people get along and live fruitful lives—that's the best thing that can happen to a teacher," she said.

Sources:

Beecher, Graciela, telephone interview with Pam Berry, August 31, 1992.

—Sketch by Pam Berry

Maria Antonietta Berriozabal
(1941-)
Government·official

At the age of 14, Maria Antonietta Rodriguez, later Berriozabal, decided she had a mission: to help her parents send her three brothers and two sisters to school and to college. She believed that by adding to the family's income, the rest of her siblings could forgo work to concentrate on their schoolwork. Her mission began in 1959, immediately after graduation from Providence High School in San Antonio, Texas. Twenty years later, long after her siblings had completed college, she received a bachelor's degree in political science from the University of Texas at San Antonio.

It is this kind of dedication and unselfishness that led to Berriozabal's venture into the world of politics. Berriozabal spent ten years as a San Antonio City Councilor, often taking an unpopular stance on issues she believed in. She was the first Hispana to be elected to a citywide post in San Antonio and in a major U.S. city. In 1991 she ran, unsuccessfully, for mayor. She lost the election, but captured 47 percent of the vote. Berriozabal is content knowing that she raised the consciousness of San Antonio citizens to include in their political vocabulary issues such as affordable housing, neighborhood development, and the empowerment of community leaders.

In September 1991, Berriozabal was awarded a fellowship at the Institute of Politics at the John F. Kennedy School of Government at Harvard, where she taught a course entitled "Women, Minorities, and Public Policy: A New American Agenda." In 1992, her self-imposed sabbatical from the public eye took her to various volunteer endeavors, including organizing programs for *Hispanas Onidas,* a network of Hispanic women, and collecting papers from her ten-year political file for inclusion in a newly-formed Hispana archive at Our Lady of the Lake University in San Antonio. Berriozabal also serves as president of the board of Visitation House, a shelter for homeless women and children in San Antonio. She is a board member of the Federal National Mortgage Association (Freddie Mae) Affordable Housing Advisory Board in Washington, D.C., the National Hispanas Leadership Institute, the National Catholic Reporter, and the Mathematics and Science Education Board of the National Academy of Sciences.

Berriozabal was born April 14, 1941, in Laredo, Texas, the daughter of Apolinar Rodriguez, a carpenter, and Sixta (Arredondo) Rodriguez. The year she was born her par-

ents, along with their first child, a son, decided to leave their home in the central Texas town of Lockhart. They wanted to return to Mexico with Apolinar's mother, who had fled to Texas in 1910 during the Mexican Revolution. But they encountered problems at the border in Laredo when they were told that if they left the United States they would not be allowed to return. Berriozabal was born at this time. The family decided to stay in Texas and to live in San Antonio, where the Rodriguez family grew to include two more sons and two more daughters.

Government Career Culminates in Mayoral Race

Berriozabal credits her hard-working parents with giving her the philosophy that children deserve the best possible attention and opportunity. In a telephone interview with Yleana Martinez, Berriozabal recalled how important it was to her parents that their children receive a private education in Catholic schools. She saw it as so important to them that she postponed her own college education to help finance her siblings's educations. Berriozabal believes that many Latinos who drop out of school do not do so out of disregard for education. "It's not the ones who are ignorant or without talent [that drop out]. I think the ones we lose are the brightest ones, the most responsible, because they see the family situation around them," she explained.

In 1979 she married Manuel P. Berriozabal, a mathematics professor, before moving to Louisiana where he was hired to teach math at the University of New Orleans. The following year, the couple returned to San Antonio when he was hired at the University of Texas. In 1979, Berriozabal finally received her bachelor of arts degree in political science, and continued to take graduate courses in environmental management.

Berriozabal ran for City Council for District One in 1980. Throughout the ten years she spent as an elected official, she said, she championed issues that dealt with the city's future: the need to stem the increase in juvenile crime and to invest in human capital. Of her failed mayoral campaign, she said: "Forty-seven percent of the vote: to me that is a wonderful victory. It means people do listen, people do understand the issues. There were just not enough of them."

The loss gave Berriozabal one thing she had never had before: time. "I have been, since I was 14, pursuing a public life, really, through church work, work in politics, and attention to community and family and their needs. I followed a path, and that path culminated in the mayor's race. I am coming to a place where I realize that for there to be followers and leaders such as I am and was ... there have to be masses of educated and informed people. There are women who believe as I do, about public life." And

Berriozabal is happy knowing she paved the way for them to follow in her path.

Sources:

Berriozabal, Maria Antonietta, telephone interview with Yleana Martinez, August, 1992.

—Sketch by Yleana Martinez

Berry, Erlinda Gonzáles
See **Gonzáles-Berry, Erlinda**

Gloria Bonilla-Santiago
(1954-)
Educator

An educator described by colleagues as "unstoppable" and "a mover and a shaker," Gloria Bonilla-Santiago has worked to further opportunities for Latinos in education, at the workplace, and throughout society. "I see myself as someone who is always building and creating spaces for Latinos," she told Ann Lopez during an interview for *Intercambios.* A professor at Rutgers University School of Social Work, Bonilla-Santiago directs the Hispanic Affairs Office, which she championed to create. When she arrived at Rutgers in 1981 as assistant director of the Academic Foundations Department, the school had no programs for Hispanic students, no office from which administrators could recruit Hispanic students, no place for Hispanic students to make their academic concerns known. Bonilla-Santiago filed grievances and fought to establish the office. "I was willing to work; I was willing to bring in the money," she told Lopez. "There was no way they could tell me no!" The Hispanic Affairs Office opened in 1983. Within four years, its officers had recruited 250 Latino students.

Born on January 17, 1954, Bonilla-Santiago is the youngest daughter of Pedro Bonilla and Nuncia Rodriguez, Puerto Rican migrant farm workers. As a child, she moved every six months to follow the crops from Florida to New Jersey. One season, when she was ten, she decided to stay in New Jersey with Marta Benavides, a Baptist minister from El Salvador, while her family migrated to Florida. "Because of her, I didn't have to leave school and work in the fields like most migrant children," she told Lopez. "She helped me to stay in one place so I could finish school and go to college." Bonilla-Santiago entered Glassboro State College in 1972 to study political science. She then went on to Rutgers University to get a master's degree in social work.

In 1982 Bonilla-Santiago applied for Rutger's Ph.D. program in sociology, but the provost refused to admit her, claiming that no minority woman had ever completed a doctorate in four years. She filed a grievance and won, finishing her doctorate in four years. While studying for her Ph.D., she married Alfredo Santiago in 1983.

Bonilla-Santiago's contributions to the Hispanic community extend beyond academic concerns. In 1985, New Jersey Governor James Florio appointed her to a commission examining sex discrimination in state laws. When Bonilla-Santiago discovered that 42 percent of New Jersey's Hispanic women lived in poverty, she shared her findings with Latina leaders and formed the New Jersey Hispanic Women's Task Force, which introduced a bill requiring the state to establish and fund three resource centers for poor Latinas. The initiative passed in a year and garnered $400,000 from the state legislature.

The New Jersey Hispanic Women's Task Force grew to 1,200 members, including many professional women who felt stifled in their careers. In 1989, Bonilla-Santiago was instrumental in creating the Hispanic Women's Leadership Institute to prepare women from New York, New Jersey, and Pennsylvania to assume leadership roles in their chosen fields and to develop career strategies. She also has served as a board member of the National Council of La Raza, of Marywood College, and of the Camden Alliance for the 21st Century. She is a member of the National Network of Hispanic Women and 1988 winner of a John F. Kennedy Fellowship from Harvard University.

Bonilla-Santiago has authored two books, including *Puerto Rican Migrant Farmworkers: The New Jersey Experience.* In 1992, she completed *Breaking Ground and Barriers: Hispanic Women Developing Effective Leadership,* which surveyed more than 100 Latina leaders nationwide. "I asked women for their experiences, what were their obstacles and barriers," she told Lopez. "They were strong women, and what they have to say is important to us. My next book will deal with domestic violence. It was an issue that came out of my interviews for this book, but I could not deal with it properly there."

In 1990, Bonilla-Santiago became a tenured professor at Rutgers. At a party held in her honor, the provost who had denied her access to the doctoral program congratulated her. "Here was a man who had never believed in me, but attended my party because he was proud of me," she told Lopez. "My mother didn't want to serve him food. I said, 'No mammi, you have to serve him because we have developed consciousness in this man.' That was a beautiful moment in my life."

Sources:

Periodicals

Intercambios, in press.
Progressive, December, 1985, p. 17.

—*Sketch by Dawn Levy*

Lucrezia Bori
(1887-1960)
Opera singer

Spanish opera singer Lucrezia Bori, known for years as the grande dame of the Metropolitan Opera, was one of its most beloved sopranos. In 19 seasons, more than 600 performances, and 29 roles with the company, her grace, style, and musicality made her a critically acclaimed and enormously popular star. Her artistic integrity, personal dignity, and lack of temperamental behavior also made her one of opera's most gracious figures. Following an illustrious stage career, her tireless dedication to fundraising efforts for the Metropolitan Opera earned her the nickname "the opera's Joan of Arc."

Bori was born Lucrecia Borja y González de Riancho on December 24, 1887, in Valencia, Spain, the daughter of a well-to-do army officer. She was a descendant of Renaissance Italy's powerful Borgia family; her name in Italian, in fact, was Lucrezia Borgia. Her family, however, insisted she change it for the stage. Bori made her first public appearance at a benefit concert in Valencia at age six. After a convent education, Bori at 16 decided to become a singer and went to Milan, Italy, for coaching. She made her professional debut at the Teatro Adriano in Rome on October 31, 1908, as Micaela in *Carmen.* Bori was subsequently hired by the Italian opera house La Scala the following season, where the promising young artist so enchanted German composer Richard Strauss that he insisted she sing the role of Octavian in the local premier of his *Der Rosenkavalier* in 1911.

Premieres at the Metropolitan Opera

Bori's long association with the Metropolitan Opera began in 1910 in Paris, when she was invited to replace an indisposed colleague as Manon in Puccini's *Manon Lescaut* with the touring New York company. After an enthusiastic response to her portrayal, two more performances were added and quickly sold out. Her first American appearance was in the same role at age 24, opposite the legendary Italian tenor Enrico Caruso, performed on the opening night of the Metropolitan Opera's 1912-13 season in New York. A critic of that era quoted in the *Record Collector* praised Bori's performance as an "exquisite exhibition of legato singing," and "exquisite diction, impeccable intonation and moving pathos."

As Bori was enjoying the peak of her success, her career took a fateful and dramatic turn. Nodules on her vocal chords required delicate throat surgery in 1915, followed by five years of lonely convalescence. In a *New York Times* article she described her harrowing period of recovery, during which she once forced herself to be absolutely silent for two months. "I felt," she said, "as must those stricken with blindness just as the sun of spring flooded the world." Her discipline and courage were instrumental in her triumphant comeback to the Met in 1921, and her career flourished in the 15 years that followed.

Bori was known for her remarkably clear, true voice and dramatic prowess, capable of expressing passion as well as vulnerability and whimsical charm. Some of Bori's most famous roles included Mimi in *La Bohème*; Norina in *Don Pasquale*; Juliette in *Roméo et Juliette*; and Violetta in *La Traviata,* among others. Of her recordings, critic C. J. Luten wrote in *Opera News:* "Not everyone takes to her somewhat acidulous voice, but who can resist what she does with it? She radiates vivacity in Juliette's waltz . . . and in the Norina-Malatesta duet from *Don Pasquale.* Her legato, long line and pathetic accent . . . are masterful."

Bori's farewell performance at the Met, on March 29, 1936, was a moving tribute to a brilliant career still in its prime. After singing selections from *La Traviata* and *Manon,* the audience stood and cheered for 20 minutes in homage, with women weeping and men stamping their feet. Bori was later quoted in the *New York Times:* "I have no illusions about the length of time a singer may sing. I want to finish while I am still at my best."

Ensures Met's Survival Through Fundraising Work

Lucrezia Bori's "second career" with the Metropolitan Opera began in the early 1930s, when the company's survival seemed threatened by the Depression. In addition to a demanding singing schedule, Bori took on many outside engagements as the head of fundraising committees, including writing letters, meeting with benefactors, and traveling. In 1933, she was praised by Paul D. Cravath, then president and chairman of the Met board, who told the *New York Times* that Bori "did more than anyone else to make opera at the Metropolitan . . . a financial possibility." In 1935, she became the first active artist and the first woman elected to the board of directors of the Metropolitan Opera. In 1942, she was elected president of the Metropolitan Opera Guild.

On May 2, 1960, Bori suffered a cerebral hemorrhage. She died in New York on May 14 at age 71, and funeral rites were held at St. Patrick's Cathedral. Bori, who never married, is buried in the Borja family plot in Valencia. Her will provided for the establishment of the Lucrezia Bori Foundation for charitable, educational, and literary purposes.

Sources:

Periodicals

Chicago Tribune, July 14, 1991, Section 13, p. 18
New York Times, May 15, 1960, p. 1; May 18, 1960, p. 41; May 22, 1960, Section 2, p. 9; May 24, 1960, p. 25.
Opera News, November, 1983, p. 68; December 19, 1987, p. 4; January 18, 1992, p. 37.
Record Collector (Ipswich, Suffolk, England), December, 1973, pp. 147-155.

—Sketch by Julie Catalano

María Brito
(1947-)
Painter, sculptor

Known for her highly personal art, María Brito has shown her work in various national and international exhibits. She has won highly coveted commissions, including the Olympic Sculpture Park in Seoul and "Art in Public Places" at the Metro-Dade Center in Miami, Florida. Among her numerous artistic awards are two National Endowment fellowships, two Cintas Fellowships, a Florida Department of State grant and a Pollack Krasner Foundation Grant.

Brito was born October 10, 1947, in Havana, Cuba. At 13, she and a younger brother were sent alone to Miami, Florida, through Operation Pedro Pan, a secret "underground railroad" used by parents who wanted their children out of communist Cuba. Her family soon joined her in Florida, where she grew up and studied. "It was a period in my life that I took as it came," she told *Miami Herald* art critic Helen Kohen. Brito continues to live and work in Miami, raising two sons there.

In her academic pursuits, Brito received two undergraduate degrees, one in art education from the University of Miami, one in fine arts from Florida International University. But it was not until she enrolled in a ceramics course to get hands-on experience that her artistic urge awakened. With encouragement from other artists and her natural ability, she eventually got a master's of fine arts degree from the University of Miami in 1979.

Brito often uses everyday household objects in her paintings and sculptures. In a framed construction of "Madonna and Child," for instance, she inserted a set of dental impressions on either side of the portrait. The teeth look like receptacles. Yet Brito can not always explain her motivation for including such items. "I'm not sure I was seeking receptacles," she said in the *Miami Herald* interview. "The teeth just went in there and became receptacles."

Kohen identified Brito's art as creations by "an artist who works intuitively" and describes viewers of these works as "likely to be hushed, somewhat in awe of art that touches them despite an impenetrable density." Brito told Kohen that her ideas are usually triggered by a word that seems rife with possibilities or by a knickknack purchased at a flea market. For a period of time, she was attracted to faucets, pipes, and electrical cords. "All these things," wrote Kohen, "are metaphoric connectors, items that work in her sculpture to join past with present, cause with effect, beginning with endings. Pipes and cords also are lines, variations of the formal elements used by artists for centuries."

Brito's work has gathered acclaim as she exhibits in various museums and galleries. She has shown her work in, among other cities, Austin, Miami, and New York City. Her art was represented in "Cuba-U.S.A.: The First Generation," a sampling of Cuban American artists that toured St. Paul, Washington, D.C., Los Angeles, Chicago and other U.S. cities. She has evolved into using more painting in her constructions instead of recycling print images. The surfaces are sleeker, too, and she is paring down incidentals. "I still work out of a gut feeling, but now I am taking away everything that is not important, anything irrelevant," she said in the *Miami Herald.*

Sources:

Periodicals

Más, May-June, 1991, p. 81.

Miami Herald, March 31, 1991, p. 61.

—Sketch by Ana Veciana-Suarez

Silvia Brito
(1933-)
Producer, actress, director

Since 1977, Silvia Brito has dedicated herself to promoting Spanish culture in the United States through the Thalia Spanish Theatre. The small, off-Broadway theatre, located in Queens, New York City, draws an enthusiastic audience made up of people from Queens, Manhattan, and even neighboring states. As executive artistic director and producer, Brito oversees three major productions a year—mostly works by Spanish playwrights. The theatre also presents Friday "folklore evenings," featuring traditional Spanish songs and dances, such as the tango and flamenco. Asked by this contributor in a telephone interview what she considers to be her greatest accomplishment, she replied, "Being able to fulfill myself as an artist and having a Spanish theatre in New York against all odds."

Born in Havana, Cuba, in 1933, Brito was first attracted to the theatre when she was a young child. She remembers writing in a school notebook that she wanted to be a great actress when she grew up. "It's something I really always wanted to be," she said. "I love the theatre. For me, it was fascinating to go to a play and see the zarzuela (traditional Spanish musical theatre). It's a kind of mystery life that I always wanted to be part of." Brito may have inherited her performance instincts from her father, Osvaldo Brito, who was a trumpet player and composer. Her mother, Lillian Garrido de Brito, was a homemaker.

Following her graduation from high school, Brito spent a year at Baldor Academy, a business school, learning some practical skills to support herself while she pursued an acting career. Upon receiving her business administration certificate, she began work as a secretary and bookkeeper for a men's clothing store in Havana. In 1959, she became an actress at Teatro Prometeo, a professional theatre, where she worked for two years. Brito immigrated to the United States in 1961 for political reasons. From 1966 to 1968, she was an actress with the Andres Castro Company, a New York City company that had originally been formed in Havana. She later became an actress with the Dume

Grupo Studio, where she worked from 1968 to 1970 and from 1975 to 1976. She also acted and directed for Repertorio Espanol from 1970 to 1972. Throughout her career as an actress, she held various secretarial jobs to supplement her income.

In 1977, Brito had the opportunity to become the head of an existing Spanish theatre in Manhattan. She named it Thalia Spanish Theatre and moved the company to Queens. Although Brito enjoyed her career as an actress, she finds directing and producing even more fulfilling. "As an actor, you only have one part but as a director, you have the part of each one," she said. Under Brito's direction, Thalia Spanish Theatre has received great reviews at "A Festival of Zarzuelis," a Spanish theatre festival held each year in El Paso, Texas. Brito's future plans for the theatre include moving to a larger facility in Queens that will have enough room to hold training classes for actors, singers, dancers, designers, and playwrights.

Brito's talents have earned her numerous awards over the years, including the Tiempo and Talia Award for Best Actress in 1970 and 1971, several ACE Awards for Best Director and Best Production, the Aplausos Award for Best Director in 1989, and a 1989 Business Council Award for Artistic Merits.

Sources:

Brito, Silvia, telephone interview with Pam Berry, August 31, 1992.

—Sketch by Pam Berry

Brito Selvera, Norma
See **Selvera, Norma Brito**

Georgia L. Brown
(1948-)
Political consultant

Since her days on Jimmy Carter's electoral campaign staff in 1976, Georgia L. Brown has served as political consultant to a number of Democratic candidates. Her list of electoral campaigns includes Gary Hart's and Richard Gephardt's bids for the Democratic Party's presidential nomination and Bill Richardson's reelection campaign for Congress. "Politics is not for people who just want to become well-known and attend a lot of parties," she noted in an interview with Michelle Vachon. "You must be willing to give up all of your free time, be completely dedicated to your candidate, and not expect any rewards. If you have the opportunity to work on a presidential campaign, hours are long, the salary low, and the working conditions usually difficult. But it becomes all worthwhile when you develop a close relationship with the candidate and his or her family. These friendships can last forever: after all these years, I'm still in touch with the Carter family."

Brown was born Georgia Lenor Ayala in Albuquerque, New Mexico, on September 6, 1948, the eldest of two children. Both her father and mother were Mexican American, born and raised in New Mexico. Brown studied at Cortez Elementary School, Cortez Junior High School, and Del Norte High School in Albuquerque. Later, she attended the University of New Mexico, again in Albuquerque, where she majored in Spanish with a minor in linguistics. Brown's entrance into politics happened more or less by accident. After her graduation from the University of New Mexico in 1971, the chairman of the New Mexico Democratic Party, who was a friend of her father, offered her a position at the party's state headquarters. "Even though my father had many political friends, this was my first experience in the field," she recalled in her interview. "Throughout my school days, I had been extremely introverted. I had joined the Spanish Club and the American Field Service, but I had never volunteered for anything. Working at the Democratic State Headquarters gave me self-confidence. I felt that I could finally be myself because I now knew that I had a job to do. This ended up being my career."

Before committing herself to politics, Brown taught Spanish to kindergarten through second grade students in Moriarty, New Mexico. "This was after working at the Democratic Party State Headquarters," she pointed out in her interview. "I had always wanted to teach. At Christmastime, my students performed Christmas carols and the second graders put on the play 'Little Red Riding Hood' in Spanish for the whole school. I was in heaven: there is no reward comparable to seeing a gleam of happiness in a child's eyes. I only taught for one year because the principal did not think that the school should have bilingual education. The parents were very disappointed. What a loss to the students."

On August 23, 1975, Brown married Chris Brown, who was New England coordinator for Jimmy Carter's campaign. The ceremony took place at the Governor's mansion in Santa Fe. In 1976, and again in 1980, they moved to New Hampshire to run Carter's campaign. "One of my fondest memories is Election Night 1976, when Jimmy won the New Hampshire state primary, which was the first one scheduled," she confided in her interview. "We had such a feeling of pride, of accomplishment, because we were convinced that there stood the next President of the United States. We had managed the first hurdle!"

Establishes Political Consulting Firm

In 1977, the Browns launched their own political consulting firm, Brown Inc. "We decided to only take on Democratic candidates," she continued. "Some people work for either party, but we don't feel that you can do a good job if you get involved in a campaign only because the candidate has money. When it comes to picking a client, Chris travels with him or her to see how the public reacts to the candidate and to make sure we agree on important issues. Then, I check how the candidate behaves in the intimacy of his or her home. I won't work for a person who is all sweetness and light with his or her family in public, and does not even pay attention to them behind closed doors." During the 1992 presidential campaign, they participated in the reelection campaigns of Senator Harry Reid of Nevada, Congressman Steny H. Hoyer of Maryland, and Congressman Bill Richardson of New Mexico.

Brown has combined her career with family responsibilities. She has two daughters, Jamie Allison and Erin Lynn, born in 1976 and 1981. "When I worked at Jimmy Carter's campaign headquarters in 1980, I used to take Jamie with me to the office," she recalled in her interview. "She was three years old then. She started playing with electronic typewriters, and before we knew, she was the one showing people how to program the machines. After the election, she found kindergarten boring—there was no machine to play with." Brown stopped travelling with candidates when Jamie entered first grade—she then began handling campaign tasks from her home office in Santa Fe, New Mexico. "I will always be a mother and a wife first," she stated. "If you ask me what I consider my biggest accomplishment, I would say that it is helping my husband become one of the most successful political consultants in this country; but even more important, it is watching my daughters grow up and helping them be proud of who they are. I always taught them to be themselves."

Looking back on her years in politics, Brown remarked in her interview that rewards come only with time and usually in the form of increased self-confidence and responsibilities. One unexpected bonus was to spend the night at the White House with the First Family during President Carter's term. Another reward was discovering that she could write poetry in Spanish. "It made me feel good to know that I was capable of anything if I set my mind to it," she commented.

In Brown's opinion, Hispanics have made strides in politics but still have a long way to go. "We need to work together, to show the world that we have intelligence, determination, a desire to succeed, and above all, pride," she concluded in her interview. "Only then shall we cease being outsiders and become major players in the political arena."

Sources:

Brown, Georgia L., interview with Michelle Vachon, July 29, 1992.

—*Sketch by Michelle Vachon*

Cheryl Brownstein-Santiago

Cheryl Brownstein-Santiago
(1951-)
Newspaper journalist

Cheryl Brownstein-Santiago is a *Los Angeles Times* news editor and associate editor of the newspaper's bilingual supplement, *Nuestro Tiempo,* which currently has a circulation of nearly 500,000. As one of the few Hispanics in the country with a long career in the newspaper business, she actively encourages her fellow journalists to hire and promote minorities in the newsroom. In her view, it is as much a matter of economics as justice, for Brownstein-Santiago insists that members of the Hispanic community want the media to reflect a more diverse view of their world.

The veteran reporter was born October 9, 1951, in New York City, the youngest of three children. Her father, Robert S. Brownstein, was the son of Jewish immigrants who arrived via Ellis Island. A World War II veteran, he was a government clerk when he met Ruth Santiago, who had left her native Puerto Rico for a similar clerical job in New York. The two eventually married, and Brownstein worked as a diamond cutter before opening his own fruit and vegetable business.

When Brownstein-Santiago was in second grade, Robert and Ruth divorced, a process that included a move to Nevada and culminated in Ruth's return to Puerto Rico after an 18-year absence. While Brownstein-Santiago and her sister stayed with their maternal grandmother, Ruth and her son lived in San Juan so that she could work as an executive secretary and save enough money to start her own business.

Successfully Copes with Culture Shock

The experience of living in a community where nearly everyone but Brownstein-Santiago and her siblings spoke Spanish came as a shock. Her teachers were perplexed;

should they put the fourth-grader into a class with younger children so that she could learn the language, or should they let her absorb Spanish naturally? After a brief but unhappy stay in a second-grade class, she was finally transferred to the fourth grade. Fortunately, Brownstein-Santiago's grandmother knew enough English to act as an interpreter, and she also taught Spanish to her granddaughters. But the entire affair was very unsettling, and as Brownstein-Santiago told interviewer Peg McNichol, "I'm a very strong opponent of total immersion [in the classroom] as a result of that experience."

After two years, the family was finally reunited in San Juan. By then, two changes had occurred. One was that Puerto Rican law required two last names, the father's followed by the mother's, and as a result Cheryl and her siblings had to take the name Brownstein-Santiago. The other was that the children were well on their way to becoming completely bilingual. But in San Juan, the language tables were turned once again. Ruth Santiago, by then an executive secretary with the Puerto Rican telephone company, was able to enroll Cheryl in Commonwealth Junior High School, a private, English-language facility for the sons and daughters of American businessmen. The school was expensive (Ruth often had to work as many as three different jobs to pay the tuition) but offered a much better education than the public system.

Later, at Academia San Jose High School, Cheryl found she was much sought after as one of the few bilingual students. By the time she graduated, she had joined the chess club, learned to play the clarinet, edited the school newspaper, and worked as yearbook photographer. Ruth Santiago had remarried and opened a pharmacy in San Juan, hoping to earn enough money to send all three of her children to college.

Leaves Puerto Rico to Attend College in Ohio

Faced with opportunities to continue her education in Puerto Rico, Spain, or the United States, Brownstein-Santiago chose Ohio University in Athens, Ohio. Her goal was to obtain a degree in commercial photography and in the process become self-sufficient, as both her grandmother and mother had in the face of numerous hardships. Seeing them triumph over difficult circumstances gave Brownstein-Santiago a great deal of inner strength and the conviction that she would always be able to support herself.

When she discovered that photography was more fun as a hobby than as a possible career, Brownstein-Santiago took stock of her choices. She wanted to switch to psychology, but it would require more than four years of school and she wanted to be independent with just a four-year degree. She then considered social work, but her counselor instead suggested journalism since she had enjoyed working on her high school newspaper. She picked newswriting and editing as a major, with a minor in psychology.

During the summer of 1972, Brownstein-Santiago combined work at her mother's pharmacy with an internship at the *San Juan Star*. One of the drugstore's customers was a teletypist who told the young woman about an opening at the San Juan bureau of United Press International (UPI). The job turned out to be "excellent experience for someone new to the profession," according to Brownstein-Santiago. Most of the work involved providing 10 to 15 stories a day on the Caribbean region to UPI's radio service.

Joins Staff of *El Miami Herald*

After graduating from college, she continued to work for UPI, but as her sister, brother, and mother left Puerto Rico one by one to settle in the United States, Brownstein-Santiago herself grew anxious to see more of the world. In 1976, she asked UPI for a transfer, and when that did not materialize, she quit and moved to Florida. Within a few months, she had secured a job as staff reporter on *El Miami Herald*, a Spanish-language newspaper for Cuban Americans. She moved up to chief assistant editor, supervising four reporters and seven translators in addition to fulfilling her own editorial duties. She also joined the National Conference of Puerto Rican Women in 1979, serving as Miami chapter parliamentarian until 1981.

Eager for the opportunity to write for an English-language newspaper, Brownstein-Santiago took a job with the *Boston Globe* editing national copy. She did not stay up north for long, however, noting that "if Boston had been in the Sunbelt, I never would have left. But I decided to get back to Miami before the second winter hit."

Secures Reporting Job with the *Miami News*

Brownstein-Santiago returned to Florida as a staff reporter for the *Miami News*, covering spot news and national trends as well as immigration stories. Her territory was the Caribbean, her old UPI beat. She made several trips to Cuba at a time when Cuban-born American journalists were banned from that country. She covered the U.S. invasion of Grenada and presidential candidate Jesse Jackson's 1984 tour of Central America. She was also among the few reporters who witnessed Fidel Castro's first public visit to a church.

Around this time, Brownstein-Santiago and some of her colleagues founded the Florida Association of Hispanic Journalists, a group whose mission is to encourage other Hispanics to consider a career in journalism. Brownstein-Santiago served as the organization's secretary in 1984 and 1985. In another attempt to reach out to young people and give back to the community, she also served as board member of the YWCA of Greater Miami from 1983 until 1985.

By the mid-1980s, Brownstein-Santiago had been promoted to editorial writer for the *Miami News;* she also did recruiting for the paper. She was active professionally in other ways as well, attending the Editors' Conference on Latin America at the Woodrow Wilson International Center for Scholars in 1984 and the Editorial Page Editors and Writers Seminar at the American Press Institute in 1987.

Heads West to Work for the *Los Angeles Times*

But in 1988 the *Miami News* folded, and Brownstein-Santiago was forced to look elsewhere for a job. She soon landed one with the *Los Angeles Times*, joining a department that produces a monthly bilingual supplement entitled *Nuestro Tiempo*. Though her work on *Nuestro Tiempo* mostly involves editing the writing of others, Brownstein-Santiago occasionally authors editorial pieces of her own, including one on the political future of Puerto Rico. She has also learned much more about the differences within the U.S. Hispanic community.

Brownstein-Santiago remains fiercely committed to drawing more Hispanics into the field of journalism. "When I started out in this business," she noted, "there were newspaper managers who would say, 'Gee we'd like to hire Latins, but we can't find any who are qualified.' That's the reason most Hispanic groups got started, as a way of saying, 'Here are some perfectly qualified people.'" As part of this effort, Brownstein-Santiago volunteers to work on writing contests and scholarship committees and makes career-day visits to schools. She is also a member of the board of directors of the National Association of Hispanic

Journalists and a member of the California Chicano News Media Association. "Being a Latina in major market new media in the U.S., I feel a strong responsibility to give back to the Latin communities that have been so supportive of me throughout my career," she explained.

When she's not busy with her editorial and civic duties, Brownstein-Santiago enjoys walking on the beach and swimming in the ocean near her condominium. A self-described "happily single" woman, she owns a cockatiel and a canary and still enjoys dabbling in photography.

Sources:

Brownstein-Santiago, Cheryl, telephone interview with Peg McNichol, September, 1992.

—Sketch by Peg McNichol

Cecilia Preciado de Burciaga

Cecilia Preciado de Burciaga
(1945-)
College administrator

Cecilia Preciado de Burciaga is one of the most influential Hispanic women in the field of higher education. As an administrator at Stanford University since 1974, Burciaga is a respected spokeswoman on issues relating to women and minorities in education.

Burciaga, who did not speak English until she entered kindergarten, is a strong advocate for better educational opportunities for Hispanics. During her career at Stanford, she has pushed the university to recruit more female and minority students, faculty, and administrative staff.

A first-generation Chicana, Burciaga was born on May 17, 1945, in Pomona, California. She describes her childhood on her family's dairy farm in nearby Chino as a time of exploration and wonder. "I had the most nurturing, magical, loving childhood," said Burciaga in an interview. "Living on a farm with all that open space allows you lots of time for exploration and introspection." At the time, Chino, a town in San Bernardino county, was a rural community, with a mixture of Dutch, Italian, Portuguese, and Chicano residents. But it was predominately Chicano, and Burciaga grew up feeling comfortable and secure.

Burciaga's father, Bernardino Preciado, was an immigrant from Jalisco, Mexico, who had worked hard to become the owner of a successful farm. He was active in the local Mexican American and business community. Her mother, Rebeca (Jimenez), also born in Jalisco, ran a

traditional Mexican household. "They really raised us as Mexican children," Burciaga said.

Burciaga always had a sense of two worlds, Mexican and Anglo. At home, she spoke only Spanish. In fact, she knew no English when she first entered school. "I knew what was appropriate at home and what was appropriate in the Anglo world," she said. The strictness of her Mexican upbringing sometimes conflicted with her outside life, especially when she was a teenager. She was not allowed to date, spend the night at girlfriends' houses, or attend football games, for example.

But her parents always allowed her to pursue her dreams. She graduated from Pomona Catholic Girls High School, where she was active in student politics and clubs, in 1963. There, she gained a lifelong respect for the potential value of a Catholic education, particularly for young girls and Hispanics. "A Catholic girls high school meant you had women role models teaching you everything from chemistry to homemaking. There was an opportunity for leadership. And the uniform helps you lessen the sense of competition among other women," said Burciaga. Later in her career, she would become a strong critic of the Catholic educational system, particularly Catholic colleges and universities, for not doing more educational outreach to Hispanics.

After graduation, she briefly attended Mount St. Mary's College for Women in Westwood, California. But she was not prepared to handle her heavy courseload and left after a year, discouraged by her poor grades and guilty about her parents' sacrifices to pay the tuition. Fortunately, she decided to attend summer school at San Antonio Community College and received good grades. The next fall, she enrolled at California State University at Fullerton. After a year as a commuter student, living at home, she took a job as a student assistant in the Spanish department and rented a house with friends.

As a child, Burciaga aspired to be a bilingual bank teller, one of the few jobs available in her town where women appeared successful and important. By the time she was in college, she had decided she would be a Spanish teacher. She received her bachelor of arts in 1968, with a Spanish major and English minor, and soon earned her teaching certificate. Burciaga then returned to Chino, where she worked as a Spanish teacher in the public high school. She quickly realized that, although she loved the students, she was not happy in the high-school environment.

A year later, Burciaga found herself in Washington, D.C., in a training program for foreign service officers at the U.S. Information Agency. While a college student, she had worked as a tutor for the Upward Bound program. One of the Upward Bound leaders told her that she would be good in the foreign service. So, on a whim, she interviewed with a recruiter in California, and she was accepted.

After a year of training, from 1969 to 1970, sponsored by a Ford Foundation Fellowship, Burciaga decided that the foreign service was not the appropriate place for her. While she had hoped to use her Spanish in her job, her first assignment was New Delhi, India; in addition, the agency had a rule that female foreign service officers were not allowed to marry. Burciaga had been volunteering on weekends at the Interagency Committee on Mexican American Affairs. When she resigned from the foreign service, she joined the committee staff.

Becomes Involved in Minority Issues

For the first time, she became active in Mexican American issues at the national level, and she greatly enjoyed her work. In 1970, after a change in presidential administrations from Johnson to Nixon, Burciaga took a position on the U.S. Commission on Civil Rights. She worked as a research analyst on a Mexican American education project.

The job at the civil rights commission marked a turning point in Burciaga's young life. The project she worked on produced six fact-finding reports on Mexican American educational attainment. Burciaga traveled around the country, helping to publicize the results of the reports, which painted a picture of the status of Mexican Americans in education. "It gave me a national perspective, a national network, and a lifelong commitment to social justice," Burciaga explained in her interview.

In her many jobs and community positions since then, Burciaga has been acutely aware of being one of few Hispanics in a prominent position. As a professional Hispanic woman, she is always a minority. "It's never easy to be the one and only anything. It's exhausting," she told the *Christian Science Monitor.* But she has never stopped trying to improve the possibilities for minorities and women.

She interrupted her work for a year to attend the University of California in Riverside, where she earned a master of arts in sociology policy studies in 1972. Burciaga then returned to her post in Washington. In 1972, she married Jose Antonio Burciaga, a poet and artist, and they soon started a family which grew to include two children, Maria Rebeca and Jose Antonio. The couple decided they did not want to raise a family in Washington, so they returned to California in 1974.

Accepts Position at Stanford University

Burciaga debated about whether to start a Ph.D. program or continue working, but when Stanford University offered her a position as Assistant to the President and Provost for Chicano Affairs, she took the job. "I embarked on an administrative career, thinking it was temporary," Burciaga noted in her interview. The job was a logical extension of her work in Washington. "It was an opportunity to work with the future, both students and faculty," she continued.

In 1974, when Burciaga first started working at Stanford, the student body was just two percent Mexican American; there were few Chicano faculty or staff. She began working to increase representation of Mexican Americans among the faculty, staff, and student body. "I was trying to enable the university to incorporate talent from my background at all levels so I wouldn't be the only one here," Burciaga said in her interview. "There were very few of us."

Three years later, Burciaga was promoted to Assistant Provost for Faculty Affairs. In that position, she searched for future faculty appointments and concentrated on efforts to hire more minority and women faculty members. Over the years, Burciaga has seen the results of her work and the work of others. In 1992, Stanford's freshman class was 11 percent Chicano. The Chicano faculty has grown steadily as well. "There's a wonderful core of talent in the Chicano faculty. Did I do it? I feel I was part of the history. You do as much to influence things as you can," Burciaga stated.

Meanwhile, Burciaga's reputation was growing. In 1976, President Jimmy Carter appointed her to the International Commission on the Observance of International Women's Year in Houston, Texas. Carter chose her as one of 40 women to comprise a National Advisory Committee for Women, where she served from 1977 to 1979, joining leaders in the women's movement such as Bella Abzug, Gloria Steinem, and Coretta Scott King. The experience was a valuable one. "I learned about brokering and trading to get what you wanted," she said. "It made me a player in the women's movement."

Burciaga also learned how difficult it was to organize Hispanic women on a national level. She found that Hispanic women represent many ethnic groups, such as Puerto Rican, Cuban, and Mexican American, and each group has a different set of realities and concerns. "It's been very difficult for Hispanic women to speak in one voice," she confirmed. While one of her dreams has been to create a national consortium of Hispanic women leaders, it is a dream that has yet to be realized. "It is too early," Burciaga said.

In 1985, Burciaga was promoted to Associate Dean of Graduate Studies at Stanford. She also served as Director of the Office of Chicano Affairs. In both positions, she continued to work on her career-long efforts to expand opportunities for women, blacks, Hispanics, American Indians, and other minorities. Her staff recruited more women and minorities into the university's Ph.D. programs. In an interview with the *Christian Science Monitor*, Burciaga said that she did not find open resistance to affirmative action at Stanford, but she did have to fight against apathy. She said that it is the faculty's responsibility to create a diverse campus: "It is the faculty that hire faculty. They know best how to find their own animals. That means faculty members have got to want it."

Burciaga worked briefly as an affirmative action officer at Stanford before being promoted in 1991 to Associate Dean and Director of Development in the Office of the Vice President for Student Resources. In this position, Burciaga raises funds for student activities, ranging from summer research projects to women in science programs and the purchase of a new X-ray machine for the health center. "This has given me an opportunity to really understand the nature of student affairs here. Now, I see how many wonderful staff and students we've got," she said in her interview. "It's made me fall in love again with the vision, mission, and purpose of Stanford."

Burciaga and her family have lived on the Stanford campus since 1985. They are resident fellows and live with 100 students in a university dormitory. Family life is very important to Burciaga, whose children are now teenagers, but her family also enjoys keeping their doors open to the students. "My husband and I have always been public

people, very social. We always have people at our house," she explained.

Burciaga is a popular public speaker on the issues of higher education, minorities, and women. She appears frequently in the media, on radio and television. "I try and say things a little different than what other people are saying. I really value public speaking," Burciaga noted in her interview. One of her favorite topics remains the unrealized potential of the Catholic education system. "The Catholic church should do more to encourage Spanish students. If the church is really going to live out its faith, it should reach out to the community that is naturally its own," she stated. She also likes to talk about affirmative action and the responsibility white women have to support minority women in the workplace: "As they gain power, they need to remember affirmative action got them where they are today."

As she looks ahead, Burciaga plans to continue her efforts to increase opportunities for minorities and women in higher education. If she ever leaves academia, she predicts it will be to work at a foundation. But she will always be involved with the nation's youngest generations and helping them to achieve their potential, as she explained in her interview: "I'm very interested in the issues of youth. I'm interested in the future and trying to discern where we are going next."

Sources:

Books

Meier, Matt. S., *Mexican-American Biographies: A Historical Dictionary 1836-1987*, Greenwood Press, 1988, pp. 32-34.

Periodicals

Christian Science Monitor, July 31, 1984, pp. 19-20.

Other

Burciaga, Cecilia Preciado de, interview with Ann Malaspina, October 3, 1992.

—Sketch by Ann Malaspina

C

Cabeza de Baca Gilbert, Fabiola
See **Gilbert, Fabiola Cabeza de Baca**

Angelina Cabrera
Non-profit executive,
business development specialist

Throughout her career as an executive of non-profit organizations and a business development specialist, Angelina Cabrera has been a staunch advocate for women, Hispanics, and African Americans. Her positions have included founder and vice president of Capital Formation, an organization to help women- and minority-owned businesses; director of the National Puerto Rican Forum, an organization that provides skills training for the Hispanic community; and assistant deputy commissioner for the New York State Department of Economic Development's Minority and Women's Business Division. "My most important accomplishment is being an advocate for the Hispanic community—the Puerto Rican community in particular—and also minorities," she told this contributor in a telephone interview. "My concern right now is that the business community and the community at large become informed of the technical assistance—the kinds of programs and services—that the city, state and federal government have that will aid them. Many of these programs and services are free of charge and they are not aware of it."

Cabrera's commitment to the Hispanic community is rooted in her early childhood. Born in Brooklyn Heights to parents who emigrated from Puerto Rico, Cabrera always spoke Spanish at home. "My parents never let me forget my language and my culture," she said. "I am bilingual and I think that's very important in today's world." Her father, Francisco Quinones, was a laborer, and her mother, Oliva Massanet, was a homemaker.

Cabrera attended Carnegie Institute of Technology in Pittsburgh, Pennsylvania, from 1951 to 1954. She later took courses in political science at Fordham University and Marymount Manhattan College, both in New York City. Her first major job was as executive secretary for the New York Office of the Economic Development Administration for the Commonwealth of Puerto Rico, where she worked from 1955 to 1965. In 1964, she became a volunteer for Robert F. Kennedy during his campaign for senator. After his election, she became his secretary and office manager.

Founds Capital Formation to Assist Minority Businesses

When one of Kennedy's volunteers suggested that Cabrera form a nonprofit organization to assist women- and minority-owned businesses, she founded Capital Formation in 1968. One of the organization's most important achievements was to launch the National Bank Deposit Program, which was designed to encourage government agencies to deposit funds in minority banks. The program has since expanded to many other states.

In 1972, Cabrera became the national director of community affairs and public relations for the National Puerto Rican Forum, another nonprofit organization developed to assist the Hispanic community. The forum focused on promoting economic development within the Puerto Rican community by providing skills training and bilingual technical assistance to businesses. "I served as an advocate for the Hispanic and Puerto Rican community," she said. "Many people would call me in regard to problems with their businesses, job training, or how to get a better education for their children."

Political Work Leads to Government Appointments

Cabrera, who had been active in state and national politics since volunteering for Robert Kennedy, was chosen by Senator George McGovern to organize his Presidential campaign within the Hispanic community in 1972. Her political involvement brought her to the attention of Congressman Hugh Carey, who was running for governor of the state of New York. He asked Cabrera to run his campaign within the Hispanic community. After his election, she was named deputy director of the Women's Division at the Executive Chamber, a position she held from 1975 to 1982. As deputy director, she was actively involved in the National Women's Conference and the New York state meeting that preceded it. The conference, held in Houston in 1978, was organized by Congresswoman Bella Abzug to get women to talk about issues that affected their lives. "It was incredible because we got a lot of issues out and there was consciousness-raising about battered women, rape—all of these things we still talk about today."

When Mario Cuomo was elected governor of New York, he appointed her to the New York State Department of Economic Development, Minority and Women's Business Division. She was initially a business development specialist and was later promoted to assistant deputy commissioner. Cabrera conducts seminars throughout the state, promoting the services and programs that New York has to offer to assist women- and minority-owned businesses. Cabrera's future plans include helping minority businesses expand into the international business arena. "If they expand that means more jobs," she said. "I think that's important—we need more jobs."

Sources:

Cabrera, Angelina, telephone interview with Pam Berry, September 2, 1992.

—Sketch by Pam Berry

Lydia Cabrera
(1900-1991)
Ethnologist, writer

Writer Lydia Cabrera was considered by contemporaries as the premiere Cuban ethnologist and the island's matriarch of letters. Her collections of Afro-Cuban folklore, both fiction and nonfiction, were a major contribution to the anthropological study of her native land. When she died in September, 1991, Miamian Marcia Morgado wrote to the *Miami Herald:* "Her death deprived us Cubans of our cultural mother. She gave birth to the offspring from the marriage between European and African myths, legends and mores. She penetrated the previously closed world of former African slaves and deciphered for us their secrets . . . she brought to life a world populated by exquisitely sensuous and mischievous deities, wise animals, and breathing rocks."

Writes Seminal Work on *Santeria*

Born May 20, 1900, in Havana, Cuba, Cabrera was the daughter of a prominent intellectual. She became interested in Afro-Caribbean culture when she left Cuba in 1927 to study Asian religions at L'Ecole du Louvre in Paris, France. She returned to Cuba in 1938, after publishing the first of her 23 books. This work, *Cuentos Negros de Cuba,* was initially issued in French in 1936, then in Spanish. Among her later writings is *El Monte,* her best-known book. Published in 1954, the volume is a seminal work on *santeria,* the hybrid of Roman Catholic and African religious practices that evolved in Caribbean countries. The Castro government reissued the book without her permission in 1991. She explored Cuba's African heritage in other works of fiction as well as in scholarly tomes. She also compiled a dictionary of the Afro-Cuban Yoruba language.

Cabrera lived in Cuba, writing and researching, from 1938 to 1960, when she left first to Madrid, Spain, and later to Miami, Florida. In exile, she continued her work, publishing more than a dozen books. Her home in Miami became a mecca for young exile writers, artists, and anyone interested in the Afro-Cuban culture. For many intellectuals, she became a guiding light. "She befriended old, former slaves in Havana and Matanzas, in the fields and hills," wrote *Miami Herald* reporter Lizette Alvarez in a 1991 article. "On their porches, inside their thatched-roof huts known as *bohios,* she heard their stories and translated them into tales, fictional stories based on folklore rooted in Africa and passed down from generation to generation."

Teaches Value of Cuba's African Roots

Various reviewers have lauded her work for being thoroughly researched firsthand and for possessing a poetic, lyrical style. In a 1991 editorial, a writer for the *Miami Herald* eulogized her: "Ms. Cabrera combined a graceful prose style with rigorous attention to the truth. With respect, humility and charm, she wrote about her country . . . its plants and animals, its folklore, its legends, its popular medicine." Ramon Mestre, a *Miami Herald* columnist, also noted: "Lydia Cabrera . . . taught me to cherish a hidden Cuba, a country that rarely appears in official histories. Enraptured by its magic, I read her work and learned to value Cuba's African roots, an essential element in their national identity that too many Cubans either scorn or ignore."

Sources:

Periodicals

Miami Herald, September 21, 1991, pp. 1A, 22A; October 4, 1991, p. 15A; October 5, 1991, p. 23A.

—Sketch by Ana Veciana-Suarez

Olivia Cadaval
(1943-)
Folklore specialist

When Olivia Cadaval was a girl, a teacher emphasized the importance of culture. Cadaval learned the lesson well, and has spent her adult life trying to enrich others by introducing them to the humanities. Her work has focused on uniting non-academic people with scholars. Cadaval explained in a interview with D. D. Andreassi that she has "always tried to bridge the scholarly community and the people community: the university and the real world."

Cadaval was born in Mexico City on September 29, 1943, to Ana Maria Ramos De Cadaval and Alfonso Gonzalez Cadaval. As a young girl Cadaval was influenced by the many intellectual Spanish refugees living in Mexico. Most important among them was a Spanish teacher who constantly told her students that they knew nothing about culture. "She thought that we should have a broader perspective," Cadaval recalled in her interview. "It became a living thing for all the students who followed her." Culture would be theirs through literature, Cadaval's teacher lectured. Learning about history and the performing arts would naturally follow.

Growing up in Mexico City, Cadaval found that "ethnicity is not a question." She discovered later, however, that "when you become an immigrant you have to define yourself. I did not have a living experience in the Southwest. My experience is not as a Chicana, but as a Latina." Cadaval lived in Mexico City until she was an exchange student at MacMurry College in Illinois. During the summers she returned home and attended the University of the Americas and the Universidad Iberoamericana, both in Mexico City. Returning to the United States, Cadaval attended Mundelein College in Chicago and George Washington University, where she earned a bachelor of arts degree in philosophy and a doctorate in philosophy in American studies folk life. Also during these years, in 1964, she married David Bosserman. They have one child, Arnold.

Begins Association with Smithsonian Institute

Cadaval gained direction after a summer job she had in 1976 at the Smithsonian Institute, where she had the opportunity to work with representatives from various parts of Mexico. "That's what sent me into the folk life field," she noted in her interview. "It got me into a whole new discipline." Two years later she was hired as project director of the National Center for Urban Ethnic Affairs. "At that time there was a Eurocentric definition of ethnicity, and it was a good time for me to come in and focus on Latin American ethnicity," she explained.

Cadaval continued promoting cultural awareness as project director of the Institute for Contemporary Culture from 1982 through 1984. Her intent was to bring people in the community together with scholars. Meanwhile, from 1980 through 1985 Cadaval also acted as executive director of Centro de Arte, a local community organization in Washington, D.C., that again promoted humanities through programs led by scholars. Workshops featured art, film, and discussion series. "It trained the young people in the community to do their own programs and give back to the community," Cadaval explained in her interview.

Although Cadaval had experiences in various arenas, one of her favorite jobs was teaching classes in introduction to folklore at George Washington University for three years. Meanwhile, she worked as a self-employed cultural consultant with various organizations, like the Smithsonian and the Library of Congress. She also acted as a humanities consultant at the Latin American Youth Center.

Among her many honors, Cadaval earned a one-year Smithsonian Institute-George Washington University graduate student fellowship in 1981, a George Washington University fellowship from 1982 through 1984, and a one-year pre-doctoral fellowship with the Smithsonian in 1987. In 1988 she was hired as a folklore specialist at the Smithsonian Institute.

Although her own education and professional affiliations are extensive, Cadaval has always insisted on the importance of learning from people in the community. "It's very important to bring the non-academic scholar into the process," she emphasized in her interview. Her work has led to a number of published articles in professional journals such as *Creative Ethnicity* and the *Journal of Folklore Research,* as well as a 1979 documentary entitled "Festival and the Politics of Culture."

In concluding her interview, Cadaval downplayed her significant role in enriching lives through cultural awareness and education. She again explained how she benefited from her contact with the people in her community: "They're not the ones with the degrees and in the institutions, but they are enriching me in many ways."

Sources:

Cadaval, Olivia, telephone interview with D. D. Andreassi, September, 1992.

—Sketch by D. D. Andreassi

Campbell, Rita Ricardo
See Ricardo-Campbell, Rita

Judy Canales
(1962-)
Journalist, urban studies specialist

An up-and-coming urban studies specialist and leader among Hispanic business and professional women, Judy Canales was born in Uvalde, Texas, on June 9, 1962, the eldest of three children. Her father, Alfonso Canales, worked for the First State Bank in Uvalde and her mother, Susana Canales, was an employee of Southwestern Telephone Company of Texas. "I was inspired by my parents' commitment to their church and their community," Canales told interviewer Graciela Beecher. "We are several-generation Texans and feel the love of the land very strongly. Both of my grandparents were pioneers involved in improving and developing their local community."

Educated in her hometown at Sacred Heart Elementary School and Uvalde High School, Canales went on to attend the University of Texas at Austin, from which she received a bachelor of journalism degree. She followed up with graduate work at Trinity University in San Antonio, Texas, earning a master of arts in urban studies. In addition to her academic training, Canales gained practical experience through several internships, including assignments with Congressman Abraham Kazen of Laredo, Texas, for the Fort Worth Telegram Newspapers; with the city of San Antonio as an economic and employment management intern; and with the city of Phoenix, Arizona, as a housing counselor.

Professionally, Canales has worked for the Low-Income Housing Information Service and for the National Council of La Raza, where she coauthored a policy report entitled "The Hispanic Housing Crisis." More recently, she has served as legislative representative for housing, community development, and economic development for the City of New York in its Washington, D.C., office.

Canales has also been active in a number of Latina organizations. During her internship in Phoenix, she became a member of the Arizona Hispanic Women's Corporation and a board member of Mujer, Inc. In Texas she joined Mexican American Business and Professional Women and Hispanas Unidas. And since 1991 she has been president of the Mexican American Women's National Association (MANA).

Canales's abilities and contributions have been honored in a variety of ways. In 1991, for example, she was part of the Hispanic delegation that met in Mexico City with President Carlos Salinas de Gortari to discuss the implications of the North American Free Trade Agreement between the United States and Mexico. In recognition of her leadership skills and participation in the policy-making process, Canales became a member of the 1992 class of the National Hispanic Leadership Institute. Also in 1992, she received the Woman of Distinction Award from the National Conference for College Women Student Leaders as well as the Achievement Award from the National Association of Cuban-American Women (NACAW).

Seeks Unity and Empowerment for All Latinas

Yet Canales believes her greatest achievement in life so far has been serving as a role model for Chicanas and all Hispanic American women in their struggle for unity and empowerment. She herself understands well the value of role models, noting in her interview with Beecher, "I have always been inspired by strong leaders such as Blandina Cárdenes Ramírez, Henry Cisneros and Raul Yzaguirre. I have looked to them for guidance in my desire to serve my people."

In addition, Canales considers herself a champion of unity in diversity since, in her view, all Hispanic American women—Chicanas, Cubanas, Puerto Ricans, and others—are still victims of prejudice and machismo and are therefore excluded from male-dominated fields, especially large corporations . The solution, says Canales, is for Latinas to strive for board memberships and policy-making positions that affect the future not only of Hispanic women but of all women in the United States.

Sources:

Canales, Judy, telephone interview with Graciela Beecher, September, 1992.

—Sketch by Graciela Beecher

Cordelia Candelaria
(1943-)
Educator, author, poet

Cordelia Chavez Candelaria has received national and international acclaim as an educator, author, and poet through her involvement with multiculturalism, languages, and literature. Candelaria, author of *Ojo de la Cueva*, has also published literary criticism, research on Chicanas, and poetry in numerous journals, as well as in encyclopedias, monographs, and anthologies. Having distinguished herself through the integrity of her interpretations, Candelaria's writing reflects an effective integration of intense, critical studies, academic experience and her own southwestern heritage which she describes as the "poet's locus of inter-

Cordelia Candelaria

est." Her expressions are a testimony to her affinity for the land and her own feminine identity forged from and with the land and a culture inextricably interwoven.

Candelaria, the fifth of eight children, was born on September 14, 1943, in Deming, New Mexico, to Eloida Trujillo and Ray J. Chavez. Her fondest childhood memories are of her profound love of reading, words, and language, which led her to study English and French at Fort Lewis College in Durango, Colorado. After graduating with an honors degree in 1970, she later went on to earn an M.A. in English in 1972 and an honors Ph.D. in American literature and structural linguistics in 1976 from the University of Notre Dame.

As a poet, Candelaria has drawn upon memories of her desert home, with its majestic southwestern sunsets and rugged terrain, to present an important theme: the relationship between humans and the land that sustains them. Candelaria's poems, which are largely autobiographical, allow the reader to see and feel the land as a source of both life and death. "Cliffs," published in *Ojo de la Cueva,* is a metaphorical expression of painful chagrin as the "cliffs of red earth," turn into "a modern day Toxcatl." The poet suggests an analogy between Toxcatl, a bloody massacre that took place during the Spanish conquest, and a strip-mining operation in Black Mesa, Arizona. In *Dictionary of Literary Biography,* Margarita Tavera Rivera discussed how Candelaria uses the cactus plant as a symbol of hardiness and survival. "The cactus sends roots down to the cave

springs in search of life-giving water, an image which functions for Candelaria as a metaphor for the Chicano writer, who has managed to survive the aridness of the desert of inattention, and which surprises the observer with the vividness and beauty of its blossoms," Rivera wrote.

Another major theme of Candelaria's work is a reaffirmation of feminine identity. Her editorial contributions continue to play a crucial role in the advancement of the economic and social condition of women in general, and Chicanas and Hispanas in particular. Her thoughts and feelings on the feminist perspective are expressed, among other places, in *Chicano Poetry* and *Latina Writing.* Multiculturalism, another concern of Candelaria's, is discussed in numerous writings, including *Forging New Artistic Traditions,* and *Piñatas of Memory.* Candelaria has also written a number of books that promote higher education as a key vehicle for overcoming disadvantages and achieving personal empowerment. One of her more critical essays, "Community Empowerment and Chicano Scholarship," was published in 1992 by the National Association for Chicano Studies.

Since 1991, Candelaria has been a professor of American literature and research associate at the Hispanic Research Center of Arizona State University. Previously, Candelaria held the position of associate professor of English and director of the Chicano Studies Program at the University of Colorado in Boulder from 1978 through 1991. As part of the Chicano Studies Program from 1986 through 1988, she was the founding director of CSERA (Center for Studies of Ethnicity & Race in America). From 1976 to 1977 she worked as the program officer for the Division of Research, National Endowment for the Humanities, in Washington, D.C.

For her academic and literary accomplishments, Candelaria has received recognition nationally and internationally. She received the 1991 15-Year Higher Education Replication Study award from the National Sponsoring Committee in Denver, Colorado. Candelaria was also the recipient of the Colorado University Equity and Excellence Faculty Award in 1989, the Boulder Faculty Assembly First Annual Service Award in 1988, and the Thomas Jefferson Award in 1983. She received the Boulder Community Pacesetter nomination in 1987 and was a speaker at the International Congress on Hispanic Literature at the University of Paris, France, in March, 1986. For her academic accomplishments, Candelaria has also received several fellowships, including an Honorary Fellowship from the National Chicano Council on Higher Education and a Woodrow Wilson Graduate Fellowship.

In addition to her many professional responsibilities, Candelaria and her husband, Jose Fidel Candelaria, operate a working ranch in Ojo de la Cueva in northwestern New Mexico. The couple have a son, Clifford Candelaria. Balancing her personal and professional life may not be easy, but Candelaria serves as an inspiration and role model to minority professionals to aspire to their highest potential by applying their cultural diversity to traditional and modern challenges.

Sources:

Books

Candelaria, Cordelia, *Ojo de la Cueva*, Maize Press, 1984.
Dictionary of Literary Biography, Volume 82: *Chicana Writers*, Gale, 1989.

—*Sketch by Alma Renee Madrid*

Cañas, Maria Martínez
   See **Martínez-Cañas, Maria**

Luisa Capetillo
(1879-1922)
Union activist, feminist, author

A leader in the political and labor struggles of the working class at the beginning of the twentieth century in Puerto Rico, Luisa Capetillo condemned the exploitation of workers by political parties, religion, and capitalism. She also was a tireless feminist crusader who denounced the cultural and social system that enslaved women in ignorance and forced them into marriages based not on love but on a financial arrangement between two sets of parents. And as a suffragist, she struggled to obtain universal voting rights for both men and women. Besides her notable leadership activities, Capetillo left behind many written works that are just now being rediscovered and studied by scholars who may well conclude that her name belongs among those of the other "greats" in the American women's movement.

Luisa Capetillo was born in Arecibo, Puerto Rico, on October 28, 1879. Her mother, Margarita Perón, was French, and her father, Luis Capetillo, was Spanish. Her biographers agree that while she might have had some formal schooling, she was primarily self-taught; the knowledge of French she gained from her mother, for example, enabled her to read the works of French writers. History remembers her as the first woman to wear pants in public, which could be considered symbolic of the personal freedom she expressed in her actions and writings.

Champions the Cause of the Female Worker

Capetillo lived in a period when the industrialization of Puerto Rico had just begun; wages were low for men and lower still for women. She believed that good wages were a worker's right and that better pay would result in happier families, less domestic violence, and more educational opportunities for children. While she acknowledged that men were as oppressed as women, she was especially concerned with the plight of the female worker. Her skill was in the way she managed to relate and interweave the issues of the private world (such as the family, single motherhood, and women's rights in general) with those of the public world (such as politics, wages, and education).

As Edna Acosta-Belén observes in her book *The Puerto Rican Woman: Perspectives on Culture, History and Society*, during Capetillo's lifetime the women's movement was "characterized by two major trends: the petit bourgeois and the proletarian." Although Capetillo was supportive and understanding of both groups, she definitely focused on the world from the perspective of the proletarian, or working, woman rather than her middle-class sisters. In her book *Mi opinión sobre las libertades, derechos y deberes de la mujer como compañera, madre y ser independiente* (title means "My Opinion on the Freedom, Rights, and Duties of the Woman as Companion, Mother and as an Independent Woman"), she pointed out that affluent women were never touched by the problems that affected working women, mainly because they didn't have to take jobs outside the home to help support their families, and they always hired another woman to take care of their children.

Joins Puerto Rican Labor Movement

Capetillo's involvement in the labor movement began in 1907 when she participated in a strike in Arecibo's tobacco factories. Within a year she was an active member of the Federation of Free Workers (FLT), and in 1910 she became a reporter for the federation's newspaper. Also in 1910 she founded the newspaper *La mujer* (title means "The Woman"), which addressed women's issues.

Over the next few years Capetillo traveled extensively, journeying to New York in 1912 and contributing some articles to the newspaper *Cultura obrera* (title means "Worker's Culture"), visiting Florida in 1913 to collaborate with some union workers, and settling in Cuba from 1914 until 1916 to lecture on how to start cooperatives . By 1918 she was back in Puerto Rico once again, this time organizing strikes by agricultural workers in Ceiba and Vieques. That same year Capetillo was arrested for violence, disobedience, and being insubordinate to a police officer.

Writings Reveal the Philosophical Basis for Her Activism

A thorough examination of Capetillo's writings from her activist days provides some insight into her opinions and the ideas for which she fought all her life. In many ways she was so far ahead of her time that the society she envisioned could exist only in her imagination.

Ensayos libertarios (title means "Libertarian Essays") appeared in 1907. Dedicated to all workers, male and female, it is a compilation of articles that Capetillo originally published between 1904 and 1907. In 1910, in *La humanidad en el futuro* (title means "Humanity in the Future"), she describes a utopian society in detail and from a broad perspective. She also discusses the power of the Church and the state, the institution of marriage, and private and common property. In her 1911 work entitled *Mi opinión sobre las libertades, derechos y deberes de la mujer como compañera, madre y ser independiente,* she analyzes the situation of women in society, focusing on what she viewed as the oppression and slavery of women and affirming that education is the key to freedom.

Also among Capetillo's writings are several dramas. According to Angelina Morfi in her book *Historia critica de un siglo de teatro puertorriqueño* (title means "Critical History of One Century of Puerto Rican Theater"), the theater provided Capetillo with an alternative way to express her ideas effectively, especially her opinions about the oppression of women and the moral codes that strangle them culturally and socially.

On April 10, 1922, Capetillo died of tuberculosis in Río Piedras at the age of forty-two. She was survived by her three children, Manuela, Gregorio, and Luis, as well as her dreams for a better world. As Yamila Azize declares in *Luchas de la mujer en Puerto Rico* (title means "Women's Struggles in Puerto Rico"), "The more we know the life of this woman and become familiar with her ideas and writings, we confirm the special importance of Capetillo in our history."

Sources:

Books

Acosta-Belén, Edna, "Puerto Rican Women in Culture, History, and Society," contained in *The Puerto Rican Woman: Perspectives on Culture, History and Society,* edited by Edna Acosta-Belén, Praeger, 1986, p. 7.

Azize, Yamila, *Luchas de la mujer en Puerto Rico, 1898-1919* ("Women's Struggles in Puerto Rico"; Spanish-language; translation by Sylvia P. Apodaca), Litografía Metropolitana, 1979, p. 80.

Azize, Yamila, *La mujer en la lucha,* Editorial Cultural, 1985, pp. 79-169.

Capetillo, Luisa, *Ensayos libertarios* ("Libertarian Essays"), Imprenta Unión Obrera, 1907.

Capetillo, Luisa, *Mi opinión sobre las libertades, derechos y deberes de la mujer como compañera, madre y ser independiente* ("My Opinion on the Freedom, Rights, and Duties of the Woman as Companion, Mother and as an Independent Woman"), Times Publishing Company, 1911.

Capetillo, Luisa, "La mujer" ("The Woman"), contained in *Voces de liberación* ("Voices of Liberation"), Editorial Lux, 1921, pp. 4-6.

López Antonetty, Evelina, *Luisa Capetillo,* Centro de Estudios Puertorriqueños (Hunter College), 1986.

Morfi, Angelina, *Historia critica de un siglo de teatro puertorriqueño* ("Critical History of One Century of Puerto Rican Theater"; Spanish-language; translation by Sylvia P. Apodaca), Instituto de Cultura Puertorriqueña, 1980, pp. 271-74.

Valle Ferrer, Norma, *Luisa Capetillo: Historia de una mujer proscrita* ("Luisa Capetillo: History of a Exiled Woman"), Editorial Cultural, 1990.

—Sketch by Sylvia P. Apodaca

Cárdenas Ramírez, Blandina
See **Ramírez, Blandina Cárdenas**

Alice Cardona
New York State government official

While working as a program associate for the New York State Division for Women in 1985, Alice Cardona became aware of the impact that AIDS was having on the Hispanic community. The following year, she founded the Hispanic AIDS Forum to educate the Spanish-speaking population about the deadly disease—a move she considers the crowning achievement of her career. "If I was to die today that's what I would want people to remember," Cardona told Pam Berry in a telephone interview. "We felt at that time we needed to get the right information out." Cardona, a lifelong activist for education and women's issues, subsequently founded two other advocacy groups to address the AIDS crisis—the Women and AIDS Project of the New York State Division for Women, which is a support group for women whose lives have been touched by the disease, and the Women and AIDS Resource Network, which provides women with information and referrals.

Cardona has been acutely aware of social issues since her early childhood in New York City. Her father, Luis Cardona, was a struggling independent businessman, and her mother, Maria Delores Tosado, was a presser in a factory. The oldest girl in a poor family of nine children, Cardona remembers rebelling against sexist attitudes toward women at a young age. "I couldn't understand why I couldn't go out and play stickball with the boys and why I had to stay home and make the beds and take care of the kids, and I protested all my life against that," she told Berry.

Although Cardona was born in East Harlem, she spent most of her youth in the Bronx and Brooklyn. She graduated in 1950 from Erasmus Hall High School ("my pride and joy"), considered at the time to be one of the country's top schools. After graduation, she took a job at a thrift shop run by the Federation of Jewish Philanthropies. According to Cardona, the 11 years she spent there were "the best years of my life." The wealthy women who donated clothing, jewelry, artwork, and books to the store also gave her frequent tickets to the symphony and the theater. "It was educational," she said. "I met lots of people from all walks of life."

Cardona saved her money and, in 1961, she decided it was time to attend college. She took a night job as a computer reconciler for a bank and attended New York University during the day, a schedule she followed for the next 12 years.

Joins Staff of ASPIRA in New York City

In 1970, Cardona received an offer to work for ASPIRA Association, Inc., a Puerto Rican educational agency dedicated to helping high school students stay in school and attend college. She worked at ASPIRA for eight years, first as an educational counselor and eventually as project coordinator. "That was another great experience," she said. "It made a big difference in my life. . . . Every part of my life is the best part of my life." As director of the ASPIRA Parent/Student Guidance Program from 1971 until 1973, she was an advocate for parents, encouraging them to be active participants in the education of their children by becoming knowledgeable about the educational system.

It was while she was researching colleges for high school students that Cardona learned about Goddard College in Plainfield, Vermont, where students created their own curriculum and studied at their own pace, only going to school for two weeks every six months. She decided that Goddard's program would make it possible for her to complete her own college education, and in 1973 she finally received her bachelor's degree in liberal arts. She continued working at ASPIRA, serving as the assistant to the executive director of community relations from 1973 until 1974. In her new role, Cardona represented the director at the New York State Education Department and was an advisor to the Commission of Education of the State of New York and the Commission of Education of the City of New York. During this same period, she also became a charter member of the National Conference of Puerto Rican Women, an organization that works for the advancement of Puerto Rican women through educational and social means.

In 1979, Cardona left ASPIRA to become an independent consultant for several Hispanic and non-Hispanic organizations, including the Institute for Puerto Rican Studies, the Office of Bilingual Education of the New York City Board of Education, the Northern and Southern Westchester Bureau of Occupational Career Educational Services, and the Citizens Committee for New York City, an organization of 40 community-based organizations. She viewed each consultantship as an opportunity to help people from all walks of life obtain the jobs and training they needed to be productive citizens.

After Mario Cuomo became governor of New York, Cardona was named a program associate for the New York State Division for Women, a post she held for five years. In 1989, she was promoted to assistant director of the division, the position she holds today. Functioning as an advocate for many different women's groups, Cardona is charged with bringing women's issues to the attention of the governor. Her future goals include becoming involved in voter registration drives and voter education, activities she believes would give her great satisfaction.

Sources:

Cardona, Alice, telephone interview with Pam Berry, September 11, 1992.

—*Sketch by Pam Berry*

Vikki Carr
(1940-)
Entertainer, singer

When President George Bush gathered with presidential predecessors Ronald Reagan, Gerald Ford, and Richard Nixon at the dedication of the Nixon library in July 1990, the event culminated a new burst of American activity for Grammy winner Vikki Carr. The longtime popular singing star, who had concentrated much of her activities in the Hispanic market, was selected as the featured singer at the event in front of four presidents whom she had individually entertained during their terms in the White House.

For Carr, it was like a return home to a country's welcoming arms. Her English language album for Sony Music, *Set Me Free,* had quickly become a popular seller, and she had just finished headlining at the famed Desert Inn Hotel in Las Vegas. And, as frosting on the cake, Carr's perennial hit, "It Must Be Him," which remains a favorite

Vicki Carr

on the airwaves, was featured in the top-grossing film, *Moonstruck.*

Hails from Musical Family

Vikki Carr—originally named Florencia Bicenta de Casillas Martinez Cardona—was born in El Paso, Texas, on July 19, 1940, the eldest of seven children of construction engineer Carlos Cardona and his wife, Florence. The young girl grew up singing. Her father played the guitar at home, and at age four Florencia made her singing debut in a Christmas play. The family moved to southern California when Carr was an infant. She grew up in Rosemead, an eastern suburb of Los Angeles, attending parochial school and then Rosemead High, where she took all of the music courses she could and participated in all of their musical productions. On weekends she sang with local bands and, upon graduating in 1958, landed a vocalist spot with Pepe Callahan's Mexican-Irish Band performing at Palm Springs' Chi-Chi Club. The petite eighteen year old with a big voice called herself "Carlita." Solo engagements followed and then a long-term contract with Liberty Records in 1961. She toured Australia and returned to become featured vocalist with the Ray Anthony television series.

From then on it was a steady rise in the night club circuit: Reno, Las Vegas, Lake Tahoe, Hawaii. Her first headlining engagement was at the world-famous Coconut Grove in Los Angeles. By the 1960s she had become one of the top female vocalists in the country, guesting on virtually every

major television variety show in the U.S., including shows hosted by Dean Martin, the Smothers Brothers, Carol Burnett, and Bob Hope. In the process she shortened her rather lengthy name to "Vikki Carr." In an interview with the *Saturday Evening Post,* she recalled that when she changed her name from "Carlita" to "Carr" and adopted the Americanized name "Vikki Carr," her father was hurt. But she promised him, "I'll be as well known as a Mexican American as an Anglo." She's kept her word.

Carr's first major recording success was in Australia with "He's a Rebel" and then in England with "It Must Be Him," which skyrocketed her to stardom. That song was later released in the United States, but it was another year before it became a hit in the U.S. Subsequently she signed a recording contract with Columbia Records.

Becomes International Singing Sensation

This was followed by successful tours to England, Australia, Mexico, Venezuela, El Salvador, and Panama. Her status as an international star was confirmed in 1967 when she was invited to perform for Queen Elizabeth II at a Royal Command Performance in London. The following year she packed the London Palladium, setting a precedent for her sold-out concerts in Germany, Spain, France, England, Australia, Japan, and Holland. The previous year Carr and Danny Kaye had toured military bases in Vietnam, which provided one of the most fulfilling experiences of her career.

In 1970 the songstress was invited to a White House concert at a dinner in honor of Venezuelan president Rafael Caldera, and another performance at the inaugural of the Kennedy Music Center, in Washington, D.C. In the States Carr became a darling of the White House, performing regularly at State dinners and at Richard Nixon's 1973 Inaugural celebration. She also performed for Presidents Ford, Reagan and Bush during their time in the White House.

Proud of her Mexican heritage, Carr reminds her audiences that she was born "Florencia Bicenta de Casillas Martinez Cardona." (Although she calls herself "Mexican American," she is second generation American. Her father was born in Texas, her mother in California. Her grandparents are from Guadalajara, Chihuahua, and Sonora.) Carr admitted to *La Opinión* that "for business I'm very American, but my heart is totally Latin."

Since making her first appearance in Mexico in 1972, a mutual love affair developed between the two. It was also the year she recorded her first album in Spanish, *Vikki Carr, en Español.* Her sojourn into the Spanish music world would add an exciting new facet to her career. Already a favorite of American audiences, she was to become one of the most recognized voices of the Hispanic musical panorama. She has been awarded Mexico's "Visiting Entertainer of the Year," has hosted television specials on the

Mexican networks and, beginning with *Vikki Carr y el amor* in 1980, has garnered gold, platinum and diamond records for her Spanish language albums.

Carr's 1992 album, *Cosas del amor,* for Sony Music, won that year's Grammy as "Best Latin Pop Album." The title song held the number one position for ten weeks on the *Billboard* charts and was named "Single of the Year" by the trade journal *Radio y música.* The album hit number one on *Billboard* charts, remaining in the top 20 for more than six months, placing number one in Puerto Rico, Costa Rica, Colombia, Venezuela, and Ecuador, going "gold" in most of these countries, and in the U.S. In March, 1992, *Cosas del amor* was named "Album of the Year" in Venezuela, that country's equivalent to the "Grammy."

Carr, who resides in Beverly Hills, has been divorced twice. She told *La Opinión:* "I wasn't ready to marry the first time. Yes, I was in love, but we were both too young." She recalls that the three years following her 1974 divorce from husband/manager Dan Moss were the best, because there was no one in her life and she could dedicate herself fully to her career. In 1978 she met her second husband. "I told him, I'd like to marry you, but I won't stop singing, I was not born to be a housewife." But eventually the success of her career and the touring which kept them apart strained the marriage and the couple separated in 1991.

Carr maintains a busy schedule of domestic and international dates with her concert show and has achieved success in all areas of entertainment: theater, television, night clubs, international concert stages, and personal appearances. In 1992 she sold out two headlining engagements at Caesar's in Atlantic City and the prestigious McCallum Hall in Palm Springs, California.

Joins Linda Rondstadt in Mariachis Revival

Having aided the resurgence of mariachis in Mexico and noting her friend Linda Ronstadt's homage to this music form in the United States, Carr joined Ronstadt to perform concerts together with mariachi groups in Los Angeles and Tucson, Arizona, including headlining at the Hollywood Bowl. *Los Angeles Times* music critic Don Heckman described Ronstadt and Carr's concert at UCLA's seventh-annual Mexican Art Series as "gifted and glossy."

In 1990 Carr made a loving return to England with a date at London's Royal Festival Hall. Sifting offers to return to the musical theater, Carr also remains open to new television and feature film scripts. In 1992 she completed an English-language television pilot entitled *Who Will Sing the Songs?* When at that time Carr was asked by *La Opinión* what she considered to be the most important aspect of her career, she answered: "My dream is the television series. It's about time that Latins have a show which treats us with the respect and dignity we deserve. Because we are not all

gardeners or drug-dealers. Besides, not everyone who lives here in the United States speaks only Spanish. There's many of us who were born here and speak English."

Carr has recorded fifty best-selling records, including seventeen gold albums. She was a Grammy nominee for *It Must Be Him* (1967) and *With Pen in Hand* (1969), and won Grammys for her Spanish language albums *Simplemente mujer* (1985) and *Cosas del amor* (1992). With respect to her *Cosas del amor* Grammy win—the popular hit was a duet with Mexican songstress Ana Gabriel—Carr told *La Opinión:* "It's like winning an Oscar, because it again placed the name of Vikki Carr very strongly everywhere."

In addition to her command performances for royalty and presidents, Carr has received numerous honors. For her contributions to Chicano education, the young lady who never went to college was awarded an honorary doctorate in law by the University of San Diego. Other prestigious awards include being named "Woman of the World" by the International Orphans Fund, the 1984 "Hispanic Woman of the Year," the 1972 American Guild of Variety Artist's "Entertainer of the Year" and the *Los Angeles Times'* highly respected "Woman of the Year" for 1970. In 1988 Carr was honored by the Nosotros group with their "Golden Eagle Award" for outstanding performer. She earned the "Career Achievement Award" of the Association of Hispanic Critics, Chicago's "Ovation Award," the YWCA "Silver Achievement Award" and was honored in 1990 by the City of Hope with the "Founder of Hope" award.

In 1968, upon hearing of the financial difficulties of Holy Cross High School in the San Antonio barrio, Carr initiated the first of a series of annual benefits that have netted more than a quarter of a million dollars for the school. In 1989 the school showed its gratitude by naming its library after her.

Initiates Scholarship for Mexican Americans

In 1971 she established the Vikki Carr Scholarship Foundation to encourage Mexican American youths to pursue higher education. By 1992 the foundation had awarded over 175 scholarships to students who went to Yale, Harvard, Radcliffe, Stanford, and other universities around the country. Carr personally participates in the final screening and selection process. "These kids have become part of my family. I don't have any children of my own, but all of these youngsters are like my own family, and I couldn't be more proud of what they are doing," she told the *Saturday Evening Post,* adding, "A good education is the most important thing all of us Americans can do for our kids." Respected as an artist and a humanitarian, she has also done benefit performances and work for a wide range of organizations: March of Dimes, Vista, Tuberculosis Association, American Cancer Society, St. Jude Children's Research Hospital and the American Lung Association.

On the musical theater stage, the petite, five-foot, two-inch dynamo has garnered high critical acclaim for her leading roles in *The Unsinkable Molly Brown* (1968) with the John Kenley Players in Ohio and *South Pacific* (1969) at the Starlight Theater in Kansas City. In 1983 her starring performance in *I'm Getting My Act Together and Taking It on the Road* was so successful it broke house records at the Westport Playhouse in St. Louis.

Enthusiastic about the prospects of doing television and feature films, the versatile star formed her own production company to pursue projects. Juggling engagements, recording sessions and charity events, the pace is frantic, but she remains cool and calm. Smart, successful, warm and engaging, Carr's energy and style are as radiant and irresistible as her voice. "God knows why He does things" she philosophized to *La Opinión*. "I lost two children, but He has given me much more, and a career to which I am married until death separates us."

Sources:

Periodicals

La Opinión (Panorama Section; translated from Spanish by Elena Kellner), April 30, 1992.
Los Angeles Times (Calendar Section), April 13, 1992.
Más (translated from Spanish by Elena Kellner), November-December, 1991, p. 91.
Saturday Evening Post, September, 1975, p. 11.

—Sketch by Elena Kellner

Ruth Carranza
(1949-)
Educational filmmaker

Ruth Carranza uses the silver screen to aid others in the understanding of difficult subjects. Crafting award-winning educational films in the fields of science and technology, she is noted for her skillful use of special effects, animation, computer graphics, music, and humor in her work. She attributes the success of her films, in part, to the fact that she had problems mastering technical subjects in school and later envisioned explaining such concepts to others in a simpler fashion via the motion picture. She also makes a point of prominently placing women and minorities in her films, using a female narrator in a documentary about computers, for instance, despite the protests of her advisory board.

The twelfth sibling in a family of 13 children, Carranza was born July 12, 1949, in the border town of McAllen, Texas. Her mother, Carmen Ferrio, worked as an arts and crafts teacher. Her father, Artemio Carranza, created an organization for revolutionaries in Mexico and founded the Mi Tierra community garden, a project involving Hispanic senior citizens in San Jose, California. Her parents had lived in Saltillo, Mexico, before moving to Mexico City for Artemio to accept a government job. Nine of the Carranza children were born in Mexico; the last four were born in Texas. Carranza remembers driving through farmlands with her father during her childhood. On such outings her Artemio would note how men had made the car they drove, the roads they traveled, and the homes they saw. Young Carranza was left to believe that all women made were babies.

Pursues Career in Film

Nevertheless, in her youth Carranza dreamed of becoming a doctor. After studying zoology at the University of California, Los Angeles, she transferred to the University of California at Davis. Earning a degree in biology but failing to gain admittance to medical school, she opted to work in the laboratory of Allied Chemical company in New York. Then she accepted a position at Stanford University's Center for Materials Research—a job that required her to learn time-lapse photography in order to film crystal growth. After taking a film class to improve her technique, she switched occupations and has been making motion pictures ever since. During her career she has made numerous short films featuring subjects such as salsa music, massage, and the proliferation of cancer cells.

In the early 1980s, Carranza began making *Silicon Run*, a film demonstrating how the integrated circuits that form the "brains" of computers are made from start to finish. Distributed by Encyclopedia Britannica to high schools, colleges, and universities, the piece has been used to instruct engineering undergraduates, industrial personnel, and even the United States Senate Budget Committee. Carranza initially produced and directed *Silicon Run* for her thesis as a film school graduate student at Stanford University. The 30-minute movie took three years to complete—a year to raise the $75,000 necessary to cover production costs and two years to research, write, film, and edit the work. Her labors have paid off as *Silicon Run* has garnered Student Emmy, Silver Apple, and Golden Eagle awards in educational filmmaking. In addition, the project helped Carranza earn her master's degree in 1986—after four years in the program—at the age of 36. She told Bernard Bauer of the *San Jose Mercury News* that her age was an advantage: "You think of the world differently [as an older student]. You've been out there. You've had to survive. The film was definitely a dream I wanted to do. But there are dreams that can be feasible."

Out of the garage of her Mountain View, California, home, which she shares with documentary filmmaker Pam

Walton, Carranza operates Ruth Carranza Productions, a video company currently producing *Silicon Run II.* The sequel will complement the original, discussing the history of the electronics industry, how personal computer boards are made, and how integrated circuits are tested and packaged. In addition to her film work, Carranza also edits *Intercambios Femeniles,* a publication of the National Network of Hispanic Women.

Sources:

Periodicals

Campus Report (Stanford University), 1986; 1987.
San Jose Mercury News, December 17, 1986, p. 1C; August 17, 1988, pp. 1-2.

Other

Carranza, Ruth, interview with Dawn Levy, 1992.

—Sketch by Dawn Levy

Lynda Carter
(1951?-)
Actress

Although many television viewers remember Lynda Carter from her years as Wonder Woman in the television series of the same name, few realize how diversely talented the actress is. Carter has starred in several movies made for television, such as *Rita Hayworth: The Love Goddess* and *Daddy.* She sings in her own nightclub show and with a rock band. She serves as a consultant and beauty director for the cosmetics company, Maybelline. Finally, this Hispanic woman contributes her time and money to several deserving causes.

As the actress herself told *Vanity Fair,* Lynda Carter is "a working person" from "humble beginnings." During the early 1950's, Lynda Jean Cordoba Carter was born on July 24 in Phoenix, Arizona, to a mother of Mexican descent, Jean, and a furniture-dealing father of English heritage. When the girl was just ten years old her father divorced her mother and left the family—Jean Carter raised her three children on her own. She worked nights at a factory in

Phoenix, assembling parts for television sets. Lynda admired her mother; she told *People,* "She taught me more than anything to survive in a dignified, honorable, gracious way."

At fifteen years of age, Carter made her acting and singing debut in a pizza parlor, and at seventeen, she began to make $400 a week acting in lounges in Reno and Las Vegas, Nevada. Upon graduating from high school she attended Arizona State University in Tempe; her academic career, however, was cut short when she became Miss World-U.S.A. in 1973. For some time, Carter trained for the stage with Stella Adler and Charles Conrad. It was not long before she won the role for which she would become the most famous, that of Diana Prince/Wonder Woman in the television series *Wonder Woman.*

Garners National Fame as "Wonder Woman"

The 25-year-old, 5'9", strikingly beautiful brunette won thousands of fans when she first appeared in the 1975 pilot for the television series as the super-powered Wonder Woman. Clad in shiny red boots, a red-white-and-blue, starred-and-eagled body suit, and a gold headband and bracelet, Lynda Carter managed to battle evildoers and impress audiences at the same time. In the words of a writer for *Vanity Fair,* Lynda Carter as Wonder Woman was "a bona fide feminist superhero, albeit an amply endowed feminist superhero who wore a skimpy spangled corset." Carter starred in both *Wonder Woman,* which aired on ABC from 1976 to 1977, and *The New Adventures of Wonder Woman,* which aired on CBS from 1977 to 1979. During that time, the actress found time to play Zelda in the 1976 NBC movie *A Matter of Wife . . . and Death* and appear in such shows as *The Olivia Newton-John Show, Battle of the Network Stars,* and *Circus of the Stars.* Carter also portrayed Bobbie Jo James in the 1976 motion picture, *Bobbie Jo and the Outlaw.*

Although her career thrived during the *Wonder Woman* years, Carter's personal life began to disintegrate. One year after her debut as Wonder Woman, Carter married an agent, Ron Samuels. Samuels directed her career and shared her $3 million annual income. The marriage, however, was an unhappy one. "It was the first thing in my life that failed," Carter told *People.* "It failed because it was based on work." Carter divorced Samuels in 1982.

When *The New Adventures of Wonder Woman* was discontinued in 1979, Lynda Carter kept herself busy with various projects. She appeared in two CBS television movies in 1980, portraying Brooke Newman in *The Last Song* and Brianne O'Neil in *Hotline.* She promoted herself with her own highly rated CBS television specials, *Lynda Carter's Special* in 1980, *Lynda Carter: Encore* in 1980, *Lynda Carter's Celebration* in 1981, *Lynda Carter: Street Lights,* in 1982, and

Lynda Carter: Body and Soul in 1984. For this last special, Carter was nominated for an Emmy Award.

Plays Rita Hayworth in Television Movie

Carter regularly appeared on television. She starred in television movies such as *Born To Be Sold* in 1981 and *Rita Hayworth: The Love Goddess* in 1983. This latter role received a great deal of attention; some friends of Rita Hayworth did not want the details of the actress's life televised. Some even objected to Carter's involvement with the show. Despite these opinions, Carter was determined and excited to portray the "Love Goddess." "I really wanted the challenge," Carter told *People* magazine. "We both had Hispanic backgrounds. We were both in show business at an early age. We both sing and dance. We were both married to our managers." One friend of Hayworth's, Gloria Luchenbill, agreed in *People* that Carter should play the part: "I know both ladies, and when you look around, who else would play the part? She has that same quality of shyness and naiveté that Rita had." Not surprisingly, the Hispanic woman who portrayed another, Rita Hayworth, won the Hispanic Woman of the Year Award in 1983. Carter has also starred in *Partners in Crime* and *Stillwatch,* and in 1986 she won a Golden Eagle Award for Consistent Performance in Television in Film.

An established television star, Carter has enjoyed similar success performing live. She developed her own nightclub act and took it to Las Vegas and Reno, Nevada, soon after the demise of the Wonder Woman series. She has since taken this show to the Palladium Theatre in London, the Sporting Club in Monte Carlo, Monaco, the Hotel de la Reforma in Mexico City, and Atlantic City, New Jersey. She won a Mexican Ariel Award for International Entertainer of the Year. Carter did not limit her live performances to large shows. For a time, she sang with the rock group, "Garfin Gathering."

Carter's career extends further still. She became the beauty and fashion director of Maybelline cosmetics and served as a consultant for the company. Carter even modeled Maybelline cosmetics for magazine advertisements. Her influence on consumers dramatically affected sales figures: Within two years of Carter's arrival at the company, sales of Maybelline cosmetics tripled. The astute businesswoman even founded her own company: Lynda Carter Productions.

Although the International Bachelors Association named Carter one of the "Ten Most Exciting Women In The World," those bachelors can be sure that the actress will have nothing to do with them. In 1984 Carter married Robert Altman, a banker from Washington, D.C. She explained in *People* her life with Altman. "My life has changed since I met Robert. I feel a sense of security with

him that I've never known before. He offers advice, but only when I ask. I think, finally, I'm finding my own life." After Lynda married Altman and joined him to live in Washington, D.C., the couple had two children, a son, Jamie Clifford, and a younger daughter, Jessica. The relocation to the capital city of the United States did not end Carter's career. She starred in two television movies in 1991, *Posing* and *Daddy.*

Despite Altman's involvement and ultimate conviction of guilt in the notorious Bank of Credit and Commerce International scandal, Carter's loyalty to her husband has not waned. In fact, Carter has been his most adamant supporter. She stated in *Vanity Fair,* "To tell you the truth, I know my husband has done nothing. I know that he is a strong and brilliant guy, a loving husband, a great father, a wonderful friend, and we love each other and are going forward." According to Blaine Trump, who spoke of Carter in *Vanity Fair,* the actress's loyalty and determination typify Carter. "Lynda is the type of person who has always worked hard to get where she is. She has very solid beliefs and commitments to her family and her life, and I think that commitment has gotten her through just about every situation she has faced in life. She's not a quitter. And she's not afraid to take chances."

Despite her success and her busy schedule, Carter has not forgotten her "humble beginnings." She has eagerly contributed to many causes. She served as the American Cancer Society's national crusade chairperson from 1985 to 1986, and worked as the honorary chairperson for the Exceptional Children's Foundation from 1987 to 1988. She was a member of the United Service Organization's board of governors, the National Committee on Arts for the Handicapped, Feed the Hungry, and the Committee for Creative Nonviolence. Carter has also been very active with charitable organizations in the Washington, D.C., area. Such activity speaks for itself; the woman who once played Wonder Woman is not just another pretty face.

Sources:

Books

Contemporary Theatre, Film, and Television, Volume 5, Gale, 1988, pp. 49-50.

Periodicals

Harper's Bazaar, January, 1985, pp. 134+.
Money, January, 1980, pp. 50+.
People, November 7, 1983, p. 109; March 19, 1984, p. 9; October 15, 1984, p. 11; February 9, 1987, p. 7.
Saturday Evening Post, May-June, 1983, pp. 42+; September 2, 1991, pp. 58+.
Teen, September, 1982, pp. 82+.

TV Guide, October 24, 1981, pp. 16+.

—*Sketch by Ronie-Richele Garcia-Johnson*

Lourdes Casal
(1938-1981)
Writer, political activist

Writer and intellectual Lourdes Casal will be best remembered for her efforts to reconcile Cuban exiles in the United States with the revolution set off by Fidel Castro in their homeland in 1959. Casal became the best and most outspoken exponent of a third alternative for young Cuban American intellectuals torn between the liberalism of their American counterparts and loyalty to their conservative elders.

Casal was born in 1938 in Havana, Cuba, to middle-class parents of mixed black and white ancestry who provided their highly studious and intelligent daughter with excellent educational opportunities. Casal studied for seven years at the Catholic University of Santo Tomas de Villanueva in Havana, where she originally majored in chemical engineering. Finding the practical application of science too confining, she devoted herself to the study of psychology. By 1957, together with other Catholic students, she was collaborating with Fidel Castro's 26th of July Movement in an effort to unseat the dictatorship of Fulgencio Batista. But the communist leanings of the triumphant revolution after 1959 forced Casal into the opposition and by 1961 she sought exile in the United States.

Exile in the United States

Established in New York, Casal completed her studies in psychology, receiving a master's degree in 1962 and a doctorate in 1975 from the New School for Social Research. During this same period she compiled her book *El caso Padilla: literatura y revolucion en Cuba* (1971), a series of documents exposing the deteriorating relationship between writers and revolutionary officials in Cuba, exemplified by the suppression of Cuban poet Heberto Padilla's work. *Los fundadores: Alfonso y otros cuentos,* a collection of short stories which some critics deemed autobiographical, was published in 1973.

Casal's unflinching interest in her homeland found outlet in such projects as the first and second Reuniones de Estudios Cubanos (Symposia of Cuban Studies), which lead to the founding of the Instituto de Estudios Cubanos (Institute of Cuban Studies) and to her participation in creating the *Revista Areito.* One of the aims of this magazine was to publish articles that would explore both the positive and the negative aspects of the Cuban government. This alternative position from a group of young Cuban intellectuals in exile lead to an invitation from the Havana government to visit the island nation. Only Casal accepted.

Accepts Cuban Government's Invitation to Return

A second trip to her homeland to participate in a gathering of intellectuals at the University of Havana came shortly after her initial visit in September, 1973. This time Casal returned to New York converted to the Castro revolution, and *Revista Areito* became the mouthpiece for those who shared Casal's point of view. A desire to share this experience of re-encounter with Cuba led Casal to foster the creation of the Antonio Maceo Brigade, which enabled young Cuban exiles to visit Cuba, and the Circulo de Cultura Cubana, which brought together artists and intellectuals who wished to establish closer ties with Cuba. In 1978 she played an important role in the dialogue with the Castro government that made it possible for exiles to visit their families in the homeland. Casal returned to Cuba permanently in 1979, and she died in 1981 from a kidney ailment. A volume of her poetry, *Palabras juntan revolucion* (1981), was published in Havana by Casa de las Americas.

Casal wrote and published extensively in the fields of psychology and the social sciences. She was on the faculty of several colleges and universities, including Dominican College in Blauvelt, New York, Brooklyn College, and Rutgers University. She was the recipient of numerous awards, including the Cintas Fellowship from the Institute for International Education (1974-75), the Social Science Research Council grant for research in Cuba (1978), a fellowship from the Woodrow Wilson International Center for Scholars (1978-79), and a grant from the Ford Foundation Competition on the Movement of Caribbean Peoples (1977-78).

Sources:

Books

Burunat, Silvia, "Lourdes Casal," in *Biographical Dictionary of Hispanic Literature in the United States,* edited by Nicolas Kanellos, Greenwood Press, 1989, pp. 49-55.
De la Cuesta, Leonel Antonio, "Perfil biografico," in *Itinerario Ideologico: Antologia de Lourdes Casal,* edited by Maria Cristina Herrera and de la Cuesta, Instituto de Estudios Cubanos (Miami, FL), 1982, pp. 3-8.

—*Sketch by Silvia Novo Pena*

Rosemary Casals
(1948-)
Professional tennis player

Winner of more than 90 tennis tournaments—including five Wimbledon doubles titles with partner Billie Jean King—Rosemary Casals has earned a reputation as a rebel ever since she first entered organized competition in the early 1960s. She has been one of the game's critics, a player whose all-consuming cause has been the betterment of tennis, especially women's tennis, for more than two decades. She was a motivating force behind many of the controversial changes that shook the tennis world and led to the tennis boom of the 1960s and 1970s. Commenting on Casals's influence on the game of tennis in *Rosemary Casals: The Rebel Rosebud*, Linda Jacobs wrote: "Along the way, there have been lots of breakthroughs—lots of 'firsts.' Rosemary Casals has been in on all of them."

Born September 16, 1948, in San Francisco, California, to poor immigrants from the Central American country of El Salvador, Casals has always considered her great-uncle and great-aunt, Manuel and Maria Casals, as her parents. A Salvadoran immigrant and former member of the country's national soccer team, Manuel took Casals (and her older sister, Victoria Casals) into his home when she was only one year old, after her parents decided they could not provide for their young daughters. Manuel, also the owner of a small stamp machine business, introduced the children to the public courts of San Francisco and later became the only coach Casals ever had.

Casals's first rebellion regarding the game of tennis occurred when she was just a teenager. She hated the established tennis tradition of having younger players compete against each other on the junior circuit. Gutsy and determined right from the start, Casals saw junior tennis as a barrier rather than a stepping-stone to her participation in women's tennis. She wanted to work as hard as possible to better her game, and she often entered tournaments for girls two to three years older than her knowing they would give her the added challenge she desired. "But in spite of all her trophies," Jacobs noted, "Rosie didn't like junior competition. It made her feel like a little girl playing polite little girl games."

Junior tennis was just the first of several obstacles Casals faced during her tennis career. At five feet two inches she was one of the shortest tennis players and at a decided disadvantage, because of her height, on the court. She also became quickly acquainted with the class distinction prevalent in tennis circles at the time. Tennis, traditionally, was a sport practiced in posh country clubs by the white upper class, and so Casals's ethnic heritage and disadvantaged

Rosemary Casals

background immediately set her apart from most of the other players. Remembering these early years of her career, Casals told *People:* "The other kids had nice tennis clothes, nice rackets, nice white shoes and came in Cadillacs. I felt stigmatized because we were poor."

Refuses to Wear Traditional Tennis Attire

An unfamiliarity with country club etiquette also made Casals feel different from the majority of other players. But traditions such as polite applause from the crowd instead of noisy cheering, or wearing only white on the courts, were concepts that were nonsensical to the future tennis star anyway. She believed in working hard to perfect her game and looked to the crowd to show its appreciation for her extra efforts. As for wearing white, in one of her first appearances at the tradition-laden courts at Wimbledon, England—site of the British tennis championships—she was nearly excluded from competition when she showed up in a dress that was not white. Later in her career, the "wearing white" tradition would be one more convention she regularly ignored, becoming known for her brightly colored outfits.

The frustrations Casals had to endure on and off the court due to her size and background had a significant impact on her playing style. Despite her delicate-sounding nicknames "Rosie" and "Rosebud," she built a reputation as a player who would do anything—even attempt a between-the-legs shot—in order to win a match. "I wanted to *be* someone," she is quoted as saying in Alida M. Thacher's *Raising a Racket: Rosie Casals.* "I knew I was good, and winning tournaments—it's a kind of way of being accepted." Through a combination of this dogged determination and natural talent, by age 16 Casals was the top junior and women's level player in northern California. At 17, she was ranked eleventh in the country and appeared in the semi-finals at Forest Hills, New York, home of the U.S. tennis championships, against the then top-ranked women's player in the world, Brazil's Maria Bueno. Although Casals lost the match, the crowd loved her aggressive playing style and gave her a standing ovation.

More experience on the national and international levels of play helped Casals continue to improve her game. In 1966, she and Billie Jean King, her doubles partner, won the U.S. hard-court and indoor tournaments and reached the quarter-finals in the Wimbledon women's doubles. The two would also dominate women's doubles play in the years to follow, becoming one of the most successful duos in tennis history. Casals also teamed with Ian Crookenden in 1966 to win the U.S. hard-court mixed doubles. She met success as an individual player that same year, being ranked third among U.S. women players. She emerged victorious twice over King (then sharing first ranking among U.S. women players with Nancy Richey) in singles play and even beat Bueno, who had continued to be regarded as the world's top women's player.

In February, 1967, Casals started out another successful year by winning the women's singles title at the Wills Invitational tournament in Auckland, New Zealand. In June, she and King won the Federation Cup in Berlin for the United States. In other tournament play, she beat King in the semi-finals of the national clay-court matches in Milwaukee, Wisconsin, and defeated Margaret Court, one of the top women tennis players of all time, in the quarter-finals of the Victoria championships in Melbourne, Australia. Although Casals was disappointed to lose at Wimbledon in the semi-finals of the women's singles tournament that year, she and King took the doubles crown there as well as at the U.S. and South African championships.

Fights to Make Tennis a Professional Sport

The next year a battle between tennis traditionalists and the new breed of tennis players like Casals culminated. For decades the philosophy of the tennis establishment had been to advocate amateur tennis in the belief that professional play was somewhat tainted because players accepted money. Critics argued that the country club set could afford to remain playing as unpaid amateurs. Many of the less wealthy players, however, were forced to take under-the-table payments for their efforts just to be financially able to stay on the tennis circuit. Many of these athletes believed they should be able to derive a living from their sport, just like professional football or baseball players. Nonetheless, the tennis players who admitted their professional status suffered when major tournaments such as

Wimbledon and Forest Hills refused to admit them into competition. All this changed, however, in December, 1967, when the governing body of British tennis, the British Lawn Tennis Association, voted to allow amateurs and professionals to compete against each other in the same tournaments. The measure was quickly seconded the following March by the International Lawn Tennis Federation (ILTF).

Fed-up with the amateur status that she and her fellow tennis players had been forced into for so many years, Casals was eager to become publicly what she truly had been all along—a professional tennis player. Almost as soon as the ILTF voiced its decision, Casals, along with King, French tennis star Francoise Durr, and British player Ann Jones became the first women in the history of tennis to become touring professionals. But Casals, and her fellow women players in particular, soon found that as women they had even more to contend with than their male counterparts. "Some people called Rosie a rebel," Jacobs observed, "because she dared to go on tour, to play tennis for money. Women didn't do such things. They played in amateur tournaments for pretty trophies and left the money to the men."

Money was the reason that Casals became one of the ringleaders in the next rebellion to rock the tennis establishment. She left the National Tennis League after a little more than a year, happy to be able to compete as a professional in nearly any tournament she wanted to enter. Since the differentiation between amateurs and professionals had faded, the distinction between women and men tennis players presented another hurdle. The vast difference in prize monies awarded to male and female tennis players in the same tournament was another point that angered the women players. Such practices seemed to indicate that female athletes were somehow inferior to their male counterparts.

Demands Better Wages for Women Tennis Players

In 1970, despite the limited financial opportunities available to women tennis players at the time, Casals earned close to $25,000, the sixth-highest amount among women players. But her level of success was available to relatively few women in the sport. That year, the female players were outraged to learn that in the season's last major tournament, the Pacific Southwest Open, the men's first-place winner would receive $12,500, while total prize money allotted for women was $7,500 to be split among the quarter-finalists. Casals and other women players warned the United States Lawn Tennis Association (USLTA; now known as the United States Tennis Association) that they planned to boycott future tournaments if three demands were not met: 1) Prize money for women be at least one third as high as that slated for men; 2) More media attention be focused on women's matches; 3) Women receive equal access to center-court play.

When USLTA ignored the women's threat, the players took their grievances to the promoter of the Pacific Southwest Open. When he also disregarded their protests, they looked for and found a strong supporter in Gladys Heldman, editor of *World Tennis* magazine. Heldman managed to organize a women's tournament to be held in Houston, Texas, at the same time as the Pacific Southwest Open. The tournament—dubbed the Virginia Slims Invitational after Philip Morris, the cigarette company, became its corporate sponsor—occurred despite strong disapproval from the USLTA. Casals, in turn, became the first winner of a women's professional tennis tournament when she took home the $1,600 top prize. Although the seven U.S. players who participated in the Virginia Slims event were suspended by USLTA, they were successful in bringing their position to light and gained a lot of attention.

The success of the invitational led to Casals's involvement with the newly formed Virginia Slims eight-tournament women's professional tennis circuit and an end to any financial problems she had experienced earlier in her career. The first year she was one of the top money winners among the sixteen women participating. In 1972, her winnings totaled $70,000. The new attention focused on women's tennis had helped Casals nearly triple her income in the space of two years. In 1973, she collected the largest prize ever awarded in women's tennis to that time. She defeated Nancy Richey Gunter in the finals of the Family Circle tournament and won $30,000.

Spirited Commentary Causes Controversy

That same year women's tennis and Casals also received much publicity thanks to Bobby Riggs, the 55-year-old former tennis star of the 1930s who challenged Billie Jean King to a match to be held in late September in the Houston Astrodome. The event was a prime-time media spectacular—billed as the "Battle of the Sexes"—that drew a crowd of more than 30,000 to the arena and a viewing audience of 59 million. Casals was seen and heard during the match as the women's color commentator for the American Broadcasting Company, Inc. (ABC-TV). A number of people found Casals's observations, however, a little too colorful. King won the match, but the next day newspapers and newscasts were filled with public debate about Casals's performance. She explained her somewhat acrid remarks about Riggs in *Raising a Racket:* "Actually, all I was doing was being honest. I said he walked like a duck because he does. I didn't say anything just to be controversial. I just said it the way I meant it."

The enthusiasm for tennis generated by the Riggs-King battle helped launch another innovation in the sport in which Casals was involved—World Team Tennis (WTT). WTT included tennis teams from cities throughout the United States, each made up of two women and four men. A meeting between two teams included men's and women's singles and doubles games as well as a mixed doubles match. Scoring for each event was on a point system with the win going to the first team to earn five points. In another change from traditional tennis, the WTT coach could take a struggling player out of a game and send in a substitute. During her years with the WTT Casals played with the Detroit Loves and the Oakland Breakers and coached the Los Angeles Strings.

While involved in team tennis, Casals continued to enter regular tennis tournaments. However, the strain of playing almost constantly took a toll on her body and she had to undergo knee surgery in 1978. The operation forced a change of direction in her career, but Casals continued to meet new challenges with the persistence that always marked her tennis court appearances. Since 1981, she has been president of Sportswomen, Inc., a Sausalito, California-based company she formed to act as an agency for new tennis players and to promote both herself and a Women's Classic tour she put together for over-30 female tennis players. She also began Midnight Productions television company and has broadened her sporting activities to include golf. Although younger women now appear at Wimbledon and other tournaments, Casals continues to search for new opportunities to improve the game to which she has been a major contributor. In 1990, she again teamed with Billie Jean King, winning the U.S. Open Seniors' women's doubles championship.

Sources:

Books

Jacobs, Linda, *Rosemary Casals: The Rebel Rosebud*, EMC Corp., 1975.
Thacher, Alida M., *Raising a Racket: Rosie Casals*, Raintree, 1976.

Periodicals

People, May 31, 1982, p. 85.

—Sketch by Marian C. Gonsior

Elena Castedo
(1937-)
Writer

Elena Castedo is an acclaimed writer of both Spanish and English literature. Her first novel, *Paradise*, was published in English in 1991 and was nominated for the National Book Award. The Spanish version, *El Paradiso*, was named 1990 "Book of the Year" by Chile's *El Mercurio* and was nominated for Spain's 1990 Cervantes Award while also being a number one bestseller for five months. Her 1991 short story "The White Bedspread" was the winner in the PEN/Syndicated fiction contest and received a Phoebe Award for best fiction of the year. It was her second Phoebe; the first was for her short story "Troopers" in 1986.

Elena Castedo was born September 1, 1937, in Barcelona, Spain, to Elvira Magña Cusdarado and Leopoldo Castedo Hernández de Padilla. Her parents fled dictator Francisco Franco's Spain for Chile, where Castedo grew up and received her primary education. She worked as an art researcher and a fashion model in Chile before going to the United States and attending the University of California, Los Angeles (UCLA) and Harvard University. From 1965 to 1966, Castedo worked briefly as a social worker while she studied for her degrees. She also taught at the English College and Nascimiento Institute in Santiago, Chile, from 1966 to 1967. She received her M.A. in Spanish from UCLA in 1968, became a teaching fellow at Harvard in 1969, and earned her Ph.D. from that institution in 1976. After earning her degree, she lectured at the American University for one year, became an editor for the *Inter-American Review of Bibliography*, and from 1980 to 1985 was a consultant for CEAL, Ltd. Throughout these years Castedo honed her writing craft, and she continues to write extensively, including articles, poems, and stories for magazines and publications such as *Afro-American Review*, *Americas*, *Anthropo's*, *Atenea*, *Hispamerica*, and *Phoebe*, among others.

Castedo's first novel, *Paradise*, is the story of a family that flees the Spanish Civil War and takes refuge with wealthy landowners in an unnamed Latin American country. The story is told through the eyes of a ten-year-old girl. Critical reaction to the novel was positive. Phoebe-Lou Adams, in an *Atlantic Monthly* review, called the novel "ingenious social satire," while Merle Rubin's review in the *Christian Science Monitor* said, "*Paradise* is a classic coming-of-age novel, in which a girl comes to understand herself, her family and the complicated social world in which they live." In the *New York Times Book Review*, Lyll Becerra de Jenkins wrote, "*Paradise* is filled with rich descriptions and vivid scenes. Ms. Castedo's language is exuberant."

Although her novel, and many of her other writings, deal with the Latino experience, Castedo does not consider herself a Latino writer. As she told *Publishers Weekly*, "I'm an immigrant who went through poverty, I waited for buses for hours. I bought day old bread. But I don't see myself as part of a Latino literary movement. My interest is in human experience and emotions. The immigrant experience is a universal one." Castedo feels that writers should have a basic concern for their craft. As Castedo expressed to *Contemporary Authors*, she believes writers have a responsibility to preserve and nurture literature and other writers: "Writers of serious fiction should pool some of their scattered efforts into common and concerted action to make sure that high quality literature stays alive and well.

I'm very thankful for the support given to me by other writers I greatly admire."

Sources:

Books

Contemporary Authors, Volume 132, Gale, 1991, pp. 63-64.

Periodicals

Atlantic Monthly, March 1990, p. 116.
Christian Science Monitor, July 18, 1990, p. 15.
New York Times Book Review, April 1, 1990, p. 8.
Publishers Weekly, February 1, 1991, pp. 20-21.

—*Sketch by Andrés Chávez*

Castillo, Adelaida Del
See Del Castillo, Adelaida

Ana Castillo
(1953-)
Poet, novelist

Initially known for her elegant feminist poetry, Ana Castillo is one of a group of distinguished Chicana writers from the Chicago area. Over the years, Castillo has broadened her artistic contributions to include musical performance and prose. Her feminist message can be found in such diverse media as high school texts and musical theater pieces.

Ana Castillo was born in Chicago, Illinois, on June 15, 1953, to Mexican American parents who had migrated from the Southwest. Her interest in different aspects of creative experience prompted her to major in art at Northeastern Illinois University, where she received her a B.A. in art education in 1975. The heady artistic, activist and intellectual climate of the 1970s fostered her interest in writing and performing her poetry. She was an early contributor to *Revista Chicano-Riquena* (now *The Americas Review*), a literary magazine edited by Nicolas Kanellos which captured the artistic ferment of Midwest Hispanics. Her first collection of poems, *Otro Canto*, was published as a chapbook in 1977 with a grant from the Illinois Art Council. Two years later, coinciding with her graduation from the University of Chicago with an M.A. in social sciences, she published a second collection of poems, the chapbook *The Invitation,* with a grant from the Playboy Foundation.

In the early 1980s, Castillo's work took on musical tones. Her interest in flamenco dancing lead her to create and manage the Al-Andalus flamenco performance group from 1981 to 1982. She adapted her collection of poems in *The Invitation* for music and they were performed at the 1982 Soho Art Festival in New York City. Castillo also wrote the play *Clark Street Counts,* performed by the Chicano Raza Group in June, 1983.

Castillo's elegant style and feminist thematic put her poems in great demand. Her work appeared in a variety of anthologies which include *Women Poets of the World,* published by McMillan in 1982, *The Third Women: Minority Women Writers of the U.S.,* published by Houghton-Mifflin in 1979, and a high school text, *Zero Makes Me Hungry,* published by Scott, Foresman in 1975. Her next two poetry collections were *Pajaros enganosos,* published by Cross Cultural Communications in 1983, and *Women Are Not Roses,* published by Arte Público Press in 1984.

In later years, Castillo has developed consistently as a writer of prose fiction. Already in 1984 one of her short stories was included in the anthology *Cuentos Chicanos.* In 1986 Castillo's first novel, *The Mixquihuala Letters,* was published by Bilingual Press. This novel, written in epistolary form, was widely acclaimed for its treatment of women. It received the Before Columbus Foundation Book award in 1987 and in 1988 won an award from The Women's Foundation of San Francisco, California. Castillo's latest work is the short-story collection *My Father Was a Toltec,* published by Bilingual Press. Castillo lives in Albuquerque, New Mexico, and continues to write, perform and lecture. She is currently working on *So Far from God,* a book about environmental racism expected to be published in 1993.

Sources:

Archives, Arte Público Press, Houston, Texas.

—*Sketch by Silvia Novo Pena*

Sylvia L. Castillo
(1951-)
Founder, National Network of Hispanic Women

Sylvia L. Castillo, a clinical social worker who has been honored by the United Nations Council on Women and the California State Assembly, led efforts in the 1980s to

Sylvia L. Castillo

encourage communication and support between Hispanic professional women across the country and find new ways to encourage young Hispanic females to pursue higher education and challenging careers. Castillo cofounded the National Network of Hispanic Women and its accompanying English-language magazine, *Intercambios.* At its height in the 1980s, the Los Angeles-based network had some 500 members, and the magazine had a circulation of 6,500 issues to students, teachers, school counselors, and professionals from all fields. The network and magazine sought to prepare Hispanic women, often first-generation Americans, for leadership positions in the public and private sector.

Castillo was born on September 2, 1951, in Los Angeles, California. Her parents, Henry and Lucille Miramontes Castillo, also born in Los Angeles, were the children of Mexican immigrants. Henry was a truck driver and Lucille worked as a retail clerk in a pharmacy and, later, as a medical representative for a home health care agency. Castillo's mother was an influential presence in her life. "She was a link between the old ways and the new ways. She helped us through her experience see there were opportunities all the time. She passed on an incredible sense of confidence," Castillo told the *Rocky Mountain News.*

Before going to college, Castillo attended an all-girls parochial school, Our Lady of Loretto High School, in Los Angeles, where she graduated in 1969 after serving as the student body president in her senior year. Castillo dreamed of becoming a psychologist and, for awhile, pursued that dream. "I always thought that I was going to be a psychologist and director of a community mental health center," Castillo told interviewer Ann Malaspina. She was especially interested in women's mental health issues. "If a mother feels good, then her daughters feel good. If a mother has good self-esteem, her children will have good self esteem," she said.

Although both her parents held jobs, Castillo found her own way through higher education and into the professional world. She earned a B.A. in social psychology at the University of California at Santa Barbara in 1973. In 1976 she received a master's degree in social welfare administration from the University of California at Berkeley, where she was a National Institute of Mental Health fellow. After graduation, Castillo received a postgraduate clinical fellowship from the University of Southern California to study how to improve child abuse programs in several communities.

Interest in Hispanic Women's Issues Piqued

Soon afterwards, Castillo joined her professor, Dr. Grant Miller, as part of a mental health team at California Polytechnic State University at San Luis Obispo. From 1976 to 1979, she worked as a career and mental health counselor at Cal-Poly, where she helped found the campus's first women's re-entry and career mentoring programs for minorities and women. This was followed by an administrative fellowship in 1979 from California State University at Long Beach to study the challenges faced by college presidents. She spent a year working under Dr. Gail Fullerton, the first woman president at California State University at San Jose. While researching upward mobility in higher education, Castillo began wondering what it takes for a student to succeed. She recalled asking herself, "What does the institution have to do? Why will one Hispanic succeed and another won't?"

Also that year, she interviewed dozens of Hispanic women in higher education. Castillo discovered a common thread: despite their outward success, these women were unhappy and dissatisfied with their careers. Many were hired in the 1970s when universities, responding to student demands, hired token minorities. Now, the women were reassessing their careers and futures. "They were very isolated and didn't know their counterparts in the system," said Castillo in her interview. It was during her research that Castillo became interested in exploring the difficulties faced by Hispanic professional women. Prior to that time, studies on Hispanic success focused on the individual and his or her background, family, and education. Castillo wondered what institutions could do to encourage young Hispanics. "I was curious about why there were so few role models," she said.

She decided to start a newsletter—to be circulated to school counselors and students—allowing Hispanic wom-

en to share their experiences and providing practical information on career choices. After the newsletter began its circulation, Stanford University offered Castillo a job advising students in the placement office. "They wanted to know why students weren't making it," said Castillo. She took the job, with the stipulation that she could also publish the newsletter, and served as assistant dean of student affairs for academic advising and counseling from 1980 to 1985.

Birth of *Intercambios* and the NNHW

The first issue of the newsletter, initially called *Intercambios Femeniles* ("Interchange of Women"), appeared in December 1980. With 14 pages per newsletter, each "issue was a resource, with a networking list, statistics, and information," said Castillo. Each issue also had a theme, such as careers in science and technology, health and the Hispanic women, and leadership. The magazine profiled successful Hispanic women, reported on the latest studies on Hispanics, and tackled topics from how to preserve cultural traditions to debating affirmative action. At first, Castillo used Stanford students to do the research, and friends and colleagues sent her information and student dissertations.

Over the years, hundreds of women contributed to *Intercambios*. Later, as the magazine, which came out four times a year, became a glossy, full-color periodical with sophisticated graphics, Castillo was assisted by executive editor and filmmaker Ruth Carranza, as well as free-lance editors and writers from around the country. But Castillo wanted to move beyond the magazine. "I wanted to develop an information clearinghouse about educational advancement, career preparation, and leadership development," she said. "I had real big dreams." She hoped to link Hispanic women across the country who could share each other's expertise. Her focus, however, always remained firm: education, careers, and leadership development for Hispanic women.

Intercambios planted the seeds for the National Network of Hispanic Women (NNHW), which was first called Hispanic Women in Higher Education. To gather ideas for the newsletter, Castillo, who worked without pay, organized a board of directors with a broad spectrum of perspectives, including Latina organization leaders, teachers, administrators, an entrepreneur, and a graduate student. They debated ways to improve opportunities for young Hispanic women and how to organize a national resource center. Gradually becoming an important force in itself, the NNHW filled a void for many Hispanic women, who often could not get the kind of support they needed from their families and community. "We're talking about perhaps the first generation of college-educated Hispanic women—the first generation of professional Hispanic women," Castillo told *Hispanic Business* magazine. The board recruited members from a cross section of professions, geographic regions, and ethnic backgrounds. Members included bank executives, university administrators, corporate vice presidents, scientists, small business owners, community activists, and others. The network, funded by corporations and foundations, conducted studies, served as an information resource, and provided networking and mentoring opportunities for Hispanic women of all ages. Always fighting an uphill battle to secure financial backing, Castillo eventually established an NNHW office in Los Angeles that was run by a part-time staff.

Hoping to provide new links between Hispanic women and the corporate world, Castillo organized seminars for companies interested in recruiting Hispanic women. Beginning in 1982, she set up what she called the Roundtable for Hispanic Women and worked with companies such as Pacific Bell, Sears Roebuck, Avon Products, Anheuser-Busch, and other large businesses to identify better ways to hire and promote Hispanic women. "I see our role as a network to be a broker between the talented Hispanic woman and the needs of corporate America," Castillo told *Hispanic Business.* In 1985, Castillo received a grant from Anheuser-Busch to study Hispanic women in business. She called her project the National Roundtable for Hispana Business and Corporate Leaders. Also that year, she resigned from her Stanford job to devote all her time to *Intercambios* and the NNHW.

The national network hosted the first National Roundtable in Denver, Colorado, in March 1985. The theme of the gathering, attended by 500 women, was "An Investment in America's Future." The conference focused on career preparation, mid-management career opportunities, and women entrepreneurs, with special focus groups on leadership issues. The meeting was so successful that the NNHW conducted two more National Roundtables: one in Miami in 1987, and another in Los Angeles in 1989. Meanwhile, Castillo was facing a personal crisis. In 1986, she was forced to resign her active leadership roles at *Intercambios* and the NNHW because of illness. She took a year off to regain her health. At the age of 32, Castillo felt she had been so busy that she had neglected her personal life and her health. "I felt my health had failed and I had failed," she told Malaspina.

During that year, she married Steven Castillo Long, a friend from childhood, and moved with him to the island of Maui, Hawaii. But she could not stay uninvolved. Castillo became active in the Puerto Rican community and women's groups in Hawaii. She helped start and direct the Children's Advocacy Center in Wailuku. She also worked part time as administrative coordinator for the graduate school of social work at the University of Hawaii at Manoa and in the business and marketing office at a private school, all the while keeping in touch with the NNHW. In 1988, she was selected as one of 60 women in the United States to participate in Leadership America, a year-long national training institute for women in public policy.

Challenges for the Future

By the early 1990s, both *Intercambios* and the NNHW faced difficulties in funding and organization. As a result, the NNHW took a hiatus from activity and *Intercambios* interrupted its publishing schedule. But Castillo and others remained determined to revive these unique efforts—perhaps in slightly different forms—to promote Hispanic women in the professions. The economic uncertainties of the 1990s that have caused problems for the NNHW and *Intercambios* also now pose new challenges for Hispanic women, according to Castillo, who returned to Los Angeles in 1990. "The word 'opportunity' is going to be redefined. I think we will have limited opportunity. We barely have started to make a presence; the opportunities as they diminish will close the doors for this generation," said Castillo. "As we're affected by down-sizing, mergers, job loss, we're going to have to redefine success, otherwise it will be easy for the Hispanic woman to internalize that she's failed."

To handle these difficult times, Castillo urges Hispanic women to reassess their values and goals and to organize and communicate with each other. "The more isolated we stay as women, the less opportunity we have," she said. She would like to build a national federation of Hispanic women's groups with fund-raising abilities and the clout to have women's voices heard on issues such as education, teenage pregnancy, and health care. Along with keeping the NNHW and *Intercambios* alive, Castillo has been involved in the Commission on Hispanic Underrepresentation and Policy at California State University and the American Council on Education's Office of Women, and she has worked as an advisor on the Ford Foundation Study: the Chicana Project. Having settled in Menlo Park, California, Castillo is considering options for her own future, such as finishing her doctorate, teaching, or becoming involved in a new organization. But whatever she does, Castillo will always have her eye on her first love: ensuring that Hispanic women get the opportunities they deserve.

Sources:

Periodicals

Hispanic Business, July, 1988, pp. 25-26.
Hispanic USA, May, 1985, pp. 14-15.
Intercambios, winter, 1990; spring, 1991.
Intercambios Femeniles, winter, 1985; spring, 1987.
Rocky Mountain News, March 12, 1985, pp. 39, 42.

Other

Castillo, Sylvia L., interview with Ann Malaspina, October 1, 1992.

—Sketch by Ann Malaspina

Lillian Castillo-Speed
(1949-)
Librarian, editor

Lillian Castillo-Speed, coordinator of the Chicano Studies Library at the University of California in Berkeley, has dedicated herself to preserving the written record of the Chicano experience. The principal editor of the *Chicano Periodicals Index*, Castillo-Speed has actively worked to modernize and update the university's comprehensive database of Chicano writings and protect the autonomy of the Chicano studies collection.

Born to Richard Garcia Castillo and Jennie Guzman on February 15, 1949, in La Puente, California, Castillo-Speed revealed in an interview with Sandra Márquez that although she liked to read as a child, it was not until she volunteered to work at a public library while taking time out from graduate school that she considered pursuing a career as a librarian. She subsequently left California State University in Long Beach, where she had been working on an advanced degree in English (she had already earned a bachelor's degree from the University of California in Riverside), and transferred to the School of Library and Information Studies at the University of California in Berkeley.

Appointed Director of the Chicano Indexing Project

Within a year after receiving her master's degree in library and information sciences, Castillo-Speed was hired to direct the Chicano Indexing Project at the Chicano Studies Library, whose staff members were then in the midst of preparing the third edition of the *Chicano Periodicals Index*. This ambitious undertaking was the work of a group of Chicano librarians who realized that Chicano writings were not being indexed by mainstream libraries. In the early 1970s, they set for themselves the task of indexing the Chicano journals that had begun to emerge during the 1960s.

As principal editor of the index, Castillo-Speed was responsible for processing the work of all those helping with the project. Citations included entries from mainstream publications as well as journal articles, books, anthology articles, reports, papers and selected newspaper articles by and about Chicanos. Its production was handled by the library's own publications unit.

In an article Castillo-Speed wrote for *Reforma* magazine, the librarian explains how such indexing quickly takes on a political connotation. "What is collected. . ., what is preserved, and even how it is shelved are political questions," she notes. "They are just as politically charged as what should be taught, what texts should be assigned, what perspective should be used."

From its inception, the *Chicano Periodicals Index* was doomed to failure, Castillo-Speed told Márquez, adding that it was not considered "standard" or "up to par." But it led to the creation of the Chicano Database, an automated database containing more than 36,000 journal article citations. The database in turn led to the creation of a variety of reference books and indexes such as a Chicano thesaurus, a bibliography on Chicano art, and an index of writings by Chicanas. Today, the database is available on CD-ROM, enabling the Chicano Studies Library to market the information it contains to other libraries.

Lobbies for Preservation of Ethnic Studies Materials

In addition to her work with the *Chicano Periodicals Index*, Castillo-Speed has been active in the effort to protect the autonomous status of ethnic studies libraries on college campuses. As past president of Biblioteca para la Gente, a group of northern California librarians who promote library services for Spanish-speaking individuals, she has also lobbied to establish ethnic research centers in state libraries. In her *Reforma* article, Castillo-Speed describes how such collections are increasingly threatened by the "growing non-white population and the realization that privilege and power will have to be shared." As a result, she states, "there is renewed pressure to incorporate or assimilate separate ethnic collections," and she calls upon ethnic studies libraries to take part in the growing assimilationist debate, because "libraries are not neutral."

As testimony to her dedication and deep sense of personal responsibility, Castillo-Speed took an unusual step one summer after learning that a graduate course on ethnic bibliographies at Berkeley's School of Library and Information Sciences would be canceled due to low enrollment. She went to the dean's office and made a proposition. "If you could offer it without paying the instructor," she asked, "would you still offer it?" The dean jumped at the chance to have Castillo-Speed teach the course without pay, and instead of the projected six students, 25 enrolled. By the end of the summer, the class had produced a bibliography for publication. The course is now offered on a regular basis.

After her brief teaching stint, Castillo-Speed contemplated pursuing a Ph.D. in ethnic studies and teaching on a permanent basis. But the idea was just a dream, she said in her interview with Márquez. For now, Castillo-Speed said she is concentrating her efforts on making the Chicano Database stand on its own and hoping that someday she can move to southern California with her husband and son and start a new collection at another university.

Sources:

Periodicals

Reforma, Volume 10, number 2, summer, 1991, pp. 8-9.

Other

Castillo-Speed, Lillian, "The Chicano Database and the CD-ROM Experience," contained in *CD-ROM and the Library Today and Tomorrow,* edited by Mary Kay Dugan, G.K. Hall, 1990.

Castillo-Speed, Lillian, interview with Sandra Márquez, September 17, 1992.

—Sketch by Sandra Márquez

Lorna Dee Cervantes
(1954-)
Poet

Lorna Dee Cervantes has the distinction of being one of only a few Mexican American poets to have been published by a major publishing company. Her work, according to Marta Ester Sánchez in *Contemporary Chicana Poetry: A Critical Approach to an Emerging Literature,* is characterized by "two conflicting but central positions." In Cervantes's poetry, the critic finds both a "desire for an idealized, utopian world" and "a realistic perspective that sees a world fraught with social problems." The tension created between these two perspectives is a central element in understanding Cervantes's work.

Cervantes was born on August 6, 1954, in San Francisco, California, but grew up in San Jose. She began writing poetry when she was eight years old and published some of her earliest poems in her high school's newspaper. In 1974, she gave her first poetry reading at the Quinto Festival de los Teatros Chicanos in Mexico City, Mexico. The poem she read that day, "Barco de refugiados" ("Refugee Ship"), was published in *El Heraldo,* a Mexico City newspaper. The following year, several of her poems appeared in the *Revista Chicano-Riqueña,* and she began contributing verse to other periodicals as well.

By the end of the 1970s, Cervantes had gained a reputation both as a poet and as the editor and publisher of *Mango,* a small literary review. In addition to her work on the magazine, she edited chapbooks composed by other Chicanos that were published through the Centro Cultural de la Gente of San Jose and Mango Publications. Her efforts soon garnered critical attention, and in 1978 she received a National Endowment for the Arts grant. While on a poetry fellowship at the Fine Arts Work Center in Provincetown, Massachusetts, in 1979, she completed the poems that make up her 1981 collection, *Emplumada.*

Poetry Depicts Alienation in Anglo Society

Emplumada is divided into three sections containing several poems. While the poetry of the first two portions deals with social conflicts, the verse in remaining third is perceived by critics as being more lyrical. Some commentators note that the alienation Cervantes feels as a Chicana in an Anglo society is evident in pieces such as "Poem for the Young White Man Who Asked Me How I, An Intelligent Well-Read Person, Could Believe in the War Between Races" and "Visions of Mexico While at a Writing Symposium in Port Townsend, Washington." Sánchez notes that in the first poem, Cervantes explains her feelings at having a "subordinate place in society as Chicana, as woman, and as poet." In the second, which deals with the theme of migration and opposing societal values, Roberta Fernández concludes in *Dictionary of Literary Biography* that Cervantes "comes to terms with herself, finding resolution for the many conflicts in her life and in her role as poet."

Emplumada also contains "Beneath the Shadow of the Freeway," which Fernández describes as "Cervantes's most celebrated poem." The work depicts a young Chicana who must formulate her own world view after learning about male-female relationships and life in general from an idealistic grandmother and a cynical mother. Sánchez maintains that the poem "not only confronts the question of Cervantes' existential voice as a woman and as a Chicana, but it also brings out the conflict between her two literary voices: a discursive one and a lyrical one. By juxtaposing these two poetic voices, 'Beneath the Shadow of the Freeway' combines the principal elements of Cervantes' style, thus suggesting that it also confronts the question of her literary voice."

Since publication of *Emplumada,* Cervantes has obtained a bachelor of arts degree in creative arts from San Jose State University. She has also taken graduate courses at the University of California, Santa Cruz. In addition, she gives readings from an unpublished poetry collection entitled *Bird Ave.*

Sources:

Books

Dictionary of Literary Biography, Volume 82: *Chicano Writers, First Series,* Gale, 1989.

Sánchez, Marta Ester, *Contemporary Chicana Poetry: A Critical Approach to an Emerging Literature,* University of California Press, 1985.

—Sketch by Marian C. Gonsior

Maggie Cervantes
(1958-)
Community and political activist

Through her involvement in various city agencies and political organizations, Maggie Cervantes is a leader in her East Los Angeles community. Shortly after the Los Angeles Riot of 1992, for example, Cervantes was among Latino community organizers actively seeking ways to help those victimized by the violence to recover. Cervantes used her position as president of the Comision Femenil Mexicana Nacional, Inc., to garner financial support. She sent a letter to businesses explaining that her bilingual organization could target those most affected by the rioting, and her efforts worked. For example, California Edison sent the Comision a check for $10,000 specifically to help Latino families.

Cervantes, working through the Latino communities, found a group of 18 families in Patico Union who had been unable to secure either state or federal aid monies in the three months after the rioting. In some cases, effects of the riot left them unable to document their cases. Others, who lost their homes in the riot, did not qualify for federal or state help. Cervantes did what she could: each family received approximately $500 toward rent and other necessities. Cervantes listened as many told their stories. "It was a very emotional thing for me," she stated in a telephone interview with Peg McNichol.

Cervantes' desire to help others improve the quality of their lives is rooted in her childhood. She understands issues poor Latinas confront because she watched her own mother struggle to support her small family and deal with ethnic discrimination. Magdalena Cervantes was born October 27, 1958, in Los Angeles County, to Albert Cervantes and Dolores Barron Cervantes. Her father was an upholsterer. Her mother worked as a bank teller and would eventually become an escrow officer. As a young girl, Cervantes remembers hearing her parents disagree about whether their children (by now Cervantes had a younger sister) should be allowed to speak Spanish. She explained that her father "was punished in school for speaking Spanish and he didn't want me to feel inferior. . . . Whereas my mom grew up speaking Spanish and had no problems." The issue resolved itself when the Cervantes children began to stay with Dolores's aunt, who was bilingual. Maggie not only learned to be fluent in both languages at her great-aunt's house, she also heard stories about her great-grandmother's daring. She had escaped the Mexican Revolution by taking her daughters to the United States, despite a confrontation with officers from the Mexican Army.

"The women in my family are very strong role models," Cervantes noted in her interview. "Many of them grew up in Los Angeles in 1920s and '30s. They were entrepreneurs in addition to raising families." The prominence of working women in her family was just one factor in young Maggie's life. Another was her father's battle with alcoholism. Her parents separated several times before the couple divorced when Maggie was 12. "I think that's why I do the kind of work I do now," Cervantes said. "It was the realization that my mom would try to leave but it was not economically feasible." That unsettling experience led to Cervantes' private vow that she would always be able to provide for herself. Her father's eventually successful treatment and recovery from alcoholism gave Cervantes hope for others as well. "I have a father now, which is very good," she proclaimed in her interview. "I always had the support of my mom as a role model and now I have both."

When Cervantes was growing up, her family lived at the border of East Los Angeles in a predominantly Latino area. She was a very good student. After her parents divorced, however, she was bused from her neighborhood to a Los Angeles suburb and a multicultural school boasting equal measures of Latino, Asian, and Anglo students. In addition to the ethnic change, Cervantes was immediately aware of an economic change. She went from an area where most struggled to make ends meet to a world in which class distinctions were made between those who lived in apartments and those who lived in comfortable homes at the top of the hill. That awareness and a natural shyness limited her after-school activities.

When it came time to decide what to study in college, Cervantes wasn't sure. "I really didn't know my options," she recalled. She decided to attend East Los Angeles Community College, where she received her Associate of Arts degree in 1979. There she met Chicano studies professor Danny Solorzano, while studying sociology. "I wanted a better understanding of the society and environment I saw around me," she noted, and Solorzano encouraged her to consider Chicano studies. She enrolled in Loyola Marymount University with the intent of becoming a bilingual teacher, but financial limitations prevented her from obtaining a teaching degree.

Founds Chapter of Latina Feminist Organization

At Loyola, a private Catholic university, Cervantes again noticed class and ethnic differences. She graduated with a bachelor of arts in Chicano studies in 1981. By then, Cervantes had developed some analytical skills and was more focused on goals. In 1980, she founded and served as first president of the Loyola student chapter of Comision Femenil Mexicana, a feminist organization for Latinas. She became corresponding secretary with Comision Femenil Mexicana Nacional in 1981. Also in 1980, Cervantes acted as conference co-coordinator to Californios for Fair Representation, a state redistricting movement. Reviewing and participating in California's redistricting process was a very important activity for her, because as a student she was exposed to Latino leaders. She also became much more involved in the political arena, in an outgrowth of the Chicano political movement, which also spawned Comision Femenil. For Cervantes, political empowerment was a key issue. Her own neighborhood, she felt, was not well-represented as a result of district gerrymandering. Though the group did not accomplish all its goals, Cervantes was confident enough in the gains made then to join a similar movement in 1991.

For Cervantes, Chicano studies highlighted her own background and meant working within organizations for improvements. She felt an even stronger need to help those who had paved the way for her college studies. "I felt responsible to people who struggled to get me to college," she said. "I knew I'd have to make it so others could stand on my shoulders." After graduation, she joined the Puente Project of East Los Angeles Community College as a mentor, offering herself as a resource for young women in college.

By 1982, Cervantes decided she wanted to study public policy. She became one of three recipients of the National Hispanic Fellowship in Public Administration, which she earned while at the University of California, Riverside. She and the two other Riverside recipients became close friends, a bond they continued after graduation. Cervantes' studies at Riverside included an internship with the City of Ontario. She also earned certification in grant and proposal writing offered through the State of California. After graduation in 1984, she was hired as administrative assistant for the East Los Angeles Health Task Force. She developed personnel policies and procedures, directed a senior citizens support program, and represented the agency at public functions.

Begins Career in City Government

Cervantes continued her activism with the Comision Femenil in the Los Angeles chapter. From 1984 to 1989, she served in various positions, including vice president, membership chair, historian, legislative chair and chapter representative to the national board. Cervantes also joined the Hispanic Consumer Advisory Panel of the Southern California Gas Company in 1984. In 1985, she was hired into the Los Angeles Department of Water and Power's Occupational Health and Benefits Section Human Resources Division as a management assistant. She wrote reports and otherwise followed the progress on occupational health testing, workers' compensation, and drug screening programs.

Cervantes moved up to administrative analyst in 1986. In this capacity, she acted as a liaison analyst overseeing Los Angeles' transportation, environmental affairs, and management-employee services. This involved budget recommendations and personnel needs evaluations. Cervantes reported to the offices of the Los Angeles Mayor and City Council. She joined the Los Angeles Department of Water and Power Hispanic Affiliates Program in 1986.

For the most part, Cervantes thought she would have a lifetime career in city government. But she also knew she would eventually have to make a choice between that and her community involvement. She remained active in grassroots politics, volunteering in 1988 for the southwest Los Angeles voter registration drive in East Los Angeles. She graduated from the Mexican American Legal and Education Fund Leadership Development Program (Class IX) in 1988. The next year, she participated in a meeting with California legislators on Latina issues. She also began a one-year term as Southwest Regional Chair for the Comision Femenil.

Cervantes simultaneously continued her pursuit of education, earning certificates through the National Hispana Leadership Program in 1990 from Harvard's government mid-management program and San Diego's Center of Creative Leadership. She also was elected secretary of the Professional Hispanics in Energy board in 1990 and president of the Comision Femenil Mexicana Nacional. With her presidency, Cervantes stepped up her community activism to include a board membership for Childwatch, part of a multi-ethnic adolescent pregnancy prevention coalition. That particular issue is close to Cervantes; she points to statistics that young Latinas are not only likely to get pregnant, they are also likely to complete their pregnancy and try to raise the child (in part due to a strong Catholicism in the community). She was elected vice president of the group in 1992.

Focuses on Community Activism

By this time, Cervantes' assumption that she would have a lifetime government career began to falter. The realities of her deep commitment to the Latina community, coupled with the fact that women, especially Latinas, are not often seen in higher government, forced her to reconsider. She started thinking about being more of an advocate than a bureaucrat, and putting her experience dealing with the city offices and her understanding of the issues in the community to use. In April of 1992, Cervantes was hired as executive director for New Economics for Women, a Los Angeles volunteer organization dedicated to helping Hispanic women improve their financial resources. Among NEW's key objectives is a housing project, Casa Loma, which addresses the needs of single parents in the Sixth Street and Union Avenue area. In a city not known for affordable housing, NEW hopes to find just that for single women who are raising families while working at minimum or below-minimum wage jobs. "NEW's philosophy is that affordable housing is a catalyst to improving quality of life for low income women," Cervantes explained in her interview. "We try to provide that and link it to social services and education programs to help them become self-sufficient." She keeps busy interviewing immigrant Latinas about their needs and wants, because she feels the program must be resident-driven.

Cervantes worked with the city government again when she coordinated both the National Hispanic Leadership Agenda Testimony on housing and health issues and the Dialogue on Diversity tour by the Women's Delegation from the Commonwealth of Independent States. "Having an impact on other people's lives is most important," she said. "I consider myself an organizer and a humanist. When I can help someone improve the quality of their life, that makes me feel good . . . the biggest kick is bringing people together to get a project done."

Cervantes' work, however, took an abrupt turn after the 1992 Los Angeles riot. She was appointed to the Rebuild LA Housing Committee and found herself writing letters for private donations. Cervantes plans to continue her political activism as well. She believes that Latinos are seen more as a growing consumer market than a political power at this point, but the signs of change are there. At the lowest level of elected office, she sees greater numbers of Hispanics in service. She also noted that more Latinas ran for state offices, and she would like to see more win.

Sources:

Cervantes, Maggie, telephone interview with Peg McNichol, October 1, 1992.

—*Sketch by Peg McNichol*

Denise Chávez
(1948-)
Playwright, short story writer

"**Y**ou don't have to go anywhere. Not down the street. Not even out of this house. There's stories, plenty of them all around." With these words the mother of a character in the title story of Denise Chávez's short story collection, *The Last of the Menu Girls*, gives advice on writing to her daughter. Chávez might have been penning these words to herself, for her short stories and plays are characterized by their focus on characters and scenes from everyday life. Chávez explains that the presence of the ordinary in her work springs from her belief that as a Chicana writer she needs to speak for those who have no one to vocalize for them. "My work as a playwright is to capture as best as I can the small gestures of the forgotten people, the old men sitting on park benches, the lonely spinsters inside their corner store," she told *Contemporary Authors*.

Daughter of Ernesto E. Chávez, an attorney, and Delfina Rede Favor Chávez, a teacher, the future dramatist was born on August 15, 1948, in Las Cruces, New Mexico. She earned a bachelor of arts degree in 1971 at New Mexico State University and in 1974 received a master's degree in fine arts from Trinity University in San Antonio, Texas. In 1984, she obtained a master's degree in arts from the University of New Mexico. While she has considered herself a full-time playwright since 1977, she has also spent much time teaching, including two years as an instructor of English at Northern New Mexico Community College, in Espanola. She has also taught at the American School in Paris, and she has served as an assistant professor of drama at the University of Houston in Texas since 1989.

Early Writings Earn Critical Acclaim

In 1970, her writing talents received early recognition. In that year she won the New Mexico State University Best Play Award for her work, *The Wait*. During the remainder of the decade, she wrote nearly a dozen plays and saw most of these produced in Taos, Santa Fe, or Albuquerque, New Mexico. Since 1980, she has added other genres to her repertoire, including a poetry anthology, *Life Is a Two-Way Street*, and a collection of short stories, *The Last of the Menu Girls*. But she has continued to write for the theater, including *Novena narrativas*, a one-woman show, and *The Last of the Menu Girls*, a one-act adaptation of her short story of the same title. Her work has been selected in several collections, including *An Anthology of Southwestern Literature, An Anthology: The Indian Río Grande*, and *Voces: An Anthology of Nuevo Mexicano Writers*.

Chávez's work has continued to draw critical recognition. She has received grants from the New Mexico Arts Division, the National Endowment for the Arts, and the Rockefeller Foundation. In 1982, she received a creative writing fellowship from the University of New Mexico and, in 1990, a creative artist fellowship from the Cultural Arts Council of Houston, Texas. In 1986, her short story, "The Last of the Menu Girls," from the collection of the same title, received the New Mexico State University's Steele Jones Fiction Award. The stories in the volume revolve around the life of Rocío Esquibel, a 17-year-old whose job is delivering menus to hospital patients. Writing in *New York Times Book Review*, Beverly Lyon Clark noted that many of the stories revealed "Chávez's strengths in dialogue and in juxtaposing evocative scenes."

Married to photographer and sculptor Daniel Zolinsky, Chávez currently resides in Houston, Texas. Throughout her career, she has demonstrated a social conscience that has led her to serve as a teacher at Radium Springs Center for Women, a medium-security prison, and as co-director of a senior citizen workshop in creative writing and puppetry at Community Action Agency in Las Cruces, New Mexico. This social conscience is also present in her written work as a continuing theme of love, a theme that Chávez finds in the landscape of the American Southwest. She explained this concept in *Contemporary Authors:* "I write about the neighborhood handymen, the waitresses, the bag ladies, the elevator operators. They all have something in common: they know what it is to love and to be merciful. . . . My work is rooted in the Southwest, in heat and dust, and reflects a world where love is as real as the land. In this dry and seemingly harsh and empty world there is much beauty to be found. That hope of the heart is what feeds me, my characters."

Sources:

Books

Chávez, Denise, *The Last of the Menu Girls,* Arte Público, 1986.
Contemporary Authors New Revisions Series, Volume 131, Gale, 1991.

Periodicals

New York Times Book Review, October 12, 1986, p. 28.

—*Sketch by Marian C. Gonsior*

Linda Chavez

Linda Chavez
(1947-)
Government official, writer

Formerly the highest-ranking woman in the Reagan administration and a Republican candidate for U.S. Senator from Maryland, Linda Chavez has made a career out of defying expectations and refusing to be classified. Although she is proud of her Hispanic heritage, Chavez has insisted on making her own way in politics and is opposed to many "traditional" policies relating to minorities, such as racial hiring quotas, comparable worth and pay equity, and bilingual education programs. Although she is a conservative Republican, Chavez has not been hesitant to speak out against problems in the Reagan administration. Commenting on the covert activities of Lieutenant Colonel Oliver North, for example, Chavez told the *Christian Science Monitor* that "Ollie North is no conservative" and added that "zealots have no place in democratic governments." "It would be easier for me to be a liberal Democrat, I guess," she explained in the *Washington Post.* "People would expect that. But I guess I'm just stubborn. I do go against the grain. I do things that are not always popular.

There's a tenacity there. I guess I've always thought of myself as different and sometimes I've gotten more attention for myself than I wanted."

While Chavez has been accused by many of abandoning the Hispanic community, she notes that her ethnic background has contributed to her conservative beliefs. Chavez was born in Albuquerque, New Mexico, in 1947, the daughter of Velma, an Anglo, and Rudy Chavez, a conservative Spanish American whose family has been established in the Southwest for over three hundred years. When she was nine the family moved to Denver, Colorado, where Chavez first began to notice racial discrimination. As a teenager she marched against segregation and recalls that in school she was never encouraged to excel or further her education. Motivated by her father, a World War II veteran who taught her to value her Spanish heritage without using it as an excuse, Chavez finished high school and entered college. As her mother, Velma Chavez, told the *Washington Post,* Linda's "dad would tell her screaming and yelling doesn't accomplish anything. You have to think about things, decide what's wrong and do something about it and that's it."

Believes in Hard Work, Not Quotas

It was in college during the late 1960s that Chavez first showed indications of the conservative views she was later to espouse as a public official. At the University of Colorado, where she told *Washington Monthly*, "I made it on hard work," Chavez began tutoring Mexican American students in a remedial program; she became disenchanted, however, when she found the students were urging the administration to lower their minimum grade requirements. After receiving a B.A. in 1970, Chavez went on to graduate study in English literature at the University of California, Los Angeles. Because of her background, Chavez found herself pressured into teaching a course on Chicano writing, despite her assertions that there was not enough material by Hispanic Americans to develop an entire course. Instead of coming prepared to work, Chavez relates, her students "sort of expected that this was the course they could take to come and 'rap,' in the jargon of the day," as she told *Washington Monthly*. She recalls that her students wanted to discuss their own experiences instead of doing class work: "They *lived* Chicano literature," she recalls, so "they didn't [want to] have to read books about it." Things took a turn for the worse when, as she states in *Hispanic*, "some of the students stood up and turned their backs to me. I had to lecture with a class of kids facing their backs to me—it was a disaster." When she failed her students for not completing the reading list, they retaliated by vandalizing her home and threatening her family. Discouraged by this experience and her treatment as a "token" Hispanic, Chavez left the university in 1972 and traveled to Washington, D.C., to join her husband, Christopher Gersten, whom she married in 1967.

In the mid-seventies, Chavez began working for Democratic and liberal causes in Washington, holding a series of jobs with the Democratic National Committee and the National Education Association. While she wanted to learn more about specific issues, she felt the organizations failed to treat her as an individual with opinions and instead saw her only as an ethnic representative: "They were specifically looking for an Hispanic woman," she reported to *Washington Monthly*. "It was very clear to me they expected me to be the Hispanic lobbyist, to be their link to the Chicano caucus inside the NEA. I balked at that." After serving with the Department of Health, Education, and Welfare as a consultant on education, Chavez joined the staff of the American Federation of Teachers (AFT), where she was allowed to express her views. While editor of the AFT quarterly, *American Educator*, Chavez wrote a series of articles urging a return to "traditional values" in American schools. These writings soon brought her to the attention of conservatives in Washington, and in 1981 she began working as a consultant for President Ronald Reagan's administration.

In 1983 Chavez was asked to become a member of the U.S. Commission on Civil Rights, a non-partisan agency designed to monitor the government's progress in enforcing civil rights laws. Dissatisfied with the offer, however, Chavez held out for a position of greater power and influence and was eventually appointed staff director of the agency. Chavez immediately stirred up controversy by issuing a memo counseling the reversal of many traditional

civil rights measures, such as racial hiring quotas, a practice she believes demeans people by reducing them to an ethnic category. She also authorized a study to explore the negative effects of affirmative action on minorities. In addition, Chavez hired many temporary employees and consultants "to promote work that would reflect her and the commission majority's views," as the *Washington Post* described it. Many civil rights activists criticized Chavez for what they perceived as changing the traditionally impartial agency into an instrument of the Reagan administration, but Chavez claimed she was only remedying the liberal bias of past years. As the *Washington Post* summarized, "Chavez counter[ed] that she helped redirect the agency toward its traditional goal of a colorblind society. . . . She maintain[ed] that her critics have been unable to separate their ideological differences from their assessments of her character and performance."

Highest-Ranking Woman in Reagan Administration

It was her performance as the commission's director, however, that helped her become the director of the White House Office of Public Liaison in 1985, a position that made her the highest-ranking woman in the administration. Appointed because of her strong conservative background, despite her Democratic affiliation, Chavez nevertheless changed parties, becoming a Republican, and began working to promote administration policy among members of Congress and public groups. Chavez lasted only ten months in the position, however, for as she noted in *Policy Review*, "I learned while in the administration . . . how little policy actually emanates from the White House, whether by design or accident. My chief reason for wanting to leave the Civil Rights Commission to join the White House staff was to be able to have a greater role in influencing administration policy on a broad array of issues. What I discovered was that the White House was more involved in process than policy." Upon leaving the Office of Public Liaison in early 1986, Chavez was encouraged to seek a political office of her own.

Chavez began campaigning for the Maryland Republican nomination for senator in 1986, and she gained attention during the primaries when she gave more correct answers than any other candidate during a television quiz on current affairs. A victor in the primaries, Chavez began to prepare for a tough race against Democratic Representative Barbara Mikulski. The contest brought the national spotlight upon Maryland, for it was only the second U.S. Senate race ever contested by two women.

Despite her success in the primaries, Chavez was at a disadvantage in a state whose voters consisted of two-thirds registered Democrats. In addition, she was drawing criticism for her conversion to the Republican party and her short term as a Maryland resident. When Chavez, married and the mother of three children, called the unmarried Mikulski a "San Francisco-style Democrat" and accused her of being "anti-male," she drew fire for her campaign tactics and was accused of mud-slinging. Her strategy backfired, and despite a successful fund-raising effort that included appearances by President Reagan, Chavez lost the election by over 20 percent of the vote.

After the long campaign, Chavez retired from public office and became president of U.S. English, a private non-profit organization lobbying to make English the official national language. In addition, Chavez has frequently appeared as a political commentator on both television and radio. She has not avoided controversy, however, for in late 1988 she resigned from U.S. English; her reasoning was that she could not work with its founder John Tanton, who, in Chavez's estimation, had demonstrated an "anti-Hispanic" and "anti-Catholic" bias. An "embarrassing question," according to Anna Maria Arias in *Hispanic*, "is how Chavez could have allowed herself to be duped by what many believe is a racist organization."

Joins Conservative Think Tank

After leaving U.S. English, Chavez went on to become a senior fellow at the Manhattan Institute for Policy Research, a conservative think tank in Washington, D.C. Her recent duties include serving as director of the Center for the New American Community, which, according to Arias, "will study a common heritage that is threatened by multiculturalism."

One of the fruits of Chavez's work for the Institute has been *Out of the Barrio: Toward a New Politics of Hispanic Assimilation*, a 1991 book that discusses such topics as affirmative action and Hispanic involvement in all levels of politics. One of the motivations for writing the work arose out of a debate she had with Arnold Torres, the former executive director of the League of United Latin American Citizens. While Torres felt that Hispanics were largely poor and disadvantaged, Chavez had a different view. "I saw lots of opportunity," she told Arias. "I saw Hispanics rapidly moving into the middle class. I saw my generation, and particularly the generation after me, making huge strides, and yet I didn't see that reflected in the rhetoric." Some have attacked the book for using oversimplifications and generalizations. Chavez defended her book, telling Arias, "I think that to the organized Hispanic movement, what I say is not in their best interest. If you were an organization out there trying to get support from the private and public sector to help Hispanics who are poor and disadvantaged . . ., my coming along and saying, 'Wait a second, we are really doing okay, we're moving into the middle class and discrimination has not been nearly as severe as it has been for blacks'—that isn't a view you want out there."

While she has frequently been criticized for her conservative views, Chavez maintains that her liberal detractors are guilty of stereotyping her; they assume that because she is Hispanic, she must hold the political views that a minori-

ty is "supposed" to espouse. Countering criticisms that she has changed her views to further her career, Chavez explained to *Washington Monthly* that her opinions have changed, in part, "from watching [the Reagan] administration. I look around, and I see things sort of working and the country working and inflation having been brought down. . . . So I moved on those kinds of issues . . . relatively recently." She also notes that many different groups are included within the "Hispanic" designation, and that her own Spanish-American background, as opposed to that of Mexican Americans or Puerto Ricans, is traditionally conservative. "I'm very proud of my heritage," she told the *Washington Post*. "I see myself as what I am. I've never run away from being Hispanic. It doesn't mean I have to endorse the whole agenda."

Sources:

Periodicals

Christian Science Monitor, December 11, 1986, p. 26.
Fortune, March 4, 1985, pp. 161-164, November 21, 1988, p. 188.
Hispanic, August, 1992, pp. 11-16.
New Republic, May 13, 1985, p. 11, February 24, 1986, pp. 8-10, August 3, 1987, pp. 12-13.
New York Times, August 31, 1986, p. A58, September 10, 1986, p. A15, October 16, 1986, p. B16.
People, November 3, 1986, pp. 115-116.
Policy Review, winter, 1988, pp. 46-47.
Savvy, January, 1987, pp. 43-48, 75.
Transition, Issue 56, 1992, pp. 112-22.
Wall Street Journal, August 15, 1986, p. 36.
Washington Monthly, June, 1985, pp. 34-39.
Washington Post, July 25, 1986, p. A1, August 15, 1986, p. A17, October 24, 1986, p. C3, p. C5, October 28, 1986, p. A15, October 29, 1986, p. A1, August 16, 1988, p. A22, October 20, 1988, p. A18.

—Sketch by Diane Telgen

Linda Christian
(1923-)
Screen actress

Linda Christian, one of Hollywood's leading ladies in the 1940s, was once billed as the "Anatomic Bomb." A curvaceous, flirtatious, headline-grabbing beauty, Christian was probably more famous for her off-screen amorous adventures than she was for any of her movie roles. Newspapers, magazines, and tabloids of the day followed her jet-setting exploits around the world, where she was usually found in the company of international playboys, fellow movie stars, or millionaire industrialists. Despite dozens of romances and numerous "engagements," however, she is perhaps best remembered for her highly publicized marriage to movie idol Tyrone Power.

Linda Christian was born Blanca Rosa Welter in Tampico, Mexico, in 1923, the daughter of Dutch oilman Gerald Welter and his half-German and half-French-Spanish wife, Blanca. The family moved around so much that Christian was educated in eight schools in five countries: Mexico, Switzerland, Holland, Italy, and Palestine. At the peak of her fame, Christian used her multi-ethnic background in a typically mischievous—and often repeated—quote, as mentioned in *Time* and *Cosmopolitan:* "I'm half Dutch, a quarter German, an eighth Spanish and an eighth French, and I speak all four of those languages plus Italian and English. That makes me sexilingual."

Discovered by Errol Flynn

The Welters were living in the Palestinian town of Jerusalem in 1942 when German Field Marshal Erwin Rommel's Nazi forces began their drive on Alexandria, Egypt. Eighteen-year-old Blanca Rosa left Jerusalem to work in the British Censorship Office, passing on letters written in German and Italian. Later that year her mother took her and a sister, Ariadne, to South America and then on to Mexico. About this time, she enrolled in a medical college and somehow met movie actor Errol Flynn, who, according to Christian in *Cosmopolitan,* said, "What? Wasting beauty like this on medicine when the world cries out for stars?" With her mother's permission, Flynn took the starstruck young woman to Hollywood.

Living in an actors' boarding house for $7.50 a week, Christian was introduced by fellow boarder and future actress Ruth Roman to the head of the casting department at RKO Studios. He in turn introduced her to studio head Charles Koerner, who put her under contract. Metro-Goldwyn-Mayer picked up her contract, and Christian debuted in *Holiday in Mexico* in 1946; she did not utter a single word. She fared somewhat better in her next two films: *Tarzan and the Mermaids* (1948), and *Green Dolphin Street* (1947). Christian had what she liked to refer to as her "fated" meeting with Tyrone Power in Rome in 1948, though he was involved with actress Lana Turner at the time. She told *Cosmopolitan* that after meeting Power, she wrote, "Tonight, I met the father of my children." Their year-long courtship ended in the tiny tenth-century church of Santa Francesca Romana on January 27, 1949, in what the Twentieth Century-Fox publicity machine dubbed the "Wedding of the Century." Pandemonium reigned at the wedding as 100 invited guests were surrounded by dozens of photographers, hundreds of reporters, and thousands of hysterical teenage fans screaming "Ty il Magnifico!" and

"Viva Linda!" According to *Time* magazine, one man suffered a broken finger, and several women fainted. Immediately afterward at the Vatican, Pope Pius received the couple along with other newlyweds, although Power's divorce from his civil marriage to the French actress Annabella would not become final until later that day.

Christian was eager to become a mother, but suffered two tragedies: her first baby was stillborn, and she miscarried the second. Later, she gave birth to Romina Francesca on October 2, 1951, and Taryn Stephanie, born September 13, 1953. Christian's pictures during this time included *The Happy Time* (1952), *Athena* (1954), and a Spanish film, *Thunderstorm* (1956). Although happily married for a few years, Christian and Power eventually separated in October, 1955. When Power died of a heart attack in 1958, Christian did not attend the funeral at his widow's request, but flew with her two children from Paris to Hollywood to pray at his grave.

Much-Publicized Affairs Follow Divorce

Following her breakup with Power, Christian embarked on a dizzying series of affairs that took her, literally, around the world: she dated heir Robert Schlesinger; daredevil racer Marquis Alfonso de Portago, who died in 1957 in a suicidal crash that killed ten others; Brazilian millionaires Francisco "Baby" Pignatari and Jorge Guinle; Aly Khan; and others. She was named by Tita Purdom in divorce action against her English actor husband, Edmund, whom Christian married in 1962 and divorced in 1963.

In 1962, Christian's autobiography, *Linda: My Own Story,* was published by Crown. Some of her last movies include *The VIPs* (1963) and *How to Seduce a Playboy* (1966). After a 15-year absence from film, she returned before the cameras in Italy in 1986 in *Amore inquieto di Maria* (*Restless Love*). She lives in Rome, Italy.

Sources:

Books

Christian, Linda, *Linda: My Own Story,* Crown, 1962.

Periodicals

Cosmopolitan, July, 1959, pp. 69-75.
Life, February 7, 1949, p. 32; April 7, 1958, p. 40.
Newsweek, February 7, 1949, p. 34; April 7, 1958, p. 46.
Time, February 7, 1949, p. 18; April 7, 1958, p. 46; May 12, 1967, p. 49.
Variety, July 9, 1986, p. 10.

—Sketch by Julie Catalano

Marlene Cintron de Frias
(1951-)
Director of Office of Latino Affairs, New York

When Marlene Cintron de Frias talks about a problem relating to New York City's Hispanic population, City Hall listens. As director of the city's Office of Latino Affairs, Cintron provides Hispanics with a voice in city government. She deals with problems as massive as the AIDS epidemic in Hispanic neighborhoods and as seemingly minor as a Latino livery driver who lost his vehicle and license due to bureaucratic red tape. "No day is the same as the day before," Cintron commented in an interview with Ann Malaspina. "Every day is a potpourri of possibilities."

Devoted to Community Involvement

Cintron has always felt obligated to help her community. "It was a part of my life ever since I was a child," she said. Born on April 14, 1951, in the South Bronx, she was raised in a Puerto Rican family with strong ties to the community. Her parents, Lorenzo and Isabel (Ramos), led a number of Pentecostal church congregations in the South Bronx. As a child, Cintron often helped translate for parishioners who could not speak English. "From there, you never turn your back. You realize that despite all the setbacks, every step you take forward will make up for the steps that fell back," she said. After graduating from Roosevelt High School in 1968, Cintron earned a bachelor's degree in urban studies in 1972 from the State University of New York at Old Westbury. In 1977, she received an M.S. in education from Fordham University. Although she never intended to practice law, she graduated from Georgetown University Law Center in 1980. "The law was a great opportunity to get the credentials to do what I wanted to do," she explained.

From 1973 to 1976, Cintron worked with the federal Model Cities program in the Bronx. In 1980, she was hired by former U.S. Representative Robert Garcia to direct three district offices in the 18th Congressional District. Cintron describes that period as "the most fascinating time in my life." Working with local politicians and community leaders, she got her first real taste of politics. After leaving that position in 1985, she switched to the private sector. Cintron took a job as branch manager of a local Citibank, and soon worked her way up to assistant vice-president for intergovernmental affairs at Citicorp/Citibank North America. In that position, she monitored legislation that impacted banking.

In 1991, Cintron was invited to apply for the job at City Hall. Already known and respected by the Hispanic community, she received a warm welcome. "I think that Marlene has the sophistication and the experience to get things done, and that's what counts," said Dennis Rivera, president of Local 1199 of the Hospital and Health Care Employees Union, in an interview with the *New York Times.* Cintron's predecessor, William Nieves, had resigned unhappily, complaining that he did not have access to Mayor David Dinkins, but Cintron forged a close working relationship with the mayor. "I make sure he knows all the things he's doing right and the things he could be doing better," said Cintron, who joined a number of other Hispanic women with top jobs in the Dinkins administration.

With a staff of four, Cintron, who reports to the Deputy Mayor for Governmental Affairs, spends much of her day fielding phone calls from city residents. Her past achievements have included lobbying to take down a mural on a Department of Corrections wall which negatively depicted Hispanics, and negotiating with rioters in Washington Heights following the slaying of a Dominican man by a police officer in 1992. Also that year, she helped settle a lawsuit between minority police officers and the city over an improperly administered lieutenants' exam. As a result, Cintron expects that more Hispanics will have opportunities for advancement in the police department. "Although the city is a majority of minorities, we do not have any black or Latino precinct captains," she said. "There's something wrong."

Faces Challenges of New York Hispanics' Problems

But the problems facing New York's Hispanic population of over two million people—predominately poor immigrants representing every Spanish-speaking country in the world—remain daunting. "We have the highest unemployment rate, the highest school dropout rate, and high teenage pregnancy," Cintron noted. "The situation of the Latino community is not a good one in the city of New York." Cintron, who is married and has one son, is especially concerned about the alarming number of Hispanic women infected with HIV, the virus that causes AIDS. "They are the ones who bring up the children and keep the family unit together," she said.

Cintron is chairman of the Bronx College AIDS Services, Inc., and sits on the board of the National Hispanic Scholarship Fund. She has received many community awards, including the Dr. Ramon Emeterio Betances Award from the Puerto Rican Parade for her work with the Puerto Rican community and an award from the Hispanic Society at Baruch College. She plans to eventually return to the private sector, where she believes it is easier to get things done. "I'm here, doing a good job and making a heck of a difference," she noted, "but I'm not a permanent government bureaucrat."

Sources:

Periodicals

New York Times, February 10, 1991, p. 36.

Other

Cintron de Frias, Marlene, interview with Ann Malaspina, August 21, 1992.

—Sketch by Ann Malaspina

Evelyn Cisneros
(1955-)
Ballerina

Although she dances with a regional dance company, Evelyn Cisneros has managed to achieve national fame—she was listed in *Hispanic Business*'s "100 Influentials" in 1992. This feat has not surprised those who have known and worked with the talented and hardworking ballerina, who has danced in classics such as *Swan Lake* and *Sleeping Beauty* and has also interpreted more contemporary works such as *A Song for Dead Warriors.*

Evelyn Cisneros was born in 1955 in Long Beach, California. As a child growing up in nearby Huntington Beach, she was very shy. To help Cisneros overcome her fears, Cisneros's mother enrolled her in a ballet class, where she captured the attention of teacher Phyllis Cyr. Recognizing the young girl's potential, Cyr encouraged her to study tap, jazz, and flamenco dancing. Cisneros was an enthusiastic pupil who soon took her lessons very seriously. By the time she reached high school, she was making daily three-hour round-trip drives to her dance classes in Los Angeles. Despite having to follow such a grueling schedule, she still managed to keep up with her homework.

Wins Spot with San Francisco Ballet

Cisneros's years of training were rewarded in 1977 when, at the age of 22, she was invited to join the San Francisco Ballet. Within two years, her mentor, Michael Smuin (who was also the dance company's artistic director), had created a ballet just for her entitled *A Song for Dead Warriors.* A tribute to Native Americans, *A Song for Dead Warriors* has been broadcast on the "Great Performances—Dance in America" television series. It is a personal favorite of the ballerina for whom it was written. "I feel very special about being able to make a statement about the Indian situation in the country," Cisneros told a reporter for *Nuestro.* "I dated an Indian guy for five years. I met his family and went to pow-wows with him. I saw how deep the sadness goes."

During the early 1980s, Cisneros's fame grew despite the fact that she only danced for a regional company. Although she was profiled in various newspapers and was the subject of cover stories in two dance journals, she did not let success go to her head. She enjoyed the many opportunities she had to perform in San Francisco and was not at all sure that she wanted to seek a position in a better-known company, even though by late 1985 her best friend, Michael Smuin, and her preferred partner, Kirk Peterson, had been fired by the San Francisco Ballet. As she explained to a *Los Angeles Times* reporter, "A dancer's career is so short that this kind of decision requires serious thought."

Cisneros, who also noted in the *Los Angeles Times* that she "never dreamed of attaining this level of dancing," has had a rewarding career. In addition to *A Song for Dead Warriors,* some of her more important performances include roles in *The Tempest, Scherzo, Mozart's C Minor Mass, Romeo and Juliet, Medea, To the Beatles,* and *Piano Concerto No. 21.*

Regards Versatility as One of Her Greatest Strengths

Cisneros's success in various roles may have to do with her perception of her work. "I see myself as a dramatic dancer," she told the *Los Angeles Times,* "one not limited to any particular kind of role. As Cinderella, I have a chance to show a whole progression of character—starting browbeaten and disowned, then becoming overwhelmed with great fortune and finally having the grace that comes with fulfillment." As far as her technique is concerned, observed the ballerina in *Nuestro,* "I feel a good dancer should be comfortable in any kind of movement flow. Whether your toes and knees are pointed out or in, you should be able to interpret what different choreographers are trying to get across."

In October, 1991, when the San Francisco Ballet traveled to New York, the spotlight was on Cisneros, the company's senior ballerina. According to the *New York Times,* her performances with Anthony Randazzo in *The Comfort Zone* and *Ballo Della Regina* were "brilliant."

One day, Cisneros—whose marriage to fellow dancer David McNaughton ended after two years—hopes to build a house on land she owns in Baja, California, and raise a family there. In the meantime, she celebrates her heritage and takes seriously her responsibilities as a notable Hispanic American. As she stated in *Nuestro,* "I'm proud to be able to represent my people, although I've never been through what many of them have."

Sources:

Periodicals

Dance, December, 1984, p. 112.
Hispanic, July, 1989.
Hispanic Business, October, 1992, p. 53.
Los Angeles Times, December 5, 1985, part VI, p. 2.
New Yorker, November 3, 1980, p. 192.

New York Times, October 3, 1991, p. B1, p. C17, October 7, 1992, p. C14.
Nuestro, August, 1985.

—*Sketch by Ronie-Richele Garcia-Johnson*

Sandra Cisneros
(1954-)
Poet, author

Sandra Cisneros is a new voice in mainstream American literature. In her poetry and fiction, Cisneros presents vivid and compelling vignettes of the lives and loves of Chicanos and Latinos from a distinctly feminine perspective. In a review of her 1991 collection of short fiction, *Woman Hollering Creek and Other Stories, Newsweek*'s Peter S. Prescott wrote that "her feminist, Mexican American voice is not only playful and vigorous, it's original—we haven't heard anything like it before. . . . Noisily, wittily, always compassionately, Cisneros surveys woman's condition—a condition that is both precisely Latina and general to women everywhere." A commentator for *Washington Post Book World* deemed Cisneros "a writer of power and eloquence and great lyrical beauty," while a *Mirabella* reviewer described her as "the foremost Mexican American woman writer."

The first Chicana to receive a major publishing contract, Cisneros is one of the leading writers in the nascent field of Latino literature. The author, who sees herself as something of a pioneer, asserted to Jim Sagel of *Publishers Weekly:* "I'm trying to write the stories that haven't been written. I feel like a cartographer. I'm determined to fill a literary void." In an interview for *Authors and Artists for Young Adults (AAYA)* Cisneros further explained that in *Woman Hollering Creek and Other Stories* she attempted "to populate [the] book with as many different kinds of Latinos as possible so that mainstream America could see how diverse we are."

Cisneros was born in Chicago, Illinois, in 1954 to a Mexican father and a Chicana mother. The only daughter of seven children, Cisneros grew up in poverty. During her childhood she developed a fear of mice—an anxiety that was "not as a female thing, but a class thing," she told Sheila Benson of the *Los Angeles Times.* "To me mice are all my poverty, the whole neighborhood I grew up in, embodied in a little skittering creature that might come to get me at any moment." Many of her early years were spent moving from place to place, with regular trips to Mexico City, Mexico, so her paternal grandmother could see her favorite son.

Sandra Cisneros

The frequent relocations were unsettling, she recalled in *Publishers Weekly.* "The moving back and forth, the new school, were very upsetting to me as a child. They caused me to be very introverted and shy. I do not remember making friends easily. . . . Because we moved so much and always in neighborhoods that appeared like France after World War II—empty lots and burned out buildings—I retreated inside myself." Being the only girl in her family also contributed to her shyness. Cisneros stated in her interview: "I spent a lot of time by myself by just the fact that I was the only daughter, and my brothers—once they became socialized—pretty much hung out with their own gender. They all kind of teamed up and excluded me from their games." Cisneros acknowledges, however, that one positive aspect of her shyness was that she became an astute observer of the people and things around her, a trait that would stand her in good stead in her later literary career.

Cisneros attended Catholic schools in Chicago. In *AAYA,* she judged her basic education "rather shabby." She added, "If I had lived up to my teachers' expectations, I'd still be working in a factory, because my report card was pretty lousy. That's because I wasn't very much interested, or I was too terrified to venture or volunteer." Not wanting to be ridiculed, she was afraid to display her creative talents because she felt the nuns dismissed the importance of the minority experience. She wrote secretly at home. Fortunately, her parents stressed education. Her mother was self-taught and saw to it that all her children had library cards; her father wanted his offspring to study hard. As Cisneros recalled in a column for *Glamour,* "My father's hands are thick and yellow, stubbed by a history of hammer and nails and twine and coils and springs. 'Use this' my father said, tapping his head, 'not this' showing us those hands."

Finds Creative Voice

It was in high school that Cisneros first began to express her creativity publicly. At first she read poems in class and then, in her sophomore year, "I had a teacher who was . . . a would-be writer," she told *AAYA.* "I started writing for her. I became more public through that class and she encouraged me to work on a literary magazine . . . which I did— and I became the editor eventually." After high school, Cisneros attended Loyola University. Her father supported her efforts, believing that college would be a good place for his daughter to find a husband. As Cisneros commented in *Glamour,* "In retrospect, I'm lucky my father believed daughters were meant for husbands. It meant it didn't matter if I majored in something silly like English. After all, I'd find a nice professional eventually, right?"

What Cisneros found was a profession: writing. In the late 1970s, one of her undergraduate teachers helped her enroll in the poetry section of the Iowa Writers' Workshop, a program which led to a master's degree. However, Cisneros found herself alienated from her surroundings and her classmates. As she explained in *AAYA,* "It didn't take me long to learn—after a few days being there—that nobody cared to hear what I had to say and no one listened to me even when I did speak. I became very frightened and terrified that first year." When these feelings finally surfaced, they lead Cisneros to a great insight.

During a seminar discussion of archetypal memories in Gaston Bachelard's "Peoeics of Space,", her classmates spoke about the house of the imagination, using their childhood homes as examples. They described houses with attics, stairways, and cellars—dwellings that were a far cry from the miserable bungalow of Cisneros's childhood. Focusing on her early poverty made her doubt herself. Who was Sandra Cisneros compared to these children of privilege from the finest schools in the country? "They had been bred as fine hothouse flowers. I was a yellow weed among the city's cracks," she recalled in *Publishers Weekly.* Describing the cultural epiphany that changed her, she added: "It was not until this moment when I separated myself, when I considered myself truly distinct that my writing acquired a voice. I knew I was a Mexican woman, but I didn't think it had anything to do with why I felt so much imbalance in my life, whereas it had everything to do with it! My race, my gender, my class! That's when I decided I would write about something my classmates couldn't write about."

Revelation Leads to *The House on Mango Street*

This revelation enabled Cisneros to write her first book, *The House on Mango Street,* in which she described her house of imagination. "It's small and red with tight steps in front and windows so small you'd think they were holding their breath. Bricks are crumbling in places, and the front door is so swollen you have to push hard to get in. There is no front yard, only four little elms the city planted by the curb. Out back is a small garage for the car we don't own yet." Published in 1984, *Mango Street* features a series of interlocking vignettes told by Esperanza Cordero, a young Chicana growing up in a Chicago barrio. Through Esperanza's eyes the reader obtains a glimpse of the lives of the people around her. She wants a better life for herself and, by end of the book, Esperanza has gained a measure of the power and determination to achieve it. "I have decided not to grow tame like the others who lay their necks on the threshold waiting for the ball and chain." However, Esperanza is reminded by one of the characters that leaving the barrio does not mean leaving one's identity: "When you leave you must remember to come back for the others. A circle, understand? You will always be Esperanza. You will always be Mango Street. You can't erase what you know. You can't forget who you are."

Students from junior high school through graduate school have used the book in classes ranging from Chicano studies to psychology. Stanford University has adopted the work as part of its new curriculum. In addition, *The House on Mango Street* brought Cisneros to the attention of literary agent Susan Bergholz, who began a search for the author. Some four years elapsed before the two would actually connect. Meanwhile, Cisneros received her master's degree from Iowa and sought employment. She worked part-time as a teacher of literacy skills to Latinos and held various positions within several universities. In 1986 she received a Dobie-Paisano fellowship and moved to Texas. During this time she finished *My Wicked, Wicked Ways,* a book of poetry. Published in 1987, the verses show an independent woman, a wife and mother to none, who says, "I've learned two things./ To let go/ clean as a kite string./ And to never wash a man's clothes./ These are my rules." She adds, "What does a woman owe a man/ and isn't freedom what you believe in?/ Even the freedom to say no?" Although the volume was well received by critics, for Cisneros herself 1987 was the lowest period of her life.

Desiring to continue living in Texas after her fellowship had ended, she was unable to make a living. She was reduced to passing out fliers in supermarkets and laundromats in a vain attempt to organize a private writing workshop. Finally, her confidence shattered and in a deep depression, she left Texas to accept a guest lectureship at California State University in Chico. She described this period in her life to *Publishers Weekly:* "I found myself becoming suicidal. . . . I was drowning, beyond help. . . . It was frightening because it was such a calm depression." Help arrived in the form of an National Endowment of the

Arts fellowship in fiction, funding which revitalized Cisneros both financially and spiritually. Her enthusiasm building, she finally contacted Bergholz, whose Manhattan phone number she had carried in her pocket for months. That call led to a contract with Random House and the publication of *Woman Hollering Creek.*

Signs with Random House

With Random House behind her, Cisneros was thrust into the national limelight, and *Woman Hollering Creek* received wide distribution. A series of short stories about the lives and loves of Chicanas on both sides of the Texas-Mexican boarder, the tales feature strong women characters. For her work Cisneros received glowing reviews from various critics, being lauded as a new star on the literary horizon. A commentator for *Los Angeles Times* called the collection "stunning," while a reviewer for the *New York Times Book Review* deemed the work's protagonists "as unforgettable as a first kiss." A *Washington Post Book World* critic said the stories were "a kind of choral work in which the harmonic voices emphasize the commonality of experience."

Although some Latinos who find success feel uncomfortable becoming a "representative" of their ethnic group, Cisneros does not mind the label. She told *AAYA:* "I don't feel any sense of self-consciousness about my role as a spokesperson in the writing, because I've taken that responsibility on from the very beginning. That isn't something I'm nervous about or begrudging about. Actually, the fact that I *can* write about the things I write about. . . . I feel very honored to be able to give them a form in my writings and to be able to have this material to write about is a blessing." In her next book, Cisneros plans to explore father-daughter relationships and aspects of growing up in the middle between Mexican and Chicano cultures.

Sources:

Books

Authors and Artists for Young Adults, Volume 9, Gale, 1992.
Cisneros, Sandra, *The House on Mango Street,* Arte Público Press, 1984.
Cisneros, Sandra, *My Wicked, Wicked Ways,* Third Woman Press, 1987.
Cisneros, Sandra, *Woman Hollering Creek and Other Stories,* Random House, 1991.

Periodicals

Glamour, November, 1990, pp. 256-257.
Los Angeles Times, May 7, 1991, p. F1.
Los Angeles Times Book Review, April 28, 1991, p. 3.
Mirabella, April, 1991, p. 46.
Newsweek, June 3, 1991, p. 60.
New York Times Book Review, May 26, 1991, p. 6.
Publishers Weekly, March 29, 1991, pp. 74-75.

Washington Post Book World, June 9, 1991, p. 3.

—*Sketch by Andrés Chávez*

Imogene Coca
(1908-)
Actress, comedienne

Imogene Coca, the woman most will remember from her performances in television's *Your Show of Shows,* has been working in show business for 80 years. Although physically petite, Coca has managed to dominate stages and captivate audiences wherever she appears. She dances, sings, and jokes; perhaps her tremendous success with *Your Show of Shows* was due to the fact that the production gave her a chance to incorporate her many talents and skills.

The only child of Joseph Fernandez y Coca and Sadie (Brady) Coca, the future performer was born in Philadelphia, Pennsylvania, on November 18, 1908. Coca's parents were in the entertainment business. Her father, who was of Spanish descent, was the conductor of the Chestnut Street Opera House, while her mother came from an Irish background and was a dancer and vaudeville actress who, as a young woman, had run away from home to join Howard Thurston's magic show. For the Cocas, the performing arts were a family affair. After starting piano lessons when she was five years old, Coca began vocal training when she was six and dancing lessons at seven. Encouraged by her parents to perform on stage, she appeared in moppet parts. At nine years of age she performed a vaudeville tap dance, and when she was 11 she sang "personality" songs at Philadelphia's Dixie Theatre. When given the choice to attend high school or to seriously develop a career in show business, the 14-year-old Coca chose the latter.

Enthusiasm Leads to Shot at Vaudeville

While the training and encouragement her parents provided enabled her to supersede the efforts of less experienced performers, Coca combined her talent and enthusiasm to follow her dream. Bold and confident, she left her parents in Pennsylvania and traveled to New York when she was just 15. Soon she found her first job in the city. She appeared in the chorus of *When You Smile* between 1925 and 1926. Next she worked in a series of nightclubs: Jimmy Durante's Silver Slipper Club, the Fifth Avenue Club, the New Yorker Club, and the Jay C. Flippen Club. She then became Leonard Sillman's dancing partner in his vaudeville act. Despite her successes, Coca was not yet close to the celebrity she sought. She appeared in some minor stage roles, and toured vaudeville as Jill Cameron, Donna Hart, and Helen Gardner.

Coca finally received her big break when Sillman chose her to appear (along with the yet-unknown actor Henry Fonda) in his 1934 revue, *New Faces*. During a rehearsal, the 5-foot-3-inch, 112-pound Coca put on a borrowed overcoat and proceeded to perform a mock striptease: when she opened the coat at the dance's conclusion, she was facing the rear of the stage. The act was so funny, Sillman added it to his show, and audiences and critics alike began to take notice of Coca. She continued to work for Sillman and toured with stock companies for the next few years.

Coca managed to enjoy a thriving personal life as she worked. In 1935, she met and married Bob Burton, who was appearing with her in Sillman's *Fools Rush In*. World War II, however, interrupted her marriage and her work with her husband. Coca moved back to Philadelphia to live with her mother and nearly retired. A jaunt to New York to audition for *Oklahoma!* renewed her desire to perform, even though she did not land a part in the musical. Instead, she began to tour clubs with her act, which included "Cavalcade of Oldtime Movie Stars" and a parody of an all-girl orchestra.

It was not until late 1948 that Coca finally found the role for which she would become the most famous. Max Liebman, who had worked with Coca during a series of weekly revues at the Taminment, believed he could make a star of the entertainer in his television project, the *Admiral Broadway Revue*. While the project proved successful for National Broadcasting Company, Inc. (NBC-TV) in 1949, the program served Coca best by pairing her with Sid Caesar, who would become her comic partner and good friend. The two shared a humorous chemistry that delighted audiences; when Liebman pioneered a new project, *Your Show of Shows*, Coca and Caesar went with him.

Audiences Delight in Coca's Comedy

Largely because of the talents of Coca and Caesar, *Your Show of Shows*, which premiered on February 25, 1950, became what many critics consider to be one of the best programs of television's "Golden Age." For 90 live minutes every week, the petite Coca and larger Caesar, along with other actors, performed hilarious sketches, exaggerated dances, silly songs, parodies, and pantomimes for enthusiastic television audiences throughout the United States. Coca's husband advised her and arranged most of the music she used in her sketches. The comedienne was named "Tops in TV" by a *Saturday Review of Literature* poll in 1951, and she was nominated for an Emmy for best television actress.

Coca was dispirited when *Your Show of Shows* was canceled in mid-1954. While she was given her own program, *The Imogene Coca Show*, the production lasted just one season. The performer suffered another blow in 1955 when her husband died. Nevertheless, she continued to entertain others. She appeared on stage in *The Girls in 509*. During the play's run she met King Donovan, and the couple married almost one year later. With Donovan, Coca starred in more than 35 stage shows, including *The Gin Game* in 1984. She also worked on television: She was a maid in the series *Grindl* in 1963, and she appeared in the series *It's about Time* in 1966 and on *Sid Caesar Invites You*. Later in the 1970s, she guest starred in episodes of television's *Love American Style*, *Night Gallery*, *The Brady Bunch*, and *Wide World of Mystery*. She also had roles in the made-for television movies *The Emperor's New Clothes* and *The Return of the Beverly Hillbillies*. Her film credits include *Under the Yum Yum Tree* in 1963, *Rabbit Test* in 1978, *National Lampoon's Vacation* in 1983, and *Nothing Lasts Forever* in 1985. In 1987, Coca continued to perform, traveling on a demanding five-month, bus-and-truck tour of *On the Twentieth Century* across the United States.

In April, 1990, at the age of 81, the actress reteamed with Caesar for a reunion show, *Together Again*, at Michael's Pub in New York City, to celebrate the 40th anniversary of their work on *Your Show of Shows*. *Together Again* featured new and old material, as well as several members from the initial production. A critic for the *New York Times* gave the new effort a favorable review and noted, "At a time when topical stand-up humor is a glut on the entertainment market, Mr. Caesar and Miss Coca offer a reassuring reminder that there is still such a thing as classic comedy . . . one happy discovery of seeing the show is that their brand of comedy is immune to age and time." As a result of the reunion's success, MTV secured the rights to the original *Your Show of Shows*, arranged sketches into 65 half-hour segments, and featured them for a young to middle-aged audience on its HA! channel. In addition, several videos featuring segments of *Your Show of Shows* entered the entertainment market.

The critic for the *New York Times* also wrote, "Miss Coca, with her goofy ear-to-ear grin, buggy eyes and diminutive stature is an eternal innocent beside Mr. Caesar's knowing and beleaguered everyman. And when Miss Coca speaks, her clear, musical voice, so evocative of laughter just below the surface, complements her air of purity." Another reviewer for the *Times* commented, "However wispy she may appear, Ms. Coca easily held her own in the raucous, Plautus-like sketches. A movement of the nose or forehead could transform her from a demure aristocrat into a vicious gun moll." Audiences also enjoyed the show: *Together Again* was produced in Westwood, California, and Chicago, Illinois, as well as in New York City.

Coca "simply loves the stage," according to a *Time* magazine commentator. Various critics contend that the performer's fans can easily discern her affection for show business through her performances. As long as she is able to do so, Coca plans to continue to keep her audiences enchanted with her comic charm and lasting enthusiasm.

Sources:

Books

Contemporary Theatre, Film, and Television, Volume 2, Gale, 1986.

Periodicals

Atlanta Journal, December 26, 1985, p. C15.
Chicago Tribune, September 2, 1990, Section 13, p. 10; September 18, 1990, Section 1, p. 20.
Life, February 2, 1951, p. 53.
Los Angeles Times, September 5, 1990, p. F1; September 19, 1991, p. F1; September 23, 1991, p. F1.
New York Times, April 15, 1990, Section 2, p. 7; April 27, 1990, p. C14.
Time, April 20, 1987, pp. 11-12.
Washington Post, June 10, 1990, Section WSP, p. 12.

—*Sketch by Ronie-Richele Garcia-Johnson*

Judith Ortiz Cofer
(1952-)
Educator, poet, novelist

"**W**e lived in Puerto Rico until my brother was born in 1954," wrote poet, essayist, and fiction writer Judith Ortiz Cofer. "Soon after, because of economic pressures on our growing family, my father joined the United States Navy. He was assigned to duty on a ship in Brooklyn Yard . . . that was to be his home base in the States until his retirement more than twenty years later." In these brief sentences from an essay published in *Georgia Review* and included as part of her *Silent Dancing: A Partial Remembrance of a Puerto Rican Childhood,* the reader is introduced to the dual reality that makes up Cofer's literary universe. Her work focuses on the effect on Puerto Rican Americans of living in a world split between the island culture of their homeland and the teeming tenement life of the United States.

Although Cofer was born on February 24, 1952, in Hormigueros, Puerto Rico, the daughter of J. M. and Fanny Morot Cofer, she was brought to the United States when quite young. The family's official residence was in Paterson, New Jersey, but whenever her father's Navy job took him to sea, Cofer and her mother and brother stayed in Puerto Rico with her maternal family. As a child Cofer spoke only Spanish at first, and later was introduced to the English language, a process she found difficult, but rewarding.

Begins Career as English Teacher

She eventually earned a bachelor of arts degree in English from Augusta College in 1973 and a master of arts in English from Florida Atlantic University in 1977. Since receiving her advanced degree, Cofer has served as an English instructor at several institutions, including the University of Miami, the University of Georgia, and the Georgia Center for Continuing Education. "It was a challenge, not only to learn English," she notes in *Contemporary Authors,* "but to master it enough to teach it and—the ultimate goal—to write poetry in it."

Cofer's first books of poetry were three chapbooks—*Latin Women Pray, The Native Dancer,* and *Among the Ancestors*—published in the early 1980s. Three more volumes of poetry followed in the same decade: *Peregrina* in 1986 and *Terms of Survival* and *Reaching for the Mainland* in 1987. Branching out from poetry by the end of the decade, Cofer saw the release of her novel, *The Line of the Sun,* in 1989, and a volume of poetry and personal essays, *Silent Dancing,* in 1990. Among the honors she has received for her work are a 1989 National Endowment for the Arts fellowship in poetry and the 1990 Pushcart Prize for Nonfiction.

Cofer's first novel, *The Line of the Sun,* was lauded by various critics for its poetic qualities. In the *New York Times Book Review,* for example, Roberto Márquez described Cofer as "a prose writer of evocatively lyrical authority." In the *Los Angeles Times Book Review* Sonja Bolle also referred to the beauty of many of the novel's passages. The book is narrated by Marisol Santa Luz Vivente who tells the story of three generations of her family. The first part of the book describes the origins of the Vivente clan in the Puerto Rican village of Salud and introduces the reader to the culture and landscape of the island. The second part of the novel is set in Paterson, New Jersey, where Marisol strives to find an equilibrium between the clashing values of her Puerto Rican ancestors and those of her new American home.

Work Delves into Dual Culturalism

The same conflict appears in the autobiographical essays and poems that make up Cofer's *Silent Dancing.* The title is derived from the author's memories of a silent home movie filmed at a New Year's Eve party when her parents were young, which ends with a silent conga line of revelers. As each of the dancers comes into view she comments on how each has responded to the cultural differences in their lives. She writes of her fascination with the short clip in the book's title essay: "The five-minute movie ends with people dancing in a circle—the creative filmmaker must have set it up, so that all of them could file past him. It is both comical and sad to watch silent dancing."

In *Contemporary Authors* Cofer explained her use of autobiographical elements in her poetry. Her words seem equally applicable to her more recent works of fiction and autobiography. "My family is one of the main topics of my poetry," she notes. "In tracing their lives, I discover more about mine. The place of birth itself becomes a metaphor for the things we all must leave behind; the assimilation of a new culture is the coming into maturity by accepting the terms necessary for survival. My poetry is a study of this process of change, cultural assimilation, and transformation."

Sources:

Books

Cofer, Judith Ortiz, *Silent Dancing: A Partial Remembrance of a Puerto Rican Childhood,* Arte Público, 1990.
Contemporary Authors New Revision Series, Volume 32, Gale, 1991.

Periodicals

Georgia Review, spring/summer, 1990, pp. 51-59.
Los Angeles Times Book Review, August 6, 1989, p. 6.
New York Times Book Review, September 24, 1989, pp. 46-47.
Women's Review of Books, December, 1990, p. 9.

—*Sketch by Marian C. Gonsior*

Margarita H. Colmenares

Margarita H. Colmenares
(1957-)
Environmental engineer

Margarita H. Colmenares is the first Hispanic engineer to have been selected as a White House Fellow since the program's establishment in 1964. During her fellowship in 1991 and 1992, Colmenares served as special assistant to Deputy Secretary of Education David T. Kearns in Washington, D.C. Prior to becoming one of only 400 who have entered the program in its nearly 30 years of existence, Colmenares was president of the Society of Hispanic Professional Engineers—the first woman to head the organization—with the status of executive-on-loan from Chevron Corporation.

Throughout her life, Colmenares has used her talents as a leader to promote education. "Thirty years ago this country made a commitment to put a man on the moon," she wrote in a *Hispanic* magazine article. "The federal government passed the National Defense Education Act, which poured monies into our nation's schools to improve science equipment and instruction.... Now we need a similar commitment from our national leaders in government, private industry, educators and students in order to produce a workforce qualified to fill the increasing number of technical positions for the labor market."

Colmenares's story is one of hard work, determination, and a constant desire to learn. "As a child, I spent hours reading all the books I could get from the library," she commented in an interview with Michelle Vachon. "They were taking me out of my environment and putting me in touch with the world." She was born on July 20, 1957, in Sacramento, California, the eldest of five children. Her parents had emmigrated from Oaxaca, Mexico, and settled a few blocks away from the state capitol. "People in the neighborhood were working-class immigrants who would go where the jobs were," she remarked. "So, families changed all the time, and I always had to make new friends." Kids on her street did not have back yards—they met and played on the sidewalk. "I realized only years later what it meant to have your own back yard," Colmenares noted. Her world was bicultural, with children speaking in both Spanish and English among themselves. Colmenares's parents insisted on sending their girls to private Catholic institutions from elementary school on. "They wanted to provide us with the best possible education, even though this meant big sacrifices on their part," she told Vachon. In her all-girl high school, she started an organization for Mexican American students. "We had to meet before school at 7 a.m. because I had part-time jobs at night," she remembered.

College Presents Opportunities in Engineering

Colmenares had to wait until college for the opportunity to learn about careers in engineering. "In high school, I got trapped in shorthand and typing courses. Our math and science program was quite weak, and I was not encouraged to prepare for college," she commented. Still, with the support of her parents, who had never doubted that she would further her education, Colmenares began a business course of study at California State University, Sacramento. In her freshman year, however, she "discovered engineering by accident" and realized that this was the career she had been looking for. Lacking the prerequisites to be admitted to an engineering program, Colmenares returned to junior college and took chemistry, physics, and calculus at Sacramento City College. In the meantime, she began looking for part-time work in engineering. She applied to the California Department of Water Resources and landed an assignment with "Project Surveillance." This consisted of inspecting and reporting on the structural conditions of dams and water-purifying plants. So after school, over holidays, and during summer vacations she wore a hard hat and boots and crawled under dams. The experience helped her in school. "I had the opportunity to see how to use classroom theories to solve problems in the field," she noted.

Colmenares secured five university scholarships—federal, state, and private—and attended Stanford University, south of San Francisco. "Those years were wonderful! The golden time," exclaimed Colmenares. "Still, it was highly competitive—you had to study hard!" During her Stanford years, she learned to focus on long-term goals while developing and maintaining a balance between work and play. "One constant in my life has been to juggle work with community activities and, at that time, school. I've done every part-time job, from flipping burgers to office tasks. Since I didn't want to give up anything, I found a way to combine what I love and make it work," she explained to Vachon. So she taught the Stanford Ballet Folklorico for a year—she was its codirector—and performed with the group at community festivals and senior citizen homes. "This kept me in touch with the real world," she noted. On weekends, she tutored and served as undergraduate research assistant for graduate students in the mechanical engineering department.

Between her junior and senior years, Colmenares entered the Chevron Corporation's Co-Op Education Program, and spent nine months working full time for the company in El Paso, Texas, and in California. Upon graduation with a B.S. in civil engineering in 1981, she joined Chevron's staff. Her first position was field construction engineer for the company's northern California office. Her duties included preparing estimates and contracts and supervising the construction of marketing facilities—gas terminals, bulk storage facilities, service stations—in the San Francisco Bay area. "The work involved a lot of interaction with the public, and it was really fun," she recalled in her interview. Already a member of the Society of Hispanic Professional Engineers (SHPE), Colmenares founded the society's San Francisco chapter in 1982 and served as its president until 1984. Away from work she also performed with Los Lupenos, a Mexican folkloric dance group of San Jose, California.

At Chevron, Colmenares served as San Francisco recruiting coordinator. Later on, she was assigned to a field construction position that entailed living in Salt Lake City, reporting to the Denver regional office, and working in Colorado, Utah, Idaho, and Nevada. "It was great! In most cases, I was the first female construction engineer with whom contractors had ever dealt. Actually, I have usually been the first woman to hold most of the positions I've had in my career," she admitted to Vachon. In 1983, Colmenares interviewed for a foreign training representative post at Chevron's world headquarters in San Francisco, and was selected for the job over other candidates with more seniority. The position involved the planning of training programs for Chevron's international visitors. Programs could last from two days to two years. Colmenares had the chance to meet engineers, lawyers, and business people from Saudi Arabia, Venezuela, and Indonesia, and to develop a global view.

Takes on Role of Compliance Specialist

Next, Colmenares was offered the position of compliance specialist at the central division of its Houston marketing operations. "I had always had an interest in environmental protection," she told Vachon. "So I jumped at the opportunity to take the job." Her duties consisted of insuring compliance with federal, state, and local environmental, safety, fire, and health regulations at Chevron's facilities. Colmenares had to keep abreast of all the ever-changing sets of regulations and guidelines, inspect the corporation's facilities, and manage and coordinate compliance activities with the managerial staff. Her territory, which was originally limited to one region, eventually covered five states. Colmenares still found time to be SHPE's regional vice president, a panelist for the Cultural Arts Council, and a member of the board of directors of the Texas Hispanic Women's Network.

Three years later, she was assigned to an $18 million environmental cleanup project at the Chevron refinery in El Segundo, near Los Angeles. As lead engineer, she was responsible for overall coordination of design and construction of the subsurface and injection system. In addition to supervising the technical staff, she acted as liaison between the refinery personnel and the air quality regulatory agencies. "I learned a lot about the problems of managing such a facility in an area with high-density population. It was exciting to be part of the solution," she remarked to Vachon. Having developed an expertise in environmental engineering, Colmenares gained a promotion to air quality specialist at the El Segundo facility in 1989. She reviewed and interpreted the impact of air regulations on refinery operations, and provided guidance in the preparation of air permit applications for the construction and operation of new and modified equipment and facilities.

Serves as President of the SHPE

In 1989, Colmenares became SHPE's national president, following her term as the society's national chairperson of civic affairs and chairperson of leadership development. Colmenares formulated an ambitious program for the society, which she saw as a strong promotional tool for engineering careers as well as a powerful professional group. But Colmenares soon realized that she could not achieve her goals if she remained president on a part-time basis. "I submitted to Chevron a short proposal outlining what I wanted to accomplish," she told Vachon. "And the corporation said yes! I became an executive-on-loan to SHPE for a year, while staying on Chevron's payroll. The corporation rarely lets go of an employee for such a long period of time."

The following months were extraordinarily busy and exciting for Colmenares. The society numbers over 30 professional and 100 student chapters throughout the country, and Colmenares wanted to visit them all. Her goals were monumental. "We need to establish the blueprint for the next ten to fifteen years for SHPE," she commented in *Hispanic Engineer*. "We need to continue what we've been doing, but we need to accelerate the pace. And we want to think big."

She first applied herself to strengthening the professional chapters and encouraging their members to take on a leadership role in their communities. Her plan was to have the society help SHPE members get elected to any positions that could have an impact on education, engineering, or policy making. Then, she undertook to tour the country's schools, colleges, and universities and inspire Hispanic students to consider careers in science and engineering. Colmenares also asked politicians at every level of government to make education a priority. "Education is the key to world leadership and [the United States is] not keeping up," she noted in *Hispanic* magazine. "Education is the key to technological superiority; yet our nation continues to lag behind. . . . Hispanics have the potential to produce the engineers of tomorrow who are going to contribute to . . . technological, economic, environmental, energy and transportation challenges. . . . Given the opportunity and the resources, Hispanics are ready to contribute to this challenge. The United States must invest today in the Hispanic community in order to secure its position in the future as a world leader."

"The months of my presidency were wonderful," Colmenares told Vachon. "It renewed my optimism and hope for our nation to discover that there are thousands of volunteers out there who believe in education and try to make a difference every day of the week." As her term was coming to an end, colleagues and peers suggested that she apply for a White House Fellowship.

Started under President Lyndon B. Johnson, the program draws exceptionally promising people to Washington for one year of personal involvement in the process of government. In the course of that year, fellows meet with heads of government departments and agencies, and build a network of powerful connections. The candidates, who come from all sectors—academic, professional, business, governmental and artistic—undergo a rigorous three-phase application process. Colmenares passed with flying colors and became one of the 16-member White House Fellowship class of 1991-1992, the first Hispanic engineer to be selected. Again, Chevron Corporation supported her. Will Price, the president of Chevron U.S.A., issued a statement expressing his pride in Colmenares as the corporation's first fellow and granted her a one-year leave of absence. Colmenares subsequently moved to Washington, D.C., to participate in the program.

Joins Department of Education for Fellowship

When asked which government department or agency she would like to join during her fellowship, Colmenares indicated as her first choice the Department of Education. "It turned out that I was also their first choice of a fellow," Colmenares told Vachon. She became special assistant to David T. Kearns, the Department of Education's deputy secretary, who had obtained a leave of absence from his position of Xerox Corporation's chairman of the board to join the department. During her school years, Colmenares had taken part in the Xerox Employee Community Involvement program and worked for the corporation part time and over the summer. "I owed my first experience of corporate business to Xerox," she commented. "Now assistant to its CEO, I had come full circle!"

Her fellow's schedule did not leave her a moment to spare. At the Department of Education, she worked on the first coordinated effort on the part of 16 governmental agencies to develop a strategic plan for science and math education. Her fellowship class attended series of meetings with heads of government departments and agencies. "These were in-depth discussions with members of the federal elite," Colmenares recalled. "We really had to do our homework and come prepared with pertinent questions." The fellows spent a few weeks in Eastern Europe, visited

Moscow and St. Petersburg, and went on a few domestic trips to meet the country's leaders in both public and private sectors. "I enjoy meeting leaders," Colmenares remarked. "I study each person's style and learn something new every time." Colmenares had always taken leadership seriously. "Good leaders strive for consistency in both their personal and public lives," she told *Hispanic Engineer* after her election to SHPE's presidency. "People will be observing how you act when you're on and off the court. Be consistent in how you behave ethically and morally. . . . Apply the same principles you live by to your elected office."

Colmenares believes in constantly improving her own leadership skills. In 1989, she participated in the National Hispana Leadership Initiative, a program designed especially for U.S. Hispanic women. It included training sessions in public policy at Harvard's John F. Kennedy School of Government and the Center for Creative Leadership. In 1990, she entered the Leadership America training program for Hispanic women leaders and attended lectures given by national public figures and experts. The same year she was a delegate at the U.S.-Mexico Emerging Leaders conference organized by the American Center for International Leadership, a delegate at the national conference of the Union Pan America de Ingenioros (the Pan-American Society of Engineers), and a member of the Hispanic women's delegation to the Encuentros Mexicanos (Mexican Meetings) conference.

Colmenares's commitment to the Hispanic community has won her widespread recognition. In 1989, she received the Community Service Award from *Hispanic Engineer* magazine, was named SHPE's Hispanic Role Model of the Year and one of *Hispanic* magazine's Outstanding Women of the Year. In 1990 and 1992, *Hispanic Business* magazine recognized her as one of the 100 most influential Hispanics in the country. And in 1991, Colmenares became the youngest recipient of the California Community College League's Outstanding Alumni Award. She was also presented with the Pioneer Award at the Hispanic Engineers National Achievement Awards Conference, and was profiled on the Public Broadcasting Service (PBS) series "Choice for Youth."

In the next few years, Colmenares plans to go to graduate school, possibly in the area of public policy connected with education and engineering. She maintains that engineers have to broaden their knowledge outside their fields of specialization in order to become effective community leaders. "When you get to the real world," she stressed in *Graduating Engineer*, "you'll need it all. It's the whole concept of the well-rounded person with depth to go along with expertise." Her life-long goal remains to increase the number of Hispanics in scientific and engineering careers. If this means reforming the U.S. educational system to improve science and mathematics teaching and better prepare students for college, Colmenares is willing to take on the challenge.

Sources:

Periodicals

Chevron Focus, April, 1990, p. 40.
Department of Water Resources News (Sacramento, CA), January, 1990, p. 14.
El Heraldo Catolico (Sacramento, CA), November 22, 1989, p. 8.
El Hispano, (Sacramento, CA), May 11, 1978, p. 1.
El Tiempo (Sacramento, CA), July 5, 1989, p. 10.
Graduating Engineer, October, 1991, pp. 39-40, 88.
Hispanic, October, 1989, p. 46; December, 1989, p. 44; March, 1990, p. 66; November, 1990, p. 32.
Hispanic Business, October, 1992, p. 78.
Hispanic Engineer, conference issue, 1989, p. 43; fall, 1989, pp. 22-24.
National Hispana Leadership Institute (Denver, CO), September, 1989, p. 11.
National Hispanic Reporter, October, 1990, pp. 1-15.
Sacramento City College Express, May 11, 1978, p. 2.
Vista, June 25, 1989, pp. 6-8; August 27, 1989, p. 3; March 17, 1990, pp. 5-10; September 30, 1990, p. 16.

Other

Colmenares, Margarita H., interview with Michelle Vachon, May 18, 1992.
Reynoso, Silvia, "Woman for All Seasons" (student essay), California State University, Sacramento, April 31, 1990.

—Sketch by Michelle Vachon

Ana Colomar O'Brien
(1938-)
Diplomat

"**A**s a Latina woman, you have to prove yourself [more] than others because you are a woman," Ana Colomar O'Brien, chief of protocol of the Organization of the American States (OAS), told interviewer Luis Vasquez-Ajmac. But Colomar O'Brien has never faced a challenge thinking that she was at a disadvantage. "I was raised up with the idea that nothing falls from heaven," she continued. "If you work hard, you can succeed at life."

Born November 16, 1938, in Havana, Cuba, Colomar O'Brien described her childhood as "privileged" in the sense that she had very loving and supportive parents, Fernando and Ana Colomar. As an only child, she was never sent away when company came; if there were financial, literary, or political discussions, she was always included. Colomar O'Brien's father, Spanish-born, was a lawyer in Cuba and became a senior high school teacher when he immigrated to the United States. Her mother, born in Cuba, was a dedicated housewife and mother.

Colomar O'Brien spent her early years in Mexico and returned to Havana to continue her education. She earned a baccalaureate degree from Vedado Institute in 1958 and a master's degree in English language and culture from Havana University in 1968. Before relocating to the United States, Colomar O'Brien taught English at the Vedado Institute from 1964 to 1968. In 1969 Colomar O'Brien moved to New York and earned a B.A. in history with distinction from Queens College of the City University of New York in 1971. While attending Queens College, she supported herself working days as a public relations assistant at AVCO Embassy Pictures, a motion picture company that eventually went bankrupt.

Colomar O'Brien's interest in the public relations field continued when she moved to Washington, D.C., in 1974. During her eight years with MacKenzie McCheyne, Inc., as vice president, Colomar O'Brien worked closely with Latin American governments and heads of state, and arranged meetings with the State Department and other private organizations. She also counseled and represented American and foreign clients before the Administration, Congress, and the public. In 1982, Colomar O'Brien was hired as special assistant to the assistant secretary for Territorial and International Affairs at the Department of Interior. Colomar O'Brien worked with government officials in the U.S. Territories and the Trust Territory of the Pacific Island and was principal advisor on matters of policy in the Caribbean area. She also developed proposals for cooperative interagency programs aimed at economic development of the Virgin Islands and American Samoa.

Colomar O'Brien, a mother of two who lives in Springfield, Virginia, took on a more visible position internationally as chief of protocol of the OAS where she has worked since April of 1986. She acts as liaison to the 34 delegations and the U.S. Department of State on numerous tasks. She also oversees signing ceremonies for treaties and organizes official and social functions given by the Permanent Council, the Secretary General, and other high officials at the OAS. Preparing for major visits at the OAS is perhaps Colomar O'Brien's more demanding responsibility in terms of logistical support and preparation. She cites President Reagan's visit as particularly difficult due to the stringent security measures. The King of Spain's visit was also complicated in terms of protocol. Acknowledged by both of these visitors for her hard work, Colomar O'Brien finds such praise rewarding despite the overall pressure to perform well.

Sources:

Colomar O'Brien, Ana, interview with Luis Vasquez-Ajmac, August 4, 1992.

—Sketch by Luis Vasquez-Ajmac

Colón, Marie Acosta
See Acosta-Colón, Marie

Miriam Colon
(1945-)
Actress, director, playwright

Miriam Colon, a pioneer of the Hispanic theater movement in New York, founded and serves as director of the Puerto Rican Traveling Theater and co-founded the Nuevo Circulo Dramatico, the first Spanish-language theater in New York. A performer in theater as well as film and television, Colon was described in the *New York Times* as "the most famous Puerto Rican actress in America."

Colon, born in 1945 to working-class parents in the city of Ponce, Puerto Rico, emphasizes the importance of her mother's influence. "My mother has been the major force in my life," she commented in an interview with Gloria Bonilla-Santiago. "To this day, I am very, very attached to her. She is my role model . . . [and] a wonderful, warm woman. I am totally sure of her love—the only thing I'm sure of in my life." Her mother's encouragement allowed Colon to pursue her career in the arts. "'If you want to, be an actor,' she would say, as long as I didn't come home too late," Colon related. "She never pushed me away from the direction I wanted to go."

A scholarship to the Dramatic Workshop and Technical Institute in New York City paved the way for Colon's entry into the theater world. After earning her degree, Colon embarked on a career that has included work both behind the scenes and in the spotlight of plays, movies, and television programs. She made her Broadway debut in 1953 with *In the Summer House,* and also appeared in *The Innkeepers* in 1956 and *The Wrong Way Lightbulb* in 1980. Her film appearances include *One-Eyed Jacks,* 1961, and

The Appaloosa, 1966, both starring Marlon Brando, *The Possession of Joe Delaney,* 1972, starring Shirley MacLaine, *Back Roads,* 1961, starring Sally Field, and the 1983 version of *Scarface,* starring Al Pacino. In addition, Colon has appeared in more than 250 television shows.

A trailblazer in her career, Colon has encountered struggles in her personal life as well. She described her second husband as "a sophisticated man, a very strong man" who supported her work. When he died, Colon related, "I was emotionally devastated." She turned to her work for comfort, "trying to turn the energy out instead of in." When she met her current husband, an actor in a play she was directing, "I really was not looking for romance. But I found I was developing an interest in him. . . . I was amazed that I still had the capacity to love and trust and to give of myself."

Works to Provide Opportunities for Hispanics

Throughout her career Colon has worked for further recognition and opportunities for Hispanics in the performing arts. She was the first Puerto Rican accepted as a member of the famed Actors Studio, and was appointed by then-Governor Nelson Rockefeller to New York's Council on the Arts, a position she held for over ten years. She also served on the Expansion Arts Panel of the National Endowment for the Arts, and acts as a cultural adviser to state and national organizations. Her Puerto Rican Traveling Theater, housed in a former fire station, has provided a stage for perhaps her most important contribution: the premieres of almost 50 plays by dramatists from Chile, Puerto Rico, Spain, Venezuela, Columbia, Brazil, and Mexico in the last 25 years.

Colon has been recognized for her achievements with awards from the National Council of Christians and Jews, the Puerto Rican Legal Defense and Education Fund, the University of the State of New York, and the Asociacion de Cronistas de Espectaculos de Nueva York. She received the Mayor's Award of Honor for the Arts and Culture in 1982 from New York City Mayor Edward Koch, and was presented with the Athena Award from the New York Commission on the Status of Women in 1985.

Colon told Bonilla-Santiago that her overriding goal in life is "to leave the Puerto Rican Traveling Theater very stable, artistically and financially. I have not achieved that—maybe on the artistic side, because we have national respect and recognition, [but] I am unhappy about the financial side. I would be happy if l could say that the theater has a reserve of half a million dollars in the bank with all expenses paid, [but] we are not in that position." With her numerous contributions to the promotion of Hispanics in the arts, as well as the monument of the Puerto Rican Traveling Theater, Colon's wish to be remembered as an artist who never forgot her people should be easily fulfilled.

Sources:

Periodicals

Daily News, August 7, 1982, p. 16.
Daily News Magazine, April 19, 1982, p. 20.
El Diario La Prensa, June 19, 1980, pp. 1-36; August 11, 1982, p. 4.
New York Times, September 12, 1971, pp. 1-2; April 8, 1987, p. 9A.
San Juan Star, April 16, 1979, p. 5.
Soho News, April 8, 1981, p. 2.

Other

Colon, Miriam, interview with Gloria Bonilla-Santiago, February 17, 1989.

—Sketch by Gloria Bonilla-Santiago

Victoria Corderi
(1957-)
Broadcast journalist

"**I** never really wanted to be famous. I never really wanted to be somebody who walked down the streets besieged with fans," Victoria Corderi said in an interview with Luis Vasquez-Ajmac. "What I really always wanted to be was respected in my field, and I think I have achieved that." The youngest reporter to have joined the CBS network in 1985 and the first Hispanic to become a national network anchor, Corderi has worked as a CBS news correspondent for the CBS news magazine series *Street Stories,* which premiered in January 1992, and serves as a frequent contributor to the CBS News series *48 Hours.*

Born in New York City in 1957, Corderi was raised in New Jersey in a very Cuban household. Growing up with American friends and Cuban parents made finding her own identity difficult. As she told Vasquez-Ajmac, "I didn't quite feel totally American, and I didn't feel totally Hispanic either because I was born here." But, in the end, Corderi identified most with her Hispanic background. She studied Spanish and Latin American culture in college, travelled to Spain for over a year, lived in Miami for ten years, and ultimately became a reporter whose specialty was covering Central America.

When growing up, Corderi always knew that she would be a writer of some kind. She majored in journalism at St.

Bonaventure University and graduated magna cum laude in 1979. One year later, Corderi landed her first job as a reporter for the *Miami News.*

In 1982, Corderi began her career in television at WPLG-TV Miami, covering the city's political and federal agencies. In 1985, CBS News offered Corderi a position as a reporter. After an assignment with the CBS News Northeast Bureau in New York, Corderi joined the CBS News Los Angeles Bureau in 1986, and began work in the network's Miami Bureau in 1987.

Chooses Hard-Hitting Assignments

Corderi returned to New York City as a correspondent in January 1990 and has remained there ever since. She co-anchored the *CBS Morning News* and news segments of *CBS This Morning* until the fall of 1991. Of all the assignments that Corderi has done, she is particularly proud of her coverage of Haiti, for which she was nominated for an Emmy Award. Spending more than a year in Haiti, Corderi covered all the events leading up to what was to be Haiti's first democratic election but instead became a bloody massacre. Admired for her talent in reporting, Corderi has been awarded numerous prestigious awards. In 1990, Corderi earned an Emmy Award for her coverage on "48 Hours: Women Doing Time" and was part of two CBS news teams receiving Emmy Awards in 1989 for "48 Hours: Showdown in Cheyenne" and "48 Hours on Gang Street." To Corderi's credit, she has also received an Emmy Award for a five-part investigative series on Cuban organized crime in the United States, a National Unity Award from the University of Missouri for a two-part series on Miami slumlords, and a United Press International Award for spot news.

Having found the success she hoped for, Corderi decided to take time off. "I am at a real crossroads in my life," she told Vasquez-Ajmac, in April, 1992. Being very family-oriented, Corderi—who is married and gave birth to her daughter Cristina in the summer of 1992—struck a balance between family and career life when in September, 1992, she began working at WABC-TV in New York City as an anchor and reporter, a job that involves no traveling and takes her just two blocks from home.

Sources:

Periodicals

Hispanic, June, 1991, p. 11.
Parade Magazine, October 6, 1991, p. 4.

Other

Corderi, Victoria, telephone interview with Luis Vasquez-Ajmac, April 23, 1992.

—*Sketch by Luis Vasquez-Ajmac*

Elaine Coronado
(1959-)
President, Hispanic Alliance for Free Trade

Elaine Coronado, named one of the United States' one hundred most influential Hispanics of 1991 by *Hispanic Business* magazine, has worked as president of the Hispanic Alliance for Free Trade, Inc., to educate Hispanic Americans in the benefits and implications of the North American Free Trade Agreement and mobilized the Hispanic business community into a strong coalition of lobbyists for its passage. She credits her previous experience as executive director of the National Hispanic Quincentennial Commission with further enlightening her to the current status of Hispanic Americans.

The eldest of four children and the only daughter, Coronado was born August 6, 1959, in San Antonio, Texas, to Col. Gil and Helen Coronado. From ages six to 22, Coronado's home was wherever her father was stationed, including military bases in Germany, Spain and Panama; she moved to San Antonio, Texas, before settling in Washington, D.C., in 1989. While in Texas, Coronado studied business at the University of Texas—San Antonio from 1977 to 1980, and was recognized as the university's Outstanding Sophomore of the Year in 1980. However, after discovering the arts and the Prado Museum in Spain, Coronado changed her academic emphasis to liberal arts while attending the University of St. Louis in Madrid. Subsequently, she earned a B.A. in history in 1983 from the University of Texas—San Antonio. Upon graduation, she began work at Automatic Data Processing, a billion-dollar company in San Antonio, where she was promoted to marketing coordinator. She received the Outstanding Young Woman of America award in 1986.

Coronado's pride in her Mexican American background and professional interest in Hispanic issues developed when she was about 20 years old and has driven her to promote Hispanic concerns ever since. In April, 1989, Coronado was hired by the National Hispanic Quincentennial Commission, Inc., to advocate Hispanic-related issues. As executive director, Coronado made strides in fund-raising, recruitment of new members, and expansion of the Commission's network. "I learned a lot about our history and left with a better understanding of where we fit into the whole public policy issue," Coronado commented in an interview with Luis Vasquez-Ajmac.

Though Coronado helped bring attention to the issues surrounding the 500th anniversary of Columbus' voyage, she felt a real frustration with the division within the community about the Quincentenary. She told Vasquez-Ajmac, "We are not as organized when it comes to our history as the black community is. . . . They have TV programs that bring attention to their history and contemporary heroes. We just don't do that. We try to, but no one wants to back us up financially."

In January, 1991, Coronado left the Quincentennial Commission to help Hispanics on a greater level legislatively as founder and president of the Hispanic Alliance for Free Trade, Inc. As the trade negotiations came to a close in 1992, Coronado planned her next career move. She wants to start her own company in 1993 and eventually get into politics at some level, perhaps helping Hispanic women into political office. What Coronado feels particularly proud of now is having her own career. "I have life experiences," Coronado remarked to Vasquez-Ajmac. "I can choose what I want and don't want to do."

Sources:

Coronado, Elaine, interview with Luis Vasquez-Ajmac, July 22, 1992.

—Sketch by Luis Vasquez-Ajmac

Lucha Corpi
(1945-)
Writer, teacher

Although born and raised in Mexico and not a resident of the United States until nearly twenty, Lucha Corpi has identified herself with the Chicano community. She has contributed her poems to Chicano journals and has seen her work included in an important anthology of Chicano literature, *Chicanos: Antología histórica y literaria* ("Chicanos: Historic and Literary Anthology"). Critic Barbara Brinson Curiel finds the focus of Corpi's work in the plight of women in modern culture. In Curiel's *Dictionary of Literary Biography* essay she writes that two of Corpi's most important "concerns are women cornered by the circumstances of their lives and a notion that fate is inescapable."

Corpi was born on April 13, 1945, to Miguel Angel Corpi and Victoria C. de Corpi, in Jáltipan, in the state of Veracruz, Mexico. She received her bachelor of arts from the University of California, Berkeley, in 1975, and a master of arts in comparative literature from San Francisco State University in 1979. Since 1973, Corpi has taught English as a Second Language through the Oakland (California) Public School system. She has also worked as an instructor at Vista Junior College and served on the board of Aztlán Cultural, a Chicano organization for the arts.

In *Dictionary of Literary Biography*, Curiel maintains that Corpi's most important contribution to Chicano literature is a series of four poems called "The Marina Poems," which first appeared in the anthology *The Other Voice: Twentieth-Century Women's Poetry in Translation*, published by Norton in 1976 and subsequently included in Corpi's *Palabras de mediodía/Noon Words*, a bilingual edition published by *Fuego de Aztlán* in 1980. These poems are meditations on Doña Marina (also known as Malintzín Tenepal and *La Malinche*), the Indian woman who served as translator to Hernán Cortés during his conquest of Mexico.

These poems include Corpi's personal vision of the woman she chooses to call Marina, her Spanish name, rather than the derisive name, *La Malinche*, with which she is usually referred. Since the woman aided the man who conquered her country, the name *La Malinche* has become synonymous with traitor in the Hispanic culture. While contemporary male Mexican writers, such as Carlos Fuentes and Octavio Paz, see Marina as a woman who was fascinated by the foreign Spanish conquerors and, therefore, allowed herself to be violated, Corpi's poetry speaks of a woman fated to be an unwilling accomplice. In *Contemporary Chicana Poetry: A Critical Approach to an Emerging Literature*, Marta Ester Sánchez explains: "Corpi's Marina does not actively resist the rape. Rather, the reader must presuppose a reluctant Marina who felt she had no other choice but to submit, as men would force sex upon her in spite of her objections."

Curiel comments on Corpi's sensitive treatment of the historical figure of Marina. "Corpi portrays Marina," she notes, "as an individual rather than as a sorceress who through her evil caused the downfall of her people. She sees her as a victim caught between an old world and a new world, a woman who had journeyed from one culture and society to another and yet who had no home." Curiel maintains that "Marina reflects the experiences of many women from many cultures through time. Through her, Corpi reinterprets the historical circumstances which have fostered the devaluation of all Mexican women." The critic finds "The Marina Poems" deal with themes expressed in "Tres mujeres" ("Three Women"), an early story by Corpi.

Corpi is primarily known as a poet but has also written award-winning short fiction and novels. Her work has appeared in numerous anthologies, including *Chicanos: Antología histórica y literaria*, published in Mexico in 1980, and *A Decade of Hispanic Literature: An Anniversary Anthology*, published in 1983. Corpi's longer works include a novel, *Delia's Song*, which deals with a female character who leaves her family to study in California, and *Eulogy for a Brown Angel*, a 1992 feminist mystery novel featuring civil-rights activist Gloria Damasco, who discovers the body of boy killed during a 1970 Chicano demonstration in Los Angeles.

Corpi has received several awards for her writing, including a National Endowment for the Arts creative writing fellowship in 1979; first place in the *Palabra Nueva* literary competition for her short story, "Los cristos del alma" ("Martyrs of the Soul"), in 1983; and first place in the Chicano Literary Contest held at the University of California, Irvine, in 1984.

Sources:

Books

Dictionary of Literary Biography, Volume 82: *Chicano Writers*, Gale, 1989.

Sánchez, Marta Ester, *Contemporary Chicana Poetry: A Critical Approach to an Emerging Literature*, University of California Press, 1985.

—Sketch by Marian C. Gonsior

Oralia Lillie Corrales
(1940-)
Activist, insurance agent

Oralia Lillie Corrales endured hardships as a child farm worker before becoming a tireless community activist, a city council member, and a successful businesswoman. Over the course of her career she has developed programs for teenage mothers, filled deserted inner city homes with immigrants, and helped immigrants learn English and obtain legal resident status.

Corrales was born to O. H. Castillon and Adela Davila on July 5, 1940, in Midland, Texas. Her parents divorced when she was six. "It wasn't a very good life," she recalled in an interview with Anna Macias Aguayo. "We got to spend summers with our father in California. We would buy our own bus tickets. As soon as we got off the bus, they were ready to take us to pick crops—cotton, peaches, potatoes, onions, garlic, and grapes. We went from one migrant camp to the next until I was 14." She remembers how poor her family was; her mother supported 16 children. "I had only one little dress to wear to school," she recalled in her interview. "But everyday I would wash it and iron it. My teacher would compliment me. That's where I got my love for doing what I could for others."

Although she enjoyed school, Corrales was forced to leave in the ninth grade to help support the family. She was hired as a saleswoman at Woolworth's because she could speak Spanish and English. Later, a clinic hired her to translate for patients, and she kept a third job at a restau-

rant. Corrales eventually found time to pick up classes at Midland Community College and took extension courses with the University of New Mexico. At the age 14, she met Jesus Corrales, the man she would marry. He offered to give her a ride as she walked to all three jobs. "He was one of those persons that you can't get rid of no matter how hard you try," she described in her interview. "Fortunately, we've been happily married for 38 years." Corrales had four children of her own, legally adopted two children of a sister who died of cancer, and raised seven of her mother's children who were having problems in their own home.

"We have a table that seats at least 20," she said. "It's normally full. Now that we have grandkids, we set up some other tables in the living room." The many children in the Corrales home were one of the incentives for her work. "My husband didn't want me to work, period," she explained in her interview with Aguayo. "I didn't mean to offend him, but the kids needed shoes for baseball, track, basketball."

After working for a short time at Gibson's Discount Store, Corrales was hired by a community center to help develop programs for teenage mothers. Her next big move was to help fill 2,500 inner city homes that were left vacant when white, middle-class families migrated to the suburbs in 1969. Corrales successfully trained hundreds of Mexican immigrants on how to be good homeowners and obtain mortgage loans. Later, she helped the same group of immigrants learn English, study for driver's license tests and gain legal residence status.

From 1970 until 1975, Corrales was a social worker at Our Lady of Guadalupe Catholic Church. She quit her job to start a lawn and garden landscaping service so that the boys in her family would have jobs. Often, Corrales herself held two or three jobs. Once while she was an insurance clerk, she got the idea that she could make more money if she were an agent. She studied for her licenses and eventually worked up to her own profitable business. "I made it a rule to always sell one policy a day," Corrales related in her interview. "One time it was snowing, and I hadn't sold anything. I asked myself: 'Am I going to let the weather be an obstacle?'" She went out into the cold and sold an insurance policy. The Corrales Insurance Co. is now managed by one of her sons.

Corrales has also been active in the community as a member of the League of United Latin American Citizens, a group which fought in federal court to make the Midland City Council more racially diverse. Corrales became the first ethnic minority elected to that five member council in 1982. While on the council, she was instrumental to bringing economic development to depressed parts of the city and led a push to name a park in honor of Dr. Martin Luther King, Jr. Corrales has also directed Midland's Big Brothers/Big Sisters program and the Midland Chamber of Commerce. She was named Woman of the Year by *Hispanic* magazine in 1986.

Sources:

Corrales, Oralia Lillie, interview with Anna Macias Aguayo, October, 1992.

—Sketch by Anna Macias Aguayo

Martha P. Cotera
(1938-)
Civil rights activist, historian, educator

Martha P. Cotera

Though the media labeled her a radical during the famous Crystal City walk-out in December of 1969, Martha Cotera knew she was partaking in the most American of democratic experiments. Cotera remembers those days as "great fun." She and her husband, architect Juan Estanislao Cotera, helped to orchestrate what amounted to a massive walk-out by students protesting their exclusion by an Anglo minority that governed Crystal City, which is located near San Antonio, Texas. Cotera, 54, says the town was 95 percent Mexican American at the time. The walk-out began with a group of school cheerleaders who had been denied access to academic courses and extracurricular activities. "It was part of a history of walk-outs that happened in relation to the civil rights movement in the 1960s." Cotera noted in an interview with Julia Edgar. "My husband and I helped to sign up tutors to do a teach-in, and we went ourselves. It was the beginning of inclusion of Mexican Americans in Texas politics. It was to show people it was possible to take control of their lives at a local level." Crystal City, still a farming community, now has a Chicana school superintendent and Hispanics in high-ranking governmental posts.

Cotera was born January 17, 1938, in Nuevo Casa Grande, Chihuahua, Mexico. In 1946, she immigrated to the United States with her mother, Altagracias Castanos, and settled in El Paso, Texas. Her sister, Velia Luna, still resides there. Cotera earned a bachelor of arts degree in English, with a minor in history, at Texas Western College (now the University of Texas at El Paso) and a master's degree in education at Antioch College in Yellow Springs, Ohio. She has also begun graduate work in history at the University of Texas in Austin.

In the late 1950s, Cotera worked as a librarian in El Paso and Austin. In 1964, she became director of documents and information at the Texas State Library in Austin, a position she held until she became director of the Southwest Educational Development Laboratory in 1968. In 1970, Cotera and her husband went to Mercedes, Texas, with the Antioch College Graduate School of Education to help found Jacinto Trevino College, which eventually split off to become Juarez-Lincoln University. The purpose of the college, which is now defunct, was to prepare teachers for bilingual education programs. Cotera and her husband were faculty members until 1975. In 1974, one year after she helped found the Texas Women's Political Caucus, Cotera founded the non-profit Chicana Research and Learning Center in Austin.

Founds Chicana Research and Learning Center

The Center, of which she serves as executive director and education coordinator, is an umbrella organization that assists in funding projects and obtaining grants for them, particularly for minority women. The Center is also an information and research center. Cotera's 28-year-old daughter Maria Eugenia, for example, received assistance for a documentary film project she and other students made about Raza Unida and the Crystal City walkout.

Out of the turbulence of the walk-out and ensuing events was born Raza Unida, a "third political party" which fielded Mexican American candidates for nearly a decade, drawing its strength from Latinos who felt discriminated against because of their heritage. Cotera herself ran for a seat on the state board of education in the Winter Garden area of Texas in 1972, and the party fielded candidates for governor and lieutenant governor of Texas. Raza Unida has remained a grassroots organization, dedicated to politicizing Hispanics and improving Hispanic-Anglo relations in Texas. Members have worked to diversify local law enforcement in Austin, whose police department is now headed by a woman. Raza also sponsors voting drives at low-income housing projects and has been instrumental in building a Mexican American cultural center in Austin for dance, art and drama.

While she lived in Crystal City, Cotera headed the Crystal City Memorial Library and her husband served as urban renewal director of the town. She published the *Educator's Guide to Chicano Resources* as a board member of the Committee for Rural Democracy. Crystal City gave Cotera and her husband, whom she married in 1963, a taste of the power imbalance they were about to experience first-hand. Her radicalization began when they moved to Austin, the capital of Texas. "We, like a lot of Hispanics, are aware of a lot of discrimination. We experienced that when we came to Austin. That radicalized us. There was a lot of police brutality, and we were very concerned because we were starting a family. We just felt that if you wanted things to be good, you had to work for it," she said during her interview.

Cotera is a writer as well. She has written extensively on the role of women in Hispanic culture, publishing *Chicanas in Politics and Public Life* in 1975 and *Dona Doormat No Esta Aqui: An Assertiveness and Communications Skills Manual for Hispanic Women* in 1984. She has contributed essays addressing the problems of Hispanic women to various books and professional journals, including *The Women Say/The Men Say: Women's Liberation and Men's Consciousness, El Caracol,* and *Twice a Minority: Mexican American Women.* Cotera's writings are directed to middle-class and educated Hispanic women, because they are less likely, ironically, to immerse themselves in community or grassroots politics. "What I wanted to do with Hispanic women was to have them feel comfortable with their position as leaders and activists in the Hispanic community and the mainstream community, for them not to believe and accept the stereotypes of Hispanic women as passive women," she explained. "The grassroots women have no hang-ups. The college-educated women bought into the stereotypes."

Cotera believes that women who are politically aware generally are feminists, but she has drawn a distinction between Anglo and minority feminists, sometimes to the chagrin of other women who would like to present an image of unity to the world. Today, she says, Latina feminists have less contact with Anglo feminists than in the 1970s, partly because the emphasis of the contemporary women's movement is rights, not liberation. Also, as Cotera stressed in her interview, there is a strain of racism among white women who would prefer to consider minority counterparts as "clients." "They don't need us at all. . . . It's not the women at fault as much as our educational system, which has never educated people about diversity and never educated people to accept diversity. These people have grown up with blinders on, so it's hard for them to see us as real people and contributing people and strong people."

Cotera's writings on education include the *Handbook on Educational Strategies and Resources for Sex-Cultural Relevant Classroom Practices and Materials,* published by the United States Department of Health, Education and Welfare, Women's Educational Equity Program, in 1980, and the *Parent Education Training Program* for the Texas Association of School Boards in 1989. With her training and background in research and resource development, Cotera began working as a special staff consultant in 1975 with the Benson Latin American Collection at the University of Texas, an important archives of Mexican American historical material. In that role, Cotera helps build the collection, traveling to places rich in Mexican American lore and "snooping around," as she explained in her interview. "We run across things all the time: civil rights material, turn of the century material. We discovered a collection on bilingual education and Cuban culture in Key West. A lot of our focus is in Texas. Texas has a long history of archival material, because the first Spanish exploration was in the 1560s, 30 years or so before Roanoke. That's our first Hispanic entrance to the United States."

Opens Publishing Company

Cotera's daughter, a graduate student at the University of Texas, shares her love of history. The two are busy compiling an encyclopedia on outstanding Hispanic women from pre-Columbian times. They now have compiled over 1,000 entries on women from Mexico, South America, and Spain. When it is finished, they will call it *Mujeres Celebre.* Cotera, who also has a 20-year-old son, Juan Javier, started a company called Information Systems Development in 1975 that publishes, among other things, the *Austin Hispanic Directory.* The bilingual guide includes local civic, individual, and business information. The company, she noted, "is as successful as I want to make it. We gross about $150,000 [annually], but it's a real fun company. I do what I like to do, which is to publish the *Austin Hispanic Directory* and other minority and women data bases. I publish things nobody else wants to publish." ISD, which has been featured on the cover of *Texas Business* magazine, also published the *Publisher's List for Adult Chicano Materials, Chicana Feminist: Essays,* and *Diosa y Hembra: History and Heritage of the Chicana in the United States.*

In 1980, Cotera co-founded the Mexican American Business and Professional Women in Austin, again to politicize women and help young Latinas get the help they needed. "We just wanted to get in and see the mayor, so we gave ourselves a real establishment name," Cotera joked. The MABPWA began a district-wide Stay in School campaign in 1981 in which members acted as mentors to junior high school students in eight public schools.

Cotera, who also teaches American history at Austin Community College, is a member of several professional and political organizations. For the past 25 years, she has conducted workshops and training sessions on subjects ranging from sexual equality to information access for low-income populations, for various community and national groups. She was named Outstanding Woman of Austin in 1975 by the *Austin American Statesman* and Outstanding Citizen of Mexican American Descent in 1975 by the International Good Neighbor Council. Cotera is also an honorary member of the Alpha Theta Phi and Sigma Delta Phi fraternities.

Cotera and her husband, although busy, are still politically active in their community, working on voter registration drives and campaigning for or against local bond issues. "Both my husband and I are very much interested in the democratic process, in the sense that there are a lot of positive things about the U.S. political process," she concluded in her interview. "We're very interested in making it work and getting people involved in it, as long as people are willing to participate."

Sources:

Cotera, Martha P., telephone interview with Julia Edgar, September 26, 1992.

—Sketch by Julia Edgar

Celia Cruz

Celia Cruz
(1929?-)
Singer

Celia Cruz is the undisputed queen of salsa. After more than 40 years of performing professionally, she continues to intrigue Hispanics and non-Hispanics alike around the world with the rhythms of her Cuban homeland. A remarkable performer and person, she loves her fans as much as she loves her music. As she said in *Más,* "Music is what gave me the courage to fight and get out of poverty and touch the universe. . . . The only important thing is music." Celia Cruz has indeed brightened the world with her songs, and in doing so she has realized her dreams. She commented in the *New York Times,* "When people hear me sing, I want them to be happy, happy, happy. I don't want them thinking about when there's not any money, or when there's fighting at home. My message is always *felicidad—*happiness."

Celia Cruz will not divulge the year of her birth. The attempts of some biographers to uncover that date have failed, and they can only estimate that she was born around 1929. It is well known, however, that Cruz's birthday is October 21, and that she was born in Havana, Cuba, to Simon and Catalina (Alfonso) Cruz. Although Simon and Catalina Cruz had only four children of their own (Celia

was the second eldest), 14 children, including nieces, nephews, and cousins, occupied the Cruz home in a poor part of Havana, the Santa Saurez *barrio,* or neighborhood.

As a young girl, Celia Cruz loved music. She was responsible for putting the children who lived in her home to sleep with lullabyes; the songs she sang not only kept the children awake, they lured neighbors to the house. It was apparent at that time that Celia was gifted with a beautiful voice. With her aunt, she listened to the radio and went to ballrooms. She made friends with Cuban musicians. Instead of aspiring to become a singer, however, Cruz prepared herself for a career as a teacher. "I wanted to be a mother, a teacher, and a housewife," Cruz recalled in the *New York Times.* Cruz's father encouraged her to become a teacher; he wanted the young woman to have a respectable job. Celia Cruz graduated from the República de Mexico public school in Havana, and went on to the Escuela Normal para Maestros.

Fortunately for salsa fans, Cruz never became a teacher of literature. Despite her father's wishes, she left school and did not return after her singing career began to take off in the late 1940s. Cruz was initially encouraged to become a professional singer while she was still in school, following her victory in a talent show called "La Hora de Té," which aired on the García Serra radio network in 1947. Cruz sang the tango "Nostalgia" in bolero tempo and, in addition to winning a cake, she became a local hit. She appeared in amateur shows and was soon sought after as a paid entertainer. One of her first jobs was to sing on the Radio Progreso Cubana for one week; she also sang on Radio Unión for some months. Cruz sang, at first, because she needed money to buy food and school books. Later, however, a teacher told her that she should forget teaching and concentrate on singing. Cruz remembered the teacher's words in the *New York Times:* "You're going to sing because you'll earn more money in a day than I will in a month."

At this point Cruz became serious about her musical career. Already noted for her pregón singing (a vocal style which evolved from the calls, chants, and cries of street vendors) and the songs "Manicero" ("Peanut Vendor") and "El Pregón del Pescador" ("The Fishmonger's Call"), Cruz enrolled at the Conservatory of Music to study voice and theory. With her own good behavior, as well as her mother's help, Cruz persuaded her father once and for all that a career as a singer would not disgrace her or the family. As a student, she worked hard, and whenever she traveled to performances, a female relative accompanied her as a chaperone. After three years at the conservatory, Cruz was equipped with the skills necessary to succeed as a musician; her baggage also included the whole-hearted support of her family.

Opens Career with Las Mulatas de Fuego

At first, Cruz sang with the dancing troupe Las Mulatas de Fuego, and kept the audience entertained while the dancers changed costumes. She also sang with the orchestra of Gloria Matancera. In 1949, she was hired to sing Yoruba songs at a radio station. Finally, in August of 1950, Cruz was chosen to replace Myrta Silva, the lead singer of La Sonora Matancera, Cuba's most popular orchestra. Although fans listening to Radio Progreso wrote angry letters about the replacement, they were soon won over to Cruz's style, and Cruz became a star. In early 1951, she began to release recordings such as "Cao Cao Mani Picao/ Mata Siguaraya," "Yerboro," "Burundanga," and "Me Voy al Pinar del Rio."

For 15 years, or Cruz's golden era, as it is called, Cruz sang with La Sonora Matancera. Headliners at Havana's world-famous Tropicana nightclub and casino, the group became popular enough to work on television and in movies as well as on radio. The orchestra appeared in five movies (*Una Gallega en Habana, Olé Cuba, Rincón Criollo, Piel Canela,* and *Amorcito Corazón*) and toured the United States and Central and South America. La Sonora Matancera's fame and frequent tours served the individuals in the group well; when Fidel Castro took power after the 1959 revolution, they were able to escape Cuba by pretending that they were going on another tour, and they were welcomed abroad. From 1960 to late 1961, La Sonora Matancera entertained audiences in Mexico. Then, the orchestra packed up its act to enter the United States.

Although the singer would come to love the United States, Cruz could never forget her homeland. She continues to remember it in song, but she cannot return to Cuba. Castro, angered by the singer's defection, would not even allow her to visit the country when her mother was sick, or when her father died. If Celia Cruz continues to be unhappy about her expatriation, she seems to have accepted the situation, and Hispanics have certainly shown their appreciation of her work in the United States. "If I die now," the singer stated in the *New York Times* in 1985, "I want to be buried here."

As the *New York Times* remembered, Cruz's "early years in the United States were less than memorable; young Latinos were more interested in rock-and-roll than in music from the old country." Cruz had to work very hard to earn her fame in the United States. One good thing, however, did occur during those early years in America. On July 14, 1962, Cruz married Pedro Knight, the first trumpeter of La Sonora Matancera; she had known him for over 14 years. Knight has served as Cruz's protector, manager, and musical director ever since. He has helped her make important decisions and has provided enthusiastic support; he gave her the golden "Salsa" engraved earrings she still wears. In 1987, Louis Ramirez, an arranger of songs for Cruz, explained Knight's role in Cruz's professional life in the *New York Times.* "When discord arises on how best to sing or play a part, everyone turns to Pedro. Pedro presides quietly in a corner, with his arms crossed. After he hears us argue back and forth, he says 'si' or 'no.'"

Although Cruz did not sell many records during the 1960s, her production was prolific. She signed with Seeco records, and recorded 20 albums of La Sonora Matancera songs in just one year. These albums included *Con Amor, La Reina del Ritmo Cubano, Grand Exitos de Celia Cruz, La Incomparable Celia, Mexico qué Grande Eres, Homenaje a los Santos, Sabor y Ritmo de Pueblos, Homenaje a Yemaya de Celia Cruz, Celia Cruz Interpreta El Yerbero y La Sopa en Botella, La Tierna, Conmovedora, Bamboleadora,* and her most popular Seeco album, *Canciónes Premiadas.* After signing with Tico Records in 1966, the woman who would later be crowned the "Queen of Salsa" recorded 13 more albums, toured South America and the United States, and, just as importantly, began to work with Tito Puente, a man who would come to be known as the "King of Latin Swing."

Puente recalled in the *New York Times,* "I was listening to the radio in Cuba the first time I heard Celia's voice. I couldn't believe the voice. It was so powerful and energetic. I swore it was a man, I'd never heard a woman sing like that." Cruz recorded eight of her 13 Tico albums with Puente, including *Cuba y Puerto Rico Son, El Quimbo Quimbunbia, Alma con Alma,* and *Algo Especial Para Recordar.* Cruz and Puente performed more than 500 times together before 1987, and countless times after.

Interest in Salsa Grows among Young Hispanics

It was not until the early 1970s that Cruz, the woman whom the *New York Times* would call "salsa's most celebrated singer," began to be appreciated by young Hispanics. She was chosen to play the role of Gracia Divina in the opera *Hommy* at Carnegie Hall in early 1973. Her remarkable voice and boundless energy captured the audience, which was just beginning to enjoy the new music called "salsa." Just as Cruz is not a limited performer, salsa is not a limited music: the word salsa can be used variously to describe guaracha, rhumba, merengue, and guaguanco rhythms. As *Time* magazine put it, salsa "is a catchall term that became current in the early '70's. . . . Instrumentation features piano brass, percussion (like the congas or the timbales). . . . The rhythm is often complex and layered, but at root there is a steady beat." *Time* also noted that "real salsa, old-country music [is] preserved in the persons of Cruz and Puente."

Older fans who remembered their lives in Cuba were thrilled to hear the music of their youth as Celia Cruz sang to the salsa beat, and younger fans were genuinely enthusiastic about Cruz's fast-paced scatting. No one could help being impressed by Cruz's costume. She was and is a flamboyant dresser. Her usual costume involves feathers, sequins, or lace, and yards and yards of brightly colored fabric. Legend has it that Cruz never wears a costume twice, that each of her costumes costs more than the amount needed to produce one of her albums, and that some of her costumes have taken up a whole stage. Cruz herself acknowledges that some of her costumes prohibited other singers from comfortably moving around the stage. The exotic, outrageously flashy costumes Cruz wears reflect the energy she radiates as she performs.

Listening to her music is not enough; to experience Cruz, one must be able to watch her as she illuminates the stage and fascinates her audience. She loves to sing powerfully and with a great deal of volume, and because of this she usually sings to large audiences in structures that can withstand the amplification. Celia Cruz is always animated and completely engaged in her performances. As a reviewer for the *New York Times* wrote, Cruz "leaps, dances, flaunts, flirts, and teases to the gyrating beat of salsa." Although Cruz has her serious, passionate moments, she is never predictable; one never knows when she will break into improvisation or joke with the audience and the band. Seemingly tireless, the singer has been known to perform at her explosive pace for more than three hours.

After Cruz's contract with Tico Records expired, she took advantage of the opportunity to work with Johnny Pacheco, a long-time admirer of Cruz. Pacheco was a rumba band leader and a flutist of the charanga style. For Vaya Records, they revised Cruz's Sonora Matancera pieces to produce *Celia and Johnny*, which was released in 1974. This record, not surprisingly, went gold as Hispanics throughout the United States snatched it up. *Tremendo Cache* and

Recordando El Ayer, Cruz's next collaborative albums, met with similar success, as did other albums she recorded on the Vaya label. Another album she recorded in 1974, with conga player Ray Barretto, won a Grammy Award.

Cruz's popularity among Hispanics began to grow. Fans throughout the world went wild when she performed. During the 1970s, she sang in concert with Johnny Pacheco in the United States, and with Tito Puente and members of the Fania All-Stars, throughout Africa and France. The *New York Daily News* named her the best female vocalist in 1977 and 1979, and *Billboard* did the same in 1978; in polls conducted by *Latin N.Y.*, the singer was similarly honored annually from 1975 to 1982.

In 1982, Cruz was reunited with La Sonora Matancera, and the group released exciting new songs on their album, *Feliz Encuentro.* Later that year, Cruz was the honored performer in a concert in Madison Square Garden. 20,000 people there, as well as television viewers throughout the world, watched and danced as she sang with those who had contributed to her career over the years: La Sonora Matancera, Tito Puente, Cheo Feliciano, Johnny Pacheco, Pete Rodríguez, and Willie Colón. Cruz was presented with a gold record (along with Ray Baretto and Adalberto Santiago) for their album, *Tremendo Trio,* by Fania Records in 1983.

Remains a Busy Performer

During the latter half of the 1980s, Cruz was as busy as ever. She met the demands of salsa fans, recorded albums, and gave concerts. In 1985, she sang with various groups and lit up the stage with music based on Yoruba religious chants which once praised West African deities. In 1986, Cruz was given an Ellis Island Medal of Honor, also known as the Mayor's Liberty Award, by the National Ethnic Coalition of Organizations. In 1987, Vaya Records released Cruz's 53rd album, a collaboration with Willie Colón entitled *The Winners.* She performed in New York's Annual Salsa Festival at Madison Square Garden, and also won a fourth Grammy nomination, a New York Music Award for Best Latin Artist, and an Obie, or Off-Broadway award, that year.

Among her many notable concerts was a 1988 tribute to Frank Grillo, or Machito, a musician who was essential to the development of Afro-Cuban jazz, and who had worked with Cruz for years. According to the *New York Times,* Cruz's performance was as dazzling as usual. Her "voice, piercing and intense, ripped through the glittery band arrangements; as an improviser, Miss Cruz phrases as if she were a drummer." Cruz gave a concert in Harlem on October 21, 1989, along with the Cuban jazz star Mario Bauza (and Machito's brother-in-law), Tito Puente, Chico O'Farill, Marco Rizo, Max Roach, and Henry Threadgill. The *New York Times* reported, "Mr. Bauza's band played one of his modernist compositions and Miss Cruz, who was celebrating her birthday, sang a set of her tunes, shouting out phrases with the authority of a trumpeter; she's one of the world's great singers, and she proved it again." Cruz ended the decade by earning another Grammy Award. In the Latin category, she won the Best Tropical Performance for *Ritmo En El Corazon,* the album she recorded with Ray Barretto.

From Manhattan to Miami, salsa is a huge element of Hispanic youth culture. Popular singers such as Gloria Estefan, who says she was inspired by Cruz, base their songs on a salsa beat. Cruz explained the lure of salsa in *Time* magazine in 1988: "We've never had to attract these kids. They come by themselves. Rock is a strong influence on them, but they still want to know about their roots. The Cuban rhythms are so contagious that they end up making room for both kinds of music in their lives." According to *Time,* "young Cuban Americans have gathered to see the reigning Reina de la Salsa, Celia Cruz, who was entertaining their parents and their parents' parents in the smoky dens and fancy nightclubs of pre-Castro Cuba long before they were born." While Celia Cruz has changed with the times, some aspects of her performances have maintained themselves despite her age. She is still tireless, she continues to dress in fantastic gowns, and she will always enthrall those who see her.

Although Celia Cruz has been exciting audiences since the late 1940s with her inexhaustible energy and her unique voice and has recorded more than 70 albums, she refuses to retire or even slow down. Cruz, who is over 70 years of age, was quoted as saying in the *New York Times,* "I have no choice, really, but to put in as much time and energy as I do. I have a lot more to do." Cruz, however, does wonder what things will be like after she can no longer sing, and wishes that more women would sing salsa. "Someday, I have to die," she mused in the *New York Times.* "I want people to say, 'Celia Cruz has died, but here is someone who can take over.'"

Sources:

Periodicals

Boston Globe, March 20, 1988, p. 48.
Chicago Tribune, October 2, 1988, Section 13, p. 14.
Los Angeles Times, June 17, 1991, p. 2F.
Más (Spanish-language; translated by Ronie-Richele Garcia-Johnson), November, 1991, p. 77.
New York Times, November, 1985; August 30, 1987, Section 2, p. 14; July 1, 1988, p. 22C; July 4, 1988, p. 16A; October 29, 1989, Section 1, p. 62.
Nuestro, May, 1980, p. 60.
Rolling Stone, September 21, 1989, p. 55.
Time, July 11, 1988, pp. 50-52.
Variety, November 27, 1985, p. 140; October 25, 1989, p. 69; November 5, 1990, p. 90.
Vogue, June, 1984, p. 70.

—*Sketch by Ronie-Richele Garcia-Johnson*

Alicia Cuaron
(1939-)
Educator, business executive

The eloquence of her words and the vitality and enthusiasm with which she delivers them have distinguished Alicia Cuaron as one of America's most influential Hispanic communicators. Using a persuasive sincerity to vividly portray her setbacks, her hopes and her triumphs as a minority woman in a competitive business world, Cuaron excites her audiences and serves as a powerful motivational force. An active feminist, she was listed in *Colorado Woman News* as a national leader and was quoted as saying: "I see the world as a place full of opportunities. Women can make major changes and influence what is going to happen in this country and universally, as well."

As founder of the Institute of Hispanic Professional Development, Cuaron conducts workshops and lectures, emphasizing prospective imagery goal-setting, cultural diversity, leadership development, and self-enhancement. "I consider myself a visionary," Dr. Cuaron said in an interview with Alma Renee Madrid. "I have always tried to attain a place of authority and policy-making in the best way possible, as an Hispanic woman, to pattern programs and lead people." She is one of the top professional keynote speakers for corporations, charitable organizations such as the United Way, community colleges, and universities; she is among the first Hispanic women ever called upon to address groups at Yale, Stanford, Berkeley, and Radcliffe/Harvard Universities. Cuaron has also gained recognition in radio broadcasting, television production, and as a show host.

Cuaron was born on March 1, 1939, in Oxnard, California, to Rosendo Alfaro and Guadalupe Valladolid Perez. Her father, who had a sixth-grade education, operated a grocery store, after which he became a salesman. Her family moved to El Paso, Texas, when she was three years old. As a first-generation Mexican American born to parents who immigrated to the United States during the Mexican Revolution, Cuaron became deeply aware early in her life of the need to develop the educational level and working conditions of Hispanics. Her strong ethnic pride and commitment to helping others was fostered by her father, a "Cristero," among the followers of Christ who helped to smuggle Catholic fathers and sisters across the Mexican border during the 1920s; and more so by her mother, who was dedicated to helping anyone in need in the community. "My whole life has been the community," said Cuaron. "My parents always emphasized the importance of education and civic involvement." As a further tribute to her parents, she added, "Most of my siblings, which include five sisters and one brother, have a higher education. . . . We all read, write and speak Spanish as well as English."

Family's Support Sets Tone for Career

Caught between two cultures early in life, Cuaron now works to encourage a cultural sensitivity that emphasizes that "for Hispanics, their most important support system is their immediate family, a critical element which must never be discounted under any circumstances." Cuaron considers herself a pioneer; she worked her way through college in the University of El Paso Library. She received encouragement and support from her family and through Hispanic role-models who stressed the importance of language, culture, and respect for the community. "We were taught to have 'orgullo' (pride) and 'respeto' (respect)," she noted.

Cuaron received a B.A. in education from the University of Texas at El Paso in 1961 and started out teaching in El Paso at Navarro Elementary School's First Grade Special Education Program, which consisted of 90 percent Spanish-surname, low-income students. She taught remedial reading and English as a second language, and also in the Head Start and adult education programs. She had a daughter, Alexis Maritza Va Cuaron, now a 23-year-old student at the University of Colorado. After moving to Colorado, Cuaron attended the University of Northern Colorado in Greeley and received her M.A. in education in 1972 and Ph.D. in 1975. While in college, she developed and implemented the bilingual/bicultural Denver Head Start program, the first of its kind in Colorado. She went on to plan, develop, and implement a bilingual, multicultural Child Development Associate Head Start Program at Metropolitan State College in Denver. Cuaron points to an irony that has developed in spite of the recent curtailment of bilingual/bicultural programs: "In 1972, the people were totally against the program and now, twenty years later, the problem has compounded; it's interesting to find that I am now being called upon by organizations from throughout the United States for multicultural training in the workplace."

Developed Successful Business

In 1980, Cuaron became the first female executive director of the Colorado Economic Development Association in Denver. Working with the Women's Bureau of the Department of Labor, she developed, implemented, and evaluated regional educational and employment community/field-based seminars for low-income, Hispanic women. She also designed and administered the first Adelante Mujer Hispana Employment and Training Conference. "I consider this one of my most significant accomplishments," Cuaron remarked in her interview. "This national education and training conference, which is geared to helping women with the education and training needed for career development, had a registration of over one thousand women. The conference model, a publication of the U.S.

Department of Labor, Women's Bureau, has been the most widely requested publication ever issued by the department. Succeeding annual conferences have been replicated in Denver and throughout the country, and have reached nearly six thousand women."

Cuaron more recently went on leave from her position as executive vice-president of Source One, a Denver-based operations and facilities management company. She is handling marketing and outreach for workshops and seminars at Queen of Peace Oratory, attributing to them "better education, better salaries and more possibilities to get more things done." She is also working with the Marycrest Franciscan sisters, who provide housing for homeless mothers with children and a food and clothing bank. Through this work, Cuaron said, "I am helping to develop and market a retreat house and seeking the spiritual realm of my career."

Cuaron has been the recipient of numerous awards and honors, including ones from the American Jewish Committee, the Big Sisters of Colorado, the Chicana Service Center, and the Denver Federal Executive Board. She was also the recipient of the Rocky Mountain Regional Women at Work Award and was named one of 100 Outstanding Women in Communication, and Woman of the Year by the Colorado Hispanic Chamber of Commerce. Cuaron was one of 15 national Hispanic leaders invited to participate in Project Intel-change, an educational seminar in Israel, and has been featured as one of the "100 Most Influential Hispanics in America" by *Hispanic Business* magazine. Despite her success, Cuaron is deeply aware of the discrepancies that exist in a multicultural society. She stated, "Many Hispanics think that in order to attain success they must assimilate into the mainstream of society. This causes conflict in not knowing who you really are. The human values and culture that you grow up with are essential and need to be retained." Conveying a spiritual dimension, she stressed in her interview "the importance of striving to be honest and genuine—qualities that make you a human being—and the inner fortitude that reflects the outer beauty of self—qualities that offer a professional lifeline."

Sources:

Periodicals

Colorado Woman News, March, 1992.

Other

Cuaron, Alicia, telephone interview with Alma Renee Madrid, July, 1992.

—Sketch by Alma Renee Madrid

D

Graciéla Daniele
(1939-)
Choreographer, director

A talented dancer and choreographer as well as an ambitious director, Graciéla Daniele has both entertained and challenged her audiences. Her choreography for *The Mystery of Edwin Drood* and *The Pirates of Penzance* won her fame; for the latter musical she was nominated for a Tony award. Her work has also drawn controversy, particularly two bold dance theater events, *Tango Apasionado* and *Dangerous Games,* which she conceived and directed.

Daniele, born December 8, 1939, in Buenos Aires, to Raul and Rosa (Almoina), has attributed many of her themes to the culture of her native Argentina. She graduated from a program at the Theatre Colon in Buenos Aires with a degree in Bellas Artes. The young woman was ballet dancing as a soloist for the Nice Opera in France when she saw *West Side Story* in Paris. Daniele told the *New York Times,* "That's what brought me to New York. I didn't even speak English." Despite this obstacle, she danced well enough to earn roles in Broadway musicals. After studying with Matt Mattox and dancing in *What Makes Sammy Run,* which he choreographed, Daniele found her way into *Promises, Promises, Coco, Follies,* and *Chicago.*

It was not long before Daniele began to choreograph her own musical numbers. Her first such job was for a Milliken industrial show at the Waldorf Astoria Hotel. She then went on to choreograph *The Most Happy Fella* and *A History of the American Film;* both of these musicals were produced on Broadway. Later, for the New York City Opera, she choreographed *Naughty Marrietta. Joseph and the Amazing Technicolor Dreamcoat* for the Brooklyn Academy and *Die Fledermaus* for the Opera Company in Boston followed. In 1981, Daniele choreographed *Alice in Concert,* a musical which starred Meryl Streep and opened at New York's Public Theater.

Recognized for Work in *Pirates of Penzance*

Her choreography for another show, *The Pirates of Penzance,* also in early 1981, brought Daniele a great deal of attention. A critic for the *New York Times* remarked, "Graciéla Daniele can take credit for making an ensemble of actors and singers, most of whom have never taken a dance class in their life, as satisfying to watch as a highly trained dance company." The critic continued, "Miss Daniele's choreography, described by Frank Rich as 'intricately batty,' is a consistently strong element in a show that has a cast of widely differing bodies and voices." The success of *The Pirates of Penzance,* which was later made into a film, was very much due to Daniele's work, and, accordingly, respect for Daniele in the world of show business increased: she was nominated for an Antoinette Perry Award and won a Los Angeles Critics Award. Daniele's next effort, the choreography for *The Rink* (1983-1984), garnered her another Tony nomination.

Daniele's choreography of *The Mystery of Edwin Drood* was rewarded with favorable reviews in late 1985. Writing for *New York,* a critic commented, "[Wilford Leach] is stoutly helped by the choreography of Graciéla Daniele, whose work has often been too minimalist or derivative for my taste but who here comes up with decorative curlicues of dance that seamlessly blend into the calligraphy of the staging, so that we are at a loss to say where direction leaves off and choreography begins, and vice versa."

Daniele's work following *The Pirates of Penzance* and *The Mystery of Edwin Drood* drew sharp criticism for its controversial content. *Tango Apasionado,* which Daniele conceived and directed as well as choreographed, appeared a little more than two years after *Edwin Drood,* in December of 1987. INTAR, the Hispanic American Arts Center, had invited Daniele to develop a show and had given her the freedom to do what she wanted to do. The result, a "cross between a musical and a dance piece," as a reviewer for *New York* called it, was based on three short stories and a prose poem written by the great Argentinian writer Jorge Luis Borges. A critic for the *New Yorker* commented, "Under the onslaught of [Daniele's] misery tangos and knife duels (every other scene seems to end with a slashing), Borges gets lost and reason takes flight."

Childhood Memories Influence Dance Projects

While some viewers could not see through the violence and the abuse of female characters in *Tango Apasionado,* such elements were meaningful for Daniele; she had remembered such a culture from her childhood, and she wanted to reflect upon it. "I'm a very nonviolent person," she told the *New York Times,* "but the first opportunity I had to do something of my own, this power and passion and violence that was inside me came out. . . . I don't want to make any judgements about violence or the treatment of women in that culture, but in presenting it maybe I'm making a statement. I realize I'm screaming against it, but I'm not doing it verbally, I'm doing it visually. It's not about intellect, this piece, it's about raw human emotions."

Daniele's next project, which appeared in late 1989 at the Nederlander, was also violent; it was not understood, and it was not well received. *Dangerous Games,* which was conceived, co-written, directed, and choreographed by Daniele, consisted of two acts, "Tango" and "Orfeo." According to a critic with *New York* magazine, "Many people are offended by the show's brutality, and indeed, it is mostly crude sex, fighting with knives, fighting with whips, fighting with boleadoras, fighting with poles, torture, and still more and cruder sex." Although this same critic acknowledged that "There is solid dancing here," he thought that "dancers, like children, should be seen, not heard." A critic for the *New Republic* wrote, "One needs a new term to describe this evening—choreopathology. I don't recall ever leaving a show with such queasy feelings about the gangrenous possibilities of dance." A critic for the *New York Times* asserted that "Ms. Daniele exposes the limits of her own talent by stretching it over too much time and space."

In late 1990, Daniele directed and choreographed *Once on This Island,* a Broadway musical about a doomed love between a beautiful peasant girl and an aristocratic boy in the French Antilles. Daniele's work for this musical did not receive many favorable reviews, with residual criticism from *Dangerous Games* influencing that of the new musical. A critic for *The Nation* wrote, "earlier this season, in *Dangerous Games,* [Daniele] did for the dance traditions of Argentina what she now does for those of the Caribbean—turns them into shticks." A *New York* reviewer decided that, considering the "fiasco" of *Dangerous Games, Once on This Island* "proves—conclusively, I think—that Miss Daniele has shot what was, at most, a slender wad." Despite these pans, a critic for the *New Yorker* found no fault with the choreographer, commenting, "All goes well under Graciela Daniele's direction."

It is to Daniele's credit that she has attempted to present her idea of a past Argentinian culture in her favorite medium, the dance. If critics have not appreciated Daniele's original works, perhaps it is because she has not yet been able to present the horror of violence without horrifying her audiences at the same time. Theatre lovers will be rewarded when Daniele finally does find the combination of dance and aggression that artfully as well as accurately represents the Argentinian culture that the choreographer remembers from her childhood.

Sources:

Periodicals

Dance Magazine, January, 1991, p. 70.
Nation, June 11, 1990, p. 834.
National Review, December 31, 1990, p. 49.
New Republic, November 20, 1989, pp. 30-31.
New York, September 2, 1985, pp. 57-58; November 23, 1987, pp. 115-116; October 30, 1989, pp. 101-102; May 21, 1990, p. 78.
New Yorker, December 21, 1987, pp. 103-104; May 28, 1990, p. 101.
New York Times, January 25, 1981; November 1, 1987, Section 2, p. 5; October 20, 1989, p. C3.
Nuestro, August, 1981, p. 63.
Time, July 11, 1988, p. 83.

—*Sketch by Ronie-Richele Garcia-Johnson*

de Arellano, Diana Ramírez
See **Ramírez de Arellano, Diana**

de Baca Gilbert, Fabiola Cabeza
See **Gilbert, Fabiola Cabeza de Baca**

de Burciaga, Cecilia Preciado
See **Burciaga, Cecilia Preciado de**

de Feldman, Susanna Redondo
See **Redondo de Feldman, Susanna**

de Frias, Marlene Cintron
See **Cintron de Frias, Marlene**

Angela de Hoyos
(1945?-)
Poet

Whether her audience consists of highly educated Chicanos, recent immigrants from Mexico, middle-class, mainstream Americans, or academics of many countries, Angela de Hoyos enthralls listeners with her poetry. As a voice for those who, until recently, have not been heard, she speaks of inequality, injustice, and oppression. She writes of alienation and the problems of assimilation. She encourages solidarity and empowerment. Finally, she instills hope with her words and phrases. Angela de Hoyos, however, is more than a poet of her people. She is an internationally known and respected writer who has made outstanding contributions to international and national literature.

Ironically, two traumatic moments of de Hoyos's childhood contributed to her success as a poet: a horrible accident and a difficult transition. The first occurred in the Mexican state of Coahuila, where she was born on January 23, 1945 (some sources say 1940). The three-year-old de Hoyos was severely burned by a gas heater; she suffered wounds on her neck and chest, and the smoke she had inhaled made her very ill. During the long, painful periods she spent in bed, de Hoyos began to create rhymes and verses in her head, and as she did, she began to develop her poetic talent. De Hoyos's mother encouraged such word-play—an artistic woman, she often read poetry to the girl. After the accident, de Hoyos's father left his dry cleaning business and moved the family to San Antonio, Texas. There, she attended local schools and academies. The move to Texas would prove to be another stimulus to de Hoyos's poetic instinct; in America, the girl would come to see the prejudice and inequality of which she would later passionately write.

De Hoyos's poetry was first published in her high school newspaper. Her work was well-received, and by her early twenties, some of the poems that were published by literary journals won international acclaim. As she seemed to have a bright future as a poet, de Hoyos wanted to enrich herself with knowledge. She did not, however, attend a four-year university program. Partially because of her health and partially because she preferred to follow her own curriculum, she did not choose a specific degree plan at any one school. Instead, she chose her own course of study in fine arts and writing. She attended classes at the University of Texas at San Antonio, San Antonio College, the Witte Museum, and the San Antonio Art Institute. De Hoyos also began to socialize with some of the leaders of the growing Chicano movement in the San Antonio area, Juan E. Cárdenas and Mía and Ceilio García-Camarillo. She was

Angela de Hoyos

asked to give readings of her poetry at Chicano gatherings throughout the Southwestern United States, such as the Festival Floricanto III, Canto al Pueblo, and Sol y Sangre. As de Hoyos educated herself, she gave readings of her poetry and continued to write. Between 1969 and 1975, she had established her reputation; she had also written enough poems to form at least two collections of her work.

The first collection, *Arise, Chicano: and Other Poems,* was published in 1975 after de Hoyos's mentor, translator, and friend, Dr. Mireya Robles, encouraged the poet to make the poems she had written in 1969 available to the public. The influence of the Chicano movement is apparent in the four politically charged poems about Chicanos of the collection; these poems promote the idea that Chicanos should empower themselves to overcome oppression. The poem "Arise Chicano" reflects the feelings of one Hispanic woman as well as the mood of a generation of Mexican Americans.

Depicts Anglo Oppression of Chicanos in Poetry

The title poem of *Arise Chicano: and Other Poems,* "Arise Chicano," provides a thematic summary of the collection as a whole. In the poem, Anglos dominate the world of the Chicano, who is consequently disgraced and degraded. Migrant workers live from "hand to mouth" and work "under the shrewd heel of exploit;" their children "go smileless to a cold bed." The migrant workers are enslaved by Anglos and locked into poverty. If they have maintained their integrity by working hard, they have lost their dignity by allowing themselves to be underpaid for exhausting and sometimes humiliating work. Accordingly, the Chicanos themselves bear some responsibility for their plight. They will have to look to themselves for salvation—"You must be your own messiah," the poet writes.

Another poem in the collection, "The Final Laugh," explores racial discrimination as it encourages Chicanos to overcome oppression. In this poem, the narrator discusses the notion that the color of Chicanos will prevent them from ever achieving equality. Whites possess power, and those whose parents are not white, or bland and "mail-order," can expect to experience hardship. Even though the Chicano may take pride in her heritage, dignity will not be enough to dispense with a tradition of ignorant prejudice. The Chicano has two choices. She may be "content with the left-overs of a greedy establishment," or rebel, and find her own place in the world. "The Final Laugh" is an internationally known and respected poem. Published separately before the other poems in the collection, it received the 1972 Diploma de Benemerenza, which is the second prize of the Italian Academia Leonardo Da Vinci.

The poem "Brindis: For the Barrio" advocates militant social protest and calls for solidarity. An answer to "La cena miserable," a poem by the great Peruvian César Vallejo, "Brindis" is about hope. If man must suffer today, surely tomorrow victory over oppression will come. Working together, Chicanos may hope to find their way out of poverty and alienation. The awkwardness and unfairness of that alienation is portrayed in the poem, "Gracias, Meester!" in which a young man agonizes over his poor English as well as his accent.

Displays Growth in Work and Concern for Chicanos

The poems in de Hoyos's second book, *Chicano Poems for the Barrio,* was also published in 1975. This collection, which discusses cultural conservation within the barrio, or Chicano neighborhood, demonstrates the increasing maturity of the poet as well as a growing concern for the plight of her people. No longer content to merely advocate a socio-economic "uprising," de Hoyos rebels herself, within the text. Instead of peppering her English with a few Spanish words, as she did in *Arise, Chicano: and Other Poems,* she uses English as a frame to display Spanish terms and phrases; Spanish words are the substance of the poems, giving them their color and meaning. De Hoyos's use of language is symbolic as well as realistic: just as Spanish is woven into an English text, Chicanos are embedded in an Anglo world. The use of Spanish in everyday life as well as in any piece of literature written by a Chicano necessarily preserves the Chicano culture. De Hoyos is obviously aware of the significance of Spanish in her poems; as she liberally and skillfully writes with Spanish words, she breaks away from the English-dominated literature of the United States.

Another of de Hoyos's literary acts of rebellion is also historical. It is found in the poem "Hermano" ("Brother"). In "Hermano," de Hoyos uses the well-known incident during Texas's battle for independence from Mexico, the fight for El Alamo, to remind her readers that, before Texas belonged to the United States, it belonged to Mexicans, and that, before the Mexicans occupied the territory, the land belonged to Native Americans. Anglos therefore have no right to tell Mexicans to "go back where you came from." De Hoyos's clever revision of history, or better, correction of history, was remarkably fresh at the time she wrote "Hermano"; the idea that Columbus did not "discover" America, and that the history books read by the children of the United States contained misleading and biased information was not widespread. The substance, then, as well as the language of de Hoyos's poems, are compelling and, to the literature of the United States, rebellious.

De Hoyos urges Chicanos to do what they can to assert themselves. In "It's the Squeaky Wheel/That Gets The Oil," she reviews the Chicano situation. Chicanos have the power to change that situation, and when they use that power, and make "progress," they will be able to incorporate themselves into society in the United States. They too will be able to enjoy economic prosperity and political influence.

Works to Preserve Chicano Culture in America

Although de Hoyos encourages assimilation, she fears that an entire culture may be lost in the process. Some Chicanos seem too eager to ignore their roots in order to emulate Northern Americans. De Hoyos wrote in "Small Comfort": "En tierra de gringo/vamos poco a poco/sepultando todo," or, "In the gringo's land, we go little by little, burying everything." Assimilation and incorporation do not require the loss of culture, especially when those of the culture appreciate its unique beauty. Other poems in de Hoyos's second collection, such as "Para una ronda agridulce" ("For a Bittersweet Round"), and "Blues in the Barrio" present the reader with this beauty. The Chicano culture that is contained within the boundaries of the barrio is precious. The poet demonstrates this as she promotes the idea that, while incorporation is important, Chicano idioms, customs, values, traditions, and foods must not be forgotten.

Once again, de Hoyos has done more than advocate. She has actively preserved a piece of her culture. As she writes, she freezes what seems to be fleeting, as well as the process of a culture's passing, in her own words. De Hoyos's poems have captured some images (such as one of a mother rolling out tortillas) that Hispanics and non-Hispanics alike may appreciate. It must be remembered, however, that de Hoyos is not a Mexican poet. She is a Chicano poet. The metaphor of the barrio serves the poet well, for just as the barrio is a Chicano space within the Anglo world, the culture de Hoyos describes in *Chicano Poems for the Barrio* is alienated, and out of place, and because of this, it is a culture in transition.

De Hoyos's next collection of poetry, *Selecciones,* was published in Mexico in 1976; it was republished with a bilingual title in 1979, *Selected Poemas Selecciones.* The poems from this collection, which all focus on life and death, were written between 1965 and 1973. Notable among them are "Mi dolor hecho canción, mi canción hecho dolor," in which the narrator struggles against the peaceful urge to die and go back to the "womb of earth/from where I came," and "One Ordinary Morning," in which the inevitability of death is explored. The introspective poems in *Selecciones* are pessimistic: everyone, regardless of race or social standing, dies, and most people don't get the chance to truly live freely. In "This Fitting Farewell" the poet suggests that, while artists and poets may attempt to overcome the problems of living in such a world, they can do no more than "laugh/in the face of pain," as they create perfect worlds that are imaginary.

Woman, Woman, de Hoyos's fourth collection, was published in 1986 by Arte Público. Poems such as "Ex Marks the Spot" and "Fairy-Tale: Cuento de Hadas" speak of experiences with which many women are familiar—the betrayal of lovers. Two other poems, "Two Poems: Inebrieties" and "Mona Lisa: Marguerite" combine Spanish and English cleverly. In the former poem, de Hoyos presents part of the poem in Spanish and part in English to relate the feelings of falling in love from the perspectives of both Hispanic and Anglo women. The poet distinguished the latter poem by writing the beginning of each stanza in English and finishing it in Spanish.

De Hoyos's work has been well-received by critics. She has won numerous prizes and awards for her poetry. Among the most prestigious are the Honorable Mention from Avalon World Arts Academy, U. S. A. (1965), the Diploma Di Benemerenza from the Centro Studi E Scambi Internazionale, Italy, (1967, 1968), a Second Prize in the International Poetry Competition, (1974), the Diploma Di Benemerenza, Accademia L. Da Vinci, Italy, (1969, 1970), and the Distinguished Service Citation, magna cum laude, from the World Poetry Society Inter-Continental, India, (1970, 1971). Her work has been included in textbooks and anthologies such as *Chicano Perspectives in Literature: A Critical and Annotated Bibliography* and *Latin American Women Writers: Yesterday and Today.* Finally, she has contributed to various journals and other publications throughout the world such as *Poema Conviadado, Quaderni Di Poesia, Ediciones Cosmos, Esparavel, El Aguila, Poetry Dial, Modern Poetry in Translation, Poet Monthly, Masters of Modern Poetry,* and *La Voz del Bronx.*

Angela de Hoyos continues to contribute to causes which concern Hispanics and women as well as the international and national literary scene. She is working on her fifth collection, entitled *Dedicatorias.* This collection will be dedicated to those who have influenced de Hoyos and her work: Rodolfo Anaya, Rolando Hinojosa-Smith, Willie Velasquez, and others. A sixth collection, *Gata Poems,* is almost complete; a relatively humorous book, it will encourage readers to laugh at themselves. Although she is an internationally recognized poet, one might have to travel to Texas to hear de Hoyos read her poetry. She usually confines her activities to the San Antonio area for reasons of health.

Although de Hoyos is considered to be one of the most important Chicana poets, and while she is known around the world by those who study literature, the inevitable critical books that follow the success of any writer have yet to appear. The critical works regarding de Hoyos that are found in literary journals are, however, generally enthusiastic about the poet's future. De Hoyos's diverse audience has much to anticipate.

Sources:

Books

Contemporary Authors, Volume 131, Gale, 1991.
Dictionary of Literary Biography, Volume 82: *Chicano Writers, First Series,* Gale, 1989.

—*Sketch by Ronie-Richele Garcia-Johnson*

Debora de Hoyos
(1953-)
Lawyer

On July 24, 1991, Debora de Hoyos made history when she was appointed managing partner of Mayer, Brown & Platt, a Chicago-based international law firm. Her appointment marked the first time that a woman had been named managing partner of any of the nation's largest law firms. When making the announcement, Robert A. Helman and Leo Herzel, co-chairmen of Mayer, Brown & Platt, noted that de Hoyos would assume her new position on October 1, 1991, and serve a three-year term.

De Hoyos is a third-generation Hispanic American. She can trace her ethnic heritage to the Cantabrian mountain region of northern Spain, where her grandfather was born.

She is proud of her Hispanic background and can speak fluent Spanish. As a youngster she spent a lot of time in Mexico but was educated in the United States. She earned her bachelor of arts degree in 1975 from Wellesley College in Massachusetts, where she was a Durant Scholar. In 1978, she received her law degree from Harvard Law School. While at Harvard, she served as editor-in-chief of the school's *International Law Journal*. Upon graduation, de Hoyos joined Mayer, Brown & Platt.

During her thirteen years with the firm, de Hoyos has concentrated on finance and banking transactions, with special emphasis on acquisition financing, securitization, and international banking. She also served on the firm's committee on associates. In her new capacity, de Hoyos will deal with the day-to-day running of the firm and take an active role in making proposals to the policy and planning committee. Mayer, Brown & Platt has changed quite a lot since her arrival in 1978. Since that time, the organization has undergone a period of growth, expanding from 150 to 560 attorneys and opening six offices worldwide. By 1991, Mayer, Brown & Platt ranked as the twelfth-largest law firm in the United States.

As news of her appointment spread, de Hoyos was overwhelmed by the quantity of congratulatory mail and phone calls she received. Like many women who have assumed a position hitherto denied to their sex, de Hoyos did not want to be looked upon as a symbol but merely as someone who was honored for her hard work. She told the *New York Times* that eventually she came to realize how significant her appointment was to so many strangers—and friends as well. "It was very important to a lot of people," she admitted.

De Hoyos, married to a fellow lawyer and the mother of three young children, has experienced first-hand the strain that accompanies being a mother who works outside the home. In the same *New York Times* article, she stressed the importance of a good support system for women who wish to succeed in their careers. She noted: "Some people have a terrible time juggling. . . . I've been lucky. I've been able to balance."

De Hoyos is a contributor to the book *Advising Illinois Financial Institutions*. She is also a member of the American Society of International Law.

Sources:

Periodicals

Chicago Tribune, July 25, 1991, section 3, p. 3.
New York Times, August 11, 1991, section 3, p. 12.

—*Sketch by Marian C. Gonsior*

Angustias de la Guerra Ord
(1815-1890)
Historian

Angustias de la Guerra Ord was born into a world in transition. Ord watched firsthand as her native California moved from Spanish-Mexican rule to U.S. statehood. Her account of those transitional years, *Occurrences in Hispanic California,* is an important documentary record and a gripping story of betrayal and political intrigue, seen through the eyes of one who knew the major actors in the drama personally. The editor of the English language edition of the work commented in the forward: "The narrative of Mrs. Ord adds considerably to our knowledge and understanding of California history for the Spanish-Mexican period."

In 1846, the year de la Guerra Ord's narrative ends, California had a population of about 12,000 people—excluding native Americans—and for years the governments of England, France, Spain, Mexico, the United States, and even Russia had been manipulating people and events in the hope of taking possession of this vast territory. De la Guerra Ord dictated her recollections of these events to Thomas Savage of the Bancroft Library in Berkeley, California, in 1878. The 156-page manuscript, which was entitled *Ocurrencias en California,* became part of the library's Hubert Howe Bancroft Collection, and was translated in English and published by the Academy of American Franciscan History in 1956 under the title *Occurrences in Hispanic California.* In the foreword to the English edition, the editor noted that "the *Ocurrencias* does much to fill out the fragmentary story we have of these complicated years" of pre-statehood. Her story is told through "the elaboration and interpretation of important events of the times, the description of familiar persons, and the listings with brief comment in most cases of unfamiliar figures, by one whose background and experiences enabled her to speak authoritatively."

A Prestigious Spanish Family

De la Guerra Ord was born in San Diego, California, on June 11, 1815, into one of California's most prestigious Spanish families. Her father, Jose de la Guerra y Noriega—called "El Capitan" by all Californians—had to obtain royal permission to marry her mother, Maria Antonia Carrillo, who was of noble blood. Forty days after de la Guerra Ord's birth, her family moved to Santa Barbara, California, where her father took command of the Presidio. Her life soon became entangled with the political events of the time.

In 1833, de la Guerra Ord married Manuel Jimeno Casarin and moved to Monterey, which was then the capital of California. During the course of his career Jimeno Casarin served as secretary of state, senior member of the Assembly and on a few occasions acting governor. Jimeno Casarin's position enabled his wife to witness the political unrest that followed the California Departmental Assembly's declaration of independence, and to report such news in her recollections. She detailed the alliance between native Californians and "a force of foreign riflemen" from the United States. This alliance eventually pushed the Mexican rulers out of the territory. De la Guerra Ord also spoke at length of the secularization of the missions implemented by Governor Alvarado upon orders from Mexico, which proved highly controversial. She strongly denies that the missionaries executed grand scale cattle slaughters to retain their hides. She emphasizes that if it were true, she would have known through her father—the well-respected "El Capitan" would have been informed—and through her two brothers-in-law, who were missionaries.

Power struggles, personal conflicts and armed rebellions continued to permeate California's daily life throughout the period of Mexican rule, which finally ended in 1846 when California fell under United States military rule. De la Guerra Ord notes in her memoirs that "the conquest of California did not bother the Californians, least of all the women. It must be confessed that California was on the road to most complete ruin. On one hand the Indians were out of hand, committing robberies and other crimes on the ranches, with little or nothing being done to curb their depredations. On the other hand were the differences between the people of the north and of the south, and between both against Mexicans and other bands. But the worst cancer of all was the plundering which was carried on generally. There had been such looting of the resources of the government, that the treasury chest was 'scuttled.' General (Jose) Castro maintained a corps of officers sufficient for an army of 3,000 men. . . . Of these officers, few offered their services when the hour came to defend the country against the [American] invasion. The greater part performed no more service than the figurehead of a ship."

California Statehood Lessens Hispanic Families' Power

With the appropriation of California by the United States, the Mexican families' political influence began to dwindle. In the latter part of the 19th century, feuds between newly-arrived Americans and established Spanish and Mexican families even led to bloodshed. The de la Guerras were among the few families that managed to keep their social identity and to retain some political influence. De la Guerra Ord's brother, Pablo, was a delegate at the state's first constitutional convention in 1849. Popular with both Americans and Hispanics, he served in the state Senate throughout the 1850s, and became California's lieutenant governor in 1860. De la Guerra Ord's prominence also persisted under American rule.

De la Guerra Ord's husband died of cholera in 1853 during a visit to Mexico. She had borne him 11 children, one of whom, Porfirio, would serve as captain of the California volunteers during the U.S. Civil War. Three years after her husband's death she married James L. Ord—a surgeon with the U.S. Army whose father was the son of King George IV of England and Maria Fitzherbert—and moved back to Santa Barbara. De la Guerra Ord and her husband visited Washington, D.C., and Mexico in 1871, and had the opportunity to meet United States President Ulysses S. Grant at the White House and Mexican President Benito Juarez at the castle of Chapultepec. In 1875, de la Guerra Ord obtained the dissolution of her marriage with Ord. After her father's death, she involved herself in a legal battle over his estate. She died on June 21, 1890, and was buried, at her request, in the Santa Barbara Mission's cemetery with the words "I wish to rest with those I loved so well" written in Spanish on her tombstone. The de la Guerras' family home, which remained in the family until 1943, now constitutes one of Santa Barbara's architectural landmarks.

Sources:

Books

de la Guerra Ord, Angustias, *Occurrences in Hispanic California*, Academy of American Franciscan History, 1956.
Thompson, Joseph A., *El Gran Capitan*, 1961.
Tompkins, Walker A., *Santa Barbara History Makers*, 1983.

Periodicals

Santa Barbara Daily News, May 20, 1922.
Santa Barbara News-Press, December 2, 1956, p. B14.

—Sketch by Michelle Vachon

Adelaida Del Castillo
(1952-)
Scholar

Adelaida Del Castillo is one of a handful of scholars involved in researching the status of women in Hispanic society, specifically those of Chicano descent. A Ph.D. in social anthropology, Del Castillo teaches at San Diego State University in California, where she has been honored with numerous awards for her work. In 1991 and 1992 she received the Outstanding Faculty Award as well as being the 1992 recipient of the prestigious Phi Eta Sigma Timeos Award for Outstanding Assistant Professor. She is the editor of "La Mujer Latina Series" for Floricanto Press, edited *Between Borders: Essays on Mexicana/Chicana History* and is the coeditor of *Mexican Women in the United States: Struggles Past and Present.* In addition, Del Castillo is the author of numerous scholarly articles on Latinas. She has received a number of prestigious research grants and academic fellowships including the Inter-American Foundation Fellowship (1988), the Institute of American Cultures Research Grant (1985), and the UCLA Program on Mexico Research Grant (1986). She has made presentations across the United States and in Mexico on topics like sex and gender issues, the history of the Mexicana and Chicana, cultural diversity, human values, and strategies for survival of the disadvantaged. Her work is linked by a strong desire to achieve equality between the sexes and between the races.

Del Castillo told interviewer Andres Chavez that she has a personal interest in history, but she chose anthropology for her professional work because she enjoys interacting with people. "I found that much more engaging than spending my time in archives, researching alone. The human interaction was always very important to me and anthropology asks that you make use of that dimension. When you go out into the field, you go into the field where you know no one, you have to negotiate your way through. I've always found that a challenge and rewarding. To discover who people are is like unpacking a present. People are interesting and fascinating to me."

Del Castillo, one of six children, is the daughter of Austin and Adelaida Del Castillo. Even as a child she sensed tension within her family regarding gender roles. Her sister was older, so most of Del Castillo's playmates happened to be her brothers and their male friends. She learned to compete successfully with them on the playground. But, as Del Castillo explained to Chavez, "As soon as I entered the house my mother would expect me to make dinner or make lunch for my brothers, iron their clothes, wash dishes. I used to think, why is it that I have to do this when I can do anything they can do and as soon as I enter the house I'm treated differently. . . . I felt that this was unfair." This was one of the major themes that would shape her career. The other was the Chicano movement.

Del Castillo became active in the Chicano movement in high school. Her father stressed education, but Del Castillo says that it was the Chicano movement that became the vehicle for her higher education. While in high school, Del Castillo attended a theater workshop conducted by El Teatro Campesino, which included a course in Chicano history. As she told Chavez, when she returned from the workshop she "was transformed . . . and because of my conscience as a Chicana I thought the world was open to me to do whatever, and as a consequence I graduated from high school and went to the University of California, Los Angeles." Del Castillo's feminist views led to her research on the role of women in Mexican society, and along with other Latinas, she established the feminist journal *Encuentro Feminil.* Del Castillo received her undergraduate degree in

linguistics and went on to graduate work in social anthropology. She became interested in working with the undocumented, people who are in the United States without proper immigration papers, particularly undocumented women in Los Angeles, California. This eventually led her to Mexico City where she conducted research for her Ph.D. She told Chavez that the results of her study showed that Mexican women are leaders, "very strong women, very powerful. . . . When we look at community organizational efforts and movements that have to interface with political power, women are in the forefront." Del Castillo's book *Negotiated Lives: The Power and Stigma of Women's Domestic Relations in Mexico City* is based on an enthnographic study of women-centered households in a Mexico City irregular settlement.

Del Castillo explained to Chavez that her feminist views do not lead to the exclusion of people because of gender. She also takes issue with the macho stereotype of Latinos: "It is a myth that Anglo men are less sexist than Chicano men. Anglo men are sexist within their own cultural patterns. Men in general have to get used to the fact that women can articulate their opinions and are capable of having valuable ideas. I don't think you can construct a hierarchy of whose more oppressive, the Latino or the Anglo. . . . I'm a feminist, but I'm definitely not antimale in any way. I have sons, I'm married [to Chicano historian Juan Gomez-Quiñones]. I have to raise males, I have to interact with males as a wife and I have to mentor males as a professor and there's no way I can discriminate against males. I guess my perspective is inclusive. I'm prohuman."

Sources:

Del Castillo, Adelaida, interview with Andres Chavez, September 23, 1992.

—*Sketch by Andres Chavez*

Jane L. Delgado
(1953-)
Health organization director, clinical psychologist

Jane L. Delgado, Ph.D., is the president and chief executive officer of the National Coalition of Hispanic Health and Human Services Organizations, the only national organization that focuses on the improvement of health and human services of the nation's Hispanic population. Delgado is also the first non-white person elected to chair the National Health Council, a 73-year-old coalition of voluntary health organizations that includes such giants as the American Heart Association and the American

Jane L. Delgado

Cancer Society. In addition, she serves on numerous boards and advisory councils which address issues such as mental health, child development, patient information and education, health insurance, drug abuse, underserved communities, AIDS, health and vital statistics, and nutrition. Delgado is also a clinical psychologist who maintains a small private practice in Washington, D.C.

In 1955, the Delgado family immigrated from Havana, Cuba, to New York City. Jane was just two years old. Her father, Juan Lorenzo Delgado Borges, was employed as a publisher of Latin American magazines. Delgado's mother, Lucila, stayed home and took care of their two young daughters. Before too long, however, Delgado's father abandoned the family, leaving his wife to raise the children.

Lucila Aurora Navarro Delgado would have been content to remain at home and raise her children. But with her husband's sudden departure, she found herself forced into the workplace with no valuable skills. Though she had completed two years of law school in Cuba, she knew little English and had to accept factory work. At one point she made watches, and later she became a keypunch operator. Somehow she balanced work with parenting and always provided her daughters with love and encouragement. It was Lucila who worked two full-time jobs in order to contribute to Delgado's college education.

When Delgado entered kindergarten, her knowledge of English was nonexistent but her curiosity and imagination

were great. She concluded that she must be from another planet based on the fact that her mother was forced to fill out alien registration forms every year and her skin, she was told, was olive (green) in color. Regardless, Delgado loved school and by the third grade was doing so well that she was placed in a "gifted" class. She was disappointed to learn, however, that receiving presents was not part of the curriculum.

Pursues Education in Psychology

By the time she reached high school, Delgado was bored and unchallenged. She desperately wanted to finish high school and ended up graduating early by developing her own plan of acceleration. She researched colleges and filled out applications on her own, as there was little guidance from the high school counselors. The State University of New York at New Paltz accepted her. Delgado said good-bye to her mother at the bus stop with a pillow in one hand and a suitcase in the other. Her mother worried about her until Jane announced, three weeks later, that she had been elected vice president of the freshman class. Her mother knew then that Jane would be just fine. Delgado was just sixteen years old.

Delgado entered New Paltz as a psychology major. She had been encouraged in grade school to become a psychologist. At the time it was suggested, she didn't even know what a psychologist was. But as she grew, she realized that it would be a good profession for her. Besides, her mother always said, "You must do for others to lead a full life." Her performance at New Paltz was outstanding, and she received a bachelor of arts with honors at the age of nineteen.

Upon her graduation, Delgado moved to New York City and launched two new projects. She began a master's degree program at New York University in social and personality psychology and also began working for the Children's Television Network. Delgado was chosen as the children's talent coordinator for the TV show *Sesame Street*. She was in charge of selecting the children who appeared on the show. Feeling strongly that the children should not be actors but "real kids," Delgado developed a test that determined which children had good TV personalities. She also initiated a campaign to recruit handicapped children to appear on the show. Delgado was very successful and so was the show, but after receiving her Master of Arts in 1975, she decided to return to school and fulfill her dream to become a clinical psychologist.

Delgado learned to perform multiple tasks from her mother, who usually had more than one job. She started working at age nine selling products in the neighborhood and continued to work throughout her educational years. She funded her education with her own earnings, contributions from her mother, and student loans. Delgado applied to the Ph.D. program at the State University of New York at Stony Brook and was accepted on her second try. At first, she was not accepted to any schools that she applied to, even though her grades and admission test scores were good. She was only 22 and it was considered a risk for a graduate program to accept such a young student. While attending Stony Brook, Delgado became an instructor at the New York Experimental and Bilingual Institute. She taught college-level psychology and sociology courses. Delgado also served as a teaching assistant for an advanced experimental psychology laboratory course at Stony Brook. She prepared and delivered lectures, designed experiments, and graded the performance of students.

From 1977 to 1979, Delgado was a consultant for the Board of Cooperative Educational Services in Westbury, New York. She provided psychological and educational services for bilingual children, their parents, teachers, and school officials. She also designed and implemented a career awareness program for bilingual Hispanic and Italian teenagers. At Stony Brook, Delgado served as project director of a three-year study focusing on language development as a predictor of learning disabilities in children. The investigation covered the United States, Colombia, and Brazil. Delgado traveled through these countries to coordinate site selection, collect data, and supervise research assistants. She designed methodologies and procedures and analyzed data leading to the final report. By 1981, Delgado had not only received her Ph.D. in clinical psychology, but had also earned a Master of Sciences in urban policy and sciences. Delgado recalled in an interview with Susan Lopez Mele that in her last year of clinical training she decided "one-on-one therapy was great, but if you want to change people's lives, you have to change institutions." Delgado, in her usual "snowplow" fashion, set out to do just that.

Joins U.S. Department of Health and Human Services

Delgado had joined the U.S. Department of Health and Human Services (HHS) in Washington, D.C., in 1979. She first served in the Office of Human Development Services, where she was responsible for a wide range of activities in the Division of Special Projects. Delgado managed $1.5 million in grants and contracts. She also managed projects including Hispanic Initiative, Private Sector Initiative, Administrative Review of Regional Operations, Black Colleges Initiatives, and Undocumented Workers. In addition, she served as liaison with the international office and met foreign dignitaries, prepared a paper for the 35th General Assembly of the United Nations, and provided staff support to the White House Rural Human Services Coordinating Committee.

Delgado then joined the newly created Office of Community Services, worth $400 million in block grants. She developed a mission statement for the office and wrote position descriptions and procedures for the staff. She served as acting chief of the branch and conducted on-site financial, administrative, and program activities assessments of selected states in the implementation of the block grants. She also conducted meetings, interviewed, and resolved concerns with high-level local, state, and federal officials, grantees, and representatives of outside groups. She prepared testimony and questions and answers for congressional hearings concerning allocation of the funds.

Before long, Delgado earned a position in the Immediate Office of the Secretary of HHS, then Margaret Heckler. Delgado was responsible for overseeing $5 billion in programs on health, mental health, alcohol abuse, drug abuse, aging, block grants, and minorities. Delgado advised the secretary on issues and recommended solutions. She dealt with officials at the federal, state, and local levels on politically sensitive issues on behalf of Secretary Heckler. She also negotiated activities between the United States and Mexico. Delgado was also the senior policy coordinator for the National Institute of Mental Health, National Institute on Drug Abuse, National Institute on Alcohol Abuse and Alcoholism, and the Alcohol, Drug Abuse, and Mental Health Administration, and was instrumental in developing the "Report of the Secretary's Task Force on Black and Minority Health."

Appointed President of National Health Organization

Delgado received numerous honors and awards from Secretary Heckler. The final vote of confidence was in 1985, when Heckler recommended Delgado for the position of president and CEO of the Coalition of Spanish Speaking Mental Health Organizations. (The organization's name became the National Coalition of Hispanic Health and Human Services Organizations in 1986, but is still known by its former acronym, COSSMHO.) Delgado accepted the position and became responsible for all phases of research, policy, program, and public affairs activities. She manages a multi-million dollar budget and a staff of 32 full-time professionals.

COSSMHO was founded in 1973 by a group of mental health professionals who recognized the need for an organization to represent all Hispanics in the United States. Under Delgado's leadership, COSSMHO has grown to an organization with over 250 member agencies and over 800 professionals serving Mexican American, Puerto Rican, Cuban American, and other Hispanic American communities. It is a private non-profit organization based in Washington, D.C., which receives federal grants and contracts, foundation support, corporate support, and membership dues. Delgado has increased non-federal support of COSSMHO from 1 percent to 35 percent. She does not, however, accept contributions from alcohol or tobacco companies.

In her first year as president, Delgado implemented a major outreach program to educate and inform Hispanics about AIDS. She has also been at the forefront of women's health. "Most of the research we have is based on one-third of the population—white males," she told Mele. Delgado also ensures that environmental health issues are addressed. She has created an interactive network between COSSMHO and community health agencies nationwide, and has implemented a computer bulletin board which serves as an information broker between the agencies themselves and/or with COSSMHO. Thirty-six sites across the country are included in the network.

COSSMHO is often called upon by Capitol Hill to provide the latest health statistics on Hispanics. Delgado has given testimony before Congress on health and human services and is a frequent public speaker. She serves on numerous health boards and councils to ensure Hispanic representation. Among them are United Way of America, Advisory Committee on Food and Drug Administration, Fighting Back Drug Abuse in America, National Advisory Council on the National Health Service Corps, and the National Council on Patient Information and Education.

Delgado has stabilized COSSMHO and sees this as her greatest achievement during her time as president of the organization. Delgado considers her greatest all-around achievement her relationships with family and friends. She married Herbert Lustig on Valentine's Day of 1981. She maintains childhood friendships and has adopted many into her family over the years. Delgado, her husband, and her mother live together in Washington, D.C.

Sources:

Periodicals

Des Moines Sunday Register, April 26, 1992, p. C-7E.

Other

Delgado, Jane L., interviews with Susan Lopez Mele, September 25, 1991, and September 16, 1992.
Delgado, Jane L., fact sheet provided by the National Coalition of Hispanic Health and Human Services Organizations, July 30, 1992.

—*Sketch by Susan Lopez Mele*

de los Angeles Torres, Maria
See Torres, Maria de los Angeles

Dolores Del Rio
(1905-1983)
Actress

The type of role offered to Hispanic actresses in Hollywood during the twenties and thirties—the most important years of Dolores Del Rio's career—is evident in the following excerpt from George Hadley-Garcia's *Hispanic Hollywood*: "In the early '30s, producer David O. Selznick informed his staff, 'I want Dolores Del Rio in a South Seas romance. . . I don't care what story you use so long as we call it *Bird of Paradise* and Del Rio jumps into a flaming volcano to finish.'" According to Hadley-Garcia, Hispanic actresses like Del Rio often had to endure changing their names, being cast as a member of another ethnic group, or pretending to be of European descent if they wanted to work. Del Rio did not change her name, but did appear in a variety of ethnic roles and was billed as a "Spanish" actress at the beginning of her career. Although often typecast in exotic parts (such as the one suggested by Selznick), Del Rio became one of the first Mexican film personalities to achieve international stardom.

Del Rio was born Lolita Dolores Asúnsolo y López Negrete in Durango, Mexico, on August 3, 1905, to Jesus and Antonia (López Negrete) Asúnsolo. The family was split apart a few years later, when Del Rio's father, who was director of the Bank of Durango, was forced to flee to the United States during the Mexican Revolution of 1910. He left his wife and young daughter behind in the comparative safety of Mexico City where Del Rio grew up. She attended a French private school, the Convent of St. Joseph, where among other subjects she studied Spanish dancing. In 1921, she married Jaime Martínez Del Rio, a lawyer 18 years her senior, and left Mexico for a two-year European honeymoon. While traveling in Spain, she had her first taste of stardom as she used her dancing skills to entertain wounded Spanish soldiers returning from the war with Morocco.

In the early twenties, Del Rio was invited to Hollywood by the American film director Edwin Carewe, who had met her through a mutual friend. In 1925, she began her film career with a small part in United Artists's *Joanne*. This was to be the first of 15 silent films the actress made between 1925 and 1929. Three of her most important films of the period include *What Price Glory?*, *Resurrection*, and *Ramona*. The first title was directed by Raoul Walsh and released in 1926. In the film Del Rio played a French peasant girl named Charmaine. It became the second best-selling film of the year, earning $2 million at the box-office. The 1927 film *Resurrection* was an adaptation of Count Leo Tolstoy's work of the same title and featured Del Rio, in her first

Dolores Del Rio

starring role, as a Russian peasant. Del Rio's performance in *Ramona,* released in 1928 through United Artists, was praised by Mordaunt Hall in the *New York Times.* According to Dorothy J. Gaiter in a *New York Times* retrospective look at Del Rio's film career, Hall had noted: "Del Rio's interpretation of Ramona is an achievement. Not once does she overact, and yet she is perceived weeping and almost hysterical. She is most careful in all the moods of the character."

Silent Films Bring Fame

Because she had yet to learn English, the silent film era was especially helpful to Del Rio's career, and she was one of Hollywood's top ten money-makers during the 1920s. Her voice was first heard in the 1929 release *Evangeline* which, although silent, included three songs sung by Del Rio in French which had been edited into the movie before its release. The year 1930 marked the release of Del Rio's first talkie and of her marriage to Metro-Goldwyn-Mayer art director Cedric Gibbons. (Her first husband had died.) Gibbons was the designer of the Academy Award "Oscar" and subsequently earned 12 of the awards himself. The couple settled into a Gibbons-designed house in Santa Monica, California, and pursued an extravagant lifestyle. While Gibbons produced the sets for films such as *The Thin Man, Mutiny on the Bounty,* and *A Tale of Two Cities,* Del Rio signed a contract with United Artists which paid $9000 a week. The marriage was to last 11 years.

A serious illness caused Del Rio to lose the contract with United Artists, but once she recovered she signed with RKO Studios. In 1932, she starred in *The Girl of the Rio* which, although very popular, angered the Mexican government for its plot line that implied that Mexican justice was something that could be bought. It was banned in Mexico, Panama, and Nicaragua. That same year Del Rio also appeared in *Bird of Paradise*—the film imagined by Selznick—in which she played a Polynesian girl who throws herself into a volcano to appease the "God in the Mountain of Fire." In 1933, Del Rio starred in the movie that brought together for the first time one of the screen's most famous dance teams: Fred Astaire and Ginger Rogers. The film, *Flying Down to Rio,* featured a scene in which Astaire and Del Rio are dance partners as well as Del Rio's introduction of the two-piece swimsuit to U.S. audiences.

Works to Build Fledgling Mexican Film Industry

In 1942, after starring in 23 U.S. films, Del Rio left the United States for her native Mexico. "By 1940 I knew I couldn't build a satisfying career on glamour, so I came home," she told Chris O'Connor in a *Modern Maturity* interview. "My father had died, and I felt a need for my country, my people. Also I wanted to pioneer with our beginning Mexican film industry." Del Rio made good on her plans and appeared in two important films of the early Mexican cinema, *Flor silvestre* ("Wild Flower") and *María Candelaria* (released in English as *Portrait of Maria*). Both titles were released in 1943 and both were the product of influential Mexican director Emilio "El Indio" Fernández. *Portrait of Maria* won the best picture award—the Golden Palm—at the first post-World War II Cannes Film Festival in France in 1946. It was also a prize winner at the international film festival held in Locarno, Switzerland, in 1947. The film, which tells the story of a Mexican beauty who is stoned to death after being falsely accused of posing for a nude portrait, introduced the fledgling Mexican cinema to international audiences and established Del Rio as an important international screen personality.

During the 1940s and 1950s, Del Rio continued on as the most important Mexican actress of the day, but she stayed away from Hollywood. According to Hadley-Garcia, Del Rio's absence from U.S. screens was due to the suspicious attitude that surrounded the movie industry during the height of the Cold-War era. "During the 1950s she was barred from the U.S., for having aided anti-Franco refugees from the Spanish Civil War," Hadley-Garcia wrote. In 1947, Del Rio played what would be her last part in an American film until the 1960s, with her appearance in the John Ford film *The Fugitive,* based on Graham Greene's novel *The Power and the Glory.* Made almost entirely in Mexico, the movie starred Del Rio as an unwed Indian mother and Henry Fonda as an alcoholic Mexican priest. Although the film received a limited distribution in the United States, the presence of Fonda in its cast and Ford as its director assured continued interest in it from movie buffs. In fact, Del Rio's role in the movie has remained one for which she is best remembered.

In the 1950s the actress combined film engagements with stage productions, including a tour through New England performing in *Anastasia* in 1956. During the same period she starred in two Mexican films based on classics of Spanish literature: *La Malquerida*, based on leading Spanish playwright Jacinto Benavente's play of the same title, and *Doña Perfecta*, based on the novel by Spanish novelist Benito Pérez Galdós. An American theater producer and director, Lewis Riley, encouraged Del Rio to make her debut on the Mexican stage in his production of *Lady Windmere's Fan*, a comedy of manners by Oscar Wilde, in the late '50s. She also appeared in Henrik Ibsen's *Ghosts* and other stage productions. On November 24, 1960, she married Riley and the two made their home in an affluent suburb of Mexico City.

During the sixties the pace of Del Rio's film career slowed considerably; she made only five films in Mexico from 1960 to 1978. She returned to Hollywood in 1961 to play Elvis Presley's Native American mother in *Flaming Star*. In 1964 she starred in what was to be director John Ford's last Western, *Cheyenne Autumn*, which featured Ricardo Montalban and Del Rio as the parents of a character played in the film by teen idol Sal Mineo. In 1966, she appeared in a Spanish film, *La Dama del Alba*, and in a made-for-television travelogue, *Dolores Del Rio's Mexico*, shown on U.S. television screens in 1968. At age 63, she appeared as the leading role in a Mexico City stage production of *The Lady of the Camellias*. As the decade drew to a close, she took a small part in Italian film director Carlo Ponti's film, *C'era una Volta* (released in English as *More Than a Miracle*), as the mother of the character played in the film by Omar Sharif. The film also starred Sophia Loren.

Opens Nursery for Performers' Children

In 1970, Del Rio announced her retirement and began to devote herself to the charitable work that would take up most of her time in her later years. In 1971, with government sponsorship and the support of the Mexican Actors' Association, she founded the Estancia Infantil, a day-care center for children of Mexican performers. As chairperson of the board of the center, Del Rio spent many hours at the nursery with her young charges. She explained the concept behind the center in *Modern Maturity*: "Babies are special in Mexico, you know, and their first six years are the most important. We play Brahms and Bach to them, teach them English, folklorico dancing—all the arts." Del Rio interrupted her retirement briefly in 1978 to make *The Children of Sanchez*, a U.S.-Mexican production co-starring Anthony Quinn, which Hadley-Garcia referred to as a "minor (and little seen in the U.S.) masterpiece."

Del Rio's role in *The Children of Sanchez* was to be her last. The actress died on April 11, 1983, at her home in Newport Beach, California, of chronic hepatitis. In *Mexican Cinema: Reflections of a Society, 1896-1988*, Carl J. Mota quotes from a *Hispanoamericano* article written upon the actress's death in which Jorge Carrasco evaluated Del Rio's contribution to Mexican cinema. In his comments, Carrasco maintained that Del Rio's impact on the Mexican film industry was "very great and much time would pass before another star of her magnitude would arise. Her death [deprived] Mexican cinema of one of the great figures that gave it an international reputation during its golden age."

Sources:

Books

Hadley-Garcia, George, *Hispanic Hollywood: The Latins in Motion Pictures*, foreword by Dolores Del Rio, Citadel Press, 1990.
Mora, Carl J., *Mexican Cinema: Reflections of a Society, 1896-1988*, revised edition, University of California Press, 1989.
Shipman, David, *The Great Movie Stars: The Golden Years*, revised edition, Hill & Wang, 1979.
Woll, Allen L., *Films of Dolores Del Rio*, Gordon Press, 1978.

Periodicals

Architectural Digest, April, 1992, pp. 128-133, 254.
Hispanoamericano (Spanish-language; translation by Carl J. Mora), April 25, 1983, pp. 44-47.
Modern Maturity, February, 1981, pp. 69-71.
New York Times, April 13, 1983, p. D23.

—Sketch by Marian C. Gonsior

del Rio, Petra Barreras
See **Barreras del Rio, Petra**

Del Valle, Sandra Ortiz
See **Ortiz-Del Valle, Sandra**

Dennis, Patricia Diaz
See **Diaz Dennis, Patricia**

Rosana De Soto

(1950?-)

Actress

A versatile and talented television and motion picture actress, Rosana De Soto has earned high praise for her convincing portrayals of both leading and supporting characters. Just four years after her film debut in *The In-Laws,* De Soto received the Golden Eagle award for best actress for her work as Carlota Munoz in the 1983 film *The Ballad of Gregorio Cortez.* De Soto garnered a best supporting actress award in 1987 from the Independent Film Makers Association for her portrayal of Fabiola Escalante in *Stand and Deliver,* with Lou Diamond Phillips and Edward James Olmos.

Born September 2, in San Jose, California, the daughter of Mexican parents from Michoacan, De Soto grew up in a large immigrant family with four sisters and four brothers and recalls handpicking fruit in the summer to help her relatives make ends meet. "It was a pleasure standing under those trees, picking apples. Every day we had a picnic. It was something very natural and I loved it," she recalled in an interview in *La Familia de Hoy.* "My parents were very passionate people," she continued. "Neither had a formal education, but they did have a big heart and a very real vitality, strength of character and love of God."

De Soto's interest in the performing arts was sparked when she played an animated daisy at the age of seven. Despite her desire for an acting career, De Soto deferred her dream to attend San Jose State University, graduating with a double major in Spanish literature and drama. Even as she was attending classes during the day, however, the aspiring actress spent her evenings rehearsing and performing with the Light Opera Company, starring in a variety of dramatic performances.

Television Roles Lead to Film Career

By the time she was 22 years old, De Soto moved to Hollywood and began her professional acting career at the Improvisational Theatre at the Los Angeles Music Center. In an interview in *La Familia de Hoy,* De Soto recalled her first impressions of the glamorous film industry capital. "Suddenly I found myself amongst the most fascinating circles, with people of enormous prestige such as Federico Fellini, and I felt stunned and overwhelmed." Once, De Soto recalled, she was approached by Mel Brooks on the 20th Century-Fox lot. Failing to recognize the influential producer, De Soto turned down what perhaps could have been an important career break. Despite the gaffe, De

Soto's talent and perseverance ensured her success. Following her stay at the Los Angeles Music Center and the New York Shakespeare Festival, she found plenty of work in television, making appearances in various series, including *Barney Miller, Punky Brewster, the Redd Fox Show, Murder She Wrote, Miami Vice,* and *The Antagonists.*

After honing her skills for television audiences, De Soto turned to the movies, appearing in such films as *Cannery Row* with Nick Nolte and Debra Winger in 1982 and *About Last Night* with Demi Moore and Rob Lowe in 1986. Other film credits include the portrayal of Dustin Hoffman's wife in *Family Business,* Lou Diamond Phillips' mother in the Hispanic market's best grossing film to date, *La Bamba,* the principal female role in *Face of the Enemy,* and an appearance in *Star Trek VI* with William Shatner and Leonard Nimoy. Always careful about the roles she selects, De Soto explained in the *New York Times:* "Until you overcome the stereotyping, you are limited to playing certain roles."

Throughout her career, De Soto has devoted her spare time to community service. Some of her activities include teaching remedial courses to ex-convicts for the federally implemented California Food Federation rehabilitation program and conducting research for the Department of Employment and Redevelopment. Today, De Soto keeps busy with her career and family, including her children Sylvana Bonifacia and Daniela, but still continues her public service as a keynote speaker, addressing students and community groups with motivational talks focused on self-discipline, determination, overcoming adversity, and finding the road to success. De Soto was also a featured speaker in a lecture series with Coretta Scott King.

Sources:

Periodicals

La Familia de Hoy (Spanish-language; translated by Elena Kellner), summer, 1992.
New York City Tribune, November 5, 1987, p. 10.

—*Sketch by Elena Kellner*

Patricia Diaz Dennis

(1946-)

Lawyer, government official

Patricia Diaz Dennis is enthusiastic about her appointment as Assistant Secretary of State for Human Rights and

Patricia Diaz Dennis

Humanitarian Affairs. "You have few opportunities to leave a legacy and change people's lives for the better besides raising healthy and sane children," Diaz Dennis told Luis Vasquez-Ajmac. "This job is one where you can't do enough," she continued. "I couldn't say no to the appointment."

Diaz Dennis's response to a new challenge is not surprising, for she has taken on many challenges in her life. She decided to pursue a career in law instead of teaching school. After building an impressive reputation in labor law, she again changed career plans at the age of 40 by becoming President Ronald Reagan's appointee as a Commissioner for the Federal Communications Commission (FCC). Although she maintains a heavy work schedule, Diaz-Dennis makes spending time with her three children and her husband, Michael John Dennis, a priority.

Born October 2, 1946, in Santa Rita, a small town outside Silver City, New Mexico, Diaz Dennis is the oldest of five children. Her father, Porfirio Diaz, and her mother, Mary Romero Diaz, were close, loving parents. Porfirio Diaz was a sergeant in the army; his job required that the family travel and relocate frequently. Diaz Dennis spent several years in Japan as a teenager and lived in Santiago, Chile, where she graduated from high school. Living in foreign countries exposed Diaz Dennis to different cultures and environments. She explained to Vasquez-Ajmac, "When you're an American living abroad, you're automati-

cally in a different social grouping even if you're not in the same economic status as the social group." As a result of her travels, Diaz Dennis believes that her world view changed dramatically.

With the encouragement of her parents, Diaz Dennis became the first in her Mexican American family to go to college. Concerned about their daughter leaving home and adjusting to the United States, Diaz Dennis's parents thought it best that she be near relatives and attend the San Francisco College for Women, a Catholic school. After several semesters at that institution, she transferred to the University of North Carolina-Chapel Hill. The young woman returned to California to marry Michael Dennis after her junior year. She completed an A.B. degree in English literature at the University of California-Los Angles (UCLA) in 1970 and received the Fouragere Honors at graduation.

Meeting Michael Dennis was a turning point in Diaz Dennis's life. She credits her husband, who is also a lawyer, as the one giving her the support and initiative to practice law. She recalled in 1989 in *Executive Female,* "I had been applying to graduate school for an advance degree in English literature when he suggested I apply to law school instead. He figured that since I won all the arguments at home I should put that skill to good use."

Diaz Dennis was admitted to Loyola University School of Law in Los Angeles and began to attend school there. She served as the Executive Editor of the *Loyola Law Review* and was on the Dean's list when she earned her J.D. in 1973. That same year, Diaz Dennis passed the California State Bar Exam. Later, she was admitted to practice before the District of Columbia Court of Appeals, and the Supreme Court of the United States.

Diaz Dennis worked at Paul, Hastings, Janofsky & Walker in Los Angeles while she was still a law student at Loyola. This job sparked Diaz Dennis's love for labor law. She told *Executive Female,* "I found I really enjoyed reconciling conflicts. There are legitimate concerns on both sides of the bargaining table—management and employee—and a labor lawyer has to reconcile them." Diaz Dennis returned to the prestigious labor law firm after graduation to become not only the first female lawyer, but also the firm's first Hispanic lawyer. It was here that she built her solid background in labor law.

When Diaz Dennis gave birth to her first child , she discovered that the long hours required by a major law firm were, as she said in *Executive Female,* "incompatible with good parenting." Though she frequently nursed her child at work while maintaining her regular heavy caseload, she opted to leave the law firm of Paul, Hastings, Janofsky & Walker in 1976 for more predictable hours at Pacific Lighting Corporation.

As a lawyer at Pacific Lighting Corporation, a holding company for a California utility that also had an agricultural subsidiary, Diaz Dennis represented management in labor negotiations with the United Farm Workers Union. That position, as explained in *Broadcasting*, "could be 'emotionally difficult' because union members, some of whom spoke only Spanish, questioned whether she [Dias Dennis] wasn't on the wrong side of the bargaining table." Dias Dennis remarked in that same article, "I guess those are the sorts of experiences that toughen you."

Traveled to Hollywood to Join ABC-TV Management

In 1978, Diaz Dennis was recruited to represent management in labor issues at ABC-TV in Hollywood, California. The change was comforting, she commented in *Executive Female*, because unlike the unaccommodating structure for women with growing families at the Pacific Lighting Corporation, ABC's structure was very conducive to balancing work and family.

After one year at ABC, Diaz Dennis was promoted to assistant general attorney. She said of her experience at ABC in *Executive Female*, "I really enjoyed my job at ABC. There's a special aura about broadcasting and I had some great cases." The magazine noted, "One of her [Dias Dennis's] more unusual cases involved negotiations with a group of inmates at Folsom Prison who had been used as extras in an ABC movie and were demanding more than Screen Actors Guild's minimum."

During her tenure at ABC, Diaz Dennis accepted a presidential appointment to the National Labor Relations Board (NLRB), an independent agency that prevents and remedies unfair labor practices. After extensive interviews, President Reagan nominated her to the NLRB and the Senate confirmed her; she moved to Washington, D.C., with her family and became the second female board member and the first Latina in the agency's history.

Diaz Dennis's nomination came, in fact, as a surprise to her since no one in Washington paved the way for her. Her connection, she told Vasquez-Ajmac, was "literally through a friend of a friend of a friend who knew someone in the White House personnel office." In *Broadcasting*, Diaz Dennis was quoted as saying, "It really is a testament to democracy. The fact that someone like me was able to walk into the White House and then take on such an important public responsibility is a testament to how wonderful our country is. In no other country could someone like me have achieved this kind of job."

Perhaps because Dias Dennis had reputation for fairmindedness and was an expert in labor law, her nomination to the NLRB did not upset unions, even though she had represented management in all her years of practice.

"I believe unions didn't oppose me," remarked Diaz Dennis in *Executive Female*, "because I had established a reputation for fairness. That is really the quality to bring to decision-making. Because if people know that you gave them a fair shot, they will ultimately give you grudging respect."

Nominated by President Reagan to Head FCC

Diaz Dennis worked at the NLRB for three years before making a major career move in 1986 at the age of 40. Nominated by President Reagan to replace former FCC Commissioner Henry Rivera, Diaz Dennis became the second female and second Hispanic commissioner in the 55 year history of the FCC. "I was leaving the familiar and secure to start all over again in an incredibly complex industry," related Diaz Dennis in *US WEST*. "Communications issues are not readily understandable. They take study. The FCC's responsibility is tremendous—shaping a vision of what we want telephony to become over the next 20 years and then setting the right path for implementation."

Though Diaz Dennis was a self-proclaimed "rookie" when she started at the FCC, she emerged as an independent-minded, hard working, and thoughtful commissioner. As an FCC Commissioner, Diaz Dennis deliberated such issues as regulation of "Indecent Broadcasts"; policy regarding racial, ethnic, and gender preferences in license assignments; Open Network Architecture (ONA) proceedings; the development of the telephone system as it interrelates to small business and other common carrier issues, while remaining a strong defender of the First Amendment.

According to Diaz Dennis, one of her greatest accomplishments at the FCC involved implementing minority preferences for broadcast licenses, an issue eventually upheld by the Supreme Court. Deeming it an important issue because minorities today hold only two percent of all broadcasting licenses in the United States, she told Vasquez-Ajmac, "One of the cornerstones of the Communications Act of 1934 is diversity of programming and viewpoint. One way to ensure diversity of programming and viewpoint is to ensure diversity of ownership."

After Diaz Dennis's three-year term with the FCC expired in June 1989, she resumed private practice as partner and chair of the communications section of the law firm of Jones, Day, Reavis & Pogue in Washington, D.C. Diaz Dennis went on to serve as Vice President of Government Affairs for U.S. Sprint's Washington office and its parent company, United Telecommunication, Inc., now called Sprint Corporation, in March 1991. Here, she represented Sprint before the FCC, Congress, and other federal agencies.

Appointed Assistant Secretary of State

Diaz Dennis has been appointed Assistant Secretary of State for Human Rights and Humanitarian Affairs by President Bush and confirmed by the Senate. She views the appointment as a "rare opportunity to make a difference, to do some good for people, to save lives." She told Vasquez-Ajmac, "There are so many parts of the world where human rights are not being observed. . . . Someone who brings passion and commitment to the job will make a difference."

To many people, Diaz Dennis is that someone with passion and commitment. As a career woman, she is known to make decisions thoughtfully, competently, and fairly; she is also a devoted wife and the mother of three children. As an active member of the National Network of Hispanic Women, she cares deeply about the Hispanic community's problems. "It is my responsibility," she told *Executive Female,* "to be involved because any time one of us is successful, it means more of us can make it." Diaz Dennis "spends much of her spare time," according to *US West,* "advising young Hispanics that getting an education. . . being as 'good as you can be' are keys to taking advantage of challenges. . . ." Most importantly, she explained to Vasquez-Ajmac, "You have to have one person in your life who says you're special. Those of us who are successful," she concluded, "are obligated to extend our hands to those who come after us."

Sources:

Periodicals

Broadcasting, March 9, 1987, p. 87; September 25, 1989, p. 34.

Business Radio, October 1987, pp. 16-27.

Communications Week, June 1, 1987, p. 8; p. 33, March 4, 1991.

Communiqué, April 1987, pp. 14-20.

Executive Female, January/February 1989, pp. 35-36, pp. 67-68.

Hispanic Business, December 1987, p. 44, p. 47; May 1991, p. 6; August 1991, p. 44.

Hispanic Review of Business, April 1987, pp. 10-15.

Michigan Chronicle Pontiac Education, June 4, 1991.

National Journal, March 2, 1991, p. 529.

Phone Plus, February 1989, pp. 19-26.

Rural Telecommunications, spring 1987, pp. 50-53; fall 1987, pp. 42-44; spring 1989, pp. 10-13.

US West, Spring 1987, pp. 29-30.

Other

Diaz Dennis, Patricia, taped interview with Luis Vasquez-Ajmac, July 23, 1992, MAYA Corporation of America, Washington, D.C.

—Sketch by Luis Vasquez-Ajmac

Remedios Diaz-Oliver
(1938-)
Entrepreneur

Remedios Diaz-Oliver has struggled against revolution, jail, exile, and poverty, not to mention gender and ethnic barriers, to become chief executive officer of one southern Florida's top companies. After founding American International Container, a supplier of glass and plastic bottles, from a trailer on January 10, 1976, her work enabled the new company to take in $800,000 in sales its first year. By 1987, according to the *Miami Herald,* Diaz-Oliver's company grossed $68 million, with revenues of $90 million in 1991. The company was listed 33rd on *South Florida Business Journal's* list of top privately owned companies. In 1991, Diaz-Oliver left American International to found a family-run competitor, All American Containers.

When Diaz-Oliver was born on August 22, 1938, her Galician father was a hotel owner in Cuba who also distributed hotel supplies throughout the island. He took his daughter along with him on his various business trips to the United States and Spain, exposing her to an international perspective at an early age. Friends and supporters of Cuban dictator Fidel Castro in the early days of the revolution, the family eventually lost everything. Diaz-Oliver recalled an encounter with Castro in early 1960 in which he spoke to her, remembering her as the daughter of a former friend. "'Nenita (which my father used to call me) how are you?,' he said. I looked at him and I said, 'Surprised that you didn't keep your promises!' He didn't throw me in jail right then and there probably because I was pregnant, but I was in jail a year later," she related. Diaz-Oliver was jailed for a short time for protesting against government imposed mail inspections; upon her release she emigrated with her husband, Fausto, and her daughter, Rosa, to the United States on May 11, 1961.

Such an experience would understandably produce feelings of anger and betrayal in the victim, yet it is Diaz-Oliver's refusal to be sidetracked by adversity or anger that sets her apart. This value was instilled in her by her mother, who brought from her native Madrid an austere work ethic. "The only way you can succeed in life is by working hard, she taught me," Diaz-Oliver related. "I graduated from high school one year before everyone else. I had to get a special government permit to do it and to study abroad one year in Miami. I think I wanted to succeed!" Chosen valedictorian of her high school class, Diaz-Oliver went on to earn a master's in business administration from Havana Business University and a Ph.D. in education from the University of Havana. She had already begun a diplomatic career, was fluent in English, French, and Italian, and had planned to begin her career as a full-time educator,

Remedios Diaz-Oliver

when circumstances obliged her to abandon her home. She believes that she would have been equally successful had she been able to stay on the island despite her admission that being a female executive may have been more difficult in Latin America.

Starts New Life in Miami

However, being a penniless Hispanic woman refugee in Miami, a sleepy provincial town in 1961, also suggested its share of difficulties. Trained first and foremost as an educator, Diaz-Oliver had no time to become certified to teach in the United States or to wait for the new school terms to begin, so urgent was the need to support her infant daughter. This led her into the job market where she accepted the first employment opportunity she could find. She took a position with Emmer Glass, which sold containers, in the accounting department, working five-and-a-half days a week for $55. The need for a Spanish-speaking employee to communicate with potential clients arriving from Cuba and other parts of Latin America motivated Diaz-Oliver to familiarize herself with the business. She began to take the company's catalogues and technical books home with her to study. Within a year she was in charge of the newly formed "International Division." She was placed in charge of exporting containers for a company that had never exported before. She handled sales in Central America, and within ten years under her control the International Division had earned the company a number-one ranking among companies exporting con-

tainers to that area, as reported by the U.S. Department of Commerce. In 1968 she was the first Hispanic to earn the "E" Award—Excellence in Export—given by President Lyndon Johnson.

As head of the International Division she rapidly acquired a market that at that time had been almost exclusively controlled by exporting container companies from France and Italy. Under Diaz-Oliver's guidance, the United States for the first time made an inroad in that area. However, her rapid road to success did not remain unimpeded by difficulties or negative encounters. Being not only Hispanic but a woman as well meant encountering double-barrelled stereotypes. Diaz-Oliver reacted with her own typical aplomb. "I was contacted on one occasion by a gentleman when I was already vice president of the company," she related. "He asked to speak to the boss, and when I told him that *I* was the boss, he said, 'Come on, let me speak to the boss. You must be the secretary.' He then said, 'My God! I will never do business with a woman and I will never do business with a Cuban!' I said, 'Don't worry; I'll transfer your call to someone who is not a woman and who is not a Cuban!' He got into some trouble about a year later with an inventory problem and he called. . . . He said, 'I don't think I have any choice. Do you have such and such an item?' The next day the containers were delivered to his door and we saved him a lot of money. A year later I received an invitation for his son's wedding. He was marrying a Cuban girl!" Diaz-Oliver's handling of the situation and her refusal to react to the customer's insults "not only saved a client," she pointed out, "but we turned out to be friends! He recommended me to a lot of people because he saw I had a sense of humor and that I could take the heat. You can't get anything accomplished with anger, because everyone discriminates."

Founds Container Company

By 1976, Diaz-Oliver and her husband had founded American International Container. Her reputation in and around southern Florida had spread so widely that the support given her by the community buoyed the fledgling corporation to almost instant success. Seeming to have an instinctual understanding of how a cyclical economy like Miami's operates, she realized the potential for stability that a container supplier could have. With her husband and two children she founded All American Container in 1991, which distributes packaging products and materials, including plastic and glass bottles and containers, to companies including Coca-Cola, Pepsi, McCormick, Kraft, and Revlon. She has sales offices in Panama City, Panama; San Jose, Costa Rica; Caracas, Venezuela; Guayaquil, Ecuador; and Santiago, Chile; as well as European locations including London, The Hague, and Sydney, Australia.

The success of All American Containers spawned more opportunity for Diaz-Oliver, who is now on the boards of directors for US West Inc., Avon Inc., and Barnet Banks. Reflecting on her achievements, Diaz-Oliver commented in *Hispanic:* "I don't think [my success] is about being a woman or a minority as much as it is going in the boardroom with the same knowledge as men."

Over the years Diaz-Oliver has been able to respond to changing markets with an acumen that has allowed her to thrive through various recessions. In the eighties, when much of Latin America was in economic crisis, she shifted much of her market concentration back to the United States, especially Texas and the Carolinas. As much of Latin America is prospering in the nineties, she has begun to re-expand those markets. She also enjoys the opportunity for family involvement provided by her company. "The whole family works together," she noted, including her daughter, daughter-in-law, son-in-law, and husband.

Diaz-Oliver attributes her success to the community that supported her and makes many attempts to give something back. In addition to her executive responsibilities, she has also been very active in the Greater Miami Chamber of Commerce, Latin Chamber of Commerce, and the City of Miami and has worked towards increased tourism and investment in the greater Miami area. She has received accolades from Presidents Lyndon Johnson and George Bush, the State of Florida, the city of Miami, and Metropolitan Dade County and was named Entrepreneur of the Year by the Latin Chamber of Commerce in 1987 and Woman of the Year by the U.S. Hispanic Chamber of Commerce. She was also named Outstanding Woman of the Year in 1983 and 1984 by the Association of Critics of Radio and Television and Woman of the Year in 1984 by Latin Business and Professional Women. Numerous other organizations, including the American Red Cross, the American Cancer Society, and the United Way, benefit from her volunteerism. One of her greatest passions of the last few years has been to support education, especially at the University of Miami's Jackson Memorial Hospital. Education is the one quality that she values above all others, and that she insists is irreplaceable.

When asked what qualities she hopes her three grandchildren will have inherited from her, she does not say "thrift" or "industriousness," as one might expect from a business owner, but rather "patriotism, and a sense of ethics and family values toward every person they meet."

Sources:

Periodicals

Hispanic, October, 1992, p. 18.
Intercambios Femeniles, spring, 1987, p. 14.
Miami Herald, January 11, 1988.
South Florida Business Journal, September 23, 1991, p. 10.

Other

Diaz-Oliver, Remedios, telephone interview with Paul Miller, July 30, 1992.

—*Sketch by Paul Miller*

Rita DiMartino
(1937-)
Businesswoman

Rita DiMartino, a top lobbyist for one of the largest telecommunications corporations in the United States, acknowledges that she breaks rank with stereotypes associated with Hispanics. "A lot of people have perceptions of what Hispanic is supposed to be. I wasn't raised Catholic and I'm not a Democrat. I'm a lifelong Republican and I'm Protestant," she told interviewer Julia Edgar.

Born March 7, 1937, and raised in Brooklyn, New York, DiMartino says she learned to be "tough." When she was eight years old, her Spanish father, Juan Dendariarena, died, leaving DiMartino's mother alone with six daughters. Her Puerto Rican mother, Paquita Cruz, took her daughters out of Catholic school and placed them in a strict school with a Pentecostal tradition. DiMartino told Edgar she appreciated the discipline instilled in her by her teachers, and recognizes that what was scorned as "foreign" when she was a child has served her well as an adult. "We were brought up in a neighborhood where you were told, 'You're in America, speak English.' They tried to make us ashamed of our culture and language. You had to be a little tough. Now, corporations are globalizing more and more each day, and culture is an absolute asset, so they're looking for people who speak other languages," DiMartino told Edgar.

Culture Key to Career

DiMartino has used her culture to fuel her career and to inspire other Hispanics. She prepared to serve as a role model for Hispanics by first earning a bachelor of arts degree in liberal arts at Richmond College in Staten Island, New York, and then a master's degree in public administration from Long Island University in New York in 1977. Continuing her education, DiMartino attended a business leadership training program at Harvard University and an executive management program at the University of California at Berkeley. Her education and her facility with Spanish helped her start her career in the Minority Business Enterprise at the United States Commerce Department. She is a member of several boards and organizations, including the Council on Foreign Relations, the National Council of La Raza, the Congressional Hispanic Council, the United States Senate Republican Task Force and the National Association of Latino Elected and Appointed Officials.

After heading American Telegraph & Telephone's (AT&T) department of International Public Affairs, and holding positions as managing director of Caribbean and Central American affairs and district manager of public affairs, DiMartino assumed the position of liaison between the company and all branches of the federal government. Working in Washington, D.C., is not new to DiMartino, however. In 1982, she was appointed by President Ronald Reagan as the first Hispanic representative to the United Nation's International Children's Fund (UNICEF). Six years later, President Reagan appointed DiMartino as the first Hispanic vice chairperson of the New York State Republican Committee, a seat she still occupies. In that role, DiMartino speaks at different events, assists in fundraising activities and recruits minorities to the Republican Party. In 1992, President George Bush appointed DiMartino to a three-year term on the World Board of Governors of the United Services Organizations.

Her various political and business dealings have earned DiMartino many awards. In 1988, her work with UNICEF was recognized with the President's Award for Distinguished Service; in 1986, she received the Corporate Achievement Award from the National Hispanic Bar Association; in 1990, the National Council of La Raza recognized her for outstanding leadership; and in 1991, DiMartino won the National Hispanic Hero Award from the Midwest/Northwest Voter Registration Project. DiMartino has been married since 1957 to Anthony Robert DiMartino, with whom she has three children, Vickie Ann, Anthony Robert, and Celeste Frances.

Sources:

DiMartino, Rita, interview with Julia Edgar, September 18, 1992.

—Sketch by Julia Edgar

María Elena Durazo
(1954?-)
Labor leader

As the first woman, let alone Hispanic woman, to head a major union in the city of Los Angeles, María Elena Durazo is more than a leader: she is a groundbreaker. Her election as president of the Hotel and Restaurant Employees Local 11, a union with a 70-percent Hispanic membership, proves that Hispanics are capable of gaining greater respect and authority. As she told *Hispanic Business,* Durazo understands how her position has affected Hispanics in the community. "I think my election is absolutely a turning point for Hispanics. . . . It would signal a new confidence in being able to decide their own future. . . . They don't have to be second-class citizens anymore."

Even before Durazo was elected president of the union, she proved that Hispanic women can excel at roles traditionally held by non-Hispanics and men. The daughter of migrant workers from northern Mexico, Durazo knew firsthand the hardships that many underpaid people face. As her parents traveled from town to town to work in the fields, the children of the Durazo family accompanied them. Durazo and her brothers and sisters slept in the back of her father's pickup truck. There was never enough money to pay for everything; despite the long hours her parents put in, they could not make enough to get out of the situation. It was Durazo's childhood that inspired her to fight for the rights of immigrants and other people forced to live as her family had.

Vows to Work for Immigrants

As a young woman, Durazo was influenced by the Chicano movement of the 1970s. Determined to educate herself and assist other Chicanos to empower themselves, she worked her way through the Los Angeles People's College of Law. As she studied, she began to utilize her knowledge and skill to advocate for immigrants who had no idea of how to protect themselves. She believed in what she was doing, and worked without pay, even though she was a single mother and had a son, Mario, to support.

It was not until 1979, when the International Ladies Garment Workers Union hired her as an organizer, that Durazo began to work professionally, fighting for the rights of those who worked in the factories of the designer-label manufacturers. She made house calls and worked in the office of that union until she was hired to work as a law clerk for Abe Levy, a labor lawyer. Levy represented Local 11, and he helped her get a job with the union over which she would later preside.

At the time, the Hotel and Restaurant Employees union was not supportive of the majority of its members. As some of its leaders were retired members, or non-minorities unfamiliar with the actual membership of the union, many disagreements occurred. One of these arguments centered on what was considered a fundamental aspect of union membership—understanding what transpired at the meetings. Although 70 percent of the union's members were Hispanic, and many of those Hispanics spoke only Spanish, the union leaders refused to run bilingual meetings. They argued that the members should learn to speak and read English instead.

Due to unsympathetic policies such as this one, the union leaders were extremely unpopular with Hispanic members. The local's membership dropped by 50 percent, or more than 12,000 members, and it failed to protect its remaining members as vehemently as other locals had across the United States. The union leader, Andrew (Scotty) Allan, had been presiding over the union for 23 years when Durazo decided that enough was enough. She was sure that the union could do a better job of representing its members, and that it could even recruit the thousands of unrepresented workers in the Los Angeles area.

Becomes Union Leader, Members' Advocate

Although Durazo had been working as an organizer and arbitrator for the union for only three years, its members already looked to her for leadership. She began to persuade them that if they used the power their numbers created and voted together they could transform the union into an organization that worked for them. "I had complete faith that there were enough workers here with the talent and the motivation to make the change," Durazo explained in the *Los Angeles Times.* By 1987, Durazo had garnered enough support from the union's members to present them with a slate of candidates to challenge Allan.

As the elections took place, however, both parties charged election irregularities. The international union seized control of the local and placed it in a trusteeship. Miguel Contreras was sent in as administrator. After weeding out many union staffers, Contreras hired Durazo as a staff director to help him return the union to its proper function. Together, the pair turned the union around.

First, they hired immigrants and other representative members as union officials. They then began to conduct union meetings in Spanish as well as English, and encouraged Hispanic members to delve into contract negotiations. By encouraging members to wear union buttons at work, to recruit new union members, and to demonstrate, Contreras and Durazo helped members to feel that they had more clout. Employers sensed this new confidence, and when new contract negotiations began, union members gained their biggest wage increase in twenty years. Existing employees were promised the benefits of seniority as well as opportunities for promotions, and illegal aliens were protected from unnecessarily hard labor. The salaries of maids would increase $1.50 more per hour over three years, and waiters would receive a raise of $.80 per hour. Finally, the local union was representing its members, and members were representing themselves.

In 1989, Durazo once again put herself and a 15-person slate up for the union's elected offices. Despite the efforts of a former friend, Javier Rodriguez, who challenged her and charged that she was merely a front for the international union and received unfair assistance for her campaign from it, Durazo was successful. She was elected president of the union, and her 15-person slate of candidates won as

well. The 85 percent of union members who voted for Durazo were pleased, and despite their positions as employers, hotel and restaurant owners in the community were not unhappy with the results. Irving Baldwin, the president of the Hotel-Restaurant Employers' Council of Southern California, told *Hispanic Business,* "We can expect [Durazo's] union to be more aggressive now, but I think she's definitely business oriented.... We look with concern at what she's doing, but I have no reason to cut her. She listens and she's realistic." Apparently, other business leaders feel the same way about Durazo. They know she intends to represent the needs of the local's members, and they also know that she understands that businesses need to be profitable in order to offer employment at all.

Foresees Bright Future for Hispanic Union Workers

Durazo works ten to 12 hours a day, six days a week, planning, working, and coordinating demonstrators. She has been arrested, along with other union members, and charged with trespassing during demonstrations. While her primary objective is to keep the union functional, she believes that there is a great amount of potential for growth. She figures that 90 percent of the present restaurant and hotel workers in the Los Angeles area are unrepresented, and that many new restaurants and hotels will be built in the future. Since many illegal aliens have been given amnesty by the United States government, and since more immigrants, or their children, are expected to enter the work force as service workers, the union may have many more Hispanics to represent. Durazo, however, knows that before any major recruiting takes place, her staff will have to be organized, and the local membership itself will need some restructuring.

While presiding over an organization with 13,000 members, a staff of 35, and an annual budget of $2.5 million has its difficulties, Durazo has made progress herself. "I'm learning that there are times when decisions have to be made that don't necessarily seem like the best decisions at first, but there are lots of ramifications—legal and financial—that have to be taken into consideration," she remarked in *Hispanic Business.* The leader, who was just 36 years of age when she was elected in 1989, has been gaining popularity within the union as well as in the Los Angeles community at large. She inspires and encourages Hispanics and non-Hispanics alike to stand up and be heard. One union member declared in the *Los Angeles Times,* "Many of us come from countries where the powerful always have their way. María Elena has made us realize that united we can take control and run things the way we want. Now we can speak up when there is an injustice. María Elena has instilled this in us."

Also, since Durazo has been working for the union, she has found some personal success apart from her career. She married Miguel Contreras, the international union representative who controlled the local for two years and who has since left the local union. While some members were suspicious of the marriage, the enthusiasm Durazo shares with Contreras for defending Hispanics is obvious. She commented in *Hispanic Business,* "We see our union work as a cause—not a job."

In addition to empowering rank-and-file members of a union, and making the lives of busboys, waiters, cooks, and maids more livable, Durazo has enabled thousands of Hispanics in the Los Angeles area to dream about their futures. Knowing that her concern for them is genuine, and that they, too, can make the contributions that she has made makes all the difference for people who once went without representation. Durazo, the woman who fights for the rights of Hispanics in the United States, who actively supports action against the United States' policy in Central America, and who even struggles in the battle for nuclear disarmament, is a working role model for Hispanics as well as evidence that a once-standard situation is in a state of transformation. As Jesus Jimenez, an international representative for the United Furniture Workers of America, noted in the *Los Angeles Times,* Durazo's presidency represents "the kind of change that is needed."

Sources:

Periodicals

Hispanic Business, May, 1990, pp. 36-40.
Los Angeles Times, May 6, 1989, Section 1, p. 1.

—*Sketch by Ronie-Richele Garcia-Johnson*

Durón, Mary Salinias
See Salinas Durón, Mary

E

Sheila E.
(1958?-)
Singer, songwriter, musician

"Sheila E. is probably the hottest female drummer in the business," Lynn Norment asserted in *Ebony*. First coming to the musical spotlight in the early 1980s as funk/pop superstar Prince's duet partner on the hit single "Erotic City," Sheila E. soon struck solo success with her debut album *Glamorous Life*. The title song proved popular enough to help earn the young drummer-vocalist a gold album, and her second long-playing effort, 1985's *Romance 1600*, also turned gold. As Pamela Bloom pointed out in *High Fidelity*, "Sheila demonstrates on *Romance 1600* how equally at home she is in fusion, funk, pop, and salsa, as well as in the traditional r & b dance mix." The critic concluded, "Hers is an innate musicality that refuses to be waylaid and is propelled by an insatiable physical energy always on the prowl."

Sheila E. was born Sheila Escovedo to Pete and Juanita Escovedo in the late 1950s in Oakland, California. Hers was a musical family—her father Pete was famed for his drum work with the rock group Santana and, later, the Latin band Azteca. Her brothers also became drummers. By the time Sheila E. was three, she became devoted to watching Pete Escovedo with his conga drums. She recalled to Bloom, "When my father practiced, I'd sit in front of him and copy him, mirror style. I was just mocking then, but later I'd come back and play by myself." Because of this "mirroring," she developed what Bloom labeled a "left-handed style" on the drums, which allows her to beat them faster and harder than most drummers.

Despite Sheila E.'s early enthusiasm for percussion, her father hoped instead that she would become a symphony performer and began sending her to violin lessons when she was ten. A competent student, she nevertheless quit five years later because, as she confided to Bloom, "my friends thought it was square and so did I." Meanwhile, Sheila E. picked up the skills of playing other instruments, including guitar and keyboards, as well as traps and timbales. She also widened her musical tastes, and she and her siblings "used to blast different music from every room in the house. That's probably why I can write [any type of music] I want." Yet she realized from an early age that female drummers were practically unheard of in the professional music business, and during her adolescence she believed she had a greater chance of becoming an Olympic athlete than a successful musician. Thus Sheila E. focused on sports, playing football with boys and constantly challenging her peers to footraces.

Joins Father's Band

Sheila E. continued to stick with drumming, however, and began to land professional gigs while still in her teens. Though her father was grateful for the extra financial help her talent brought him, he gently scoffed at her ability, telling her she was too young to be a drummer. But eventually Pete Escovedo let his daughter fill in for an ailing percussionist in his band. She soloed in her first appearance with her father, and met with an overwhelming response from the audience. Sheila E. told Bloom: "When I heard that ovation, I had this feeling I had never had in my whole life. . . . It felt like the ultimate." Soon after, she quit high school to concentrate on her musical career.

In addition to touring Europe and Asia with her father's band, Azteca, and cutting two albums as part of that group, Sheila E. also got work as a studio musician for artists such as Herbie Hancock, Lionel Richie, Diana Ross, and the late Marvin Gaye. In 1978 she was touring the United States with George Duke when she met the man who has perhaps had the biggest impact on her career: Prince. He had just released his first album, and, as Sheila E. related to Bloom, "I heard about this kid who was writing and producing his own stuff, and I was impressed. When I first saw him, I just thought he was this cute guy standing against the wall. But when we met, he was impressed, too, because he had heard about *me*. We've been friends ever since."

Begins Work with Prince

Although the two often worked on songwriting together, Sheila E. did not record with Prince until 1984, when she sang a duet with him on the hit single "Erotic City." She also worked for Prince on Apollonia's album, *Apollonia 6*, and it was during this project that Prince advised her to go solo. He showed her how to compose songs faster than she had been doing, and helped her create a sexy new image. Although he was not listed in the album's credits, he helped produce Sheila E.'s debut solo album, 1984's *The Glamorous Life,* and its title-track hit single. In addition, Prince helped her gain even more exposure by hiring her as the opening act for his "Purple Rain" tour. While the drummer initially hesitated to climb into the spotlight—she told Karen Schoemer in *Interview* that "I get kind of scared when I hear my voice"—she soon learned to enjoy her new role. "I love it," she told Kurt Loder in *Rolling Stone.* Her new image and status as a headliner, she continued, "is something I've always wanted to do. Playing Latin jazz, you can't do what I'm doing now—the dress and the shows I'm putting on."

Sheila E.'s subsequent albums, while not multi-million-sellers, have established her as a songwriter and performer to watch. Her 1985 album, *Romance 1600,* included another duet with Prince, "Love Bizarre," which shot up the charts. As for the rest of the album, it led Bloom to acclaim Sheila E. for her "mastery of studio technique, by which she turns everything in sight—including her own barks, snorts, and trills—into a percussion instrument." On the percussionist's third album, simply titled *Sheila E.,* the musician turned to her family for backup; her father, mother, brothers, and sister sing or play on many of the songs. And on her 1991 effort, *Sex Cymbal,* Sheila E. returned to her musical roots: "I've always wanted to incorporate a lot of the Latin into the albums, but I didn't know how," she related to Schoemer. "I thought that if I put in too much Latin, people wouldn't like it. I think that it was a mistake to think that people wouldn't accept me as I was." Whatever she turns her talents to, whether salsa-rhythmed dance numbers, teasing pop tunes, or hot percussion licks, Sheila E. is, as a *People* reviewer concluded, "a hot property as a performer."

Sources:

Periodicals

Chicago Tribune, November 20, 1987, Section 7, p. K62.
Ebony, September, 1985, p. 31; November, 1987.
High Fidelity, January, 1986, pp. 64-65, 79.
Hispanic, July, 1991, p. 54.
Interview, March, 1991, p. 24.
Los Angeles Times, March 8, 1986, p. V5; November 15, 1987, p. C104.
People, November 19, 1984, p. 169; April 13, 1987, p. 30; May 6, 1991, pp. 29-30.
Rolling Stone, September 13, 1984, pp. 41, 50; November 21, 1985, p. 97.

—*Sketch by Elizabeth Wenning*

Rita Elizondo
(1953-)
Political educator

Starting a lifelong career in politics in the early 1970s, Rita Elizondo has worked to increase the number of Hispanics assuming leadership roles in government. She began with a school board election campaign in her hometown of San Antonio, Texas, eventually moving on to Democratic Party headquarters during Walter Mondale's bid to beat Ronald Reagan for the presidency in 1984. After a stint with the Washington office of the National Association of Latino Elected and Appointed Officials (NALEAO) in the mid-1980s, she later became executive director of the Congressional Hispanic Caucus Institute (CHCI), a non-profit, non-partisan organization dedicated to forming and informing future generations of Hispanic leaders. She joined the CHCI in 1990 because, "The development of leadership is the single most important tool that will empower Hispanics to register our will on legislations or policies that affect our community," she told *Patriots Magazine.* "This is more important than ever, as we prepare to make our contribution to life in the America of the 21st century."

According to Elizondo, nothing in her upbringing had prepared her for a life in politics. "My family was not interested in such matters," she recalled during an interview with Michelle Vachon. "In fact, I don't believe that my mother ever voted until I became involved in politics and registered her to vote." Born in Laredo, Texas, on February 23, 1953, Elizondo grew up in San Antonio. In high school, her teachers encouraged her to prepare for secretarial school. "They suggested typing, which I took, and I'm grateful for that because it has proven quite useful," she commented. "But they did not mention college. I admit that I was not a very good student—in fact I was an average student at best. I remember scoring rather low on my SATs, and I can honestly say that I was not terribly interested in being at the top of my class. My teachers probably did not think that I was capable of obtaining a college degree." But her mother disagreed. "She was the only one who inspired me to pursue my studies, probably because she had been forced to leave nursing school in her second year—she had married and my father did not want her to have a career," Elizondo explained. "That's why she always valued education."

Begins Political Career by Chance

After high school graduation in 1970, she enrolled in junior college, but decided to withdraw and savor her youth for a time. She returned a few years later. "My interest in politics did not really surface until I was in my

Rita Elizondo

early 20s," she told Vachon. "A chance incident triggered it. A friend, whose father was a school board member, recruited me to help at the polls on election day. After talking to voters for a few hours, I discovered that I really liked it." She subsequently participated in local electoral campaigns, and upon completing two years of college, took political science courses at the University of Texas. "I thoroughly enjoyed learning about the sociological aspects of government, the legislative process and the science of politics," she recalled. "It fascinated me." She graduated in 1978 with a B.A. in political science.

In 1977, during her student days, the Southwest Voter Research Institute (SVRI) contacted Elizondo to work as a volunteer on its voter registration project. "I canvassed door-to-door on weekends, and loved the contact with voters," she observed. "So I continued volunteering with the institute." In 1980, the SVRI offered her a staff position as voter registration coordinator for the San Antonio mayoral race. "Henry Cisneros was running for the first time, and the institute wanted to enlist the Hispanic community into electing its own Hispanic candidate," she remembered. "I was flattered to be entrusted with the responsibility of the whole campaign. I had to handle every detail, from organizing a Hispanic and mainstream media blitz to building coalitions with community organizations in order to reach as many Hispanic voters as we could. We toiled away 7 days a week, 18 hours a day, but it paid off. An incredible number of Hispanics registered to vote, and

Henry Cisneros became the first Hispanic mayor of San Antonio in this century."

After the election, the Cisneros organization recruited Elizondo to handle the precincts with a Hispanic majority, that is, 25 percent of the city's precincts. "Arnold Flores ran the campaign and taught me everything there is to know about grass roots organizations and field work," she related. "We held rallies, met with all local clubs and associations, and visited community centers and residences for the elderly. Cisneros won again." In the same year, Elizondo served as South Texas field organizer for Edward Kennedy's presidential nomination campaign. "We really believed in him," she said. "We managed to beat the odds of the incumbency and the party in South Texas politics, and we delivered delegates for Ted Kennedy, which astounded many political insiders."

Succeeds in Field Once Limited for Hispanics

In 1981, Elizondo relocated to Washington, D.C. She secured temporary employment with various offices, and in the process became acquainted with Washington. Two years later, she joined the Walter Mondale organization. "I was assigned to what we call the 'advance school'—the team of people who travel ahead of a candidate to prepare his or her visit in a given town," she reported. "I soon realized that I was one of a handful of Hispanics, three or four at the most, who were in the national campaign structure. Although Mondale wanted to bring minorities on board, Democratic Party operatives did not follow through. The situation improved during the 1988 presidential campaign, and I was happy to hear that Bill Clinton had Hispanics at the decision-making level during his campaign. But in 1984, there were only a few of us on staff. Was I readily accepted? Yes, because I quickly established myself as a professional. When you do advance work, people don't care what color you are as long as you deliver and pull off events. I'm happy to say that I was pretty successful: before the election, the Geraldine Ferraro people asked me to join their side. So I had to choose between Ferraro and Mondale. It was rather fun to be needed." She ended up working for both Democratic candidates.

In 1985, Elizondo interviewed with the National Association of Latino Elected and Appointed Officials. The organization was seeking a person with political skills to expand the membership and liaise with the board of directors. "NALEO's national director, Harry Pachon, hired me and gave me the task of learning about fund-raising and non-profit organizations," she told Vachon. "He became comfortable enough with my ability to administer the association that, when we received the funds to open a Los Angeles office in California, Harry moved to Los Angeles and left me in charge of the Washington, D.C., office." In 1989, NALEO opted to open an office in San Antonio, and Elizondo eagerly returned to Texas. She spent a year establishing the association's presence in the Southwest. In July of 1990, she left her position. "I felt that

I had achieved all my goals with NALEO," she said. "I had increased its membership, ran the Washington office, and in doing so I had learned about non-profit entities. I was now ready for a new challenge."

Elizondo returned to Washington, D.C. Two months later, Congressman Solomon Ortiz, who had just become chair of the Congressional Hispanic Caucus Institute, approached her about assuming the position of CHCI's executive director. Elizondo accepted and her appointment was approved by the congressional and private board members. In her capacity with CHCI, she coordinates fund raising efforts—the institute is fully supported with corporate and community funds—and oversees daily operations. "The institute has developed a dual approach," Elizondo explained in *Patriots Magazine*. "First, [we] offer talented young Hispanics an opportunity to come to the nation's Capitol to learn firsthand how public policy is made and how the federal legislative process works; secondly, [we] provide comprehensive information on educational programs and financial aid opportunities through its national clearinghouse."

Urges Hispanics to Get Involved

Elizondo considers it vitally important to prepare future Hispanic leaders. "We must work towards ensuring that our community is represented by our own, and that legislations affecting us are made by Hispanic leaders," she judged. "Non-Hispanic decision-makers are often well-meaning but don't understand our problems enough to offer the right solutions. It's up to us to elect Hispanics to local, state and national offices. But I also believe that it is crucial for Hispanics to become integrated into the political system, and make our Hispanic representatives accountable to the community. If they don't strive to answer our needs, we should boot them out and elect other Hispanics. I'm proud to see that more women are running for office. Whether or not they are Hispanic, women usually show a greater sensitivity than men to issues that are dear to Hispanics—such as housing, education and health care—and affect our daily lives. I would expect women to be amiable to compromises by opposition to political deal-cutting."

In the spring of 1991, Elizondo accompanied a U.S. delegation to El Salvador as an official electoral observer. During the 30-day visit, she traveled throughout the country to scrutinize the democratization of its electoral process. In addition to her career, Elizondo keeps busy caring for her son, Luis Joaquin, who was born in 1978. "To me, my son comes first," she emphasized to Vachon. "It will always be his soccer game or his school activity before any task that I have to handle. I admit that it's hard to juggle at times; it's even hard to make some people understand. But my family remains my first priority." In the next few years, she plans to continue her work with the CHCI. "This is the perfect time to be in Washington, and

support the growth of the Congressional Hispanic Caucus and the implementation of its legislative agenda."

Sources:

Periodicals

Patriots Magazine, Heroes and Heritage Edition, 1991, p. 8.

Other

Elizondo, Rita, interview with Michelle Vachon, October 2, 1992.

—*Sketch by Michelle Vachon*

Escobar, Marisol
See **Marisol**

Margarita Esquiroz
(1945-)
Judge, lawyer

In 1979, Margarita Esquiroz became the first Hispanic woman to be appointed judge in the state of Florida. When named to serve as circuit judge in 1984, she retained that position some months later with a sweeping electoral victory that included over 90 percent of the Hispanic vote in Dade County. "It is an accomplishment of which I am particularly proud," she reflected in a personal interview, "because it is quite a compliment to win the respect and love of your own people. I am very proud to think of myself as the first Cuban woman judge." The mayor and city commission of Miami honored her on January 26, 1979, by declaring that day "Margarita Esquiroz Day." In addition to her juridic career—which has spanned almost 20 years, and which includes publishing of various casenotes as well as the authoring of several appellate opinions—Judge Esquiroz serves on the Florida Bar, is member and honorary president of the Cuban Bar Association, is member of the Florida Association of Women Lawyers, and serves as judicial director of the University of Miami Law Alumni Association Board. She has been the recipient of the "Floridiana" award, was named "Outstanding Woman of 1984" by the Miami City Ballet Society, and was awarded the 1991 Hispanic Heritage Award for Leadership given by the Host committee of Hispanic organizations.

Born in Havana, Cuba, on February 7, 1945, Esquiroz immigrated to the United States when she was 17. Supporting herself primarily through secretarial work, she obtained her high school diploma through correspondence courses. However, her education had only just begun; she was awarded an associate of arts degree from Miami-Dade Junior College in 1969 and a bachelor of business administration from the University of Miami (Florida) in 1971. She carried on at the University of Miami Law School, graduating in 1974, where she was ranked in the top ten percent of her class and graduated cum laude. It is precisely the breadth and quality of her education to which she attributes her success, and which she prescribes for all women as a prerequisite for success: "Good training, good teachers, hard work and consistency is the formula which worked for me." Also, while she acknowledges that she undoubtedly encountered sexual and ethnic barriers, she hastens to add that she never dwelled on them and, in fact, tried to handle them with grace.

She began her professional legal career in 1965 as a legal secretary with attorney Robert J. Jewison, and was named law library assistant at the University of Miami School of Law in 1970. Two years later she was named a law graduate fellow at the University's Center of Urban and Regional Studies. In 1973, she was appointed student instructor of freshman research and writing, one of the youngest law students to be appointed to this position; her efforts were further rewarded in 1976 when she was named instructor of essay writing.

From 1974 to 1979 Esquiroz served as assistant attorney general for the state of Florida. Her practice in that capacity was principally appellate, with an emphasis on criminal cases. Appearing in both appellate and federal courts, she defended the State from claims made by litigants who claimed inheritances that otherwise would have gone to the state. In June, 1979, Esquiroz was appointed Judge of Industrial Claims of the State of Florida by then-Governor Bob Graham. For five years she presided over many workers' compensation claims. She was often obliged to serve as both judge and jury in these cases, which ran the gamut of technical, legal and medical matters. She insists that her personal history or philosophy shouldn't influence her juridical decisions: "If you are well trained and have good legal sense there should be very little divergence; it's a question of applying the law to the facts."

Judge Esquiroz presently serves as Appointed Circuit Judge on the Eleventh Judicial Circuit. She was appointed to this position by Governor Bob Graham on January 29, 1984. She has presided over a wide variety of cases and legal matters, including personal injury, commercial litigation, marriage annulments and dissolutions, and even "extraordinary remedies." The personal and professional successes of Judge Margarita Esquiroz are reflected in her dual commitment to the community and civic organizations as well as her juridical philosophy of individual justice. She quotes American poet Henry Wadsworth

Longfellow as an inspiration for success: "The heights by great men reached and kept / were not obtained by sudden flight, / but they, while their companions slept, / were toiling upwards in the night." Judge Esquiroz, who is unmarried, amends that passage to "Height by great men and *women*."

Sources:

Periodicals

Hispanic, September, 1991, p. 41.

Other

Esquiroz, Margarita, interview with Paul Miller conducted August, 1992.

—Sketch by Paul Miller

Rita Esquivel
(1932-)
Educational administrator

Rita Esquivel can claim many "firsts" in her life. As a youth, she was the first on either side of her family in the United States to graduate from high school. In 1963 she was the first Hispanic to teach at the elementary schools in the Santa Monica-Malibu Unified School District in California. She became the first female assistant superintendent at the district and is currently the first female director of the Adult Education Center, also a part of the Santa Monica-Malibu Unified School District. Esquivel worked for the United States Department of Education from 1989 to 1992 and was the first Chicano ever to head the Office of Bilingual Education and Minority Language Affairs (OBEMLA).

Like her mother, Esquivel was born in San Antonio, Texas. She is the oldest daughter, born November 4, 1932, to Juan and Juanita Esquivel, who are of Mexican descent. Her father, a self-employed radio repairman, and her mother, a homemaker, were the biggest influences in her life when growing up. It is they who assumed she would go to college. The second biggest influence in Esquivel's formative years was her high school teachers, Catholic nuns. Throughout her school days, she attended private

Rita Esquivel

schools for girls and women in San Antonio and saw the sisters as paradigms of female success. They were women with doctorate degrees, acting as principals and college presidents. Attending private girls' schools also allowed Esquivel to take on leadership roles and to be elected to various offices, positions that might otherwise go to boys. For these reasons, Esquivel remains an advocate of all women's schools.

Reluctant Teacher Finds Success

Teaching was not Esquivel's first career choice. When Esquivel graduated from high school, she wanted to become an attorney. But "in 1949 Mexican girls didn't go to law school," she remarked in an interview with Luis Vasquez-Ajmac. Taking her father's advice, she pursued a B.A. in social work at Our Lady of the Lake University in San Antonio and graduated in 1953. After searching for a job in her area of study for almost two years, Esquivel took her first elementary teaching position in 1955 while teaching swimming lessons at the local pool in San Antonio. In great need of teachers, the personnel director of San Antonio's Independent School District offered Esquivel a job. Desperate for work at that time, she accepted the offer. Esquivel recalled, "I was literally soaking wet in my swimsuit as I signed the contract in the superintendent's office."

Her first year in teaching did not go as smoothly as she anticipated. After one month, she was ready to resign.

"Kids were jumping out the window," Esquivel told Vasquez-Ajmac, and she was exasperated. Refusing her resignation, the school principal brought in a supervisor from the Central Office who taught her how to teach and helped her through the first year of a long, industrious career in education. In 1963, Esquivel left San Antonio to work in California's Santa Monica-Malibu Unified School District where she has remained for 26 years in various schools and positions. First hired as the only Hispanic elementary teacher at the John Muir Elementary School, she moved on to teach secondary education at the Lincoln Junior High School from 1965 to 1971 as a Spanish-language teacher and school counselor. She later became a school principal in 1973 at the Will Rogers Elementary School. Esquivel found the Santa Monica-Malibu Unified School District a very positive experience and nurturing environment with room for professional growth. After becoming the principal of the Will Rogers Elementary School in 1973, she worked her way up to coordinator of community relations from 1973 to 1976 and to supervisor for state and federal projects for five years thereafter. In 1981, Esquivel became the first woman assistant superintendent of education and later assistant to the superintendent from 1987 to 1989.

Named OBEMLA Director by President Bush

The next three years were to become Esquivel's most significant professionally. In 1989 she moved to Washington, D.C., chosen by President George Bush as the first Chicano appointee to the Office of Bilingual Education and Minority Language Affairs (OBEMLA) in the United States Department of Education. Her responsibilities there involved managing the largest fund in the United States Department of Education, a budget of $225 million, for discretionary funds. It was her duty to direct English as a Second Language (ESL) and bilingual education programs for the nation. In so doing, Esquivel identified model projects to fund and produced models for other schools to replicate. She also became deeply involved in research, and headed two major evaluation centers and 16 multifunctional centers across the nation. As director of OBEMLA, Esquivel also assisted the secretary of education in setting policy for children with limited English proficiency and worked with other assistant secretaries in the education of non-English-speaking children.

Esquivel is very proud of her three years as OBEMLA director. "I feel I've done something meaningful and that I have instituted change," she commented in the *National Hispanic Reporter*. Esquivel believes that she bridged the ill feeling between the Department of Education and the community in the field during her tenure, helped build relationships with professional associations, and took positive steps in regard to the Academic Excellence Program, a plan that enables OBEMLA to publicize excellent work accomplished by school districts. Esquivel is equally pleased that she helped expand the development of bilingual education programs and further developed the fellowship program to include almost 500 participants including institutions like Harvard University. Esquivel also played a major role in establishing a research symposium for practitioners in the educational field and set policy on a national level. "That," Esquivel explained to Vasquez-Ajmac, "is the greatest thing I've done in my profession."

Thoroughly enjoying her experience in Washington, Esquivel stayed with OBEMLA longer than her 18-month appointment. Esquivel was drawn to the city's vitality, the challenge of her job, seeing the capital at night and driving through Rock Creek Parkway to work. But after three years in Washington, she felt she had served her party and country well and wished to return to the basis of what education is about: people. Esquivel resumed her career with the Santa Monica-Malibu Unified School District as the first female director of the Adult Education Center in May of 1992. As director, Esquivel took on a new direction and role, a change from educating children. "I am now into mentoring and fostering adults so that they can go upward and onward," Esquivel noted. She hopes to also teach at a local university or college so that she can further influence adults and teachers to enter the administrative ranks. Simply encouraging an individual to believe that he or she can achieve success is important in Esquivel's mind. Reflecting back on her early days as an elementary teacher at the San Antonio Independent School District, she recalled what an impact mentoring had on her and how that support helped her to obtain a master's degree in education at Our Lady of the Lake University in July of 1960.

Promotes Parenting Classes for Immigrants

What is immediately notable about Rita Esquivel when speaking to her about education is her enthusiasm for it. After 39 years as an educator, school administrator, and policy maker, she can still find challenges. One of Esquivel's major goals at the Adult Education Center is to change the focus of the program while maintaining the ESL programs for adults. She wants to provide parenting classes for Hispanic parents at the school and provide a model for every school to adopt. Esquivel believes that offering parenting classes will teach Hispanic parents how the U.S. educational system functions as well as enable them to assist their kids at home and to feel comfortable in a school setting. Her most ambitious goal is to make the Adult Education Center in Santa Monica a showcase for the entire nation by the mid-1990s.

In addition to offering parenting classes at the Adult Education Center, Esquivel will also be running the General Equivalency Diploma (GED) program. Because of the large number of newly arrived immigrants in the area, Esquivel wants to look into the possibility of conducting the test in Spanish with hopes of improving the number of GED Hispanic graduates. This, she believes, would give Hispanics incentive to learn English faster in order to go to community college and beyond.

While working to improve the educational system in the United States, Esquivel has been awarded numerous honors. In 1991 Esquivel was selected as one of the 100 most influential Hispanics in America by *Hispanic Business* magazine and was chosen a NABE Honoree by the National Association for Bilingual Education. She also received the American Council on the Teaching of Foreign Languages' President's Award in 1990 and was presented the Hispanic Woman of the Year award from the Mexican-American Opportunities Foundation in 1989. More recently, Esquivel was awarded a Doctor of Letters, *honoris causam,* by Our Lady of the Lake University in May of 1991. Although Esquivel has accomplished a great deal in the field of education on a local and national level, she still sees room for improvement. She would like to see bilingual education expanded to help the growing number of immigrants adjust to a new educational system and democratic society. More importantly, Esquivel would like to reiterate to people fearful of bilingual education that its primary purpose is to teach children English. As she noted in *Hispanic National Reporter,* "Changing people's minds about bilingual education will always be a challenge."

Sources:

Periodicals

National Hispanic Reporter, June, 1992, p. 1.

Other

Esquivel, Rita, interview with Luis Vasquez-Ajmac, July 16, 1992.

—Sketch by Luis Vasquez-Ajmac

Gloria Estefan
(1958-)
Pop singer, songwriter

From Hispanic roots to the pop music mainstream, Gloria Estefan and the Miami Sound Machine are the embodiment of the American dream come true. The Miami Sound Machine was originally a Cuban American quartet that performed popular music with decidedly Latin influences. The band grew from being a sensation in Spanish-speaking countries to international best-seller status, due to the talent and hard work of Estefan and the

Gloria Estefan

sound business sense of her husband, Emilio, a onetime member of the band and later its manager.

Estefan was born Gloria Fajardo in Cuba in 1958; as a toddler she fled Cuba with her family when Communist dictator Fidel Castro rose to power. Her father, José Manuel Fajardo, had been a Cuban soldier and bodyguard of President Fulgencio Batista. After coming to the United States, Fajardo was recruited into the 2506 Brigade, a Central Intelligence Agency-funded band of Cuban refugees that was involved in the unsuccessful 1961 Bay of Pigs invasion. After President John F. Kennedy negotiated the release of the captured soldiers, Fajardo rejoined his family. He eventually joined the U.S. Army and served for two years in Vietnam.

As a child Estefan liked to write poetry, and though she took classical guitar lessons, she found them tedious. She had no inkling that she would some day become a popular music star, but music played a very important role for her as a teenager. After her father's return from Vietnam, he was diagnosed as having multiple sclerosis, possibly as a result of having been exposed to the herbicide Agent Orange while serving in the army. Estefan's mother, who had been a teacher in Cuba, worked to support the family during the day and attended school at night. Young Gloria was left to take care of her father and younger sister. She had little social life, and because she felt the weight of such responsibilities she turned to music as a release. "When my father was ill, music was my escape," Estefan told *Washing-*

ton Post reporter Richard Harrington. "I would lock myself up in my room for hours and just sing. I wouldn't cry—I refused to cry. . . . Music was the only way I had to just let go, so I sang for fun and for emotional catharsis."

Joins Future Husband's Band

In 1975 Gloria met keyboardist Emilio Estefan, a sales manager for the rum dealer Bacardi who also led a band called the Miami Latin Boys. The band played popular Latin music, but because there was no lead singer, the quartet members took turns singing. A mutual friend asked Emilio to advise Gloria and some friends about organizing a band for a special event. Emilio heard Gloria sing, and when he met her again at a wedding at which the Miami Latin Boys were entertaining, he asked her to sit in with the band. A few weeks later Emilio asked Gloria to perform as lead singer with the band, and she accepted. At first Gloria sang only on weekends, because she was still attending the University of Miami. A year and a half after Gloria joined the group, by then renamed the Miami Sound Machine, the band recorded its first album for a local label. *Renacer* was a collection of disco pop and original ballads sung in Spanish.

Although Estefan was somewhat plump and very shy when she joined the band, she slimmed down with a rigorous exercise program and worked to overcome her natural reticence. After several months on a professional level, Emilio and Gloria's professional relationship turned personal, and on September 1, 1978, they were married. Their son Nayib was born two years later, about the time that Emilio quit his job at Bacardi to work full time with the band, then made up of bassist Marcos Avila, drummer Kiki Garcia, keyboardist, arranger, and saxophonist Raul Murciano, keyboardist Emilio, and soprano Gloria.

By 1980 the group had signed a contract with Discos CBS International, the Miami-based Hispanic division of CBS Records. Between 1981 and 1983 the Miami Sound Machine recorded four Spanish-language albums made up of ballads, disco, pop, and sambas. The Miami Sound Machine first met with success in Spanish-speaking countries. The group had dozens of hit songs around the world—particularly in Venezuela, Peru, Panama, and Honduras—but enjoyed little recognition in the United States.

Finds Success in North America with First English Songs

The Miami Sound Machine's first North American hit was from the band's first English album, *Eyes of Innocence*. The disco single "Dr. Beat" went to the top of the European dance charts. The song's popularity prompted CBS to move the group to Epic, a parent label, and inspired group members to write songs in English, first with a couple of numbers on the otherwise Spanish-language record *Conga.*

The rousing dance number "Conga" itself became the first single to crack *Billboard*'s pop, dance, black, and Latin charts simultaneously. Estefan reminisced to Jesse Nash of the *New York Tribune*, "I'll never forget when we first did 'Conga.' A producer told us that the song was too Latin for the Americans and too American for the Latins. 'Well, thank you,' I said, 'because that's exactly what we are!'" Estefan and the group, the membership of which has changed over the years, pride themselves on the combination of Latin rhythms, rhythm and blues, and mainstream pop that makes up their hybrid sound.

In 1986 the album *Primitive Love,* the band's first recording entirely in English, set off a string of hit singles. "Bad Boys" and "Words Get in the Way" made their way onto Billboard's Top 10 pop chart. Behind the scenes was the work of the trio known as the "Three Jerks"—producer-drummer Joe Galdo and his partners Rafael Vigil and Lawrence Dermer—who wrote, arranged, and performed the majority of the music on *Primitive Love* and the follow-up album, *Let It Loose.*

As a band, the Miami Sound Machine developed a split personality. In the studio the "Three Jerks" and session players made records, and for concerts the road band, which included Garcia and Avila, performed. Estefan was the common denominator. Extensive tours, concerts in 40,000-seat stadiums, and music videos on MTV and VH-1 made the Miami Sound Machine a leading American band. Estefan gradually became the star attraction, and the act came to be billed as Gloria Estefan and the Miami Sound Machine or sometimes simply Gloria Estefan. Some commentators on the popular music scene called Estefan a demure, Hispanic version of Madonna.

After the *Let It Loose* album, Galdo and friends quit working with the Miami Sound Machine, so the band was on its own creatively. Early in its evolution, the band's biggest hits were rousing dance numbers, but by the end of the 1980s it was Estefan's ballads that engendered its success. "Ballads are basically what I'm about," Estefan confessed to Dean Johnson of the *Boston Herald.* "I just feel you can express yourself more completely and eloquently in a ballad. It's easier to identify with someone else and form a closer bond with the audience." From the *Let It Loose* album the singles "Rhythm Is Gonna Get You," "Betcha Say That," and "1-2-3" made it to *Billboard*'s Top 10 list, but it was the ballad "Anything For You" that topped the charts.

Despite the group's popularity with English-speaking listeners, the Estefans have not forgotten their roots. There are always Spanish-language projects in the works, and the title of their 1989 album *Cuts Both Ways* attests to their intention to live up to their international reputation. Estefan contributed to *Cuts Both Ways* in more capacities than as just the lead singer. She was involved in its planning and production, composed some of the music, and wrote lyrics to most of the songs. The rollicking salsa finale "Oye Mi Canto" ("Hear My Song") rivaled "Conga" for its appeal.

Fractures Spine in Traffic Accident

Emilio Estefan relinquished his position as keyboardist with the Miami Sound Machine after the birth of son Nayib. He then devoted his considerable energy and managerial talent to promoting the band and the other enterprises that were to eventually make the Estefans producers of their own and others' records. While Estefan toured with the band, her husband ensured that Nayib would have at least one parent at home. A close family, the Estefans would arrange to meet as often as possible during tours. While traveling together on March 20, 1990, the band's bus was involved in an accident with a tractor trailer on snowy Interstate 380 near the Pocono Mountains of Pennsylvania. While Nayib suffered a fractured shoulder and Emilio received minor head and hand injuries, Gloria suffered a broken vertebra in her back. In a four-hour operation several days later, surgeons realigned Estefan's spine and implanted steel rods to buttress the fracture. With a prognosis for complete recovery doubtful, Estefan retired to her home on Star Island, near Miami, to begin her long recovery.

Thanks to extensive physical therapy, intense determination, and the support of her family and fans, Gloria Estefan made what many consider a miraculous comeback. She marked her return to performing with an appearance on television's American Music Awards in January of 1991, and beginning in March, she launched a year-long tour to tout her comeback album *Into the Light.* According to *People,* her "long, sometimes uncertain recovery" gave the singer-songwriter "a renewed feeling about life," as she told writer Steve Dougherty. "It's very hard to stress me out now. It's hard to get me in an uproar about anything because most things have little significance compared with what I almost lost." She added that "so many people got behind me and gave me a reason to want to come back fast and made me feel strong. Knowing how caring people can be, how much they gave me—that has changed me forever."

Sources:

Periodicals

Boston Herald, March 7, 1990; March 14, 1990.
Detroit Free Press, August 1, 1988.
Los Angeles Daily News, September 12, 1989.
Los Angeles Herald Examiner, January 29, 1989.
Miami Herald, September 30, 1988; May 7, 1989; July 9, 1989; May 27, 1990.
New York Post, July 25, 1988; February 28, 1990; March 21, 1990; March 22, 1990; March 23, 1990.
New York Tribune, September 14, 1988; December 13, 1989.

People, October 27, 1986; February 18, 1991.
Rolling Stone, June 14, 1990.
Washington Post, July 17, 1988.

—Sketch by Jeanne M. Lesinski

Clarissa Pinkola Estés
(1943-)
Writer, Jungian analyst

Clarissa Pinkola Estés

In her first book, Clarissa Pinkola Estés tells stories with the warmth and compassion of a mother to her child at bedtime. And like that mother, Estés hopes lessons will be learned. Her message in *Women Who Run with the Wolves: Myths and Stories of the Wild Woman Archetype* is clear: women must trust their powerful and often neglected instincts. *Women Who Run with the Wolves* achieved a great deal of acclaim, appearing on the *New York Times* bestseller list only five weeks after it was officially published by Ballantine Books in the summer of 1992. "In fact, its success could even be termed a 'sensation' or even a fullfledged phenomenon," according to her publicist, Malka Margolies, in a press release. Estés is also a Jungian analyst and an artist-in-residence for the state of Colorado.

Estés was born in January of 1943 to Cepción Ixtiz and E. M. Reyés, who were mestizos (Mexicans of Spanish and Indian decent). She was adopted by Maria Hornyak and Joszef Pinkola, immigrant Hungarians living in the United States. Estés was raised in Michigan near the Indiana state line. There she was surrounded by woodlands, orchards, farmland, and the Great Lakes. Her community was filled with people of different Eastern European cultures, as well as Mexicans, Puerto Ricans, African Americans, and families from the backwoods of Tennessee and Kentucky. While growing up, however, Estés "carried in her blood" the mestizo stories, according to a *San Francisco Chronicle* article. She told the *Chronicle* that after World War II her foster father brought his four widowed sisters from Eastern Europe to America. These women, Estés recalled, treated her as though she "was the future, and they tried to pour everything they knew" into her. That folklore along with a love of nature—especially wolves—became an integral part of her life.

She began to better understand herself when she was in her thirties and found her original family, who "not only embraced me but recognized my poetic spirit and told me all the stories that I already knew," she stated in the *San Francisco Chronicle.* "But receiving them orally is different from finding them through dreams and the inner imagination." Estés also told the *Chronicle* that when she was young she thought it was tragic that she was torn from her family. But as an adult she saw it as a miracle: "People who are twice born as adoptees, especially if they are adopted into another culture, have the special ability to bridge those groups."

In the 1960s Estés migrated west toward the Continental Divide and lived amidst Jewish, Irish, Greek, Italian, African American, and Alsatian "strangers who became kindred spirits and friends," Estés said in *Women Who Run with the Wolves.* In 1976 she graduated with a bachelor of arts degree in psychotherapeutics from Loretto Heights College in Denver, Colorado. Five years later she earned her doctorate in philosophy in ethno-clinical (multicultural) psychology from the Union Institute in Cincinnati, Ohio. Ethno-clinical psychology is the study of both clinical psychology and ethnology, the latter emphasizing the study of the psychology of groups, particularly tribes. In 1984 Estés was awarded her post-doctoral diploma in analytical psychology from the Inter-Regional Society of Jungian Analysts in Zurich, Switzerland. This post-doctorate diploma certified Estés as a Jungian analyst.

Jungian Theory Informs Storyteller's Work

Estés, who is married and the mother of three daughters, practices analysis in Colorado and Wyoming. She has served as the executive director of the C. G. Jung Psychoanalytic Institute in Denver, Colorado. A senior Jungian analyst, Estés is a specialist in cross-cultural mythology. In the early 1900s, Carl Jung used storytelling for studying archetypal patterns as an opening to the unconscious. Estés uses Jung's work as a springboard into writing a new psychology for women.

Estés won a grant and apprenticeship from the Rocky Mountain Women's Institute at Denver University for work on the manuscript *Las brujas* ("The Old Healers"). She explains in *Women Who Run with the Wolves,* "My life experience as a *cantadora-mesemondo,* poet, and artist informs my work with analysands equally." Estés went on to describe what she does in her consulting room to help women return to their wildish nature: "I place substantial emphasis on clinical and developmental psychology, and I use the simplest and most accessible ingredient for healing—stories." She added that she also follows the patient's dream material, which contains many plots and stories. "The analysand's physical sensations and body memories are also stories which can be read and rendered into consciousness," she asserts.

Estés teaches a form of powerful interactive trancing that is proximate to Jung's theory of active imagination. This produces stories which further the client's psychic journey. "We contact the wildish Self through specific questions and through examining fairy tales, folktales, legends, and mythos. Most times we are able, over time, to find the guiding myth or fairy tale that contains all the instruction a woman needs for her drama. It is like a play with stage instructions, characterizations, and props," Estés maintains in *Women Who Run with the Wolves.*

As a *cantadora* ("keeper of old stories") in the Hispanic tradition, Estés is an artist-in-residence for the state of Colorado. Her work is funded by the National Endowment for the Arts. *La invitada* ("a guest" or "the empty chair"), Estés explains in *Women Who Run with the Wolves,* "is always present at storytelling. Sometimes during a telling the soul of one or more of the audience comes and sits there for it has a need. Although I may have a whole evening of material prepared, I often change it to mend or play with the spirit that comes to the empty chair. The guest always speaks to the needs of all."

An award-winning writer, Estés has created best-selling audio tapes in the Jungian storyteller series, including *The Creative Fire,* on incubation and creativity; *The Wild Woman Archetype,* on the instinctual nature of women; and *In the House of the Riddle Mother.* Her poetry has been published in *Exquisite Corpse, Los mochis, The International Signal, Fennel Stalk, Icon, Palabras,* and *Muse.* Her conversations with Dr. James Hillman, poet Robert Bly, and artist Nicole Hollander were published by *Bloomsbury Review.*

Draws on Archetypes to Help Women

She earned the most acclaim, however, with *Women Who Run with the Wolves,* a book based on 20 years of researching, writing, and collecting countless stories from diverse ethnic groups. In the first few pages of *Women Who Run with the Wolves,* Estés explains her inspiration for the work: "Traditional psychology is often spare or entirely silent about deeper issues important to women; the archetypal, the intuitive, the sexual and cyclical, the ages of women, a woman's way, a woman's knowing, her creative fire. This is what has motivated my work on the Wild Woman archetype for the better part of two decades." A *Library Journal* contributor observed that the book, written in a "clear, richly evocative style," was a "perceptive study of women's deep nature."

In *Women Who Run with the Wolves* Estés remembers that growing up in the northern woodlands she always felt close to wolves. She states, "Healthy wolves and healthy women share certain psychic characteristics: keen sensing, playful spirit, and a heightened capacity for devotion. Wolves and women are relational by nature, inquiring, possessed of great endurance and strength. They are deeply intuitive, intensely concerned with their young, their mate, and their pack. They are experienced at adapting to constantly changing circumstances, they are fiercely stalwart and very brave. So that is where the concept of the wild woman archetype crystallized for me, in the study of wolves." A review in *Publishers Weekly* noted that this comparison "defines the archetype of the wild woman, a female in touch with her primitive side and able to rely on gut feelings to make change."

Estés' stories are designed to show women to trust their instincts. The story "La loba" in *Women Who Run with the Wolves* teaches the transformative function of the psyche; "Bluebird" talks about wounds that will not heal; and "Skeleton Woman" gives the reader a glimpse of the mystical power of relationship and how dead feelings can be revived. Together the stories advocate "wolf rules for life: eat, rest, rove in between; render loyalty; love the children; cavil in moonlight; tune your ears; attend to the bones; make love; howl often."

Estés tells her readers that the wild woman "passed through" her spirit twice: once by her birth into a "passionate Mexican-Spanish bloodline," and later through "adoption by a family of fiery Hungarians." In an interview with her publisher she asserted that she comes from "a long line of storytellers. I've spent many hours seated at the feet of old Hungarian and Latina women who storytell in plain voices. For them, story is a medicine which strengthens and arights the individual and community. From them I learned that story greases and hoists the pulleys, shows us the way out, down, in and around, cuts for us fine, wide doors in previously blank walls—doors that lead us to our own knowing as wildish women."

Estés' work delves into the healing power of the female psyche. She avoids, however, denigrating men, saying in a *USA Today* article that she is "tired of divisiveness." In *Women Who Run with the Wolves,* Estés shows how the "wild woman archetype" is damaged by a stifling culture that discounts what is feminine. By using stories and myths from Inuit, Asian, European, Mexican, and Greek traditions, Estés shows her readers how they can reclaim their soul life. She claims that women who study the meaning of the stories can find inner-power of self-determination and creativity that will lead to power and freedom. Through the tales she explores the female power in sex, love, money, marriage, birthing, death, and transformation.

The first in a proposed trilogy, *Women Who Run with the Wolves* is scheduled to be followed by *The Dangerous Old Woman and the Power of Age* and *The Mother-Daughter-Sister Relationship.* She ends her first book with the following message: "I hope you will go out and let stories happen to you, and that you will work them, water them with your blood and tears and your laughter till they bloom, till you yourself burst into bloom. Then you will see what medicine they make, and where and when to apply them. That is the work. The only work."

Sources:

Books

Estés, Clarissa Pinkola, *Women Who Run with the Wolves: Myths and Stories of the Wild Woman Archetype,* Ballantine, 1992.

Periodicals

Library Journal, June 15, 1992.
Publishers Weekly, May 11, 1992; October 5, 1992.
San Francisco Chronicle, August 2, 1992.
USA Today, August 13, 1992.

Other

Ballantine Books press release, 1992.

—*Sketch by D. D. Andreassi*

Sandra María Esteves
(1948-)
Poet

Sandra María Esteves is a poet affiliated with the Nuyorican group of writers. Her work reflects the conflicts of living between two languages and two cultures, as well as the problems of surviving as an Hispanic woman in a world dominated by Anglo males. She has been compared to Julia de Burgos, a poet from a previous generation of émigrés whose double burden as a woman and as a Puerto Rican living in New York led to her untimely death.

The child of immigrants, Esteves was born in the Bronx, New York, on May 10, 1948. Her mother, a garment factory worker from the Dominican Republic, and her father, a sailor from Puerto Rico, separated when Esteves was very young; at age six the child was sent to a Catholic boarding school. The seven years she spent at Holy Rosary Academy left an indelible mark on the poet's psyche. Subjected to the strictures of Irish-based American Catholicism, she was not permitted to speak Spanish at the Academy, where she remained during the week. Weekends, she returned to the Puerto Rican world of her family, specifically the home of her paternal aunt, who cared for the girl so that her mother could go to work. Esteves's early experiences formed an awareness of living in two cultures which would later be manifested both in the themes and in the bilingualism of her early poetry.

After graduating from high school in 1966 and attempting to study art at the Pratt Institute, Esteves went to Puerto Rico, where she intended to remain. She returned to New York after a few months, however, now fully conscious of her ethnicity and proud of it. Esteves was soon participating in various protest movements of the 1970s and expressing her new awareness through poetry. After Nuyorican poet Jesus Papoleto Melendez introduced her to the world of young Hispanic artists, she became one of a group of young Nuyorican poets which included Tato Laviera and Miguel Algarin. She also became part of "El Grupo," a collective of Nuyorican socialist poets, performers and musicians committed to taking the message of protest throughout the eastern United States. Her work as a painter followed a similar course through her contact with the Taller Boricua art collective.

In 1978 Esteves received her bachelor's degree in fine art from the Pratt Institute. In 1980 her first collection of poetry, *Yerba buena*, was published by Greenfield Review Press and selected as the Best Small Press Publication for 1981. At this time Esteves began to write almost exclusively in English to express her experiences as an urban Hispanic woman living in the United States. The following decade was one of intense creativity and cultural involvement for Esteves. Among her many accomplishments were her participation in the Cultural Council Foundation of the CETA Artistic Project (1978-80) and her appointment as executive artistic director of the African Caribbean Poetry Theater. Two other collections of Esteves's poetry have been published, *Tropical Rains* (1984), and *Bluestown Mockingbird Mambo* (1990). Esteves resides in New York City and is the mother of three daughters.

Sources:

Books

Gordils, Yanis, "Sandra María Esteves," *Biographical Dictionary of Hispanic Literature in the United States,* edited by Nicolas Kanellos, Greenwood Press, 1989, pp. 85-94.

Other

Archives, Arte Público Press, Houston, Texas.

—Sketch by Silvia Novo Pena

Ernestine D. Evans
(1927-)
Legislator

Ernestine D. Evans used to tell people that her middle initial stood for Democrat. She is a former legislator, gubernatorial secretary, and secretary of state for New Mexico, with a public service career spanning some 40 years. Today, she is a retiree who travels, writes, and maintains an optimistic outlook on life. "I'm 75 and still standing up," she commented in an interview with Anna Macias Aguayo.

Evans was born on September 5, 1927, in Alamosa, Colorado. But her love for New Mexico will not allow her to admit that she is not a native. "I was temporarily out of state when I was born," she explained in an interview for the *Santa Fean.* "I was only gone for about ten days." Every fall she returns to the ranch where she grew up in El Rito, New Mexico. "It's beauty appeals to me, and the mountains, the freedom and horses are fond memories to me. Of course, I will not get on a horse, because they build them so much higher."

The daughter of a rancher and a schoolteacher, Evans studied at the Spanish American Normal School, where she graduated valedictorian of her class of 35 students and earned a teaching certificate in the same year. Her first job was teaching fifth through eighth grade students in a two-room school house at a remote sawmill camp. She eventually married Alcadio Griego, the Rio Arriba County treasurer, and had a son. Griego died of spinal meningitis while he was running for the state legislature in 1941, and Evans was asked by the Democratic party to replace him in the race. "He was the love of my life," recalled Evans in her interview with Aguayo. "He died in between the primary and the general election. I said to myself that I was going to try to fulfill the unfinished business that he had in mind."

Evans was one of five women elected to the State Legislature that year. After a two-year term, she took a job as administrator of a military hospital that treated soldiers wounded in World War II. In 1945, she became an administrator in the New Mexico land office, and in 1953 she was a manager for the board of education finance. Public service and politics became a way of life for Evans. She served as an administrative secretary under two governors and worked for the legislative council, often known as the "first" Spanish American to hold the various posts. The highlight of her career was becoming secretary of state.

"I had to travel night and day to campaign," Evans said in her interview with Aguayo. "I told the people the secretary of state is nothing but a super-duper county clerk. It's the mother of county clerks. The funniest thing is that the year I was elected, 1967, most of the other elected officials were Republicans." Evans used her position to reform the regulations for notary publics. In 1978, she was re-elected to the secretary of state seat and was responsible for providing automatic voting booths for poor counties in New Mexico, which was supposed to standardize the equipment being used statewide and prevent cheating. A *Santa Fean* contributor characterized Evans's efforts: "Ernestine is encouraging officials in each county to hold school for voters, and she has cleaned up a good deal of local color in voting procedures. She is justifiably proud of her arrangement." "Being secretary of state helped me a lot," related Evans in her Aguayo interview. "I met people from throughout New Mexico. My name was a household word throughout the state."

Evans turned to writing in 1986 with the publication of *Turquoise and Coral,* a book about real people in northern New Mexico. She spends most of her free time traveling and looking for ways to enjoy life. She admits, however, that retirement is sometimes dull. "There's no industry in Santa Fe," she pointed out in her interview with Aguayo. "All jobs are state-related. My son wants me to go into real estate. Selling things is not my thing. My field was state government."

Sources:

Periodicals

Santa Fean, April, 1978, pp. 18-19.

Other

Evans, Ernestine D., interview with Anna Macias Aguayo, October, 1992.

—Sketch by Anna Macias Aguayo

F

Gigi Fernández
(1964-)
Professional tennis player

Born in 1964 in San Juan, Puerto Rico, Gigi Fernández was first introduced to tennis on her eighth birthday, when she received lessons as a gift from her parents. That present has led to a stellar career in tennis that already includes accomplishments such as an Olympic gold medal, a world doubles championship, a doubles crown at Wimbledon, and a championship at the French Open. A strong server and volleyer, Fernández reached the number-one ranking in the world in doubles in 1991.

Almost as soon as Fernández first picked up a tennis racket, she found that the game came naturally to her. She was ranked number one in Puerto Rico as a junior player despite the fact that she didn't practice a lot. It wasn't until she arrived at South Carolina's Clemson University as a scholarship student that she began to work hard at her game. During her freshman year, Fernández made the finals in the NCAA singles championship, which fueled her decision to turn professional in 1985. That same year, Fernández was recognized by *Tennis* magazine as a "player to watch" for achieving a singles ranking of twenty-third in the world. Six years later, with a singles victory in Albuquerque, a semifinal finish in Eastbourne, and a quarterfinal finish at the U.S. Open—her best finish at a Grand Slam event—Fernández was ranked seventeenth in the world, her highest singles ranking to date.

Despite her success as a singles player, many observe that her strong serve and volley game are actually better suited to doubles playing. She has garnered six Grand Slam women's doubles titles to date, including the U.S. Open in 1988, 1990, and 1992, the French Open in 1991 and 1992, and the Wimbledon Championships in 1992. In 1991, she and her partner were ranked number one in doubles tennis. At Barcelona in 1992, Fernández and partner Mary Joe Fernández (who is no relation) captured the doubles title, making Gigi the first Puerto Rican ever to win an Olympic gold medal.

Chance Meeting with Martina Navratilova

Fernández credits an encounter with tennis great Martina Navratilova as giving her focus as a professional tennis player. The two first met at a players' party at Wimbledon when Navratilova approached Fernández, then an unknown on the tour, and asked if she had received a note Navratilova had sent in which she praised the young woman's performance against Navratilova's doubles partner, Pam Shriver. Fernández had not yet seen the note but was shocked that the best player in the world had taken the time to write to her. When she later read what Navratilova had written, she was even more surprised, for Navratilova had gone on to state that if Fernández worked hard and was disciplined, she had the potential to be among the game's best players.

"It was thrilling to me," Fernández later recalled in the *New York Times.* "I was ranked about 150 in the world and I weighed about 170 pounds. I had lost about 14 matches in a row in the first round and I was eating in frustration, porking out on ice cream and chocolate chip cookies—anything I could get my hands on. But when I read the note, I decided to change my diet and habits. I went home for a week and thought about what kind of tennis player I wanted to be."

Although Fernández said she took Navratilova's words to heart—the two even played doubles together for a time—she still intends to have as well-rounded a life as possible while maintaining her competitive edge. Her interests outside tennis include skiing, board-sailing, and modeling. She is also a promotional spokesperson for Avia clothing and footwear and Yonex racquets, and she frequently endorses products native to Puerto Rico.

While tennis is not considered a major sport in Puerto Rico, Fernández has nevertheless captured her countrymen's admiration with her winning ways. She has come under some criticism, however, for her decision to compete for the United States in the Federation Cup and Olympic tournaments. This choice, which she said in *Más* was "the most difficult of her life," was based solely on professional reasons. "Representing Puerto Rico I would have lost in the first round," she explained. The comments of her detractors are "like criticizing Raúl Julia for going to work in Hollywood or Justino Díaz for singing at the Metropolitan Opera of New York."

Her success—28 doubles titles, two individual titles, and $1.8 million in lifetime prize money—has nevertheless made her an object of pride on her home island. Also, as the first female Puerto Rican athlete to turn professional, she has paved the way for a new generation of female athletes on her island home. "In a way, it's kind of neat," she remarked in *Hispanic* magazine, "because it's opening a door for female athletes in Puerto Rico. Before, it was taboo for a female to make a living out of a sport. Girls are supposed to get married and have kids, so now maybe this opens the door."

Sources:

Hispanic, July, 1988.
Más (translated from Spanish by Diane Telgen), November, 1992, p. 53.
New York Times, February, 1985, pp. 180-181.

—Sketch by Rosalva Hernandez

Giselle Fernandez
(1961-)
Journalist, network correspondent

Giselle Fernandez's journalistic abilities allowed her to advance quickly through the ranks of radio and television news to become a correspondent on the *CBS Evening News* in 1992. She had earlier worked as a news anchor on *CBS This Morning* and at a number of local stations in California, Illinois, and Florida.

Fernandez was born on May 15, 1961, in Mexico City, Mexico. At the age of four, her family relocated to East Los Angeles. Her father worked as a flamenco dancer and her mother was a folklorist and professor at the University of California, Los Angeles (UCLA). In a telephone interview with Sally Foster, Fernandez recalled spending summers with her mother doing research in isolated Mexican villages. In her studies of mystical and mythological traditions and stories of Mexican traditions, Fernandez's mother interviewed hundreds of villagers. Fernandez attributes her ambition to "get the story from the people" to her experiences with her mother in Mexico.

At the age of 15, Fernandez moved to West Lake Village, California, where she attended and graduated from the public schools. When selecting a college, she was attracted to Goucher College in Baltimore, Maryland, because of its reputation as a women's college and the recommendation of a number of friends. However, an internship in Wash-

ington, D.C., and the absence of family drew Fernandez back to California and the strong journalism program at the University of Southern California, Sacramento. There she participated in many internships in radio news. In 1983, she was awarded her bachelor of arts degree.

Fernandez's first job in television following graduation was as a reporter at KRDO, an ABC affiliate. Offered advancement at KEYT in Santa Barbara, she was promoted to reporter and weekend anchor. In 1986, Fernandez had the opportunity to move to a larger media market in Los Angeles. KTLA, the largest independent broadcaster in Los Angeles, hired her as a reporter and weekend anchor.

Wishing to expand her experience, Fernandez moved to Chicago in 1988 to work as a weekend anchor and reporter at a CBS affiliate. Her next major step was to take the position of weeknight anchor with a Miami station in 1989. In October, 1991, Fernandez came to national attention as one of the anchors of *CBS This Morning*. Her talent was quickly recognized by the company, and she was promoted to correspondent on the *CBS Evening News* within only six months.

Fernandez revealed to Foster that she felt that all of the stories she had covered had importance. Several, however, brought a special satisfaction. While serving as local news anchor in Miami, her coverage of the role of Israel in the Gulf War was of particular importance to the large Jewish community in the Miami area. The ability to furnish timely coverage on a major world event with a significant local perspective was very rewarding to both Fernandez and the viewing audience. More recently, Fernandez was able to make use of her special knowledge of the Miami area in the CBS coverage of the devastation caused by Hurricane Andrew, a storm classified as one of the most destructive in history. During her ten days on site in Miami, Fernandez significantly contributed to the CBS news team's outstanding coverage—recognized even by their network competitors.

When asked about future trends in journalism, Fernandez predicts that "technology is heading to regionalize the news business, using special segments from networks. Culture and changing family patterns will change the way news will be delivered." She believes that the news is a service industry providing the down to earth information people need in their daily lives. In spite of the trend toward cutbacks in network news departments, Fernandez believes that there has already been a return to thorough and aggressive reporting on important issues and a movement away from the "star" industry.

Sources:

Fernandez, Giselle, telephone interview with Sally Foster conducted on September 14, 1992.

—Sketch by Sally Foster

Mary Joe Fernández
(1971-)
Professional tennis player

A well-known name on the women's professional tennis circuit, Mary Joe Fernández has been playing professionally since the age of 14. It has only been since 1990, when she started playing the women's circuit full-time, that Fernández has begun to make a serious bid to become the world's top-ranked female player. Probably her brightest moment in tennis thus far was when she and doubles partner Gigi Fernández of Puerto Rico captured the gold medal for the United States at the 1992 Olympics in Barcelona, defeating Spain's own Arantxa Sánchez Vicario and Conchita Martínez with King Juan Carlos looking on.

Born in 1971 in the Dominican Republic to José and Sylvia Fernández, Mary Joe moved with her family to Miami when she was six months old. At age three she began to play tennis. Her sister Sylvia recounted to the *New York Times* that when her father took her to play tennis, Mary Joe would often tag along. To keep Mary Joe occupied, José bought her a racquet so she could bounce tennis balls off of a wall. Two years later, Fernández started taking lessons from a professional tennis player.

Wins Succession of Youth Tournaments

Fernández showed talent for the game very early on. At age ten, she won the United States Tennis Association Nationals for players 12 and under. At 11, she won the Orange Bowl singles title for players 12 and under and proceeded to win the title again at age 14 for 16-and-under and at age 14 for 18-and-under players. She also won the United States Tennis Association championship for 16-and-under players and the U.S. Clay Court Championship for her age in 1984. She played in her first professional tournament when she was 13, participating as an amateur. She beat her first round opponent, 33-year-old Pam Teeguarden, but lost the following match. That same year, she defeated the world's 11th-ranked player, Bonnie Gadusek.

As a 14-year-old freshman at Carrollton School of the Sacred Heart, Mary Joe began to feel pressure to turn pro and play the professional circuit full-time. Despite financial considerations, she resisted and became a straight A student at Carrollton. "I just decided that if I was going to go to school, I was going to do it right," she told *Sports Illustrated* in 1991. "And I wasn't ready to sacrifice being with my friends." Fernández did, however, enter four Grand Slam tournaments and various other tournaments over the next three-and-a-half years, working them in

around her high school classes. "If Mary Joe doesn't want to study, we make her study," her father José told *Sports Illustrated*. "If she doesn't want to play tennis, we don't make Mary Joe play."

Many credit that balanced approach with preventing her from burning out on the game too soon or pushing her body too early as some of her contemporaries such as Tracy Austin and Andrea Jaeger have done. But she did gain valuable experience in the few Grand Slam events in which she competed. In her very first Wimbledon match as a 14-year-old, she faced her idol, Chris Evert Lloyd, losing in straight sets. She also missed her high school graduation because she was competing in the French Open.

Experiences Highs and Lows During Professional Debut

The year 1990, Fernández's first as full-time participant on the pro tour, proved both encouraging and discouraging. She won 40 of 50 singles matches and two tournaments, including her first ever professional tournament championship in the Tokyo Indoors. With endorsements, her earnings topped $1 million that year. However, Mary Joe received several injuries during the year. In March of 1990, she tore a hamstring in a Virginia Slims match against rival Gabriela Sabatini; two months later her back went out during a third-round match in the German Open; prior to Wimbledon, a severe knee sprain prevented her from competing in that tournament; finally, after losing in the final of the Australian Open to Steffi Graf, she returned home with tendinitis in her right shoulder. Many speculated and Fernández herself acknowledged that some of the injuries may have resulted from her lack of a consistent conditioning program. Her coaches often encouraged her to build her upper body strength. Since her injuries, she has begun a conditioning regimen using a strength coach.

The conditioning has paid off: Fernández, consistently ranked among the top seven women players in the world, reached as high as fourth in late 1990 through early 1991. One of the roadblocks she has had to overcome to maintain her competitiveness with the top women has been mental toughness. "[Steffi] Graf and [Monica] Seles go into tournaments expecting to win," former coach Tom Gullickson told *Sports Illustrated*. "Mary Joe hopes she'll win . . . when she does, I think she's still a little bit surprised."

With an Olympic gold medal under her belt, Fernández is still moving toward her goal: becoming the top female player in the world. In 1992, she reached the semifinals in the singles at the U.S. Open before losing to eventual champion Seles. Observers say she has had more success in doubles, winning eight tournaments with various partners, including the 1991 Australian Open with Patti Fendwick, Lipton with Zina Garrison, and Toyko Nichirei with Pam Shriver. In 1991, at age 17, she became the 33rd woman to earn more than $1 million; her career earnings top $2.1 million.

Sources:

Periodicals

Los Angeles Times, June 25, 1986, section II, p. 1.
New York Times, September 21, 1984.
Sports Illustrated, February 11, 1991, pp. 76-79.
World Tennis, February, 1991, pp. 25-26.

—Sketch by Jonathan J. Higuera

Sally Garza Fernandez
(1958-)
Corporate relations director

Sally Garza Fernandez, director of corporate relations for Anheuser-Busch, reached the top of the corporate ladder by way of an indirect path. Originally interested in politics, Fernandez later changed career paths and eventually found herself directing a staff of eleven to manage the image of the beer distributor. In addition to her duties as head of corporate relations, Fernandez also advises the executive staff about marketing to the Hispanic community.

Fernandez was born on March 5, 1958, in Port Huron, Michigan, a Canadian border town on the east side of the state. Her lawyer grandfather, Cornelius Gutierrez, had settled in the small city in the 1920s. "He created a Mexican credit union there," Fernandez said in a telephone interview with Carol Hopkins. "We have a lot of history in my hometown," she added. Fernandez's father, Pedro Garza, was a migrant worker and her mother, Emma, was a bank manager. Fernandez remembers growing up as a "typical all-American kid" in a predominately Anglo American community. "There were probably only ten other Hispanic families in town," she recalled for Hopkins. The lack of cultural diversity, however, did not prevent Garza from getting involved in student government, cheerleading and the homecoming court. "I'm sure [my life today] has a whole lot to do with things coming a little easier for me in the beginning," she told Hopkins.

When Fernandez decided to attend college, a high school counselor told her that her grades were too low and she would never be admitted. "But I was one of those kids that all you've got to do is tell them that they can't do something and, of course, they do it," Fernandez told Hopkins. She was accepted by Michigan State University in the mid-70s. Although, as a child, Fernandez had decided she wanted to follow in her grandfather's footsteps and go into law, a college internship as a legislative aide in Lansing ended that dream. "I wanted to work in Texas," she explained to Hopkins, "because I always had this concern about the abusive behavior that went on, particularly toward Hispanics." Her experience at the state capital, however, left Fernandez totally disillusioned with law and politics. "I thought the legislators didn't represent the people," she told Hopkins.

In an effort to find a satisfying career, Fernandez held jobs in several other fields while in college, including teaching preschool and monitoring a job training program. She credits her early work experiences with giving her a head start in the "real world." Those experiences, she told Hopkins, "taught me to have a better sense of the world and to be a little more perceptive about things than the people who just go through school."

After graduating in 1980 with a degree in political science and pre-law, Fernandez spent time designing career counseling and placement programs for educational institutions. In 1982, she was hired by the General Motors Institute admissions department to recruit new students. Later, General Motors Corporation hired Fernandez to prepare a position paper on the company's relationship with the Hispanic community. From there, she went on to be staff assistant in the company's placement and college relations division.

In 1989, Fernandez was recruited by Anheuser-Busch in St. Louis, Missouri, and became director of corporate relations. Fernandez, who told Hopkins that her perspective on politics has changed now that she's older, is considering life beyond the corporate job she holds today. "It'll either be in the political arena or in my own business," she said. When asked how she might advise today's young people, Fernandez said: "I'd tell them that when they're in school to get out there and do other things. Everybody's got a degree. It's the experiences that set you apart."

Sources:

Fernandez, Sally Garza, telephone interview with Carol Hopkins, October 4, 1992.

—Sketch by Carol Hopkins

Ana Maria Fernandez Haar
(1951-)
Advertising executive

Ana Maria Fernandez Haar knew what it took to be a success as a sixth grade student. Years later, she took that same formula to become successful in the highly competitive world of advertising, eventually becoming president of IAC Advertising Group, Inc.

Fernandez Haar came with her parents Gilberto and Esmerald Emiliana (Diaz) to Miami, Florida, from their native Cuba in 1960, when she was only nine years old. She found herself in an entirely different world. "New language, new country, new rules. It was tough," she said during a telephone interview with Carol Hopkins. Her struggles with English in the sixth grade were frustrating to the young girl, who had been a top student in her classes in Cuba. She later told the *Miami Herald,* "I could have done two things as a kid: I could have sulked, I could have given up; or I could have stood back and figured out what I had to do to get that teacher's attention." She chose the latter approach. Instead of just fulfilling an assignment to find and read a poem, for example, she memorized the entire poem—in English— and got an A.

When it came time to decide upon a career, Fernandez Haar was certain of one thing: "I wanted to be anything but broke." She attended college classes at night, graduating from Miami Dade Community College in 1971. By day, Fernandez Haar worked at Miami's Flagship Bank (now Sun Banks), where she was promoted from administrative assistant to assistant vice president. In the mid-1970s, she took a job at another local bank as the new vice president of commercial lending divisions. On one assignment, she worked as a marketing advisor, mounting a campaign to market the Miami Beach Chamber of Commerce to three Latin American countries. In the course of this project she realized that no one within the bank's lending staff knew either the domestic Hispanic or Latin American markets.

Creates IAC Advertising Group

In 1978, at the age of 27, Fernandez Haar decided to open her own advertising and marketing agency, IAC Advertising Group, Inc. Her plan was to target the multilingual consumer market in Miami, which has the nation's third largest Hispanic population. To get her agency going, she approached a financial backer she knew from her banking days. He agreed to help finance her efforts, and Fernandez Haar opened her agency with three employees. IAC's first five years were "absolutely dreadful," she said. Her schedule was demanding and her life became very hectic. Still, her banking experiences helped her manage. She told the *Miami Herald,* "I made a budget; I was a banker. I knew how long the agency would run if I didn't get any business, and I knew how quickly I had to get business."

The hard work has paid off. IAC Advertising Group, Inc. has a growing list of clients that includes Barnett Banks, Publix Super Markets, Bell South, and Mervyns. Fernandez Haar now employs 25 people. Her award-winning agency has filled a niche: "We wanted to have a place that was

more focused on marketing and strategic planning than [just operating] a creative boutique."

Fernandez Haar looks upon her career and realizes she has persevered under extreme conditions. "You grow up in this country noticing that there are ample opportunities. You just have to figure out which way to go."

Sources:

Periodicals

Advertising Age, September 28, 1987.
Miami Herald, October 19, 1987; July 11, 1988, p.1.
Miami Today, October 10, 1991, p. 108.

Other

Fernandez Haar, Ana Maria, telephone interview with Carol Hopkins, October 1, 1992.

—Sketch by Carol Hopkins

Loida Figueroa
(1917-)
Educator, historian, writer

From her days as an undergraduate at the Interamerican University of Puerto Rico's San Germán campus until the present, Loida Figueroa has researched and written about the history of Puerto Rico. She majored in history and French at the Interamerican University, majored in history at Columbia University in New York City, where she received her master's degree, and received her doctorate in philosophy from Universidad Central de Madrid, where she concentrated on Puerto Rican studies. Figueroa taught Puerto Rican, Spanish, and Latin American history at the University of Puerto Rico's Mayagüez Campus for 14 years, Puerto Rican history and studies at the City University of New York's Lehman College and Brooklyn College for a total of three years, and is currently teaching Puerto Rican history at the Interamerican University of Puerto Rico. Despite her academic achievements, though, Figueroa considers her greatest achievement the three volume book *Brief History of Puerto Rico,* a not-so-brief look at the history of Puerto Rico before 1900.

Figueroa's academic and literary accomplishments are particularly impressive considering that her parents had no formal schooling. She was born in Yauco, Puerto Rico, in 1917 to Emeteria Mercado, a domestic worker, and Augustine Figueroa, a sugar cane cutter. Both parents impressed upon their children the importance of getting a good education. Figueroa received her bachelor's degree from the Interamerican University of Puerto Rico, then called the Polytechnic Institute, in 1941. From 1942 to 1943, she taught English and social studies in elementary and junior high schools in Fajardo and Guánica, Puerto Rico. She then taught English, French, and history at Guánica High School from 1944 until 1947. In 1947, Figueroa received a scholarship from the government of Puerto Rico to pursue a master's degree from Columbia University in New York City; she received her degree in 1948 and resumed teaching at the high school until 1957.

Publishes Three Volumes of *Brief History of Puerto Rico*

Figueroa became an instructor at the University of Puerto Rico's Mayagüez Campus in 1957, eventually being promoted to professor. There she taught the history of Puerto Rico, Spain, Latin America, and the West Indies. In 1961, the University of Puerto Rico gave her a scholarship to pursue her doctorate at the Universidad Central de Madrid in Spain—she received her doctorate in philosophy in 1963.

Figueroa published the first volume of her work, *Brief History of Puerto Rico,* in 1968. The following year, she published the second volume, which grew out of her doctoral thesis, "Puerto Rico Facing the Offer of Special Laws by Spain." From 1971 to 1972, she took a leave of absence from the university to begin researching and writing the third volume of *Brief History of Puerto Rico* and also to teach at the City University of New York's Lehman College. The third volume was published in 1976.

Figueroa retired from the University of Puerto Rico in 1974. She then taught at the City University of New York's Brooklyn College for three years, retiring from there in 1977. She came out of retirement in 1992 to teach three courses in Puerto Rican history at the Interamerican University of Puerto Rico's San Germán Campus. Figueroa, who has been married three times and has four daughters, 12 grandchildren, and four great-grandchildren, also writes a column on Puerto Rican history for a local newspaper. Her future plans include trying to secure funding to do investigation and research for the fourth volume of her work, to cover the history of Puerto Rico from 1900 to 1970.

Sources:

Figueroa, Loida, telephone interview with Pam Berry, October 1, 1992.

—*Sketch by Pam Berry*

María Irene Fornés
(1930-)
Playwright

Although she is not well known by casual theatergoers, María Irene Fornés is often ranked among the most original contemporary writers and producers of plays. She has been dubbed the "Picasso of theatre" by *Hispanic* magazine, and has earned six Obie Awards, presented for the year's best Off-Broadway shows. Her list of achievements is all the more impressive when one considers that she did not begin to write until she was 30 years old.

Fornés was born in Havana, Cuba, on May 14, 1930, to Carlos Luis and Carmen Hismenia (Collado) Fornés. Although he had worked for the government at one time, Carlos Fornés was what *Hispanic* described as an "intellectual rebel." Descended from a family of educators, Fornés's father read a great deal. He made sure that his daughters could do so as well, and taught them at home. While María Fornés attended Escuela Publica No. 12 in Havana from the third to the sixth grade, her intellectual growth was a result of her father's caring instruction.

After the death of her husband, Carmen Fornés packed up her family of six daughters and left Cuba for New York. María Fornés was just 15, and she could not speak English. She found her first job as a worker in a ribbon factory, where she kept military decorations in their proper positions on an assembly line. Two weeks was enough of that job. Fornés learned to speak English, and she found work as a translator. Even this, however, would not suit Fornés. Eventually working as a doll maker to support herself, Fornés began to paint seriously. She became a naturalized citizen of the United States in 1951, and some years later she left the country to paint in Europe. After three years Fornés returned to New York in 1957; she worked there as a textile designer until 1960. Although Fornés's works went unacclaimed, the ten years she painted were well spent— her painting contributed to the structures of the award-winning plays she would later write.

Painting Paves Way for Later Writing

In an interview for *Contemporary Authors* (*CA*), Fornés explained how her concept of dramatic structure was linked to her experience as a painter: "Hans Hofmann always talked about push-and-pull . . . the dynamics created between colors when you place one color very close to another or anywhere else in the canvas. . . . The color and shape of the form would create this tension . . . that had a very strong impact on my play writing, because I compose my plays guided not by story line but more by energies that take place within each scene, and also the energies that take

María Irene Fornés

place between one scene and the scene that follows." While she was painting, however, Fornés had no idea that one type of art would lead to another. She only knew that she had difficulty disciplining herself to paint. "I thought that it was normal for a young person to prefer being in coffee houses to working at home," she recalled in the interview.

In retrospect, Fornés understood her trouble. She told *CA,* "I think the reason I was having a hard time painting was that it wasn't the form of art that was best suited for me." Fornés discovered her calling around 1960. Legend has it that in an effort to help her roommate, the now famous philosopher and critic, Susan Sontag, break her writer's block she began to write a play. *Hispanic* even asserted that for this play Fornés borrowed "her words from a cookbook." Whatever precipitated her first attempt to write, Fornés acknowledges that the urge to write consumed her, and she spent 19 days working on her first play. As she explained to Rachel Koenign and Kathleen Betsko in *Interviews with Contemporary Women Playwrights,* "I loved [writing] it, it was such a thrill. I started writing late; I was around thirty. I had never thought I would write; as I said, I was an aspiring painter. But once I started writing it was so pleasurable that I couldn't stop." Fornés's first published play, *La Viuda,* or *The Widow,* appeared in 1961 in *Cuatro Autores Cubanos;* she subsequently received a John Hay Whitney Foundation fellowship in 1961, and a Centro Mexicano de Escritores fellowship in 1962. Fornés's inspiration and enthusiasm soared. She had seen Zero Mostel perform in *Ulysses,* and unconsciously she imagined him as

a character in what became her first produced play, *There! You Died.* "It wasn't that I saw the play [*Ulysses*] and thought, I'm going to write plays," Fornés insisted in *CA.* She had intended to write a play about a power struggle between a man and a computer, but she realized that the computer would be better replaced by a person, a Zero Mostel-like character. In the play, two male lovers battle as father and son, teacher and pupil, in a seemingly endless tango, until Leopold murders Isidore in a bullfight. *There! You Died* (or *Tango Palace*) finally appeared in 1963 and was a success. Fornés's career as a serious playwright had begun.

Her next important play, *The Successful Life of 3,* won Fornés acclaim when it appeared with *Tango Palace* in January of 1965 in Minneapolis. In *The Successful Life of 3,* He, She, and 3 become entrenched in a love triangle which is presented in ten short vignettes over a 16-year period. The standards of time and space in this play are jumbled, and parodies abound; the use of "freeze" shots contributes to the destruction of traditional theatrical molds. According to Bonnie Marranca in *American Playwrights,* this play, which "represents Fornés at her comic best," is "beautifully orchestrated." Fornés's musical, *Promenade,* first shown in April of 1965 Off-Off-Broadway, was also a hit. A comedy about two escaped prisoners, 105 and 106, who return to prison after they experience the outside world, *Promenade* strongly criticizes a society in which those with the most money and the most power are the most cruel. A critic for the *New York Times* remarked, "One definition of *Promenade* might be that it is a protest musical for people too sophisticated to protest." Fornés won an Obie, or Off-Broadway theatre award, for distinguished play writing in 1965 for *The Successful Life of 3* and *Promenade.* Another play which Fornés produced in 1965 was *The Office,* which previewed on Broadway but which never officially opened. Also in 1965, Fornés received an award from the University of Minnesota.

Fornés was very active from 1966 to 1970. She received a Yale University fellowship in 1967-68, a Cintas Foundation fellowship in 1967, and a Boston University-Tanglewood fellowship in 1968. She produced her play *A Vietnamese Wedding* in 1967 and 1969 Off-Broadway as a protest to American involvement in the Vietnam War. The play, which was first performed during Angry Arts Week, utilized members of the audience to demonstrate the universal elements of a Vietnamese tradition. *The Annunciation* was produced with *The Successful Life of 3,* in 1967 Off-Off-Broadway. *Dr. Kheal* appeared in the spring of 1968 Off-Off-Broadway in the United States and in London in 1969. One of Fornés's most frequently produced plays, it portrays a single character, Dr. Kheal, as he gives eccentric lectures on ancient intellectual questions. *The Red Burning Light: or Mission XQ,* was also written to protest the Vietnam War. It was first produced in Zurich, Switzerland, in 1968 for the Open Theatre European Tour, and then at La Mama Experimental Theatre Off-Off Broadway in the spring of 1969. *Molly's Dream,* which demonstrates cinema's influence on people's expectations, was produced

Off-Off-Broadway in 1968. In the play legendary movie-star characters interact with a saloon waitress, Molly, in her daydreams; while Molly is caught in her dreams a man who could have fulfilled her longing comes into the saloon and then departs before she can awake to find him. All of these plays, including *Tango Palace* and *Promenade*, were published in a book entitled *Promenade and Other Plays* by Winter House in 1971. Fornés won a Rockefeller Foundation grant that same year.

Founds New York Theatre Strategy

In 1972, Fornés founded the New York Theatre Strategy with a few other playwrights. Serving as the group's president from 1973 to 1978, and in other offices until 1980 when the group dissolved, Fornés hoped to help make opportunities available for playwrights whose works would not otherwise be produced. The New York Theatre Strategy's efforts have contributed to the production of countless experimental productions. From 1972 to 1973 Fornés also found a second way to assist playwrights like herself: she became a teacher with Theatre for the New City in New York City.

In 1972, Fornés received a Guggenheim fellowship as well as a Creative Artist Public Service grant. Her next play, *The Curse of the Langston House*, was first produced in Cincinnati in late 1972. It was followed by *Aurora*, which appeared Off-Off-Broadway in 1974. Fornés won a grant from the National Endowment for the Arts this same year, and in 1975, she received another Creative Arts Public Service grant. *Cap-a-Pie*, written in Spanish and with music by José Raúl Bernardo, was produced in May of 1975 at INTAR (International Arts Relations), the native Spanish theatre of New York. *Washing* appeared Off-Off-Broadway in late 1976. Also in 1976, Fornés received a grant from the New York State Council on the Arts. In 1977, *Lolita in the Garden*, also written in Spanish, was first shown at INTAR. *Fefu and Her Friends*, one of Fornés's most successful plays, was produced Off-Off-Broadway at New York Theatre Strategy in 1977.

According to a reviewer in *Performing Arts Journal*, "one could say that *Fefu* and the plays that followed it . . . have paved the way for a new language of dramatic realism, and a way of directing it." The critic continued, "Fornés brings a much needed intimacy to drama, and her economy of approach suggests another vision of theatricality, more stylized for its lack of exhibitionism." Many critics recognized these traits in *Fefu and Her Friends*. About a gathering of eight friends in the New England home of Fefu in 1935, this play symbolically discusses feminism and a host of other interrelated issues. *Fefu and Her Friends* is noted for its originality; for the second act, the audience is asked to travel to four different rooms to view four different scenes. This enables the audience to share an intimate, personal space with the characters and get to know them up close as

they ponder alone in bed or review a lost lesbian love affair. Fornés won an Obie for *Fefu and Her Friends* in 1977.

Fornés went on to write and produce *In Service* at the Claremont, California, Padua Hills Festival in 1978. *Eyes on the Harem* was her next project. Produced in 1979 Off-Off-Broadway at INTAR, this play exploits feminist themes in legends from the Turkish Ottoman empire. A critic for the *New York Times* wrote that while it was "farfetched" at times, the play was "hardly ever ponderous." The critic noted that there was a "deliberate fragmentation of chronology and tone," and that "some of the sketches" were "very funny." Critics enjoyed the "Meet Me in St. Louis" scene which, according to a reviewer for the *New Yorker,* was "indelible." For this play, Fornés won another Obie Award for distinguished direction.

During the early 1980s, Fornés continued her rapid pace; she wrote (or adapted) and produced plays prolifically. In 1980, Fornés produced *Evelyn Brown (A Diary)* Off-Off-Broadway. She next adapted two plays, *Blood Wedding,* by Spain's leading 20th-century poet and playwright, Federico García Lorca, and the surreal *Life Is Dream,* a famous play written during Spain's Golden Age by the great Pedro Calderon de la Barca, in 1980 and 1981 respectively. Both were produced at INTAR. *A Visit* and *The Danube,* both Fornés's own works, were produced for the Padua Hills Festival in California and later Off-Off-Broadway. The former, which appeared in 1981, was a musical comedy which, according to the *New York Times,* juxtaposed "lascivious behavior and ornate dialogue." Its main character is a young girl who flits about the home of a family in Lansing, Michigan, in 1910, and allows herself to be seduced by various men and women. The latter play, *The Danube,* was produced in 1982, 1983, and 1984; in it, Paul and Eve fail to communicate with each other and thus destroy their relationship. Frequent backdrop changes and foreign language tapes contribute to the idea that men and women speak different languages. To top off 1982, Fornés won another Obie Award for sustained achievement.

Mud, which is about another, more violent love triangle, was produced in 1983, for the Padua Hills Festival in California. As with every play Fornés wrote for this festival, *Mud* was designed for its set. It was performed outdoors, and it ended near sunset—freezes were used to end scenes instead of blackouts, and the fading light made the costumed characters look drab. Fornés liked these effects and kept them even when the play was produced in New York. *Sarita* tells the story of a young girl so obsessed with a man that she kills him and ends up in a mental institution; it was produced at INTAR in 1984. *No Time* was produced at the Padua Hills Festival in 1984. Fornés's hard work during these years paid off: in 1984, Fornés received an Obie Award for *The Danube, Mud,* and *Sarita,* and won grants from the Rockefeller Foundation and the National Endowment for the Arts.

In 1985, Fornés received the prestigious American Academy and Institute of Arts and Letters Award in Literature. Fornés's play *The Conduct of Life,* a story about a Latin American man who is forced to perform violent acts as a government torturer and who acts just as violently within his own home, was produced Off-Off-Broadway, and it received an Obie for best new play. She then adapted and translated Virgilio Pinera's *Cold Air,* and it was produced at INTAR; for her translation she won a Playwrights U.S.A. Award. *Mud, The Danube, Sarita,* and *The Conduct of Life* were published in *María Irene Fornés: Plays* in 1986 by PAJ Publications. The book's preface was written by Fornés's former roommate, Susan Sontag.

In March of 1986, *A Matter of Faith* appeared Off-Off-Broadway, and *Lovers and Keepers,* actually three one-act musicals, was produced in April at INTAR. This latter play featured music by the famous Latin-jazz musicians Tito Puente and Fernando Rivas. Fornés's next project was an adaptation from Anton Chekhov's story, "Drowning." She produced this adaptation, also entitled *Drowning,* as a one-act play with six other one-act plays by other authors in 1986 under the title *Orchards. Art* was produced Off-Off-Broadway in 1986, and *The Mothers* was produced at the Padua Hills Festival that same year. *Abingdon Square,* a shocking play about a 15-year-old girl who, married to an older man, seeks a real love, was produced by Fornés Off-Broadway in 1987; it won her yet another Obie. Also in 1987, Fornés adapted Chekhov's "Uncle Vanya" for a play of the same name and produced the play Off-Broadway. In 1989, the playwright wrote *Hunger,* a play set in a warehouse that explores an imaginary future of socio-economic collapse and its human consequences; it was first produced Off-Off-Broadway by En Garde Productions. *And What of the Night,* a show which included *Hunger, Springtime, Lust,* and *Charlie* (previously entitled *The Mothers*), was produced in Milwaukee, Wisconsin, in 1989.

Works with Novice Playwrights

Fornés told *CA* that, although there is "a rich Spanish tradition of classic theater . . . there hasn't been a strong modern Hispanic theater—by that I mean since the turn of the century." According to Fornés, the "Hispanic American doesn't have a model yet. . . ." She believes that it is "very important to try to work with Hispanic playwrights at a level where they are just beginning to write, so that they don't dismiss possibilities of ways of writing that would be very original to them but ways they would not see models for in the active American or English or German theater." Fornés does more than advocate such instruction; she is an active teacher of young Hispanic writers. She has continually instructed students at the Padua Hills Festival in California and at INTAR; in 1988, she taught a workshop at Manhattanville College in Purchase, New York.

A leader as well as a playwright, Fornés has made an invaluable contribution to the arts. Her plays are remarkable for their exciting and unusual forms, their striking contents, and their memorable characters. Besides writing and producing plays, Fornés is an instructor of young playwrights. She has assisted countless authors as they struggle to find their own voices, or even a theater in which to produce their plays. Finally, Fornés is a champion of Hispanics and women; she writes to inspire and acknowledge both groups, and serves as an extraordinary role model for them.

As a critic for the *Chicago Tribune* wrote, Fornés is "one of the art form's most cherished secrets. Ask playgoers about her, and they are apt to answer with a blank look. Mention Fornés to those who work in the theater, and their faces light up." Many critics assert that Fornés is one of the best playwrights the United States has to offer, and that her work will one day be widely known and respected. Whether or not the public appreciates her work, Fornés enjoys the process of creation. As she told *CA,* "I find more pleasure in the creating part of [my work], and I think that's the reason why I am always willing to keep experimenting and inventing things."

Sources:

Books

Betsko, Kathleen, and Rachel Koenig, *Interviews with Contemporary Women Playwrights,* Beech Tree Books, 1987, pp. 154-67.
Contemporary Authors New Revision Series, Volume 28, Gale, 1990.
Contemporary Literary Criticism, Volume 61, Gale, 1990.
Contemporary Theatre, Film, and Television, Volume 1, Gale, 1984.
Dictionary of Literary Biography, Volume 7: *Twentieth-Century American Dramatists,* Gale, 1981.
Fornés, María Irene, *Lovers and Keepers,* Theatre Communications Group, 1987.
Fornés, María Irene, *María Irene Fornés: Plays,* PAJ Publications, 1986.
Fornés, María Irene, *Promenade and Other Plays,* Winter House, 1971.
Marranca, Bonnie, and Guatam Dasgupta, *American Playwrights: A Critical Survey,* Volume 1, Drama Books Specialists, 1981.

Periodicals

Chicago, April, 1990, p. 89.

Chicago Tribune, June 14, 1969; February 8, 1988, Section 5, p. 3; February 9, 1988, Section 2, p. 10; May 27, 1988, Section 5, p. 4.
Hispanic, July, 1988, pp. 44-46.
Los Angeles Times, August 2, 1989, Section 6, p. 7.
Nation, April 6, 1985, p. 412; April 23, 1988, p. 580.
Newsweek, January 25, 1982, p. 73.
New Yorker, May 7, 1979, p. 131; January 4, 1988, p. 59.
New York Times, April 17, 1968; June 5, 1969; February 22, 1972; January 14, 1978; January 22, 1978; April 25, 1979; December 30, 1981; October 25, 1983; March 13, 1984; March 20, 1985; April 17, 1986; April 23, 1986; December 15, 1987, p. C21; October 17, 1989, p. A16.
Performing Arts Journal, Number 1, 1984.

—*Sketch by Ronie-Richele Garcia-Johnson*

Frias, Marlene Citron de
See **Cintron de Frias, Marlene**

G

Nely Galán
(1964-)
Television anchor, producer

Nely Galán has transcended the usually tedious process of achieving success in the television industry. By 1991, when she was 27 years old, she had her own syndicated talk show, which was produced in both Spanish and English and aired throughout the United States. She had appeared on news programs around the country, managed a television station, and owned her own production company. Talented as well as persistent, Galán is determined to help shape the future of television produced for Hispanic viewers.

Born in Cuba in 1964, Nely Galán was raised in a traditional Catholic family and educated in Catholic schools. While the young woman wanted to become a writer, her family thought she should set her sights on getting married. As Galán told *Hispanic,* "My mother wanted me to be a wife and a concert pianist—but only play the piano at home." Not surprisingly, considering Galán's professional ambitions, she protested when her family attempted to steer her down traditional paths. One such protest, an article bemoaning the pain of being sent to a strict Catholic school, found its way into the hands of *Seventeen* magazine editors. Impressed, these editors published Galán's article and offered her an editorship. Galán's career as a writer seemed to be well underway.

Instead of continuing to write, however, Galán began to focus on television work. When her editorship with *Seventeen* ended, she became an anchor on *Checking It Out,* a news show for teenagers. As she worked for *Checking It Out,* Galán traveled throughout the United States interviewing guests and filming stories. During these two years Galán began to understand the power of television, and those in the business began to recognize her talent. Galán decided to become a producer.

One of her first jobs was to assist with the production of the special *Since JFK: The Last 20 Years;* that special won an Emmy. Her next position gave her much more authority, if not a luxurious work setting. As she recalled in *Hispanic,* she worked in a "one-room shack" as the station manager for WNJU-TV in Teterboro, New Jersey, and dealt with "asbestos falling from the ceiling." Despite the dilapidated condition of the station, Galán stayed at WNJU-TV for three years. She was responsible for a $15 million budget and a staff of some 100 people. Galán was only 22 years old when she entered that position; she was the youngest television station manager in the United States.

The ambitious young woman began to dream of buying her own television station, but she realized that, even if she could come up with the required funds, she did not have the authority needed to own a station herself. Perhaps she could gradually gain this authority. CBS had made her a very tempting offer to anchor a show aired from WCAU-TV in Philadelphia. At first, Galán scorned the offer. She explained in *Hispanic,* "I didn't want to be anchor-woman. Puhleassse. I had a chip on my shoulder. . . . I thought, 'Oh, these people just want a token Hispanic.'" Although she hesitated, she decided to take the offer—on her own terms. Galán was also contracted to host a television talk show. She ensured that the syndication rights to her English and Spanish shows, called *Bravo,* would belong to her.

Buys Television Production Company

Finally, Galán began to earn the authority she sought to become a respected businesswoman in the television industry. Audiences loved Galán and her show, which dealt with serious and intriguing topics. Both Galán and her show began to receive favorable attention. By 1988, *Bravo* was airing on 31 different television stations. The 26-year-old Galán found herself in the position to buy and lead her own television production company, Tropico Communications. By the end of the decade, Galán had another talk-show, *Nely,* which was aired from WBBM-TV. She also became the co-anchor of *House Party* on NBC-TV.

During the early 1990s, Galán became more and more concerned about the future of television shows produced for Hispanic audiences. It was apparent to her that, while some Hispanic viewers appreciated Spanish shows, other, younger Hispanics preferred English-speaking shows. She told *Hispanic,* "I asked 30 kids, when you think of Spanish TV what do you think of? And they said things like, 'Ugh, it's embarrassing. I would never watch it.' It embarrasses them! I was heartbroken!" Galán recognizes the need for two kinds of television aimed at Hispanic audiences; she wrote to one of the networks to explain her realization. "There is a tremendous gap between the Hispanic market that watches Spanish language television and the untapped market that knows who Gabriel García Márquez is. You need one for survival; you need the other for our future. The gap must be bridged." Already providing both types of television shows, Galán is beginning to build that bridge herself.

Sources:

Periodicals

Chicago Tribune, March 3, 1990, section 1, p. 10.
Hispanic, November, 1988, pp. 50-51; November, 1991, pp. 18-24.

—Sketch by Ronie-Richele Garcia-Johnson

Catalina Esperanza Garcia
(1944-)
Anesthesiologist

The first Hispanic woman to graduate from the University of Texas medical school, Catalina Esperanza Garcia is also a founding member of two Hispanic women's organizations: Mexican-American Business and Professional Women and the Dallas Women Foundation. Both groups seek to foster a sense of unity among Hispanic women and encourage them to further themselves professionally and personally.

Garcia was born in El Paso, Texas, on October 18, 1944, the daughter of Arturo Ramos and Catalina Galindo Garcia. After attending the University of Texas, from which she received a bachelor of science degree in 1964 and a Ph.D. in 1969, she interned at Baylor University Medical Center in Dallas and was an anesthesia resident at Parkland Hospital. Garcia then became a partner in the Dallas Anesthesiology Group, working primarily out of the Baylor University Medical Center. She is also a government appointee to the Texas State Board of Medical Examiners, a position in which she helps review and regulate medical licensing in the state.

In addition to pursuing her career in medicine, Garcia is active in a variety of business and community affairs, especially those that bring her into contact with other Hispanic women. In 1975, for example, she was a founding member of Mexican-American Business and Professional Women, which promotes the professional development of Hispanic women by holding seminars and furnishing opportunities to network. Ten years later, she was a founding member of the Dallas Women Foundation, a nonprofit organization that helps raise money for various women's groups and projects, including halfway houses and shelters. Another goal of the Foundation that is of particular interest to Garcia is its crusade for salary regulation, which would ensure that women's earnings equal those of men in the same job . These and other efforts to empower women led the Women's Center of Dallas to present Garcia with its Women Helping Women Award.

The future of Hispanic youth is also of concern to Garcia, who once served as chairperson of the Dallas Independent School System's Hispanic Advisory Committee. In this position, she traveled to schools with large numbers of Hispanic students, bringing together parents and teachers for discussions on what the schools needed and what the parents could provide. In recognition of her leadership role on the committee, Garcia was named the school system's "Volunteer of the Year" in 1985. "Since there are so few Hispanic women physicians, I represent my gender and my people wherever I go," Garcia related in *Vista.* "This doesn't make me behave in a different fashion, but I realize the meaning of this awesome responsibility."

In 1992, Garcia returned to her hometown to attend a Hispanic Women Professions workshop at El Paso County Community College. Talking with students about women in health care, she reiterated her belief that any Hispanic woman can accomplish what she has with the proper encouragement and inspiration. "Often parents are too busy to remember how fragile a young woman's self-esteem can be," she later explained to Stephanie Poythress in an interview. "I travel to schools, telling young women that we sometimes have to build our own self-confidence. I like to inspire people. My message is: develop yourself to the fullest."

Sources:

Periodicals

Vista, March 7, 1992.

Other

Garcia, Catalina Esperanza, telephone interview with Stephanie Poythress, September 17, 1992.

—Sketch by Stephanie Poythress

Cristina Garcia
(1958-)
Journalist, novelist

Cristina Garcia climbed the ranks at *Time* magazine before she decided to change career paths and write her first novel, *Dreaming in Cuban,* which was nominated for a National Book Award. Her characters delve into issues her parents faced during the Cuban Revolution of the 1950s. Garcia, who tells the story of three women who have very different perspectives of the revolution, was favorably received by critics. "Her special feat is to tell it in a style as warm and gentle as the 'sustaining aromas of vanilla and almond,' as rhythmic as the music of Beny More," maintained a *Time* reviewer.

Garcia was born July 4, 1958, in Havana, Cuba, to Frank M. Garcia and Hope Lois Garcia. Her family fled to the United States when she was two years old, and she grew up with American friends and English as her primary language. Garcia earned a bachelor of arts degree in political science from Barnard College in 1979, and went on to graduate from the Johns Hopkins University School of Advanced International Studies in Latin American studies in 1981. She married Scott Brown December 8, 1990. As a youth, Garcia wanted to join the foreign service; her life took a different path, however, and the written word became her vehicle.

Garcia's first career move was to land a job at *Time* magazine in 1983 as a reporter and researcher. During the next seven years she held various positions at *Time,* including bureau chief and correspondent. In 1990 she decided to change direction again. Instead of reporting facts, Garcia wanted to bring the images in her imagination to life with her words in *Dreaming in Cuban.* In an *Ann Arbor News* story Garcia said she remembered growing tired of "telling the truth." One day, she wrote a poem about three crazy women who kill themselves, and soon she was at work on her novel. She took a leave of absence from *Time,* returned three months later, and endured another six months before she quit for good. Garcia related that she was "frustrated with the constraints of journalism and the journalism of *Time.*" She was living in Miami, immersed in Cuban culture and meeting Cubans. "All the issues of my childhood came bubbling up."

Dealing with these issues was a means for Garcia to understand her ancestors and their special struggles. Like many of those who left the country, Garcia's parents were vilified by Cuban president Fidel Castro in a hard exile. "First generation Americans, they live cut-off from a homeland their parents cannot forgive and their new country forbids them to visit," a *Time* reporter noted in a review of Garcia's book. "In her impressive first novel, *Dreaming in Cuban,* Garcia takes back her island."

Explores Cuban Revolution in Novel

Garcia's story concerns three generations of Cuban women and their different reactions to the revolution. The book takes the reader to 1972 on the beach in Cuba. Celia del Pino, a staunch believer in communism, volunteers for stints in the sugarcane fields and as the local civilian judge. Meanwhile, her daughter Lourdes Puente in Brooklyn owns a bakery and is dependent on capitalism to make her business survive. Celia's other daughter, Felicia, is delusional and spouts politics for santeria, a religion that uses voodoo and Christian symbolism.

Garcia explained in an *Ann Arbor News* story that as a child she heard many anti-Castro sentiments. "When I was growing up, I was in a virulently anti-Castro home, so Cuba was painted for me as a very monstrous place, an island prison. . . . Writing this helped me to understand my parents and their generation a little better." Her book also shed new light on Latin Americans for her readers. A reviewer in *Publishers Weekly* praised Garcia's characters. "Embracing fantasy and reality with equal fervor, Garcia's vivid, indelible characters offer an entirely new view of a particular Latin American sensibility."

Sources:

Periodicals

Ann Arbor News, April 23, 1992.
Publishers Weekly, January 13, 1992.
Time, March 23, 1992.

—*Sketch by D. D. Andreassi*

Frances Garcia
(1938-)
Mayor of Hutchinson, Kansas

Frances Josephine Garcia still remembers the racial discrimination her family experienced when she was a child. They were not allowed to eat in certain restaurants, and when they went to the movies, they had to sit in the balcony. These immigrants from Mexico were not even able to enjoy malteds inside the drug store—they were expected to drink them outside. "Times," however, "are changing," said Garcia during an interview with Ronie-Richele Garcia-Johnson. Garcia, who has served two terms as the mayor of Hutchinson, Kansas, has been a part of this change. Hutchinson's population of 41,000 people is just 2% Hispanic—clearly, her political success has had more to do with her confidence, her qualifications, and her dedication to her community than with her ethnicity.

Frances Garcia's parents were born in Mexico; seeking better lives, their families immigrated to the United States and settled in Hutchinson, Kansas. While neither Garcia's mother or father graduated from high school, they were hard workers and believed in education. Her father, Joe G. Calvillo, who found a job in manufacturing during the war, became a naturalized citizen and educated himself. He was a voracious reader, and he loved math. He told his daughter, who was born on June 4, 1938, in Hutchinson, "You can do anything you want to with hard work and common sense," but advised her to "never expect anything to be given to you."

Garcia's mother, Micaela (Chavez) Calvillo, who was raised to be a good wife and mother, understood the value of education as well as the meaning of community. As Garcia recalled in the *Hutchinson News,* her mother continually assisted those who came from the nearby train tracks. "My mother was always feeding someone who got off the train. . . . [She] would always sit them down on the porch and give them a meal." Micaela Calvillo did not hesitate to invite travelers in for Thanksgiving dinner. While Micky instilled her daughter with the traditional values she had learned from her own mother, she earned her United States citizenship and encouraged Garcia to seek education and a good life.

After Garcia graduated from Hutchinson High School in 1956, she attended a junior college near her home. Garcia could not decide whether she wanted to study business or become a teacher (she had received a Business Certificate from Salt City Business College in 1954), so she earned an Associate bachelor's degree in liberal arts from Hutchinson Community College in 1958. During this time in school, she dated the man who was to become her husband, John T. Garcia. The couple were married on August 27, 1960. Today, they have two sons, John Jr. and Geoffrey.

While her husband worked as a farm machine operator, Garcia stayed at home to raise her children. In 1966 she went to work at the Wells Department Store Credit Office as a credit officer. By 1968, she had left that job to become a clerk/typist at the Reno County Clerk's Office. Then, in

Frances Garcia

1972, Garcia became a savings consultant and Loan Secretary. She earned a Savings and Loan Training for Savings Consultant certificate the next year. Garcia worked as a consultant until 1981, when she suffered back problems which necessitated surgery. In 1983, she became a volunteer outreach worker and interpreter with the Hutchinson Methodist Ministry; she served in this position until 1990.

Launches Political Career

It was not until the mid-1980s that Garcia, who had two grandchildren by that time, became seriously involved in Hutchinson politics. A friend of hers, Tony Flores, encouraged her to run for one of the three seats available on the city council. According to Garcia, she thought she might "give it a try." Her family was generally supportive of her decision to run for the council. During an interview with Garcia-Johnson, Garcia laughed when she recalled the advice of her youngest son. When he asked her, "Mother, do you know that your life will never be your own?" she knew he was right, but she also knew that the question was motivated from his own self-interest as well. Her sons, who had been blessed with a wonderfully caring mother, were beginning to realize that they would have to share her with the entire town if she won the election. That, however, was fine with Garcia. She knew that she had some valuable contributions to make to her community.

When Garcia first made the commitment to run for city council, she did not know how to run a campaign. Harkening back to her father's advice about "hard work and common sense," she utilized both. It made sense to her to reach out to the people of Hutchinson, and the best way to do that was to walk the streets of the town, going door to door and introducing herself. It was a lot of work, but Garcia was determined to allow voters to get to know her before election day. She explained in *Vista,* "I worked hard and I didn't promise anything except to try to do a good job and create a good, healthy living environment for Hutchinson."

Garcia's father was correct—she could do anything with hard work and common sense. In the interview with Garcia-Johnson, Garcia spoke of the moment when she was told just how effective her door-to-door canvassing tactic had been. "Mrs. Garcia," began the official who had called her to his office, "Has the newspaper contacted you?" Garcia shook her head, "No." "Well," continued the official, "you better have a seat. You are the top vote getter—you could be the next mayor." Garcia, who had been unknown before her campaign, was one of six candidates and had not expected to do very well in this first election. The news that she might very well become mayor of her home town left her shocked. Her supporters and her family were elated.

Garcia was featured in the *Hutchinson News* on that Tuesday, March 26, 1985, when she was named the top vote getter. The newspaper explained why the elected council person with the most votes would probably become the mayor: "Traditionally commissioners choose the top vote-getter as mayor, although it is not mandatory. . . ." Garcia's stands on campaign issues were also emphasized in the newspaper. She was concerned about employment, commerce, crime, and the city's growth, and she insisted that she could be a fair representative in Hutchinson. "Comments from people tell me the city as a whole is not being represented. I think I can represent all the people. People need to know you're there ready to listen any time." Garcia also mentioned the Hispanics in the community who made up just 2% of the population. "Maybe they (Hispanics) could relate a little better to the commission if I were elected."

Wins Mayoral Race

Garcia was still surprised when she won a spot on the city council and the mayor's seat. When she took office in April, 1985, she became the first Hispanic woman mayor in the Midwest. Hispanics throughout the country were proud of Garcia. Her parents felt honored. Her husband and sons were thrilled. Garcia continued to earn the praise of those who knew her as she began to work.

Garcia served as Hutchinson's mayor from April 1985 to April 1986 and continued as a city commissioner for the next three years. At the Midwest Voter's Registration Conference in 1987, she presented a workshop on "Women's Involvement." She also spoke during the Topeka, Kansas Hispanic Heritage Week held in 1985. Garcia told Garcia-Johnson that, as mayor, she enjoyed working with the people of Hutchinson, her fellow commissioners, and the town's chamber of commerce.

In 1988, Garcia decided to run for the Kansas Senate. Explaining this decision in a campaign leaflet, she wrote, "the issues regarding the quality of our education, and availability of health care services, our environment and our ability to help small businesses grow, are simply too critical to sit back and not at least try to make a difference." She emphasized the need for quality education, economic development, environmental protection, and accessible health care in Kansas as she campaigned. Garcia's approach to the problems facing the state of Kansas was best summed up by a statement she wrote for this piece of campaign literature: "For our people to fulfill their capacities by their own hard work and determination, we must provide them with the best educational training and re-training opportunities possible. I believe the citizens of Kansas are ready for bold leadership in the areas of education, economic development, health care and environmental protection if it will lead to real progress." Once again, Garcia promised to give the average person the opportunity to voice her or his own concerns.

Despite the backing of Reno County and many supporters, Frances Garcia did not win the election. She did, however, win a good proportion of votes, especially considering that she ran against a well-known businessman who was seeking a second term as a state senator for the 34th Senatorial District. Garcia did win her bid for re-election to the city council. Once again, from April 1989 to April, 1990, she led the city as its mayor. In 1992, she was still a Hutchinson City Commissioner. Former City Manager George Pyle explained the reason for Garcia's success as a mayor and commissioner when he spoke to the *Hutchinson News* in mid-1990. "She listens, she sympathizes, she empathizes," he said of the leader. "I do remember how impressed I was with her ability to stand up in front of a group and communicate." Garcia herself confirmed her willingness to learn about and from the people of Hutchinson. "My phone is always open to anybody," she told the *News.*

While occupying a seat as a city commissioner is in itself a full-time commitment, Garcia serves her community in other ways. She has been a vice-president of the Kansas Art Commission as well as a member of such groups as the American Business Women Association, the Hutchinson Symphony Board, and the Committee for the National League of Cities. In the past, Garcia has been an active member of numerous community advisory boards and has also served as the president and vice president of the Kansas League of Municipalities—she is the second person from Hutchinson to have ever done so.

Balances Career and Family

As busy as she is, Garcia always finds time to spend with her family. Her husband is understanding and supportive of her work. While the couple often meet each other as they are coming and going through the door of their home, John occasionally travels with Frances to her various meetings in Kansas and throughout the United States. Frances Garcia also enjoys spending time with her parents, who have always encouraged her to excel, her sons, who have been as proudly supportive of her efforts as their father, and her six grandchildren.

Garcia has won many awards of recognition for her efforts. Among the most notable was that from the League of United Latin American Citizens, which awarded Garcia with a plaque and certificate of recognition at the 1985 1st Annual Mayors Ball held in Denver, Colorado. Garcia was also honored at LULAC's 1986 Women's Symposium. The Kansas Advisory on Hispanic Affairs presented her with a Certificate of Recognition in 1987, and the American GI Forum State Convention praised her with an Outstanding Award the next year. In 1989, she was awarded a certificate of recognition for her work with the Hutchinson Leadership Program. Finally, Garcia was chosen as one of 47 "outstanding" representatives of Kansas Hispanics and profiled in the book, *El Camino Real: The King's Highway,* by the Kansas Advisory Committee on Hispanic Affairs in 1990. According to the *Hutchinson News,* the book "chronicles the stories of Hispanic heroes who have led the way for others" and was to be distributed to schools and libraries throughout Kansas.

"Only in the United States," remarked Frances Garcia during her interview with Garcia-Johnson, "could the daughter of a migrant from Mexico be the mayor of the city." While the environment in which she was raised contributed to this Hispanic woman's political success, most of the credit for her accomplishments belongs to Garcia and her supportive family. "It has been an honor and a learning experience," the leader says of her time as mayor and city commissioner, "and I hope that I have opened the door for young people and especially women."

Sources:

Periodicals

Hutchinson News, March 26, 1985; July 22, 1990, pp. 45, 48. *Vista,* July 5, 1986.

Other

Garcia, Frances, campaign literature, 1988.
Garcia, Frances, telephone interview with Ronie-Richele Garcia-Johnson, August, 1992.

—*Sketch by Ronie-Richele Garcia-Johnson*

Juliet Villarreal García
(1949-)
University president, educator

Juliet Villarreal García has established a national reputation as an outstanding educator and innovative college administrator. With her appointment as president of Texas Southernmost College in Brownsville, Texas, she became the first Mexican American woman college president in the United States.

Born May 18, 1949, in Brownsville, Texas, García was second of three children in her family. The value of education was always stressed in her parents' household. The family took great pride in her mother's achievement of being the salutatorian of her high school graduating class. As García remembered in a telephone interview with Sally Foster, "There was always money for books or any supplies needed for school." At a time when the public schools sent children home for speaking Spanish in class, the Villarreals consciously emphasized a bilingual household: García's mother, a native Texan, always spoke to the children in English, and her father, originally from Mexico, spoke in Spanish. Bilingualism and cultural awareness were part of the children's daily life. García's mother died at the age of 40, and her father became both mother and father to the three young children and continued to encourage their pursuit of education.

After graduating from Brownsville High School, García entered the University of Houston. While at college, she met and fell in love with Oscar García. At the age of 19 and in her junior year of college, the young couple wanted to marry. García's father insisted that marriage should not end his daughter's education, but that she must complete her bachelor's degree as a condition for his blessing. After one year of marriage, García received her B.A. in speech and English from the University of Houston. The young couple continued their graduate studies at the University of Houston. While completing her master's degree, García was granted a university-sponsored teaching fellowship. After García received her M.A. in speech and English in May, 1972, she and her husband returned home to Brownsville.

García's first teaching job following her master's studies was at Pan American University in Edinburg, Texas, in the spring of 1972. Balancing a home life with two young children and a roundtrip commute of 120 miles from Brownsville was very difficult. When García was approached by Texas Southernmost College (TSC), a community college in Brownsville, for a full-time instructor's position, she gladly accepted. García continued to teach in the English Department of TSC for two years.

Juliet Villarreal García

The Garcías relocated to Austin so that Juliet could attend the University of Texas at Austin for her Ph.D. studies. There she was selected as a Ford Foundation Fellow in Doctoral Studies and worked as a teaching assistant. She was granted her Ph.D. in communications and linguistics and was also elected to the Phi Kappa Phi Honors Society in 1976.

Develops Administrative Skills

Returning to Texas Southernmost College upon graduation, she began to teach in the English Department. While maintaining her teaching schedule, in 1979 García was appointed the Director of the TSC Institutional Self-Study for the Southern Association of Colleges and Schools (SACS), a non-governmental, regional accrediting association for educational institutions. The position involved assessing all aspects of the school's existence, including inventories of libraries, plant facilities, curriculum, faculty, staff and mission, a project which took more than a year.

After the completion of the self-study process, the transition from faculty member to administrator seemed to be a natural one for García. In 1981, she was appointed Dean of Arts and Sciences at TSC. She was very eager to use the information and insights gained through the self-study for TSC. Her enthusiasm paid off when in 1986, García was appointed president of Texas Southernmost College and became the first Mexican American woman college presi-

dent. Using her intimate knowledge of the workings of the college combined with the strategic plans developed as a result of the self-study process, President García launched a series of major campaigns to address vital college concerns.

Working with college and community leaders, García successfully directed the effort to raise $13.5 million through a general obligation bond issue underwritten by the community of Brownsville. The passage of this bond issue marked the first time the community had ever voted to give bond money to TSC. These funds were used to build new campus structures and restore existing ones. The expansion program doubled both the instructional capacity of TSC and the library over a five year period.

Initiates Innovative Scholarship Program

One of the most effective ways of providing accessibility to higher education is through early intervention and the guarantee of financial support for college. Using this premise, work began on the establishment of the Texas Southernmost College Endowment Scholarship. To create this endowment, García directed an aggressive campaign to raise $1 million through private and community sources to match a grant of $2 million provided by federal government funds. To qualify for a scholarship at TSC under this program, junior and senior high school students in the lower Rio Grande valley have to enroll in academically rigorous classes and receive grades of As or Bs. By providing both encouragement and motivation at the junior and senior high level, TSC, under the leadership of García, has developed a highly innovative and successful scholarship program which has been recognized with state, regional, and national awards.

In anticipation of the North American Free Trade Agreement (NAFTA) and to further expand the educational resources and opportunities in the Brownsville community, a new coalition of college and political figures developed. This informal group began work to forge a relationship between the University of Texas at Brownsville and Texas Southernmost College. The community expects that the Brownsville area will be pivotal in the developing trade and commerce as well as an entry point for educational and cultural exchange. A bill was passed by the legislature and signed by Governor Ann Richards that allowed a merger of the two educational institutions. In this cooperative measure, TSC would continue to provide technical and vocational curriculum, freshman and sophomore level classes, continuing education classes, and associate degrees. UT-Brownsville would provide upper division and graduate level curriculum and award bachelor's and master's degrees. As García told Shawn Foster of the *Brownsville Herald,* "We're the first institution in Texas to try this kind of partnership. We have heard the UT systems say the eyes of Texas are upon us." By combining both educational institutions, students will benefit by the four-year university atmosphere with a unified degree plan, catalogue, and simplified administrative procedures.

It is also hoped that the creation of what President García describes as a "community university" will address the problems of students whose families have never attended college. Community colleges have traditionally been the means by which these students enter higher education. The combination of the open admissions policy of a community college with the programs and course offerings available at a university will encourage these students to complete not only their certificate or associate degree, but their baccalaureate and master's degrees as well.

Named University President

In October, 1991, Juliet García was appointed the President of the new University of Texas at Brownsville and assumed office in January, 1992. Her work reflects her belief that strong commitment to the community is an integral part of any educational institution. In another interview with Shawn Foster of the *Brownsville Herald,* García explained, "The university here cannot hide behind red brick walls covered with ivory. It must affect the community in a positive way. . . . The majority of Hispanics enter higher education through junior colleges." The curriculum at the new University of Texas at Brownsville is designed to stress the value of the students' experience and emphasize bilingualism. Remembering her own experiences of being prohibited from speaking Spanish in her early education, García hopes to reestablish bilingualism and bi-literacy. "Our goal is not to replicate any of the other UT schools, but to exceed them. We have the raw resources here in the people that we have left undeveloped," stated García in her interview with Sally Foster. It is hoped that the University of Texas at Brownsville model will inspire similar development in other educational institutions in Texas.

García was elected to the board of trustees of the Southern Association of Colleges and Schools in 1991. The board serves as the administrative body which oversees higher education institutions. In addition she serves on the boards of the American Council on Education, the Academy for Educational Development, the Texas Commerce Bank, the Gladys Porter Zoo, and the Oblate School of Theology. García has received many awards in addition to her academic honors. She was named Outstanding Young Woman in America in 1976 and Outstanding Young Texas-Ex Award in 1986. She has also been honored with a 1989 "Hall of Fame" Education Award by the National Network of Hispanic Women, a 1991 Distinguished Citizenship Award by the Grand Lodge Order of Elks, and as Outstanding Alumnus by the University of Texas-Austin College of Communication in 1991.

In a telephone interview, García discussed the issues that she felt were the most important facing education. She stated that educational institutions are charged with vigilantly guarding a democratic society and environment. The security of that society rests on the educated voter who is an active participant. García, who lives in Brownsville, Texas, with her husband, Oscar, and her son and daughter, sees her historic appointment as president of a newly formed university as a first step in opening doors to Hispanics in academia. Drawing on her own strengths and the support of her family, she has achieved career success at an early age. Aware that she is a standard bearer for many, she said in her telephone interview, "There is extra responsibility. . . . If you succeed, people will then be willing to give others a chance." García is a community-spirited educator and administrator with a clear vision for providing accessible education and the skills to make that vision a reality.

Sources:

Periodicals

Brownsville Herald, June 7, 1991, p. 1; September 2, 1991, p. 1; October 28, 1991, pp. 1, 8; November 17, 1991, pp. 1, 12; December 28, 1991, p. 1; January 1, 1992, p. 1.
Valley Morning Star, June 9, 1991, pp. 1, 14.
Vista, July, 1987, pp. 6-8.

Other

García, Juliet Villarreal, telephone interview with Sally Foster, September 11, 1992.

—*Sketch by Sally Foster*

Garcia, Maria Emilia Martin
See **Martin-Garcia, Maria Emilia**

Norma García
(1950-)
Government official

Norma G. García broke with tradition to become the first woman to be elected mayor of Mercedes, a small south Texas town with a population of about 12,000 situated in

Norma García

the bountiful citrus bowl of the lower Rio Grande Valley. The surprise of García's victory was due to more than her sex, however. In Hidalgo County politics, where family bloodlines and political alliances can make or break a candidate, García had two more strikes against her. First, she ran as an independent, and second, she was not a Mercedes native. Her success as a three-term mayor earned her the title of Mayor of the Year from the Association of Hispanic Municipal Officials.

García was born October 5, 1950, in nearby Donna, Texas, an agricultural and livestock center slightly smaller than Mercedes. The daughter of Zacarias H. Garza, a mechanic, and Olivia Cavazos Garza, a teacher's aide, she was the eldest in a family of four sisters and three brothers. As a youngster, she never thought of a career in politics, she told Yleana Martinez in a telephone interview. Her family, however, had a history of political activity. An uncle on her mother's side was a school board member for 16 years, and her father's brother had served as a municipal judge. García's maternal grandfather was active in local and state campaigns. García began her own foray into the political arena at the age of 18 by working as an elections clerk.

In 1969, after studying stenography at a community college in San Antonio, García returned to Donna to work as a interviewer for the Texas Employment Commission. She moved to Mercedes in 1978 after marrying Jorge Antonio García, the owner of a funeral home. The couple

has three children, Martha Ann, Lucas Aaron, and Jorge Antonio II. In 1983, she took real estate courses at Southmost College in Brownsville, Texas, and earned a sales agent license from the American College of Real Estate in 1984.

Decides to Run for Office

That same year, García threw her hat into the ring to run for a post with the city council. She lost the race by 150 votes. She continued to work the real estate market, which she described as being "not exactly booming at the time." García then joined the Hidalgo County Women's Political Caucus to further extend her community contacts and groom herself as a candidate, for she believed her next step would be to run for a county-wide position. She fondly remembers a high point of her involvement with the Caucus when she met Atlanta Mayor Andrew Young and former Vice Presidential candidate Geraldine Ferraro in 1985 at the annual conference of the National Women's Political Caucus.

García's political career really began to take off when she left real estate work in 1985 to take a position as assistant director with the CBM Education Center. A year later, she was hired as a legislative assistant to State Representative Juan J. Hinojosa. She was named Chair of the Hidalgo County Urban County Association, and served on a state-wide committee that sought to find ways to help Texas residents obtain affordable housing. In 1986, while still acting as Hinojosa's administrative aide, García ran successfully for mayor, a post she would hold for three terms, the maximum permitted by the city charter.

Undertakes 'Second Choice' Mayoral Bid

In an interview with Martinez, García recalled that running for mayor of Mercedes was not her first choice. "When I first ran I ran because I wanted to do my civic duty. I had been looking at another position, which was county clerk," she said. "I felt I was a little more polished than in 1984, and that's why I was looking for a county-wide position." However, the mayor at the time caught wind of her plans and approached her. After a cordial discussion, García decided to postpone her bid for county clerk. "Because of the way politics were at the time, only one of us could run," she told Martinez, adding that the current county clerk had 14 years seniority as an elected official. "I was taught to respect my elders, I grew up that way. He so graciously asked me to please let him run," García said. Instead, she opted for the mayor's race, using a campaign slogan that played on her name—"Normalize Mercedes." She defeated her opponent in a run-off by a comfortable margin; she later appointed him to a post on the local housing authority. Although critics pointed out that allowing a defeated opponent an opportunity to remain in a visible position amounted to political suicide, García told the *Valley Morning Star* she did it as a "gesture of good faith." A firm believer in extending an open hand of friendship to supporters and foes alike, García proved her detractors wrong when she won a second term in 1988 and a third in 1990. "In the long run, now that I look back I see I've definitely grown as a person," she told Martinez. "I've acquired a lot of experience with people. I've built networks around the state, including other elected officials and at state agencies."

Makes Significant Contributions to Mercedes

García's numerous contacts have certainly helped the city of Mercedes. García can claim as accomplishments during her mayoral tenure almost $2 million in grant awards for municipal improvements. Projects from these funds included $1 million for new water and sewer lines and paving, which helped about 2,000 residents. A $320,000 state grant from the Texas Parks and Wildlife Department was used for the renovation of a park and the Mercedes Boys Club. A $400,000 low interest loan was obtained through the Texas Department of Community Affairs to expand a local grocery store, which resulted in new jobs in the small town.

During her first term, she continued to work as administrative aide to Hinojosa. The work helped her in many ways, she said, because she was able to get a better handle on issues that affected her constituents. Hinojosa also has been hailed for his work to reform the Texas Open Meetings Act, a bill that seeks to ensure that all elected officials conduct public business in the open. Hinojosa received awards and citations from several citizens groups for this work, an honor that he is quick to share with his staff members. As he told the *Valley Monitor*, "Any recognition that I have received is a reflection of my staff . . . Norma knows which buttons to push and who to call to get things done. She is a leader and a team player all rolled into one."

García's civic and community accomplishments are numerous. In 1988, García was honored as Woman of the Year by both the McAllen Business and Professional Women's Association and by the Mercedes Chamber of Commerce. In 1992, she was named Mayor of the Year by the newly-formed Association of Hispanic Municipal Officials, an organization for which she served as president that same year. In addition, she is past chairman of the Hidalgo County Women's Political Caucus and of the Hidalgo County Urban County Advisory Committee and she has served as secretary and president of the Lower Rio Grande Valley Development Council. She is a member of the Texas Municipal League Board, and was appointed by Governor Ann Richards to the Texas Environmental Agencies Transition Committee. The committee is charged with organizing a natural resource conservation commission by combining forces from three state environmental agencies. Despite her hectic schedule, García still takes time to study the organ and practice cake decorating. Of course, there is always the politicking for other candidates that comes with the territory of being a city's chief executive officer. "I wanted to do my civic duty, pay something back to the community, corny as it sounds," she told the *Valley Morning Star*. "Everybody should do it once. You get a different perspective on the inside. People don't understand how the system works. It's easy to point a finger."

Mercedes, the so-called Queen City of the Rio Grande, may be small in size, but to García its problems are just as important as that of any major urban center. García acknowledges that her husband, Jorge Antonio, has been a tremendous help in keeping the household functional while she keeps the city on track. He is the owner of García-Trevino Funeral Home, which has been operated by his family since 1933. Unfortunately for him, in this corner of South Texas the old-world style of turning to a man to get business done persists. García claims that he is constantly being approached by citizens who ask him to tell his wife about some problem that needs attention. Some even call the funeral home with messages about mayoral business. Norma García admits that meetings with her constituents, which often include her husband, take place in the most unlikely settings. "We'd go to the grocery store together, and people would stop me and talk about pot holes, brush that needed to be picked up," she told Martinez. "We'd go with a shopping list but wouldn't get through half of it because we'd need to leave. Then he'd have to go to another store and do the rest of the shopping."

Sources:

Periodicals

Mercedes Enterprise, May 7, 1986.
Monitor, (McAllen, Texas), March 13, 1988.
Valley Morning Star, April 22, 1992.

Other

García, Norma G., telephone interview with Yleana Martinez, August, 1992.

—*Sketch by Yleana Martinez*

Carmen Lomas Garza
(1948-)
Visual artist

Paintings, etchings and lithographs are Carmen Lomas Garza's tools to portray her vision of the traditions and customs of her rural Chicano community in Texas. Mining her remembrances of a strong and vibrant culture, the nationally honored artist recreates the image of her personal history.

Garza was born in 1948 in Kingsville, Texas, a small town located southwest of Corpus Christi. In an interview with Jose Adan Moreno in *Caminos*, Garza described her ambitions as a young girl: "I remember doing a lot of drawing in elementary school, but the turning point came when I made the decision to concentrate on being a professional artist when I was about 13 years old." Her parents, Mucio B. Sr. and Maria Lomas Garza, were artistic and she felt their influence; her mother was a self-taught artist and her father was an artisan who worked in both sheet metal and wood. Garza began her college education at Texas Arts and Industry University. While still an undergraduate, some of her prints were featured in the journal *El grito* in 1971. By the time she received her bachelor of science degree in 1972, Garza had developed a highly individualistic style. After graduation, Garza went to study at Antioch Graduate School and was granted her Master of Education degree in 1973.

Relates Chicano Culture in Art

Garza has largely concentrated on weaving a pictorial depiction of the traditions of Chicano culture. Drawing on her childhood memories, she captures the magic in daily life found in the gathering of cactus during Lent, children playing, family and neighborhood activities, and the maintaining of home altars using a stylized depiction of figures called monitos. Rather than distance herself through commentaries, she shares her private visions with her audience. Prints from her earliest period are dominated by the use of stark black and white modified only by the limited use of aquatints. Strong contrast is evident in both the monochromatic color scheme and in the use of tightly executed patterns. Increasingly, Garza has begun to add more color to her work, employing water colors to enhance skin tone and to accentuate special objects in her prints.

Relocating to California, Garza entered the master's program at San Francisco State University. She also worked as a curator administrative assistant at the Galeria/Studio 24 in San Francisco until 1981. Her master of arts degree was conferred in 1980. Although Garza worked to establish herself in the California arts community, she continued to exhibit work in her native Texas, especially in San Antonio, Mission, and Houston. At one of her earlier shows, "Tejano artists," Mimi Crossley of the *Houston Post* cited Garza as "one of the true 'finds' of the exhibit." She also participated in the group exhibitions of "Los quenandos" (1975), "Dale Gas: Give It Gas" (1979) and "Fire! An Exhibition of 100 Texas Artists" (1979). Always interested in the Mexican Museum, Garza was commissioned to create the cover for the "Los Primeros Cinco Anos," a celebration of the Museum's fifth anniversary exhibition in 1980. Later in

1984, the Museum named Garza as its artist-in-residence, a position she retained until 1987.

Garza continued to display her work at public museums and private galleries throughout California and the West Coast. She participated in a two-woman show with Margo Humphrey at the San Francisco Museum of Modern Art, displaying her skills in both gouache paintings and printmaking. Her regional and national reputation was enhanced when she received a National Endowment for the Arts Fellowship in printmaking (*intaglio*) in 1981. She also continued to exhibit among increasingly established artists in the "Califas Exhibition" and the "Saved Stuff" Exhibit at the Helen Euphrat Gallery. Garza's work is part of several permanent collections, including the McAllen International Museum, Texas Women's University, and University of Texas Library at Austin.

Introduces Full-Color Works

Between 1982 and 1984, Garza began to expand her media by using full spectrum color in her paintings. During that time, she was commissioned by the City of San Francisco to do a series of paintings based on the theme of the development of the daily use of water throughout history. The style of her paintings was described by noted art critic Tomas Ybarra-Frausto in *Imagine* as "small and full of luminous details and keen perceptions . . . they are charged with rich reservoirs of meaning and expressive power." Garza was awarded a second National Foundation for the Arts Fellowship, for painting, in 1987.

Through the beauty of her work, Carmen Lomas Garza records her own history as a young Chicana and extends her hand to all those who wish to experience it. In her career as an artist, as well as a cultural educator and recorder, Garza has a bright future. In 1990, Garza's work *Family Pictures,* a bilingual children's book, was published; in it she describes and illustrates childhood daily activities. A *Publishers Weekly* reviewer noted, "The vibrant, canvaslike illustrations, accentuated with papel Picado-images on the text pages, evoke Garza's love for family and community despite the hardships she encountered while growing up. Readers of various ethnic origins should use this exemplary bilingual book as a litmus test for exploring diversities of multicultural lifestyles."

Sources:

Periodicals

Booklist, June 1, 1990, p. 1907.
Caminos, November, 1984, pp. 44-45, 53.
El grito, summer, 1971, pp. 2, 70-73.
Houston Post, August 19, 1976, p. 7BB.
Imagine, summer/winter, 1986, pp. 129-32, 231-32.
Publishers Weekly, July 13, 1990, pp. 54-55.

—Sketch by Sally Foster

Lila Garza
(1953-)
Entrepreneur

When Lila Garza founded the Michigan Hispanic Chamber of Commerce in 1989 she wanted to help minority entrepreneurs overcome some of the problems she faced as a business owner. "If you don't know how to run your own business, you're not going to succeed," she told interviewer D. D. Andreassi. Garza wrote in a Michigan Hispanic Chamber of Commerce brochure that she believed the "path to obtaining Hispanic empowerment is through the collective means of educating, networking, and assisting one another in obtaining contractual opportunities." Motivated by strong religious teachings, Garza's work guided hundreds of minority business people to overcome obstacles that might have otherwise proven insurmountable.

Lila Hernandez Garza was born December 5, 1953, in Meoqui, Mexico, one of five children of Antonio Hernandez and Herlinda Rodriguez. "My parents were very interested in building our characters," Garza told Andreassi. "I came from a close and united family. If I had to give credit, it would be to God first and secondly to my mother. She is very strong and she kept our family together." Garza, a born-again Christian, told Andreassi that the evangelistic church she attended in Detroit was an important part of her life. "People go to this church because they want to, not because they are brainwashed," Garza said in an interview with the *Detroit News.* "We lead the life stated in the Bible, whereas other religions make adjustments and say, 'It's OK, you can do it.'"

Garza attended the Roman Catholic church until she was 15 years old and she decided to change her religion and her lifestyle. Accompanied by her mother, Garza started going to a Christian evangelistic church. "We really felt that we fit in that church," she told this interviewer. "It really interested me a lot in the teaching of the Bible." A few years later Garza graduated from a Michigan high school and in 1977 she earned a bachelor of arts degree in business administration from Michigan's Northwood Institute. Garza married and was divorced after three years. Eleven years later she married Jesus Garza with whom she had one child, Antonio. Meanwhile she started her career as a manager for Elias Brothers Restaurants and in 1978 Garza became a manager at the Woold Shoe Company. One year later she joined Ford Motor Company as a systems coordinator in the purchasing department. Garza spent the next seven years supervising a system that tracked daily plant production.

In 1986 Garza was feeling confined in her career growth, so she decided to venture out on her own. She established the Airex International Freight Service, Incorporated, an air freight transportation and forwarding company. During the next two years Garza's company earned a revenue growth of more than $4.5 million. Buoyed by the company's overwhelming success, she continued to expand. However, she closed the business a couple of years later when its major contractors, Ford Motor Company and General Motors, reduced fast-track shipping.

In 1990 Garza started a new business and became partial owner of L & C Assemblers, an automotive seat cover and industrial uniforms manufacturer. Relying on the information gained from this experience, she joined the development of a new sporting apparel manufacturing company, Textrim Inc., which sold the rights to all of its lines to a group of investors. Hungry for new opportunities, a few months later Garza created a full-talent communications company that specialized in industrial, education, and business development videos. In addition to the many hours she spent running her businesses, Garza was a board member of the Michigan Hispanic Chamber of Commerce and a member of the United States Hispanic Chamber of Commerce. In 1990 she was awarded the Hispanic Business Woman of the Year award for Region IV in Michigan. Garza, a sorority sister in Tau Delta Rho, also won an award from the National Chamber of Commerce. But the accolades held little significance for her. "I'm not interested in titles or awards," she told Andreassi. "I'm interested in doing the work and making progress with it."

In late 1992 she was still seeing signs of progress with the Michigan Chamber of Commerce, including a grant from the Michigan Department of Commerce and the development of affiliate chambers around the state. The chambers offer programs such as teaching business techniques and matching Hispanic entrepreneurs with mentors. "If they don't know how to do business with Chrysler they will know how to when they get out of this," Garza commented to Andreassi.

Another of Garza's goals is to start an investment company that helps minority and women entrepreneurs. "I'm very committed to helping minorities, not just Hispanics," she told Andreassi. "Without economic achievements you can't go anywhere. It's so important to have a close relationship with God and your family. In the good times and the bad times it's very helpful." Always planning new projects, Garza also hopes to blend her business knowledge with her spiritual devotion by establishing a small school for minority children that will incorporate Montessori teaching with Christian instruction.

Sources:

Periodicals

Detroit News, December 23, 1990.

Other

Garza, Lila, telephone interview with D. D. Andreassi, August, 1992.

Michigan Hispanic Chamber of Commerce, publicity materials.

—Sketch by D. D. Andreassi

Garza, Sally Fernandez
See **Fernandez, Sally Garza**

Irma Gigli
(1931-)
Medical researcher

Irma Gigli is one of few women in the world to chair a university department in a medical discipline. Since 1982, she has headed the dermatology division at the San Diego School of Medicine of the University of California. "Administrative duties would never constitute my first choice," she told Michelle Vachon in an interview. "But when the university offered me this position, there were no women heading dermatology departments in the United States, and only a few in other countries. I felt compelled to accept the appointment." In the course of her career, Gigli has conducted dermatology and immunology research at Harvard Medical School and New York University in the United States, Universitat der Stadt Frankfurt in Germany, and the University of Oxford in England. She now divides her time between the University of California at San Diego and the Bernhard Nocht Institute for Tropical Medicine in Hamburg, Germany.

Gigli started her medical studies more than four decades ago in her native Argentina. Born in Cordoba on December 22, 1931, she had already achieved a teacher's degree, a bachelor's degree, and a doctor of medicine degree when she arrived in the United States in 1958. She spent her first three years at Cook County Hospital in Chicago, Illinois, where she completed one year of internship and two years of residency in dermatology. Her initial exposure to the United States proved difficult. "I had to play intellectual tricks with myself in order to survive," she recalled to Vachon. "I came from a very protective family, and had never been away from home. I was really not prepared for this gigantic hospital." But she learned quickly. During her first month of internship, for example, she found herself on call every weekend. "I soon realized that the 'boys'—

there were very few female interns at the hospital—would befriend secretaries, take them to dinner, and consequently have their names removed from weekend duty lists." She, however, found other means to fix her schedule.

In 1960, Gigli obtained a post-doctoral fellowship to study at New York University's School of Medicine in New York City. One year later, she received her certification in dermatology and moved to Miami, Florida, to attend the Howard Hughes Medical Institute on an immunology fellowship. "My mentor at the institute was a very talented and extremely demanding man—we toiled away seven days a week," she emphasized to Vachon. "But everything I eventually accomplished was motivated by my early experience at this laboratory." In 1964, Gigli's student visa expired and she had to return home. "Argentina was already in the midst of political turmoil," she explained. "My family advised me to leave. So I accepted an invitation from the department of dermatology at the University of Frankfurt, and spent two years in Germany as a visiting scientist. The director, Dr. F. Hermann, allowed me to undertake whatever I wanted. This gave me the opportunity to get my feet wet setting up a laboratory and working independently."

Studies with Nobel Laureate

Gigli returned to the United States in 1967. During the following seven years, she held research positions in immunology and teaching positions in dermatology at Harvard Medical School in Cambridge, Massachusetts. She also served as chief of dermatology service at Peter Bent Brigham Hospital and Robert B. Brigham Hospital in Brookline, Massachusetts, and worked as clinical associate in dermatology at Massachusetts General Hospital in Boston. In 1974, she took a sabbatical and studied with Nobel laureate Rodney Porter at Oxford University in England. "This year enriched both my life and my career," she remembered fondly. "Porter was a first-class human being. Harvard offered me a full-time position, and Porter tried to make the offer as attractive as possible. But I was not willing to undergo the adjustment of living in yet another foreign country." So in 1976, Gigli accepted a dual appointment at New York University, as professor of dermatology and experimental medicine and member of the Irvington House research institute. Six years later, she joined the University of California at San Diego as professor of medicine and head of the dermatology division and associate chair for research in the department of medicine.

Gigli has published more than 100 research papers and more than 100 research abstracts. A guest speaker throughout the United States, Latin America, and Europe, she also belongs to more than 15 foundations and associations—such as the American Association of Immunologists, the American Association for the Advancement of Science, the International Society of Dermatology, and the Lupus Foundation. "As I advanced in my career, I began to appreciate the necessity of having a strong professional network," she told Vachon. "In medicine, membership to some organizations is highly respected in academic circles. But you can only join these organizations by invitation, thus the importance of having colleagues to sponsor you. Being good in your field is not enough; without a professional network, you might not make it."

In 1985, Gigli married Hans Müller-Eberhard, an immunochemist who was affiliated with the Scripps Clinic in La Jolla, California. He became director of the Bernhard Nocht Institute for Tropical Medicine in Hamburg, Germany, in 1988. Gigli spends six months in Germany every year, conducting research at her husband's institute. "I have become interested in diseases related to underdeveloped countries," she noted to Vachon. "Because of my husband's work, I have had the opportunity to travel in Africa and to get involved in tropical medicine. If we were more aware of the unbelievable hardship the Third World endures, we would perhaps show more compassion. We cannot view ourselves as sheltered from what happens in those countries. Our experience with AIDS is the biggest indication that we should not shelter ourselves from health problems in other parts of the world." In addition to her growing interest in tropical diseases, Gigli plans to become active in science education at the international level within the next few years.

Sources:

Gigli, Irma, interview with Michelle Vachon, October 5, 1992.

—Sketch by Michelle Vachon

Fabiola Cabeza de Baca Gilbert
(1898-)
Home economist, author

Fabiola Cabeza de Baca Gilbert has combined her interest in food and Hispanic culture in a number of fiction and nonfiction books based on her experiences as an extension worker in the Hispanic and Pueblo villages of New Mexico. Filled with historical and culinary highlights, Gilbert's writings include *Historic Cookery, The Good Life,* and *We Feed Them Cactus.*

Gilbert was born on May 16, 1898, on her family's northeastern New Mexico land grant. She was raised by her paternal grandmother after her mother, Indalecia (Delgado) Cabeza de Baca, died when Gilbert was four years old. While growing up, Gilbert spoke fluent Spanish and English and two Pueblo dialects—Tewa and Tiwa. The author attended schools in Las Vegas, New Mexico, and earned a degree in pedagogy from New Mexico Normal University in 1921. After studying for a year in Spain, Gilbert returned to New Mexico to teach in public schools for six years. She was assigned to teach domestic science—a subject that would become her life's work.

Gilbert continued her education, earning a bachelor of science degree in home economics from New Mexico State University, Las Cruces. She then began working with the New Mexico State Extension Service as a home demonstration agent. In this capacity she traveled to Hispanic and Pueblo villages of northern New Mexico where she organized clubs for women and children, taught nutrition and canning techniques, trained the citizens in craft skills, and helped them to market their products.

In 1939, she married Carlos Gilbert, an insurance agent. The same year, in cooperation with the Extension Service, Gilbert published her book *Historic Cookery*. The cookbook sold more than 100,000 copies and has been reissued several times. The recipes in the book were derived from Gilbert's observation of cooks in the New Mexico villages and experimentation in her own kitchen to get precise measurements.

Gilbert's personal life has presented her with some discouraging obstacles: her marriage ended in separation and she lost her right leg in an automobile accident. But these tragedies did not hinder her career goals. She hosted a bilingual weekly radio program on food and nutrition and wrote a column in Spanish for *El Nuevo Mexicano,* a Santa Fe newspaper. In 1949, Gilbert penned *The Good Life,* a portrayal of the yearly cycle of seasons and festivals in a fictitious Hispanic village in New Mexico. The last half of the book includes the recipes described within the text. In 1954, Gilbert published *We Feed Them Cactus.* Her first publication without a culinary theme, the book describes the life of settlers on the plains in the late nineteenth and early twentieth centuries.

Writing books did not detract from Gilbert's teaching activities. UNESCO sent her to Mexico in 1951 to establish a home economics program among the Tarascan Indians and to instruct Latin Americans in cooking and preservation techniques. She also set up nutrition centers in the Lake Patzcuaro region of Mexico. Gilbert retired from the Extension Service in 1959 and went on to train Peace Corps volunteers in her methods during the 1960s. She has continued to lecture and write articles on folklore and food. Gilbert has received a number of awards, including a 1957 Superior Service Award from the U.S. Department of Agriculture.

Sources:

Books

Alford, Harold, J., *The Proud Peoples,* New American Library, 1973.

Mainiero, Lina, editor, *American Women Writers: A Critical Reference Guide from Colonial Times to the Present,* Volume 2, Ungar, 1980.

Perrigo, Lynn I., *Hispanos: Historic Leaders in New Mexico,* Sunstone Press, 1985.

—*Sketch by Stephanie Poythress*

Arlene F. Gillespie
(1936-)
Economist, public servant, activist

Arlene Fullana Gillespie considers her goal in life to always have been to improve the quality of life, not only of Hispanic Americans, but of all disadvantaged people who contact her for help. Having been at the forefront of defending Hispanics' and other poor peoples' right to avail themselves of the needed health care, housing, educational and social services at the local, state, and national levels, she has seen her goal fulfilled during her lifetime. "I was the only one in my family more interested in public service than in making money," she explained in a telephone interview with Graciela Beecher. "I guess I was born with this urgent need to serve others."

Born in San Juan, Puerto Rico, on September 24, 1936, to a well-to-do middle class family, she was the second in a family of five children. Her father, Pedro Fullana Serra, was of Hispanic ancestry and her mother, Arlene Birela Coffey, was of British descent. Gillespie feels indebted to her parents for giving her an excellent education, which enabled her to fulfill her dream of serving those less fortunate than herself.

After graduating in 1958 from the University of Puerto Rico at San Juan with a bachelor of arts degree in economics and social sciences, she attended the London School of Economics, from which she received her master of arts degree. She later attended the University of Munich in Germany, where she completed all the requirements for her doctoral degree except the dissertation.

Two important posts held by Gillespie in her native Puerto Rico included serving as special assistant to the Secretary of Labor and as chief of planning, research and evaluation for the Office of Economic Opportunity (OEO).

As special assistant to the Secretary of Labor she helped establish the Commonwealth Office of Economic Opportunity. As chief of planning, research, and evaluation at the OEO she was in charge of the planning, implementation, and evaluation of a variety of programs such as Head Start, Follow Through, Foster Grandparents, Upward Bound, Legal Services of Puerto Rico, Drug Rehabilitation Center, the Aguadilla Community Health Center and other social, educational, and economic programs.

Leaves Puerto Rico

Talking about her life in Puerto Rico, Gillespie recalled in her interview: "I felt some kind of claustrophobia living in Puerto Rico. I loved the island, but I considered that it was too small for me. I longed to spread my wings in a larger territory, that of mainland United States. Sometimes I felt nostalgia, but I knew I was capable of doing more. Yearning to reach more people, I decided to move to Washington, D.C., where decisions made by the government affect the entire nation."

So in 1962 Gillespie moved to Washington, D.C., to serve in the Alliance for Progress under President Kennedy. In 1966 she married Dr. George Gillespie and accompanied him to the South American country of Colombia, in a diplomatic capacity. Her only child, Marjorie, was born in Colombia in 1969. Recalling the situation of women in Colombia at that time she noted that "women were still trapped at home, being housewives and dreaming of nothing else. Now, after almost thirty years, it is gratifying to see Colombian women beginning to take a more active role in politics and public life in general." Returning to the nation's capital during that same year, she participated in many important projects and organizations promoting the betterment of the Puerto Rican and Hispanic communities.

In 1979 she was appointed deputy director of the Mayor's Office on Latino Affairs (OLA) and was in charge of budget development and administration. During her tenure as deputy director she became interested in expanding and improving health care services for the Hispanic community in Washington, D.C. Her advocacy role in this area continued when she was appointed executive director of the OLA in April of 1984.

Heads District of Columbia's Office of Labor Affairs

As executive director she expanded her staff in order to better serve the Hispanic and other disadvantaged communities in the District of Columbia through improved monitoring and outreach services to assure poor people the access to needed city services. The community at large also benefitted from her work as consultant to the Office of Economic Opportunity through her efforts to implement and evaluate Head Start and other related programs throughout the country. "Wherever I worked I felt compelled to improve things, to use the talents the Lord gave me for the benefit of my fellow countrymen. I wanted to become a role model for all public servants in the United States," she recalled to the interviewer of her years with the OLA. Gillespie left the Mayor's Office in 1991 to become vice president of the National Puerto Rican Coalition, Inc., an organization devoted to advancing the social, educational, economic, and political well-being of fellow Puerto Ricans.

Throughout her life Gillespie has received numerous awards and honors for her years of service and devotion to her fellow countrymen. Most recently, the National Association of Cuban American Women presented her with an achievement award at its Ninth Annual Achievement Awards dinner held at the Fort McNair Officers' Club on July 24, 1992.

Sources:

Gillespie, Arlene F., telephone interview with Graciela Beecher, September, 1992.

—Sketch by Graciela Beecher

Elsa Gomez
(1938-)
College president

As the first Hispanic woman to become president of a four-year liberal arts college in the United States, Elsa Gomez has proven her dedication to the educational process while emphasizing the particular importance of quality education for minorities. "With a horrendous drop-out rate for high school students there are not enough Hispanics in the pipeline to attend school," Gomez said in a telephone interview with Stephanie Poythress. "It is not enough anymore to have a high school degree. Having a college degree is required for almost anything you want to pursue now. I try to get across to Hispanics that it is important to stay in school—not only for themselves, but to bring the Hispanic perspective higher into businesses."

Gomez was born on January 16, 1938, in New York City to Juan and Francisca Gomez. The 1940s and 1950s were an exciting time to grow up in New York, she recalled for Poythress. "It was much like it is now, but people didn't talk about the issues that affected them," Gomez said. "There

were obvious prejudices, but every racial group was called something." Gomez, who spent much of her spare time at her father's business, attended a private Catholic school and led a somewhat sheltered childhood, she recalled.

Gomez later attended College of St. Elizabeth in New Jersey and graduated with a bachelor of arts degree in 1960. She went on to earn her master's degree from Middlebury College in Florence, Italy, in 1961. At both schools, Gomez studied Italian language, culture, and literature. "I started as a chemistry major, hoping someday to be a research chemist," Gomez told Poythress. "I decided during my sophomore year to change my major to Italian. I think it was a result of my elementary education. The nuns at my school were Italian and I learned the language as a child."

When she returned to the United States, Gomez wanted to find a job that would repay her family's hard work and efforts that enabled her to attend college. She joined the faculty at the University of Puerto Rico (Mayaguez) in 1962, teaching Italian and Western Civilian Culture. From 1979 until 1982, Gomez was the chairperson of the University's Department of Humanities. In 1982, she was appointed associate dean of the University of Puerto Rico's college of arts and sciences. In 1983, Gomez joined the Massachusetts Board of Regents of Higher Education as director of academic programs. She left the position in 1987 to become dean of the college of arts and sciences at Lock Haven (PA) University. In 1989, she accepted an offer to become president of Kean College in New Jersey. As president, Gomez is involved in community organizations and events as well as administrative tasks. For example, she is on the board of directors for Summit Trust Corporation and the Union County Chamber of Commerce. "My involvement and appointments are in recognition of the importance of education," Gomez said in her interview with Poythress. "It also is a statement of the growing importance of the Hispanic perspective." Gomez is also active as a speaker, addressing various organizations about issues such as women's leadership and the future of Hispanic women.

For her efforts and accomplishments, Gomez has received numerous awards from civic, community and educational organizations, including the National Puerto Rican Congress Hispanic Women's Achievement award and the March of Dimes Virginia Apgar award.

Sources:

Gomez, Elsa, telephone interview with Stephanie Poythress, October 5, 1992.

—Sketch by Stephanie Poythress

Sylvia Alicia Gonzáles
(1943-)
Educator, author

Activist, educator, and author Sylvia Alicia Gonzáles believes Latinas must overcome their differences and concentrate instead on forming coalitions with other like-minded groups to ensure their continued personal and professional growth. In a *Contemporary Authors* statement, she notes that her own world view has been shaped by her identity as a Latina. "As a minority in this country, caught between two worlds of language, culture, and history, it was important to have a voice. . .," Gonzáles explains. "My own predicament inspired me to seek, understand, interpret the broader experience of humankind in order to find my place in the world. I grew to love people, cultures, differences, in a way that I had not been loved or accepted. I wrote of my experiences, my perceptions. I traveled to Latin America seeking my roots, Europe in search of my universality, and the barrios of the United States to share with my people."

Born in Arizona on December 16, 1943, to accountant Nazario Antonio Gonzáles and Aida López, Gonzáles earned a bachelor's degree from the University of Arizona and a doctoral degree in education from the University of Massachusetts. She began her career in 1968 as a social science analyst for the U.S. Civil Rights Commission in Washington, D.C. Six years later, she became an assistant professor of Mexican American Studies and bilingual education at San Jose State University in California.

Outside the classroom, Gonzáles served as executive director of the National Association of Bilingual Education in 1974 and has been actively involved with the Mexican American Women's National Association and the National Women's Political Caucus. In 1977, she was a delegate-at-large at the U.S. State Department's International Woman's Year Conference.

Gonzáles's writings have consistently dealt with feminist themes and Chicano self-empowerment. Commenting on her book *La Chicana piensa*, reviewer Enid Zimmerman observed: "Through her short stories, essays and poetry, the author explores herself and her milieu, from her love relationships to her place as a woman within the Chicano culture. In all spheres she finds change necessary; her tone is not militant, however, but contemplative."

Of major concern to Gonzáles is the divisiveness she sees among Latinas. In an article she wrote for *Nuestro* magazine, the educator analyzed the factionalism that occurred at a 1980 Hispanic feminist conference in San Jose, describing it as an example of Latinas acting out the undermining and hostility "taught to us by the system in which we live." Latinas must move away from the model given to them, insists Gonzáles. "If we aspire to leadership," she states, "then let it be the leadership of cooperation and group consciousness to change our destinies and that of all people."

Sources:

Books

Contemporary Authors, Volumes 77-80, Gale, 1979.

Periodicals

Bilingual Review, Volume 9, 1982, p. 227.
Nuestro, August/September, 1981, p. 45.

—*Sketch by Sandra Márquez*

Erlinda Gonzáles-Berry
(1942-)
Educator, novelist

Erlinda Gonzáles-Berry has worked to create an enriching environment not only for students who are native Spanish speakers, but for all pupils. Her many activities have earned her a reputation as a dedicated, conscientious educator, as well as a role model for Chicano and other students. A teacher of Spanish at the college level since the mid-1970s, Gonzáles-Berry was elected head of the Spanish department at the University of New Mexico in 1992, becoming the first Chicana professor to hold that post. In addition to her teaching duties, she has written a novel and has worked as an editor on other volumes.

Gonzáles-Berry was born August 23, 1942, on the family ranch outside Roy, a small rural community in northern New Mexico, where her cultural roots were established and her creative imagination received its initial influences. She describes her early years on the ranch as living in a garden of Eden, secure and comfortable. A severe water shortage forced the family to move into town, however, beginning a difficult time in her life. Her extended family of cousins, aunts, and uncles helped her cope with the racist remarks made against her and her family after the relocation. Later, the family moved to Rosebud, New Mexico, where Gonzáles-

Berry's mother was hired to be the community's school teacher.

Overcomes Racial Discrimination

The future educator attended grades five through eight in the one-room school, helping her mother with the younger students. She remembers that her creative impulse found an outlet in school plays. After Gonzáles-Berry's mother was forced out of her teaching job because of racial discrimination, her family members were the only Chicanos in the community. As a result, Gonzáles-Berry's parents decided to send her and one of her sisters to boarding school in El Rito, New Mexico, 200 miles away. At the facility, the faculty and the student body were predominately Chicano. The school proved to be a successful experience for Gonzáles-Berry, as she excelled in her studies and became the president of the student body. She recalls that her experience at the University of New Mexico, where she earned her undergraduate degree in physical education, was not nearly as positive. Gonzáles-Berry quickly learned that not all students were accepted and treated equally. After graduation, she briefly taught dance at a high school in California and later returned to Albuquerque to teach physical education at a middle school.

Deciding to change careers, Gonzáles-Berry enrolled as a graduate student at the University of New Mexico. She earned her master's and Ph.D. degrees in Spanish in 1971 and 1974 respectively. She taught Spanish for four years at Earlham College, a small Quaker school in Indiana, before returning to New Mexico. She then taught at New Mexico State University for one year before she was hired in 1979 to teach Spanish at the University of New Mexico. There, Gonzáles-Berry created a program for native Spanish speakers in an effort to bridge the gap between the Chicano students' culture and the academic environment.

In 1983, Gonzáles-Berry received an outstanding teacher award and was promoted to full professor. Then came her election as chair of the Spanish department some nine years later. In 1991, Gonzáles-Berry saw the publication of her first novel, *Paletitas de guyaba,* by El Norte Publications. The work received critical attention, with commentators pointing to its unique subject matter and engaging style. She has also edited *Pasó por aquí: Critical Essays on the New Mexican Literary Tradition, 1542-1988* and *Las mujeres hablan: An Anthology of Nuevo Mexicana Writers.* Gonzáles-Berry is married to Edward Berry and has one daughter. She continues to live in Albuquerque, New Mexico.

Sources:

Gonzáles-Berry, Erlinda, interview with Teresa Márquez, August 21, 1992.

—Sketch by Teresa Márquez

Patricia Gonzalez
(1958-)
Artist, painter

Artist Patricia Gonzalez has made a name for herself as a creator of inventive, intense paintings of flowers and landscape scenes. Reminiscent of the "magical realist" writers of her native South America, Gonzalez's paintings combine the extraordinary with the everyday, presenting a truly individual vision. "I'm more interested in how things exist in one's own mind," the artist told Susan Chadwick of the *Houston Post.* "What's happening is what's happening in your mind."

Gonzalez was born April 3, 1958, in Cartagena, Colombia, and her memories of her childhood there include an abundance of vegetation such as that she found in her grandmother's gardens. But when she was eleven, Gonzalez moved with her family to the cooler climate of London, England. Gonzalez grew up there, eventually studying art at the Central School of Art and Design and receiving a bachelor of fine arts degree from the Wimbledon School of Art in 1980. She had not yet developed the imaginative, almost mystical style that was to become her trademark.

After her graduation, however, Gonzalez returned to the city of her birth; she was surprised to find it drier and less fertile than she remembered. Her new awareness of the contrary nature of human memory and of her own cultural heritage led her to paint vivid yet dreamlike scenes of flowers and landscapes that were often occupied by mysterious human figures. After teaching art and English in Colombia for several months, Gonzalez moved to Houston in 1981. There she studied briefly at the Glassell School of Art and continued her painting.

Presents One-Woman Show at Graham Gallery

In 1984 Gonzalez secured her first one-woman show, at Houston's Graham Gallery. Subsequent shows led to a National Endowment for the Arts fellowship in 1987, and a solo exhibition at the Contemporary Arts Museum of Houston in 1989. The works of this exhibition, according to *Houston Post* critic Chadwick, are "suggestive not so much of place but of atmosphere and mood." Employing unusual perspectives and unconventional techniques, Gonzalez "is courageous in her determination to break the rules in order to express her thoughts and feelings," Chadwick writes. "Why should you always abide by a rule?" the artist added. "You don't get a good painting by formula."

While Gonzalez has continued to use florals and landscapes as her subjects, her paintings have become "softer, more ethereal and more appealingly decorative," Chadwick comments in a 1991 *Houston Post* article. Including animals and various imaginary figures, paintings such as "Enlaced" and "Shimmer" illustrate the "overtly mystical qualities" and "poetry" that characterize Gonzalez's style, the critic adds.

Besides various galleries and museums in Houston, Gonzalez's work has appeared in Los Angeles, New York, Austin, and Cartagena, Colombia; her works were also included in the traveling exhibit, "Hispanic Art in the United States." Gonzalez is the recipient of the Grumbacher Award, a Synergy Purchase Award, and of a grant from the Anne Giles Kimbrough Fund. Married to fellow painter Derek Boshier and the mother of two children, Gonzalez lives and works in Houston.

Sources:

Books

Brown, Betty Ann, and Arlene Raven, editors, *Exposures: Women and Their Art*, Newsage Press, 1989.

Periodicals

Houston Post, January 17, 1989, p. D4; March 11, 1991, p. B1.

—Sketch by Diane Telgen

Consuelo González Amezcua
(1903-1975)
Artist, writer

Texas artist Consuelo González Amezcua distinguished herself with fanciful, detailed ink drawings that reflect her interest in religion, mysticism, and magic. She spent a lifetime following her muse, which, in addition to her art, included writing poetry, composing songs, playing various instruments, and singing. She remained a local talent in her hometown of Del Rio until 1968, when she had her first major exhibition at the McNay Art Institute in San Antonio, Texas. Since then, her works have appeared in several individual, group, and traveling exhibits in galleries in New York, Texas, and Massachusetts.

Born in Piedras Negras, Mexico, on June 13, 1903, Chelo (her lifelong nickname) was the daughter of two teachers, Jesus González Galván and Julia Amezcua de González. She lived in Mexico for ten years before moving to Del Rio, Texas, where she would live until her death in June of 1975.

Whether in Mexico or Texas, Chelo's dominant influence was her family. "My parents were poor, but they always tried to create happiness for us," González Amezcua revealed to Amy Freeman Lee, author of the catalogue for the McNay exhibit. "They played the guitar and sang with joy. . . . My father and mother told me stories, and my dear sister Zare, who took special care of me, sang to me and was the inspiration of many of my musical compositions."

Worked from Direct Inspiration

González Amezcua grew up dreaming and drawing, taking inspiration from nature, the Bible, and figures from ancient history, particularly characters from ancient Mexico, Spain, and Egypt. Although she won a scholarship to attend the Academy of San Carlos, she never made it to art school due to her father's untimely death. González Amezcua stayed home with her mother and remained self-taught in her art, writing, and music. Living and working in the house in Del Rio she shared with her mother and older sister Zaré, González Amezcua spent countless hours at the dining room table creating ball-point pen drawings. Each work took about 18 days to complete. There were no plans or miniature studies; she worked from direct inspiration without studying or copying the work of other artists. "She was a very hard worker; she worked all the time," remembered Zaré González Amezcua in a 1992 telephone interview.

Most of González Amezcua's early works use colors sparingly, though her later works show a great deal more color. Often birds, gardens, or hands are featured in overflowing, playful detail. "Chelo lovingly called her art 'filigree art,' for her work is full of those little, intricate details that were also a part of the jewelry she loved to wear, called '*filigrana*,'" remembered the artist's niece Livia Fernandez. Equally at home with language and images, González Amezcua included her poems in some drawings. She was also fond of depicting Aztec and Egyptian rulers and kings in all their fineries. Lee reflected on the inspiration for and impact of the artist's varied subjects: "As a Latin, her strong attraction to Mexican and Spanish sources is self-explanatory; as a cosmic spirit, she finds Egypt an equally comfortable homeland—perhaps it was for her in other times. Regardless of the ethnic source of her figures or their attitudes whether they are dancing, scudding across a highly designed sky or manifesting themselves as apparitions—they are universal in scope, commanding in appearance, dramatic in gesture and grandiose in overall effect."

On a personal level, González Amezcua was "very unconventional," according to her sister Zaré. "She was a lovely person who did whatever she pleased," said Zaré. "She was a real character." Fernandez agreed, recalling how her aunt would entertain her when she was young. "In the summer, Chelo would wear these flowing dresses and enjoy the weekend by having all the neighborhood children, along with my mother's nieces and nephews, over.

She'd put on a show or teach us to mold statues made of mud or starch. Sometimes she would get tortilla dough and mold nonsense figures to make us laugh and enjoy the hot sun. While working with her hands, she would tell jokes, ask nonsensical questions, and make us feel that we were the best of any and everything on earth."

González Amezcua's works are currently on a two-year traveling exhibition in cities throughout Texas.

Sources:

Books

The Latin-American Spirit, Art, and Artists in the U.S.A., 1920-1970, Abrams, 1988.
Mexican American Art: Twentieth Century, University of Texas Press, 1973.
Texas Women: A Celebration of History, Texas Foundation for Women Resources, 1981.

Other

Fernandez, Livia, correspondence with Jim Kamp, October 9, 1992.
González Amezcua, Zaré, telephone interview with Jim Kamp, September 28, 1992.
Lee, Amy Freeman, *The Hidden Eye: Filigree Drawings by Consuelo Gonzalez Amezcua* (catalogue), Marion Koogler McNay Art Institute (San Antonio, Texas), February 11 - March 10, 1968.
Quirarte, Jacinto, and Rolando Hinojosa-Smith, *Mystical Elements/Lyrical Imagery: Consuelo González Amezcua* (catalogue), Del Rio Council for the Arts, 1991.

—Sketch by Jim Kamp

Maria Grever
(1894-1951)
Composer, songwriter

Maria Grever, a pioneer in the field of twentieth-century popular music, was the first Mexican woman to become a successful composer. Her romantic songs and ballads, like "Jurame" and "What a Difference a Day Makes," achieved widespread popularity beginning in the 1920s among audiences in Spain, South America, Mexico, and the United States. Although a few of her songs remain international favorites today, Grever has been accorded scarcely a footnote in the pages of music history. She is not even mentioned in most listings and encyclopedias of composers. Yet many of her songs, estimated to number in

the hundreds, live on, kept alive by recording stars like Placido Domingo and Aretha Franklin.

Grever was born to a Spanish father and Mexican mother on September 14, 1894, in Mexico City. Her maiden name was Maria de la Portilla. She spent much of her childhood in Spain and travelled widely in Europe with her family. At the age of 12, she returned to Mexico. According to a *New York Times* article, Grever composed her first piece of music—a Christmas carol—when she was four years old. Grever settled in New York after marrying Leo A. Grever, an American oil company executive, who was best man in her sister's wedding. She was wed to Grever four days after her sister's nuptials.

She studied piano, violin, and voice, although one account of her life suggests that she learned to read music only in her later years. In fact, most of her songs were written in one key. Grever was said to have the gift of perfect pitch. A 1919 review of one of her first New York City concerts in the *New York Times* mentions that Grever, a soprano, performed opera in Madrid early in her career.

Grever was an extraordinarily versatile musician. She frequently wrote both the melodies and lyrics of her pieces and then performed the pieces in live concerts. During her career, which peaked in the 1930s and 1940s, she wrote film scores and lyrics for Broadway shows, and organized concerts combining theatre, music, dance, and song. She was also a voice teacher. But Grever's strongest legacy is her songs. Often based on the folk rhythms and styles of Latin American music, particularly Mexican or Spanish tangos, the lyrics are lushly romantic, full of feeling, and easy to recall. Her message is always direct. For example, her song "Yo No Se" ("I Know Not") begins with the stanza: "When at night my thoughts are winging / To you, my dear, / Then your voice, an old song singing, / I seem to hear; / You are kneeling by me, blending, / Though far away, / Your voice with mine ascending, / In a song of love's first day."

Grever often worked with American lyricists, who translated the songs from Spanish to English to make them accessible to audiences in the United States. In fact, Grever collaborated with three of the leading songwriters of her day—Stanley Adams, Irving Caesar, and Raymond Leveen.

Eighteen-Year-Old's First Hit Became Million-Seller

Her first published song, "A una Ola" ("To a Wave"), appeared when she was 18 and sold some three million copies, according to a biography on a 1956 retrospective album of Grever's work. Grever published "Besame" ("Kiss Me") in 1921, and in 1926, Grever's Spanish tango "Jurame" ("Promise, Love") found a large audience. Grever's first major hit was "What a Difference a Day Makes," or "Cuando Vuelva a Tu Lado," written in 1934. That song is one of Grever's longest-lasting hits; it is included on many currently available recordings by artists as diverse as Chet Baker, Ray Conniff, Dinah Washington, and Bobby Darin.

The same year Ella Fitzgerald sang "A-Tisket A-Tasket" and Cole Porter won over the nation with "My Heart Belongs to Daddy," Grever scored one of her biggest sensations, a nonsensical tune entitled "Ti-Pi-Tin." One account of Grever's music claims that "Ti-Pi-Tin," written in 1938, broke with her usual style, and her publisher rejected it. But bandleader Horace Heidt and his orchestra, performing on NBC radio, took the song to the air and contributed to its eventual hit status.

Grever's songs, broadcast frequently on the radio during her time, include "Lamento Gitano," "Lero, Lero from Brazil," "Magic Is the Moonlight," "Make Love with a Guitar," "My First, My Last, My Only," "Rosebud," "Thanks for the Kiss," "My Margarita," "Andalucia," "Cancionera," and many more. Estimates of her musical output range from 200 to 500 songs, depending on the source.

One of the reasons Grever's songs became well-known was that leading performers of her era adopted them in their repertoires. Singers like Enrico Caruso, Lawrence Tibbett, Tito Schipa, Nino Martina, and Jessica Dragonette helped popularize Grever's work. Along with other albums which included Grever's tunes, the 1956 album "The Bobby Hackett Horn," a Columbia label, adapted "What a Difference a Day Makes," and the 1959 Columbia Classic album "Happy Session," performed by Benny Goodman and his orchestra, featured "Cuando Vuelva a Tu Lado."

Grever also wrote film scores, including the music for the 1944 movie "Bathing Beauty," featuring her song "Magic Is the Moonlight," or "Te Quiero Dijiste." In 1941, "Viva O'Brien," a musical with music by Grever and lyrics by Leveen, had 20 performances on a New York stage. Some of the show's songs were entitled "El Matador Terrifico," "Mood of the Moment," "Broken Hearted Romeo," and "Wrap Me in Your Serape."

Enjoyed International Acclaim

Grever apparently enjoyed performing before live audiences and organizing concerts of her work by other musicians. In 1919, one of her earliest New York recitals of Spanish, Italian, and French music, at the Princess Theatre, received positive reviews from critics. During the height of her fame, she made concert tours in Latin America and Europe. In New York, Grever's music was heard live in many of the city's concert halls. In 1927, she organized a concert at the Little Theatre, which featured an Argentine cabaret, song dramas complete with costumes, scenery, dialogue, and dancing, and a short play, "The Gypsy." The evening opened with performances by a jazz orchestra. One of her first successful New York concerts took place in 1928 at the Pythian Temple before an audience that included the ambassadors of Spain, Mexico, Cuba, and Argentina.

The *New York Times* reviewed a 1939 concert at the Guild Theatre, in which Grever presented popular songs and a miniature opera, entitled "El Cantarito." She performed a few songs, but was assisted by dozens of other singers and musicians, including a large chorus, dance troupe and orchestra. The *Times* critic praised her "innate gift of spontaneous melody," and commented that, while some of Grever's music is not to be taken too seriously, "her more earnest endeavors were sincere and effective."

In the late 1930s, she was threatened with blindness as a result of an eye infection. In 1942, Grever hosted a benefit for the Spanish-American Association for the Blind, with headquarters in New York City. She served as mistress of ceremonies for a program which included musical performances by students at the New York Institute for the Education of the Blind. The funds raised were to benefit the blind in Spanish-speaking countries.

At the time of her death at the age of 57, on December 15, 1951, following a lengthy illness, she was living in the Wellington Hotel on Manhattan's Seventh Avenue. She was survived by her husband and two children, son Charles Grever, a New York music publisher, and daughter Carmen Livingston of Chicago, according to her obituary in the *New York Times*. Following her death, she was honored by a musicale at the Biltmore Hotel by the Union of Women of the Americas. She was named "Woman of the Americas," 1952, by the UWA before her death. Grever was a member of the prestigious American Society of Composers, Authors, and Publishers.

In 1956, RCA released a retrospective album, "Songs of Maria Grever," with 12 songs performed by Argentine singer Libertad Lamarque, accompanied by the orchestras of Chucho Zarzosa and Mario Ruiz Armengol. Along with her more famous songs, the album featured "Volvere" ("I Will Return"), "Eso Es Mentira" ("That Is a Lie"), and "Asi" ("Thus"). The album jacket, written by Bill Zeitung, argues that Grever never enjoyed widespread name recognition, despite the fact that her songs achieved "an immensely deserved run of popularity." Her music "is on every hand," wrote Zeitung. "Yet the name is familiar to only a few."

Sources:

Books

Lewine, Richard, and Alfred Simon, *Songs of the Theatre*, Wilson, 1984, p. 828.

Mattfeld, Julius, *Variety Music Cavalcade 1620-1961*, Prentice-Hall, pp. 420, 493, 521-26, 551.

Spaeth, Sigmund, *A History of Popular Music in America*, Random House, 1962, pp. 516-17.

Periodicals

New York Times, December 15, 1919, p. 15; February 14, 1927, p. 14; February 27, 1928, p. 16; March 6, 1939, p. 11; December 16, 1951, p. 90; May 5, 1952, p. 18.
Variety, July 31, 1940.

Other

Music research collections, New York Public Library for the Performing Arts at Lincoln Center.
"Songs of Maria Grever," RCA record album, 1956.

—Sketch by Ann Malaspina

Linda Griego
(1935-)
Deputy Mayor of Los Angeles, restaurateur

Linda Griego's organizational and business skills are put to work in her restaurants as well as in the city of Los Angeles where she serves as deputy mayor. Griego was born on October 10, 1935, in Socorro, New Mexico. The daughter of Juan B. and Terisita Gonzalez, Griego grew up in the city of Tucumcari, New Mexico, and didn't speak English until she was six years old. Although Griego's family lived below the poverty level, education was a priority for them. Griego attended schools in New Mexico, and after graduating from high school, she left her hometown and moved to Washington, D.C., where she attended George Washington University and worked for U.S. Representative Tom Morris for two years. That was just the first taste of politics for Griego. She later worked for eight years for California Senator Alan Cranston in both Washington, D.C., and Los Angeles.

After graduating with a bachelor's degree in history from the University of California, Los Angeles, Griego was hired by Pacific Bell to manage installation and repair crews. "I was one of two women in a 90-man garage out in the San Gabriel Valley. There was some resentment about picking a woman off the street and putting her in charge of technical crews, but I loved it," Griego said in an interview in *L.A. Executive.* Griego worked for Pacific Bell for three years until the company asked her to relocate to San Francisco. Instead, Griego decided to take her first step into the restaurant business.

Griego opened the Chili Stop, a Mexican eatery and deli. The Chili Stop was intended to be a carryout operation with just 16 seats. Its popularity soon turned it into a full-service restaurant. Quickly outgrowing her space, Griego had to find a new location for her business. In 1983, she formed a partnership with Peter Mullin and purchased an old firehouse that had been abandoned for 15 years. The firehouse was slowly transformed into the Engine Co. 28, a one million dollar project. In designing the interior, Griego solicited the help of Jerry Magnin, who had designed several Los Angeles-area restaurants. Magnin eventually became Griego's second partner. Through overseeing the extensive renovations, Griego acquired tremendous knowledge about the building trade. This information and experience allowed her to take and pass the state contractors licensing exam.

Griego has found that the key to success in the restaurant business is feeling comfortable asking for help. "When I started the Chili Stop, I went to City Restaurant and asked them to show me what they did right and wrong. They were unbelievable. People are willing to help. I always take the time for others because people did it for me," she told *L.A. Executive.* Griego manages the business end of Engine Co. 28 and has hired a competent managerial staff to operate the business on the many occasions when she can't be there.

Often when Griego is absent from the restaurant, it is because she is working with one of the numerous committees to which she belongs. She has served on the Downtown Strategic Plan Committee as well as the boards of the Constitutional Rights Foundation and the Los Angeles Conservancy. In 1990, Griego was named to Los Angeles' Cultural Affairs Commission. "I don't go on boards just for the sake of it. I have to make a difference and the board has to make a difference in the community," she commented in *L.A. Executive.* Griego feels that volunteerism is one way for her to give back some of what she has received from others.

In January of 1991, Griego opened her second restaurant—The Red Car Grill in West Hollywood. Shortly after opening her new business, Griego was named by Los Angeles Mayor Tom Bradley to the Community Redevelopment Agency. In September of 1991 she was named deputy mayor. Her duties as deputy mayor include luring new businesses to Los Angeles. As a owner of two thriving restaurants, she knows much about the ingredients of success. Her work in City Hall enables her to pass that recipe on to others.

Sources:

Periodicals

Gourmet, March, 1992.
L.A. Executive, November/December, 1991.

—Sketch by Stephanie Poythress

Stella G. Guerra

Government official

After her appointment by President George Bush, Stella G. Guerra became assistant secretary of the interior for territorial and international affairs in 1989. In this position, she is responsible for coordinating federal policy in the territories of American Samoa, Guam, the U.S. Virgin Islands, and the Trust Territory of the Pacific Islands (Palau). She also oversees all federal programs and funds in the freely-associated states of the Republic of the Marshall Islands and the Federated States of Micronesia.

Guerra was born in Corpus Christi, Texas, the daughter of Eva Valerio and Víctor García. Although she was close to her parents, she was raised by her maternal grandparents beginning at an early age. Her father died when she was only 13.

Like many other Hispanic children living in the United States, Guerra didn't speak English when she started elementary school. In particular, she remembers always having problems differentiating between the vowels "e" and "i" in words like "Tim" and "team." One day in junior high school, a teacher made her stand in front of the class and repeat those words for more than half an hour. When she was finally able to pronounce them correctly, she was allowed to go home with her classmates. This incident affected her greatly. "An embarrassing experience like that does something to you," she told a reporter for *Airman*. She later came to realize that the teacher might have been trying to help her understand how important it is to communicate.

Studies Hairdressing to Help Finance Education

Despite her occasional difficulties with the English language, Guerra was an energetic and outgoing girl who was popular with other students. Her school activities included cheerleading and serving on the student council. For being named the first runner-up in a Miss Texas High School Pageant, Guerra won a free cosmetology course and didn't hesitate to take the classes even though it meant attending classes every Saturday throughout the summer.

The money Guerra earned as a hairdresser helped finance her studies at Texas A & I University in Kingsville, where she majored in education, art, and history and received a bachelor of science degree. She subsequently earned a master of arts degree in communication disorders at Our Lady of the Lake University in San Antonio and an associate of arts degree in business at Del Mar College in Corpus Christi. While she was still in college, Guerra had to take time out to undergo open heart surgery, an experience that gave her a genuine appreciation for life.

Her career as a business owner and educator began in San Antonio. From 1974 until 1980 she owned and managed a successful chain of record and tape stores called the Gramophone Shops. From 1967 to 1980 she worked for the Northeast Independent School District, first as a regular classroom teacher, then as a special education teacher, and finally as an administrator of testing programs.

Guerra's government career started in 1980 when she obtained a position in the State Department as a staff assistant to the White House Chief of Protocol. As special assistant for international affairs in the Department of Education from 1981 until 1983, she represented the department on various task forces, including the 1982 UNESCO World Conference on Cultural Policies in Mexico City, the 1982 World Assembly on Aging in Vienna, the 1982 World Food Day meeting in Rome, and the 1985 United Nations World Conference on Women in Nairobi. She also represented the United States in the First International Days on the Development of Human Intelligence, held in Caracas in 1982.

Moves into Executive Ranks of Federal Government

In 1983 Guerra joined the Pentagon as Air Force deputy for equal opportunity and director of Equal Employment Opportunity (EEO). As an acting director of the EEO program she gave all civilian employees what she called "a fair shot," convinced that "once given that opportunity, it is up to the person to be prepared to take advantage of it," as she told an interviewer for *Airman*. And she added that she "wholeheartedly believes equal employment opportunity is not a special program for minorities and women. . ., it is for everyone, and simply a matter of management officials doing what is morally and legally correct." Since 1987, Guerra has also served on the Presidential Task Force for Women, Minorities, and the Handicapped in Science and Technology.

In addition to her professional responsibilities, Guerra is active in a number of organizations. She is a member of the board of directors of Wolf Trap Foundation for the Performing Arts (Vienna, Virginia), the Japan-Hispanic Institute (Washington, DC), and the American Cultural Center (San Antonio) and is advisory council cochair of the Friends of the Arts Americas Museum of the Americas. She is also a member of the National Association of Hispanic Women.

Guerra has been the recipient of many awards. In 1986, for example, she was first runner-up in WRC Communications' Washington Woman of the Year contest. That same year, she received the Woman of the Year Award of Merit from the Governor of California for the Mexican American Opportunity Foundation Award. In 1987, the Valley Forge Freedom Foundation awarded Guerra its George Washington Honor Medal for Public Address. Also that year, she was recognized by the Beethoven Society and given the Washington "Mover and Shaker" Award for her outstanding support for the performing arts and the hearing impaired. And in 1992 she was named by *Hispanic Business Magazine* as one of the top 100 most influential Hispanics in the United States. In her capacity as a government official, Guerra also addresses many different groups and has had her speeches published in *Vital Speeches of the Day, The Executive Speaks, Speech Writer's Newsletter,* and the *Congressional Record.*

Believes in Serving as a Mentor for Young Hispanics

Guerra's success has not made her forget her modest upbringing nor her Hispanic roots; she is aware of the responsibility she has as a Hispanic role model. She feels it is important for today's successful Hispanic women to serve as mentors for younger Hispanics, just as the heroes of previous generations did for her and others. For Guerra the term "heroes" has a different connotation than the traditional one, because in her view this word means something unique to each person. Her heroes, for example, include the grandparents who raised her. Through their innate wisdom and the values they passed along, Guerra explained to interviewer Sylvia P. Apodaca, they instilled in her a love for education and a sense of achievement that she has carried throughout her life.

Guerra also remembers learning from her father that "if something is worth doing, it was worth doing right," as she remarked in *Airman.* When asked by Apodaca what she would say to a young woman who is starting a career, Guerra declared, "Opportunities are always there. We must learn to recognize them but more importantly, take advantage of them. We must stay on course and never give up, so that we can become all that we want to be. Equal opportunity does not warrant success. What it does warrant is that we have a fair shot in life."

Sources:

Periodicals

Airman, September, 1985, p. 39.
Congressional Record, September 15, 1986, pp. 726-29.

Other

Guerra, Stella, written interview with Sylvia P. Apodaca, September 8, 1992; telephone interview with Sylvia P. Apodaca, September 14, 1992.

—*Sketch by Sylvia P. Apodaca*

Guerra Ord, Angustias de la
See de la Guerra Ord, Angustias

Dolores "Lolita" Guerrero
(1941-)
Restauranteur

Dolores "Lolita" Guerrero is one of the most prosperous female restaurateurs in Houston, Texas. The popularity of her business, in part, is due to her secret recipes for home-cooked Mexican food. Ironically, her success has come from preparing the same *fideo, arroz con pollo,* and *calavazita* she "stretched" to feed her parents and three siblings as she was growing up in poverty.

Guerrero was born in Beaumont, Texas, on July 19, 1941, to Salvador and Santos Guerrero, an iron worker and egg grader. As a child, Guerrero was assigned to prepare meals for her family while her parents worked. "I learned to cook when I was 11 years old," Guerrero recalled in an interview with Anna Macias Aguayo. "My mother used to call me from work and tell me what I was going to make for dinner." Her fondest memories are of how she waited on her father when he came home exhausted from work.

When the elder Guerrero found himself unemployed one day, he decided to open a small taco stand at a vacant gas station in Beaumont, near where the family lived. "The business was started out of necessity because my father became ill with asthma," she explained. "We sold enchiladas, tacos, and tostadas. I liked helping my parents with the business."

Achieves Success as Restauranteur

Guerrero graduated from St. Anthony High School in Beaumont. She also earned a certificate from Miss Angelo School of Business and briefly studied at Lamar University. But rather than pursue a degree, she felt pressure to work to help support the family. In 1972, Guerrero and her sister opened a 12-table restaurant in Houston named Las Dos Hermanas. By 1985 her financial success led her to open her very own restaurant, Lolita's on the Park. The large facility, which seats up to 200 people and offers a full-service bar, is located a few miles south of downtown Houston.

In recent years Guerrero gained the exclusive rights for the sale of Mexican food at Houston Intercontinental Airport, where she has opened two cafeteria-style restaurants named Lolita's and plans a third. "I've had a very colorful career," Guerrero said. "My father taught me that I'm just as good as the next guy. I've never felt like I've been held back. I once asked my dad why he worked so hard, and he said, 'It's because I don't have an education. But our people have always been hard workers. We are a proud people.'"

Guerrero believes that her widespread recognition in the Houston business community is the result of her hard work ethic. But she also asserts that her involvement in Hispanic organizations, such as the Hispanic Chamber of Commerce and the League of United Latin American Citizens, has helped her career. "I've had the support of a lot of groups," she acknowledged. "I don't feel like I could have made it past a certain plateau without my friends."

In turn, Guerrero is committed to giving back to her community. Her volunteer work in voter registration drives has been recognized with the Willie Velasquez Award. She also serves on the board of directors of the George I. Sanchez School, a private program that helps high school dropouts receive education and drug rehabilitation. On the political front, Guerrero's help has been sought out by both Republicans and Democrats alike.

Although she considers herself an independent, she has served on an advisory panel to Republican senator Phil Gramm and previously co-chaired the Houston campaign for the Democratic presidential ticket in 1988. In October 1992, she and a panel of Hispanic business leaders met with President George Bush in Dallas to discuss their views on police brutality, entrepreneurship, and the U.S.-Mexico-Canada Free Trade Agreement. "Nothing good comes easy," Guerrero opined. "But it's always a pleasure to know that I have survived as a Hispanic woman."

Sources:

Guerrero, Dolores "Lolita," interview with Anna Macias Aguayo, October 6, 1992.

—Sketch by Anna Macias Aguayo

Lena Guerrero

Lena Guerrero
(1957-)
Politician

Lena Guerrero is the first Hispanic woman to chair the Texas Railroad Commission. During the course of her political career, she has also directed a city-wide campaign and was elected the Democratic State Representative from Austin District 51 in Mission, Texas. In an interview for *Austin,* Guerrero explained that she sees her involvement in politics as a natural progression. "I decided when I was fifteen that what I wanted to do was be in a position to help a lot of people who didn't know I had really helped. . . . So, somewhere along the line, people were an important factor in what I wanted to do and that's the public side of this service. The other was that I wanted to use what I knew,

because I had lived in a very poor barrio in South Texas. I understood that people didn't start out at the same point, that the disadvantaged got more disadvantage and that those with opportunities got richer with opportunities. Somehow I felt the responsibility at age fifteen to use that information."

Guerrero was born in 1957, the fifth child of Alvaro and Adela Guerrero, who had nine children altogether. Her father managed a lumber yard but died of cancer when he was 51 and Guerrero was eleven. After his death, her mother took a job in the school cafeteria in Mission, Texas, where she is still employed. During an interview with Gloria Bonilla-Santiago, Guerrero recalled the period following her father's death: "My mother was not prepared in any way to deal with his death. . . . She had never worked outside the house for pay. It was not at all easy for her. It was a very traumatic experience for all of us." At the time of her father's death, two of Guerrero's older siblings were already married, and about six months later the other two were also beginning their own families. "Instantly," she explained in her interview with Bonilla-Santiago, "I became the one person that my mother could depend upon. My responsibility was the younger children, especially the three-year-old."

In an interview for *Austin,* Guerrero remembered that her mother viewed education as "the most important thing, her bottom line was a high school education." While completing this education, Guerrero and her brothers and sisters also spent their summers working—as migrant farm workers—to help support the family. Following high school, Guerrero began attending the University of Texas in 1976. She became very active in politics, working on campaigns at local, state, and national levels, serving for three years as legislative staff, and interning with U.S. Senator Lloyd Bentsen in Washington.

In 1979, Guerrero became the youngest person elected state president of the Texas Young Democrats, and the first Mexican American. She served on the Democratic National Committee representing the National Young Democrats, and also served as a member of the American delegation to the International Conference on Peace, Detente and Disarmament in Helsinki, Finland. Guerrero's political career continued to rapidly progress when she became the first Mexican American to direct a city-wide political campaign for a non-Hispanic candidate (Austin mayoral candidate Ron Mullen).

In addition to being active politically, Guerrero has also been involved in a number of civic activities. She served on the boards of the Austin Area Urban League, Planned Parenthood, the Austin Independent School District Textbook Advisory Committee, and the Arthritis Foundation. She also co-chaired the Austin Sesquicentennial Committee and was a member of the Chamber of Commerce Leadership Austin Program. Guerrero's activities have not passed unnoticed. In 1982 she was selected by the Mexican-American Business and Professional Women's Association for its outstanding Woman of the Year award in public affairs.

Elected to House of Representatives

Guerrero's political career took another step forward in January of 1985 when she was sworn into the House of Representatives for Austin District 51; she was only the second Hispanic woman to win a seat in the House. She commented on the experience in her *Austin* interview: "I know that, individually, I've been able to touch some lives, to stop a hurt. . . . Leo [Guerrero's husband] taught me to play golf, every time you hit a nice shot, it brings you back to play. And every time you help a family in a small way, that brings you back, too."

During her years in office, Guerrero has taken a special interest in issues of health and human services, environmental protection, and economic development. She is also known as a voice for women and children. "It becomes important for me to address issues where voids are, a lot of issues tend to be women's issues," pointed out Guerrero in *Austin*. "Every woman who serves in public life has a responsibility to address those issues." In another interview with *Austin* she went on to explain: "I want to address the concept that women who are active in politics and see a

future for themselves and other women in that arena are not trying to be men. We do not want to be better, we do not want to be less, we just want an opportunity to participate in the same kind of arenas that men have participated in historically."

In 1987 Guerrero was selected by the National Network of Hispanic Women as the recipient of their leadership award in the area of government. During this time, she was also elected to the Southern Regional Council of Legislators, an organization promoting equal opportunity throughout the South. Guerrero was recognized again in 1989 when *Texas Monthly* voted her one of "the best legislators of the year." While earning this recognition, Guerrero had passed successful legislation on child care, groundwater management, teenage pregnancy, and had created centers for medical coverage for single heads of households by winning the confidence of the people most likely to oppose her. In 1991, Guerrero was appointed the first Hispanic woman to chair the Texas Railroad Commission by Governor Richards. And in 1992, she was one of the keynote speakers at the Democratic National Convention.

Controversy erupted during Guerrero's 1992 reelection campaign when it was revealed that she did not graduate from college, as she had claimed (she is short by nineteen credits). Although she lost the 1992 election and was forced to resign from the commission, Guerrero has not lessened her commitment to Latina issues.

In her interview with Bonilla-Santiago, Guerrero explained her concerns for the Latina women's movement. "We came after the women's movement, after civil rights. Our movement was not a movement in separation of ourselves, our families. Our movement was an advancement and an opportunity to succeed. It's a struggle of lateness, largely because we have a gender barrier and a cultural barrier. I'm known as a three-fer. First I'm a woman, I'm young, and I'm a minority."

Sources:

Periodicals

Austin, February, 1985, pp. 20-22; December, 1987, pp. 28-30.
Texas Monthly, July, 1989, pp. 86-97.

Other

Guerrero, Lena, interview with Gloria Bonilla-Santiago, January 13, 1989.

—Sketch by Gloria Bonilla-Santiago

Ana Sol Gutiérrez

(1942-)

Aeronautical engineer, public servant

Ana Sol Gutiérrez is a woman of many accomplishments. She is the first elected Hispanic member on a board of education in Maryland and the first Hispanic of Salvadorean descent ever elected to public office in the history of the United States. "The time has come simply because there is a critical mass of immigrant or ethnic minority students," she said to Amy Goldstein of the *Washington Post*. She has attained her position and the support of the people in Montgomery County, Maryland, because of her dynamism, assertiveness in community affairs, and commitment to education.

Gutiérrez was born Anna Emma Sol in Santa Ana, El Salvador, on January 11, 1942, the daughter of Ana Pérez, a homemaker, and Jorge Sol-Castellanos, El Salvador's first finance minister, director of the World Bank and the International Monetary Fund, and an economist for the Organization of American States. Divorced from Fernando Gutiérrez, she is the mother of three sons: Fernando, Alejandro (Alex), and Rodrigo.

A resident of Montgomery County since she was five years old, Gutiérrez attended various local schools, including Chevy Chase Senior High School. She then studied liberal arts and chemistry at the University of Geneva in Switzerland before graduating from Pennsylvania State University with a bachelor of science degree and later from American University with a master of science in management and computer sciences.

At the time Gutiérrez began her career in aeronautical engineering, her work didn't fit the traditional role model expected for a women. Mercedes Olivera observed in *Vista,* "A woman as an astronaut, aerospace engineer or electrician was a rare sight three decades ago, rarer still if she had a Spanish surname." When asked by contributor Sylvia P. Apodaca if her parents had some influence in her career, Gutiérrez declared: "Absolutely! My father was especially supportive and a strong role model to achieve to my fullest potential both professionally and individually."

After completing her education, Gutiérrez moved to Bolivia and then Venezuela. In Bolivia, she taught as a professor of mathematics and computer sciences at the Universidad Mayor de San Andrés, and in Venezuela she taught undergraduate- and graduate-level courses in systems engineering and computer systems. Also in Venezuela, Gutiérrez served as a manager at INTEVEP, the Venezuelan Petroleum Research Institute, where, in 1976, she developed a computer-based technical information system to support the company's research and development laboratory activities. In addition to her teaching and managerial responsibilities, Gutiérrez worked as an international management consultant in Venezuela, Bolivia, and Peru.

After returning to the United States, Gutiérrez continued to work in the aerospace field. Until mid-1992 she was a systems engineer for Loral Aerosys in Seabrook, Maryland. As a senior consultant engineer for Computer Sciences Corporation (CSC) since 1992, she is an operations manager of the FAA (Federal Aviation Administration) Advance Automation System Program. In this position, Gutiérrez is responsible for managing two departments, Product Assurance and Configuration Management. She also serves as senior consultant on Total Quality Management (TQM) to other CSC corporate centers and has worked on programs for the National Aeronautics and Space Administration (NASA) and the Goddard Space Flight Center in Greenbelt, Maryland.

Gutiérrez's many civic activities primarily focus on education. She has long been active in the Montgomery County PTA and other community-based organizations, including the education committee of the League of United Latin American Citizens (LULAC), and the National Council of La Raza. She is also a member of Senator Barbara A. Mikulski's academic review board, the National Coalition of Education Activists, the Hispanic Education Issues Committee of Montgomery College, and the National Science Foundation Advisory Committee for the Minority Education Project. In her view, education is a very important issue for everybody, but it is especially important for Hispanics. Schools are "the instruments for not just the individual to succeed, but for us as a community to succeed," Gutiérrez told *Washington Post* reporter Retha Hill.

Gutiérrez is currently pursuing her Ph.D. in engineering at George Washington University. Her future plans include serving out her term on the Montgomery County Board of Education while continuing to work as a senior consulting engineer.

Sources:

Periodicals

Vista, October 5, 1991, p. 20.
Washington Post, November 3, 1990, p. B5; May 9, 1991, section MDM, p. 1.

Other

Gutiérrez, Ana Sol, telephone interview with Sylvia P. Apodaca conducted on August 22, 1992.

—Sketch by Sylvia P. Apodaca

Nancy C. Gutierrez
(1941-)
Government official

When California Governor Pete Wilson appointed Nancy Gutierrez as director of the state's Department of Fair Employment and Housing, he put someone in charge who knew the meaning of diversity. Gutierrez was born in Santa Fe, New Mexico, on June 5, 1941, the fifth child and first daughter of Lorenzo and Coy Lincoln Thompson Gutierrez. Gutierrez's understanding of diversity can be traced to her own ethnic heritage: her father was Hispanic, her mother, French, Irish, and German. Her father (eldest son of Santa Fe judge Lorenzo Gutiérrez, Sr.) was Santa Fe's assistant postmaster. He dropped out of college as a young man to work and help pay for his younger brother's college education. Coy Thompson was a nurse.

Nancy Gutierrez attended parochial schools in Santa Fe until she was a teenager. By then her parents had divorced and her mother returned to her hometown in California's San Fernando Valley, along with Nancy and two of Nancy's brothers. There, Gutierrez developed an even stronger relationship with her maternal grandmother, whose sense of humor and egalitarian attitude inspired her.

After graduating from John Francis Polytechnic High at age 17, Gutierrez went to work as an operator for American Telephone and Telegraph (AT&T). By 1963, she was supervising her mostly female coworkers. Gutierrez started moving into non-traditional positions when, as she told Peg McNichol in a telephone interview, "I recognized that if I wanted to be competitive, I needed to go to the technical side of the business and perform there." In the early 1970s, when many companies set affirmative action standards, Gutierrez accepted a position supervising installation crews, a typically all-male section of the company. Gutierrez, drawing on her experience with four older brothers, was not intimidated by the prospect of supervising men. She wasn't intimidated by the possibility of failure, either. "There's a tendency in my life to be the pioneer," she remarked in the same interview. "I was very fortunate to be raised with parents, grandparents, and siblings who reinforced self-esteem and confidence."

Makes Strides in Affirmative Action Practices

Gutierrez found that she enjoyed her work as a supervisor so much that when, nearly a decade later, an opportunity arose to coordinate new offices in Southern California for what is now Pacific Bell, she hesitated. "When (management) gave me an opportunity to come into human resource," she noted, "I didn't really want to do it." She reluctantly accepted the offer. After completing the initial project, Gutierrez was tapped to head a state-wide recruitment program started by Pacific Bell to find more technically trained staff. As the head of human resources, Gutierrez, who had not obtained a college degree, found herself supervising workers who had more formal education than she. Aware that women were not motivated to pursue careers in engineering and science, Gutierrez worked to create an affirmative action program that went beyond legislation and mere good faith effort.

Gutierrez joined the National Women's Employment and Education Foundation in 1982 and the National Network of Hispanic Women in 1984. These groups focused on recruiting women who were on welfare for private sector jobs. Gutierrez's involvement with them took her to leadership seminars throughout the southwest United States. In 1985, through Pacific Bell, she hosted a forum of management recruitment that resulted in the formation of the National Hispanic Council. Gutierrez became active in groups outside the company as well, joining the Society of Hispanic Professional Engineers and the Mexican Engineering Association.

In 1990, after 31 years of service, Gutierrez took advantage of an early retirement program to care for her ailing mother. (Her father had died three years earlier.) But she remained active. With her interest in child development, she accepted membership on the board of directors for the Los Angeles Girls Scout Council and started a small consulting company, Gutierrez and Associates, as part of the Leadership America program.

Takes Reins at Consumer Affairs Department

While Gutierrez had no intention of going back to work full time, her mother's recovery and a friend's suggestion changed her mind. The friend heard that the California Department of Consumer Affairs needed a director for the Fair Employment and Housing Department and suggested Gutierrez as the best candidate. The director would be responsible for enforcing civil rights laws for all Californians and would have plenty of input on new legislation. Gutierrez was not reluctant this time about a new job.

Gutierrez was sworn in on August 19, 1991, and took office on October 1, 1991. Her immediate concerns were slashing $2 million from the budget while maintaining high standards for protecting and safeguarding civil rights for employment, housing, services and public accommodations. She had to deal with issues pertaining to the state's family leave policy (which Wilson signed), fallout from the Clarence Thomas/Anita Hill sexual harassment hearings, the Los Angeles riots, and political positioning from both parties. With an eye toward fairness, Gutierrez fielded all these issues as challenges to be met. She looks forward to continuing service in this line until 1994.

As she approached her first anniversary on the job, the Society for Institutional and Organizational Psychologists asked her to write about Pacific Bell's employee programs. *Beyond Good Faith Commitment: Recruiting Management Diversity at Pacific Bell,* which Gutierrez coauthored with Dr. Lori Wilberson, was published as part of the Diversity in the Work Force series in 1992.

Sources:

Gutierrez, Nancy C., telephone interview with Peg McNichol, October 2, 1992.

—Sketch by Peg McNichol

H

Rita Hayworth
(1918-1987)
Actress

Whether illuminating the screen with a song and dance or beaming from a magazine photo, Rita Hayworth was an unforgettable sight. Capitalizing on her inherited beauty and talent to become a legendary motion picture star, Hayworth captured the hearts of countless American servicemen during the 1940s. At her peak, she epitomized American beauty, and her career produced several memorable moments: dance routines with Fred Astaire in *You'll Never Get Rich* (1941); a glamorous photo in *Life* magazine; a scandalous striptease in *Gilda* (1946); and mature sophistication in *The Lady From Shanghai* (1949). While Hayworth's death in 1987 saddened America, it alerted the nation to the plight of those threatened by Alzheimer's disease, the illness that slowly killed her.

Born Margarita Carmen Cansino to Eduardo and Volga Haworth Cansino on October 17, 1918, in New York City, Rita Hayworth was no stranger to show business. Her father, a headliner on vaudeville, was descended from a line of famous Spanish dancers, and her mother, a Ziegfeld showgirl, came from a family of English actors. When the girl was nine years old, the family moved to Los Angeles, California, where the motion picture industry was rapidly growing. There, Eduardo taught dancing and directed dance scenes for various studios. She began her education at the Carthay School and later spent her first and only year of high school at Hamilton High. Throughout her school years, she continued family tradition by taking acting and dancing lessons.

At eleven, the girl found her first acting role in a school play, and by 1932, she had made her professional debut. She appeared in a stage prologue for the movie *Back Street* at Carthay Circle Theater. At this point, Eduardo Cansino decided that his attractive twelve-year-old daughter was ready for work. The perfect dance partner, she was introduced as Eduardo's wife when they danced at the Foreign Club in Tijuana, Mexico, for a year and a half, and then later on a gambling boat off California's coast. The "Dancing Cansinos" performed twenty times per week.

Makes Film Debut in *Dante's Inferno*

Rita Cansino, as she was called during this time, received her first big break when she was noticed dancing with her father in Agua Caliente, Mexico. Winfield R. Sheehan of the Fox Film Corporation hired the young woman, then sixteen, for a role in a movie starring Spencer Tracy entitled *Dante's Inferno* (1935). Though the film was not successful, Rita Cansino was given a year-long contract with Fox. During this year she held minor, ethnic roles in the motion pictures *Charlie Chan in Egypt* (1935), *Under the Pampas Moon* (1935), *Paddy O'Day* (1935), and *Human Cargo* (1936), in which she played Egyptian, Argentinean, Irish, and Russian dancers respectively. When her contract expired and was not renewed, the actress spent a year playing Mexican and Indian girls; she earned $100 for each role.

When Rita Cansino was 18, she married Edward C. Judson, a car salesman, oil man, and businessman who became her manager. According to the *New York Times*, Judson "transformed" the actress "from a raven-haired Latin to an auburn-haired cosmopolitan" by altering Rita's hairline and eyebrows with electrolysis and changing her professional name. Rita Cansino took her mother's maiden name, added a "y" to ensure its proper pronunciation, and became Rita Hayworth. Magazines and newspapers captured the image of the new Rita, who won the favor of Harry Cohn and a seven-year contract with his Columbia Pictures.

After fourteen low-budget movies, Hayworth was finally given a leading role. She was hired by Howard W. Hawks to portray an unfaithful wife in *Only Angels Have Wings* (1939), which starred Cary Grant. Good reviews of her performance attracted attention: she was borrowed from Columbia by Warner Brothers Pictures for the film *Strawberry Blonde* (1941) with James Cagney, and in that same year, she made *Blood and Sand* (1941) with Fox. Hayworth began to shine. According to *Time*, "something magical happened when the cameras began to roll"; the woman who was "shy" and "unassuming" offstage "warmed the set." The *New York*

Times wrote that Hayworth "rapidly developed into one of Hollywood's most glamorous stars."

Hayworth achieved celebrity status when she starred as Fred Astaire's dance partner in *You'll Never Get Rich* (1941) for Columbia. She appeared on the cover of *Time* and was dubbed "The Great American Love Goddess" by Winthrop Sargent in *Life*. In 1942, she made three hit movies: *My Gal Sal, Tales of Manhattan* and *You Were Never Lovelier,* with Fred Astaire. As her career skyrocketed, however, Hayworth's marriage failed; she divorced Edward Judson that same year.

Marries Orson Welles

During the early forties, Hayworth's personal life improved and she established her professional allure. She married Orson Welles, the famous actor, director, and screenwriter, in 1943; they had a daughter, Rebecca, two years later. Hayworth was earning more than $6,000 a week as Columbia's leading actress. After she starred in *Cover Girl* (1944) with Gene Kelly, *Life* presented a seductive photograph of the actress wearing black lace which, according to the *New York Times,* "became famous around the world as an American serviceman's pinup." The *Times* also noted that, in what was "intended . . . as the ultimate compliment, the picture was even pasted to a test atomic bomb that was dropped on Bikini atoll in 1946."

Hayworth's fame continued to grow after she made *Tonight and Every Night* (1945) and *Gilda* (1946). Of these films, critics contend that *Gilda* is the most memorable. A scene in which Hayworth sang "Put the Blame on Mame" and stripped off her long, black gloves scandalized conservative viewers. It was testimony to her popularity that her 1947 film, *Down to Earth,* was included in a twentieth-century time capsule despite the fact that the film itself received some bad reviews.

Hayworth did not mind the attention she garnered. "I like having my picture taken and being a glamorous person," she was quoted as saying in the *New York Times.* "Sometimes when I find myself getting impatient, I just remember the times I cried my eyes out because nobody wanted to take my picture at the Trocadero." Hayworth's daughter Yasmin Aga Khan confirmed this in *People:* "Mother was very good with her fans, very giving and patient."

While Hayworth starred as a sophisticated short-haired blonde in *The Lady From Shanghai* (1948) with her husband Orson Welles—who also directed the movie—she was in the process of divorcing him. She was later quoted in *People* as saying, "I just can't take his genius anymore," and in *Time,* she noted, "I'm tired of being a 25-percent wife." After making *The Loves of Carmen* (1948), she married Prince Aly Kahn, with whom she had been having an affair, in 1949. This was an off-screen scandal, for Hayworth was already pregnant with their daughter, the Princess Yasmin Aga Kahn. Although she was quoted in *Time* as saying,

"The world was magical when you were with him," this marriage did not last as long as her second; the couple divorced in 1953.

Hayworth's career began to wane. After making the movies *Affair in Trinidad* (1952), *Salome* (1953), and *Miss Sadie Thompson* (1953), she once again entered a marriage (1953-1955) that would prove to be unsuccessful as well as destructive. This fourth husband, the singer Dick Haymes, "beat her and tried to capitalize on her fame in an attempt to revive his own failing career," said Barbara Leaming, a Hayworth biographer, in *People.* While Hayworth came out of her temporary retirement after her divorce to make *Fire Down Below* (1957), which met with some positive reviews, she had only a supporting role in the film *Pal Joey* (1957). Failing to maintain her glamour, this movie was Hayworth's final appearance as a contracted actress.

At this point in the actress's life, Hayworth's personal life seemed to parallel her professional career. She married producer James Hill in 1958 and divorced him in 1961. *People* reported that Hill had wanted Rita to continue to make movies instead of "play golf, paint, tell jokes and have a home." After the failure of this fifth and final marriage, it was apparent that Hayworth did not have good luck with the men in her life. While Hayworth was quoted in *People* as saying, "Most men fell in love with *Gilda* but they woke up with me," biographer Barbara Leaming asserted that these "doomed" relationships were due to Hayworth's abusive father, Eduardo Cansino. Leaming told *People,* "Eduardo raped her [Hayworth] in the afternoons and danced with her at night." In her biography of Hayworth, *If This Was Happiness,* Leaming elaborates on this revelation, which she says was given to her by Orson Welles.

Develops Alzheimer's Disease

While critics agreed that Hayworth gave one of her best performances as a traitorous American in *They Came to Cordura* (1959), they also noted that her trademark beauty was fading. As a free-lance actress, Hayworth found fewer roles. *The Story on Page One* (1960), *The Poppy Is Also a Flower* (1967), and *The Wrath of God* (1972) were some of her last films. Hayworth's 1971 attempt to perform on stage was aborted; the actress could not remember her lines.

Biographers, relatives, and friends now believe that the first stages of Alzheimer's disease were responsible for Hayworth's memory lapses, alcoholism, lack of coordination, and poor eyesight during the last three decades of her life. Although Alzheimer's, a disease which was relatively unknown at the time, was not diagnosed as the source of Hayworth's problems, it was obvious that Hayworth was ill. In 1981 she was legally declared unable to care for herself. Her daughter, Princess Yasmin Aga Kahn provided shelter, care, and love for her mother, and sought to enlighten the public to the symptoms of the obscure neurological disease by helping to organize Alzheimer's Disease International and serving as its president.

Hayworth's mind slowly began to deteriorate. When she died in her New York apartment on May 14, 1987, she did not even know her own family. Nevertheless, the "All-American Love Goddess," as *Time* called her, was not forgotten by her fans. The *New York Times* reported at the time of her death that President Ronald Reagan, a former actor, stated: "Rita Hayworth was one of our country's most beloved stars. Glamorous and talented, she gave us many wonderful moments . . . and delighted audiences from the time she was a young girl. [First Lady] Nancy and I are saddened by Rita's death. She was a friend whom we will miss."

Sources:

Books

Leaming, Barbara, *If This Was Happiness*, Viking, 1989.

Periodicals

American Film, July, 1986, pp. 69-72.
Good Housekeeping, August, 1983, pp. 118-27; September, 1983, pp. 74-82.
Harper's Bazaar, November, 1989, pp. 156-59.
Ladies' Home Journal, January, 1983, pp. 84-89.
Ms., January, 1991, pp. 35-38.
New York Times, May 16, 1987.
People, November 7, 1983, pp. 112-17; June 1, 1987, pp. 72-79; November 13, 1989, pp. 129-32.
Time, May 25, 1987, p. 76.
Variety, May 20, 1987, pp. 4-6.

—*Sketch by Ronie-Richele Garcia-Johnson*

Antonia Hernández

Antonia Hernández
(1948-)
Civil rights lawyer

As president and general counsel for the Mexican American Legal Defense Fund (MALDEF), a Hispanic civil rights organization, Antonia Hernández has become a highly visible advocate for the nation's large and growing Hispanic community. Her opinions and advice on how a given issue will affect U.S. Hispanics have often been featured in newspaper editorial pages, national magazines, television talk shows, and numerous other media outlets. Immigrant rights, employment discrimination, education-al inequities, U.S. Census figures, redistricting, voting and language rights, are among her regular topics of concern.

Leader in Civil Rights Activism

Hernández began working for MALDEF in 1981 as a staff attorney in its Washington, D.C. office. Two years later she became employment litigation director in the Los Angeles office. During those years she sought greater opportunities for Hispanics in federal employment and promoted affirmative action in private and public sector jobs. It was also a period when MALDEF initiated several lawsuits to get employers to compensate bilingual workers whose second language capabilities were part of their job. In 1985, Hernández became president and general counsel of MALDEF, succeeding Joaquin Avila. "Every person who heads [MALDEF] gives it his or her flavor," Hernández told *Hispanic*. "My flavor has been taking the helm of an organization and helping it into institutional maturity."

Her tenure with MALDEF has been marked by controversy. In 1987, an executive committee of the MALDEF Board of Directors abruptly terminated her, citing questionable administrative and leadership abilities. Hours later they appointed former New Mexico Governor Toney Anaya to the post and gave him a $100,000 salary—$40,000 more than Hernández had been making. But Hernández refused to be dismissed, maintaining that only the full board had the power to fire her. A state judge from Texas agreed, requiring that the full board determine her status. They voted 18 to 14 to retain her.

Since then, she has gone on to become an organizational mainstay and MALDEF's most visible spokesperson. A public interest lawyer since graduating from the University of California at Los Angeles (UCLA) Law School in 1974, her advocacy is informed by her personal experiences of growing up as an immigrant in East Los Angeles, California. For example, her experiences as a child learning English by the "sink or swim" method has made her an effective advocate of bilingual education. "I made it. But just because I made it cannot be used as an example that it works," she told the *Los Angeles Daily Journal.* "I say 'Don't look at me, look at all those who didn't make it.' Because you're not judged by whether you made it, whether the minority made it. You're judged by whether the majority makes it." Because of her work, the situation "will be much better for my children," she told *Hispanic.* "They will have the opportunities I had to fight for. As a consequence, they'll have a bigger responsibility to give to their community."

Born on May 30, 1948, in the Mexican state of Coahuila in the town of Torreón, Hernández came to the United States with her family when she was eight. They settled in East Los Angeles. Her father, Manuel, was a gardener and laborer. Her mother, Nicolasa Hernández, was a homemaker raising her six children but she also took on odd jobs whenever possible. As the oldest child, Antonia was often called upon to help raise her younger siblings and to do unconventional tasks for young women of that time period such as car maintenance. "In my time, women didn't have the freedom that women have today," her mother told *Parents,* "but I wanted my daughters to have that, to learn, to travel, to work, to do whatever they wanted to do." While the Hernández family was not rich in material possessions, they provided a nurturing environment, says the younger Hernández. "I grew up in a very happy environment but a very poor environment," she told *Parents.*

Hernández credits her early upbringing in Mexico as instilling pride in her Mexican roots. "When I came to the United States, I was very proud of who I was. I was a Mexican. I had an identity. I had been taught a history, a culture of centuries of rich civilization so I had none of the psychoses of people who don't know who they are," she told the *Los Angeles Daily Journal.* Her belief in the extended family can be seen in her daily life. She, her husband, and their three children now live in Pasadena, near her mother and her sisters.

All of her brothers and sisters have earned college degrees and several are teachers. "My parents instilled in us the belief that serving the public interest was a very noble thing to do," Hernández told *Parents.* Hernández was on her way toward earning a postgraduate degree in education when she decided she could be more useful to her community with a law degree. She had already received her bachelor's degree and a teaching certificate from UCLA in 1973. She was working in a counseling program, she told *Parents,* when she "realized that we couldn't help the kids as teachers unless we did something about the laws that were holding them back."

Although her professors encouraged her to attend Harvard or Stanford, she chose UCLA so she could remain near her family. "I was the oldest in our family, and my parents were sacrificing everything they could to help me with school," she explained to *Parents.* "They were looking forward to me graduating and working as a teacher so I could help them with the rest of the kids. So my feeling was that if I were to ask them to sacrifice three more years, moving away would be too drastic."

Although Hernández was not a straight-A student in law school, her professors recall her as bright and articulate. "She had the ability to get her point across without alienating other people and people respected her for that," recalled one professor in the *Los Angeles Daily Journal.* Hernández acknowledges her priority wasn't top grades but the organizations and issues she cared about. During law school, she served on the admissions committee and several Chicano student organizations. "I wasn't out there to make the law firm roster," she told the *Los Angeles Daily Journal.* "I knew I was going to be [in] public interest [law]. . . . To me, to be a really good lawyer, you have to be a well-rounded person."

A Lawyer on Her Own Terms

After receiving her juris doctorate, she became an attorney for the East Los Angeles Center for Law and Justice, where she handled criminal and civil cases, often involving police brutality. After a year there, she became directing attorney of the Lincoln Heights office for the Legal Aid Foundation, where she directed a staff of six attorneys and took part in case litigation and fought for bills in the state legislature.

By then she had already married Michael Stern, an attorney she met while a law clerk for California Legal Rural Assistance in 1973. Two years later Stern came to Los Angeles as the deputy public defender in the federal Public Defender's Office. An old friendship turned to courtship and they were married in 1977, though not before receiving her father's permission. Stern practices with a private law firm.

In 1978, Hernández was offered a job as staff counsel to the United States Senate Judiciary Committee, which was chaired by Senator Ted Kennedy. After initially declining, Hernández took the position, with a little prodding from her husband. "I was very happy doing poverty law and being near my family," Hernández told *Parents.* "They called me back because they thought it was the salary, and so they raised it. I didn't want to explain what the problem was so I said yes. As a professional woman you just don't say 'My mother said I shouldn't do this.'" Her husband took a more pragmatic view, telling *Parents:* "We didn't have children; we had very little furniture and few responsibilities. I figured I'd get a job."

Political Experience Shapes Career

Overcoming her reluctance to leave her hometown, Hernández gained valuable experience in the nation's capital. At the Senate Judiciary Committee, she drafted bills and briefed committee members, specializing in immigration and human-rights work. She even took a brief leave of absence to coordinate Kennedy's Southwest campaign during his unsuccessful bid for the Democratic presidential nomination. "In that degree I played the Hispanic role," she told the *Los Angeles Daily Journal.* "But on other issues, I was just another staff member who had to do the work that had to be done."

Soon after the Democrats lost control of the Senate in 1980, Hernández was out of work. Within days, MALDEF asked her to join their Washington, D.C. staff. Her progress there was steady, working as associate counsel, director of the employment litigation program, executive vice president, and deputy general counsel before moving into the top slot. One of her brightest moments was her role in defeating the Simpson-Mazzoli immigration bill, which would have required Latinos to carry identification cards. Immigrant rights has been one area that Hernández has been especially effective in pushing the federal government to recognize. Throughout her tenure at MALDEF, the organization has created historic changes through court litigation for the U.S. Hispanic community, including the creation of single member election districts and favorable public school equity court decisions in Texas, and successful challenges to district boundaries in Los Angeles County.

Hernández says her time in Washington, D.C. has given her a broader understanding of the diversity within the U.S. Latino community. "Living on the East Coast has helped me transcend the regional aspect of the organization by mixing with Puerto Ricans, Cubans and other groups," she told *Hispanic.* She has sought to increase the cooperation among civil rights organizations across racial and ethnic lines. "If we allow ourselves to be sucked into believing we should fight over crumbs, we will." Her resolve on that issue was tested in late 1990 when the Leadership Conference on Civil Rights failed to support the repeal of employer sanctions found in the 1986 Immigration Reform and Control Act. Citing the government's own General Accounting Office study showing that the provisions led to increased discrimination against Hispanic-looking job applicants, Hernández threatened to pull MALDEF out of the coalition, which was gearing up for an intense lobbying campaign for what would later become the 1992 Civil Rights Bill. In the end, the National Associa-

tion for the Advancement of Colored People (NAACP) voted to support the repeal.

As much as her performance is measured by court decisions, she understands the human element of her work. "A court victory is important but just the beginning of the process. It must translate into empowerment. It is the people that have the power to give life to those court victories," she told *La Paloma.* However, despite her professional success, she acknowledges that the 1980s were not the best of times for the U.S. Hispanic community. "The 1980s was not the decade of the Hispanic," she told *Hispanic.* "Madison Avenue put up the expectation and said we failed. The 1990s is a threshold decade. We need to move. Otherwise, we'll develop into a community with a small middle class and a large poverty class."

Antonia says family comes first despite her high-powered job. She describes her children as "my greatest accomplishment." Balancing the needs of her family with a career has been a continual struggle, but one she has become adept at. She's often gone from home for long stretches of time, testifying before Congress or addressing other national organizations. "I try to balance my life and it has worked," she told *Hispanic.* "But I have little time to myself and very few good friends." She acknowledges that having a husband who is familiar with her culture through his work with farmworkers and able to speak Spanish has helped. Although of Jewish descent, Stern has embraced his wife's strong cultural ties. "I don't want him to feel uncomfortable because he's living our way," Hernández told *Parents.* "But he's very accommodating. I don't know if I could be as accommodating if it was the reverse."

Her community involvement includes serving on the boards of California Tomorrow, Quality Education for Minorities Network, California Leadership, Latino Museum of History, Art, and Culture, and Los Angeles 2000. And, after the 1992 riots in Los Angeles, Hernández began recruiting others into community service. Appointed by Mayor Tom Bradley to the Rebuild L.A. commission to spearhead revitalization efforts in the beleaguered city, Hernández has been adamant in calling for immigrants and Hispanics to be involved in the rebuilding process.

Sources:

Periodicals

Hispanic, December, 1990, pp. 17-18.
Hispanic Business, February, 1992, p. 10.
Intercambios Femeniles, spring, 1988.
La Paloma, December, 1991.
Los Angeles Daily Journal, September 3, 1985, p. 1.
Los Angeles Times, August 5, 1985, section II, p. 1.
New York Times, March 2, 1987, p. A15.
Parents, March, 1985, pp. 96-100, 170-174.

Vista, August, 1992, pp. 6, 28.

—Sketch by Jonathan J. Higuera

Christine Hernandez
(1951-)
Texas State Representative

"**T**he Southwest has always been known for strong women," said sociology professor O.Z. White of San Antonio's Trinity University. A specific example of this might be Christine Hernandez, a Texas politician who is not only a woman of strong character, but an individual whose accomplishments exceed those of a person twice her age.

Hernandez was born on July 23, 1951, to Joe Hernandez and Aurora Zapata in San Antonio, Texas. She attended high school and college in that city, receiving her bachelor of arts degree in sociology and her elementary teaching certificate at Our Lady of the Lake University. As a young girl she wanted to emulate the dedicated teachers she so admired. This ambition led to a ten-year career as an elementary school teacher. As a teacher, she tutored students after school, sponsored a Cub Scout pack, helped the PTA, acted as a mentor to first-year teachers, and generally offered assistance whenever and wherever she could. During this time, Hernandez earned her master's degree in bilingual teacher education from the University of Texas in San Antonio in 1981.

Although she eventually left the classroom in order to become full-time president of the San Antonio Federation of Teachers, Hernandez continued to have an impact on students and the teaching profession. The position allowed her to lobby both the school board and the legislature directly. When the San Antonio Independent School District converted to single-member trustee districts in 1986, she successfully ran for the seat representing her southwest-side community. In her campaign she stressed the need for continued education reforms, dropout prevention efforts, and substance abuse prevention programs. In addition, Hernandez was the first Hispanic woman named to the Texas Association of School Boards and the first Hispanic woman to sit on the Board of Directors of the Star Bar of Texas.

Hernandez continued to be a pioneer. She became the first Hispanic woman in San Antonio's history to be elected to the Texas House of Representatives. She defeated a St.

Mary's University political science professor with a 53 percent share of the vote and was sworn into office in January of 1991. As a member of the Texas House of Representatives, Hernandez has assisted on a wide range of committees. She served as vice chair of research and development on the science and technology committee, was a member of the Mexican-American Legislators Policy Issues Committee, and chaired the Education Issues Committee in 1992. In 1988 Hernandez acted as a delegate at the Democratic National Convention in Atlanta.

While her career continues down different roads, Hernandez always remembers where she has been. Her interest in elementary school children inspired Hernandez to propose in the state legislature a program that came to be known as "Mama Patrols." The project required Dallas, Houston, and San Antonio to provide school crossing guards using funds from specified school-zone traffic violations. "It would allow for the additional $20 to be placed on top of such violations as speeding in a school zone or passing a school bus stopped in a school zone," Hernandez told the *San Antonio Express-News.*

In addition to her many job-related responsibilities, Hernandez gives generously to community involvement. She has chaired the state's Task Force for Indigent Health Care and has been on numerous commissions for the improvement of public education, health care, economic development, and environmental protection. She has also been active in the United Way.

Hernandez was selected by *Good Housekeeping* magazine in May of 1985 as one of the "100 Young Women with Promise." She recalled in an interview published in *Lake Alumni:* "I found out about [the honor] when one of my friend's saw me in the magazine." She was named Hispanic Woman of the Year by the Mexican American Democrats of San Antonio in September of 1984 and received the Mexican American Women's National Association Award in July, 1988. Her advice to today's youth, as quoted from her profile in *Patriots,* follows the principles she has used in her life: "Get a good education, believe in yourself, set your goals, and reach for the stars. The only limits any of us have are the ones we set on ourselves."

Sources:

Periodicals

"Christine Hernandez: President, San Antonio Federation of Teachers," *Patriots,* Hispanic American Heritage Month, 1990 Commemorative Issue, p. 76.
San Antonio Express-News, June 5, 1988; May 14, 1991, p. A8.
San Antonio Light, March 9, 1990, p. A4.
"Seal of Approval," *Lake Alumni,* Our Lady of the Lake University of San Antonio, Volume 11, number 3.

—Sketch by Bill Evans

Maria Latigo Hernandez
(1893?-1986)
Community leader, civil rights activist

Maria Latigo Hernandez is best known for her life-long efforts to achieve justice, equality, and educational opportunity for Hispanic Americans. Her work with organizations such as Orden Caballeros de America, La Liga por Defensa Escobar, and La Raza Unida Party virtually chronicles the Mexican American civil rights movement in Texas. She documented her social philosophy in her book, *Mexico y los cuatro poderes que dirigen al pueblo.*

Hernandez was born at the end of the nineteenth century in Mexico. Because of the political unrest in that country following the Great Revolution of 1910, her parents sought safety in the United States, bringing Hernandez and her five siblings to Texas. They settled in Hebbronville. In 1915, she met and married Pedro Hernandez, who became an extremely influential part of her career as an activist. In 1918 the young couple moved to San Antonio, where they opened a grocery store and bakery. At this time, the Hispanic community had already developed many societies for burial services and health assistance. The Hernandez family set out to make a special study of the civic-oriented groups, such as Los Hijos de Texas and La Orden Hijos de America.

Pedro Hernandez described their reasons for exploring the ideals of these new organizations in *A War of Words:* "Born in the mind of my wife and I was the idea of organizing a civic group to awaken more and more the civic consciousness of our own . . . toward the end increasing the number of voters in the elections, and thereby making good use of civic rights. We shall take to power those responsible elements of our community." In 1924, Maria and Pedro Hernandez joined La Orden Hijos de America.

Provided Medical Services for Community

While both Pedro and Maria continued their roles as civil rights leaders and advocates for better quality education, in the 1920s Maria Hernandez began to care for her ill and aging father. She worked for her father's physician, who was impressed with her natural abilities and encouraged Hernandez to further her medical training. "She entered training as a midwife. She served in that capacity for years serving people who couldn't afford medical care," recalled her son, Pedro, in an article in the *San Antonio Express-News.*

During this time, a compatriot of Maria and Pedro, Alonso Perales, was also establishing a new organization in

south Texas. In 1927, Perales formed the Liga de Ciudadanos Latino Americanos from chapters of other established groups. With an expanding membership, Perales changed the name of the organization to League of United Latin American Citizens (LULAC) two years later.

The local La Orden chapter in San Antonio refused to join the LULAC organization. Both Maria and Pedro Hernandez, members of the original group, disagreed with the LULAC goals and strategies. "They didn't have what I mostly was interested in, fraternal and civic activity for both sexes. Other groups exclude their women, form auxiliary women's groups. To my view, the sexes are different but equal in their rights," explained Pedro Hernandez in *A War of Words.* Both Pedro and Maria promoted a well-developed feminist viewpoint at a time when American women had only recently been granted the right to vote. There was also disagreement with the implications involved in changing the organization name from the Spanish language to the English language. Furthermore, the emphasis on voting, political accountability of leaders, and a "Pan Americanism" vision as set forth by Pedro and Maria Hernandez did not fit with the precepts set by the LULAC.

Advocated Bilingual Education

By restricting many of her speeches and articles to the Spanish language, Maria Hernandez contrasted with the assimilationists who advocated the almost exclusive use of English to increase acceptance of Hispanics in American society. Assimilationists felt that the increased acceptance of English-speaking Hispanics would expand their civil rights. By her dogged insistance on using the Spanish language and maintaining Hispanic cultural awareness, Hernandez became a pioneer in the applications of bilingualism in education today.

In 1929, Maria and Pedro Hernandez founded a new organization, the Orden Caballeros de America, which focused on civic and civil rights. "From that date to [the 1970s], they have participated in the most important events of Chicano history in Texas," stated Martha Cotera in *Profile on the Mexican American Woman.* Maria Hernandez was in the forefront of expanding educational opportunities for Hispanic children. In 1934, Hernandez formed La Liga Por Defensa Escolar en San Antonio. Its purpose was to challenge the deplorable conditions in the schools for Mexican children: the outrageous teacher to student ratio of 1/130, lack of heat, and uninhabitable facilities. Marches and rallies were used to gain public awareness and to force the State Board of Education to receive a list of complaints.

One event illustrating Hernandez's oratory skills, ability to inspire, and commitment to education occurred at a rally sponsored by Liga por Defensa Escolar and LULUC at

Lanier High School. The demonstration was attended by the superintendent of public schools, L.L. Woods. Among the featured speakers, Hernandez was the only one who addressed the crowd of 5000 in Spanish. A dynamic orator, she inspired parents to rise to her call against injustice. As quoted in *A War of Words,* Hernandez then addressed the superintendent and challenged him: "[The students are] not at fault for being born with black eyes and brown hair and not with blue eyes. We are all supported by the stripes and stars of the flag. I want you to take this gesture of this community as a protest and disgust over the terrible conditions." In response to the crowd of parents and community leaders who applauded Hernandez's statements, the superintendent promised to return to Austin and work to improve the classroom conditions.

Hosted Radio and Television Shows

Using her skills as a great communicator, Hernandez embarked on another career beginning in the 1930s. She was the host of one of the first Spanish-speaking radio programs in San Antonio. Her afternoon program, "La Voz de las Americas," was aired daily on KABC-radio. It began as a half-hour program but was soon expanded to one hour. Later, in the 1960s, Hernandez ventured into another media, television. She hosted a weekly television program called "La Hora de la Mujer" on station KWEX.

In 1939, Hernandez was appointed goodwill ambassador to Mexico by several San Antonio organizations. She met with President Lasaro Cardenes and his wife. As a gesture of his country's esteem, President Cardenes presented Hernandez with an Aztec calendar design engraved on a large silver platter. This tribute was publicly displayed in San Antonio.

As the United States entered World War II, Hernandez vigorously supported the war effort. With two sons in military service, she sold war bonds, raised funds, and wrote articles for Spanish-language newspapers. A supporter of Franklin Delano Roosevelt, she campaigned for him in the Hispanic community.

In 1945, Hernandez wrote a book entitled, *Mexico y los cuatro poderes que dirigen al pueblo.* In the work, she discussed the importance of family and political action. She emphasized the importance of home life as the foundation of society and the basis of the formation of individual character. While society tests everyone's character and citizenship, Hernandez noted, it also reflects on the quality of the community's leaders. She expressed no tolerance for those leaders who have used a community agenda for personal aggrandizement, stating in the book that by acting politically, citizens will increase the awareness of social problems. She declared in *Mexico y los cuatro poderes que dirigen al pueblo* that political activism is a moral responsibility to one's family, one's community, and one's country.

Campaigned with Husband for La Raza Unida Party

Both Hernandez and her husband, Pedro, served among the vanguard of the Mexican civil rights movement for more than 50 years. Long after they had reached "retirement age," both continued their political and social involvement in the Chicano movement of the late 1960s and 1970s through the political party La Raza Unida Party (RUP). The RUP was formed by 300 Mexican-Americans in Crystal City, Texas in 1970 as a political party. Other organizations had also used the name "La Raza Unida" ("The People United"). The RUP of 1970 was founded to organize unregistered Mexican Americans into an independent voting bloc. It was hoped that the party would be able to elect candidates in areas or districts where Mexican Americans voters formed a majority. Furthermore, La Raza Unida Party would be an effective voice representing Mexican American issues in elections where they did not have a voting majority and act as a balance of power between major political parties.

While the RUP was initially denied ballot access, it was able to help elect its first officeholder through the skillful organization of a write-in campaign. Other RUP candidates won victories in municipal, school district, and nonpartisan elections. As the party became increasingly established, RUP was able to win majorities on the Crystal City and San Juan city councils in southern Texas. Hernandez first became involved with RUP when she was the featured speaker at a statewide conference in 1970. Both Pedro and Maria were active and strong supporters in the development of this separate party. In 1972, the two activists traveled throughout southern and central Texas at their own expense to campaign on behalf of the RUP gubernatorial candidate, Ramsey Munoz, and Martha Cotera, the RUP State Board of Education candidate.

After the death of her husband in 1980, Hernandez continued to live at the ten-acre ranch in southwest Bexar County that she and Pedro had purchased in 1955. She always acknowledged the importance of her husband as a positive force in her life. Their lifetime of partnership and work was a union of the heart, mind, and soul. At the time of her own death in 1986, she was survived by one son and four daughters, 19 grandchildren, 23 great-grandchildren and eight great-great-grandchildren.

Hernandez's life was dedicated to her family, her community, and her country. Whether nursing her father, campaigning for political candidates, selling war bonds, or championing educational opportunities for Hispanic children, her life's work stressed the importance of family and the power of citizen advocacy. In assessing her contribution to the Mexican American community, Hernandez related in Cotera's book, "I feel my husband and I have worked very hard since 1924 for the betterment of our people. I feel we have not accomplished very much because of our limited resources. But when a person dedicates all his life to the movement, that in itself is worth more than money."

Sources:

Books

Cotera, Martha, *Profile of the Mexican American Woman,* National Educational Laboratory Publishers, 1976.

Hammerback, John C., Richard J. Jensen, and Jose Angel Gutierrez, *A War of Words: Chicano Protest in the 1960s and 1970s,* Greenwood Press, 1985.

Hernandez, Maria L., *Mexico y los cuatro poderes que dirigen al pueblo,* Imprinta Munguia de San Antonio, 1945.

Lewels, Franciso Jr., *The Uses of the Media by the Chicano Movement: A Study in Minority Access,* Praeger Press, 1974.

Munoz, Carlos, *Youth, Identity, Power,* Verso, 1989.

Perales, Alonso, *Are We Good Neighbors?,* Artes Graficas, 1948.

Pinon, Fernardo, *Of Myths and Realities: Dynamics of Ethnic Politics,* Vantage Press, 1978.

Periodicals

San Antonio Express-News, January 11, 1986.

—*Sketch by Sally Foster*

Sally B. Hernandez-Pinero
(1952-)
New York City official

As chair of the New York City Housing Authority, Sally B. Hernandez-Pinero has come full circle. One of her surprise visits to public housing projects included a trip to the Bronx's Twin Parks West project and the apartment in which she was raised. A tenant of the building, Doris Massenburd, told the *New York Times,* "When you have lived in public housing, you gain something special inside you that you never forget. This lady has it."

Born in 1952 in the Bronx, Hernandez-Pinero is the daughter of immigrants who came to the United States from Moca, Puerto Rico. Her father labored as a building superintendent and as a dishwasher, and her mother was a school lunch worker at a local junior high. Along with her four siblings, Hernandez-Pinero attended Junior High School 44 and the Bronx High School of Science. She received her undergraduate degree from Wesleyan University, an independent college located in Middletown, Connecticut. It was while at Wesleyan that Hernandez-Pinero first displayed her activist side. "I officially came out, fighting one cause or another," explained Hernandez-Pinero in a *New York Times* interview. From there, Hernandez-Pinero went on to New York University's School of Law where she received a graduate degree.

What followed were the first steps of a fast-rising career in city politics. Hernandez-Pinero's various job titles included: Deputy President of the Borough of Manhattan, attorney for the City of New York's Legal Services Department, Commissioner of the City of New York's Financial Services Corporation, and the Deputy Mayor of Finance and Economics for the City of New York.

Appointed Deputy Mayor of New York City

With all this experience, Hernandez-Pinero was appointed Deputy Mayor in December of 1989 by the recently-elected Mayor of the City of New York, David Dinkins. She made the leap from Commissioner of Financial Services to join three others (Norman Steisel, Bill Lynch, and Barbara Fife) as Deputy Mayor. Among the issues that Hernandez-Pinero dealt with as Deputy Mayor was industrial aid. In September of 1991, her office released a report that called for a shift in financial support. Instead of the City of New York concentrating on financial aid to keep old manufacturers in the city, the report stated that more of an effort should be made to lure new businesses. It was reported in the *New York Times* that new businesses, between 1976 and 1986, generated nearly 464,000 jobs, while companies that left the city produced just 37,000 jobs.

By November of 1991, Hernandez-Pinero announced her decision to move to a less demanding position to spend more time with her family. Married to Hector Pinero, a vice president of a real estate company, Hernandez-Pinero gave birth to her first son in 1986 and a second in 1989. When she left her post, Hernandez-Pinero was the lone person of Hispanic descent in Mayor Dinkins's cabinet.

Hernandez-Pinero found a new position in New York City government when she was appointed chair of the city's Housing Authority in February of 1992. She replaced Laura Blackburne who had resigned under the pressure of questions about spending excessive money on trips and office renovations. One of the first goals Hernandez-Pinero set was to improve the city's housing projects. As she asserted in the *New York Times,* "These are the most austere times we have seen, and I plan to make sure that every agency dollar is spent wisely on public housing tenants and not bureaucrats." Within days of being hired to her new post, Hernandez-Pinero canceled all agency American Express cards, making employees pay their own expenses and be reimbursed after evaluation. The new Housing Authority chair also began a series of surprise visits to public housing projects and a reduction in the department's number of managers.

Sources:

Periodicals

Hispanic Link Weekly Report, March 2, 1992.
New York Times, December 9, 1989, p. 28A; September 24, 1991; November 28, 1991, p. 1B; February 25, 1992; February, 28, 1992.

—*Sketch by Bruce MacLeod*

Florence Hernández-Ramos
(1950-)
Public radio executive

As the first Hispanic female president and general manager of a public radio station, Florence Hernández-Ramos has been a pioneer in shattering stereotypes about radio, audience preferences, and Hispanics and women in media. With no prior media experience, activist-turned-executive Hernández-Ramos organized and took the helm of KUVO, the first bilingual radio station in Denver, Colorado, in 1985. "Our greatest challenge then, as it is now, was to define what an Hispanic-owned station is," Hernández-Ramos explained in an interview for *Odyssey West.* In a city where Hispanics account for only 13 percent of the population, KUVO's unique blend of jazz fusion, rhythm and blues, salsa, and other Latin sounds has successfully crossed ethnic boundaries, appealing to the community's Hispanic, black, and Anglo listeners.

Born May 3, 1950, in Lamar, Colorado, to Dora Castillo and Jesus Hernández, Hernández-Ramos was one of seven children. She was the first Hispanic valedictorian student at Lamar High School. After graduating from the University of Colorado at Boulder in 1973 with a teaching certificate in secondary education and a major in Spanish, Hernández-Ramos participated in a federally funded program to introduce Chicano studies in universities across the country.

College life was Hernández-Ramos's first exposure to prejudice, leading her to pursue activist causes for the working class. "When I got really involved in the lettuce and grape boycotts," she remembered in a *Rocky Mountain*

News interview, "I saw people taunting us on the picket line simply because of the color of the skin." For two years, she worked as a punch press operator for an auto parts shop in Denver to avoid, she said in the same interview, "high money-making positions."

Spurred by her interest in civil rights, Hernández-Ramos attended the University of Colorado School of Law from 1974 to 1977. She spent the year of 1975 working for the Colorado Rural Legal Services as a summer intern in the farm worker program. In 1982, when she was a paralegal in the Colorado attorney general's office, she was introduced to radio station executive Hugo Morales, who was visiting Denver to investigate the possibility of setting up a public radio station. Hernández-Ramos began researching the viability of such a venture, and two grants totaling $510,000 helped to launch the station. The 89.3 FM frequency was acquired in 1983 by Denver Educational Broadcasting, a group of Hispanic-controlled public radio stations in the United States.

Bilingual KUVO Begins Broadcasting

On August 29, 1985, after 22 intense months of organizing, fund-raising, and promotion, KUVO signed on the air. Hernández-Ramos had orchestrated a major effort to obtain professional training and orientation, assemble a board of directors, purchase and install broadcasting equipment, and recruit and train volunteers for every facet of operations. "People have a stereotype about a Hispanic controlled station," Hernández-Ramos maintained in *La voz Hispana de Colorado.* "They are shocked to discover we have a jazz format." Although the station broadcasts primarily in English, Hernández-Ramos is committed to serving the minority communities by ensuring that news and public service announcements relating to minority issues get priority airing. Information programs with a focus on the special accomplishments of Hispanics and other minority communities are an essential part of the station's programming.

Hernández-Ramos's leadership in the development of KUVO as a station responsive to the Hispanic community has been recognized by National Public Radio, the Corporation for Public Broadcasting, the National Federation of Community Broadcasters, and the National Endowment for the Arts. She has served on committees and panels for each organization, as well as for numerous other organizations relating to broadcasting and minority issues. Her awards include the Mary Bock Award for Excellence in Media from the Denver chapter of American Women in Radio Television, and the Colorado Hispanic Media Association's management award. In 1986, KUVO was voted the Best Hispanic Station in Denver, and the Best Jazz Station in Denver in 1987 and 1988. A special concern of Hernández-Ramos is the future establishment of Five Points Media Center, a project where minorities would get extensive training in the electronics media and become a pool of candidates for management positions.

Married to attorney Manuel Ramos, Hernández-Ramos has a stepson, Diego Ramos, and two godsons, Roberto Santos and Gabriel White.

Sources:

Periodicals

La voz Hispana de Colorado, January 24, 1990, p. 8.
Odyssey West, July/August, 1990, pp. 24-25.
Rocky Mountain News, May 25, 1992.
Up the Creek, March 24, 1986.
Weekly Issue, July 16, 1992, p. 2.

—*Sketch by Julie Catalano*

Carolina Herrera

Carolina Herrera
(1939-)
Fashion designer

When she introduced her first collection in 1981, Venezuelan socialite Carolina Herrera stunned high society and stirred the fashion industry with her innovative creations. The deep necklines and exaggerated sleeves featured in her collection reminded audiences of traditional beauty while promoting a contemporary elegance. The renowned designer Bill Blass recognized her talent. "I think she has tremendous potential," he was quoted as saying of Herrera in *People*. "She is going to be a force in the fashion world." Since that time, Herrera has invigorated fashion design and dressed some of the world's most famous women. A recipient of the 1987 MODA Award for Top Hispanic Designer, she has secured her place among the world's most heralded fashion designers.

Herrera's success as a designer has much to do with her upbringing as a member of fashionable society. Born in Caracas, Venezuela, in 1939, to Guillermo Pacanins, an officer in the Venezuelan Air Force and, later, a governor of Caracas, Maria Carolina Josefina Pacanins y Nino was raised by people who enjoyed hosting parties in their glamorous homes and reveled in wearing the latest fashions. As a young girl, she designed garments for her dolls, and as a young woman, she designed for herself and for her friends. As *People* noted, she was "very sad" because she was not allowed to dress "like a vamp" in red as a child. Her grandmother introduced the stylish thirteen-year-old to the famous couturier Cristobal Balenciaga at a fashion show in Paris; at her first ball she wore a white gown from the House of Lavin.

When the elegant young woman married Reinaldo Herrera, her childhood friend and the eldest son of Mimi Herrera, in 1969, she found even more incentive to dress glamorously. Her mother-in-law was a wealthy art patron as well as the owner of "La Vega," an enormous house built in 1590 in Caracas. Herrera suited herself to her classically luxurious surroundings. She first made the Best Dressed List in 1971, and has been a perennial listee since. She won a spot in the Fashion Hall of Fame in 1981.

Diversion Becomes a Career

As Herrera told an interviewer with *Hispanic,* she began her professional career as a designer because her children were grown and she "wanted to try something new." She felt capable of designing successfully. When Armando de Armas, a Venezuelan publishing magnate, provided the financial backing Herrera needed for a venture into the business world of fashion, she "changed from being a mother with nothing to do but arrange flowers and parties to being a professional who works twelve hours a day at the office," she told *Newsweek*. While Herrera was optimistic about her chances for success, some of her societal peers and members of the fashion industry supposed that Herrera's designs would not merit a second glance.

Ellin Saltzman, the fashion director for Saks Fifth Avenue, recalled in *People* that she had her own doubts about

Herrera when she first heard of her 1981 collection. She had assumed that Herrera was "another socialite designing a fly-by-night collection no one will ever buy or wear." Herrera, however, proved that she was not an amateur. Herrera's work, which utilized layers, diverse fabrics, and various lengths, was received with enthusiastic praise. The skeptical fashion director from Saks Fifth Avenue found Herrera's collection to be "sensational," as she remarked in *People,* and experts with authority agreed. According to *People,* Herrera was dubbed "Our Lady of the Sleeves" by *Women's Wear Daily* because of the "exaggerated shoulders" on her fanciful evening gowns. While features such as fairy-tale sleeves and plunging necklines attracted attention, the industry respected the classic taste and superb tailoring of Herrera's work. The fashion world was buzzing—Herrera's collection promised to inspire other designers as well as incite new trends.

Popularity Spawns Success

By the end of 1982, Herrera's creations were widely acclaimed. Royal personalities, such as Princess Elizabeth of Yugoslavia, Spain's Duchess of Feria, and Countess Consuelo Crespi, were wearing Herrera's designs. Other public figures, First Lady Nancy Reagan and well-known actress Kathleen Turner among them, were donning Herrera gowns. Reagan and Turner sported the same silver-blue, one-shouldered gown of coupe de velours, which was paired with a marvelous maribou feather cape. Garments such as these, and other, sleek, striped, silver and gold gowns, captured the fancies of many women and made Herrera a star designer.

It is Herrera's understanding of the socialite's lifestyle and her extraordinary talent, along with her social contacts, that attract some of the world's most famous celebrities to her clothing. As Ivana Trump, ex-wife of the wealthy Donald Trump, explained in a *Newsweek* article, Herrera's designs catch the fancies of people like herself because she "is in society, she travels and goes to the same restaurants and parties as the women who buy her clothes." Ellin Saltzman, the fashion director at Saks Fifth Avenue, noted in the same article that Herrera contributed "dressy lunch and evening clothes that women couldn't find anywhere else" to the market. The fine quality and unique design of Herrera's works make her originals highly desirable. There is a great demand for her clothing despite exclusive prices. A luncheon suit might cost anywhere between $1,500 to $3,800. Pajamas of silk made especially for lounging at the pool were tagged at $1,200 in 1982. Herrera's exquisite gowns were priced at $2,100 to $4,000 in the same year.

Designs Garner Accolades

During the 1980s, Herrera continued to establish herself as a respected designer. As she understood the desire for slim clothing, she produced dresses and outfits that were less exaggerated than those she had previously designed;

she contributed to the trends of the mid-eighties with her own adaptations of the sleek style. In 1986, Jacqueline Kennedy Onassis, a Herrera client who as the First Lady set the standard for American fashion in the 1960s, asked Herrera to create a wedding dress for her daughter Caroline Kennedy. Finally, Herrera won the MODA Award as the Top Hispanic Designer in 1987 from Hispanic Designers, Inc., an award which had been previously won by the prestigious designers Adolfo and Oscar de La Renta.

1988 was the year that Carolina Herrera introduced her own perfume. "Carolina Herrera," as it is called, has been enthusiastically received by consumers. According to *Hispanic,* this perfume is her "most accessible and perhaps personal product." The perfume's odor of jasmine and tuberose is reminiscent of Herrera's happy childhood—a jasmine vine in the family's garden scented the girl's bedroom—and denotes her success as an adult. Herrera has been wearing this original mixture for years, and it permeates the atmosphere of her New York office.

While by late 1989 Herrera had been designing leather goods, eyewear, and furs for Revillon, and developed a less expensive line of clothing which she named "CH," her most exclusive apparel was featured along with those of the likes of designer Bill Blass in the media's fashion reports. Her collection for the fall of 1989 exemplified the reason for her fame: her creations were fun yet functional, elegant yet bold. Herrera was among those designers who utilized animal prints in their collections for the season. Herrera's particular adaptation of the theme was daring: she mixed the prints with crimson sequins and velvet. *Hispanic* displayed a "leopard print wool challis dress with a black persian velvet jacket lined with the same leopard spots" which could make "the switch from daytime into night" that was unusually stunning and versatile.

Collections Showcase Unique Designs

The *New York Times* reported on Herrera's 1989 fall show at the Plaza and emphasized other aspects of the collection: shorts that were "styled with a ripply fullness that makes them almost impossible to differentiate from skirts," "graphic black and white cotton pique suits" with combinations of hearts and stripes, dresses and jackets in pastel shades which were "harbingers of a new suit look to come," and "trouser outfits" with pants "either wide or narrow." Especially striking was Herrera's "upwardly mobile version" of the motorcycle jacket; in pink, chartreuse, or orange satin and with rhinestones instead of nailheads, these jackets contributed to "fun" outfits. Herrera's various evening gowns were characteristically beautiful, whether they were long and black, reminiscent of Fabergé eggs, or white with crystal beading. Herrera's diverse designs are testimony to her ideas. She told *Hispanic,* "Nowadays, everything [in fashion] is accepted. . . . There's a craziness going around the world." Despite this "craziness," Herrera acknowledges that odd designs are not as marketable as designs that take the needs of the buyer into account. In the same interview, she quipped, "Nobody wants to look like a costume. . . . The thing to do is to have a sensational simple dress."

Herrera continues to produce versatile, elegantly designed clothing. The *New York Times,* discussing her fall fashion show at the Plaza in 1991, noted that she had highlighted red plaids for daytime, and lamé, wool crepe, and "bold checks" for night. She utilized opaque tights in mustard and red for daytime, and feathers, silver sequins, and rhinestones with her evening wear. According to the *Times,* the "basic Herrera look is slick and uncomplicated, expressed in lamé jumpsuits and jersey dresses," yet her designs were not "shy and retiring." The *Times* observed that Herrera offered women the choice to wear a suit or a dress "in the same fabric," slim long gowns, or puffy short ones. "Clearly she is thinking about the different figures and needs of her followers."

Herrera's life is very busy. She has, however, managed to balance her roles as a designer and businesswoman, as a wife, a mother to four daughters and grandmother to three grandsons, as well as homes in New York and Caracas and an active social schedule. Although she believes that it is imperative that a designer observe and involve herself in social activity, she commented in *Newsweek,* "I never go to lunch anymore. It interrupts my day and it's boring." While it is obvious that Herrera is very serious about her work, she insists that she loves it. "The more I do the more I like it," she told *Hispanic.*

Herrera has earned her place as a distinguished fashion designer, and she is prepared to continue to dress women beautifully, refresh the world of fashion, and introduce exciting new products. As she confessed in an interview in *Hispanic,* "I am never satisfied. I'm a perfectionist. When I see the show is ready and the collection is out and they're quite nice, I still say, 'I could do much better.'"

Sources:

Periodicals

Americas, September-October, 1990, p. 30.
Architectural Digest, April, 1987, p. 128; September, 1988, p. 178.
Boston Globe, September 15, 1988, p. 65.
Harper's Bazaar, August, 1986, p. 152; September, 1989, p. 380.
Hispanic, March, 1989, pp. 28-30; October, 1989, pp. 36-37.
Newsweek, June 30, 1986, pp. 56-57.
New York Times, October 31, 1989, p. B8; April 9, 1991, p. B8.
Nuestro, October, 1985, p. 60.
People, May 3, 1982, p. 122.

Vogue, March, 1987, p. 342; June, 1990, p. 270; January, 1991, p. 132.

—*Sketch by Ronie-Richele Garcia-Johnson*

Hilda Hidalgo
(1928-)
Educator, social activist

Hilda Hidalgo is an educator, a social worker, and a political activist whose distinguished work involves empowering New Jersey's Hispanic community with political influence, higher education, and leadership skills. Hidalgo has been instrumental in setting up regional and national organizations that promote higher education and goals among Hispanics. Her many professional, political, and community activities underscore her commitment to the principles of social justice and equality.

Born to a middle-class Puerto Rican family on September 1, 1928, Hidalgo spent several years teaching at Colegio de Nuestra Senora de Valvanera in Coamo, Puerto Rico. She earned her bachelor's degree from the University of Puerto Rico in 1957, traveling to the mainland in 1958 to study for a master's degree at Catholic University of America, which she earned in 1959. Hidalgo then went on to earn a master's in social work from Smith College in Northampton, Massachusetts, in 1968. And in 1971, she earned her doctorate from Union Graduate School in Yellow Springs, Ohio.

It was while studying at Catholic University of America that Hidalgo began her fight against racial and social prejudice. During a visit to a friend in Big Spring, Texas, she walked into a shop to buy a soft drink. A prominently displayed sign (using expletives) warned that service would not be given to certain minorities. "The man at the counter looked at me," recalls Hidalgo in a telephone interview with Cheryl Beller. "I realized in that second, that in this society, I was all of those things. I think [the man] saw the fury in my eyes. He gave me a Coca-Cola; I broke the bottle on the counter." With a bleeding hand, Hidalgo boarded a bus for Washington, D.C. "That was the turning point for me," she says. "I knew that I had my work cut out for me: sexism, racism, homophobia—anything that put people into categories and targeted them for lack of opportunities."

Hidalgo has been active in political, social, and educational arenas in New Jersey since 1964 when she began serving as director of the Group Work and Tutorial Division of the Child Service Association in Newark. She was a visiting lecturer at the Graduate School of Social Work in Northampton, Massachusetts, and professor and chairperson in the Department of Community Development and Urban Studies at Livingston College in New Brunswick.

Founds Puerto Rican Congress of New Jersey

In 1975, Hidalgo became the first president and a founding member of the Puerto Rican Congress of New Jersey. The organization serves as a state-wide umbrella for coordinating leadership, and creating an agenda of priorities which address concerns of the Hispanic community. The Puerto Rican Congress secures grants and funding for programs which aid Hispanics. Its key priorities include child welfare, housing, migrant labor, education, and health care issues. "When I graduated and came to Newark, I had a degree and a job, but I couldn't sign an [apartment] lease because I was Puerto Rican," explains Hidalgo in her interview.

Hidalgo began teaching at Rutgers University in Newark, New Jersey, in 1977. In her early years, she was the chair of undergraduate social work at Rutgers, and coordinator of Puerto Rican studies. Hidalgo eventually became a full professor in public administration and social work, and held several administrative positions at the university prior to her retirement in 1992. As the director of Rutgers' Master's of Social Work Bilingual Program, Hidalgo was distressed to find that in 25 years, Rutgers (New Jersey's only graduate school of social work) had fewer than eight Hispanic graduates. Hidalgo was instrumental in creating an experimental master's program in social work for Hispanics. "It was an innovative program," she points out in her interview with Beller. "In order for a student to earn an 'A,' she had to help another student. We held classes at night and all day Saturday. In four years, 50 Latinos graduated with master's degrees in social work."

As director of Hispanic, bilingual, and bicultural master's of public administration at Rutgers, Hidalgo set up a similar program for Hispanic students. "In a period of 10 years, we were able to have a nucleus of more than 100 Puerto Ricans, Latinos, and students from El Salvador, Mexico, and Peru earn their master's degrees. There was no magic to it; the students worked hard. We cared about the students and they succeeded." Hidalgo believes that similar programs can be developed for elementary, high school, and college students. "It takes the belief that you can do it and hard work," she continues in her interview. "The concept of cooperation and working together are very important. The value of education is extremely important—education in a broader sense where people have the ability to critically think and analyze situations."

Aside from her education experience, Hidalgo was also the first vice president of the New Jersey Chapter of the National Association of Social Workers, and she served as commissioner for the Council on Social Work Education. She is licensed as a certified marriage counselor and a clinical social worker, and her many contributions include offering free social services for 25 years to non English-speaking clients. "Some of my clients have become professionals; some of them were on the verge of suicide when they came to me," she states in her interview with Beller. Hidalgo believes she has an obligation to give something back to society. "I believe when you have had the opportunity for an education, you owe something to society. No one makes it exclusively on their own merit. We are not isolated islands; we live in society. We have to have a commitment to pay back society . . . otherwise, you're a very arrogant person . . . the center of the universe."

Experiences Prejudice During Political Convention

Continuing to add to her community service experiences, Hidalgo served as the secretary for the first black and Puerto Rican convention in 1970, which was aimed at electing a minority for mayor of Newark. "Corruption in local government was rampant at the time," she asserts in her interview. On the Monday following the weekend convention, Hidalgo's personal car was destroyed by a bomb. "Ten years after it happened, I was finally able to talk about it in public," she continues. The same day of the car bombing, Hidalgo received telephone calls which warned, "'You will be next. You will be hurt or killed,'" she recalls. "It made me even more angry." In 1970, Kenneth Gibson was elected as Newark's first African American mayor. "Eventually, we won the election," says Hidalgo. "You cannot give [racial prejudice] the power to hurt you. Only the people you love and work with can hurt you."

Hidalgo believes in celebrating diversity, and lends her support to many minority causes, including Hispanic education and welfare issues, and gay and lesbian issues. She has written numerous articles relating to Hispanics, Puerto Rican perspectives, and feminism. In 1982, she published a resource manual titled *Rehabilitation in the 80's: Understanding the Hispanic Disabled,* and in 1985 she co-authored *Lesbian and Gay Issues: A Resource Manual for Social Workers.* Hidalgo also served on editorial boards for the *Journal of Gay and Lesbian Psychotherapy, Affilia: The Journal of Women in Social Work,* and *Society and Culture,* a journal published by the State University of New York at Albany.

In 1992, Hidalgo received another one of her numerous honors and awards for distinguished public service. The Puerto Rican Congress of New Jersey bestowed its highest honor, the CEMI Award, which signifies the God of Goodness in Spanish. Hidalgo says more significant than receiving the honor was the presentation of it, by a young Puerto Rican woman who is a Newark judge. Municipal Judge Myrna Milan was in high school, and a member of Aspira, when she and Hidalgo first met. Hidalgo was the first president and founder of Aspira, a national organization which promotes higher education for Hispanics. She founded the New Jersey Chapter of Aspira (which means "to aspire" in Spanish). Aspira works closely with the Puerto Rican Congress of New Jersey in promoting higher education among Latinos. Aspira also promotes scholarship programs for high school and college students, and vocational programs.

Hidalgo says the most difficult aspect of her current work is promoting benefits of an education to young Puerto Ricans and minorities. "Hundreds of young people are blossoming, and doing great things," she maintains in her interview. "But I don't think we have a significant commitment to really provide the kinds of opportunities that are essential. I have a hard time telling graduating students that they will have a great future. I have young men who tell me they can make more money and help their families by selling drugs. That's the reality. We need to talk to them about the risks, about what will happen to their little brothers. I believe we need to look at better ways to give them a sense of self-worth."

Sources:

Hidalgo, Hilda, telephone interviews with Cheryl Beller, October 4 and 18, 1992.

—Sketch by Cheryl Beller

Maria Hinojosa
(1961-)
Radio reporter

Perhaps because she has always recognized the powerful beauty of her cultural inheritance, Maria Hinojosa has made a point of making it accessible to others. She has captured the opportunity to celebrate Mexican and Mexican American culture as she works, writes, and creates, and she is determined to make the most of that opportunity. With her radio reports and shows, her artwork, and her social and organizational activities, Hinojosa continues to contribute to the cohesiveness of a booming New York City community.

The fourth child of Raul and Berta (Ojeda) Hinojosa, Maria de Lourdes Hinojosa was born on July 2, 1961, in Mexico City. When she was 18 months old, the Hinojosa family moved to the United States, where her father, a medical research doctor, studied and worked. After spending some time in New England, the family settled in Chicago. According to the reporter, instead of forgetting about their roots, the elder Hinojosas maintained strong ties with their family in Mexico; each summer, the family took a car trip to a different part of the country. Those exciting trips to her native land instilled a love of Mexican culture in Hinojosa and gave her a profound sense of pride in her heritage. "I was very, very proud to be a part of this huge country," she explained during an interview with Ronie-Richele Garcia-Johnson.

While the trips Hinojosa took to Mexico made her aware of her cultural roots, they also opened her eyes to socioeconomic inequity. She noticed that the poverty she had witnessed in Mexico was present in areas of Chicago, and she began to become politically active. When she went to a private school for the first time, at the University of Chicago High School, she created the organization Students for a Better Environment. It was important to her that the students there realize that not everyone lived the privileged life that they enjoyed, and that they should be thankful.

At that point in her life, however, Hinojosa had no idea that she would pursue a career as a socially committed radio reporter. She wanted to be an actress. She applied to Barnard, a women's college at Columbia University in New York City, and was accepted. Hinojosa was enthusiastic about school and New York, but she became increasingly frustrated as an aspiring actress. As she was just five feet tall and couldn't be described as looking either Mexican or white, there didn't seem to be a place for her in theatre. While her failure as an actress was disappointing, it allowed Hinojosa to get involved in radio when friends suggested that she try it.

It was just by chance that Hinojosa heard about an opening for a Latino show on Columbia's 24-hour student radio station, WCKR-FM. She started out with the radio show *Nueva cancion y demas*. As producer and host of this program, Hinojosa spent three hours each week on the air playing alternative Latin American music, announcing the news and discussing Latin American issues in a talk show format. While she continued to produce *Nueva cancion y demas* Hinojosa went on to become the program director of WCKR. While serving in this demanding position, she maintained excellent grades and majored in both Latin American studies and political economy.

Joins National Public Radio

In 1985, when Maria Hinojosa graduated magna cum laude from Barnard, she wasn't quite sure what she should do. She applied for an internship with the National Public Radio and was given a position as a production assistant in the Washington, D.C., office. For the *Weekend Edition-Saturday* show, Hinojosa produced mini-documentaries and news stories. Her next position, which she accepted in late 1986, was associate producer of *Enfoque nacional,* National Public Radio's weekly Spanish language national news program, at KPBS in San Diego, California. Hinojosa lived in Tijuana, Mexico, during her time in this position. In 1986, for her work on "Immigration and Detention," she won a Silver Cindy Award.

By 1987, however, Hinojosa was ready for a change. She returned to New York to become a producer with CBS News. For CBS, she produced the network radio broadcasts *The Osgood File, Where We Stand, with Walter Cronkite, Newsbreak, Today in Business, First Line Report,* and *Newsmark.* January of 1988 found Hinojosa working as a researcher/producer on live segments of *CBS This Morning.* In August of 1988, Hinojosa returned to National Public Radio (NPR) as a free-lance reporter/producer in Washington, D.C. She worked as a contract reporter for NPR's *Latin File* and programs such as *All Things Considered, Morning Edition, Weekend Edition, Crossroads, Latino,* and *Horizons* documentary series, and *Soundprint of American Public Radio.* Hinojosa won a 1989 Corporation for Public Broadcasting Silver Award for the piece "Day of the Dead."

Hinojosa returned to New York City in January, 1990, to work general assignments as a staff member of WNYC Radio. In August of that year, she began to work as a general assignment reporter for NPR's New York Bureau. By September, Hinojosa was ready to take on another challenge. She began to host her own live call-in public affairs prime-time television talk show, *New York Hotline,* which aired on WNYC Television. She was the first Latino to host a prime-time public affairs news television show in New York.

Hinojosa has quite a bit of television experience. She hosted a national broadcast called "Beyond the Browning of America," which was produced in conjunction with the Center for Puerto Rican Studies and aired on public television stations throughout the United States. Another program, "Crosswalks," aired on the municipal cable system and featured the Democratic National Convention. Finally, Hinojosa has moderated and hosted the public access television show *Latinos in accion.*

Hinojosa did not go unrecognized for the outstanding work she produced in the early 1990s. In 1990, she won an International Radio Festival of New York Silver Award for "Drug Family," and a fellowship from the New York Foundation for the Arts for work in radio. In 1991, for "Crews," a piece about members of youth gangs, she won the Unity Award from Lincoln University, a Top Story and First Place Radio Awards from the National Association of Hispanic Journalists, and a First Place from the New York Newswomen's Club. Also in 1991, she earned a First Place Award from the Associated Press for her coverage on WNYC of Nelson Mandela's visit to New York City. Her 1992 distinctions include a Kappa Tau Alpha Award for Excellence in Journalism from New York University, a Latino Coalition for Fair Media Award for Outstanding Service in Journalism, and a first place, radio, from the

National Association of Hispanic Journalists for "Body Bags."

Dedicated to Community Involvement

In late 1992, Hinojosa was working for NPR as a New York Bureau Staff Reporter. Her beats as a general assignment reporter included latino and multicultural affairs, race relations, youth issues, and labor and politics. She also hosted the show she had begun in 1980, *Nueva cancion y demas,* for WCKR-FM. She is a member of the boards of the Northstar Fund, the Committee for Hispanic Children, and Families 10th Year Anniversary Program. Hinojosa is a frequent guest lecturer at Princeton University, Haverford College, the Ohio Statewide Hispanic Conference, Mujeres Latinas en Accion/Chicago, and the City University of New York.

Known in New York for her artistic talent as well as for her radio personality, Hinojosa has been building altars in celebration of the Day of the Dead, a traditional Mexican holiday, since 1988. One of these, dedicated to undocumented immigrants, is especially moving. It features paper bags, which are symbolic for those bags carried by the people who cross the border into the United States, as well as tiny skeletons. Hinojosa has also highlighted the plight of those victimized by the AIDS virus in her altars. One of Hinojosa's altars was installed in the Bronx Museum of Art. Hinojosa told Garcia-Johnson that, in addition to enjoying the actual construction of each altar, she considers their creation and presentation as a way of establishing a Mexican American cultural presence in New York City and as a method of reaching out to the Mexican American community in the city. She wants the city to realize that Mexican Americans are a social and cultural force in the city, and she wants the Mexican Americans themselves to revel in their cultural heritage.

Hinojosa seems to thrive on her schedule. While she spends a great deal of her day working, she always manages to find time for her friends and for her husband, Gérman Perez, whom she married on July 20, 1991. Perez, who was born in the Dominican Republic, is a painter of large-scale acrylic works and shares Hinojosa's devotion to Hispanic American culture and her love of New York City.

The influx of Mexicans and Dominicans into New York during the 1980s and their growing cultural influence has contributed to the Pan-American community which enthralled Hinojosa during her first years in the city. She finds the cultural transformation taking place in the city exciting. That transformation is part of the reason why Hinojosa enjoys her job as a reporter. She told Garcia-Johnson that she loves "being on the street" and allowing "those [Hispanic] voices to be heard." Radio reporting to Hinojosa is "a part of my life." Hinojosa intends to continue enjoying her "dream job" in New York—she is not interested in administrative work in radio. She is collaborating on a video production about Latinos in the United

States called "The U.S. Mambo: One Step Forward, Two Steps Back." Finally, she is determined to finish a book she has started about the Crews, or Latino gangs, she has been studying.

Hinojosa's remarkable contributions to Mexican and Pan-American culture in New York City are becoming increasingly important as that community grows and as people throughout the United States become aware of the influence of Hispanics in the country. Young Hispanics, especially, will benefit from the appreciation of the historical and actual culture in transformation that Hinojosa promotes. With her determined effort to celebrate the culture that she loves, Hinojosa has not only achieved personal success, she has given voice to the concerns of a community.

Sources:

Hinojosa, Maria, telephone interview with Ronie-Richele Garcia-Johnson, August, 1992.

—Sketch by Ronie-Richele Garcia-Johnson

Hoyos, Angela de
See **de Hoyos, Angela**

Hoyos, Debora de
See **de Hoyos, Debora**

Dolores Huerta
(1930-)
Labor leader, social activist

Cofounder and first vice president of the United Farm Workers union, Dolores Huerta (sometimes referred to as Dolores "Huelga" [strike]) is the most prominent Chicana labor leader in the United States. For more than thirty years she has dedicated her life to the struggle for justice, dignity, and a decent standard of living for one of our country's most exploited groups, the women and men who toil in the fields. The recipient of countless community service, labor, Hispanic, and women's awards and the subject of many newspaper articles, as well as *corridos* [ballads] and murals, Huerta serves as a singular role model for Mexican American women living in the post

Dolores Huerta

World War II era. Although Huerta is widely acclaimed and celebrated, her early history, family life, transformation from volunteer to labor activist, and career are barely known.

Dolores Fernández Huerta, the second child and only daughter of Juan and Alicia (Cháves) Fernández, was born on April 10, 1930, in the small mining town of Dawson in northern New Mexico. On her mother's side of the family, Huerta is a third-generation New Mexican. Like her mother, Huerta's father was born in Dawson but to a Mexican immigrant family. The young couple's marriage was troubled, and when Huerta was a toddler her parents divorced. Her mother moved her three children—John, Dolores, and Marshall—first to Las Vegas, New Mexico, and then to Stockton, California, where she had relatives.

Raised Primarily by Mother and Grandfather

As a single parent during the Depression in California, Alicia Chávez Fernández experienced a difficult time supporting her young family. Describing her mother in an interview with this author, Huerta noted, "She was a very genteel woman, very quiet but very hard working," as well as very "energetic, motivated, and ambitious." To make ends meet, her mother worked at a cannery at night and as a waitress during the day. For child care, Alicia Fernández depended on her widowed father, Herculano Chávez, who had followed her to Stockton. In the same interview, Dolores Huerta recalled his importance: "My grandfather kind of raised us. . . . He was really our father. . . . My grandfather's influence was really the male influence in my family." The gregarious Huerta enjoyed a close relationship with her grandfather Chávez in a happy childhood with attentive supervision, respect for one's elders, Mexican *corridos,* and rosary recitations. Considering herself to be a dutiful but playful child, she remembered in the interview, "My grandfather used to call me seven tongues . . . because I always talked so much." Verbal skills would serve her well in later life.

The family's economic fortunes improved during the war years. Alicia Fernández ran a restaurant and then purchased a hotel in Stockton with her second husband, James Richards, with whom she had another daughter. Particularly during the summers, Dolores Huerta and her brothers helped run these establishments located on the fringes of skid row, catering to working-class and farmworker clientele. Huerta relished the experience and believed she learned to appreciate all different types of people, as she conveyed in the interview. "The ethnic community where we lived was all mixed. It was Japanese, Chinese. The only Jewish families that lived in Stockton were there in our neighborhood. . . . There was the Filipino pool hall . . ., the Mexican drug stores, the Mexican bakeries were there." While Huerta was exposed to a vibrant community life, her relationship with her stepfather was strained, and eventually her mother's marriage ended in divorce.

In the early 1950s, Alicia Fernández Richards married a third husband, Juan Silva. This happy union produced another daughter and endured until her mother's death. Huerta spoke admiringly of her mother's entrepreneurial and personal spirit and her expectations for her children. Again she reminisced, "My mother was always pushing me to get involved in all these youth activities. . . . We took violin lessons. I took piano lessons. I took dancing lessons. I belonged to the church choir. . . . I belonged to the church youth organization. And I was a very active Girl Scout from the time I was eight to the time I was eighteen." Mother and daughter shared a caring relationship extending into Huerta's adult years.

Although Huerta's primary family influences derived from her mother and grandfather, she did not lose contact with her father. His work history and activities inspired her. Like most people in Dawson, Juan Fernández worked in the coal mines. To supplement his wages, he also joined the migrant labor force, traveling to Colorado, Nebraska, and Wyoming for the beet harvests. Indignant over inferior working conditions, frequent accidents, and low wages, Fernández also became interested in labor issues. Leaving Dawson after the dissolution of his marriage, he continued his labor activism by becoming secretary-treasurer of the CIO local at the Terrero Camp of the American Metals Company in Las Vegas. Using his predominately Hispanic local union as a base, he won election to the New Mexico state legislature in 1938, representing San Miguel County.

He worked with other sympathetic members to promote a labor program, including the proposal of New Mexico's "Little Wagner Act" and a wages-and-hours bill. Yet due to his independent demeanor and his outspoken temperament, he lasted only one term in the state house.

After her parents' divorce, Huerta had only sporadic contact with her father, but as a sickly eleven-year-old she spent a summer traveling around New Mexico with him while he made a living as a pots-and-pans sales representative. In her adult years she had more contact with her father, particularly after he settled in Stockton, where he lived in a labor camp for a time, worked in the asparagus fields, held other odd jobs, and returned to school for a college degree. Huerta remained proud of her father's union activism, political achievements, and educational accomplishments. Remembering her father she revealed in the interview, "He was always supportive of my labor organizing," but she added he was less approving of her personal lifestyle. Their relationship remained aloof and distant until the end of his life.

As a youngster growing up in Stockton and especially after her mother's improved economic circumstances and remarriage, Huerta experienced a more middle-class upbringing. She attended Lafayette grammar school, Jackson Junior High, and graduated from Stockton High School. A former high school classmate recalled in an article in the *Stockton Record,* "When we were in school, she was very popular and outspoken. She was already an organizer, but I didn't think she'd get so serious and work for such a cause." Unlike most Hispanic women of her generation, the outgoing Huerta continued her education at Stockton College, interrupting her studies temporarily with her first marriage to Ralph Head. After her divorce, and with financial and emotional help from her mother in raising two daughters, Celeste and Lori, she returned to college and received an A.A. degree.

Huerta held a variety of jobs in Stockton before, during, and after her brief marriage. Before her marriage she managed a small neighborhood grocery store that her mother had purchased but which eventually went bankrupt. Then she obtained a job at the Naval Supply Base as the secretary to the commander in charge of public works. During and after her first divorce, she worked in the sheriff's office in records and identifications. Dissatisfied with this employment option, she resumed her education, pursuing a teaching career and obtaining a provisional teaching credential. An interview published in *Regeneración* in 1971 revealed her subsequent frustrations with this profession: "I realized one day that as a teacher I couldn't do anything for the kids who came to school barefoot and hungry."

Influenced by Postwar Activism

A part of her aroused consciousness grew out of a new wave of civic activism that swept through Mexican American communities after World War II. The postwar organization that would eventually alter her life course was the Community Service Organization (CSO), a Mexican American self-help association that was founded in Los Angeles—it was instrumental in electing Edward Roybal, the first Hispanic member of the Los Angeles City Council in the twentieth century—and then spread throughout California and the Southwest.

Huerta's transformation to social and labor activism occurred gradually. Initially suspicious of the CSO and its chief organizer, Fred Ross, when he came to Stockton in the mid 1950s, Huerta reported to *Regeneración,* "I thought he was a communist, so I went to the FBI and had him checked out. . . . See how middle class I was. In fact, I was a registered Republican at the time." Her misgivings allayed, Huerta soon became very active. Changing her party affiliation, she participated in the civic and educational programs of the CSO, registering people to vote, organizing citizenship classes, pressing local government for barrio improvements. As a result of her skills, she was hired to lobby in Sacramento for CSO legislative initiatives, such as the ultimately successful old-age pensions for noncitizens.

During the course of these activities she met and married her second husband, Ventura Huerta, who was also involved in community affairs. This relationship produced five children: Fidel, Emilio, Vincent, Alicia, and Angela. The marriage deteriorated, however, because of incompatible temperaments, but also because of disagreements over Dolores Huerta's juggling of domestic matters, child care, and her interest in civic activism. Huerta summed up the contention in an article that appeared in *The Progressive.* "I knew I wasn't comfortable in a wife's role, but I wasn't clearly facing the issue. I hedged, I made excuses, I didn't come out and tell my husband that I cared more about helping other people than cleaning our house and doing my hair." During trial separations (that eventually ended in a bitter divorce), Huerta's mother again provided her with important emotional and financial support as well as backing her CSO career, contributing baby sitting, housing, and household expenses. Speaking with this interviewer more than twenty years after her mother's early death from cancer in 1962, Huerta disclosed the depth of her loss. "When she died, it took me years to get over it. In fact, I still don't think I'm over it. . . ."

Cofounded UFW Union with César Chávez

At the same time that Dolores Huerta was struggling to balance a failing marriage, family, and work with a commitment to social concerns in the late 1950s, she became drawn to the conditions of farm workers. She joined a northern California community interest group, the Agricultural Workers Association (AWA), founded by a local priest, Father Thomas McCullough, and his parishioners. It later merged with the AFL-CIO-sponsored Agricultural

Workers Organizing Committee (AWOC), for which Huerta served as secretary-treasurer. During these years she also met César Chávez, another CSO official who shared her interests in farm labor. The two cooperated to bring rural labor issues to the attention of the more urban-oriented CSO. Frustrated with CSO unresponsiveness, first Chávez and later Huerta left the group to devote their time to organizing field workers and thus to change the course of agricultural and labor history in California with the founding of the Farm Workers Association (FWA), the precursor to the UFW, in Delano in 1962.

The full extent of the Chávez-Huerta close collaboration has only recently been documented with the availability of correspondence between the two and others. Writing to his CSO mentor, Fred Ross, in 1962, Chávez communicated, "Dolores was here [Delano] for one and a half days. I filled her in on all the plans and asked her to join the parade. . . . While here we did some work on the list of towns to work in throughout the valley. . . . Also she, Helen [Chávez's wife], and I decide [sic] on the name of the group. 'Farm Workers Assn.'"

From the founding of the union, Huerta has held decision-making posts and maintained a highly visible profile. As second in command to Chávez, she has exerted a direct influence on shaping and guiding the fortunes of the UFW. In the 1965 Delano strike, she devised strategy and led workers on picket lines. She was the union's first contract negotiator, founding the department and directing it in the early years. In these and other positions Huerta fought criticism based both on gender and ethnic stereotyping. Reacting to Huerta's uncompromising and forceful style, one grower exclaimed in a 1976 story in *The Progressive,* "Dolores Huerta is crazy. She is a violent woman, where women, especially Mexican women, are usually peaceful and calm." Such attacks highlighted the extent of her challenge to the political, social, and economic power of California agribusiness, as well as to patriarchy.

Another major responsibility for Huerta was the directorship of the table grape boycott in New York City and later her assignment as the East Coast boycott coordinator in 1968 and 1969. Her critical leadership there, the primary distribution point for grapes, contributed to the success of the national boycott effort in mobilizing unions, political activists, Hispanic associations, community organizations, religious supporters, peace groups, student protestors, and concerned consumers. In New York Huerta also became aware of the potency of the emerging feminist movement through her contacts with Gloria Steinem. As a result of this influence, Huerta began to incorporate a feminist critique into her human rights philosophy. As reported in Ronald Taylor's book on the union, Huerta explained her approach: "The whole thrust of our boycott is to get as many supporters as you can." After five years, the growing power of this grassroots coalition across the nation finally forced Coachella and Delano grape producers to negotiate the historic contracts of 1970.

Huerta's organizing expertise and inspiration were felt again when she returned to New York to administer the lettuce, grape, and Gallo wine boycotts of the 1970s. The concerted pressure of the renewed cross-class and cross-cultural cooperation in New York City and in other major cities across the U.S. resulted in the passage of the Agricultural Labor Relations Act (ALRA) in 1975, the first law to recognize the collective bargaining rights of farm workers in California.

In the midst of boycott duties and a heavy traveling and speaking schedule, Huerta began a third relationship—with Richard Chávez, César's brother. This liaison produced Juanita, María Elena, Ricky, and Camilla, bringing the total number of her children to 11. Huerta alluded in her interview to the sacrifices her position placed on all her children as a result of her frequent absences: "I don't feel proud of the suffering that my kids went through. I feel very bad and guilty about it, but by the same token I know that they learned a lot in the process."

During the late 1970s, Huerta assumed the directorship of the union's Citizenship Participation Day Department (CPD), the political arm of the UFW, as she carried the union's battle to protect the new farm labor law into the legislative arena in Sacramento. In the 1980s she was involved in another ambitious UFW project, the founding of Radio Campesina, the union's radio station, KUFW. Her schedule continued to accommodate speaking engagements, fund raising, publicizing the renewed grape boycott of the 1980s, and testifying before state and congressional committees on a wide range of issues, including pesticides, health problems of field workers, Hispanic political issues, and immigration policy.

Severly Injured During Peaceful Demonstration

At great personal cost Huerta has committed her energies to the UFW as an outspoken leader, executive board member, administrator, lobbyist, contract negotiator, picket captain, and lecturer. She has been arrested more than 20 times and suffered a life-threatening injury in a 1988 peaceful demonstration against the policies of then presidential candidate George Bush, who was campaigning in San Francisco. Rushed to the hospital after a clubbing by baton-swinging police officers, Huerta underwent emergency surgery in which her spleen was removed. She remained hospitalized to recover from the operation and six broken ribs. According to a 1991 report in the *Los Angeles Times*, the incident caused the police department to change its rules regarding crowd control and police discipline; another result was a record financial settlement to Huerta as a consequence of the personal assault.

Recovering from this medical setback, Huerta gradually resumed her work for the farm workers in the 1990s, a period of time when conservative political forces seemed triumphant, awareness of the farm workers' cause had dimmed, and the union itself went through a difficult process of internal reassessment and restructuring. Still Huerta asserted that the UFW legacy remains strong for the Hispanic community and beyond. Towards the end of her interview with this contributor, she affirmed, "I think we brought to the world, the United States anyway, the whole idea of boycotting as a nonviolent tactic. I think we showed the world that nonviolence can work to make social change. . . . I think we have laid a pattern of how farm workers are eventually going to get out of their bondage. It may not happen right now in our foreseeable future, but the pattern is there and farm workers are going to make it."

Sources:

Books

Day, Mark, *Forty Acres: Cesar Chavez and the Farm Workers*, Praeger, 1971.

Dunne, John Gregory, *Delano: The Story of the California Grape Strike*, Farrar, 1976.

Levy, Jacques, *Cesar Chavez: Autobiography of La Causa*, Norton, 1975.

London, Joan, and Henry Anderson, *So Shall Ye Reap*, Thomas Crowell, 1970.

Majka, Linda C., and Theo J. Majka, *Farm Workers, Agribusiness, and the State*, Temple University Press, 1982.

Matthiessen, Peter, *Sal Si Puedes: Cesar Chavez and the New American Revolution*, Random House, 1969.

Meister, Dick, and Anne Loftis, *A Long Time Coming, The Struggle to Unionize America's Farm Workers*, Macmillan, 1977.

The New Mexico Blue Book, State Official Register, 1939-1940, Optic Publishing Company, 1941.

Taylor, Ronald B., *Chavez and the Farm Workers*, Beacon Press, 1975.

Periodicals

Baer, Barbara L., "Stopping Traffic: One Woman's Cause," *The Progressive*, September, 1975, pp. 38-40.

Baer, Barbara L., and Glenna Matthews, "'You Find a Way': The Women of the Boycott," *Nation*, February 23, 1974, pp. 232-38.

Bakersfield Californian, January 25, 1991, p. A1-2.

Carranza, Ruth, "From the Fields into the History Books," *Intercambios Femeniles*, winter, 1989, pp. 11-12.

Coburn, Judith, "Dolores Huerta: La Pasionaria of the Farmworkers," *Ms.*, November, 1976, pp. 11-16.

"Dolores Huerta Talks About Republicans, Cesar, Children, and Her Home Town," *Regeneración*, Volume 2, number 4, 1975, pp. 20-24.

"Labor Heroines: Dolores Huerta," *Union W.A.G.E.*, July-August, 1974, p. 6.

Los Angeles Times, January 25, 1991, p. A3; February 14, p. E5.

Murphy, Jean, "Unsung Heroine of La Causa," *Regeneración,* Volume 1, number 11, 1971, p. 20.

Rose, Margaret, "'From the Fields to the Picket Line: Huelga Women and the Boycott,' 1965-1975," *Labor History,* summer, 1990, pp. 271-293.

Rose, Margaret, "Traditional and Nontraditional Patterns of Female Activism in the United Farm Workers of America, 1962 to 1980," *Frontiers,* Volume 11, number 1, 1990, pp. 26-92.

Santa Fe New Mexican, November 10, 1938.

Stockton Record, March 2, 1986.

"A Woman's Place Is . . . on the Picket Line!," *El Malcriado,* July 1, 1970, pp. 16-18.

Other

Huerta, Dolores, interviews with Margaret Rose, March 16, 1984, February 4, 1985, February 8, 1985, February 12, 1985, February 19, 1985, (La Paz) Keene, California, and February 26, 1985, Bakersfield, California.

Rose, Margaret Eleanor, "Women in the United Farm Workers: A Study of Chicana and Mexicana Participation in a Labor Union, 1950 to 1980" (dissertation), University of California, Los Angeles, 1983.

—*Sketch by Margaret Rose*

I-K

Marta Istomin
(1936-)
Artistic director

Marta Istomin's artistic talent, language abilities, and administrative cunning distinguish her as one of the top art administrators in the world. During her decade-long tenure as artistic director at the Kennedy Center for the Performing Arts in Washington, D.C., she elevated the stature of the performing arts center in the areas of music, opera, dance, and ballet. With an integrated offering pairing promising young musicians with established stars, Istomin used her position to broaden the Kennedy Center's audience and to silence those critics who insinuated that her only achievement prior to her Kennedy Center post was being twice married to famous men. "In general I think more needs to be done to encourage the appreciation of music for itself rather than through superstars," she once told the *Baltimore Sun*. In 1992 she was named president of the Manhattan School of Music in New York City, the largest private conservatory in the United States. "Ultimately, I think all conservatories have the same goal," she observed in *New York Newsday*. "We want to produce a few students of world quality—that's all there are in any generation. And then we want to develop students who will go out and fill those places in orchestras and conservatories throughout the world."

Born on November 2, 1936, in Humacao, Puerto Rico, Istomin grew up in a musical family, with parents and relatives playing in chamber groups. Her father, Aguiles Montañez, was a lawyer and accountant and her mother, Angelica, had secretarial skills. Together they started a school teaching accounting and secretarial skills. The oldest of three children, Martita began playing the violin when she was five and her talents grew under the tutelage of her uncle, a music critic, who helped found a music society and brought many professional musicians to Puerto Rico to perform. This uncle encouraged her to switch to the cello when she was nine because "there was no female cellist on the island, and he thought it was so beautiful and romantic," Istomin told the *Washingtonian*. With ensembles gathering in her parent's home on weekends, Istomin began

Marta Istomin

receiving accolades from gathering musicians for her playing.

Istomin was 12 when her uncle took her to New York City to audition at the prestigious Mannes School of Music. She was accepted and given a scholarship to study under Lieff Rosanoff, a renowned cellist whose mentor had been the internationally acclaimed Pablo Casals. The summer of her first year in school, she went with her uncle and Rosanoff to a music festival in Prades, France, where she first met Casals, who was presiding over an annual music festival. Because Casals' mother was Puerto Rican, the two immediately had something in common besides the cello. Istomin auditioned for him and he agreed to take her on as a student after she finished her training at Mannes.

Life with Pablo Casals

When Istomin turned 17 she became Casals' pupil. She moved with her mother to Prades, France, the village where the expatriate Casals, who left Spain during the Spanish Civil War, had taken residence. Casals was both a musical legend and an international symbol of liberty and courage. As a show of support for Spaniards, Casals left the concert stage permanently following World War II after the Allies refused to depose Spanish dictator Francisco Franco and the United Nations officially recognized him. It was Istomin who eventually convinced Casals to return to the performance stage on behalf of world causes, leading to his 1962 performance in the White House for John F. Kennedy.

Istomin recalls Casals as a "taskmaster. He taught me to really understand the science of technique," she told the *Washingtonian.* "He used to say that music, each note, was like nature, always different. You would never see the sun rise the same way." Istomin was her own taskmaster as well, as Casals remembered in his biography, *Joys and Sorrows: Reflections:* "Of all the pupils I have taught, Martita was one of the best. I was impressed from the outset not only by her musical talent, but by her remarkable aptitude—I have never had a student who learned more rapidly or worked with greater discipline."

Istomin offered to help Casals with his correspondence, and soon she became his secretary and assisted him with his annual Prades Festival. Convincing him to go Puerto Rico to establish a musical festival, Istomin used his name and her administrative acumen to establish the international Casals Festival, the Puerto Rico Symphony Orchestra, and the Conservatory of Music. During the rehearsal of the first annual Casals Festival, Casals had a heart attack. Marta nursed him back to health and vowed never to leave him.

They were married four months later. He was 80 and she was 20. "People were gossiping," Istomin told *Washington/ Baltimore Theatre Guide.* "My parents were dead set against it. They did not come to the wedding and my father did not speak to me for several years." Although not performing himself, Casals presided over many festivals. Indeed, Prades had become a mecca for the world's greatest instrumentalists and pianists. Because Casals always wanted Istomin at his side, she learned a great deal about musicians and how to work with artists. "I never remember leaving him for more than a day in 17 years," she told *United Press International.*

Istomin's own career as a musician was short. She explained her decision to stop performing to the *Washingtonian,* saying: "To be a musician you have to be a slave to the instrument. You cannot wing things. . . . Music exists in the moment only, so everything must be exactly right." Her last recital was in 1965 at a ceremony in Puerto Rico honoring her father and allowing her to reconcile with him.

Two years after Casals died in 1973 at the age of 96, Istomin married another internationally acclaimed musi-

cian, pianist Eugene Istomin. After Casals died, many of the widow's friends were concerned about her. Eugene Istomin, a Casals protégé and the youngest musician ever to perform at Casals' Prades Festival, was one of those friends. "He would call. But a lot of people would call," recalled Marta Istomin in *Musical America.* "Other people kept calling less and less often, as naturally happens. But Eugene kept calling consistently—even more. So one day we discovered there was more than just that."

The couple has not let Casals' legacy overshadow their lives together: "There was no jealousy," Istomin told *Washingtonian,* "because we both loved Casals. He is a common denominator." In fact, Marta Istomin is Casals' primary chronicler in her role as cofounder and vice president of the Pablo Casals Foundation in Barcelona, Spain. She maintains the Casals Archives, a collection of photographs, letters, clippings, programs, manuscripts and music. The archives will eventually be divided and donated to the Casals Museum in Spain and to another museum in Puerto Rico.

"[My husband] has added other dimensions to my life, in art, in literature," Istomin told *Musical America.* "But most important, he gave me a sense of reality. I had been living in Casals' world, an unreal world, the world of his perceptions. . . . But with Eugene, he says: 'This is the world. You must do in it what you feel you must do.'" She credits him with giving her the confidence to accept the Kennedy Center post.

Kennedy Center Years

At the Kennedy Center for the Performing Arts, Istomin truly developed her own talents. Concentrating on American composers, musicians, and ballet companies as well as small scale orchestras and ensembles, chamber and string music, new and avant-garde music, and up-and-coming young artists, she brought the center much closer to its congressional mandate of being the nation's cultural center. In the *Washingtonian,* Istomin recalled being "intimidated" when first offered the job. "But the challenge got to me, how can I turn it down? It will mean so much to my people to have a Latin American in this job."

Soon she initiated the successful Terrace Concerts chamber music series, exposing audiences to lesser-known, but promising singers and instrumentalists and reviving interest in chamber music. She also coordinated the "Washington Front and Center!" series showcasing the best local musicians. In 1989, as part of her commitment to American artists and companies, she initiated a commissioning project that would enable six major American ballet companies to premiere original works at the Kennedy Center. Many viewed this as a bold step, considering the rarity of ballet commissions.

Her international experience and ties enabled her to attract many international groups and artists as well. Fluent in English, Spanish, French, Catalan, and conversational in German and Italian, she became known as Washington, D.C.'s undeclared cultural ambassador. One of her biggest musical coups was attracting Richard Wagner's colossal *Der Ring des Nibelungen,* the German masterpiece of the romantic period. The series of four operas was one of the most complex programs to be staged at the Kennedy Center. Negotiations with the Berlin Opera and the West German government took more than three years.

Her rapport with the performers also earned her praise. As acclaimed violinist Isaac Stern once told the *Washingtonian,* "Everyone knows that there is now someone at the Kennedy Center you can talk to in professional music terms and who will take chances. There is a language and knowledge that goes into making music that you cannot learn. You have to grow up in the field as she did." Istomin approaches her administrative responsibilities with a performer's sensitivity in mind. "I feel that one of the responsibilities of the arts leaders is to encourage and be firm and determine to present what they, as leaders, feel is true art and not be led mainly by trends and sometimes media-fabricated publicity," she declared in the *Washingtonian.* Moreover, Istomin told *United Press International* in 1981, "I know what artistic expression is. I've lived with it all my life. Perhaps I have that little extra understanding and feeling that I can contribute to the other part of artistic endeavor which is putting all those elements together so that unique moment can happen."

Following her resignation from the Kennedy Center in 1990, Istomin commented in *Lear's:* "I feel I've lived four lives, so I'm ready for my fifth." Shortly thereafter she accepted the position of director general of the Evian Music Festival in France, an internationally acclaimed annual event featuring world-class orchestral and chamber music, chamber opera, and soloists. She has also acted as a consultant on a number of independent projects, including the Casals Festival in Puerto Rico, before joining the Manhattan School of Music in July of 1992. Istomin has won many awards in her long career, including the Distinction Award from the National Conference on Puerto Rican Women in 1990 and the Hispanic Achievement Award for the Arts in 1991.

Sources:

Books

Casals, Pablo, *Joys and Sorrows: Reflections,* Simon & Schuster, 1970.

Periodicals

Christian Science Monitor, August 3, 1976.
Lear's, November, 1990, pp. 88-92, 146.
Morning Sun (Baltimore), May 4, 1980.
Musical America, November, 1986, pp. 4-7, 36-37.
New York Newsday, March 19, 1992.
United Press International, May 31, 1981.
Vista, June 4, 1989.
Washington/Baltimore Theatre Guide, winter/spring, 1989.
Washingtonian, December, 1987.
Washington Post, March 24, 1980.

—*Sketch by Jonathan J. Higuera*

Amparo Iturbi
(1899-1969)
Concert pianist

The younger sister of one of the world's most famous, brilliant, and flamboyant pianists, Amparo Iturbi had a hard act to follow most of her life. A polished, well-known, and gifted pianist in her own right, Iturbi nevertheless spent most of her musical career in the shadow of her celebrated brother, José. Despite world tours, hundreds of concerts, record albums, widespread critical and popular acclaim, and performances on radio, in movies and on television, little information exists on Iturbi in comparison to José. Although they were extremely close, and José considered her one of the top women musicians in the world, he was fond of repeating one of his favorite quips, quoted in *Time:* "I am my sister's worst enemy."

Iturbi's life and career were inexorably entwined with her brother's from her birth in Valencia, Spain, on March 12, 1899. Her mother was Maria Theresa Baguena Iturbi and her father was a pianomaker and tuner. By the time she was three, she had developed an unusual musical talent for singing, but seven-year-old José's prowess at the piano was already well established throughout the neighborhood. When Amparo was six, José was already earning a living as an accompanist at a singing academy. For Iturbi, the piano soon won out over her dreams to become an opera singer, and she studied diligently under her first teacher, Maria Jordan, and later, José. Although she occasionally bristled in later life when being referred to as her brother's pupil, she recalled idolizing José in her youth. In 1937, she told a reporter for the *New York Times,* "When we were small I used to follow him around everywhere. Everything he did, I did. That is why I play with the same technique he uses. My hands are like his."

When José left for the Paris Conservatory at 15, Iturbi wanted to follow him, but her brother rejected the idea. Many years later, he told *Time* the reason for his refusal: "It's all work. One gets nothing but exhaustion. And [for her] it's not necessary." At 14, Iturbi gave her first piano recital at the Valencia Conservatory of Music, then another in Barcelona under the tutelage of Eduardo Chavarri. In

Amparo Iturbi

the audience was the renowned Spanish composer, Enrique Granados, who so delighted in her performance that he invited her to play for his pupils at his Academia Granados. Following the recital, Granados performed some of his own compositions for the young girl. At the peak of her career, Iturbi was considered one of the foremost interpreters of Granados's music (particularly his difficult *Goyescas*), an accomplishment some critics believe was inspired by this early experience. A 1957 review in the *New York Times* was typical of those received for her performance of the Granados piece: "It took real courage to present in its entirety so demanding a suite, and the results could be greeted with admiration."

Makes Concert Debut in Paris

At 18, Iturbi arrived in Paris and gave her first concert six years later in 1924. The performance met with such success that she was soon in demand all over Europe, giving solo concerts in France, Holland, Belgium, Italy, England, and Spain. She lived in Paris until 1937, when she and her mother moved to the United States. Reunited with her brother, who achieved celebrity as the most famous Spanish pianist during the period immediately prior to World War II, Iturbi was enthusiastically received in the United States. She made her New York debut at Lewisohn Stadium on July 7, 1937, appearing with José before an audience of 12,000. They performed 18th-century Austrian composer Wolfgang Amadeus Mozart's concerto for two pianos in E flat, a work that Mozart allegedly wrote for himself and his sister. The evening, according to many commentators, was an unqualified success. Iturbi performed two encores for the cheering crowd, and critic Noel Straus wrote in the *New York Times:* "Her attainments so closely rival [José's] that there was little to choose between them. Her tone, feeling for phrase and nuance, and even her approach to her work were strikingly akin to those of her brother."

Iturbi did not fare as well in her December 24 concert with the Philharmonic Orchestra that same year. Called in as a last-minute replacement for ailing Brazilian pianist Guiomar Novaes, Iturbi attempted the solo part in 19th-century German composer Ludwig van Beethoven's concerto in G major. Recalling her triumphant debut at Lewisohn, Straus wrote in the *New York Times:* "[The musical selections at her debut] were more congenial to her talents than the Beethoven concerto, which made far greater demands on her powers as interpreter. Possibly no woman should ever attempt this particular creation of the Bonn master, for in spite of its restrained character, it is completely masculine in essence."

Occasional mixed reviews aside—many of them contrasting her more delicate style with that of her more dazzling brother—Iturbi was immensely popular during a performing career that spanned four decades. She played in nearly every state in the union, with major orchestras under the batons of John Barbirolli, Otto Klemperer, Ignace Strasfogel, Eugene Ormandie, Alexander Smallens, Frederic Stock, and many others. During World War II, she played hundreds of concerts for the United States Army and Navy, and in 1944 alone she performed 304 concerts in seven months, covering 57,000 miles over the African front. Although she told *Time* in 1948 that concertizing "is a crazy life," she had lined up a 30-concert tour for that fall. In one season she crossed and recrossed the Atlantic three times for concert tours in England and Europe. Various critics praised her impeccable technique and musical phrasing. In one solo concert in New York in 1944, a writer for the *New York Times* stated that Iturbi "again showed her remarkable talent and extraordinary similarity to her brother as an artist. . . . Miss Iturbi's technique is comprehensive and sure, notable for its fleetness, distinctness and ease. She received an ovation at the end of the Fantasia and played three encores . . . with dash and brilliance."

Performs with Brother José Iturbi

Audiences turned out in droves to see the Iturbis play as a team. Of their program at Carnegie Hall in 1938, a commentator for the *New York Times* said, "Miss Iturbi's methods of applying color and nuance, her attacks and her tone resembled those of her brother, and the result was balance and cohesiveness of the two instruments. Mr. Iturbi was perhaps the dominant personality in the concerted works, but his sister held up her share with poise and assurance." Some commentators believe that such reviews appropriately described the siblings' offstage relationship as well. Iturbi—poised, gracious, and somewhat shy—was a distinct counterpoint to the more outspoken, charming José who loved the limelight. In her autobiography *September Child*, Jean Dalrymple—who later became the duo's personal manager and publicist—described Iturbi as "slim and beautiful, like a Spanish painting." José, in addition to receiving more press for his performing abilities, often made headlines for his opinions regarding women's unsuitability for musical careers, describing the feminine gender in the *New York Times* as "temperamentally limited, making it impossible for them to attain the same standards as male musicians." Despite such statements, Iturbi never publicly refuted her brother.

In 1940 Iturbi's life was shaken by the death of her mother. More tragedy followed with the suicide of her niece Maria, José's only child, in 1946. The incident occurred after years of hearings in which José petitioned the court to grant him full custody of his two granddaughters. According to a report in the *New York Times,* he asserted that his daughter was "not the proper person" to have charge of the children. Following this saga, 28-year-old Maria shot herself in her father's Beverly Hills home. Iturbi and her daughter Amparin had also moved to the city and lived nearby. In the same year, however, Iturbi began to share briefly in her brother's more extensive movie career, appearing in the Metro-Goldwyn-Mayer (MGM) film, *Holiday in Mexico*. She later had a role in MGM's *That Midnight Kiss* in 1949. Iturbi and José also recorded numerous albums together for RCA Victor and Angel Records, although she described the recording process in *Time* as "the ultimate torture of our century."

In later years, Iturbi turned to teaching full-time. Dalrymple, in an interview with Julie Catalano, said that Iturbi "didn't care about wandering around and going places to make a small amount of money. She preferred to stay in Beverly Hills where she had a beautiful home and lots of very fine pupils." Among her students was pianist, composer, and teacher Bruce Sutherland. Iturbi's final concert was in Los Angeles on October 2, 1968. She made her last concert appearance in New York in November of that year. On Christmas Day, however, she was hospitalized at Cedars of Lebanon Hospital in Los Angeles with a brain tumor. She died in her home on April 22, 1969, at age 70. One of her last visitors was Spanish guitarist Andres Segovia, who played at her bedside. On November 14, 1971, her brother performed a memorial concert in her honor in Los Angeles. José died of a heart attack at age 84 on June 29, 1980. In 1986, Marion Seabury, José's longtime secretary, established the Iturbi Foundation in Beverly Hills, a non-profit organization which helps young professionals in all artistic fields.

Sources:

Books

Dalrymple, Jean, *September Child*, Dodd, 1963.

O'Connell, Charles, *The Other Side of the Record*, Knopf, 1947.

Periodicals

Newsweek, May 5, 1969, p. 78.
New York Times, January 23, 1936, p. 25; May 2, 1937, section XI, p. 10; July 8, 1937, p. 21; September 19, 1937, section XI, p. 12; December 24, 1937, p. 21; February 6, 1938, section X, p. 7; February 8, 1938, p. 16; May 8, 1939, p. 20; January 3, 1940, p. 21; July 24, 1944, p. 18; April 18, 1946, p. 29; April 23, 1969, p. 47; June 29, 1980, p. 20.
Time, July 5, 1948, p. 46; May 2, 1969, p. 80.

Other

Dalrymple, Jean, interview with Julie Catalano, August 18, 1992.
Seabury, Marion, correspondence with Julie Catalano, September 18, 1992.

—Sketch by Julie Catalano

Cleofas Martínez Jaramillo
(1878-1956)
Writer, folklorist, businesswoman

The writings of Cleofas Martínez Jaramillo are significant to Hispanic culture for their depiction of cultural tradition. Her books range from her 1955 autobiography *Romance of a Little Village Girl,* to a collection of her mother's oral stories, to her cookbook of traditional Mexican and Spanish cuisine. Jaramillo's writings are linked by her concern for the preservation of Spanish customs and rituals in her home of New Mexico, which she saw vanishing as Hispanics moved into the modern American age.

Jaramillo was born to Martina Lucero Martínez and M. Martínez on December 6, 1878, in Arroyo Hondo, a small northern New Mexico village. Her family was influential in New Mexico; her paternal great-grandfather, Manuel Martínez, had a Tierra Amarilla land grant. Her father was a man who prospered because of his energy and his various business interests, which included sheep and cattle raising, farming, and mercantile. In *Romance of a Little Village Girl,* Jaramillo remembers her mother working as hard as her father in the store the family owned in Arroyo Hondo, "If my father was out busy . . . and someone came who wanted something at the store, mother dropped her work and went and waited on the customers. Our store supplied the simple needs of the people, from dry goods and groceries to patent medicines, which mother would tell the people how to use."

At the age of nine, Cleofas attended the Loretto Convent School in Taos, New Mexico, and later was enrolled at the Loretto Academy in Santa Fe, New Mexico. On July 27, 1898, she married wealthy Venceslao Jaramillo, an influential businessman, legislator, and politician in Santa Fe. They lived a life of comfort but also one of tragedy: two of their children died young and a third child, Angelina, was only four years old when Venceslao Jaramillo died. Although he had been very wealthy, Venceslao left his business affairs in disarray and his widow in debt. Jaramillo became an astute businesswoman, managing his affairs after her husband's death. Her tragedies continued, however, when Angelina was murdered at the age of seventeen. Cleofas was devastated and recorded this difficult time in her autobiography.

In *Romance*, Jaramillo describes nearly seventy years of her life. She narrates the descent from her edenic girlhood in northern New Mexico to her old age, where she laments the diminishing traditions of New Mexican Hispanic culture. The book documents the Spanish customs and rituals that governed Jaramillo's life, including the religious ceremonies, holidays, courtships, weddings, and funerals.

Because Jaramillo was interested in the history and culture of New Mexico, she wrote several books that detail her concern with the disappearance of Hispanic cultural traditions. Her mother was a storyteller, and in *Spanish Fairy Tales* Jaramillo translates twenty-five of her mother's stories into English. She actively participated in the preservation of Hispanic culture, not only through her writing but also by founding the Sociedad Folklórica in Santa Fe. She recalled in *New Mexican* that in 1935 she saw an article in *Holland Magazine* about Spanish and Mexican food and reflected: "Now, why don't we who know our customs and dishes do something about preserving the knowledge ... we who know the customs and styles of our region are letting them die out." In her cookbook, *The Genuine New Mexico Tasty Recipes* (1939), she preserved that aspect of culture embodied in native foods. In *Shadows of the Past* (1941), she describes vignettes of Hispanic culture, including a portraits series of the women in her family.

Jaramillo's work is notable for her concern and production in a time when most Hispanic women had little leisure or encouragement to write. Her narratives and stories are valuable because they preserve folk life. Her publications seek to preserve a facet of Hispanic life that she saw slipping away.

Sources:

Books

Jaramillo, Cleofas, *Cuentos del hogar* ("Spanish Fairy Stories"), The Citizen Press, 1939.

Jaramillo, Cleofas, *Shadows of the Past*, Seton Village Press, 1941.

Jaramillo, Cleofas, *The Genuine New Mexico Tasty Recipes: Potajes sabrosos*, Seton Village Press, 1939.

Jaramillo, Cleofas, *Romance of a Little Village Girl* (autobiography), The Naylor Company, 1955, pp. 11-12.

Rebolledo, Tey Diana, "Las Escritoras" in *Pasó por Aquí*, edited by Erlinda Gonzales-Berry, The University of New Mexico Press, 1989.

Periodicals

Journal of Narrative Technique, Volume 20, number 2, 1990.
New Mexican, February 26, 1954, p. 26.
New Mexico Historical Review, Volume 58, number 2, 1983.
Santa Fe Scene, August, 1958.

—Sketch by Tey Diana Rebolledo

Mari-Luci Jaramillo
(1928-)
Educator, ambassador, businesswoman

Mari-Luci Jaramillo holds the position of assistant vice president for Educational Testing Services, one of the largest non-profit testing corporations in the world. Her career in education spans nearly four decades, though Jaramillo took a brief break from her educational career to serve as U.S. ambassador to Honduras under U.S. President Jimmy Carter. "Being able to serve my country at that level was a wonderful experience," she recalled during her interview with contributor Michelle Vachon. "I knew that everything I said or did reflected on the United States. I had the opportunity to carry the best of my country and translate the best of my host country towards making the two nations understand each other." Jaramillo's post at the Honduras American Embassy had come as a surprise to her. "I was not rich and had never participated in party politics, two things I thought were essential to political appointments. The only explanation I can offer is that many Chicano representatives close to President Carter were aware of my involvement in Latin American educational projects." Jaramillo handled her diplomatic duties in her usual way: "I worked like a fool. I'm a workaholic and I don't mind being labelled as such."

Jaramillo was born in Las Vegas, New Mexico, on June 19, 1928. Her father was originally from Durango, Mexico, and her mother from Las Vegas. The second of three children, she grew up in Las Vegas, then a small town of 14,000 inhabitants. When she was still a child, Jaramillo

Mari-Luci Jaramillo

developed her life-long habit of getting up at four or five o'clock in the morning. "We were poor and did not have enough wood to keep the house warm at night," she remembered in her interview. "So my mother would get up and bundle me up in the chair, with only my hands sticking out to do my homework." She attended public school and won all the awards conferred by her high school. "My father demanded academic perfection. After graduation, I pursued the education track to become a teacher because it was the only career opportunity in town—I could complete the program in four years and my friends had already enrolled in it. Luckily for me, I loved teaching once I started."

After her first year in college, Jaramillo quit her studies to marry a school teacher. They moved to a small rural town where she held a series of odd jobs while raising her three children. Although she had earlier given up the idea of going back to college, she resumed studying on her own, and soon began classes. "For years, I was taking care of my children, holding a job, and studying, all at the same time. During my last semester, a teacher helped me financially, which allowed me to concentrate on school." In 1955, she obtained a baccalaureate from the New Mexico Highlands University in Las Vegas, with a major in education and a minor in Spanish and English. Shortly after, she secured a position with the West Las Vegas school system where she was to remain for a decade. She served as an elementary school teacher and eventually as language arts supervisor for all of the county's schools.

Reaches Out to the Hispanic Community

While she was teaching elementary school, Jaramillo had been working actively to increase the level of education in the Hispanic community. "Growing up where I did and seeing the desperate need for education among people who looked like me made me believe that we could break the poverty hold on Chicanos if we educated ourselves," she told Vachon. "I started reaching out to help and it became a way of life. I did all I could on my own, trying to teach English and reading, and trying to reach adults as well as children. When I got out of my small community, I realized that the problem was everywhere, that Hispanics were not really getting their fair share in educational and professional opportunities." In 1965, Jaramillo started lecturing at the University of New Mexico, in Albuquerque. She first taught English as a second language and conducted classes in Spanish for Latin American students. Later, she joined the Department of Elementary Education as assistant professor, eventually becoming a professor and chairperson for the department.

Jaramillo greeted the emergence of the civil rights movement in the late 1960s and early 1970s with enthusiasm. "Suddenly, I had the chance to take on larger projects. Among others, I took part in the university's Cultural Awareness Center activities. We would meet with administrators, counsellors, teachers, parents and anyone else willing to listen to tell them that maybe Chicanos and Hispanics are not your average father, mother, two-point-three children and a dog and a cat and a white fence families; that they bring a beautiful language and a unique culture with them; that we shouldn't try to kill it off, but instead that we should look for these qualities and nurture them while we teach English." Through these activities, Jaramillo extended her involvement nationally and internationally. In conjunction with the U.S. Agency for International Development and the university's Latin American educational programs, she travelled to Argentina, Columbia, Ecuador, Venezuela, and to every country in Central America to train teachers and to hold workshops on education and school development. "I saw similarities in the needs of the poor across the world. I did everything I could to call attention to it and to be part of the solution."

Appointed U.S. Ambassador to Honduras

When Jimmy Carter became president in 1976, he asked Jaramillo to serve as ambassador to Honduras. "I could hardly believe my ears when I got the phone call," she said in her interview. "During the presidential election campaign, the Democrats had created a talent bank that included the names of minorities and women to be considered for appointment. A friend of mine put my curriculum vitae in it without my knowing. Since I had not revised it for a long time, I was not expecting anything out of it. But many Chicanos working on the Carter campaign knew that I spoke Spanish fluently, that I was bicultural, and that I had repeatedly visited Latin America." Between 1977 and 1980,

Jaramillo and her second husband lived in Tegucigalpa, Honduras. She served as chief of mission for six government agencies and 500 Peace Corps volunteers operating in the country, and attended to the American community of about 2,000 people. "It was a fairy tale," recalled Jaramillo in her interview. "It was also hard work. The Central American region was starting to flare up. When the trouble began in Nicaragua, many Nicaraguans fled to Honduras, which is next door. Also, the Honduran military establishment had just abdicated power. We undertook to assist in holding the first free election in years. It was so exciting to watch a country go from military rule to a democracy. The election took place after my departure, but I am proud to say that Honduras has been choosing its president through democratic elections ever since."

Jaramillo returned to Washington, D.C., in 1980 to become deputy assistant secretary for inter-American affairs at the U.S. Department of State. Two months later, Jimmy Carter lost the presidential election. "I stayed at the Department of State until March 1981 and then left of my own accord," she pointed out during her interview. "I would have liked to continue representing my country abroad, but I really belonged to the Carter administration. I believed in human rights and in the work done by the administration. It would have been difficult to represent a government with which I disagreed on major issues. Besides, I was not asked to stay." Upon leaving the State Department, Jaramillo returned to the University of New Mexico. "I was not expecting to get a job in the middle of the semester. But they told me that they had been waiting for my return and that they had a position for me." Jaramillo became special assistant to the president. "I had been a university professor and administrator, but this was a novelty. My tasks included representing the president whenever he could not attend a function. The position was interesting and it gave me time to get my bearings and settle down." In 1982, she was named associate dean for the university's College of Education and in 1985 the university's vice president for student affairs.

Enters the Corporate World

Two years later, Educational Testing Services (ETS) hired Jaramillo as vice president for its San Francisco Bay area office, located in Emeryville, California. "ETS has one of the most specialized staffs in the field of developing and administering tests. Headquartered in Princeton, New Jersey, the non-profit corporation contracts with universities, departments of education, and professional organizations worldwide." In 1992, Jaramillo secured the position of assistant vice president for field services at ETS, and now administers the corporation's eight U.S. field offices.

Jaramillo admits that her concept of education has changed throughout the years. "I used to think that if you educate people, they will be able to make it," she explained in her interview. "I found out that it isn't so. Some highly educated people cannot get into the system for a variety of reasons. Today I counsel students to learn about the importance of economics and the political aspects of our democracy regardless of their field of expertise. 'Know the system and make it work for you,' I tell them. You have to understand how the business world operates and what it means when our government talks about protecting American interests in a foreign country. You have to see yourself in relation to currents events in order to participate. Politically, I believe that our American system works as long as you participate in it. You must vote and make your voice heard. Otherwise you will be left out."

Jaramillo has accumulated numerous awards in the course of her career. In 1986, Jaramillo was named co-recipient of the Harvard Graduate School of Education's Anne Roe Award honoring leading educators who have contributed, in the field of education, to women's professional growth. In 1988, the Miller Brewing Company recognized her as one of the country's Outstanding Hispanic Educators, and *Hispanic Business* magazine named her one of the 100 Most Influential Hispanics in the United States. In 1990, the Mexican American Women's National Association conferred on Jaramillo the Primera Award for being the first Hispanic woman to be appointed U.S. ambassador to Honduras, and the American Association for Higher Education granted her an award for Outstanding Leadership in Education in the Hispanic Community. Jaramillo participates actively in community and professional organizations. She sits on the board of directors of the Children's Television Workshop in New York, the board of trustees of the Tomas Rivera Center at Claremont University in Claremont, California, and on the board of directors of the New Mexico Highlands University Foundation. She also serves as a minority recruiter for the U.S. Department of State.

Jaramillo is divorced and lives in Emeryville, California. "Looking back—would I do it again?," she wondered during her interview. "I think that I have occasionally made a difference in my children's and students' lives. Many of my students call me after all these years, and I am close to my children and grandchildren. Yes, I have enjoyed every minute of it!"

Sources:

Jaramillo, Mari-Luci, interview with Michelle Vachon, September 20, 1992.

—*Sketch by Michelle Vachon*

Jimenez Maes, Petra
See **Maes, Petra Jimenez**

Michelle Kearney

(1945-)

Banker, sales executive

Throughout her career, Michelle Kearney has found success in several different fields. She's been a translation supervisor for the Spanish Unit at the United Nations, an account officer with the international banking group of a major bank, and a vice president of two successful film studios. Since 1978, she has concentrated her attention on the entertainment industry—first as the vice president of international sales for Lorimar Telepictures in New York City, and later as the senior vice president of Carolco pictures, also located in New York City. Kearney is considered a specialist in foreign television sales to the Latin American markets and was featured in the October, 1991, issue of *Hispanic Business* magazine as one of the 100 most influential Hispanics in the United States. "I believe that probably my most important accomplishment was to have been able to operate in the American society with no problems at all," explained Kearney in a telephone interview with Pam Berry. "If you come here and intend to live in this society, you must blend and be part of this society. You have to retain your culture but you have to blend and enrich the American culture also."

Kearney attributes much of her success to being brought up in a family of professionals who firmly believed in the value of education. She was born in Soato, Colombia, in 1945 to Maria Ayala, an elementary school teacher, and Carlos Estpinan, a businessman. Kearney attended the Ponticia Universidad Javeriana in Bogata, Colombia, for two years prior to getting married and moving to the United States in 1970. Her husband, Gerald Kearney, works for the airline industry, and the couple has one son.

Begins International Sales Career

Kearney worked as a translator in the United Nations' Spanish Unit from 1973 to 1975. Although she was only there for a brief period, she found the experience very rewarding. "It's a place where you have the opportunity to meet people from all over the world," she said. "It gives you a better perspective of the whole world because you come in contact with other cultures." Because there were few opportunities for advancement at the United Nations, Kearney decided to investigate other career options. A friend told her that Citibank in New York City was looking for someone with a Latin American background to work as an account officer in their international banking group; she applied for the job and was hired. "Citibank was really the company that opened up the American opportunity for me," she maintained in her interview with Berry. "They really believed in me. They gave me the opportunity to

prove what I could do and, in the beginning, it was difficult because my English was not very good."

In 1978, Kearney took advantage of an opportunity to join a start-up venture—Telepictures Corporation, which later became Lorimar Telepictures, one of the most successful syndicators in the United States. She started with the company as an officer manager and later, as the company became established, moved into sales. She was responsible for several territories in Central and South America, selling television rights to broadcasters. Eventually, she was promoted to vice president of Latin American sales.

When Lorimar Telepictures was acquired by Warner Brothers and the decision was made to move the company's operations to Los Angeles, Kearney decided to resign. She joined Carolco Pictures, one of the most successful independent film studios, in 1989. Carolco produced and distributed such big hits as *Basic Instinct, Rambo,* and *Terminator 2.* As senior vice president of international sales for the studio, Kearney was instrumental in organizing the international television department. She manages all activities related to the sale of pay and free television in Latin America and Asia (excluding Japan). She also negotiates for the acquisition of television rights from independent producers. Someday, she hopes to own her own film distribution company.

Sources:

Kearney, Michelle, telephone interview with Pam Berry, September 23, 1992.

—Sketch by Pam Berry

Louise Año Nuevo Kerr

(1938-)

Educator, administrator

While other high-school teachers ignored Louise Año Nuevo Kerr, a typing instructor helped her fill out a scholarship application that forever changed the young girl's life. "I was always grateful for that, and I've always seen the irony," Kerr told interviewer D. D. Andreassi. She won the four-year *salsipuedes* ("get out if you can") scholarship, which allowed her to attend college and eventually pursue a career as a history professor and dean. Even though her professional life has revolved around universities, Kerr stated that she is not "just an ivory tower scholar. I see the university as needing to contribute in the larger world and to know what is going on out there."

Kerr was born December 24, 1938, in Denver, Colorado, to Roseana Bertha Lopez and Bonifacio Benjamin Año Nuevo. Her mother was Mexican American and her father was a native Filipino. The oldest of four children, Kerr grew up in California where her family worked on farms. "We were all migrants for a while," she said in her interview. Her father eventually became a sedentary farm worker and a sharecropper in California.

Traumatic Incident with Immigration Officers

Kerr vividly remembered a traumatic incident that occurred when she was working in a field at the age of thirteen. At the time, in the mid-1950s, there were a lot of Mexican farm workers and "often times they were not documented," Kerr said in the interview. "Immigration people came to the field doing roundups, and they stopped me and it was a terrifying experience, because you had to prove you were a citizen. . . . It was important in that day and time not to have an accent. They asked me where I was born, and I said 'St. Anthony's Hospital in Denver.' It was telling in my view of the unfair treatment of Mexicans. The idea of the oppression was for me unfair and it raised a lot of anger, because it was governmentally imposed. It was very significant in my life and maybe I've never come to grips with it."

Her life took a turn for the better when Kerr, the first person in her family to graduate from high school, won a scholarship and began attending the University of California. She graduated with a bachelor of arts degree in sociology in 1960. Six years later she earned a master's degree in history. She married Howard H. Kerr on October 4, 1963, and they had two children, Catherine and Sarah. The family moved to Illinois when Howard was offered a teaching position at the University of Chicago. "I had always assumed that what you aspired for was not to work," Kerr told this interviewer. "I was happily enjoying being home with my kids." One day in 1970, however, she was listening to the radio and was surprised to find a Spanish station. She learned there were 250,000 Hispanics living in Chicago. "I arranged to take a course to find out more about it," she recalled in the interview.

A short time later she was offered an assistant teaching post at the University of Illinois, a job she held through 1972. Kerr became a member of the Organization of American Historians in 1973 and later chaired the group's membership committee from 1982 to 1984. She also became a member of the American Historical Association in 1973. Meanwhile, she finished her course work and earned her Ph.D. in history in 1976 from the University of Illinois.

After completing her Ph.D., Kerr was offered a teaching position and fellowship at Loyola University. Luckily she was able to accept the teaching position and take a leave of absence to work on the fellowship. As a teacher she led classes focusing on United States history and the role of Hispanics in the United States. Kerr was active in many organizations, including the Illinois Humanities Council, which she was a member of from 1973 to 1982, serving as vice-chair the last two years. She was also a member of the National Council on the Humanities from 1980 to 1987.

In 1980 Kerr received a National Research Council Ford Foundation Fellowship. About the same time she was offered the position of assistant dean in the college of arts and science at Loyola. She told this interviewer that one of the reasons she took the offer was because her daughter, Catherine, was starting college and it was an opportune time to make extra money. She soon became associate dean at Loyola and continued teaching until 1988. Kerr went on to become the associate vice-chancellor of academic affairs at the University of Illinois at Chicago.

Kerr has not limited herself to academic activities. In 1986 she joined the Committee on the Status of Women and in 1989 she became involved with the Committee on Decent and Unbiased Campaign Tactics (CONDUCT). Regarding CONDUCT, Kerr told this interviewer that "its exclusive purpose is to make sure that campaigns remain on a high plain. That's been a very important organization in Chicago, especially since the election of [Chicago Mayor] Harold Washington." Her civic involvement has included work with the Salvation Army in Chicago and 4-H clubs. "In a larger professional sense, I've always seen myself as an active participant in the civic community and the community at large," Kerr related.

She has strived to maintain her work as a historian by contributing to various books and periodicals. She served as editor of *Mid-America: An Historical Review* in 1981, and in 1984 her work appeared in both *Illinois History* and *Ethnic Chicago*. Kerr has served on the editorial boards of scholarly journals, including the *Journal of American Ethnic History, Aztlan: International Journal of Chicano Studies,* and the *Journal of National Public History.* In addition, Kerr has had articles published in *Mexican-Americans in Multi-Culturalism in the United States* and *Chicanas in the Urban Mid-West: Crossing Borders.* When asked about her writing, Kerr noted that she has always considered herself a historian: "I've never given up my work in history and have in fact continued recently to publish."

Kerr's achievements have been acknowledged with several accolades including the Congressional Hispanic Caucus Humanities Award in 1979, the Illinois Humanities Council Public Humanities Award in 1984, the Mexican American Business and Professional Woman Pioneer Award in 1979, and the Young Women's Christian Association (YWCA) Metropolitan Chicago Leadership Award in Education.

In 1992, Kerr attended a Harvard University course for creative academic leadership. "I'm in the process of rethinking where I want to go next, whether I want to remain an administrator or go back to the classroom,"

Kerr said. She asserted that her goal is to "open opportunities to others, particularly to young people to help them find many options for themselves and to do the same for myself and perhaps in that respect to be a role model." Kerr maintained that she wants to raise the hopes and expectations of young people "in a way that mine had been raised for me by my family, by those who did support me and, I suppose, by myself."

Sources:

Kerr, Louise Año Nuevo, interview with D. D. Andreassi, October 6, 1992.

—Sketch by D. D. Andreassi

L

Carmela Gloria Lacayo
(1943-)
Social worker, community organizer

Carmela Gloria Lacayo first became involved in social work as a missionary for an order of nuns. Her work with the poor and elderly in California inspired her to establish the National Association for Hispanic Elderly, a nonprofit organization that provides a variety of services such as housing, job placement, and other aid to Hispanic senior citizens. She has also been appointed to a number of political positions, including vice-chair of the Democratic National Committee, member of the Census Bureau on Minority Populations, and an advisor on Social Security reform.

Lacayo was born June 28, 1943, in Chihuahua, Mexico. Her Nicaraguan father, Enrique Lacayo (now deceased), although born into a "blueblood" family, lost his fortune when he immigrated to the United States. Her Mexican mother, Mary Louise, came to the United States to work as a fashion model and dress designer. She met Lacayo's father when they both were working in Hollywood's garment industry. Lacayo told Julia Edgar in an interview how her parents provided her with the values that have shaped her life: "Even though we were really poor when we were kids, my father, because of the family he came from, had a real respect for culture and education. My mother, even though she had a third-grade education, saved money to buy an encyclopedia and put me through parochial school. None of us have ever had the wherewithal—I'm the only one in family who finished college—but there was some kind of sense of the value of education as being a leaping point for success in life. I think there is something of a desire that your parents give you to do better than they did. That's why I have such a mission to help Latino parents to understand the importance of education, to fight for decent education for kids in schools, because that's the only chance they have to change the cycle of poverty."

Joins Catholic Nunnery

When she was seventeen, Lacayo joined an order of Roman Catholic nuns that was founded in Hungary at the

Carmela Gloria Lacayo

turn of the twentieth century. She graduated in 1961 from Immaculate Heart College in Los Angeles with a bachelor of arts degree in sociology and theology. The convent's liberal teachings placed a great emphasis on social service—which Lacayo took to heart. But her personal experience also shaped her sensibilities. She became a missionary, hoping that she would be sent to Mexico, land of her mother's ancestors and her own birthplace. Instead, Lacayo was assigned to run a community center in west Oakland, California, an impoverished area filled with social and political unrest. There she became particularly active in helping the elderly, a focus that was to become her life's work. "One of the problems was that seniors were being totally ignored. Our seniors, because it was a terrible ghetto, were the isolated ones. They needed special attention," she recalled. In response to these needs, Lacayo developed a pilot program to construct senior citizen housing in Oakland and created a senior citizen group which was eventually named after her.

After a stint in Rome, Italy, where she formed a "sister senate" to act as a liaison between nuns and bishops, Lacayo left the convent at the age of twenty-seven. Returning to Los Angeles in 1975, Lacayo founded the nonprofit National Association for Hispanic Elderly (NAHE), a research and training agency that now has offices in ten states and the District of Columbia. With an annual budget of $15 million, the NAHE is one of the largest Hispanic organizations in the country.

Works for the Elderly

Aside from providing social and housing services, the NAHE serves as a job placement agency for Latinos fifty-five and older, primarily in community service settings such as schools, hospitals, and day care centers. The program is funded by United States Labor Department grants which subsidize the seniors' wages. Each year, twenty percent of the elderly find permanent employment through the NAHE. "It's getting people, especially those who are low-skilled, a second chance. All they want is an opportunity to be of service. Our elderly are our best heritage, so if we lose touch with them, we lose our roots and connections," Lacayo said in her interview.

During and after the riots in Los Angeles in the spring of 1992, an NAHE subsidiary, El Pueblo Community Development Corporation (the first Hispanic economic development corporation in Los Angeles), served as a link between schools in the hardest-hit areas and parents of elementary school children. "Because we have our elderly in so many agencies and schools, we have an entree. You can really make an impact educating people through elders. It's kind of fun," Lacayo says. In addition to the NAHE, she helped to establish the Area Agency on Aging in Los Angeles, serving as an administrative coordinator for Mayor Tom Bradley.

In 1976, a year after Lacayo established the NAHE, she was nominated by President Jimmy Carter and then elected as one of two vice-chairpersons of the Democratic National Committee. With Detroit Mayor Coleman Young, she served as vice-chair—the first Hispanic woman to hold the position—until 1980. Although this was a highly respected post, Lacayo found she did not entirely enjoy the internal politicking within the Democratic Party. She tried to organize a women's division within the Democratic National Committee, but encountered much resistance, primarily from the white feminists in the party. Noted feminist Bella Abzug, according to Lacayo, wanted the vice-chair position. "They made my life pretty miserable. I learned a lot about inclusive and exclusive politics," Lacayo stated.

Views Herself as Philosopher, Not Fighter

After Carter lost the presidency to Ronald Reagan in 1980, Lacayo decided that, as a director of a nonprofit agency, she ought to stay out of partisan politics. "I came to

it because I knew President Carter when he was governor and nobody knew him. I did it because he asked me. I took a citizen's position and stayed in Los Angeles. You have to be a street fighter, but I'm more of a philosopher," she explained. "I'm happier being in a constituency-based organization where I can demand from either parties issues that need to be represented."

Although she has not returned to party politics (she declined to work on the 1992 Democratic presidential campaign), she has accepted certain government appointments. In 1990 the Bush administration asked her to serve as one of about thirty experts on the Supplemental Security Income advisory panel. The group revised the social security program for the blind, aged, and disabled. In an interview she described the conflicts involved in this project: "The Bush people came in and decided to reform it, but some people on the committee were not trickle-down types. A number of us had a broader perspective of what government's responsibility is to the poor." Lacayo was also appointed by the U.S. Secretary of Commerce to the Census Bureau Committee on Minority Populations in 1990.

Lacayo has remained involved in local and state organizations in California as well. She was appointed to the Los Angeles County Housing Commission in 1991. She has also served as a member of the advisory committee of the Roybal Center on Gerontology at California State University in Los Angeles and as chair of the Forum of National Hispanic Organizations.

The activist's interests have continued to expand. In 1985, Lacayo founded Achvah/Amistad, a friendship exchange program in which Hispanic leaders have visited with counterparts in Israel and Jewish leaders have visited Mexico. "The project is very close to my heart," Lacayo said in an interview. "The two communities have a lot in common. I think it's very important for us to have intergroup relations. I've spent a lot of time trying to build bridges." Lacayo attributes her concern with Hispanic/Jewish relations to her family. Her parents, who made frequent trips to Mexico during the 1930s and 1940s, worked for the Jewish underground in Mexico City during World War II. After the war, they provided information to underground leaders about former Nazi officers who had migrated to South America. Following the assassination of one of these officers, Lacayo's parents were warned to return to the United States. Lacayo's mother, now in her eighties, vividly remembers their adventures, and Lacayo plans to write a history based on those memories.

Another of Lacayo's areas of concern is the field of women's issues. In 1989, Lacayo was invited to join the prestigious Women's Trusteeship, the Los Angeles affiliate of the International Women's Forum, a 3,000-member group of women leaders from a wide spectrum of professions. Lacayo also cofounded Hispanas Organized for

Political Equality (HOPE), a nonprofit organization dedicated to the political education and participation of Hispanic women; she continues to serve on the group's board of directors.

Lacayo's work within the various communities she serves has earned her several awards. She became the first Hispanic fellow of the Gerontological Society of America in 1981 and was named "Outstanding Professional of the Year" by the National Society of Fundraising Executives in 1991. Lacayo also received in 1991 the SAGE award in Consumer Education for effective marketing and communications targeted toward older consumers. In addition, she was named "Latina Woman of the Year" by the Spanish-speaking media in Los Angeles and was made honorary mayor of San Antonio. Despite her many accomplishments, Lacayo still has more projects planned for the future. Although she has taken graduate courses throughout the years, Lacayo would like to earn a Ph.D. or law degree so that she can teach.

Sources:

Lacayo, Carmela Gloria, telephone interview with Julia Edgar, September, 1992.

—Sketch by Julia Edgar

Latigo Hernandez, Maria
See **Hernandez, Maria Latigo**

Romy Ledesma
(1935-)
University administrator, scientist

Romy Ledesma is the only woman in the country to administer a Materials Research Center of Excellence (MRCE). Each of the eight MRCEs in the country, all located on university campuses, supports the research efforts of minorities and operates outreach programs designed to encourage high school students to pursue scientific careers. In 1992, the National Research Foundation, which provides funding for the MRCEs, honored Ledesma for her success in fulfilling the center's scientific research

and minority outreach mandates. In that same year, Ledesma was inducted into the El Paso Women's Hall of Fame for her contribution to the field of science and for providing a role model for future generations of leaders. At the induction, she was recognized for her pioneering efforts in encouraging minority and female students to pursue science and engineering careers.

Ledesma has lived most of her life in El Paso, Texas, where she was born on November 17, 1935, the youngest child and the only girl of four siblings. A Mexican American who did not speak English when she started school, her excellent grades enabled her to complete elementary and high school three years ahead of schedule. She taught Spanish until her marriage. "Then I became a homemaker, taking care of my husband and four children," she explained during an interview with Michelle Vachon. "I also gave private music lessons at home. I had inherited a taste for music from my father and I played piano, French horn, trumpet, baritone horn, oboe and saxophone." When her children neared school age, Ledesma entered the International Business College, received her professional certification in 1963, and worked in accounting and secretarial positions.

Four years after receiving her certification, Ledesma enrolled as a full-time student at the University of Texas at El Paso and took her B.S. in biological sciences, concentrating on botany, with minors in geological science, Spanish, and education in 1971. She immediately secured the position of research technician and herbarium curator at the Texas A & M Research Center in El Paso. In addition to conducting crop physiology and entomology research, Ledesma developed a desert herbarium and served as liaison and translator at international meetings of experiment station scientists.

After completing her M.S. in biological sciences (emphasizing plant ecology) in 1977, she received a job offer from Texas A & M University in College Station, Texas. "This meant moving 700 miles away from home. But my children were now in college and my husband offered to come with me," she recalled in her interview. So in 1978, Ledesma joined Texas A & M University's department of horticultural sciences as a graduate assistant, teaching about native plants of Texas, fruit and nut culture, and plant propagation. She soon decided to resume her studies, but, as she told Vachon, "As I started taking courses, I realized that the business side of things still appealed to me. So I made a move into the administrative part of higher education and took on college and university administration." Between classes, she worked as a non-teaching graduate assistant for the university's department of educational administration, and later held a similar position with the Dean's Office at the College of Education.

This busy schedule was interrupted by two full-time internships. For the first, in 1983, Ledesma came back to the University of Texas at El Paso and was assigned to the president's office. She told Vachon, "My internship project was to find out how a university operates. Through interviews with administrative staff at lower levels of the organization, I was able to get information that never appears in reports. I asked workers their opinions on how their departments functioned, what could be improved and how. It was quite interesting. The president, Dr. Haskell Monroe, took me to most of his meetings and truly supported me with this project. He was an excellent mentor and role model." For her second internship in 1984, Ledesma went to Austin to become a management intern at the Office of Budget and Management of the Texas State Governor's Office.

In 1987, Ledesma graduated with a Ph.D. in college and university administration and a minor in industrial engineering. She decided to take a hiatus from work in 1988 to spend time with her 13 grandchildren. "At one point during the summer, I had nine of them with me for a whole month," she remembered fondly. "It was like having a little school in your own house—it was terrific!" The following year, she joined the MRCE at the University of Texas at El Paso. "The center was launched in November of 1988. I came on two months later and had to build it from the ground up," she told Vachon. As project coordinator, Ledesma administers the center's $1 million annual budget, supervises the activities of more than 100 people—ranging from undergraduate students to university professors conducting scientific research—and directs the outreach program.

Disapproves of Stereotypes of Women

In the course of her career, scientists and engineers have always accepted Ledesma readily, but administrative colleagues have proven more difficult. "When people see a woman sitting behind a desk in an administrative office, they assume that she is a secretary," she told Vachon. "But you have to find a way to overcome this." In one instance, Ledesma invited a young male employee to attend a meeting with her in order to introduce him to administrative processes. Throughout the meeting, a university official addressed the young man, unaware that Ledesma was the one in charge. Such experiences have taught Ledesma to react neither aggressively nor defensively, but to find a diplomatic way to correct the error. Looking back on her educational path, Ledesma corrected another misconception. "If you enter a field of study and realize that this is not where you want to be, change your major," she remarked to Vachon. "Don't listen to people who say that it can't be done. I have done it numerous times myself. Believe me, it's never too late."

In the next few years, Ledesma intends to complete her doctorate in horticultural sciences and to publish a research report on an insect that has not been documented since it was discovered in the late 1800s, the name of which

she wishes to keep confidential until her report is finished. In 1992, Ledesma was elected to the executive committee of the most recently formed regional chapter of the Texas Association of Chicanos in Higher Education, a civic organization devoted to assisting Chicanos pursuing degrees and addressing issues important to them. As the association's first recipient of a graduate fellowship, Ledesma is pleased to be helping the organization that once helped her.

Sources:

Periodicals

El Paso Times, March 20, 1992, p. 16.

Other

Ledesma, Romy, interview with Michelle Vachon, September 28, 1992.

—*Sketch by Michelle Vachon*

Lehtinen, Ileana Ros
See Ros-Lehtinen, Ileana

Aliza Lifshitz
Physician, reporter

Aliza Lifshitz served as the 1992 president of the 1,300-member California Hispanic American Medical Association. One of the first Latina physicians to become involved in the struggle against AIDS, she devotes about one third of her Los Angeles practice to the care of people diagnosed with the HIV virus. Many of her patients are undocumented workers, so-called illegal aliens. "They come here seeking the American dream," she observed in an interview with Diana Martínez. "Most of them are very young. And now they are alone, frightened and devastated by this dreaded disease." In a public service ad taken out by the American Medical Association, Lifshitz stated that "the first principle of medical ethics is to offer compassion and respect for human dignity. For me, this pledge includes the illegal alien dying of AIDS. . . . It is so easy to stereotype these people simply as 'illegals with AIDS.' But I want people to know they are human, too. That they have a mother or a father or a child who will miss them when they are gone." As part of her work she participates on AIDS

Aliza Lifshitz

committees for both the California Medical Association and the Los Angeles Medical Association, as well as other state and private organizations.

A private-practice physician specializing in internal medicine, clinical pharmacology, and endocrinology, Aliza Lifshitz likens herself to an old fashioned doctor. She has worked with community-based organizations to offer low-cost treatment to indigents, and she works with patients who can not afford payment. Her 'old fashioned' style has made her popular. Some of her patients travel great distances to see her and bring small tokens of their appreciation. As she explained in an interview with Diana Martínez, "I really like my patients, and sometimes some of the patients that I see will either knit something, or make something I can hang on the wall or they bring some cookies that they prepared or some fruit. . . . I guess that's old fashioned too, but I love it." She says communicating and giving time to her patients is very important to her. She explained, "Recently, I had a new woman patient, and I did her medical history and her physical examination, as I do with all my patients. As I was examining her, I was explaining what I was doing and describing the laboratory tests I would be asking for. As I was finishing up, I asked her what she did for a living. When she told me she was a neurologist, I almost died. I apologized for explaining things the way I did. And she said, 'Oh no, I loved it,' and later wrote me a letter that said it was nice to see that there were still some old fashioned doctors around. I felt very complimented by her letter."

Lifshitz was born in Mexico City to Jewish-Mexican parents. Her father, in addition to being an engineer, graduated from the Music Conservatory in Mexico as a classical pianist. Her mother, a painter, would occasionally work with him. Her parents enrolled Lifshitz in the American elementary school in Mexico City to expose their daughter to culturally diverse children and to learn English. She attended Mexico City's Jewish High School before studying at the Catholic Institute of LaSalle. She received her B.S. with honors from the Colegio Israelite de Mexico in 1969 and opted for a medical career. As she explained to Martínez, "I wanted to do something that was creative and would help people. . . . I've always seen medicine as an art that is based on a science. The greatest majority of the healing that we do is actually through listening to the patient and communicating with them." She enrolled at the Universidad Nacional Autonoma de México, graduating cum laude in 1976. She completed her medical training and residency in the United States, attending Tulane University and University of California at San Diego.

Follows Example Set by Parents

Lifshitz's subsequent patients have often referred to her as compassionate. She attributes this trait to her parents. She told Martínez, "Both my parents were dedicated to helping people. My mother had more time to practice it. It was one of those things I always admired about her. She was always there for people, and I thought 'Wow if I could ever be like that!' My mother had a tremendously big heart for people. I remember her taking care of everything from a limping dog on the street to making sure she bought food for people who she saw needed it. That's what my mother was all about."

Known for communicating with her patients one-on-one, Lifshitz also deals with the media in the same manner. As she told Martínez, "I can reach so many more people and get so much more information out through the media. With one written article or one television health report, I'm able to reach more people than I would be able to reach in an entire year with my practice." Lifshitz believes the Latino community, in particular, needs more information on the HIV virus and other health concerns. In an interview published in *Unidos* magazine, she said "In 20 to 30 years, AIDS will be primarily a minority disease. It is evident the gay community has been more effectively reached regarding AIDS education and awareness." Echoing these sentiments, Lifshitz told Martínez, "There is so much information out there for someone who speaks English. In very many instances it has been said, and it continues to be said, that Hispanics are not interested in preventive health. But many times it's simply because Hispanics don't have access to that information. Once data are made available to them, they are very interested."

Lifshitz is currently the health reporter for the Spanish-language Univision, a television network, and local television in Los Angeles. In addition to reporting, she has produced prime-time specials on various health-related topics. She is also a charter and board member of the National Association of Physician Broadcasters, editor-in-chief of *Hispanic Physician,* and medical editor of *Más,* a national Spanish-language magazine. Recalling the beginning of her media career, which began in 1986 on KSCI-TV in Southern California with a live 30-minute call-in program, she told Martínez: "I received hundreds of calls and would spend my weekends answering mail. That's when I saw the wealth a program like that was for our community." She added, "I enjoy everything I do. I enjoy contact with my patients, so when you like something so much it's not difficult to do it. It's what keeps me going. I feel that I'm very privileged that I have been able to accomplish a lot and I am able to do what I'm doing. Sometimes I'm tired but I'm always excited about my work."

Advocates Universal Basic Health Care System

Lifshitz is very concerned with the state of health care in the United States. She explained to Martínez some of her principal concerns. Like many health care professionals, she sees a need for universal basic health care. "We have more working poor without insurance, we have more elderly retired with health care needs. We have less people carried through government aid." She continued, "And there has been a lot of cross shifting to insurance companies to cover for uncompensated care. We have overloaded hospitals, and hospitals are closing their emergency rooms. We need to be able to provide basic health care for everyone, in a country that is supposed to be a developed country. If we are going to rate how civilized a country is according to how they treat their poor, I think we're becoming more and more uncivilized."

Additionally, Lifshitz is concerned about issues regarding women's health. In an interview for the Spanish-language publication *Vanidades* she said, "I believe that things are changing. However, I think that as a woman, one still has to work twice as hard to receive recognition for your merits. But I believe that women who come after us will have a slightly easier road than we have now." She postulates that as women attain greater recognition in the health field, more attention will be paid to women's medical issues. In an interview with *Hispanic* magazine, Lifshitz noted, "The impact that women have had on health care beyond nursing has not been recognized. People don't realize that there are some really interesting and great women in health care. Most research projects in the past have focused on men; the medical world needs to focus more on women."

When asked what drives her, Lifshitz concluded: "I would basically like in some way to leave this world a little bit better than what I found it." She has received community recognition awards, including the University of South-

ern California Los Amigos De La Humanidad of the School of Social Work's "Distinguished Contributor to Social Welfare," 1992; Multicultural Area Health Education Center's "Physician of the Year," 1991; Comision Femenil's "Women Making History Award," 1991; and Comision Femenil's "Women in the Health Sciences Award," 1991.

Sources:

Periodicals

Hispanic, October, 1991, p. 15.
Unidos, April, 1992, pp. 16-18.
Vanidades (Spanish-language; translation by Diana Martínez), August, 1992, pp. 100-01.

Other

Lifshitz, Aliza, interview with Diana Martínez, 1992.

—Sketch by Diana Martínez

Lisa Lisa
See **Velez, Lisa**

Lomas Garza, Carmen
See **Garza, Carmen Lomas**

Diana López
(1948-)
Novelist

Diana López, who writes as Isabella Ríos, is the author of *Victuum,* one of the first Chicana novels published in the United States. The work is a bildungsroman which tells the story of Valentina Ballesternos from pre-birth experiences to her marriage and birth of her children. Interweaving her narrative with glimpses of cultural and historical detail,

López transforms her novel from a mere fictional account to an examination of the growth of the Hispanic presence in southern California during the first half of the twentieth-century.

López was born on March 16, 1948, in Los Angeles, California, the first child of Louis H. and Valentine (Ballesteros) López. Her ancestry includes the Native American heritage of the Chihuahua and northern New Mexican tribes on her father's side and an early Californio family on her mother's side. Family stories and historical anecdotes played an important role in López's childhood. From her great-aunts, many of whom lived to be more than one hundred years old, López developed the fascination for the Hispanic cultural roots evident in her novel.

Although López began her university studies with the hopes of becoming a lawyer, she soon discovered a love of storytelling and instead decided to pursue a degree in English literature. She earned a bachelor of arts from San Francisco State University and later a master of arts in English and creative writing. In 1979, she received a doctor of education in bilingual higher education from Nova University. While at San Francisco State, López joined with the five other Chicano students to raise Chicano enrollment at the campus. She personally developed a tutorial program to help minority students with their studies. She also cultivated her literary pursuits by giving readings of her poetry and short stories. Since 1970, she has had a teaching position with the English Department at Moorpark College in Ventura.

Victuum is an experimental novel which begins with its protagonist still in her mother's womb. We are introduced to Valentina through a fetal stream of consciousness: "I watch. I listen. For sound am I, silenced by the human ear at present; shaped matter unseen by the human eye at present." The first two-thirds of the book, entitled "Part 1," tell the story of Valentina's life from birth to marriage. "Part 2" is dominated with dreams and psychic images in which she meets Isaiah, Ulysses, Pope Eusebius and other figures from history and mythology. Valentina is led through these events by Victuum, a being from another solar system.

In *Dictionary of Literary Biography*, Annie Olivia Eysturoy notes that the absence of references to Valentina's daily life near the end of the novel may lead readers to speculate if she has left the realm of reality completely, or not. "López explains," Eysturoy comments, "that these visions represent the epitome of Valentina's state of mind. She wanted to create an atmosphere in which the reader is forced to question the nature of reality." The experimental form and content of the novel led some critics, including Francisco Lomelí in *Minority Voices*, to question the nature of the work. Some felt that calling it a novel stretched the boundaries of the genre. In an unpublished interview with Eysturoy, López describes her work as "a nonfiction novel and

drama." Eysturoy observes that through the use of dialogue, López's unique work "tries to draw the attention away from the individual in favor of the community and present the individual as an integral part of the collective whole."

Sources:

Books

Dictionary of Literary Biography, Volume 82: *Chicano Writers, First Series*, Gale, 1989.
Ríos, Isabella, *Victuum*, Diana-Etna, 1976.

Periodicals

Minority Voices: An Interdisciplinary Journal of Literature and the Arts, spring, 1980, pp. 49-61.

—*Sketch by Marian C. Gonsior*

Josefina López
(1969?-)
Playwright

At the age of three, Josefina López knew that she was going to be a writer. "I've always known it," she declared in the *Ann Arbor News*. By the age of 17, this confident young woman had written her first nationally-renowned play, *Simply Maria*. She was just 21 when another one of her plays, *Real Women Have Curves*, was produced in various cities across the United States. Before most young people have even chosen careers, López had become a fresh and exciting new presence in the theater. Reflecting on the possible reasons behind her success, she concluded in the *Los Angeles Times*, "I've taken our beautiful hot and fiery colors of Mexico and mixed them with American feminism and freedom of speech."

Josefina López was born in Cerritos, a town in the Mexican state of San Luis Potosi. Seeking a better life, her parents moved their eight children to Los Angeles when Josefina was just six years old. The journey to the United States was frightening for the little girl; she was allowed to cross the border only because she was using her sister's American birth certificate. Her parents had green cards but Josefina did not, and consequently her childhood years were marred by the fear of being sent back to Mexico. As a teenager, she had to lie about having a social security number in order to gain employment. This precarious status left her feeling as if she did not fit into American society.

Garners National Acclaim for Debut Effort

While the nightmarish existence of living as an undocumented person in an inhospitable country has left its mark on López, the young playwright might contend that her fears have worked to her advantage. After seeing Luis Valdez's moving play *I Don't Have to Show You No Stinking Badges*, the teenage López was inspired to write her own story, which she entitled *Simply Maria, or the American Dream*. A frank look at López's life as a young Mexican in the United States that examines how difficult it can be to reconcile loyalty to one's heritage with the hope of achieving the American dream, *Simply Maria* is not a typical interpretation of the adolescent experience. "I wrote *Maria* because I had to," she explained in the *Los Angeles Times*. "I just poured out my guts."

López entered *Simply Maria* in two contests—the Young Playwrights Festival in New York, in which she was a semifinalist, and San Diego's Gaslamp Quarter Theatre California Young Playwrights Project, in which she captured first place. *Simply Maria* was subsequently produced in San Diego in January, 1988.

López's blossoming talent attracted a great deal of attention. In 1990, an adaptation of her play aired on public television and won the Vocal Program Award for Excellence in the children's category. Since 1990, López has written two other plays of note—*Food for the Dead*, which deals with homosexuality and machismo, and *Real Women Have Curves*, which, according to López in the *Ann Arbor News* (Ann Arbor, Michigan), "deals with empowerment and self-pride, and acceptance by women of their physical selves and their inner selves." She went on to note that the latter title "is a little exaggerated in terms of some of its comedy, but it's very realistic in its emotions." *Real Women Have Curves* has met with favorable reviews in the many different cities in which it has been produced. A critic writing for Ann Arbor-based *Current* observed, "This ambitious play thumbs up its nose at societal presumptions that women are supposed to be tall, model-esque, and painfully nipped at the waist, while delivering other powerful messages."

Looks Forward to Achieving "American Dream"

Despite her success as a playwright, López still has not found living in the United States any easier. Although she has residency and green cards that allow her to live and work in America, she has to wait to apply for citizenship and therefore cannot vote. She also has been thwarted in her attempts to enroll in a four-year university. Her father makes too much money for her to receive financial aid but not enough to pay for her education, and López herself is not eligible for aid because she is not yet a citizen.

López is nevertheless beginning to overcome the feelings of alienation she felt as a teenager and is confident that she will one day attend college and continue to gain fame as a playwright. She is determined to write despite the fact that her parents, whom she adores, do not completely understand why—or what—she writes. But as López asserted in the *Los Angeles Times*, writing "has been my ticket out of the barrio, out of the house, and out of the old ideas."

Sources:

Periodicals

Ann Arbor News, April 3, 1992, pp. D1-2.
Current, April, 1992, p. 23.
Los Angeles Times, July 29, 1990, section CAL, pp. 48+.

—*Sketch by Ronie-Richele Garcia-Johnson*

Lourdes Lopez
(1958-)
Ballet dancer

Although she was pigeon-toed as a child and once feared she would never become a respected ballerina, Lourdes Lopez is now a principal dancer with the New York City Ballet Company. She has mastered classic dances such as the demanding *Theme and Variations* from Tchaikovsky's Suite No. 3, *Serenade*, and *La sonambula*, and she has brightened contemporary ballets such as *Réjouissance* and *Sonate de Scarlatti*. Ballet enthusiasts and critics have come to adore Lopez's dramatic face and elegant line, and those with authority predict that she may achieve even greater status as a ballerina.

In 1959, one year after Lourdes Lopez was born in Havana, Cuba, her family fled Fidel Castro's regime. Her father, an accountant, had served in deposed Cuban leader Fulgencio Batista's army, and he was no longer safe in the country. The family came to the United States and settled in Miami, Florida. It was in that city that Lopez first began to dance. At the time, the young girl wore orthopedic shoes to counter her flat feet and pigeon-toes; her parents thought that ballet would strengthen her legs. Ballet for Lopez, however, was more than physically rewarding. As her talent for the dance surfaced, she became increasingly passionate about the art.

Wins Coveted Scholarship

At the age of 11, Lopez won a scholarship for a coveted spot at New York's School of American Ballet. George Balanchine, the late director of the school, noticed her potential. At fourteen, she earned the opportunity to study ballet at the school full-time. Although she was still very young, Lopez left home for New York, where she lived with her older sister. Lopez's determination and perseverance in school won her a spot in the corps de ballet in 1974, when she was just 16. When she joined the company, according to *Time*, the ballerina felt out of place. She explained in the magazine in 1988, "It is hard when you've got all those blond girls and you're darker than everyone and your mother speaks a different language."

Lopez did not look like the other ballerinas in the company, and she certainly did not dance like them—she was extraordinarily talented. By the time she was twenty-two she was a soloist for the company. At that time, in 1980, she said in *People*, "I'm working hard now, and I'm seeing results." Once again, Lopez's discipline was rewarded. Although she had once thought that she would never become the star of the ballet, she became a principal ballerina for the company in 1984.

Captures Attention with Unique Style

One of Lopez's first performances as a principal dancer for the company was in *Réjouissance*, a ballet by Peter Martins. While she did not receive much attention for that effort, she did earn a somewhat favorable review for her work in the *Finale (Theme and Variations)* of Tchaikovsky's Suite No. 3 in 1985. Noting her "dark, glamorous looks," and acknowledging her gift for dancing, a critic for the *New Yorker* commented, "Lopez is strong and talented . . . yet the beauty she brings onstage isn't amplified and dramatized by her dancing." The critic continued, "I also feel that she [Lopez] habitually dances with less than her full impact." According to the critic, Lopez, who reminded her of the "ballerinas of the forties who had large dramatic faces and moonlighted in the movies" could be even more striking if she could polish her footwork.

Lopez has modeled her dance technique after those of her favorite dancers, Kay Mazzo and Patricia McBride. Her training by the famous Balanchine is also apparent in her work. This education, combined with Lopez's natural affinity for the dance, has given her the distinct style which some critics and ballet enthusiasts greatly appreciate. Dancer-choreographer Peter Martins was quoted as saying in

People that Lopez is the "new Alicia Alonso." This was a tremendous compliment; Alonso is the legendary Cuban ballerina who stunned the United States with her charm and popularized ballet in Cuba and other countries in Latin America. It was Martins who gave Lopez roles in his *Réjouissance* and *Sonate de Scarlatti*. In addition to Martins's ballets, Lopez has appeared in *Apollo*, *Firebird*, the *Four Seasons*, the *Goldberg Variations*, *Serenade*, *La sonambula*, and other ballets. She also appeared in *Dance in America*, a series on television's Public Broadcasting System.

Lopez is as graceful off the stage as she is on the stage. When she was approached by a couple who wanted to name their race horse after the ballerina, she agreed that the idea was a good one. As *Sports Illustrated* reported in 1987, the couple wanted the horse to gain the "speed and dignity" as well as the "superior athletic ability" that one of their favorite ballerinas possessed. According to the magazine, Lopez, on a whim, bet twenty dollars that the horse "Lourdes Lopez" would win her race. The horse came through for her namesake, and the ballerina won eighty dollars. Winning the eighty dollars, however, was not the most exciting event of 1987 for the ballerina Lourdes Lopez—on July 26th of that year she married Lionel Saporta, an attorney.

Lopez continues to dance for the New York City Ballet. If her past performances provide any indication of her future, ballet lovers have reason to hope that she will emerge as one of America's great ballerinas of the twentieth century.

Sources:

Periodicals

Dance Magazine, May, 1985, p. 22.
New York, June 4, 1984, p. 84-85.
New Yorker, March 18, 1985, p. 121-22.
Nuestro, November, 1981, p. 14.
People, October 13, 1980, p. 75.
Sports Illustrated, September 21, 1987, pp. 94-96.
Time, July 11, 1988, p. 74.

—Sketch by Ronie-Richele Garcia-Johnson

Mara Awilda López
(1951-)
Government official

As a lifelong employee of the District of Columbia, Mara Awilda López has drawn on her academic background in cultural geography and on insights gained from her government service to aid the local Latino community, the focus of her attention for more than a decade. Of Puerto Rican and Honduran descent, she was born in New York City on December 12, 1951, the daughter of Otilia Rodríguez and merchant marine Hermenegildo Briceño, and is now married and the mother of two children. Her close ties to the Latino residents of the nation's capital date back to the late 1970s, when she conducted 170 interviews that formed the basis of her master's thesis for the University of Maryland, a report entitled "The Perception of the Barrio and Community Boundaries by Hispanic Residents of Washington, D.C." Her training also includes studies in cultural geography at the University of Puerto Rico.

López's tenure in district government has included several posts in the Department of Housing and Community Development, including special assistant to the director, women's program manager, and management analyst. She has also served with the D.C. Department of Transportation and with the Council of Hispanic Community Agencies.

Yet as López told interviewer Sandra Márquez, her most satisfying position to date was the eleven months she spent as acting director of the Mayor's Office of Latino Affairs, an agency charged with ensuring that Washington's Latino community has access to city government services and a voice in city affairs. A cabinet-level appointee within the government of Mayor Sharon Pratt Kelly, López administered a yearly budget of $1.3 million and managed a staff of twelve. In May, 1991, the same month she assumed her new post, she faced a major test of her academic training and skills as a liaison when civil unrest broke out in a predominantly Latino suburb of Washington. "It was a very difficult time," López recalled in her interview with Márquez. "There was a need for a lot of healing. Listening needed to happen on both sides."

The culmination of López's efforts in serving Washington's Latino community came with the creation of a "multicultural initiative," a document she described to Márquez as "the most tangible product of my tenure" at the agency. Envisioned by López as a blueprint for guiding city services in the Latino community, the initiative calls for the translation into Spanish of public announcements and signs, the collection of data from city service recipients by ethnicity and race, and cultural sensitivity on the part of government employees.

After leaving the Mayor's Office of Latino Affairs, López became a program analyst for the Department of Employment Services, a job that requires her to relocate displaced workers and implement job training programs devised by the U.S. Labor Department. Explaining to Márquez her motivation for pursuing the position, López said, "I wanted to learn a new field. Understanding labor and economics will help me as a person." One day she hopes to apply her expertise in local issues to problems at the national level.

Sources:

Periodicals

Washington Post, May 25, 1991, p. B8; July 3, 1991, p. A4; February 11, 1992, p. A1.

Other

López, Mara Awilda, interview with Sandra Márquez, September 1, 1992.

—*Sketch by Sandra Márquez*

María Cristina López
(1944-)
Health educator

When María Cristina López was a child, she was fascinated by the gold scales that weighed medicines, herbs, and homemade remedies in her mother's drug store. Those memories are especially dear to her today because they played such a major role in shaping her professional life in the field of health education. As one of the founders of the private, nonprofit Santa Fe Health Education Project, López has made it her mission to teach women (mostly Latinas) about their bodies.

López was born August 1, 1944, in a mining town just south of the border between Mexico and the United States. Her father died when she was only two years old, the victim of a mining accident. Her mother then assumed the role of the village pharmacist and town physician in order to support her two daughters.

Looking back on her youth, López admits she took her mother for granted, not realizing until many years later that her own interest in chemistry and math could be traced to her mother's influence. "[She] would administer shots, mix medicines, dispense antibiotics and fix scrapes," López remarked in an interview with Marilyn Stein. "She learned pharmacy from working with a cousin in a drug store for two years and then she went out on her own. There were some directions to follow in prescribing medicine, but she had no formal education."

López, on the other hand, eventually earned a degree in chemistry from Albuquerque College of St. Joseph on the Rio Grande, a small Catholic school that had awarded her a scholarship. Her plans to return to Mexico were sidetracked when she fell in love with a doctor and decided to remain in the United States, where she became active in the health education field. Her first efforts involved organizing groups of minority women and educating them on their health and the health of their families. In 1975, she co-founded the Santa Fe Health Education Project, a program intended to serve primarily (but not exclusively) Hispanic women. The project's offerings include workshops for senior citizens and sex education for teenagers. Staff members have also published a book on menopause and a health newsletter, both of which are printed in English and Spanish.

López is proud of the accomplishments of the Santa Fe Health Education Project but frustrated by the inequities of the U.S. health care system. She favors a universal system that would make quality care available to everyone. "That is what we are fighting for," she told Stein.

In 1992, López's life took yet another direction after she received a master's degree in Spanish from the University of New Mexico and accepted a teaching position there. Her decision to pursue language studies grew out of her love for Spanish and her native culture and her "need to immerse myself in it," as she put it.

Sources:

López, Cristina María, telephone interview with Marilyn Stein, September 21, 1992.

—*Sketch by Marilyn Stein*

Nancy Lopez

Domingo and Marina Lopez, took up the game for her mother's health. By the age of 11, she was a better golfer than either of her parents. Her father became convinced that Nancy was champion material and began to groom her for tournament play. The family scrimped on its own needs to finance her golfing. The family's dedication seemed justified by her performance on the golf course. At the age of 12, she won the first of three state women's tournaments. While still in high school, she finished second in the Women's Open. In 1972 and 1974, she won the U.S. Girls Junior title. And as a student at the University of Tulsa, she won the intercollegiate title before dropping out of school to turn professional.

Record-Breaking First Year

During her first year on the professional circuit, Lopez broke several standing records. She began the year by winning the Bent Tree Classic at Sarasota, Florida, in February, then went on to win a record five tournaments in succession, including the prestigious LPGA title. (Lopez has since won her second and third LPGA titles as well as a Nabisco Dinah Shore title.) By August of 1978 she had surpassed the highest earnings record, $150,000, set by Judy Rankin in 1976. Lopez went on to earn more than $200,000 by the end of the year. She also endorsed or made commercials for various golf products.

Since her initial appearance on the pro circuit, Lopez has always been ranked at the very top of her sport. In

Nancy Lopez
(1957-)
Professional golfer

Since becoming a professional golfer in 1978, Nancy Lopez has consistently ranked among the top women on the circuit. She is one of only five women in the sport to have earned more than $1 million in her career. In addition, she has won over 40 tournament victories and was the youngest woman ever to be named to the Ladies Professional Golf Association (LPGA) Hall of Fame.

Born January 6, 1957, in Torrance, California, Lopez first became a golf enthusiast as a child when her parents,

1979, she won 8 of the 19 tournaments she entered, a feat Bruce Newman of *Sports Illustrated* called "one of the most dominating sports performances in half a century." Lopez had her best year in 1985, when she earned more money— over $400,000—than any other player on the circuit. She won five tournaments and set a record-high scoring average of 70.73 percent. In 1987 Lopez was named to the LPGA Hall of Fame, "which has the most difficult requirements for entry of any sports Hall of Fame in the nation," as Gordon S. White, Jr., noted in the *New York Times*. Thirty tournament victories, two of them major titles, are needed for Hall of Fame inclusion. Also in 1987, she authored a book, *Nancy Lopez's the Complete Golfer*.

Through it all, Lopez has managed to balance the demands of a sports career with those of a wife and mother. In fact, she told Joseph Durso of the *New York Times:* "I like being a wife and mother more than I like professional golf." She and her husband, baseball player Ray Knight, share the necessary domestic duties between them. "We complement each other," Knight told Durso. "We help each other with the chores." And Knight occasionally caddies for his wife. Because of their respective status in golf and baseball, Lopez and Knight are "probably the most prominent married couple in sports," according to Durso. They are also among the happiest. Lopez told Jaime Diaz in *Sports Illustrated:* "I'm so happy with my life, that now when I play, there is no pressure. It's just all fun, and when it's fun, you perform better."

Sources:

Periodicals

Hispanic, June, 1989, pp. 15-16.
New York Times, March 31, 1985; May 19, 1988.
People, April 25, 1983.
Sports Illustrated, August 5, 1985; August 4, 1986; February 9, 1987; May 29, 1989, p. 65.

—*Sketch by Denise Wiloch*

Priscilla Lopez
(1948-)
Actress, singer, dancer

After years of working on stage and screen, Priscilla Lopez has become a sought-after actress, receiving Obie

Priscilla Lopez

and Tony awards as well as an additional Tony nomination. The Puerto Rican American woman has starred in numerous Broadway musicals, appeared in movies, and performed in several television series, but theater-goers know her best for her portrayal of the energetic Diane Morales in the musical *A Chorus Line.*

Lopez was born on February 26, 1948, to Francisco and Laura (Candelaria) Lopez in the Bronx, New York. The family of six was poor. Although Laura Lopez had her hands full with her four children, she managed to inspire young Priscilla with her collection of Hit Parade songbooks and the song, "Secret Love." Lopez assured Judy Klemesrud in the *New York Times,* that, while her mother "put the acting bug in my head," she was not the stereotypical pushy stage mother. Acting was something that the young girl "wanted to do. In fact, performing was my only satisfaction in those days. The only approval or attention I ever got came from performing."

Strives for Stardom

Lopez wanted to become a professional performer, and she did not hesitate to pursue her goal. When a man visited her neighborhood to sell dance lessons, she jumped at the chance to learn. Lopez was just six years old. As a twelve-year-old, she waited for five rainy hours to audition for a role in *Gypsy;* although she failed to win a part, her determination to become an actress persisted. She studied theater at the Performing Arts High School in New York, where she won the lead in the spring drama festival and a $200 award for her acting. By the time Lopez was eighteen, she had obtained a part in her first Broadway show.

This show, *Breakfast at Tiffany's,* closed after two previews, and while the actress was able to garner other parts, she did not appear in any successful plays for some time. As Lopez later explained in the *New York Times,* tryouts for such plays were excruciating. The actress was usually just another number in a crowd of hopefuls, the competition was merciless, and directors were often heartless. "It's agonizing, it's absolutely agonizing," she lamented in the *Times.* "When you do get the job, they never tell you. They say, 'We'll be getting in touch with you.' It's very cruel." Fortunately for Lopez, directors got in touch with her often and she appeared in numerous productions, including *Henry, Sweet Henry, Lysistrata, Company, Her First Roman, The Boy Friend,* and *Pippin.* Despite the number of plays she danced in, Lopez did not win a speaking role until 1969's *Your Own Thing.* After replacing Leland Palmer in this role, Lopez's confidence soared, and she decided that she wanted to be a serious actress as well as a dancer.

Lopez's professional success and optimistic attitude were complemented by her marriage to Vincent Fanuele, a trombonist. The actress and the musician, who met while working on a production of *Company,* were married on January 16, 1972. Lopez went on in 1973 to appear in *What's a Nice Country Like You Doing in a Place Like This,* another Off-Broadway production. In 1974, the actress was given an opportunity to appear on television. Lopez accepted the job, playing the part of Rita, a waitress, in the series *Feeling Good.* It would be another year before she would return to the stage to star in the musical that made her famous, *A Chorus Line.*

Relates Dance Experiences for *A Chorus Line*

In January of 1974, Lopez, along with other dancers, met with choreographer/director Michael Bennett. The director wanted know about their lives as professionals, and the dancers eagerly told their stories. Lopez's memories of her dancing experiences were vivid. She told of her trouble with Karp, a drama teacher who had asked class members to describe how they felt as they imagined themselves riding a bobsled or pretending to be an ice cream cone. Lopez recalled that she could never feel anything; she deplored the method acting exercises and found them useless. "It was a horrible time for me," she recalled in the *New York Times,* "and it got so bad that the teacher even suggested I transfer to another school."

Lopez's unspoken reply to the instructor inspired the song "Nothing" in *A Chorus Line,* Bennett's musical; in fact, her experiences served as the basis for a character. "Everything about Morales in the show is true about me. Especially the song about the class," Lopez said in the *New York*

Times. Lopez remained with Bennett as he developed the musical, and she was chosen to play the character created from her stories—Diane Morales, a poor, Puerto Rican Broadway hopeful.

Bennett produced two versions of the play in experimental workshops, and then the musical opened at Joseph Papp's Off Broadway Public Theater. The musical begins with an audition where a group of dancers has gathered to try out for parts in a Broadway show. More than just previous job experience is revealed, however, when each one steps forward to talk about him or herself. The hopes, dreams and desires of each dancer are revealed throughout the course of the musical. Lopez, who, in effect, played herself, convincingly related the frustrations and triumphs she had been experiencing since she was a child. A *New Yorker* critic called the play "the most original, joyous, generous-spirited, and dynamic new musical to come along in years." The critic went on to praise Lopez just as highly: "Every number, every routine is good, and at least two of them—as performed by the magnetic Priscilla Lopez, in the character of a crackling, spunky, funny Puerto Rican girl named Diana—are show-stoppers." Laudatory reviews such as this one rocketed the musical to Broadway, and Lopez's salary went from $150 per week to $650.

Ironically, the very incident that had threatened to dash Lopez's dreams while she was still in high school actually led to their fulfillment; Lopez and her song about the terrible teacher became instant hits. "What I Did for Love," also sung by Lopez, was another favorite with critics. In this song, as a critic from the *New Yorker* wrote, Lopez "refutes the cheap cynicism of every show-business exposé you ever saw in movies or on the stage." Critics and audiences enjoyed the passionate portrayal of Lopez's character as much as her voice. "Bouncy 27-year-old Priscilla Lopez, probably the best singer in the show, is the pure spirit of this theatricality," wrote a *Newsweek* reviewer. The *New York Times* featured a story about her entitled, "Priscilla Lopez: The Leggy Kid on the Far Right." Finally, Lopez won an Obie award for her performance in the musical, and she was nominated for an Antoinette Perry, or Tony, Award.

Career Expands after *A Chorus Line*

Lopez's next role was in a television series called *A Year at the Top.* She then portrayed Sister Agnes in the CBS television series, *In the Beginning.* After playing the role of Theresa in the film *Cheaper to Keep Her,* Lopez returned to the stage. She appeared in *A Day in Hollywood / A Night in the Ukraine.* In this play, Lopez portrayed a transsexual Harpo Marx. While a *New York* magazine critic wrote that her character was "less than entrancing," as well as "not so interesting," a critic for the *Nation* commented, "Priscilla Lopez, whom I liked so much in *A Chorus Line,* is cutely nuts as the silent Harpo Marx." Others also found her efforts engaging—Lopez won a Tony Award for that performance.

Lopez's next role was as Lisa in *Key Exchange,* produced at the Orpheum Theatre in New York in 1982. As this play received little attention, so did Lopez. In 1983, however, she appeared in a play which was taken more seriously. *Buck,* written by Ronald Ribman, told the story of a television producer and his desire to reenact crimes for a cable television show. While a *New Republic* critic wrote that the play was, "after David Mamet's *Edmond,* the most courageous new American work thus far this season. . .," he also commented that it "lurches wildly from film noire to Pirandellian theatricality to domestic sentiment to media satire to surreal nightmare, without ever finding a congenial place to rest." A *New Republic* reviewer was more complimentary as he discussed Lopez. "The production is even more confused about its purpose, though some of the acting—particularly Priscilla Lopez as the murdered girl—is strong."

In *Extremities,* which was performed at the Westside Arts Center and the Cheryl Crawford Theatre in New York in 1983, Lopez played Terry. Later in 1983, she appeared as Norina in *Non-Pasquale* at the New York Shakespeare Festival at the Delacorte Theatre. A *New York* magazine critic did not find much to praise about the play. "Little, in fact, has any bite to it, or charm, or less than leaden wit," the critic wrote, adding that "as Norina, Priscilla Lopez is spunky and funky as usual, though spit curls do not flatter her." From 1982 to 1983, Lopez worked as a special assistant to Tommy Tune for the production *Nine.*

During the latter half of the 1980's, Lopez found an abundance of work on screen as well as on the stage. She played Nelly Gardato in the television movie, *Doubletake.* In early to mid-December, 1985, Lopez choreographed the *Times and Appetites of Toulouse-Lautrec,* by Jeff Wanshel. Lopez also portrayed the roles of La Goulue and Paulette in this two-act musical set in nineteenth-century Paris. From late December, 1985, to the early days of January, 1986, Lopez appeared in *Be Happy for Me* as Elizabeth at the Douglas Fairbanks Theater. This play, a comedy, was set on the Caribbean island of Aruba. Later in 1986, Lopez portrayed Wanda Orozco in *Intimate Strangers,* another made-for-television movie. Her next role was that of the character Rosa Villanueva, an emergency room nurse in the television series *Kay O'Brian.* In September of that year, Lopez discussed in the *Los Angeles Times* her reasons for deciding to join a television series; apparently, some felt such a decision would put her acting career at risk. In 1987, Lopez captured the role of Aldonza in the movie, *Revenge of the Nerds II.* In 1988, she appeared in two more television movies, *Jesse* and *Alone in the Neon Jungle.* That same year, Lopez found time to take part in an Off-Broadway production entitled *Marathon '88,* which was actually twelve one-act plays in three series. Lopez appeared in series B; plays in that series included "Mango Tea," "Human Gravity," and "Door to Cuba."

In 1989, the actress portrayed Dr. Gail Gitterman in the movie *Simple Justice.* She then succeeded Mercedes Ruehl in the play *Other People's Money,* as the character Kate Sullivan. 1989 also marked the year Lopez was honored with a part in the special, *Night of One Hundred Stars III.* This all-star show, presented for the Actors' Fund of America, was performed in Radio City Music Hall in May of 1990, and later that month, it appeared on television. Included in the list of stars in the show were celebrities such as Muhammad Ali, Jane Fonda, Richard Gere, Gladys Knight, Olivia Newton-John, Brooke Shields, and Sylvester Stallone. Lopez performed two songs, "What I Did for Love" and "One."

If Lopez's career has been rewarding, her performances have rewarded countless audiences. The inspiration she provided for the character of Diana Morales in *A Chorus Line* continues to delight audiences in theaters all over the United States, as well as in a movie adaptation. Lopez herself has also demonstrated the ability to adapt from stage to screen and back again. Talent and versatility, Lopez's keys to success early in her career, continue to capture roles for the dancer, actress, and singer years after she first impressed the theatrical world with her emotional and realistic portrayal of a character who was, essentially, herself.

Sources:

Books

Contemporary Theatre, Film, and Television, Volume 3, Gale Research, 1986.

Periodicals

Dance Magazine, August, 1980, p. 88.
Horizon, August, 1980, pp. 24.
Los Angeles Times, September 4, 1986, section VI, p. 10.
Nation, June 14, 1980, pp. 731-32.
New Republic, April 18, 1983, pp. 25-27.
Newsweek, June 9, 1975, pp. 85-86.
New York, May 19, 1980, pp. 58-61; September 5, 1983, pp. 65-66.
New Yorker, June 2, 1975, p. 84; March 21, 1983, p. 98.
New York Times, September 28, 1975.
Theatre World, 1985-1986, pp. 69, 84; 1988-1989, pp. 46, 49; 1989-1990, p. 39.

                                                    —*Sketch by Ronie-Richele Garcia-Johnson*

los Angeles Torres, Maria de
See Torres, Maria de los Angeles

Mónica Cecilia Lozano
(1956-)
Newspaper editor

As the associate publisher and editor of the largest Spanish-language daily newspaper in the United States, Mónica Cecilia Lozano is determined to keep the 450,000 readers of *La opinion* aware of and interested in the news. In an interview with Ronie-Richele Garcia-Johnson, Lozano explained that there is an overlap between "straight journalism and journalism with a sense of commitment," and she is definitely committed to the readers of *La opinion*. It is important to her that Hispanics, and especially politically neglected Spanish-speaking Hispanics, empower themselves. "As a group," Lozano believes, "we can have power if we are informed and educated. . . . I really believe in what I am doing."

The editor, whose grandfather founded *La prensa* in San Antonio, Texas, in 1913, and then *La opinion* in 1926 in Los Angeles, remarked in her interview that "you can't separate my success from my family." Lozano was born the third of four children, to Ignacio E. and Marta (Navarro) Lozano, on July 21, 1956, in Los Angeles, California. While her parents were very strict and sent her to Catholic schools through high school, they did not necessarily expect that she would eventually work for the family business. Although Ignacio Lozano published the newspaper that his father had begun in 1926, *La opinion*, from the time of his father's death in 1953 to 1986, and Jose Lozano, Mónica's brother, began to serve as publisher in 1986, and her sister also worked for the paper, Lozano did not think that she would get involved with the newspaper. The self-described overachiever wanted to excel on her own; she did not want to dwell in the shadows of her grandfather, father, brother, and sister.

After earning her bachelor's degree from the University of Oregon, Lozano decided to live in San Francisco. Although she did not know anyone in that city, she soon began to feel at home. For over five years, she worked at a large printing company, first as a press operator and then as a manager of a company branch, as well as on local community newspapers. While working these full-time jobs, she also attended San Francisco City College at night. According to Lozano, she wanted to help her community, and she realized that she needed to use any resources, including the power of the print medium, which might facilitate her goals. She also became intrigued with the workings of the newspaper business and was determined to learn every procedure involved in running a paper— including pre-press and press operations. She eventually received a degree in printing technology from San Francisco City College.

Mónica Cecilia Lozano

Destined to Join Family Newspaper, *La opinion*

Looking back on her decisions to work for the printing company in San Francisco and to earn a degree in printing technology, Lozano wonders if she knew, subconsciously, that she wanted to join the family business. "I guess there is such a thing as [having] ink in your veins," she laughed during her interview. By the time she returned to Los Angeles and began working for *La opinion*, she had prepared herself to supervise and even manually complete every step of the paper's production. In addition, she was well equipped to provide the newspaper's Hispanic readers with the valuable information she learned working on community projects in San Francisco.

While *La opinion* was a source of employment for several members of Lozano's family, Lozano did not just inherit a career in the newspaper business from her father and grandfather. They imparted their sense of dedication, moral responsibility, and ethical ideals to the young woman. "I wanted to do something to help my community," Lozano stressed in her interview. "I wanted to use whatever resources I had to help. . . . It became clear that there was this vehicle. . . . If I wanted to be useful—I should come back to L.A. to work for *La opinion*."

When Lozano became managing editor of *La opinion* in November, 1985, she immediately began to focus on the needs and concerns of her readers. One of her first major projects was to ensured the publication of a special tabloid which discussed the threat of the AIDS virus in the Hispanic community. The Hispanic Coalition of AIDS honored the publication with an advocacy award in June, 1988, for this life-saving, educational contribution to the community. The publication was also awarded the Inter-American Press Association's award for the best public service publication. As a result of her hard work and dedication, Lozano was named associate publisher of *La opinion* on September 16, 1989. In August of 1990, Lozano was appointed publisher of the widely read and respected weekly Spanish newspaper, *El eco del valle*. In November, 1991, she became the paper's editor. When asked to describe her responsibilities as editor of such an influential newspaper, Lozano picked up a paper and pointed at it. She was responsible, she told her interviewer, "for everything except the advertisements."

Spanish-speaking Hispanics who live in Southern California have indeed benefitted from Lozano's commitment to the community and her readers. Largely because of her efforts, *La opinion* has published public service supplements, tabloids, and other publications which discuss such important issues and topics as drug abuse prevention, prenatal care, education, AIDS, and immigration issues. Lozano's seemingly tireless determination to keep the readers of *La opinion* well-informed have been praised and admired by many community leaders.

Lozano, who is a member of the National Association of Hispanic Journalists, the California Chicano News Media Association, and the American Society of Newspaper Editors, has also received state-wide, national, and even international recognition for her newspaper work. In 1987 and 1992, she was named one of the 100 most influential Hispanic women by *Hispanic Business* magazine. The DIME, or Distinction in Media Excellence award, was presented to her by the March of Dimes for a supplement she published on prenatal care. In 1992, she was elected vice president of the California Hispanic Publishers Association.

Family Takes Top Priority in Life

Although Lozano feels a "tremendous sense of tradition" as she works for *La opinion* and is dedicated to the newspaper and its readers, her children, Santiago Centanino and Gabriella Centanino, take priority over all else. Lozano believes that spending quality time with her children is better than spending great amounts of time with them. Her children, she says, understand that she loves them more than anything despite the fact that she works long hours. Lozano also noted in her interview: "Most mothers are not traditional homemakers. Most are forced into working." As an experienced working mother, Lozano readily acknowledges that combining working and mothering is difficult. "The most challenging thing is finding time for your family." Lozano's daily life necessitates a "tremendous balancing act." She feels she is in the "rhythm that working mothers get into."

Lozano's chosen profession, however, is very demanding and her working hours can be quite unpredictable. Responsible for the contents of almost the entire paper, she cannot return home at the end of the day and leave her work in the office. Her days, which are filled with deadlines, begin early in the morning and end late at night. There is no telling when an important news item will occur. A large gas explosion in Mexico, for example, sent reporters and staff members rushing. They all knew that it was important that readers, who might have families in that area, get the facts about the disaster. Such an event, explained Lozano in her interview, requires thorough yet quick work. "This is what you are here to do," Lozano stated. "You go into a different gear."

Another high-gear situation involving Lozano and her newspaper was the Los Angeles Riot of 1992. This time Lozano was not surprised, and she was definitely not unprepared. It was clear to her before the Rodney King verdict that an acquittal of the four policemen accused of unnecessary force would incite violence in the city. She called her editors together and told them that if the policemen were found innocent, "there's no reason to think that the city is not going to burn."

Los Angeles, Lozano pointed out in her interview, has "real deep social problems, the kind of problems that need real deep structural changes." The riots, to her, were expressions of the city's problems. She remarked: "We so easily ignore real serious problems.... Los Angeles is literally segmented by economic boundaries.... You don't get much mix there." And when asked if the riots were heartbreaking to her, Lozano replied no, but said that she would be "disheartened if we didn't learn from this. It's such a critical time. My biggest fear . . . is that we will move forward as if nothing happened." The city, according to the newspaper woman, "has to think seriously about these sort of issues. We have to prepare ourselves [for the future] and we aren't doing that. I think the lesson to learn is that we really need to be serious about our future. We have to integrate more people into it."

Working Toward a Better Future for Los Angeles

Lozano continues to work to better Los Angeles. She is one of seven members and the only woman on the board of the Community Redevelopment Agency (CRA). The mandate of this organization is to "eliminate blight" in neighborhoods that are needy. Since a major purpose of the CRA is to motivate and empower neighborhoods with funding, Lozano believes this is exactly the type of community building project that "I think the government should buy into." The CRA, she commented to her interviewer, has the "opportunity to do something concrete . . . for the homeless population in the city." Lozano feels that with a budget close to 400 million dollars, the CRA has the ability and power to accomplish good things for the community of Los Angeles.

Despite the troubles the city is having, Lozano loves Los Angeles. When she was younger, she revealed in her interview, she "really didn't want to live in L.A." because it seemed to her that the city was "big," "impersonal," and "difficult." During this time in her life, Lozano felt that San Francisco was "a perfect medium" between urban and rural life. These days Lozano feels the energy expended in an effort to revitalize Los Angeles and to prepare it for the future makes the place very exciting. "So much is going on," continued Lozano. Latinos especially are "really trying to do something" for the future of the city. Lozano also believes that she can contribute to a better future with *La opinion.* "There is so much I'd like to do with the newspaper," she declared. "Now that I'm here [in Los Angeles], I couldn't see myself living anywhere else. . . . I can't foresee myself doing anything but [this.]"

In addition to contributing to the city she loves as she works for *La opinion* and the Community Redevelopment Agency, Lozano is an active member of the Los Angeles community. For instance, she is a member of the board of trustees of the University of Southern California. She also sits on the board of directors of the Venice Family Clinic, a non-profit facility which provides health care to low income, minority patients. Lozano works with the Central American Refugee Center and the Center for Human Rights and Constitutional Law. She also serves on the national advisory board of the Scott Newman Center.

Lozano has been recognized on many occasions for her community service. In 1988, the Central American Refugee Center (CARECEN) presented her an award for her contribution to immigrant rights. Some of the other honors Lozano has received for her work include the Outstanding Woman of the Year Award from the Mexican American Opportunities Foundation in 1989, Northern Trust of California's "Hispanic Excellence" award in 1990, the annual award from Comision Femenil of Los Angeles for outstanding contribution as a woman in media in 1990, and the National Organization of Women (NOW) Legal Defense and Educational Fund annual award in 1992.

Lozano is well aware of the example she has created for young Hispanic women; she stated in her interview that as an influential Latina, she feels a "real sense of responsibility" for them. While she encourages young Hispanic women to excel, she knows that it takes a great amount of courage and persistence to succeed. "If you are going to do it," she cautioned, "you should be prepared to go all the way."

Sources:

Periodicals

Hispanic, March, 1992, p. 60.

Other

Lozano, Mónica, personal interview with Ronie-Richele Garcia-Johnson, conducted on August 31, 1992.

—Sketch by Ronie-Richele Garcia-Johnson

Wendy Lucero-Schayes
(1963-)
Olympic athlete, broadcaster

In over ten years of competitive diving, Wendy Lucero-Schayes has had a distinguished career that includes participation in the 1988 Olympic Games. A member of the U.S. Diving National Team for eight consecutive years, Lucero-Schayes is the winner of nine national titles, three U.S. Olympic Festival titles, and several medals in international competition, including a silver at the 1991 World Championships. Her accomplishments are not limited to athletics, however; she has also begun a career in television broadcasting, appearing on national networks as a sports commentator and hosting a local talk show in her hometown of Denver. Her ability to develop her athletic talents, providing herself with opportunities to travel the world and get an education, has made Lucero-Schayes an example for those who would also succeed through hard work and determination.

Wendy Lucero-Schayes was born on June 26, 1963, in Denver, Colorado, to Shirley and Don Lucero. The son of Spanish immigrants, Lucero-Schayes's father worked as an electrician; he was able to work steadily because employers thought he was Italian, not Hispanic. Her mother, of Irish extraction, maintained the household, raising Lucero-Schayes and her sister and brother. The family was active and athletic; Lucero-Schayes began swimming and dancing at an early age, and she picked up gymnastics, tennis, and diving while tagging along to her older sister's lessons. She became competitive in each of her endeavors; sports provided an opportunity for a tomboy to excel, in contrast to school, where she felt teachers frowned upon her because of her energetic nature.

Her sister provided an additional motivation to excel, for the two often ended up competing in the same age group at meets. Their two-year age difference doomed her to being second best, Lucero-Schayes revealed in a personal interview. "For me to compete with my sister—well, she's my older sister, she's always going to win because she's two years older." Always being the runner-up "kept me in a 'trying to achieve' mode," she explained. "I would always strive to be the best I could be because I wanted to

Wendy Lucero-Schayes

grasp what my sister was attaining—but I wanted it now, even though I was two years younger." When Lucero-Schayes began to close the gap between them, her sister moved on to other activities; but the young athlete still felt driven to excel.

Ice Skating Star Inspires Olympic Dream

Part of Lucero-Schayes's ambition was to fulfill a dream she had harbored since she was nine: to compete in the Olympic Games. At first, she thought she would compete in gymnastics, but she realized her late start in the sport would limit how far she could go. Then, she related in her interview, "I fell in love with ice skating. After I saw Dorothy Hamill in 1976 win the Olympic gold, that really inspired me. I knew I wasn't going to be an Olympic gymnast; so I thought 'Well, I'll make it in ice skating.'" Besides providing her an outlet for athletic endeavors, figure skating gave Lucero-Schayes a chance to express herself artistically. "I did enjoy it because of the aesthetic ability" the sport required, she explained. "Being able to dance to the music and perform, and be creative that way— I just fell in love with that aspect."

After competing for four years, however, she came to the conclusion that she would not attain her Olympic dream through ice skating. Not only did she come late to the sport, which left her at a disadvantage in the exacting school figures portion of competitions, but her family lacked the financial resources needed to be successful in

national competition. "As far as getting into the Ice Capades, I probably could have done that," Lucero-Schayes recalled, "but I wanted to get a college education, and ice skating wouldn't have done that." In the early 1980s, at the time she was thinking about continuing her education, a series of federal laws and court decisions had mandated that universities give women equal access to athletic scholarships. By competing in a varsity sport, Lucero-Schayes would be able to take advantage of the full-ride scholarships being made available to female athletes.

While in high school Lucero-Schayes returned to diving, which she had tried for a time as a preteen. Her gymnastics training served her well, and she quickly became very competitive on the springboard events. She placed fourth in her state's championships as a sophomore, and came in second as a senior. By the time she finished high school, she was competing in the Junior Olympic Championships, where she placed sixth in the three-meter event, and the Phillips 66 National Diving Championships, where in both the indoor and outdoor competitions she finished in the top twenty on the one-meter springboard. Her success led her to be named 1981's Hispanic Athlete of the Year, citation as an Academic All-American, and also resulted in a scholarship offer from the University of Nebraska.

Lucero-Schayes was looking forward to the challenges of college; although she had encountered problems with teachers as a very young student, her competitive nature soon emerged and she was earning top grades by the time she entered high school. In addition, her parents had instilled in her the value of an education; because neither of them had been to college, they wanted their children to have the advantages higher education could give them. "My parents were great role models to me, my mother was *the* highest role model that I had," Lucero-Schayes stated in her interview. "I had other role models, the sports role models like the Dorothy Hamills and the Peggy Flemings and the Olga Korbuts. But my mother was always the one I respected and that I thought of as the most wonderful; and I had a dad that was very supportive and tried to give his kids whatever he could with the limitations that he had. They were successful enough with what they had done, but they wanted me to be as self-confident as I could be, because they knew the outside world wasn't going to give that to me."

College Scholarship Spurs Athletic Career

While attending the University of Nebraska Lucero-Schayes had the difficult task of balancing her classes with a demanding schedule of training and competition. She had to work particularly hard to master the three-meter springboard, a new event for her. "I was born and raised in a climate that really was for winter sports," the athlete explained in her interview. "I was really lucky they had some high school pools, but they only had the lowest springboard [one-meter] available to me and that's what you dove in high school anyway. So I really didn't learn the

Olympic springboard event [three-meter] until college, which is a very late date to start out. I've been trying to play catch-up ever since." After two years she transferred to Southern Illinois University, seeking a more compatible coach and better opportunities to compete nationally. The move proved quite successful; she won the 1985 NCAA championship on the one-meter event and earned her first national titles, placing first at the 1984 and 1985 Phillips 66 Outdoor Championships. During these years she was also named an Academic All-American for her performance in the classroom.

Lucero-Schayes had goals outside of athletics, however, and worked hard to achieve those as well. To complement her education—she earned a B.S. in television sales and management in 1986—with hands-on experience, she sought opportunities to work in broadcasting and television production. "As I was training for the Olympic Games in 1988 and the few years before that, I would try to be a production assistant for golf tournaments, horse tournaments, Monday Night Football—anything I could do," she related in her interview. She worked as a freelance sportscaster for NBC, ABC, and ESPN—including a stint as a commentator for the 1991 World Championships—and hosted a talk show, "Focus Colorado," in her hometown of Denver. She particularly enjoyed that experience, she revealed, "because then I could get involved with people that have helped shape not only the state, but eventually the U.S. and what we think."

Training and competing in preparation for the 1988 Olympic Trials was her immediate focus coming out of college, however, and Lucero-Schayes was making great progress. Although she felt she had the potential to dive well on the ten-meter platform, she relinquished the opportunity to learn the event in order to focus on what would be her best shot to make the Olympic team, the three-meter springboard. Her rigorous training for the Olympic event began paying off; in 1987 she won her first three-meter diving titles, at the U.S. Olympic Festival and the American Cup II; she was also attending more international meets, winning bronze in one-meter events at the McDonald's International and at a competition between the U.S. and the Soviet Union.

Mother's Illness Interrupts Olympic Training

But during the time Lucero-Schayes was making great strides toward her Olympic goal, two separate incidents hindered her training: her mother, who had been a constant source of encouragement throughout her career, was diagnosed with an advanced form of breast cancer; meanwhile, her coach was undermining her self-confidence. Although she had won the HTH Classic early in 1988, in three subsequent competitions she placed no better than fourth—and she needed to finish second at the trials to make the Olympic team. She related her difficulties in her interview: "I had people in my life that basically didn't believe in me; I had a coach, a top Olympic coach who told me, 'I'm sorry, but you remind me of me and you'll never make it.' I didn't stay with that person and I ended up realizing that I wanted to prove him wrong."

Lucero-Schayes switched coaches and continued training for the trials; her previous coach's lack of faith only deepened her determination. Another motivating factor was her mother, who had completed chemotherapy for her cancer and would be able to attend the Olympic trials. Lucero-Schayes cites this meet as her most memorable, for the recovery of her mother and her presence at the meet allowed her to enjoy the competition. She turned in one of the best performances of her career and finished second, just eighty-one hundredths of a point ahead of the next diver. She had made the Olympic team, vindicating herself in the face of her former coach's doubt. "To try to believe in myself and surpass what other people think was a big step for me, and I ended up competing and winning, overcoming his top people that he thought *would* succeed."

Lucero-Schayes competed at the 1988 Olympics in Seoul, Korea, finishing sixth. Although she didn't win a medal, she recalls the trip fondly for other reasons: "One of my favorite incidents was with the Russian coach—her name was Tatiana—she gave me a wonderful gift," the athlete remembered in her interview. "We had been creating a nice friendship throughout my couple years of seeing her in international competitions, and I really liked her. After the Olympic games were over, she ended up giving me this wonderful china bowl. And that friendship and that bond—I'll never forget that. I think that is one of the neatest things that could have ever happened, because you cross boundaries through sports that you could not do with anything else."

Employs Tale of Success to Motivate Others

After competing in the Olympics, Lucero-Schayes continued her work in communications, increasing her involvement in public speaking. She has participated in conferences and charity events, and has visited schools. Although she enjoys her work in television, she gets a special reward from speaking to people in person. "I end up being able to touch people's lives that way," she said in her interview, "and I think it's more important because people really need to see you face-on—to talk to you and be able to touch you. The experience may be a short span of time but enough to give them one positive thought that maybe will change their lives for the better." Lucero-Schayes has served as a spokesperson for the American Cancer Society, and often appears as a motivational speaker, periodically in front of Hispanic organizations. "The success I've had in sports overcoming those people who didn't think that I could [succeed] has made me like myself better and find out, 'Yeah, I am capable and I'm not going to let them determine what I can do.' Hopefully I can share that with others."

Public appearances also introduced the diver to her husband, professional basketball player Dan Schayes. The two were appearing at a benefit for a charity promoting organ donation; he gave her a note, joking "I will share my organs with you anytime," and she gave him her number. They began dating, and two years later, in late 1991, they married. The couple often trains together; but more important is the support they provide as each undergoes the strains of competition. "I had dated athletic guys before, but not elite athletes, and it makes a big difference," Lucero-Schayes revealed to Michelle Kaufman of the *Detroit Free Press.* "Danny understands what it feels like to be under pressure, to win and to lose."

The pressure was certainly on Lucero-Schayes going into the Olympic year of 1992. She had continued to improve her diving, winning Olympic Festival titles in 1989 and 1990, and capturing one-meter and three-meter championships those same years. She followed those performances with her best year ever in 1991: she took both springboard events in the indoor championships, placed first in the one-meter and second in the three-meter outdoors, and garnered silver medals at the Sixth World Championship and Alamo International competitions. For her efforts she was voted the U.S. Female Diving Athlete of the Year in both 1990 and 1991. Although a severe parasitic intestinal infection prevented her from competing in late 1991 and hampered her training time going into 1992, Lucero-Schayes was still considered a likely Olympian and a medal contender for Barcelona. These expectations were harder on her than the physical difficulties of training, she commented in her interview. "It's definitely more mental than it is physical, because as much as I have trained, my body now knows [what to do]; it's letting the mind relax and do what I have trained it to do for years. It is more of a mindset, whether or not I feel I'm capable of getting out there and performing to the best of my ability and overcoming the stress and the pressure. But I think this is good," she explained, "because in a way if you're not learning or growing or achieving in that aspect then it's not fun to do it."

Lucero-Schayes finished third in the 1992 Olympic trials, one place short of making the team. Although competing in a second Olympics, in the country of her ancestors, would have been "a dream come true," the athlete still finds much to be satisfied with her career. "Diving has been wonderful to me; not only did it pay for a college education, but I was able to travel around the world, nothing that my parents were ever financially capable of doing. Not only did it expand my horizons and make me understand what the world is all about," she added, it gave her the opportunity to experience "camaraderie, getting to create friendships with [athletes from] other countries." At the end of the 1992 season, she was still investigating the possibility of combining competitive diving with lecturing and various opportunities in broadcasting. In the long term, Lucero-Schayes and her husband plan to return to Denver, where she will continue her career in communications. Now that she has made her mark in the world of athletics, she wants to inspire others on a broader scale. "I always felt that communications—whether radio and television, or through newspapers and journalism—it's going to shape our world, it is the up-and-coming future. I really believe that instead of being on the other side just watching it happen, I want to be involved with helping in a positive way."

Sources:

Periodicals

Atlanta Constitution, July 28, 1989, p. F3; August 2, 1990, p. F7.
Detroit Free Press, April 14, 1992, p. D1.

Other

Lucero-Schayes, Wendy, interview with Diane Telgen conducted April 15, 1992, Ann Arbor, MI.

—*Sketch by Diane Telgen*

Luz Villanueva, Alma
See **Villanueva, Alma Luz**

Naomi Lynn
(1933-)
University president, public affairs specialist

The first Hispanic to serve as a president in the Illinois public university system, Naomi B. Lynn strongly believes in the interdependence of government and education. "Government is absolutely dependent on education . . . to provide educated and concerned voters," she told Sally Foster in a telephone interview. "Education promotes democracy."

The second of three girls, Lynn was born in New York City on April 16, 1933, to Camelo Burgos and Maria Lebron Berly. She attended New York City public schools until reaching her teens, at which time she opted to transfer to a private preparatory high school. In a home where the value of education was constantly stressed, her decision was met with support and encouragement from her parents.

After graduation, Lynn, who had grown up in a devoutly Presbyterian household, followed in the footsteps of her older sister, Ruth, and enrolled at Maryville College, a small religious school in Tennessee. In 1954, shortly after receiving her bachelor of arts degree in political science, she married fellow student Robert Lynn and moved with him to Illinois, where both began their graduate studies at the University of Illinois. Four years later, Lynn received her master of arts degree in political science.

In 1970, following a two-year stint (from 1966 until 1968) as an instructor in political science at Central Missouri State College in Warrensburg, Lynn moved to Kansas with her family (which eventually included four daughters), where she joined the faculty of Kansas State University in Manhattan as an assistant professor of political science and earned her Ph.D. Around the same time she wrote and published *The Fulbright Premise*. In 1975, she was promoted to associate professor, and in 1980 received her appointment to full professor. She was named head of the political science department in 1982, a position she held until 1984.

First Female Academic Dean at Georgia State

Lynn advanced further in her career at Georgia State University in Atlanta, where she accepted a post as dean of the College of Public and Urban Affairs, making her the first female academic dean in the university's history. During her tenure, the college expanded and developed a higher profile in the community, thanks in part to Lynn's own personal involvement in a variety of causes. Besides her memberships in United Way and Leadership Atlanta, she advised the Atlanta city government as well as the state of Georgia, and served on Governor Zell Miller's Commission on Economy and Efficiency in Government. In 1990, she also co-edited a book entitled *Public Administration: The State of Discipline*.

Lynn's strong belief in the need for effective partnerships between government and the academic community has created a demand for her services as a consultant. While she was still based in the Kansas-Missouri area, she accepted Governor John Carlin's challenge to work with the largest umbrella bureaucracy in Kansas, the Department of Social and Rehabilitation Services. There her assignments included helping restructure the department to make it more effective and responsive to its clientele and serving as a member of the oversight committee on mental health facilities.

Lynn's research on women in public administration (done in conjunction with the Association of Public Service Administrators, or APSA) created an opportunity for Lynn to work with the United Nations. At APSA's request, she attended the International Conference on the Decade of the Woman, held in Mexico City, and later edited the *United Nations Decade for Women*. In 1987, the United Nations appointed her as a consultant for a training program in Bangkok, Thailand, that focused on preparing women to enter personnel and civil service jobs in developing nations.

Assumes Presidency of Sangamon State University

Lynn's increasing visibility in academia and public affairs eventually resulted in many offers to assume the presidency of a college or university. As she remarked to Foster, "I seemed to be on everyone's list." But it was not until she was contacted by representatives from Sangamon State University (SSU) in Springfield, Illinois, that she decided to accept the challenge for a combination of personal and professional reasons. Her husband's mother, who lived just outside of Springfield, was very ill, and the Lynns wanted to be involved in her care. Furthermore, SSU is known for its public affairs studies, and, as Lynn noted, its location in the state capital furnishes her with a "natural laboratory." Upon her appointment to the presidency in July, 1991, she became only the second woman and the first Hispanic to head a school in the Illinois public university system.

In her new role, Lynn hopes to enhance the prestige of SSU by improving and enlarging the curriculum, which is currently geared toward graduate and upper division (juniors and seniors) students only. Her intent is to open the doors to freshmen and sophomores and offer more comprehensive programs of study. The major hurdle Lynn faces is locating the resources to fund this ambitious plan.

Lynn has been the recipient of many honors. In 1986, she was elected a fellow of the National Academy of Public Administration and received the Distinguished Alumni Award from Maryville College. She is the former president of the American Society of Public Administrators, and in 1992 she assumed the presidency of the National Association of Schools of Public Affairs and Administration. She is also president of Pi Sigma Alpha, the national political science honorary society.

Sources:

Lynn, Naomi, telephone interview with Sally Foster, September 24, 1992.

—Sketch by Sally Foster

M

Petra Jimenez Maes
(1947-)
Judge

A specialist in juvenile and family law who was instrumental in establishing New Mexico's first family court, Petra Jimenez Maes has always been motivated by a desire to "help the underdog," as she told interviewer Sally Foster. The type of court she pioneered uses non-judicial specialists to help streamline the custody process in Santa Fe.

Maes was born on October 5, 1947, in Albuquerque, New Mexico, the eldest in a family of three girls and two boys. Her parents, who owned a television repair shop, were first-generation U.S. citizens; her mother was born and raised in Albuquerque, and her father was born in Texas but grew up in New Mexico.

Maes's interest in the law dates back to her childhood. Whenever she accompanied her parents on visits to the family attorney, she recalls being greatly impressed by his ability to help people and by the respect his profession enjoyed.

Education was always stressed in the Jimenez household, and it was a family goal that all the children at least graduate from high school. As one of only a few Hispanic students in her public school in Albuquerque, however, Maes often found herself being steered toward vocational education classes. When she discussed her desire to become an attorney with her shorthand teacher, for example, she was told that aiming for a career as a legal or executive secretary would be more realistic. Maes told her mother about the lack of encouragement she received from this particular instructor, and Mrs. Jimenez never forgot it. In later years, she made a point of visiting the shorthand teacher and letting her know about each of Maes's educational and career advancements.

In 1966, Maes entered the University of New Mexico as a political science major. While she was still an undergraduate, she obtained a part-time position with an Albuquerque law firm, where she became familiar with court proce-dures and the drafting of wills. At the university, her business law professor encouraged her to pursue law as a profession. He also offered Maes excellent advice on selecting classes, directing her toward ones that emphasized writing and the development of analytical thinking skills.

Makes History at New Mexico Law School

After earning a bachelor's degree in political science in 1970, Maes entered the University of New Mexico Law School. As part of her studies, she became actively involved in a special program known as Central Legal that ran a legal clinic for indigent clients. In 1973, Maes was one of the first two Hispanic women to receive a J.D.L. degree from the university. As she later recalled in an interview with a *Journal North* reporter, "When I graduated from law school, Mom said, 'Honey, I'm so glad you fulfilled your dream.' But I answered, 'This isn't all of it, Mom. I want to be a judge.' My mom just groaned."

After graduation, Maes set up an office in the South Valley section of Albuquerque. With only the help of a part-time secretary, she maintained a general practice, spending a great deal of her time doing pro bono work in the surrounding community. She also taught undergraduate courses at her alma mater, including Women in Law and Chicanos in Law.

In 1975, Maes married Ismael "Sonny" Maes and closed her Albuquerque office to take a position with Northern New Mexico Legal Services in Santa Fe. When the firm decided to expand its operations, Maes and a colleague were sent to open a satellite facility in Espanola, a ranching and farming community approximately 30 miles north of Santa Fe. Her practice focused mainly on laws dealing with domestic, property, and water rights issues, but the presence of eight pueblos nearby also presented her with an opportunity to practice Indian law.

Realizes Dream When Appointed Judge

In 1981, Maes was appointed to the district bench by Governor Bruce King to fill a vacancy, thus fulfilling another dream. Being a judge held great appeal for her, she told Foster, because "a judge is where the real power is.... Lawyers can only present a case.... A judge is responsible to all of the litigants." At the end of her term Maes faced a tough opponent in her bid to be elected to the bench in her own right. She credits her husband with ensuring her victory in that contest. "Besides being my number one supporter," she continued, "he took care of getting signatures on petitions, arranged for advertising, and put up signs." She also attributes her success in subsequent elections to his superb campaign management skills.

In 1983, the Maes family—which by then included three children and a fourth on the way—moved from Sonny's ranch to a home in Santa Fe after Maes grew weary of the long commute to work. Then tragedy struck when Sonny was killed in an automobile accident. His wife was in labor at the time of his funeral; she delivered their youngest child the following day.

Establishes New Mexico's First Family Court

Upon her return to work, Maes began devoting more and more of her attention to juvenile and family law. She analyzed how the judges did their work in order to develop a court system that would be more responsive to the litigants. In 1984, she established New Mexico's first family court and agreed to help launch it by serving as presiding judge.

Specializing in divorce, custody arrangements, and related issues, the family court makes use of non-judicial specialists to streamline the legal process. Despite the fact that she met with opposition in some quarters, Maes eventually saw her initiative and tenacity recognized by her colleagues, who voted her to a two-year term as chief judge in 1985 and charged her with overseeing the administrative capacity of the court.

As chief judge, Maes took note of the trend toward legal specialization among the lawyers who appeared before the bench. Through her leadership, the court also began to specialize, focusing on criminal and civil law in addition to family law. This administrative change allowed judges to concentrate on the specific types of law involved in the cases that were presented to them.

In 1987, Maes transferred to the civil division of the court to fill a vacancy, returning in 1990 to family court, where she helped to make additional refinements to procedures. By 1992, all of the changes had been finalized, and other courts in the state began to model themselves after the Santa Fe example.

In 1988, Maes ran unsuccessfully for the State Supreme Court, hoping to fill a vacancy created by a female justice. This remains one of her goals, but in the meantime she is concentrating on her new three-year appointment as chief judge in the first district.

Outside the courtroom, Maes works within the community to develop programs for young people and promote awareness of the difficulties they face in contemporary society. She is active on the boards of the National Center of Family Law and the Hispanic Women's Council. She is also a member of the New Mexico Women's Bar Association and the Capital City Business and Professional Women's Organization.

Maes has been the recipient of numerous honors, including the Firestarter Award from the Greater Southwest Boy Scout Council in 1981, the Distinguished Service Award from the Mexican American Legal Defense and Education Fund (MALDEF), also in 1981, and the Award of Excellence from the National Network of Hispanic Women in 1989. She was named an Outstanding Young Woman of America in 1983 and was honored by the Southwest Miss Teen Pageant in 1992.

Sources:

Periodicals

Journal North, May 13, 1989.

Other

Maes, Petra Jimenez, telephone interview with Sally Foster, September 18, 1992.

—Sketch by Sally Foster

Irma Maldonado
(1946-)
Public relations consultant

Irma Maldonado is the executive vice president of HDI-National Hispanic Education and Communications Projects and the creator of the National AIDS Education Leadership Council. Her involvement with AIDS education includes the creation of public service announcements that have run on a number of stations, including MTV. Maldonado's business sense and leadership abilities have brought her numerous awards for service to the Hispanic community, including Coca Cola Woman of the Year (1989), the "Hermana Award" from the Mexican American Women's National Association (1987), Washington Metropolitan Woman of the Year (1982), and the Census '90 Award. Maldonado was also elected president of the Mexican American Women's National Association in 1988.

Maldonado was born in Oxnard, California, on March 14, 1946, to Celia Valverde and Joseph Cusick; she was three years old when they divorced. Celia later remarried and opened a Mexican restaurant in Santa Paula, California, where Maldonado and her sisters served as waitresses and kitchen help. Maldonado's involvement in politics began at an early age. She was elected vice president of her elementary school and held the office of secretary/treasurer of her junior high. In high school she became the first Mexican American to be elected president of the sophomore class. Maldonado recalls, "I was a quiet child, but I always wanted to be in the group that made the decisions that affected my world, so I ran for office."

Despite good grades in high school, Maldonado was not encouraged to continue her education. One counselor actually discouraged Maldonado from applying to a four year institution. Luckily, an English teacher inquired of her plans and wrote her a letter of reference. As a result, Maldonado was accepted to Mount Saint Mary's College in Brentwood, California, where she majored in English literature. On July 9, 1966, Maldonado married Daniel C. Maldonado. They moved to Washington, D.C., when he was accepted to Georgetown University, and Maldonado began working as an editorial assistant for United Press International. They moved back to Southern California for a period of time, and Maldonado gave birth to a daughter and son. Upon returning to D.C., she took a job as business manager of the New City Montessori School where her children were enrolled.

Supports AIDS Education through Television

In 1974, Maldonado was hired as manager of the congressional relations office of the American Library Association (ALA), where she stayed for fourteen years. The ALA supports the rights of citizens to gain information through the library system. Maldonado gathered and disseminated evidence affecting libraries throughout the country, and she addressed issues such as literacy, pay equity, and tax legislation. Maldonado left ALA to help her husband start MARC Associates, a government relations and strategy consulting firm.

As President of the Mexican American Women's National Association, Maldonado's responsibilities included fundraising, leadership conferences, newsletter production, scholarship and training programs. Her keen business sense and leadership qualities brought newfound stability to the organization. In 1988, Maldonado joined HDI-National Hispanic Education and Communications Projects as executive vice president. She created the National AIDS Education Leadership Council and oversees the Council's direction, publications, and activities. Maldonado is co-project director of the AIDS Education Campaign and has developed award-winning television public service announcements on AIDS. She serves as creative director and producer for the announcements which have aired on MTV, Univision, and Telemundo.

Sources:

Books

Crocker, Elvira Valenzuela, *Mana: One Dream, Many Voices— A History of the Mexican American Women's National Association,* DegenBela Graphics, 1991, p. 57.

Periodicals

American Libraries, December, 1983, p. 712.

Other

Fact sheets and curriculum vitae provided by HDI-National Hispanic Education and Communication Projects, September 29, 1992.
Maldonado, Irma, telephone interview with Susan Lopez Mele, September 29, 1992.

—Sketch by Susan Lopez Mele

Sonia Manzano
(1950-)
Actress, writer

Sonia Manzano, an actress and writer for *Sesame Street,* brings a positive role model for Hispanic children to popular television. When she was growing up in the United States, Manzano recalls never seeing Hispanic images in children's books or in the media. "I think it has a terrible impact when you don't see yourself reflected in the society because then you get the feeling you don't exist—like Richard Wright's *Invisible Man,*" Manzano said in a telephone interview with Luis Vasquez-Ajmac. "That's why I love being on *Sesame Street* so much. I'm happy to be in a situation where I'm not asked to be like anyone else."

Born June 12, 1950, in New York City and raised in the South Bronx, Manzano grew up in a very close-knit, Spanish-speaking community. Of Puerto Rican descent herself, Manzano is one of four children. Her father, Bonifacio Manzano, is a roofer by trade while her mother, Isidra Rivera, is a seamstress. Growing up, Manzano never thought of pursuing a career in show business until she was a junior in high school. With the help of a supportive teacher, Manzano went to the prestigious High School for the Performing Arts in Manhattan. Subsequently, she attended Carnegie Mellon University in Pittsburgh, Pennsylvania, on a scholarship and majored in drama. While there, Manzano was cast in the musical *Godspell* and was later part of the original cast when the production came to Broadway. During her performance in *Godspell*, an agent noted her talent and helped her obtain an audition at *Sesame Street*.

Creates Role Model for Hispanic Children

When Manzano began working at *Sesame Street*, the emphasis of the TV series was on helping black inner city children. But with the addition of the character "Maria," Manzano brought to the show a new role model for Hispanic children. Each year, *Sesame Street* focuses on a different ethnic group. Manzano will have a particularly challenging year in 1993, when the show's emphasis will be on the diverse Hispanic culture. She looks forward to writing for and about Hispanics on the show.

After ten years on *Sesame Street* as "Maria," Manzano began writing scripts for the show with hopes of making her character more visible. Understanding the importance of incorporating Hispanic culture into the show's plot line, Manzano often wrote material based on her own real-life experiences, particularly as she developed the relationship, marriage, and eventual parenthood of "Luis" and "Maria." To date, she has earned seven Emmy awards as a member of the *Sesame Street* writing staff as well as an award in 1991 from the Hispanic Congressional Caucus in Washington, D.C.

Television is not a mere stepping stone for Manzano. She is very content acting and writing for *Sesame Street*. By enriching children's lives and expressing her ideas, Manzano feels that she has made a positive impact. Manzano enjoys working with her daughter, Gabriela, on *Sesame Street* and has been married since 1986. When time allows, she also lectures on the importance of Hispanic role models.

Sources:

Periodicals

Atlanta Constitution, May 10, 1989, p. B1.
Boston Globe Magazine, May 7, 1989, p. 8.

Other

Manzano, Sonia, telephone interview with Luis Vasquez-Ajmac, April 23, 1992.

—*Sketch by Luis Vasquez-Ajmac*

Marisol
(1930-)
Sculptor, painter

Not content to work with one medium or to limit her creativity to one style, Marisol began to carve wooden figures and adorn them with unexpected materials. The results of this innovative technique have been carried away to museums and private collections around the world. Marisol is arguably one of the most influential artists of the latter 20th century. Known for works such as *Baby Boy, Baby Girl, The Kennedys, The Party,* and *The Last Supper,* she has simultaneously challenged viewers of her works to ponder the essence of art as well as the messages she conveys with each piece.

Marisol Escobar was born in Paris, France, on May 22, 1930, to wealthy Venezuelans Gustavo and Josefina (Hernandez) Escobar. Given a continental upbringing, Marisol traveled with her parents and her brother throughout Europe, Venezuela, and the United States; it was not until the death of Josefina Escobar during World War II that Gustavo Escobar decided to settle in one place. Escobar, with Marisol, moved to Los Angeles, and Marisol was promptly enrolled in the Westlake School for Girls.

Despite some unhappiness that stemmed from her disapproval of the life-style her parents had led and a phase in which she had visions of becoming a saint, Marisol began to study art in earnest. She wanted to be a painter, and her instructor, Howard Warshaw at the Jepson School, helped her develop her talent. It was not long before the sixteen-year-old woman required further instruction. In 1949, with the encouragement of her father, she left Los Angeles to study at the Académie des Beaux Arts in Paris. She went on to the Art Students League in New York City, and then, from 1951 to 1954, she studied at the New School with the noted impressionist Hans Hofmann in New York and Provincetown. In New York, Marisol frequented the Cedar Bar, where Jackson Pollock, Willem de Kooning, Franz Kline, and Philip Guston, who would become major American painters, often chatted. Marisol came to know de Kooning, and he became a sort of mentor to the young woman. Marisol found herself less involved with traditional impressionism and increasingly intrigued with sculpture, pre-Columbian figures, and South American folk art.

The figures Marisol created of metal, carved of wood, or molded of terra cotta, were first shown in a gallery on Tenth Street, and later at the Leo Castelli Gallery, in New York in 1957. Critics were enthusiastic about the artist's work; her pieces were fresh and engaging. Marisol (who, by this time, had dropped her last name, which she thought sounded too masculine) began to earn a reputation for originality. At this point in her career, however, Marisol decided she needed time to review her feelings about her newly successful career. After a year alone in Rome, the artist returned to New York, and began to work even more productively than she had before.

Uses Commonplace Materials in Art

When Marisol saw a sack full of wooden forms used by a hatmaker, she was inspired to make a sculpture with them; they became *Tea for 3*. After that creation, she began to carve figures herself. As she told *Smithsonian*, "I first started drawing faces on wood to help me carve them. Then I noticed that drawing looked like carving, so I left it. Then, once, I couldn't get a drawing the way I wanted it, so I put a photograph up to help me. I liked it there. So I thought, 'Why not use a photograph?'" Marisol did. She used glass, metal, wire, old clothing, wigs, hats—anything she found in the street could find its way into her creations. Marisol turned a beam she found in the gutter into a representation of the *Mona Lisa* and a couch into a piece she called *The Visit*. For this latter piece, the artist even parted with her favorite coat and her own purse; one of the wooden figures needed it more than the Marisol did.

Marisol was also intrigued by the possibilities of the self-portrait. At first, she made casts of her body parts and took photos of herself, because she often worked late at night and was a convenient model. Later, however, she realized that the reproductions of herself—whether they were hands sprouting from blocks of wood, photographed smiles tacked to a wooden image, or even full-body, miniature Marisol figures in the arms of a larger wood figure—could make statements. In *The Party*, for instance, fifteen permutations of Marisol, fifteen figures, congregate in a social setting. The possibilities of interpretation for this piece are endless.

By the early 1960's, Marisol's fame was growing. She became increasingly involved in the New York art scene. Andy Warhol, the celebrated Pop artist, was a good friend who featured her in his movies. In 1961 Marisol was invited to exhibit her work in the Museum of Modern Art's "Art of Assemblage" show. *Life* magazine carried photos of her work to readers throughout the United States. One of Marisol's carved portraits, *The Family*, which represented a dust bowl farm family in wood and mixed media, was purchased by New York's Museum of Modern Art after it appeared in 1962 at Marisol's exhibition at the Stable Gallery. The Albright-Knox Art Gallery of Buffalo bought another piece, *The Generals*, which featured representations of George Washington and Símon Bolivar astride horses with barrels for bodies. Marisol was well on her way to becoming an influential artist. She was given a room at the Museum of Modern Art for the show, "Americans, 1963;" viewers of the show found that Marisol, more than any of the other fifteen artists, delighted them with her work.

Attracts Attention with Looks and Lifestyle

While Marisol's artwork was engaging, the media seemed to be more intrigued with her stunning looks and interesting lifestyle. Who was this Marisol? The artist herself was not very willing to answer this question. In 1961, she arrived at an artists' panel meeting wearing a white, Japanese mask. By the end of the evening, the audience was screaming at Marisol to take off her mask. When Marisol finally did remove the mask, the audience was more surprised and amused than disappointed—the artist had painted her face to resemble the mask which covered it. What was a statement about art and the self became a mystery about the artist instead. *Vogue, Glamour,* and *Cosmopolitan* magazines featured her, and the public still wanted more.

Smithsonian commented on the "Marisol myth:" Marisol was thought to be "an enigmatic 'Latin Garbo,' someone who wouldn't mind being marooned on a desert island with only herself." Of course, this perception of Marisol was misleading. Marisol kept quiet in an attempt to save herself from the demands of the media; she did not wish to appear mysterious and secretive. Nevertheless, the myth of the "Latin Garbo" maintained itself and managed to divert attention from the seriousness of Marisol's work.

During America's Vietnam War years, the increasingly politicized atmosphere influenced Marisol's work. The London *Telegraph Sunday Magazine* commissioned the artist to portray Prime Minister Harold Wilson and the British Royal Family, along with de Gaulle, Francisco Franco, and Lyndon Johnson. As *Smithsonian* recalled, this was a "hit list" because the resulting creations involved an "interplay of ridicule and menace; the good-natured spoofing of *The Kennedys* (1960) had vanished with the upheavals of the era." Perhaps the emotions that inspired Marisol to work on the political figures were strong enough to persuade her to leave the United States. Instead of showing her work in New York between 1967 and 1973, Marisol traveled. She explored the lands throughout the Western Hemisphere and, camera in hand, she began to scuba dive in the waters of these lands. Underwater photographs and fish-sculptures with Marisol-like features resulted from these travels.

When Marisol showed her latest works in the Sidney Janis Gallery in 1981, her work, as *Smithsonian* noted, had changed. "Instead of offering sly generalized criticism of the rituals of American social and political life as she had before, Marisol focused on more pointedly personal ruminations in delineating beings she views as mentors and beacons." There were portraits, in aged, chipped wood, of Georgia O'Keeffe, Louise Nevelson, Picasso, Marcel Duchamp, and other artists. Finally, there was Marisol's interpretation of Leonardo da Vinci's *The Virgin and Child*, which had taken the artist five years to complete.

Interprets the Work of Leonardo da Vinci

Fascinated with da Vinci's work, Marisol was inspired to create *Madonna and Child with St. Anne and St. John* in 1978, and in 1984, she showed a work she created after another of da Vinci's masterpieces, *The Last Supper*. This latter piece gave the artist favorable attention. A critic for *New York* wrote, "She [Marisol] is a commanding craftsman who can endow relief sculpture with more elegant pathos than is currently fashionable. Her effortless brilliance at joining seemingly unjoinable forms and materials puts to shame the relative awkwardness of Louise Nevelson's endless wood collages."

In her first show since 1984, in May of 1989 at the Sidney Janis Gallery in New York, Marisol featured sculptures of the Archbishop Desmond Tutu and Emperor Hirohito. The former sculpture involved a panel, a portrait bust, and a scepter, while the latter had bulbs for eyes and a carved and painted, wooden block body. Another piece, *John, Washington and Emily Roebling Crossing the Brooklyn Bridge for the First Time,* depicted a famous family of pioneers. There were also portraits of impoverished families. Her "most amusing" sculpture, as the *New York Times* declared, was "a rendition of a working woman who is the embodiment of grim determination. Dressed in a business suit, she grips in one hand a briefcase while holding in the other a baby who appears destined to make millions selling junk bonds." By 1991, the respect for Marisol's work had grown. That year she was given the honor of exhibiting her sculptures at the National Portrait Gallery in Washington, D.C.

While Marisol is constantly working on pieces for her upcoming shows, she has not been too busy to keep up with current events or to contribute to her community: in 1991, her face was posted in the subways of New York City in bilingual advertisements that encouraged healthful, anti-AIDS behavior. The woman who once inadvertently intrigued the public by concealing her face behind a mask, and who replicated that face countless times in her artwork, had once again taken advantage of its beauty. Whatever the context in which the artist has placed herself, viewers of Marisol's face and artwork are always rewarded.

Sources:

Periodicals

Harper's Bazaar, August, 1981, pp. 163+.
New York, June 4, 1984, p. 70.
New York Times, April 16, 1988, p. A11; May 19, 1989, p. C33.
New York Times Magazine, March 7, 1965, pp. 34+.
Smithsonian, February, 1984, pp. 54+.
Washington Post, April 5, 1991, p. WW59.

—*Sketch by Ronie-Richele Garcia-Johnson*

Marrero, Martika
See **Martika**

Martika
(1969-)
Singer, dancer, actress

Marta Marrero, the daughter of Cuban immigrants, insists that she has always wanted to be a famous. She told the *Los Angeles Times,* "My mom asked me when I was two what I wanted to be when I grew up. I told her, 'I wanna be a star.'" By the time she was 19, Martika was well on her way to achieving her dream. Her single, "Toy Soldiers" became a pop sensation, hitting number one on the charts, and other singles from her gold debut album, entitled *Martika,* were also doing well. Martika is not surprised at her success. She unabashedly told *People:* "I knew stardom would happen and I never questioned it. I had no doubt. I just knew I wanted to live on a bigger scale. I wanted to be a household name. All I had to do was to catch up to my destiny."

Martika was born Marta Marrero to Gil and Marta Marrero on May 18, 1969, and was raised in the San Gabriel Valley of Southern California along with her three older brothers. As her mother's own show business ambitions were dashed by strict parents, the young girl was given the opportunity to follow her dreams. Marta, whose nickname Martika is derived from the Spanish diminutive Martica for Marta, started to take music and dance lessons when she was four years old. At the age of eleven, she began to look for an agent. She recalled in *Hispanic,* "I just looked in the phone book and started calling agents."

Childhood Dreams Begin to Come True

Martika's independent and resourceful attitude won her an agent and a small part in the film *Annie.* Martika's next jobs included appearances on television. She was seen in episodes of *Silver Spoons, Hardcastle & McCormick,* and *Diff'rent Strokes,* and she starred in *Kids, Incorporated,* a popular children's series. According to *Hispanic,* it was at that point in her career that Martika changed her mind about acting. She explained in the magazine, "My acting was really taking off . . . when I sort of changed gears, and went into music. I just felt it was really where I wanted to be, where my strength would lie. And music was my first love."

Although Martika was eager to make an entrance onto the music scene, she waited until she had a good producer and a satisfactory contract. "I didn't want to sign just to put

Martika

out a record. I wanted to write my own songs, to be involved creatively. I wanted to be sure that when I brought my music to the world I was saying something," she asserted in *People*. When Martika met Michael Jay, the record producer who had help make the hit group Miami Sound Machine a success, she found a partner who complemented her strong melodies and lyrics with his musical direction. Together, they produced a debut album which lived up to Martika's creative goals and became a smash hit. *Martika* was released in January, 1989, by CBS/Columbia.

Martika wrote five of the songs on this album. One of these, "Toy Soldiers," made her famous when it hit the number one spot on the pop charts. Martika said in *Hispanic* that the song "was just right: it sort of wrote itself, actually." She and Michael Jay "had the title and the hook first," she said in *Hispanic*, and then she decided that the song should focus on addiction. Martika was inspired by a personal experience—one of her friends was dependent on cocaine. She had seen the terror addiction could create and the emotion she felt found its way into her voice as she sang.

"Toy Soldiers" was not *Martika's* only powerful song. Her cover of "I Feel the Earth Move," a Carol King song, was exciting, and the song "More Than You Know" moved teenage listeners. Both "I Feel the Earth Move" and "More Than You Know" made the top 30 singles in the pop charts, and later in 1989, those songs, along with "Toy Soldiers," became top twenty hits. The album *Martika* went

gold. Martika had achieved the fame that she had always sought.

The singer began to receive media attention in local as well as nationwide magazines and newspapers. The *Los Angeles Times*, after noting Martika's insistence that she was not a "limited" "dance-music singer," acknowledged that Martika's talent truly was not "limited." "If you cut through the layers of production on *Martika . . .*," the *Los Angeles Times* reviewer wrote, "you can see that she has a point. Her rousing version of Carole King's 'I Feel the Earth Move' is particularly impressive. Martika . . . does have a decent voice." Fans throughout the United States agreed: they danced to her music, bought her records, and asked for more.

Hit Album Brings Fame

Martika revelled in the attention. She has not been shy about letting everyone know that she loves her fame. "To be the center of attention is great," she told the *Los Angeles Times*. "Other people who love it won't admit it—but I do, very willingly. And I love driving in limos and wearing nice clothes and having people fuss over me and stare at me." Martika actively cultivates the garden of popularity she has so carefully planted. One aspect of this cultivation is the maintenance of her image. Her dark hair is cut short, and her heavy bangs frame a face that is strong, yet elegant. While red lipstick accentuates her mouth, Martika's bold features sport little makeup. Martika's wardrobe is bright and flashy. On stage, once, she wore the costume of a pirate: a kerchief covered her head, a huge hoop hung in her ear, and a large ruffled shirt raged beneath a long vest.

When she's off stage, Martika wears fashionable clothing. Black dresses with scores of bead necklaces, short dresses, cowboy boots, crosses, vests, and tie-dyed shirts. At one time, she sported a temporary rose tattoo on her bosom. Although Martika's look and mood resemble those of Madonna, the undisputed queen of pop and dance music, Martika is clearly her own person. It is true that Madonna is one of Martika's favorite singers, but Martika doesn't need to copy anyone to make a striking impression.

Stardom Leads to Change

In an interview with *People* in 1989, Martika and her mother discussed the changes in the young woman's life since she has become a star. In some ways, she is like any other young woman her age, and in others, she differs drastically. Martika lives at home. She drives a Celica convertible (she bought it herself when she was sixteen), she attends parties, and she obeys her parents. She loves to shop. On the other hand, Martika is continually faced with serious decisions. She is always busy. Finally, she does not date; she doesn't have time.

While Martika's comments, isolated and separated from the young woman herself, might lead one to believe that she is just another shallow show girl, it is apparent that Martika is introspective and thoughtful. The lyrics of "Toy Soldiers" and the maturity she demonstrates as she advances her career convey that impression. Martika herself reminds her fans that she is not an empty-headed performer. She told *People*, "There are times when I'm a girl who loves to laugh and giggle. Other times I get serious and concerned about world hunger, the ozone layer, the homeless and issues like that." Martika's maturity is also evident in the way she treats her fans. When approached, she is very considerate, and generous with her time.

A supportive family may be one reason why the singer maintains a gracious attitude. The influence of her family has benefitted Martika in many ways. Her parents have encouraged her efforts and supported her as she made many career moves. Her mother, Marta, who understands the pain of having one's show business aspirations cut short by conservative parents, has been enthusiastic about Martika's plans. She has been especially helpful; she has even served as Martika's manager. Gil Marrero, Martika's father, does what he can to ensure that things run smoothly. Martika's youngest brother is also eager to work for her; as her personal assistant, he provides moral support as well as practical help. Another, older, sibling manages the singer's fan club. Of course, Martika's parents, siblings, and relatives are some of her biggest fans. When the young woman performed near her home in Southern California, her grandparents and other relatives were in attendance at the concert. They had good reason to be proud of the singer who has been called "Cuban American dynamite."

Martika began her concert tour, with her own band, to promote her already successful album. Opening for Rick Astley, the deep-voiced British pop star, Martika's energetic performances delighted audiences. Her bold moves were fresh, and her voice was exciting—the talent Martika had wanted to display illuminated the stage. While a *Hispanic* critic remarked that Martika's "looks and moves are reminiscent of an early Madonna," and that her "singing in Spanish—verses from her bilingual song, 'Water' brings images of Gloria Estefan," the critic concluded that the singer's "delivery" was uniquely her own.

After the public's response to Martika, her album, and her performances, the young singer was inspired to seek new heights. She was planning a tour of Europe to promote her album, and she even hoped to make a reverse "crossover" into the Latin American market. She revised her album for release in that part of the world by recording four of its songs, including "Toy Soldiers," in Spanish.

While many stars from Latin America aspire to fame in the United States, Martika intends to do the opposite and make herself famous in Spanish-speaking countries. Or, as an *Interview* writer put it, Martika would like to use "her mainstream Anglo success to reach the burgeoning Latino market." Whether she targets Hispanics abroad or in the United States, Martika's Cuban American ethnicity brings much to her work and makes it desirable to Hispanics everywhere.

However successful her album *Martika* was, in October of 1989, Martika was not satisfied: she was already planning her next album, which she expected to be a hit. She told *People* "I have my next album up here, in my head." That album, entitled *Martika's Kitchen*, was released in August of 1991 by Columbia Records. This second album was not the instant smash that *Martika* was; it did not produce any hit singles. Although the popularity of her second album may have been a disappointment for Martika, she continues to plan her next project with the unwavering ambition she has displayed since childhood. If her past is any indication, she will continue to dream and plan her next move into the spotlight.

Sources:

Periodicals

Hispanic, December, 1989, pp. 12.
Interview, August, 1989, p. 61.
Los Angeles Times, March 5, 1989, p. C58; September 15, 1991, p. CAL-69.
People, October 30, 1989, p. 75.
Teen Magazine, November, 1989, p. 56.

—*Sketch by Ronie-Richele Garcia-Johnson*

Arabella Martinez
(1937-)
Community leader, government official

Arabella Martinez has been a lifelong advocate for the advancement of minorities and women. Her passionate beliefs combined with her skills and experience has led her to a key position in President Jimmy Carter's Administration and to a role as one of the most influential and successful community leaders in Oakland, California.

Born July 31, 1937, in Trinidad, Colorado, Martinez moved to San Francisco at the age of five with her parents, who sought war industry jobs. In a telephone interview with Sally Foster, Martinez described her mother as a woman of many talents "who could have been a great designer" and as someone who loved reading. Her mother gave her a "thirst to get ahead." When selecting a college career, Martinez looked to the role models available to low-income Latino girls: teacher, social worker, or probation officer. Deciding that she was not suited for either teaching or probation work, Martinez emphasized social work in her undergraduate studies at the University of California. She felt that it offered an opportunity to "help people" even though she had a secret love for anthropology. Martinez received a bachelor of arts degree in 1959. After graduation, she began her career in social work as a case worker for the Alameda County Welfare Department in Oakland, California. She assisted the elderly, disabled, and Aid to Families with Dependent Children (AFDC) households. In 1963, she accepted a position with the Contra Costa Social Services Department in Pleasant Hill, California. Her case work focused on the Aid to Families with Dependent Children Program.

After hearing a rousing speech given by an organization member, Martinez joined the Mexican-American Community Service Organization (CSO). The CSO's goal was to build ties to other Hispanic community organizations as well as develop its own programs to assist local Mexican Americans in need of aid. In response to the need of an organization that coordinated community efforts and provided a forum for communication, the Spanish Speaking Unity Council (SSUC) was formed in 1964 with Martinez as its first chairperson. With the passage of the federal War on Poverty legislation, the SSUC believed that coordinated community effort would increase the funds available to the community as well as its effectiveness. Encouraged by a SSUC board member to return for her master's degree to advance her career in community leadership, Martinez entered the University of California, Berkeley. She received a Haywood Fellowship and pursued graduate studies in community organization and administration. She was awarded a master's degree in social work in 1966.

Immediately, Martinez accepted a position as the executive director of the Valley Communities Economic Opportunity Organization (VCEOO) in Livermore, California. During her two years of service with the group, she directed community action programs. Her responsibilities involved the design, implementation, and management of new programs. In many ways, Martinez's work on the VCEOO prefigured her role in the SSUC. Martinez's appointment as the executive director of the SSUC in Oakland, California, caused a degree of controversy. When asked about the "specter of machismo" in her position at SSUC in a *La Luz* interview, Martinez replied, "Oh yes. Interestingly enough, not with the older Chicanos but with young Chicanos, many of whom thought the job ought to have gone to a man." Martinez recalled the level of enthusiastic support she did receive and "just ignored the rest . . . I've always been independent and that has set me apart."

Accomplishes Goals During Tenure at SSUC

From 1969 until 1974, Martinez sought to fulfill her goal of combining the common interests of fragmented Chicano community groups. Her tenure at SSUC was highlighted by many accomplishments in the community. In the business community, Martinez developed and managed programs of small business assistance, job creation, and

venture development. She was also involved in programs of overall economic development. In the area of education, Martinez directed training and placement programs, adult education, and developed special instructional programs for Chicano youth. She also planned and managed major housing and office development projects in the community. To accomplish these goals, it was necessary for her to raise more than $3 million. She was also able to forge strong alliances with local, state, and federal governments as well as other minority development organizations. In addition, she also designed the planning strategies, personnel policies, fiscal record keeping, and office management of SSUC. In reviewing her years at SSUC, Martinez reflected in her interview that her greatest accomplishment was that "we've built an effective economic base of operations for the council and we've also developed community leadership. . . . In fact, the council has been used as the leadership model by other organizations."

Martinez left SSUC for several years to travel and begin work as an independent consultant. Her consultancy provided management, financial, and program advice and recommendations to private and public organizations. Among her clients were the Ford Foundation, National Opinion Research Corporation, K. S. Sweet Associates, the Stanford Research Institute, and the National Center for Economic Alternatives.

In January, 1977, Martinez was appointed by President Jimmy Carter to the position of assistant secretary for the Office of Human Development Services, a part of the U.S. Department of Health, Education, and Welfare (HEW). The Carter Administration made a special effort to place female and minority candidates in key policy positions within the federal government. Martinez was one of the highest ranking Hispanics in government service. HEW was one of the most important departments during the Carter years. The administration set forth many initiatives regarding civil rights enforcement, health care delivery reform and cost containment, controversial restrictions on Medicaid abortions, and welfare reform. There was also a strong commitment to address the effects of poverty on children.

Joseph Califano, the new HEW secretary, wanted to restructure what many people felt was one of the government's largest bureaucracies. He hoped the major changes he had planned would lead to the more efficient administration of the department. Unfortunately, many key supporters of the department on Capitol Hill resented his changes without their consultation. Congressman John Brademas had protected many HEW programs involving the handicapped, aged, and underprivileged children from the Nixon and Ford Administration's attempt to dismantle them. When Secretary Califano chose Martinez rather than his suggested selection, the Congressman appeared to resent the appointment. When restructuring placed Martinez in charge of areas of special concern, Brademas responded by deriding her qualifications publicly. Martinez was caught between a Congress which was overly sensitive to slights of minorities after the Nixon-Ford years and an administration which did not recognize the importance of training its staffers in working more effectively with Congress. It was a trait that bedeviled the Carter Administration with its congressional relations. As one anonymous congressional staffer explained to the *New York Times:* "It's demeaning for bureaucrats to come up here and shuffle, but they simply have to do it sometimes. It's an art, and Arabella doesn't seem to know it." In responding to this statement, Martinez replied, "If shuffling means to be servile—then that's not my style."

In an address to a women's political caucus in October, 1977, Martinez reflected on her experience in government service. While the Carter Administration had a good record on appointing women to important jobs, she felt that any women entering a high level position would face criticism and charges of being unqualified. She stated in her interview that "even though I had 18 years of experience in the field in which I was going to work," her credentials were ignored or dismissed. The situation was exacerbated by the press who "never bothered to check or ask for a resume. I don't think they would have done that to a white male." She also acknowledged that she and Congressman Brademas became friends once he had the opportunity to witness her abilities. "I think he was most impressed with my honesty and integrity," Martinez recalled. The Office of Human Development Services managed the social services and rehabilitation programs of HEW, such as the seniors' program, Meals on Wheels, and Head Start for disadvantaged children. Assistant Secretary Martinez was responsible for the management of a $5 billion annual budget and 2000 employees. She was involved in policy formulation, program design, agency development, budgeting, research, and evaluation of policies. In her duties, it was also necessary to develop relations with state and municipal governments, other federal agencies, and public interest groups.

Advances Rights of Minorities

In 1979, Arabella Martinez left HEW for the private sector to continue her work as a consultant. In a statement released to the press at the time, Martinez stated that she could "be more effective in furthering the cause of social justice outside the government rather than inside." Her resignation did not reflect a break with the Carter Administration because she continued to express her support of President Carter. Martinez created a nonprofit corporation, the Center for Policy Development (CPD) in 1980. In her role as president of the center, Martinez assisted foundations and corporations in the development of their community policies and programs, especially those working with women and minority economic advancement. Clients included the ARCO Foundation, Ford Foundation, Carnegie Corporation of New York, Port of Oakland, the California State Library, and National Institute for Dispute Resolution. The CPD also was active in fund raising cam-

paigns. It raised over $800,000 for the Oakland Young Women Christian Association's (YWCA) capital campaign. The CPD also helped advance the Women's Initiative for Self Employment by raising $300,000 to provide support for low and middle income businesswomen in the San Francisco Bay area. Another significant accomplishment was the role played in the development and implementation of the California Regional Capital Project which was designed to provide a pool of loan funds for female entrepreneurs.

At the end of 1989, the board of directors of SSUC requested that Martinez return as its chief executive officer. Her agenda for the revitalization of the SSUC included the development of short- and long-term planning strategies to increase the financial capacity and the traditional leadership building role of the council. Martinez began to redevelop strong relationships with banks and other lenders, local business leaders, political leaders, and philanthropic organizations. She also began the process of rebuilding the board of directors. In addition to the public duties, there were also internal administrative tasks to perform. It had become necessary to restructure debt and to develop computerized accounting systems to redesign the SSUC's financial organization. As a result of these efforts, more than $3 million was raised in a period of only 22 months. Monies raised were for specific programs as well as the rebuilding of administrative support at the council. The SSUC was once again a premier organization providing and training leadership in the Hispanic community. One of SSUC's biggest projects was the Transit Village, a multimillion dollar ten year program. Transit Village will develop the area around the Bay Transit (public transportation) to generate multi-use buildings for housing and office space as well as provide facade improvement for retail sector. Coordinating government, private sector, and foundation funds, SSUC hopes to completely redevelop a blighted area of the community.

Quoted in an interview with *La Luz*, Martinez explained her viewpoint of minority economic advancement: "We've never been hard-line ideologue in the council. Basically we've been pragmatic in our approach to problem solving. I think some people confuse ideology with reality. Of course we're passionately concerned with wanting to make life better for Chicanos. But there's no way you're going to change the system by just throwing rocks at it. The net effect of throwing rocks is zero. We've found that we can exert changes by becoming part of those agencies we seek to make more responsive to our needs."

Martinez has been the recipient of many awards and honors, including the DIANA Award from Epsilon Sigma Alpha in 1975, a commendation from the National Association of Social Workers in 1979, a special award from the Spanish Speaking Unity Council in 1979, a commendation from the City of Oakland for community service in 1979, a leadership award from Adelante Mujer Hispana in 1982, a community leadership award from the Oakland, California

YWCA in 1985, the Woman Power Award from the Women's Yellow Pages in 1989, and the National Concilio in San Francisco in 1991.

Martinez has long believed that the pathway to self-sufficiency and empowerment of women and minorities has its foundations in economic advancement. She has spent her life working to establish strong community-based organizations to promote economic progress in job development, creation of loan pools for small business, and training and placement of youth and adults through alliances with corporations, foundations, and lenders. When asked to describe herself, she modestly stated in the telephone interview: "I bring people, ideas, and money together. . . . I energize and motivate a diverse group of people." Her successful leadership is a model which is emulated by many other national and community leaders.

Sources:

Periodicals

La Luz, November, 1974, p. 16; September, 1977, p. 34.
New York Times, January 19, 1977; March 24, 1977, p. A17; July 16, 1977; September 10, 1977, p. A8; October 24, 1977, pp. A1, A24.
Washington Post, October 24, 1979, p. A24.

Other

Martinez, Arabella, telephone interview with Sally Foster on October 2, 1992.

—Sketch by Sally Foster

Demetria Martinez
(1960-)
Author, poet, journalist

Demetria Martinez is an award-winning poet and author who began her career as a journalist. She gained widespread attention as the defendant on trial in a sanctuary case, the first such involving federal prosecution against a journalist. Martinez was acquitted in this landmark case.

Martinez's grandmother was Lucy Jaramillo, elected county clerk in Albuquerque, New Mexico in the 1940s. Jaramillo remained politically active through the 1980s, holding several elective posts in New Mexico. Her father, Theodore Martinez, was president of Technical Vocational Institute, a community college in New Mexico. Recognized as a pioneer in the Hispanic community, he was the first

Hispanic to sit on the Albuquerque School Board, winning two terms during the 1960s. The governor of New Mexico appointed Theodore Martinez to the state Board of Educational Finance. A Peace Corps volunteer, he served two years in Belize. Dolores Jaramillo Martinez, Demetria's mother, is a kindergarten teacher.

After graduating from Princeton University, Martinez returned to New Mexico and became a freelance writer, covering religious issues for the *Albuquerque Journal* and the *National Catholic Reporter.* The latter, a nationwide newspaper that Martinez describes as independent from the Catholic Church, has published more than 100 of her stories and columns. As a reporter Martinez became involved in the case that led to her indictment on one count of conspiracy and two counts each of transporting and inducing two alien women to illegally enter the United States.

The case resulted from Martinez's work for the *Albuquerque Journal,* for which she wrote a weekly article or story. In August 1986, the Rev. Glen Remer-Thamert of the Evangelic Lutheran Church of America contacted Martinez to tell her about two El Salvadoran women who wanted to enter the United States to deliver their babies and give them up for adoption. He said the babies were due around Christmas time and suggested that it would make a good Christmas story for the newspaper. Martinez drove to El Paso, from where she and Remer-Thamert walked across the international bridge into Cuidad Juarez, Mexico, where the minister had made arrangements with a Juarez family to help the two women cross the border. Once the women arrived in El Paso, Remer-Thamert drove them back to Albuquerque on back roads while Martinez interviewed the pair. Martinez eventually decided not to write the story, explaining that she became concerned that "their anonymity would be endangered and they could end up with deportation." Instead, she wrote a poem about their plight.

Involvement with Salvadoran Women Leads to Charges

Much to Martinez's surprise, the interview resulted in her indictment on the five counts of violating federal immigration laws. Because it was the first time the federal government had charged a journalist in a sanctuary case, Martinez became the subject of newspaper stories across the country, including the *New York Times.* In one story in the *New York Times* Martinez summed up the importance of the case, observing that "At one level it is a concern for reporters who are attempting to gather information about a topic which the current administration would deem politically incorrect. At another level, there's the whole relationship between the reporter and the source."

To officials of the sanctuary movement (consisting mainly of church-related groups who provided haven for refugees from Central American conflicts), the case was viewed as a breakthrough in their mission. The federal prosecutors argued, however, that Martinez was a criminal, comparing her actions with those of a drug dealer who asked to be allowed to break the law because he intended to write about it. Martinez believes the government's intention was to send a warning to the sanctuary movement and to intimidate other journalists from reporting events in El Salvador. "Religion writers were following closely the U.S. policy in El Salvador," she noted. "The U.S. was sending a million dollars a day in military aid, basically that was going to kill people. Middle-class white church people were questioning why we were backing this government which was a pariah in international eyes." The *National Catholic Reporter* had played a key role in bringing Salvadoran government atrocities to public attention, beginning with the 1980 assassination of Archbishop Oscar Romero. This incident, says Martinez, "opened many Christians' eyes."

Witnesses Defend Martinez's Free Speech Rights

During the nationally-publicized trial, the government obtained a copy of Martinez's unpublished poem about the two women who came with her to the United States. The poem, written in a reporter's voice and addressed to Salvadoran women, drew geographical detail from the journey from El Paso to Albuquerque. Defense witnesses, including U.S. journalists with background in ethics, testified that freedom of the press includes the right to research a story—and the right to choose not to write it. Witnesses pointed out that Martinez took a separate car, was taking notes throughout the trip from El Paso to Albuquerque and followed the rules of journalism throughout the event. Literary experts testified that it is common historically for writers to cover a story and later write books or poems about the experience. They cited examples, including that of John Steinbeck, who after reporting on the Depression wrote *The Grapes of Wrath*. Also testifying in defense of Martinez were a rabbi and other theologians who swore to the historical importance of the sanctuary movement and its importance in religious life today. Said Martinez in a telephone interview with Carol von Hatten, "It would make perfect sense for a religion writer to be covering a sanctuary story."

The defense succeeded, said Martinez, in showing that the two Salvadoran women, who were persuaded to become prosecution witnesses, were "powerless in the United States. Their fate rested in the hands of the immigration department." She noted, "we were able to show how they could easily have been coerced into testifying. I think the jury discounted most of their testimony because of this." The 1988 acquittal came after only a few hours of deliberations. The *New York Times* reported that one juror told the Associated Press that "from the start of deliberations jurors had agreed that Ms. Martinez was involved solely as a reporter." Martinez bears no ill will toward the two Salvadorans who testified against her; she believes they had no choice. The women have remained in the United States. One did give up her baby for adoption, but the other decided to keep her child.

Lessons of the Trial

What impact did the trial have on her? Martinez explained that "The end result shows how small on the scale of things it was . . . a footnote to a much larger drama—the struggle of the El Salvadoran people. It helped to keep [the trial] in perspective. It was nothing compared to the El Salvadoran experience in the 1980s when any knock on the door could have you dragged away and never seen again."

Martinez's experiences also helped her form some personal insights into the challenges faced by individuals who act according to conscience. "For those engaged in political struggle in this country, it's not easy. They are up against a lot. There's a lot that needs to be changed, including our foreign policy. Definitely our domestic policies. And when people are committed to change [the failure to achieve change] can be very discouraging. But their discouragement and pain is very small on a global scale of things. This is what the trial gave me, a global perspective."

In 1989, a year after the trial ended, Martinez's poem, "Turning," was published by *Bilingual Press Review*. It was one of three poems included in the volume, which is entitled "Three Times a Woman." The poem won first prize in the Thirteenth Annual Chicano Literary Arts Contest in 1989. Martinez subsequently traveled across the country giving readings and lecturing at several universities, including MIT, Stanford, the University of California, the University of Utah, Long Island University, and numerous campuses in Arizona and Texas. She taught a summer session in Boulder, Colorado, at the Naropa Institute. In March of 1990, she spent a month as writer-in-residence at Hedgebrook Cottages, Whidby Island, Washington. "They nurture women writers there and are committed to helping women's literature," said Martinez.

In addition to "Turning," Martinez has published poetry in *The Christian Century*, the journal *River Styx* and in several anthologies. In 1990, she moved to Kansas City and became the national news editor for the weekly *National Catholic Reporter*. Martinez and her husband, photographer Jeff Scott, plan to move to Tucson in 1993, where they will work for the *National Catholic Reporter* on its Southwest project. She will write columns about environmental racism and Hispanic women's issues, and he will provide photographs.

Sources:

Periodicals

New York Times, June 7, 1988; August 3, 1988, p. A8.

Other

Martinez, Demetria, telephone interview with Carol von Hatten, September 30, 1992.

—Sketch by Carol von Hatten

Elizabeth Martinez
(1943-)
Library administrator

As city librarian for Los Angeles, California, Elizabeth Martinez administers an operating budget of more than 37 million dollars, and supervises a staff of 1,200 employees assigned to 63 library branches. Martinez, who started her career as a children's librarian, is the only Hispanic woman heading one of the largest library systems in the United States. She admits that her ascent to the position of administrative head was arduous. "Being a woman, and a Mexican American woman at that, I had to be the best at all times in order to gain professional acceptance," she explained in an interview with Michelle Vachon. "I was perceived as representing all Hispanics, and strongly felt the responsibility of showing what the entire Hispanic population could accomplish." In 1966, there were only five Mexican American librarians in the country and "we all knew each other." There are now approximately 420 Hispanic librarians working in academic and public libraries. "One of my efforts since I became a librarian has been to recruit more Hispanics into the profession," related Martinez in the *Los Angeles Times*. "There are very few Hispanics who go into the library profession, and one of the reasons is that they don't have a tradition of library services in their community."

Martinez was born April 14, 1943, in Pomona, California, where she grew up in the poorest part of town. "I was a library kid," she recalled in an interview for the *Orange County Register*. "Books were a kind of escape. I visited places I'd never seen." Her local children's librarian developed an interest in her, and encouraged her to read and learn about the world; Martinez ended up going to the library as much for the librarian as for the books. After graduating from high school with excellent grades, "I was turned down at the local private college because of my ethnic background," she told Vachon. But she tried again, entered the University of California at Los Angeles in 1961, and received her bachelor of arts in Latin American studies in 1965. The following year, Martinez secured her master's in library and information science from the University of Southern California (USC) in Los Angeles (she later obtained a certificate in management from USC in 1978, and

an executive management program certificate from the University of California at Irvine in 1986). "I more or less chose this career by accident, because I did not want to be a teacher," Martinez commented in her interview with Vachon. She was determined to make a difference in people's lives, and realized that she could accomplish that by being a librarian. In 1966, Martinez joined Los Angeles County Public Library as California's first Mexican American librarian. One day, a young Hispanic girl brought her mother to the library to meet Martinez. "'See mom, she looks just like me,'" the child said. "You never understand how much a role model you are until something like this happens," remarked Martinez in her *Orange County Register* interview.

In 1972, the Los Angeles County Public Library promoted Martinez to the position of regional administrative librarian for the west and central county regions. During the following seven years she administered 12 to 15 libraries with a personnel budget of more than one million dollars. Among other accomplishments, Martinez established a Chicano resource center in East Los Angeles and an Asian cultural center in Montebello; she also developed a multilingual telephone information center. From 1974 until 1976, Martinez lectured at the California State University's School of Library Science at Fullerton, served on its advisory committee, and contributed to the school's success in obtaining a federal grant for the creation of a Mexican American librarians' institute.

Supervises Construction of New Libraries

After serving for a short period of time as the Los Angeles County Public Library's chief of public services, Martinez accepted the position of county librarian for the Orange County Public Library in 1979. She handled the system's $24-million budget and oversaw its 600 employees. During her tenure, Martinez also supervised the construction of eight new community libraries, including the San Juan Capistrano regional library (its concept earned architect Michael Graves national and international acclaim); implemented one of the largest computerized circulation control systems; established multicultural services and a books-by-mail loan service; created the Friends of the Library Foundation; and set an annual recognition day for the library's friends and volunteers. In June of 1990, Martinez returned to the Los Angeles Public Library as city librarian. In addition to the library's 63 existing branches, Martinez has had to supervise the construction of 26 new branches, including the central library built at an estimated cost of 212 million dollars.

Martinez's achievements have earned her numerous awards throughout her career. She received the George I. Sanchez Award from the National Association of Spanish Speaking Librarians in 1976, the Edmund D. Edelman Certificate of Commendation from the Los Angeles County Board of Supervisors in 1977, the Hispanic Women's Recognition Award from Orange County's League of United Latin American Citizens in 1982, Orange County's Women of Achievement award in 1988, and Orange County's Women's Alert Award in 1990. The Hispanic Book Distributors named Martinez Hispanic Librarian of the year in 1990, and since 1987, by governor's appointment, she sits on the board of trustees of the California State Summer School for the Arts.

In spite of her past accomplishments, Martinez is constantly planning to improve current services and to prepare for the future. She believes that libraries will either provide the instant information required in this age of personal computers and fax machines or become expendable. But evolving library techniques and their certain evolution into the next century have not altered the personal requisites to pursue a librarian's career. "You must enter the profession with a sense of responsibility as well as a love of literature and knowledge," she noted in her interview with Vachon. "You must yearn to share a vision, a quest for knowledge with people, and long to impart information that will enable them to improve their lives."

Martinez has written extensively on racism. In a 1988 article published in *Library Journal,* she stressed that "Racism is an epidemic, like AIDS. It . . . permeates every aspect of our society." Mentioning incidents from her personal life—"I didn't look 'American'"—she concluded: "I continue to be an optimist—a cautious, sometimes suspicious, but still vigilant optimist. And my message is this: Now that we know what was, and what is, think about what if? What if we worked together to overcome racial bias?. . . What if we dialogued and learned about each other so as to lessen sensitivity and hostility? What if we gave each other the benefit of the doubt?. . . What if we begin today?"

Martinez has two children, Nicolas and Maya, born in 1973 and 1977. Divorced, she lives in Upland, California.

Sources:

Periodicals

Library Journal, November 1, 1988, pp. 35-39.
Los Angeles Times (Orange County edition), April 7, 1986, pp. V1, V3.
Orange County Register, March 15, 1989, pp. K1, K4; September 12, 1989, p. B2.

Other

Martinez, Elizabeth, interview with Michelle Vachon, August 28, 1992.

—*Sketch by Michelle Vachon*

Lissa Ann Martinez
(1954-)
Ocean engineer, consultant

Ocean engineer Lissa Ann Martinez credits luck for the success that she has achieved in her life. Whether it was receiving a quality education at a young age, attending the Massachusetts Institute of Technology (MIT) on a scholarship, or being selected the first National Academy of Engineering fellow, she told contributor Sandra Márquez in an interview: "Autonomous acts lined up and I consider that just my good fortune." Martinez manages her own marine environmental consulting firm outside of Washington, D.C. Her job requires her to advise federal agencies such as the Environmental Protection Agency and her former employer, the U.S. Coast Guard, on how to implement international ship pollution agreements. While excited to be part of a small cadre of professional marine protection experts, Martinez acknowledges she is basically dealing with the age-old problem of "what to do when people throw garbage in the ocean."

Martinez was born on July 15, 1954, in Cherry Point, North Carolina, the daughter of Molly and Edmund Ovalle Martinez. Her father's career in the marines took the family to many different states during her youth, but as she told Márquez, being on the move so much actually proved to be a benefit. Unlike many Latino children, especially ones she later observed in the Texas public school system, she never had to deal with teachers who had lower expectations of her just because she was Hispanic.

Applying to MIT on the advice of a close family friend and high school counselor who had been invited by the university to visit the campus, Martinez noted in her interview with Márquez that "in retrospect the pivotal influence of one individual made the difference." She went on to earn her bachelor's degree in ocean engineering from MIT and her master's degree in technology and public policy from the same institution.

Establishes Scholarship at MIT

Martinez has maintained close ties to her alma mater, teaming up with her husband, Brian Hughes, the chief executive officer of a company that designs rocket engines, to establish a scholarship fund for economically disadvantaged students. The idea took shape in 1988, when Hughes was preparing to sell his privately-owned telecommunications company. He and Martinez decided to donate stock to MIT, a gift that at the time of the sale was valued at more than $200,000. The endowment has made it possible for some of the school's neediest students to replace a portion of their loans with grants. "I was pleased that MIT had identified a group of students that needed more help than is usually available," Martinez remarked to Carla Lane of *MIT Spectrum,* "and I am proud to be able to help them."

Between running her own business and raising her two sons, Martinez leads a busy life. Yet she still finds time to engage in a variety of professional and community activities. She is a founding member of the Washington, D.C., chapter of the Society of Hispanic Professional Engineers, and in 1991 she was a member of a 15-person task force that created six new election districts for her hometown of Takoma Park, Maryland. Out of that effort grew a successful campaign to extend voting rights in city elections to all Takoma Park residents, regardless of their citizenship. As Martinez explained to Márquez, "For our town, the fairest voter representation was to allow everyone to vote."

As one of only a few women working in her field, Martinez is constantly charting new territory. She looks forward to the day when more women enter the field of engineering.

Sources:

Periodicals

Hispanic Engineer, fall, 1987, pp. 30-34.
MIT Spectrum, January, 1992, p. 16.

Other

Martinez, Lissa Ann, interview with Sandra Márquez, September 12, 1992.

—*Sketch by Sandra Márquez*

Vilma Martinez

Vilma Martinez
(1943-)
Attorney, public speaker

Vilma Socorro Martinez is a nationally known and respected attorney and lecturer who has been committed to the cause of civil rights her entire life. She decided long before law school that this would be the focus of her career and her life. "I didn't think my parents were treated fairly and I don't think I was treated fairly," said Martinez in a telephone interview with Carol von Hatten.

Martinez was born in San Antonio, Texas, the daughter of Salvador and Maria Pina Martinez. During high school she served as an officer in the National Honor Society and planned to continue her education. But her counselor tried to dissuade her from going to college, advising her that avocational school would be more appropriate for a Mexican American. That was not the first time the young student had encountered prejudicial thinking. She recalled in an interview with the *Los Angeles Daily Journal* that some well-meaning teachers referred to her as Spanish, presuming that calling her Mexican might hurt her feelings. Martinez, however, rejected her counselor's advice and attended the University of Texas in Austin. To help finance her education, Martinez worked at the university. One of her jobs was in the biochemistry lab. There, a professor took an interest in her and encouraged her to leave Texas and pursue graduate education at an Eastern liberal university. She did follow that advice and after obtaining her degree in Austin, she enrolled in law school at Columbia University in New York City.

Recalling her early days encountering prejudice against Mexican Americans while growing up, Martinez acknowledged in her interview: "I was bitter. I remember ranting to my mother, who told me, 'If you're going to let them destroy you like that you will be the only one hurt and no one will listen to what you have to say.'" Determined to make people listen to what she had to say, Martinez, fresh from law school in 1967, took a position with the Legal Defense and Education Fund of the National Association for the Advancement of Colored People (NAACP). Her clients were minorities and poor people living in New York City and the South. One of her most noted cases during her years with the NAACP was Griggs vs. Duke Power. In this case, Martinez won a ruling establishing that it is a violation of Title VII of the U.S. Civil Rights Act for a company to require a high school diploma and intelligence tests because of their disproportionate impact on minority job applicants.

Becomes President of MALDEF

In 1970, Martinez joined the New York State Division of Human Rights as an equal employment opportunity counselor. She helped draft and implement new regulations and administrative procedures on employment rights. The following year she joined the prestigious New York law firm of Cahill, Gordon & Reindel and worked as a labor lawyer. While at Cahill, Gordon & Reindel, Martinez and Notre Dame Law School graduate Grace Olivarez became the first women to join the board of the Mexican American Legal Defense and Education Fund (MALDEF). In 1973, at the age of 29, Martinez was appointed general counsel and president of MALDEF. During her presidency she advocated diversification of the organization. "You can accomplish only so much if you join hands only with those from your own background," Martinez stated in her interview.

One of her major accomplishments during her years with MALDEF was her tireless work expanding the U.S. Voting Rights Act to include protection of Mexican Americans. The original act, passed in 1965, applied only to blacks and Puerto Ricans. Typical violations of the U.S. Voting Rights Act had included polling places that suddenly ran out of ballots when Mexican Americans tried to vote, and ads that ran on Spanish language stations warning Mexican Americans that they would be fined or arrested if they voted. Her endeavor met some opposition from Clarence Mitchell, head of the NAACP Washington office, who argued that expanding the U.S. Voting Rights Act would dilute voting rights enforcement for blacks. However, Martinez skillfully enlisted the help of a coalition of groups to aid this important case. Supporting her effort to expand voter protection were organized labor, the Congressional Black Caucus, and Japanese Americans. Congress responded to her efforts and in 1975 extended voting protection to Mexican Americans. That victory came on the heels of a ruling the previous year in which MALDEF secured a guarantee of bilingual education for non-English speaking children attending public schools.

Another one of Martinez's important MALDEF achievements was her ground-breaking work on the Plyler vs. Doe case which challenged a Texas law denying free public school education to undocumented children—children of illegal aliens. Before this 1982 legal decision, public school tuition of $1,000 was required for each undocumented child. As Martinez declared in her interview: "This put school out of reach for many of these children, basically our children—American children who had lived here for years but who weren't citizens. Without that educational opportunity those kids wouldn't have a chance." Plyler vs. Doe set a precedent in extending rights to undocumented aliens.

However, Martinez believes her greatest executive accomplishment at MALDEF was to institutionalize the organization. "I was able to create a mechanism for MALDEF to exist through fund-raising, recruiting, and learning to juggle resources so it could continue to grow year in and year out," Martinez told her interviewer. When she arrived at MALDEF in 1973, the organization had no endowments and Martinez spent many restless nights worrying about how to meet the payroll. But she was determined to build MALDEF into an organization that would continue to be capable of furthering the cause of Mexican Americans. When she left MALDEF in 1982, the organization had been transformed into a force that operated with a $4.9 million annual budget and a staff of 23 attorneys working nationwide.

Joins Los Angeles Law Firm

"Personally and professionally it was time to move on," said Martinez in her interview. But she was uncertain what to do next. She considered running for elective office or teaching at the college level. Eventually she decided to join the Los Angeles law firm of Munger, Tolles & Olson. Becoming a partner in the large law firm would give her real independence in her career, she concluded. However, it was a move that required some thought for Martinez. During her years at MALDEF she frequently had been questioned during lectures at law schools by students worried about "selling out" to corporate institutions. That was not an issue in her move from MALDEF, Martinez decided. "People should be free to grow up and be whatever type of lawyer they want to be." At Munger, Tolles & Olson, she litigates labor disputes, including wrongful termination, employment discrimination and insurance bad-faith cases.

As a result of her extensive and successful work on behalf of civil rights, she is a sought-after speaker and has addressed groups at the University of California (All-University Faculty Conference), Yale University, Rice University, University of Notre Dame, and her alma mater, the University of Texas. She has also lectured at a number of law schools, including the law schools affiliated with Harvard University, Yale University, Stanford University, and the University of Michigan. She was a guest speaker at the

Ditchley Foundation in Oxfordshire, England. She also has addressed the National Association of Hispanic Journalists and the California Newspaper Publishers Association.

Throughout her career, Martinez has been extraordinarily active in community, legal, educational, and public service projects. Many of those positions have enabled her to continue her lifelong efforts to expand opportunities for minorities. Martinez has generously given her time and expertise to serve as a board member or officer for a wide array of institutions and corporations. She is chair of the UCLA Board of Visitors and is a co-founder of its Achievement Council. The council, formed after she discovered low eligibility rates of Mexican Americans in the University of California system, seeks to increase the number of minority students attending college. She is active with Claremont College's Tomas Rivera Center, a Hispanic think tank. Continuing her 17-year campaign in the voter rights area, she serves as vice chair of the Southwest Voter Registration and Education Program. She has been a member of the board of Anheuser-Busch since 1983, and in 1984 she became vice chairman of the board of the Edward W. Hazen Foundation in Los Angeles. In 1990, she joined the board of the Sanwa Bank of California and is a member of its Community Reinvestment Committee. She also serves on the board of People for the American Way, which she joined in 1991. Martinez is a member of the advisory board of the Asian Pacific Women's Network, the Loyola Law School's Institute for Latin American Legal Studies, and the Asian Pacific American Legal Center of Southern California. Martinez is also a member of the Council of Foreign Relations and Columbia University's Law School Board of Visitors.

Martinez served from 1975 to 1981 as an unpaid consultant to the U.S. Census Bureau, chairing a panel that persuaded the bureau to add a question on the census form asking if a person is of Hispanic origin. As a result, the heritage of Hispanics now is included in the official count of the American population; states include such information in their demographics studies; and the information has led in part to the redrawing of some electoral districts. During the Carter Administration, Martinez served as a member of the advisory board on ambassadorial appointments. In 1976, she was appointed by Governor Jerry Brown to the California Board of Regents, serving 14 years including a two-year term as chairman.

Martinez's service and achievement have not gone unnoticed or unappreciated. She has earned a number of awards, including the Jefferson Award in 1976 for public service from the American Institute, a medal of excellence from Columbia University's Law School, in 1978, and again in 1992 as a major figure in civil rights, a distinguished alumnus award from the University of Texas, 1988, and the Valerie Kantor Award for Extraordinary Achievement in 1982 for her work with MALDEF. In the early 1990s,

Martinez returned to MALDEF, this time as a member of its board of directors.

Despite her busy schedule, Martinez is not solely occupied with her career and public service. She and her husband of more than two decades, Stuart Singer, also an attorney, keep busy raising their two sons, Carlos and Ricardo Singer.

Sources:

Periodicals

Los Angeles Daily Journal, January 6, 1992.

Other

Martinez, Vilma, telephone interview with Carol von Hatten, September 19, 1992.

—Sketch by Carol von Hatten

María Martínez-Cañas
(1960-)
Photographer

María Martínez-Cañas has made a name for herself as a photographer whose work is characterized by collages of shapes and images that reinvent traditional photography. "Shadows, mountain ranges, even benches make us question their identity," wrote Elissa Turner in the *Miami Herald* of Martínez-Cañas's work. "The literal world, like photography itself, has been mapped out in new directions."

Martínez-Cañas was born in Havana, Cuba, May 19, 1960. When she was three months old, her family moved to Puerto Rico, where she spent most of her childhood and adolescence. Though both her native Cuba and adopted Puerto Rico are Caribbean islands with similar cultures, her work expresses a particular longing for her homeland. "Like a baby adopted at birth who eventually yearns to know all about her biological mother, Martínez-Cañas became a woman in search of her Cuban cultural identity," explained Larry Thall in the *Chicago Tribune*.

Experiments with New Forms of Photography

Martínez-Cañas received an undergraduate degree in photography from the Philadelphia College of Art and a master of fine arts degree from the School of Art Institute in Chicago. As early as 1981, Martínez-Cañas began to experiment with amberlith, a photographic material that blocks light. By cutting and scoring this material, then printing the incisions on white paper, the innovative photographer achieved a truly unique effect. "It looked like printouts of an oscilloscope, the machine that reads the beats of music, then reproduces it," she told Turner in the *Miami Herald*. Martínez-Cañas continued to experiment with her photography, sometimes drawing inspiration from the early maps and documents she studied in Seville, Spain during a Fulbright-Hayes grant. When working, Martínez-Cañas does not make a preliminary sketch of her work, nor does she plan anything more than the actual physical size of her finished photography. Thall called her "an artist with the hand of a neurosurgeon."

Writing in the *Chicago Tribune*, Thall found her work many-layered: "On one level they are like visual folktales passing along the culture of Cuba. . . . On the second layer reside elements of Spanish history and early cartography, tropical botany, religion and female symbolism. Finally, there exists a layer that seems to question established Eurocentric values." In addition to several exhibits in the United States, her work has also appeared in Bibliotheque Nationale in Paris, in Sendar, Japan, and in Madrid. Her photographs were also included in a traveling exhibit, "Cuba-U.S.A.: The First Generation." A recipient of a National Endowment photography fellowship and a Cintas Foundation grant, she lives and works in Miami.

Sources:

Periodicals

Chicago Tribune, May 3, 1991, p. 89.
Más, Mayo-Junio 1991, p. 81.
Miami Herald, January 16, 1992, p. F7.

—*Sketch by Ana Veciana-Suarez*

Martínez Jaramillo, Cleofas
See **Jaramillo, Cleofas Martínez**

Martínez Tagle, Tessa
See **Tagle, Tessa Martínez**

Martinez Tatum, Grace
See **Tatum, Grace Martinez**

Maria Emilia Martin-Garcia
(1951-)
News reporter, radio producer

Maria Emilia Martin-Garcia became a social worker in Northern California in order to help people. But when she discovered the limitations of social work and saw the potential of radio as a means to inform and assist individuals, Martin worked her way into public radio, becoming a guiding voice on Hispanic issues.

Martin-Garcia was born in Mexico City, Mexico, on January 28, 1951, one of the six children of Charles McGlynn Martin (of Irish descent) and Adela Garcia Rios, a Mexican. Spending her formative years in California, Martin-Garcia was introduced to radio while attending Sonoma State College. She recalled in *Express News,* "The Chicana group I belonged to was asked to have a show on the local radio station—seven or eight young women with no experience in radio. But, we had something to share—our excitement about our new-found identity as Chicanas . . . our history as Mexican American women."

Later setting college aside, Martin-Garcia began working for the social service department in Sonoma County while volunteering at KBBF, a local public radio station. Eventually Martin-Garcia acquired a grant to become the station's news director on a full-time basis. Her experience at KBBF convinced her of the importance of public radio and informative programming. In an interview Martin-Garcia commented that "KBBF grew out of a need to serve a community of Mexican farm workers, single men whose only world was the field and the bar and who had little information outside of that."

Martin-Garcia's interest in public radio and Latino issues continued long after leaving KBBF. While working with California Public Radio in 1980, Martin produced "Sacramento en Revista," which focused on legislative activities of interest to the Latino community. She also produced a weekly state-wide Spanish-language magazine in San Francisco from 1981 to 1983. Martin later moved to Seattle, Washington to produce "Revista Latina," a weekly bilingual music and information magazine program, for KUOW-FM. Then in 1987 and 1988 she produced "Latin American Week in Review" for KXCR-FM in El Paso, Texas. She joined National Public Radio (NPR) in Washington, D.C. as editor of "Latin Files" in 1989. After the show lost its funding in 1990, Martin became responsible for ensuring good consistent coverage of Latino issues on NPR's major mainstream news programs, such as *All Things Considered* and *Morning Edition*. As assignment editor, she helped make NPR more responsive to the public as a whole.

Martin has taken a sabbatical from NPR to work with the Center for Mexican-American Studies at the University of Texas at Austin on Latino news and cultural affairs programming as senior producer. After completing her sabbatical, Martin intends to return to public radio in some capacity. "National Public Radio," Martin told an interviewer, "does the best kind of journalism and reflects the reality of what is going on in communities all over the world." It is her continued goal to be involved in that process—of using public radio to make different communities better understand each other.

Sources:

Periodicals

Express News, March 4, 1992, p. D5.

Other

Martin-Garcia, Maria Emilia, interview with Luis Vasquez-Ajmac, July 20, 1992.

—Sketch by Luis Vasquez-Ajmac

Carmen Maymi

(1938-)

Director, Office of Equal Opportunity

Throughout her life, Carmen Maymi has worked to make the world a fairer, more equitable place to live. As a community organizer in Chicago and later as a high-ranking Washington government official, Maymi has worked to improve social policies affecting equality in the work force, labor standards, civil rights, and women's rights. "The issue of Hispanic women is one that deserves special consideration because of the double jeopardy of sexism and racism," said Maymi in a telephone interview with Luis Vasquez-Ajmac. "Those things have been prevalent in my life," she added, "in the same ways as they have been for other Hispanic women's lives. . . . How we take those challenges and make them into incentives to succeed make us stronger and make our careers ever more significant."

An only child, Maymi was born March 17, 1938, in Santurce, Puerto Rico, to Luis Maymi Garcia and Socorro Sierra Maymi. Her father, an accountant by profession, held various political positions in Puerto Rico while her mother taught school. At the age of 15, Maymi moved to Chicago and continued her education, eventually receiving a B.A. in 1959 and an M.A. in 1961 from DePaul University. She later received an honorary doctorate degree from Lewis University in recognition of work that improved the status of women in the work place and helped women in prison obtain college degrees.

Launches Government Programs

Beginning her career in 1959 in Chicago as a community organizer, Maymi joined the Commonwealth of Puerto Rico's migration division as a career counselor and later became a regional supervisor for the community organization. "There were extraordinary needs to help the community," she recalled for Vasquez-Ajmac. "It was an extension of myself to improve the life of all of us." Known for her hard work, Maymi joined the government in 1966 as a community service specialist with the former Office of Economic Opportunity where she helped launch programs on a national scale. She subsequently combined her public service career with various executive and management positions in the private sector. Returning to government work in 1972, Maymi worked with the President's Cabinet Committee for Spanish Speaking People developing program goals in the employment of Hispanics for federal cabinet agencies.

Seeks to Improve Status of Women in the Workforce

From 1973 to 1977 Maymi focused her attention on the welfare of working women. As Director of the Women's Bureau for the Department of Labor and Deputy Assistant Secretary for Employment Standards, she implemented policy and legislation, such as the Equal Pay Act, that would have long-lasting positive effects on women in the work place. She also became a U.S. representative to the United Nations and held a post at the National Labor Organization in Geneva where she worked to improve the conditions of working women globally. From 1980 to 1986 Maymi directed the Office of Equal Opportunity within the Office of Personnel Management. Since 1986 Maymi has been the director of Equal Opportunity for the U.S. Department of the Interior where a top priority of hers has been to enforce the Disability Rights Program and to make its programs fully accessible to persons with disabilities.

Despite her busy schedule, Maymi has still found time to build a house in the mountains, a project she oversaw in every phase until its completion. She now enjoys her beautiful home, being outdoors, hiking, and studying nature. Maymi also values time spent with her daughter, Rosa, and takes pride in watching Rosa's career prosper.

Sources:

Periodicals

Milwaukee Journal, October 13, 1974, p. 149.

Other

Maymi, Carmen, telephone interview with Luis Vasquez-Ajmac, August 18, 1992.

—*Sketch by Luis Vasquez-Ajmac*

Rachel McLish
(1958-)
Bodybuilder, actress

Rachel Livia Elizondo McLish, the woman credited with bringing glamour to women's bodybuilding, first gained fame when she won first place in the 1980 U.S. Women's Bodybuilding Championships. Other titles include Ms. Olympia in 1980 and 1982 and the World Championship in 1982. McLish left bodybuilding competition when the use of steroids became a factor, prompting her to crusade against steroid use and drug abuse in general. Although she has since turned her attention to acting, writing, and the fashion world, McLish remains dedicated to promoting physical fitness, especially among women.

Born in Harlingen, Texas, to Rafael and Rachel Elisondo, McLish's interest in fitness was first sparked simultaneously by the study of ballet and her father's weight-lifting hobby. Even as a child, she was fascinated with the strength and the grace of the human form. These two diverse activities set the foundation that would later enable her to encourage women to appreciate feminine muscularity as a new physical ideal. During her high-school years, she won a spot on the cheerleading team and found herself forced to choose between cheering and ballet. She opted for cheerleading. The immediate gratification of popularity and a full social schedule overshadowed her childhood dream of becoming a professional dancer. By the time she enrolled at Pan American University in Texas, she regretted giving up dance and feared that, at age seventeen, she was too old to pursue it again. McLish missed the physically active lifestyle she had known all her life and decided to pursue her other love—working with weights. At the time, weight-training wasn't very popular with the general public and exercise clubs were scarce. McLish eventually found a spa called the "Shape Center" and fell in love with the atmosphere. Unfortunately, as an impoverished college student putting herself through school, she couldn't afford the membership dues. Instead, McLish applied for and was offered a job at the spa. She started by teaching exercise classes and eventually became a manager.

Becomes First Female Body Building Champion

In 1978, McLish earned a degree in health and physical education and formed a partnership to build the "Sport Palace," the first and largest health club facility in south Texas. The club was so successful, it eventually expanded to Corpus Christi and Brownsville, Texas. In 1980 McLish read about the first U.S. Women's Body Building Championship being held in Atlantic City. She was interested for two reasons: to promote her fitness centers but, more important, if she could win the first title she could serve as a positive "feminine" example of a bodybuilder. She entered and walked away with the title.

As the first female bodybuilding champion, Rachel McLish was hailed as a new female role model. She appeared on magazine covers and television programs worldwide. She became a sought-after personality and traveled extensively to lecture on physiology, diet and beauty under the title of the World's First Female Body Building Champion. Her dedication and effort paid off. She won the Ms. Olympia title in 1980 and 1982 and the 1982 World Championship. When the emphasis in body-building shifted in the mid-1980s from muscle tone to massive muscular development, however, McLish decided to stop competing. While she wasn't winning bodybuilding titles, McLish wasn't idle, either. She accepted a part in the documentary *Pumping Iron II: The Women.* McLish also starred in the CBS prime-time television special *Women of the 21st Century,* a documentary exploring a woman's commitment to a physical lifestyle. She made her feature film debut in 1992 in *Aces: Iron Eagle III* opposite Academy Award-winner Louis Gossett, Jr. McLish continues to pursue a career in films, but is very selective about the roles she chooses, refusing any that she feels are demeaning to women.

Enters Fashion World

In 1985 McLish became spokesperson for the Health and Tennis Corporation of America. Her continuing dedication to fitness and nutrition also prompted her to write two books, *Flex Appeal* and *Perfect Parts. Flex Appeal* addresses all aspects of health and fitness, including psychological conditioning, dietary responsibility, nutrition and sports medicine. *Perfect Parts* is a fitness guide on spot reducing. In 1990, McLish and K-Mart department stores joined forces to create a line of bodywear that would offer comfort, fit and fashion for active women. The collection, "Rachel McLish for The Body Company," made its debut in K-Mart's 2,200 stores on January 1, 1990. As with every other aspect of her professional life, McLish took a hands-on approach and was actively involved with the project from its conception. In a 1992 interview with Elena Kellner, McLish commented: "It's not like I'm just a spokesperson. And I feel really lucky that my mother was a seamstress and she taught me how to sew at a very early age. So when I had my first meeting in New York with the manufacturers, the pattern-makers, the fit models and all the people involved in making a line of clothing, they were pleasantly shocked in that I knew exactly how to construct a garment." She proudly added that in 1991 her line of bodywear accounted for 28% of the total sales of sportswear in the United States.

McLish was briefly married in the early 1980s to John McLish, her sweetheart at Pan Am University in Texas. They had no children. In 1990 she wed Ron Samuels, a successful Los Angeles artists' manager and film producer who, in an interview with the *Dallas Morning News,* described his wife as a settling force: "She has an inner strength and spirituality that is very uplifting and strengthens me. She has tremendous self-esteem without any sense of arrogance."

Through her campaign against steroid abuse and unique image as a "feminine bodybuilder," Rachel McLish has become a role model for many women and has helped make weight-training and body shaping one of the fastest growing women's exercise activities. In an interview in the *Los Angeles Times,* McLish expressed her thoughts: "The point of physical fitness is not narcissism or egotism. It's well-being. Most people have no idea what it's like to feel good all over. All the time. People unfortunately take drugs to do it part of the time. But the ultimate rush is the feeling you can get from intelligent exercise. It's addictive. In the best way."

Sources:

Periodicals

Dallas Morning News, October 1, 1989.
Hispanic, September, 1992, pp. 50-54.
Hispanic Business, July 1992, p. 24.
Los Angeles Times, June 26, 1987.

Other

McLish, Rachel, interview with Elena Kellner, April 1992.

—*Sketch by Elena Kellner*

Concha Meléndez
(1892-?)
Scholar, poet

As a poet, Concha Meléndez has expressed her most personal thoughts, and as a scholar, she has contributed to the fields of Puerto Rican and Latin American literature with her interpretations of serious literary works. Although she was a prolific writer, it was the quality of her work, and not the quantity of it, that so impressed her colleagues. Hector O. Ciarlo, who wrote a book about Meléndez's work entitled *El escritor y su obra,* spoke of Meléndez with both admiration and affection: "Hay en Concha Meléndez ciertos símbolos y una rara dimensión mística, que penetran profundamente su vida y su obra." Ronie-Richele Garcia-Johnson translated his comment: "There are, in Concha Meléndez, certain symbols and a rare mystical dimension that profoundly penetrate her life and work."

Expresses Loss through Poetry

Meléndez, born on November 23, 1892, in Caguas, Puerto Rico, began to write when she was still quite young and her first published work appeared before she was thirty. While Meléndez dedicated *Psiquis doliente,* a book of poetry, to her father, the collection includes poems written about her mother, who must have died when Meléndez was very young. In "Autobiografía," which is dedicated to the poet's sister Rafaela, the woman laments her loss, and in "Para ti, Madre," the poet writes of her sadness that her mother did not live to read her poetry: "Tú no escuchaste nunca mis versos, eras/ un lirio agonizante cuando yo vine, y Dios quiso temprano que te me fueras. . . / ¡ya no hay sol en tus ojos que me ilumine!" As translated by Garcia-Johnson: "You never heard my verses, you were/ a dying lily when I arrived, and God wanted you to leave me early/ already the sun that shines on me is not in your eyes." The poet credits her mother for inspiring her: "Porque es mía tu pena, mío el amor/ de tu alma pura y noble, tu fuerza mía,/ son mis tres fuentes/ de poesía/ como torrentes/ de un río único de armona." As translated by Garcia-Johnson: "Because your pain is mine, mine is the love/ of your pure and noble soul, your strength mine,/ they are my three fountains/ of poetry/ like torrents/ of one unique river of harmony."

Meléndez, who counts the Mexican poet Amado Nervo as one of her favorites, wrote her first published scholarly work, *Amado Nervo,* on Nervo's life and poetry. The book appeared in 1926 and was followed in 1934 by *La novela indianista en Hispanoamérica,* possibly Meléndez's best known work. *Signos de Iberoamérica* was published in 1936. From 1940 to 1950, Meléndez served as the chair of the department of Hispanic studies at the University of Puerto Rico at Río Piedras. During this time she published several works, including *Entrada en el Perú* in 1941, *Asomante: Estudios hispanoamericanos,* in 1943 and *La inquietud sosegada poética de Evaristo Ribera Chevremont* in 1946. Meléndez wrote the introduction and notes and served as the editor of *Cuentos hispanoamericanos,* which appeared in 1953. She also wrote *Ficciones de Alfonso Reyes* in 1956 and edited *El cuento* in 1957. Her work, *Figuración de Puerto Rico y otros estudios,* was published in 1958.

After 1959, Meléndez became a professor emeritus at the University of Puerto Rico, Río Piedras. She also served as a consultant for the Institute of Puerto Rican Culture while she continued to write. Her works during this time period include *El arte del cuento en Puerto Rico* in 1961, *José de Diego en mi memoria* in 1966, *Literatura Hispanoamericana* in 1967, and *Literatura de ficciín en Puerto Rico: Cuento y novela* in 1971. *Palabras para oyentes: Conferencias, presentaciones de escritores, exposiciones de pintura,* and *Poetas hispanoamericanos diversos,* notable for an essay on Chile's famous poet, Pablo Neruda, appeared in 1971. The *Complete Works of Concha Meléndez* appeared in 1979. In addition to publishing her own books, Meléndez contributed to various periodicals such as *Asomante, Alma Latina, Puerto Rico Ilustrado, El Mundo, Brújula,* and *La Torre.*

Meléndez's efforts have not gone unrecognized. She was named the Puerto Rican Woman of the Year by the Association of American Women in 1971 and she has received citations of merit from the Institute of Puerto Rican Literature, the Puerto Rico Atheneum, the Commonwealth of Puerto Rico, and the Mexican Academy of Language. By 1982, the aging poet and scholar was too ill to do the work that she loved. She had, however, already made a substantial contribution to Hispanic literature. Meléndez's writings as a poet and scholar have helped Hispanics around the world celebrate their cultural history.

Sources:

Books

Ciarlo, Hector O., *El escritor y su obra: al encuentro de Concha Meléndez y otros ensayos,* Editorial de la Universidad de Puerto Rico, 1982.
Hispanic Writers, Gale Research, Inc., 1991, pp. 309-10.
Meléndez, Concha, *Amado Nervo,* Instituto de las Españas, 1926.
Meléndez, Concha, *Psquis doliente,* 1923.

—*Sketch by Ronie-Richele Garcia-Johnson*

Margarita B. Melville

Margarita B. Melville
(1929-)
Scholar, activist

Scholar and activist Margarita Melville has devoted her life to the struggle for social justice, both by personally intervening to improve the conditions of the oppressed and by voicing their plight through her scholarly works. Her long history of activism began during her years as a teacher in Guatemala, and expanded to include resistance to the Vietnam War and support for the rights of Mexican Americans. Much of her writing in support of these issues has been done in conjunction with her husband, Thomas Melville.

Margarita Bradford Melville was born on August 19, 1929, in Irapuato, Guanajuato, Mexico. She was one of five children in a family of mixed United States/Mexican ancestry and, by virtue of her birth, has experienced the phenomenon of living in two worlds. Melville's paternal grandfather, an American, went to Mexico to work on the construction of the national railroad system (Ferrocarriles Nacionales de Mexico) and married into a Mexican family. After spending her early childhood in her provincial Mexican town, Melville was sent to Loreto Academy in El Paso, Texas, for her high school education. Mexican families in the late 1940s saw no reason to provide higher education for their daughters, assuming that women would devote their lives to serving their families.

Yet Melville, like other Hispanic women of her generation who felt the challenge of improving the world around her, of going beyond the family circle to assist the less fortunate, sought another alternative. This and her desire for further education prompted her to join a religious order, and in 1949 in St. Louis, Missouri, she took her vows as a Maryknoll sister and became a Catholic nun. Historically in Latin America, the only alternative to marriage or family concerns open to young women of good families was to become a nun. Melville's choice in entering Maryknoll was fortunate, for this American congregation of missionary nuns and priests was active the world over in the struggle for social justice.

Serves as Missionary in Guatemala

Melville left the convent to attend Mary Rogers College in Ossining, New York, where she received a bachelor of education degree in 1954. That same year, she was sent by her order to teach in Guatemala. Guatemala was a cultural shock for the young nun. Poverty was rampant, and 95 percent of the arable land was held by 2 percent of the population. The wealthy landowners considered any attempt to alter this state of affairs as subversive, since the landless peasantry provided cheap labor for their labor-intensive coffee and cotton plantations. During her thirteen years in Guatemala, Melville taught at all levels of a Catholic girls school. One of her accomplishments was establishing a model school where her students could do practice teaching.

Outside of the classroom, with student volunteers, Melville traveled to the countryside to teach the people to read and write. She directed a group of university volunteers in health and literacy programs, from which the Cursillos de Capacitacion Social were born. The Cursillos were workshops geared to empowering the peasantry, leading them to the awareness of their rights and developing the leadership and community interaction skills that would enable them to change an unjust system. Such social activism by Catholic men and women was encouraged by the spirit of the Second Vatican Council (1961-63), which proposed that the Church had a place in this world. Despite the fact that the changes that Melville and others like her were attempting to accomplish in Guatemala were grounded in accepted religious teachings, they were declared subversive. In 1967, at the request of the Guatemalan government, the United States embassy, and the bishop of the capital city, Melville, along with others, was asked to leave the country.

Imprisoned for Protesting U.S. Policies

Back in the United States Margarita married Thomas Melville, a former priest who was part of the Guatemala struggle. One of the couple's pressing concerns was to make the American public aware of the presence of U.S. troops in Guatemala. Melville compared the situation to U.S. involvement in Vietnam, for in both cases she thought that troops placed abroad as "advisors" were in fact supporting a repressive campaign against the peasantry. Having joined the growing anti-war movement, the Melvilles participated in the burning of Selective Service records in

the Baltimore, Maryland suburb of Catonsville. They were arrested as a result of this action and became part of a group that would come to be known by the time of their court trial as the Catonsville Nine. Margarita was one of two women in the group and the only Hispanic. Her testimony in court was utilized in the writing of the drama, *The Catonsville Nine,* later adapted for film. Margarita was sentenced to a year in federal prison and her husband to two years. While serving her sentence—which was reduced to nine months for good behavior—in a West Virginia facility, Margarita and her husband completed a joint thesis for their M.A. degrees in Latin American studies from the American University in Washington, D.C. This work, *Guatemala: The Politics of Land Ownership,* was published in 1971. The previous year, a joint autobiography of the Melvilles, stressing their social justice activism, was published by Knopf under the title *Whose Heaven, Whose Earth?*

After their release from prison, the Melvilles decided to pursue doctorates in anthropology at the American University. In 1973, research for their joint dissertation took them to Chile for two years to study the social organization of the Mapuche Indians during the government of Salvador Allende. It was during this period that their two children were born. After the military coup that overthrew Allende's socialist government, the Melvilles were asked to teach at the Catholic University in Temuco, Chile, to fill in some of the many gaps left by their Chilean colleagues who were either forced into exile, kidnapped, or killed by agents of the Augusto Pinochet dictatorship.

After receiving her doctorate in 1976, Melville accepted a position at the University of Houston as assistant professor of anthropology. There, Melville turned her attention to the concerns of women and Chicanos. In 1977 she served as member of the Houston executive committee for the International Women's Year Commission. She helped organize activities for Chicanas and joined the board of directors of the Centro para Immigrantes, a non-profit organization which provided legal services to immigrants seeking to legalize their status or, in many cases, fight deportation. She served as chair of this organization from 1982-83, during the peak years of the exodus of people from Central America who were fleeing civil war in El Salvador and Guatemala. Her interest in this issue is revealed in her contribution to David Haines' 1985 collection *Refugees in the United States.*

Studies Mexican American Issues

Melville's engagement in Mexican American issues has deepened over the years. She is the editor of two important studies, *Reflections of the Mexican Experience in Texas* (1979), and *Twice a Minority: Mexican-American Women* (1980), and led the University of Houston's Mexican American Studies Program in 1978-79. The author of numerous scholarly articles on Mexican American issues, Melville also served on the editorial board of *Aztlan,* an international journal of Chicano studies, between 1981 and 1985 and was a member of the board of directors of the National Chicano Research Network between 1980 and 1982. In 1986 Melville left the University of Houston to become associate professor at the University of California at Berkeley, where she serves as Coordinator for Chicano studies and, since 1988, has held the position of Associate Dean for the Graduate Division.

Regardless of her involvement in Mexican American affairs, Melville's preoccupation with Guatemala continues. Although she has never returned to that Central American nation she continues to speak for the oppressed in the region. In the early 1990s, Melville spent time in Guatemalan refugee camps in the Mexican states of Chiapas and Campeche as part of her research for a book. Interviewing the children in these camps she discovered that the policies of scorched earth—the destruction of villages and fields—are in operation for the purpose of suppressing any efforts towards a viable way of life by the peasants. Melville has reported some of her findings in articles appearing in *Children: Guatemala's Human Resource for the Future,* edited by M. Howard, and in scholarly journals.

Melville supports Hispanic women's issues through her participation in the group Mujeres Activas en Letras y Cambio Social (Women Active in Literature and Social Change), a California-based organization that supports young Hispanic women who want to pursue higher education and retain their community and ethnic ties. Melville was named 1992 Scholar by the National Association of Chicano Studies for her significant contributions to scholarly research and writing in the area. Melville resides in Berkeley, California with her husband, Dr. Thomas Melville, and their two children.

Sources:

Melville, Margarita B., interview with Silvia Novo Pena, 1992.

—Sketch by Silvia Novo Pena

Corine Mendoza
(1952-)
Police sergeant

Corine Mendoza is one of only four Hispanic women in the Chicago Police Department (CPD) who has attained the rank of sergeant. Mendoza, who has been an officer for 14 years, started her career at a time when female police officers were scarce, and Hispanic female police officers were even scarcer. The total number of women in the CPD still comprise less than 20 percent of the 12,000 officers but, as Mendoza said in an interview with Julie Catalano, "the numbers are definitely increasing. We're not a novelty anymore."

Mendoza's upbringing in a traditional Mexican American family could hardly have predicted her career as a law enforcement officer. As one of five children born to Dolores Heredia Sanchez and Jesus Jose Sanchez, Mendoza remembers her childhood in the Pilsen area, one of Chicago's oldest Hispanic *barrios,* as "poor," but, as she told Catalano, "my mother always made sure we did the best we could." Describing her feelings at the time about police work, Mendoza stated: "I always admired police officers, but it was something I never thought seriously about because as a female there was no encouragement for any kind of professional career. I was taught your lot in life was to grow up, get married, and become a wife and mother." Mendoza eventually did marry and become a mother to three children, Daniel, Jr., Aaron, and Elizabeth. She and her husband, Daniel, divorced in 1988.

Mendoza attended Richards Vocational High School and received her associate's degree from City College in 1979. About that time, she read an article in a women's magazine about law enforcement becoming a promising field for women. She decided to explore the possibilities. After passing the entrance test, Mendoza was accepted into the six-month Chicago Police Academy course in December, 1978. In 1979, she began her first assignment in the patrol division in the 13th district, primarily Puerto Rican, and one of the "hottest" (most dangerous) areas at the time. As she described the district to Catalano, "It was very volatile, with a lot of rioting and protesting. It was a really bad area." In addition, women had been allowed in the patrol division for only four years when Mendoza joined the department, and she described to Catalano her early years on the force as "a big culture shock. It wasn't a hostile environment, but the guys were still a little leery and hesitant about accepting us."

From 1980 to 1984, Mendoza worked on the department's mass transit unit as a decoy, apprehending pickpockets, assailants, muggers, and other felons on buses and trains and during public special events. From 1984 to 1985, she worked in neighborhood relations in the ninth district, where she describes her work with the Police Explorers as one of the highlights of her career. The program, an extension of the Boy Scouts of America, exposes children to various careers such as medicine, law, and science by teaming them with professionals in those fields. The group Mendoza worked with were primarily inner city minority boys and girls aged 12 to 17, many of them gang members leaving their neighborhood for the first time, who were taken on field trips and camping excursions organized by the Police Explorers.

Mendoza's next job with the CPD was as a teacher. During her two years as an instructor at the Chicago Police Academy, Mendoza was instrumental in developing a new course called Cultural Awareness, which sensitized officers to the cultural differences and idiosyncracies among minority groups that they might encounter in their jobs. Following a year with the Street Narcotics Impact Program (SNIP), Mendoza was promoted to the rank of detective in 1989, working in the violent crimes unit.

Mendoza has been commended for her outstanding service to the community of Chicago through her work with the police department. She received a community award in 1984 for her efforts (along with two fellow officers) in rescuing a 68-year-old woman from the second floor of a burning building. She received a department commendation in 1982, a unit citation in 1983, and numerous honorable mentions.

In addition to the many benefits her intelligence brought to the job, Mendoza also found her ethnicity to be a boon to her career. Being bilingual, Mendoza told *Vista* magazine, "is the biggest single advantage" in performing her duties. "When I was a detective, I was one of only two people in that department who spoke Spanish. Believe me, in Chicago, that is really an asset."

Mendoza was promoted to sergeant in July, 1990, and works in the patrol division in Marquette, the 10th district, which is roughly 70 percent Hispanic. Of her career and the changes that have accompanied the public image of women officers, she told Catalano: "Women are not rarities anymore. We're in every level of patrol, gang crime specialists, detectives, narcotics—we're everywhere—and because we're part of the scheme of things, we're more accepted among the rank and file. I believe that the more advances I make as a female, the more doors I open for my daughter."

Sources:

Periodicals

Vista, March 3, 1991, p. 10.

Other

Mendoza, Corine, interviews with Julie Catalano, January 10, 1991; October 8, 1992.

—*Sketch by Julie Catalano*

Lydia Mendoza
(1916-)
Singer, musician

Singer and musician Lydia Mendoza is the first interpreter of rural popular Tejano and border music to acquire star status through her many recordings. As such she made this music known beyond the borders of her region and throughout Latin America.

Mendoza was born in Houston, Texas, in 1916 to Leonor Zamaripa Reyna and Francisco Mendoza Espinosa, both from the northern Mexican state of Nuevo Leon. Until 1927, when the Mendozas settled permanently in Texas, the family traveled back and forth to Monterrey, Mexico, following Leonor, who worked for the Ferrocarriles Nacionales de Mexico as a mechanic. Mendoza's parents were lovers of music. Her father had a collection of opera records which included performances by Enrico Caruso; while in Monterrey he often took his children to the theater to see traveling artists and zarzuela companies. Mendoza's mother, in turn, was an accomplished guitar player and singer.

From the time she was four years old Mendoza remembers wanting to learn the guitar and even constructing her own instrument with rubber bands. In time she mastered the guitar and mandolin, and became proficient with the violin. Although the Mendoza adults had always played and sung for their own enjoyment, when her father was forced to leave his job with the railroad for health reasons, music became their mainstay. The family of eight traveled the border towns performing at barber shops, restaurants, and street corners. The older children—Lydia was the second child—played some of the instruments as part of the accompaniment to their parents' voices. Their first big break came in 1928 when they recorded 20 songs for the Okeh Record Company in San Antonio for $140. Mendoza's father named their group the Cuarteto Carta Blanca after the Monterrey brewery where he once worked. Shortly afterwards they traveled to Michigan as migrant workers, experiencing for a brief period the hardships of this way of life. Soon, however, the family was spared the back-breaking field work; singing in Mexican restaurants and in local parties in Pontiac, as well as a job her father providentially found at a Ford Motor Company plant, supported the Mendoza brood.

The Great Depression of 1929 brought the Mendozas back to Texas. They eventually settled in San Antonio. By 1933 Lydia was well-known in South Texas because of her frequent participation in radio contests. In 1934, she was asked to record as a soloist for New York City-based Blue Bird Records. Her recording of the song "Mal hombre" became an instant hit and she was asked to sign a contract with Blue Bird. In 1935 she married Juan Alvarado, a shoemaker by trade who she had met three years earlier. At first her husband, pressured by his family, was reluctant to let his wife perform, particularly after they had a daughter, but the big record sales and royalties convinced him otherwise. Now Alvarado, as the driver, joined the Mendozas in touring the Southwest, doing variety shows which included comedy skits, dancing, and singing. Lydia began to be known as "La alondra de la frontera" (the Lark of the Border), beloved by the common people, especially the working men, and known in Latin America through her records.

With the coming of World War II, the rationing of gasoline sent Lydia into retirement, with occasional performances for local fiestas. For a while she sang at a club in spite of a storm of criticism from family and friends who argued that clubs were no place for a decent woman. In 1947 the Mendozas were back on the road performing under the name of Grupo Variedad. The group was formed by Lydia, brothers Andrew and Manuel, and sisters Maria and Juanita. As before the war, they did variety shows, sometimes making stops in three different towns in one night. Maria's marriage and the death of her mother in 1952 brought about the disintegration of the group. From then on, Lydia always performed solo. She toured the Southwest continually and Mexico for six months. She recorded under the Azteca, Ideal, Falcon, and Columbia labels. In 1961 Lydia's first husband died—the couple had three daughters—and in 1964 she married another shoemaker, Fred Martinez.

With the growing interest in ethnic roots beginning with the 1960s, Lydia Mendoza was recognized as a repository of traditional Mexican and Mexican American popular music. In 1971 she performed at the Smithsonian Festival of American Folklife at the World's Fair in Montreal. In 1977 she participated and performed in the Library of Congress Ethnic Recordings in America Conference. In 1984 she received the National Heritage Award and in 1985 she was welcomed into the Tejano Music Hall of Fame and the Texas Women's Hall of Fame. Mendoza presently resides in Houston, Texas.

Sources:

Mendoza, Lydia, interviews with Chris Strachwitz for a forthcoming volume on the musician's life to be published by Arte Público Press, Houston, Texas.

—*Sketch by Silvia Novo Pena*

Mendoza Schechter, Hope
See Schechter, Hope Mendoza

Amalia Mesa-Bains
(1943-)
Artist

"To me, an artist is someone who speaks of the world, not as it is, but as it could have been or as it could be," Amalia Mesa-Bains remarked in an interview with Michelle Vachon. "I deal very much in the past and in memory but only for the sake of shedding light on what the future might be, trying to reshape the future, to lend meaning and to give people courage." Mesa-Bains, whose work has appeared in numerous national and international exhibitions, has never sold a piece. "When I first started, I used my grandmother's hair and the keys to her front door in some of my installations," she recalled. "Actually, many of my current ones contain some of my own belongings, personal materials from my life. My installations and altars are narrations of parts of my life, of my ideas and convictions. There is no sense, no reasoning in selling work that is made from that: you can't sell your life."

Mesa-Bains was born in Santa Clara, California, on July 10, 1943, to Mexican American parents. She obtained a bachelor's degree in painting from San Jose State University in 1966 and a master's degree in interdisciplinary education from San Francisco State University's School of Education in 1971. Pursuing her studies at the Wright Institute's School of Clinical Psychology in Berkeley, California, she first completed her master's degree, and then her doctorate in clinical psychology in 1983. Her dissertation was a study of culture and identity among Chicana women artists.

Mesa-Bains first exhibited in the 1967 Phelan Awards show held at the Palace of the Legion of Honor in San Francisco. Shortly thereafter, she discovered the Chicano movement. "The movement, which roughly began in the late 1960s, was a period during which young artists like myself, coming into early adulthood, put their energy into some kind of political and social change," she recalled in her interview. "Almost all the artists that I know who went to work in the movement developed or reframed their artistic roles through that lens. . . . From that point on, I changed my concept of the role of an artist." Mesa-Bains defines herself as an artist and a cultural worker "because when I came into being an artist, it was exactly at the period of my life as an adult in which I came into understanding my own identity as a woman but, more importantly, as a member of a [Chicano] cultural identity. We were a cultural identity that was exploited and we still continue to be."

In 1973, Mesa-Bains joined the Galeria de la Raza, an alternative Chicano gallery in San Francisco opened "because mainstream galleries and museums were not at all interested in exhibiting our work. They thought it was too ethnocentric or too political or simply not relevant to what they considered art to be." In 1975, she started her altar installations as a reflection of the ceremonial aspects and spiritual beliefs of her community. She participated in the Fifth Sun Chicago exhibition at the University of California—Berkeley's University Museum in 1977 and in the Posada exhibition at the San Francisco Museum of Art in 1980, and held her only one-person show—"Grotto of the Virgins"—at INTAR gallery in New York City in 1987.

In 1989 and 1990, Mesa-Bains was among the 13 Chicano artists selected to tour internationally with the exhibition "Le démon des anges" (Angels' Devil). "It was so exciting," she remembered in her interview. "I travelled back and forth for over two years. We exhibited in Nantes and Lyon in France, in Barcelona in Spain and in Stockholm in Sweden, and received incredible press coverage—radio, television, national magazines and newspapers—in every country we visited." In 1990, she took part in "The Decade Show," which "tackled social issues related to artists of diverse background," at the Studio Museum of Harlem in New York City, and started touring the country with "CARA—Chicano Art: Resistance and Affirmation," a retrospective and social history of the Chicano movement.

In 1992, the John D. and Catherine T. MacArthur Foundation awarded Mesa-Bains a five-year fellowship to allow this "exceptionally gifted individual" the freedom to create without economic constraints. Mesa-Bains received the INTAR-Hispanic Arts Center's Golden Palm Award in 1991, the Association of American Cultures' Artists Award and the Chicana Foundation of Northern California's Distinguished Working Women Award in 1990, and the San Francisco Mission Cultural Center's Award of Honor in 1989. She was appointed to the San Francisco Arts Commission by the city's mayor, and has been invited to sit on several panels of the National Endowment for the Arts.

Mesa-Bains, who admits to carrying on careers in four or five different fields simultaneously, taught elementary school as a bilingual and multicultural education teacher, and served as project manager at the Division for Integration of the San Francisco Unified School District. She produced and hosted the television program "Latin Tempo" at KPIX in San Francisco, and is consultant to Far West Laboratories in San Francisco. She writes extensively and regularly lectures at colleges and universities. Since 1967 Mesa-Baines has been married to Richard Bains, an ethnomusicologist with the San Francisco Symphony Orchestra.

Sources:

Books

Lippard, Lucy R., *Mixed Blessings: New Art in Multi-Cultural America*, Pantheon, pp. 82-84.

Periodicals

Art in America, January 1991, p. 61.
Artweek, November 9, 1989, pp. 19-21.
Dallas Morning Star, February 17, 1990, p. C2.
FACE B (France), January, 1990, pp. 37-39.
Más, July-August, 1991, p. 72.
San Francisco Chronicle, July 19, 1990, p. E3.

Other

Mesa-Bains, Amalia, interview with Michelle Vachon, September 11, 1992.

—Sketch by Michelle Vachon

Myrna Milan
(1954-)
Municipal court judge

As a municipal court judge in busy Newark, New Jersey, Myrna Milan must listen and judge hundreds of cases that come before her. She does not merely decide on the guilt or innocence of an individual, but instead works closely with the court system to develop alternative sentences for youths. "In my particular court, I'm judge and jury," explained Milan in a telephone interview with Julia Edgar. "We do non-jury trials, so you're in a position where you have to hear facts and you have to make a ruling on a case. When you find someone guilty, you have to mold a sentence. You have to look at an individual, their background, and what it is you hope to accomplish by the sentence. I am very much for alternative sentencing. The goal has got to be to rehabilitate, not just penalize." Sometimes, that means ordering the defendant to pay restitution to the victim, attend counseling, usually for a drug problem, or perform community service work.

Milan's attention to social ills evolved from her parents' involvement in politics. Born January 28, 1954, she grew up in Hoboken, New Jersey, an immigrant community that boasted Puerto Rican, Polish, Czechoslovakian and Italian populations. In the late 1960s, her parents would hold meetings in their home to discuss the race riots in their community and lament the scarcity of Hispanic leaders in local government. Milan's mother, Vidalina, was more educated than the average Puerto Rican woman in Hoboken, and she worked in a model cities program as a social worker. Her father, Pedro, also from Puerto Rico, became the first Hispanic mayor's aide in 1971.

Perhaps as a result of listening to the political discourse around her, Milan thought of becoming a lawyer. After her graduation from Douglass College in New Brunswick, New Jersey, an adjunct of Rutgers University, Milan worked as a high school counselor with Aspira, a national organization that provides tutoring and career counseling and encourages cultural awareness. Although Aspira was offering wonderful opportunities to Hispanic teens, it did not receive federal or state funding because of a clause in state legislation. That's when Milan became "fascinated" with the law. She decided to go back to school, and in 1981 she earned a law degree from Rutgers Law School in Newark.

After graduation, Milan worked as a lawyer in the private and public sectors, taking a job in 1983 as city prosecutor in Elizabeth, New Jersey. She returned briefly to private practice before she was appointed to the bench in 1988 by Newark Mayor Sharpe James. Milan believes she is the first Hispanic woman on New Jersey's municipal court bench. She currently serves on two Supreme Court task forces, one on alternative sentencing and the other on women in the courts. Of the latter, the committee looks into gender bias in the courts, specifically how women are treated as litigants and attorneys, and issues reports to the Supreme Court. Milan was twice appointed to the task force, and just completed her first three-year term. She is now on "holdover" while judges are selected to ascend to the Superior Court—Milan is among six hopefuls for a position on the court.

Most of the cases Milan hears involve disorderly conduct, street fights, trespassing and drug possession. "I find that I'm in a position where at times you can do something for a victim and a defendant. There are times when they come back to you and thank you for what you did. That is part of what I think is the challenge of the job."

Milan is a member of the Union County Bar Association, the Hispanic Bar Association and the Puerto Rican Congress of New Jersey. When she was appointed to a judgeship, she withdrew from CURA, Inc., a drug and alcohol rehabilitation program, because of a possible conflict of interest. She and her husband, Jose Rivera-Benitez, a deputy attorney general with the New Jersey Attorney General's office, have one three-year-old daughter, Adriana Erin Rivera.

Sources:

Milan, Myrna, telephone interview with Julia Edgar, September 20, 1992.

—Sketch by Julia Edgar

Nicholasa Mohr
(1935-)
Writer, illustrator

As an impoverished young girl, Nicholasa Mohr used her imagination to temporarily escape her often shocking surroundings. As an adult, she uses this same creativity to relate her feelings as a woman and an American Puerto Rican, to present the reality of a people and to express her artistic talent. Once an aspiring fine arts painter and printmaker, Mohr became a writer and illustrator of her own books and received immediate acclaim. While her realistic novels and stories have won many awards and have garnered her a following among readers, Mohr has found satisfaction in being able to utilize her many talents and assist people she cares about at the same time. She explained in her *Something about the Author Autobiography Series* (*SAAS*) essay, "As a writer I have used my abilities as a creative artist to strengthen my skills and at the same time in small measure have ventured to establish a voice for my ethnic American community and our children."

Mohr was born on November 1, 1935, to Pedro and Nicholasa (Rivera) Golpe. Her parents migrated from Puerto Rico during the Great Depression to a barrio in Manhattan with their four children; Mohr was the last of three children later born in New York City and the only girl. Before long, the family moved to the Bronx. When she was just eight years old, Mohr's father died. Often ill herself, Mohr's mother struggled to ensure that her family stayed together, and she constantly encouraged her children to develop their talents and work hard themselves. As the author related in her *SAAS* essay, it was her mother who gave Mohr paper, a pencil, and some crayons—and with them, Mohr learned that "by making pictures and writing letters I could create my own world . . . like 'magic.'" In the same essay, Mohr remembered her mother telling her, "*Mi hijita* [My little daughter], you are special with these God-given talents. Someday you must study so that you can become an important artist . . . make an important contribution to the world and really be somebody."

Imagination and Talent Offer Escape from Reality

Although her mother died before Mohr began high school, her mother's influence did not. "My mother's strength and independence served as a strong role model for me," the author stated in her *SAAS* essay. "As I look back, she was the first feminist I knew." Mohr had to be strong herself, and she continued to excel in school despite a lack of emotional support from her guardian aunt. Mohr's artwork in school, she believes, allowed her to partially escape the bigotry other Puerto Rican children had to endure. The gifted child was respected. Her abilities gave her confidence and the hope that she would overcome poverty and prejudice. "I used my imagination and was able to create something interesting and pleasing where previously there had been a sense of despair," she said in *SAAS*. Also, as Mohr developed her writing, drawing, and painting skills, she garnered the experience that would allow her to portray the situations and characters that later appeared in her books.

Mohr was determined to become an artist. When it was time for her to attend high school, she was mortified by her guidance counselor's insistence that she, as a Puerto Rican girl, did not need a solid academic education. The counselor wanted to send Mohr to a school to learn how to sew. Nevertheless, Mohr managed to find a school with a department in fashion illustration, and she was able to practice drawing. Upon graduation from high school, Mohr enrolled in the Arts Students' League in New York, and attended from 1953 to 1956. She attended school while working to support herself as a waitress, a clerical factory worker, and a translator.

Although she had saved enough money to study art in Europe, Mohr decided to travel to Mexico City. There, at the Taller de Gráfica Popular, she studied the works of Jose Clemente Orozco, the murals of Diego Rivera, and the paintings of Rivera's wife, Frida Kahlo. The colors, figures, and methods that these artists used to express their feelings about their cultures greatly influenced Mohr. "In a profound way their work spoke to me and my experiences as a Puerto Rican woman born in New York," she wrote in *SAAS*. "The impact was to shape and form the direction of all my future work."

Mohr returned to the United States, and began to study at the New School for Social Research in New York City. It was there that she met the man who would become her husband, Irwin Mohr; he was working on a doctorate in clinical psychology. She married the native New Yorker on October 5, 1957, and they soon had a son, David. Mohr continued studying fine art at the Brooklyn Museum Art School, from 1959 to 1966, and then she began to study printmaking and silkscreening at the Pratt Center for Contemporary Printmaking from 1966 to 1969.

A second son, Jason, was born to the Mohrs in 1970, and, with the help of a grant for the artist's work, the couple moved to a home in the suburb of Teaneck, New Jersey. There, Mohr worked in her huge art studio. According to Mohr's quote in *SAAS* her prints are not "just . . . literal scenes of social injustices, . . . or aesthetically abstract . . . [they were] filled with bold figures, faces, and various symbols of the city . . . numbers, letters, words, and phrases . . . a kind of graffiti." Her bold innovations brought Mohr some measure of notoriety in the New York art scene. Mohr was also an art teacher. In 1967, she had become an art instructor in art schools in New York and New Jersey, and from 1971 to 1973, she worked as an art instructor at the Art Center of Northern New Jersey. From 1973 to 1974, she was also an artist-in-residence with the New York City public schools.

As a successful artist with her own one-woman exhibitions and an art agent, Mohr had never considered writing when she was asked by a publisher to write about her life as a Puerto Rican American. Mohr thought she might try when she had time, and she wrote fifty pages of vignettes. Although the publisher liked the piece, she did not want to publish it. Mohr remembers this well in her interview with Paul Janeczko: "I think what she expected was something much more sensational, the sort of stereotypical ghetto person. So I told her that much to my embarrassment I had never stolen anything, taken hard drugs, been raped or mugged. So I guess she thought my life was uneventful."

Mohr put away her pen and continued to work as an artist until Harper and Row Publishers asked her to do a cover for one of their books. Instead, Mohr brought them her vignettes. Ellen Rudin, an editor for the company, was enthusiastic, and she encouraged Mohr to develop what she had written: Mohr was given a contract. She spent time writing at the MacDowell Colony in New Hampshire, and finished her first book, *Nilda*, which appeared in 1973. Mohr recalled in her interview with Janeczko that she "fell very much in love with writing" although she was "a little bit nervous." While it was difficult for her to make the transition from being primarily an artist to a writer, she recalled in the same interview that she "found that I could do certain things in writing and there was a crying need for what I had to say as a Puerto Rican, as someone living here, and as a woman." She found that she "could draw a picture with words, and it was extremely stimulating and eye-opening to realize what one could do with words."

First Book Impresses Readers and Critics

While Mohr found herself intrigued with writing, readers were fascinated with what Mohr wrote. They were touched and enlightened as they read *Nilda*, the autobiographical story of a poor Puerto Rican girl living in New York's Spanish Harlem. While the story is set during the time of World War II, emphasis is given to the situation at home. Puerto Ricans, already American citizens, were called "spics" and animals by the very people who were supposed to guide, uphold, and assist their youth. Teachers, social workers, nurses, and even policemen referred to Puerto Ricans as "you people" in the book, and the young girl's peers behave just as cruelly. Particularly effective are two scenes, one in which a very poor girl is taunted for her lack of a real suitcase at camp, and another in which a girl who has just given birth to a baby is denied entrance to her home by her own embarrassed mother. One young girl found this episode to be almost overwhelming. She said in *Newsweek*, "When I found out Petra was pregnant, I had to put down the book, get myself a glass of milk, turn up the heat and cuddle up in my quilt." The book was powerful in other ways too; according to Mohr, it would demonstrate how one could escape reality through imagination. "Once there [in her imagination], she [Nilda], would also find relief from an environment she, in fact, is powerless to change in any other way," wrote the author in *SAAS.*

Nilda was a great success. Critics praised the story's fresh characters, content and style, as well as the cover and eight illustrations Mohr had provided. One critic, Donald B. Gibson, lauded the work in *Children's Literature:* "There is no pity here, for the author is too much aware of the humanity of her characters and of the other implications of pity to be in any way condescending." He wrote that *Nilda* was "what I would call a significant book, a touchstone by which others may be judged." Mohr was given the Outstanding Book Award in Juvenile Fiction from the *New York Times* in 1973. She received the Jane Addams Children's Book Award from the Jane Addams Peace Association, also for *Nilda,* in 1974. She won another MacDowell Colony writing fellowship, this one for the summer of 1974. Finally, the Society of Illustrators presented Mohr with a citation of merit for *Nilda*'s book jacket design. The book eventually made *School Library Journal*'s "Best of the Best 1966-1978" list in 1979.

After her experience with *Nilda,* Mohr felt that she had to write more. Her next book, a collection of short stories complete with a book jacket of her own creation, was published in 1975. The twelve stories and the novella in *El Bronx Remembered* are set in post-war New York, and deal with once-delicate subjects frankly. One story, for example, features a doomed marriage between a pregnant teenager and an aging homosexual. Another story is about a lonely, dying old Jewish man who is befriended by a Puerto Rican family. Other stories deal with racism, religion, as well as sexuality and death. All of the stories, spiced with Spanish words, are realistic. "If there is any message at all in these stories, any underlying theme," wrote a critic in the *New York Times Book Review,* "it is that life goes on."

For *El Bronx Remembered,* Mohr was awarded the Outstanding Book Award in Teenage Fiction from the *New York Times* in 1975, and she received the Best Book Award from *School Library Journal* that same year. *El Bronx Remembered* also was a National Book Award finalist for the "most distinguished book in children's literature" in 1976. Finally, Bantam Books chose to publish Mohr's books in paperback form. Mohr realized that she could combine her love of art with her talent for writing, and reach more people, by writing books. She enjoyed her work, and she had been very successful. She made the decision to continue writing, and did so as a writer-in-residence at the MacDowell Colony.

Continues to Write for Adults and Children

Her next self-illustrated book, *In Nueva York,* was very similar to *El Bronx Remembered.* First published in 1977, *In Nueva York*'s related short stories featured mature subjects.

In one story, a woman who searches for her son finds that he is a dwarf. In another, a homosexual woman marries a homosexual man. Both "The Robbery" and "Coming to Terms" deal with the violent death of a teenage thief shot by a store owner and its consequences. "Mohr creates a remarkably vivid tapestry of community life as well as of individual characters," wrote one critic in the *Bulletin of the Center for Children's Books.* She continued, "Tough, candid, and perceptive, the book has memorable characters, resilient and responsive, in a sharply-eyed milieu." Mohr was given the Best Book Award from the *School Library Journal* and the Best Book Award in Young Adult literature from the American Library Association. The book was selected as one of the ten "Paperbacks: New and Noteworthy" books by the *New York Times* in January of 1980. It won the distinction of being named a Notable Trade Book in the Field of Social Studies by the joint committee of the National Council for the Social Studies and the Children's Book Council.

Mohr's third self-illustrated book, *Felita,* which was published in 1979, also won this last award, in 1980. A novel for younger children, *Felita* related the story of a Puerto Rican girl whose parents decide to move to a better part of town. Felita missed her old friends, and the neighbors would not let their children befriend her. Discouraged by discrimination and harassment, Felita's family returned to their old neighborhood, and Felita was forced to readjust. *Felita,* well-received by critics, won an American Book Award from the Before Columbus Foundation in 1981.

From 1977 to 1980, Mohr attempted to contribute to her community through more than her writing and artwork. She was a lecturer in Puerto Rican studies in 1977 at the State University of New York at Stony Brook, and a visiting lecturer in creative writing for various groups, including the University of Illinois Educational Alliance Program in Chicago, the Cedar Rapids, Iowa, community schools, a writers-in-residence seminar at the University of Wisconsin at Oshkosh, and the Bridgeport Connecticut public schools from 1977 to 1978. Mohr served as the head creative writer and co-producer of the television series, "Aqui y Ahora," (Here and Now,) and as a member of the New Jersey State Council on the Arts. She was a member of the board of trustees as well as a consultant for the Young Filmmakers Foundation, and a consultant on bilingual media training for Young Filmmakers Video Arts.

When Mohr's husband died and her sons went to off to college, the author moved to a small townhouse in Brooklyn in 1980. In 1981, Mohr's brother Vincent, to whom she was very close, also died. Mohr did not publish another book until 1985. *Rituals of Survival: A Woman's Portfolio,* a collection of short stories and a novella written for adults, was published by Arte Público Press. For this work, Mohr was presented a Legislative Resolution from the State of New York, commending her for her "valuable contributions to the world of literature."

By 1986, Mohr had written another children's book, *Going Home,* a sequel to *Felita.* In *Going Home,* Felita takes a trip to Puerto Rico with her family, and is sad to leave by the end of the summer despite the problems she had encountered with the children there at the beginning of her vacation. This book garnered a warm reception. A critic for the *School Library Journal* commented, "Felita is a vivid, memorable character, well realized and well developed. It is a pleasure to welcome her back."

Mohr has a broad list of writing and teaching experience. She has had selections of her work published in *Family in Harmony and Conflict,* edited by Peter Reinke. Her short stories have appeared in *Children's Digest, Scholastic Magazine,* and *Nuestro.* She is a member of the board of contributing editors of *Nuestro,* and is a member of both the Authors Guild and the Authors League of America. She is the author, with Ray Blanco, of the screenplay, "The Artist," and she has contributed to textbooks and anthologies such as *The Ethnic American Woman: Problems, Protests, Lifestyles,* which was edited by Edith Blicksilver. Finally, she wrote a piece for the radio entitled, "Inside the Monster," for the Latino Writers Symposium. Also, from 1988 to 1990, Mohr was a distinguished visiting professor at Queens College in New York City.

Mohr, who has been awarded an honorary doctorate from the State University of New York at Albany, is currently working on another novel and a screenplay. In her writing, Mohr strives to challenge readers of all ages to view the world with open eyes, to encourage them to alter their perception, and to entertain them. Mohr, who escaped reality as a child through her imagination, today uses her creative talents to try to change reality through her readers.

Sources:

Books

Authors & Artists for Young Adults, Volume 8, Gale, 1992.
Contemporary Literary Criticism, Volume 12, Gale, 1980.
Mohr, Nicholasa, interview with Paul Janeczko, *From Writers to Students: The Pleasures and Pains of Writing,* edited by M. Jerry Weiss, International Reading Association, 1979, pp. 75-78.
Mohr, Nicholasa, *Nilda: A Novel,* Harper, 1973, 2nd edition, Arte Público, 1986.
Mohr, Nicholasa, *El Bronx Remembered: A Novella and Stories,* Harper, 1975, 2nd edition, Arte Público, 1986.
Mohr, Nicholasa, *In Nueva York,* Dial, 1977.
Mohr, Nicholasa, *Felita,* Dial, 1979.
Mohr, Nicholasa, *Going Home,* Dial, 1986.
Mohr, Nicholasa, *Rituals of Survival: A Woman's Portfolio,* Arte Público, 1985.
Sadker, Myra Pollack, and David Miller Sadker, *Now upon a Time: A Contemporary View of Children's Literature,* Harper, 1977, pp. 210-30.
Something about the Author Autobiography Series, Volume 8, Gale, 1989, pp. 185-94.

Periodicals

Best Sellers, December, 1975, p. 266.
Bulletin of the Center for Children's Books, June, 1976, p. 161; July-August, 1977, p. 178; May, 1986, p. 178.
Children's Literature, Volume 3, 1974, pp. 230-34.
English Journal, February, 1978, p. 100.
Essence, May, 1980, p. 25.
Horn Book, February, 1976, p. 57; February, 1980, p. 56; September-October, 1986, pp. 591.
Interracial Bulletin of Books for Children, November 4, 1976, p. 15.
The Lion and the Unicorn, fall, 1978, pp. 6-15.
Newsweek, March 4, 1974, p. 83.
New York Times, January 20, 1980.
New York Times Book Review, November 4, 1973, pp. 27-28; November 10, 1974; November 16, 1975; May 22, 1977.
Publishers Weekly, July 25, 1986, p. 190.
School Library Journal, April, 1977, p. 79; August, 1986, p. 105.
Vista, May 14, 1989, p. 3.

—Sketch by Ronie-Richele Garcia-Johnson

Gloria Molina
(1948-)
Los Angeles County Supervisor

Gloria Molina's political career has been a series of firsts: the first Chicana elected to the California State Assembly, the first Chicana elected to the Los Angeles City Council (and only the third Chicano elected in this century), and the first woman ever elected to the L.A. County Board of Supervisors, the most powerful local government in the country. She is also the first Latino since 1875 to serve on the Board of Supervisors and the first Latina to be the co-chair of the campaign committee of the Democratic presidential nominee. Molina has built her political career by grassroots campaigning and by resisting being "one of the boys" with other politicians. In a characteristic statement, reported by the *New York Times* the day after her election to the L.A. County Board of Supervisors, Molina said, "I can't go into the Board of Supervisors and start acting like them. I did not get elected to meet their needs. I got elected to meet the needs of the people of the first district."

In an interview with *Hispanic,* Molina characterized the politicians she's known as "people who don't serve the community, who don't resolve problems, people who ex-

Gloria Molina

pect to be respected by virtue of their positions, but call them to the table and they don't get involved in partnerships with their constituents. And meanwhile the people are suffering." It was statements like these which led *Hispanic* magazine in a July, 1991, cover story to describe Molina as "the confrontational fighter, the outsider who asks tough questions, speaks her mind against dirty politicians, and demands answers with an insistence that makes enemies feel attacked by a pit bull that won't let go." These attitudes have given Molina great popularity with the public. A 1991 national survey of Latinos conducted by L.A.'s Spanish language newspaper *La opinión* and Univision, a Spanish-language television network, found that Molina is the most admired Latino leader in the nation.

Molina's legendary tenacity is the result of her life experiences. The oldest of Leonardo and Concepcion Molina's ten children, Gloria Molina was born May 31, 1948, in a suburb of Los Angeles, California. Her parents had migrated from Mexico a year earlier. After attending high school in Pico Rivera, a suburb of Los Angeles, she enrolled in Rio Hondo College to study design. In 1967, when she was 19, Molina's father had an accident and she took a full-time job as a legal assistant to support her family. She continued her education by going to school at night, graduating from East Los Angeles College in 1968, and attended California State University, Los Angeles until 1970. In 1971, she became a job counselor for the East Los Angeles Community Union (TELACU), an economic development corporation.

Although involved in the Chicano movement in the 1960s, it was in the '70s that Molina's deep involvement in community affairs blossomed. She was active in the Latin American Law Enforcement Association and was a boardmember of United Way of Los Angeles. In 1973 a group of Chicana activists organized the Comision Femenil de Los Angeles, an organization dedicated to meeting the needs of the women of the Chicano/Latino community, with Gloria Molina as the founding president. During her presidency, the Comision developed many badly needed social programs for Chicanas in the Los Angeles area. Molina was the national president of the Comision Feminil from 1974 to 1976. Molina was also a founding member of Hispanic American Democrats, the National Association of Latino Elected and Appointed Officials (NALEO), and Centro De Niños, an organization which helped children.

Takes First Position in Politics

In 1974, Molina took the first step in her professional political career by becoming the administrative assistant to California State Assemblyman Art Torres. Three years later, President Jimmy Carter appointed her as director for region nine of Intergovernmental and Congressional Affairs in the Department of Health and Human Services. In 1980, Molina returned to California to become chief deputy to the speaker of the California Assembly, Willie Brown. When the 1982 election season began, she made the fateful decision to run for the state assembly.

Gloria Molina's 1982 assembly race contained all the elements that make her the politician she is. The local Chicano politicians informed Molina that she didn't have the qualifications to run for assembly, emphasizing that the community wasn't ready to elect a woman and the funding and endorsements would go to another candidate. Angered, Molina decided to buck the establishment but admitted she had fears. "I was shaking in my boots," she told *Hispanic* magazine in 1991, "but I had to tell them, 'I will have all those things,' otherwise I would have folded. I had reservations about a good deal of it but I wasn't going to let them deny me the opportunity." Molina put together the kind of aggressive, grassroots campaign that has become her trademark. Her opponent had more money and more endorsements but in the end, it was Gloria Molina who had more votes and became the first Chicana ever elected to the California state assembly.

Molina's two terms in the assembly established her reputation as a political maverick. Molina told this story to the *San Antonio Light* newspaper: "When I went to the Assembly [in 1982], one man said to me 'Oh, I'm so glad we have you, we need someone like you to work on bilingual education and child care.' I said, 'I want to work on insurance and taxation issues.'" Although a liberal Democrat, Molina once supported a bill to add work requirements for welfare because she thought it a sensible way to help people get jobs. She defied her former boss, Assembly Speaker Willie Brown, the second most powerful politician in California, by refusing to cut deals. It made it more difficult for Molina to get her bills passed, but as *Ms.* magazine reported, she feels, "Anytime you take a position, you run the risk of offending another legislator. You have to take risks." Nonetheless, Molina was able to have two laws passed of special concern to her district. One prevents discrimination against immigrants in auto insurance and the other requires notification if a neighborhood is to be sprayed for agricultural pests. Molina's work has been recognized with numerous awards, including Woman of the Year in 1983 from the Mexican American Opportunity Foundation and in 1984 from *Ms.* magazine. In 1983, she was named Hispanic of the Year by *Caminos* magazine and Democrat of the Year by the Los Angeles County Democratic Central Committee.

In 1986, California Governor George Deukmejian selected a site in East Los Angeles, a predominantly Chicano area, to build a new prison. Outraged residents appealed to their political leaders for help to stop the prison from being built and Molina responded. Governor Deukmejian was determined to see the prison built before he left office but he badly underestimated the depth of feeling against the prison in the East L.A. community and the skill of political leaders like Gloria Molina. A series of political and legal maneuvers stopped the construction plans. Although there were other politicians, lawyers, and community organizations involved, Molina's leadership convinced many voters that she was a politician who would not betray the interests of the community. Molina would continue fighting against the prison even after she left the assembly.

Elected to Latino City Council

In 1987, the City of Los Angeles and the Mexican American Legal Defense and Education Fund (MALDEF) reached a settlement on a gerrymandering suit which called for the creation of a new Latino City Council seat and a special municipal election to fill the seat. Molina decided to run for the seat and once again she was opposed by a candidate of the local political establishment, along with two lesser known candidates. Molina, and her political consultant planned what the *Washington Post* called "a letter-perfect special election campaign." With four people running, most political observers expected a runoff. Molina won with 57 percent of the vote.

This victory marked a change in Molina's thinking about her future. As she told a reporter for the *San Antonio Light* in 1987, "I used to be a fatalist. Even when I was elected in 1982, I didn't think of going any farther. Now I am goal-oriented."

Works for Better Response to Citizens' Needs

One of her goals as a city councilwoman was to make the city departments more responsive to the citizens. When people in her district complained about trash pickups, she

followed trash trucks and street sweepers around the district. She confronted drug dealers on the streets and donated $75,000 from her office budget to create MASH-LA (More Advocates for Safe Homes), an attempt to organize people to clean their own neighborhoods and take back the streets from the gangs and drug dealers. She also worked to develop public/private partnerships to increase affordable housing, improve traffic flow and increase open space in the central city. As she had when she was in the assembly, Molina continued to fight the building of a state prison in East L.A. Dr. Rudolfo Acuña, a columnist for the *L.A. Herald Examiner,* describes this scene from a 1988 hearing by the state Department of Corrections: "Attention, however, quickly shifted to Councilwoman Gloria Molina. . . . She combatively addressed the English-speaking panel members in Spanish. Translated, she said, 'This community, which already houses 75 percent of the county's inmates, does not deserve another lockup in its midst. . . . (The proposed site is located) in a community that houses 870,000 people within a five-mile radius.'" Acuña noted, "Significantly, the 'No Prison in East L.A.' movement has given [Molina] a forum to showcase alternatives to the 'Let's make a deal' politics of the Latino male establishment." The struggle against the prison would continue for four more years before the Chicanos in the state legislature would effectively kill the bill to build a prison in East L.A.

In a case that went all the way to the U.S. Supreme Court, MALDEF successfully sued the Los Angeles County Board of Supervisors for gerrymandering and forced the creation of a Latino district and a special election to fill it. The five-member Board of Supervisors has an annual budget of over $10 billion and represents nearly 10 million people. It is the most powerful locally elected governmental body in the United States. Molina decided to run for the seat and was opposed by the man who gave her her first job in politics, Art Torres. Molina won a hotly contested race and assumed office March 8, 1991, becoming the first woman ever elected to the Board of Supervisors and the first Latino since 1875 to serve as Supervisor. Molina's election changed the Board of Supervisors in more than one way. She broke the monopoly that white males have had on the job, she changed the political composition from conservative to liberal, and the county bureaucracy discovered that there was a supervisor who would unmercifully grill them if they came to board meetings unprepared to explain their actions or how the taxpayer's money was being spent. The other Supervisors are not above Molina's criticism. In a widely reported debate over the distribution of bleach kits and condoms to drug users, a move advocated by public health officials to slow the spread of AIDS, Molina interrupted a conservative Supervisor speaking against the measure to accuse him of talking "absolute nonsense." On a different occasion, when an oil company was granted a drilling project in her district but had not bothered to inform the citizens who would be affected by it, an angry Molina confronted the officials in a public hearing. As the *Washington Post* reported, she said, "You have demonstrated disrespect for this community. Turn around and look at them. Be respectful to this community."

Molina's abilities caught the eye of the national Democratic leadership and in July, 1992, Democratic presidential candidate Bill Clinton appointed her co-chair of the National Campaign. In a press release, Clinton said, "I'm grateful that Supervisor Molina has accepted the position. Her experience and commitment to grassroots organizing brings added energy to this campaign."

Sources:

Books

Meier, Matt S., *Mexican-American Biographies: A Historical Dictionary, 1836-1987*, Greenwood Press, 1988, pp. 142-43.

Periodicals

Hispanic, July, 1991, pp. 13-15.
Los Angeles Herald Examiner, August 5, 1988, p. A10.
Ms., January, 1985, pp. 80, 114.
New York Times, February 17, 1991, p. A17.
San Antonio Light, May 1, 1987, p. B8.
Vista, February 4, 1992, p. 10.
Washington Post, April 14, 1987, p. A4; June 17, 1991 p. A5.

Other

Press release, Clinton/Gore presidential campaign, July 28, 1992.

—*Sketch by Andrés Chávez*

Molina, Marilyn Aguirre
See Aquirre-Molina, Marilyn

Pat Mora

promoted cultural exploration by others. Mora, who has led many to ponder their own cultural backgrounds, has worked variously as an instructor, an assistant to administrators, and a museum director, given poetry readings and presentations, served on various committees, written, and performed as a wife and mother simultaneously; she provides an excellent model for young Hispanics who are just beginning to understand the past and are about to experience promising futures.

Mora was born January 19, 1942, to Raul Antonio and Estella (Delgado) Mora. She grew up in the town of her birth, El Paso, Texas, where her father was a practicing optician. Mora's mother, Estella, stayed home to care for her children. As many young minorities do, Mora eschewed family customs. The knowledge that some mainstream Americans thought that Mexican Americans were inferior fed her preference to look and feel "American." The young Mora would speak Spanish at home to her grandmother and her aunt, but she would try to ignore her ethnicity in school, and would cringe when her father played Mexican music on the radio. She would not realize that assimilation meant a loss of cultural identity until later.

Shortly after receiving a bachelor's degree from Texas Western College in 1963, Mora married William H. Burnside. With Burnside, she had three children, William, Elizabeth, and Cecilia. Mora began to teach at a school in the El Paso Independent School District, where she stayed until 1966. By 1967, Mora had earned her master's degree

Pat Mora
(1942-)
Poet, educator

While Pat Mora has earned distinction as both a poet and an educator, she is best known for the cause that requires all of her talents: cultural appreciation and conservation. Mora has been essential to the movement to understand and uphold Mexican American culture. As an poet, she has explored her ethnicity, and as an educator, she has from the University of Texas at El Paso, and from 1971 to 1978 she taught English and Communications part-time at El Paso Community College. Changing to a part-time lecturer in 1979, Mora remained in this position until 1981, the same year that she and her first husband divorced. It was also during 1981 that she became the assistant to the vice president of academic affairs.

Discovers Value of Mexican Heritage

Living near the Mexican border, surrounded by Mexican American relatives and friends, Mora could not fight the influence of Mexican culture. She finally began to appreciate her birthright for the gift that it was. As she explained in the *Christian Science Monitor,* she is now devoted to her culture. "I revel in a certain Mexican passion not for life or about life, but *in* life, a certain intensity in the daily living of it, a certain abandon in such music, in the hugs, sometimes in the anger."

Mora's intense concern for her culture needed an outlet; she began to express her feelings in writing. She related her desire to write in *Contemporary Authors.* "For a variety of complex reasons, anthologized American literature does not reflect the ethnic diversity of the United States. I write, in part, because Hispanic perspectives need to be part of our literary heritage; I want to be part of that validation process. I also write because I am fascinated by the pleasure and power of words." Mora believes that Hispanic writers need to make their mark on American Literature, and that Hispanic culture can be preserved by and in literature.

Despite the stress that inevitably accompanies a divorce and a change in career, Mora managed to establish a reputation in literary circles during the early 1980s. She contributed to *Revista Chicano-Riquena: Kikiriki/Children's Literature Anthology,* which was published by Arte Público Press in 1981 under the editorship of Sylvia Cavazos Pena. Mora's career as a writer and advocate of cultural appreciation began to take off. From 1983 to 1984 she hosted the radio show, *Voices: The Mexican-American in Perspective,* on KTEP, a National Public Radio affiliate. She received her first important literary award for her creative writing in 1983, when she was recognized by the National Association for Chicano Studies.

Gains Fame as Writer

Mora's next award came from New America: Women Artists and Writers of the Southwest, for her poetry, in 1984. She found time to serve on the board of her local YWCA, and did so until 1988. 1984 was a year of professional and personal triumph for Mora. In addition to the New America award, she was honored with the Harvey L. Johnson Book Award from the Southwest Council of Latin American Studies. Her first poetry collection, *Chants,* was published by the Arte Público Press of the University of Houston. And finally, she married Vernon Lee Scarbo-

rough, an archaeologist who studies the Maya of Central America.

For Mora, the latter half of the 1980s proved to be just as fruitful as the first half. Two years after *Chants* was published, in 1986, Arte Público released *Borders,* Mora's second collection of poetry. Both *Chants* and *Borders* won Southwest Book Awards from the Border Regional Library Association. In 1986, Mora once again contributed to a children's literature anthology edited by Pena, *Tun-Ta-Ca-Tun.* That same year, she also received a Kellogg National Fellowship. With this aid, she began to study international and national issues of cultural conservation. Mora's work made her an invaluable source of information—she was asked to become a consultant to the W. K. Kellogg Foundation on U.S.-Mexican youth exchanges, and to serve on the advisory committee for the Kellogg National Fellowship program. She served as a member of the Texas Commission on the Arts's Literary Advisory Panel from 1987 to 1988, and as a poetry judge for the Texas Institute of Letters in 1988. Mora was named to the El Paso Herald-Post Writer's 1988 Hall of Fame.

While Mora was gaining fame as a writer, she continued to distinguish herself as an educator at the University of Texas at El Paso. She won a Leader in Education Award from El Paso Women's Employment and Education, Inc., in 1987. Later that year she was recognized with the Chicano/Hispanic Faculty and Professional Staff Association Award for her outstanding contribution to the advancement of Hispanics at the University of Texas at El Paso. Finally, in 1988 Mora became the director of the University Museum as well as the assistant to the University's president.

Continues Efforts to Conserve Heritage

In September, 1989, Mora gave up her life in El Paso to move to Ohio. While she did miss the food and company she was used to, Mora admitted that she began to crave the sound of the Spanish language in an article she wrote for the *Christian Science Monitor:* "When I hear a phrase in Spanish in a Cincinnati restaurant, my head turns quickly. I listen, silently wishing to be part of that other conversation—if only for a few moments, to feel Spanish in my mouth."

Mora did, however, began to appreciate her new Midwestern environment. She enjoyed the lush greenery and the cold snow in the winter. She also began to recognize the differences between her new home in the Midwest and her old home in the desert. She wrote in the *Monitor,* "No forest conceals the shacks on the other side of the Rio Grande. . . . I miss that clear view of the difference between my comfortable life as a U.S. citizen and the lives of my fellow human beings who also speak Spanish. . . ." Instead of losing her affiliation for and loyalty to her culture, Mora was able to view it from a fresh perspective.

The decade of the 1990s presents many more opportunities for Mora to contribute to cultural conservation. She has already made a great start: her third collection of poetry, *Communion*, was published by Arte Público Press in 1991. And by 1992, her illuminating work had been included in many anthologies and textbooks: *Woman of Her Word: Hispanic Women Write*, *The Norton Introduction to Literature*, *Sisters of the Earth* (Vintage), *American Mosaic* (Houghton Mifflin), *New Worlds of Literature* (Norton), *Literature: Reading, Reacting, Writing* (Holt), *Mexican American Literature* (HBJ), *Adventures in Reading* (HBJ), *Face to Face* (Scott, Foresman), and *Hispanics in the United States* (Bilingual Review Press). Mora, who is a member of the Poetry Society of America, the Academy of American Poets, and the Texas Institute of Letters, has also contributed articles and stories to periodicals, including *Hispanics in the United States: An Anthology of Creative Literature*, *New America: Women Artists and Writers of the Southwest*, *Kalliope: A Journal of Women's Art*, and *Calyx*. Mora's poems and stories have been translated into Spanish, Italian, and Bengali.

Mora has many other projects in mind for the rest of the 1990s. *A Birthday Basket for Tia*, a children's book, will be published in 1992 by Macmillan. A collection of personal essays entitled *Nepantla: Essays from the Land in the Middle*, will be published in 1993 by the University of New Mexico Press. Another children's book, *Pablo's Tree*, is due out the same year from Macmillan, and still another, *Tomas and the Library Lady*, will be published that year by Knopf. Clarion books is also preparing to publish some of Mora's works for children. Meanwhile, the author will continue to work on her fourth collection of poetry, which has tentatively been titled, *The Narrow Rim*, and more books for children.

As a successful Hispanic writer, and a writer who writes about and for Hispanics, Mora is an exemplary role model for the young people of an increasingly multi-cultural America. Mora is aware of the influence she may have on minority youths. While she noted in *Horn Book* that some young minorities are "proud of their cultural roots," she acknowledges that advertisements "convince us that our cars, clothes, and even our families aren't good enough," and that "being beautiful is being thin, blond, and rich, rich, rich." Mora hopes to counter the influence of a post-literate, consumption-oriented and often prejudiced society. She wrote of her battle against destructive and misleading conceptions and values in *Horn Book*: "I write to try to correct these images of worth. I take pride in being a Hispanic writer. I will continue to write and to struggle to say what no other writer can say in quite the same way."

Sources:

Books

Contemporary Authors, Volume 129, Gale, 1990.

Periodicals

Christian Science Monitor, July 18, 1990, pp. 16-17.
English Journal, September, 1990, pp. 40.
Horn Book, July-August, 1990, pp. 436-37.
National Catholic Reporter, May 10, 1991, p. 24.
Nuestro, March, 1985, p. 51.

—*Sketch by Ronie-Richele Garcia-Johnson*

Cherríe Moraga
(1952-)
Writer

Frank and undaunted, Cherríe Moraga has managed to express feelings that many Hispanic women share. Although she could "pass" for a white woman, and did not experience the pain of prejudice that some Hispanics face, Moraga had to cope with another type of discrimination: homophobia. As a lesbian, Moraga began to understand what her darker mother had always felt, and this realization, coupled with her passion for writing, incited Moraga to textually communicate the feelings that generations of minorities, regardless of specific race, gender, or sexual orientation, have experienced. The results of Moraga's hard work, a book of poems, collections of writings by other minorities and feminists, and several plays, have startled readers and made American literary history; in addition to encouraging women and minorities, especially Hispanics and Chicanas, to seriously consider their cultural and sexual situations, she has assisted other culturally cognizant writers to revise the norm in contemporary literature. Moraga was a central figure in feminist, lesbian, Chicana, and American literature during the decade of the 1980s.

Moraga was born on September 25, 1952, in Whittier, California. As the product of a mixed-race marriage, she was influenced by two cultures. Her father's family was from Missouri and Canada, and her mother's family was from California, Arizona, and Sonora, Mexico. Moraga's family moved to live near her mother's relatives in San Gabriel, California, when she was nine years old. Like Moraga, Southern California is the product of Mexican and Anglo influence. Moraga was surrounded by the Spanish language, and a mixture of Spanish and English, as well as English; she experienced Mexican customs at home, and American traditions in school.

Moraga was a good student; she intended to become a teacher. In college, however, when Moraga began to study writing, her aspirations began to change. The people who

Cherríe Moraga

to be heterosexual—homosexual intimations would be unsettling. Instead of persuading Moraga to write a lie, however, the reading group incited Moraga to write specifically as a lesbian, and about homosexual issues. Moraga decided to commit herself to writing what she wanted to write—her readers would just have to change their expectations.

Moraga's commitment to at least try to become a serious writer conflicted with her job as a teacher. She had taught for two years when she left the profession and Southern California for San Francisco in 1977. In San Francisco, she could avoid the influence of her family, and immerse herself in a community which is known for its liberal attitude as well as its artistic atmosphere. Moraga promised herself that, if she did not excel as a writer after a year of total devotion to the art, she would return to teaching.

The year in San Francisco proved to be rewarding and fruitful. As Moraga supported herself with odd jobs and unemployment, she read and wrote. Finally, she had the time to explore the world of lesbian literature. Books such as Radclyffe Hall's 1928 *The Well of Loneliness* and the works of Djuna Barnes inspired and enlightened Moraga. She also found time to talk with other aspiring artists, lesbians, and feminists in cafés. This diverse community of women supported Moraga's endeavor to write. Her poetry began to mature.

Begins Writing Career

By the time Moraga's year was up, she had written enough outstanding poems to read in front of an audience. With the Los Angeles poet Eloise Klein Healy, she read to a packed coffeehouse. Moraga realized that she was more than a writer—she was a good writer; she had something valid to say, and she knew how to say it. She also found that, as she had hoped, audiences would appreciate the content of her poems as much as her poetic voice. Moraga's success after this first year assured her that she should continue to write.

At this point in her career, Moraga began to think and write more about being, specifically, a lesbian of color. She was not just a lesbian, she was a Chicana lesbian. Instead of just being discriminated against for being a woman, or of Mexican American descent, she could experience prejudice for her sexual orientation as well. This sort of bias could come from anyone, even other women, feminists, and lesbians. One poet, Judy Grahn, wrote of being a lesbian of color. Her poems spoke to Moraga; they expressed something that she had been trying to pinpoint herself, and they did so simply and elegantly. Determined to meet this inspirational poet, Moraga arranged a meeting. At this meeting, Grahn gave Moraga a piece of advice which she still follows. Yvonne Yarbro-Bejarano, writing in the *Dictionary of Literary Biography,* quoted Grahn as saying, "do what nobody else can do, which is to write exactly from your own voice, the voices you heard growing up." Grahn's

wrote fascinated her as much as writing itself; she began to develop a love for art and artists. Despite this new interest in art and writing, Moraga was determined to finish school and become a teacher. When she earned her bachelor of arts from a small private college in Hollywood in 1974, she became one of the few people in her family to hold a degree.

Reveals Sexual Preference

Following graduation, Moraga began to teach. Her first job was as an instructor of English at a private, Los Angeles high school. Moraga might have kept teaching if she had not enrolled in a writing class through the Los Angeles Women's Building. This class stimulated her artistic instincts, and she became more and more enthusiastic about her writing. At the same time she began to blossom as a writer, Moraga "came out" as a lesbian. As she no longer had anything to hide from herself or others, Moraga was finally able to express herself freely; some of her first works were lesbian love poems.

Although Moraga was happy with her personal revelation and progress as a writer, she soon found that not everyone would be willing to accept her textual expression of her sexuality. Some of the first challenges she received as an open lesbian were from members of her inspirational writing group. These members argued that, in her writing, Moraga should not refer to her lover as "she." A reading audience, they said, expected loving, sexual relationships advice, as well as her political orientation, gave Moraga a new direction.

By the time Moraga was ready to begin her thesis for her master's degree in feminist writing at San Francisco State University, she was also ready to tackle the issue of being a feminist and/or lesbian of color. She did so by agreeing to work with Gloria Anzaldúa as she collected writings of women of color for a book. The women included essays, poems, letters and conversations that discussed feminism and lesbianism from the perspectives of women of color in the book; they even added a foreword by the well-known writer, Toni Cade Bambara. The result of this collaboration not only fulfilled Moraga's thesis requirement, but also made her a recognizable figure in the feminist world and stimulated the minds of women of color.

Writings Recognized and Honored

Moraga received her master's degree in 1980, and *This Bridge Called My Back: Writings by Radical Women of Color* was published the next year. This "groundbreaking collection of Third World feminist theory," as Barbara Smith called it in the *New England Review,* was "solidly based in personal recollection and self-revelation." A critic for *Ms.* magazine commented, "*This Bridge* marks a commitment of women of color to their *own* feminism—a movement based not on separatism but on coalition. . ." *This Bridge Called My Back* was republished in 1983, and it won the 1986 Before Columbus Foundation American Book Award. A revised, bilingual edition of the book was published as *Esta puente, mi espalda: Voces de mujeres tercermundistas en los Estados Unidos* in 1988.

Moraga included a preface, two poems and one essay in the book she edited. The essay, entitled, "La Güera," deals with the writer's anxiety over being a lesbian as well as a minority, her guilt for not understanding the prejudice her mother faced, and, most importantly, her anger that such bias would occur at all in the free society the United States claims to be. "It wasn't until I acknowledged and confronted my own lesbianism in the flesh, that my heartfelt identification with and empathy for my mother's oppression—due to being poor, uneducated, and Chicana—was realized," writes Moraga in "La Güera." "My lesbianism is the avenue through which I have learned the most about silence and oppression, and it continues to be the most tactile reminder to me that we are not free human beings." "In this country," she continued," lesbianism is a poverty—as is being brown, as is being a woman, as is being just plain poor."

The anger, frustration, and the knowledge that change must be instigated by the oppressed themselves that are found in Moraga's essay also appear in her poems in *This Bridge.* In "For the Color of My Mother," which Moraga had written during her first year in San Francisco, the poet speaks of the anguish that her mother had never expressed, and by doing so gave her mother a voice. She wrote: "I am a white girl gone brown to the blood color/of my mother/speaking for her. . ." In "The Welder," Moraga expresses her belief in solidarity and empowerment. "I am a welder./Not an alchemist./I am interested in the blend of common elements to make/ a common thing. . . . I am the welder./ I understand the capacity of heat' to change the shape of things. . . . I am the welder./I am taking the power into my own hands." Moraga not only advocates action in her poems, she is politically active herself.

In 1981, while attempting to find a publisher for her thesis, Moraga went to Boston and then to New York. The feminist scene in these cities was exciting at the time, and Moraga found many feminists and Hispanics (especially Puerto Ricans) who shared her ideas. It was not long before she became politically involved in her new communities. She spent time with local activists, joined an organization which sought to end sexual violence, and cofounded the Kitchen Table/Women of Color Press, which would allow still more feminists and women of color to express themselves textually.

When Moraga edited one of the group's first published books, *Cuentos: Stories by Latinas,* with Alma Gómez and Mariana Romo-Carmona, she once again broke ground for Hispanic feminists and lesbians. Like *This Bridge, Cuentos* was a revolutionary anthology: it was the first collection of writings by feminist Latinas. Also, once again, Moraga included some of her own work in an anthology. The two stories in *Cuentos,* "Sin luz," and "Pesadilla" deal with sexuality, racism, homophobia, and the attempts of women to cope with all three.

In "Sin luz," which means "without light," a young girl married to an old man has trouble feeling anything, physically or emotionally. Although she never feels fulfilled with her marriage, the girl becomes pregnant. The loss of her baby at seven months thus has various symbolic implications: Can a child be created without love, or light? Is a homosexual union, which cannot produce a child, different from a union which is neither loving nor fruitful? Moraga's other story, "Pesadilla," or nightmare, describes a fictional lesbian relationship. In it, Cecilia, a Chicana, and Deborah, a black woman, attempt to love each other and live together despite the interruptions of the pervasive outside world. The symbolic violation which occurs when a man breaks into their apartment and paints homophobic slurs on the walls penetrates the souls of the women and almost spoils the love between them.

Moraga's next project was to collect some of the work that she had produced herself since just before she left Southern California. The result of this effort was *Loving in the War Years: (Lo que nunca pasó por sus labios).* As Raymund Paredes in the *Rocky Mountain Review* wrote, the pieces in this collection are "notable for their passion and intelligence." Included in *Loving* is the poem, "For the Color of My Mother," and the essay, "A Long Line of Vendidas." This latter piece, written while Moraga was in New York, discusses Chicana sexuality in light of the Chicana's cultural heritage. According to Moraga, Chicanas were always taught to think of the needs of their men before their own; Chicana's must understand their particular situation, and free themselves from this sexual and cultural oppression. Once again, Moraga had given American literature another first. As Yarbro-Bejarano noted, *Loving in the War Years* was the first published book of writing by an avowed Chicana lesbian.

Presents Lesbian Themes in Plays

Moraga's desire to express her feelings and ideas about being a minority as well as a lesbian intensified. She began to work on a play. *Giving Up the Ghost* was read in mid-1984 at a feminist theater in Minneapolis, and later that year Moraga took her play to INTAR, the Hispanic-American Arts Center in New York City. At INTAR, the playwright-residency program directed by the renowned Off-Broadway playwright María Irene Fornes, Moraga began to develop the specific skill needed to produce a good play and started working on other plays and musicals.

Moraga's experience at INTAR contributed to her success as a playwright. *Giving Up the Ghost: Teatro in Two Acts* was published by West End Press in 1986, and has been produced twice, in 1987 in San Francisco and in Seattle. Moraga has written two other plays that have not been published, *La extranjera*, which she wrote in 1985, and *Shadow of a Man*, which she wrote in 1988. Another of Moraga's plays, *Heroes and Saints*, was produced in Los Angeles in 1989.

Giving Up the Ghost is Moraga's most celebrated play. In this work, Amalia and Marisa share a homosexual relationship after Marisa is raped and Amalia's male lover dies. The play is set in an East Los Angeles barrio, and has an English script peppered with Spanish; it seems to accurately reflect the Chicana culture the audience expects. The homosexual relationship, however, as well as Moraga's symbolic treatment of it, makes the play remarkable. Raymund A. Paredes, in the *Rocky Mountain Review*, succinctly describes this underlying symbolism. He writes, "*Giving Up the Ghost* represents the most radical element of contemporary Chicana writing. Moraga portrays heterosexual love as inherently abusive, an act of violent penetration which in the context of the excessively masculine culture of Mexican Americans becomes more brutal still." Despite the negative aspects of the culture, explains Paredes, Moraga "clings to her ethnic identity fiercely, demanding in her work that the culture transform itself in behalf of women's rights of self-determination."

In 1986, Moraga returned to teaching. This time, however, she instructed students in the art of writing instead of in English. At the Chicano Studies Department at the University of California at Berkeley, Moraga could finally combine her initial desire to teach, her passion for writing, and her study of Chicana culture. She could also live in the

intellectually stimulating San Francisco Bay area. Although she is teaching, Moraga continues to write: in 1989, she was working on a collection of poems which are to be entitled, *Dreaming of Other Planets*. Moraga is also working to develop her knowledge of theater, and to stage some of the plays she has written. Finally, Moraga maintains her determination to speak out against various kinds of oppression while upholding the Chicano culture she has both chided and cherished.

Sources:

Books

Dictionary of Literary Biography, Volume 82: *Chicano Writers, First Series*, Gale, 1989.
Moraga, Cherríe, and Gloria Anzaldúa, editors, *This Bridge Called My Back: Writings by Radical Women of Color*, Persephone Press, 1981, revised bilingual edition (edited with Ana Castillo) published as *Esta puente, mi espalda: Voces de mujeres tercermundistas en los Estados Unidos*, Spanish translation by Castillo and Norma Alarcón, ISM Press, 1988.

Periodicals

Essence, January, 1982, p. 17.
Mother Jones, January-February, 1991, p. 15.
Ms., March, 1992, p. 39.
New England Review, summer, 1983, pp. 586-87.
Rocky Mountain Review of Language and Literature, Volume 41, number 1-2, 1987, pp. 125-28.

—*Sketch by Ronie-Richele Garcia-Johnson*

Luisa Moreno
(1907-1990?)
Labor organizer

In the 1950s, at the height of Joseph McCarthy's hunt for communist sympathizers, Luisa Moreno was deported from the United States under the terms of the McCarran-Walter Immigration Act. A labor organizer for nearly three decades, she had risen through the ranks to become international vice president of the United Cannery, Agricultural, Packing and Allied Workers of America and state vice president for the Congress of Industrial Organizations (CIO). In the 1930s, Moreno pioneered the first Mexican American civil rights coalition, thereby bringing upon herself the scrutiny of the House of Representatives Un-American Activities Committee. She never returned to the United States after her deportation.

Moreno was born in Guatemala in 1907. "She came from an upper middle class family," explained University of California in Santa Barbara history professor Zaragosa Vargas, a labor-history specialist researching Mexican American labor organizers and union struggles in the 1930s for an upcoming book. "She studied in the United States and graduated from a very select parochial school—the College of the Holy Names—in Oakland, California."

Moreno's first effort as a labor organizer took place in New York City in the early 1930s, working with Hispanic garment factory workers in Spanish Harlem. Later, she joined the American Federation of Labor (AFL), and organized cigar workers in Florida. "But she grew disillusioned with the conservative posture of the AFL, and switched to the CIO," noted Vargas in his interview with Michelle Vachon. She soon served as editor for the newspaper of CIO's affiliate United Cannery, Agricultural, Packing and Allied Workers of America (UCAPAWA), and travelled throughout the southwest to organize workers. During the pecan shellers' strike in San Antonio, Texas, the UCAPAWA sent her to replace Emma Tenayuca as strike leader. "Union executives wanted to take the limelight away from a known Communist party member. Moreno managed the situation quite successfully, became the official voice of UCAPAWA in San Antonio, and achieved prominence within the union."

Focuses on the Rights of Mexican Americans

By the end of the decade, Moreno had focused more on Mexican Americans' civil rights. In 1938, she participated in the launching of El Congresso de los Pueblos de Habla Espanol, or the National Congress of the Spanish Speaking People, also known as El Congresso. Moreno gained support from a cross-section of the Hispanic population and organized labor, including the stevedores, copper miners, butchers and meat packers, seamstresses, and construction workers, in addition to UCAPAWA members. El Congresso's first conference was to take place in Albuquerque, New Mexico, in April of 1938. But the House of Representatives Un-American Activities Committee, accusing the organizers of communist sympathies, created such an uproar in Albuquerque that the conference was postponed until December and moved to Los Angeles, California. There the delegates finally met and committed themselves to the economic, social, and cultural betterment of the Mexican people. "El Congresso constituted the first Mexican American civil rights organization, and remained active from about 1938 until 1941," stated Vargas in his interview with Vachon. "Its membership numbered about 70,000 within 73 Mexican American organizations, and reached out to Puerto Ricans, Cubans, and other Latinos. It fizzled out right around World War II, when many of its members wound up in uniform."

Moreno continued her labor activities, organizing cotton workers in South Texas, pecan shellers in San Antonio, beet workers in Colorado and Michigan, and more than 60,000 cannery workers in California. She held the position of international vice president for UCAPAWA and state vice president for the CIO, and also chaired the California committee against discrimination in the labor movement. In the 1950s, she was forced to leave the United States. "There is a question about her background—was she a communist or not," explained Vargas in his interview. "It's very hard to find out whether these individuals in the 1930s were actually Communist party members. But that's beside the point. The thing to remember is that many progressive organizations of the 1930s, such as the Communist party, were instrumental in making the CIO successful in all its endeavors." Following deportation, Moreno stayed in Mexico, then in Cuba, where she participated in the first years of the revolution. Returning to Mexico, she lived in Guadalajara. Towards the end of her life, she sojourned in her native Guatemala. Moreno died destitute, "like many party members and luminaries of the 1930s."

Sources:

Books

Mirande, Alfredo, and Evangelina Enriquez, *La Chicana: The Mexican-American Woman*, University of Chicago Press, 1979, pp. 230, 232.

Other

Vargas, Zaragosa, interview with Michelle Vachon, October 12, 1992.

—*Sketch by Michelle Vachon*

Rita Moreno
(1931-)
Actress, singer, dancer

A remarkably versatile performer, Rita Moreno has received all four of show business's top awards. For her acting in *West Side Story*, Moreno won an Oscar in 1962. A Grammy followed her vocal performance on the *Electric Company Album* for children in 1972. Her role as Googie Gómez in *The Ritz* (1975) on Broadway won her a Tony. And finally, Moreno has been awarded two Emmys: one for guest appearances on *The Muppet Show* in 1977, and another for an episode of *The Rockford Files* in 1978. Although impressive, this long list of prestigious awards merely suggests the variety of Moreno's excellent performances, and it cannot convey the determination with which she has worked to become a respected actress.

Rita Moreno

Moreno, a woman who has illuminated the screen and charged the stage since she was a teenager, had to fight to win roles that merited talent. Too often, the need to earn a living as an actress forced her to take parts which were stereotypical and sometimes even debasing; for quite some time she was cast as either a "Latin Spitfire" or an "Indian Princess." Moreno struggled to exorcise these images, especially after the media referred to her as "Rita the Cheetah" because of her roles and her personal life. When Moreno finally received the recognition she deserved after winning an Oscar for her portrayal of Anita in *West Side Story*, she became one of the few Hispanics to "cross over" into stardom and become internationally famous. She commented in an interview for *Hispanic* magazine, "I have crossed over, but never, not for one minute, have I forgotten where I came from, or who I am. I have always been very proud to carry the badge of honor as a Hispanic." While Moreno has utilized her Hispanic identity to her advantage to portray characters such as that of Anita, she has also managed to poke fun at stereotypes on stage and screen with her wit and talent, as she did as Googie Gómez in *The Ritz*.

Moreno, or Rosa Dolores Alverio, was born to Paco Alverio and Rosa María Marcano Alverio in the small town of Humacao, Puerto Rico, on December 11, 1931. Moreno's parents divorced soon after her birth, and her mother left her with relatives while she went to New York to work as a seamstress. When Moreno was five years old, her mother returned for her, and, along with other members of the family, they found a home in a Manhattan tenement. It was at this point in Moreno's life that she began to take dancing lessons. Paco Cansino, an uncle of the legendary actress and dancer Rita Hayworth, was a very effective dance teacher: the young Moreno soon began to dance professionally.

Moreno, who attended New York Public School 132, soon found herself performing in the children's theater at Macy's Department Store and entertaining at weddings and bar mitzvahs. By the time she was thirteen, Moreno had exchanged the life of a schoolgirl for that of an actress. As "Rita Cosio," she had her first role on Broadway as Angelina in Harry Kleiner's *Skydrift*. Later, she performed in nightclubs in Boston, Las Vegas, and New York, and dubbed in the Spanish for Elizabeth Taylor, Margaret O'Brien, and Peggy Ann Garner in their movies. Moreno's first film, *So Young, So Bad* (1950), led to a meeting with Louis B. Mayer, who contracted her with Metro-Goldwyn-Mayer (MGM).

Gains Recognition with Stereotypical Roles

Under the name Rosita Moreno (her stepfather's surname), and later, Rita Moreno, the actress garnered minor roles in some twenty-five movies. The most notable of these included *The Toast of New Orleans* (1950) and *Pagan Love Song* (1950), with Esther Williams. Freelancing after she lost her contract with MGM, Moreno found only stereotypical, ethnic roles. With the exception of her part as Zelda Zanders in *Singin' in the Rain* (1952), Moreno portrayed Latin vamps in *The Fabulous Senorita* (1952), *The Ring* (1952), *Cattle Town* (1952), *Latin Lovers* (1953), and *Jivaro* (1954). She was hired to play an Arab in *El Alamein* (1953), and an American Indian in both *Fort Vengeance* (1953) and *The Yellow Tomahawk* (1954).

Although Moreno became a recognizable actress after these movies, the "Latin Spitfire" roles created a troublesome and unfair image for her. She became known as "Rita the Cheetah"; her highly publicized relationships with Marlon Brando, the famous actor, and Geordie Hormel of the Hormel meat family, exacerbated this image. Disheartened with these roles which, she later told a *New York Times* contributor, she "played . . . the same way, barefoot, with my nostrils flaring," the physically petite actress attempted to return to the stage. She lost a part in *Camino Real* because the playwright, the renowned Tennessee Williams, did not think her voice was suitable.

It seemed as if Moreno's career had taken a turn for the better when she was featured on the cover of *Life* magazine. She immediately signed a contract with Twentieth Century-Fox, singing in *Garden of Evil* (1954), and doing a Marilyn Monroe takeoff in *The Lieutenant Wore Skirts* (1955). Once again, however, she was given stereotypical roles which failed to challenge the serious actress. The casting was difficult for Moreno emotionally as well as professionally. As she recalled in the *New York Times,* she spent six and a half years in therapy "trying to get my ethnic problems untangled." Moreno was not the only one who was disappointed with her acting opportunities. After her performance in *Untamed* (1955), a writer for the *New York Post* voiced the frustration of Moreno and her fans: "Will the powers in Twentieth Century-Fox wait patiently until Miss Moreno loses half of her youth, vitality and beauty before they get around to giving her a romantic break?"

In *Seven Cities of Gold* (1955), Moreno was still not treated as a serious actress; she did not find a truly satisfying role until she was given a part as a Burmese slave girl in the hit musical *The King and I* (1956). As Tuptim in the Rogers and Hammerstein film adaptation, she sang "We Kiss in a Shadow" and "I Have Dreamed" with Carlos Rivas. Moreno also narrated "The Small House of Uncle Thomas," which was choreographed by Jerome Robbins, for the film.

Wins Academy Award for *West Side Story*

Despite these professional successes, Moreno found the latter half of the 1950s to be less rewarding; she made few movies from 1956 to 1960. In 1956, she won a role in *The Vagabond King,* followed by *The Deerslayer* in 1957, and after her contract with Twentieth Century-Fox expired she appeared in *This Rebel Breed* (1960). Once again, Moreno sought to return to the stage; she performed in Arthur Miller's *A View from the Bridge* in theaters in Seattle, Washington and La Jolla, California. Although she was well-received during this summer theater tour, Moreno could no longer cope with the frustration she had been experiencing—she attempted suicide with sleeping pills. When she woke in the hospital, however, she realized that she wanted to live. She recovered beautifully, and went on to star in the movie for which she is most famous, *West Side Story* (1961).

Moreno had been asked by Jerome Robbins a year after her performance in *The King and I* to try out for the role as Maria in the original theater production of *West Side Story,* but Moreno, busy as well as intimidated, did not. By the time the movie version of the play was being made, Moreno's face had matured, and she was better suited to the character of Anita, the more experienced friend of Maria, who was ultimately portrayed by Natalie Wood. As Anita, Moreno illuminated the screen with her singing and dancing. Especially memorable is the scene in which Moreno sang "America," a facetious piece in which life in America is satirized. *West Side Story* was an instant success. It won ten Academy Awards, one of which was Moreno's Oscar for best supporting actress.

During the ten years from 1961 to 1971, Moreno found that she could not rest on her laurels. While she played Rosa Zacharias in Tennessee Williams' *Summer and Smoke* (1961), and a camp follower in *Cry of Battle* (1963), she did not find these parts entirely rewarding; seeking better roles, she left Hollywood for London. There, in 1964, she

portrayed Ilona Ritter in Hal Prince's *She Loves Me.* Forced to return to the United States because of British performance laws, Moreno made her way to Broadway once again. This time she won the role of Iris Parodus Brustein in Lorraine Hansberry's *The Sign in Sidney Brustein's Window,* a play which ran for 101 performances. Marlon Brando, the man whom Moreno had dated on and off for eight years, assisted Moreno as she renewed her movie career with her portrayal of a drug addict in *The Night of the Following Day* (1969). This led to appearances in various movies; she found roles in *Marlowe* (1969), *Pop!* (1969), a comedy focused on East Harlem, and *Carnal Knowledge* (1971), in which she played a prostitute visited by Jack Nicholson. And in 1970 she returned to the theater to portray Sharon Falconer in *Gantry* on Broadway, and replaced Linda Lavin in *Last of the Red Hot Lovers,* by Neil Simon, in New York.

Marries and Launches Television Career

It was during these ten years that Moreno met and married Dr. Leonard Gordon, a cardiologist and internist at Mount Sinai Hospital in New York. When they were introduced near the end of 1964, Gordon asked Moreno to attend a New Year's party with him. When she accepted, Moreno instructed Gordon to pick her up at the Henry Miller Theater, but as Gordon later told a *Hispanic* contributor, he "couldn't figure out the sense of it." "Why would this attractive young lady be going to the theater on New Year's Eve? Was she going on a date with some other guy and then planning to dump him and go out with me?" Gordon, still perplexed, waited and waited for Moreno to leave the theater long after the audience exited, while an angry Moreno waited inside her dressing room, thinking she had been stood up. It was not until Gordon checked the marquee to see if he was at the right theater and saw Moreno's name in lights that he realized his date was *the* Rita Moreno. Moreno and Gordon finally went on their date, and they were eventually married in June of 1965. A *Hispanic* contributor explained, "On the surface it might seem that a Hispanic actress and a Jewish doctor are an unlikely combination, but . . . their successful partnership in all things . . . is based on the wide range of interests they have in common." The happily married couple celebrated their twenty-fifth anniversary in 1990.

Moreno took a break from both theater and film to perform for television in 1971. When the Children's Television Workshop, which produces the popular educational series for pre-school children, *Sesame Street,* asked Moreno to star in *The Electric Company,* a television series for older children, she was enthusiastic. "I jumped at the chance," she told a *New York Times* writer. "I love doing that show. It's just like vaudeville, except that we play to four million kids every day. I get to do some zany characters—and not a Latin in the bunch." As Pandore, a bratty blond girl, and Otto, a movie director, she encouraged children to develop reading skills. Moreno's performance was delightful, and in 1972 her participation, with Bill Cosby and others, in the soundtrack recording of *The Electric Company* won her a Grammy award for the best recording for children.

Laughs at Stereotypes in *The Ritz*

This success did not develop into any other television ventures, though. Moreno's next role was that of the Shoplifter in the play *Detective Story,* which ran in Philadelphia in 1973. She then portrayed Staff Nurse Norton in *The National Health,* first in New Haven, Connecticut, from 1973 to 1974, and then in the Circle in the Square, New York City, in 1974. It was around this time that Moreno displayed the character that would eventually win her the Tony Award to playwright Terrence McNally at a party. Singing "Everything's Coming up Roses" with her mother's Spanish accent and the mannerisms she had developed during the filming of *West Side Story,* she was hilarious. McNally later invited Moreno to attend his new play, *The Tubs,* at the Yale Repertory Theater, and she was shocked to see the character she had created singing on stage. McNally asked her to portray this character, which he named Googie Gómez, when the play, renamed *The Ritz,* came to Broadway in 1975, and she accepted.

Moreno was a hit. While the *New York Times* noted that her performance as the Puerto Rican singer was "variously hailed as 'pure beauty,' 'wonderfully atrocious' and 'a comic earthquake,'" a writer for the *White Plains Reporter Dispatch,* quoted in *Current Biography Yearbook,* said it best: "In fractured English, she [Moreno] creates a portrait of tattered glory. . . . Hot, cold, tempestuous, wiggling, seething, cursing,. . . so that she tears the house down every time she opens her mouth or does a bump and grind, she is showing a new generation of theatergoers what stars are all about." *The Ritz* ran for 400 performances, and it was no surprise when Moreno received the Antoinette Perry, or "Tony," Award, for best supporting actress.

Although some in the audience worried that the performance would offend Hispanics, Moreno was not among them. She felt that the character she and McNally had created made fun of the stereotypical roles she had always been cast to play. Saying that she had not received any "feedback flak from her own people," Moreno told a *New York Times* writer, "The Spanish people who come backstage say they love what I'm doing. Of course, some *Latins* might take offense, but I don't want to meet them. I don't want to talk to anyone who doesn't have a sense of humor about themselves. . . . I have had to learn to laugh at myself—otherwise there would be lines of sorrow from my forehead to my toes."

Moreno's next appearance was in the motion picture version of *The Ritz.* While this performance was not as appreciated as the one on Broadway, many believed this was the fault of the director, Richard Lester. Later, however, guest appearances on *The Muppet Show* in 1977 won her an Emmy for outstanding continuing or single performance by a supporting actress in variety or music. She won

another Emmy for outstanding lead actress for a single appearance in a drama or comedy series in 1978 for her appearance in "The Paper Palace" episode of the series *The Rockford Files.* Moreno went on to portray a Jewish mother in *The Boss's Son* (1978), and to develop a nightclub act which she has since performed in Chicago, New York City, Lake Tahoe, Toronto, Atlantic City, and on various cruise ships. Her next motion picture role did not come until 1980, when she played an Italian American mistress in *Happy Birthday, Gemini.* And in 1981, Moreno was given the opportunity to star with Alan Alda and Carol Burnett in the motion picture comedy *The Four Seasons.*

In 1982 Moreno found herself on television once again. She appeared as a secretary named Violet Newstead in ABC's *Nine to Five.* This situation comedy, based on Jane Fonda's movie of the same name, promoted the rights of working women. While it did relatively well from 1982 to 1983, its ratings fell after a time-slot change, and it was taken off the air. Despite the failure of the series, Moreno was nominated for an Emmy. Moreno's next career move was to return to the stage. With James Coco and Sally Struthers, she appeared in *Wally's Cafe* on Broadway for twelve performances in June of 1981. In 1985, she was again starring with Struthers, this time as the slobby Olive Madison in a revision of Neil Simon's comedy, *The Odd Couple,* on Broadway. The play, which was originally written for two male principals, was not well received despite its talented cast.

Since then, Moreno has been involved in a variety of activities. Although she loves to spend time with her family in their homes in Pacific Palisades, California, and Manhattan, Moreno also finds ways to spend time with Leonard Gordon and Fernanda Luisa professionally. She has appeared several times with her daughter, Fernanda, in theaters around the nation in *Steel Magnolias* and *The Taming of the Shrew.* She was a member of the board of directors of Third World Cinema and the Alvin Ailey Dance Company, and she was included on the theater panel of the National Foundation of the Arts. With her husband Gordon as her manager and partner, she is committed to the Hispanic community. She remarked in *Hispanic:* "Lenny and I are very involved in trying to make the Hispanic community understand that education is everything."

While Moreno is aware of the responsibility she has as a Hispanic role model, she is, as she explained in *Hispanic,* an actress with career aspirations. It is to Moreno's credit that she attempts to combine her love of acting with her desire to assist the Hispanic community. In 1989 she worked on two movies which would provide inspiration to Hispanics. It was her aspiration to play the part of a Hispanic woman who created an organization to fight gang warfare. Before she won one of *Hispanic*'s ten 1989 women of the year awards, Moreno spoke of this character: "She's the kind of Hispanic woman I want desperately to portray on television, and that is a woman of some sophistication, who speaks English very well, who is quite political. She is the emerging Hispanic woman, the one that nobody has gotten to see yet on television." Whether she portrays them in television movies or provides an example with her own career and personal life, Moreno is a leader of these emerging Hispanic women. She told another *Hispanic* interviewer, "When I was a young starlet, I wanted to be an all-American girl. . . . But when I grew up and developed a sense of self-esteem as a Hispanic, I learned how essential it was to cling to one's own heritage, for only in that way can we truly understand our ancestors, our culture, and ultimately understand ourselves."

Sources:

Books

Current Biography Yearbook, H. W. Wilson, 1985.

Periodicals

Boston Globe, September 5, 1986, p. 62; September 8, 1986, p. 26.
Chicago Tribune, May 3, 1988, section 5, p. 3; November 15, 1988, section 5, p. 8.
Cosmopolitan, August 1981, p. 14.
Harper's Bazaar, May, 1981, pp. 160-61; September, 1981, pp. 309-11.
Hispanic, October, 1989, pp. 30-33; December, 1989, p. 40; September, 1990, p. 56.
Los Angeles Times, November 17, 1988, section 6, p. 1.
Ms., January-February, 1991, pp. 93-95.
Newsweek, May 25, 1981, p. 74.
New Yorker, June 22, 1981, p. 86; June 24, 1985, p. 78.
New York Post, March 13, 1955.
New York Times, March, 1975.
Nuestro, October, 1981, pp. 44-46; March, 1986, pp. 16-25.
People, May 3, 1982, pp. 105-07.
TV Guide, January 15, 1983, pp. 26-29.
Variety, February 26, 1986, p. 60.
Washington Post, March 19, 1990, p. C5.

—*Sketch by Ronie-Richele Garcia-Johnson*

Trish Moylan-Torruella
(1953-)
Organization executive

As National Director of Education for Planned Parenthood Federation of America, Inc., in New York City, Patricia Moylan-Torruella is responsible for overseeing the educational programs of the organization's 169 affiliates and more than 900 clinics in the United States. An innovative leader in the health education field for years, Moylan-Torruella has designed courses for a wide range of clients, from doctors to patients to prison inmates. Her success, she says, is rooted in her bicultural background and lifelong interest in human relationships.

Moylan-Torruella was born November 8, 1953, in San Juan, Puerto Rico, to Edward F. Moylan, an administrator in bookkeeping from Boston, and Aida Torruella, a native Puerto Rican and psychiatric social worker, who divorced when Moylan-Torruella was still a child. Growing up in San Juan, the young girl looked up to her mother and two older brothers as her primary role models. Enveloped by her mother's large extended family, Moylan-Torruella watched as her brothers followed the path of traditional Latino men while she, encouraged by her mother, began to explore the bicultural aspects of her identity.

After graduating from high school in 1970, Moylan-Torruella left Puerto Rico for South Hadley, Massachusetts, where she attended Mount Holyoke College and received a bachelor of arts degree four years later in psychology and education. In an effort to learn more about her roots in Hispanic culture, Moylan-Torruella spent her junior year at the University of Madrid studying Spanish arts, literature and history. After graduating in 1974, she began working with learning-disabled children in the Augusta, Maine, school system. A year later, however, she moved to New York City and spent the next year working on her master's degree in public health at the City University of New York's Hunter College. While at Hunter College, she was nominated by the directors of her program and was selected by the Richter Foundation as the recipient of the Richter Award for Academic Excellence and Professional Potential.

Designs Courses for Diverse Groups

Upon graduation in the summer of 1976, Moylan-Torruella became a consultant at the Metropolitan Correctional Facility in Manhattan, where she designed the first human sexuality course taught in prisons and also developed an interviewing program to assess the adjustment abilities of incoming inmates. The program was especially focused on the needs of non-English speaking prisoners.

From 1976 to 1980, Moylan-Torruella worked as a health educator at the Lutheran Medical Center in Brooklyn, where she organized a program designed to train resident doctors and nurses how to communicate with their patients about health care and prescriptions. Near the end of 1980, during a sabbatical, Moylan-Torruella taught health education at Hunter College and assisted author Mike Carrera in research for his book on human sexuality, *The Facts, The Acts and Your Feelings.* Later, she went to work for the United Cerebral Palsy organization. At first, she worked as a sexuality specialist, but in 1984 she was promoted and became the organization's Director of Professional Education.

Researches Cultural Assimilation and Addiction

In 1986, Moylan-Torruella moved to the Alcoholism Council of Greater New York as the Deputy Director of Education and Training. While most of her efforts focused on certifying human service professionals, Moylan-Torruella also conducted a study of the interrelationship between sexuality and addictions and between Latinos and addictions. One of the significant findings of this study was a correlation between Latino families' cultural assimilation into American society and greater levels of alcoholism and addiction. "It's a reaction to the tremendous stress involved with families moving to the United States," she said during an interview with Suzanne L. Parker. "They have to learn the English language and the family begins pulling apart because the children leave their culture behind."

Moylan-Torruella joined the Planned Parenthood Federation of America, Inc., in 1989. As Director of Education, Moylan-Torruella draws upon not only the many years of experience and knowledge she has garnered in the health care field, but the strong values she developed as a child. "As a kid I had a very strong sense of rights and unfairness and to this day I have such a strong sense of the cruelty of discrimination," she told Parker. "In the same sense, I think children are warped by the withholding of information about sex education. Lack of access to information shouldn't be a barrier and so often it is." Moylan-Torruella attributes her own success in overcoming barriers to her bicultural upbringing and well-educated mother. "I was the youngest of my generation of 12 cousins and so as we were growing up I would measure myself against the choices my cousins were making for their lives," she recalled for Parker. "There was a lot of sexism in the family, which is culturally traditional, but because of my background, I did not believe the same constraints applied to me."

Sources:

Moylan-Torruella, Trish, telephone interview with Suzanne L. Parker, August 4, 1992.

—Sketch by Suzanne L. Parker

N-O

Evelyn Nieves
(1959-)
Journalist

Evelyn Nieves came from a neighborhood in the Bronx, New York, where most kids did not think about college. But with the backing of supportive parents, Nieves overcame a poor educational system and landed a job on one of the most prestigious newspapers in the world, the *New York Times.* She became one of the first Hispanic journalists at the paper. Nieves wanted to be a social worker, but changed her mind when she realized she excelled in English with little effort. She knew she would be able to reach more people and make a bigger impact with her writing. "It wasn't until I got to college that I realized I could combine a social activism with writing, and that is the definition of journalism that I had," she told this interviewer in a telephone interview. "It wasn't a lifelong dream. It was very natural."

She was born November 3, 1959, in the Bronx the youngest of four children to Antonia Martinez and Angelo Nieves. Her parents emigrated from Puerto Rico and instilled in their children a strong allegiance to their heritage. "The first trip I took to Puerto Rico was when I was nine," she said in her interview. Her father wanted his children to "know where we came from and where he came from."

He made sure, too, that his children understood where they were going. "From the time we were in kindergarten, there was no question that we would go to college," Nieves said. When her father's friends complimented him on having four children who attended college, his common response was that he was sorry he could not have given them more when they were growing up, because they would have attended Harvard University.

Nieves excelled in school and graduated from Adlai E. Stevenson High School two months after her fifteenth birthday with enough credits that she could have gotten her diploma six months earlier. She went on to graduate from New York State University with a bachelor of arts degree and a master's degree in English. She did well even though the public schools in the Bronx did not provide the best education. "Sometimes when I look at my education I get upset because the schools weren't better," she related in her interview. "I think if I accomplish anything, it's in spite of where I grew up."

Feels Affinity towards the Poor

Nieves always felt a strong tie to the Bronx and other poor neighborhoods. "I feel an empathy towards groups that are poor." And at the same time, the Bronx is where she feels most comfortable. "When I go to Union City and back to the Bronx, I feel happy. I feel I don't have to explain to these people. I feel they already know what I'm about." Her father, who owned restaurants in the Bronx, had that same type of bond. "He was the cook and the food was really good," Nieves proudly explained. "People told him that if he moved the restaurant he would make a fortune. But he didn't want to leave the neighborhood."

Sometimes when Nieves visits her parents in the Bronx she uncovers stories just by being in the neighborhood, knowing the problems people face and the emotions they feel. And having grown up in an impoverished area, she brings to her writing an understanding that reporters without that rearing would not know.

Nieves also adds a Hispanic perspective to the paper that might otherwise be overlooked. She explained that Hispanic reporters naturally tend to draw on Hispanics for story information, because, like all journalists, they turn to the people and organizations with whom they are familiar. "Until you see more Hispanic journalists, you won't see Hispanic surnames and the guy at the corner store being quoted," she told this interviewer. "I don't want to use a political word, but it's empowering. I get calls from people, and they say maybe you will want to do this story—and it's strictly from my name. You don't see too many Hispanic journalists." Other times she feels helpless because the callers are reaching out, but the ideas do not lend themselves to stories. In those cases, her instincts toward social work surface and she finds herself giving advice.

Her first experience as a reporter was with her high school newspaper. After college she worked at various small papers before she landed a job at the *Middle Town Times Herald Record* in Orange County, New York. She stayed there for three and half years before she applied at the *New York Times.* "I had to do a lot of selling, because I came from a small newspaper," and the *New York Times* customarily hires reporters from large papers, she said in her telephone interview. She was hired in July 1990.

Nieves is drawn to stories that reveal an injustice or in some other way influence people to make improvements for the oppressed. One story she wrote uncovered the plight of Newark, New Jersey, residents who were living in housing complexes that appeared to be abandoned. She wrote another story about a group of people in the Bronx, mostly immigrants from Central America, who took over an abandoned building and got kicked out by the city officials. "I went into journalism to do those kinds of stories."

In addition to her newspaper work, one of her goals is to write about Latinos and Puerto Ricans "and not just as a subculture, but about Puerto Rican lawyers and other groups." Someday, she also hopes to write a book about Puerto Ricans in the Bronx to illustrate some of the obstacles they face daily. "It's the poorest Hispanic group in the country. When I go back there and see a train station that hasn't been fixed, it angers me, because these people don't complain."

Sources:

Nieves, Evelyn, telephone interview with D. D. Andreassi, August, 1992.

—*Sketch by D. D. Andreassi*

Antonia Novello

Antonia Novello
(1944-)
Surgeon General of the United States

When C. Everett Koop announced in late 1989 that he would retire from the post of United States Surgeon General, speculation about who his predecessor would be was particularly lively. During his eight-year tenure, Dr. Koop played an unusually prominent role in American public life, elevating the previously soft-spoken voice of the Surgeon General to a forceful, opinionated one that people paid attention to. Koop gained national prominence and respect by speaking out on controversial issues, sometimes colliding openly with the views of the administrations of presidents Ronald Reagan and George Bush on such topics as sex education and the use of condoms to prevent the spread of AIDS.

When Dr. Antonia Novello, the deputy director of the National Institute of Child Health and Human Development at the National Institutes of Health (NIH), was cho-

sen for the Surgeon General post, many observers noted that following in the illustrious footsteps of Dr. Koop would not be easy. The first woman and the first Hispanic to hold the position, Dr. Novello brought with her a reputation for hard work and dedication, but her ability to fight for her convictions was unproven. Both Novello and administration officials admitted that questions about her views on abortion—she opposes it—had been a part of the selection process. This so-called "litmus test," allegedly applied to candidates for this and other high-level health care appointments, was a subject of widespread controversy. But Novello claimed, as reported in the *Washington Post* several months after she was sworn in, "I'm for the people who deserve help . . . how I vote is not relevant. I think that as a woman, as a Hispanic, as a member of a minority . . . I bring a lot of sensitivity to the job." Voicing a concern that echoed in other quarters, California Democratic Representative Henry Waxman told the *Post,* "I hope she's a fighter, because it's a bad time for infant mortality, for AIDS, for the homeless, for the uninsured, and this administration hasn't shown much interest in these problems . . . she can do a lot."

Novello was born in Fajardo, Puerto Rico, on August 23, 1944. She and her brother were raised by their mother, a school teacher, after their parents' divorce. Novello suffered from a painful congenital colon condition until she was 18 years old, when it was finally corrected. She has said that one of the reasons she became a doctor was to help others who were suffering as she had. Novello received both her B.S. and M.D. degrees from the University of Puerto Rico, where she was—as described by her teacher Dr. Ivan Pelegrina in the *Detroit Free Press*—"one of our brightest students." Ana Flores Coello appears to have been a major motivating force in her daughter's life at this stage; Novello told *Glamour:* "I wasn't allowed to work until I graduated from medical school because my mother felt that once I earned money I might be sidetracked by material rewards before I got to my real work."

Develops Early Interest in Pediatric Care

Novello did get to her "real work," beginning with an internship and residency in pediatrics from 1970 through 1973 at the University of Michigan (UM) Medical Center in Ann Arbor. She served as a fellow in pediatric nephrology at UM in 1973 and 1974, and she remembered this "first job" in *Glamour* as germinal in her eventual decision to enter government work; she "learned how many people slip through the cracks." Monitoring the progress of patients waiting for kidney transplants, Novello was dismayed at the number who could not be helped. Those cases in which she, personally, was powerless to help were especially affecting: "You become a true caring physician when you're able to share the pain."

In 1971 Novello was the first woman to receive the UM Pediatrics Department's Intern of the Year award. Her classmate Dr. Samuel Sefton, who is now a neonatologist in Kalamazoo, Michigan, told the *Detroit Free Press,* "It was difficult for women to be accepted [in the medical field] then, and I always was impressed with the way she handled situations." Barbara Lanese, head nurse (then and now) of the UM perinatal unit, concurred with Sefton: "[Antonia] was a resident when female physicians weren't as readily accepted as they are today. . . . She was a wonderful physician, and she was warm, friendly and well-respected. She was able to break the tension just by the kind of person she is."

In 1974 Novello joined the staff of Georgetown University Hospital in Washington, D.C., as a pediatric nephrology fellow. She served as a project officer at the NIH's National Institute of Arthritis, Metabolism and Digestive Diseases in 1978 and 1979, a staff physician at NIH from 1979 through 1980, and the executive secretary in the Division of Research Grants at NIH from 1981 through 1986. She earned a master's degree in public health from Johns Hopkins University in 1982.

From 1986 until her appointment as Surgeon General, Novello served as deputy director of the National Institute of Child Health and Human Development, where she nurtured a special interest in children with AIDS. Concurrently, Novello was a clinical professor of pediatrics at Georgetown University Hospital. Her colleague there, pediatric department chairman Dr. Owen Rennert, told the *New York Times* that Novello "is tremendously concerned about the medical and social problems of children and she

has a way of drawing others into that concern." In 1982 and 1983 Novello was a Congressional fellow on the staff of the Labor and Human Resources Committee chaired by Senator Orrin Hatch, a Republican from Utah. As reported in the *Washington Post,* Hatch later commented that she had "given good advice on several bills . . . including legislation on organ transplants and cigarette warning labels."

Accepts Appointment to Surgeon General Post

Novello's appointment to the post of Surgeon General came at a time of controversy and hostility between some scientists involved in public health issues and the Bush administration. Several candidates for top jobs at such organizations as the NIH, the Center for Disease Control, and the Health Care Financing Administration had withdrawn their names from consideration, complaining that their interviews had included questions about their views on abortion and on the use of fetal tissue in research (another controversial practice opposed by the Bush White House). Dr. Burton Lee, the President's personal physician, might have been a contender for Surgeon General, but took himself out of the running because his views on abortion did not coincide with Bush's. In so doing, he echoed the administration's contention that it is important and appropriate that the appointee defend Bush's positions with conviction.

During Novello's two-hour interview, she was able to convince administration officials that her view on abortion was the approved one. Some observers speculated that Novello's reputation for cooperative, dedicated and essentially low-key work made her a particularly desirable choice after the outspoken reign of Dr. Koop. Yet Novello claimed at a press conference covered in the *Washington Post* that "as long as the data can be trusted and is not just hearsay, I'll say it like it is. . . . I was never told I have to keep a low profile. I really intend to be like Dr. Koop when the data is there."

As head of the 5,700 commissioned officers of the Public Health Service, Novello promised to focus her energies on AIDS-infected children, smoking (she opposes particularly the glamorous portrayal of smoking in advertisements) and such women's health issues as breast cancer and heterosexual AIDS. Other areas of concern for Novello include teenage drinking, drinking and driving, and finding ways to diminish the stigma of mental illness.

Strives for Better Health Care

The Surgeon General's is an essentially public role, and Novello—who receives several hundred invitations to speak per month—spends much of her time on the road, promoting the cause of better health. She talks with Louis Sullivan, Secretary of Health and Human Services, three or four times a week and meets with him monthly. Sullivan, with whom Novello has pledged to work closely, described her (as quoted in the *Detroit Free Press*) as "a very commanding woman who has a tremendous ability to reach out to communities." To what extent and to what ends she will put that ability to use is a subject of concern for some, like the Congressional official (a Democrat) quoted in the *Washington Post* who said, "Toni Novello is a nice, talented, hard-working woman. But she has never stood up and shouted for the programs she directs. . . . If she wants to play anything like the role Koop did, she is going to have to learn to speak up."

Novello's own perception of the potential power and impact of her new job became more sharply defined, she told the *Washington Post,* when she visited her birthplace, Puerto Rico, shortly after becoming Surgeon General: "When I got off the plane, kids from my mother's school lined both sides of the road handing me flowers. . . . I went to the VA hospital to speak. When the veterans saw my gold braid [she is a Vice Admiral in the Public Health Service] they all stood and saluted. . . . I realized that for these people, for women, I have to be good as a doctor, I have to be good as a Surgeon General, I have to be everything."

Since her appointment to the Surgeon General post in 1989, Novello has addressed and attempted to solve many of the problems which concern her, including teenage drinking. In late 1991, she met with some of the largest beer and wine companies in the United States and asked them to stop aiming their advertising at children and teenagers. "The ads have youth believing that instead of getting up early, exercising, going to school, playing a sport or learning to be a team player, all they have to do to fit is learn to drink the right alcohol," remarked Novello during a press conference covered in the *New York Times.* The marketers of beer and wine do not see their ads as being aimed at children, and will not voluntarily back down—there may be laws in the future requiring them to include warnings in their advertisements.

In addition to her attempts to lessen teenage drinking problems, Novello has also aspired to provide better health care for children, women, and minorities. As she stated in an *Hispanic* interview shortly after her appointment: "I hope that being the first woman and minority Surgeon General since the post came into being—and the visibility the post confers—enables me to reach many individuals with my message of empowerment for women, children, and minorities."

Sources:

Periodicals

Detroit Free Press, October 30, 1990.
Glamour, August, 1990.
Hispanic, January/February, 1990, p. 20; October, 1991, p. 15.
Newsweek, October 30, 1989.
New York Times, October 18, 1989, section A, p. 20; November 2, 1989; June 27, 1991, section D, p. 20; November 5, 1991, section A, p. 16; November 6, 1991, section A, p. 25.
Parade, November 11, 1990.
People, December 17, 1990.
Washington Post, October 18, 1989; October 24, 1989; May 8, 1990.

—*Sketch by Kelly King Howes*

Nuevo Kerr, Louise Año
See **Kerr, Louise Año Nuevo**

O'Brien, Ana Colomar
See **Colomar O'Brien, Ana**

Adriana C. Ocampo
(1955-)
Planetary geologist

Adriana C. Ocampo has worked since high school for the National Aeronautics and Space Administration (NASA). Now a planetary geologist, she is involved in NASA's ambitious mission to Jupiter, Project Galileo, and in the Mars Observer venture. "Space exploration holds the secret to the evolution of our planet and the origin of life on earth," she told Michelle Vachon in a telephone interview. "It is part of the future of human beings. We need to study asteroids and comets, and we need to go to the Moon and Mars to try to establish a colony."

"Her love of stars and planets goes back to childhood," recalled Ocampo's mother, Teresa Uria Ocampo, in an interview with Vachon. "Instead of playing with dolls like other little girls, Adriana was making astronauts out of them, using my kitchen appliances to build spacecraft." Born on January 5, 1955, in Barranquilla, Columbia, Ocampo grew up in Buenos Aires, Argentina, where her family had moved when she was only a few months old. The year she turned fifteen, Ocampo and her family immigrated to the United States and settled in Pasadena, California. During her junior year in high school, she jumped at the opportunity to take a summer job at the Jet Propulsion Laboratory, the NASA facility in Pasadena. At the end of the summer, this became a part-time position that Ocampo kept during her studies in aerospace engineering at Pasadena City College and in geology at California State University in Los

Angeles (CSULA). When she received her bachelor's degree in geology from CSULA, Ocampo had already been working at the prestigious laboratory for ten years. The transition from part-time to full-time employee seemed only natural—she joined the Jet Propulsion Laboratory staff in 1983.

Researches Distant Planets

Her tasks on the Jupiter and Mars probing missions will keep her busy for years to come. On project Galileo, Ocampo serves as science coordinator for the near-infrared mapping spectrometer, one of the four remote-sensing instruments mounted on the spacecraft to analyze Jupiter's atmosphere. She holds a similar position on the Mars Observer project—experiment representative for the thermal emission spectrometer. During the Viking mission to Mars, she produced a photo atlas of Mars's moon that, to date, is the only atlas of this moon in existence.

Ocampo is a member of the Chicxulub Consortium, an organization regrouping American, Canadian and Mexican representatives for the study of a crater in the Yucatan Peninsula in Mexico. Scientists think that this crater might have been formed by a meteorite believed to have caused the extinction of dinosaurs sixty-five million years ago. Its fall is presumed to have created clouds of dust and gasses in the Earth's atmosphere that produced acid rain and diminished the dinosaurs' food supply.

Ocampo's membership involvement with the Chicxulub Consortium is just one aspect of her international work in space resarch. A few years ago, she came up with the idea of an international gathering for North and South American scientists to share information on space exploration. "I made phone calls," she explained in an interview with Vachon, and as a result the Space Conference of the Americas took place in Costa Rica in 1990 and is scheduled to occur in Chili in 1993. Ocampo has given workshops on planetary sciences in Mexico, Costa Rica, and Columbia as part of her involvement with the Planetary Society and the United Nations. A member of the Society of Hispanic Professional Engineers, she has served as national secretary for one term and national vice president for two terms. She presides over the society's international affairs committee, and is a member of the space committee.

In 1989, Ocampo married archeologist Kevin O. Pope, whose company conducts remote-sensing geological and ecological research. In the future, "I still would like to be an astronaut as a mission specialist," she admitted in her interview. Although her application was previously rejected, she is not giving up. "I also want to start a research foundation for the exchange of information on science and technology on a good-will basis. Together we could improve the standard of living in the Americas."

Sources:

Periodicals

Hispanic Engineer, Fall, 1987, pp. 22-24; Fall, 1989, p. 24.

Other

Ocampo, Adriana C., telephone interview with Michelle Vachon, May 5, 1992.
Ocampo, Teresa Uria, telephone interview with Michelle Vachon, April 27, 1992.
Pope, Kevin O., telephone interview with Michelle Vachon, April 27, 1992.

—Sketch by Michelle Vachon

Ellen Ochoa
(1958-)
Astronaut

When Ellen Ochoa became the first female Hispanic astronaut in July, 1990, she decided that being a role model for young girls and Hispanics would be one of her top priorities. She would show them that if they study hard and reach far enough the possibilities are endless. Ochoa is among the selected few who will explore the mysteries of outer space, and like other astronauts who have ventured into space, her work is destined to influence scientists for generations. Before Ochoa turned thirty-three, she had also left a mark on the science world by developing special techniques in optical processing; she holds three patents in the field.

Immediately after the National Aeronautics Space Administration (NASA) selected Ochoa to become an astronaut, she began speaking to groups, especially young girls and Hispanics, advocating the importance of education. She emphasized her Hispanic heritage hoping they would see a part of themselves in her. "It may encourage them to do something like someone who is similar to them," Ochoa explained to D. D. Andreassi in a telephone interview. Otherwise, she said, her gender and heritage have no influence on her work. "When I'm at work, I don't consider myself any different from any other astronaut," related Ochoa. "I consider myself one of the astronauts in the office."

Ochoa was born May 10, 1958, in Los Angeles to Rosanne (Deardorff) and Joseph Ochoa, who was born in California

Ellen Ochoa

and was of Mexican descent. Ochoa, whose parents were divorced when she was in junior high school, grew up with her mother, three brothers and one sister in La Mesa, California, in a close-knit family of high achievers. When her brother, Tyler Ochoa, a lawyer in Palo Alto, California, heard his thirty-one-year-old sister was selected by NASA, he told a *Houston Post* interviewer that she worked incredibly hard to be chosen among thousands of other applicants. "She's always been very diligent about studying and working for what she wanted to do," remarked Tyler. He described his sister as calm, rational and thoughtful, all qualities that would be useful to her as an astronaut.

Education Values Instilled

Ochoa's mother instilled the value of education in her at an early age. "From my mother we were all encouraged to do whatever we wanted to do," Ochoa told Andreassi. "She placed a high premium on going to college." Rosanne, a living example of her own advice, took college courses for twenty-three years, according to the *Houston Post.* The studying finally paid off when Rosanne finished a triple major in business, biology, and journalism, a field that Ochoa considered, but later decided against in favor of physics.

Ochoa was just as dedicated to school work. She did exceptionally well in math and science, but easily mastered all of her other courses as well. When Ochoa was thirteen

years old she won the San Diego County spelling bee; and in junior high school she was named outstanding seventh and eighth grade girl—from then on she consistently went to the head of her class. Ochoa was valedictorian at Grossmont High School in La Mesa, and achieved the same honor at San Diego State University where she earned a bachelor of science degree in physics. "I try to work hard for whatever I try to do," she commented in her interview with Andreassi. "That's what I tried to do in school and that's what I'm trying to do now on my job."

Ochoa went on to Stanford University where she earned a master's degree and a doctorate in electrical engineering. She was the recipient of the Stanford engineering fellowship and IBM predoctoral fellowship. Ochoa told a *Hispanic* magazine interviewer that she demonstrates the value of education. "If you stay in school, you have the potential to achieve what you want in the future," she maintained. "Education increases career options and gives you a chance for a wide variety of jobs." This is often a theme of her speeches to school children; Ochoa stresses the importance of children studying math and science to increase their worth in the job market.

During all of her scholastic achievements, Ochoa kept active with her music. In high school, she became an accomplished flutist. She captured the top musician recognition at Grossmont High School and she was the student soloist winner at the Stanford Symphony Orchestra in 1983. Ochoa considered playing the flute for a career, but opted for something more stable. "I like to eat," she pointed out to Andreassi, adding that she personally knows musicians who have a hard time paying bills. When she was out of school, Ochoa expressed her love for the instrument during many hours of playing in her spare time. "I still play a lot whenever I can on the side," she continued, "so it's something that you can do as a hobby as well."

Research Projects Lead to Patents

Ochoa took on another hobby when her older brother got his private pilot's license. She decided to follow his lead, and in 1988, two years before she would become an astronaut, she got her pilot's license for small engine planes. "I wanted to be an astronaut and I thought I should learn more about aviation," she told Andreassi. Ironically, after she became an astronaut she found that she would have little time to fly, or for her other hobbies—playing volleyball and bicycling.

During the course of her career, Ochoa has always kept busy with research projects. From 1985 through 1988 she was a research engineer in the Imaging Technology Branch at Sandia National Laboratories in Livermore, California. While scientists, artists, and inventors struggle their lifetimes to patent their ideas, Ochoa was not even thirty-three years old when she held three patents in optical processing. She developed a process that implements optics for image processing that is normally done by computer. For instance, one method she devised removes noise from an image through an optical system rather than using a standard digital computer to do the work.

While research always interested Ochoa, she observed to Andreassi that she had a difficult time trying to decide what career to pursue. Even in college she was unsure. In fact, while Ochoa was an undergraduate she changed her major five times, from music to business to journalism to computer science, before deciding on physics, according to the *Houston Post.* It was while she was a graduate student at Stanford, when friends applied to NASA, that she realized she had the qualifications to be an astronaut.

Ochoa would not have been able to consider this career before 1978, the year that NASA graduated the first six women ever selected to the program. She told a *Houston Post* interviewer that when women were accepted into the program a milestone had been reached and a lot of people were influenced. "We realized, 'Oh, it's really open to real people, not just an elite group of test pilots,'" she recalled. Little did the twenty-year-old college student know in 1978 that twelve years later she would be blazing new trails by becoming NASA's first female Hispanic astronaut.

Earns Spot at NASA

It was a combination of Ochoa's many qualifications and persistence that won her a spot at NASA. She first applied to the program in 1985, and in 1987 she was named one of the top 100 finalists. Ochoa graduated in the astronaut class of 1990, which included eighteen men and five women, according to the *Houston Post.* That year Ochoa reached another turning point in her life by marrying Coe Fulmer Miles of Molalla, Oregon.

Just as she had done in school, Ochoa made a name for herself at NASA, beginning in 1988 as a researcher, and later as chief of the Intelligent Systems Technology Branch at the National Aeronautics and Space Administration/ Ames Research Center at Moffet Field Naval Air Station in Mountain View, California. Her progression through the ranks was rapid. Ochoa began as a researcher, and she was soon supervising almost 40 scientists before her selection as an astronaut. "She was assertive," remembers her deputy Nancy Sliwa, quoted in the *Houston Post.* "She defended (her) branch needs within NASA." Ochoa's accomplishments were acknowledged in 1989 when she was awarded the Hispanic Engineer National Achievement Award for most promising engineer in government. A year later she was given the pride award by the National Hispanic Quincentennial Commission in Washington.

Ochoa plans to put her expertise to test in space. In late 1992 her title was missions specialist civilian and she was preparing to go on her first flight, ATLAS 2 (Atmospheric Laboratory for Applications and Science). The shuttle mission, scheduled for take-off in March of 1993, plans to utilize a set of instruments to measure chemical composition, temperature, and pressure of the earth's atmosphere. The astronauts will set out to measure solar radiation and how it varies across different wavelengths. "What the scientists are hoping to do is measure what effect and variability the sun would have on the earth's atmosphere and determine values for concentration of chemical species in the atmosphere," explained Ochoa to Andreassi.

Prepares for Space Flight

Ochoa faces tremendous challenges as she follows in the footsteps of Sally Ride, the first female the United States sent on a space flight. During the ten-day ATLAS 2 mission, Ochoa will be one of two scientists on board the shuttle. She was chosen to play a key role by deploying instruments into space that will enable scientists to look at the sun's corona. Ochoa will be one of two astronauts operating the deployment arm under stressful conditions, because there will be limited chances to achieve proposed tasks during the short mission.

Ochoa revealed to Andreassi that while she is excited about reaching her goal of flying in space, she is also aware there will be a lot to learn before the ATLAS 2 take-off. "But there's nothing else I'd rather be doing," she said. Ochoa also stated that she is not worried about an accident in space, even as she recalled the Challenger shuttle disaster in January of 1986. All seven Challenger crew members, including teacher Christi McAuliffe, died when the shuttle exploded shortly after take-off as friends and family watched horrified from the ground. "I'm sure on flight day I'll think about a lot of different things, but we train for a lot of different things," Ochoa commented in her interview, adding that every precaution will have been taken to make the mission as safe as possible. Ochoa did point out, however, that there are always some unknown elements and that risks are part of the equation that everyone who becomes involved with a space flight understands.

After she achieves her short term goal of flying in space, Ochoa told Andreassi that she hopes to continue her work as an astronaut for "quite a number of years and beyond that I'll have to wait and see what I will do." She plans to continue making public speeches, to explain her responsibilities as an astronaut, and most of all to maintain her duties as a role model. She related to Andreassi that her emphasis will be with school children, because they are at an impressionable age and are most easily influenced. "I think that's where I can make a difference." And she always remembers that her achievements are noticed especially by Hispanic groups. "A lot of those kids have come up to me and said, 'Wow, it's inspiring to see that you made it, because it shows what I can do.'" "Anything I can do along those lines is important for those people and for the country in having an educated work force." She already made an impact on youngsters shortly after she became an astronaut. According to the *Houston Post*, Ochoa gave a speech at a San Francisco Bay Area Catholic school when a Hispanic youngster, who was among a group of students who surrounded her, said: "'I'm glad you came. You've inspired us.'"

Sources:

Periodicals

Hispanic, May, 1990, p. 19.
Houston Post, July 17, 1990, p. A9; July 22, 1990, p. A9; July 23, 1990, p. A9.

Other

Ochoa, Ellen, telephone interview with D. D. Andreassi, August, 1992.

—*Sketch by D. D. Andreassi*

Virginia F. Ojeda
(1945-)
Franchise owner

Virginia Ojeda is a third-generation Chicagoan and the first native Chicago Hispanic to own a McDonald's franchise in the city that is home to the fast-food company's headquarters. Ojeda and her husband, Ernest, own four McDonald's restaurants in the Chicago area.

Ojeda, whose father worked in the steel mills in Chicago, attended Chicago public schools and Northeastern Illinois University. "I've had five careers," Ojeda told this interviewer. She first worked in the adult division of the Illinois Department of Corrections and then moved into the juvenile division. She also worked as a contract negotiator for the Illinois Department of Children and Family Services, where she developed her lifelong interest in helping children. In 1976, Ojeda became the regional affirmative action manager for the A & P food stores.

It was during this time that she and her husband purchased three apartment buildings and a laundromat, investments which financed their entry into the restaurant business. It was not easy. The Ojedas were turned down by McDonald's twice, but they persevered. They finally were awarded a franchise on their third application and opened their first restaurant in 1980. In an interview, Ojeda stated that all the personnel for their restaurants come from the surrounding community, which is 98 percent Hispanic. Ojeda told this contributor that staff morale is high and the turnover is only 90 percent—a source of pride in an industry where the turnover rate is often 300 to 500 percent. Ojeda attributes this achievement to "mutual respect for each other. We recognize where people are going. We try to use their potential, give them a little power, listen to their thoughts, and this makes for really good teamwork. People working for you often have better ideas than you do."

The business owner has a special affinity for the women who work for her and she pays special attention to developing their potential. Ojeda commented: "When we hired them, these women were very much the stereotype. They were timid. They were confused about how smart they were because they weren't supposed to be that bright. I've taught them how it's okay to be a strong woman. Now 50 to 60 percent of our managers are women. I have never been disappointed in the people I have as managers." Her managers annually receive McDonald's management awards.

Ojeda remains very active in her community. She serves as the commissioner of the Human Relations Commission for the city of Chicago. She is a board member of both the Chicago Capital Fund, which raises money to help finance new development in the city, and the Ronald McDonald's Children's Charities for the Chicago region. She is also a board member of the Development Committee for Old St. Pat's, a historical church the committee is trying to save. In addition, she is a founding member of SER Jobs for Progress, a past chairperson of the Youth Service Project, a committee member of the Illinois Woman's Agenda, and the former marketing chairperson of the Chicago Council of Urban Affairs.

Ojeda, who lives in the Chicago area with her husband and two grown sons, said she is at an interesting point in her life, explaining that she is interested in both future business development and personal development. These goals have inspired her to enroll in writing classes. Ojeda is a fine example for women in business, according to Jose Nino, president of INAMCO Trading Company, a Chicago international business firm. Nino told *Hispanic Business*, "She succeeds in helping women achieve as much as they can in business. Virginia and Ernie are among the best role models we could present to our youth."

Sources:

Periodicals

Hispanic Business, July, 1990.

Other

Ojeda, Virginia F., telephone interview with Carol von Hatten, September 1, 1992.

—*Sketch by Carol von Hatten*

Graciela Olivárez
(1928-1987)
Government official, educator

Although she dropped out of high school, Graciela Olivárez went on to become one of the most high-profiled Hispanics in the nation. As the first woman to graduate from Notre Dame School of Law, President Carter's Director of the Community Services Administration, and a senior consultant for the United Way, Olivárez paved the way for other women and Hispanics with her actions as well as her example.

Olivárez was born on May 9, 1928, in a town near Phoenix, Arizona, to Damian Gil Valero and Eloisa Solis Valero. Although she dropped out of high school when her family moved to Phoenix in 1944, Olivárez did not let her lack of a degree affect her confidence. She attended business school and aggressively sought a job. By 1952, she held a position as the women's program director of KIFN, a Spanish-language radio station. She became locally famous as Phoenix's first female disc jockey.

During the 1960s, Olivárez became increasingly active with the social and political movements of the time. As she wrote in *New Catholic World* in 1984, that was a time when "we [her generation] believed that we could do almost anything we set out to do." Olivárez's youthful optimism and determination to help the impoverished won her an influential position as the State Director of the Office of Economic Opportunity (OEO) for Arizona in 1965. With its commitment to eradicate poverty, the OEO provided a wonderful work place for Olivárez, who deeply cared about the plight of the impoverished. In 1984, she reminded readers in *New Catholic World* that the OEO "created programs such as Head Start, Legal Services, VISTA volunteers, Job Corps, Community Action Agencies, programs for migrant farm workers and their families, community development corporations and the weatherization program."

Olivárez did not work in this position for long. During the civil rights movement, the president of Notre Dame University, Reverend Theodore Hesburgh, had met Olivárez and was impressed with her intelligence and her record. He encouraged her to attend the university's law school. Although Olivárez was already in her late thirties and did not have the usual educational qualifications, she courageously decided to take the Reverend up on his offer. At the age of forty-two, in 1970, Olivárez graduated from the Notre Dame School of Law—she was the first woman ever to do so.

Fights Poverty

Following her graduation, Olivárez returned to the Southwestern United States. There, she taught law and worked for various government agencies. By 1972, she had been appointed the director of the University of New Mexico's Institute for Social Research and Development. From 1973 to 1975 she was a professor at the law school at that University. Next came a position as New Mexico's State Planning Officer in 1975. Olivárez's efforts to decrease poverty eventually caught the attention of the President of the United States, Jimmy Carter. When he appointed her as the director of the Community Services Administration in 1977, she became the highest-ranking female Hispanic in Carter's administration.

In 1980 Olivárez left the Carter administration to return to her home in New Mexico and to run her own business, the Olivárez Television Company, Incorporated. That same year, she began to serve as a senior consultant with the United Way of America. By 1984, Olivárez was the owner of a management consulting/public relations firm in Albuquerque. At that time she continued to discuss the poverty situation in the United States. She wrote in an article for the *New Catholic World:* "To solve the nation's growing numbers of poor, we need (1) rational analysis and practical programs, (2) the cooperation of both the public and private sectors and (3) sincere concern for the future of all Americans. Short-sighted ideological and political posturing, coupled with simplistic approaches, won't do."

Olivárez received many honors for her work over the course of her career. The American Cancer Society presented her with an Outstanding Leadership Award in 1960, and during the early 1970s the League of Mexican-American Women named Olivárez an Outstanding Woman of the Southwest. Amherst College in Massachusetts awarded her with an honorary Ph.D. in 1973, and Olivárez went on to receive another honorary doctorate from Michigan State University in 1976, and still another from her alma mater, Notre Dame, in 1978. The Woodlawn Organization honored her with its Leadership Award in 1978, and she won the Mexican American Opportunity Found Aztec Award the next year. And in December of 1985, Olivárez was honored by the Mexican American Legal Defense and Educational Fund for her contributions to the Latino community.

When she died in 1987, Olivárez left a legacy of hope to a generation of young Hispanic woman who are now influential scholars, professionals, and politicians. Just as importantly, she left a tremendous contribution of effort, ideas, and optimism to those who continue to fight poverty in the United States.

Sources:

Periodicals

Los Angeles Times, December 5, 1985, section I (H), p. 1.
National Catholic Reporter, November 6, 1987, p. 2.
New Catholic World, July-August, 1984, p. 183.
Redbook, April, 1975.
Washington Monthly, April, 1980, p. 60.

—*Sketch by Ronie-Richele Garcia-Johnson*

Oliver, Remedios Diaz
See **Diaz-Oliver, Remedios**

Gilda Oliveros
(1949-)
Mayor

Gilda Cabrera Oliveros holds the unique honor of being the first Cuban-born, female mayor in the United States. President George Bush invited her to the White House in 1991 to acknowledge her accomplishment in becoming Mayor of Hialeah Gardens, Florida, and the key to her small city now hangs in the Oval Office.

Born on August 14, 1949, in San Antonio de las Vegas, Cuba, Oliveros was raised there for seventeen years by her parents, Juan Jose Cabrera and Angela Maria Ginart. Although her father once owned his own trucking company in Cuba and her mother was a satisfied housewife, they fled Cuba in 1966 with their only child, fearing the wrath of the Cuban government. Oliveros admits that the reason her family left Cuba was because she was a rebel. "I didn't like the Castro regime, and was very outspoken," she said in an interview with this contributor. "My parents decided to get me out of Cuba before I got them and myself in trouble." In Miami, her father became a boat builder and her mother a factory worker. Many years later, as the mayor of a small Hispanic community in the Greater-Miami area, she remains as outspoken as she was then.

Although she cried through her struggles with the new language and being away from friends and family, Gilda adapted to her new home and graduated from Miami Central High School in 1969. She married Aldo Oliveros soon after graduation and had her first daughter, Yesenia, two years later. But marriage and child-rearing didn't deter her from pursuing her childhood dream of helping people through a career in the medical field. She attended night school while raising her two daughters, Yesenia and Jesebelle, and running the family business with her now ex-husband. She eventually received certification as a medical assistant from Miami/Dade Community College in 1973.

However, her interest in community affairs and her outspokenness sidetracked her medical career and drew her into politics. According to the Mayor, "I didn't give up my idea of being in medicine until the moment I decided to run for city council." She credits her decision to run for city council in 1987 to her dislike for what was going on around her politically and socially.

Becomes Mayor after Serving on City Council

She won a seat on the city council in 1987 and was appointed Finance Director for the City of Hialeah Gardens. Oliveros took a liking to politics during her stint as a councilwoman and decided to run for mayor in 1989. She was elected mayor over three male competitors who were well known in local politics. She credits her work as a councilwoman and her unorthodox approach to politics as the key to winning the race. "I was new blood and had proven myself to be honest and a go-getter in the city council," she related. "I brought something different to the arena: In politics, you're not supposed to tell people what you think. I tell people the truth whether they like it or not."

Oliveros is proud of being the first Cuban American woman mayor in the country, but she admitted in her interview, "it is also a weight on my shoulders because everything I do is watched carefully, and I'm in the public eye all of the time." Although Mayor Oliveros carries the weight of her position comfortably on her shoulders, she concedes that showing the strength that she has to show to do her job well is the hardest part of her job. Referring to recent personnel cuts, she said, "Firing so many employees, many of whom I liked, was very hard. . . . Having to be the tough guy, and showing strength all the time even when you don't feel like it is hard."

In contrast, she finds that the most pleasure she gets from her position lies in the simple things. A word of gratitude from one of her constituents is enough to make the hard political fights and the lack of privacy all worth while. "It's nice to meet someone you've helped and who appreciates what you are doing."

Since Mayor Oliveros assumed her position, the city of Hialeah Gardens has blossomed. Once known only by a few as a small suburb of a larger city, Hialeah Gardens has taken on its own persona. According to the Mayor, "When I took over, no one at the state or county level really knew Hialeah Gardens. Now developers are coming in, and we even have money for a park which we haven't had for twenty-five years." She feels that one of her greatest contributions to the city is that she has helped it to grow, while allowing it to retain that small-town atmosphere that she fondly remembers from her days in Cuba.

Mayor Oliveros has been honored repeatedly by her community, receiving the "Dynamic Woman of the Year," and the "Principal Award of Excellence" in 1989, as well as the "Distinguished Leadership Award" and the "Woman of the Year" award in 1990. She intends to run for a third term in office after her current term expires; after that, she has her sights set on winning a seat in the state legislature.

Sources:

Oliveros, Gilda Cabrera, interview with T. A. Niles, August 18, 1992.

—*Sketch by T. A. Niles*

Olvera Stotzer, Beatriz
See **Stotzer, Beatriz Olvera**

Lupe Ontiveros
(1942-)
Social worker, actress

Actress Lupe Ontiveros has performed in film, television, and theater. Endearing humor is her trademark. She is well-known in entertainment-industry circles for her commitment to advancing the positive image of Latinos. Childhood memories from growing up in El Paso, Texas, to episodes from her more than thirty years in Hollywood, have given Ontiveros the ability to draw from her life's experiences in portraying a diverse array of characters. Ontiveros calls herself a "rebel." Her lifestyle reflects a mix of both traditional and avant-garde beliefs with humor and ambition interspersed.

Born September 17, 1942, Ontiveros is the only surviving child of Juan Moreno and Lucita Castañon. She was named for the Virgen de Guadalupe because her parents, having suffered the loss of four other children (two sets of twins) due to premature births and inadequate medical care, promised to name her in the Virgen's honor if she survived. Her parents also pledged to raise their daughter in the Catholic faith.

"It was beautiful growing up in the '50s," Ontiveros told Oralia Michel in an interview. "We were coming out of a war, people were connecting again and making babies, and the soldiers coming back from the war were trying to recoup their lives. The whole country was coming of age again rebuilding morally and financially. My mother was a very progressive woman and together with my father, they were very ambitious." They started out selling sodas, sombreros, and shoes from a Ford pick-up with a home-built shell. They sold their wares at migrant workers camps in El Paso. Later, her parents' hard work paid off, and they came to own a tortilleria and two restaurants.

Ontiveros was eager to begin her education at a young age. She started kindergarten early because she insisted on going to school. Subsequently, she attended Texas Woman's University. Never having been away from home, Ontiveros recalls that college life was a rude awakening. She remembers feeling totally out of her element. She was used to the warmth of her parents' home, the security of the businesses they had built, and the rapport she had with all their customers—people she describes as being like her older sisters and brothers. Despite being homesick and having trouble with her grades (she didn't know how to study), she stayed and finished college at the insistence of her mother. She graduated with a bachelor of science degree in sociology and plans to become a nurse. Later, Ontiveros would attribute her wittiness and sense of humor, in part, to the fact that she had been raised within two cultures. She had seen some of the poorest people living in some of the worst conditions find reasons to laugh and be happy. The humor of these Mexicans and the comedy she saw as a young girl performed by the famous Mexican movie star/comedian, Cantinflas, influenced her.

After marrying she moved to San Diego in 1968 and then to Los Angeles where she worked as a social worker for 16 years. It was during the last few years as a social worker that she also took up acting. While still nursing her youngest son, Ontiveros decided to audition for a part as an extra in a movie and landed her first role. Her transition from social work to acting full-time came when she was selected to perform in the play *Zoot Suit*, which ran in Los Angeles and New York. Since then, her many film credits include *Born in East L.A., California Suite,* and *Goonies.* She is most proud of her lead role in the motion picture *El norte.* She also made appearances in television's *Once a Year for a Lifetime, Chicken Soup, Stones for Ibarra,* and *Who's the Boss,* and in theater's *Stone Wedding* and *Rooster.*

Ontiveros, who considers herself a strong woman, has had to use that strength to overcome two of the biggest difficulties of her life. First, she endured and fully recovered from a bout with arthritis that caused paralysis for six months. She also overcame the depression that set in when her mother died while she was appearing in *Zoot Suit.* Her latest challenge is battling the stereotyping and racism prevalent within the entertainment industry. A witness to the struggle of fellow actors and filmmakers, she says too little change has occurred regarding these issues, and she fears that she may not be able to affect a change in her lifetime. Like many actors, Ontiveros says she has a lot more to give. "I'm still waiting for that ultimate role in a series or movie. However, if I die today,"Ontiveros told Michel, "I'd feel very fulfilled with what I've been able to do in film."

Sources:

Ontiveros, Lupe, interview with Oralia Michel, June 30, 1992.

—Sketch by Oralia Michel

Ord, Angustias de la Guerra
See **de la Guerra Ord, Angustias**

Katherine D. Ortega

Katherine D. Ortega
(1934-)
Former U.S. Treasurer, banker

Katherine Davalos Ortega came to national prominence in the fall of 1983 when President Ronald Reagan nominated her for the position of Treasurer of the United States. Her nomination was confirmed by the Senate and she served as Treasurer for six years. Her role as U.S. Treasurer was preceded by a series of no less admirable achievements, including being the first woman bank president in California and guiding an Alamogordo, New Mexico, financial institution to a point where it could claim $20 million in assets. In her acceptance speech following her appointment as Treasurer, Ortega is quoted in the *New York Times* as referring to her Hispanic background as a source of pride and inspiration. "I am the product of a heritage," Ortega commented, "that teaches strong family devotion, a commitment to earning a livelihood by hard work, patience, determination and perseverance."

Ortega was the ninth child of Donaciano Ortega, a blacksmith and cafe owner, and Catarina Davalos Ortega of Tularosa, New Mexico, where she was born on July 16, 1934. Her paternal grandparents had brought their family to New Mexico from Texas in the late 1880s. Ortega grew up in Tularosa, a tiny village of less than three thousand inhabitants, nestled in the shadow of the Sacramento Mountains not far from the Alamogordo atomic bomb testing site. It was here that Ortega learned Spanish—her first language—and, then, English. During her early years she excelled at mathematics and was so skilled with numbers that she was allowed, even as a ten-year-old youngster, to use the cash register at her family's restaurant business. As she got older she found special pleasure and a high measure of success in her mathematics and accounting classes at school. In her last year of high school, she worked at the Otero County State Bank in Alamogordo.

Experienced Job-Related Discrimination

After graduation from high school, Ortega took a two-and-a-half year break in her education and obtained a position at a bank where she worked in order to earn money for college. She eventually entered Eastern New Mexico State University at Portales where she majored in business and economics and graduated with honors in 1957. Ortega explained what happened after her college graduation in an interview with Marian Christy of the *Boston Globe:* "When I graduated from college, I planned to teach typing and shorthand at the high-school level. I was told by the chairman of the business school that I need not apply in the eastern part of New Mexico, where such a job was open, because of my Hispanic background. My immediate reaction was: 'That's it. I won't teach.'"

Disgusted with the discrimination that would keep her from following her chosen career path, Ortega quickly decided to create her own career opportunity. She and one of her sisters, who was a certified public accountant, started an accounting firm in Alamogordo. During the 1960s and 1970s she held several different positions in accounting in New Mexico and later in California, to where she moved in 1967. From 1969 to 1972 she was a tax supervisor at the firm of Peat, Marwick, Mitchell & Co. in Los Angeles, and from 1972 to 1975 she served as vice-president and cashier at the Pan American National Bank also in that city. In 1975, she became the first woman president of a California bank when she accepted the position of director and president of the Santa Ana State Bank.

In 1979, Ortega moved back to New Mexico to help run the family accounting business, which eventually became the Otero Savings & Loan Association. She served as consultant to the firm from 1979 to 1982. Ortega also became a California certified public accountant in 1979. About this same time, Ortega intensified her involvement in politics, although according to a *New York Times* contributor, she once declared, "I have often said that I was born a Republican." At first, her political work was on the local and state level, with the party calling on her to play a liaison role with Hispanic and women's organizations. She was also active in the campaigns of Pete V. Domenici, a Republican senator from New Mexico; he later returned the favor when, as chairman of the Senate Budget Committee, he suggested Ortega to then-President Reagan when he needed someone to fill the treasury position.

Nominated Treasurer of United States

Ortega received her first taste of national recognition from the Republicans in April of 1982 when Reagan selected her to be part of a ten-member Presidential Advisory Committee on Small and Minority Business Ownership. Eight months later, Reagan appointed her a commissioner on the Copyright Royalty Tribunal. This five-member panel is the Federal agency that determines what royalty fees cable companies throughout the nation pay for use of copyrighted material. The tribunal, which was created in 1978, also establishes royalties paid by jukebox operators to the musicians whose music they provide. In September of 1983, Ortega learned that she would be nominated to be U.S. Treasurer and she received Senate confirmation several weeks later.

Ortega was officially nominated as Treasurer of the United States on September 12, 1983, in a ceremony marking the beginning of Hispanic Week celebrations in the nation's capital. According to the *New York Times,* in President Reagan's nominating remarks he claimed that Ortega was "symbolic of the values the Hispanic community represents" and added that "nothing is a better influence on America than the strength and decency of the Hispanic family." On October 3, 1983, Reagan again praised his appointee as she was sworn in to her post by Treasury

Secretary Donald T. Regan in the Rose Garden of the White House. In *New York Times* coverage of the event the President is reported as saying, "It's important that key positions within an Administration be filled by people who reflect the goals and ideals for which the people voted. . . . And this is certainly true today." During the ceremony Ortega signed special forms that were used to add her signature to plates from which U.S. currency would be printed during her tenure, an estimated 5.5 billion bills in the first year.

The position of U.S. Treasurer has in recent years nearly always gone to a politically prominent woman. Romana Acosta Bañuelos, appointed by President Nixon in 1974, was the first Hispanic woman to serve in this capacity; Ortega was the second. Although the post is deemed to be for the most part ceremonial, the U.S. Treasurer supervises the Bureau of Engraving and Printing, the United States Mint, and the United States Savings Bond Division. Some of Ortega's duties included maintaining an account of government spending, handling claims for lost, stolen or counterfeit Government checks, and burning unusable U.S. currency. When Ortega took office, she was responsible for handling the nation's $220 million budget and overseeing 5,000 employees. In 1985, Ortega was given the added responsibility of promoting the sale of U.S. Liberty Coins, three gold and silver commemorative coins designed to raise $40 million to help pay for the restoration of the Statue of Liberty.

In 1984, Ortega flew more than 60,000 miles to speak at Hispanic and Republican events. Her most important speaking engagement came in August of that year when she flew to Dallas, Texas, to deliver the keynote address at the Republican National Convention. That this important convention role was given to a comparatively new member of the Reagan Administration surprised a lot of long-time convention observers who had expected to see Elizabeth Dole, a member of the Reagan Cabinet, or Nancy Kassebaum, a senator from Kansas, fill the bill. Ortega was undaunted by the assignment and gave a stirring speech later reprinted in *Vital Speeches of the Day.* In the address, she referred to her Hispanic heritage several times and—to the joy of Spanish-speaking delegates—even included several Spanish phrases in the text. "To those millions of Democrats abandoned by their national leadership . . .," she declared, "we Republicans here in Dallas say: we welcome you to our home. Nuestra casa es su casa. Our home is your home."

Ortega's high-profile image at the convention served to remind those feminist groups who had complained about a lack of female appointments during Reagan's administration that he had indeed filled many positions with qualified women. Ortega mentioned in a *New York Times* article that one of her goals was "to get the message out. . . . There is a perception that Ronald Reagan has not named women to his Administration. When I'm out there, I talk about all the subcabinet appointments. I want to set the record straight." Ortega credited her father for inspiring her quest for success in the male-dominated worlds of banking and politics. She noted in the *New York Times:* "My father taught me we were as good as anybody else, that we could accomplish anything we wanted. . . . He encouraged all three of his daughters to make a living for themselves so we would never have to be dependent on anybody."

Ortega served as Treasurer of the United States until 1989. Since that time she has been for the most part self-employed. After completing her work at the Treasury, she has served as an alternative representative to the United Nations and is on the board of directors of several major corporations, including the Ralston Purina Company, the food and animal feed firm, and the Kroger Company, the grocery chain, both of which appointed Ortega to their boards in 1992. She is also on the advisory boards of Leadership America and the National Park Service and a member of Executive Women in Government and the American Association of Women Accountants. On February 17, 1989, she was married to Lloyd J. Derrickson. Her leisure activities include travel, reading and golf.

Ortega's distinguished career has brought her many awards and honors. In 1977, Eastern New Mexico University presented her with its Outstanding Alumni of the Year Award. She has also received several honorary degrees, including honorary doctor of law degrees from her alma mater, Eastern New Mexico University, in 1984, and from Kean College of New Jersey, in 1985, and an honorary doctor of social science from Villanova University in Pennsylvania in 1988. Other awards Ortega has received include the California Businesswoman's Achievement Award and the Outstanding Woman of the Year Award from the Damas de Comercio.

Ortega is quite willing to serve as an example to other Hispanics who find themselves facing the obstacle of racial bigotry. "I think of myself as a role model for my people. . .," she told a *Boston Globe* contributor. "I hope they see me and say: 'Hey, there's hope. We can accomplish.' I think people can look at me and see what I've accomplished and pursue careers for themselves. Everyone encounters obstacles. I tell people if one road is closed, take another. I'm a stubborn person."

Sources:

Periodicals

Atlanta Constitution, May 13, 1986, p. B1.
Boston Globe, November 24, 1985, p. B25.
Ms., August, 1984, p. 22.
New York Times, September 13, 1983, p. B14; October 4, 1983, p. A19; August 24, 1984, p. A20.
Vital Speeches of the Day, September 15, 1984, pp. 712-13.

—*Sketch by Marian C. Gonsior*

Carmen Ortiz
(1948-)
Business executive

Carmen Ortiz, the founder in 1988 of the Hispanic Women's Chamber of Commerce, is committed to the belief that entrepreneurship is the way of true advancement in American society. The Chamber teaches Hispanic women how to become successful businesspeople. Ortiz is also a certified financial planner and registered investment adviser with the Securities and Exchange Commission, as well as the owner and president of C.D. Ortiz Financial Management Group in New York City.

Born in Puerto Rico, the daughter of Fausto and Carmen Ortiz, Carmen Ortiz graduated from the University of Puerto Rico and received her advanced degree in 1974 from Texas Woman's University. Recognized as one of the leading American experts in bilingual education for disabled children, Ortiz first taught at Bank Street College of Education in New York City, a leading graduate school, where she was the first Hispanic faculty member in the school's history. She later worked for the U. S. State Department as a consultant in South America.

Upon Ortiz's return to the United States, however, her interests took a decided turn. Ortiz returned to Columbia University School of Business and in 1984 received her M.B.A. and became a certified financial planner. "Dr. Ortiz strongly believes that the vehicle for advancement is through entrepreneurship," said colleague Carmen Luciano during a telephone interview with this contributor. "She recognized that Hispanic women had greater difficulty in starting their own businesses, and faced double discrimination as women and Hispanics."

Founds the Hispanic Women's Chamber of Commerce

Because of the difficulties faced by Hispanic women who wished to go into business, Ortiz founded the Hispanic Women's Chamber of Commerce in 1988. This organization brings Hispanic women together and introduces them to federal and state officials who deal with minority business development. The chamber holds seminars in accounting, personal dynamics, legal structures of business and responsibilities of management. The response has been enthusiastic. Women from all walks of life have attended. "The membership base includes a range of businesswomen, from CPAs to researchers to beauty salon owners to public relations directors," said Luciano. In New York state alone, there are now some six hundred Hispanic women operating their own businesses. The long-range goal of the group is to open the way for Hispanic women to gain appointments to boards of directors of Fortune 500 companies.

In addition to owning and leading the C. D. Ortiz Financial Management Group, Ortiz is working on the formation of a joint venture to provide financial education in the work place and is publishing a Spanish-language workbook on money management. The joint venture will contract with corporations to provide financial planning to their workers as an employee benefit. Ortiz says that initially the venture will target companies in New York, then expand across the country. Her workbook, "probably the first such publication," she tells this contributor, will contain "very basic concepts about finances, a financial planning guide for the Hispanic community in succeeding in the U. S. economy."

While Ortiz is excited about the work she has done and her new business ventures, the center of her life has become spirituality. "I reached the realization," she tells this contributor, "that there is something more to life than making money. In searching for what else there is in life, I confronted my spirituality. And out of that I was transformed." Now, she said, "I execute my business from the principles of spirituality. I bring to my clients a sense of well being out of financial security."

Because of her work assisting Hispanic businesswomen to become successful entrepreneurs, Ortiz was named Hispanic Businesswoman of the Year by the New York Department of Economic Development in 1991. She also was nominated as Woman Entrepreneur of 1991 by *Inc.* magazine. In addition, Ortiz serves on the Advisory Board of the Small Business Administration, Region Two, and is a member of the advisory board of New York City's Minority Business Development. Ortiz is very optimistic about the future of Hispanic businesswomen, said Luciano. She sees the Hispanic Women's Chamber of Commerce as a way for them to "consolidate a power base, break down discrimination, build up a knowledge base and self-confidence for Hispanic women."

Sources:

Luciano, Carmen, telephone interview with Carol von Hatten, September 10, 1992.
Ortiz, Carmen, telephone interview with Carol von Hatten, October 1, 1992.

—Sketch by Carol von Hatten

Ortiz, Judith Cofer
See Cofer, Judith Ortiz

Sandra Ortiz-Del Valle
(1951-)
Basketball referee

Sandra Ortiz-Del Valle is one of the few women basketball referees working men's professional leagues. She has quietly broken boundaries in the sporting world by succeeding in a male-dominated profession. Her skills and determination have led to her work as a referee for the United States Basketball League (USBL) and earned her membership in the Naismith Basketball Hall of Fame.

Ortiz-Del Valle was born in New York on April 23, 1951, to Puerto Rican parents. Growing up in the Bronx was an educational experience that affected the course of her life. She watched her mother, Delia Ortiz, striving to improve herself. Her mother was the sole Hispanic American on the local school board in an almost completely African American neighborhood in Harlem. Ortiz-Del Valle considers her mother a pioneer in the educational system in Harlem and New York City. From her, Ortiz-Del Valle learned determination. Her father, Esteban, an electrician with the Transit Authority, taught her the importance of completing a task once it has been undertaken.

As a child, Ortiz-Del Valle turned to sports as a way to stay out of trouble and was introduced to basketball while attending high school in the Bronx. She was "instantly hooked on the game," the referee said in a telephone interview with this contributor. She graduated from City College in 1974 with a bachelor of science degree in education and completed her master's degree in administration and supervision in 1983. It was while playing women's college basketball that Ortiz-Del Valle first started refereeing, beginning with youth games in 1978.

Eager to train as a referee, she took courses to learn the skill and is now a member of the International Professional Basketball Officials Association. She started working in the pro-am leagues in 1984, and by 1989 her ability and reputation were recognized by the USBL, which hired her as a referee. The USBL is composed of some of the best basketball players in the United States. A number of the men who play in the league could make it to the National Basketball Association. That is clearly a path Ortiz-Del Valle has her eyes on. Her goal and her vision are clear: she has her sights set on the NBA.

Even after 14 years as a referee, Ortiz-Del Valle still finds that she is expected to prove herself as a legitimate basketball official because she is a woman. She has met with some resistance. She told this interviewer, "When I am faced with people new to the idea of a woman referee in a men's league, they think I have to pay my dues, and many think I am into it for the novelty. The players and coaches who know me recognize that I am serious and respect me."

Media coverage of her career has served as a positive influence on the girls attending the Humanities High School where she teaches, and they are very supportive of her efforts, said Ortiz-Del Valle. Working full-time as a physical education teacher and a bowling and boys' baseball coach in the New York City school, Ortiz-Del Valle has found that the philosophy of using sports as a positive influence in youngsters' lives keeps her involved and motivated.

Sources:

Ortiz-Del Valle, Sandra, telephone interview with Robyn Kleerekoper, August 29, 1992.

—Sketch by Robyn Kleerekoper

Carmen Otero
(1933-)
Judge

Overcoming a shyness that began in her youth, Carmen Otero has dabbled in a number of professions. After stints as a teacher, librarian, and lawyer, Otero became a judge in Seattle, Washington, in the mid-1970s. Several years later she became chief criminal judge of King County Superior Court, a post she has held for more than a dozen years. As the head magistrate, she supervises 22 other judges. Otero is especially interested in the Hispanic Bar Association, which she supports financially and with her time. She serves as mentor to many Hispanic law students.

Otero was born June 7, 1933, at home on a cattle ranch in remote, northern New Mexico. "Those were hard times," recalled the judge during a telephone interview with Carol von Hatten. "People were very poor. Most didn't have jobs." Her mother, Grace Arceo Otero, had worked as a maid during the Great Depression to support her husband, Bernie Otero, while he earned a degree in education from the University of New Mexico. While her parents worked and studied, Otero grew up on the ranch with her grandparents, aunts, and uncles—all of whom spoke Spanish. Because Otero did not speak English when she initially entered public school, she was sent home by representatives of the school district due to the language barrier. As a result, the start of Otero's education was delayed one year until she was seven years old. "I had a very strong mother who only had a fifth grade education, but her strong belief in education spurred us on," Otero explained.

Overcomes Intense Shyness

When Otero's father graduated from the university, he obtained a job as a mathematics teacher and athletic coach. Eventually, he ran successfully for election as county school superintendent of Santa Fe, New Mexico. After three years, her father became a field worker for the state employment service commission. By the time Otero graduated from Santa Fe High School, she had struggled throughout her youth to overcome an intense shyness. Then she attended the University of Colorado, receiving her bachelor's degree in education in 1955. "Even as a teacher I was very shy and was uncomfortable speaking at teachers' meetings," she remembered. "I had to force myself to get over this shyness."

After working several years as a teacher, Otero decided to expand her professional experience and studied library science. As a librarian, she found that her intellectual curiosity continued to grow and she eventually settled on law school. While studying law, she received a Ford Foundation fellowship and wrote a legal analysis entitled "Outdoor Recreation in Urban Areas." The foundation published the piece, which dealt with legal aspects of the inequity of funding the maintenance of parks in urban areas. Some time later, she moved to Washington State and began a new career as a lawyer. This new job eventually led her to a position as assistant attorney general in the Consumer Protection Division of the Department of Motor Vehicles.

In 1976, she became a judge in Seattle's Northeast District Court. Three years later she moved to King County Superior Court where, as chief judge, she later began revising the Superior Court system's procedures as a means of clearing up the backlog of cases. She also started writing a criminal manual, which will include guidelines for both judges and attorneys.

Otero has developed numerous professional affiliations, including service to the Washington State Juvenile and Family Law Committee. The director of the Washington State Magistrates Association, she also maintains membership in the Superior Court Judges Association and the National Women Judges Association. "As I got older," Otero noted, "I found a renewed interest in my heritage, and six years ago I reclaimed my birth name." Her renewed interest also prompted greater activity in the Hispanic community. She serves on the Hispanic Sea-fair Board and the League of United Latin American Citizens' Education Service Center Board.

"I will continue to serve as a judge as long as the people continue to elect me to be one," she related. "I have had other careers and this won't be my last." Otero plans to pursue a career in the non-profit public sector after retiring from the bench. The judge is married to Frank James, a retired judge, and has two grown children and four grandchildren.

Sources:

Otero, Carmen, telephone interviews with Carol von Hatten, September and October, 1992.

—Sketch by Carol von Hatten

Nina Otero-Warren
(1882-1965)
Writer, educator

Maria Adelina Emelia "Nina" Otero-Warren opened the way for women and Hispanic women in every field into which she ventured. In 1917 she chaired New Mexico's suffragettes' chapter. In 1922 she won her district's Republican nomination in the House of Representatives electoral race. And in 1936, with the publication of her book *Old Spain in Our Southwest,* she joined the first generation of Hispanic women writers in New Mexico to speak of their heritage and their threatened cultural identity.

Otero-Warren was born in Los Lunas, New Mexico, in 1882. The youngest child of Eloisa and Manuel B. Otero, she belonged to an old and well-established New Mexican family. She attended elementary and secondary private schools in New Mexico, and studied at the all-women Maryville College of the Sacred Heart in St. Louis, Missouri. After her graduation, she chose to pursue a career in education, and in 1917, her dedication earned her the position of school superintendent for Santa Fe County, New Mexico. In that same year, as American women were fearlessly demanding the right to vote, Otero-Warren moved to the forefront of the battle. She became chair of New Mexico's chapter of the Congressional Union—the national suffragist organization. An active member of the Republican Party, she obtained her party's district nomination for the House of Representatives in 1922.

Otero-Warren left the Santa Fe County school superintendency in 1929. During the following years, she served as adult education supervisor for Indian Services and education director for the Civilian Conservation Corps. In 1941, she joined President Franklin Delano Roosevelt's Works Progress Administration, and accepted the position of director of adult education in Puerto Rico.

During the 1930s, a few southwestern writers took advantage of the Federal Writers Projects to record the oral history and folklore of the region. They collected Amerindian recipes, folktales and, in the case of Hispanic writers, stories of Spanish colonial times. Inspired by their work, Otero-Warren published *Old Spain in Our Southwest* in 1936. Speaking of Otero-Warren and two other writers of her generation—Cleofas Jaramillo and Fabiola Cabeza de Baca Gilbert—Tey Diana Rebolledo explained in the *Journal of Narrative Technique,* "This generation of women writers document their lives and the lives of Hispanic New Mexicans during the time when the land and society in New Mexico were shifting from Hispanic to Anglo control. These writers came from old landed upper class New Mexican families. The perspectives presented in their stories therefore generally reflect these class origins. They extol the Spanish (and not the Mestizo or Indian) heritage, and see the past as a utopia in the pastoral tradition where humans were integrated with nature and tied to the land. . . . The narrative accounts often extend back into the 19th century."

Otero-Warren wrote about her feelings of isolation and alienation at the disappearance of a way of life and the suppression of traditions and values of her Spanish heritage. She said in her book: "This southwestern country, explored and settled nearly four hundred years ago by a people who loved nature, worshipped God and feared no evil, is still a region of struggles." Although she presented highly romanticized vignettes evoking a lost era of fiestas and caballeros, "The fact that all (these writers') books focus on the loss of land and the despoiling of the Hispanic culture is ipso facto the first resistance; they are not forgetting the 'details' of the domination," maintained Rebolledo. Otero-Warren, like most writers of this period, mourned an idealized Spanish past while trying to survive the transition to an Anglicized world. It was not until the Chicano movement of the 1960s that writers talked about a future for Hispanics in this country, the richness of their bilingualism and biculturalism, and the necessity to struggle to preserve and promote culture and language.

In 1938, Otero-Warren received an honorary doctorate degree in literature from her old College of the Sacred Heart. After her term in Puerto Rico, she returned to New Mexico, and served as director of the Office of Price Administration in Santa Fe. After World War II she remained active in state politics and sat on numerous boards and commissions, eventually operating a realty company and an insurance company in Santa Fe. Otero-Warren died in January of 1965 in Santa Fe.

Sources:

Books

Norwood, Vera, and Janice Monk, editors, *The Desert Is No Lady: Southwestern Landscapes in Women's Writing and Art,* Yale University Press, 1987, pp. 98-99, 105.
Otero-Warren, Nina, *Old Spain in Our Southwest,* Harcourt, 1936.

Periodicals

Journal of Narrative Technique, spring, 1990, pp. 135, 138.

—*Sketch by Michelle Vachon*

P-Q

Antonia Pantoja
(1922-)
Founder of Universidad Boricua, activist, educator

An educator who has never been content with merely standing in front of a class and imparting her vast knowledge, Antonia Pantoja is the founder of many organizations dedicated to serving the Puerto Rican community and promoting community relations. A union organizer and activist as well as a teacher, Pantoja has been a pioneer and leader among Puerto Ricans by motivating them politically and intellectually. Her "dare to dream" message is the impetus behind every project with which she becomes involved.

Born in Puerta de Tierra, San Juan, Puerto Rico, in 1922, Pantoja benefitted from her parents' desire to give her a good education and also from their involvement in workers' rights. She was sent to live in Barrio Obrero ("the workers' neighborhood") with her grandfather, a cigar maker and union organizer at the America Tobacco Company. In *Portraits of the Puerto Rican Experience*, Pantoja described Barrio Obrero as "a poor slum, it had an internal social order, and people were conscious of their rights and of the need for education." In the late 1920s, Pantoja witnessed her family's strong conviction and fight for the cigar workers' rights—one of the first successful strikes in Puerto Rican history. She discovered firsthand the importance of the workers' movement, a belief she would carry with her through her life's work. In *Portraits of the Puerto Rican Experience*, Pantoja remembered her childhood in Puerto Rico as a time in which she "learned the relation between struggle and progress."

Pantoja graduated from the University of Puerto Rico, earning her Normal Diploma—a two-year education program—and began work as a teacher in the rural mountain area between the towns of San Lorenzo and Las Piedras. While the job was rewarding, the pay was very low. Pantoja sought alternatives to helping her family obtain an improved economic life, and she decided to go to America.

Antonia Pantoja

Moves to America and Sees Worker Inequalities

In 1944, with World War II in progress, Pantoja journeyed with her grandfather and younger brother to Old San Juan. At the docks she boarded the SS *Florida* and, amid enemy submarines that were scattered throughout the water, completed a dangerous ten-day ocean-liner journey across the Atlantic. She finally landed in New Orleans and boarded a train for her final destination, New York City. There, weakened from her long journey—she suffered from asthma—she began work as a welder in a factory that built radios for submarines. She lived in a small apartment in the Bronx and labored in the factory from seven a.m. to ten p.m.—long hours that threatened her health further. At one point she was so tired that her welding tool fell from her hand and burned her, causing her foreman to label her accident-prone.

Leaving the radio factory, Pantoja found a job at another factory, making children's bedroom lamps. It was during this period that she realized the oppression of the Puerto Ricans in the city. Puerto Ricans were discriminated against and paid sub-minimum wage, mainly because of their lack of knowledge and political power. With the memories of her grandfather's fight against the tobacco company still vivid in her mind, and with an inherent sense of leadership, Pantoja organized her coworkers, informed them of their rights, and taught them about unions. "As a teacher in Puerto Rico, I knew the value of education," she stated in an interview published in *A Guide to Celebrate Puerto Rican Heritage and Culture*. "Once you acquire some knowledge, the doors to opportunity are open for you."

After organizing its workers, Pantoja left the factory and became acquainted with a new circle of friends: a group of artists and performers from a theatrical troupe. Leaving the Bronx, Pantoja moved to New York City's East Village. She soon adapted their bohemian lifestyle and would stay up until dawn discussing politics with her new friends. "I separated completely from my people," she remarked in *A Guide to Celebrate Puerto Rican Heritage and Culture*. "I discovered New York from the life of artists, painters, dancers and ballerinas. I was very happy with my friends . . . However, I missed my people and decided to return to a job that would bring me closer to them."

Pantoja found a job working with the 110th Street Community Center, and during her lunch hour evenings, she took courses at Hunter College. Trying to balance her schedule of work and school was very difficult. Through extensive library research, she was able to learn of and obtain a scholarship. With it, she could continue her college education full time and do volunteer work for the Puerto Rican community. "This was the turn around of my life," she says in *A Guide to Celebrate Puerto Rican Heritage and Culture*.

Volunteers Time for Puerto Rican Community

Pantoja earned her bachelor's degree from Hunter College in pre-social work and received a fellowship to attend Columbia University's School of Social Work. While at Columbia, she and other Puerto Rican students formed a group whose goal was to explain why so many of their people suffered from poverty and rejection in New York. Group members volunteered their time in Puerto Rican neighborhoods—cleaning, painting, seeking donations, and getting people to vote. In this project, Pantoja had started what would be the mission of her work.

In 1953, Pantoja worked as a director of a pilot project on Puerto Ricans with the Associated Charities in Connecticut. It was her job to collect data on problems facing Puerto Ricans in Bridgeport, Connecticut, and report her findings and recommendations to the mayor's committee. That same year, Pantoja and friends organized the Hispanic Young Adult Association (HYAA) with a membership of mostly second-generation Puerto Rican college students concerned about their community. Since the organization

was of and for Puerto Ricans, the name was changed to the Puerto Rican Association for Community Affairs (PRACA). Its goal was to provide services to children and families, and to train the community's leaders to become influential within the power structure.

While working on her master's degree at Columbia University's School of Social Work, Pantoja was involved in a student practice at the Hudson Guild in New York City during the mid-1950s. The Guild's goal was to improve the community and develop positive relations between Irish, Jewish, Greek, and Italian residents and the African Americans and Puerto Ricans. Pantoja's special student project was to establish a housing clinic and a neighborhood committee.

Pantoja earned her master's degree in 1954 and was appointed supervisor of the adult division for the Union Settlement. She was responsible for direct supervision of staff members, development of leadership skills, and program direction at the summer camp. Later in her career, Pantoja was chosen as director of the Community Relations Division for the City of New York's Commission of Intergroup Relations. Her activities involved the establishment of objectives, programs, and budgets, as well as the supervision of staff who were assigned to respond to tense situations in the city. Pantoja strived to reduce racial conflict and enhance intercultural and interracial relations. "Everyone has the ability to grow and to succeed if they try," she remarked in *A Guide to Celebrate Puerto Rican Heritage and Culture*.

Community Work Leads to Creation of Aspira

In 1958, Pantoja and a group of young professionals organized the Puerto Rican Forum, Inc., an agency for business and career development dedicated to creating Puerto Rican institutions in New York City. The largest and oldest Puerto Rican community social service agency, the Puerto Rican Forum led to the development of the Aspira Club of New York—an educational agency, and Pantoja's dream.

The Aspira (meaning "strive" or "aspire" in Spanish) Club promoted higher education for Puerto Ricans. Founded in 1961, its goal was to provide inspiration and guidance to Puerto Rican youths continuing their education in the professional, technical, or artistic fields. It also provided a vehicle to encourage self-confidence and identity among Puerto Ricans. Aspira Clubs have been formed in many high schools throughout New York, conducting workshops and conferences for both educators and youth. Between 1961 and 1968, Pantoja devoted almost all of her time to Aspira.

While Aspira was devoted to the intellectual needs of Puerto Ricans in New York, work yet needed to be done in the communities. Shortly after the founding of Aspira, the Puerto Rican Community Development Project was formed.

Its goal was to promote a sense of identity among Puerto Ricans and help them develop community strength. The leading figure in this movement was also Pantoja.

By July of 1967, Pantoja was working as an assistant professor at Columbia's School of Social Work. She taught a course in community organization and supervised students working directly in the neighborhoods on community issues. In addition to her university duties, Pantoja continued her work in Puerto Rican organizations. She was selected as a delegate-at-large for the 1967 Constitutional Convention of New York State, serving for four months. As a member of the Bundy Panel, she fought for the decentralization of the New York City public school system. Pantoja was also a part-time lecturer. She spoke at the New School of Social Research, Center for New York Affairs.

Due to her asthma, Pantoja returned to Puerto Rico in 1968, where she taught at the University of Puerto Rico's School of Social Work. She also developed Aspira Clubs while in Puerto Rico, and acted as a consultant on private and public projects. She returned to the United States in 1970.

Establishes Universidad Boricua

That same year Pantoja wrote a proposal and secured funds to establish the Universidad Boricua and Puerto Rican Research and Resource Center in Washington, D.C. Its purpose was to develop an informational base of resources and art objects about Puerto Ricans. With the resource center as a base, she developed the theoretical foundation for a university that would serve Puerto Ricans in the United States and provide innovative, bilingual, career-oriented programs for professionals, technicians, and workers—a foundation that would also be her doctoral thesis.

Through grants, the university was realized. In 1973, Pantoja became the Chancellor of the Universidad Boricua—the university's first president. The Universidad Boricua is the only bilingual institution of higher learning that was established and controlled by Puerto Rican academicians.

Pantoja's asthma worsened, and she was advised by her doctor to move to a different climate. Relocating from Washington, D.C., to San Diego, California, Pantoja took a position as associate professor at San Diego State University, teaching social policy and community development. However, battles with the college bureaucracy led her to depart from the university. She and fellow educator Wilhelmina Perry founded the Graduate School for Community Development in San Diego, of which Pantoja was president. Serving communities and neighborhoods nationwide, its main objective was to teach people to develop institutions in society, change them, or create new ones.

In the mid-1980s Pantoja returned to Puerto Rico and participated in the development of Producir, Inc., with the collaboration of Perry. The company promotes Puerto Rican self-sufficiency through a community-based organization that creates jobs for the local economy. In 1989, Pantoja was honored by being asked to return to her alma mater, Hunter College, and deliver the keynote speech at the Bella Abzug Conference. She addressed the "erasing of the footsteps" of Puerto Rican woman in their struggle to achieve social and economic justice. In the early 1990s Pantoja received the John W. Gardner Leadership Award from Independent Sector, the national association of nonprofit organizations, as well as the Hispanic Heritage Award for leadership.

Sources:

Books

Fitzpatrick, Joseph, *Puerto Rican Americans,* Prentice-Hall, 1973.
Maldonado, Adal, *Portraits of the Puerto Rican Experience,* IPRUS, 1984.

Periodicals

Centro, winter, 1989-90, pp. 48-52.

Other

A Guide to Celebrate Puerto Rican Heritage and Culture (manual), Hunter College, November 1991, pp. 12-25.

—Sketch by Stephanie Poythress

Adelina Patti
(1843-1919)
Opera singer

Outside of opera aficionados with a true appreciation of history, Adelina Juana Maria Clorinda Patti is not widely known. If she were alive today, that slight probably would not have offended Patti, one of the greatest sopranos of all time. One of the first true prima donnas, the highly regarded opera singer preferred castles and private railroad cars to widespread fame and the intrusions that accompany it.

Born in Madrid, Spain, on February 10, 1843, to Italian parents, Patti came from a musical family. Her sister Carlotta was a well-known concert singer, her mother Caterina sang for various opera companies, and her father Salvatore managed opera houses. Patti toured America as a child prodigy, already singing at the age of four and performing publicly for the first time at eight. First arriving in London in 1861 at age 18, Patti sang every season at Covent Garden until 1884—thus giving her name to an era. "The peak of her career was when, in 1876, she became the first Covent Garden Aida," wrote a critic in *Grand Opera*. "This role seemed to open up to her hitherto unsuspected resources in dramatic representation, assuring her a place in history as one of the greatest prima donnas of all time. Something of the unique quality of her voice can still be gleaned from gramophone recordings."

She was to become, according to *Notable American Women, 1607-1950*, "The epitome of the prima donna." Patti used a private railroad car to travel the world like a queen, sometimes commanding the then phenomenal sum of $5,000 for a performance before an audience of a few thousand. "Patti was a prima donna in the truest sense, revelling in the public adoration and embellishing her singing with extraordinary agility, as well as mastering the lyrical legato style," wrote Mary Hamilton in *A-Z of Opera*. "She never lacked spirit and once sang Rossini's aria, 'Una voce poco fa' to the composer complete with her own florid trills and ornamentation," Hamilton continued.

Although Patti sang in the great opera houses of the world, she also performed contemporary concerts, including a rendering of *Home, Sweet Home* that had the audience in tears when she sang it for the last time at a Red Cross benefit at Royal Albert Hall in London in 1914. Other famous roles included Lucia in *Lucia De Lammermoor*, and Juliet in *Romeo and Juliet*. In fact, Henry W. Simon, in *Festival of Opera*, called her "the most famous of Juliets."

Patti, who called herself a citizen of the world, married three times. Her first husband was a French nobleman, the Marquis de Caux. They separated in 1877 and divorced in 1885. In 1886 she married tenor Ernest Nicolini, who often had sung to her. Once, during a performance of *Romeo and Juliet* at the Metropolitan Opera House in New York, Patti "imprinted 29 real kisses" on Nicolini during the balcony scene, reported the *New Kobbe's Complete Opera Book*. A year after Nicolini's death in 1898, Patti married Swedish Baron Rolf Cederstrom. She had no children and died of heart disease in 1919 at her Victorian castle Craig-y-Nos in Wales.

Her last performance was at the Metropolitan Opera House on April 9, 1892. Just as contemporary musicians are known to do, Patti often seemed to be giving a final performance somewhere—a strategy designed to draw a big crowd. Irving Kolodin, writing in *The Metropolitan Opera, 1883-1966*, referred to a highly promoted *Fledermaus* final performance as a "Patti farewell," perhaps suggesting it was not a farewell at all. And the Earl of Harewood, in the *New Kobbe's Complete Opera Book*, said, "Unfortunately she was heard by too many long after her days had passed. She had too many 'farewells.' But those who heard her at her best will always remember her as the possessor of a naturally beautiful voice, exquisitely trained." Patti's legacy in the opera world is as "the most celebrated

diva of her time, especially in coloratura roles," wrote Alan Wagner in *Prima Donnas and Other Wild Beasts*. One of the greatest sopranos of all time, she will also be remembered as "one of the most adored prima donnas of the 19th or any other century," Wagner concluded.

Sources:

Books

Blum, Daniel, *A Pictorial Treasury of Opera in America*, Grosset & Dunlap, 1954, pp. 8, 35, 208.

Concise Oxford Dictionary of Opera, edited by Harold Rosenthal and John Warrack, Oxford University Press, p. 304.

Grand Opera, edited by Anthony Gishford, Viking Press, 1972, pp. 180-81.

Hamilton, Mary, *A-Z of Opera*, Facts on File, 1990, p. 157.

Kolodin, Irving, *The Metropolitan Opera, 1883-1966*, Knopf, 1966, p. 574.

New Kobbe's Complete Opera Book, edited by George Henry Hubert Lascelles, 7th Earl of Harewood, Putnam, 1976, pp. 81, 461, 793.

Notable American Women, 1607-1950, edited by Edward T. James, and others, Harvard University Press, 1950, pp. 30-31.

Simon, Henry W., *Festival of Opera*, Hanover House, 1957, p. 516.

Wagner, Alan, *Prima Donnas and Other Wild Beasts*, Argonaut Books, 1961, pp. 13-15, 246.

—Sketch by Lawrence J. Paladino

Elizabeth Peña
(1959-)
Actress

Her performances in movies such as *Down and Out in Beverly Hills*, *La Bamba*, and *Jacob's Ladder* and in the television shows *I Married Dora* and *Shannon's Deal* have won Elizabeth Peña respect and recognition. While Peña has always been perceived as sexy, directors are realizing that she is also extraordinarily versatile: Peña has been hilarious in some roles and serious and somber in others. Hard work and determination, combined with a gift for acting and a striking face, have made Peña a sought-after actress.

The first daughter of actor, writer, and director Mario Peña and producer Estella Marguerita Toirac Peña, Peña was named after the city in which she was born on September 23, 1959: Elizabeth, New Jersey. It was in this city that the family lived while Mario studied drama at Columbia

University. Despite their affection for the city and the United States, the young family went back to Cuba four months after Peña's birth. The Cuban Revolution was new and promising, and they wanted to rejoin their families during what seemed to be an exciting time.

Unfortunately, Mario was imprisoned when he returned home; he had written a poem which the government considered to be "antisystem." When he was able to talk himself out of prison, he found that he had no choice but to flee the country and return to the United States. Estella Marguerita, Peña, and her younger sister, Tania, were not allowed to follow him and leave Cuba until 1968, when Peña was nine years old. Even as they were ready to board their plane, the officials harassed the family; their papers were in English, and no one was willing to acknowledge their authority. Finally, one official waved them through the red tape. Although, as Peña recalled in a *People* interview with Tim Allis and Nancy Matsumoto, the plane's "motors were running," Peña, her mother, and her sister, made their flight.

Family Reunited in United States

When the family was reunited and settled in New York, the elder Peñas' careers began to take off. Mario founded New York City's Latin American Theater Ensemble with Estella, and they both became respected figures in New York's theater scene. Elizabeth owes her love of acting as well as her determination to succeed as an actor to her parents. She told an *Interview* contributor in 1987, "My father and mother are the biggest influences in my life. They've been able to survive as actors in the theater in New York and have instilled that same sense of survival in me." While she was inspired by her parents, Peña also remembers that her mother did not want her to become an actress. When she was accepted to New York's renowned School of Performing Arts, Peña recalled in her *People* interview, her mother fell to her knees as she wailed, "If you become an actress, you'll kill me." Peña retorted, "Well, you better start arranging your funeral." Aside from graduating from the School of the Performing Arts, Peña also studied acting with Curt Dempster at the Ensemble Studio Theater and Endre Hules at La Mama ETC. And in addition to acting, she studied clowning with Mark Stolzenberg and speech and voice with Lynn Masters. Despite her initial dismay, Estella soon began to support her daughter's efforts to become an actress.

Peña's mother was not the only one to be persuaded by her daughter's determination to utilize her gift for acting. Peña aggressively pursued roles in motion pictures and on stage. In 1979 she played Aurelita in the movie *El Super*, and in 1980 she landed a part in *Times Square*. Her next role was that of Rita in the movie *They All Laughed*, which she followed with a number of stage appearances in New York. Included among these many roles were the parts of Jesse in *Dog Lady*, Maria in *Bring on the Night*, Cynthia in *Shattered Image*, Teresa in *La Morena*, Juliet in *Romeo and Juliet*, Beba

in *Night of the Assassins*, and Teresa in *Italian-American Reconciliation*. By 1984, Peña had landed another movie role, that of Liz (Rubén Blades's girlfriend) in *Crossover Dreams*.

Acting Career Launched

At this point in her career, Peña felt she was ready to take on Hollywood. She moved to the famous town and began to search for roles. The casting director for *Down and Out in Beverly Hills* (1986), a movie starring Richard Dreyfuss and Bette Midler, found himself deluged with photos and messages from Peña. Although she had just arrived in Hollywood and had no agent, Peña was determined to get the part, and determined to do it by herself. By the time she was given a screen test, Peña was almost broke. She gave the test her best, and the casting director was impressed. He cast Peña in her first high-profile role as the Salvadoran maid, Carmen. Peña's sexy as well as funny performance in *Down and Out in Beverly Hills* received favorable attention, and she was soon an actress in demand.

This success made 1987 a very busy year for Peña. She won a role in another hit movie, *La Bamba;* she portrayed the abused yet loyal wife, Rosie, of Richie Valens's elder brother. Later in that year, Peña earned a role in a television situation-comedy about a man who marries his Central American maid so she won't be deported, *I Married Dora*. While Jeff Jarvis, writing in *People*, asserted that the show should receive a grade of "D", he also acknowledged Peña's talent. "Only one small asset rescues this sludge-brained idea from an instant F: Elizabeth Peña's charm." Still in 1987, Peña excelled in another movie, Steven Spielberg's *Batteries Not Included*.

Although she took a break from acting after she married William Stephan Kibler on July 2, 1988, Peña stayed busy. In 1988, she accepted a number of awards, including the Hispanic Women's Council Woman of the Year Award, the New York Image Award, the U.S. Congress Congressional Award, and the Nosotros Golden Eagle Award. Peña's career picked up pace again in 1990, with what a *Newsweek* contributor calls a "warm and gritty" performance as Jezzie, the girlfriend of Jacob Singer (Tim Robbins) in the eerie movie *Jacob's Ladder.* That same year, she was cast as a client/secretary of a heartbroken lawyer in the television show *Shannon's Deal.* Tom Shales, writing in the *Washington Post* and quoted in *People*, maintained that Peña's "so assertive and gutsy. . . . Maybe the show should be about *her.*"

The *Post's* critic had a point. While Peña has brightened many productions, including the television shows *Hill Street Blues, TJ Hooker, Cagney and Lacey, As the World Turns, Tough Cookies* and *Saturday Night Live,* the made-for-television movies *Drug Wars: The Camarena Story* and *Found Money,* and the movies *Blue Steel* and *Fat Chance,* she has yet to find a role in which she is the star. She is not discouraged, however. "I like who I am," she tells Allis and

Matsumoto. "I don't have a problem with it; I think everybody else does. That's part of *their* growing up." She went on to add: "I've never thought of [being Hispanic] as an obstacle. I think it's good. There are certainly enough five-foot-seven blonds."

Sources:

Books

Contemporary Theater, Film and Television, Volume 5, Gale, 1988.

Periodicals

Interview, April, 1987, p. 34.
Más, fall, 1990, p. 14.
Newsweek, November 12, 1990, pp. 77-78.
New York, February 3, 1986, pp. 82-83; April 16, 1990, pp. 97-98.
People, September 30, 1985, p. 10; October 19, 1987, p. 15; May 13, 1991, pp. 107-108.

—*Sketch by Ronie-Richele Garcia-Johnson*

Maggie Peña
(1959-)
Entrepreneur

"**I** have an inner drive to give back to my community and to try to influence youth in a positive way," said Maggie Peña in an interview with Michelle Vachon. A cofounder of the National Society of Hispanic MBAs in 1988, she has worked to increase the enrollment of Hispanics in graduate business schools and to improve their professional advancement. She served as the society's vice president in 1990 and president in 1991. "Much has been written about the sad state of Hispanic education," she told *Hispanic* magazine in July of 1991. "As Hispanics, we need to take a more aggressive leadership role with respect to finding and contributing to the solution of this problem. We can no longer afford to stand on the sidelines." During her presidency, the society launched a scholarship program for Hispanic pupils and joined forces in the high school environment with Junior Achievement, an organization designed to introduce students to business education.

Peña was born in Bogota, Colombia, on January 29, 1959. She moved to Los Angeles, California, with her family when she was seven years old. She attended school in Los Angeles until the 11th grade and completed her last two years in Bogota. "My parents wanted me to get in touch with my cultural roots," she remembered to Vachon. In 1976, Peña won a four-year California State scholarship, enrolled at Immaculate Heart College in Los Angeles, and graduated with a B.A. in biology in 1980. For the following three years, she worked as a biology lab assistant and high school chemistry lab teacher, and she ran the family's juice outlet business. "I was planning to make a career in scientific research," she explained. "But after working in a laboratory for a while, I realized how lonely a life this would be. So I switched fields of study." In 1983, she took up marketing and finance at the University of California in Los Angeles and in 1986 received her master of business administration degree.

After obtaining her MBA, Peña kept the position that she had held at Paramount Pictures Corporation for a year. As financial analyst for the video division, she managed a multi-million dollar budget. "My experience in the corporate world opened my eyes to what was an unknown to me: the mysterious world of big business and big money," she recalled to Vachon. "I gained the confidence to handle large and complicated projects and acquired management skills that are invaluable for running a successful business, be it a profit or non-profit entity." In 1987, Paramount Pictures promoted her to finance manager for the video division. Her responsibilities included developing a computer-database system to evaluate the performance of home video products, analyzing the worldwide marketability and profitability of all the corporation's pictures, and implementing the annual budgeting and forecasting system.

In 1988, Peña participated in the launching of the National Society of Hispanic MBAs (NSHMBA). "We felt that there was a tremendous void of support for Latinos who wanted to pursue graduate studies in business," she told Vachon. Her involvement with the society increased steadily and led to her election as its president in 1991. By then, the NSHMBA had established seven chapters throughout the country and raised $500,000 to promote educational opportunities for Hispanics. Among her other achievements is her establishment of a summer enrichment program for junior high school students in Chicago, Los Angeles, and Washington, D.C. "My work with the society proved extremely rewarding," she observed. "I developed a stronger sense of my Latino roots and discovered the tremendous network of Hispanic leaders nationwide. One of the most important lessons for me was to learn the power of organizing and working together. I met many people willing to do their share for the community if only they knew where to start—they just needed leadership and a small push to get going."

In 1991, Peña left Paramount Pictures to join her family's business—The Juice Fountain. "My mother has always been an entrepreneur, and I wanted to follow in her footsteps," she noted to Vachon. She has since opened the family's third freshly squeezed juice outlet in the Los Angeles area. In addition to her activities with the NSHMBA,

Peña is a committee member of the United Way, the Music Center, and Artes de Mexico in Los Angeles, and she is a member of the National Women's Political Caucus. She also serves on the Los Angeles's Racial Harmony Task Force created by the Rebuild L.A. mayoral project. In the next few years, she plans to become active in youth organizations to reduce school absenteeism and gang-related problems in Los Angeles. Additionally, she hopes to raise funds to help the plight of children in Columbia.

Sources:

Periodicals

Hispanic, March, 1992, p. 20.
Hispanic Business, February, 1991, p. 21.

Other

Peña, Maggie, interview with Michelle Vachon, September 8, 1992.

—Sketch by Michelle Vachon

Rosie Perez

Actress, dancer, choreographer

Rosie Perez, whose closest revelation of her age has been "under 25," claims to be having a hard time sleeping these days—her career is not moving fast enough for her. In just a few short years, she went from being a science student to becoming one of the most sought-after pop music choreographers in the industry and a rising actress. "I'm very happy with the way things are going for me right now," she relates in an interview with Frank Spotnitz for *Entertainment Weekly,* "but I still feel like they're going too slow. I want it all."

Rosa Mary Perez was born at Greenpoint Hospital in Brooklyn, New York, daughter of Ismael Serrano and Lydia Perez. Raised in Brooklyn's mostly Puerto Rican Bushwick district, Perez is one of ten brothers and sisters who grew up watching their parents dance "salsa" on weekends and holidays. Her mother was a singer in Puerto Rico, and music always filled the house. In her *Entertainment Weekly* interview, Perez reminisced: "Growing up with nine brothers and sisters was an early lesson in assertive-

ness training. In a family like that, you have to compete for attention."

A good student who excelled in science, Perez moved to Los Angeles at the age of 18 to attend college, where she studied marine biology as a biochemistry major. It was while dancing at a trendy Los Angeles latin club that she was first invited to dance on the television show *Soul Train.* After doing a couple of shows, Perez quit, but while she was there she met Louis Silas, Jr., senior vice president of black music at MCA Records. Silas asked if she wanted to be in a recording group, and although Perez declined, she kept in touch with him.

Launches Choreography Career with Bobby Brown

One day Silas asked if she would choreograph one of his artists who was coming out with his third solo album. Silas wanted him to have a younger appeal and asked Perez to find some dancers who could dance "hip-hop" with him. Perez at first refused because she had no experience, but after hearing the music decided to go ahead. The artist's name was Bobby Brown and the project was a success.

After seeing Brown on the television program *Soul Train,* a new Motown recording group (The Boys) asked Perez to choreograph their show. With the double successes of Bobby Brown and The Boys, offers poured in. She and her partners, Heart & Soul, found themselves busy creating the stage and/or video choreographies for many artists, including Diana Ross and rappers Al B. Sure, LL Cool J, Heavy D & the Boyz, and for such record labels as Motown, Polygram, and Capitol. The next step was the small screen, with Perez choreographing the Fox television program *In Living Color.* When a *GQ* contributor asked her to define her dancing style, Perez (who considers herself a better choreographer than a dancer) replied, "Clearness. Quickness. Difficult combinations. I'll never do a move for a four count—usually just a two and move on. That's what earns me respect with the club people." She then laughingly adds: "Here's my dancer's arrogance. I haven't seen anybody who can articulate hip-hop the way I do, in such a lean, crisp way, and still be authentic. There are a lot who try and do it, and it comes off very corny. I still got the flavor."

Takes on Acting in *Do the Right Thing*

In her official "biography," Perez tells how her movie career was launched. "While I was choreographing The Boys, I was dancing at the Funky Reggae Club in Los Angeles. Spike Lee was having his birthday party there and the band EU was performing. The band asked me to dance on stage; afterwards Spike introduced himself to me. His partner, Monty Ross, gave me their phone number and asked me to call. I forgot all about it until I was leaving to go back to Brooklyn (the school semester had finished) and decided to call them. They were really excited and asked me if I would be in Los Angeles long. When I told them that I was returning to Brooklyn in a couple of days, they started screaming and Spike said, 'This is fate.' I didn't know what he meant by that, because he never mentioned the possibility of a movie until a month later. When I told him I had to return for the new school semester in Los Angeles, he offered me the role of Tina in *Do the Right Thing.* Instead of finishing that semester, I decided to do the movie, and it changed my life."

In an interview with *Newsweek,* Perez described her movie debut experience as possibly the best and worst thing that happened to her. There was a nude scene involving an ice cube that, she has said, made her feel like she was "raped" by the camera. When Hispanic groups criticized her for promoting a stereotype, Perez defended the film— "I was not portraying something that's not really out there"—but informed her agent she didn't want to play any "Tinas" in the future.

Film Career Rapidly Progresses

By contrast, her role as Woody Harrelson's feisty girlfriend in the basketball-themed film *White Men Can't Jump,* was originally written for a white woman who'd gone to an Ivy League school. But writer/director Ron Shelton was so impressed by the instant chemistry between Perez and Harrelson that he hired her and, without making major changes to the script, the role was transformed from that of a Barnard graduate to a former Brooklyn disco queen.

In quick succession, Perez's acting credits went on to include the films *Baboon Heart* and *Night on Earth.* Television appearances include *21 Jump Street, Criminal Justice,* and a recurring role in the CBS series *WIOU.* With a successful acting career well under way, Perez concluded in a *Preview* interview: "Minorities can play regular roles too. And being a minority you have a responsibility to help other minorities along the way."

Sources:

Periodicals

Entertainment Weekly, April 3, 1992, p. 11.
GQ, August, 1992, pp. 49-58.
Newsweek, May 4, 1992, pp. 64-65.
Preview, April, 1992, p. 25.
Rolling Stone, May 14, 1992.

Other

Biography of Perez, provided by Baker-Winokur-Ryder Public Relations.

—Sketch by Elena Kellner

Janice Petrovich
(1946-)
Educational researcher, policy analyst

Frustrated with simple solutions to a failing educational system for minorities and appalled by the disparity of the ways schools are financed, Janice Petrovich is dedicated to increasing the understanding of barriers to excellence, equity and educational opportunities. Moreover, as the national executive director of the ASPIRA Association, Inc., and director of the ASPIRA Institute for Policy Research, Petrovich is well-respected for her commitment to Latino youths in the United States.

Petrovich was born December 6, 1946, in Puerto Rico to Enrique Petrovich Quinones and Miriam Beiso-Mojica, both of whom are from Puerto Rico. She first came to the United States at the age of three when her father moved to Georgia to train for the Korean War. Though Petrovich subsequently lived in many cities during her youth, she still regards San Juan, Puerto Rico, as her home.

When it came time for college, it was a fascination with the sciences that prompted Petrovich to study chemistry and mathematics at the University of Puerto Rico. She earned a bachelor of science, magna cum laude, in 1968, and then obtained a position at a pharmaceutical company in Puerto Rico. One year later, she changed jobs and began teaching chemistry and physics at the Puerto Rico Junior College, a job which lasted until 1972. While teaching, Petrovich noticed a general disinterest among students in learning math and science. This observation led her to study social and educational theories to determine why some students were motivated to learn and succeed in school and why others were not. Ultimately, Petrovich went beyond seeking explanations and began studying theories on developing self-esteem, social change, and empowerment to help students succeed and take control of their lives.

Focuses on Minorities in Higher Education

Petrovich's interest in minority and educational research further developed as she earned a doctor of education in 1979 from the University of Massachusetts's Amherst Graduate School of Education, Division of Educational Policy and Research. As a research associate for a Ford Foundation Project in 1981, Petrovich studied the role of minorities in higher education at the Higher Education Research Institute. She later became director of the Research Institute at the Inter American University in Puerto Rico, and founder of the Center for Research and Documentation on Women.

Leaving Puerto Rico for Washington, D.C., in 1984, Petrovich was hired by the American Council on Education as director of Research Studies for the Division of Policy Analysis and Research. Here, her goal was to expand research on minority issues, particularly as they pertain to higher education. She executed research studies on higher education from a national and campus-based perspective and developed a policy research agenda for the organization.

In 1986 Petrovich made another career change, becoming the director of the ASPIRA Institute for Policy Research and national executive director of the ASPIRA Association, Inc., the only national organization dedicated to helping Latino youths. As national director she is able to fulfill her quest to eliminate barriers to success and educational opportunity for minorities. She has been instrumental in expanding the ASPIRA Math/Science Initiative (an academic enrichment effort), mentoring programs, and other services to Latinos on a national scale. As director of the ASPIRA Institute, Petrovich has also directed a major study on the needs of Northeast Latinos, testified at Congressional hearings, and initiated the ASPIRA Advocacy Network.

Having recently published "Mentors: Effective Role Models, Advisors,'Gate Openers'" in *A Special Report on Mentoring,* Petrovich enjoys writing on educational issues affecting minority students and women. Having no fixed career moves planned for the immediate future, Petrovich currently lives in the Washington, D.C., metropolitan area with her thirteen-year-old daughter.

Sources:

Petrovich, Janice, interview with Luis Vasquez-Ajmac, August 6, 1992.

—Sketch by Luis Vasquez-Ajmac

Paloma Picasso
(1949-)
Fashion designer

As the daughter of one of the twentieth century's most influential artists, Paloma Picasso hesitated to enter the world of design. She did not want to be compared to her father, nor did she relish the unavoidable notoriety his name would provide. Once she began to show the jewelry she created, however, authorities were genuinely impressed. The success of the pieces she produced for Tiffany & Company encouraged Picasso to design and market items

Paloma Picasso

ranging from fashion accessories to china. These items, including eyewear, cosmetics, and leather goods, may be identified by their bold shapes and brilliant colors, and are sold and appreciated throughout the world. Picasso's face is just as easily recognized. Posing in glossy magazine advertisements with her perfume, *Paloma,* the designer is, according to *Hispanic,* "her own best model." While Pablo Picasso transformed aesthetic standards in the fine arts, his trend-setting daughter has independently introduced fresh perspectives in fashion design.

Born April 19, 1949, Paloma Picasso has always been surrounded by art and artists. Pablo Picasso, the Spanish painter who was instrumental in the development of cubism, and Françoise Gilot, the French painter, named their daughter after the "paloma," or dove, that Picasso had created for the posters announcing an International Peace Conference in Paris, France. Although the young girl was not formally instructed by her unmarried parents, she was encouraged to draw; while she was not allowed to touch her parents' brushes, paints, and canvases, she and her older brother Claude frequently found themselves serving as models. Despite Pablo Picasso's separation from his children in 1961, his passion for art and his reputation clearly influenced his daughter. Paloma Picasso told *Hispanic:* "Once, when I was six, he couldn't resist the clean white canvas of my espadrille shoes. He took them from my feet, picked up his crayons, and did drawings all over them." Picasso remembered feeling depressed at the loss of her clean shoes, but she remembered in *Newsweek,* "At the same time, I was aware that he *was* Picasso, and that anybody else would be thrilled."

As a teenager developing her own tastes and styles, Paloma Picasso was reluctant to pursue artistic goals. She felt alienated from her father, who, at the request of his second wife, Jacqueline Roque, refused to see his children by Gilot—Claude and Paloma. Paloma Picasso also did not want to be judged in her father's overwhelming shadow. "In the beginning, I tried not to think that I would have to do anything artistic," she related in *Hispanic*. "From the time I was fourteen, I stopped drawing completely. . . . I thought, 'I don't want to become a painter like my father,' but I didn't know what else I wanted to become." Picasso's urge to create soon surpassed her hesitation; she began to study jewelry design and fabrication while still in her teens.

Establishes Reputation with Innovative Jewelry

Picasso's creativity was also expressed in the way she dressed herself. She became known throughout Paris for the flea-market finds that she paired with designer items to create her own, bold look during the 1960s. She was friends with the likes of the designer Yves St. Laurent, and she met John Loring, of Tiffany & Company, when she was sixteen. The stylish young woman decided to design jewelry professionally when she was referred to as a designer in a newspaper article reporting on the necklace she had improvised from an outlandish Folies-Bergeres bikini for a costume in a play. Yves St. Laurent commissioned her to design her own collection of jewelry in 1969, and later, she began designing gold jewelry for Zolotas, a Greek firm.

After the elder Picasso died, Paloma Picasso lost interest in designing. "I had given up designing when my father died in 1973," she recounted to the *New York Times*. "I didn't feel like doing anything. I just looked at all the paintings, and there was the sense of being overwhelmed." Picasso's father had left no will, and his illegitimate children, Paloma, her brother Claude, and her half-sister Maya, brought suit for their share of the estate, which was valued at $250 million. When Paloma Picasso finally won her share of the inheritance, which was estimated to be close to $90 million, she chose some of her father's works, which included a set of dolls painted with her own visage, and a sculpture entitled *Girl Jumping Rope*, made from a basket and cake pans, for herself. As the French government had also received a huge sum and a collection of works as taxes from the estate, Picasso consented to assist it in the creation of the Musée Picasso in Paris.

Although Picasso had temporarily given up designing, she began another artistic endeavor. She starred in a motion picture that won the Prix de l'Age d'Or, *Immoral Tales (Contes Immorreaux)* (1974). Directed by Walerian Borowczyk, the movie was praised by critics, and Picasso's performance as a Hungarian countess with eccentric sexual desires was met with enthusiasm. The *New York Times* reported, "Paloma Picasso, the late Pablo's daughter . . .

has a magnificent figure and a face as beautiful as her father's drawings from his classical period." While Picasso has not since pursued acting, she has often expressed her hope to portray the designer Coco Chanel in a motion picture.

Picasso expects her husband, Rafael Lopez-Cambil (known by his pen name Rafael Lopez-Sanchez), to write the screenplay for this movie about Coco Chanel. Picasso met the Argentine playwright and director, whom she had admired, after her father's death. When she began to work again, it was for Lopez-Cambil; Picasso designed the sets for some of his productions. The relationship between Picasso and Lopez-Cambil became personal, and the couple married in 1978.

The wedding was an event. Wearing a red, black, and white Yves St. Laurent original for the ceremony, and a heart-shaped, red, Karl Lagerfeld gown for the disco reception, Picasso once again excited the fashion world. The *New York Times* stated that during these years, Paloma Picasso had become "something of a muse to Paris couturiers," and especially to the designers of her wedding gowns. The petite woman had once again impressed the design world.

Begins Association with Tiffany & Company

In 1979, John Loring, senior vice-president of Tiffany & Company, asked Picasso to produce a table setting. Replete with silver ribbon and topped off with a mushroom-shaped cake, the setting, entitled the "End of Summer," was well received. Tiffany & Company was so pleased with it that they asked Picasso to create jewelry for the company. "When Tiffany's asked me about doing jewelry, I was thrilled," Picasso told the *New York Times*. She had always wanted to design for an American store. "I went into all the great jewelry shops of Paris. They are so grand, the salespeople seem to look down on you. As a customer you feel threatened. Tiffany is a great place because all kinds of people come in, just like Woolworth's." The company was equally enthusiastic about Picasso, whose pieces are priced from just over one hundred dollars to a half a million dollars. Loring spoke of her in *Hispanic*, "Paloma has taken the gaudiness out of jewelry but kept the glitter," and Henry B. Platt, Tiffany's president, proudly exclaimed in *Newsweek* that "for the first time, people can hold a Picasso in their hands and try it on."

While designing for Tiffany & Company is an honor bestowed on the likes of Elsa Peretti and Angela Cummings, both well-known designers, Picasso has honored the company by designing for it. She has brought the company a strikingly bold jewelry that merits the name Picasso. Brilliant gems framed in blocks of gold, large stones or metal pendants on simple cords, and gold or silver "hugs and kisses," or X's and O's, are characteristic of Picasso's work. Unusual combinations of pearls, vibrant semi-precious stones, and metals are also prominent. Although her creations portend a new aesthetic for jewelry, Picasso, says *Newsweek*, "rejects fine-art pretensions." The designer told the magazine, "This [jewelry] is something people can wear, rather than hanging it on the wall or putting it on the table. I like things to be used." In the *New York Times*, Picasso remarked that while "jewelry should be jewelry, something that you wear," it "is more permanent, less superficial than fashion."

Resolves to Forge Own Path in Design and Business

Picasso is a determined woman. Although she inherited enough money and fame from her father to live leisurely or to fund her business ventures, Picasso has insisted that she earn her own laurels. While she has resigned herself to the fact that even taking her mother's last name would not hide the fact that she was Picasso's daughter, she is adamant about not using her inherited wealth. "My road was paved for me by my mother," Picasso once explained to *Vogue*. "My mother always worked, and I was raised to believe women were independent. My idea of femininity is a strong femininity."

Such demanding expectations of herself have incited Picasso to diversify her activities and increase her creative energy. Since the enthusiastic reception of the 85 pieces she designed for Tiffany & Company in 1980, she has ventured into various projects. The most accessible of these is the fragrance line she introduced in 1984. It seemed natural for her to come up with her own designer scent; her grandfather, Emile Gilot, was a chemist and perfume manufacturer. Picasso's perfume, which she named simply *Paloma*, was carefully developed, and Picasso made sure that this product was presented beautifully. The resulting packaging is eye-catching. The circle of a bottle, surrounded in a red and black box, is as bold and bright as Picasso's jewelry. Picasso, who habitually clothes herself in red, black and gold, stated in *Vogue* that the perfume resembles herself: "What you see is what you get. I wanted my fragrance to be like that, too." She made a similar remark in the *New York Post* when she announced that her perfume, which is priced at over $150 an ounce, is a "fragrance for a strong woman like myself."

After Picasso introduced *Paloma* there seemed to be no end to her production of new items. Like her jewelry, these may be identified by their distinctive Paloma Picasso look. In 1988, Picasso began to design her own accessories. In 1989, she designed china which is marketed by Villeroy & Boch. She introduced By Paloma Picasso, her own, relatively less expensive line of accessories, including leather goods, in 1990. Picasso plans cosmetics which, along with her perfume, are marketed by Cosmair, she sells the famous blue-red lipstick she wears, *Mon Rouge*, she styles eyewear which is marketed by Optyl, and she even designs ceramic tiles. In 1990 Picasso opened boutiques in Paris and Tokyo, and she hopes to open more. Picasso continues to design fabulous jewelry for Tiffany & Company. Her tenth anniversary collection, which was presented in 1990,

was described in *Mirabella* as "having the raw power of just-cut stones and just-mined minerals. Her gems are deep pools of color hung on thick veins of gold."

Keeps Pace with Rigorous Schedule

Managing existing products and designing new ones keeps Picasso very busy. She sleeps as a Spaniard—rising before noon and retiring between four and five o'clock in the morning. She breakfasts with her husband, who is also her business partner and manager, and her lawyer, and then she races to begin her day. Picasso's schedule is computerized, and she routinely flies from her homes in New York and Paris to Italy. While she is traveling, she keeps her fax machine ready to transport any ideas she may have. At this pace, Picasso has managed to prosper without funds from her late father. The royalties from her many design projects garner the company she owns with her husband, Lopez-Cambil, Ltd., $3 to $5 million per year.

The woman who won the MODA Award for design excellence in 1988 has affected the world of design since she was a teenager. Picasso's strikingly elegant face is internationally famous and her whims set trends. The media revels when she formally introduces her products and finds a story even when she remodels her kitchen. Whether she is seen in a magazine advertisement with a bottle of her perfume, or in Paris walking the bulldog she has named Martha Phillipson, Picasso gets attention, and deservedly so. If her past creations are any indication of her future works, Paloma Picasso is well worth watching.

Sources:

Books

Newsmakers, Volume 1, Gale, 1991, pp. 89-92.

Periodicals

Harper's Bazaar, December, 1989, pp. 144-150; January 1991, pp. 123-126.
Hispanic, October, 1988, p. 36; December, 1988, pp. 28-33; May, 1991, pp. 20-26.
House and Garden, November, 1990, pp. 236-276.
House Beautiful, February 1989, pp. 103-104.
Mirabella, November, 1990; December, 1990.
Newsweek, October 20, 1980, p. 69.
New York Post, March 26, 1984.
New York Times, March 11, 1976; June 9, 1980, p. B16; April 22, 1990, p. S38.
New York Times Magazine, April 22, 1990, p. 38.
Vogue, April, 1981, pp. 229-231; December, 1985, pp. 318-331; January, 1990, pp. 190-197.
Working Woman, October, 1990, pp. 140-145.

—*Sketch by Ronie-Richele Garcia-Johnson*

Pinero, Sally B. Hernandez
  See **Hernandez-Pinero, Sally B.**

Pinkola, Clarissa Estés
  See **Estés, Clarissa Pinkola**

Piñon, Evangelina Vigil
  See **Vigil-Piñon, Evangelina**

Mary Helen Ponce

Mary Helen Ponce
(1938-)
Writer, scholar

Writer Mary Helen Ponce married soon after she graduated from high school; and she chose to stay home and care for her four children until her youngest son entered kindergarten. At that time, to the benefit of her readers and students, Ponce decided to educate herself and to write about her culture. While in her work the courageous Ponce embraces this culture, she has not hesitated to fictionally discuss its more problematic aspects in her collection of short stories, *Taking Control*, and her novel, *The Wedding*.

Ponce was born January 24, 1938, to Tranquilino Ponce and Vincenta (Solis) Ponce in Pacoima, California. While, in a telephone interview with Ronie-Richele Garcia-Johnson, Ponce acknowledged that Pacoima was a bit like Taconos, the fictional town in *The Wedding*, she emphasized that *The Wedding* is not autobiographical; Ponce did not grow up as Blanca of her novel did. Pacoima was, for Ponce, a good town, with "many nice families." Ponce also credits her parents, who had a "terrific sense of humor," and her very intelligent sisters, who served as role models for the young girl, for her "very happy childhood."

As she told Garcia-Johnson, Ponce realized that "learning" was her "happiness," and, because of this, she was determined to educate herself when her youngest son was old enough to enter school in 1974. After earning her bachelor's degree from California State University in 1978, Ponce went on to receive a master's degree from the same university in 1980. Ponce studied from 1982 to 1984 at the University of California at Los Angeles, where she was the recipient of the History Department's Danforth Fellowship, and worked toward her Ph.D. at the University of New Mexico in 1988. Ponce then served as an instructor of Chicano studies from 1982 until 1987 at UCLA; she was an adjunct professor from 1987 to 1988. Ponce also taught at California State University of Northridge, and she was a member of the adjunct faculty at the University of New Mexico in the Women Studies Program from 1988 to 1992. In addition to studying women and Mexican American culture, Ponce has served on organizations which focus on the same subjects, including the Mexican American National Women's Association, the National Association of Chicano Studies, the Western Association of Women Historians, and Mujeres Activas en Letras y Ciencias Sociales.

Although studying, teaching, participating in various organizational activities, and caring for a family keep Ponce busy, she has managed to find time to write. She has contributed stories to magazines throughout the Southwestern United States and Mexico; during the early to mid-1980s, *Nuestro* magazine published several of her stories. In 1987, Ponce had written enough good stories to publish her first collection, *Taking Control*, and by 1989, she had finished her first novel, *The Wedding*. Ponce's short stories and *Taking Control* have been warmly received, and women have especially enjoyed *The Wedding*.

As the book's title suggests, the nine stories in *Taking Control* are about Hispanic women who do or do not take control of their lives. One of the most striking stories of this collection is "La Josie." La Josie inadvertently frightens a young, divorced mother when, every weekend, she pounds on her door to escape her abusive husband. The narrator of the story can not believe it when, the morning after every fight, La Josie once again appears to be in love with Pete, her husband. The narrator has her own problems with men; her second husband expects her to wash his jeans in hot water so they will fit him more tightly and then runs off with a seventeen-year-old girl. Upon seeing La Josie some years later, the narrator recounts, "Yesterday I saw La Josie . . . and I saw myself."

While another story, "The Painkillers," deals with the suffering of a mistreated woman and her passive response, it presents a healthy relationship as a contrast. Mary Lou Lopez is sure that her husband will leave her after she fails to give birth to a boy and has a hysterectomy; after she undergoes the same procedure, Crista knows that although her family will be disappointed, the love of her husband is secure and reassuring. Crista, along with the assertive Ave in "The Campout" and Concha, the woman who decides to take control of her life in "El Marxista," is one of Ponce's exemplary Hispanic female characters.

Explores Problems of Assimilated Mexican Americans

More than presenting problems specific to women, some of the stories in *Taking Control,* such as "The Campout," "The New Affirmative Action Officer," and "The Permanent," deal with a Mexican American dilemma: How can the Mexican American live comfortably in American society while maintaining respect for her culture? How should the educated or assimilated Mexican Americans react to criticism of those who persist in speaking Spanish and continue to work in the fields? How should those Mexican Americans who have "made it" in America treat those who have not?

The last story in the collection, "The Permanent," seems to answer these questions. After becoming angry and embarrassed at the sight of Mexican Americans who could not speak English and who dressed like Mexicans, and after pretending not to understand Spanish herself, an elderly Mexican American woman finds herself defending them. She realizes that she was wrong to feel anger and embarrassment: "Her anger was spent. But she felt guilty. Very guilty." She thinks, "I will no longer impose my value system on other Mexicanos. I will not think of them as different, as them, but as us. And, I will be of some help." In addition to presenting more assimilated Mexican Americans with a solution, the author of "The Permanent" seems to have created a guideline for herself: with her writing, Ponce is being "of some help."

Not everyone, however, would agree that Ponce positively contributes to Mexican American literature. Alejandro Morales, an instructor of Chicano literature at the University of California of Irvine discussed Ponce's first novel, *The Wedding* (1989), in the *Los Angeles Times.* According to Morales, the book presents a "vision" which is "grotesque satire, naturalistic caricature that tends to bolster already damaging stereotypes of Mexican Americans and Americans." "'The Wedding,'" wrote Morales, "is not an uncommon story. It has been told too often. Ponce's version is sadly naive, contradictory and insulting. Her story ignores the positive contributions of Chicano blue-collar workers, takes away their dignity, pride, and history. 'The Wedding' is best left unread."

In her interview with Garcia-Johnson, Ponce answered such criticism, insisting that *The Wedding,* which was originally a longer work, is first and foremost a "love story." She also stated that she wouldn't apologize for her work because "it's honest." While many people cannot understand how Blanca could love Cricket, Ponce reminds readers that, during the 1950s, there were not many expectations for women. Blanca had no hope of educating herself, and she had no choice but to marry. Growing up in the environment he did, Cricket never had a chance either. The couple, according to the author, "didn't know any different."

Portrays Hope and Tradition in *The Wedding*

Ponce wanted to write a realistic story about a love like Blanca's, the love of family, of tradition, independence, and of hope, which are, according to Ponce, timeless. She also wanted to write about a wedding. When Ponce was growing up near Hollywood during the late 1940s and early 1950s, a young woman's dream was to wear a Civil War-era dress, like Scarlett O'Hara in *Gone with the Wind,* at her wedding, and there were many weddings during those years.

The Wedding's plot centers on the preparation for a wedding and the wedding itself; as the story progresses, the reader is introduced to the bride-to-be, Blanca, the groom-to-be, Sammy-the-Cricket, and their friends and family. Instead of being determined to educate herself and work her way out of poverty, Blanca drops out of school and seeks a husband. She is attracted to Sammy-the-Cricket not because he is intelligent, or because he is kind to her, but because he fights well and is a gang leader. Getting married is more important to Blanca than marriage itself; she dreams of having a wedding that will make her family proud and impress the people of her small town.

The choice of cushions, wedding dresses, flowers, bridesmaids, and even the groom are described in great detail. The wedding itself, rather than the marriage, is important to Blanca; she does not consider canceling the wedding when she realizes that Cricket will always be cheap, because to cancel the wedding would disappoint her family. While it is true that a wedding is one of the most important events in a person's life (if a person decides to marry), the symbolic significance of the union is lost in the process of planning Blanca's wedding. Although, the morning of her wedding, Blanca was "transformed and excited," this fictional character could not escape reality. The moment before she was to walk down the aisle, Blanca's "armpits" were "damp with sweat" and "beads of perspiration" were "on her upper lip."

A perspiring, weeping bride, a groom destined for jail—the ending of *The Wedding* demonstrates that if the event was truly the "best wedding in the barrio" as Blanca wanted it to be, that is all it was. By using the pivotal social event in a young person's life, the event that unifies the sexes, as a vehicle, Ponce has presented what she seems to loathe the most: male ignorance and disrespect for females, and female ignorance and passivity. If there is any social commentary in *The Wedding*, perhaps it is a feminist one.

Many readers may not understand why Ponce chose to represent "her people" as she did. Why didn't she feature any exemplary characters, like those in *Taking Control*, to serve as foils for the "one-dimensional, abnormal puppets" (as Morales calls them) in *The Wedding*? Ponce's character Ave from "The Campout" in *Taking Control* could explain why Mexican American barrio culture, in this novel, is anything but glorified. When asked by her husband and her white friends why she destroyed a sketch of poor, clam-digging Mexican children on the beach, she told them that she did not want to romanticize her subjects. "David, what you and Bitsey and Biff call beauty, art is not. Not really. It's the reality. I mean you think it's graceful, artistic . . . I mean all those words is romanticizing, distorting the reality, making suffering look noble, artistic. . . ." If Ponce's works can enable families to understand the devastation misogynic and masochistic attitudes cause, then the novel is well worth reading even if it isn't written in the style of more popular Hispanic works.

Ponce told Garcia-Johnson that, since 1990, there has been a "terrific conflict" between her work as a writer and her scholarly work: she loves to write as well as study history and literature. Consequently, since the publication of *The Wedding*, Ponce has continued to write as well as teach. She contributed to *Phoebe: An Interdisciplinary Journal of Feminist Scholarship Theory and Aesthetics* in 1990, and to *Frontiers: A Journal of Women Studies*. A monograph Ponce has written, *The Lives and Works of Five Hispanic New Mexican Women Writers 1978-1991: Short Biographies*, and an autobiography, *Hoyt Street*, will soon be published. In 1992, Ponce was teaching at the University of California at Santa Barbara in the Chicano Studies Department as a member of the adjunct faculty; she was also working on her dissertation.

Sources:

Books

Ponce, Mary Helen, *Taking Control*, Arte Público Press, 1987.
Ponce, *The Wedding*, Arte Público Press, 1989.

Periodicals

Los Angeles Times, November 19, 1989, p. 10.
Nuestro, December, 1983, p. 44; March, 1985, p. 54; April, 1985, p. 43; June-July, 1985, p. 50.

Other

Ponce, Mary Helen, telephone interview with Ronie-Richele Garcia-Johnson, August 10, 1992.

—Sketch by Ronie-Richele Garcia-Johnson

Estela Portillo Trambley
(1936-)
Writer

Estela Portillo Trambley is noted for being the first Chicana to publish a short story collection and the first to write a musical comedy. Like many Chicano writers, she draws on her ethnic background for the themes that dominate her literary creations, but instead of condemning the demoralizing forces present in the poor Chicano neighborhoods she has known, she finds the *barrio* to be a source of joy and spiritual awakening for its inhabitants. She explained her position to Juan Bruce-Novoa in *Chicano Authors: Inquiry by Interview*: "When I was a child, poverty was a common suffering for everybody around me. A common suffering is a richness in itself."

Portillo Trambley was born on January 16, 1936, in El Paso, Texas, and has spent most of her life living and working in the same city. She holds both bachelor of arts and master of arts degrees in English from the University of Texas at El Paso, and followed a career in education before deciding to seriously apply herself to writing. She worked as a high school English teacher in El Paso from 1957 to 1964. She has also served as chairperson of the English department of the El Paso Technical Institute and, since 1979, has worked in the Department of Special Services of the El Paso public school system.

Her flair for the dramatic arts won Portillo Trambley a position as resident dramatist at El Paso Community College, and as such she produced and directed the college's dramatic productions and served as a drama instructor. Concurrently with her work as a dramatist, she hosted a talk show, *Estela Sez*, for one year on Radio KIZZ and wrote and hosted a cultural program, *Cumbres*, for KROD-TV in El Paso. Her experience with television writing made her realize that she wished to pursue writing as a full-time career. A year after making this decision, in 1971, her first play, *The Day of the Swallows,* was published. The following year she won the prestigious Quinto Sol Award, a literary award presented by Quinto Sol Publications.

Blends Tradition and History in Writings

Since then, Portillo Trambley has contributed a varied and important body of work to the world of Chicano literature. Her historic collection of short stories, *Rain of Scorpions and Other Writings,* appeared in 1975, and her musical comedy, *Sun Images,* was first produced in 1976. Subsequently, she has seen *The Day of the Swallows* appear in *Contemporary Chicano Theatre,* edited by Roberto Garza, in 1976, and her play, *Puente Negro,* published in the anthology *Sor Juana and Other Plays,* in 1983. She is also the author of numerous unpublished plays and of the novel, *Trini,* published by Bilingual Press in 1986.

Drawing from her Hispanic background and its nearly mythic traditions of *machismo* and female subservience, Portillo Trambley's work often focuses on the plight of women in a male-dominated society. In *Rain of Scorpions and Other Writings,* for example, she speaks of a world where "it had been decreed long ago by man-made laws that living things were not equal. It had been decreed that women should be possessions, slaves, pawns in the hands of men with ways of beasts. It had been decreed that women were to be walloped effigies to burn upon the altars of men." A similar feminist content is found in what is considered her best play, *The Day of the Swallows,* which ends with the suicide of its desperate protagonist Josefa, who fears revelation of her lesbianism.

Although her work contains feminist sympathies, Portillo Trambley is steadfast in her desire to keep her writing from being political. She told Bruce-Novoa: "Political literature, no matter how clever it might be, tends to make stereotypes of the evil exploiter and the poor, innocent victim. That is not life. The exploiter is a human being too. He might be violent and selfish and greedy and mean, but down deep, despite having mutated into a Machiavellian oddity, he is still human. Once you take this away from your character in literature, you've taken away his life. Political literature assassinates characters."

Sources:

Books

Bruce-Novoa, Juan, *Chicano Authors: Inquiry by Interview,* University of Texas Press, 1980.
Portillo Trambley, Estela, *Rain of Scorpions and Other Writings,* Tonatiuh International, 1976.

—*Sketch by Marian C. Gonsior*

Preciado, Cecilia de Burciago
See **Burciaga, Cecilia Preciado de**

Dolores Prida
(1943-)
Playwright

Dolores Prida is one of the most important Hispanic playwrights in the United States. Armed with a fine sense of satire and a good sense of humor, she writes plays which bring to the stage the problems of racism, social injustice, feminism and the search for identity by Hispanics torn between two cultures.

Born in Caibarien, Cuba, on September 5, 1943, Dolores Prida came to the United States with her family as part of the wave of exiles who fled Fidel Castro's pro-communist government. Settling in New York, she attended Hunter College from 1965 to 1969, majoring in Spanish American literature. During her first fifteen years in the United States, Prida worked in different capacities for publishing houses and periodicals as editor and journalist. These jobs included managing editor of the Spanish-language New York daily newspaper *El tiempo,* New York correspondent for *Vision,* the Latin American magazine, from 1977 to 1980, and executive senior editor of *Nuestro* magazine, a national English-language magazine for Hispanics. Linked to the *Revista areito,* the publication of young Cuban intellectuals who sought a new understanding with the Havana government, Prida traveled to Cuba in 1978 and 1979 to participate in a dialogue that eventually allowed visitation of the island nation by exiles who had relatives there. Although Prida's work never touched upon the area of Cuban politics, her involvement in this project have lead to death threats on the part of the more militant anti-Castro exiles and created a climate that has made it impossible for her works to be presented in parts of New Jersey and Southern Florida.

Prida made her debut as a playwright in 1977 with her bilingual musical comedy *Beautiful Senoritas,* produced by Duo Theater in New York. The work's call for the liberation of Hispanic women from the dual repression of males and the Catholic Church has made it a favorite. In 1980 it was presented as a special performance at the National Organization for Women convention in San Antonio. In 1981, Prida's *Coser y cantar* premiered at the Duo Theater. Its two characters, She, the English speaker, and Ella, her Spanish counterpart—the two sides of an uprooted Latin woman—argue throughout the one-act play, exposing the problems of living in two worlds. *Coser y cantar* has been performed repeatedly since its debut, while as a radio play it has been broadcast throughout the United States. Prida's first collection of plays, *Beautiful Senoritas and Other Plays,* was published in 1991 by Arte Público Press of Houston, Texas.

In addition to her work as a playwright and journalist, Prida has also taught a play-writing workshop at Hostos Community College and written scripts for documentary films. She has received a variety of recognitions, among them a Doctor of Humane Letters from Mt. Holyoke College in 1989, the Cintas Fellowship Award for Literature in 1976, and the Creative Artistic Public Service Award for Play-writing for 1979-1980. Prida continues to work in New York City where she is active in the theater.

Sources:

Books

Escarpenter, Jose, and Linda S. Glaze, "Dolores Prida," in *Biographical Dictionary of Hispanic Literature in the United States,* edited by Nicolas Kanellos, Greenwood Press, 1989, pp. 244-49.
Weiss, Judith, "The Theaterworks of Dolores Prida," in Dolores Prida's *Beautiful Senoritas and Other Plays,* Arte Público Press, 1991, pp. 9-16.

Other

Archives, Arte Público Press, Houston, Texas.

—Sketch by Silvia Novo Pena

Leticia Quezada
(1953-)
President, Los Angeles Board of Education

Leticia Quezada was the third Latino—and the first Latina—to be appointed to the Los Angeles Board of Education. Elected to the Board in 1987, Quezada's main goal was to set up a bilingual education program for Spanish-speaking children. Since her election, she has held a number of different posts while attempting to achieve this goal, and in 1992 she was elected president of the organization.

Quezada was born in Santa Barbara, Chihuahua, Mexico, on July 12, 1953. Her father, Feliciano Quezada, worked as a miner and suffered from tuberculosis. Only able to achieve a second-grade education during his lifetime,

Feliciano died in 1962 at the young age of 33. Four years later, Quezada immigrated to California from Juarez, Mexico, with her widowed mother, Maria Delores Prieto, and her younger sister.

Before he died, Feliciano Quezada instilled in his daughter the importance of getting a good education—a value she has carried with her throughout her life. Staying true to this important value, Quezada earned a bachelor's degree in psychology from the University of California, Santa Cruz in 1975. And in 1976 she went on to earn a master's degree in education from California State University, Sacramento, becoming a certified teacher in California, specializing in bilingual (English/Spanish) studies.

Following her graduation from California State University, Quezada worked for the City of Los Angeles as an administrative assistant and a grants management specialist. In 1981, she joined Carnation Co. as manager of community relations and Latino marketing. It was also in 1981 that she married Steven Uranga, a city management analyst for the Community Development Department of Los Angeles. Quezada's experience as an education administrator continued to grow when she was chosen to fill the unexpired term of Rick Tuttle as a Los Angeles Community College District Trustee in 1985. A part-time position, it is the role of the trustees to design programs that will bring more money and more students into Los Angeles' two-year colleges.

Works Toward Goal of Bilingual Education

In 1987, Quezada rallied a major campaign and was elected as a board member on the Los Angeles Unified School District. Representing District Five (comprised of 540,000 Angelenos, including 150,000 students), Quezada's goal as a board member was the implementation of a bilingual education system to educate Spanish-speaking children and encourage Latino parent involvement. This mission stems from Quezada's experiences as a child: When her family moved to Pittsburg, California, the school she attended taught only in English, which, to her, was a foreign language. Going from a straight-A student in Mexico to a straight-F student in the United States made her angry and embarrassed. "Because of my own experiences as a child who was Spanish-speaking and struggling, poor and powerless, I want to help make a change," she explains in an interview for the *Los Angeles Times.*

Some of Quezada's critics claim that she only cares about Latino children. Disputing the charge, Quezada defended herself, maintaining in the *Los Angeles Times:* "I think all the children should be bilingual. It makes sense in this, a multicultural city in a multicultural state in a multicultural nation." This criticism, though, is balanced out with the positive recognition Quezada receives. In 1983 *Cominos* magazine named her "Hispanic of the Year," and she was also awarded the title of "Unsung Hero of the Latin Community" by the *Los Angeles Times* in 1985.

Quezada's fierce commitment to represent the Latino children is evident in her "Master Plan for the Education of the Limited English Proficient Students." It addresses the need for more bilingual teachers and spells out how the district can train teaching assistants to become bilingual teachers. The plan was adopted by the Los Angeles Board of Education in 1987, just a few short years before Quezada was elected president of the organization.

Sources:

Periodicals

Los Angeles Times, July 26, 1985, section 2, p. 1; January 28, 1990 p. E1; July 7, 1992, p. B1.

—Sketch by Stephanie Poythress

Naomi Quiñonez
(1951-)
Poet, editor, educator

Naomi Quiñonez is best known as a gifted poet and writer. Her book *Invocation L.A.: Urban Multicultural Poetry,* edited with Michelle T. Clinton and Seeshu Foster, won an American Book Award in 1990. Quiñonez's poetry draws on history, folk mythology and Hispanic culture and traditions. In reviewing the poetry collection *Sueno de Colibri Hummingbird Dream Poems,* Lorna Dee Cervantes writes: "Naomi Quiñonez has created a dream book of survival. Her women are all women, and her book is for all of us who have looked inside ourselves and found something else beside the prison, the privy, the blood factory, or the coffin." Quiñonez has also devoted her life to political activism and to education.

Born in Los Angeles on May 25, 1951, Quiñonez is the second of three daughters. Her parents, originally from Chihuahua, Mexico, emigrated to Texas in the years following the 1910 Mexican Revolution. After World War II, they moved to Los Angeles. Quiñonez began writing poetry as a child and gave her first poetry reading at the age of seven. She attributes her love of books as the inspiration behind her writing.

The Quiñonez family was traditional in their values and ambitions for their daughters. But as a "child of the '60s," Quiñonez was anxious to expand her horizons. She started college at California State University, Los Angeles, and later transferred to San Jose State College, where she majored in English and Journalism. While at San Jose State, she worked in the Ethnic Pride Program. This special program, funded by the Dean of Students, allowed students to trace their cultural history and begin teaching cultural awareness programs in the San Jose elementary public schools. The program's goal was to instill pride of culture at an early age. Balancing her college course work with active participation in the Ethnic Pride Program, Quiñonez also edited the Mexican American Service Agency Newsletter. She graduated from San Jose State College in 1975.

Works with the Disadvantaged

Following graduation, Quiñonez accepted a Director of Programs position at University of California, Santa Cruz. Under her management, the University's tutorial center worked to assist disadvantaged students improve testing performances through a variety of services. She also began to work in Watsonville among the migrant workers, helping to develop better social programs and medical services for impoverished rural Californians. At this time she met Chris Matthews, an activist and political reformer, who ran for election as County Supervisor in 1978. When he won election, he appointed her as his assistant.

In 1980, Quiñonez returned to Los Angeles to become the managing editor, director and writer of *Caminos,* an alternative magazine. While working on a shoestring budget, she and a dedicated group of writers were able to explore the many facets of Los Angeles. Urged by a *Caminos* board member, Quiñonez entered a new public administration program at the University of Southern California. Selected as a fellow in the Hispanic Field Service Program, she realized that her work experience of managing people, budgets and programs was greatly complemented by her new studies. Her master's degree was awarded in 1983. She continued a year of post-graduate studies in telecommunications at USC.

In 1984, Quiñonez began teaching at California State College at Northridge in the Chicano studies program and coordinated a special college writing program. During her tenure at North Ridge, she wrote and published *Sueno de Colibri Hummingbird Dream Poems.* In 1986, Quiñonez accepted the position of director of the Adult Literacy Programs of Los Angeles. Working to eradicate the 20 percent illiteracy level, she developed a large community-based program that was geared to the adult learner, especially the problems of Spanish-speaking learners. Using libraries as a center of learning, librarians were primary players in the program. In 1988, Quiñonez organized the first state-wide Latino Literacy Conference.

Wins American Book Award for *Invocation L.A.*

Returning to academia in 1988, Quiñonez resumed teaching at California State College, Long Beach, in the Chicano studies department. In her teaching and writing, she sought to merge both literary and cultural roots. In 1990, she edited *Invocation L.A.: Urban Multicultural Poetry* with Michelle Clinton and Seeshu Foster. *Invocation L.A.* is an anthology of poetry from several ethnic groups in the Los Angeles area. The collection was awarded the American Book Award in 1990. In late 1990, Quiñonez left CSC, Long Beach to begin work on her Ph.D. in American Studies at the Claremont Graduate School. She hopes to blend her studies of history, literature and feminist studies into this unique program. She began teaching part-time at California State University, Los Angeles. As she stated in a telephone interview with this contributor, "Literature and history are inseparable."

In the wake of the Los Angeles Riot of 1992, she submitted an educational and cultural proposal to the Los Angeles City Government. "Mestizo Voices" (literally meaning mixed races) focuses on the healing of the Los Angeles community by learning about all of its peoples' cultures. As Quiñonez explained, "Culture is incredibly important in transcending social problems." The program will involve writers and performing artists and work with high school students from South Central and East Los Angeles. She feels that the "stakes are now higher and there is a great importance in coming together."

Sources:

Books

Invocation L.A.: Urban Multicultural Poetry, edited by Naomi Quiñonez, Michelle T. Clinton, and Seeshu Foster, West End Press, 1989.

Quiñonez, Naomi, *Sueno de Colibri Hummingbird Dream Poems,* West End Press, 1985.

Periodicals

Caminos, December, 1980, pp. 6-7, 10, 16-19, 20-22, 39, 46; February, 1981, pp. 32-36; March, 1981, pp. 34-36, 62.
Chismerte, September, 1983, p. 17.
Latina, Volume 1, number 3, 1983, p. 58.
Maize, fall/winter, 1982-83, pp. 31-33.

Other

Quiñonez, Naomi, telephone interview with Sally Foster, September 26, 1992.

—Sketch by Sally Foster

R

Blandina Cárdenas Ramírez
(1944-)
Educational administrator, association executive

"The recurring theme in [Blandina] Cárdenas Ramírez' professional experience," said Margaret Cerrudo in *Intercambios Femeniles*, "is her life long commitment to education, Hispanic culture, children, and the rights of individuals." Indeed, for much her life, Blandina (Bambi) Cárdenas Ramírez has been part of the vanguard for civil rights and education. Appointed to the United States Commission on Civil Rights, she told Cerrudo that she is "fighting for equal access laws and the development of human capital."

Born October 25, 1944, in Del Rio, Texas, Ramírez is the youngest of three daughters who grew up in a supportive and traditional household. As Ramírez described her home life to Connie Paige in *Ms.*, "My family was very traditional about the maternal role. On the other hand, that did not diminish my family's respect for women and the clear aspirations that the next generation would do something. For us there was a strong sense of responsibility to make a contribution to improve the position of Hispanics." Also recollecting a childhood memory of her father to Cerrudo in *Intercambios Femeniles*, Ramírez recalled her father's words: "There is nothing my daughter can't do."

Ramírez's father, a civil service employee, and her mother, a homemaker, as well as the local church and school, were major influences in her life. Ramírez followed in the footsteps of her parents as a strong proponent of bilingual and bicultural education. In fact, by the time she entered first grade, she could read both English and Spanish. Completing elementary and secondary school at the San Felipe Independent School District in Del Rio, Texas, Ramírez graduated at the age of 16 in 1961. She subsequently went to Texas Women's University until 1962, when she resumed her studies at the University of Texas at Austin, where she completed a B.A. in journalism and public relations in 1967. She later obtained a doctoral degree in educational leadership and administration from the University of Massachusetts in 1974.

As a student and thereafter, Ramírez earned many academic honors and awards. Beginning in 1962, she earned

Blandina Cárdenas Ramírez

the Freshman Writer of the Year from Texas Woman's University. In 1971 she was awarded the Ford Foundation Fellowship in Educational Leadership and the Rockefeller Fellowship in Leadership and Public Policy in 1974. Ramírez was also the recipient of the Chancellor's Medal from the University of Massachusetts and received an Honorary Degree from Kean College of New Jersey in 1991.

Ramírez has also received numerous accolades as a leader in her community and advocate of civil rights, including "El Aguila Azteca," the highest honor given to a non-citizen by the President of Mexico. She was also named Outstanding Hispanic Woman in Texas by the National Hispanic Woman Institute, won awards from the American Educational Research Association and the National Education Association, and was honored by the National Council of La Raza and the San Antonio City Council.

Interest in Education Leads to Politics

Ramírez began her professional career as a teacher and educational administrator in 1967, when she started teaching migrant pre-school, third grade, and high school English at San Felipe Independent School District in Del Rio, Texas. She also developed innovative methodology for teaching disadvantaged children. In 1969, Ramírez continued her assistance to migrant children as assistant coordinator of the Texas Migrant Educational Center within the Southwest Educational Development Laboratory in Austin, Texas.

Moving to San Antonio, Texas, Ramírez began work in 1969 at the Edgewood Independent School District as special assistant to the superintendent and as director of the Career Opportunities Program. Her responsibilities as special assistant included the development of all innovative programs in the school district and fundraising. The programs, developed to serve the needs of a highly disadvantaged population, received wide national recognition, and the Career Opportunities Program, which Ramírez oversaw, included teacher training programs designed to enable 125 teacher aides to become teachers.

While completing her doctoral degree from 1971 to 1974, Ramírez advised numerous national projects as a consultant. Exposed to civil rights issues, she consulted for the Office of Civil Rights of the Department of Health, Education, and Welfare and the United States Justice Department. She also assisted the Southwest Education Development Laboratory Bilingual Children's Television project and the National Education Association.

Upon the completion of her Ed.D. from the University of Massachusetts, Ramírez became a Rockefeller fellow assigned to the U.S. Senate Committee on Children and Youth, chaired by then Senator Walter F. Mondale, from 1974 to 1975. As a fellow, she drafted legislation, coordinated external relations, and organized hearings. The major leadership development program of the Rockefeller Foundation also identified four minority individuals for placement on key policy making settings.

Before returning to San Antonio, Texas, Ramírez was hired as commissioner for the Administration for Children, Youth, and Families and chief of the Children's Bureau within the Department of Health, Education, and Welfare from 1977 to 1979. Shortly thereafter, she began working as director of training and development for the Intercultural Development Research Association in San Antonio from 1979 to 1985. There, Ramírez focused on improving the quality of instruction and the quality of education opportunity for all children, particularly in the state of Texas. As director, she was responsible for the development of products and strategies to assist school districts in comprehensive planning to meet state and federal regulations for developing programs in parent education and involvement, school board and administrator training, and faculty and staff training.

Works as Civil Rights Commissioner

One of Ramírez's most visible civil rights ventures came in 1980 when she was appointed to the eight-member U.S. Commission on Civil Rights. Originally appointed by then-President Jimmy Carter, she was the first Hispanic to ever serve on the commission. Established in 1957, the U.S. Commission on Civil Rights monitors the enforcement of civil rights laws by the executive and provides recommendations to the president and Congress on the need for policies and procedures to advance civil rights in the nation. As a commissioner responsible for overseeing the government's compliance with civil rights laws, Ramírez became a vocal opponent of President Ronald Reagan and criticized his civil rights record.

In 1983, President Reagan tried to remove her, along with two other commissioners, by appointing replacements considered more politically conservative. But Ramírez would not go willingly. She sued for an injunction forbidding the termination, and a federal court reinstated her position as commissioner, a role Ramírez still holds. Ramírez recalled the incident to Paige in *Ms.:* "The furor over the Civil Rights Commission has been difficult and painful, but from an individual standpoint very growth-producing. One did not imagine there would be a civil rights movement, or a Women's Movement. And suing the President of the United States and winning—and even though winning is not easy—it was a miracle of our democracy." Devoted to her work as a commissioner, Ramírez said to Cerrudo in *Intercambios Femeniles*, "It's my love. . . . It's what it's all about."

In 1988, Ramírez began working at Our Lady of the Lake University, a small private liberal arts institution in San Antonio, Texas, as vice president for Institutional Advancement. As vice president, she was responsible for the Offices of Development, Alumni Affairs, and Public Affairs. Subsequently, in 1989 Ramírez became director of the Office of Minorities in Higher Education at the American Council on Education in Washington, D.C.

The American Council on Education is considered the umbrella membership organization for institutions of higher education in the country. Her priority as director is increasing the participation of minorities in higher education. As director, she represents the association before Congress and the president. She also provides leadership, information, and service on minority issues to more than 50 higher education organizations which make up the Washington Higher Education Secretariat. Ramírez is frequently requested to make presentations on educational issues, diversity, and minority participation before a broad spectrum of audiences. Some of the notable organizations to which Ramírez has spoken include the New Jersey Education Association, the Center for Adolescent Schooling, and the National Conference on Black Student Retention.

In addition to speaking to organizations on educational and minority issues, Ramírez participates and continues to be active in major commissions, committees, and task forces on a national and international scale. She has been selected as a board member of numerous organizations, including the National Foundation for the Improvement of Education in Washington, D.C., the National Resource Center for Children in Poverty in New York and Quality Education for Minorities in Washington, D.C. Ramírez is also founding chairperson of the Mexican American Women's National Association, in Washington, D.C.

Ramírez is involved in many organizations and issues, and she is regarded as a professional willing to take risks. As related to Paige in *Ms.,* "There comes a time in a person's life when you almost have no choice. You cannot shirk the responsibility. You come to understand that the things you care about have much more to do with the process of history and the development than with yourself."

Sources:

Periodicals

Intercambios Femeniles, summer, 1989.
Ms., April, 1986, p. 68.
Nation, November 12, 1983, p. 451.
Time, November 7, 1983, p. 68.

—*Sketch by Luis Vasquez-Ajmac*

Sara Estela Ramírez
(1881-1910)
Revolutionary, poet, feminist

Although she has lost the fame she once possessed in Texas, Sara Estela Ramírez's story has not lost its significance. In fact, as Hispanic women increasingly influence politics in the United States, Ramírez's work as an activist and writer has become even more meaningful. During the course of her career as an educator, Ramírez was associated with the Partido Liberal Mexicano, a political party which fought for the rights of Mexicans and Mexican Americans. And in addition to her political affiliations,

Ramírez also used her literature to express her feelings regarding minority rights.

Ramírez was born in Progreso, Coahuila, Mexico, in 1881. Although her mother died when she was still a young girl, she managed to run her household and educate herself. She first studied in Monterrey in the Mexican state, Nuevo Leon, and later, she worked to become a teacher at Ateneo Fuentes, a teachers' institution in Saltillo. By 1898, she had her first job as a teacher in Laredo, Texas, at the Seminario de Laredo.

It was in Laredo that Ramírez began to promote the rights of Mexicans and Mexican Americans in Texas and where she was associated with the Partido Liberal Mexicano (PLM). Ironically, the fact that Ramírez was a woman worked to her advantage as she became more and more politically involved. According to Emilio Zamora, who has reintroduced Ramírez to Hispanics with his paper, "Sara Estela Ramírez: Una Rosa Roja en El Movimiento," women who propagandized and communicated the party's policies were not harassed in the same manner as men who performed the same activities. Ramírez was an especially courageous worker for the party. Zamora writes that she was "a central figure" in the party who had a "close working relationship" with at least one of the party's leaders.

Uses Literature for Revolutionary Message

Zamora reveals that Ramírez was most influential because of her literary works. From 1898 until the year she died, she wrote poems, essays, and articles which were published in *La Crónica* and *El Demócrata Fronterizo,* and the local press featured her challenging, inspirational speeches. Not content to have her work published by others, Ramírez published her own daily literary periodicals, first *La Corregidora* and then *Aurora,* during the last six years of her life. Ramírez also wrote and starred in a play, *Noema,* which was produced in and around Laredo.

Zamora, who can be credited for reminding Hispanics of the woman who, until his paper, was "a heretofore unknown political and literary figure of the early 1900's in South Texas," presents three samples of Ramírez's writing in "Sara Estela Ramírez: Una Rosa Roja en El Movimiento." One of these, "Alocución," is a speech which was read at the twenty-fourth anniversary of the founding of the Sociedad de Obreros (Society of Workers) and which was published by *El Democrata Fronterizo* on April 17, 1909. In this speech, Ramírez charged the members of the society to work together: "El obrero es el brazo, el corazon del mundo. . . . Que vosotros, obreros queridos, parte integrante del progreso humano, celebreis aun, incontables aniversarios, y que con vuestro ejemplo enseñeis a las sociedades a quererse para ser mutualistas, y unirse para ser fuertes." As translated by Ronie-Richele Garcia-Johnson, this passage reads, "The worker is the arm, the heart of the world. . . . Let us, dear workers, integral parts of human progress, celebrate yet, innumerable anniversaries, and with our example let us teach societies to want to be mutualists, and to unite to be strong."

Articulates Feminist Views

Another work included in Zamora's paper is ¡Surge!, a poem written by Ramírez "A la mujer," or to the woman, shortly before her death. The first verse indicates the attitude that women should aspire to any height. "¡Surge! Surge a la vida, a la actividad, a la /belleza de vivir realmente; pero surge radiante/y poderosa, bella de cualidades, esplendente/ de virtudes, fuerte de energias." Roughly translated into English by Garcia-Johnson, this reads "Rise! Rise to life, to activity, to the beauty of really living; but rise radiantly and powerfully, beautiful with qualities, splendidly with virtues, strong with energy." Clearly, the pre-feminist Ramírez was ahead of her times; words such as "surge," "poderosa," and "fuerte" suggest that she advocated that women be as politically active as she was herself and that they take control of their lives.

Despite her tenacity as a political figure, Ramírez also had a more sentimental side to her character. According to Zamora, in "La Pagina Blanca," the final work included in Zamora's paper, the poet "confronts rejection by the man/ men she loves." She speaks of a metaphorical album in which there is a seemingly forgotten blank page. This page, however, is the one that the poet reads most often: "¡Leo mas que en las otras del Libro!" The poet concludes with the line, "Esa pagina blanca en que leo/Tu desden y el cariño de mi alma!" The translation by Garcia-Johnson is, "This blank page that I read/Your disdain and the love of my soul!"

Although Ramírez died when she was just twenty-nine years of age, she made a permanent mark on Mexican and Texan politics. She also left enough literary works to allow critics like Zamora and Ines Hernandez Tovar to assess her talent. Finally, with the help of such critics, Ramírez may pass her courage as well as her passion for literature to a new generation of Hispanic women.

Sources:

Books

Tovar, Ines Hernandez, *Sara Estela Ramírez: The Early Twentieth Century Texas-Mexican Poet*, University of Houston, 1984.
Zamora, Emilio, "Sara Estela Ramírez: Una Rosa Roja en El Movimiento," in *Mexican Women in the United States: Struggles Past and Present*, edited by Adelaida R. Del Castillo and Magdalena Mora, with translations by Ronie-Richele Garcia-Johnson, Chicano Studies Research Center Publications, University of California, 1980.

—Sketch by Ronie-Richele Garcia-Johnson

Susan Elizabeth Ramirez
(1946-)
Educator, author

Susan Ramirez's resume includes enough honors and fellowships to satisfy an entire school of academic hopefuls. A professor of history at DePaul University in Chicago, where she has taught since 1982, Ramirez is an expert in the ethno-history of Peru and other Hispanic cultures. She has written several scholarly books in her field, including *Provincial Patriarchs: Land Tenure and the Economics of Power in Colonial Peru* (which has been translated into Spanish) and *The World Upside Down: Essays on Cross Cultural Contact and Conflict in Colonial Peru*. Ramirez is the editor of *Indian-Religious Relations in Colonial Spanish America* and has also presented her work in periodical articles, symposiums, and conferences.

Ramirez was born October 11, 1946, in Toledo, Ohio, to Eduardo Ramirez and Helen McCartney Ramirez. Her father was a typewriter repairman and salesman who felt that a woman needed no more than a high school education. Ramirez recalled that as a child she could not leave the house without permission, so "I studied a lot. If you stay home and study you get good grades. I had none of the normal outings that normal students have. I went to one basketball game, but that was against my father's wishes," she related in a telephone interview with Larry Paladino. In spite of his opposition to her interest in education, Ramirez's father helped to pave the way for her successes by taking the family on frequent trips to his native Mexico where Ramirez spent most of her time studying. Her enduring interest in Latin America, she maintained, is a result of her family's vacations to Mexico.

It was her mother, Ramirez said, who had the most influence on her career, especially while she was a pupil at York Community High School in Elmhurst, Illinois. "The most crucial thing that ever happened to me was that my father wouldn't let me go to college," the educator recalled in an interview. "But my mother schemed with the high school counselor and she got me accepted at the University of Illinois-Urbana. I was so thrilled to be tapped for college. I was packed before I graduated."

After earning a bachelor of arts degree in Latin American studies (with honors and distinction) in 1968, Ramirez went on to get her master's degree in history in 1973 at the University of Wisconsin, where she also completed her doctorate in 1977. "I wanted to study political economy," stated Ramirez. She noted that while she was a student, "A lot of times I discovered things I didn't realize, because I was naive. The so-called justice system is politicized. In essence, there's little justice for the common person. That goes for Latin America and the United States, too." Out of the many disciplines that she studied, Ramirez found that history "gave me the most freedom to do what I want." The historian didn't stop her education process with a Ph.D.; she also received a certificate in business administration from the Wharton School of the University of Pennsylvania in 1982, studied demography at Cornell University for three years, and studied anthropology for a summer in Cuernavaca, Mexico, at Centro Intercultural de Documentación.

"It was a struggle," she said in her interview. "For me to have gotten my Ph.D., it was a little short of a miracle, given my father's attitude towards women. He thought high school was enough and women should go on to become housewives." Of particular pride to Ramirez is the fact that she earned her doctorate before any affirmative action programs existed.

Before embarking on her scholarly career, Ramirez had been involved with synchronized swimming and at one point worked as a lifeguard. She continues to swim for pleasure and collect stamps—but mostly she works. "I'm always behind," she declared. "I'm over-committed. I like to write in the morning. In the afternoon I teach. And in the evening I think about what I'm going to write in the morning."

Sources:

Ramirez, Susan Elizabeth, interview with Larry Paladino, August 25, 1992.

—Sketch by Larry Paladino

Tina Ramirez

Dancer, choreographer, educator

When Tina Ramirez was growing up in both Venezuela and Mexico, her parents opposed her aspirations to be a dancer. Despite this opposition, however, Ramirez has gone on to a successful career in dance, choreography, and teaching, which has culminated in her role as the Artistic Director of Ballet Hispanico. Her "pan-Hispanic" vision unites flamenco, classical and modern techniques, and under her energetic guidance and direction, the Ballet Hispanico has become one of the most successful dance companies in the United States.

Born in Caracas, Venezuela, Ramirez's family moved to New York City when she was seven. Her father was a famous Mexican bullfighter, Jose Ramirez, and her Puerto Rican mother was a teacher. Ramirez's training did not begin at the traditional young age; her family opposed her youthful aspirations to begin dance lessons. As Ramirez recalled in an interview with Glenn Loney for *Dance* magazine, "The family said I'd have to be a teacher . . . I didn't have any dance lessons until I was 13." Fortunately, when the lessons started, she was able to study with such diverse dance luminaries as Lola Bravo, Anna Sokolow, Chester Hale and the Cansinos.

Ramirez's career began as a dancer with the Frederico Rey Dance Company, a group which toured nationally and in Canada and Cuba. She quickly established her reputation as a Spanish dancer, and to further refine her art, she studied with Luisa Pericet in Spain during the 1950s and continued to perform in Madrid. Upon her return to the United States, Ramirez and her sister, Coco, formed a duo and toured with Xavier Cugat. While in New York, she also appeared in Broadway productions of *Kismet* and *Lute Song*, and performed in the first television version of *Man of La Mancha*. And in 1963, she embarked in a new direction at the Puerto Rica Heritage Theater. Succeeding her former teacher and mentor, Lola Bravo, Ramirez dedicated herself to teaching and choreographing for low income teens in this special educational program.

Founded Ballet Hispanico

In 1970, Ramirez furthered her career by founding the Ballet Hispanico with a small grant from the New York State Council of the Arts. Established both as a company of performing dancers and a school, Ballet Hispanico emphasizes strong dance technique and Hispanic heritage. "What I'm looking for—and what I want to develop—are dancers who are alive, dynamic. . . . Emotions should come from the inside and be revealed by the body in motion. That's why I see dance as 'painting in space,'" described Ramirez in a telephone interview with Sally Foster.

The Ballet Hispanico reflects Ramirez's "pan-Hispanic" vision as well as a repertoire unrestricted by dance style. As she explained to Richard Thompson in an interview for *Horizon,* "I believe in united. Why not draw from 21 nations instead of two? One of the things that influenced me greatly is the fact that I dislike the separation of ballet and other forms of dance." The Ballet Hispanico of Dance school teaches 600 students at all levels of dance training. Ramirez remarked in her interview with Foster that "everything is done for the children . . . this is my life." Ramirez's work "for the children" has received numerous honors over the course of her career, including the New York Governor's Arts Award in 1987 and the New York City Mayor's Award of Honor for Arts and Culture in 1983. She has also been the honoree of the National Puerto Rican Forum and the Hispanic Institute for the Performing Arts.

The Ballet Hispanico began touring nationally in 1974 and internationally in 1978. While performances are critically renowned, the tours reveal the multiplicity of work done by Ballet Hispanico. Tours usually combine performance, lectures and demonstrations, master classes, and workshops representing a blending of the artistic and educational missions of the company and school.

Sources:

Periodicals

Dance, March, 1980, pp. 76-80; November, 1981, pp. 45-46; February, 1985, p. 100; November, 1985, p. 68; March, 1991, p. 96.
Horizon, November/December, 1988, pp. 60-61.
New York Times, October 31, 1991, pp. B3, C15, C18.

Other

Ramirez, Tina, telephone interview with Sally Foster, August 26, 1992.

—*Sketch by Sally Foster*

Diana Ramírez de Arellano
(1919-)
Poet, literary scholar, educator

Named poet laureate of Puerto Rico in 1958, Diana Ramírez de Arellano is a poet of intense imagery. Since the publication of her first collection *Yo soy Ariel* ("I Am Ariel") in 1947, Ramírez de Arellano has received numerous awards for her work, including special citations from the governments of Bolivia and Ecuador, as well as various groups in Puerto Rico. Her verse is rooted in the scenes and culture of her childhood in Puerto Rico; in this piece from *Arbol en vísperas* ("Tree at Vespers"), the poet extols the Jobo tree native to the island: "Not the poplar or the laurel do I exalt here/ nor the fir nor the spruce or the aspen or the juniper/ planted in Castille's rugose palm/ or in the fertile shores of another triumph/ by my friend's magic hand/ Nor do I sing her Alfonsa-Lark's resin bearing pines/ in distant Cuellar's forests/ Nor even don Antonio's centenary elm-tree/ in Soria's unblemished hillsides/ do I invoke though I possess a little bit of it./ Love summons here, common to none, a tree unknown,/ throbbing, trembling." The passion of the poem mirrors a passion for Puerto Rico.

Born June 3, 1919, in New York City, Ramírez de Arellano moved to Ponce, Puerto Rico, with her parents, Enrique Ramírez Brau and María Teresa Rechani Ramírez de Arellano, and attended primary and secondary schools there. Her father was a noted poet and journalist, and her great-grandfather was the prominent journalist and historian Salvador Brau. She gives both of these forebears, who demonstrated how the written word could be used as an artist's palette, credit for her talents. She has also acknowledged the role of her mother in developing her work, which frequently examines various female figures in the Spanish-speaking world.

The poet has had a diverse education. She received her bachelor's degree from the University of Puerto Rico in 1941; she then attended Columbia University's teacher's college and got her master of arts degree in 1946. For the next six years she worked as an instructor of Spanish at the University of North Carolina and at Rutgers University while simultaneously working on a Ph.D. from the University of Madrid. After receiving her Ph.D. in 1952, she became an assistant professor at Rutgers; six years later she moved to the City College of the City University of New York, where she would teach until her retirement as professor emeritus in 1984. 1958 was also the year she was named poet laureate and earned first prize in literature from the Institute of Puerto Rican Literature, a citation from Club Cívico de Damas, and diploma de honor from Ateneo Puertorriqueño de San Juan, all for her volume of poetry, *Angeles de ceniza* ("Angels of Ashes"). She won the Institute of Literature's first prize again in 1961, this time for a volume of criticism on contemporary Spanish-language poetry.

Poetry Examines Universal Themes

In her numerous poetical works Ramírez de Arellano examines literary themes themes of love, life, hope, memory, and exile and return to one's homeland. According to the *Diccionario de literatura puertorriqueña,* her style is based in the tradition of other Latin American poets, and shares the post-modernistic sensibilities of modern Spanish masters such as Miguel de Unamuno. In addition, works such as her 1955 poem *Albatros sobre el alma* ("Albatross over the Soul") have been cited as building on the symbolism of the English poet Samuel Taylor Coleridge. Her critical work has also been praised for combining her poetic imagination with a clarity of expression.

A member of several international and national teaching and writing associations, including PEN International, the poet frequently lectures and makes appearances at colleges and literary organizations; she also has served as a consultant to arts councils in the United States and Canada, including the Ford Foundation. Ramírez de Arellano, who has remained single throughout her life, is now retired from teaching and divides her time between New York, Puerto Rico, and Spain. She currently serves as President of the Josefina Romo Arregui Memorial Foundation, an organization dedicated to the memory of the late Spanish poet who served as Ramírez de Arellano's mentor.

Sources:

Books

Hispanic Writers, Gale, 1991, pp. 393-94.
Ramírez de Arellano, Diana, *Arbol en vísperas/Tree at Vespers* (bilingual edition), Ediciones Torremozas, 1987.
Rivera de Alvarez, Josefina, *Diccionario de literatura puertorriqueña,* 2nd edition, Instituto de Cultura Puertorriqueña, 1974, pp. 1285-87.

Periodicals

Bulletin of Hispanic Studies (Liverpool University), Volume 35, number 2, 1958.
Modern Language Notes, February, 1959.

—*Sketch by Bill Evans*

Ramos, Florence Hernández
See Hernández-Ramos, Florence

Tey Diana Rebolledo
(1937-)
Critic, educator

Literary critic and educator Tey Diana Rebolledo is renowned for her research on literature by Chicana and Latin American women writers, especially the study of early work by such authors. Her interest in 19th- and early 20th-century literary works and unpublished manuscripts by Hispanic writers was fueled by her mother's writings—work that went unpublished and languished in the family trunk for many years. The silencing of women's voices either through neglect or lack of publishing opportunities has strongly influenced Rebolledo's research.

Rebolledo was born April 29, 1937, in Las Vegas, New Mexico, to Esther Vernon Galindo and Washington Antonio Rebolledo. Both parents were creative writers; her father was also a professor of Spanish at Highlands University in Las Vegas and the author of a book of short stories and other literary works. Her parents' creative influence marked her life. Rebolledo recalls accompanying her fa-

ther to the local Spanish-language radio station where, as host of a talk show, he would discuss Hispanic culture. The family's trips to Mexico reinforced the strong cultural roots that they had established in northern New Mexico. When Rebolledo was ten, her family moved to New London, Connecticut, where her father was to teach Spanish at Connecticut College. She remembers that the relocation was a culture shock because few Spanish-speaking people lived in the community and the lifestyle was so different from what she experienced in New Mexico. Her world was further disrupted when her father died in 1951.

In 1959 Rebolledo received her B.A. in Spanish from Connecticut College and began graduate work in Latin American studies at the University of New Mexico. She obtained her M.A. in 1962, a year before her daughter was born. Rebolledo next moved to Portland, Oregon, where she was a homemaker, rearing her daughter before she resumed teaching Spanish at a community college for two years. In 1974, Rebolledo resettled in Tucson, Arizona, and began doctoral studies at the University of Arizona. She received her Ph.D. in Spanish in 1979. Rebolledo wrote her thesis on Rosario Castellano, a feminist Mexican poet. An educator at the University of North Carolina, Chapel Hill for one year, Rebolledo also served as a member of the Department of Foreign Languages at the University of Nevada in Reno from 1978 and 1984. She returned to the University of New Mexico in 1984 as director of the women's studies program, with a joint appointment in the Spanish department. In 1988 she became a full-time professor of Spanish and Chicana literature.

Chicana Poet Influences Academic Work

Rebolledo's interest in Chicana literature had begun when she was a graduate student in Arizona and she met Margarita Cota Cárdenas, a Chicana poet who invited her to poetry readings. Her casual introduction to Chicana/o literature became a consuming interest and her first published paper was on Cota Cárdenas's work. Her scholarship focused on Chicana authors and trends and connections in the literature. In *Infinite Divisions: An Anthology of Chicana Writers,* Rebolledo presents the historical development of Chicana writing from 1880 to the early 1990s. And in the compilation *Las mujeres hablan: An Anthology of Nuevo Mexicana Writers,* she includes the work of many emerging authors.

Such works and accomplishments have earned Rebolledo a reputation for being a respected Chicana literary critic and scholar. Acknowledged for her academic achievements, she has received the University of New Mexico Scholar award, the New Mexico Commission on Higher Education Eminent Scholar award, and grants from the New Mexico Quincentennial Commission and the National Endowment for the Humanities. Rebolledo lives and works in

Albuquerque, New Mexico, is married to Michael Passi, and is the mother of Tey Marianna Nunn.

Sources:

Rebolledo, Tey Diana, interview with Teresa Márquez, September 18, 1992.

—*Sketch by Teresa Márquez*

Susanna Redondo de Feldman
(1913-)
Director, educator

Susanna Redondo de Feldman is the Director of the Hispanic Institute in the United States. The Institute is a cultural extension of the Department of Spanish and Portuguese at Columbia University in New York City. Beginning her career as a teacher, Redondo de Feldman's administrative duties quickly grew. And though she is now somewhat retired, she continues to support Hispanic literature and culture.

Redondo de Feldman was born on September 27, 1913, in the Camguey Province of Cuba. Her father was a well-known mechanical engineer and her mother was a housewife who had always longed to be a teacher. As the first of five children, Redondo de Feldman's plans to become a doctor were discouraged by her mother, who wanted her to be a teacher, and by her father, who was working to finance the educations of her younger siblings.

While married to a young army officer who studied medicine, Redondo de Feldman was able to indulge her love of science while studying with him. Pursuit of a career in medicine was abruptly halted when she was exposed to the body of a child in anatomical studies. The child bore a striking resemblance to her young daughter. Thoroughly shaken by this incident, she resumed literary studies begun earlier at the University of Havana.

She completed her Ph.D. in literature at the University of Havana in 1945. In October of that year, Redondo de Feldman arrived in New York and sought a teaching position at Columbia University. The chairman of the Spanish and Portuguese department and founder of the Hispanic Institute, Frederico de Onis, interviewed her.

This meeting was the beginning of a long association. Unable to give her a teaching position in mid-semester, he offered Redondo de Feldman a secretarial job at the Institute, then called Instituto de las Espansas. Within three weeks, a teaching vacancy occurred and Redondo de Feldman was teaching at night and working at the Instituto de las Espansas during the day.

Appointed Director of Hispanic Institute

She continued to teach in the Spanish and Portuguese department, her departmental advancement culminating in her appointment as department chairman. During this time, Redondo de Feldman also worked at the Hispanic Institute with Dr. de Onis, who became her mentor. Upon his retirement, he beseeched her to "take care of the Institute . . . it is the labor of my life," remembered Redondo de Feldman in a telephone interview with Sally Foster. She was appointed director soon after and continued her teaching duties.

The Hispanic Institute provides research programs in Spanish and Portuguese literature as well as lectures and concerts. Through a trust established for the Institute, it bestows the Vernon Prize for the best literary essay on Spanish literature by a non-Spanish speaking college student. It maintains a library and archives of Spanish and Portuguese literature and linguistics as well as its own extensive publications. The Hispanic Institute's scholarly journal, *Revista Hispanica Moderna,* is published in Spanish, Portuguese, and English on a bi-annual basis and has an international circulation.

Although Redondo de Feldman retired from her teaching and chairmanship duties in 1981, she continues to promote the knowledge of Spanish, Spanish American and Portuguese literature and culture through her work at the Hispanic Institute. Married to an engineer, she has one daughter who is a university teacher, three grandchildren, and two great grandchildren.

Sources:

Periodicals

Revista Hispanica Moderna, January, 1991; June, 1991; January, 1992; June, 1992.

Other

Redondo de Feldman, Susanna, telephone interview with Sally Foster, August 26, 1992.

—*Sketch by Sally Foster*

Shirley Rodríguez Remeneski
(1938-)
Political activist

Shirley Rodríguez Remeneski has spent her life working within the political system to improve conditions in the Hispanic communities of New York. Beginning her career as a volunteer in New York City borough politics and subsequently serving under United States Congressman Herman Badillo and New York Mayor Ed Koch, Remeneski now heads the New York Governor's Office for Hispanic Affairs. In this position she works to develop community-based programs in Hispanic neighborhoods throughout the state, to expand educational opportunities for Hispanic youth, and to encourage political activism among a population that she insists is underrepresented in public office. She has focused primarily on programs for the young, she told contributor Tom Pendergast, because "we have to build the future leadership for our community."

Remeneski was born on January 15, 1938, and raised in an ethnically mixed neighborhood on the West Side of Manhattan. Her father, Armando Rodríguez, had immigrated to New York from San German, Puerto Rico when he was nineteen and, when his first wife died of tuberculosis, he returned to Puerto Rico and married Remeneski's mother, Providence. Armando worked as an inventory man in the kitchen of the prestigious Gotham hotel and Providence became a union representative in a leather factory. Her parent's relative poverty didn't keep Remeneski from enjoying her childhood among her close-knit extended family. Her grandmother, who lived with the Rodríguezes in their large apartment, sold her Puerto Rican home so that she could pay for relatives to come to the United States. Remeneski fondly recalls the constant stream of family members who lived with them while her father helped them find jobs and apartments.

Remeneski told Pendergast that she started to work when she was fourteen years old because she wanted pretty clothes and the extra spending money her parents couldn't give her. In 1956 she attended New York's City College, but she dropped out in 1957 and took a job as a secretary for Mills Music in order to help her family through some financial difficulties. She was married to Richard Remeneski in 1960, and the couple had two children before divorcing in 1970. When she was twenty-six, Remeneski made a decision that was to change her life. Noticing that Hispanics had little political representation in her Bronx community, she volunteered to work for the political campaign of Herman Badillo. Badillo was an "incredibly intelligent man," she told Pendergast, and he was able to unite different groups—Jews, Hispanics, and Italians—to win the post of Bronx borough president. Badillo asked

Remeneski to create a department of social services in the Bronx to serve the community's needs for health, employment, and educational services. She filled this post from 1965 to 1971, and her career as a political activist was launched.

Began Career in U.S. Government

In 1971, Badillo was elected to the U.S. House of Representatives, and he asked Remeneski to work as his district administrator in an area that included the Bronx, Queens, and Manhattan. During the four terms that Badillo served, Remeneski worked with him to "defend Latino political rights, to extend bilingual education, and to make the ballots bilingual," she remarked. But Badillo was frustrated by the difficulties of advancing his legislative agenda in an atmosphere hostile to minority needs and in 1978, despite the objections of Remeneski and other of his aids, he returned to New York City politics by joining the mayoral administration of Ed Koch. Remeneski continued to work with Badillo, however, accepting the position of assistant deputy mayor. Though she worked within the Koch administration, Remeneski saw herself as "an advocate for the community," and she helped community organizations attain city funding. Remeneski's association with Badillo ended when he left the Koch administration in 1979.

Remeneski continued to serve the community when she accepted the post of legislative coordinator for the South Bronx Development Organization. Working with Edward Logue, a nationally known urban developer, she lobbied city, state, and federal governments for funding and legislative support for their projects. Her greatest success, she related to Pendergast, was the Charlotte Gardens project, where her group secured low interest loans and an urban development grant to buy and restore a group of homes in the Bronx. They in turn sold the homes to poor families for a reasonable price. "To this day the area is kept beautifully," she says proudly, "and poor people who could never have afforded a house now own their own home." In 1980 the United Bronx Organization voted Remeneski Woman of the Year.

Heads New Office for Hispanic Affairs

In 1986, after five years of work as district administrator for the New York State Department of Social Services, Remeneski was asked by New York Governor Mario Cuomo to head his newly created Office for Hispanic Affairs, which was formed to address the declining status of the Hispanic community. Although the Office provides many services, Remeneski is most proud of their Hispanic mentoring program. Hispanic children identified as "at risk"—those whose grades are slipping, who come from dysfunctional families, or who are unmotivated—are paired with successful Hispanic adults of the same sex. The program requires a great deal from the mentors; they must commit to staying with that child for a period of three years. At the end of the three-year period, the children attend a week-long camp where they take leadership and enrichment courses to prepare them for high school. "Hispanic children often lack self-esteem and confidence, and feel like outsiders in a society that doesn't address the needs of its ethnic minorities," Remeneski noted. "This program provides them with positive role models and gives them the tools they need to succeed." The program has since been adopted statewide, with Mrs. Cuomo as its head.

Remeneski has served as a delegate at two Democratic national conventions and received numerous accolades for community service, including having the 1990 Puerto Rico Day parade in New York dedicated to her. Throughout her long career as a political activist she has maintained the desire to build up the Hispanic communities of New York. Asked about her goals for the future, Remeneski told Pendergast: "I want to continue to concentrate on educating Hispanic youth, for that will take care of many problems that now exist, and I want to continue my efforts to get Latino women elected to state and federal office, and to increase Latina representation in the corporate world."

Sources:

Remeneski, Shirley Rodríguez, interview with contributor Tom Pendergast conducted on September 8, 1992.

—*Sketch by Tom Pendergast*

Hermelinda Renteria

Hermelinda Renteria
(1960-)
Construction engineer

A construction engineer with the Pacific Gas and Electric Company, Hermelinda Renteria spends her life in a hard hat and construction boots overseeing million-dollar projects in California. In her capacity as contracts and technical services supervisor at the San Francisco Bay Power Plant, she puts construction packages together, assigns contracts, and supervises the work until completion. However, Renteria had to fight to get a field job and faced repeated battles to escape the office positions traditionally reserved for women engineers. "It's up to you to decide what you want to do with your career," she stressed in an interview with Michelle Vachon, "and don't let anyone tell you otherwise." Renteria regards community service as a duty for a successful career person. "We can't just sit back and enjoy our money and comfort. We need to help others share this good life—it's only fair." Her involvement ranges from sitting on both the business

advisory board of the San Francisco's Human Rights Commission and the board of directors of the San Francisco Girl Scouts to serving as chapter vice president for special programs of the Latina Women's Network.

Renteria was born on June 8, 1960, in Llamas Zacatecas, Mexico. In 1963, her family moved to Chico, California, and in 1966 to Watsonville, California, where she grew up with her sister and two brothers. "Our parents were farm workers, and had to go wherever they could find work," she explained in the interview. "We lived in shared housings in labor camps." When Renteria and her sister reached high school age, her father insisted on sending them to a private Catholic school. "Anything we needed for education, our parents would provide, no matter what." After high school, Renteria chose to pursue university studies in Guadalajara, Mexico. "I wanted to know more about my cultural heritage," she said. The experience was difficult at first. "I've always been a tomboy and at my Catholic high school, we had been told that we girls could do anything we wanted career-wise. Suddenly, I was at the Universidad Autonoma de Guadalajara in a class composed of three women, and 120 male students with old-fashioned views on women. They did not make life easy for the three of us." Renteria became active in student organizations, such as the Women's Affairs Committee of the Student Affairs Council. To spoof the Miss University pageant, she launched a "King Ugly" contest on the campus. This caused a stir among her teachers who were used to unobtrusive engineering students. But in 1983, the three women were among the 52 students in her class who graduated with baccalaureates in science.

Renteria found her first engineering position with the Jalisco State Department of Public Works in Guadalajara. "I'm often asked whether being Hispanic creates difficulties in my field," she stated in her interview. "My answer is that being Hispanic is no problem, being a woman is." Although she held the title of engineering aide, Renteria nevertheless received flowers and was treated to lunch on Secretary's Day. In 1984, she returned to California. "I came back to help my parents on the farm and supervise their 170 employees. They had just come out of retirement to save their old strawberry farm that the new owner, a relative, had let deteriorate." When the crisis subsided, Renteria took positions related to engineering—engineering aide for the City of Ventura, California, draftperson for the County of Ventura's Road Maintenance Department, and draftperson for Gerald Graebe & Associates in Salinas, California. "I had to prove that my degree and my field experience were valid. I was willing to accept any offer to gain credibility," she recalled in her interview. Then she met Joseph McGowan, a vice president with the multinational firm Granite Construction, who recommended her for a position with Pacific Gas and Electric Company (PG&E). So in 1984, Renteria joined the utility company's staff of 26,000.

Ascends through Ranks of PG&E

She first served as field engineer; to her displeasure, this amounted to desk work. After a few months on the job, she met with her supervisor, Tom Allen, and expressed her strong desire to work in the field. With his support, she was soon put in charge of a million-dollar construction project. "It makes such a difference when a supervisor stands by his employees," she remembered in her interview. "Occasionally, contractors tried to go over my head. But my supervisor would tell them that he trusted my decisions. It really built up my confidence." Renteria progressed within the company; she served as field engineer at the Diablo Canyon Nuclear Power Plant in San Luis Obispo, California, then she trained in project management in San Francisco, and later she was assigned to contracts administration. One of her projects consisted of remodelling a PG&E building in San Francisco, which meant keeping the edifice's outer shell while rebuilding the inside in its entirety. On a subsequent assignment, Renteria remodelled the computer floor of the company's billing department. "We had to work at night so we wouldn't interrupt the department's activities," she remembered in her interview. "The company was nervous about this—if anything went wrong, it could have been disastrous." Renteria received the PG&E's 1988 Performance Recognition Award for the project.

Her next post was assistant to the construction superintendent for the Diablo Canyon Power Plant in San Francisco. Afterwards, she joined the marketing department and attended to the company's special clients—the U.S. Army,

universities, the school district. Finally in 1992, Renteria became contracts and technical services supervisor for the San Francisco Bay Power Plant, a position she truly enjoys. It requires dealing with outside contractors and insuring that the work be executed according to PG&E's specifications.

Renteria draws upon her own experience in the work force when she gives talks in elementary and high schools. "I tell schoolgirls that if they are interested in working on site, they have to be careful when they accept office duties, whether or not they are of a technical nature," she emphasized in her interview. "It can be very difficult for a woman to switch back after she has been identified with desk duties for a period of time." Her work with young people extends to being involved with the educational programs of the League of Latin American Citizens (LULAC), as well as to serving as chapter president of LULAC's National Education Service Centers from 1989 to 1992.

Serves as a Role Model for Hispanic Girls

Renteria's commitment to young people prompted her to accept an appointment to the board of directors of the San Francisco Bay Area Girl Scouts. "The organization was looking for role models to inspire Hispanic girls. I was so impressed by the board's achievements that I couldn't refuse," she explained to Vachon. "There are more than 23,000 girl scouts in the San Francisco area, and the organization's activities—pregnant teen programs, conferences on multicultural relations—really focus on the issues they face today." Renteria was also appointed to the business advisory board of the San Francisco Human Rights Commission due to her work on behalf of minority businesses. "Our goal is to insure that women-owned and minority businesses get their fair share of city contracts." In the Hispanic community, she served as vice president in charge of special projects for the San Francisco Latina Women's Network. One of her undertakings was a seminar for women contemplating the second part of their lives. "We wanted to help women in their thirties and forties decide what they will do with the rest of their lives," she said in her interview. "I met many women who planned to completely change direction. It made me think about my own life."

Renteria has played an important role locally as well as nationally in the Society of Hispanic Professional Engineers (SHPE). She was San Francisco's chapter president for four terms between 1988 and 1993, and national secretary from 1989 to 1991. According to an article in the society's publication *Hispanic Engineer,* "Renteria's positive attitude and gregarious nature, along with her dedication to hard work, ensured her development as a leader." In 1988, she received an award from SHPE and the Asociacion Mexicana de Ingenieros Mecanicos y Electricistas (Mexican Association of Mechanical and Electrical Engineers) for her contribution in organizing the Third International Conference on Engineering and Technology, which took place in Juarez, Mexico. In 1991, Renteria was recognized by SHPE for her "Outstanding Leadership and Dedication." She also belongs to the American Society of Civil Engineers and the Society of Women Engineers. A member of the PG&E Employees Association, her participation earned her the company's Community Service Award in both 1989 and 1990.

In another arena, Renteria has been a Big Sister in the youth-support organization Big Brothers/Big Sisters of America since 1987 and has guided the same "little sister" for years. "I was used to dealing with my brother who is sixteen years younger than me," she confided in her interview. "So I asked to support a girl of his age, and it has worked well. I have seen them grow up. The three of us have gone on numerous outings together." Renteria also takes part in various mentor programs. So far she has followed three students from high school to college and has encouraged them to enter graduate school. "I really believe in education. It's a stepping stone to everything in life, especially today since the simplest job requires technical training. I have seen what happens to students who drop out of school. Education opens doors, creates possibilities. You don't have to complete college right away—attend for a few years and complete later if you have to. But do it."

In 1989, the Anti-Defamation League of B'nai B'rith awarded Renteria the "Woman on the Move" Certificate of Honor for her service to the community. The following year, her work with the Mission Girls's Services Program at the Young Women's Christian Association (YWCA) of San Francisco/Marin/San Mateo earned her a Certificate of Merit "for dedication and commitment to the YWCA Mission—the empowerment of women and girls and the elimination of racism." And in 1991, the Skyline College of San Bruno, California, presented Renteria with a Certificate of Appreciation for "encouraging the education of young women and nurturing their interest in science and mathematics."

Renteria admits that she is constantly looking for challenges. She plans to pursue her studies either in engineering or in education—she would like to teach one day. She also sees marriage in her future. But "I wouldn't give up my career or my activities. I think that you can have it all—a happy marriage and family life, a successful career and community involvement—and I intend to prove it!"

Sources:

Periodicals

Hispanic Engineer, fall, 1989, pp. 24-25.
Newsline (Lawrence Livermore Laboratories newsletter, Livermore, CA), September 14, 1990, p. 2.
Society of Hispanic Professional Engineers (newsletter), September/October, 1990, p. 8; November/December, 1990, p. 3.

Vanidades, August 7, 1990, p. 100.

Other

Renteria, Hermelinda, interview with Michelle Vachon conducted on May 9, 1992.

—Sketch by Michelle Vachon

Rita Ricardo-Campbell
(1920-)
Economist, government official, writer

Rita Ricardo-Campbell launched her career in the 1940s by becoming the first woman to teach economics at Harvard University in Cambridge, Massachusetts. In 1968, she was the first woman to be appointed senior fellow at Stanford University's Hoover Institution in Stanford, California. A few years later, she joined the board of directors of the Watkins-Johnson Company and the Gillette Company, the only woman director of these two *Fortune*-500 organizations. And in the 1980s, she served as the only woman member of the President's Economic Policy Advisory Board. "I have been lucky," said Ricardo-Campbell in an interview with contributor Michelle Vachon. "I had the energy to pursue a career and raise my family. Most importantly, I could always count on the support of my husband."

A collateral descendant of 19th-century economist David Ricardo, Ricardo-Campbell was born on March 16, 1920, in Boston, Massachusetts. She first attended Simmons College in Boston, which she described to *Hispanic Business* as "a very interesting college—all women—whose motto was 'to prepare women for work, marriage, and family.'" In 1941, she obtained her B.S. in library sciences, then quickly secured a scholarship and enrolled at Harvard University. During World War II "opportunities for women were much greater than at other times," Ricardo-Campbell told *Hispanic Business.* "I was there at the right time." She took her master's degree in 1945 and her Ph.D. in economics the following year. Upon receiving her doctorate, Ricardo-Campbell was promoted to university instructor—she had been working at the university since 1942, first as fellowship and research assistant and afterwards as teaching fellow and tutor.

In 1946, she married Wesley Glenn Campbell, who also taught economics at Harvard University. "I decided to hyphenate my name because I didn't want to loose my Sephardic roots," she mentioned to *Intercambios Femeniles.* In 1948, she joined Tufts University in Medford, Massachusetts, as an assistant professor. Three years later, Ricardo-Campbell and her husband moved to Washington, D.C., where her husband had been offered a position. She served as economist for the Wage Stabilization Board in 1951 and for the U.S. House of Representatives' Ways and Means Committee in 1953; she worked as a consulting economist from 1956 until 1960, when her family moved to California and her husband assumed the directorship of the Hoover Institution at Stanford University. Ricardo-Campbell taught at San Jose State University in San Jose, California, for one year and joined the Hoover Institution in 1961. She held the positions of archivist and research fellow until she was named senior fellow in 1968.

"As a senior fellow here at the Hoover Institution, I can research whatever appeals to me," she explained to *Intercambios Femeniles*. Interested in public policy, economics and the politics of health care, in 1976 Ricardo-Campbell wrote the book *Social Security: Promise and Reality*, which is still considered the primary source of information on the social security system. In 1982, she published *The Economics and Politics of Health*, and in 1988 *Issues in Contemporary Retirement* (coedited with Edward Lazear of the Hoover Institution). Her next book is to be on the hostile takeover attempt against the Gillette Company.

Joins the President's Economic Policy Advisory Board

Ricardo-Campbell has been repeatedly asked to serve as advisor on public policy. From 1967 through 1975, she held the post of California commissioner for the Western Interstate Commission for Higher Education and took on its chairmanship for one term in 1970. She served as a member of the President's Economic Policy Advisory Board from 1981 through 1989, as a member of the National Council on the Humanities from 1982 through 1988, and was elected member of the President's Committee on the National Medal of Science in 1988. Two years later, she chaired, in New York City, a chief-executive roundtable on health care costs containment, and spoke at the World Congress on Health Economics in Zurich. She is also a member of SRI International's advisory council and a director of the Mont Pelerin Society.

Ricardo-Campbell sits on the board of directors of Watkins-Johnson Company, the Samaritan Medical Center Management Group and the Gillette Company. "I was invited to these boards because of my understanding of economics and finance," she said to this contributor. "Surprisingly, these appointments have established my status in the business community in ways that I had never achieved while I was a President's economic advisor. Executives immediately accept me on a different level because I'm a director of *Fortune*-500 companies."

In a 1988 interview with the *Hoover Institution Newsletter*, Ricardo-Campbell predicted that the United States would be struggling until the turn of the century with the economic impact of social security, the cost of medical care,

services requested by an aging population, the growth of entitlements and world trade competition. "I would add the U.S. deficit to this list of domestic issues," she remarked in her interview. "Internationally, I find these so-called ethnic cleansings that have been carried out in Eastern Europe, these so-called 'wars of conscience' extremely disturbing. This idea of ethnic groups claiming the right to live apart and by themselves spells trouble all over the world. I'm also deeply disturbed by the existence of a Russian army without leadership, and I don't see any decline necessarily in the numbers of people who are starving. These global issues will have to be addressed in the coming years."

Ricardo-Campbell, who is the mother of three daughters, expects to see women in the United States rise to higher levels in business. "Women will solidify whatever gains they have made and will increase them," she stated in her interview. "I think that it's an upward trend." Ricardo-Campbell, a grandmother, lives with her husband in Los Altos Hills, California.

Sources:

Periodicals

Atlanta Journal/Atlanta Constitution, July 5, 1987, p. C1.
Hispanic Business, March 1988, pp. 33-34.
Hoover Institution Newsletter, winter 1988-1989, p. 3.
Intercambios Femeniles, spring 1987, pp. 10-11.
Science, September 16, 1988, p. 1516.
U.S. News & World Report, July 27, 1981, p. 35.

Other

Ricardo-Campbell, Rita, interview with Michelle Vachon, July 15, 1992.

—*Sketch by Michelle Vachon*

Riddell, Adaljiza Sosa
See Sosa-Riddell, Adaljiza

Rio, Dolores Del
See Del Rio, Dolores

Rio, Petra Barreras del
See Barreras del Rio, Petra

Ríos, Isabella
  See López, Diana

Chita Rivera

Chita Rivera
(1933-)
Actress, dancer

Although the general public would be most likely to recognize Chita Rivera as Anita from the musical *West Side Story* and as Rosie from *Bye Bye Birdie,* theatergoers and those in the business know that Rivera has the ability to make or break a musical. The woman of Puerto Rican descent has been illuminating theaters with her energetic, explosive dancing, her powerful voice, and her comic gestures as well as her serious expressions since she graduated from high school. In addition to headlining in numerous musicals, she has starred in movies and appeared on television. Although she has already inspired a new generation of actresses, Rivera is as radiant as ever.

The third child of Pedro Julio Figueroa and Katherine del Rivero, Dolores Conchita Figuero del Rivero was born on January 23, 1933, in Washington D.C. Her father, Pedro, a Puerto Rican musician who played the clarinet and the saxophone in the U.S. Navy Band, died when she was only seven years old. To provide for her family, Katherine del Rivero, who was of Puerto Rican and Scots-Irish descent, found a job as a government clerk. The widowed mother, however, did more than put food on the table; she enrolled the young Rivera in singing, piano, and ballet lessons.

Rivera was most enthusiastic about ballet. She performed in shows her brother Julio arranged in the basement of their home, and she demonstrated so much promise in class that her instructor, Doris Jones, encouraged her to audition for a scholarship to Balanchine's School of American Ballet. Dolores won the scholarship in 1950. In order to attend the school, which was located in New York City, she went to live with her uncle's family in the Bronx.

Makes Debut in *Call Me Madam*

The young dancer graduated from Taft High School in 1951, and the very next year landed her first professional job as a dancer. She had accompanied a friend from the School of American Ballet to an audition for *Call Me Madam,* which was to be choreographed by Jerome Robbins, and she won a part instead of her friend. Dolores, or

Conchita del Rivero, as she called herself, had been touring the country with the musical for almost a year when she decided to return to New York; she had accepted an offer to replace Onna White in *Guys and Dolls* as a principal dancer.

Conchita was on her way to becoming a sought-after performer. After her Broadway debut in *Guys in Dolls,* she found herself in the chorus of *Can-Can* in 1953 and then on television's *Imogene Coca Show* in 1954. Friends involved with the production of *Can-Can* persuaded the young woman to change her name. After three days of referring to herself as Chita O'Hara, she finally settled on Chita Rivera. It was Chita who became a singer, actress, and dancer and joined *Shoestring Revue,* which was produced Off-Broadway, in 1955. The revue received some good reviews, and Rivera was given special attention. It was not long before she was cast as Fifi, a French prostitute in *Seventh Heaven* on Broadway. That same year, she was chosen to tour with the Oldsmobile Industrial Show.

In 1956, Chita captured the role of Rita Romano in *Mr. Wonderful,* a musical produced for Sammy Davis, Jr., on Broadway. She began to appear as a guest on variety shows at this point in her career, including such programs as *The Garry Moore Show, The Ed Sullivan Show, The Arthur Godfrey Show, The Sid Ceasar Show, The Dinah Shore Show,* and *The London Palladium Show.* Rivera's performances that year led to one of her best parts ever—that of Anita in *West Side Story.*

Wins Acclaim with Role in *West Side Story*

A major musical conceived by Jerome Robbins, *West Side Story* is William Shakespeare's *Romeo and Juliet* in a contemporary setting; a young couple falls in love despite their dissimilar and antagonistic backgrounds, and their love is tragically ended. In *West Side Story* Romeo is Tony, a "white, American" gang member, while Juliet is Maria, the Puerto Rican sister of a rival gang member. The nurse who helps Juliet marry Romeo is transformed into Maria's brother's girlfriend, Anita. Cast as the fiery Anita, Rivera sang "A Boy Like That" and "I Have a Love," as well as the song which has become a musical classic, "America."

West Side Story and Chita were instant hits in 1957. The musical ran for 732 performances, and besides an offer of marriage, Chita garnered a Tony nomination. Although Chita did not win a Tony, she married Anthony Mordente, one of the dancers in *West Side Story*. When Chita became pregnant with their daughter, Lisa Angela Mordente, she left the production of the musical. After the birth of the baby, who grew up to become an actress herself, the acting couple resumed their roles when *West Side Story* found its way to London in 1958.

After the musical closed in England in 1959, Rivera starred in another hit musical on Broadway and in London. In *Bye Bye Birdie*, which ran from 1960 to 1961, Chita portrayed Rosie Grant and performed along with Dick Van Dyke. In the musical, Rosie, a secretary who wants save her advertising agency employer, hatches a contest that allows one girl to kiss a rock star, Birdie, goodbye as he leaves for military service. As she enthralled the audience with her clever acting, Rivera sang "Spanish Rose," "How to Kill a Man," and "Shriners' Ballet"; her dynamic presentation earned her another Tony nomination. She then went on to play Athena Constantine in *Zenda*, a short-lived play in California in 1963, and to act in a television show benefit with the immensely popular British rock group the Beatles in 1964 in England. Her next appearance was as Anyanka, the gypsy princess, in *Bajour* in 1964. That performance won her a third Tony nomination, a citation from Best Plays, and an invitation to become the official hostess of the "World's Fair and Summer Festival Season" in New York City.

Develops Solo Cabaret Act

By this time, Chita Rivera was a celebrated stage star; she decided to venture out on her own. With the help of her friends Fred Ebb and John Kander, a lyricist and composer that Chita would team up with throughout her career, she developed a cabaret act. In 1966, she traveled throughout the United States and Canada with this act. However, even though the cabaret was well received, she decided to return to the stage. She went on to perform as Jenny in *The Threepenny Opera*, as Linda Low in *Flower Drum Song*, as Charity in the national tour of *Sweet Charity*, as Nickie, Charity's roommate, in the motion picture version of *Sweet Charity*, and as Christopher Columbus's mistress in the flop *1491*.

The early 1970s found the actress on tour once again, appearing in *Jaques Brel Is Alive and Well and Living in Paris*, as well as performing in standing productions like *Born Yesterday*, *Milliken Breakfast Show*, *The Rose Tattoo*, and *Sondheim: A Musical Tribute*. In 1974, she performed in the serious play *Father's Day* in Chicago; Oliver Hailey, the author of the play, had asked her to play the part of the divorcée. Next, she starred with Hal Linden as she portrayed Katherine in *Kiss Me Kate*, which toured cities in the United States. In 1975, she took her cabaret act on the road once again. "Chita Plus Two" stirred audiences at the Grand Finale nightclub in New York and at Studio One in Los Angeles. After the conclusion of her tour, Rivera played Velma Kelly in *Chicago* in New York City; for that performance with Gwen Vernon and Jerry Orbach she earned a fourth Tony nomination. Although the musical was extremely successful and ran for more performances than even *West Side Story*, Rivera left the production to begin another tour with her cabaret act. She spent the latter part of the 1970s and the first year of the 1980s traveling throughout the United States, Canada, and Europe. For her act she was given an award for the best variety performance in 1980 by the National Academy of Concert and Cabaret Arts.

During the early 1980s Rivera continued to perform on stage and screen. In 1981 she starred in two musicals. One, *Hey Look Me Over*, received little attention. The other, *Bring Back Birdie*, the sequel to *Bye Bye Birdie*, was not received well; however, Rivera received her fifth Tony nomination for her dancing as Rosie in "A Man Worth Fighting For" and "Well, I'm Not." Rivera then appeared on television, on the PBS special *Broadway Plays Washington: Kennedy Center Tonight* in 1982, and in *Night of 100 Stars* that same year. In 1983 she portrayed the Queen in magician Doug Henning's *Merlin*; while the musical was unsuccessful, Rivera won another Tony nomination for her performance. From 1983 to 1984, she shined in the musical *Pippin*, which was produced for the cable television network Showtime.

Costars on Stage with Liza Minnelli

In the mid-1980's Rivera performed in two outstanding musicals and finally won a Tony Award. The first of these musicals, *The Rink*, was created specifically for Rivera by her friends Ebb and Kander. Rivera played Anna, a woman faced with closing a skating rink left to her by her husband. Starring the famous singer Liza Minnelli (as Anna's daughter Angel) along with Rivera, the musical tells the story of a strained mother/daughter relationship. Rivera and Minnelli had been friends since 1975, when Minnelli replaced Gwen Verdon for five weeks during the run of *Chicago*. Minnelli was quoted in *People* as saying of Rivera, "She's a force and she thinks I'm a force. It's like two grounding poles, and there's this electrical thing that goes VROOM." Rivera said of Minnelli in the same article, "I look at Liza and I see my Lisa." Partly because Rivera had just lost her mother, as Minnelli had lost her own mother, *Wizard of Oz* star Judy Garland, and partly because Minnelli had been inspired to become an actress in musicals after seeing Rivera perform in *Bye Bye Birdie*, the two performers sang and danced with more than their usual passion.

The Rink received some so-so reviews, but critics raved about Rivera. Richard Corliss commented on her performance in *Time* magazine: "Packing 30 years of Broadway savvy into the frame of a vivacious teen-ager, the 51-year-old entertainer could by now sell a song to the deaf; she commands the audience like a lion tamer with a whip snap in her walk; and, by the forces of magnetism and sheer will, she eats co-stars for breakfast." While one critic from *New York* magazine was less enthusiastic, he acknowledged Rivera's talent: "Miss Rivera's performances are knowing and efficiently executed. . . . [She] is an able singer, authoritative dancer, and clear enunciator, with an emotional range that has gradations as well as extremes, and a projection of gags with a certain zing—more vibration than punch—that is idiosyncratic and winning." The judges for the Antoinette Perry Awards recognized Rivera's achievements by awarding her a Tony as outstanding actress in a musical.

After releasing 1984's *The Rink*, an album recorded with Minnelli and the rest of the singers from the musical, and appearing in *Night of 100 Stars II* and in a televised coverage of *Macy's Thanksgiving Day Parade*, Rivera moved on to *Jerry's Girls*, a revue produced in New York City beginning in 1985, the year Rivera was inducted into the Television Academy Hall of Fame. Once again, Rivera was lauded. A critic for *New York* magazine commented, "the ageless Chita Rivera does some rousing things vocally and pedally." Unfortunately, Rivera suffered an accident that left her unable to finish the musical's run, and members of the chorus had to fill in for her. In April of 1986 she suffered another accident: as Rivera made a U-turn in New York City, her car collided with a taxi. Doctors predicted that she would fully recover in three to six months. Rivera had to work very hard to overcome the compound fractures in her left leg—although she was more than fifty years of age, she bounced back from her injuries.

In the late 1980s Rivera mixed television roles with theater performances, appearing in *The Mayflower Madam* and *Can-Can* on stage, and *Celebrating Gershwin* and *Broadway Sings: The Music of Jule Styne*, among other shows, on television. By 1992, although she was almost sixty years of age, Rivera starred in *Kiss of the Spider Woman*, a musical written by the team of Kander and Ebb. Based on the novel written by the late Manuel Puig, *Spider Woman* deals with the dilemmas of those involved in revolutionary movements, and while it speaks to the world, it is especially pertinent to situations in some Latin American countries. In the book and the play (which Puig helped develop), two prisoners share a cell; one of them describes the movie

musicals he has seen. In the play, these movie-musical scenes are acted out. Rivera, who portrayed a beautiful symbol of death, was challenged as she played such a complex character.

Rivera is worth watching in any vehicle in which she may be performing in the future. A high kick, a vivacious nod, and a soaring voice packed with emotion—all of these elements have combined in her to create an acting force who will long be remembered by those who have seen or heard her.

Sources:

Books

Contemporary Theatre, Film, and Television, Volume 8, Gale, 1990.

Periodicals

Atlanta Journal/Atlanta Constitution, March 13, 1988, sec. J, p. 2, sec. PM, p. 8.
Boston Globe, March 13, 1988. sec. PAR, p. 13; June 19, 1988, sec. A, p. 1; July 22, 1989, p. 6.
Chicago Tribune, April 8, 1986, sec. 1, p. 4; February 7, 1988, sec. 13, p. 14; February 10, 1988, sec. 2, p. 11.
Dance Magazine, May, 1984, pp. 146+.
Globe and Mail, (Toronto), February 1, 1992, p. C3.
Horizon, October, 1984, p. 56.
Los Angeles Times, December 4, 1988, sec. C, p. 5; December 15, 1988, sec. VI, p. 1.
Ms., December, 1984, p. 34.
New York, February 20, 1984, pp. 86-87; January 13, 1986, p. 50.
New York Times, November 26, 1989, sec. 1, p. 71.
People, March 5, 1984, pp. 61-64.
Time, February 7, 1983, p. 63; February 20, 1984, p. 84; April 21, 1986, p. 72.
Variety, June 5, 1985, p. 54; December 25, 1985, p. 62; June 4, 1986, p. 47; February 17, 1988, p. 180.

—*Sketch by Ronie-Richele Garcia-Johnson*

Mireya Robles
(1934-)
Poet, short story writer, novelist, critic

A native of Guantanamo, Cuba, Mireya Robles is a writer whose work reflects her feminist beliefs and strong sense of heritage. While few of her writings have thus far been translated into English, they have nevertheless attracted the attention of readers and critics in the United States, Latin America, Europe, and India.

Robles was born on March 12, 1934, the daughter of Antonio Robles and Adelaida Puertas. She came to the United States in 1957, shortly before Fidel Castro assumed power in Cuba, and became a naturalized citizen in 1962. Beginning in 1963, Robles was affiliated with Russell Sage College in New York as both a student and a teacher; she received her bachelor of arts degree in 1966 and served as an instructor in Spanish until 1973. She also began writing, initially experimenting with poetry and then moving on to short stories, articles, and opinion pieces.

Robles gained significant recognition for her poetry in 1971, when she won first prize from the Iberoamerican Poets and Writers Guild of New York for a collection entitled *Tiempo artesano,* later translated as *Time, the Artisan.* In short-story competitions held in 1973, her "Hidra" placed second with the *Silarus Literary Review,* and her "Trisagio de la muerte" placed second with the University of Maine at Orono. That same year, her work was reprinted in the anthology *Voces de mañana,* published by Harper. In 1974, L'Academie Internationale de Lutece awarded Robles a gold medal for several of her poems, stories, and essays. Also in 1974, "La relatividad de la realidad," was singled out by the Circulo de Escritores y Poetas Iberoamericanos de New York for first prize.

Robles's growing literary success coincided with several career moves. In 1973, she left Russell Sage College and joined the faculty of Briarcliff College in New York, serving as assistant professor of Spanish until her promotion a year later to associate professor. She remained at Briarcliff until 1977, when she decided to make writing her top priority.

Since the mid-1970s, Robles has produced another poetry collection, *En este aurora,* published in 1976, and a novel, *Hagiografia de Narcisa la Bella,* published in 1985 by Ediciones del Norte of Hanover, New Hampshire. She has also translated a number of works from English into Spanish, including the bilingual collection *Levantate, Chicano!/ Arise, Chicano!, and Other Poems* and *Selecciones,* both compiled by Angela de Hoyos. Robles has also contributed articles, reviews, stories, poems, and translations to a variety of journals, among them *International Poetry Review, Opinion, Poet,* and *Star West.*

Robles has not confined her interest in literature strictly to writing, however. In 1973, for example, she served as a panel member at the First Congress of Cuban Literature. She also attended the 1975 Conference on Women Writers from Latin America, the 1976 Congress of Inter-American Women Writers, and the 1978 Conference of Inter-American Women Writers. In addition, Robles has made personal appearances in South America and Europe, guested on television and radio programs in the United States and Spain, and given poetry readings in New York City.

Sources:

Books

Contemporary Authors, Volumes 81-84, Gale, 1979, p. 473.

—Sketch by Peg McNichol

Belgica Rodriguez
(1941-)
Art critic, museum curator, writer

As an internationally known art critic, museum director, and educator, Belgica Rodriguez strives to promote Latin American art. Her challenge, according to Rodriguez in a telephone interview with Luis Vasquez-Ajmac, is to work for artists from Latin America and to do whatever she can to put the development of Latin American art into history. Rodriguez's primary means of promoting Latin American art is through her writings as an art critic.

Born July 25, 1941, in Barcelona, Venezuela, and raised in Caracas, Rodriguez was one of eight children. Her mother, Belgica Campos de Rodriguez, raised her children alone, without assistance from family or friends. Despite a difficult childhood, Rodriguez was a happy, active child who had a liking for both the sciences and the arts. After finishing middle school in Caracas at age 17, Rodriguez first attended medical school, but was forced to leave her studies due to insufficient funds.

Rodriguez's first significant job in the arts began in 1964 when she became general secretary of the Ateneo de Caracas and supervisor of its gallery, where she remained for nine years. After her first year working at the art institute, Rodriguez began her studies in liberal arts. She completed a bachelor of arts in literature at the Central University of Caracas in 1969 and, three years later, pursued her interests in art history at the University of London, Morley College, obtaining a master of arts from the Courtauld Institute of Art at London University in 1976. Specializing in Latin American contemporary art, Rodriguez finished her doctorate in art history at the University of Paris I, La Sorbonne, in 1979. And upon completing her studies in Paris, she returned to Caracas to teach art history at the Central University of Venezuela, a position she still holds.

Since 1978, Rodriguez has been active in many national and international art events as both a member of juries and as a curator of important exhibitions. She is particularly proud of the exhibitions she has organized, including "Perspective from the Present," which was shown in Japan in 1991; "Culture of the Americas into the Nineties," held in connection with the international sculpture conference in 1990 in Washington, D.C.; and "Latin American Photography in the 1980s," also shown in Washington, D.C., in 1989.

Rodriguez is the author of published articles, catalogues, and books. Her most outstanding written works include *Breve historia de la escultura contemporanea en Venezuela* ("A Brief History of Contemporary Sculpture in Venezuela"), *La pintura abstracta en Venezuela 1945-1965* ("Abstract Painting in Venezuela, 1945-1965"), *Venezuela en la Bienal de Venecia* ("Venezuela in the Biennial of Venice"), and *Ramon Vazquez Brito: el hombre, el artista* ("Ramon Vazquez Brito: The Man, The Artist"). She contributes regularly to magazines abroad, including *Cologuio Arte* of Lisbon, Portugal, and *Arte en Colombia,* published in Bogota, Colombia, and is a columnist for *El Nacional,* as well as co-founder of the art magazine *Arte Plural de Venezuela.*

In March 1988, Rodriguez began her position as director of the Art Museum of the Americas, Organization of the American States, in Washington, D.C. She hopes that her reputation as an art critic and her connections as president of the International Association of Art Critics (AICA) will enable her to put the museum in the forefront internationally. At the same time, however, Rodriguez has not forgotten her main concern: writing about Latin American art. She is in the process of finishing a book on Central American art and continues to publish articles.

Sources:

Rodriguez, Belgica, telephone interview with Luis Vasquez-Ajmac, April 24, 1992.

—Sketch by Luis Vasquez-Ajmac

Gloría Rodríguez

provide low-income Hispanic mothers in Texas with basic parenting skills. As founder, executive director, and CEO of Avance—a Spanish word meaning "advance"—Rodriguez has helped thousands of minority women break the cycle of poverty, ignorance, and abuse through classes and programs designed to develop healthy relationships with their children, and to assist the women in taking control of their own lives through increased independence and enhanced self-esteem. As a result of years of dedication and steady fundraising efforts, Avance is regarded as a unique and phenomenal national success story among social service organizations. Considered a national model by the federal government, Avance is one of ten national family literacy models cited in the Barbara Bush Foundation for Family Literacy book, *First Teachers*. As Rodriguez told the *West Side Sun* in 1991, "My greatest accomplishment is that we have kept the mission alive against all odds . . . after 18 years Avance is still expanding and in the national forefront."

Rodriguez grew up in the predominantly Hispanic and economically disadvantaged West Side of San Antonio, Texas, where she was born on July 9, 1948. Her father, Julian Garza, died when she was two, leaving her mother, Lucy Villegas Salazar, to raise eight children alone. Because the family had only $96 a month to live on, Rodriguez and her sisters often sold their mother's homemade earrings at restaurants and drive-ins. At age nine she got a job cleaning a neighbor's house, and, when she entered Kennedy High School, she worked as a department store

Gloria Rodriguez
(1948-)
Executive director

Teaching parents how to raise their children was a philosophy unheard of in 1973, and yet Gloria Rodriguez took that idea and turned it into a lifelong mission to salesgirl. Rodriguez excelled in school and became a popular cheerleader and beauty queen who graduated in 1967 with a solid academic record.

Upon graduation, Rodriguez was undecided about her future. She wanted to be a teacher but had resigned herself to a secretarial position and applied for a clerical job at City Hall. "But my life was changed," she told the *San Antonio Light,* "when I got a letter from Our Lady of the Lake University saying I was one of 30 students selected for Project Teacher Excellence." The federally funded pilot program had been designed to give disadvantaged students an opportunity to study bilingual education in exchange for their returning to the community to teach. Rodriguez had competed against 300 applicants for one of the coveted spots. She almost lost her chance, she recalled in the *Light,* when her high school principal declined to give her a recommendation, stating that she was not "college material." Rodriguez persuaded the committee to give her a chance and set out to prove the principal wrong.

"I knew college would be difficult," Rodriguez told the *West Side Sun.* "Other college students were better prepared academically and could express themselves better in the English language." Rodriguez credits her grandfather, who came to live with the family after her father died, with fostering in her a profound spiritual awareness that helped her through troubling times at college and has remained an important facet of her everyday life. "The first two years of college," she told the *West Side Sun,* "I went daily to the chapel to pray. I vowed that if I did well, I would use my training to help others."

Discovers Link between Education and Parenting

Rodriguez completed her bachelor of arts degree in 1970 and received her master of education degree in 1973. She was hired by the Northside School District in San Antonio as its first bilingual teacher in 1970 and given a class of 35 first graders labeled "problem learners." She was warned by school administrators not to expect much success. Rodriguez wrote in the *San Diego Union:* "Initially I thought they had a 'language problem' and assumed they simply needed a bilingual teacher. But, I found, they were as deficient in Spanish as they were in English." Rodriguez drew on her own experiences in a family that was poor and yet managed to instill respect, independence, and determination in Rodriguez and her siblings. She knew that some children blossomed even in poverty, while others were crushed by it.

"It was like a light bulb went on: It all starts with the family," Rodriguez told the *Dallas Morning News.* "Children from a strong family had a better chance at surviving. Parents must be in the front line of preparing kids for success." From that point on, Rodriguez focused on the concept of parent education. Returning to college, she enrolled in a research class and began surveying the mothers of the children in her class. She discovered that even though the mothers valued education, they did not see themselves as educators and expected the schools to begin the process of education.

"Education begins at home and the first and most important teachers are the parents," Rodriguez told the *Express News.* "I was in the wrong place. I realized that parents needed assistance in this very important area." Coincidentally, two doctoral students from Cornell University had submitted a proposal to the Zale Foundation in Dallas to fund the first Avance in that city, and the company wanted to replicate the program in San Antonio after the program's highly successful first year. Rodriguez interviewed for the job, and was hired as its first—and only—director. The organization's first site was in the Mirasol Housing Projects, a few blocks from where Rodriguez was raised.

Launches Avance in San Antonio

Avance's beginnings were humble, to say the least. Rodriguez and three assistants went door to door in the projects to see who wanted to get off welfare and become better parents at the same time. A handful of skeptical women signed up, almost all high school dropouts and single mothers living on public assistance. Because the field was so new, Rodriguez and her associates designed the program from scratch, loosely modeling it after Houston's Parent Child Development Center, which had closed from a lack of funds. As Rodriguez studied factors contributing to child abuse and neglect, she found deep rooted problems. Isolation, depression, stress, hopelessness, and helplessness were recurring themes among the mothers. She discovered that the traditional image of a loving, close-knit, Hispanic family was often clouded by overwhelming economic and social conditions. "All of us have the potential to be warm, caring, and nurturing parents," Rodriguez told *Vista* magazine. "But environmental conditions are often adverse to growth . . . parents are under a great deal of stress, channeling all their energy into basic survival. Sometimes they take it out on their children."

Avance's nine-month program gives mothers and their preschool children a support system many have never known. Weekly three-hour sessions are geared to the mental, physical, and social health of the family in a clean, relaxed, safe, and friendly environment. While children play in supervised groups according to age, mothers construct simple toys and picture books to stimulate their child's learning environment and attend classes in child development, discipline techniques, problem-solving skills, nutrition, childhood diseases, and safety procedures. With their children, they take field trips, plant gardens, build friendships, and learn to communicate. Followup visits at home are videotaped, so mothers can watch themselves interacting with their children. "This is a prevention program," Rodriguez told *Vista.* "Before the 1970s, all treatment went to the child. But you can't separate the child from the environment, so you start with the family."

The Dallas Avance program folded after several years, but Rodriguez was determined that the San Antonio program would not meet the same fate. With grants from the City of San Antonio, the United Way, the Carnegie Corporation of New York, the Mailman Foundation, and other private and government sources along the way, Avance grew. In 1989, Avance received a $5 million grant from the Federal Head Start Bureau of the Administration for Children, Youth, and Families, allowing the agency to begin intensive prenatal services and continue them through the child's first five years.

Expands Avance Programs

In 1988, Rodriguez launched the groundbreaking Fatherhood Project, a program for Hispanic fathers, many of whom had been initially wary, indifferent, and occasionally hostile toward their wives' involvement with Avance. Rodriguez's goal with the pilot project was identical to the women's programs: Get the men involved in their children's education and in the process motivate them to pursue their own education and job skill training. Additional Avance programs include literacy training and job placement services for parents.

Rodriguez supervises a staff of 120 (many of them Avance graduates) and operates on a $2.7 million annual budget with six sites in San Antonio and one in Houston. Avance has attracted national attention from organizations hoping to duplicate its success. Visiting dignitaries include first lady Barbara Bush, Great Britain's Prince Charles, Texas governor Ann Richards, the Reverend Jesse Jackson, and Mexico's first lady Cecilia Occelli de Salinas, who plans to use Avance as a model for a program in Mexico. Expansion into the *colonias* of the Lower Rio Grande Valley in Texas began in 1992 and future programs are planned for Dallas, El Paso, and Puerto Rico.

In 1979, Rodriguez received her second masters degree from the University of Texas at San Antonio, and her Ph.D. in early childhood education from the University of Texas at Austin in 1991. From 1979 to 1982, she was project director for Project C.A.N. (Child Abuse and Neglect), a national demonstration research project. In 1988 Rodriguez was selected by *Hispanic* magazine as one of the 100 Most Influential National Hispanic Leaders. In 1990, she received the first Attitude award, presented by the Lifetime Cable Network show *Attitudes* for changing public attitudes toward family service. She has served as a charter board member of the National Family Resource Coalition, and as a consultant to the Harvard Family Research Project, Georgetown University, and the Yale Bush Center.

As an advocate for children, Rodriguez has participated in the White House Conference on Families, and present-

ed testimony at several congressional hearings. She serves on the Council of Governors Policy Advisors and the Carnegie Corporation of New York Task Force in Early Childhood Education. She is a frequent contributor to the *San Antonio Light* and *Hispanic Link News Service,* and is on the advisory boards of *La Familia de Hoy* magazine, the Council of Families in America, and Parent Action.

Rodriguez married engineer Salvador C. Rodriguez, Jr., on June 17, 1972, and has three children: Salvador Julian Rodriguez, born April 18, 1975; Steven Rene Rodriguez, born September 6, 1980; and Gloria Vanessa Rodriguez, born November 15, 1983.

Rodriguez never forgot her college-days vow to God to use her training to help others, and her responsibility to her ethnic roots in particular: "Some don't believe child abuse exists in the Hispanic community because traditionally we have close family units," she told the *Express-News.* "But that's a fallacy. Child abuse is everywhere—it knows no ethnic or economic barriers." Her faith in God and dedication to Avance's mission guide her in her goal to reach as many impoverished children as possible. She writes in the *San Antonio Light*: "We cannot afford to lose one child or one family to poverty and lack of education. . . . When one child gets hurt, eventually all children can get hurt. When one child hurts, we are all vulnerable."

Sources:

Periodicals

Business Week, February 20, 1989, p. 151.
Dallas Morning News, February 16, 1992, p. 41A.
Express-News (San Antonio), September 4, 1982, p. 1C; April 10, 1983, p. 6E; October 25, 1989; March 27, 1990, p. 11B; March 28, 1990, p. 13A; April 13, 1991, p. 1D; March 22, 1992, p. 1A.
Fort Worth Star Telegram, August 25, 1991.
New York Times, January 1, 1988, p. 16; January 25, 1988, p. 22; March 8, 1988, p. 8Y.
Our Kids (San Antonio), July, 1990, p. 28.
San Antonio Light, September 3, 1982, p. B3; January 13, 1988, p. B5; May 22, 1988, p. K1; October 2, 1988; October 24, 1988, p. F2; May 9, 1989, p. B2; May 14, 1989, p. F1; June 11, 1989, p. F1; June 12, 1989, p. E5; September 20, 1989; October 25, 1989; June 6, 1990; June 12, 1990; October 28, 1990; April 11, 1991, p. A1; January 18, 1992, p. A1; January 20, 1992, p. D1; March 8, 1992, p. A1; April 19, 1992; May 10, 1992; July 19, 1992, p. E1; September 3, 1992.
San Diego Union, November 26, 1989, p. C8.
San Juan Star (Puerto Rico), August 1, 1992.
Vista, May 20, 1990, p. 16.
West Side Sun (San Antonio), August 30, 1979, p. 38; October 5, 1989; May 16, 1991.

—Sketch by Julie Catalano

Helen Rodriguez
(1929-)
Doctor, community activist

Helen Rodriguez is a leading spokesperson on issues regarding women in medicine. A physician, Rodriguez was on the pediatrics faculty of Albert Einstein Medical School and an attending doctor at Lincoln Hospital in the Bronx for many years. She has developed many programs in ambulatory pediatrics that provided continuity for thousands of inner-city children. She has served on hundreds of task forces, consultant teams, and committees concerned with the development of children's health education. Some of her professional affiliations include the American Board of Pediatrics, National Resource Center for Children in Poverty, the Board of American Professional Society on the Abuse of Children, the American Public Health Association, the Center for Constitutional Rights, and many others.

Helen Rodriguez

Rodriguez was born in 1929 in New York City, but during the first years of her life she moved with her family back to Puerto Rico. Her family grew up on a coffee plantation, which belonged to Helen's grandparents in Cayey, Puerto Rico. Her grandparents, who migrated from Venezuela to Puerto Rico during the 1860s, were part of a wave of counterrevolutionary movements that have hit Puerto Rico throughout its history. During this time, Puerto Rico was thought of as a well safeguarded place and loyal to Spain. In a personal interview with this contributor, Rodriguez recalled the influence of Puerto Rico on her life and career. "My personal trajectory into work as a physician in social medicine is that of a girl who grew up in Puerto Rico in the thirties, New York in the forties, and who, as a woman, is still growing as a member of that half of our nation that lives in the United States. Puerto Ricans share with other rural peoples an intimacy with the land. No one is really more than a one-generation urban dweller. Our relatives are in the small towns, villages, and countryside; the mountains and shorelines are never totally lost from view."

In 1939, at the age of ten, Rodriguez moved back with her mother to New York City, where she spent the remainder of her formative years. She returned to her homeland for college, marriage, the beginning of her family, and then, after an interruption of several years, premedical and medical study. After completing her B.S. in 1957 at University of California, Berkeley, she graduated in 1960 from the University of Puerto Rico Medical School with the highest honors, first in her class. Rodriguez started her postgraduate training as conventional academic with specialty training in pediatrics and research credentials in neonatology.

Ironically, Medical school and pediatrics training left Rodriguez no time to spend with her own children. The work load was overwhelming, so she blocked out everything but her work. Taking care of the children became her husband's responsibility. In her 1988 interview, Rodriguez said that "it was totally a matter of survival." When asked in school about her parents' occupations, Rodriguez's six-year-old daughter Laura replied that her father was an economist and "my mother studies and sleeps."

After her residency, Rodriguez became aware of the marital problems she had been blocking out during the intense years of medical school. Her husband, who initially joked about her earnings, became increasingly irritated by each of her raises and her dedication to her work. Eventually the jokes stopped, and the marriage dissolved after sixteen years.

Discovers Conflict in Health Care System

As her career developed, Rodriguez was struck by the serious contradictions between a physician's dedication to quality health care for everyone and the reality of a dual-track health care system—one system for the rich and one for the poor. This disturbing situation led her to seek a new career in community medicine, which in 1970 brought her to Lincoln Hospital in the South Bronx; she became director of the Department of Pediatrics in an embattled hospital in an embattled neighborhood.

Her job at Lincoln turned out to be the most difficult and challenging work she had ever done. In an interview with Helen Benedict published in *Women Making History*, Rodriguez related her experience with passion and a touch of nostalgia, for at Lincoln she became caught up in a medical revolution—the introduction of patient and community participation in health care. She recalled that at Lincoln she learned to question and change the traditional patriarchal method of practicing medicine: the big, white doctor in the big, white coat who tells you what to do as if you were a child. But arriving at this position was, at times, painful, even for someone as radical as Rodriguez, for it was not easy to disregard her training that taught her to think of doctors as superior beings who always know best. In her 1988 interview with this contributor, Rodriguez recounted a 1976 lecture she gave at Barnard College in which she told the story of her first encounter as a patient with the American health care system. It was an experience in which she "was the unwitting control subject in an experiment involving women with first pregnancies, with and without emotional support." This cruel experience left her with a special feeling for the victims of health care. "My awareness grew out reality," she said in that lecture.

As a result of the Lincoln appointment, Rodriguez embarked upon a career change from which she says there was no turning back. "I felt I had literally crossed a bridge. I could never lead the quiet, respectable life of an academic again, nor did I want to." Recognizing that she was not fulfilling her aspirations at Lincoln Hospital, Rodriguez quit her directorship in 1974 and went to work for Lukes Roosevelt Hospital Center. At Roosevelt too, she encountered racial and sexist problems. In a hospital where sixty percent of the patients were Hispanics, she engaged in a battle for more bilingual social workers. Rodriguez remembers her white colleagues refusing to make eye contact in meetings with her, preferring instead to meet the eyes of her white female assistant. "Racism is the hardest nut to crack in this country," she said to a *Savvy* interviewer. "It will get cracked by people becoming conscious of their own need to change society."

From Roosevelt Hospital, Rodriguez went to the faculty of the Biomedical Program at City College in 1975. There her course in social medicine brought students in direct contact with the living contradictions of their future patients. Under her supervision, students walked through the neighborhood, conducted a census, observed the services that existed, and listened to the people of the community describe their situations. When these students ultimately completed their basic science and clinical rotations, they had an extra dimension of exposure and understanding, unique in medical education in United States.

However, there was a lot of hatred brought out by her appointment; students were advised not to study in the rotation because they wouldn't learn anything. But Rodriguez learned not to take the abuse personally. "As a physician, you cannot respond to hostility," she remarked in *Savvy*. "It is important to acknowledge people's anger without fanning it." In the midst of it all, Rodriguez was running a service with over 4,000 admissions and 100,000 outpatient visits each year.

For Rodriguez another major career hurdle was understanding the nature of leadership: "Leadership means encountering hostility," commented Rodriguez in her 1988 interview with this contributor. "Even if you are a beloved leader, there will be enemies. A lot of us women are unprepared not to be loved or even to be hated."

Rodriguez is a strong advocate of abortion rights and an advocate of the movement to combat illegal sterilization and sexual abuse of children. She devotes much time and energy to these two causes and others. There are not enough hours in the day for Helen, nor are there many multi-talented people like her. Rodriguez is sought out throughout the country for many speeches and public appearances, and she always responds to the demands from the public.

Some of Rodriguez's most precious moments come from spending time with her family, friends, and grandchildren. These people became vitally important to Rodriguez when she re-evaluated her life after learning that two of her closest friends had cancer. Today, she is busy taking care of herself and enjoying her family in California. For Helen, finding a degree of comfort in her work and life is crucial. She left her position with the Department of Health in New York City in 1990 so that she could spend more time with her grandchildren. She is now a pediatrician and consultant in health programming, giving speeches and lectures on Latino women, reproductive rights, and abortion issues to audiences around the country.

Sources:

Books

Benedict, Helen, "Helen Rodriguez-Trias, Mixing Pediatrics with Politics," *Women Making History, Conversations with Fifteen New Yorkers*, edited by Maxine Gold, New York City Commission on the Status of Women, 1984, pp. 83-84.

Periodicals

Savvy, September, 1981, pp. 40-43.

Other

Rodriguez, Helen, interview with Gloria Bonilla-Santiago, New York, NY, October, 29, 1988, tape recording, Cherry Hill, NJ.

—Sketch by Gloria Bonilla-Santiago

Lina S. Rodriguez
(1949-)
Judge

Lina S. Rodriguez

Lawyer Lina S. Rodriguez was appointed to the Arizona Superior Court as a Judge in 1984. The daughter of an Arizona copper miner, she had been the first of her family to graduate from college. Although she was determined to pursue her studies beyond high school, Rodriguez had not planned a judiciary career. "There were no lawyers or judges in Oracle, the small Arizona town where I grew up," she recalled in an interview with contributor Michelle Vachon. "I did not have a role model to inspire me. It took the off-hand remark of one of my 11th-grade teachers, Walter Wdowiak, to make me consider law. One day when we were discussing our future, Mr. Wdowiak told me that I would make a good lawyer. He advised me to look into it and never to forget that I could do anything I wanted to do. I followed his advice."

Rodriguez was born in Salt Lake City, Utah on September 27, 1949. A Mexican American, she grew up in Oracle, Arizona, with her five brothers and sisters, and attended San Manuel High School. A top student, she secured four scholarships, and in 1968 entered the University of Arizona in Tucson where she collected a number of honors. She received the university's Outstanding Freshman Scholarship Award in 1969, the Phi Kappa Phi Certificate of Merit in 1969, 1970, 1971, and 1972, and the Alpha Lambda Delta National Scholastic Honorary for 1969-1972. "My parents encouraged me to excel," she pointed out during her interview. "They were always there for me, offering support whenever I needed it." Rodriguez graduated with a B.A. in Education with an English major and a Spanish minor in 1972. She taught at the Apollo Junior High School in Tucson for two years, and in 1974 enrolled at the University of Arizona's College of Law to obtain her law degree. After winning the 1977 Perry Writing Award—a statewide competition for law students—she graduated in 1977 and was admitted to the Arizona State Bar a few months later.

Fulfills Her Dream of Becoming a Lawyer

Immediately following her Bar examination, Rodriguez joined the Tucson law firm of Bilby, Shoenhair, Warnock & Dolph, where she had worked as a law clerk during her legal studies. "It was difficult at first," she admitted in her interview. "It was like being in a foreign country with a language of its own. I had to learn to speak 'legalese.' Also, since I was the first female attorney at the firm, some clients treated me as a secretary. But the firm was truly behind me. My colleagues even gave up their membership to a men-only private club because I was barred from it. The club later changed its policy and now allows women members." A few years later, Rodriguez's colleagues suggested that she apply for a Superior Court judgeship, which she did. She was nominated in 1983 and sworn in as judge of the Arizona State Superior Court on January 3, 1984. "The firm told me that I would be welcome back if I wanted to return to private practice. But I love being a judge—it suits me." She is assigned to the Pima County Superior Court, Division One, in Tucson, Arizona.

In addition to her extensive judicial activities—she is a member of the Arizona Board of Pardons and Paroles search committee, the Arizona Supreme Court permanent judicial performance committee, and chairs the jury management committee of the Council on Judicial Administration—Rodriguez participates in numerous community organizations. She sits on the Tucson Committee on Foreign Relations, the Diocese of Tucson issues committee, and the advisory boards of the Tucson Association for Child Care and Resources for Women. She also frequently addresses student audiences. "I tell them to work hard from the very beginning," she explained in her interview. "They will need good high school grades to secure scholarships. If they are thinking of a career in law, I tell them to get in touch with a judge or a lawyer and learn about the profession before making a decision. It's a very competitive field."

A founding fellow of the Arizona Bar Foundation, Rodriguez belongs to national, state and county Bar associations and to the Arizona Law Women's Association. She is also the recipient of numerous awards, including the 1988 Woman of the Year Award from the Hispanic Professional Action Committee and the 1988 Young Women's Christian Association Woman on the Move Award for her outstanding work in government. In 1986, she was recognized by the National Council of Hispanic Women for High Achievement. Married to Lloyd E. Graves since 1990, she gave birth to Logan Rodriguez Graves on June 16, 1991. She lives with her husband and her son in Tucson, Arizona.

Sources:

Periodicals

San Manuel Miner, December 21, 1988, p. 1.

Other

Rodriguez, Lina S., interview with Michelle Vachon, July 17, 1992.

—Sketch by Michelle Vachon

Patricia Rodriguez
(1944-)
Artist, educator

Since her first display in 1970, Patricia Rodriguez has seen her work appear in more than 90 group exhibitions and in nearly 12 solo shows. The Arts Council of the Museum of Modern Art in New York City and the Mexican Museum in San Francisco, California, have acquired her work for their permanent collections. The Department of Art of the University of California at Berkeley keeps a slide archive of her pieces. In 1988, a commentator for the Mexican Museum described her creations in the exhibit "Cajas: Containers of Remembrance and Belief," noting that "Rodriguez is a master of intuitive composition, devising intricate relationships seemingly at random but always directed in their discourse. Her compositions present myth in strange shrines where legend and the unconscious work together." In the program "Salad Bar," an exhibition held at the Bayview Opera House in San Francisco in 1990, Rodriguez described her work presented there as "very much a part of my cultural heritage. Also known as 'Nichos' in Mexico, they are a synthesis of Mayan, Aztec, and the Catholic church. . . . I have always believed that my works are a vehicle where spiritual messages are expressed. Each construction has its own self consciousness that is a personal, spiritual, and social-feminine statement."

Born in Marfa, Texas, on November 8, 1944, Rodriguez lived with her grandparents until she was seven years old. In an interview with Michelle Vachon, she explained that she "became interested in art at the age of nine or ten. I loved making art in church, and I was lucky to be encouraged by the Baptist church programs for children. I remember having wonderful role models who really cared about the children in the community, and helped us build our self-esteem." The year she turned 12, her Mexican American parents became migrant workers and traveled with their children throughout Texas, Arizona, New Mexico, and California. They settled in Oxnard, California, where Rodriguez finally attended school full time. "By then I was 13 years old, and I could not read nor write," she assessed. "They kept me in sixth grade doing art projects and bulletin boards to keep me busy and out of trouble. How I made it through high school, I'll never know. But I loved to learn and I loved discovery and life."

One of her junior high school teachers incited her to pursue her art studies. "He saw something in my ability," she recalled. "But my parents did not understand why I would be interested in art when I could be a secretary or a manager or adopt any other profession that would inspire respect." Despite her parents' concern, Rodriguez took her teacher's advice. She received her bachelor of fine arts degree from the San Francisco Art Institute in 1972 and her master's degree in painting from the Sacramento State University in 1975. She also secured her California Community College Instructor Credential in 1977 and her English-as-a-Second-Language Certificate of Authorization for Service in civics, arts, and humanities in 1991. According to Rodriguez, teaching constitutes an integral part of an artist's career. "Art plays an important role in the Hispanic community," she observed. "It serves as the embodiment of our history and cultural values that should be transmitted to our children in order to give them self-esteem and the courage to succeed professionally. I regularly see Chicano artists teaching children and teenagers, working with handicapped people and senior citizens, and in doing so bringing our Hispanic heritage to life."

Develops Course on Chicano Art History

Rodriguez has taught art since the beginning of her exhibiting career. While she served as art instructor at the University of California at Berkeley, she became the first Chicano art instructor to be featured in art books and magazines while teaching in the University of California system. During her five years with the university, she developed the first course on Chicano art history—the class has been used as a model for subsequent courses at the University of California at Los Angeles and at the University of Texas at Austin.

Of all her exhibitions, Rodriguez fondly remembers two as having been especially rewarding. The first—entitled "The Fifth Sun, Contemporary/Traditional Chicano & Latino Art"—took place at the University Art Museum at

Berkeley in 1977. "I spent a whole year meeting the museum curator once a week to insure that the exhibit would respect Chicano artists' wishes," she stressed to Vachon. "We negotiated and discussed to determine what would give the show power. The museum eventually allocated enough money to produce a fine paperback catalogue. The opening was a total success: 15,000 persons attended, and we received extensive media coverage."

The other exhibition that stands out in her mind was a solo show that she dedicated to her mother and held at the Inter-Cultural Center Gallery at Sonoma State University's Student Union in Sonoma, California. "As my career progressed, my mother became very proud of my accomplishments," she admitted. "She even quietly bragged about me." That exhibition occurred in 1990 shortly after her mother's death. Despite her successes, Rodriguez believes that Chicano artists still have difficulty being included in museums' mainstream exhibitions and publications. "We pay for these public institutions with our tax dollars; therefore we should have equal voice and opportunities. Up-and-coming Chicano artists should be prepared to obtain their rightful places in museums. As an art instructor, I have seen young Chicanos much more aggressive and uninhibited about their future than I was. So I feel that there is hope. Young Chicano artists can always reach to us for moral support and direction. We are also still young and strange."

Sources:

Books

Lippard, Lucy R., *Mixed Blessings: New Art in a Multicultural America,* Pantheon Books, 1990, p. 54.

Other

Rodriguez, Patricia, interview with Michelle Vachon, October 5, 1992.

—Sketch by Michelle Vachon

Rita M. Rodriguez
(1942-)
Director, Export-Import Bank of United States

Cuban-born Rita M. Rodriguez never dreamed she would hold such an important position as director of the Export-Import Bank of the United States. She told *Intercambios Femeniles,* "I never really thought about it nor did I seek it out. An executive search firm found me and,

the next thing I knew, I got a call from the White House." When formally confirmed in her position by the U.S. Senate on October 1, 1982, Rodriguez became one of five directors of the bank. The Export-Import Bank is an independent agency of the United States under the executive branch.

Rodriguez is the daughter of Tomas Rodriguez and Adela Mederos. She was born in Oriente, Cuba, on September 6, 1942, and came to the United States when she was fifteen. She holds a bachelor's degree in business administration from the University of Puerto Rico, and both a master's degree in business administration and a Ph.D. from the New York University Graduate School of Business. While completing requirements for her advanced degrees, Rodriguez worked as a lecturer in economics and as a research assistant for the National Bureau of Economic Research.

Before accepting her banking position, Rodriguez had a highly-successful academic career. When she was hired to teach at the Harvard Business School in 1969, she was the first female to ever do so. She started at Harvard as an assistant professor of business administration, a post she held from 1969 to 1974. In 1974, she became an associate professor, remaining at Harvard until 1978 when she accepted a position as professor of international finance at the University of Illinois.

Appointed Director of Export-Import Bank

Her coming to the United States, her career, and her marriage to E. Eugene Carter on January 7, 1972, all contributed to making Rodriguez a well-traveled individual. She has resided in Florida, Puerto Rico, New Jersey, and Massachusetts, eventually moving to Chicago in the late 1970s to be with her husband after he accepted a position there. Subsequently, she spent the first year of her present appointment commuting between Washington, D.C., and Chicago, until her husband discovered a career opportunity in the nation's capital. Subsequently, they moved to the nation's capital with their now teenage daughter, Adela-Marie.

Rodriguez is the author of several works written during her years as an university professor. With Heinz Riehl, she authored *Foreign Exchange Markets: A Guide to Foreign Currency Operations,* published in 1977, and *Foreign Exchange and Money Markets,* published in 1983. In 1980, her *Foreign Exchange Management in U.S. Multinationals* was published and, in 1984, her *International Financial Management,* written with her husband, E. Eugene Carter, appeared. Rodriguez's *The Export-Import Bank at Fifty,* published the year she took her directorial position, tells the story of the institution.

The Export-Import Bank of the United States, known as Eximbank, was created in 1934 by an executive order. Although previously a governmental agency, in 1945 it was incorporated as an independent entity. Its chief purpose is to improve U.S. trade with other countries by providing the necessary loans, guarantees, and insurance to promote economic exchange. Rodriguez's position as director is a presidential appointment and is based on continuing support from the executive branch. She meets with other members of the board of the directors of the bank on a regular basis to discuss questions of bank policy.

Sources:

Books

Who's Who among Hispanics, 1992-93 edition, Gale, 1992.

Periodicals

Intercambios Femeniles, spring, 1987, p. 19.

—*Sketch by Marian C. Gonsior*

Rodríguez Remeneski, Shirley
    See **Remeneski, Shirley Rodríguez**

Linda Ronstadt

Linda Ronstadt
(1946-)
Singer

Few performers in any medium have proven more daring than Linda Ronstadt, a singer who has made her mark in such varied styles as rock, country, operetta, and mariachi. In the 1970s Ronstadt churned out a veritable stream of pop hits and heartrending ballads that delighted country and rock fans alike. Just when she seemed pegged as a pop idol, however, she turned her talents to opera—in *The Pirates of Penzance* and *La Bohème*—and to torch songs accompanied by the Nelson Riddle Orchestra. Almost every Ronstadt experiment has met with critical acclaim and, surprisingly, with fan approval and hefty record sales. *Newsweek* contributor Margo Jefferson attributes this success to Ronstadt's voice, which she describes as having "the richness and cutting edge of a muted trumpet." Jefferson concludes, "In a field where success is often based on no more than quick-study ventriloquism, Linda Ronstadt stands out. She is no fad's prisoner; her compelling voice wears no disguises."

Time reporter Jay Cocks calls Ronstadt "gutsy," "unorthodox," and a challenger of creeds. As the singer tells it,

she developed a habit of rebellion early in life and stuck to it with singleminded determination. Ronstadt was born and raised in Tucson, Arizona, the daughter of a hardware store owner who loved to sing and play Mexican music— she later made an album of his favorite songs. Ronstadt herself enjoyed harmonizing with her sister and two brothers—she was proud when she was allowed to take the soprano notes. At the age of six she decided she wanted to be a singer, and she promptly lost all interest in formal schooling. Aaron Latham, a classmate at Tucson's Catalina High School, wrote in *Rolling Stone* that by her teens Ronstadt "was already a larger-than-life figure with an even larger voice. She didn't surprise anyone by becoming a singer. Not that anyone expected her fame to grow to the dimensions of that voice. But the voice itself was no secret."

Ronstadt attended the University of Arizona briefly, dropping out at eighteen to join her musician boyfriend, Bob Kimmel, in Los Angeles. With Kimmel and guitar player Kenny Edwards, Ronstadt formed a group called the Stone Poneys, a folk-rock ensemble reminiscent of the Mamas and the Papas and the Lovin' Spoonful. The Stone Poneys signed a contract with Capitol Records in 1964 and released a single, "Some of Shelley's Blues," in early 1965. Their only hit as a group came in 1967, when "Different Drum," a cut from their second album, made the charts. By that time, intense touring, drug abuse, and a series of disappointing concert appearances as openers for the Doors caused the Stone Poneys to disband. Ronstadt told

Rolling Stone that her band was "rejected by the hippest element in New York as lame. We broke up right after that. We couldn't bear to look at each other."

Embarks on Solo Career after Breakup of Stone Poneys

Ronstadt fulfilled her Capitol recording contract as a solo performer, turning out some of the first albums to fuse country and rock styles. On *Hand Sown . . . Home Grown* (1969) and *Silk Purse* (1970), Ronstadt teamed with Nashville studio musicians for an ebullient, if jangly, country sound. The latter album produced her first solo hit, the sorrowful "Long, Long Time." In retrospect, Ronstadt has called her debut period the "bleak years." She was plagued by the stresses of constant touring, difficult romantic entanglements, cocaine use, and critical indifference—and to make matters worse, she suffered from stage fright and had little rapport with her audiences. "I felt like a submarine with depth charges going off all around me," she told *Time.* Ronstadt eluded failure by moving to Asylum Records in 1973 and by engaging Peter Asher as her producer and manager. Asher collaborated with her on her first bestselling albums, *Don't Cry Now* and the platinum *Heart Like a Wheel.*

Heart Like a Wheel was the first in a succession of million-selling albums for Ronstadt. By the mid-1970s, with hits such as "When Will Be Loved?," "Desperado," "You're No Good," "Blue Bayou," and "Poor, Poor Pitiful Me," the singer had established herself as rock's most popular female star. Stephen Holden describes Ronstadt's rock style in a *Vogue* magazine profile. Her singing, according to Holden, combined "a tearful country wail with a full-out rock declamation. But, at the same time, her purity of melodic line is strongly rooted in folk." A *Time* contributor elaborates: "She sings, oh Lord, with a rowdy spin of styles—country, rhythm and blues, rock, reggae, torchy ballad—fused by a rare and rambling voice that calls up visions of loss, then jiggles the glands of possibility. The gutty voice drives, lilts, licks slyly at decency, riffs off Ella [Fitzgerald], transmogrifies Dolly Parton, all the while wailing with the guitars, strong and solid as God's garage floor. A man listens and thinks 'Oh my, yes,' and a woman thinks, perhaps, 'Ah, well. . . .'"

A leap from rock to operetta is monumental; few voices could make it successfully. In 1981 Ronstadt astonished the critics and her fans by trilling the demanding soprano part of Mabel in a Broadway production of *The Pirates of Penzance.* Her performance led *Newsweek* correspondent Barbara Graustark to comment, "Those wet, marmot eyes turn audiences on like a light bulb, and when her smoky voice soars above the staff in a duet with a flute, she sends shivers down the spine." Ronstadt's appearance as Mimi in *La Bohème* off-Broadway in 1984 was received with less enthusiasm by the critics, but the singer herself expressed no regrets about her move away from rock. "When I perform rock 'n' roll," she told *Newsweek,* "it varies between antago-

nistic posturing and to-the-bones vulnerability. I wanted to allow another facet of my personality to emerge. . . . I've gained confidence in knowing that now . . . I can handle myself in three dimensions, and even if never use my upper extension except in the bathtub, I've gained vocal finish."

That "vocal finish" was applied to yet another Ronstadt experiment—three albums of vintage torch songs, *What's New?, Lush Life,* and *For Sentimental Reasons,* featuring the Nelson Riddle Orchestra. Jay Cocks calls *What's New?* a "simple, almost reverent, rendering of nine great songs that time has not touched. . . . No one in contemporary rock or pop can sound more enamored, or winsome, or heartbroken, in a love song than Linda Ronstadt. Singing the tunes on *What's New,* or even just talking about them, she still sounds like a woman in love." Holden writes, "One of the charms of Ronstadt's torch singing is her almost girlish awe in the face of the songs' pent-up emotions. Instead of trying to re-create another era's erotic climate, she pays homage to it with lovely evenhanded line readings offered in a spirit of wistful nostalgia." Holden adds that *What's New* "revitalized Ronstadt's recording career by selling over two million copies, and, coincidentally, defined for her generation the spirit of a new 'eighties pop romanticism.'" Ronstadt also earned several prestigious awards for her 1986 album *Trio,* a joint country music venture with Dolly Parton and Emmylou Harris.

Records Album Reflecting Mexican Heritage

More recent Ronstadt projects have departed even further from the pop-rock vein. In 1987 the singer released *Canciones de mi padre,* an album of *mariachi* songs that her father used to sing. "When we were little, we spoke Spanish at home, but the schools pounded it out of us pretty early," she told James Brady in *Parade.* "There was an antibilingual attitude then. So my Spanish is very rudimentary—child's Spanish, really." *Newsweek* critic David Gates calls the work "Ronstadt's best record to date," noting that "its flawless production is the only concession to Top 40 sensibilities. And Ronstadt . . . has found a voice that embodies not merely passion and heartache, but a womanly wit as well." *Mas canciones,* Ronstadt's follow-up to *Canciones de mi padre,* appeared in 1991. Also in 1991 Ronstadt starred in *La Pastorela,* an updated version of a traditional Mexican holiday play, aired on PBS's *Great Performances.* "I loved the idea of doing a work particular to Mexico," she told Edna Gunderson in *TV Guide.* "*La Pastorela* is not found in Cuba or Venezuela. People tend to lump Hispanic cultures together. They think Ricky Ricardo would have been happy dancing the tango in a mariachi band."

While Ronstadt will not rule out recording more rock, she seems far more fascinated by other forms and other, more remote, historical periods. Gates finds the raven haired artist "the most adventurous figure in American popular music," concluding that, at the very least, Ronstadt is "commendable in her refusal to bore herself."

Sources:

Books

The Illustrated Encyclopedia of Country Music, Harmony Books, 1977.

Stambler, Irwin, *The Encyclopedia of Pop, Rock, and Soul,* St. Martin's, 1974.

Periodicals

down beat, July, 1985.

Esquire, October, 1985.

Newsweek, October 20, 1975; April 23, 1979; August 11, 1980; December 10, 1984; February 29, 1988.

Parade, December 22, 1991, p. 22.

People, October 24, 1977; April 30, 1979.

Rolling Stone, December 2, 1976; March 27, 1977; October 19, 1978; November 2, 1978; August 18, 1983.

Saturday Review, December, 1984.

Time, February 28, 1977; March 22, 1982; September 26, 1983.

TV Guide, December 21, 1991.

Vogue, November, 1984.

Washington Post Magazine, October 9, 1977.

—*Sketch by Anne Janette Johnson*

Margarita Roque
(1946-)
Political activist

Margarita Roque, the current executive director of the Congressional Hispanic Caucus, always knew she would work in the political arena in some capacity to improve the inequities experienced by minorities. Often feeling like a victim of discrimination while growing up, Roque was determined to make life better, if not for herself, then certainly for her children and grandchildren.

A Mexican American native of El Paso, Texas, Roque was born November 13, 1946, and raised in a small farming community outside El Paso where 99 percent of the population was Hispanic. There, her parents José Matias Roque and Dolores Rincon owned a farm and ran a small grocery store. With the death of her father, Roque began working at age 11 to help her mother and six siblings make ends meet.

Roque's childhood was characterized by negative experiences, particularly in terms of her educational upbringing.

She recalls vividly the disparity of resources between her poor farming community's high school and those available at El Paso High School, which she desperately wanted to attend. She also remembers the overt discrimination she received from teachers who judged her unfairly in comparison to other white classmates.

After graduating from high school in Castillo, Roque entered the University of Texas—El Paso, but soon dropped out, disappointed with her experience. She married young and moved to the Washington metropolitan area with her family in 1971. A later move to Gaithersburg, Maryland, became a turning point in Roque's life. She divorced, had her first taste of local politics, and re-entered college at the age of 37. After listening to a radio announcement one day about Hood College, something inside Roque told her that it was time to complete her education. She enrolled in Hood College in Frederick, Maryland, majored in political science, and graduated in 1984.

Career Dreams Realized

Roque began her career in Washington, D.C., as an intern for Senator Paul Sarbanas in 1983. She went on to work with the Churches' Committee for Voter Registration and the Women's Vote project. But, technically, Roque's first foray into political activism began when she moved to a problem-ridden neighborhood in Gaithersburg. Organizing neighbors to write their city council, Roque was ultimately the one selected by the group to meet with the council members about their concerns. "I was always the trouble maker. If you don't speak out about your problems, you're not going to get results," relates Roque in a telephone interview with Luis Vasquez-Ajmac.

For the past six years, Roque has been the executive director of the Congressional Hispanic Caucus, a bipartisan organization consisting of 13 Hispanic members of Congress and 84 associate members of the House and Senate. On a day-to-day basis, Roque organizes and implements an agenda of policy that Caucus members have put together and provides information to constituents. It is her duty to see that the Caucus remains dedicated to advancing issues affecting Hispanic Americans in the United States through the legislative process. Roque expects the Caucus to grow and sees the growth of the Hispanic community as one of the challenges government must face during the next decade. Although Roque believes that Hispanics have made progress, she explains in her interview: "We have a long way to go. . . . To say there is no discrimination today certainly is not the real world."

In addition to working at the Hispanic Congressional Caucus, Roque also serves in an ombuds capacity for education issues in the Hispanic community. During her free time she enjoys seeing her three children and grandchildren, and getting together with the Hispanic community, "sharing good food, good talk and music."

Sources:

Roque, Margarita, telephone interview with Luis Vasquez-Ajmac, July 29, 1992.

—Sketch by Luis Vasquez-Ajmac

Ileana Ros-Lehtinen
(1952-)
U.S. Congresswoman

Being first has become something that Ileana Ros-Lehtinen does quite well. In 1982, she became the first Cuban-born female to be elected to the Florida state legislature. Seven years later, after a successful career as a state legislator, she won a special election held on August 29, 1989, to fill the seat left vacant by the death of long-time Miami political powerhouse Claude D. Pepper. A few days after her victory, Ros-Lehtinen was sworn in as the first Cuban American, as well as the first Hispanic woman, ever elected to the U. S. Congress. "As the first Cuban-American elected to Congress," *Boston Globe* commentator Chris Black noted, "she also will be likely to become one of the most visible, most quoted Cuban-born politicians in the nation."

Ros-Lehtinen (pronounced ross-LAY-teh-nin), who is known as Lily to her family and friends, was born July 15, 1952, in the Cuban capital city of Havana, to Enrique Emilio Ros, a certified public accountant, and Amanda Adato Ros. In 1960, she and her family—including her parents and a brother—fled to Miami from Cuba, a year after political leader Fidel Castro's revolution rocked that tiny island nation. Almost immediately, Ros-Lehtinen's parents became involved with other recent refugees in plotting the downfall of the Castro regime. But after the failure of an invasion attempt by anti-Castro forces at Cuba's Bay of Pigs in 1961, the possibility of returning to Cuba became more and more remote, and Ros vowed to raise his children as loyal Americans. His wife recalled in a *Boston Globe* article how strongly her husband felt about his decision: "He said you cannot educate two kids without a flag and a country. This is going to be their country and they have to love it."

Ros-Lehtinen earned her associate of arts degree from Miami-Dade County Community College in 1972 and her bachelor of arts degree in English from Miami's Florida International University in 1975. Eleven years later she completed requirements for a master of science in educa-

Ileana Ros-Lehtinen

tional leadership from the same institution. Since then, she has continued her studies as a doctoral candidate in educational administration at the University of Miami. Before embarking on her political career, Ros-Lehtinen worked as a teacher and was principal for ten years at Eastern Academy, a school she founded. Her love of politics came as a legacy from her father who had concentrated so much of his life on the hope of restoring democracy to his native land. He is said to have been the chief architect of her political career and was at her side when she announced her victory in her U.S. Congressional race.

Launches Political Career as State Representative

Ros-Lehtinen's first elected office was in the Florida state legislature, where she served as a representative from 1982 to 1986 and as a state senator from 1986 to 1989. While in the state legislature she met her future husband, Dexter Lehtinen, who was also at the time a member of that legislative body. Although early in her career Ros-Lehtinen showed a tendency to focus on issues of a global nature rather than on those affecting her constituents in a personal way, Black wrote in the *Boston Globe* that Ros-Lehtinen eventually became "a politician of the opposite extreme, a pragmatic legislator focused almost exclusively on the most parochial of issues. One Miami political reporter now describes her as 'a pothole kind of legislator,' much more concerned with the specific needs of individuals and businesses in her district than broader changes in public policy."

When Ros-Lehtinen resigned her seat in the state senate shortly before the August 3, 1989, primary, it appeared—much to the dismay of the Miami area's non-Hispanic voters—that the race to fill Florida's 18th congressional district seat might be a head-to-head battle between two Cuban American women. Early favorites included Ros-Lehtinen on the Republican side and Miami City Commissioner Rosario Kennedy for the Democrats. However, the opponent who emerged from the primary was Gerald F. Richman, an attorney, a former president of the Florida Bar Association, and a Jew. The Ros-Lehtinen-Richman campaign was marked by deep cultural and racial tensions and came to be one of the most ethnically divided congressional races in Florida's history. A highlight of an otherwise brutal contest came from President George Bush who not only gave Ros-Lehtinen his personal endorsement, but made a special trip to Miami to deliver a speech on her behalf.

Most of the controversy surrounding the campaign grew out of a response to Republican party chair Lee Atwater's announcement that since the district was 50 percent Hispanic, electing a Cuban American to the seat was of utmost importance. Richman, the Democratic candidate, was quoted in a *Time* article as having countered Atwater's claim with the assertion, "This is an American seat." Cuban American and other Hispanic voters were deeply offended by Richman's reply and the implication it carried that Hispanics are not truly Americans. Spanish-speaking radio stations in the Miami area assured their listeners that a vote for Richman would be the equivalent of voting for Castro. Another source of division during the campaign came from the National Republican Congressional Committee (NRCC) which, according to reports in *National Review,* attempted to run Ros-Lehtinen's campaign from Washington. William McGurn explained the problem with a quote from a Republican insider: "The NRCC treated this district like a colony. . . . Their attitude was that they knew Florida's 18th better than the people who live here."

Wins Turbulent Race for U.S. Congressional Seat

Triumphing over the bitterness of the campaign, Ros-Lehtinen emerged victorious from the race, capturing 53 percent of the vote. Post-election analysis showed that voters largely seemed to cast their ballot based on their ethnic heritage: 96 percent of blacks and 88 percent of non-Hispanic whites voted for Democratic candidate Richman; while 90 percent of Hispanics, who voted in record numbers, voted for Ros-Lehtinen. In her victory speech, the new congresswoman maintained that she would work to heal the wounds caused by the campaign. "It's been a terrible divisive campaign," she told the *New York Times.* "But now it's time for healing. I know that there are a lot of people out there who feel alienated." Ros-Lehtinen's win was also seen as a victory for the Republican party because the seat she had captured had belonged to the Democrats for 26 years. When Ros-Lehtinen's seat came up for

election in 1990, she received 60 percent of the vote and a decisive mandate to continue her political career.

During her tenure, Ros-Lehtinen has been a member of the Foreign Affairs committee and has served on its subcommittee on Human Rights and International Organizations as well as its subcommittee on Western Hemisphere affairs. She has also been involved with the subcommittee on Employment and Housing, where she is the ranking minority member. In an article focusing on Hispanic political candidates, which appeared in *Hispanic,* Anna Maria Arias described Ros-Lehtinen's stand on issues important to voters in her district. According to Arias, Ros-Lehtinen supports bilingual education, is "in favor of a seven-day waiting period for the purchasing of guns, and voted for a bill that would improve veterans' benefits." Ros-Lehtinen is also vehemently anti-abortion, except to save a woman's life, favors a constitutional amendment to ban flag burning, and advocates the death penalty for convicted organizers of drug rings.

True to her ethnic roots, Ros-Lehtinen remains a staunch adversary of Castro and an equally outspoken champion of a free Cuba. In 1990, she expressed her strong opposition to South-African leader Nelson Mandela's visit to Florida during his eight-city tour of the U. S., a trip which engendered a virtual hero's welcome for him in the other states to which he traveled. While there seemed to be a near unanimous outpouring of praise for Mandela and his efforts to end apartheid (racial segregation) in his native country, Ros-Lehtinen felt she could not honor a man who had not only publicly embraced such advocates of violent revolution as the Palestine Liberation Organization's Yasser Arafat and Libya's Muammar Gaddafi, but who also was on record as a strong supporter of Castro. She pointed out that Cuban Americans longing for a return to democracy in their country of origin could not forget that members of Mandela's African National Congress had received military training on Cuban soil.

Voices Opposition to 1991 Pan American Games

Ros-Lehtinen again spoke out against Castro when she condemned participation in the Pan American Games, an Olympics-like international sports competition, held in Cuba during the first two weeks of August in 1991. She argued that Castro's bid to have the Games in his country was merely a ploy to bolster Cuba's ailing economy and to provide ready propaganda supporting his regime. In a *Christian Science Monitor* article on the topic, the congresswoman wrote: "Castro has his circus for now, but despite the fanfare of the Pan American Games, he is an anachronism in a world that values democracy and freedom. It will not be long till he follows the path of the dinosaurs into extinction. Cuba's economic crisis is so desperate that Castro would shave his own beard if that would give him the American dollars which he holds so dear."

The ethnic pride Ros-Lehtinen inherited from her father remains strong in the politician, and perhaps because of this, she is very conscious of her position as a role model for Hispanics. She also values the achievements made by other Hispanic women, and when presented with a special award from *Hispanic* magazine in 1992, she praised their successes. "[The Hispanic woman] is an accomplished writer, or a computer programmer, or an attorney, or a doctor, as well as a loving wife and mother." She also believes that Hispanic women will continue to make contributions in the future. "Now, more than ever," she wrote in *Vista*, "we Hispanic women must re-energize and refocus our efforts to realize the vast potential that lies within our grasp."

Sources:

Periodicals

Boston Globe, August 31, 1989, p. 3.
Christian Science Monitor, August 9, 1991, p. 18.
Hispanic, September, 1990, p. S5; October, 1990, p. 26; August, 1992, p. 28.
Ladies' Home Journal, November, 1991, p. 182.
National Catholic Reporter, April 19, 1991, p. 1.
National Review, November 24, 1989, p. 39.
New York Times, August 31, 1989, p. A16.
Time, September 11, 1989, p. 31.
Vista, February 4, 1992, pp. 6, 22.
Washington Post, July 30, 1989, p. A4; August 17, 1989, p. A4.

—*Sketch by Marian C. Gonsior*

Lucille Roybal-Allard

Lucille Roybal-Allard
(1941-)
U.S. Congresswoman

Lucille Roybal-Allard is the first woman of Mexican American ancestry to be elected to the United States Congress. She became the 33rd Congressional District's representative in November 1992. The oldest daughter of a political family, Roybal-Allard's father is the highly esteemed California Congressman Edward Roybal. After 30 years of Congressional service, Ed Roybal, often called the dean of California Latino legislators, retired in 1992. Congresswoman Roybal-Allard, a Democrat, previously served in the California State Assembly, representing the 56th District from 1987 to 1992. There she served on a number of influential committees, including the Assembly Rules committee and the very powerful Ways and Means committee, which oversees the distribution of public monies.

She was also the chair of the Ways and Means subcommittee on Health and Human Services. Her political style, described as quiet and conciliatory, has contributed to her many legislative victories. She won passage of what some have hailed as landmark environmental legislation, as well as new laws in the areas of domestic violence and sexual harassment. Roybal-Allard is especially proud of her work to empower local communities. As she related in an interview with Diana Martínez: "People often don't know how their lives are impacted by what's going on in Sacramento or Washington, D.C. People can take control of their lives. They can be involved in the political process and make a difference."

Roybal-Allard was born and raised in the Boyle Heights section of Los Angeles, California, a predominately Mexican American area. She attended Saint Mary's Catholic School before she earned her B.A. from California State University, Los Angeles, in 1961. She has warm memories of working on her father's campaign; he was a great example to her, but Roybal-Allard is quick to give equal credit to her mother. "My mom has been a tremendous role model," she revealed to Martínez. "She's really the one who has helped to support and spearhead my father's career. She used to run his headquarters, which used to be our home when we were kids because they couldn't afford a headquarters. So she has always been there, helping him get elected, walking precincts, registering voters, doing all the things that needed to be done. At the same time, she'd be at his side whenever he needed to be at public events.

She's worked very hard and is greatly responsible for his success, because it really does take a partnership. In politics it takes the cooperation of your family; otherwise it's almost impossible to succeed."

In an interview with the *Civic Center News Source*, Roybal-Allard says she remembers working on her father's political campaigns as early as age seven. "We used to fold and stuff and lick stamps. When I got a little bit older they used to call us 'bird dogs,' and we would do voter registration. So I was a bird dog for a few years."

There was a downside to political involvement as well. As Roybal-Allard explained to the *Civic Center News Source*, "I think for me the main part of it was the lack of privacy and lack of personal identity. When my sister and I would go to a dance where people might not know who we were, we used to decide on a different last name so we could just be anonymous and have fun . . . I remember as a freshman in college in a political science class I raised my hand to answer a question and after I finished the professor said 'Well, now we know what your father thinks,' and went on to the next student."

Experiences such as these led Roybal-Allard to the conclusion that she did not want to be a politician. She continued to be involved in her father's campaigns and those of other Latino politicians but chose a career of community and advocacy work for herself. As Roybal-Allard explained to Martínez, her decision to work in community service was a direct result of her upbringing. "When I think you have a role model like both my father and my mother who have really dedicated their lives to the community and have taught human values and understand the value of people, it really has an impact on one's life." She served as the executive director of the National Association of Hispanic CPAs, in Washington, D.C., was the assistant director of the Alcoholism Council of East Los Angeles, and worked as a planning associate for United Way. She enjoyed community work, but as time went on she became more and more frustrated by the barriers created by political policy makers. In 1987 a combination of political opportunity and personal circumstances changed Roybal-Allard's mind about running for office.

Decides to Pursue Political Career

The 1987 election of Assemblywoman Gloria Molina to the newly created seat on the Los Angeles City Council left Molina's assembly position vacant. Roybal-Allard knew Molina through their mutual community activities and she had worked on the assemblywoman's campaign. Molina asked Roybal-Allard to consider running for the vacant assembly position. Her personal situation and the request of her friend led to her decision to run. As she explained to *Hispanic*, "The timing was just right for me. My children were grown and my husband's job called for a lot of travel." Roybal-Allard's second husband, Edward Allard III, has his

own consulting firm whose clients are mostly on the East Coast. Roybal-Allard told Martínez that she received no pressure from her father to run. "I'm sure that his involvement in politics ultimately was one of the reasons . . . that I wound up getting involved in politics. But, he has always been one that believed that we needed to be independent and make decisions on our own, and if we need guidance he will be there." Once she decided to run for California's State Assembly, she received help from both her father and Gloria Molina. She easily defeated nine other candidates and won with 60 percent of the vote.

As a newly elected assemblywoman, one of Roybal-Allard's first tasks was to continue the fight against building a prison in East L.A. A tremendous challenge for a new politician considering that her principal foe was the Governor of the State of California. In 1986, California Governor George Deukmejian proposed a site near a heavily Mexican American residential area as the location for a State prison. Deukmejian tried to steamroll the opposition to get the prison built but had his plans flattened instead. For seven years Roybal-Allard, along with Gloria Molina and other local Latino politicians, worked with grassroots organizations, professional groups, and church leaders to prevent the prison from being built. As an expression of her philosophy of local empowerment, Roybal-Allard assisted community women in organizing "The Mothers of East L.A." which was implacable in its opposition to the prison. A series of legal maneuvers halted construction of the prison but did not kill it. Deukmejian left office in 1990, but the struggle against the prison continued until September, 1992 when Governor Pete Wilson signed a bill, amended by Roybal-Allard, which eliminated the funds for the construction of the East L.A. prison. This victory, coming as Roybal-Allard left the California Assembly for the U.S. Congress, gave her cause to reflect on her own feelings and what the political struggle meant to her community. As she stated in a press release, "I started my assembly career when the East Los Angles prison bill was approved and it feels great to be leaving the assembly on this victory note. . . . This is a victory for the entire community. For seven years our community has marched against the prison, we have fought in the courts and in [California capital] Sacramento—this fight has empowered us. This community was once viewed as powerless. However, the Mothers of East Los Angeles and other community groups have served notice to the state's powerbrokers that ignoring the desires of the East Los Angeles community will no longer be accepted."

The prison wasn't the only struggle Roybal-Allard waged to improve the quality of life in her district. She fought against a toxic waste incinerator, again aided by the highly respected grass roots organization, Mothers of East Los Angeles. As a result of that struggle, Roybal-Allard authored a bill which entitles every community in California to an environmental impact report before a toxic incinerator is built or expanded, a protection that was often omitted prior to her efforts. This bill, along with her strong voting record on the environment, earned her the Sierra Club's California Environmental Achievement Award.

Takes Action on Women's Issues

Roybal-Allard has also authored a series of laws which place her in the forefront of women's issues. Included is a requirement that the courts take into consideration an individual's history of domestic violence in child custody cases. She has also worked for legislation requiring colleges to provide information and referrals for treatment to rape victims and enacted two laws that strengthen the legal position of sexual assault victims by redefining the meaning of "consent." Another of her bills requires the California State Bar to take disciplinary action against attorneys who engage in sexual misconduct with their clients. This is the first such law adopted by any state in the country.

For her legislative efforts, Roybal-Allard has received a number of prestigious awards and commendations, including honors from the Los Angeles Commission on Assaults Against Women, the Asian Business Association, and the Latin American Professional Women's Association. Roybal-Allard was also honored in 1992 by the Mexican American Women's National Association (MANA) in Washington D.C. She was presented with the "Las Primaras" Award for "her pioneering efforts in creating a better future for the community through the political process." In addition, Roybal-Allard was named in *Hispanic Business*'s 1992 list of "100 Influentials."

Ironically, when Roybal-Allard was first elected to the California Assembly many thought her to be too demure to be effective. But as she explained to *Hispanic* her conciliatory style is long-range effective, "People may be your enemies today on one issue, but they may be your allies tomorrow on another issue. So I've learned to work well with groups on both sides of the aisle, even with those who I oppose bitterly on particular issues." Her track record on political effectiveness to date has been impressive. A number of community members, and political observers, have speculated that when the senior Roybal left Congress in 1992, his daughter followed in his steps, continuing the Roybal legacy of effective representation.

Sources:

Periodicals

Civic Center News Source, January 13, 1992, pp. 1, 8, 12.
Hispanic, March 9, 1992, p. 20.

Other

News release from the office of Lucille Roybal-Allard, September 16, 1992.

Roybal-Allard, Lucille, interview with Diana Martínez, September 2, 1992.

—Sketch by Diana Martínez

Vicki Ruiz
(1955-)
Professor of humanities, historian

In a very short time, Vicki Lynn Ruiz has risen to the top of her profession, fueled, she told interviewer Tom Pendergast, "by insomnia and a drive to succeed." Ruiz, an educator and oral historian who has attempted to understand the lives of Mexican women in the twentieth century and to transmit that knowledge to her students, is the Andrew W. Mellon Professor of the Humanities at the Claremont Graduate School, a position that allows her the utmost flexibility as a scholar and as a teacher. Ruiz's goals at Claremont, whose faculty she joined in 1992, are to complete a groundbreaking history of Mexican women in the United States and to build a strong graduate program.

Ruiz's interest in Mexican history springs directly from her own past. She was born on May 21, 1955, in Atlanta, Georgia, the daughter of Robert Mercer and Ermina Ruiz. Robert's parents disowned him for marrying a Hispanic woman, so when he and his wife started a family, their children took the surname Ruiz.

Ermina was proud of her heritage and enjoyed sharing it with her children. Besides recounting stories of working in the coal mines and beet fields of southern Colorado, she told them of her father, who had come to the United States during the Mexican revolution and was once an active member of the Industrial Workers of the World (a radical union that was organized between 1905 and 1920), and of her mother, a proud woman whose family had emigrated to Colorado from Mexico early in the nineteenth century.

Ruiz, however, grew up in Florida, far from her Mexican roots. Her father owned a large sport fishing boat and moved the family back and forth from Marathon to Panama City, depending on the season. Ruiz told Pendergast: "I grew up on the water, and I particularly loved the time we would spend in the Florida Keys. I loved to get lost in the different colors of the parrot fish, and squirrel fish, and angel fish." The family's nomadic existence meant that Ruiz attended many different schools as a child, but by the time she reached the eighth grade her mother insisted that they stay in one place.

Living in what Ruiz only half-affectionately calls the "Redneck Riviera"—Panama City, Florida—posed its share of difficulties. Some local parents did not want their sons dating a Mexican girl, and Ruiz was denied a Daughter of the Confederacy academic scholarship because she could not trace her ancestry to the pre-Civil War South. By the time she finished high school, she knew she wanted to escape her small town, and education provided the quickest way out.

Examines Role of Women Cannery Workers

Ruiz entered Florida State University believing that she wanted to be a high school teacher, but her professors eventually convinced her to pursue graduate studies instead. "I applied to Stanford University on a whim," she related to Pendergast, "and a professor named Al Camarillo called me and told me he would support my application." Camarillo proved to be a huge source of support and guidance for Ruiz, introducing her to the history of the women's cannery unions in California and to Luisa Moreno, an early union organizer who had been deported from the United States for her activism. "I went to Guadalajara, Mexico, to interview Moreno," Ruiz said, "and I came back knowing what I would study."

Ruiz received her master's degree in 1978 and her doctorate in 1982, both from Stanford. Her subsequent examination of the cannery workers was published by the University of New Mexico Press in 1987 as *Cannery Women, Cannery Lives: Mexican Women, Unionization, and the California Food Processing Industry, 1939-1950*. In a *Southwestern Historical Quarterly* review, Yolanda G. Romero called the book "an outstanding addition to the historical literature on labor," and William Flores, writing in the *Oral History Review*, deemed it "essential reading for anyone engaged in research on Chicanos and Mexicans, on cannery workers, and more broadly on issues of gender and work."

Ruiz's first academic post was at the University of Texas in El Paso. "I felt lucky that there was a job in my field," she told Pendergast, "and I kept thinking how lucky I was to be teaching, because I was learning so much from my students." She left El Paso in 1985 for the University of California at Davis, where she enjoyed the support of a community of Chicano scholars, and stayed at Davis until 1992, when she accepted a position at the Claremont Graduate School near Los Angeles.

Shifts Research Focus to Mexican Women's History

During this entire period Ruiz continued to work in the field of Mexican women's history, co-editing *Women on the United States-Mexico Border: Responses to Change* and *Western Women: Their Land, Their Lives*. In 1992 she began working on *Form Out of the Shadows: A History of Mexican Women in the United States, 1900-1990*, which will examine, Ruiz told Pendergast, "the changing cultural landscape created out of the interaction of two distinct cultures, examining the different ways that Mexican women have responded to American culture."

Besides teaching and writing, Ruiz has pursued a variety of other interests. For example, she served as a consultant to the National Women's History Project and coordinated a portion of the Texas Sesquicentennial Oral History Workshop. She has also served on the advisory board of the Research Clearinghouse on Southern Women and Women of Color.

Ruiz cites Luisa Moreno as one of her role models for her strength and bravery in organizing women in the California food processing industry. But she reserves the greatest praise for her mother, whose enthusiasm for life never wavered despite the fact that she often had to work long hours at difficult jobs to help support her family. "My mother was a survivor," Ruiz recalled, "and she found great joy in working and helping out. She was also a wonderful storyteller."

Ruiz herself is the mother of two boys, Miguel and Daniel, from her first marriage, which lasted from 1979 until 1990. She married Victor Becerra in 1992.

Sources:

Periodicals

American Historical Review, April, 1989.
Journal of American History, June, 1988; December, 1988; December, 1989; December, 1990.
Ms., July/August, 1990.
New Republic, October 22, 1990.
Oral History Review, spring, 1989.
Southwestern Historical Quarterly, April, 1989.

Other

Ruiz, Vicki, interview with Tom Pendergast, September 9, 1992.

—Sketch by Tom Pendergast

S

Martha Saenz
(1942-)
Immigration lawyer

Martha Saenz is an inspiration for women seeking to integrate family and career goals successfully. She is not only the mother of three, a former legal assistant at the Inter-American Development Bank and past president of the Human Relations Council of Prince Edward County, Virginia, but also has a private practice in immigration law in Washington, D.C., and is the first Hispanic president of the Women's Bar Association of the District of Columbia. Representing more than 400 clients from 70 different countries, Saenz assists immigrants in attaining legal residency and avoiding deportation. A self-described guide to U.S. law and society, she stated in an interview with Sandra Márquez: "I serve as an interpreter of the American system for my clients. Latinos are coming from a different point of reference. What I can do is be sensitive to their cultural background."

Born May 30, 1942, in Bogota, Colombia, Saenz was only seven when she moved to the United States with her mother, Irene Gómez de Saenz, who had separated from Martha's father, Alfonso Saenz. Martha Saenz credits her mother's idealism and her father's pragmatism for her own success. Irene, who had a master's degree in Spanish literature and a love of books and education that she passed along to her daughter, chose to leave her native country because of the greater opportunities available to women in the United States. Alfonso, a businessman in Colombia, supported his daughter emotionally and financially throughout her undergraduate years at Middlebury College in Vermont and later while she pursued her law degree from American University in Washington, D.C.

Saenz's success did not come without its challenges. She decided to give law school a try following a divorce from her first husband. But it was not until two years after she first applied that she finally received acceptance notices from three programs, including American University, the school she eventually chose to attend. Once enrolled, she had to schedule her classes around day care for her children. Later, occasional family crises such as her son's broken arm or a flooded basement interrupted important court appearances.

Now married to an economist with whom she has a daughter, Saenz described the personal satisfaction that can be derived from balancing family with career in an article she wrote for the *Washington Lawyer*. "It is incredibly sad for a woman to have to give up a brilliant legal career or not have children because she feared she could not do both," she observed. "It is that very mixture of personal and professional that can benefit a practice of law." According to Saenz, women have a special contribution to make to the legal profession. In a field dominated by men and their emphasis on "material values," women are more likely to focus on the intellectual challenge of solving a client's problem and offer understanding and compassion to help the client through a crisis.

In the future, Saenz told Márquez she would like to apply the knowledge gained from her legal practice by serving in public office and by writing a book based on the experiences of her clients. As testimony to her sense of commitment to others, she described her mission as one of "helping people to help themselves," adding, "We really have to look within ourselves for our inner strength. The good that you do does come back to you."

Sources:

Periodicals

Executive Female, March/April 1988, pp. 26-27.
Washington Lawyer, Volume 3, number 1, September/ October, 1988, pp. 48-49.

Other

Saenz, Martha, interview with Sandra Márquez, August 26, 1992.

—Sketch by Sandra Márquez

Mary Salinas Durón
(1952-)
Banker

Mary Salinas Durón realized early on that true empowerment for the Latino community would require more than just political participation and consciousness-raising exercises—it would require financial strength. "When I was in college, being part of the Chicano movement, I began to feel that the missing link was that there wasn't any emphasis on the economic development of our community," she told interviewer Sandra Márquez. As vice president of urban and community affairs for First Interstate Bank of California, Salinas Durón makes sure that Latinos and other ethnic and racial groups have access to capital for community development projects and personal investment needs. She manages the bank's community development loan program and oversees her employer's compliance with the Community Reinvestment Act (CRA), a federal law requiring banks to meet the credit and deposit needs of their clientele, including low and moderate income individuals. Under her stewardship, First Interstate Bank has been one of the few financial institutions nationwide to receive an "outstanding" CRA rating from federal regulators.

Born to José Salinas and Lupe Martinez on April 30, 1952, Salinas Durón joined First Interstate as an intern while completing her M.B.A. at the University of California in Los Angeles. She then served as a commercial loan officer before creating the Hispanic marketing unit in 1981. Regarded as a pioneering effort by a California bank, the unit affirmed the significance of the Hispanic market.

Tailors Special Marketing Unit for Hispanics

To launch the marketing unit, Salinas Durón traveled to Mexico to find out what kinds of banking services members of California's predominantly Mexican American Latino community were accustomed to using. After determining which First Interstate branches served a Hispanic population, she then translated brochures and made sure that bank personnel reflected the diversity of the communities in which the branches were located. Her involvement with the marketing unit positioned Salinas Durón as a liaison between community groups and the bank. "Unless I had a pulse on the community, I couldn't really devise those kinds of programs," she explained in her interview with Márquez.

In addition to her responsibilities at First Interstate, Salinas Durón serves on the boards of several community organizations. She is a past president and founding member of the Hispanic Bankers Association, an organization she and four other women established to attract more Latinos to the banking profession. She is also a member of the corporate advisory committee for the Hispanic Women's Council, a leadership development organization dedicated to Latina empowerment.

On a more personal note, Salinas Durón and her husband, Armando, residents of Montebello, California, are the parents of three daughters. It is the successful combination of family and professional life, Salinas Durón told Márquez, that has brought her the greatest satisfaction. "I think it makes for a full person. Having my children has helped other facets of my life. That's what makes life fruitful." Salinas Durón also takes pleasure in various forms of Chicano art and artistic expression. She is, for example, a former board chairperson of the Los Angeles-based Bilingual Foundation of the Arts, a theater group that brings previously unproduced Latino works to the stage in both English and Spanish.

Salinas Durón acknowledges that much work remains to be done in the area of economic empowerment in the Latino community. To remedy the Latino population's general lack of capital, her future career goals include addressing economic issues in the political arena.

Sources:

Periodicals

Hispanic Business, March 1991, p. 28.
Vista, April 7, 1991, p. 3.

Other

Salinas Durón, Mary, interview with Sandra Márquez, September 18, 1992.

—*Sketch by Sandra Márquez*

Carol A. Sanchez
(1961-)
Industrial engineer

Carol A. Sanchez's accomplishments at Hughes Aircraft Company have earned her the Superior Performance Award, Hughes's highest recognition to be conferred upon an individual, and the 1990 National Hispanic Engineer Achievement Award for the Most Promising Engineer. She serves as senior industrial engineer at Hughes's Missile Systems Group in Tucson, Arizona. "My work consists of offering production support to the team of experts who build missiles," she explained to this contributor in a 1992 interview. "The tasks include analyzing and developing manufacturing machinery and equipment, methods and standards, and evaluating and establishing simplified production process and motion patterns for greater output and less fatigue for the workers." Sanchez admits that she did not plan to make a career in engineering. "All I knew was that I wanted to attend the University of Arizona and do something with computers. I didn't know anything about engineering."

Sanchez was born in Tucson, Arizona, on April 24, 1961, the third child of a family of four children and a third generation Mexican American. Her parents regarded education as crucial. "You had to be sick and dying to be excused from school," she recalled in her interview. Her fondest memories of elementary school are the field trips her class took to the museum. "I loved to learn about the role American Indians and Hispanics played in our history." In high school, she shunned science and mathematics and concentrated on typing and shorthand classes. But she became interested in computer sciences at a career information fair organized by her school. "This was the early seventies and computers were up and coming. The sheer novelty of it fascinated me." So when the time came to choose a field of study, she thought of computers but without anything more specific. "I virtually came to engineering by process of elimination," she confessed. "Upon entering the University of Arizona, I had the choice to take on liberal arts, business, or engineering. The first two fields of study did not appeal to me, and the engineering courses seemed interesting. So, I took engineering." In 1984, Sanchez graduated with a B.S. in systems engineering. The following year, she joined Hughes Aircraft.

Stresses the Importance of Communication

Sanchez is assigned to the company's Advanced Medium Range Air to Air Missile Program (AMRAAM). The project incorporates the latest digital technology and micro-miniaturized solid-state electronics to improve air-to-air capability of U.S. fighter aircraft. Sanchez provides industrial engineering support to the program. She is also on the Continuous Measurable Improvement (CMI) team for improved productivity and on the CMI tool system team. "Besides handling equipment and material, engineering means dealing with people," she stressed in her interview. "Communication, both verbal and written, might be the most important skill in an engineering career. You must learn to work with people from different cultures and backgrounds, and to respect the workers who build a unit according to your specifications as much as the managers who use your report to make a decision."

This is one tip Sanchez gives students in her lectures. She regularly visits elementary and high schools, takes part in the pre-engineering workshops held every year at the University of Arizona, and speaks at the annual Youth Convention of the League of United Latin American Citizens (LULAC). "My message is simple," said Sanchez in her interview. "I tell students to focus on education, to develop people skills and to take advantage of internship programs to acquire experience in the workplace." Sanchez is co-chairperson of the Education Committee for Hughes Hispanic Employees Association (HHEA). With the help of two HHEA members, and in cooperation with the Tucson Professional Women's Network, she has launched a mentor program to support Hispanic students at Tucson's Cholla High School.

Sanchez belongs to the Society of Hispanic Professional Engineers. In 1990, she was recognized by *Professional* magazine as one of the top twenty minority engineers in the country. In 1991, the corporation AT&T selected her as a role model to be featured in an exhibit honoring Hispanic achievers. Besides getting Hughes's prestigious Superior Award in 1987, she received two of the company's High Performance Team Awards in 1989.

Sanchez has taken part in Hughes's career development program offered to employees with a promising future with the company. She plans to earn a master's degree in business administration or in a technical field and later join Hughes's management staff. In October of 1992 she married Michael W. Conrad, an industrial engineer at Hughes Aircraft Company.

Sources:

Periodicals

Hispanic Engineer, conference issue, 1990, p. 60.
Engineering Horizons, women's edition, 1991-1992, p. 109.
Professional, winter, 1990, p. 27.

Other

Sanchez, Carol A., interview with contributor Michelle Vachon, conducted on May 8, 1992.

—*Sketch by Michelle Vachon*

Dolores Sanchez
(1936-)
Publisher

Publisher Dolores Sanchez holds the distinction of being the first Hispanic American to own a newspaper chain. Born April 3, 1936, and raised in Los Angeles, California, Sanchez has deep roots in the community where she publishes the eight weekly papers that form

Eastern Group Publications. The papers have a combined staff of 18 reporters and a circulation of 12,000, and generally carry information about jobs and community activities in east and northeast Los Angeles, though some major stories first appeared in them. Sanchez stated in a telephone interview with Julia Edgar that she is sincerely committed to providing the kind of information that caters to the sizable Hispanic population in Los Angeles, as well as to Eastern Group readers living in places as diverse as Yokohama, Japan, and San Juan, Puerto Rico—"wherever people have an interest in what's going on in the Hispanic community, since there is a feeling that most trends begin here," she explained in the interview.

Sanchez, the mother of four children and one stepdaughter, did not begin her career intent on working in the publishing industry. She studied nursing, earning a bachelor of science degree from Mount St. Mary's in Los Angeles, and went on to become a partner in her first husband's grocery business. Later she formed her own food brokerage company, then served as president of the Chicana Service Action Center (CSAC) in the mid-1970s. At the CSAC, she initiated job training programs for Hispanic women who were re-entering the work force.

Appointed Head of Unemployment Commission

Sanchez's work at the center, along with a fleeting conversation in a Los Angeles airport about women's problems in business, helped propel her into her next position. Future First Lady Rosalynn Carter was impressed by the woman she met briefly at the airport, and her recollection was backed up by other activist groups in the southwest that knew of Sanchez's dedication to providing a voice for women. When Jimmy Carter was elected president, he selected Sanchez to head the National Commission on Unemployment Compensation. For the next four years Sanchez spent two weeks a month living and working in Washington, D.C. She was in charge of evaluating programs that had not undergone revision since the late 1930s.

"Our charter was to look at the program and suggest solutions to some of the problems that were legislative or administrative," Sanchez stated during the interview with Edgar. "At the time, half of the state trust funds had gone bankrupt, so there was a great need to reassess the program, even what short-term unemployment is. Much of the legislation we proposed is being enacted now." The Commission was due to expire in 1979, about the same time Sanchez learned the Eastern Group newspapers were in serious trouble. "I decided it was a voice of the community we couldn't afford to lose and now was the time to have a locally owned and operated newspaper," she explained. She rescued the weeklies from bankruptcy.

In 1980, former California Governor Jerry Brown selected Sanchez to lead the transition team that evaluated the California Employment and Training Act and helped write the more inclusive Job Employment Training Program. Sanchez, who was responsible for overseeing the governor's 40 million dollar discretionary fund, said government funds had previously gone only to community groups. The new Job Employment and Training Act drew in private industry, which provides the kind of training individuals "never would have gotten through community services."

In 1984, well into her tenure as Eastern Group's new leader, Sanchez was chosen to serve as a member of the Fine Arts Commission for the Los Angeles Olympics Organizing Committee. In 1986, she was honored as one of California's Outstanding Women Entrepreneurs at the second annual Governor's Conference on Women in Business. A year later, she was awarded the Business and Industry Silver Achievement Award by the YWCA. In 1990, Eastern Group's *Eastside Sun* won the "Award of Excellence" from the Great Los Angeles Press Club. The same year the entire newspaper chain received an award for its efforts in the field of crime prevention.

Sanchez also serves as a board member of the regional Institute of Southern California, a consortium that provides research and solutions to regional problems like air and water quality, transportation and waste disposal.

Sources:

Sanchez, Dolores, telephone interview with Julia Edgar conducted on August 10, 1992.

—Sketch by Julia Edgar

Sanchez, Laura Balverde
See **Balverde-Sanchez, Laura**

María E. Sánchez
(1927-)
Educator, administrator

María E. Sánchez, a teacher and educational administrator, was instrumental in efforts to establish bilingual education in the New York City public school system. She was among a handful of Puerto Rican women teachers in the 1960s and 1970s who helped develop the first classroom programs and community outreach services for non-English-speaking students.

From her earliest days in the Puerto Rican mountain community of Cayey, where she was born on February 25, 1927, Sánchez considered herself a teacher. The daughter of Julio Rodriguez Sánchez, a farmer, and Modesta Rivera, a homemaker, Sánchez grew up teaching catechism at her church and helping neighborhood children with their homework. "I was always a teacher," said Sánchez in an interview. While her two older sisters left school early to marry, Sánchez broke with cultural traditions and convinced her parents to allow her to attend high school and, eventually, college. "In my time, very few females went to high school. But I insisted I had to go," she said. She was one of only four women in her high school class who went on to college.

With the support of a government scholarship, Sánchez studied education at the University of Puerto Rico in Rio Piedras. At that time, many male teachers in the country were serving in World War II, leaving classrooms without teachers. Sánchez accepted a job in her hometown after her second year of studies. She taught English, social studies, and Spanish to sixth and seventh graders, returning to Rio Piedras for classes on weekends and during the summers. In 1952, she graduated magna cum laude with a B.A. in education.

The following year, Sánchez married Jose Miguel Sánchez and followed him to New York City where he was a student. Although the move was expected to be temporary, the couple started a family and settled permanently in New York. For five years, Sánchez stayed home with their three young daughters, one of whom was disabled and died at a young age. But when her husband became ill temporarily, Sánchez returned to work.

Pioneer in Bilingual Education

Her desire to teach in the public school system was stymied by a strict oral English test, which she and other Puerto Rican teachers could not pass because of their Spanish accents. Instead, Sánchez found a new niche, created by the post-World War II "Great Migration" of Puerto Ricans to New York. The schools were struggling to accommodate the children, many of whom did not speak English. At the urging of a Bronx elementary school principal, the schools created a new position, "Substitute Auxiliary Teacher," for Spanish-speaking teachers who would counsel new students, assist teachers, and serve as liaisons between schools and the Puerto Rican community. In 1958, Sánchez became an auxiliary teacher, assigned to P.S. 24 in Brooklyn.

It was a challenging job, requiring workdays that stretched into the late evening hours, but Sánchez was answering a desperate need. The auxiliaries were educational pioneers, developing and advocating better classroom programs and services for children without English skills. Sánchez helped organize the Society of Puerto Rican Auxiliary Teachers, which achieved licensure for the educators. "We started

fighting for our rights," stated Sánchez. "And that was the beginning of bilingual education." In the late 1960s and early 1970s, Sánchez helped secure federal grants provided by the 1968 Bilingual Education Act to establish the city's first bilingual kindergartens.

Sánchez went on to supervise auxiliaries, later renamed "bilingual teachers in school community relations," at the Central Board of Education and for three school districts in Brooklyn and the Lower East Side. In 1970, she was appointed supervisor of bilingual teachers in Brooklyn's District 14. "We were experts in Puerto Rican issues and history. We were consultants, lecturers, trainers, teachers," recalled Sánchez.

During summers, Sánchez lectured on bilingual education and Puerto Rican history and culture at colleges and universities. She led workshops, chaired parent meetings, and participated in media panels on bilingual education. Meanwhile, she earned an M.S. in education from Hunter College in 1965. In 1973, she received a professional diploma in Administration and Supervision from Richmond College, CUNY.

In 1972, Brooklyn College invited Sánchez to start a bilingual education major for teacher trainees. It would be the first undergraduate bilingual teacher training program in New York, although other schools had graduate-level programs. Sánchez worked with the Department of Puerto Rican Studies and School of Education to develop the program. Best of all, she was back in the classroom, doing what she loved best: teaching students.

Students and Faculty Demand Sánchez Appointment

In 1974 the college's Department of Puerto Rican Studies lost its chairperson. When the college president appointed a new chair from outside the school, without consulting the faculty, the students and faculty mounted a protest. They wanted Sánchez for the job. Creating a flurry of media attention, four professors and 40 students were arrested in the fall of 1974 after taking over the registrar's office. The president yielded and Sánchez was appointed the new chair. While Sánchez served as chair of the Department of Puerto Rican Studies at Brooklyn College, she never lost her love of classroom teaching. Until she retired in 1990, Sánchez continued to teach as well as perform her administrative duties and act as a consultant and lecturer on bilingual education.

Under Sánchez, the Department of Puerto Rican Studies flourished, offering an undergraduate major, graduate history and literature courses, and undergraduate and graduate degrees in elementary education with a bilingual specialty. Sánchez, a fervent believer in the power of organizing, also started the Student Union for Bilingual Education, the Graduate Association for Bilingual Education, the Latino Faculty and Staff Association, and the Puerto Rican Students Alumni Association. "I try to bridge the gaps between groups so that they can fight together for what is good," she declared.

But perhaps Sánchez's proudest accomplishment as a teacher and administrator has been her role as mentor to hundreds of students and young faculty. "I love to see people go up and do things," she commented. "People often say they owe their career to me. I tell them 'Don't thank me. Go do this for someone else.'" She recalled with pride encountering a former kindergarten student at P.S. 24, then just arrived from Puerto Rico, as a student at Brooklyn College. Former students she remains in touch with include a Puerto Rican judge, a minister, college professors, and many others. "This is my little contribution for the Puerto Rican community, empowering people, helping them get an education," acknowledged Sánchez. "Once they have that power, they can do it for someone else."

During her career, she has been active in dozens of organizations, including the Puerto Rican Educators Association, the Catholic Teachers Association, the National Association of Teachers of English as a Second Language, and the National Association of Bilingual Education. At her retirement in 1990, Brooklyn College named her Professor Emerita. The college also created an endowment fund in her name for the Center for Latino Studies, an adjunct of the Department of Puerto Rican Studies, which she helped create. Sánchez lives on Staten Island with her husband, Jose Miguel, a retired store planner for J.C. Penney. They have two daughters, Annabelle Sánchez Jastremski and Madeline Sánchez, and two grandchildren.

Sources:

María E. Sánchez, interview with Ann Malaspina, October 1, 1992.

—Sketch by Ann Malaspina

Milcha Sanchez-Scott
(1953-)
Playwright

As an author of a large number of successful plays that have been presented nationally and internationally, Milcha Sanchez-Scott has become one of the preeminent playwrights in the United States. Although Sanchez-Scott is known for interjecting Spanish sentences or expressions in her play's dialogue, her theatre is directed toward English-speaking audiences worldwide. She has achieved and excelled in her work, leaving prejudices behind and embrac-

ing fully her Spanish roots, a rich heritage that, at the same time, is American. As she explains in the *Latin American Theater Review*, "I feel I am an American writer who has been influenced by the places I've lived or where my parents were born."

Milcha Sanchez-Scott was born on the Island of Bali in 1953. Her mother is Indonesian, and her father is from the city of Santa Marta in Colombia, South America. As a young girl, Sanchez-Scott was sent to a Catholic school near London, England, where she learned to speak English. In the summers, she would return to her home in Santa Marta, "running around with my cousins" as she recalls in *On New Ground: Contemporary Hispanic-American Plays.*

Sanchez-Scott has fond memories of her childhood. One of Sanchez-Scott's most vivid childhood recollections is visiting a Latin American church built by Indians. As in many areas in Latin America, these villagers were profoundly devoted and humble and believed in miracles. In her travels later in her life, Sanchez-Scott found similar beliefs and devotion among the Hispanics she met in sections of New Mexico and California. This fervent faith fascinated her.

When she was about fourteen years old, Sanchez-Scott and her family moved to La Jolla, California. Subsequently, she went to the University of San Diego, a Catholic woman's college, and majored in literature, philosophy, and theater. Enchanted with acting and the workings of the theater, Sanchez-Scott auditioned for a role in a drama project that was to be produced at a prison in Chino, California. Accepted for the part, Sanchez-Scott began working with a fellow theater lover named, Doris Baizley. As Baizley became better acquainted with the young actress, she learned of Sanchez-Scott's interest in writing. Baizley encouraged Sanchez-Scott to combine her love for the theatre and her writing talents to explore her play writing ability. Inspired, Sanchez-Scott began what would become a very successful career as a playwright.

Debut Play Produced in Los Angeles

In 1980, at the age of twenty-seven, Sanchez-Scott's first play, *Latina,* premiered in Los Angeles. The play highlighted Hispanic working-class women. Sanchez-Scott got her material for *Latina* from her experiences working at an employment agency for maids in Beverly Hills, California. These women, she states in *On New Ground,* "had their feet on the ground, and their eyes on the stars, and their hearts full of love. . . . It was like meeting at the river."

Four years later, *The Dog Lady* and *The Cuban Swimmer,* Sanchez-Scott's two one act dramas, were presented by International Art Relations (INTAR) in New York City with Max Ferra as artistic director. In April of 1987, the two plays were also produced at the Gate Theater in London. Another of her plays, *Evening Star,* was produced by Theater For A New Audience under the direction of Jeffrey Horowitz as artistic/producing director, and directed by Paul Zinmet. The play later premiered at the Cubículo in New York. Mel Gussow in the *New York Times*, maintains that this "play stands by itself as a wistful study of adolescent yearning." Additional plays written by Sanchez-Scott include *Stone Wedding*, which premiered in Los Angeles, *The Architect Piece*, and *Carmen*, an adaptation of the opera of George Bizet's of the same name, which was first produced at the Los Angeles Theater Center in December, 1988.

One of Sanchez-Scott's best known dramas, *Roosters*, premiered at INTAR in New York in 1987, under the direction of Jackson Phippin. This two-act play also opened in San Francisco at the Eureka Theater and was filmed for *American Playhouse* in Los Angeles in 1988. It was published first by Theater Communications Group in the *American Theater* magazine. In 1989, it was included in *On the Ground*, an anthology of contemporary Hispanic American plays. The play is a story of a fifth-generation Mexican American family that raises roosters for cockfighting. The plot starts when the father returns home after being in prison. Janice Arkatov, in her article reviewing *Roosters* for the *Los Angeles Times*, points out: "We all have to leave our parents. We all have to grow up and leave home, face the various stages of life, grow old. These people in this play are mythical, archetypal characters: mother/father, madonna/whore, son/daughter. And they are Americans."

For Gussow writing in *New York Times*, *Roosters* "moves gracefully to its conclusion, a moment in which the illusory becomes tangible." Gussow also notes that "Ms. Sanchez-Scott has a natural theatrical talent and an ability to ensnare an audience in a tale." The extraordinary magic of the Sanchez-Scott style is praised by the *Chicago Tribune* as Sid Smith describes *Roosters* as "an unusual, provocative drama . . . and a glimpse into a Southwestern society. . . . The style is 'magic realism'—the mingling of ordinary life and fairy tale fantasy widely employed by Latin and South American writers."

Sources:

Books

Osborn, M. Elizabeth, editor, *On New Ground: Contemporary Hispanic-American Plays*, Theater Communications Group, 1987, pp. 244-280.
Sanchez-Scott, Milcha, *Dog Lady* [and] *The Cuban Swimmer*, Dramatists Play Service, 1988.
Sanchez-Scott, Milcha, *Evening Star*, Dramatists Play Service, 1989.

Periodicals

Chicago Tribune, March 9, 1989, section 5, p. 7.

Latin American Theater Review, spring, 1990, pp. 63-74.
Los Angeles Times, June 15, 1988, p. 3; April 22, 1991, p. 1.
New Statesman, May 15, 1987, pp. 25-26.
New York Times, May 16, 1988, p. C13; March 24, 1987, p. C15; May 10, 1984, p. C32.
Time, July 11, 1988, p. 82.

—*Sketch by Sylvia P. Apodaca*

Alicia Sandoval
(1943-)
AFL-CIO communications director, education expert

In her various roles as the director of communications for the AFL-CIO in Los Angeles and as the first Hispanic executive at the National Education Association (NEA), Sandoval has broken numerous barriers for young Hispanics. "It's clear there is something special about her—something that has made her a *bona fide* maverick for most of her working life," wrote Darryl Figueroa about Sandoval in *Hispanic*.

The second oldest of three daughters, Alicia C. Sandoval was born on the second day of May, 1943, in Glendale, California, to Mexican American parents, Crescento Domingas and Lucy Sandoval. She was raised in Burbank, where her father worked as an aerospace engineer. Sandoval recalled experiencing racism, which manifested itself in fights and name-calling, when she was young. "In those days," Sandoval told Luis Vasquez-Ajmac in a telephone interview, "people were very ignorant of ethnic differences."

Sandoval's desire to help other Hispanics developed while she attended college. Two mentors, Dr. Julian Nava, former Ambassador to Mexico under President Jimmy Carter, and historian Dr. Rudy Acuna, made her aware of institutional racism and the importance of women getting educational degrees. Sandoval went on to complete a B.A. in English and education in 1966 from the University of California at Los Angeles and an M.A. in educational administration from the University of Southern California in 1970. She later helped Acuna set up the first Chicano studies department at California State University at Northridge.

In 1968 Sandoval launched a career in education in East Los Angeles, where she taught at predominately Hispanic schools. She later changed gears when she took a leave of absence from teaching to work on a 12-part educational television series for KNBC-TV called "Mexican American Heritage," the first educational series ever done on the subject. Approving of her work, which consisted of script writing and production, an NBC representative suggested that she audition at Metromedia TV in Hollywood to host a public affairs television talk show. This move led to a 13-year career in broadcasting. As co-producer and host at Metromedia TV (now Fox TV, KTTV-TV, Channel 11), Sandoval became one of the first Hispanics to host a daily talk show. She researched, wrote, and selected guests and topics, which ranged from interviews with Jane Fonda to saluting outstanding minority community leaders.

A strong union supporter, Sandoval left Metromedia TV and became the public relations director for the AFL-CIO in Los Angeles from 1985 to 1987. There, her primary duties were to train labor union leaders to be more effective on television and radio and to help recruit new members.

Becomes First Hispanic NEA Executive

In 1988 Sandoval moved to Washington, D.C., to become the first Hispanic executive of the NEA, the largest independent union outside the AFL-CIO. As director of communications, Sandoval believes her greatest accomplishment was to open doors for other Hispanics. During her three years there, she kept Hispanic issues in the forefront and launched a $14 million outreach campaign which made Hispanics more aware of educational issues.

In 1991 Sandoval began working at Renny Martin Companies, a public relations firm in Washington, D.C. She is enthusiastic about a program she designed for public and private organizations called "Work Force Diversity Training," which finds ways to reprogram thoughts on discrimination. Sandoval is also looking forward to combining her educational and entertainment background in other creative projects. Seeing endless opportunities ahead, Sandoval told Vasquez-Ajmac, "I live in a world of ideas."

Sources:

Periodicals

Hispanic, May 1988, pp. 17-19.
Hispanic Business, November 1988, p. 35.

Other

Sandoval, Alicia, interview by Luis Vasquez-Ajmac conducted on September 2, 1992.

—*Sketch by Luis Vasquez-Ajmac*

Irma Vidal Santaella
(1924-)
Lawyer, judge

The Honorable Irma Vidal Santaella is the first Puerto Rican woman to become a lawyer in New York state and the first Puerto Rican from the Latino-rich county of Bronx to ascend to New York's Supreme Court. She is a "pioneer for the Puerto Rican-Hispanic community," according to New York State Senator Efraim Gonzalez, a longtime associate. Despite all of Santaella's accomplishments, Gonzalez and other friends still affectionately refer to her as "mom." Senator Gonzalez noted in a telephone interview with Julia Edgar that the judge is a woman who arrived at the judicial pinnacle by "breaking down barriers. To us, she's great, because she has a sensitivity to people she presides over. She was like our mother. She still is." In a telephone interview, Carmen Pacheco, a Puerto Rican attorney and founding partner of New York City's first Hispanic women's law firm, likened Santaella to Spain's Queen Isabella, who made possible Christopher Columbus's first voyage to the Americas in the 15th century. "She has set our sails. She is somebody we should look at and try to model ourselves after."

Born in New York City October 4, 1924, and raised by her mother and aunts in Puerto Rico, Santaella has an extensive and diverse educational background. After graduating in 1942 from the Modern Business College in Ponce, Puerto Rico, she immediately undertook two years of pre-medical school classes at the Inter-American University in San German, Puerto Rico. She began her professional life as a licensed public accountant, graduating with a bachelor of arts degree from Hunter College in New York in 1957. While she worked, she put herself through law school and graduated from the Brooklyn Law School in New York in 1961. She then commenced a practice of civil law in the South Bronx until 1963.

Since then, Santaella has tirelessly championed the rights of minorities and women and children, serving on the New York City Commission on the Status of Women from 1975 to 1977 and heading the Children's Camp in South Bronx in 1967. Since 1982 she has been a member of the New York City Advisory Council on Minority Affairs. Santaella is also the founder of the National Federation of Puerto Rican Women, the National Caucus of Puerto Rican and Hispanic Women, the Hispanic Community Chest of America, Inc., and the National Association for Puerto Rican Civil Rights. As founder in 1962 and chairperson until 1968 of the Legion of Voters, Inc., Santaella played a significant role in advising the late New York Senator Robert F. Kennedy and Senator Jacob Javits on legislation involving Puerto Ricans in the provisions of the Voting

Irma Vidal Santaella

Rights Act of 1965. The senators sought her counsel because she helped draft an amendment which ultimately eliminated English literacy tests for non-English speaking American citizens.

In 1968, Santaella launched her second campaign for a congressional seat while Senator Robert Kennedy, a friend, ran for the presidency. When Kennedy, who had served as United States Attorney General under his brother, President John F. Kennedy, was assassinated during a speech, her campaign fizzled because Santaella was so dejected at her close friend's demise. "Something disappeared. We went through the exercise of the election, but our heart was no longer there," she said in an article printed in *Manhattan Lawyer* magazine in 1989.

Despite a personal and political setback, Judge Santaella's idealism was still intact. She continued her work for the Legion of Voters, and in 1975, New York Governor Hugh L. Carey appointed her as chairperson of the state Human Rights Appeal Board, of which she had been a member since 1968. In 1976, Judge Santaella helped found the National Association for Puerto Rican Civil Rights, the same year she served as a delegate to the Democratic National Convention for the third time.

Becomes New York Supreme Court Justice

In 1983, Santaella won a seat on the New York Supreme Court, where her rulings have reflected her social activism,

particularly for minority rights. In the summer of 1987, for example, she refused to allow the eviction of a doctor who practiced in a luxurious apartment building on Manhattan's Park Avenue. The landlord claimed Dr. Geoffrey Richstone had improperly made renovations to his office without permission. Judge Santaella not only found that the doctor had openly added equipment and modified his office, but she learned that the building's tenants did not like the presence of Dr. Richstone's minority patients and had asked them to use the back door of the building to enter and leave. In refusing the eviction request, the judge said she could not understand why the landlord sought relief that would "deny black senior citizens access to their doctor's office—for no apparent reason other than their age and race—in a state that is a citadel of freedom."

In early 1991, Judge Santaella ordered the New York State Board of Elections (NYSBE) to implement a program to sign up more poor people and minorities as voters when they registered for a driver's license or applied for a government position. The program, initiated a year earlier, was stymied because of fighting between Democrats and Republicans on the NYSBE over whether state employees could answer questions from registrants. In her opinion, Judge Santaella reasoned that the goal of the program was to give "New York City citizens, especially minorities, the opportunities to elect representatives of their choice" in an important City Council election the following September.

Judge Santaella is also a strong advocate of First Amendment rights. While she is a practicing Catholic and has served as a board member of the Catholic Interracial Society, she refused to allow the church to stop the production of a play which it found blasphemous. In October, 1990, Judge Santaella told the Roman Catholic Archdiocese of New York it could try to evict the RAPP Arts Center and its play, *The Cardinal Detoxes,* from a parochial school building, but could not stop the production in the meantime. "I am not a censor, and I'm not going to engage in any act of censorship," she wrote in her opinion, reprinted in part in the *New York Times* in October, 1990.

Urges Settlement in Ross Perot-General Motors Case

Santaella "once again sided with the underdog," wrote Shaun Assael in *Manhattan Lawyer* magazine, when she refused to move a lawsuit against General Motors Corporation to Delaware. A company stockholder sued the corporation in New York State Supreme Court, contending General Motors (GM) breached its fiduciary duty by paying Texas billionaire and presidential candidate Ross Perot more than his stock was worth to surrender his seat on the company's board of directors. In a "remarkable scene" in her chambers, said an attorney who was present, Judge Santaella "made a forceful, careful statement" urging settlement between the plaintiff, Perot and former GM Chairman Roger Smith. The Appellate Division of the New York Supreme Court, however, reversed Judge Santaella's ruling in that case, deciding that GM, because it does business in every state, is subjected to the laws of each state.

Aside from numerous citations and awards she has received for her non-judicial work—including the National Puerto Rican Coalition Life Achievement award and Governor Mario M. Cuomo's Recognition Award—Judge Santaella was cited by the New York State Assembly in 1989 for attaining the highest disposition rate of cases in Manhattan Supreme Court a year earlier. In fact, from 1983 to 1990, the judge heard and closed 21,000 cases, and from 1984 to 1989, she was reversed by higher courts only 24 times. Judge Santaella, said Assembly members in their commendation of the judge, "so truly personifies that commitment to excellence which so distinguishes the Hispanic tradition of law, to that visible and honored predilection for the orderly disposition of concerns so essential to a just society. . . ."

In 1990, Judge Santaella, a divorced mother of two, received an honorary law degree from Sacred Heart University in Connecticut. She is a board member of dozens of organizations, including the Community Service Society, Puerto Rican Crippled Children's Fund, Talbott Perkins Children's Services, the American Judicature Society, Planned Parenthood, Inc., and the New York City Steering Committee for Quality Education. Judge Santaella's civic achievements were noted in citations from former New York Govs. Nelson Rockefeller in 1972 and Carey in 1982. Other awards include the 1991 National Council of Hispanic Women's Life Achievement award and the 1992 National Latinas Excellence Award of Leadership.

Sources:

Books

The Women's Book of World Records and Achievements, edited by Lois Decker O'Neill, Anchor Press, Doubleday Books, 1979, p. 364.

Periodicals

Assael, Shaun, "Santaella: Up from the Bronx Clubhouse," *Manhattan Lawyer,* February 21, 1989.
Hentoff, Nat, "The Wrong Set of Patients," *Washington Post,* July 7, 1987, p. A15.
Heveski, Dennis, "Court Orders Voter Registration Plan to Begin," *New York Times,* February 24, 1991, p. 32.
Sullivan, Ronald, "Church Loses Bid to Bar Play It Contends Is Blasphemous," *New York Times,* October 12, 1990, p. B2.

Other

Gonzalez, Efraim, telephone interview with Julia Edgar, August 12, 1992, Berkley, Michigan.
Pacheco, Carmen, telephone interview with Julia Edgar, August 6, 1992, Berkley, Michigan.

State Assembly of New York Legislative Resolution commending the Honorable Irma Vidal Santaella, June 1, 1989.

—*Sketch by Julia Edgar*

Santiago, Cheryl Brownstein
See **Brownstein-Santiago, Cheryl**

Fabiola Santiago
(1959-)
Newspaper editor, journalist

Fabiola Santiago is managing editor of *El Nuevo Herald,* one of the largest Spanish-language daily newspapers in the continental United States. *El Nuevo Herald* is published by the Miami Herald Publishing Company and has a daily circulation of over 100,000 and a Sunday circulation of over 120,000. Since the creation of *El Nuevo Herald* (formerly *El Miami Herald*) in 1987—for which Santiago was one of the architects—the daily has been repeatedly praised for excellence in journalism. The *Wall Street Journal* in 1992 specifically commended *El Nuevo Herald* for the depth of its journalism and its success in reaching and informing the Spanish-speaking community.

Santiago was born in 1959 in Cuba and came to the United States with her parents and her brother in 1969. She received a bachelor's degree in journalism from the University of Florida. In 1980, Santiago began her professional career as an intern for the *Miami Herald.* Her base was the city of Hialeah, the seventh largest in Florida. During this period she covered the historical Mariel boatlift of refugees from Cuba in 1980, and Miami's Liberty City riots the same year. Between 1981 and 1985 Santiago served as a reporter for the *Herald,* focusing on South Florida's community of Cuban exiles for the paper's Spanish-language supplement. In 1985 and 1986 her capacity was expanded to general assignment reporter. While focusing primarily on immigration issues, her other assignments included hurricanes, civil disturbances, and Cuban political prisoners. In 1986 Santiago was named assistant editor of the "Neighbors" section of the *Herald.* She supervised coverage and edited reports in three different South Dade and two North Dade editions.

Cofounds Spanish-Language Newspaper

In 1987, Santiago created *El Nuevo Herald*'s City Desk at the time of the paper's inception and birth. Her responsibilities included hiring and training reporters, grounding a perspective of local and international coverage with an emphasis on Latin America. Since 1989, Ms. Santiago has served as the managing editor of the newspaper. The daily operations of the newsroom, which includes eighty employees, are under her charge. She also presides over two assistant managing editors and seven department heads. She oversees all hiring, recruiting, and budget administration, and since 1991 has participated as an officer of the Miami Herald Publishing Company.

Among Santiago's other activities, the editor has taught news reporting and writing at Miami's Barry College and has been a speaker on various panels and conferences in Latin America, Canada, and the United States. Her areas of expertise are attracting minorities, the mainstream press, and bilingual publishing, among others. In addition, she serves on the Board of Directors of the National Association of Hispanic Journalists, the Associated Press Managing Editors, the National Association of Hispanic Editors, and the Society of Professional Journalists. She is also an appointed member of the National Advisory Board to the Polynter Institute for Media Studies.

Along with her enterprise reporting—including the reports on the Cuban radio establishment in Miami—Santiago has also written several articles for both the Travel section of the *Miami Herald* and the "Viajes" section of the *El Nuevo Herald.* These include her descriptions of trips to Aruba and Niagara. Santiago is married to Wayne Wragg, an engineer. They have three daughters.

Sources:

Periodicals

Miami Herald, February 19, 1989, p. J1; April 7, 1989, p. A8; November 18, 1990, p. K10.
Wall Street Journal, April 23, 1992, p. A1.

—*Sketch by Paul Miller*

Santiago, Gloria Bonilla
See Bonilla-Santiago, Gloria

Isaura Santiago
(1946-)
Educator, college president

Hostos Community College president Isaura Santiago has dedicated herself to removing the barriers that slow the educational and professional development of New York City's large Spanish-speaking populations. Throughout her career, Santiago has directly challenged bureaucratic problems, whether they be in a school system that refuses to educate non-English speaking children, or in an adoption system that denies children to non-English speaking families. She has forged workable solutions to reshaping those bureaucracies to meet the needs of all members of the community. As the president of a Brooklyn, New York, college that has dedicated itself to providing higher education to a bilingual population, Santiago has been able to promote the needs of her community on a larger scale by training people for jobs in health services and technology and providing them with the language skills they need to succeed in the workplace.

Santiago's parents, Americo and Carmen Santiago, left their native Puerto Rico to come to the United States for one reason, Santiago told contributor Tom Pendergast in a telephone interview: they wanted to provide the best possible education for their children. Americo came first, and when he had earned enough money he sent for his wife and daughter. Isaura was born in the Williamsburg section of Brooklyn on January 19, 1946, the youngest of the Santiagos' three daughters. Santiago explained to Pendergast that the three girls were "latchkey kids—we quickly learned to take care of ourselves." Her parents worked long hours to provide for their children, and their difficulties were compounded when Americo contracted cancer, which forced him to quit working. Eventually he lost his eyesight, and Carmen took over responsibility for providing for the family.

"My mother did everything," said Santiago. "She helped us kids with our homework and taught us to read and write, she taught Sunday school, lead a Girl Scout troop, worked in the community, and became a shop steward at the factory where she worked." Her mother also taught the girls that the best occupation they could pursue was teaching. In fact, Santiago's first experience as a teacher came when she and her sisters "adopted" a neighbor girl who had Down's syndrome, a disorder that includes mental retardation and delayed development. Santiago told Pendergast: "My mother didn't see any reason why we shouldn't teach this girl, so she assigned me and my sisters the task of teaching her to read and write, and teaching her manners. I thought that I had done such a wonderful job teaching her to read using the nursery rhyme section of our

Isaura Santiago

encyclopedia, but when my mother asked her to read it she discovered that the girl had just memorized all the rhymes I had taught her. But eventually we did teach her many things, and her parents were thrilled."

Santiago attended public schools in Brooklyn, and did well despite holding numerous jobs to bring in extra money for the family. Her mother told her that good grades would make all the hard work worthwhile, and Santiago worked hard to prove her right. She took a double major in secretarial and college preparatory classes, the first because teachers kept advising her to study something practical, the second because she knew she wanted to go on to college. Not surprisingly, Santiago chose to pursue a degree in teaching when she entered Brooklyn College in the fall of 1963, and she decided that she wanted to teach science. "The first year was very difficult," she remembered. "I had never before been challenged and I found out that my ghetto schooling left me unprepared for the tough competition from students from New York City's best schools. Also, I was the only woman in the science curriculum, which was filled with sexism and discrimination." She switched to liberal arts and graduated in 1967.

Santiago paid for her schooling by working for a temporary employment service, and in her junior year at Brooklyn College she was assigned to a neighborhood legal services firm. The firm had few Hispanic lawyers, so Santiago soon became an indispensable translator and secretary. "These lawyers adopted me," she related to Pendergast,

"and I don't know how I would have gotten through college without them." Santiago also learned a great deal about the law while working for the firm, information she would put to good use in her later civil rights and community rights work. She so enjoyed the work that she considered becoming a lawyer, but when she told her father of her idea, he was appalled, for he thought that girls should only go into teaching or social work. "A woman lying is a terrible thing," Santiago remembers him telling her, "and lawyers have to lie." Though Santiago thought her father was being old-fashioned, she too decided that she truly did want to teach.

Santiago's student teaching experience at Brooklyn was extremely unpleasant. Her first assignment at a school in Bedford-Stuyvesant was with a young, white teacher "who looked like she had stepped off the cover of *Vogue* magazine," said Santiago. "She acted like none of these African American and Hispanic kids could touch her. She was icy and we did not get along." Santiago spent her lunch hour at the playground with the children instead of in the faculty lounge and was soon reprimanded for being unprofessional. She asked to be transferred to another school, but there, she recalled, "I did the undoable: I refused to do what the teacher asked of me." Santiago chafed at being used as a translator between Hispanic kids and their English-speaking teachers, so when a teacher suggested that one quiet little boy was retarded simply because he did not speak English, Santiago refused to translate a test they wanted to give him. "Hispanic children were being mistreated," she said, "and I was not going to be any part of it."

Fights for Rights of Young Hispanics

Turned off by the lack of support given to teachers in the public schools, Santiago went to work for Aspira, a community-based educational organization that provided support services for young Hispanics. The Brooklyn-based Aspira, which means "to aspire" in Spanish, encouraged neighborhood youths to go to college, and Santiago was impressed by their innovative programs, by the clubs they formed, and by the storefront activities they promoted. "Teaching for Aspira became a labor of love for me," stated Santiago, "because I could teach in a setting where there was absolute freedom, and I felt that I was making a difference." Santiago eventually became the executive deputy director of Aspira.

Santiago was extremely busy between the time she received her bachelor of arts in 1967 and her doctorate of philosophy in 1977. She left Aspira in the late 1960s to teach at Hunter College in New York City, and it was there that she decided to go into teacher education. Santiago received her master of arts in education from Brooklyn College in 1969, and in 1972 she took a position at the City University of New York, where she taught elementary education and developed a graduate bilingual education program. She stayed at City University until 1979. In these years, Santiago also became increasingly involved in community activities and in promoting bilingual education. The lawyers with whom she had once worked had formed a Puerto Rican legal defense fund and Antonia Pantoja urged Santiago to help them initiate a lawsuit to protect the rights of non-English speaking children in the city school system. Santiago, who had seen firsthand the neglect that non-English speaking children endured, plunged herself into the gathering of evidence and the endless paperwork that the suit entailed. But she claimed that it was all worth it, for the suit, known as Aspira vs. the Board of Education, prompted the beginnings of bilingual education in New York schools.

Santiago began to study for her doctoral degree at Fordham University in 1972, but her involvement in the lawsuit made writing her dissertation difficult, since the school principals did not want her studying in their schools. Instead of doing a study of schools, Santiago documented the history of the lawsuit for her dissertation, and that work was published by Educational Testing Services as *A Community's Struggle for Bilingual Education: Aspira vs the Board of Education.* "I am very proud of the book," Santiago told Pendergast, "because now, when minority communities try to develop an educational system, they have a history to look back on." Assisted by funding from the Ford Foundation, Santiago received her doctorate of philosophy in 1977. Her parents, who had achieved their goal of educating their children, returned to Puerto Rico on the day their youngest daughter, Isaura, defended her dissertation.

In 1979, Santiago was contacted by Columbia University president Larry Cremin, who asked her to apply for a newly formed professorship in bilingual education at the university's internationally-recognized Teachers' College. But there was one catch, he explained. The department of language and literature refused to countenance bilingual education, so this professor would have to work out of the international studies department. Santiago agonized over the decision: on the one hand she felt that it was important for her to go there, to help people, especially women and Hispanics, pursue graduate work; on the other hand, taking a position that the language and literature department had refused could be damaging to her university career. But Santiago refused to be intimidated by the political uncertainty, and vowed to Cremin that she would make the language and literature department wish they could have her on their staff.

"There is one thing in society that always works," Santiago told Cremin, "and that is money, so I'll go out and get money to bring students in." In her first three years at Columbia, Santiago brought in 23 endowed scholarship programs, and was then officially invited to join the language and literature department. Santiago enjoyed working under Cremin, who assumed that bilingualism was a way of life, but she was not afraid to differ with him over principles. Invited by Cremin to serve on the university's affirmative action committee, Santiago refused, and told Cremin that though she supported him and thought it was wonderful that he wanted to involve minorities in a university where they had traditionally been excluded, having only minorities serving on the committee would make it look like they were only looking out for their own people. "I wanted power people on the committee, tall, white, gray-haired men, not just minorities," she remembered. Santiago credits Cremin for having the bravery to change the institution he served, and said that he was always there to support her.

Works for Bilingual Education at Hostos

In 1986 Santiago learned that the presidency of Hostos Community College was open. Hostos is part of the multi-college City University of New York system, and it serves the primarily Hispanic population of the South Bronx, where the college is located. Formed in 1968, the college has three principal goals, according to Arthur Levine and Deborah Hirsch, who interviewed Santiago for *Change: The Magazine of Higher Learning:* "to provide bilingual education in order to remove the linguistic barriers to higher education; to provide career and technical programs that lead to employment and socioeconomic mobility; and to provide knowledge and critical thinking skills for life, senior-college transfer, and professional advancement through the liberal arts." Given Santiago's training and interests, it seemed a natural place for her to go. "People urged me to take the position," Santiago told Pendergast, "and going there felt like going home, for the university was formed in response to community demands that came out of families just like my own."

Since taking the presidency in 1986, Santiago has led the college, which enrolls over 5,000 students, through a period of immense growth and change. During tough economic years, Santiago fought to get funding for the college, lobbying the mayor and the state legislature for money to continue her program of growth. She realizes that her efforts have paid off, she says, when she looks around her and sees the many new buildings and facilities that make the university an oasis in a desert of poverty and hopelessness. Santiago admits that being an administrator has placed her at a distance from the profession that she loves, and says wistfully that she would like to be a teacher again someday. But she also acknowledges that the presidency of Hostos has allowed her to continue the community building that has characterized her career. And, she told Pendergast, "we only need fifty million more dollars to complete our plan for growth."

Santiago is proud of the new computer labs that will make Hostos one of the most high-tech universities in the City University program, and of their flourishing health services and bilingual education programs. But she is most proud of the students who attend Hostos. Eighty percent of the students are women, and most of them work full-time while attending school. "When I sit out on a bench in front of the library and talk to female students who work so hard, get up at six in the morning, take their kids to school, and then succeed at school, it makes it all worthwhile," she explained to Pendergast. "To go into one of the poorest communities in the nation and see these buildings is to see a gateway, a ray of hope for people in poverty."

Santiago told Levine and Hirsch that what other colleges could learn from Hostos "is that the role of educational institutions is to provide opportunities through education for groups who haven't been able to share in the wealth of our society by appreciating and building on the linguistic and cultural diversity that the students bring to the institution." In her interview with Pendergast she added: "This college community is a special community. They have had a history of struggle, a history of doing creative things in an incredibly difficult environment. I have a tremendous sense of faith that the faculty here will continue to serve the community in the best way they know how. They have provided instruction to generations of immigrants when no one else would have done it. I always tell the legislature that each of our graduating classes pays the state budget each year, because we get people off welfare and into good jobs."

Santiago has received many awards but, she told Pendergast, "I am embarrassed by awards so I often turn them down. The biggest reward I get is helping people." She met her husband, William Santiago, at a party given by the Puerto Rican Association for Community Affairs, and they were married in 1972. "Even though he has an MBA and has always worked for large firms, I get him involved in community politics," Santiago said. The couple have a twelve-year-old son and a seventeen-year-old daughter. Not surprisingly, Santiago's sisters also work in education, one as a superintendent of schools in Jackson, Michigan, the other as the director of continuing education at a community college. Though she always knew that she would be involved in education, Santiago told Pendergast that she sometimes finds it odd that she is a college president: "People know me for building communities, for being one of the soldiers. I never thought of myself as a leader, but I am proud to have been responsible for making changes in bilingual education."

Sources:

Periodicals

Change: The Magazine of Higher Learning, May/June, 1988, pp. 49-53.
New York Times, June 1, 1987; September 14, 1987.

Other

Santiago, Isaura, telephone interview with Tom Pendergast, October 9, 1992.

—*Sketch by Tom Pendergast*

Saundra Santiago
(1957-)
Actress

Actress Saundra Santiago is known to viewers throughout the United States for her role on the popular television series, *Miami Vice*. She is also recognized among audiences for her appearances in such plays as *A View from the Bridge, Road to Nirvana,* and *Evita,* and for her performance in the 1984 film *Beat Street.* Renowned for her talent as well as her beauty, Santiago is a sought-after actress.

Born to a Cuban father and a Puerto Rican mother in the Bronx, New York, in 1957, Santiago was given a strict Catholic upbringing. Her family lived in New York, where her father worked as a supervisor in a candy and cookie factory and where her mother was a key-punch operator. Santiago attended elementary school at Our Lady of Victory School in the Bronx. When Santiago was thirteen years old, in 1970, her father decided to move the family to Florida, where he would work as a supervisor in a Miami bread factory. The young woman had no trouble making the transition; at South Dade High School, the young Santiago became a cheerleader, a homecoming queen, and the student body president. She did not discover her talent for acting, however, until her sophomore year at the University of Miami.

When she saw a flyer announcing auditions for *West Side Story,* a musical Santiago loved, she decided to try out for a part. Although she was not given a role in that production, Santiago found herself attending other auditions, and she was soon a popular actress on campus. She could sing as well as act, and it was not long before she "just plain got the bug," as she explained in the *New York Times.* Santiago's love of acting inspired her to continue her education after she graduated from the University of Miami with a B.A. in drama in 1979. She attended Southern Methodist University's graduate professional-acting program in Dallas, Texas, and while she was badgered for her slouching shoulders and chided for her persistent New York accent, she began to excel.

Santiago graduated with an M.F.A. in 1981 and headed for New York. Once there, Santiago worked as a singing waitress, and lived with seven eccentric, aspiring entertainers in a five-room flat. It was at this time that she met Merwan Mehta, the actor son of Zubin Mehta; the couple would date for three-and-a-half years. Santiago had an agent and went to audition after audition. It was not long before she was offered her first professional role.

The role was that of Catherine in Arthur Miller's *A View from the Bridge,* which was produced at the Long Wharf

Theatre in New Haven, Connecticut, in November of 1981. Santiago, like Miller's Catherine, had grown up in New York as well as in a male-dominated environment. Although at first Santiago "started analyzing Catherine too much," as she explained in the *New York Times,* she began to portray her role wholeheartedly after a talk with her director, Alvin Brown. He told her, "'Saundra, you know Catherine inside out. All you have to do is let her be.'" The actress did so. "I stopped holding on to her [Catherine], and she came back to me."

Although the play made its way to Broadway in 1983, at least one critic found fault with it. One such reviewer, writing for *New York* magazine, did not appreciate Santiago's talents. He wrote, "As Catherine, Saundra Santiago tries desperately hard, but is utterly charmless throughout." There were, however, some who did enjoy Santiago's portrayal of Catherine. The *New York Times* thought enough of her to interview her; that newspaper noted, "Miss Santiago's Broadway debut in [*A View*] was critically well received." According to *People,* Santiago received "glowing reviews." Also, Santiago did well enough to be noticed by a television director, Bonnie Timmerman. By 1984, Santiago had been given a part in *Miami Vice,* a television series which achieved tremendous success during the 1980s.

Attains Fame with *Miami Vice* Role

In *Miami Vice* Santiago played an efficient, hard-working detective, Gina Calabrese, and worked opposite stars Don Johnson, Philip Michael Thomas, and Edward James Olmos. As Gina and Don Johnson's character became romantically involved, Santiago received more and more attention from audiences. She began to be recognized in public. She was the envy of female *Miami Vice* lovers throughout the United States; she had to kiss the star of the show. Santiago did not complain about the script. "Don's a good kisser," she told *People.* She also, however, assured the magazine that she had no romantic interest in anyone on the *Miami Vice* set. "It's not a good idea to date a co-worker," she explained.

Around the same time that she was cast in *Miami Vice,* Santiago was given a chance to appear in a movie, 1984's *Beat Street.* Also, while working on *Miami Vice,* she continued to act on the stage. She illuminated the musical *I Love My Wife* for three weeks in Miami. This diversity in Santiago's career would serve her well as *Miami Vice* inevitably lost its popularity. In 1989, she starred as Eva Peron in the musical *Evita* at the Fox Theatre in Atlanta. She went on to costar in *Spike Heels,* another play, with actor Kevin Bacon, and to shine in *Road to Nirvana* in 1991. Discussing the latter production, which opened in New York, a critic from the *New Yorker* wrote, "I also enjoyed the beautiful Saundra Santiago as Lou."

In addition to being successful professionally, Santiago utilizes her fame to help her community. She serves as a volunteer worker with the police department in Miami.

The speeches she gives at schools help convince fans of *Miami Vice,* as well as children who have never seen the show, to stay out of trouble. Many people recognize this contribution to the youth across the country as well as in Miami. As Don Johnson commented in *People,* Santiago is a "great role model for the Latin community."

Sources:

Periodicals

Atlanta Constitution, July 31, 1989, p. B1.
New York, February 21, 1985, pp. 52-54.
New Yorker, March 18, 1991, p. 82.
New York Times, March 11, 1983.
People, April 21, 1986, pp. 107-08.
Time, February 14, 1983, p. 87; July 11, 1988, p. 73.

—Sketch by Ronie-Richele Garcia-Johnson

Miriam Santos
(1956-)
City official, lawyer

As the *Christian Science Monitor* noted, Miriam Santos "champions making opportunities for women and minorities." The city treasurer of Chicago understands the difficulties women and minorities face—as the child of Puerto Rican immigrants who could not speak English, Santos has struggled to become a respected and successful member of her community. She earned this respect first as an attorney, then she set her sights on public service, becoming the first female Hispanic ever elected to citywide office. These triumphs have made Santos a role model for career-minded Hispanics and women alike.

Santos was born to Manolin and Ana Santos, both Puerto Rican immigrants, in Gary, Indiana, on January 6, 1956. While Manolin Santos was a hard worker and held a job in the steel mills that allowed the family of seven to live in a small apartment above a machine shop, he could not speak English. Consequently, Santos frequently found herself translating for her father and mother. She became upset when judges and other officials condescended to her parents for not learning to speak English. "I remember my anger at it," she told the *Christian Science Monitor.* At that point in her life, the newspaper reported, "Santos knew she would be a lawyer."

Santos's determination accelerated her natural talent; after skipping a grade in high school, she graduated with

Miriam Santos

honors. She was just as enthusiastic and successful in college. At DePaul University in Chicago, she studied political science and worked to help support her family at the same time. After winning the Saint Vincent DePaul Academic Scholarship Award in 1974 and 1975, and with the help of the Model Cities Education Support Grant, which she received from 1974 to 1979, Santos earned a bachelor's degree in political science from DePaul University in 1977. Her education was by no means complete, though. The DePaul University College of Law Scholarship and the ASPIRA Scholarship Award, along with the assistance of the Notre Dame University Council on Legal Education Opportunities Program, allowed her to attend the DePaul University School of Law, where she earned a J.D. in 1980. Santos passed the Illinois Bar exam that same year.

Santos immediately went to work as a law clerk for Robert E. Mann, a lawyer and state legislator. Mann remembered in the *Christian Science Monitor* that Santos was "bright and very dogged and thorough in her work" as well as "extremely devoted to her parents." Santos moved on to become the statewide Hispanic coordinator for the Stevenson/Stern Campaign in 1982. From 1981 to 1982 she also served as a director with the Aspira Center for Educational Equity. A year later she became the deputy director of child support enforcement for Cook County State's Attorney Richard M. Daley, the man who would later become the mayor of Chicago. She left that job to become a highly paid senior attorney for Illinois Bell. Santos's father's work had

disabled him, and her mother was similarly indisposed; Santos had to pay their medical bills.

Although she was busy caring for her parents and involved with her demanding career, Santos was becoming a leader in her community. She won recognition from the Institute for Educational Leadership in Washington, D.C., in the early 1980s, then served on the Mexican American Legal Defense and Education Fund's Board of Directors, beginning in 1987, and on the Board of Directors for Travelers and Immigrants Aid. In 1989, her former boss, Daley, won a special election to complete the remainder of Mayor Harold Washington's term after the latter official passed away. Santos cochaired Daley's transition team as he took office.

Appointment by Daley Launches Political Career

By this time, Santos's career was taking off. She had just been promoted to division manager of customer and community relations at Illinois Bell. As she told the *Christian Science Monitor,* she was excited about "this great job where I felt I could be Santa Claus at Illinois Bell and give to every cause that I ever dreamed of." Although she was enthusiastic about the position, she could not pass up another opportunity—in April, 1989, Daley appointed her acting city treasurer, as the current officer had become the state's acting attorney.

Santos welcomed the chance to serve her community as well as to further her career; she accepted the appointment and became responsible for the management of $40 billion in city revenue, five pension funds (for fire personnel, police personnel, municipal employees and laborers, and public school teachers) worth $8.5 billion, and 23 employees. Santos worked quickly and thoroughly, and in the process received a great amount of attention.

Her first acts in office involved eliminating inefficient operations, computerizing money management, halving bank fees, investing funds in interest-bearing accounts, and working to impede embezzlement opportunities. In June of 1990, she made an anti-apartheid statement by instructing her staff to ignore the bids of the Xerox Corporation and IBM because the companies in question had ties to the South African government. That September, Santos charged that the Chicago Teachers Pension Fund had lost more than $136 million in stock value since July of that year and took steps to make corrections. As she worked, Santos generated seven million dollars for the city of Chicago.

Instead of neglecting her previous community activities, Santos found a way to incorporate them as she worked to keep the city prosperous. She persuaded banks, businesses, and community organizations to ensure that the city deposited its money in banks that lend to businesses owned by minorities and women as well as to new businesses. The plan was to facilitate bidding for city projects by such businesses and encourage their growth. The plan was realized in early January of 1991, when Santos announced that up to $25 million in city funds were designated to the financial institutions that met the requirements discussed. *Más* magazine praised Santos for the enterprise: "Miriam Santos has notably increased the opportunities for minority businesses to work with the city."

Santos began to shine as a public figure. She joined the Chicago Council on Foreign Relations, the Board of Directors of the Make-A-Wish Foundation, and the Advisory Board of the Chicago Junior League, all in 1990. The efforts she contributed to her community were recognized with various awards. In 1990 she was given the Distinguished Hispanic Professional Award by the Hispanic Alliance for Career Enhancement, and she was named as one of *Hispanic Business* magazine's 100 Hispanic Influential Leaders. To top it all off, she finally earned the Master's of Business Administration from Northwestern University's Kellogg School of Management that she had been working on before becoming acting city treasurer.

Santos's achievements during this time as acting city treasurer were scrutinized as well as highlighted as early as November of 1990, when it was announced that she would attempt to be elected to her office in the upcoming local elections. Challenger Edward Murray created a stir when he demanded that Santos account for the profit from a soda pop machine located in her office in early February of 1991. Santos was then faced with a controversy involving two vice presidents at Chicago's largest bank who wanted her ousted. Despite the efforts of her opponents, Santos continued to receive widespread support.

The *Chicago Tribune* endorsed Santos in an editorial shortly after the trouble with Murray and the bankers. By mid-February, the newspaper was reporting that Hispanic Santos, along with an African American, Joe Gardner, would affect the mayor's own efforts to be elected to his office; the mayor was hoping that white citizens on the northwest and southwest sides of the city would vote for his running partner and current treasurer, Santos, instead of Edward Murray, who had once been the mayor's ally.

Becomes High-Profile Politician in Chicago

Daley's hopes were more than realized—while Hispanics represented only 8.3 percent of Chicago's voters, Santos won 69.6 percent of the vote in primaries held on February 26, 1991. Ironically, she had received a higher percentage of the votes than Daley himself, who won 63 percent of the votes in the mayoral primary. The *Chicago Tribune* did not fail to recognize this evidence of Santos's popularity with the voters: "Though some people thought [Santos] would win the Democratic nomination for the city treasurer's post on Mayor Richard Daley's coattails, the results [of the primary election] could be facetiously interpreted to mean that, in fact, he rode in on her skirt hem."

Santos's success was heralded by the press. The *Chicago Tribune* wrote, "Since the demise of former Mayor Jane Byrne, the vivacious attorney is often mentioned as the most likely candidate to become the highest profile female politician in Chicago." Juan Andrade, president of the Midwest-Northeast Voter Registration Education Project, told the paper, "This [election] looks great for Miriam. It certainly puts her on a track potentially leading to national prominence."

As personal as Santos's victory might have been, her win in the Democratic primary was also a great achievement for Hispanics across the country. While, at the time, Santos was already known as the first Hispanic woman to hold citywide office, many observers noted that victory in the final election would make her the first Hispanic woman elected to a citywide office in the United States. Santos acknowledged the effect that her ethnicity had on her campaign, but also cited her contributions to the city as an individual in the *Chicago Tribune:* "Well, because I'm an Hispanic woman, as well as a professional, competent person, I was able to go out in all communities and reach other communities. I'm very proud of my Hispanic background, but I'm also very proud of what I've been able to do in the treasurer's office for the last 22 months."

Apparently, voters were impressed with those 22 months. In April of 1991, she was elected as Chicago's city treasurer and became the first female Hispanic to be elected to a post in a citywide race. 1991 was a year of effort and achievement for Santos for other reasons as well. Her program of using city deposits as incentives for community banks to loan to minority-owned small businesses was doing well by May of 1991. In July, however, Daley sought to eliminate her as an ex-officio member of the city's pension boards because of her independent stance; Santos fought back with gusto, setting off a highly publicized controversy. The governor of Illinois eventually vetoed the proposed legislative provision removing Santos from the boards, but observers noted that the feud may have jeopardized Santos's political future with Daley. Santos, however, declared to *Hispanic:* "I am not going to make peace at the cost of my integrity. I came here to do a job and to do it exceptionally well." The city was proud of its treasurer; the *Chicago Tribune* featured her in an article which focused on her efforts to serve as mentors to women beginning their careers.

Santos was still very active out of her office; in 1991 she became a member of several organizations and received recognition from others. She joined the Finance Council of the Archdiocese of Chicago and the Executive Committee of the Board of Directors of Illinois, the Democratic Leadership Council, and the Advisory Board for the Cabrini Green Tutoring Program. She then received the Woman of the Year Award for 1991 from the Puerto Rican Chamber of Commerce and Industry of Chicago, the Women in Government Award from Operation PUSH, and Chicago Jaycee's Outstanding Citizen Award.

Santos, who as a girl worked on a Christmas ornament assembly line to support her family while she attended college, has not only achieved her dream of becoming a lawyer, she has received national recognition. While, during her campaign to be elected as Chicago's city treasurer, she did not voice any hopes of becoming the city's mayor someday, various observers believe that she has the potential to become the mayor, or even to seek national office. Whatever position she may hold in the future, it is certain that Santos will continue to be a leader and source of inspiration to Hispanics and women.

Sources:

Periodicals

Chicago Tribune, April 27, 1989, p. 6; June 29, 1990, section 2C, p. 5; September 11, 1990, section 2C, p. 1; November 11, 1990, section 2, p. 1; January 8, 1991, section 2C, p. 2; February 6, 1991, section 1, p. 1; February 8, 1991, section 2C, p. 4; February 12, 1991, section 1, p. 14; February 17, 1991, section 2C, p. 1; February 17, 1991, section 4, p. 4; February 28, 1991, section 2C, p. 2; March 21, 1991, section 2C, p. 1; May 15, 1991, section 3, p. 3; June 16, 1991, section 6, p. 9; July 10, 1991, section C, p. 2.
Christian Science Monitor, March 20, 1991, p. 8.
Hispanic, May, 1992, pp. 10-12.
Más (Spanish-language; translation by Ronie-Richele Garcia-Johnson), Julio-Agosto, 1991, p. 10.

—Sketch by Ronie-Richele Garcia-Johnson

Cristina Saralegui

Cristina Saralegui
(1948-)
Television talk show host, editor

With her Spanish language talk show, Cristina Saralegui has become Hispanic television's answer to Oprah Winfrey, Sally Jesse Raphael, and Phil Donahue. The writer and talk show host is not afraid to face controversy and insists that she only has one objective: to inform Hispanics. Saralegui emphasized her concern for Hispanics during an interview with *Hispanic* magazine: "We do the show to help Hispanics here. Once you cross the border you are an immigrant, not a tourist. This is where our kids grow up and we have to be concerned about our community."

Cristina Maria Saralegui was born January 29, 1948, in Havana, Cuba, to Francisco and Cristina Saralegui. Her grandfather, the publishing tycoon Don Francisco Saralegui,

was the dominant influence in her early life. Recognized throughout Latin America as "the Paper Czar," or "Don Pancho," her grandfather introduced young Saralegui to his business. "I was four or five," Saralegui recalls in her official biography, "when I would stroll by the hand of my grandfather visiting the huge rotary presses and the editorial departments of our family owned and operated magazines, *Bohemia, Carteles,* and *Vanidades.* They were the three most successful magazines published out of the island."

In 1960, at the age of 12, Saralegui and her family left their comfortable life in Havana and started a new life in Miami's Cuban exile community. "I remember my last day in Havana," Saralegui relates in her biography. "Looking out of the balcony at the beautiful sea, and thinking as my vision became blurry with tears, that this was probably the last time I would see my friends and this magnificent view, which I loved so much."

In Miami, Saralegui prepared herself to enter the family's traditional business by studying mass communications and creative writing at the University of Miami. During her last year at the university, she began an internship with *Vanidades Continentel,* the number one ladies' service magazine in Latin America. In her biography, Saralegui recalled that she worked hard at *Vanidades Continentel:* "At the time it was a huge challenge. I had to teach myself to write in Spanish. Having attended high school and college in the United States, and receiving all my formal training in English, I was more fluent in the English language."

Saralegui, however, was determined enough to earn a position as the features editor of *Vanidades Continental.* She maintained that position from 1970 to 1973, when she became the editor of *Cosmopolitan-en-Español.* In 1976 she took a position as the entertainment director for the *Miami Herald* newspaper. By 1977, Saralegui was the editor-in-chief of *Intimidades* magazine.

Editor of *Cosmopolitan-en-Español*

In 1979, Saralegui was named Editor-in-Chief of the Spanish language version of Hearst's *Cosmopolitan* magazine. The internationally distributed *Cosmopolitan-en-Español* circulated in all Latin American countries and all major cities in the United States. Saralegui held this position for ten years, until resigning in 1989 to become executive producer and host of Univision Network's *El show de Cristina.*

Host of *El show de Cristina*

Saralegui admits it was not an easy transition adapting to the demands of television. After 23 years as a journalist, where appearance is irrelevant, Saralegui could not understand the importance of looks for the visual medium. A size 18, she had never exercised, spending most of her time behind a desk. But good friends Emilio and Gloria Estefan sent her their personal fitness trainer. "They saved my life" she told the *Miami Herald.* Saralegui started jogging three miles a day, watched her weight, changed her hair, and shrank six dress sizes.

El show de Cristina, in the style of *Phil Donahue* and *Oprah,* became known for discussing controversial topics, such as sex, previously considered "taboo" in Spanish language media. Soon Saralegui went from being dubbed "the Latin Helen Gurley Brown" to "Oprah con salsa." While Saralegui did not mind such comparisons, she was disturbed by those who voiced early objections to her blonde looks. "People would write me hate letters. How dare I try to represent Hispanics when I was so white? I tried to make them see it was racism," she told the *Chicago Tribune.* In an interview with the *Los Angeles Times,* Saralegui recalled, "At the beginning they said 'it won't work. You're a Cuban woman. You have a Cuban accent. How dare you represent us [the Hispanics] because you're so white? I understand that brown is beautiful, but so is white, pink, or whatever you are. We're a cultural minority. We go from [the darker skin tones of] Celia Cruz to me, and everything in the middle."

Saralegui was also worried that she'd have a hard time finding Hispanic guests willing to talk about personal or controversial issues. "Everybody thought the Hispanics wouldn't talk about their problems, but they just needed a forum to discuss these things," Saralegui told the *Chicago Tribune.* "After the first show letters started coming in and they told me stuff that I would not tell my pastor, my gynecologist or my husband."

Emmy Award for *El show de Cristina*

It turned out that the objections regarding Saralegui's complexion and her worries about the show did not matter. *El show de Cristina* was a huge success. It has been rated the number one day-time television show and ranked among the top ten Spanish-language programs in the United States. Moreover, it won an Emmy Award in 1991.

Later in 1991 the outspoken Saralegui launched a three-minute daily radio show entitled *Cristina opina.* Prior to the debut of the nationally syndicated program, distributed through the Cadena Radio Centro Network, Saralegui said in her biography, "I am very excited about *Cristina opina* because it is going to give me an opportunity to share my thoughts, my feelings, my concerns, the experiences I have gathered working hands-on with Hispanics of every country in the past 29 years, and will be a great addition to the work we have accomplished on television."

When asked by *La opinion* if there have been changes in her personal life since she began to work on television, Saralegui replied, "Yes, for good. The routine of my private life has remained almost the same. I've never been a pretentious person, since childhood I got used to leading a tranquil and healthy life. I've always dedicated myself to writing, I love to read a lot, especially biographies. I consider myself a very private person and my family respects this behavior from me. Even if it doesn't seem so, I am a person with time for herself. Be it at home, on the plane, in the hotel, at the studio, wherever I may be, I'll always find five or ten minutes to study, because I like to do so. This routine has remained the same with or without the programs."

In November 1991, Saralegui launched another project, *Cristina la revista* ("Cristina the Magazine"). She is executive director of this monthly lifestyle magazine which is an off-shoot of her television program, distributed by Editorial America. "The magazine is more trouble than the two TV shows put together. Print is always harder to do than television," the former journalist confessed to the *Miami Herald.*

By 1992 Saralegui had achieved another of her professional goals by adding one more dimension to her career. She became the executive producer and host of *Cristina,* an English-language version of her Spanish talk show, making Saralegui the first Hispanic to host daily television programs in two languages. She is quick to point out that any *Cristina* show is unmistakably a Cristina production. She chooses the subjects. "I tell the producers what angles I want. I OK all the angles. I'm very hands on," she explained to the *Miami Herald.*

In addition to her own television series, Saralegui has been a guest on numerous national and local television programs. She has made frequent appearances on the Spanish-language program *Sabado gigante,* acted as creative consultant for *TV mujer* and appeared in the Univision soap opera *Amandote*. She also produced a series of television specials in the style of *This Is Your Life*, celebrating the lives of leading Latin entertainers. "The reason we do these programs," Saralegui told *Hollywood Latinews*, "is because celebrities many times are people who started off in life very poor and they don't have the opportunities that middle class people have, yet they reach such heights. And we want to see, motivationally speaking, how they have made it. They are super-achievers. So when I do these special programs what I stress is that aspect that if they could do it, we can do it too." As was noted in *New York Newsday*, she once shared with a friend the secret to her own success: "To be absolutely fearless and plow ahead, no matter what."

Saralegui told *La opinion* that future goals include to appear in a movie, learn to pilot a plane, and learn deep-sea diving. "I want to have fun while I work. Life is not only work and work, you also have to do what most appeals to you." She also admits two of her virtues are being much too honest and being consistent, but reveals her biggest flaws are being "intolerably perfectionistic, much too honest and not too patient."

Saralegui is managed by her second husband, Marcos Avila, eleven years her junior, a former bass player and part founder of the music group Miami Sound Machine. In an interview with the *Chicago Tribune* she recalled: "I got married the first time because I wanted to have a family. I thought romance was for foolish ladies. I met Marcos when I was 35, and I thought, God sent me this to show me how wrong I was before. I was eleven years older than him, I wore a suit, I was the editor-in-chief of a ladies' magazine and I had a big staff. He was a little musician with a ponytail and an earring. Imagine him at an editorial cocktail party! Everybody's family had a fit!"

They married in 1964 and Avila heads Cristina Saralegui Enterprises, Inc., the company that handles all of Saralegui's operations and business ventures. "That's the secret of our marriage" she told *Más* magazine. "Be together and talk about everything twenty-four hours a day." She also told *Hollywood Latinews*, "I think the most important thing I learned from my failure in my first marriage is that you nave to have the same dreams and you have to go in the same direction. It's really important you work in the same kind of job."

The green-eyed blonde has over twenty-five years of journalism experience and has received numerous distinctions. In addition to being listed as one of *Hispanic Business*'s "100 Influentials" in 1992, she was named one of the "Legendary Women of Miami," received the Corporate Leader Award from the National Network of Hispanic Women, and has addressed organizations ranging from Women in Communications to the Union of American Women of Puerto Rico. She has served on international juries of beauty pageants, has participated as Celebrity

Grand Marshal at several national parades and has been awarded the keys to many cities in the United States and Latin America. As the Hispanic spokesperson for Crest Toothpaste, Saralegui has yet another reason to smile.

When Cristina Saralegui is not writing, taping, touring, consulting, or exercising, she can be found with her husband, her two daughters, Cristina Amalia and Stephanie Ann, and her son, Jon Marcos, in their Miami home.

Sources:

Periodicals

Chicago Tribune, May 31, 1992.
Hispanic, November 1991, pp. 18-24.
La opinion (translated from Spanish by Elena Kellner), Panorama section, October 20, 1991.
Los Angeles Times Calendar, June 22, 1992; June 25, 1992.
Más (translated from Spanish by Elena Kellner), July-August 1991, pp. 43-50.
Miami Herald, June 21, 1992, pp. 11-31.
New York Newsday, April 2, 1992, June 22, 1992.

Other

Hollywood Latinews (television program), interview with Elena Kellner, October 16, 1991.
Saralegui, Cristina, official biography provided by Magikcity Communications.

—*Sketch by Elena Kellner*

Schayes, Wendy Lucero
See **Lucero-Schayes, Wendy**

Hope Mendoza Schechter
(1921-)
Labor leader

Hope Mendoza Schechter's career has played itself out in two very different but related areas. She spent the first part of her life actively involved in labor and community organizations and then, after her 1955 marriage to Harvey Schechter, became equally active in Democratic party politics on the national and local level, as well as in running her own business. Throughout her life she has been devoted to the concerns of the Mexican American community in her hometown of Los Angeles, California.

Born in the Arizona mining town of Miami in 1921, Hope Mendoza moved to Los Angeles with her family when she was a child. Her education was interrupted in 1938 when she dropped out of high school to work in the garment industry. After a period of working in defense factories during World War II, Mendoza returned to the garment industry, and soon became an active organizer for the International Ladies Garment Workers Union, for which she served as business officer until the mid-1950s. During the late 1940s and early 1950s Mendoza also became involved in community and state politics, serving on committees of the state Democratic party and the Central Labor Council, and founding, with others, the Los Angeles Community Services Organization, on whose board she served for seven years.

Mendoza's 1955 marriage to Harvey Schechter prompted her to finish her high school education. In 1961 she used the skills that she had learned as a shorthand reporter to establish the Schechter Deposition Service. In 1972, Schechter was inducted into the Los Angeles Justice Lodge of B'nai B'rith as a court reporter, becoming one of the first females to enter the all male organization. She managed her business until 1973, when she merged it with another firm. Schechter's devotion to community and political causes only increased after her marriage, as she became a member of the board of directors of the Council of Mexican-American Affairs and the Mexican-American Youth Opportunities Foundation. She was also a delegate to two national Democratic conventions, once serving as president of the Democratic Women's Forum. And, in 1964, Schechter was named to the Peace Corps National Advisory Council by United States President Lyndon Johnson.

Sources:

Books

Meier, Matt S., *Mexican-American Biographies: A Historical Dictionary, 1836-1987*, Greenwood Press, 1988, pp. 213-14.

Periodicals

Los Angeles Times, May 2, 1972.
New York Times, April 14, 1964.

—Sketch by Tom Pendergast

Isabel Schon
(1940-)
Educator, literary critic

Isabel Schon has abided by a belief learned early in her life: Children will have a love of books if their parents do. As a former librarian and current director of the Center for the Study of Books in Spanish for Children and Adolescents at the San Marcos campus of California State University, Schon has devoted her life to enriching the lives of Spanish-speaking children with literature.

Born January 19, 1940, Schon recalls that both her parents served as role models for her during her childhood in Mexico City. Her mother, Anita, was a professor, while her father, Oswald, was an attorney, and Schon remembers tagging along with him when he visited the only library in town, an adjunct of the United States Embassy. "My papa loved to read," she related in a telephone interview with Julia Edgar. "I didn't even know what I was reading, but I was talking to him, anyway."

Schon graduated from high school in 1958 and "rushed" to get a job as a librarian at the American School (where she eventually founded the school's Educational Media Center). She later continued her education and earned a bachelor of arts degree at the Universidad Nacional Autonoma de Mexico. In 1972 she emigrated to the United States, where she graduated cum laude from Mankato State College in Minnesota with a bachelor of science degree. She went on to earn a master of arts degree in elementary education at Michigan State University and then a Ph.D. from the University of Colorado. She taught for a time at Arizona State University in Tempe, beginning as an assistant professor and becoming a professor of library science. In the mid-1980s, she left the university for California.

Schon, who is married to R. R. Chalquest and has one daughter, Vera, has dedicated her professional life to the study of literature. She calls herself a "horrible" writer of children's books and maintains that she does not possess a natural flair for them. Nevertheless, she has published a collection of nursery rhymes and games that she played with her seven siblings as a child; authored a bilingual filmstrip and teaching guide series on Mexican history, art, and culture; and contributed more than 40 articles and book reviews to education and library journals. The purpose of the CSU center, which Schon founded in 1989, is to study children's literature throughout the Spanish-speaking world and provide reference materials and books to university students, parents, and teachers.

Schon's ground-breaking work has gained momentum, and she looks toward a "renaissance" in the area of children's Spanish literature. "Up to a few years ago, literature was impoverished," she remarked in the interview, noting that as late as three years ago bookshelves around the country carried about 15 books in Spanish for children. "This year, I don't know of any major publisher that is not publishing in Spanish or planning to." She added that she feels Americans take for granted the "wonderful" books and libraries available to them. "The U.S. has resources. That's not true in many Spanish countries. Even today, Mexican schools do not have libraries."

Sources:

Books

Contemporary Authors, Volume 110, Gale, 1984, pp. 458-59.

Other

Schon, Isabel, telephone interview with Julia Edgar conducted on August 27, 1992.

—*Sketch by Julia Edgar*

Scott, Milcha Sanchez
See **Sanchez-Scott, Milcha**

Norma Brito Selvera
(1947-)
Deputy Director, U.S. Department of Labor

Norma Brito Selvera worked her way through college as a secretary at a job corps office, an experience that prepared her for responsibilities as deputy director of the U.S. Department of Labor. She advanced through the ranks at various job corps offices and finally reached her lifetime goal when she was named director of a job corps center. Then, without her knowledge, Selvera was sought out by the director of the U.S. Department of Labor to work as his deputy. She told D. D. Andreassi in a telephone interview that she was drawn to the job corps career

because she wanted to guide people who otherwise would have floundered in life. "I'm the kind of person who is drawn to the underdog," Selvera said in the interview.

Selvera was born March 9, 1947, to Maria Christina Rodriguez Brito and David Nieto Brito in Alice, Texas. Both her parents, born in Texas, were of Mexican descent. She had one sister, Maria Theresa Brito, an attorney. Selvera, who grew up in San Antonio, credits a twelve-year education at a Catholic school with giving her the basic tools she needed to succeed. "The self-discipline that I think goes hand in hand with a Christian or Catholic organization and the learning of setting priorities are traits that I carry with me throughout life," she told this interviewer.

Selvera attended Southwest Texas State University, where she received a bachelor of science degree with honors in 1971. She earned a masters degree in education three years later. She married Baldemar (Baltimore) Selvera in 1973, and the couple had one child, Daniel.

While in college, Selvera worked as a secretary for a job corps. From 1971-74 she worked as a counselor at Gary Job Corps Center in San Marcos, Texas, which serves primarily youths 16 to 21 years old. About 4,000 youths go through the program annually. The next three years Selvera worked as an assistant to the center director, and from 1977 through 1981 she took on the responsibilities of assistant director of residential programs.

Nearly eighty percent of the youths Selvera worked with were minorities. She told this interviewer that she was drawn to her work because she thought she could make a difference in these young people's lives. "They were not educated well enough to carve out the future for themselves and their potential families, and I wanted to influence their decision-making so they would be able to have good jobs. . . . I wanted them to have a good set of values, family values, and home values." Her goal was to show young people how to enhance their self-esteem and to understand good work ethics.

Selvera told this interviewer that she was proud of many of her students, including one young man who went on to teach college in Oklahoma. But her students did not have to become college professors to make her proud. "Job corps is a success if you take youngsters and help them get their GED (General Equivalency Degree), and train them, and they go on to hold jobs and pay taxes every year," she told this interviewer. "Keeping them off of welfare to me is a success."

Selvera's career as a job corps worker took her to many locations where she assumed various positions. She worked as Singer Career Systems Development Corporation director of residential programs in the Little Rock, Arkansas job corps from 1981 to 1983. The next two years she worked as center director of the Susquehanna, Maryland job corps and for the next five years she worked as the Texas Educational Foundation staff training coordinator.

Referring to her career change from counselor to director of the job corps programs, Selvera told this interviewer she left counseling "because I realized as a counselor I could impact 80 to 100 youngsters on my case load. But if I moved to management I could make decisions that would affect even more."

Takes Position with the Federal Government

In 1990, Selvera was recruited by the U.S. Department of Labor, Office of Job Corps in Washington, D.C., where she worked as deputy director until 1992. Later that year she left Washington to return to Texas, where she became deputy regional administrator of employment and training administration.

The transition from the job corps to the labor department was a big one. "I left the job corps with lots of mixed feelings," she told this interviewer. "I had the opportunity to go into the area that will give me a much broader base to deal with." Selvera supervises job training partnership act programs, employment services, unemployment services and alien certification. Her goal is to draw on her job corps experience and make customers the prime focus. "I want to get my staff and the state staff more focused on the client," she added.

Selvera has given her time to several organizations. From 1979 to 1981 she worked as a volunteer on a steering committee at the Palmer Drug Abuse Program. From 1983 to 1985 she served on the board of directors for the Cecil County Training Center, an organization that locates jobs for handicapped people. She also volunteered with the Texas Hays County Red Cross board of directors, the Hays County Crisis Center and the Association of Hispanic Federal Executives.

Selvera's advice to young people is to take advantage of every learning opportunity and to accept any new challenge an employer might offer, even if it does not fit the job description. "You don't learn only in a college classroom," she observed.

Sources:

Other

Selvera, Norma Brito, telephone interview with D. D. Andreassi, September, 1992.

—Sketch by D. D. Andreassi

Lupe Serrano
(1930-)
Ballerina

Affiliated for nearly two decades with the American Ballet Theatre (ABT), prima ballerina Lupe Serrano has enjoyed a long and rewarding career in the field of dance, first as a performer and most recently as a teacher. Indeed, dancing has been the focus of her life for almost as long as she can remember.

Serrano's father, Luis Martinez Serrano, was a musician and songwriter from Barcelona, Spain, who was raised in Buenos Aires, Argentina. On a tour that took him to Mexico City, he met Luciana Desfassiaux, a Mexican native whose parents had come from France. The success of his tour detained Serrano in Mexico long enough for him to marry Luciana and start a family. But in 1930, Luis, eager to take his expectant wife home to meet his parents, agreed to conduct an orchestra that was traveling through South America. The group was in Santiago, Chile, when Lupe arrived on December 7. During Luciana's recovery from the birth, Luis fell ill. The tour moved on, but the Serranos remained in Chile for the next 13 years.

Even as a small child, Lupe was oblivious to anything other than dancing. Family legend has it that she danced constantly, and according to her parents, on her third birthday she made all her guests sit down while she performed for them. Luis and Luciana eventually decided their daughter should have formal lessons, and despite the rather limited educational choices they faced in Chile, they managed to find a suburban school that offered some training in modern dance, oriental, soft shoe, pointe work, and castanets.

Begins Formal Ballet Training in Mexico City

The Serranos returned to Mexico City when Lupe was 13, and it was then that her formal ballet training began. "I had terrible habits by then!," Serrano remembered in an interview with Peg McNichol. "But I had been in so many recitals that I had a sense of how to fill the stage." She studied seriously with a ballet company in Mexico City and soon earned a position in the Corps de Ballet—"the very last row of the corps," as she recalled. Her efforts paid off, however, and at the age of 14, she debuted in the company's production of *Les Sylphides*.

Serrano worked especially hard in high school, condensing the work of her last two years into one so she would be free to tour. Her devotion to ballet left no time for a college education, but she studied extensively on her own to prepare for the dances themselves and to learn about the

Lupe Serrano

places to which she traveled. At the Palacio de Bellas Artes, for example, Serrano broadened her knowledge of English and French and took courses in such subjects as drama, history, music, and folklore.

Around the time she was 18, Serrano went on a tour with Cuban prima ballerina Alicia Alonso that took her through Central America and Colombia. When she returned to Mexico City, she found that her teacher had formed a ballet company. The experience provided Serrano with a harsh lesson in the economic realities of being a dancer. "Ballet is not a self-supporting art anywhere in the world," she observed in her interview. "It has to be sponsored. A person like my ballet teacher, who was devoted to the art of ballet, of course would not have the ability to raise funds." The company folded after only 18 months, unable to bear the weight of expenses for toe shoes, costumes, and other needs.

Seeks Her Fortune in New York City

Serrano then joined the government-sponsored Ballet Folklorika of Mexico, but she soon felt the pull of New York City and the promise it held out to young dancers. Having saved a little money, she arrived there at the age of 20 and obtained a position with the Ballet Russe de Monte Carlo, where she was featured in her first solo performances and had the opportunity to travel throughout North and South America.

But that company went bankrupt, too, and Serrano returned to Mexico City and a starring role on a television program about the classical arts. It was 1952 and television was still fairly new, so Serrano had to make adjustments for the cameras. "We had to rearrange the way we covered space on the floor, because the cameras were not very mobile," she recalled in her interview. "And you had to be much more subtle in expression, because the camera brings you much closer to the audience. On the stage, you have to think of projecting yourself a block away. Television is much more intimate."

One day Serrano's phone rang with a long distance call from New York. On the other end of the line was the former road manager of the Ballet Russe de Monte Carlo. He was now with the ABT in New York, and he wanted to know if Serrano was interested in auditioning for the troupe.

Auditions Successfully for the ABT

Serrano wasted little time returning to the United States. She took classes and auditioned several times. When she was accepted in 1953, she joined as principal dancer, a position of great honor. "I remember having such respect for the company itself," she said to McNichol. The first time she led her fellow dancers in a big finale, Serrano thought to herself, "'Well, look at you now, leading this group of wonderful dancers.' I felt a great sense of pride." During the nearly two decades Serrano performed with the ABT, she appeared in more than 50 different roles ranging from classics such as *Swan Lake* and *Giselle* to a variety of contemporary works.

One of Serrano's most memorable experiences as a member of the ABT came in 1961, when the troupe visited the Soviet Union as part of a cultural exchange. They had to deal with many cultural and linguistic barriers (many eventually settled on French or German as a common language), but when they danced, everyone understood. During their 11-week tour, the ABT performed portions of Balanchine's *Theme and Variations* and excerpts from other American ballets such as *Rodeo, Fancy Free,* and *Combat* as well as classical pas de deux such as *La Fille Mal Gardee.* Serrano enchanted the audience in Leningrad so completely that they insisted she repeat her solo performance rather than just take a bow for it.

The tour also included dates in parts of Europe. Serrano remembers being in Athens and standing in the Acropolis under the full moon during a party hosted by the American Embassy. At one point, staff members invited the dancers to stroll around the ruins. For Serrano, it was a magical evening, "to be stepping on those stones that had been laid down so many years ago."

In 1963, Serrano and her husband since 1957, ABT conductor Kenneth Schermerhorn, welcomed their first child, Erica. The ballerina noted to McNichol that returning to dancing after having a baby was "not that difficult," but she did notice that she had "a completely different feeling, as though dancing was a wonderful self-indulgence. I had a much more relaxed approach to it then." By this time, Schermerhorn was affiliated with the New Jersey Symphony. The family lived in New Jersey, and a busy Serrano commuted to New York for classes and rehearsals.

In 1967, the ballerina experienced perhaps the most active year of her entire career. She danced excerpts from *Raiymonda* at a White House performance for President Lyndon Johnson, toured the Soviet Union for a second time and was met with a reception as enthusiastic as the first, and gave birth to her second daughter, Veronica.

Serrano then took a year off, returning to the ABT as a permanent guest artist and choosing her own performances. After Kenneth Schermerhorn accepted a position with the Milwaukee Orchestra, the family moved to Wisconsin.

Serrano continued to make guest appearances with the ABT and also started teaching at the University of Milwaukee and the Conservatory of Milwaukee. She found teaching to be a superb way to communicate her love for ballet. She enjoyed watching young dancers blossom and professional dancers refine their skills under her tutelage.

Retires from the Stage

In 1970, Serrano turned 40. The press began referring to her as a "veteran ballerina" and making references to her age before commenting on her performances with the ABT. Despite her desire and ability to perform, the remarks unsettled her, so in 1971 she decided to retire from the stage. At the same time, her marriage ended in divorce. Her family urged her to return to Mexico City, but she felt the United States was her home, especially since she had her two young daughters.

Serrano soon accepted her first full-time teaching position as assistant director at the National Academy of Arts in Illinois. Like many ballet companies, the school struggled with overwhelming financial demands before it was finally forced to close. In 1974, the Pennsylvania Ballet School named Serrano company teacher and director of the apprentice program. A year later she became school director, a position she held until 1983. Among her students during this period were her daughters; only Veronica, however, opted to continue her lessons and pursue a career in dance, eventually becoming a soloist with the ABT as her mother had before her.

In addition to her duties with the Pennsylvania Ballet School, Serrano taught master classes for professional dancers. She also judged dance events and was invited to guest teach at the San Francisco Ballet, Minnesota Dance Theatre, Cleveland Ballet, Washington Ballet, Cincinnati Ballet, Rome Opera Ballet and the American Ballet Theatre.

In 1988, Serrano left Philadelphia to become the artistic associate for the Washington (D.C.) Ballet. She continues to dance, but only within the confines of the classroom, where she concentrates on instructing advanced students aged 13 to 18 and professionals. "I have never lost my love for that," she declared in her interview. "It still gives me great pleasure."

Sometimes Serrano thinks she should try choreography, or perhaps develop a video or write a book about ballet technique. But most of her time is devoted to teaching. She says she has reached a point in her life where she no longer feels driven to be the best at everything she does. For now, insists Serrano, it is enough to do her best with three classes a day and individual coaching sessions.

Sources:

Serrano, Lupe, interview with Peg McNichol, September, 1992.

—Sketch by Peg McNichol

Faustina Solís
(1923-)
Health educator, social services consultant

Faustina Solís has dedicated her life to improving social conditions in poor communities throughout California. From the settlement houses of inner-city Los Angeles to the migrant camps of the state's agricultural regions, Solís has displayed the insight, dedication, and stubborn persistence that have earned her recognition as an expert in the field of community medicine. She also served as the first full professor at the University of California at San Diego School of Medicine with neither a medical degree nor a doctorate.

One of twelve children of Cutberto Silva and Maria Fernandez Solís, who had fled their native Mexico in 1911 to escape the chaos of the revolution, Faustina Solís was born in Compton, California, on April 28, 1923. Although Cutberto had managed his mother's store in the Mexican town of Durango, upon his arrival in Pasadena, California, he could only find work as a farm laborer. Soon he and his family moved to Compton, and there Cutberto took a job in a lumber company, a position he held for the rest of his life.

A firm believer in the value of education, Solís's father read to his children each night before they went to bed and taught them about Mexican history and literature. Her grandmother, who had urged the entire family to convert from Roman Catholicism to Methodism, insisted that the children learn to read the Bible. As a result, Solís entered school with stronger reading skills than many other students.

Although she experienced discrimination during her student years, Solís told interviewer Tom Pendergast that she was most influenced by "the teachers and school personnel who didn't discriminate against [me], that accepted [my] intelligence and encouraged [me]." After graduating from high school, she attended Compton Junior College until the United States' involvement in World War II led her to interrupt her education and go to work.

When Solís was finally able to resume her studies, she enrolled at the University of California in Los Angeles. "I didn't know what I wanted to do," she commented to Pendergast. "I would have liked to go into anthropology but it was not in my realm of imagination to ever get a Ph.D. I chose sociology because I knew I wanted to work with people." Having completed her undergraduate degree in the mid-1940s, Solís went to the University of Southern California to pursue graduate studies and, with the help of a psychiatric scholarship from the National Institute of Mental Health, she earned her master's degree in social work in the late 1940s.

Gains Practical Experience in Social Work

Solís had decided early in her life that she would not marry. As she explained, "I didn't want to be held back in my career by a husband and a family, and most Mexican men don't want a wife who is more educated than them." She also knew that she didn't want to work at a single job for a long time; she wanted to be able to move at will and take any job that sounded interesting. For the next twenty years Solís did just that, and in the process she gained a wealth of experience in the California social service system.

Her first job was in early childhood education, but from there she moved on to a settlement house in urban Los Angeles, a hospital for the developmentally disabled in Pomona, and then a small town in the California desert. In 1963 Solís joined the State Health Department and subsequently developed groundbreaking programs for agricultural migrant workers that provided them with education and day care for their children, health care, and housing.

Launches a Successful Academic Career

In 1971, the University of California in San Diego asked Solís to help establish their comprehensive health center on the Mexican border. Thus began a long affiliation with the university that saw Solís become actively involved in teaching courses in community medicine and in developing the health sequence of the undergraduate curriculum. Working out of the department of community and family medicine, she became a full professor and served as provost of her division of the university beginning in 1982. She also worked as a consultant on rural health programs in the United States and for programs in Ecuador and Venezuela.

Solís has been honored for her commitment to social services in numerous ways, including having a lecture hall on the San Diego campus of the University of California named after her. And upon her retirement from teaching in 1988, she was named professor emeritus in recognition of her service to the university.

Looking back at her many accomplishments, Solís told Pendergast that her work with migrant populations was "the most intense and the most rewarding, because I saw the beginning of what are now common programs for migrants." Though she encountered considerable discrimination along the way, she did not let it interfere with her mission. "I took my commitment and focused on what needed to be done, not to combat the discrimination but to empower people for their own development," she remarked. "I wanted to focus on positive goals and not get slowed down by other peoples' problems."

Sources:

Solís, Faustina, interview with Tom Pendergast, September 9, 1992.

—Sketch by Tom Pendergast

Adaljiza Sosa-Riddell
(1937-)
Professor of Chicano studies

Educator, activist, and author Adaljiza Sosa-Riddell believes Chicanos in this country will only experience true empowerment through the establishment of an independent nation-state. "It may take several lifetimes," she told interviewer Sandra Márquez. "It's not something that can happen overnight." According to Sosa-Riddell, a Chicano revolution will have to be a spontaneous event occurring when the situation is ripe. In the interim, Chicanos must go on with their daily lives, she noted. "While we are waiting for the revolution, we have to eat."

Sosa-Riddell sees her role in the Chicano independence movement as that of an educator, teaching Chicanos who they are and where they are going. She stresses the importance of political and geographic autonomy in preserving

Adaljiza Sosa-Riddell

identity and asserts that an armed struggle may be required to carry out this goal, for as she maintains, "This world only recognizes nation-states."

Sosa-Riddell's world view was profoundly influenced by her early life experience. Born December 12, 1937, to Luz Paz Sosa and Gregoria López Sosa, she worked in the fields with her migrant-worker parents and eight siblings. Summers were spent in California's Silicon Valley picking prunes and apricots. At the start of the school year the family would return to their Colton, California, home for the remainder of the year. As Sosa-Riddell remembers it, that home was little more than a barn or a shack; the walls were knocked out, there was no hot water, and they sometimes had to sleep on a dirt floor. Yet the harsh physical environment was made more bearable by the warm bond that existed between members of the family.

Sosa-Riddell's parents, who had not received any formal education beyond the first grade, were nevertheless self-taught and highly literate people who constantly pushed their children to do well in school. Politics also played a prominent role in the household. Sosa-Riddel's father, a young revolutionary in Mexico, was arrested several times in the United States for his radical socialist activities. Both Luz Pas Sosa and his wife encouraged their children to be free thinkers at an early age.

In 1955, following in an older sister's footsteps, Sosa-Riddell went to the University of California in Berkeley.

She worked 30 hours a week in the library in order to supplement her $200 scholarship and lived with her sister for about a year before moving into a dormitory.

While the curriculum at Berkeley did not speak to her life experience, Sosa-Riddell reflected in her interview with Márquez, she did not find that troublesome at the time. "Our life experience was so difficult that I didn't want to have that reinforced," she explained. Instead, Berkeley served as an introduction to a world she had never known—a world that "was so cosmopolitan and international, a place where I could experience everything." Sosa-Riddell was especially influenced by the various Third World liberation movements then emerging.

Sosa-Riddell nevertheless recalls feeling somewhat alienated at times. In particular, she cites a course on the state's history that depicted California as an empty land made habitable by the Spanish and the British. "I never asked, 'Where were the native American people?'" she said. As one of only about four Chicano students on campus, Sosa-Riddell was also subjected to anti-Mexican sentiment in the classroom. These experiences eventually prompted a search for identity, she told Márquez. She grew increasingly interested in Mexico and began to ask herself how it could be that "this country had its own culture and we had nothing to do with it?"

Although she had wanted to study law, Sosa-Riddell was discouraged from doing so by advisors who insisted that no one could work and go to law school at the same time. So during her junior year in college, Sosa-Riddell married fellow Berkeley student William Riddell, and together they pursued their master's degrees. She majored in political science and submitted a dissertation on Mexican nationalism.

By the time they had obtained their degrees, Sosa-Riddell and her husband had several student loans that needed to be paid off. They returned to Sosa-Riddell's hometown of Colton, where she taught elementary school for seven years. It was during this period that she accomplished what she regards as her greatest life achievement—building her parents a comfortable home and providing for them emotionally and financially until their deaths. "They never had to worry about money any more," Sosa-Riddell told Márquez. "[And] I was able to take care of my mother when she was sick."

Heads Chicano Studies Program

In 1971, after receiving a doctorate from the University of California at Riverside for a dissertation entitled "Who Cares Who Governs? A Historical Analysis of Local Governing Elites in Mexicali, Mexico," Sosa-Riddell began lecturing in the department of political science at the University of California at Davis. Two years later she was named director of the Chicano studies program, responsible for course development, faculty recruitment, budget decisions, and community outreach efforts. She created and taught courses such as Introduction to Chicano Studies, Chicanos in Contemporary Society, Women in Politics, Political Economy of Chicano Communities, and U.S.-Mexican Border Relations.

Sosa-Riddell's lifelong commitment to improve the lives of Chicanos in the United States and her personal identity as a feminist merged together when she became a founding member of Mujeres Activas en Letras y Cambio Social (MALCS) in 1981. The mission of the organization is to foster the development of Latina scholarship and to confront the predominantly white and male academic world with that body of knowledge. The educator has dedicated herself to MALCS, serving as editor for the group's newsletter, *MALCS Noticiera,* and launching its summer institute program, which provides a forum for discussing policy concerns, research results, and native methodologies. Since its inception in 1985, the institute has held sessions across the United States in cities such as Chicago, Los Angeles, and Boulder. The success of the group's publication series has led to plans to create the first journal of Chicana studies.

Lobbies for Chicana/Latina Research Institute

In 1990, MALCS kicked off a system-wide effort to call attention to Latina concerns at the University of California by forming the Chicana/Latina Research Project. From the very start, one of the project's long-term goals has been to establish a permanent Chicana/Latina Research Institute on the Davis campus that would serve the entire country. That dream is now close to reality thanks to MALCS and Sosa-Riddell's own lobbying efforts. When the professor learned that the all-male committee established by the California state legislature to study the status of Latinos in California had no plans to address the condition of women as separate area of inquiry, she convinced the legislators to insert in their final report a chapter that she had written on the status of Chicanas. Among her recommendations was the creation of a research center to address Latina issues. MALCS expects the Chicana/Latina Institute to be operational in Davis by the mid-1990s.

Sosa-Riddell has also been active with the National Association for Chicano Studies. A founding member of the group, she was instrumental in reviving the organization by bringing its national conference to Davis in 1985. According to Sosa-Riddell, participation was up, women's issues garnered the spotlight, and the community's involvement was revitalized.

Besides her activities with MALCS and the Chicana/Latina Research Project, Sosa-Riddell has had a long-standing interest in the subject of reproductive technologies and their impact on Latinas. As she explained in her interview with Márquez, infertility treatments are often unavailable to Latinas because of financial constraints, yet genetic engineering looms as a threat against them in the form of genocide against the poor. "The technology is way ahead of our thinking," she noted. "We have to ask ourselves, 'Who is in control of how our technology is applied?'" Sosa-Riddell has delivered numerous public speeches on this topic and intends to continue writing about it as well.

In recognition of her activism, Sosa-Riddell has received numerous honors, including a Scholar of the Year Award from the National Association for Chicano Studies northern California region in 1988 and, that same year, a Woman of the Year Award from the Business and Professional Women's Association for her activities on behalf of Chicanas, Latinas, and other women of color. In 1989, the Comision Feminil gave her its Latina Leadership Award.

Sosa-Riddell resides with her family in Sacramento, California. Her husband, William, works for the California Air Resources Board, and their daughter, Citlali Lucia Sosa, is a feminist who enjoys the study of history. The educator's future plans include a possible book on electoral reform in school districts and a biography of Dolores Huerta, the vice president of the United Farm Workers Union.

Sources:

Periodicals

Aztlan, spring/fall, 1974, pp. 156-166.
Western Political Quarterly, December, 1975, pp. 739-743.

Other

Sosa-Riddell, Adajliza, interview with Sandra Márquez, September 27, 1992.

—*Sketch by Sandra Márquez*

Soto, Rosana De
See **De Soto, Rosana**

Shirlene Ann Soto
(1947-)
Professor of Chicano history

Shirlene Ann Soto, a professor of history in the Chicano studies program at California State University at Northridge, underscores her commitment to her field by recounting an incident that occurred in one of her classes. As she told contributor Tom Pendergast, she once explained to her students that some countries allow very young children to stay with their mothers if the women are imprisoned. Soto then asked her students if they thought this was a policy that the United States should adopt. Noting that their opinions were clearly divided along ethnic lines, with the Hispanic students unanimously declaring that children should remain with their mothers no matter what, she realized that "Hispanicness pervaded [her] life." As an educator and writer Soto now tries to make sense of the Hispanic historical experience and to encourage all Hispanics, especially Hispanic women, to persevere in their quest for education.

Soto was born on January 22, 1947, in San Luis Obispo, California, and grew up on the cattle ranch that her parents, Vernon and Althea Soto, ran outside Cambria, California. Though they were not rich, they were "hardworking and economically responsible," said Soto, who describes her childhood as "idyllic" because she was surrounded by a very supportive and loving extended family.

From her earliest years in school, Soto was identified as a very bright child; she scored high on tests, skipped grades, and captured the attention of her teachers. Despite the fact that no one else in her family had attended college, Soto told Pendergast that "going to college was not much of a decision. I was a cheerleader and the student body president, and I realized that without a degree I could go nowhere."

She began her schooling at Santa Clara University but soon transferred to San Francisco State University, where she received her bachelor's degree in 1969 and the encouragement to continue her education. Attracted to the University of New Mexico's strong program in Mexican history, Soto—with the help of a Ford Foundation fellowship—earned her Ph.D. in 1977.

Fights to Gain Support for Her Research

Getting that degree was not without its problems, however. Her advisor actively discouraged her from pursuing her interest in the contributions of women to Mexican history, suggesting that she focus instead on constructing a negative picture of a prominent male figure. Soto refused to give up, however, remarking to Pendergast that her grandmother's lifelong example of optimism and practicality was of great comfort and inspiration during those trying times. Eventually she convinced her advisor to support her research, the results of which were published in her doctoral dissertation, "The Mexican Woman: A Study of Her Participation in the Revolution, 1910-1940."

In 1977, Soto became an assistant professor in the department of history at California Polytechnic State Uni-

versity and continued her study of the role of women in the Mexican revolution. Despite her success in establishing that women of all socioeconomic classes were actively involved in the struggle, she still encountered resistance to her work. So in 1980, Soto left California Polytechnic State University and accepted a one-year administrative fellowship position with the California State University system.

Spearheads Efforts to Broaden Curriculum

At the end of her fellowship, Soto was named assistant vice president for academic affairs at California State University at Northridge. In this position she coordinated and set policy in educational equity programs, encouraged the development of women's studies courses in a local community college, and furthered the development of the Chicano studies program, the largest such program in the nation and one that is especially active in addressing the needs of the Hispanic community. Soto joined its faculty as a full professor in 1985, returning to teaching with renewed vigor and commitment to promoting the needs of Hispanic students. And in an atmosphere more conducive to her research, Soto was able to expand on her doctoral thesis and in 1989 published *Emergence of the Modern Mexican Woman, 1910-1940: Her Participation in the Revolution and Her Struggle for Equality.*

In addition, Soto regularly contributes articles to professional journals and presents papers at regional and national conferences. One of the highlights of her developing career, she says, is the fact that she has produced some of the first work in English dealing with women in the Mexican revolution. Looking back over her career, Soto credits her family with supplying a great deal of support and motivation—more evidence of her strong Hispanic identity. "One advantage of the Latino family is that they are very supportive," she explained to Pendergast. "They may not have the resources, but they have the soul."

Sources:

Periodicals

Hispanic American Historical Review, November, 1991, pp. 903-904.
Journal of Latin American Studies, February, 1992, pp. 210-211.

Other

Soto, Shirlene Ann, interview with Tom Pendergast, September 9, 1992.

—Sketch by Tom Pendergast

Marta Sotomayor
(1939-)
Gerontologist, educator

Marta Sotomayor has devoted her life to improving the quality of life for Latinos in the United States, particularly in the area of health care. An educator, author, and advocate of the Latino elderly, Sotomayor is president of the National Hispanic Council on Aging (NHCoA) in Washington, D.C., and first vice president of the National Council of La Raza.

Born in San Diego, California, on December 7, 1939, Sotomayor is one of four daughters of Venancio Sotomayor, a grocer, and Catalina Gonzalez, a schoolteacher. During the Depression, the Sotomayors moved to Mexico and did not return to California until the 1940s, at which time Venancio Sotomayor once again assumed ownership of the family's supermarket chain.

In an interview with Sandra Márquez, Sotomayor recalled that her parents placed a very strong emphasis on education. "I don't remember any other option but that I would attend college and do well," she said. Following in one of her older sister's footsteps, she enrolled at the University of California in Berkeley in 1955 to study economics and social welfare. Completing her education meant enduring cultural isolation, however; as Sotomayor told Márquez, she does not remember meeting any other Chicano students during her years at Berkeley or later while she pursued her master's degree in social sciences.

Awakens to Need for Latino Empowerment

The realization that Latinos lacked political and economic power eventually spurred Sotomayor to action. "I had a sense that something had to give," she explained to Márquez. "Things had to change for us. Ever since then I've been an agent for change."

Sotomayor decided to combat powerlessness with knowledge. In 1970, for example, she went to Colombia as a Fulbright scholar to study that country's higher education system. And in 1973, she earned a doctorate in social policy and planning from the University of Denver with a dissertation entitled "Status and Tradition: A Study of Chicano Grandparents in an Urban Barrio." It was the first such work to address the issue of the Hispanic elderly.

Prior to becoming president of the National Hispanic Council on Aging in 1986, Sotomayor held a variety of academic positions. She taught in the school of social work and urban planning at San Jose State University in California and in the schools of social work at both California

Marta Sotomayor

State University in San Diego and Howard University in Washington, D.C. She has also taught community psychiatry at Baylor School of Medicine in Houston and urban planning at Metropolitan State College in Denver. In addition, she is a former assistant dean and associate professor in the graduate school of social work at the University of Houston.

Sotomayor also has a long record of service in public health, including various positions with the Administration for Mental Health, Drug Abuse and Alcohol and the National Institute of Mental Health. In 1979, she was appointed to the U.S. Commission to UNESCO, and from 1984 until 1986 she served with the National Institutes of Health as the senior policy advisor on the secretary's task force on minority health.

In Sotomayor's view, Latino health care concerns have reached a critical point in the United States. Factors such as poverty, inadequate outreach, language barriers, overcrowding in homes, and cultural insensitivity among health care providers discourage access to health care services and have resulted in what she terms a "prohibitive" system that ignores the needs of a growing segment of the population.

Assumes Presidency of Hispanic Council on Aging

Since the mid-1980s, Sotomayor has tried to address some of those needs as president of the National Hispanic Council on Aging, or NHCoA. Founded in 1980, its stated mission is to eliminate the social, civic, and economic injustices that impact negatively on the quality of life for elderly Hispanics and their families. In an article Sotomayor wrote for *California Sociologist,* she describes NHCoA's philosophy: "The programs of the organization are to be based on self-help. . . . The long range goal of the organization is to make available to the elderly the necessary resources required to create changes and to enhance their capacity to make the process of self-help, self-sufficiency, and independent living a reality."

NHCoA relies on family support, community involvement, and intergenerational linkages to fashion its programs, which not only pass along information but provide opportunities for leadership development as well. And in keeping with Sotomayor's belief that the current U.S. health care system is too disease- and illness-oriented—a focus she would like to see changed—NHCoA health promotion campaigns all stress the benefits of preventive medicine.

Assisting Sotomayor with these tasks is a full-time staff of four in NHCoA's Washington, D.C., office plus six others who do grass roots work in various communities across the country. They operate with an average annual budget of $800,000.

Writings Examine Hispanic Health Care Needs

Sotomayor has edited several books that address the topic of health care for Latinos. In *Hispanic Elderly: A Cultural Signature,* for instance, she points out that the role of culture cannot be overlooked when considering the needs of elderly Latinos. The Hispanic population is not a homogeneous one; there are many sub-groups that share a common cultural and linguistic heritage. According to Sotomayor, these unique cultural traits are often ignored or misunderstood by most policy makers and health care providers.

Rapidly changing demographics will necessitate increased attention to the health care needs of Latinos, states Sotomayor in *Empowering Hispanic Families: A Critical Issue for the '90s.* "Because of their tremendous growth rate and the diminishing birth rate of the majority society," she declares, "the well-being of this society depends on the well-being of this one group, for Hispanics will constitute the bulk of the labor force in the next two decades." She goes on to explain that the challenge in helping professionals meet the needs of the Hispanic population is in finding tools that address the relationship between family and society, for the problems of one cannot be viewed separately from the other.

Poverty, a condition that often results from social factors and is later perpetuated by kinship ties, is often the root cause of Latino disenfranchisement, maintains Sotomayor. "At the emotional level, poverty leads to self-blame, which is usually followed by a sense of powerlessness. . . . Power-

lessness and the subsequent inability to believe in the possibility of change preclude people's ability to mobilize local helping resources." This point underscores her fundamental belief that one cannot "empower others"; instead, individuals empower themselves in the process of improving their own lives. By linking elderly Latinos with an array of health care services meeting their self-identified needs, Marta Sotomayor is helping Latinos take a very critical step toward personal and communal empowerment.

Sotomayor brings her commitment to improving the quality of life for all segments of society to her many different personal and community interests. Besides serving as a member and vice chair of the governor's commission on Hispanic affairs for the state of Maryland, she is also on the board of the YWCA of Washington, D.C. In addition, she continues to monitor the status of the mentally ill, explaining to Márquez that "it's an area I follow closely. I feel a lot of us don't want to look at that."

Sotomayor lives in the Washington, D.C., metropolitan area with her husband, Guillermo Chávez, director of the human and political rights division of the United Methodist Church. Her only child, Carlos Schatter, is a trained classical guitar player who now heads his own music center in Corpus Christi, Texas. A member of a family known for its long life spans, Sotomayor says she looks forward to the day when she can slow down her busy pace and relish the many years ahead.

Sources:

Books

Curiel, Herman, and Marta Sotomayor, editors, *Hispanic Elderly: A Cultural Signature,* Pan American University Press, 1988.
Sotomayor, Marta, editor, *Empowering Hispanic Families: A Critical Issue for the '90s,* Family Service America, 1991.

Periodicals

California Sociologist, winter, 1989, pp. 65-89.

Other

Sotomayor, Marta, interview with Sandra Márquez, September 14, 1992.

—*Sketch by Sandra Márquez*

Speed, Lillian Castillo
See **Castillo-Speed, Lillian**

Beatriz Olvera Stotzer

(1950-)

Manager, Los Angeles Department of Water and Power

Beatriz Olvera Stotzer believes in causes: justice, gender equality, cultural sensitivity among races, and empowerment of the disadvantaged. Her values are reflected in her work as manager of multicultural affairs for the Los Angeles Department of Water and Power and in the various jobs she has held throughout her life. Dedicated to helping others in need, she assisted coworkers left homeless during the Los Angeles Riot of 1992 and participates in the Rebuild L.A. project.

Stotzer was born in El Paso, Texas, on July 14, 1950, to Guadalupe Rios and Gilberto Olvera. The descendant of a general who fought in the Mexican Revolution, she attributes her fighting spirit to this part of her heritage. The second of six children, she grew up in poverty in East Los Angeles. Her father had been a noteworthy big band musician in Mexico, but was unable to find comparable work in the United States. "We lived in a one bedroom frame house in Boyle Heights," Stotzer told Anna Macias Aguayo in an interview. "I slept on the porch. My parents slept on the kitchen floor."

Stotzer's mother became concerned when several of her children had not learned to read after nearly six years in public schools. As a result, Stotzer was transferred to Catholic schools where she was tutored intensely by nuns and taught to read. She began working odd jobs such as babysitting and housekeeping at the age of 12. At 16, she loaded trucks at a U.S. Post Office. In 1968, she made what she recalls as a disappointing entry into East Los Angeles Community College. "I flunked out because I was trying to go to school full-time and work full-time," she explained.

Becomes Activist in Chicano Movement

A year later, Stotzer again tried her hand at education, entering a special program at Cal State Northridge. She graduated with a B-average in political science and Chicano studies. While at school, her social conscience was nurtured by the Chicano movement. She became an activist in various student groups, including one that she founded. "I started a group called Chicanos in Law because I thought if our people were going to be empowered it would be through lawyers," she related. But Stotzer never studied law. Instead, she went to San Jose State University to obtain a master's degree in political science. In graduate school, Stotzer became involved in the creation of a program for children to learn Chicano history, a curriculum which is still in existence today.

In 1976, Stotzer returned to Los Angeles to administer an anti-poverty program for the City of Los Angeles. She was elected as local and national president of the Comision Femenil Mexicana Nacional, a group that defended women's rights. "I had an incredible mother who believed that we should be grateful for the riches the U.S. had to offer," Stotzer told Aguayo. "My grandmother believed that no man had the right to determine the destiny of any woman." She also found inspiration in her sister, a woman who suffered from Down's Syndrome. Before she died at 27, Stotzer's sister managed to publish two plays, correspond with 30 pen pals around the world, and advocate rights for the disabled. "I come from a lineage of rabble rousers and feminists," she said.

Later Stotzer managed the largest community outreach program for a Public Broadcasting Service (PBS) station at KCET in Los Angeles. After less than two years in the position, she increased revenues from $187,000 to $1.2 million. Her job involved promoting the programming produced by the station. "We did an outreach program to help minorities become more interested in math and science," she reported. "We sent packets to teachers with study guides and worksheets." After a time she became frustrated that not enough Latino-related programming was offered and left the station. "Programs at a public broadcasting station should mirror the population it serves," she asserted to Aguayo.

Stotzer has also founded the New Economics for Women project, which built 110 homes for single mothers. The program managed to turn a $97,000 grant into a $20 million funding base for the housing development. Stotzer also chaired a study on critical issues facing Latinos for the Tomas Rivera Center in Los Angeles.

In her most recent post, Stotzer offers cultural sensitivity training to the 11,000 employees of the Los Angeles utilities company. "This is the city that has the most Latinos, the most Cambodians, the most Koreans outside of their native country," she informed Aguayo. "In order for our service to be efficient, we can't continue pretending that we're living in the 1950s when everyone was monolingual. Unless we're able to serve that diversity, we will not have an efficient product. Our product, water and electricity, is essential to business development and life."

Stotzer's skills in understanding people were useful when the riots broke out in Los Angeles in April, 1992. She helped raise money for her fellow employees left without food and shelter. She now serves on the Rebuild L.A. board. "I was there to get people connected with the services they needed," she explained. "That was my role."

Sources:

Stotzer, Beatriz Olvera, interview with Anna Macias Aguayo,
October 6, 1992.

—*Sketch by Anna Macias Aguayo*

T

Carmen Tafolla
(1951-)
Poet, educator

Poet Mary Carmen Tafolla came to the attention of the literary world with her appearance at the Floricanto Festival held in Austin, Texas, in 1975. Although she no longer resides in Texas, she has been considered one of the most important Chicano poets from that state. Her move to California in 1983 may have changed her point of reference, but left intact the important presence of the past—what Yolanda Broyles González in *Dictionary of Literary Biography* calls the "intense sense of rootedness in her heritage"—in her writing.

A native of San Antonio, Texas, Tafolla was born on July 29, 1951, on the city's west side. She attended Chicano schools for nearly ten years as a youth and began writing poetry when she was a teen. She continued her education at Austin College in Sherman, Texas, where she earned a bachelor of arts degree in Spanish and French, as well as a master of arts in education. By 1981 she had also been awarded a Ph.D. in bilingual education from the University of Texas at Austin. She has taught high school and university classes and served for several years as director of the Mexican Studies Center at Texas Lutheran College in Seguin, Texas. Since 1984, she has been associate professor of women's studies at California State University at Fresno.

Tafolla's first poetry collection, *Get Your Tortillas Together*, which also contains contributions from Reyes Cardenas and Cecilio Garcia-Camarillo, appeared in 1976. Many of these poems are also included in her 1983 collection entitled *Curandera* ("Healer Woman") and in the portion dedicated to her work in the 1985 anthology *Five Poets of Aztlán*, edited by Santiago Daydí-Tolson. She has contributed poems to numerous anthologies, including the Mexican Cultural Center of San Antonio's *Chicano Literature Anthology* and the University of Texas Press' *Floricanto II: An Anthology of Chicano Literature*. Her poetry has appeared in periodicals as well.

Ethnic Background Influences Poetry

The poet's emphasis on her ethnic heritage in her work is evident in the characters she chooses to populate her poems. This is especially true of the female voices heard in her work. For instance, in "444 Years After" she speaks of Our Lady of Guadalupe, a spiritual patroness of Mexico and also a very important image in Chicano culture. In "La Malinche" she speaks of the historic figure of La Malinche, an Indian woman who served as Hernán Cortés's interpreter and advisor during his conquest of Mexico. Tafolla's female figures, whether historical or contemporary, are seen as persons of great inner strength. Broyles Gonzalez contends that "even in the most adverse situations—such as impoverishment or prostitution—Tafolla's women generate an indomitable will to endure and survive. Through her women figures Tafolla redefines the concept of strength."

Tafolla explains her use of women in her poetry and her views in general on women's issues in her prose work, *To Split a Human: Mitos, machos, y la mujer chicana*, published by the Mexican American Cultural Center of San Antonio in 1975. The book also deals with the effects of sexism and racism on Chicano society. In 1976, Tafolla contributed two chapters exploring the historical significance of the Catholic presence in Texas to *The Spanish Speaking Church in the U.S.*, published by Our Sunday Visitor Press.

Tafolla's manuscript for an unpublished poetry collection, *Sonnets to Human Beings*, won first prize in poetry in the University of California at Irvine's Chicano literature competition in 1987. Her papers are included in the Nettie Lee Benson Collection of the Latin American Collection at the University of Texas at Austin.

Sources:

Books

Daydí-Tolson, Santiago, *Five Poets of Aztlán*, Bilingual/Editorial Bilingüe, 1985.
Dictionary of Literary Biography, Volume 82: *Chicano Writers*, Gale, 1989.

—Sketch by Marian C. Gonsior

Tessa Martínez Tagle
(1947-)
College president

As the president of Miami/Dade Community College Medical Center Campus since 1988, Tessa Martínez Tagle has established herself as one of the more prominent figures in Dade County, Florida. She has provided "dynamic leadership" in Florida's largest county for the "primary educator and trainer of health professionals below the M.D. level," according to Bob McCabe, district president of Miami/Dade Community Colleges. In an interview with T. A. Niles, McCabe remarked that "Tagle has revitalized this institution and reached out to the community in unprecedented ways."

Born July 15, 1947, in San Antonio, Texas, Tagle, an only child, was raised by her two grandmothers and an aunt after her mother's death when Tessa was two years old. Despite the early loss of her mother, Tagle recalls a pleasant childhood that included many visits with her father in Mexico, where he worked in the mountains and jungles for the U.S. Department of Agriculture. She remembers fondly the times she spent with some of the ancient Indian tribes that lived there, becoming fluent in Totonac, one of the native dialects.

Tagle credits her success to those early days with her grandmothers, as well as to a promise that her father made to her mother that resulted in the "personal drive" that she has exhibited in obtaining her professional status. "When my mother was dying, she made my father promise that I would be surrounded by women and that I would go to college," Tagle told Niles in an interview. "He made sure of both and that I had the will to succeed."

Discovers Enthusiasm for Teaching

As a high school student Tessa believed that she would be a journalist one day because one of her teachers had told her that she was a talented writer. After high school, Tagle earned a bachelor's degree in journalism from the University of Texas at Austin in 1969 and was married that same year. However, instead of a journalism career, circumstances led her to a teaching position. According to Tagle, she was rejected upon applying for a job at a television station because, being female, she was not considered a good risk. She recounted to Niles: "I was so dejected that I went home and sobbed." Convinced by a friend to give teaching a try, she eventually secured a high school teaching position in San Antonio and found the experience to be "the best time of my life."

Building upon that early experience in the classroom, Tagle sought new challenges in the field of education and spent fifteen of the next sixteen years in several positions, including lecturing and administering, at San Antonio College. Her career at San Antonio was highlighted when she became dean of Occupational, Technical and Continuing Education in 1984. While at San Antonio College, Tagle continued her education, receiving a master of arts in education/business from the University of Texas at San Antonio in 1975, and a doctor of philosophy in educational administration from the University of Texas at Austin in 1988.

With her only child, a daughter, in school, and a marriage struggling to survive, Tagle had no plans to relocate, but she was lured to south Florida by the challenge of the president's position and the nearby ocean. Despite the difficulties of acclimating to a new city, a new job, and a new family situation, she was still able to do "a superior job," McCabe related to Niles. She enjoys the challenges of her position, and finds overcoming the difficulties inherent in providing a good health care education the most satisfying part of the job.

In a community comprised of a large minority population plagued by high poverty, drug use, and crime rates, the campus has experienced marked increases in minority student enrollment under Tagle's leadership. These increases have resulted in more career opportunities for those high-risk groups with limited options. An obvious example of Tagle's commitment to the community is her initiative to open up the campus to a comprehensive community-enhancing project: the Overtown Neighborhood Partnerships (ONP). The ONP project addresses the social causes of individual and community pathology in inner-city neighborhoods, and is envisioned as a model for the rest of the country.

Respected by Associates and Community

Tagle's commitment to community service and her leadership style is applauded by her colleagues. Sylvia Edge, Dean of Nursing Education, told Niles in an interview that she heralds Tagle's ability to lead by "identifying areas that need change, and identifying people and ways of working together, while allowing you to implement change in ways you think appropriate." Kym Hubert, one of her assistants, also attested to Niles that "Tagle is a role model, the most dynamic and powerful person I've ever met, and everything a career woman would want to be." Tagle has received honors including being named "Outstanding Hispanic Educator" and "Leader of the 80's." She was appointed to the Policy and Priorities committee of the Education Commission of the States in 1991, and holds memberships in such organizations as the National Institute for Leadership Development, the National Advisory Committee/

Expanding Leadership Opportunities for Minorities in Community Colleges, and the American Council on Education's National Identification Program.

As Tagle continues her distinguished service as an educator and community leader, more accolades and job offers are bound to accumulate. However, she says that she doesn't worry about what to do next. Her philosophy, she told Niles, is "If you do a good job with what's on your plate, the next thing will take care of itself." If her history is any indication, one can look forward to Tagle making health education policy decisions at the state and national level.

Sources:

Edge, Sylvia, interview with T. A. Niles conducted on August, 14, 1992.

Hubert, Kym, interview with T. A. Niles conducted on August 12, 1992.

McCabe, Robert, interview with T. A. Niles conducted on August 14, 1992.

Tagle, Tessa Martínez, interview with T. A. Niles conducted on August 12, 1992.

—Sketch by T. A. Niles

Grace Martinez Tatum
(1960-)
Engineer

When the United States began its air war against Iraq in 1991, engineer Grace Martinez Tatum saw the fruits of her labor. As a supervisor in the Naval Air Warfare Center in Point Magu, California, she oversees a staff of 45 engineers and technicians that test many of the U.S. Navy and Air Force missiles. "Our primary concern was the safe carry and safe launch of a missile—safe in terms of protecting the pilot and the ground troops," Tatum explained in an interview with Anna Macias Aguayo. "We don't frame what we do in the context of whether we're destroying anything. We are asked to keep that perspective."

Born November 11, 1960, Tatum began her engineering training around her family's dinner table in San Antonio, Texas, where her father Jose C. Martinez, an engineering technician for the government, would explain the intricacies of a salt shaker. Tatum's mother, Alice Martinez, would never miss an opportunity to preach about going to college. "If we were in the car, waiting at a red light, and saw a construction crew, my mother would point out the sweaty, dirty guy with the jack hammer and the man in the business suit with a clip board," recalled Tatum in her interview. "She would ask us: 'Which one of those do you think has a college degree?'" Thus, Tatum's aspiration for an education in a subject she found fascinating was instilled.

"I think we were brainwashed into going into engineering," continued Tatum in her interview with Aguayo. "My brothers also went into that. There wasn't a lot of thought that went into it. It was just assumed that I would do it too." After finishing her primary studies in Catholic schools, Tatum earned two academic scholarships that helped her obtain an engineering degree from Trinity University in San Antonio. She immediately went to work in what was formerly called the Pacific Missile Testing Center in Point Magu. She began as a journeyman engineer in 1983, but rose quickly through the ranks. "I went from handling individual projects to managing the entire branch," Tatum remarked in her interview. Later, she became head of a division, and Tatum and her employees were charged with redesigning and updating some of the missiles used by American forces during the Persian Gulf War, specifically the Mavericks and Sidewinders.

Tatum has earned commendations for her work almost annually. She attributes her career success to her attitude. She said she has never considered her status as a woman or a Hispanic to be a limitation. "I've only stayed in positions that I've felt good about, where I have had managers that have believed in me." Tatum tries never to let her life as a wife or mother interfere with work. "I have seen another woman trying to come up in the ranks, but she was having trouble with how people perceived her," related Tatum in her Aguayo interview. "She would say she couldn't attend a late meeting because she needed to be with her children. I've seen other women who abuse their leave, saying, 'Oh, my stomach hurts.' I don't make excuses." Tatum likes to project the image of a dedicated, serious-minded professional. When she speaks to youths about how she rose to the level of a general manager earning $60,000 a year, Tatum confidently tells them that they need to make a career plan and stick to it.

Sources:

Tatum, Grace Martinez, interview with Anna Macias Aguayo, October 6, 1992.

—Sketch by Anna Macias Aguayo

Emma Tenayuca
(1916-)
Community activist

Emma Tenayuca began her career as a community activist at the age of 16 by participating in the famous Finck Cigar Strike. Intensifying her activities in the 1930s, she reached the position of executive secretary for the Workers Alliance of America. Her influence in San Antonio, Texas, was such that workers insisted on naming her honorary strike leader when union officials ousted her from her leadership position because of her Communist party affiliation. Blacklisted by the House of Representatives Un-American Activities Committee at the beginning of World War II, she left San Antonio to return a few years later, never to leave again.

Tenayuca was born in San Antonio in 1916. Her mother was a Cepeda, one of the Spanish families that founded San Antonio during Spanish rule, her father an Amerindian from South Texas. "Her strong Texas roots made Tenayuca identify herself as a Texan first and a Hispanic second," explained University of California at Santa Barbara history professor Zaragosa Vargas, a labor-history specialist who has researched Tenayuca's life. "Although she worked as a labor organizer, she described herself as a community activist. At the youthful age of 16, she joined the Finck Cigar employees in their walk-out, and ended up in jail. This strike became a landmark because the strikers were mostly women, and this was the first strike of the so-called National Recovery Administration (NRA) strikes of 1933 and 1934."

Shortly after the cigar strike episode, Tenayuca assisted in the establishment of an International Ladies' Garment Workers' Union chapter in San Antonio. But she soon found herself devoting most of her time to the Workers Alliance, which was an extension of the Communist party at the neighborhood level. She staged demonstrations to demand jobs for Spanish-speaking people, and sent letters to Washington, D.C., to draw some of President Roosevelt's New Deal funds to San Antonio. Tenayuca also kept watch on U.S. immigration officers to prevent the deportation of Mexican American union activists. She became secretary to 11 Workers Alliance chapters in the San Antonio area and served as the national organization's executive secretary.

Becomes Involved in Communist Party

"Tenayuca joined the Communist party fairly late, and remained a member for only a year and a half," related Vargas in his interview with Michelle Vachon. "She took an active part in it because of her husband, Homer Brooks, a former engineering student from Pennsylvania and the Communist party's secretary in Texas." In 1939, Tenayuca and Brooks published an analysis of the Mexican Americans' situation. Entitled "The Mexican Question in the Southwest," the study appeared in *Communist.* Outlining a strategy for action, they recommended to direct the struggle "(1) Against economic discrimination—extra-low wages; expropriation of small land holders (2) For educational and cultural equality ... (including) the use of Spanish as well as English in the public schools (3) Against social oppression—for laws making illegal the various forms of Jim Crowism (this struggle must be linked with that of the Negro people) and (4) Against political repression." Their analysis constituted the only effort on the part of the Communist party to answer Mexican American issues in a policy statement.

Throughout the 1930s, Tenayuca played an active role in the pecan shellers' fight and, when they came out on strike, she became a vital force behind their protest. Her involvement triggered strong opposition from unexpected quarters. "The United Cannery, Agricultural, Packing and Allied Workers of America (UCAPAWA)—which was part of the Congress of Industrial Organizations (CIO) and represented the pecan shellers—wanted to gain legitimacy and draw attention away from Communist activists," Vargas pointed out in his interview with Vachon. "The UCAPAWA replaced Tenayuca with Luisa Moreno as strike leader, but the pecan shellers insisted on keeping her as honorary strike leader."

On the eve of World War II, the Communist party decided to hold a rally at the Veterans Hall in San Antonio. "Mayor Quinn and Chief of Police Kilday saw this event as their opportunity to get rid of Tenayuca once and for all," Vargas told Vachon. "These two old-time political bosses were being challenged by Tenayuca's influence over Mexican Americans that they had repressed. Therefore, they launched a smear campaign, using her Communist party affiliation to turn public opinion against her." A near-riot took place in downtown San Antonio and the rally was canceled.

Immediately following the rally incident, the signing of the Nazi-Soviet pact changed Tenayuca's political affiliation forever. "The Communist party had done a complete turnaround in regard to its politics," commented Vargas. "San Antonio was up in arms over the news. Tenayuca's brother and many of her Mexican American friends had already joined the military. She could not endorse the Soviet Union's alliance with Hitler. Consequently, she dropped out of the party." Soon afterwards, the House of Representatives Un-American Activities Committee investigated her Communist party connection, and she started feeling the effects of being blacklisted. "Tenayuca could not find work; she was totally destroyed. In spite of the fact that she was a devout Catholic, the Church completely turned its back on her." She survived due to the kindness of a Jewish woman who admired her militancy and offered her a job sewing military uniforms during the Second World War.

Tenayuca then moved to San Francisco, California, and attended San Francisco College. She graduated magna cum laude and returned to San Antonio during the Cold War years to pursue her studies. She received her master's degree and became an elementary school teacher. She still lives in San Antonio.

Sources:

Books

Mirande, Alfredo, and Evangelina Enriquez, *La Chicana: The Mexican-American Woman,* University of Chicago Press, 1979, pp. 230-31.

Periodicals

Communist, Number 18, 1939, pp. 257-68.
Tamiment Institute, winter, 1983, pp. 43-44.
Texas Observer, October 28, 1983, pp. 7-15.

Other

Vargas, Zaragosa, interview with Michelle Vachon, October 12, 1992.

—*Sketch by Michelle Vachon*

Isabel Toledo
(1963?-)
Fashion designer

"**I**sabel Toledo is one of the most inventive American designers of the under-30 generation," writes *New York Times* contributor Anne-Marie Schiro. Toledo first appeared on the New York fashion scene in the mid-1980s, when her husband and business partner Ruben Toledo showed some of her hand-sewn designs to trend-setting fashion retailers Patricia Field and Henri Bendel. By the late 1980s, Toledo's designs were appearing in numerous fashion magazines, including *Cosmopolitan* and *Women's Wear Daily,* and she was no longer sewing everything

herself. Though she is now widely recognized for her innovative designs that contrast fabrics and shapes to produce whimsical effects, Toledo told *Cosmopolitan:* "I design for myself. If people buy my clothes, they're telling me they like how I look. It's very personal."

Toledo was born in Cuba in the early 1960s, and her family immigrated to the United States when she was five, settling in West New York, New Jersey. When her three daughters objected to going to a babysitter, Toledo's mother convinced the girls that they were actually going to sewing lessons. Toledo took her mother seriously, she told *Cosmopolitan,* and really learned to sew. She started sewing her own wardrobe, and the first clothes that her husband sold he lifted directly out of her closet. Though she never intended to become a fashion designer, Toledo took courses at the Fashion Institute of Technology and at the Parsons School of Design, both in New York City. In the mid-1980s she worked at the Costume Institute of the Metropolitan Museum of Art, where she restored and designed period clothing for mannequins and did research.

The first appearance of Toledo's designs in fashion stores attracted immediate attention: people called to place orders and to see her seasonal collections. Soon she and her husband, childhood friends who married in 1985, had enlisted the help of their parents in the effort to keep up with increasing demand for Toledo's clothes. Finally they found a financial backer who helped them get her designs sewn at a Brooklyn, New York, factory that he owned. By 1987 Toledo's designs were selling at exclusive fashion stores such as I. Magnin in California and Bergdorf's and Barneys in New York, at prices ranging from $120 to $450.

Toledo's trademark is denim, which she complements with such fabrics as linen, organza, and mohair to produce a look that *Hispanic* magazine called "young" and "energetic," and which, according to Schiro, makes "her development fascinating to fashion watchers." Her stylistic trademarks are circles and curves, which she integrates into the structure of the design, whether it be a foldable mini-skirt made out of two-circles or a balloonlike sleeve on a long, billowy shirt. Her designs are unusual, but Toledo is not designing for everyone. "Women don't like to be told by other women what to wear," she told Michael Gross of the *New York Times,* but "the fact is, I'm a woman and I know what's best for me."

Sources:

Periodicals

Cosmopolitan, June, 1987, pp. 240-41.
Hispanic, October, 1989.
New York Times, April 16, 1987; April 6, 1990; April 13, 1991.

Women's Wear Daily, November 6, 1989; April 9, 1990;
November 5, 1990; April 16, 1991.

—*Sketch by Tom Pendergast*

Maria Elena Toraño
(1938-)
Consultant

Maria Elena Toraño has lived a life of contrasts. She
arrived in the United States in the early 1960s, among the
first wave of immigrants to leave communist Cuba. Twenty-
six years later she became the first Cuban American appointed to high federal office by a United States President
when she took the position of associate director for public
affairs in the U.S. Community Services Administration
under President Jimmy Carter. In 1980, Ronald Reagan
took office and cleaned house, forcing Toraño to look for a
job; that search led her to found META Inc., a multi-
million-dollar consulting agency in Miami, Florida. Along
the way Toraño has gained recognition as a hard-working,
conscientious business woman, a passionate advocate for
Miami, and a leader in advancing the interests of Hispanic
women.

Toraño was born February 13, 1938, in Havana, Cuba, to
Julio Diez-Rousselot and Sira Diez-Rousselot. Little is
known of her early life in Cuba, except that her first visit to
the United States was to attend high school in New Orleans, Louisiana. She returned to Cuba, attended college,
and married Arturo Toraño on February 9, 1958. She
taught home economics at the University of Havana, where
she had earned her bachelor of arts degree. When the
Communist regime of Fidel Castro came to power, the
Toraños fled to the United States. Arturo's later involvement in the U.S.-backed Bay of Pigs invasion—a failed
1961 attempt to overthrow Castro—landed him in a
Cuban prison and forced Toraño to work a succession of
menial jobs to support her family, which by then included
two young sons. She quickly moved into positions of
responsibility, teaching in the Dade County, Florida, public school system and serving as a caseworker for the
Florida Department of Public Welfare. Following those
positions, she began a lengthy affiliation with Eastern
Airlines.

Toraño joined Eastern Airlines in 1968 as a ticket agent,
but she rapidly advanced in the company. She eventually
served as program manager of Latin American affairs,
where she worked to increase Eastern's share of the U.S.
Hispanic market. "Eastern was such a glamorous job,"
Toraño told *Nuestro* contributor Raquel Puig Zaldivar,
"but I felt jealous of people who were getting things done. I
wanted to be involved in social problems." After a brief
stint as director of Latin American Affairs at Miami's
Jackson Memorial Hospital in 1976, Toraño was recruited
by Jimmy Carter's administration to be the associate director of its Community Services Administration.

The period from 1976 to 1980 marks the emergence of
Toraño as both a regional and a national force in promoting the interests of minorities and women. Part of the
importance of her Presidential appointment, she told
Zaldivar in 1977, was "achieving Cuban American representation in Washington. But the importance to me goes
beyond that. I equate success with power—power to *do* for
yourself and others, power to do things that are needed,
power to make good things happen." Not only did she
increase awareness of Hispanic interests within Washington, she also found time to establish the National Association of Spanish Broadcasters, which lobbied for Hispanic
interests in the communication industry, and the National
Hispana Leadership Institute, a corporate-sponsored group
that seeks to promote the interests of Hispanic women.

Ronald Reagan dissolved the Community Services Administration after he was elected in 1980, and Toraño
returned home to Miami uncertain of her future. She told
New Miami contributor Ken Ibold: "I gave myself this great
line: After you've worked for the President of the United
States, who can you work for? And the answer was: You
work for yourself." She received encouragement from her
new husband, Leslie Pantin, whom she married in 1980
after divorcing Arturo Toraño in 1978. Pantin, a successful
Miami business executive, taught Toraño the essentials of
running a business, and she soon launched her public-
relations consulting firm, META Inc. Toraño courted big
name clients like Adolph Coors and the Miami Dolphins,
but while she was working on a project for the South
Florida Small Business Administration, she realized the
money-making potential for minority-owned businesses
in government contracts. She immediately began pursuing
U.S. government contracts and changed the company's
focus from public relations to management services. In
1990, META—whose name alludes to its founder's initials
and to the Spanish word for "goal" or "objective"—landed its biggest contract, managing $88 million in residential
real estate, commercial properties, and non-performing
loans for the Resolution Trust Corporation, a government
agency assigned to clean up in the aftermath of the Savings
and Loan scandals of the late 1980s.

Toraño told Ibold: "When you've been through life and
you have had the experience of being poor like I was, you
get horrified about ending up in the poorhouse. So I have

to make this company successful and profitable." She has certainly succeeded at that goal. Along the way she has become an asset to Miami's business and cultural community, serving on the International Health Council and the City of Miami International Trade Committee, as well as the Florida Arts Council. Toraño has been honored for her efforts with numerous awards, including the Coalition of Hispanic American Women's 1991 Woman of the Year award and the South Florida Small Business Administration's 1991 Minority Business Person of the Year award.

Sources:

Periodicals

Hispanic Business, March, 1985.
New Miami, November, 1991.
Nuestro, December, 1977, p. 57.

—Sketch by Tom Pendergast

Celia G. Torres

Celia G. Torres
(1936-)
Businesswoman, community leader

Highly respected both in her community and nationally in leadership circles, Celia G. Torres describes herself as an "agent of change." Cofounder of the National Network of Hispanic Women, Torres is among a few Latina women who have made a difference overcoming both personal and public challenges. "Since high school I have often found myself being the only one doing what I was doing," she explained to Oralia Michel during a telephone interview. "I seemed to be making a path for others; I was always ahead of my time."

An only child and the granddaughter of Mexican immigrants from a small community near Guadalajara, Torres was born on February 28, 1936, in Los Angeles to Angelina Gonzales and Francisco Estrada. She was raised in an all-female household at the end of the Depression. Her mother, a garment worker, became seriously ill and was hospitalized for three years, leaving her eight-year-old daughter to be raised by her invalid grandmother and married aunt. Torres says that some of her early influences for her social consciousness were from her aunt and uncle, who were foster parents, and from her uncle's involvement in unions.

Uses Education to Leave Barrio Behind

At a young age, Torres saw one way out of the barrio—education. Her mother and her aunt, who was also her godmother, combined their resources to send Celia to Catholic schools. In addition to her family, Torres credits her teachers, the sisters of St. Joseph of Carondolet, for teaching her the values she lives by today. This investment in her future paid off in more ways than one. From St. Mary's Academy, where in the fifth grade she learned parliamentary procedure, Torres went on to St. Vincent's Parish school, where in the sixth grade she was asked to be sodality prefect (leader of a religious-oriented student organization). With this role, her skills as a leader began to develop.

From sixth grade through her college years at Mount St. Mary's College, Torres held at least one office per year. She worked her way through high school and college, paying for transportation, tuition, and books from the age of 15. Sometimes holding down three jobs at a time, she worked as a babysitter, sales clerk, waitress, and library assistant. When Torres's mother returned from the hospital, she developed a new reliance upon her daughter, believing that when she finished high school, she would help her raise her two children from a subsequent marriage, which did not last. Though Torres went against her mother's wishes and was determined to pursue a career, an understanding between mother and daughter soon developed.

While pursuing her bachelor's degree in sociology at Mount St. Mary's, Torres represented her college at state and national conferences, which contributed to her "hands on" interest in community and civic affairs.

As a Catholic woman in the 1950s, Torres did what was expected of her. She became a social worker and got married. Marrying Julio Torres, she helped her husband start his medical practice, their business, and had five children. Drawing from her childhood and education, Torres enjoyed raising her children. "I used a lot of creativity," she related in the *Los Angeles Times*. "We had art shows in which the neighborhood children could sell their artwork." She was always active in parent-teacher groups and participated in her children's extracurricular activities, having no regrets about the years she spent mothering; she chose to re-direct her life to accommodate her family. In the midst of giving so much of herself to her husband and family, Torres promised herself that she would one day pursue her graduate education. Deriving strength from the spiritual and human values instilled by her family and the Carondolet Sisters, she never lost sense of where she was going. "I was determined to keep my identity and not be known as 'Mrs. Dr. Torres,' as someone from the hospital once called me," Torres related in her telephone interview.

Resolving to focus on herself, she became increasingly involved in civic and community work in her hometown of Rancho Palos Verdes, California, a conservative Anglo community. In 1974 she became the first Hispanic woman to serve as the President of the local Parent, Teachers Association (PTA), a high-profile position. "That was a difficult time because getting elected required being under so much scrutiny. But once I made it, I became known by Hispanics as 'the hand that can reach the Anglo community.' Through me, Hispanics now had access to the private sector," Torres remarked in her interview. The position marked a turning point in her career—attaining a position of power in an Anglo community gave her the determination and confidence to work for other changes. At age 42 Torres fulfilled her promise to herself by commencing work on a master's degree, and in 1980 she graduated from the University of Southern California with a master's in social work.

Finds Success in Real Estate Business

Before and after her graduate studies, Torres joined her husband in developing a successful group of real estate holdings in the Southwest. "We didn't set out to be in business," Torres declared in her telephone interview. "We wanted to help people. We lived during a time when opportunities were available, and we managed to build on them." Torres's duties as executive vice president included financial reporting and portfolio development. She traveled around the country for site visits, conducting research and inspection of new properties.

In addition to being a businesswoman, Torres volunteers time working for the Hispanic community. Some of the issues Torres has advocated are fair housing, police utilization, various women's issues—including women in the church—and the prevention of substance abuse, teen pregnancy, and child abuse. She helped institutionalize Latino student support groups at several colleges and universities and has successfully raised funds for such projects as child abuse prevention, AIDS, the homeless, scholarship, and political candidates. She also helped establish and chaired the National Network of Hispanic Women (NNHW). Among what Torres considers her greatest contributions are her support of education through participation on educational boards, the scholarships she and her husband have given, funding of new projects, and her work with the NNHW. "We put many pieces of the puzzle together to empower Latinas, the work of NNHW has its place in history."

Along with her success, Torres has also experienced difficult lessons and has had to overcome several barriers. She pointed out in a *Latina* magazine interview that these barriers are invisible and sometimes so subtle that one might spend half a career without ever quite knowing they exist. "But they do," she said. "I think you can recognize them when you find yourself swimming upstream as hard as you can, knowing you're just as good as anyone else, and getting nowhere." These barriers she believes are cultural and structural. She explained in *Latina* that Hispanic women have "been raised with religious and family values that are a little tighter and stronger [than those of Anglo women]. The Latina is very much expected to fulfill a mothering female role in some way. There is tremendous pressure form both inside and outside. I'm not sure that the same pressure from family and religion exists for the Anglo woman."

According to *Latina*, Torres speaks from the collective experience of the many women she was in touch with as cofounder of NNHW, an organization that seeks to find and advance "outstanding Hispanic women for leadership positions in education, industry, business and government." What Hispanics need most, according to Torres, is a support system. "With the kind of bicultural lives we lead, we need to have a place to express both those parts. Otherwise there is a part of us that doesn't develop, that shuts down." She learned much from her own experience in college. "Our culture is a very warm culture," she said. "We relate people-to-people, person-to-person, face-to-face, and that's an important value to us. Institutions of higher learning are traditionally very cold, unfriendly places where the attitude is sink or swim. So, someone coming from a warm family environment, and particularly a female who has been protected by her family, many times finds the transition difficult."

In 1989 health problems led Torres to redirect her path when, as she says, cancer gave her a wake up call. "My husband and I are making a transition into the next phase of our lives," she stated in her telephone interview. Torres calls it the "research and development" phase and says she believes in second beginnings. "We are looking for the best way to use our talent and experiences but without being in the fast lane." Torres hopes to write a book and continue giving counseling and support to those seeking empowerment and transformation, particularly women.

Sources:

Periodicals

Latina, November, 1985, pp. 51-52.
Los Angeles Times, November 3, 1986, Section 5, pp. 1, 6.

Other

Torres, Celia G., telephone interview with Oralia Michel, September 1, 1992.

—Sketch by Oralia Michel

Maria de los Angeles Torres
(1955-)
Professor, political activist

When she was only six years old, Maria de los Angeles Torres was alone and frightened as she boarded a plane in Cuba destined for the United States during the heart of the Cuban Revolution of the 1950s. The trip marked the beginning of a life directed by political activism. Torres became politically active in high school fighting the Vietnam war and working on civil rights causes. After college she was named executive director of Chicago Mayor Harold Washington's Commission on Latino Affairs. A few years later she fought for civil rights while working with the 1988 Democratic Platform Committee. Her next move was to the classroom, where she taught political science at DePaul University in Chicago. Her goals are to develop Latin American rights in the United States and to foster a better relationship between Cuba and the United States. "I see myself as an intellectual and an activist and I don't see a contradiction in those two things," she stated in a telephone interview with D. D. Andreassi.

Torres' life was dramatically touched by the short time she spent as a young girl in Cuba. She was born July 1, 1955, to Maria Vigil Isabel Torres and Alberto Torres. She came to the United States through the Peter Pan Operation, a State Department program that encouraged children to use a visa waiver allowing them to later claim their parents when they arrived in the States. Her family supported the

revolution. She explained in her interview that the State Department policy was a way to scare the Cuban middle class and "bleed the country of a lot of professionals." Her father was an ophthalmologist and her mother was a chemistry professor. "I remember the U.S. invading Cuba and I was sent to the United States. It was scary, but it was sort of exciting. I have wonderful memories of Cuba with a lot of light, family, and cousins," she recalled in her interview.

Torres, her parents, and three sisters lived in Miami for one year before they moved to Cleveland. After two winters her parents decided they preferred a warmer climate and the family moved to Texas, where there was a medical association shortage. Her father quickly landed a job. When Torres was a high school student she started to rebel against her parents. Wanting to leave home, she graduated early from Robert E. Lee High School in Midland, Texas.

Torres moved to San Antonio, where as an undergraduate she went from university to university until she settled at St. Mary's University. Along with other students, Torres worked with a coalition of professors on civil rights issues. She earned her bachelor of arts degree in psychology and Spanish and did a master's thesis on social research. Torres then attended the University of Michigan and delved into political science studies. She dropped out for one year and worked with the International Ladies Garment Workers Union before returning to the University of Michigan to finish her course work. Meanwhile, she married Matthew Piers, a civil rights attorney, and had two children, Alejandra and Paola Pierce-Torres, both bilingual.

Torres landed a job as coordinator of bilingual studies at Mundelein College in Chicago. She also became involved in Chicago Mayor Harold Washington's election campaign. When he won, Washington asked Torres to work with his Commission on Latino Affairs. That job ended when she decided to take a position teaching political science at DePaul University, which fulfilled her lifetime goal to teach and do research work. Torres was also a member of Latino Scholars, an inter-university program for Latino research.

Meanwhile, in 1978 Torres returned to Cuba as a member of a radical youth organization. It had only been a year since the United States had allowed Cubans to return to their homeland. Fourteen years later, she explained in her interview that she had returned "a million times since then in a lot of different ways. I sort of feel I'm at home in both places. Part of my goal is to be in both places, emotionally and professionally, without there being such a schism."

Promotes Cuban American Relations

In 1988 Torres worked on the Democratic Platform Committee to promote improvements for Latin Americans, including access to quality and bilingual education, job development, a respectful relationship between the

United States and Latin America, independence for Puerto Rico, and better immigration laws. Torres wrote in a *Nation* article that a popular myth portrays Cuban Americans as political exiles, economically successful—and conservative: "Yet not even in Miami do all Cuban Americans live up to the stereotype. While the community undeniably bears the scars of thirty years of failed U.S. policies toward Cuba, and of the island government's intolerance toward those who have left, Cuban American politics are now in transition, and there are many positive signs of change," she stated.

Torres believes the future of Cuba needs to be negotiated by the people who live there and those who have left. "My research and work is about that," she explained in her interview. "It's about Cuban American politics and what happens to people and how do we negotiate our identity and politics. We're caught between two countries—our home country and our host country. Cuba needs to include people who have left and who will leave. In a sense we have a lot to give back and a lot to gain with a respectful relationship." Torres, partly through her work on the board of the Cuban American Committee, hopes to lobby Cuban officials to be more humane in the way they treat people who have left the country and to convince government officials to permit return visits.

Torres emphasized the importance of change in U.S. policies toward Latin America in a *Nation* article: "The fact that the Southwest is even part of the United States; that Puerto Ricans are U.S. citizens, or that there are more than one million Cubans in this country—all these are conse-quences of past U.S. policies toward Latin America." Coming full circle, Torres is working on a MacArthur research and writing grant reconstructing the history of the Peter Pan Operation. Her work will document the program responsible for bringing her and other Cuban youngsters to the United States during the revolution.

Sources:

Periodicals

Nation, July, 1988; October, 1988.

Other

Torres, Maria de los Angeles, telephone interview with D. D. Andreassi, September, 1992.

—*Sketch by D. D. Andreassi*

Torruella, Trish Moylan
See Moylan-Torruella, Trish

Trambley, Estela Potillo
See Portillo Trambley, Estela

U-Z

Teresa Urrea
(1873-1906)
Mystic, *curandera*

A gifted, enigmatic, and highly complex young woman, Teresa Urrea achieved notoriety with her extraordinary psychic abilities and healing powers rarely heard of in her time. She lived and practiced her healing arts at the Cabora ranch in northern Mexico, which for a time became known as the Lourdes of Mexico. In her brief life she cured tens of thousands of people of real or imaginary ills and became known as the Saint of Cabora, even though the title was not conferred on her by any church authority. She is as well known for the part she may have innocently played in the inception of the Mexican Revolution as she is for her extrasensory powers. Contemporary Mexican historians call her the Mexican Joan of Arc.

Urrea was born on October 15, 1873, on Rancho Santana, north of Ocoroni in the state of Sinaloa, Mexico. Her mother was 14-year-old Cayetana Chavez, a poor Yaqui Indian girl, and her father was Don Tomas Urrea, a Mexican patron of the ranch. Her parents were not married, and Teresita (the diminutive form of her name) was half-sister to all of her father's 18 children and her mother's four.

Discovers Healing Powers

In 1888, Urrea moved to her father's ranch in Cabora, and it was here that the sensitive, fragile girl learned from one of her father's Indian servants, Maria Sonora, the use of herbs in caring for the sick and injured. Shortly after her arrival at Cabora, Urrea lapsed into an inexplicable catatonic state that lasted three months and eighteen days. After three disoriented months of recovery, she began to experience trances and believed she had been charged by the Virgin Mary to cure people. She demonstrated her powers on a few nearby patients—many of her reported cures were spectacular—and a slow but steady stream of devotees began to make their way to the ranch.

The news of the beautiful girl of Cabora who could cure all illnesses spread quickly, and soon Teresita had a large following, especially among the Tarahumaras, Yaqui, and Mayo Indians, who regarded her with awe. Her reputation caused great concern among the Mexican government and the Catholic church. Mexican president (and later dictator) Porfirio Diaz in particular was troubled by the influence that one young woman could exercise over the tribes, although it was a power she apparently neither wanted nor encouraged. The Indians sought her blessing for a series of revolts over land boundaries, but Urrea would only remark, according to the *Southern California Quarterly,* "God intended for you to have the lands, or He would not have given them to you." Although no evidence has ever been uncovered that Urrea or her father inspired these rebellions, the Mexican government exiled both of them in 1892.

Flees North with Followers

Political controversy followed Teresa to Nogales, Arizona, where the thousands of pilgrims flocking to see her became recruitment prospects for the revolutionists plotting to overthrow the government of Diaz. The household later relocated to Solomonville in eastern Arizona in 1895, and then to El Paso in 1896. Continued harassment from the Mexican government forced the family to move away from the border to Clifton, Arizona. Throughout the moves, Urrea, known by this time as the "santa de Cabora," continued to minister to the sick and the poor. The Indians who followed her became fanatical, attacking a customs house in Nogales, Mexico, with shouts of "Viva la Santa de Cabora," resulting in the deaths of 14 people.

Urrea publicly refused to have any part in the affairs of Mexico. According to *Voices: Readings from El Grito,* she issued a statement in 1896 printed in the *El Paso Herald,* one of only three documents in existence that contain direct quotations from her. It says, in part, "I have noticed with much pain that the persons who have taken up arms in Mexican territory have invoked my name in aid of the schemes they are carrying through. But I repeat I am not one who authorizes or at the same time interferes with these proceedings."

Urrea's life took an uncharacteristically commercial turn in 1900 when she joined forces with a medical company in New York that would tour the United States on a "curing crusade." She agreed to accept the $10,000 contract on the condition that none of her patients would be charged for her help. When she discovered that scheming promoters were indeed collecting hefty fees, Urrea found a lawyer to terminate her contract. In the meantime, she had a one-day marriage to mine worker Guadalupe Rodriguez, who was later tried for a crime, found insane, and sent to an asylum. She later married John Van Order of Arizona, and had two daughters, Laura in 1902 and Magdelena in 1904.

Urrea returned to Clifton, Arizona, where her health began to fail. On January 11, 1906, Urrea died peacefully of consumption (pulmonary tuberculosis) at the age of 33. Many of her followers insisted she had simply worn out her spirit in the service of her people. Hundreds of mourners followed her casket in a funeral procession to Shannon Hill Catholic cemetery, where she was buried beside her father, Don Tomas.

Sources:

Books

Holden, William Curry, _Teresita,_ Stemmer House, 1978.
Voices: Readings from El Grito, A Journal of Contemporary Mexican American Thought, 1967-1973, Quinto Sol, 1973.

Periodicals

Historia Mexicana (Durango, Mexico), April-June, 1957, pp. 627-644.
New York Times, August 13, 1896, p. 1; August 14, 1896, p. 1; August 15, 1896, p. 1; August 20, 1896, p. 1.
Southern California Quarterly, September, 1963.

—_Sketch by Julie Catalano_

Nydia Margarita Velázquez

Nydia Margarita Velázquez
(1953-)
U.S. Congresswoman

Nydia Margarita Velázquez, the daughter of a poor sugar-cane cutter, is the first Puerto Rican woman to be elected to the United States House of Representatives. Velázquez, a Democrat, won her seat in Congress in November, 1992, after a grueling and controversial Democratic primary that pitted her against longtime incumbent Stephen J. Solarz and a crowded field of Hispanic challengers. Velázquez now represents the 12th Congressional District in New York City, a heavily Democratic and Hispanic district that was created in 1992 to encourage the election of a Hispanic representative. The district of just over 500,000 people encompasses poor and working-class neighborhoods in Queens, Manhattan, and Brooklyn.

As a Puerto Rican woman raised in a hardworking rural household with few modern conveniences, Velázquez brings a unique perspective to national politics. She was born March 23, 1953, in Yabucoa, Puerto Rico. Once famous for its sugar-cane industry, Yabucoa is located in a lush valley on the island's southeast coast. Velázquez and her twin sister were among nine children raised by Benito and Carmen Luisa (Serrano) Velázquez, who lived at the edge of town in a small, wooden house, surrounded by sugar-cane fields and the Rio Limon River.

To support the family, Carmen sold _pasteles,_ a traditional Puerto Rican food, to cane cutters in the fields. Benito, who had a third-grade education, cut sugar cane and later became a butcher and the owner of a legal cockfighting business. A local political leader, Benito founded a political party in his town and, significantly, passed on to his daughter Nydia a strong social conscience, according to the _New York Times._ During Nydia's childhood, dinner conversations often revolved around workers' rights and other political issues. "I always wanted to be like my father," she said in an interview with the _New York Times._

Always eager to learn, Velázquez convinced her family to allow her to start school at the age of five. She proved to be a bright student, skipping several grades to graduate early and become the first in her family to receive a high school diploma. At 16, Velázquez was already a freshman at the University of Puerto Rico in Rio Piedras. She graduated magna cum laude in 1974 with a bachelor's degree in political science. After teaching briefly in Puerto Rico, she won a scholarship to continue her studies in the United States. She left the island, with her family's reluctant support, to enter New York University. Velázquez earned a master's degree in political science in 1976, then returned to the University of Puerto Rico in Humacao to teach political science. Leaving Puerto Rico again in 1981, she became an adjunct professor of Puerto Rican studies at Hunter College at the City University of New York, where she taught for two years.

In a September 21, 1992, interview with *Newsday,* Velázquez revealed that she left Puerto Rico for more reasons than simply to advance her education and career. "I was harassed when I was a professor at the University of Puerto Rico, when the [conservative] New Progressive Party took power in Puerto Rico," she said. Velázquez said that she was accused of being a Communist and leftist. She eventually made her home in New York, but her career in politics and public service has subsequently included work in both the U.S. and Puerto Rico.

She received her first taste of New York City politics in the early 1980s. In 1983 she served as special assistant to former U.S. Representative Edolphus Towns, a Democrat from Brooklyn. As a special assistant, Velázquez was in charge of immigration issues, and part of her job included testifying before Congress on immigration legislation. In 1984, Velázquez was appointed to the New York City Council, filling the vacancy left when former Councilman Luis Olmedo was convicted on charges of federal conspiracy and attempted extortion. At the age of 31, Velázquez became the first Latina to serve on the council.

After losing her council seat in the next election in 1986, Velázquez returned to Puerto Rico to serve as the national director of the Migration Division Office of the Department of Labor and Human Resources of Puerto Rico until 1989. In that year the governor of Puerto Rico appointed Velázquez secretary of the Department of Puerto Rican Community Affairs in the United States, a cabinet-level position that functions as a major link between Puerto Rico and the U.S. Government. Responsible for the New York City headquarters and four regional offices, Velázquez advised the Puerto Rican government on Puerto Rico's public policy and its commitment to the Puerto Rican community in the United States. She exercised her political influence in 1989 when Hurricane Hugo devastated Puerto Rico. Velázquez personally called General Colin Powell, head of the Joint Chiefs of Staff, and shortly after, the Commonwealth received a promise of federal assistance. During her tenure as secretary, Velázquez also led success-

ful voter registration drives that led to the registration of more than 200,000 voters in Puerto Rican communities in the Northeast and Midwest, and in 1991 she initiated *Unidos contra el sida* (United against AIDS), a project to fight the spread of AIDS among Puerto Ricans.

Velázquez's close ties with the Puerto Rican Government came under scrutiny during her 1992 bid for Congress. Her critics charged she was more concerned with Puerto Rican politics than with the problems of her constituents—an accusation she repeatedly denied. During the campaign, it was disclosed that Velázquez, while working for the Puerto Rican Government, had personally supported the pro-Commonwealth position in the fierce ongoing debate over the island's colonial status. During the race, she took a neutral stance on whether Puerto Rico should become a state or nation or continue as a commonwealth. "My responsibility as a member of Congress is to support whatever pledge Puerto Ricans make to resolve the situation," she told *Newsday.* Acknowledging that she is concerned about Puerto Rico, she related to a *Newsday* reporter during the campaign: "I say that, yes, we have been oppressed and disenfranchised for too long."

Velázquez's bid for Congress came at a time of national efforts to bring Hispanics and other minorities to the polls. The 12th Congressional District was one of nine new districts created in 1992 to increase minority voting power under the Voting Rights Act. The district includes a patchwork of Hispanic neighborhoods in three boroughs, including Corona, Elmhurst, and Jackson Heights in Queens, the Lower East Side in Manhattan, and Williamsburg, Bushwick, Sunset Park, and East New York in Brooklyn. According to the *New York Times,* the average income in the district is $22,500, more than $10,000 less than the state average. Some 22 percent of the people are on public assistance, and 27 percent are non-citizens. While a majority of the district's population is Hispanic—including Puerto Ricans, Dominicans, Colombians, and immigrants from other Spanish-speaking countries—the region also includes whites, blacks, and Asian Americans

Former Representative Solarz's Brooklyn district, which was heavily Jewish, was dissolved by the redistricting process. As a non-Hispanic, Solarz was criticized for seeking to represent a district designed for minority leadership. But he insisted that he was the best person for the job. "I categorically reject that only a black can represent a black district, or a Hispanic an Hispanic district," he told the *New York Times.* Although Solarz was a respected foreign policy expert in Congress, he was one of many legislators caught in the House bank scandal in the early 1990s, after it was revealed that he had written 743 overdrafts, according to the *New York Times.*

The 1992 Democratic primary in the 12th district was a bitter battle, pitting five Hispanic candidates against the popular Solarz, a nine-term Congressman. Velázquez ran an old-fashioned, grassroots campaign, pounding the pavement, making phone calls, and garnering support from family and friends. She could not afford much campaign literature or television advertisements. Although she raised just a fraction of Solarz's campaign fund of over two-million dollars, she had the endorsements of New York City Mayor David Dinkins, the Hispanic union leader Dennis Rivera, president of Local 1199 of the Drug, Hospital and Health Care Workers Union, and the Reverend Jesse Jackson. Dinkins's support was in part a political thank-you for Velázquez's 1989 voter registration efforts, which helped Mayor Dinkins win the Hispanic vote in the mayoral election.

Still, with four Hispanic opponents, one of her biggest challenges was to unite the district's diverse and politically fractured Hispanic community. Not only did Velázquez have to prove that she could represent all Hispanics in her district—not just the Puerto Ricans—she also had to fight the prejudice that often separates Puerto Ricans raised on the island from those with roots on the mainland. Even Velázquez's supporters describe her as controversial. "I think that Nydia just provokes very strong opinions of love and hate from people because she's so passionate herself," said Luis A. Miranda, Jr., president of the Hispanic Federation of New York City, in an interview with the *New York Times.*

Velázquez won the September 15 primary. Soon after, she returned to Puerto Rico and her hometown, where she was given a heroine's welcome. According to an account in the *New York Times,* she rode into Yabucoa in a pickup truck, accompanied by Mayor Angel Luis Ramos and a state senator. A loudspeaker proclaimed: "She's back! Our Nydia Velázquez, who will be the first Puerto Rican woman in Congress, is back in Sugartown!" Velázquez told the crowd that she dedicated her victory to her mother and the women of Puerto Rico. In an interview with *Newsday,* Ramos commented, "She represents a good example for the children. She came from a poor family and went to public school."

The low point of the 1992 campaign came in early October, when an anonymous source sent information to news organizations detailing Velázquez's attempted suicide and hospitalization the previous year. The incident was given much attention by the *New York Post,* which broke the story, and spread to the national media. Velázquez never denied the charges. Instead, she held a press conference, where, surrounded by friends and family, she acknowledged that she had suffered serious depression as the result of personal problems, including her mother's illness and a brother's drug addiction. "In 1991, in a troublesome period of my life, I attempted to commit suicide," said Velázquez, as reported by the *New York Times.* "It was a sad and painful experience for me, and one I thought was now in the past." She noted that she was

"appalled" and "outraged" that privileged medical information in the form of confidential hospital records had been released to the public, in violation of state law.

Velázquez's supporters must have recognized their candidate as a survivor who had overcome personal adversity and proven her potential to lead their communities. Velázquez, at the age of 39, defeated both Republican and independent challengers in the November election, taking more than three-quarters of the vote. At her election-night party in Williamsburg, Brooklyn, surrounded by "Fair Housing" signs, Velázquez said, in Spanish, that her victory was important for herself, her parents, and her people in the 12th District. "For you, I'm going to fight to gain better jobs, better lives, and better opportunities," she said.

As a non-traditional politician, Velázquez does not fit the standard conservative or liberal labels; instead, she often calls herself progressive. She hopes to concentrate her congressional career on the problems confronting her urban district, including jobs, the economy, child care, and housing. She supports federal construction projects to create jobs and government loans to help small businesses. Shortly before her election day victory, Velázquez told the *New York Post* that she wanted to improve the educational system and stem the tide of crime and drugs. On the international front, she opposes Jewish settlements on the West Bank and favors increased economic aid to Latin America.

Velázquez also plans to prove that Hispanic women can serve proudly in the political arena. "We are the ones who go out and collect signatures, but when it came to the final process, we were not good enough to run for office," said Velázquez in *USA Today.* She is one of 47 female representatives in the 103rd Congress. Frequently described as outspoken, independent, and determined, Velázquez is likely to breathe fresh air into Washington politics. "New blood is good," she told the *New York Times* on election day. Along with providing a new voice for Hispanics in Congress, she pledges to work with other minority and progressive members of Congress to improve the quality of life for all people in the nation's inner cities.

Sources:

Periodicals

Newsday, September 21, 1992, p. 37; September 26, 1992, p. 10; September 27, 1992, p. 18; October 10, 1992, p. 13.
New York Post, November 4, 1992, p. 4.
New York Times, July 9, 1992, p. B3; September 7, 1992, pp. 21-22; September 27, 1992, p. 33; October 10, 1992, p. 25; October 29, 1992, p. B7; November 2, 1992, p. B1, B4; November 4, 1992, p. B13.
Noticias del Mundo, November 4, 1992, pp. 1A, 4A.
USA Today, October 27, 1992, p. 2A.

Washington Post, October 9, 1992, p. A12.

—Sketch by Ann Malaspina

Lisa Velez
(1967?-)
Singer

With her sweet voice and infectious energy, singer Lisa Velez—known as Lisa Lisa—has captured the affections of thousands of teenagers throughout the United States. Her songs "I Wonder If I Take You Home" and "Lost in Emotion" have rocketed to the top of the pop charts, and at least one of her albums, written and produced by Full Force, has gone platinum. Remarkably enough, the aspect of Velez's personality that contributed to her success—her innocent honesty—has remained intact since she has become a star. As she was quoted as saying in *Newsweek:* "I don't consider myself a star. I'm an entertainer. I like to do my job. If I'm a star, it shows that I'm doing my job right."

The youngest of ten children, Velez was raised in the tough part of Manhattan, New York, known as Hell's Kitchen. From an early age she wanted to become a singer. Although, according to *Newsweek,* the young girl says she was "no angel," she joined her church's choir, became involved with her high school's musical theater, and when a California prune company sought actors to sing and parade about in prune costumes in Penn Station, Velez jumped at the chance. Velez's opportunity to become a star, however, did not manifest itself until she met Mike Hughes at the Fun House, the dance club that pop singer Madonna haunted just as she began her rise to stardom. Hughes introduced Velez to his Brooklyn production team, Full Force, and she was given an audition with the group in 1984. Full Force had been searching for a sexy yet sweet voice, a voice like that of Diana Ross during her days with the group, The Supremes, and Velez had just what they needed to create the sound they desired. As a critic for *Newsweek* wrote, "What the musicians in Full Force fell in love with . . . was a voice of guileless charm and ingenuous ardor—the kind of voice you don't hear much of in pop music today." After nicknaming her Lisa Lisa, the group began to record with the singer. Full Force is more than pleased with the success Velez has helped them obtain. Band member Mike Hughes proudly explained her popularity in *People:* "The Latin female thing started back with Madonna. She was part of the Fun House [club] crowd, playing the Puerto Rican role, dressing that way, hangin' out with that crowd. She was accepted and became the Latin queen. Now Madonna and everyone knows that Lisa is the new queen."

First Album Features Top 40 Hit

Indeed, after Lisa Lisa and Cult Jam (two members of Full Force, percussionist and rapper Mike Hughes and keyboardist-guitarist Alex Mosely, or "Spanador") had released their first album with the single "I Wonder If I Take You Home," the group seemed to be well on its way to stardom. The single did well in the Top 40 Pop Chart; teens loved Velez's innocent voice as much as the words she sang, and the song's beat was catchy. Although a critic for *People* thought that "with the exception of 'You'll Never Change', a number that contains attractive harmonies, the rest of the album [*Lisa Lisa & Cult Jam with Full Force,* Columbia, 1985] is uninspired, mechanical neodisco," Debby Bull, writing for *Rolling Stone,* thought that Lisa Lisa and Cult Jam's songs were refreshing.

Bull best described the song "I Wonder If I Take You Home": "What a perfectly conceived pop confection: Lisa Lisa's trying to make a decision ('Lately, you've been expressing to me/Just how much you want to make love/I want it just as much as you do/But will you still keep in touch?') while the guy puts pressure on in the background ('Take me, take me, take me home')." As Bull noted, the conversation between the girl and her boyfriend is the group's standard plot. It is the basis of songs like "You'll Never Change" and "All Cried Out." Bull also described the group's sound: she wrote that it is "clever collages of electronic blips and doodles, smooth pop ballads, street raps and funky bass riffs."

Second Album Goes Platinum

After "Head To Toe" was released and became Cult Jam's third Top 40 single, and after that song hit the number one spot on the pop chart, Velez seemed to be the queen of the funky pop sound. The group's second album, *Spanish Fly* (Columbia Records), went platinum after just ten weeks on the market; it had sold nearly two million copies by mid-1988. As a critic for *People* commented, "'Head to Toe' is strikingly reminiscent of the Supreme's 'Back in My Arms Again,' and 'Lost In Emotion' has a throwback tinge too. While Lisa doesn't have Ross's sense of style—not many people do—she does have a rich, versatile sound and the vocal strength to penetrate the album's percussion-heavy arrangements." The romantic song the critic mentioned, "Lost in Emotion," sent the group's popularity soaring once more.

Wearing her usual costume of a miniskirt, a short, tight, jacket, and flat shoes, Velez enthralled and excited audiences around the country. The *New York Times* reported that Velez "struts, she emotes, she talks to her audience as one teen-ager to another. . . . It becomes more and more evident that she is shaping a distinctive singing style as well as a vivid stage personality and a much-imitated look."

The group's next album, *Straight to the Sky,* was very successful the year it was released, 1989. Like all of Lisa

Lisa and Cult Jam's albums, this one was written and produced by Full Force. A critic for the *New York Times* noted that "the album works as a dialogue between Lisa Lisa and Full Force (and her two regular sidekicks, Cult Jam), in which the men sometimes play her lovers and at other times answer as her producers, with sound. . . . The record is alive with this interplay . . . and with the triumph of the underdog Lisa Lisa beating the men down, only to call them back as her home-boys."

In 1991, Lisa Lisa and Cult Jam (with Full Force and C+C Music Factory) released another album, *Straight Outta Hell's Kitchen* (Columbia). This album included the songs "Don't Say Goodbye," "Let the Beat Hit 'Em," and "I Like It, I Like It" and was received enthusiastically by fans of the group. A critic for *People*, however, was not impressed with the "creative fusion." He wrote, "Their [Full Force and C+C Music Factory] handiwork didn't give Lisa a bad record, just not a very distinctive one." He continued, "You'll probably hear lots of *Hell's Kitchen* on the radio. You just won't remember much of it two months from now."

Despite her status as pop-music royalty, Velez has not forgotten her roots. She still lives with her mother in her old neighborhood, and she is true to her Federal Express delivery man boyfriend. Velez understands that she is a role model for teens, and she acts accordingly. She told *People*, "I want my fans to know that I'm not over at Saks buying furs. I want them to look at us and think, 'If they were able to do it, we can, too.'" Velez is enthusiastic about encouraging other Hispanics, especially Puerto Ricans, to excel in whatever they do. One way she contributes to this cause is by working to fight illiteracy with the Coors Foundation. "Step back and watch out!" she was quoted as saying in *Time* magazine. "I want to bring the Puerto Ricans out. Boom!"

Sources:

Periodicals

Más, November-December, 1991, p. 9.
Newsweek, June 22, 1987, p. 77.
New York Times, October 31, 1987, p. A14; May 7, 1989, section 2, p. 27.
People, October 21, 1985, p. 24; May 11, 1987, p. 29; September 14, 1987, pp. 53-54; September 23, 1991, p. 21.
Rolling Stone, October 10, 1985, pp. 62-63.
Time, July 11, 1988.

—*Sketch by Ronie-Richele Garcia-Johnson*

Vidal Santaella, Irma
See **Santaella, Irma Vidal**

Evangelina Vigil-Piñón
(1949-)
Poet

Careful craftsmanship and the delicate interweaving of detail and gentle satire have made the work of poet-performer Evangelina Vigil-Piñón an index of feminism and Hispanic life in the United States. She was born in San Antonio, Texas, on November 29, 1949, to Mexican American parents. The old Alamo City, with its barrios, close-knit families, dusty streets, and particularly the Tejano and Norteno popular music that filled the city's plazas, cafes, and street corners, left an indelible mark on the future poet. As a child Vigil-Piñón loved music and song. Her initial desire to sing later gave way to her poetry writing.

Vigil-Piñón, who received her B.A. in English in 1974 from the University of Houston, attributes her desire to write poetry to the influence of contemporary American writers she encountered while in college. She started writing in 1975, and in 1976, after her return to San Antonio, she published her first poem in the magazine *Caracol*. This magazine, edited by Cecilio Diaz Camarillo, served as a mouthpiece for young Chicano writers, especially those from Texas. Some of its best known contributors included Abelardo, Angela de Hoyos, Carmen Tafoya, and Ricardo Sanchez.

In the next few years Vigil-Piñón's poetry was published in several Chicano, Southwestern, and Hispanic national journals. Her first collection of poems, a chapbook entitled *Nade y Nade*, was published in San Antonio in 1978. The following year the National Endowment for the Humanities awarded Vigil-Piñón a fellowship for creative writing, which allowed her to devote herself full-time to writing. Her work from this period is included in her second book of poetry, *Thirty an' Seen a Lot*, published in 1982 by Arte Público Press in Houston, Texas. The book won an American Book Award in 1983 from the Before Columbus Foundation of San Francisco, California.

Vigil-Piñón's third book of poetry, *The Computer is Down*, published by Arte Público Press in 1987, reveals the poet's new thematic interests. Whereas the first two collections dealt heavily with family, feminism, and nostalgia for childhood, her new poems showed greater concern with the urban experience. By this time Vigil-Piñón had moved to the metropolitan area of Houston, had married graphic artist Mark Piñón, and had a son, Marc-Anthony, born in 1984. A concern manifest in her current work is the changing of Hispanic culture due to the influx of immigrants from Latin America. Vigil-Piñón continues to give poetry readings which are increasingly combined with singing and guitar playing. Some of the songs she performs are her own compositions; the majority, however, are written by others and have inspired her poems. Often lines of poetry and lyrics are juxtaposed.

Vigil-Piñón has edited two anthologies: a collection of children's writings, *From Inside, Out,* published in 1978 by M & A Editions of San Antonio, Texas, and *Woman of Her Word: Hispanic Women Write,* published by Arte Público Press in 1983. In 1988 she wrote the definitive English translation of Tomas Rivera's classic . . . .*y no se lo trago la tierra and the earth did not part* for Arte Público Press. Vigil-Piñón currently works in public information for the Cultural Arts Council of Houston, teaches Hispanic poetry at the University of Houston, and is assistant editor of *The Americas Review* (formerly *Revista Chicano-Riquena*).

Sources:

Archives, Arte Público Press, Houston, Texas.
Vigil-Piñón, Evangelina, telephone interview with Silvia Novo Pena, September, 1992.

—Sketch by Silvia Novo Pena

Alma Luz Villanueva
(1944-)
Poet

In *Contemporary Authors,* poet Alma Luz Villanueva writes of "the paradox, the mystery of writing," and explains that for her the mystery is "when we touch the most personal, the most hidden within ourselves, we touch the other, the outer, the universal." Villanueva's poetry is an exploration inward to discover her roots as a female, as a Chicana, and as a poet. Perhaps her most personal work is her 1978 collection of poems, *Mother, May I?,* which Marta Ester Sánchez described in *Contemporary Chicana Poetry: A Critical Approach to an Emerging Literature* as an account of "the important phases of [Villanueva's] life from childhood to her early thirties." Villanueva's other major works of poetry, *Bloodroot* and "Poems" (included in *Third Chicano Literary Prize, 1976*), are also autobiographical.

Villanueva was born in Lopoc, California, on October 4, 1944. Her father was of German descent; her mother's name was Lydia Villanueva. Alma Villanueva lived with her Mexican grandmother in San Francisco, California, until she was eleven years old. In *Contemporary Chicana Poetry*

Sánchez stressed the importance of the relationship between Villanueva and her grandmother: "Since [Villanueva's] closeness to her grandmother is part of her childhood, her Chicana, or Mexican American, identity plays a minor role in her adult poetic persona, which lies more within a community bounded by gender than within one bounded by race or ethnicity." The poet's childhood ended abruptly when, at age fourteen, she discovered she was pregnant with her own first child.

Although she wrote poems as a teenager, Villanueva only took up writing seriously as she approached her thirtieth birthday. Her major works of poetry, *Bloodroot,* "Poems," and *Mother, May I?,* were all produced while the poet was in her thirties. During this period of her life she also wrote several allegorical plays, including *The Curse* and *La Tuna,* and contributed short stories to periodicals. The 1980s and 1990s have seen more poetry from Villanueva and also two novels, *Ultraviolet Sky* and *Naked Ladies,* but, in 1985, Sánchez maintained that *Mother May I?* was Villanueva's "most interesting and dynamic work." The collection also sets Villanueva apart from her more famous male Chicano poet counterparts and other female Hispanic poets because, as Sánchez noted, Villanueva "is the only one to write a poetic autobiography."

Explores Feminist Issues in Work

In *Chicano Literature* Charles M. Tatum praised Villanueva's poetry for "its tone of undaunted exploration of a wide variety of themes." James Cody, the editor of her 1977 collection, *Bloodroot,* notes in his preface to the volume that "there are no subjects that she does not embrace unhesitatingly." Although these critics see Villanueva's poetry as multi-thematic, it is often written from a feminist point of view. So important is the idea of femaleness to Villanueva's work that Sánchez writes that "the poetic enterprise of *Mother, May I?* is to create from concrete experience a personal myth of universal womanhood." In the book Villanueva looks at the cast of females who have influenced her, including her mother, her grandmother (identified as "mamacita"), and her daughter. The work's closing passages express the deep need of the author to find a sense of empowerment through fellowship with other women: "the thread, the story/ connects/ between women;/ grandmother, mothers, daughter/ all women/ the thread of this story."

Villanueva won first prize for poetry in the Third Chicano Literary Prize competition held at the University of California at Irvine in 1977, and the American Book Award in 1989 for her novel, *Ultraviolet Sky.* In 1984 she received a master of fine arts from Norwich University. Villanueva can be heard on several recordings, including *Like the Free Spirit of Birds,* from New Radio and Performing Arts of New York City, and *Women's Spirituality* and *Hispanic Poets Read,* two tapes in the "Poetry Archives" series of San Francisco State University.

Sources:

Books

Contemporary Authors, Volume 131, Gale, 1991, pp. 466-67.

Sánchez, Marta Ester, *Contemporary Chicana Poetry: A Critical Approach to an Emerging Literature,* University of California Press, 1985.

Tatum, Charles M., *Chicano Literature,* Twayne, 1982.

Villanueva, Alma Luz, *Bloodroot,* preface by James Cody, Place of Herons Press (Austin, TX), 1977.

Villanueva, Alma Luz, *Mother, May I?,* Motheroot Publications (Pittsburgh, PA), 1978.

Periodicals

Carta Abierta, June, 1978, p. 19.

Revista Chicano-Riqueña, fall, 1978, pp. 75-76.

—*Sketch by Marian C. Gonsior*

Villarreal García, Juliet
See García, Juliet Villarreal

Helena Maria Viramontes
(1954-)
Writer

Helena Maria Viramontes is one of a new generation of Hispanic women fiction writers. She is known for her striking use of language and her realistic portrayal of women—for creating characters that are far from the idealized versions of feminists successfully battling patriarchy, as the critic Yvonne Yarbro-Bejarano has observed.

Viramontes was born February 26, 1954, in East Los Angeles, California, where she attended Chicano schools. She began writing in college while studying English literature at Immaculate Heart College, where she received her B.A. in 1975. Her first attempts were in poetry, but she soon determined she was better suited for fiction writing, particularly short stories. Her tales initially revolved around those close to her. "Whenever I finished a story, I would read it to my friends, and they would tell me how these things had also happened to them. It made me realize that I was not just writing about myself but about a whole community of women," Viramontes explained in a telephone interview with Silvia Novo Pena. As a result, the author began to record in her short fiction some of the stories other women were telling her about their own lives.

Before long she entered her work in contests and achieved recognition. Her stories began to appear in several national and regional publications, and in 1977 she won first prize for fiction from *Statement Magazine,* a publication of California State University in Los Angeles, for her short story "Requiem for the Poor." The following year she again won first prize in the *Statement* contest for her short story "The Broken Web." In 1979 she won first prize for fiction in the University of California at Irvine Chicano Literary Contest for her short story "Birthday." In 1983 her stories "Snapshots" and "Growing" appeared in the anthology *Cuentos: Stories by Latinas,* published by Kitchen Table/Women of Color Press. Her award-winning story "The Broken Word" appeared in the 1984 Arte Público Press anthology of Hispanic women writers, *Woman of Her Word,* edited by the poet Evangelina Vigil. Viramontes's first collection of short stories, *The Moths and Other Stories,* was published by Arte Público Press in Houston, Texas in 1985.

Viramontes's fiction centers on women of different ages, mainly Chicanas from the Southwest, struggling against all economic obstacles to raise their children. One of her themes is the violence women endure as a result of being dominated by men. Her writing, she believes, is a way of condemning oppression, whether it involves racism or sexism. Her work has been influenced by such black writers as Toni Morrison, Alice Walker, and Ntozake Shange, as well as by contemporary Latin American writers, especially Gabriel García Márquez. Chicana feminist writers Ana Castillo and Sandra Cisneros have also had a great impact upon Viramontes, who considers herself a feminist. "If we are going to improve as a society, we have to re-teach ourselves as well as the men to develop the feminine side of our natures, something that has been lost. It is the feminine aspect that will strive to save the environment, making the world safe for all creatures," she remarked in her interview.

Viramontes has collaborated on two non-fiction projects. In 1983 she edited with Maria Herrera Sobek the anthology *Chicana Writers: Word and Film,* published by Third Woman. With the same author in 1988 she produced another non-fiction anthology, *Chicana Creativity and Criticism: Charting New Frontiers in American Literature,* published by Arte Público Press.

In 1989 Viramontes received a National Endowment for the Arts fellowship to attend a workshop on story-telling by Nobel winner Gabriel García Márquez offered at the Sundance Institute. She was one of eight writers nominated from a national pool for this honor. In 1991 Viramontes adapted one of her stories for film. Picked up by director Ana Maria Garcia and produced by the Film Institute, this half-hour film was scheduled to be released in 1992 or 1993.

Viramontes has organized a number of readings and panels aimed at attracting attention to her work and that of her fellow professional writers. She has also been instrumental in the creation of the Southern California Latino Writers and Film Makers group, the first attempt to organize Latino writers in the Los Angeles area.

The writer resides in Irvine, California, with her husband and two children. She has plans to complete her master of fine arts in creative writing at the University of California at Irvine and is currently working on a novella, tentatively titled *Their Dogs Came with Them,* about the domination of women by men.

Sources:

Books

Yarbro-Bejarano, Yvonne, "Introduction," *The Moths and Other Stories,* by Helena Maria Viramontes, Arte Público Press, 1985.

Other

Archives, Arte Público Press, Houston, Texas.
Viramontes, Helena Maria, telephone interview with Silvia Novo Pena, September, 1992, and November, 1992.

—Sketch by Silvia Novo Pena

Nelly Vuksic
(1939-)
Conductor, musician

Argentinean-born conductor and vocalist Nelly Vuksic unites classical and contemporary music from Latin America and the United States to create a musical experience that is both enjoyable and educational. Vuksic's eclecticism has taken her throughout the Western Hemisphere in search of new conducting experiences and new music. She proudly informed Tom Pendergast during a telephone interview that in every performance of her musical group, Americas Vocal Ensemble, there is at least one premiere performance for the United States. In addition to her work with various choral groups, Vuksic also performs regularly with her husband, pianist Cesar Vuksic. Her journey from a small town in rural Argentina to New York City is as interesting as the music her groups have performed.

Nelly Perez Trevisan de Vuksic was born to Emilio and Lydia Perez on August 19, 1938, in Totoras, Argentina, a small town outside of the larger city of Rosario. Rosario, a

Nelly Vuksic

port city on the Parana River upstream from the coastal city of Buenos Aires, is one of the largest cities in the Santa Fe province of Argentina. The Perez Trevisan family enjoyed a great deal of prestige in Totoras where, Vucksic recalled in her interview, "everyone knew everyone else": her grandmother had been the first schoolteacher in town, and her grandfather had founded what was once the town's largest general store and grocery. Her parents were not rich, however, for the family store, which her father managed, no longer did a booming business. Her mother was a seamstress and taught sewing to a group of young neighborhood girls which included her daughter.

Vuksic's education was not very organized. She studied in her grandmother's private school until she was eight years old, when she began to attend the public schools. She finished her primary schooling, but it was years before she could attend secondary school. If her formal education was scattered, her musical education was more thorough, disciplined, and continuous. "My family was very musically oriented," Vuksic explained in her interview. "My dad played guitar and loved Argentinean tangos, and he and mom organized musical evenings, where everyone in the family would gather and sing popular songs." In addition to singing at home, she sang from a very early age at the Catholic church she attended, where she also learned to play the harmonium, an instrument similar to the organ. Revealed Vuksic, "I learned two important things about music under the supervision of the nuns: how to sing in a group and how to sing a Gregorian chant."

When she was eight, Vuksic began to take piano lessons under the supervision of a teacher she characterized as "mean but talented." Vuksic learned rapidly and was soon an accomplished pianist. The teacher had many students in the bigger town of Rosario and Vuksic would play at the concerts and challenges her teacher organized at the El Circulo Theatre. Vuksic remembered the theatre as being "very beautiful, very lavish, and very French, and I went there to play music by Schuman, Beethoven, Chopin, difficult pieces by the classical composers." After she had been playing for a time she got a piano of her own, which her family in Argentina still uses, and she practiced until late at night. "Piano was my job," she told her interviewer, "and it made my mother very proud."

Since her family could not afford to send her to the secondary school in a neighboring town, Vuksic spent all her time with music, playing and teaching. Eventually she had earned enough money to pay her own way through school, though she did not finish secondary school until she was in her early twenties. "Luckily," she remembered, "I looked young enough to fit in with the teenagers." Even while she was in the American equivalent of high school, Vuksic began attending courses at nearby Rosario University, where she attracted attention with her musical talents. Urged to study the practical field of music education, Vuksic began to learn to conduct and was invited to be a conductor with the Coro Estable de Rosario's prestigious youth choir.

Discovers Fulfillment in Conducting

Despite the fact that she had won numerous prizes for her piano playing and was building a reputation in Rosario as a fine pianist, Vuksic began to devote herself to conducting. "I discovered I could conduct, that I was a conductor," she stated in her interview. "It was a new way of expressing myself. A conductor can shape the music with her hands, where in teaching you don't get that fulfillment." She became very interested in choir, and also assisted the conductor of the university's adult chorus. But her progress as a conductor was interrupted briefly when, shortly after her graduation, Vuksic married a young pianist named Cesar Vuksic. The musical couple was married on February 14, 1969, in her hometown of Totoras, and they soon began a joint career of travel and music that has continued for over twenty years.

Cesar was supported in his musical career by his family, but he wanted to leave the country "to gain experience and to grow," explained Vuksic. In 1972, the renowned pianist Pia Sebastiani offered Cesar a scholarship to Ball State University in Muncie, Indiana. He accepted, and his wife followed a year later with their young son, Alejandro. Though she knew little English, Vuksic was also offered a scholarship in the School of Music where, she said, she "did everything that could be done—taught piano, sang, accompanied people and, most of all, learned English." Soon, however, she was offered the conductorship of the

women's chorus and assisted with the concert choir as well. By 1978 she completed her doctoral studies in conducting from Ball State University and was twice awarded the university's Music Concerto Night Award, in 1976 and 1977. In 1978 she followed Cesar to Western Michigan University, where he had received a visiting musicianship. There she conducted the choir and several chamber orchestras and taught piano.

In 1979, Vuksic accepted a position that would change her musical life forever; she left the United States to work at the Conservatorio del Tolima, in Colombia, South America. In her interview Vuksic declared: "In Colombia, I became Latin American. They played Latin American music, both contemporary and traditional, along with European music and I discovered the charm of folk music." Vuksic was offered the conductorship of the well-known Los Coro de Tolimo and the Coro Ibague; with this last group she won the Concurso Polifomico Internacional Colombia, a prestigious international music award, in 1980. More important than the award, claimed Vuksic, was the widening of her musical horizons. After her experience in Colombia, she became committed to musical eclecticism, to understanding all the different varieties of music produced in all the Americas, North, Central, and South.

Despite their success in Colombia, Vuksic and her husband felt that it was "important to keep growing—musically, professionally, and spiritually"—and so they moved to New York City in 1982. Yet New York City was not, at first, all they had hoped it would be. "It was not easy finding work in New York," Vuksic told her interviewer. "I did all kinds of work, cleaning houses, menial jobs, just to keep busy. I would not have done this in my country, but in the United States doing these things was acceptable. I felt resentful, but at the same time I learned that I could do anything." Her first job in New York came almost by accident. She went to an Italian poetry reading—though she did not know Italian—and ran into an Italian tenor who was singing at the same place. She offered to accompany him on piano, he hired her, and soon they were working in restaurants and night clubs, playing Broadway music, Italian songs, and songs from operas.

Soon other jobs came Vuksic's way. When she first came to the city, she had visited the Americas Society and there had met "her angel," Lucille Duncan, the director of the performing department. Duncan mentioned her name to Hugh Ross, a well-known New York City choral conductor and, some time later, Ross contacted Vuksic and asked her to assist him in performing some works of a contemporary European musician. "I was thrilled at the thought of working with him," explained Vuksic, "but it turns out he wanted me as a singer, not a conductor." However, a friend who Vuksic met doing this job became very interested in Vuksic's desire to conduct performances of contemporary and traditional Latin American music and encouraged her to form the choral group that became Americas Vocal Ensemble.

Founds Americas Vocal Ensemble

Vuksic founded the Ensemble in 1982 and soon the group recorded some choral works of Colombian composer Luis Antonio Escobar. Escobar was so thrilled by *Las Cantatas Madrigales* that, in a note he wrote for the album cover, he praised Vuksic for picking up ideas that he thought were not perceived by any other conductors. "I was very gratified to receive his admiration," noted Vuksic. The Ensemble has also recorded *Opus One: Americas Vocal Ensemble Performs the Music of Joel Wallach* and *Music of the Americas,* and it plans to release a compact disc titled *Hispanic Christmas Collection.* When the group was beginning, it relied on individual contributions for support but, as its reputation has grown, the group has received enough recognition to secure grants. The Ensemble has begun to perform throughout New York City and the east coast, including a performance at the American Music Festival in Washington, D.C. The growth of Vuksic's reputation in the 1980s and early-1990s has allowed her to conduct other New York choral groups, including the United Nation Singers.

During the time that she was struggling to establish the reputation of Americas Vocal Ensemble in New York, Vuksic also happened onto a teaching job. A friend encouraged her to introduce herself to a New York music school director, and she told the director that she was looking for work. It just so happened that he was looking for a bilingual music teacher, and he hired her on the spot for a position at the Bloomingdale House of Music in 1982. Later Vuksic worked for the Friends Seminary, where she taught voice, first on the high school level and later on all grade levels. She taught there from 1985 to 1990, when she took a job at Columbia University's program for teaching music to gifted children. Although teaching has always been Vuksic's second love, she admitted during her interview that "teaching people to sing fulfills my soul. One of my favorite lyrics in a song is 'Keep my heart in tune, I want to teach the world to sing.'" Though she has often taught in organized schools, she prefers teaching voice to individuals.

Vuksic's greatest joy in conducting Americas Vocal Ensemble is that she is able to introduce people to a wide variety of music. She is as likely to present music by a contemporary Colombian composer as she is by a seventeenth-century U.S. composer. She is pleased that every performance she presents is a premiere for at least one of the pieces she plays. "Each piece of music has its moment," Vuksic claimed, "and I am interested in working in all kinds of music." Another consistent pleasure in her life has been the opportunity to often work alongside her husband. Together they perform a program of Argentinean tangos and sambas, in both traditional and classical arrangements and often accompanied by their commentaries on the pieces. In addition, Cesar is the pianist of the Americas Vocal Ensemble and the United Nations Singers and frequently performs as a soloist. Nelly is always on the lookout for new opportunities, especially if they further

her professed mission of "expanding and disseminating Latin American music." Asked to name her favorite music to perform, Vuksic said without hesitation: "My favorite music is the music that I am preparing for my next performance."

Sources:

Periodicals

Imagen, December, 1990, p. 42.
Más, October, 1990, p. 11.

Other

Vuksic, Nelly, telephone interview with Tom Pendergast conducted on September 14, 1992.

—*Sketch by Tom Pendergast*

Warren, Nina Otero
See **Otero-Warren, Nina**

Raquel Welch
(1940-)
Actress, singer, producer, writer

Since she first appeared in *Life* magazine in 1964, Raquel Welch has had little difficulty garnering attention. By 1966, the internationally known actress had become so popular that *Life* named her the most photographed woman of the year. The winner of various California beauty contests, Welch suddenly found herself on magazine covers, in movies, and in her own television specials. She later expanded her career as she maintained her company, Raquel Welch Productions, produced films, performed on stage, wrote a fitness book, and recorded a pop single. While Welch has been celebrated as a sex symbol, she has proven that she is a serious actress and has won the respect of critical audiences with her performances in the Broadway musical *Woman of the Year* and in the television movie *Right to Die.* Welch described her current status in *Hispanic:* "I've won my stripes. . . . I've gone from just being a sex symbol to being thought of as a legitimate actress."

Welch was born Raquel Tejada, the daughter of Armand Tejada, a Bolivian immigrant of Spanish heritage, and

Raquel Welch

American Josephine Hall Tejada, in Chicago, Illinois, on September 5, 1940. Two years later, her family relocated to La Jolla, a beach town in southern California, where Armand Tejada was employed as a structural engineer at a General Dynamics plant. At the public high school in La Jolla, Tejada, or "Rocky," as her friends called her, was a cheerleader, a member of the dramatic club, and the vice president of her senior class. She took ballet lessons and began to enter and win beauty contests; after her first victory at the age of fifteen, Welch became Miss La Jolla, Miss San Diego, and Maid of California. After her 1958 graduation she tried to pursue a career as an actress but with no success. So she took a job as a weather girl with a local television station in San Diego and spent a year studying acting at San Diego State College.

On May 8, 1959, Raquel Tejada became Raquel Welch when she married her high school sweetheart, James Westley Welch. The couple later separated and then divorced in 1964. Leaving her children, Damon and Tahnee, in California to live with her parents, Welch went to Texas, where she modeled for Neiman-Marcus and worked as a cocktail hostess. Welch's dream was to move to New York City to better her chances of finding acting jobs, but she could not raise enough money for a trip to New York City. Welch returned to southern California, where she collected her children and found a home in Hollywood. Welch once again looked for work as an actress, and by the end of 1964, she had found minor parts in the film *A House Is Not a Home* and in the Elvis Presley movie *Roustabout.*

When publicist Patrick Curtis, a former child actor, met Welch, he left the public relations firm of Rogers & Cowan to head his own firm, Curtwel Productions. He devoted much of his time to managing Welch's career. His promotion of Welch gave her the opportunities she needed to rise to fame. She won a role in *A Swingin' Summer,* which brought her notice. In 1964, Welch appeared as a billboard girl in ABC-TV's *The Hollywood Palace,* and later that same year, Welch was featured in *Life* magazine. Twentieth Century-Fox contracted with Welch and designed a part especially for her in the memorable science fiction film, *Fantastic Voyage.* However, it was the image of Welch in a tight skin-diving suit, rather than her performance, which garnered the most media attention.

Achieves International Stardom

Although Welch "had a very Puritan upbringing," she said in *Hispanic,* she was well on her way to becoming a sex symbol by 1967. Welch explained in the same article that she thought it fun "to strut my stuff," and didn't complain when Twentieth Century-Fox loaned her out to Hammer Film Productions for the making of *One Million Years B.C.* in 1967. Cast as Loana Shell, a cavewoman, Welch almost speechlessly romped around the set in a fur bikini, to the delight of European audiences. While Welch's role in this film was not very challenging, it won her fame, especially after Curtis advertised Welch as America's Ursula Andress. The actress appeared on some 92 European magazine covers, and Welch's popularity soon spread to the United States, where her image graced at least sixteen American magazine covers. By the time Welch starred as a prostitute in the Italian comedy *Shoot Loud, Louder . . . I Don't Understand You* and as a spy in *Fathom,* she had definitely achieved international star status. When she and Curtis married on Valentine's Day in 1967, in Paris, the media had a field day trying to capture the romantic image of Welch in a tiny, white crocheted dress.

Welch's next assignments were to portray a gang member in *The Biggest Bundle of Them All* and to star in the British comedy *Bedazzled,* a Faustian film in which Welch played the role of a deadly sin, Lillian Lust. While the former film was not well-received by critics, it did not damage Welch's image, and the latter film enhanced her sex-symbol status. Welch created a stir with the daring costume she wore to the 1967 Academy Awards, and her tour of South Vietnam with Bob Hope brightened what had been a dreary Christmas for many American soldiers.

From 1968 to 1970, producers capitalized on Welch's fame and beauty to entice audiences to theaters, and she was cast in many films. In 1968, Welch starred in *The Queens: The Oldest Profession,* a film about prostitution, *Bandolero,* a western with James Stewart, and *Lady in Cement,* one of Frank Sinatra's Tony Rome movies. In 1969, the actress portrayed a go-go dancer in the suspense film *Flare Ups* and traveled to Spain to make *100 Rifles.* As Welch's character made love in a scene in *100 Rifles* with a black character, played by actor Jim Brown, the actress found herself enmeshed in controversy, and a great box office success.

A cameo role as a driver whipping her slaving oarswomen in *The Magic Christian* followed in 1970. Welch then chose another controversial role, that of Myra, the man-like female personality of the transsexual Myron, in the film *Myra Breckenridge*, which also featured Rex Reed, Mae West, and John Huston. Unfortunately, the movie, based on Gore Vidal's novel about homosexuality in Hollywood, failed to win the admiration of critics, and it was rumored that Welch's disagreements with the director and Mae West had contributed to the disastrous product. Disputing the label of being a "difficult" actress, Welch explained in *Hispanic:* "All I ever fought for was quality in my films. I really felt I was being penalized for being the sex symbol they had created, and that made my Spanish blood boil." Despite the disappointing reception of *Myra Breckinridge*, and her unfair portrayal in the media, Welch met with some positive response in the same year with her CBS television special, *Raquel.*

Enjoys Decade of Professional Success

Although 1971 brought the actress personal turmoil as she divorced Patrick Curtis, 1972 was a productive year for Welch. She starred in *Fuzz Bluebeard, Hannie Caulder,* and *Kansas City Bomber.* In 1973 she made *The Last of Sheila,* and in 1974 she won a Golden Globe Award for best actress in *The Three Musketeers.* The movies she made in the mid to late seventies included *The Wild Part, The Four Musketeers, Mother, Jugs, and Speed, Crossed Swords, The Prince and the Pauper, Restless,* and *L'Animal.* In 1979, Welch made a guest appearance on the very popular television series, *The Muppet Show.*

It was during the filming of *L'Animal* in Paris in 1977 that Raquel Welch met her third husband, screenwriter-producer Andre Weinfeld. Welch and Weinfeld were married in a small ceremony in Mexico in 1980. In *People* magazine, Welch praised Weinfeld's "funny, generous, sensual spirit." Although, according to a *People* article, Welch had vowed never to mix business and marriage again, her new husband worked on her next television special, *From Raquel with Love,* that appeared on ABC-TV shortly after their wedding and was rated very highly. *Hispanic* reported that the couple had "a wonderful working relationship" managing Welch's production company; however, they separated in late 1989.

In 1981, Welch professional career took a substantial and very public blow when she was replaced by Debra Winger after production had already begun on the film *Cannery Row.* While Metro-Goldwyn-Mayer (MGM) claimed that Welch had behaved unprofessionally on the set, Welch believed that she had been unfairly fired to cut the cost of the film's production. She filed a $20 million lawsuit against the company, and a lengthy legal battle ensued. In

1986, she finally was awarded $10.8 million by the court, an award which was later overturned. The experience traumatized Welch. She told people that she felt that she had been "blackballed" by Hollywood, and she explained in the *New York Times* that the episode had "stunned" her. "After that, I thought I was completely dead. . . . I never want to feel that way again—I'd rather die for real," she lamented.

As it turned out, Welch's experience surrounding *Cannery Row* led her to accept some serious and challenging acting roles. The actress acknowledged in *People* that the rough experience incited her to defend herself, "I operate on the premise that you always have to fight for what you want." She confided in the *New York Times* as well, "If it hadn't been for the 'Cannery Row' experience, I wouldn't have been predisposed to stick my neck out on 'Woman of the Year.'"

Creates Sensation with Broadway Role

Welch's performance in the hit musical *Woman of the Year* in 1981 marked a turning point in her career and a transformation of her reputation. When Lauren Bacall needed a vacation from the role she made famous on Broadway, Welch was asked to replace her for two weeks. Welch's years of presenting her nightclub act, "Live in Concert," in Atlantic City, Las Vegas, Rio de Janeiro, and other entertainment hot spots had given her the experience she needed to excel, singing and dancing, on stage. The popularity of her act suggested to the play's producers that Welch was capable of filling Bacall's shoes for two weeks. Her performance in *Woman of the Year* was lauded. After creating a sensation, Welch was asked to return later when Bacall took a six-month break. Welch was elated with this exciting revision of her acting career and felt that she had finally won the respect she deserved. She declared in the *New York Times:* "When we got the reviews—the only way I can describe it is the phrase, 'The thrill of a lifetime.' I'm totally hooked. I can't wait to get back."

Before she returned to Broadway for her six-month stint in *Woman of the Year,* Welch starred in *The Legend of Walks Far Woman* a movie made for television. Her "dramatic debut," as a *People* magazine critic dubbed the appearance, was to portray an independent, tough Native American woman who witnesses the battle of Little Big Horn and survives. Welch related her enthusiasm for the role to the *New York Times:* "I like the idea of heroines who survive and struggle. It's important to have your own principles, to have dignity and follow your own code, as Walks Far does. I like a woman character with backbone." A *People* magazine critic found the movie "solemn but worthwhile." Welch's reputation as a legitimate actress was beginning to solidify.

Despite these changes in her work and reputation, Welch's sex symbol image stubbornly maintained itself. Welch was well aware of this, and she was quoted in *People* as saying: "Why hate it? It doesn't do me any good. The sex symbol image is there. I don't dislike it. I don't love it. It's like

Mount Rushmore. It's not going to go away." As perpetual as her image, Welch's beauty was intact, and she capitalized on her amazing vitality by writing a book about it in 1984. Entitled *The Raquel Welch Total Beauty and Fitness Program,* the book focused on retaining one's physical and mental health with yoga, specialized diets, and exercise, and was released with an accompanying videocassette. Welch's work was a bestseller—at least 100,000 copies of the book had been sold by the end of 1985. Despite a $1 million damage suit by Bikram Choudhury, Welch's former yoga instructor and good friend who charged that the actress had stolen his moves and format and claimed her instructions could lead to injuries, Welch continued to introduce fitness programs on video. She produced and starred in the home exercise video, *Raquel: Lose 10 Lbs in 3 Weeks,* and *Body and Mind: Total Relaxation and Stress Relief Program.* In 1987, she released another video, *A Week with Raquel,* which also became a top seller.

1987 was a productive year for Welch. She starred in a made-for-television movie, *Right to Die,* which dramatized the trauma of decision-making in life and death situations. Welch's portrayal of a woman dying of amyotrophic lateral sclerosis, better known as Lou Gehrig's Disease, won her praise. Instead of playing a glamorous, sexy woman, she effectively characterized a pale, suffering woman in a state of rapid physical decay. Although a *People* magazine critic berated the movie and described it as "an inappropriate and exploitive exercise in emotional voyeurism," a reviewer for the *New York Times* wrote, "Ms. Welch gives an enormously affecting performance as Emily Bauer, not only uncompromising but also admirably sensitive to the intentions of the film."

Welch was pleased with her performance as well. She remarked to the *New York Times,* "I wasn't making a conscious search for something like this, but I had always known I had a whole part of my being and my professional ability that I'd never had a chance to use fully, and this satisfied that." She continued: "Everything that was the public Raquel Welch, I got rid of . . . in this role. . . . There was a great freedom in knowing for myself how much there was without all that, and what a range of things I can look forward to personally, as well as for myself as an actress. I'm very grateful I found that out." One of the things Welch was looking forward to was the European release of an energetic pop single—and the continental tour that would promote it—later in 1987. Entitled "This Girl is Back in Town," Welch's song communicated her renewed confidence. A *Hispanic* writer quoted a portion of its lyrics: "Well, now I know right from wrong, and . . . the only place where I belong. No more fooling around / This girl's back in town."

In 1988, during the production of another critically acclaimed television movie, *Scandal in a Small Town,* Welch commented in *Hispanic,* "I've always thought the older I got the more people would see that I have more to me than just my good looks." Many would agree that, while Welch is

finally receiving the recognition that she deserves, she hasn't lost her good looks. Although she is over fifty years of age, she maintains the image that made her famous and intends to create her own acting opportunities. Welch's physical vitality, her determination to emerge as a serious actress, and her clever utilization of all of her talents have made her an inspirational figure. The Los Angeles Hispanic Women's Council confirmed her status by naming her Woman of the Year in 1990.

Sources:

Books

Haining, Peter, *Raquel Welch: Sex Symbol to Super Star,* St. Martin's Press, 1984.

Periodicals

Chicago Tribune, June 25, 1986, p. 4.
Cosmopolitan, May, 1983, pp. 250-56; May, 1990, pp. 320-24.
Good Housekeeping, October, 1984, pp. 116-20.
Harper's Bazaar, August, 1982, p. 116; November, 1984, pp. 244-48.
Hispanic, April, 1988, pp. 20-24.
Los Angeles Magazine, January, 1985, p. 18.
Los Angeles Times, March 23, 1985, section V, p. 1; June 25, 1986, section 2, p. 1.
Life, August 26, 1966; July, 1982, pp. 74-78.
New York Times, May 30, 1982; October 7, 1987, p. C1; October 12, 1987, p. C18.
Mademoiselle, March, 1988, p. 86.
People, July 21, 1980, p. 51; December 7, 1981, pp. 127-28; February 11, 1985, p. 40; October 12, 1987, p. 9.
Redbook, May, 1983, pp. 10-11; February, 1985, pp. 98-99.
Time, August 16, 1982, p. 62.
TV Guide, May 29, 1982, pp. 18-22; October 10, 1987, pp. 26-29.
Woman's Day, November 11, 1984, pp. 124-25.

—*Sketch by Ronie-Richele Garcia-Johnson*

Mary Rose Wilcox
(1949-)
Politician

Mary Rose Wilcox's victory in the 1992 primary for District Five Maricopa County, Arizona, Supervisor was typical of her political career. Since winning a spot on the Phoenix, Arizona, City Council in 1982, Wilcox has had consistent success. In addition to becoming the first His-

Mary Rose Wilcox

panic woman to serve on the council, she won her seat five consecutive times. Wilcox has been a key figure in Phoenix housing and is known for her strong commitment to the improvement of her community.

Wilcox grew up in Superior, a rural mining town about 60 miles east of Phoenix. Her maternal grandparents cofounded Superior, which included a population of 5000 that was more than 80 percent Hispanic. Her father, John Garrido, was a copper miner involved in unionization. Her mother, Betty Nunez Garrido, was a homemaker active in the Roman Catholic Church and the public school system. Family pride and a strong sense of community duty were stressed in the Garrido household. Wilcox was deeply influenced by the political activism of her parents, who were part of the first Hispanic generation that began to reject racial discrimination.

Wilcox remembers hearing stories of her father's World War II service while she was in elementary school. Having served the United States in war, her father returned with a new perspective, and he no longer wanted to be treated like a second-class citizen. Wilcox watched her father and miners form a union in the 1950s. Changes in the adult world were mirrored in her own transition from a segregated to integrated school. Like her parents, Wilcox became an active participant in the community, especially at Superior High School. While attending the school, she played clarinet in the band and served on the student council. Through her parents' and her own activities, Wilcox felt a

strong Hispanic influence in the community. "We were on the student council, in the band, on the football and basketball teams," Wilcox remembered in a telephone interview with Peg McNichol.

When Wilcox attended Arizona State University, however, she abruptly discovered her minority status. She expected to transfer the sense of community responsibility and interaction from Superior to Phoenix. Instead, she and the three other minority women in her dorm were relegated to a single room and otherwise ignored. Wilcox didn't remain invisible for long. In 1967 the Chicano movement was sweeping the nation. She joined the on-campus activism and participated in a strike to improve working conditions for the university's laundry workers, the majority of whom were Hispanic. Wilcox had witnessed how the unionization of the copper miners in Superior had provided her family with health insurance and education, and she was convinced solidarity would provide the laundry workers with similar benefits.

While working towards a degree in social work, Mary met Earl V. Wilcox. He came from the southeast section of Phoenix, a heavily Hispanic area mottled with poverty and crime. His sensibilities and commitment to the community were met and matched by hers—he was a youth project director. The couple married in 1971, and she left school to support his efforts toward a master's degree in education.

The Wilcoxes joined the Hispanic political movement and campaigned for Alfredo Guitierrez, an Arizona politician. Wilcox also worked in Scottsdale, Arizona, as a job developer for the Maricopa County Manpower Program, helping create career ladders for people in the private sector. Much of Wilcox's work involved members of the Yaqui, a Native American tribe with Hispanic influences that had unhappily relocated to Scottsdale from northern Arizona due to a flood control project. Relocating the entire village meant finding more than jobs. Wilcox's attempts to identify new housing and support systems for the Yaqui caught the attention of U.S. Senator Dennis DeConcini. DeConcini invited her to become a caseworker with his office.

Wilcox joined DeConcini's staff in 1977, eventually attaining the status of special assistant and later serving as liaison to the Small Business Administration and the U.S. Immigration and Naturalization Service. In 1978, Wilcox's casework led to an association with Friendly House. Patterned after the old Settlement Houses of Chicago, Friendly House is a 75-year-old nonprofit organization devoted to helping immigrants. Wilcox helped develop an educational arm for Friendly House that extends to local school districts. Programs supported by Friendly House target at-risk children during after school hours. Some help youngsters improve their grade point average by raising their level of literacy. Others work with adults to improve parenting skills. By 1992, Wilcox was a Friendly House Foundation board member and had watched the group expand from a $100,000 annual working budget to $4 million. It remains one of her favorite organizations.

Cofounds Hispanic Woman's Corporation

In 1983, Wilcox and five other women cofounded the Hispanic Woman's Corporation, a group that offers annual day-and-a-half long seminars to help Hispanic women upgrade their careers and educations. In Arizona it is the largest conference of its kind, drawing up to 1,800 women. The conference is privately funded by corporations that use the event as a recruiting opportunity. Also in 1983, Wilcox helped create IMAGE, a coalition of Hispanic government employees at the federal, state, and local level. From 1983 to 1986, Wilcox served as the group's president. Though membership averaged 60, Wilcox saw the number of luncheon attendees mushroom due to speakers who discussed civil rights, politics, and social changes. One of the key issues was Arizona state politics.

Republicans have dominated the Arizona political scene since the mid-1950s (the last Democratic president Arizona chose was Harry Truman), but strong pockets of Democrats remain, many of them in cities like Phoenix. Until 1982, Phoenix had been represented primarily by middle-aged Caucasian men, many of them business owners from the city's central district. Wilcox's work for DeConcini put her at the heart of the community and resulted in her election to the Human Resources Commission. In that post she campaigned to restructure Phoenix's city council from at-large representation to districts (expanding the council from six to eight members), with the mayor elected at-large. By this time, Wilcox was a working mother feeling the effects of the women's movement. The success of her districting campaign inspired her to run for the District Seven position, which she won in 1982. It was a time she remembered in her interview as "the most satisfying in my life."

Wilcox took office with liberal reform Mayor Terry Goddard and Calvin Goode, a black colleague who was one of the few survivors of the reform campaign. Some of her key projects were chairing the city council's housing commission and working to pass a $37 million bond for affordable housing in 1988. The bond issue funded projects dedicated to safe, affordable single family housing and transitional housing for the impoverished and aged.

Wilcox gained a reputation as a housing advocate with the bond's passage and by teaming up with Goode in 1987 to establish a $1 million fund for an anticrime program called Neighborhood Fightback. The monies were granted to strong community associations willing to upgrade the community. The grants were as high as $250,000 and paid for repairs, house painting, and street lighting. Crime rates in neighborhoods with these programs dropped as much as 22 percent. After three years, the program was adopted on a state-wide level.

Becomes Vice Mayor of Pheonix

In 1988, Wilcox was chosen vice mayor by other members of the city council. During that two year-term, which was concurrent with her seat on council, she became very visible. Wilcox credited Goddard for his confidence in her abilities to do more than the traditional vice mayor. It appeared that Wilcox would become a near institution in city politics. She won a four-year term of office in 1989 after an uncontested campaign in which she called for a ban on semiautomatic weapons like the AK-47 assault rifle, a weapon commonly used by gang members on the city's south side. She also supported a proposition to build a baseball stadium in her district, on the premise that it would draw new jobs and more money into the area.

Wilcox's main thrust as a candidate, however, continued to be that she was the grassroots choice. She described herself as someone not glamorous or mysterious but more like a member of the voter's family. Her campaign speeches often included comparisons between herself and her constituency. "Look at me," she would ask. "Don't I look like your sister or your daughter or the woman next door?" Despite her appeal as an 'average' woman, Wilcox has demonstrated her political savvy. After Goddard left his post to seek a state office, there were rumors that Wilcox planned to run for mayor. In May of 1991, however, Wilcox's name was on the short list as a possible replacement for Maricopa County District Five Supervisor Ed Pastor.

Her decision to seek another term on the city council was greeted with some speculation that she wouldn't finish the four-year term. Wilcox vowed to do so, but in June, 1992, she did resign. Among the factors cited by the press was her disappointment over not receiving the supervisory appointment in 1991 and her frustration with conservative Phoenix Mayor Paul Johnson. The move, which forced a $95,000 special election, created some negative feelings in the community, but Wilcox managed to assuage those with the explanation that her efforts toward neighborhood improvement and better health care services for low income families would have greater strength at the county level.

Wilcox faced a tough primary. She didn't have the luxury of an unopposed campaign. This time, she faced four challengers: two Democrats and two Republicans. She won by targeting members of the Democratic community who knew her well: Hispanic women over age 35, telling them "our voice counts." Discussing her success, Wilcox noted in her interview, "If I'd been a male doing the stuff I'd done in the last nine years, there is no way another male would have run against me." Wilcox anticipated a significant win in November, 1992, that would make her the first Hispanic woman to serve as a supervisor.

Though politics play a vital role in Wilcox's life, she has other priorities. The importance of family is a constant theme. She has remained supportive of her husband's career—he was a state representative before accepting the role of Maryvale justice of the peace in 1991. The couple started a joint venture, as publishers of the quarterly *Aqui Magazine* for the Hispanic community. They consciously limited their own family to one child, daughter Yvonne, due to busy schedules. Yvonne has started her own family, and the Wilcoxes take great delight in their grandson, born in 1991. Wilcox credits motherhood with making her a well-rounded person. Her experience as a child with many siblings and her large extended family (her husband comes from a family of 13) convinced her that, regardless of structure, strong family connections are important. She has transferred her feelings for strong family commitment to the Hispanic community in general. She is committed to being a role model not just for Hispanic women but for women in general. She sees it as a responsibility that never lets up, but she is gratified when she meets a woman who has entered politics citing Wilcox's career as inspiration.

When Wilcox has time to herself, after the board meetings and family commitments, she occasionally plays her clarinet, but she is more likely to read or do some light impact aerobics. She still harbors hopes of finishing her degree. Since her three-and-a-half years at Arizona State, she has returned to college periodically. Even without her degree, her accomplishments and contributions to the Phoenix area are significant.

Sources:

Periodicals

Arizona Republic, September 13, 1989; April 10, 1992; June 18, 1992; June 30, 1992; July 2, 1992.
Arizona Republic/The Phoenix Gazette, April 29, 1991.
Arizona Republic Voter's Guide, Oct. 2, 1989.
Phoenix Gazette, May 25, 1992; June 17, 1992; June 19, 1992.

Other

Wilcox, Mary Rose, telephone interview with Peg McNichol, September, 1992.

—Sketch by Peg McNichol

Judith Zaffirini
(1946-)
Texas state senator, communications specialist

The first Mexican American woman elected to the Texas state senate, Judith Zaffirini assumed in 1986 that to win the office, she would be forced to spend upwards of $350,000 on a campaign. "I didn't have a last name that worked for me," she quipped in a telephone interview with Julia Edgar. Mexican Americans in the southern part of the 20-county district were liable to vote for the candidate with the Mexican name, she supposed, while voters in the north would likely choose the candidate with the Anglo-Saxon name. However, Zaffirini easily won her first term against five male candidates—the Democratic incumbent who had occupied the seat for 14 years withdrew from the race—and became one of only four women in the 31-member senate. She ran unopposed for a third term in 1992, and represents a 200-square-mile area stretching from Laredo, her hometown, to San Antonio, to El Paso.

Born February 13, 1946, to Nieves Mogas and George Pappas, a railroad clerk, Zaffirini developed an interest in politics at an early age. When she was five, one of her two sisters recruited her help in calling people who needed transportation to the voting polls. "It was a matter of helping our parents because my father was politically active and my grandfather was on the city council," Zaffirini recalled in the interview. "I just grew up in it and enjoyed it." As a 15-year-old Catholic school student in Laredo, Zaffirini was elected president of the All-Cities student council. During those years, she met the president of the Texas Association of Parents of Retarded Children, an important encounter which helped shaped her politics. At the first fundraiser she organized, the high school raised $700 for the organization. By 1978 Zaffirini had earned a Ph.D. in communications from the University of Texas at Austin.

Zaffirini now sits on the education, health, and human services and finance committees of the senate. More than 100 bills she personally sponsored have become law in Texas; one that she is particularly proud of passed when she was ranked 30 of 31 in seniority. The bill, which Zaffirini remarked did not entertain widespread support at the beginning, compels the state to store radioactive waste on state property rather than on private land. Under two other laws she helped write, adults who are convicted of selling drugs to children must serve jail terms, and adults who do not report child abuse can be criminally charged.

In addition to her senatorial duties, Zaffirini is also founder and chairperson of the Texas Office for the Prevention of Developmental Disabilities, an appointed member of the Legislative Education Board, which oversees the state board of education, and a member of the Texas Press Women, the Cancer Treatment Advisory Board, and the Stop Child Abuse and Neglect honorary board. She has been married for more than 25 years to attorney Carlos Zaffirini—with whom she was named one of ten "power couples" in the state by *Texas Monthly* magazine—and is the mother of Carlos, Jr. She plans to resume her career as a public relations consultant, she told Edgar, after serving 12 years in the senate, during which time she plans to examine such issues as providing tuition-free education in the state, allowing more students to earn college credit on the job, and requiring second-language courses in elementary and secondary schools.

Sources:

Zaffirini, Judith, telephone interview with Julia Edgar conducted on August 24, 1992.

—Sketch by Julia Edgar

Bernice Zamora
(1938-)
Poet

Bernice Zamora's most important contribution to the world of Chicano literature is *Restless Serpents,* a book of poems which also contains poetry by José Antonio Burciaga. The work expresses Zamora's anger at being a victim of a dual system of repression; as a Chicana Zamora feels oppressed both by the dominance of the male within the context of her own Latino culture and by the dominance of Anglos in society at large. "Zamora's poetry in *Restless Serpents,*" wrote Nancy Vogeley in *Dictionary of Literary Biography,* "explores such topics as Chicano cultural traditions, the experience of women in that culture, language, and the power of poetry." In her role as poet, Zamora finds the strength to resist Anglo and male domination.

Zamora was born Bernice Ortiz on January 20, 1938, in the rural environment of Aguilar, a small farming community in the sparsely populated southeastern portion of the state of Colorado. Her ancestors from both sides of the family had made their living in the area for generations. Her father was a coal miner, farmer, and automobile painter; her mother (whose maiden name was Valdez) spent some time employed by an optical company. When Zamora was seven, she moved with her family to the more urban setting of Pueblo, Colorado, but returned to Aguilar during summer vacations from school. Pueblo was to be the poet's home for most of the years she spent in Colorado, until her move to California in the mid-1970s.

As a child Zamora spoke Spanish with her family, but attended Catholic schools in Pueblo where English was the language of instruction. Although she excelled in art in high school, she left the traditional educational system to work at a bank and take classes at night. She married (Zamora was her husband's name) and had two daughters, Rhonda and Katherine. The poet didn't begin working toward her college degree until she was nearly thirty, when she enrolled at Southern Colorado University. She earned a bachelor of arts degree in English and French, then began graduate studies at the Colorado State University in Fort Collins. She received her master of arts degree in 1972, writing her thesis on the poetry of Wallace Stevens and Francis Ponge, and spent the next year pursuing additional studies at Marquette University.

After her marriage ended in 1974, Zamora moved with her two daughters to California. She decided to continue work on her doctorate in English and American literature at Stanford University. During the seventies, she contributed poetry, short stories, and critical articles to various publications. In 1976, she published *Restless Serpents* and appeared at that year's national conference of the Modern Language Association. At the meeting Zamora delivered a paper entitled "Archetypes in Chicana Poetry" (later published in the journal *De colores*), focusing on work she was preparing for her doctoral dissertation. The following year, she was invited to be guest editor for the summer issue of the Chicano review *El fuego de Aztlán.* As she continued her studies she also taught at Stanford and at the University of San Francisco, and was an instructor in Chicano studies at the University of California at Berkeley.

As the 1980s began, Zamora moved to Albuquerque, New Mexico, to work on *De colores.* In 1980, she and José Armas coedited an anthology of works gleaned from the *Flor y Canto* festivals held in the late 1970s in Albuquerque and Tempe, Arizona. The publication, entitled *Flor y Canto IV and V: An Anthology of Chicano Literature,* was to be her last before she suffered a serious illness in Houston, Texas. In 1982, she returned to California where she has continued to write poetry, but has refrained from publishing. She was granted her Ph.D. from Stanford University in 1986.

Although her most important book, *Restless Serpents,* was issued in an edition of only two thousand copies, the poetry collection is considered a "seminal work" by *Dictionary of Literary Biography* contributor Vogeley, who quoted from several other critics to substantiate her claim. Vogeley noted, for example, that in *Caracol* Juan Bruce-Novoa wrote about *Restless Serpents:* "Like those serpents, Zamora's poetry fascinates: inscrutable signs of life and death in beautiful form, capable of demonic possession; gods of mysterious, lost worlds, only accessible to us in the surface of the images they themselves are." Vogeley also included a statement from poet Lorna Dee Cervantes's review of *Restless Serpents,* originally published in *Mango.* Cervantes claimed that with the book's "carefully crafted poems, [Zamora] proves herself to be one of the most (if not *the* most) outstanding Chicana poets today."

Sources:

Books

Bruce-Novoa, Juan, *Chicano Authors: Inquiry by Interview,* University of Texas Press, 1980.

Dictionary of Literary Biography, Volume 82: *Chicano Writers: First Series,* Gale, 1989, pp. 289-94.

Sánchez, Marta Ester, *Contemporary Chicano Poetry: A Critical Approach to an Emerging Literature,* University of California Press, 1985.

Periodicals

De colores, 4, Number 3, 1978, pp. 43-52.
El fuego de Aztlán, summer, 1977, p. 4.

—*Sketch by Marian C. Gonsior*

Carmen Zapata

Carmen Zapata
(1927-)
Actress, producer, community activist

Often referred to as "The First Lady of the Hispanic Theatre," Carmen Zapata has been the cofounder, president and managing producer of the non-profit Bilingual Foundation of the Arts (B.F.A.). This Los Angeles-based performing arts organization is dedicated to bringing the Hispanic experience and culture, through the medium of bilingual theatre, to both English and Spanish-speaking audiences. Zapata has received much acclaim for these productions from the community as well as from critics and reviewers. She works closely with the Los Angeles Unified School District to introduce the works of great Hispanic authors to the students.

Carmen Margarita Zapata was born in New York City on July 15, 1947, to Julio Zapata, a Mexican immigrant, and Ramona Roca, a woman from Argentina. Zapata and Roca had met and married in New York; they lived with their three daughters in Spanish Harlem. As the family spoke Spanish exclusively in their home, Zapata's first day of school was so traumatic that even now she cannot remember her first years of schooling. Despite the language her family spoke, and the neighborhood in which they lived, Carmen Zapata was not well informed about Mexican culture as a child.

Zapata's talent manifested itself at an early age; the youngster played the piano and the violin at family gatherings, sang in the school choir, and appeared in school plays. Although, in the beginning, she did not approve of her daughter's desire to have a career in show business, Carmen Zapata's mother sacrificed much to give young Carmen dancing and music lessons. That sacrifice was not made in vain. After studies at the Actors Studio and with Uta Hagen, Zapata was on her way to success.

Zapata made her debut in the chorus of the hit 1946 Broadway musical *Oklahoma.* Zapata graduated to a lead role in *Oklahoma* when the play went on the road. When she finally returned to Broadway, she took over one of the principal roles in *Stop the World, I Want to Get Off.* She also appeared in *Bells are Ringing* and *Guys and Dolls.*

Zapata performed in musicals for twenty years. Between plays, she worked at night clubs as "Marge Cameron" in a singing and comedy act she had created. At one point she emceed for strippers at a burlesque house in Toledo, Ohio. She explained this job to the *Los Angeles Times:* "At the time it was not 'in' to be Hispanic. I had a hard time getting club owners to hire me, unless I shook my fanny and played the maracas."

A brief marriage to comedy writer Roy Freedman ended in divorce after five years. In 1967, following her mother's death, Zapata moved to California and began what would become an extensive film and television career. Her first film role was as a prostitute in the 1968 movie *Sol Madrid.* When producers claimed that "Marge Cameron" didn't look "all-American," and that she looked "ethnic," Zapata began to use her real name once again. As a result, she now found herself stereotyped in the role of a maid or a mother.

This displeased her, despite the fact that she made good money and received a great deal of visibility.

Recognizing the need for change within the Hollywood entertainment industry, Zapata helped form the initial minority committee of the Screen Actors Guild. She was also one of the original members of the Hispanic actors organization called, "Nosotros," which was begun by actor Ricardo Montalban.

While television and films kept her busy, Zapata was dissatisfied with the roles she was finding. She also missed the theatre. When a daring Cuban director, Margarita Galban, offered Zapata the opportunity to return to the theatre, the frustrated actress was enthusiastic. At that time, Galban's company, "Seis Actores," was producing a Spanish-language play. Galban offered Zapata the opportunity to play the lead in *Cada quien su vida* ("To Each His Own"), but Zapata was hesitant. She recalled to the *Los Angeles Times,* "She invited me to do a piece in Spanish. I'd never acted in Spanish before; I was petrified." But Galban reassured her that the character was that of a drunkard, so mistakes in speech were permissible. "And after I did it, I became very interested in Spanish-language theater. Why? It's beautiful! There are some glorious pieces that non-Spanish speaking people are not aware of. When I realized that, I started doing my translations."

Translates the Work of Federico Garcia Lorca

Zapata delved further into her Hispanic roots and co-translated some of the classics of Hispanic literature. Dissatisfied with the plays available in Spanish, the actress set out to create her own stage works. She accomplished the formidable task of bringing into English Federico Garcia Lorca's trilogy: *Blood Wedding, Yerma,* and *The House of Bernarda Alba,* as well as Fernando de Rojas's *La celestina* and J. Humberto Robles Arenas's *Uprooted.* Zapata and her partner, Michael Dewell, were appointed by the Lorca Estate as official translators. Their translation of the trilogy was published by Bantam Books in 1986.

In 1970 Zapata, Galban, and scenic designer Estela Scarlata joined forces. With $5,000 provided by Zapata, the trio rented a theatre in downtown Los Angeles and borrowed sets, lights, and costumes from the studios. They then launched their theatre which, in 1973, became the Bilingual Foundation of the Arts.

Interviewed by the *Los Angeles Times,* Zapata pointed out there now exists a trend toward Hispanic theatre, something her B.F.A. has been doing for years. "That was always the idea—to have everyone learn about, share and become part of our literature, our tradition." This is done at the B.F.A. theatre where, on different nights, performances alternate between English-speaking and Spanish-speaking versions. "We decided in 1979 to go bilingual, because that

would make us unique as a theater. We also thought it would be nice if we reached into the non-Hispanic community and had them enjoy the beauty of our literature."

Zapata, who confesses that the theatre is her "baby" and that running it leaves her little time for acting, nonetheless has extensive credits, which include more than 300 appearances in television programs such as *Marcus Welby, Owen Marshall, Medical Center, Mod Squad, The Rookies, The Bold Ones, Bonanza, Treasury Agent, Streets of San Francisco, MacMillan and Wife, Switch, Charlie's Angels, Chico and the Man, Barreta, Fantasy Island, Archie Bunker's Place, Trapper John, M.D.,* and many others. She appeared regularly in the Anthony Quinn series for ABC, *Man and the City,* and had recurring roles on *The Dick Van Dyke Show* and the NBC soap-opera *Santa Barbara.* In 1976 she starred in her own ABC television series *Viva Valdez,* and from 1981 to 1982 she had a recurring role in the series *Flamingo Road.* Zapata admitted to *Hollywood Latinews* that she is most proud of the nine seasons in which she starred as the matronly "Doña Luz" in the PBS bilingual children's television show, *Villa Alegre.*

Garners Emmy Nominations

Zapata's professional recognitions include the 1984 Best Actress Award for best dramatic performance in the play *Blood Wedding,* given by Dramalogue, a local Emmy for her 1973 documentary *Cinco Vidas,* and a 1971 Emmy nomination for the television series *The Lawyers.*

As a guest speaker, Zapata has addressed audiences at various California universities and at fund-raising functions for charitable groups. Her community involvement includes service on the board of the National Conference of Christian and Jews, the United Way, the Boy Scouts of America, the National Repertory Theatre Foundation and the Mexican-American Opportunity Foundation. She is also a member of the Mayor's Committee on the Arts (Los Angeles), the California Arts Council's Ethnic Advisory Minority Panel and many other organizations. She has served as a panel member of the Expansion Arts Program of the National Endowment for the Arts, the Los Angeles Special Olympics Events Committee and other programs.

Zapata, a tireless activist, has received countless awards for her efforts. These awards include an Outstanding Woman in Business Award from Women in Film, the Boy Scouts of America Community Leadership Award, a Mexican-American Foundation award, and recognition from the Hispanic Women's Council. She was granted an Honorary Doctorate Degree in Human Services from Sierra University. In 1990 Carmen Zapata received what she admits is her favorite award—the Civil Order of Merit (*El Lazo de Dama de la Orden del Merito Civil*) by His Majesty Juan Carlos I, King of Spain. The Order recognizes Zapata's commitment to Hispanic concerns within the arts and in the realm of community service. Only a few have been honored with this Order of Knighthood from the Spanish Head of State, an honor which could be likened to the Knighthoods bestowed upon Dame Judith Anderson and Sir Laurence Olivier by the Queen of England. Finally, on November 22, 1991, in recognition of her outstanding contributions to the arts in the state of California, Carmen Zapata was among nine Californian artists, arts organizations and patrons to receive the prestigious 1991 Governor's Award for the Arts presented by Governor and Mrs.Pete Wilson.

At the Bilingual Foundation, Zapata is involved with the newly developed Teen Theatre Project (*Teatro Para Los Jovenes*), an innovative theatre-in-education program designed by B.F.A. to meet the needs of junior and high school students who have been identified as "at risk." Play productions are performed in the schools by professional, ethnically diverse actors chosen for their ability to relate to and communicate with students. Performances are followed by an open discussion of the issues affecting teenagers. This program is made possible through grants from the Seaver Institute and Kraft General Foods Foundation. Zapata feels it is one of the most important steps in addressing the needs of the student population of many urban schools. In a television interview with *Hollywood Latinews,* Zapata pointed out that a 1990 study of New York City schools showed arts programming to be the single most effective deterrent to drop-out rates. The Teen Theatre Project was modeled after B.F.A.'s highly successful theatre-in-education program for elementary students, which has served nearly one million children since its inception in 1985.

During an interview with *La opinion,* the busy actress/producer who makes her home in Van Nuys, California, admitted, "If I stop working I die. Work keeps me alive. I need to have something to do when I get up in the morning, to have a place to go, and that place is my theater."

Sources:

Periodicals

Los Angeles Times, Calendar section, February 5, 1989.
La opinion (translated from Spanish by Elena Kellner), Panorama section, December 29, 1991.

Other

Hollywood Latinews (television program), interview with Elena Kellner, February, 1992.
Zapata, Carmen, biography provided by the Bilingual Foundation of the Arts, 1992.

—Sketch by Elena Kellner

Iris M. Zavala
(1936-)
Poet, educator, literary critic

Iris M. Zavala is the prolific author or editor of more than thirty books, the majority written in her native Spanish language. The author maintains that her work represents an effort to effectively combine imagination with erudition. Zavala told *Contemporary Authors New Revisions Series* that because of this goal "the reader (if any) will find that my books of poetry and my novella make wide use of history, philosophy, art, literature and foreign languages." In the same source, Zavala lists Spanish poet Dante, German economic philosopher Karl Marx, Spanish novelist Miguel de Cervantes, Dutch scholar Erasmus, and German poet Johann Wolfgang von Goethe, as just some of the "friends" who have assisted her in the writing of her books.

Zavala was born on December 27, 1936, in Ponce, Puerto Rico, the daughter of Romualdo and Maria M. Zapata Zavala. She was a bright student who earned her bachelor of arts degree from the University of Puerto Rico in 1957, and her master of arts in philology and her Ph.D. from the University of Salamanca in 1961 and 1962, respectively. She then launched a long academic career which has taken her to Puerto Rico, the United States, and the Netherlands. Her first position was at the University of Puerto Rico at Río Piedras, where she served as assistant professor of Spanish literature from 1962 to 1964.

After moving to the United States, Zavala was briefly associated with Hunter College of the City University of New York beginning in 1968, where she served as assistant professor of Hispanic literature. A year later she joined the faculty of the State University of New York at Stony Brook, where she remained for more than a dozen years. While at Stony Brook, she served as associate professor of Hispanic and comparative literature from 1969 to 1971, and as full professor from 1971 to 1983. She was also director of graduate studies for two years and joint professor of comparative literature from 1976 to 1983.

Since leaving Stony Brook in 1983, Zavala has filled several different positions at the University of Utrecht in Utrecht, Netherlands, a historic cultural center about twenty miles southeast of Amsterdam. She has been chair of the department of Hispanic literature as well as chair and director of the school's Spanish Institute. Reflecting her keen interest in the field of literary criticism, she has also served as director of the Utrecht Summer School of Critical Theory and Semiotics since 1983, and coordinator of the Semiotics and Theory, Text and Content research group since 1984.

Writings Encompass Several Genres

Zavala's work is as rich and varied as the countries to which her career has taken her. Along with nonfiction, she has produced several volumes of fiction and poetry. She is one of a group of Puerto Rican poets who began publishing their poems in the early 1960s in the literary magazines *Guajana* and *Prometeo*. Her first poetry collection, *Barro doliente* ("Repenting Clay"), was published in 1965. Other volumes include *Poemas prescindibles* ("Dispensable Poems"), *Escritura desatada* ("Unattached Writing"), and *Que nadie muera sin amar el mar* ("That No One Die without Loving the Sea"). Her first novel, *Kiliagonia,* originally published in 1982, was released by Third Woman Press of Indiana University in English translation as *Chiliagony* in 1984. Another novel, *Nocturna mas no funesta,* was published in 1987.

She has also written numerous volumes of literary criticism and other nonfiction works. Her most important works in the genre are her studies on Spanish writers of the late nineteenth and early twentieth centuries. These include *Ideología y política en la novela española del siglo XIX* ("Ideology and Politics in the Nineteenth-Century Spanish Novel"), published in 1971, *Romanticismo y costumbrismo* ("Romanticism and *Costumbrismo*"), published in 1989, and *Unamuno y el pensamiento dialógico* ("Unamuno and Thought in Dialogue"), published in 1990. She has edited many works of literary criticism, such as *Libertad y crítica en el ensayo puertorriqueño,* which she edited with Rafael Rodríguez. The work was published in English translation as *The Intellectual Roots of Independence: An Anthology of Puerto Rican Political Essays* by Monthly Review Press in 1979.

Zavala is also a frequent contributor to publications throughout Europe, the United States, and Latin America, and has edited several book series. Her work has earned her numerous honors including grants from the Social Science Research Council and the State University of New York at Stony Brook. She has been awarded a National Literary Prize from Puerto Rico several times, and in 1983 her novel *Kiliagonia* was a finalist in the Premio Herralde competition in Spain. Perhaps her greatest honor came in 1988, when King Juan Carlos of Spain awarded her the Lazo de Dama de la Orden de Mérito Civil for her contributions to Spanish culture.

Sources:

Books

Contemporary Authors New Revisions Series, Volume 32, Gale, 1991.

—*Sketch by Marian C. Gonsior*

Patricia Zavella
(1949-)
Anthropologist, educator

Patricia Zavella has used her training as an anthropologist and her interest in promoting Hispanic activist organizations as the basis for her scholarly examinations of the role of gender in the workplace and of the relation between women's work and family. Much of her work has focussed on women who work in the food-processing industry in northern California; her 1987 book, entitled *Women's Work and Chicano Families: Cannery Workers of the Santa Clara Valley* was an ethnography that combined personal interviews with statistical patterns of work-related behavior to explain the culture of Chicana workers, and many of her scholarly articles treat the same issue. Her next book, *Sunbelt Working Mothers: Reconciling Family and Factory in the Sunbelt,* co-authored with Louise Lamphere and Felipe Gonzales, with Peter B. Evans, was published in 1993.

Born on an United States Air Force base near Tampa, Florida, on November 28, 1949, Zavella moved frequently as her father was shifted to different bases. What she remembers about her early schooling, she told contributor Tom Pendergast in an interview, was that she was never able to attend a full year of school and that teachers always assumed that, because she came from a Mexican American family, she was not as smart as the other kids. "The first time I did well on a spelling test was a surprise for my teachers," she commented, "and their negative attitude made me very competitive." When she was in sixth grade her schooling stabilized, however, for her father left the Air Force to become an electronics technician in Ontario, California. Her schoolwork, and especially her love of reading, acted as a refuge from the responsibilities that went along with being the oldest girl in a family that included twelve children, for her mother needed her help to care for the large family.

When she was in high school, Zavella began to receive the encouragement that would eventually prompt her to continue her education through graduate school. Upon completing high school, she received her A.A. degree from Chaffey College in Alta Loma, California, in 1971 and then got her A.B. in anthropology from Pitzer College in Claremont, California, in 1973. Her interest in anthropology is not surprising: A sociologist for whom she had worked in a high school work/study program told her that she was an excellent researcher, and she had an influential anthropology professor at Pitzer named Jose Cuellar who urged her on. She also became involved in Hispanic activist organizations while getting her undergraduate degrees, she told Pendergast, and "this raised [her] consciousness about the way Mexicans were treated in the United States."

Zavella continued her study of anthropology at the University of California at Berkeley.

Researches Chicana Workers

For her dissertation field research, Zavella moved to San Jose, California, where she was intrigued by a discrimination suit being filed by women cannery workers against the food processing plants where they worked. The workers won the suit and Zavella decided to study the ways that Chicana workers were tracked into female job categories. She spent fifteen months living in the same community as the workers, interviewing people, taking notes, and trying to understand their lives. This study became her first book.

After completing her M.A. in 1975 and her Ph.D. in 1982 at Berkeley, Zavella accepted the position of assistant professor at the University of California at Santa Cruz in 1983 and became associate professor in 1989. She is affiliated with the interdisciplinary Community Studies Board at the university, and her teaching interests include the anthropology of work, changing family structures, and research methods.

Most important to Zavella, however, is her commitment to the Chicana movement, which is reflected in both her teaching and in her scholarship. "The consciousness I developed in my political activities," she told Pendergast, "urges me to incorporate all kinds of people into academia. I would like to see more Chicano studies programs, because they provide a base of support for people who do my kind of work and interdisciplinary work that examines elements of culture traditionally excluded from academic study." In addition to her work at the university, Zavella has served as a consultant to various family studies projects in the west and southwest, and is a regular contributor to scholarly journals. She is the mother of two children from a previous marriage, and currently lives in Santa Cruz with her partner, Jim Jatczynski.

Sources:

Periodicals

American Ethnologist, August, 1989.
Feminist Studies, spring, 1990.
Journal of American Ethnic History, spring, 1989.
Journal of American History, December, 1988.
Oral History Review, spring, 1989.
Technology and Culture, October, 1988.

Other

Zavella, Patricia, interview with contributor Tom Pendergast conducted on September 28, 1992.

—*Sketch by Tom Pendergast*

Zinn, Maxine Baca
See Baca Zinn, Maxine

Teresa Zubizarreta
(1938-)
Advertising executive

Teresa Zubizarreta is the president and owner of one of Miami's largest Hispanic advertising agencies, Zubi Advertising Services. Her agency specializes in Spanish-language advertising, an area not served by mainstream agencies who have failed to attach importance to the tremendous growth in the Spanish-speaking market. Although not planned as such, the agency is an all female organization. Zubizarreta stated in the *Miami Herald:* "Women don't have [hang-ups] about titles, their output is greater. . . . I believe women are superior. I don't want to be equal because that would be a step down." Her motto, she added, is creation, not translation, from English-language advertising campaigns.

Zubizarreta was born September 7, 1938, in Havana, Cuba. Memories of her younger days include images of a happy childhood, a protected life, and the exclusive schools she attended. She studied at Saint Mary's Dominican High School in New Orleans and at Tarbox School of Business in Havana. Like many other Cubans, she was not allowed to bring anything with her when she left her country as an exile in 1960. At first, she was on welfare and got her first coat from Goodwill Industries. On a suggestion from her husband, and because they were desperate for money, she began looking for a job.

Although in Anglo society a woman employed outside the home is almost the norm, Zubizarreta found looking for such a position difficult due to her Hispanic background. She referred to this problematic aspect of her life in a *Chicago Tribune* interview with Carol Kleiman. "Hispanic women have so many doctrines to live up to. . . . We have to overcome the moral labyrinth of the mind that says a woman is born to take care of the man, children and house but does not go out to the work force," Zubizarreta noted. "As much as I love my culture and my family, I feel much more rewarded internally because I've been able to prove I am worth something, which I may not have been able to do if I had stayed in Cuba." Her own determination allowed her to take on the additional role of an executive at work, while continuing to fulfill the traditional role of a homemaker.

After making the decision to look for work, there was yet another unexpected obstacle that stood between Zubizarreta and her hopes for gaining economic security. When she first looked for a job, she was abruptly told by an employer that the company did not hire Cubans. Eventually she was hired as a secretary at McCann Marshalk, an advertising agency, in 1962. She subsequently moved to J.M. Mathes Advertising, where she worked for Bill Ryder and Dick Schild. In 1970 she took a position with EHG Enterprises, a development firm, as advertising director for property in Puerto Rico. Zubizarreta soon found this job to be taking away most of her cherished time with her family, so she decided to accept a less demanding position—with an accompanying substantial cut in salary—as an advertising director at Flagship Bank.

Opens Own Advertising Agency

Zubizarreta began her career as owner of her own agency in 1973. Since opening the agency she has acquired some important clients, including the *Miami Herald,* Pepsi Cola Bottling of Miami, Amoco Oil Co., General Motors Corporation's Cadillac division, and the U.S. Peace Corps. Among her public service advertising clients are the United Way Campaign, FACE (Facts about Cuban Exiles), and the South Florida Blood Drive. At first, her zealous dedication and commitment to her job left her little time for her marriage. She and her husband, real estate executive Octavio E. Zubizarreta, divorced in 1979, but remarried in 1983. The couple have two children, Octavio and Michelle.

Zubizarreta has a long list of awards and achievements. She was honored as an outstanding businesswoman at the National Alliance of Hispanic Women's conference in Miami. In 1988 she was nominated Woman of the Year by the Latin Business and Professional Women organization. In 1989 she and her family were nominated in an Hispanic Family of the Year competition. The following year she received an Honorable Mention for her work in management from the National Association of Women Business Owners.

Zubizarreta refuses to be inferior and rejects the word "can't." She believes she has the strength to overcome all disadvantages and to succeed in a strange land. As she declared to Laurie Baum of the *Miami Herald,* although she arrived in the United States not knowing what "media" meant or how to type on an electric typewriter, she readily credits her success to being able to say, "I'll learn." Her ability to absorb and use new information has made all the difference.

Sources:

Periodicals

Baum, Laurie, "Coolness under Fire," *Miami Herald,* Business Monday Magazine, January 8, 1986, pp. 9-10.
Chicago Tribune, September 7, 1987, Section 3, p. 6.
"Making a Name in Marketing," *Miami News,* Money section, April 27, 1987, pp. 12-14.

—Sketch by Sylvia P. Apodaca

Subject Index